THE CIA WORLD FACTBOOK

VOLUME 1

FULL-SIZE
2019 EDITION

Introduction, Maps, World, Afghanistan ~ Gabon

Central Intelligence Agency

The CIA World Factbook Volume 1: Full-Size 2019 Edition

Giant Format, 600+ Pages: The #1 Global Reference, Complete & Unabridged - Vol. 1 of 3, Introduction, Maps, World, Afghanistan ~ Gabon

Central Intelligence Agency

This edition first published 2019 by Carlile Intelligence Library. "Carlile Intelligence Library" and its associated logos and devices are trademarks. Carlile Intelligence Library is an imprint of Carlile Media (a division of Creadyne Developments LLC). The appearance of U.S. Government visual information does not imply or constitute U.S. Government endorsement. This book is published for information purposes only.

Published in the United States of America.

ISBN-13: 978-1-79299-738-9
ISBN-10: 1792997388

WWW.CARLILE.MEDIA

Central Intelligence Agency Headquarters, Langley, Virginia

Photographs in the Carol M. Highsmith Archive, Library of Congress, Prints and Photographs Division.

TABLE OF CONTENTS

HISTORY OF THE CIA WORLD FACTBOOK

A Brief History of Basic Intelligence and The World Factbook

The Intelligence Cycle is the process by which information is acquired, converted into intelligence, and made available to policymakers. ***Information*** *is raw data from any source, data that may be fragmentary, contradictory, unreliable, ambiguous, deceptive, or wrong.* ***Intelligence*** *is information that has been collected, integrated, evaluated, analyzed, and interpreted.* ***Finished intelligence*** *is the final product of the Intelligence Cycle ready to be delivered to the policymaker.*

The three types of finished intelligence are: basic, current, and estimative. Basic intelligence provides the fundamental and factual reference material on a country or issue. Current intelligence reports on new developments. Estimative intelligence judges probable outcomes. The three are mutually supportive: basic intelligence is the foundation on which the other two are constructed; current intelligence continually updates the inventory of knowledge; and estimative intelligence revises overall interpretations of country and issue prospects for guidance of basic and current intelligence. *The World Factbook, The President's Daily Brief,* and the *National Intelligence Estimates* are examples of the three types of finished intelligence.

The United States has carried on foreign intelligence activities since the days of George Washington but only since World War II have they been coordinated on a government-wide basis. Three programs have highlighted the development of coordinated basic intelligence since that time: (1*) the Joint Army Navy Intelligence Studies* (JANIS), (2*) the National Intelligence Survey* (NIS), and (3) *The World Factbook.*

During World War II, intelligence consumers realized that the production of basic intelligence by different components of the US Government resulted in a great duplication of effort and conflicting information. The Japanese attack on Pearl Harbor in 1941 brought home to leaders in Congress and the executive branch the need for integrating departmental reports to national policymakers. Detailed and coordinated information was needed not only on such major powers as Germany and Japan, but also on places of little previous interest. In the Pacific Theater, for example, the Navy and Marines had to launch amphibious operations against many islands about which information was unconfirmed or nonexistent. Intelligence authorities resolved that the United States should never again be caught unprepared.

In 1943, Gen. George B. Strong (G-2), Adm. H. C. Train (Office of Naval Intelligence - ONI), and Gen. William J. Donovan (Director of the Office of Strategic Services - OSS) decided that a joint effort should be initiated. A steering committee was appointed on 27 April 1943 that recommended the formation of a Joint Intelligence Study Publishing Board to assemble, edit, coordinate, and publish the *Joint Army Navy Intelligence Studies* (JANIS). JANIS was the first interdepartmental basic intelligence program to fulfill the needs of the US Government for an authoritative and coordinated appraisal of strategic basic intelligence. Between April 1943 and July 1947, the board published 34 JANIS studies. JANIS performed well in the war effort, and numerous letters of commendation were received, including a statement from Adm. Forrest Sherman, Chief of Staff, Pacific Ocean Areas, which said, "JANIS has become the indispensable reference work for the shore-based planners."

The need for more comprehensive basic intelligence in the postwar world was well expressed in 1946 by George S. Pettee, a noted author on national security. He wrote in *The Future of American Secret Intelligence* (Infantry Journal Press, 1946, page 46) that world leadership in peace requires even more elaborate intelligence than in war. "The conduct of peace involves all countries, all human activities - not just the enemy and his war production."

The Central Intelligence Agency was established on 26 July 1947 and officially began operating on 18 September 1947. Effective 1 October 1947, the Director of Central Intelligence assumed operational responsibility for JANIS. On 13 January 1948, the National Security Council issued Intelligence Directive (NSCID) No. 3, which authorized the *National Intelligence Survey* (NIS) program as a peacetime replacement for the wartime JANIS program. Before adequate NIS country sections could be produced, government agencies had to develop more comprehensive gazetteers and better maps. The US Board on Geographic Names (BGN) compiled the names; the Department of the Interior produced the gazetteers; and CIA produced the maps.

The Hoover Commission's Clark Committee, set up in 1954 to study the structure and administration of the CIA, reported to Congress in 1955 that: "The National Intelligence Survey is an invaluable publication which provides the essential elements of basic intelligence on all areas of the world. There will always be a continuing requirement for keeping the Survey up-to-date." The *Factbook* was created as an annual summary and update to the encyclopedic NIS studies. The first classified *Factbook* was published in August 1962, and the first unclassified version was published in June 1971. The NIS program was terminated in 1973 except for the *Factbook*, map, and gazetteer components. The 1975 *Factbook* was the first to be made available to the public with sales through the US Government Printing Office (GPO). The *Factbook* was first made available on the Internet in June 1997. The year 2019 marks the 72nd anniversary of the establishment of the Central Intelligence Agency and the 76th year of continuous basic intelligence support to the US Government by *The World Factbook* and its two predecessor programs.

The Evolution of The World Factbook

National Basic Intelligence Factbook produced semiannually until 1980. Country entries include sections on Land, Water, People, Government, Economy, Communications, and Defense Forces.

1981 Publication becomes an annual product and is renamed *The World Factbook*. A total of 165 nations are covered on 225 pages.

1983 Appendices (Conversion Factors, International Organizations) first introduced.

1984 Appendices expanded; now include: A. The United Nations, B. Selected United Nations Organizations, C. Selected International Organizations, D. Country Membership in Selected Organizations, E. Conversion Factors.

1987 A new Geography section replaces the former separate Land and Water sections. UN Organizations and Selected International Organizations appendices merged into a new International Organizations appendix. First multi-color-cover *Factbook*.

1988 More than 40 new geographic entities added to provide complete world coverage without overlap or omission. Among the new entities are Antarctica, oceans (Arctic, Atlantic, Indian, Pacific), and the World. The front-of-the-book explanatory introduction expanded and retitled to Notes, Definitions, and Abbreviations. Two new Appendices added: Weights and Measures (in place of Conversion Factors) and a Cross-Reference List of Geographic Names. *Factbook* size reaches 300 pages.

1989 Economy section completely revised and now includes an Overview briefly describing a country's economy. New entries added under People, Government, and Communications.

1990 The Government section revised and considerably expanded with new entries.

1991 A new International Organizations and Groups appendix added. *Factbook* size reaches 405 pages.

1992 Twenty new successor state entries replace those of the Soviet Union and Yugoslavia. New countries are respectively: Armenia, Azerbaijan, Belarus, Estonia, Georgia, Kazakhstan, Kyrgyzstan, Latvia, Lithuania, Moldova, Russia, Tajikistan, Turkmenistan, Ukraine, Uzbekistan; and Bosnia and Hercegovina, Croatia, Macedonia, Serbia and Montenegro, Slovenia. Number of nations in the *Factbook* rises to 188.

1993 Czechoslovakia's split necessitates new Czech Republic and Slovakia entries. New Eritrea entry added after it secedes from Ethiopia. Substantial enhancements made to Geography section.

1994 Two new appendices address Selected International Environmental Agreements. The gross domestic product (GDP) of most developing countries changed to a purchasing power parity (PPP) basis rather than an exchange rate basis. *Factbook* size up to 512 pages.

1995 The GDP of all countries now presented on a PPP basis. New appendix lists estimates of GDP on an exchange rate basis. Communications category split; Railroads, Highways, Inland waterways, Pipelines, Merchant marine, and Airports entries now make up a new Transportation category. *The World Factbook* is first produced on CD-ROM.

1996 Maps accompanying each entry now present more detail. Flags also introduced for nearly all entities. Various new entries appear under Geography and Communications. *Factbook* abbreviations consolidated into a new Appendix A. Two new appendices present a Cross-Reference List of Country Data Codes and a Cross-Reference List of Hydrogeographic Data Codes. Geographic coordinates added to Appendix H, Cross-Reference List of Geographic Names. *Factbook* size expands by 95 pages in one year to reach 652.

1997 *The World Factbook* introduced onto the Internet. A special printed edition prepared for the CIA's 50th anniversary. A schema or Guide to Country Profiles introduced. New color maps and flags now accompany each country profile. Category headings distinguished by shaded backgrounds. Number of categories expanded to nine with the addition of an Introduction (for only a few countries) and Transnational Issues (which includes Disputes-international and Illicit drugs).

1998 The Introduction category with two entries, Current issues and Historical perspective, expanded to more countries. Last year for the production of CD-ROM versions of the *Factbook*.

1999 Historical perspective and Current issues entries in the Introduction category combined into a new Background statement. Several new Economy entries introduced. A new physical map of the world added to the back-of-the-book reference maps.

2000 A new "country profile" added on the Southern Ocean. The Background statements dramatically expanded to over 200 countries and possessions. A number of new Communications entries added.

2001 Background entries completed for all 267 entities in the *Factbook*. Several new HIV/AIDS entries introduced under the People category. Revision begun on individual country maps to include elevation extremes and a partial geographic grid. Weights and Measures appendix deleted.

2002 New entry on Distribution of Family income - Gini index added. Revision of individual country maps continued (process still ongoing).

2003 In the Economy category, petroleum entries added for oil production, consumption, exports, imports, and proved reserves, as well as natural gas proved reserves.

2004 Bi-weekly updates launched on *The World Factbook* website. Additional petroleum entries included for natural gas production, consumption, exports, and imports. In the Transportation category, under Merchant marine, subfields added for foreign-owned vessels and those registered in other countries. Descriptions of the many forms of government mentioned in the Factbook incorporated into the Definitions and Notes.

2005 In the People category, a Major infectious diseases field added for countries deemed to pose a higher risk for travelers. In the Economy category, entries included for Current account balance, Investment, Public debt, and Reserves of foreign exchange and gold. The Transnational issues category expanded to include Refugees and internally displaced persons. Size of the printed *Factbook* reaches 702 pages.

2006 In the Economy category, national GDP figures now presented at Official Exchange Rates (OER) in addition to GDP at purchasing power parity (PPP). Entries in the Transportation section reordered; Highways changed to Roadways, and Ports and harbors to Ports and terminals.

2007 In the Government category, the Capital entry significantly expanded with up to four subfields, including new information having to do with time. The subfields consist of the *name* of the capital itself, its *geographic coordinates*, the *time difference* at the capital from coordinated universal time (UTC), and, if applicable, information on *daylight saving time* (DST). Where appropriate, a special note is added to highlight those countries with multiple time zones. A Trafficking in Persons entry added to the Transnational Issues category. A new appendix, Weights and Measures, (re)introduced to the online version of the *Factbook*.

2008 In the Geography category, two fields focus on the increasingly vital resource of water: Total renewable water resources and Freshwater withdrawal. In the Economy category, three fields added for: Stock of direct foreign investment - at home, Stock of direct foreign investment - abroad, and Market value of publicly traded shares. Concise descriptions of all major religions included in the Definitions and Notes. Responsibility for printing of *The World Factbook* turned over to the Government Printing Office.

2009 The online *Factbook* site completely redesigned with many new features. In the People category, two new fields provide information on education in terms of opportunity and resources: School Life Expectancy and Education expenditures. Additionally, the Urbanization entry expanded to include all countries. In the Economy category, five fields added: Central bank discount rate, Commercial bank prime lending rate, Stock of narrow money, Stock of broad money, and Stock of domestic credit.

2010 Weekly updates inaugurated on the *The World Factbook* website. The dissolution of the Netherlands Antilles results in two new listings: Curacao and Sint Maarten. In the Communications category, a Broadcast media field replaces the former Radio broadcast stations and TV broadcast stations entries. In the Geography section, under Natural hazards, a Volcanism subfield added for countries with historically active volcanoes. In the Government category, a new National anthems field introduced. Concise descriptions of all major Legal systems incorporated into the Definitions and Notes. In order to facilitate comparisons over time, dozens of the entries in the Economy category expanded to include two (and in some cases three) years' worth of data.

2011 The People section expanded to People and Society, incorporating ten new fields. The Economy category added Taxes and other revenues and Budget surplus (+) or deficit (-), while the Government section introduced International law organization participation and National symbols. A new African nation, South Sudan, brings the total number of countries in *The World Factbook* to 195.

2012 A new Energy category introduced with 23 energy-related fields. Several distinctive features added to *The World Factbook* website: 1) playable audio files in the Government section for the National Anthems entry, 2) online graphics in the form of a Population Pyramid feature in the People and Society category's Age Structure field, and 3) a Users Guide enabling visitors to navigate the *Factbook* more easily and efficiently. A new and distinctive Map of the World Oceans highlights an expanded array of regional and country maps. Size of the printed *Factbook*'s 50th anniversary edition reaches 847 pages.

2013 In the People and Society section five fields introduced: Demographic profile, Mother's mean age at first birth, Contraceptive prevalence rate, Dependency ratios, and Child labor - children ages 5-14. In the Transnational Issues category, a new *stateless persons* subfield embedded under the Refugees and internally displaced persons entry. In the Economy section two fields added: GDP - composition by end use and Gross national saving. In the Government category the Judicial branch entry revised and expanded to include three new subfields: *highest court(s)*, *judge selection and term of office*, and *subordinate courts*.

2014 In the Transportation category, the Ports and terminals field substantially expanded with subfields for *major seaport(s)*, *river port(s)*, *lake port(s)*, *oil/gas terminal(s)*, *LNG terminal(s)*, *dry bulk cargo port(s)*, *container port(s)*, and *cruise/ferry port(s)*. In the Geography section, the Land boundaries entry revised for all countries, including the total country border length as well as the border lengths for all neighboring countries.

2015 In the Government category, the first part of the Legislative Branch field thoroughly revised, expanded, and updated for all countries under a new *description heading*. This subentry includes the legislative structure, the formal name(s), the number of legislative seats, the types of voting constituencies and voting systems, and the member term of office. Area Comparison Maps introduced online for about half of the world's countries. (More to follow when they become available.)

2016 In the Government section for all countries, a new Citizenship field added to describe policies related to the acquisition of citizenship and to the recognition of dual citizenship. Also, under the Country Name entry, *etymologies* (historical origins) added to explain how countries acquired their names. A new Electricity Access field added to introduce the Energy category. A Population Distribution field included in both the People and Society and the Geography sections. A major addition to the Transportation category is National Air Transport system with subfields on a country's *registered air carriers, inventory of registered aircraft, annual passenger traffic, and annual freight traffic.*

2017 In the Government category the Constitution entry revised and expanded with new subfields for *history* and *amendments.*

GUIDE TO COUNTRY PROFILES

These are the **Categories**, **Fields**, and **subfields** of information generally recorded for each country. For more information about each entry, see the **Definitions and Notes** section.

INTRODUCTION

Background:

GEOGRAPHY

Location:
Geographic coordinates:
Map references:
Area:
- total
- land
- water

Area - comparative:
Land boundaries:
- total
- border countries
- regional borders

Coastline:
Maritime claims:
- territorial sea
- exclusive economic zone
- contiguous zone
- continental shelf
- exclusive fishing zone

Climate:
Terrain:
Elevation:
- mean elevation
- elevation extremes

Natural resources:
Land use:
- agricultural land
- agricultural land: arable land
- agricultural land: permanent crops
- agricultural land: permanent pasture
- forest
- other

Irrigated land:
Population distribution:
Natural hazards:
Environment - current issues:
Environment - international agreements:
- party to
- signed, but not ratified

Geography - note:

PEOPLE AND SOCIETY

Population:
Nationality:
- noun
- adjective

Ethnic groups:
Languages:
Religions:
Demographic profile:
Age structure:
- 0-14 years
- 15-24 years
- 25-54 years
- 55-64 years
- 65 years and over

Dependency ratios:
- total dependency ratio
- youth dependency ratio
- elderly dependency ratio
- potential support ratio

Median age:
- total
- male
- female

Population growth rate:
Birth rate:
Death rate:
Net migration rate:
Population distribution:
Urbanization:
- urban population
- rate of urbanization

Major urban areas - population:
Sex ratio:
- at birth
- 0-14 years
- 15-24 years
- 25-54 years
- 55-64 years
- 65 years and over
- total population

Mother's mean age at first birth:
Maternal mortality rate:
Infant mortality rate:
- total
- male
- female

Life expectancy at birth:
- total population
- male
- female

Total fertility rate:
Contraceptive prevalence rate:
Health expenditures:
Physicians density:

Hospital bed density:
Drinking water source:
improved: urban
improved: rural
improved: total
unimproved: urban
unimproved: rural
unimproved: total
Sanitation facility access:
improved: urban
improved: rural
improved: total
unimproved: urban
unimproved: rural
unimproved: total
HIV/AIDS - adult prevalence rate:
HIV/AIDS - people living with HIV/AIDS:
HIV/AIDS - deaths:
Major infectious diseases:
degree of risk
food or waterborne diseases
vectorborne diseases
water contact diseases
animal contact diseases
respiratory diseases
soil contact diseases
aerosolized dust or soil contact diseases
Obesity - adult prevalence rate:
Children under the age of 5 years underweight:
Education expenditures:
Literacy:
definition
total population
male
female
School life expectancy (primary to tertiary education):
total
male
female
Unemployment, youth ages 15-24:
total
male
female
People - note:

GOVERNMENT

Country name:
conventional long form
conventional short form
local long form
local short form
former
abbreviation
etymology
Dependency status:
Government type:
Capital:
name
geographic coordinates
time difference
daylight saving time
capital
Administrative divisions:
Dependent areas:
Independence:
National holiday:
Constitution:
history
amendments
Legal system:
International law organization participation:
Citizenship:
citizenship by birth
citizenship by descent only
dual citizenship recognized
residency requirement for naturalization
Suffrage:
Executive branch:
chief of state
head of government
cabinet
elections/appointments
election results
head of state
Legislative branch:
description
elections
election results
Judicial branch:
highest courts
judge selection and term of office
subordinate courts
Political parties and leaders:
International organization participation:
Diplomatic representation in the US:
chief of mission
chancery
telephone
FAX
consulate(s) general
consulate(s)
embassy
honorary consulate(s)
Diplomatic representation from the US:
chief of mission
embassy
mailing address
telephone
FAX
consulate(s) general
branch office(s)
consulate(s)
Flag description:
National symbol(s):

National anthem:
name
lyrics/music
Government - note:

ECONOMY

Economy - overview:
GDP (purchasing power parity):
GDP (official exchange rate):
GDP - real growth rate:
GDP - per capita (PPP):
Gross national saving:
GDP - composition, by end use:
household consumption
government consumption
investment in fixed capital
investment in inventories
exports of goods and services
imports of goods and services
GDP - composition, by sector of origin:
agriculture
industry
services
Agriculture - products:
Industries:
Industrial production growth rate:
Labor force:
Labor force - by occupation:
agriculture
industry
services
industry and services
manufacturing
construction
commerce
other services
Unemployment rate:
Population below poverty line:
Household income or consumption by percentage share:
lowest 10%
highest 10%
Distribution of family income - Gini index:
Budget:
revenues
expenditures
Taxes and other revenues:
Budget surplus (+) or deficit (-):
Public debt:
Fiscal year:
Inflation rate (consumer prices):
Central bank discount rate:
Commercial bank prime lending rate:
Stock of narrow money:
Stock of broad money:
Stock of domestic credit:
Market value of publicly traded shares:
Current account balance:
Exports:
Exports - partners:
Exports - commodities:
Imports:
Imports - commodities:
Imports - partners:
Reserves of foreign exchange and gold:
Debt - external:
Stock of direct foreign investment - at home:
Stock of direct foreign investment - abroad:
Exchange rates:

ENERGY

Electricity access:
population without electricity
electrification - total population
electrification - urban areas
electrification - rural areas
Electricity - production:
Electricity - consumption:
Electricity - exports:
Electricity - imports:
Electricity - installed generating capacity:
Electricity - from fossil fuels:
Electricity - from nuclear fuels:
Electricity - from hydroelectric plants:
Electricity - from other renewable sources:
Crude oil - production:
Crude oil - exports:
Crude oil - imports:
Crude oil - proved reserves:
Refined petroleum products - production:
Refined petroleum products - consumption:
Refined petroleum products - exports:
Refined petroleum products - imports:
Natural gas - production:
Natural gas - consumption:
Natural gas - exports:
Natural gas - imports:
Natural gas - proved reserves:
Carbon dioxide emissions from consumption of energy:

COMMUNICATIONS

Telephones - fixed lines:
total subscriptions
subscriptions per 100 inhabitants
Telephones - mobile cellular:
total subscriptions
subscriptions per 100 inhabitants
Telephone system:
general assessment
domestic
international
Broadcast media:
Internet country code:
Internet users:

total
percent of population
Broadband - fixed subscriptions:
total
subscriptions per 100 inhabitants
Communications - note:

TRANSPORTATION

National air transport system:
number of registered air carriers
inventory of registered aircraft operated by air carriers
annual passenger traffic on registered air carriers
annual freight traffic on registered air carriers
Civil aircraft registration country code prefix:
Airports:
total
Airports - with paved runways:
total
over 3,047 m
2,438 to 3,047 m
1,524 to 2,437 m
914 to 1,523 m
under 914 m
Airports - with unpaved runways:
total
over 3,047 m
2,438 to 3,047 m
1,524 to 2,437 m
914 to 1,523 m
under 914 m
Heliports:
Pipelines:
Railways:
total
standard gauge
narrow gauge
broad gauge
dual gauge
Roadways:
total
paved
unpaved
urban
non-urban
Waterways:
Merchant marine:
total
by type
Ports and terminals:
major seaport(s)
oil terminal(s)
container port(s) (TEUs)
lake port(s)
LNG terminal(s) (export)
LNG terminal(s) (import)
river port(s)
dry bulk cargo port(s)
bulk cargo port(s)
Transportation - note:

MILITARY AND SECURITY

Military expenditures:
Military branches:
Military service age and obligation:
Maritime threats:
Military - note:

TERRORISM

Terrorist groups - home based:
Terrorist groups - foreign based:

TRANSNATIONAL ISSUES

Disputes - international:
Refugees and internally displaced persons:
refugees (country of origin)
IDPs
stateless persons
Trafficking in persons:
current situation
tier rating
Illicit drugs:

DEFINITIONS AND NOTES

ABBREVIATIONS

This information is included in **Appendix A: Abbreviations**, which includes all abbreviations and acronyms used in the *Factbook*, with their expansions.

ACRONYMS

An acronym is an abbreviation coined from the initial letter of each successive word in a term or phrase. In general, an acronym made up solely from the first letter of the major words in the expanded form is rendered in all capital letters (NATO from North Atlantic Treaty Organization; an exception would be ASEAN for Association of Southeast Asian Nations). In general, an acronym made up of more than the first letter of the major words in the expanded form is rendered with only an initial capital letter (Comsat from Communications Satellite Corporation; an exception would be NAM from Nonaligned Movement). Hybrid forms are sometimes used to distinguish between initially identical terms (ICC for International Chamber of Commerce and ICCt for International Criminal Court).

ADMINISTRATIVE DIVISIONS

This entry generally gives the numbers, designatory terms, and first-order administrative divisions as approved by the US Board on Geographic Names (BGN). Changes that have been reported but not yet acted on by the BGN are noted. Geographic names conform to spellings approved by the BGN with the exception of the omission of diacritical marks and special characters.

AGE STRUCTURE

This entry provides the distribution of the population according to age. Information is included by sex and age group as follows: *0-14 years (children), 15-24 years (early working age), 25-54 years (prime working age), 55-64 years (mature working age), 65 years and over (elderly)*. The age structure of a population affects a nation's key socioeconomic issues. Countries with young populations (high percentage under age 15) need to invest more in schools, while countries with older populations (high percentage ages 65 and over) need to invest more in the health sector. The age structure can also be used to help predict potential political issues. For example, the rapid growth of a young adult population unable to find employment can lead to unrest.

AGRICULTURE - PRODUCTS

This entry is an ordered listing of major crops and products starting with the most important.

AIRPORTS

This entry gives the total number of airports or airfields recognizable from the air. The runway(s) may be paved (concrete or asphalt surfaces) or unpaved (grass, earth, sand, or gravel surfaces) and may include closed or abandoned installations. Airports or airfields that are no longer recognizable (overgrown, no facilities, etc.) are not included. Note that not all airports have accommodations for refueling, maintenance, or air traffic control.

AIRPORTS - WITH PAVED RUNWAYS

This entry gives the total number of airports with paved runways (concrete or asphalt surfaces) by length. For airports with more than one runway, only the longest runway is included according to the following five groups - (1) *over 3,047 m* (over 10,000 ft), (2) *2,438 to 3,047 m* (8,000 to 10,000 ft), (3) *1,524 to 2,437 m* (5,000 to 8,000 ft), (4) *914 to 1,523 m* (3,000 to 5,000 ft), and (5) *under 914 m* (under 3,000 ft). Only airports with usable runways are included in this listing. Not all airports have facilities for refueling, maintenance, or air traffic control. The type aircraft capable of operating from a runway of a given length is dependent upon a number of factors including elevation of the runway, runway gradient, average maximum daily temperature at the airport, engine types, flap settings, and take-off weight of the aircraft.

AIRPORTS - WITH UNPAVED RUNWAYS

This entry gives the total number of airports with unpaved runways (grass, dirt, sand, or gravel surfaces) by length. For airports with more than one runway, only the longest runway is included according to the following five groups - (1) *over 3,047 m* (over 10,000 ft), (2) *2,438 to 3,047 m* (8,000 to 10,000 ft), (3) *1,524 to 2,437 m* (5,000 to 8,000 ft), (4) *914 to 1,523 m* (3,000 to 5,000 ft), and (5) *under 914 m* (under 3,000 ft). Only airports with usable runways are included in this listing. Not all airports have facilities for refueling, maintenance, or air traffic control. The type aircraft capable of operating from a runway of a given length is dependent upon a number of factors including elevation of the runway, runway gradient, average maximum daily temperature at the airport, engine types, flap settings, and take-off weight of the aircraft.

APPENDIXES

This section includes *Factbook*-related material by topic.

AREA

This entry includes three subfields. *Total area* is the sum of all land and water areas delimited by international boundaries and/or coastlines. *Land area* is the aggregate of all surfaces delimited by international boundaries and/or coastlines, excluding inland water bodies (lakes, reservoirs, rivers). *Water area* is the sum of the surfaces of all inland water bodies, such as lakes, reservoirs, or rivers, as delimited by international boundaries and/or coastlines.

AREA - COMPARATIVE

This entry provides an area comparison based on total area equivalents. Most entities are compared with the entire US or one of the 50 states based on area measurements (1990 revised) provided by the US Bureau of the Census. The smaller entities are compared with Washington, DC (178 sq km, 69 sq mi) or The Mall in Washington, DC (0.59 sq km, 0.23 sq mi, 146 acres).

BACKGROUND

This entry usually highlights major historic events and current issues and may include a statement about one or two key future trends.

BIRTH RATE

This entry gives the average annual number of births during a year per 1,000 persons in the population at midyear; also known as crude birth rate. The birth rate is usually the dominant factor in determining the rate of population growth. It depends on both the level of fertility and the age structure of the population.

BROADBAND - FIXED SUBSCRIPTIONS

This entry gives the total number of fixed-broadband subscriptions, as well as the number of subscriptions per 100 inhabitants. Fixed broadband is a physical wired connection to the Internet (e.g., coaxial cable, optical fiber) at speeds equal to or greater than 256 kilobits/second (256 kbit/s).

BROADCAST MEDIA

This entry provides information on the approximate number of public and private TV and radio stations in a country, as well as basic information on the availability of satellite and cable TV services.

BUDGET

This entry includes *revenues*, *expenditures*, and capital expenditures. These figures are calculated on an exchange rate basis, i.e., not in purchasing power parity (PPP) terms.

BUDGET SURPLUS (+) OR DEFICIT (-)

This entry records the difference between national government revenues and expenditures, expressed as a percent of GDP. A positive (+) number indicates that revenues exceeded expenditures (a budget surplus), while a negative (-) number indicates the reverse (a budget deficit). Normalizing the data, by dividing the budget balance by GDP, enables easy comparisons across countries and indicates whether a national government saves or borrows money. Countries with high budget deficits (relative to their GDPs) generally have more difficulty raising funds to finance expenditures, than those with lower deficits.

CAPITAL

This entry gives the *name* of the seat of government, its *geographic coordinates*, the *time difference* relative to **Coordinated Universal Time (UTC)** and the time observed in Washington, DC, and, if applicable, information on *daylight saving time* **(DST)**. Where appropriate, a special *note* has been added to highlight those countries that have multiple time zones.

CARBON DIOXIDE EMISSIONS FROM CONSUMPTION OF ENERGY

This entry is the total amount of carbon dioxide, measured in metric tons, released by burning fossil fuels in the process of producing and consuming energy.

CENTRAL BANK DISCOUNT RATE

This entry provides the annualized interest rate a country's central bank charges commercial, depository banks for loans to meet temporary shortages of funds.

CHILDREN UNDER THE AGE OF 5 YEARS UNDERWEIGHT

This entry gives the percent of children under five considered to be underweight. Underweight means weight-for-age is approximately 2 kg below for standard at age one, 3 kg below standard for ages two and three, and 4 kg below standard for ages four and five. This statistic is an indicator of the nutritional status of a community. Children who suffer from growth retardation as a result of poor diets and/or recurrent infections tend to have a greater risk of suffering illness and death.

CITIZENSHIP

This entry provides information related to the acquisition and exercise of citizenship; it includes four subfields:

citizenship by birth describes the acquisition of citizenship based on place of birth, known as *Jus soli*, regardless of the citizenship of parents.

citizenship by descent only describes the acquisition of citizenship based on the principle of *Jus sanguinis*, or by descent, where at least one parent is a citizen of the state and being born within the territorial limits of the state is not required. The majority of countries adhere to this practice. In some cases, citizenship is conferred through the father or mother exclusively.

dual citizenship recognized indicates whether a state permits a citizen to simultaneously hold citizenship in another state. Many states do not permit dual citizenship and the voluntary acquisition of citizenship in another country is grounds for revocation of citizenship. Holding dual citizenship makes an individual legally obligated to more than one state and can negate the normal consular protections afforded to citizens outside their original country of citizenship.

residency requirement for naturalization lists the length of time an applicant is required to live in a state before applying for naturalization. In most countries citizenship can be acquired through the legal process of naturalization. The requirements for naturalization vary by state but generally include no criminal record, good health, economic wherewithal, and a period of authorized residency in the state. This time period can vary enormously among states and is often used to make the acquisition of citizenship difficult or impossible.

CIVIL AIRCRAFT REGISTRATION COUNTRY CODE PREFIX

This entry provides the one- or two-character alphanumeric code indicating the nationality of civil aircraft. Article 20 of the Convention on International Civil Aviation (Chicago Convention), signed in 1944, requires that all aircraft engaged in international air navigation bear appropriate nationality marks. The aircraft registration number consists of two parts: a prefix consisting of a one- or two-character alphanumeric code indicating nationality and a registration suffix of one to five characters for the specific aircraft. The prefix codes are based upon radio call-signs allocated by the International Telecommunications Union (ITU) to each country. Since 1947, the International Civil Aviation Organization (ICAO) has managed code standards and their allocation.

CLIMATE

This entry includes a brief description of typical weather regimes throughout the year.

COASTLINE

This entry gives the total length of the boundary between the land area (including islands) and the sea.

COMMERCIAL BANK PRIME LENDING RATE

This entry provides a simple average of annualized interest rates commercial banks charge on new loans, denominated in the national currency, to their most credit-worthy customers.

COMMUNICATIONS

This category deals with the means of exchanging information and includes the telephone, radio, television, and Internet host entries.

COMMUNICATIONS - NOTE

This entry includes miscellaneous communications information of significance not included elsewhere.

CONSTITUTION

This entry provides information on a country's constitution and includes two subfields. The history subfield includes the dates of previous constitutions and the main steps and dates in formulating and implementing the latest constitution. For countries with 1-3 previous constitutions, the years are listed; for those with 4-9 previous, the entry is listed as "several previous," and for those with 10 or more, the entry is "many previous." The amendments subfield summarizes the process of amending a country's constitution – from proposal through passage – and the dates of amendments, which are treated in the same manner as the constitution dates. Where appropriate, summaries are composed from English-language translations of non-English constitutions, which derive from official or non-official translations or machine translators.

The main steps in creating a constitution and amending it usually include the following steps: proposal, drafting, legislative and/or executive branch review and approval, public referendum, and entry into law. In many countries this process is lengthy. Terms commonly used to describe constitutional changes are "amended," "revised," or "reformed." In countries such as South Korea and Turkmenistan, sources differ as to whether changes are stated as new constitutions or are amendments/revisions to existing ones.

A few countries including Canada, Israel, and the UK have no single constitution document, but have various written and unwritten acts, statutes, common laws, and practices that, when taken together, describe a body of fundamental principles or established precedents as to how their countries are governed. Some special regions (Hong Kong, Macau) and countries (Oman, Saudi Arabia) use the term "basic law" instead of constitution.

A number of self-governing dependencies and territories such as the Cayman Islands, Bermuda, and Gibraltar (UK), Greenland and Faroe Islands (Denmark), Aruba, Curacao, and Sint Maarten (Netherlands), and Puerto Rico and the Virgin Islands (US) have their own constitutions.

CONTRACEPTIVE PREVALENCE RATE

This field gives the percent of women of reproductive age (15-49) who are married or in union and are using, or whose sexual partner is using, a method of contraception according to the date of the most recent available data. The contraceptive prevalence rate is an indicator of health services, development, and women's empowerment. It is also useful in understanding, past, present, and future fertility trends, especially in developing countries.

COORDINATED UNIVERSAL TIME (UTC)

UTC is the international atomic time scale that serves as the basis of timekeeping for most of the world. The hours, minutes, and seconds expressed by UTC represent the time of day at the Prime Meridian (0º longitude) located near Greenwich, England as reckoned from midnight. UTC is calculated by the Bureau International des Poids et Measures (BIPM) in Sevres, France. The BIPM averages data collected from more than 200 atomic time and frequency standards located at about 50 laboratories worldwide. UTC is the basis for all civil time with the Earth divided into time zones expressed as positive or negative differences from UTC. UTC is also referred to as "Zulu time." See the Standard Time Zones of the World map included with the **Reference Maps**.

COUNTRY DATA CODES

See **Data codes**.

COUNTRY MAP

Most versions of the *Factbook* provide a country map in color. The maps were produced from the best information available at the time of preparation. Names and/or boundaries may have changed subsequently.

COUNTRY NAME

This entry includes all forms of the country's name approved by the US Board on Geographic Names (Italy is used as an example): *conventional long form* (Italian Republic), *conventional short form* (Italy), *local long form* (Repubblica Italiana), *local short form* (Italia), *former* (Kingdom of Italy), as well as the *abbreviation*. Also see the **Terminology** note.

CRUDE OIL - EXPORTS

This entry is the total amount of crude oil exported, in barrels per day (bbl/day).

CRUDE OIL - IMPORTS

This entry is the total amount of crude oil imported, in barrels per day (bbl/day).

CRUDE OIL - PRODUCTION

This entry is the total amount of crude oil produced, in barrels per day (bbl/day).

CRUDE OIL - PROVED RESERVES

This entry is the stock of proved reserves of crude oil, in barrels (bbl). Proved reserves are those quantities of petroleum which, by analysis of geological and engineering data, can be estimated with a high degree of confidence to be commercially recoverable from a given date forward, from known reservoirs and under current economic conditions.

CURRENT ACCOUNT BALANCE

This entry records a country's net trade in goods and services, plus net earnings from rents, interest, profits, and dividends, and net transfer payments (such as pension funds and worker remittances) to and from the rest of the world during the period specified. These figures are calculated on an exchange rate basis, i.e., not in purchasing power parity (PPP) terms.

DATA CODES

This information is presented in Appendix D: Cross-Reference List of Country Data Codes and Appendix E: Cross-Reference List of Hydrographic Data Codes.

DATE OF INFORMATION

In general, information available as of January in a given year is used in the preparation of the printed edition.

DAYLIGHT SAVING TIME (DST)

This entry is included for those entities that have adopted a policy of adjusting the official local time forward, usually one hour, from Standard Time during summer months. Such policies are most common in mid-latitude regions.

DEATH RATE

This entry gives the average annual number of deaths during a year per 1,000 population at midyear; also known as crude death rate. The death rate, while only a rough indicator of the mortality situation in a country, accurately indicates the current mortality impact on population growth. This indicator is significantly affected by age distribution, and most countries will eventually show a rise in the overall death rate, in spite of continued decline in mortality at all ages, as declining fertility results in an aging population.

DEBT - EXTERNAL

This entry gives the total public and private debt owed to nonresidents repayable in internationally accepted currencies, goods, or services. These figures are calculated on an exchange rate basis, i.e., not in purchasing power parity (PPP) terms.

DEMOGRAPHIC PROFILE

This entry describes a country's key demographic features and trends and how they vary among regional, ethnic, and socioeconomic sub-populations. Some of the topics addressed are population age structure, fertility, health, mortality, poverty, education, and migration.

DEPENDENCY RATIOS

Dependency ratios are a measure of the age structure of a population. They relate the number of individuals that are likely to be economically "dependent" on the support of others. Dependency ratios contrast the ratio of youths (ages 0-14) and the elderly (ages 65+) to the number of those in the working-age group (ages 15-64). Changes in the dependency ratio provide an indication of potential social support requirements resulting from changes in population age structures. As fertility levels decline, the dependency ratio initially falls because the proportion of youths decreases while the proportion of the population of working age increases. As fertility levels continue to decline, dependency ratios eventually increase because the proportion of the population of working age starts to decline and the proportion of elderly persons continues to increase.

total dependency ratio - The total dependency ratio is the ratio of combined youth population (ages 0-14) and elderly population (ages 65+) per 100 people of working age (ages 15-64). A high total dependency ratio indicates that the working-age population and the overall economy face a greater burden to support and provide social services for youth and elderly persons, who are often economically dependent.

youth dependency ratio - The youth dependency ratio is the ratio of the youth population (ages 0-14) per 100 people of working age (ages 15-64). A high youth dependency ratio indicates that a greater investment needs to be made in schooling and other services for children.

elderly dependency ratio - The elderly dependency ratio is the ratio of the elderly population (ages 65+) per 100 people of working age (ages 15-64). Increases in the elderly dependency ratio put added pressure on governments to fund pensions and healthcare.

potential support ratio - The potential support ratio is the number of working-age people (ages 15-64) per one elderly person (ages 65+). As a population ages, the potential support ratio tends to fall, meaning there are fewer potential workers to support the elderly.

DEPENDENCY STATUS

This entry describes the formal relationship between a particular nonindependent entity and an independent state.

DEPENDENT AREAS

This entry contains an alphabetical listing of all nonindependent entities associated in some way with a particular independent state.

DIPLOMATIC REPRESENTATION

The US Government has diplomatic relations with 190 independent states, including 188 of the 193 UN members (excluded UN members are Bhutan, Cuba, Iran, North Korea, and the US itself). In addition, the US has diplomatic relations with 2 independent states that are not in the UN, the Holy See and Kosovo, as well as with the EU.

DIPLOMATIC REPRESENTATION FROM THE US

This entry includes the *chief of mission*, *embassy* address, *mailing address*, *telephone* number, *FAX* number, *branch office* locations, *consulate general* locations, and *consulate* locations.

DIPLOMATIC REPRESENTATION IN THE US

This entry includes the *chief of mission, chancery address, telephone, FAX, consulate general* locations, and *consulate* locations. The use of the annotated title Appointed Ambassador refers to a new ambassador who has presented his/her credentials to the secretary of state but not the US president. Such ambassadors fulfill all diplomatic functions except meeting with or appearing at functions attended by the president until such time as they formally present their credentials at a White House ceremony.

DISPUTES - INTERNATIONAL

This entry includes a wide variety of situations that range from traditional bilateral boundary disputes to unilateral claims of one sort or another. Information regarding disputes over international terrestrial and maritime boundaries has been reviewed by the US Department of State. References to other situations involving borders or frontiers may also be included, such as resource disputes, geopolitical questions, or irredentist issues; however, inclusion does not necessarily constitute official acceptance or recognition by the US Government.

DISTRIBUTION OF FAMILY INCOME - GINI INDEX

This index measures the degree of inequality in the distribution of family income in a country. The index is calculated from the Lorenz curve, in which cumulative family income is plotted against the number of families arranged from the poorest to the richest. The index is the ratio of (a) the area between a country's Lorenz curve and the 45 degree helping line to (b) the entire triangular area under the 45 degree line. The more nearly equal a country's income distribution, the closer its Lorenz curve to the 45 degree line and the lower its Gini index, e.g., a Scandinavian country with an index of 25. The more unequal a country's income distribution, the farther its Lorenz curve from the 45 degree line and the higher its Gini index, e.g., a Sub-Saharan country with an index of 50. If income were distributed with perfect equality, the Lorenz curve would coincide with the 45 degree line and the index would be zero; if income were distributed with perfect inequality, the Lorenz curve would coincide with the horizontal axis and the right vertical axis and the index would be 100.

DRINKING WATER SOURCE

This entry provides information about access to improved or unimproved drinking water sources available to segments of the population of a country. *Improved* drinking water - use of any of the following sources: piped water into dwelling, yard, or plot; public tap or standpipe; tubewell or borehole; protected dug well; protected spring; or rainwater collection. *Unimproved* drinking water - use of any of the following sources: unprotected dug well; unprotected spring; cart with small tank or drum; tanker truck; surface water, which includes rivers, dams, lakes, ponds, streams, canals or irrigation channels; or bottled water.

ECONOMY

This category includes the entries dealing with the size, development, and management of productive resources, i.e., land, labor, and capital.

ECONOMY - OVERVIEW

This entry briefly describes the type of economy, including the degree of market orientation, the level of economic development, the most important natural resources, and the unique areas of specialization. It also characterizes major economic events and policy changes in the most recent 12 months and may include a statement about one or two key future macroeconomic trends.

EDUCATION EXPENDITURES

This entry provides the public expenditure on education as a percent of GDP.

ELECTRICITY - CONSUMPTION

This entry consists of total electricity generated annually plus imports and minus exports, expressed in kilowatt-hours. The discrepancy between the amount of electricity generated and/or imported and the amount consumed and/or exported is accounted for as loss in transmission and distribution.

ELECTRICITY - EXPORTS

This entry is the total exported electricity in kilowatt-hours.

ELECTRICITY - FROM FOSSIL FUELS

This entry measures the capacity of plants that generate electricity by burning fossil fuels (such as coal, petroleum products, and natural gas), expressed as a share of the country's total generating capacity.

ELECTRICITY - FROM HYDROELECTRIC PLANTS

This entry measures the capacity of plants that generate electricity by water-driven turbines, expressed as a share of the country's total generating capacity.

ELECTRICITY - FROM NUCLEAR FUELS

This entry measures the capacity of plants that generate electricity through radioactive decay of nuclear fuel, expressed as a share of the country's total generating capacity.

ELECTRICITY - FROM OTHER RENEWABLE SOURCES

This entry measures the capacity of plants that generate electricity by using renewable energy sources other than hydroelectric (including, for example, wind, waves, solar, and geothermal), expressed as a share of the country's total generating capacity.

ELECTRICITY - IMPORTS

This entry is the total imported electricity in kilowatt-hours.

ELECTRICITY - INSTALLED GENERATING CAPACITY

This entry is the total capacity of currently installed generators, expressed in kilowatts (kW), to produce electricity. A 10-kilowatt (kW) generator will produce 10 kilowatt hours (kWh) of electricity, if it runs continuously for one hour.

ELECTRICITY - PRODUCTION

This entry is the annual electricity generated expressed in kilowatt-hours. The discrepancy between the amount of electricity generated and/or imported and the amount consumed and/or exported is accounted for as loss in transmission and distribution.

ELECTRICITY ACCESS

This entry provides information on access to electricity. Electrification data – collected from industry reports, national surveys, and international sources – consists of four subfields. *Population without electricity* provides an estimate of the number of citizens that do not have access to electricity. *Electrification – total population* is the percent of a country's total population with access to electricity, *electrification – urban areas* is the percent of a country's urban population with access to electricity, while *electrification – rural areas* is the percent of a country's rural population with access to electricity. Due to differences in definitions and methodology from different sources, data quality may vary from country to country.

ELEVATION

This entry includes both the *mean elevation* and the *elevation extremes*.

ELEVATION EXTREMES

This entry includes both the highest point and the lowest point.

ENERGY

This category includes entries dealing with the production, consumption, import, and export of various forms of energy including electricity, crude oil, refined petroleum products, and natural gas.

ENTITIES

Some of the independent states, dependencies, areas of special sovereignty, and governments included in this publication are not independent, and others are not officially recognized by the US Government. "Independent state" refers to a people politically organized into a sovereign state with a definite territory. "Dependencies" and "areas of special sovereignty" refer to a broad category of political entities that are associated in some way with an independent state. "Country" names used in the table of contents or for page headings are usually the short-form names as approved by the US Board on Geographic Names and may include independent states, dependencies, and areas of special sovereignty, or other geographic entities. There are a total of 267 separate geographic entities in *The World Factbook* that may be categorized as follows:

INDEPENDENT STATES

195 Afghanistan, Albania, Algeria, Andorra, Angola, Antigua and Barbuda, Argentina, Armenia, Australia, Austria, Azerbaijan, The Bahamas, Bahrain, Bangladesh, Barbados, Belarus, Belgium, Belize, Benin, Bhutan, Bolivia, Bosnia and Herzegovina, Botswana, Brazil, Brunei, Bulgaria, Burkina Faso, Burma, Burundi, Cambodia, Cameroon, Canada, Cape Verde, Central African Republic, Chad, Chile, China, Colombia, Comoros, Democratic Republic of the Congo, Republic of the Congo, Costa Rica, Cote d'Ivoire, Croatia, Cuba, Cyprus, Czech Republic, Denmark, Djibouti, Dominica, Dominican Republic, Ecuador, Egypt, El Salvador, Equatorial Guinea, Eritrea, Estonia, Ethiopia, Fiji, Finland, France, Gabon, The Gambia, Georgia, Germany, Ghana, Greece, Grenada, Guatemala, Guinea, Guinea-Bissau, Guyana, Haiti, Holy See, Honduras, Hungary, Iceland, India, Indonesia, Iran, Iraq, Ireland, Israel, Italy, Jamaica, Japan, Jordan, Kazakhstan, Kenya, Kiribati, North Korea, South Korea, Kosovo, Kuwait, Kyrgyzstan, Laos, Latvia, Lebanon, Lesotho, Liberia, Libya, Liechtenstein, Lithuania, Luxembourg, Macedonia, Madagascar, Malawi, Malaysia, Maldives, Mali, Malta, Marshall Islands, Mauritania, Mauritius, Mexico, Federated States of Micronesia, Moldova,

Monaco, Mongolia, Montenegro, Morocco, Mozambique, Namibia, Nauru, Nepal, Netherlands, NZ, Nicaragua, Niger, Nigeria, Norway, Oman, Pakistan, Palau, Panama, Papua New Guinea, Paraguay, Peru, Philippines, Poland, Portugal, Qatar, Romania, Russia, Rwanda, Saint Kitts and Nevis, Saint Lucia, Saint Vincent and the Grenadines, Samoa, San Marino, Sao Tome and Principe, Saudi Arabia, Senegal, Serbia, Seychelles, Sierra Leone, Singapore, Slovakia, Slovenia, Solomon Islands, Somalia, South Africa, South Sudan, Spain, Sri Lanka, Sudan, Suriname, Swaziland, Sweden, Switzerland, Syria, Tajikistan, Tanzania, Thailand, Timor-Leste, Togo, Tonga, Trinidad and Tobago, Tunisia, Turkey, Turkmenistan, Tuvalu, Uganda, Ukraine, UAE, UK, US, Uruguay, Uzbekistan, Vanuatu, Venezuela, Vietnam, Yemen, Zambia, Zimbabwe

OTHER

2 Taiwan, European Union

DEPENDENCIES AND AREAS OF SPECIAL SOVEREIGNTY

6 Australia - Ashmore and Cartier Islands, Christmas Island, Cocos (Keeling) Islands, Coral Sea Islands, Heard Island and McDonald Islands, Norfolk Island

2 China - Hong Kong, Macau

2 Denmark - Faroe Islands, Greenland

8 France - Clipperton Island, French Polynesia, French Southern and Antarctic Lands, New Caledonia, Saint Barthelemy, Saint Martin, Saint Pierre and Miquelon, Wallis and Futuna

3 Netherlands - Aruba, Curacao, Sint Maarten

3 New Zealand - Cook Islands, Niue, Tokelau

3 Norway - Bouvet Island, Jan Mayen, Svalbard

17 UK - Akrotiri, Anguilla, Bermuda, British Indian Ocean Territory, British Virgin Islands, Cayman Islands, Dhekelia, Falkland Islands, Gibraltar, Guernsey, Jersey, Isle of Man, Montserrat, Pitcairn Islands, Saint Helena, South Georgia and the South Sandwich Islands, Turks and Caicos Islands

14 US - American Samoa, Baker Island*, Guam, Howland Island*, Jarvis Island*, Johnston Atoll*, Kingman Reef*, Midway Islands*, Navassa Island, Northern Mariana Islands, Palmyra Atoll*, Puerto Rico, Virgin Islands, Wake Island (* consolidated in United States Pacific Island Wildlife Refuges entry)

MISCELLANEOUS

6 Antarctica, Gaza Strip, Paracel Islands, Spratly Islands, West Bank, Western Sahara

OTHER ENTITIES

5 oceans - Arctic Ocean, Atlantic Ocean, Indian Ocean, Pacific Ocean, Southern Ocean

1 World

267 total

ENVIRONMENT - CURRENT ISSUES

This entry lists the most pressing and important environmental problems. The following terms and

abbreviations are used throughout the entry:

Acidification - the lowering of soil and water pH due to acid precipitation and deposition usually through precipitation; this process disrupts ecosystem nutrient flows and may kill freshwater fish and plants dependent on more neutral or alkaline conditions (see acid rain).

Acid rain - characterized as containing harmful levels of sulfur dioxide or nitrogen oxide; acid rain is damaging and potentially deadly to the earth's fragile ecosystems; acidity is measured using the pH scale where 7 is neutral, values greater than 7 are considered alkaline, and values below 5.6 are considered acid precipitation; note - a pH of 2.4 (the acidity of vinegar) has been measured in rainfall in New England.

Aerosol - a collection of airborne particles dispersed in a gas, smoke, or fog.

Afforestation - converting a bare or agricultural space by planting trees and plants; reforestation involves replanting trees on areas that have been cut or destroyed by fire.

Asbestos - a naturally occurring soft fibrous mineral commonly used in fireproofing materials and considered to be highly carcinogenic in particulate form.

Biodiversity - also biological diversity; the relative number of species, diverse in form and function, at the genetic, organism, community, and ecosystem level; loss of biodiversity reduces an ecosystem's ability to recover from natural or man-induced disruption.

Bio-indicators - a plant or animal species whose presence, abundance, and health reveal the general condition of its habitat.

Biomass - the total weight or volume of living matter in a given area or volume.

Carbon cycle - the term used to describe the exchange of carbon (in various forms, e.g., as carbon dioxide) between the atmosphere, ocean, terrestrial biosphere, and geological deposits.

Catchments - assemblages used to capture and retain rainwater and runoff; an important water management technique in areas with limited freshwater resources, such as Gibraltar.

DDT (dichloro-diphenyl-trichloro-ethane) - a colorless, odorless insecticide that has toxic effects on most animals; the use of DDT was banned in the US in 1972.

Defoliants - chemicals which cause plants to lose their leaves artificially; often used in agricultural practices for weed control, and may have detrimental impacts on human and ecosystem health.

Deforestation - the destruction of vast areas of forest (e.g., unsustainable forestry practices, agricultural and range land clearing, and the over exploitation of wood products for use as fuel) without planting new growth.

Desertification - the spread of desert-like conditions in arid or semi-arid areas, due to overgrazing, loss of agriculturally productive soils, or climate change.

Dredging - the practice of deepening an existing waterway; also, a technique used for collecting bottom-dwelling marine organisms (e.g., shellfish) or harvesting coral, often causing significant destruction of reef and ocean-floor ecosystems.

Drift-net fishing - done with a net, miles in extent, that is generally anchored to a boat and left to float with the tide; often results in an over harvesting and waste of large populations of non-commercial marine species (by-catch) by its effect of"sweeping the ocean clean."

Ecosystems - ecological units comprised of complex communities of organisms and their specific environments.

Effluents - waste materials, such as smoke, sewage, or industrial waste which are released into the environment, subsequently polluting it.

Endangered species - a species that is threatened with extinction either by direct hunting or habitat destruction.

Freshwater - water with very low soluble mineral content; sources include lakes, streams, rivers, glaciers, and underground aquifers.

Greenhouse gas - a gas that"traps" infrared radiation in the lower atmosphere causing surface warming; water vapor, carbon dioxide, nitrous oxide, methane, hydrofluorocarbons, and ozone are the primary greenhouse gases in the Earth's atmosphere.

Groundwater - water sources found below the surface of the earth often in naturally occurring reservoirs in permeable rock strata; the source for wells and natural springs.

Highlands Water Project - a series of dams constructed jointly by Lesotho and South Africa to redirect Lesotho's abundant water supply into a rapidly growing area in South Africa; while it is the largest infrastructure project in southern Africa, it is also the most costly and controversial; objections to the project include claims that it forces people from their homes, submerges farmlands, and squanders economic resources.

Inuit Circumpolar Conference (ICC) - represents the roughly 150,000 Inuits of Alaska, Canada, Greenland, and Russia in international environmental issues; a General Assembly convenes every three years to determine the focus of the ICC; the most current concerns are long-range transport of pollutants, sustainable development, and climate change.

Metallurgical plants - industries which specialize in the science, technology, and processing of metals; these plants produce highly concentrated and toxic wastes which can contribute to pollution of ground water and air when not properly disposed.

Noxious substances - injurious, very harmful to living beings.

Overgrazing - the grazing of animals on plant material faster than it can naturally regrow leading to the permanent loss of plant cover, a common effect of too many animals grazing limited range land.

Ozone shield - a layer of the atmosphere composed of ozone gas (O3) that resides approximately 25 miles above the Earth's surface and absorbs solar ultraviolet radiation that can be harmful to living organisms.

Poaching - the illegal killing of animals or fish, a great concern with respect to endangered or threatened species.

Pollution - the contamination of a healthy environment by man-made waste.

Potable water - water that is drinkable, safe to be consumed.

Salination - the process through which fresh (drinkable) water becomes salt (undrinkable) water; hence, desalination is the reverse process; also involves the accumulation of salts in topsoil caused by evaporation of excessive irrigation water, a process that can eventually render soil incapable of supporting crops.

Siltation - occurs when water channels and reservoirs become clotted with silt and mud, a side effect of deforestation and soil erosion.

Slash-and-burn agriculture - a rotating cultivation technique in which trees are cut down and burned in order to clear land for temporary agriculture; the land is used until its productivity declines at which point a new plot is selected and the process repeats; this practice is sustainable while population levels are low and time is permitted for regrowth of natural vegetation; conversely, where these conditions do not exist, the practice can have disastrous consequences for the environment.

Soil degradation - damage to the land's productive capacity because of poor agricultural practices such as the excessive use of pesticides or fertilizers, soil compaction from heavy equipment, or erosion of topsoil, eventually resulting in reduced ability to produce agricultural products.

Soil erosion - the removal of soil by the action of water or wind, compounded by poor agricultural practices, deforestation, overgrazing, and desertification.

Ultraviolet (UV) radiation - a portion of the electromagnetic energy emitted by the sun and naturally filtered in the upper atmosphere by the ozone layer; UV radiation can be harmful to living organisms and has been linked to increasing rates of skin cancer in humans.

Waterborne diseases - those in which bacteria survive in, and are transmitted through, water; always a serious threat in areas with an untreated water supply.

ENVIRONMENT - INTERNATIONAL AGREEMENTS

This entry separates country participation in international environmental agreements into two levels - *party to* and *signed, but not ratified.* Agreements are listed in alphabetical order by the abbreviated form of the full name.

ENVIRONMENTAL AGREEMENTS

This information is presented in Appendix C: Selected International Environmental Agreements, which includes the name, abbreviation, date opened for signature, date entered into force, objective, and parties by category.

ETHNIC GROUPS

This entry provides an ordered listing of ethnic groups starting with the largest and normally includes the percent of total population.

EXCHANGE RATES

This entry provides the average annual price of a country's monetary unit for the time period specified, expressed in units of local currency per US dollar, as determined by international market forces or by official fiat. The International Organization for Standardization (ISO) 4217 alphabetic currency code for the national medium of exchange is presented in parenthesis. Closing daily exchange rates are not presented in *The World Factbook*, but are used to convert stock values - e.g., the market value of publicly traded shares - to US dollars as of the specified date.

EXECUTIVE BRANCH

This entry includes five subentries: *chief of state; head of government; cabinet; elections/appointments; election results. Chief of state* includes the name, title, and beginning date in office of the titular leader of the country who represents the state at official and ceremonial functions but may not be involved with the day-to-day activities of the government. *Head of government* includes the name, title of the top executive designated to manage the executive branch of the government, and the beginning date in office. *Cabinet* includes the official name of the executive branch's high-ranking body and the method of member selection. *Elections/appointments* includes the process for accession to office, date of the last election, and date of the next election. *Election results* includes each candidate's political affiliation, percent of direct popular vote or indirect legislative/parliamentary percent vote or vote count in the last election.

The executive branches in approximately 80% of the world's countries have separate chiefs of state and heads of government; for the remainder, the chief of state is also the head of government, such as in Argentina, Kenya, the Philippines, the US, and Venezuela. Chiefs of state in just over 100 countries are directly elected, most by majority popular vote; those in another 55 are indirectly elected by their national legislatures, parliaments, or electoral colleges. Another 29 countries have a monarch as the chief of state. In dependencies, territories, and collectivities of sovereign countries - except those of the US - representatives are appointed to serve as chiefs of state.

Heads of government in the majority of countries are appointed either by the president or the monarch or selected by the majority party in the legislative body. Excluding countries where the chief of state is also head of government, in only a few countries is the head of government directly elected through popular vote.

Most of the world's countries have cabinets, the majority of which are appointed by the chief of state or prime minister, many in consultation with each other or with the legislature. Cabinets in only about a dozen countries are elected solely by their legislative bodies.

EXPORTS

This entry provides the total US dollar amount of merchandise exports on an f.o.b. (free on board) basis. These figures are calculated on an exchange rate basis, i.e., not in purchasing power parity (PPP) terms.

EXPORTS - COMMODITIES

This entry provides a listing of the highest-valued exported products; it sometimes includes the percent of total dollar value.

EXPORTS - PARTNERS

This entry provides a rank ordering of trading partners starting with the most important; it sometimes includes the percent of total dollar value.

FISCAL YEAR

This entry identifies the beginning and ending months for a country's accounting period of 12 months, which often is the calendar year but which may begin in any month. All yearly references are for the calendar year (CY) unless indicated as a noncalendar fiscal year (FY).

FLAG DESCRIPTION

This entry provides a written flag description produced from actual flags or the best information available at the time the entry was written. The flags of independent states are used by their dependencies unless there is an officially recognized local flag. Some disputed and other areas do not have flags.

FLAG GRAPHIC

Most versions of the *Factbook* include a color flag at the beginning of the country profile. The flag graphics were produced from actual flags or the best information available at the time of preparation. The flags of independent states are used by their dependencies unless there is an officially recognized local flag. Some disputed and other areas do not have flags.

GDP (OFFICIAL EXCHANGE RATE)

This entry gives the gross domestic product (GDP) or value of all final goods and services produced within a nation in a given year. A nation's GDP at official exchange rates (OER) is the home-currency-denominated annual GDP figure divided by the bilateral average US exchange rate with that country in that year. The measure is simple to compute and gives a precise measure of the value of output. Many economists prefer this measure when gauging the economic power an economy maintains vis-à-vis its neighbors, judging that an exchange rate captures the purchasing power a nation enjoys in the international marketplace. Official exchange rates, however, can be artificially fixed and/or subject to manipulation - resulting in claims of the country having an under- or over-valued currency - and are not necessarily the equivalent of a market-determined exchange rate. Moreover, even if the official exchange rate is market-determined, market exchange rates are frequently established by a relatively small set of goods and services (the ones the country trades) and may not capture the value of the larger set of goods the country produces. Furthermore, OER-converted GDP is not well suited to comparing domestic GDP over time, since appreciation/depreciation from one year to the next will make the OER GDP value rise/fall regardless of whether home-currency-denominated GDP changed.

GDP (PURCHASING POWER PARITY)

This entry gives the gross domestic product (GDP) or value of all final goods and services produced within a nation in a given year. A nation's GDP at purchasing power parity (PPP) exchange rates is the sum value of all goods and services produced in the country valued at prices prevailing in the United States in the year noted. This is the measure most economists prefer when looking at per-capita welfare and when comparing living conditions or use of resources across countries. The measure is difficult to compute, as a US dollar value has to be assigned to all goods and services in the country regardless of whether these goods and services have a direct equivalent in the United States (for example, the value of an ox-cart or non-US military equipment); as a result, PPP estimates for some countries are based on a small and sometimes different set of goods and services. In addition, many countries do not formally participate in the World Bank's PPP project that calculates these measures, so the resulting GDP estimates for these countries may lack precision. For many developing countries, PPP-based GDP measures are multiples of the official exchange rate (OER) measure. The differences between the OER- and PPP-denominated GDP values for most of the wealthy industrialized countries are generally much smaller.

GDP - COMPOSITION, BY END USE

This entry shows who does the spending in an economy: consumers, businesses, government, and foreigners. The distribution gives the percentage contribution to total GDP of *household consumption, government consumption, investment in fixed capital, investment in inventories, exports of goods and services, and imports of goods and services*, and will total 100 percent of GDP if the data are complete.

household consumption consists of expenditures by resident households, and by nonprofit institutions that serve households, on goods and services that are consumed by individuals. This includes consumption of both domestically produced and foreign goods and services.

government consumption consists of government expenditures on goods and services. These figures exclude government transfer payments, such as interest on debt, unemployment, and social security, since such payments are not made in exchange for goods and services supplied.

investment in fixed capital consists of total business spending on fixed assets, such as factories, machinery, equipment, dwellings, and inventories of raw materials, which provide the basis for future production. It is measured gross of the depreciation of the assets, i.e., it includes investment that merely replaces worn-out or scrapped capital. Earlier editions of *The World Factbook* referred to this concept as Investment (gross fixed) and that data now have been moved to this new field.

investment in inventories consists of net changes to the stock of outputs that are still held by the units that produce them, awaiting further sale to an end user, such as automobiles sitting on a dealer's lot or groceries on the store shelves. This figure may be positive or negative. If the stock of unsold output increases during the relevant time period, *investment in inventories* is positive, but, if the stock of unsold goods declines, it will be negative. *Investment in inventories* normally is an early indicator of the state of the economy. If the stock of unsold items increases unexpectedly – because people stop buying - the economy may be entering a recession; but if the stock of unsold items falls - and goods "go flying off the shelves" - businesses normally try to replace those stocks, and the economy is likely to accelerate.

exports of goods and services consist of sales, barter, gifts, or grants of goods and services from residents to nonresidents.

imports of goods and services consist of purchases, barter, or receipts of gifts, or grants of goods and services by residents from nonresidents. *Exports* are treated as a positive item, while imports are treated as a negative item. In a purely accounting sense, *imports* have no direct impact on GDP, which only measures output of the domestic economy. Imports are entered as a negative item to offset the fact that the expenditure figures for consumption, investment, government, and exports also include expenditures on imports. These imports contribute directly to foreign GDP but only indirectly to domestic GDP. Because of this negative offset for imports of goods and services, the sum of the other five items, excluding imports, will always total more than 100 percent of GDP. A surplus of exports of goods and services over imports indicates an economy is investing abroad, while a deficit indicates an economy is borrowing from abroad.

GDP - COMPOSITION, BY SECTOR OF ORIGIN

This entry shows where production takes place in an economy. The distribution gives the percentage contribution of *agriculture, industry*, and *services* to total GDP, and will total 100 percent of GDP if the data are complete. Agriculture includes farming, fishing, and forestry. Industry includes mining, manufacturing, energy production, and construction. Services cover government activities, communications, transportation, finance, and all other private economic activities that do not produce material goods.

GDP - PER CAPITA (PPP)

This entry shows GDP on a purchasing power parity basis divided by population as of 1 July for the same year.

GDP - REAL GROWTH RATE

This entry gives GDP growth on an annual basis adjusted for inflation and expressed as a percent. The growth rates are year-over-year, and not compounded.

GDP METHODOLOGY

In the **Economy** category, GDP dollar estimates for countries are reported both on an official exchange rate (OER) and a purchasing power parity (PPP) basis. Both measures contain information that is useful to the reader. The PPP method involves the use of standardized international dollar price weights, which are applied to the quantities of final goods and services produced in a given economy. The data derived from the PPP method probably provide the best available starting point for comparisons of economic strength and well-being between countries. In contrast, the currency exchange rate method involves a variety of international and domestic financial forces that may not capture the value of domestic output. Whereas PPP estimates for OECD countries are quite reliable, PPP estimates for developing countries are often rough approximations. In developing countries with weak currencies, the exchange rate estimate of GDP in dollars is typically one-fourth to one-half the PPP estimate. Most of the GDP estimates for developing countries are based on extrapolation of PPP numbers published by the UN International Comparison Program (UNICP) and by Professors Robert Summers and Alan Heston of the University of Pennsylvania and their colleagues. GDP derived using the OER method should be used for the purpose of calculating the share of items such as exports, imports, military expenditures, external debt, or the current account balance, because the dollar values presented in the *Factbook* for these items have been converted at official exchange rates, not at PPP. One should use the OER GDP figure to calculate the proportion of, say, Chinese defense expenditures in GDP, because that share will be the same as one calculated in local currency units. Comparison of OER GDP with PPP GDP may also indicate whether a currency is over- or under-valued. If OER GDP is smaller than PPP GDP, the official exchange rate may be undervalued, and vice versa. However, there is no strong historical evidence that market exchange rates move in the direction implied by the PPP rate, at least not in the short- or medium-term. Note: the numbers for GDP and other economic data should not be chained together from successive volumes of the *Factbook* because of changes in the US dollar measuring rod, revisions of data by statistical agencies, use of new or different sources of information, and changes in national statistical methods and practices.

GEOGRAPHIC COORDINATES

This entry includes rounded latitude and longitude figures for the centroid or center point of a country expressed in degrees and minutes; it is based on the locations provided in the Geographic Names Server (GNS), maintained by the National Geospatial-Intelligence Agency on behalf of the US Board on Geographic Names.

GEOGRAPHIC NAMES

This information is presented in Appendix F: Cross Reference List of Geographic Names. It includes a listing of various alternate names, former names, local names, and regional names referenced to one or more related *Factbook* entries. Spellings are normally, but not always, those approved by the US Board on Geographic Names (BGN). Alternate names and additional information are included in parentheses.

GEOGRAPHY

This category includes the entries dealing with the natural environment and the effects of human activity.

GEOGRAPHY - NOTE

This entry includes miscellaneous geographic information of significance not included elsewhere.

GINI INDEX

See entry for **Distribution of family income - Gini index**

GNP

Gross national product (GNP) is the value of all final goods and services produced within a nation in a given year, plus income earned by its citizens abroad, minus income earned by foreigners from domestic production. The *Factbook*, following current practice, uses GDP rather than GNP to measure national production. However, the user must realize that in certain countries net remittances from citizens working abroad may be important to national well-being.

GOVERNMENT

This category includes the entries dealing with the system for the adoption and administration of public policy.

GOVERNMENT - NOTE

This entry includes miscellaneous government information of significance not included elsewhere.

GOVERNMENT TYPE

This entry gives the basic form of government. Definitions of the major governmental terms are as follows. (Note that for some countries more than one definition applies.):

Absolute monarchy - a form of government where the monarch rules unhindered, i.e., without any laws, constitution, or legally organized opposition.

Anarchy - a condition of lawlessness or political disorder brought about by the absence of governmental authority.

Authoritarian - a form of government in which state authority is imposed onto many aspects of citizens' lives.

Commonwealth - a nation, state, or other political entity founded on law and united by a compact of the people for the common good.

Communist - a system of government in which the state plans and controls the economy and a single - often authoritarian - party holds power; state controls are imposed with the elimination of private ownership of property or capital while claiming to make progress toward a higher social order in which all goods are equally shared by the people (i.e., a classless society).

Confederacy (Confederation) - a union by compact or treaty between states, provinces, or territories, that creates a central government with limited powers; the constituent entities retain supreme authority over all matters except those delegated to the central government.

Constitutional - a government by or operating under an authoritative document (constitution) that sets forth the system of fundamental laws and principles that determines the nature, functions, and limits of that government.

Constitutional democracy - a form of government in which the sovereign power of the people is spelled out in a governing constitution.

Constitutional monarchy - a system of government in which a monarch is guided by a constitution whereby his/her rights, duties, and responsibilities are spelled out in written law or by custom.

Democracy - a form of government in which the supreme power is retained by the people, but which is usually exercised indirectly through a system of representation and delegated authority periodically renewed.

Democratic republic - a state in which the supreme power rests in the body of citizens entitled to vote for officers and representatives responsible to them.

Dictatorship - a form of government in which a ruler or small clique wield absolute power (not restricted by a constitution or laws).

Ecclesiastical - a government administrated by a church.

Emirate - similar to a monarchy or sultanate, but a government in which the supreme power is in the hands of an emir (the ruler of a Muslim state); the emir may be an absolute overlord or a sovereign with constitutionally limited authority.

Federal (Federation) - a form of government in which sovereign power is formally divided - usually by means of a constitution - between a central authority and a number of constituent regions (states, colonies, or provinces) so that each region retains some management of its internal affairs; differs from a confederacy in that the central government exerts influence directly upon both individuals as well as upon the regional units.

Federal republic - a state in which the powers of the central government are restricted and in which the component parts (states, colonies, or provinces) retain a degree of self-government; ultimate sovereign power rests with the voters who chose their governmental representatives.

Islamic republic - a particular form of government adopted by some Muslim states; although such a state is, in theory, a theocracy, it remains a republic, but its laws are required to be compatible with the laws of Islam.

Maoism - the theory and practice of Marxism-Leninism developed in China by Mao Zedong (Mao Tse-tung), which states that a continuous revolution is necessary if the leaders of a communist state are to keep in touch with the people.

Marxism - the political, economic, and social principles espoused by 19th century economist Karl Marx; he viewed the struggle of workers as a progression of historical forces that would proceed from a class struggle of the proletariat (workers) exploited by capitalists (business owners), to a socialist"dictatorship of the proletariat," to, finally, a classless society - Communism.

Marxism-Leninism - an expanded form of communism developed by Lenin from doctrines of Karl Marx; Lenin saw imperialism as the final stage of capitalism and shifted the focus of workers' struggle from developed to underdeveloped countries.

Monarchy - a government in which the supreme power is lodged in the hands of a monarch who reigns over a state or territory, usually for life and by hereditary right; the monarch may be either a sole absolute ruler or a sovereign - such as a king, queen, or prince - with constitutionally limited authority.

Oligarchy - a government in which control is exercised by a small group of individuals whose authority generally is based on wealth or power.

Parliamentary democracy - a political system in which the legislature (parliament) selects the government - a prime minister, premier, or chancellor along with the cabinet ministers - according to party strength as expressed in elections; by this system, the government acquires a dual responsibility: to the people as well as to the parliament.

Parliamentary government (Cabinet-Parliamentary government) - a government in which members of an executive branch (the cabinet and its leader - a prime minister, premier, or chancellor) are nominated to their positions by a legislature or parliament, and are directly responsible to it; this type of government can be dissolved at will by the parliament (legislature) by means of a no confidence vote or the leader of the cabinet may dissolve the parliament if it can no longer function.

Parliamentary monarchy - a state headed by a monarch who is not actively involved in policy formation or implementation (i.e., the exercise of sovereign powers by a monarch in a ceremonial capacity); true governmental leadership is carried out by a cabinet and its head - a prime minister, premier, or chancellor - who are drawn from a legislature (parliament).

Presidential - a system of government where the executive branch exists separately from a legislature (to which it is generally not accountable).

Republic - a representative democracy in which the people's elected deputies (representatives), not the people themselves, vote on legislation.

Socialism - a government in which the means of planning, producing, and distributing goods is controlled by a central government that theoretically seeks a more just and equitable distribution of property and labor; in actuality, most socialist governments have ended up being no more than dictatorships over workers by a ruling elite.

Sultanate - similar to a monarchy, but a government in which the supreme power is in the hands of a sultan (the head of a Muslim state); the sultan may be an absolute ruler or a sovereign with constitutionally limited authority.

Theocracy - a form of government in which a Deity is recognized as the supreme civil ruler, but the Deity's laws are interpreted by ecclesiastical authorities (bishops, mullahs, etc.); a government subject to religious authority.

Totalitarian - a government that seeks to subordinate the individual to the state by controlling not only all political and economic matters, but also the attitudes, values, and beliefs of its population.

GREENWICH MEAN TIME (GMT)

The mean solar time at the Greenwich Meridian, Greenwich, England, with the hours and days, since 1925, reckoned from midnight. GMT is now a historical term having been replaced by UTC on 1 January 1972. See **Coordinated Universal Time**.

GROSS DOMESTIC PRODUCT

See **GDP**

GROSS NATIONAL PRODUCT

See **GNP**

GROSS NATIONAL SAVING

Gross national saving is derived by deducting final consumption expenditure (household plus government) from Gross national disposable income, and consists of personal saving, plus business saving (the sum of the capital consumption allowance and retained business profits), plus government saving (the excess of tax revenues over expenditures), but excludes foreign saving (the excess of imports of goods and services over exports). The figures are presented as a percent of GDP. A negative number indicates that the economy as a whole is spending more income than it produces, thus drawing down national wealth (dissaving).

GROSS WORLD PRODUCT

See **GWP**

GWP

This entry gives the gross world product (GWP) or aggregate value of all final goods and services produced worldwide in a given year.

HEALTH EXPENDITURES

This entry provides the total expenditure on health as a percentage of GDP. Health expenditures are broadly defined as activities performed either by institutions or individuals through the application of medical, paramedical, and/or nursing knowledge and technology, the primary purpose of which is to promote, restore, or maintain health.

HELIPORTS

This entry gives the total number of heliports with hard-surface runways, helipads, or landing areas that support routine sustained helicopter operations exclusively and have support facilities including one or more of the following facilities: lighting, fuel, passenger handling, or maintenance. It includes former airports used exclusively for helicopter operations but excludes heliports limited to day operations and natural clearings that could support helicopter landings and takeoffs.

HIV/AIDS - ADULT PREVALENCE RATE

This entry gives an estimate of the percentage of adults (aged 15-49) living with HIV/AIDS. The adult prevalence rate is calculated by dividing the estimated number of adults living with HIV/AIDS at yearend by the total adult population at yearend.

HIV/AIDS - DEATHS

This entry gives an estimate of the number of adults and children who died of AIDS during a given calendar year.

HIV/AIDS - PEOPLE LIVING WITH HIV/AIDS

This entry gives an estimate of all people (adults and children) alive at yearend with HIV infection, whether or not they have developed symptoms of AIDS.

HOSPITAL BED DENSITY

This entry provides the number of hospital beds per 1,000 people; it serves as a general measure of inpatient service availability. Hospital beds include inpatient beds available in public, private, general, and specialized hospitals and rehabilitation centers. In most cases, beds for both acute and chronic care are included. Because the level of inpatient services required for individual countries depends on several factors - such as demographic issues and the burden of disease - there is no global target for the number of hospital beds per country. So, while 2 beds per 1,000 in one country may be sufficient, 2 beds per 1,000 in another may be woefully inadequate because of the number of people hospitalized by disease.

HOUSEHOLD INCOME OR CONSUMPTION BY PERCENTAGE SHARE

Data on household income or consumption come from household surveys, the results adjusted for household size. Nations use different standards and procedures in collecting and adjusting the data. Surveys based on income will normally show a more unequal distribution than surveys based on consumption. The quality of surveys is improving with time, yet caution is still necessary in making inter-country comparisons.

HYDROGRAPHIC DATA CODES

See **Data codes**

ILLICIT DRUGS

This entry gives information on the five categories of illicit drugs - narcotics, stimulants, depressants (sedatives), hallucinogens, and cannabis. These categories include many drugs legally produced and prescribed by doctors as well as those illegally produced and sold outside of medical channels.

Cannabis (*Cannabis sativa*) is the common hemp plant, which provides hallucinogens with some sedative properties, and includes marijuana (pot, Acapulco gold, grass, reefer), tetrahydrocannabinol (THC, Marinol), hashish (hash), and hashish oil (hash oil).

Coca (mostly *Erythroxylum coca*) is a bush with leaves that contain the stimulant used to make cocaine. Coca is not to be confused with cocoa, which comes from cacao seeds and is used in making chocolate, cocoa, and cocoa butter.

Cocaine is a stimulant derived from the leaves of the coca bush.

Depressants (sedatives) are drugs that reduce tension and anxiety and include chloral hydrate, barbiturates (Amytal, Nembutal, Seconal, phenobarbital), benzodiazepines (Librium, Valium), methaqualone (Quaalude), glutethimide (Doriden), and others (Equanil, Placidyl, Valmid).

Drugs are any chemical substances that effect a physical, mental, emotional, or behavioral change in an individual.

Drug abuse is the use of any licit or illicit chemical substance that results in physical, mental, emotional, or behavioral impairment in an individual.

Hallucinogens are drugs that affect sensation, thinking, self-awareness, and emotion. Hallucinogens include LSD (acid, microdot), mescaline and peyote (mexc, buttons, cactus), amphetamine variants (PMA, STP, DOB), phencyclidine (PCP, angel dust, hog), phencyclidine analogues (PCE, PCPy, TCP), and others (psilocybin, psilocyn).

Hashish is the resinous exudate of the cannabis or hemp plant (*Cannabis sativa*).
Heroin is a semisynthetic derivative of morphine.
Mandrax is a trade name for methaqualone, a pharmaceutical depressant.
Marijuana is the dried leaf of the cannabis or hemp plant (*Cannabis sativa*).
Methaqualone is a pharmaceutical depressant, referred to as mandrax in Southwest Asia and Africa.
Narcotics are drugs that relieve pain, often induce sleep, and refer to opium, opium derivatives, and synthetic substitutes. Natural narcotics include opium (paregoric, parepectolin), morphine (MS-Contin, Roxanol), codeine (Tylenol with codeine, Empirin with codeine, Robitussin AC), and thebaine. Semisynthetic narcotics include heroin (horse, smack), and hydromorphone (Dilaudid). Synthetic narcotics include meperidine or Pethidine (Demerol, Mepergan), methadone (Dolophine, Methadose), and others (Darvon, Lomotil).
Opium is the brown, gummy exudate of the incised, unripe seedpod of the opium poppy.
Opium poppy (*Papaver somniferum*) is the source for the natural and semisynthetic narcotics.
Poppy straw is the entire cut and dried opium poppy-plant material, other than the seeds. Opium is extracted from poppy straw in commercial operations that produce the drug for medical use.
Qat (kat, khat) is a stimulant from the buds or leaves of *Catha edulis* that is chewed or drunk as tea.
Quaaludes is the North American slang term for methaqualone, a pharmaceutical depressant.
Stimulants are drugs that relieve mild depression, increase energy and activity, and include cocaine (coke, snow, crack), amphetamines (Desoxyn, Dexedrine), ephedrine, ecstasy (clarity, essence, doctor, Adam), phenmetrazine (Preludin), methylphenidate (Ritalin), and others (Cylert, Sanorex, Tenuate).

IMPORTS

This entry provides the total US dollar amount of merchandise imports on a c.i.f. (cost, insurance, and freight) or f.o.b. (free on board) basis. These figures are calculated on an exchange rate basis, i.e., not in purchasing power parity (PPP) terms.

IMPORTS - COMMODITIES

This entry provides a listing of the highest-valued imported products; it sometimes includes the percent of total dollar value.

IMPORTS - PARTNERS

This entry provides a rank ordering of trading partners starting with the most important; it sometimes includes the percent of total dollar value.

INDEPENDENCE

For most countries, this entry gives the date that sovereignty was achieved and from which nation, empire, or trusteeship. For the other countries, the date given may not represent "independence" in the strict sense, but rather some significant nationhood event such as the traditional founding date or the date of unification, federation, confederation, establishment, fundamental change in the form of government, or state succession. For a number of countries, the establishment of statehood was a lengthy evolutionary process occurring over decades or even centuries. In such cases, several significant dates are cited. Dependent areas include the notation "none" followed by the nature of their dependency status. Also see the **Terminology** note.

INDUSTRIAL PRODUCTION GROWTH RATE

This entry gives the annual percentage increase in industrial production (includes manufacturing, mining, and construction).

INDUSTRIES

This entry provides a rank ordering of industries starting with the largest by value of annual output.

INFANT MORTALITY RATE

This entry gives the number of deaths of infants under one year old in a given year per 1,000 live births in the same year. This rate is often used as an indicator of the level of health in a country.

INFLATION RATE (CONSUMER PRICES)

This entry furnishes the annual percent change in consumer prices compared with the previous year's consumer prices.

INTERNATIONAL DISPUTES

see **Disputes - international**

INTERNATIONAL LAW ORGANIZATION PARTICIPATION

This entry includes information on a country's acceptance of jurisdiction of the International Court of Justice (ICJ) and of the International Criminal Court (ICCt); 59 countries have accepted ICJ jurisdiction with reservations and 11 have accepted ICJ jurisdiction without reservations; 122 countries have accepted ICCt jurisdiction. Appendix B: International Organizations and Groups explains the differing mandates of the ICJ and ICCt.

INTERNATIONAL ORGANIZATION PARTICIPATION

This entry lists in alphabetical order by abbreviation those international organizations in which the subject country is a member or participates in some other way.

INTERNATIONAL ORGANIZATIONS

This information is presented in Appendix B: International Organizations and Groups which includes the name, abbreviation, date established, aim, and members by category.

INTERNET COUNTRY CODE

This entry includes the two-letter codes maintained by the International Organization for Standardization (ISO) in the ISO 3166 Alpha-2 list and used by the Internet Assigned Numbers Authority (IANA) to establish country-coded top-level domains (ccTLDs).

INTERNET USERS

This entry gives the *total* number of individuals within a country who can access the Internet at home, via any device type (computer or mobile) and connection. The *percent of population* with Internet access (i.e., the penetration rate) helps gauge how widespread Internet use is within a country. Statistics vary from country to country and may include users who access the Internet at least several times a week to those who access it only once within a period of several months.

INTRODUCTION

This category includes one entry, **Background**.

INVESTMENT (GROSS FIXED)

This entry records total business spending on fixed assets, such as factories, machinery, equipment, dwellings, and inventories of raw materials, which provide the basis for future production. It is measured gross of the depreciation of the assets, i.e., it includes investment that merely replaces worn-out or scrapped capital.

IRRIGATED LAND

This entry gives the number of square kilometers of land area that is artificially supplied with water.

JUDICIAL BRANCH

This entry includes three subfields. The *highest court(s)* subfield includes the name(s) of a country's highest level court(s), the number and titles of the judges, and the types of cases heard by the court, which commonly are based on civil, criminal, administrative, and constitutional law. A number of countries have separate constitutional courts. The *judge selection and term of office* subfield includes the organizations and associated officials responsible for nominating and appointing judges, and a brief description of the process. The selection process can be indicative of the independence of a country's court system from other branches of its government. Also included in this subfield are judges' tenures, which can range from a few years, to a specified retirement age, to lifelong appointments. The *subordinate courts* subfield lists the courts lower in the hierarchy of a country's court system. A few countries with federal-style governments, such as Brazil, Canada, and the US, in addition to their federal court, have separate state- or province-level court systems, though generally the two systems interact.

LABOR FORCE

This entry contains the total labor force figure.

LABOR FORCE - BY OCCUPATION

This entry lists the percentage distribution of the labor force by sector of occupation. *Agriculture* includes farming, fishing, and forestry. *Industry* includes mining, manufacturing, energy production, and construction. *Services* cover government activities, communications, transportation, finance, and all other economic activities that do not produce material goods. The distribution will total less than 100 percent if the data are incomplete and may range from 99-101 percent due to rounding.

LAND BOUNDARIES

This entry contains the *total* length of all land boundaries and the individual lengths for each of the contiguous *border countries*. When available, official lengths published by national statistical agencies are used. Because surveying methods may differ, country border lengths reported by contiguous countries may differ.

LAND USE

This entry contains the percentage shares of total land area for three different types of land use: *agricultural land, forest, and other*; *agricultural land* is further divided into *arable land* - land cultivated for crops like wheat, maize, and rice that are replanted after each harvest, *permanent crops* - land cultivated for crops like citrus, coffee, and rubber that are not replanted after each harvest, and includes land under flowering shrubs, fruit trees, nut trees, and vines, and *permanent pastures* and meadows – land used for at least five years or more to grow herbaceous forage, either cultivated or growing naturally; *forest* area is land spanning more than 0.5 hectare with trees higher than five meters and a canopy cover of more than 10% to include windbreaks, shelterbelts, and corridors of trees greater than 0.5 hectare and at least 20 m wide; land classified as *other* includes built-up areas, roads and other transportation features, barren land, or wasteland.

LANGUAGES

This entry provides a listing of languages spoken in each country and specifies any that are official national or regional languages. When data is available, the languages spoken in each country are broken down according to the percent of the total population speaking each language as a first language. For those countries without available data, languages are listed in rank order based on prevalence, starting with the most-spoken language.

LEGAL SYSTEM

This entry provides the description of a country's legal system. A statement on judicial review of legislative acts is also included for a number of countries. The legal systems of nearly all countries are generally modeled upon elements of five main types: civil law (including French law, the Napoleonic Code, Roman law, Roman-Dutch law, and Spanish law); common law (including United State law); customary law; mixed or pluralistic law; and religious law (including Islamic law). An additional type of legal system - international law, which governs the conduct of independent nations in their relationships with one another - is also addressed below. The following list describes these legal systems, the countries or world regions where these systems are enforced, and a brief statement on the origins and major features of each.

Civil Law - The most widespread type of legal system in the world, applied in various forms in approximately 150 countries. Also referred to as European continental law, the civil law system is derived mainly from the Roman *Corpus Juris Civilus*, (Body of Civil Law), a collection of laws and legal interpretations compiled under the East Roman (Byzantine) Emperor Justinian I between A.D. 528 and 565. The major feature of civil law systems is that the laws are organized into systematic written codes. In civil law the sources recognized as authoritative are principally legislation - especially codifications in constitutions or statutes enacted by governments - and secondarily, custom. The civil law systems in some countries are based on more than one code.

Common Law - A type of legal system, often synonymous with"English common law," which is the system of England and Wales in the UK, and is also in force in approximately 80 countries formerly part of or influenced by the former British Empire. English common law reflects Biblical influences as well as remnants of law systems imposed by early conquerors including the Romans, Anglo-Saxons, and Normans. Some legal scholars attribute the formation of the English common law system to King Henry II (r.1154-1189). Until the time of his reign, laws customary among England's various manorial and ecclesiastical (church) jurisdictions were administered locally. Henry II established the king's court and designated that laws were "common" to the entire English realm. The foundation of English common law is "legal precedent" - referred to as *stare decisis*, meaning "to stand by things decided." In the English common law system, court judges are bound in their decisions in large part by the rules and other doctrines developed - and supplemented over time - by the judges of earlier English courts.

Customary Law - A type of legal system that serves as the basis of, or has influenced, the present-day laws in approximately 40 countries - mostly in Africa, but some in the Pacific islands, Europe, and the Near East. Customary law is also referred to as"primitive law," "unwritten law," "indigenous law," and "folk law." There is no single history of customary law such as that found in Roman civil law, English common law, Islamic law, or the Napoleonic Civil Code. The earliest systems of law in human society were customary, and usually developed in small agrarian and hunter-gatherer communities. As the term implies, customary law is based upon the customs of a community. Common attributes of customary legal systems are that they are seldom written down, they embody an organized set of rules regulating social relations, and they are agreed upon by members of the community. Although such law systems include sanctions for law infractions, resolution tends to be reconciliatory rather than punitive. A number of African states practiced customary law many centuries prior to colonial influences. Following colonization, such laws were written down and incorporated to varying extents into the legal systems imposed by their colonial powers.

European Union Law - A sub-discipline of international law known as"supranational law" in which the rights of sovereign nations are limited in relation to one another. Also referred to as the Law of the European Union or Community Law, it is the unique and complex legal system that operates in tandem with the laws of the 27 member states of the European Union (EU). Similar to federal states, the EU legal system ensures compliance from the member states because of the Union's decentralized political nature. The European Court of Justice (ECJ), established in 1952 by the Treaty of Paris, has been largely responsible for the development of EU law. Fundamental principles of European Union law include: *subsidiarity* - the notion that issues be handled by the smallest, lowest, or least centralized competent authority; *proportionality* - the EU may only act to the extent needed to achieve its objectives; *conferral* - the EU is a union of member states, and all its authorities are voluntarily granted by its members; *legal certainty* - requires that legal rules be clear and precise; and *precautionary principle* - a moral and political principle stating that if an action or policy might cause severe or irreversible harm to the public or to the environment, in the absence of a scientific consensus that harm would not ensue, the burden of proof falls on those who would advocate taking the action.

French Law - A type of civil law that is the legal system of France. The French system also serves as the basis for, or is mixed with, other legal systems in approximately 50 countries, notably in North Africa, the Near East, and the French territories and dependencies. French law is primarily codified or systematic written civil law. Prior to the French Revolution (1789-1799), France had no single national legal system. Laws in the northern areas of present-day France were mostly local customs based on privileges and exemptions granted by kings and feudal lords, while in the southern areas Roman law predominated. The introduction of the Napoleonic Civil Code during the reign of Napoleon I in the first decade of the 19th century brought major reforms to the French legal system, many of which remain part of France's current legal structure, though all have been extensively amended or redrafted to address a modern nation. French law distinguishes between"public law" and "private law." Public law relates to government, the French Constitution, public administration, and criminal law. Private law covers issues between private citizens or corporations. The most recent changes to the French legal system - introduced in the 1980s - were the decentralization laws, which transferred authority from centrally appointed government representatives to locally elected representatives of the people.

International Law - The law of the international community, or the body of customary rules and treaty rules accepted as legally binding by states in their relations with each other. International law differs from other legal systems in that it primarily concerns sovereign political entities. There are three separate disciplines of international law: public international law, which governs the relationship between provinces and international entities and includes treaty law, law of the sea, international criminal law, and international humanitarian law; private international law, which addresses legal jurisdiction; and supranational law - a legal framework wherein countries are bound by regional agreements in which the laws of the member countries are held inapplicable when in conflict with supranational laws. At present the European Union is the only entity under a supranational legal system. The term"international law" was coined by Jeremy Bentham in 1780 in his *Principles of Morals and Legislation*, though laws governing relations between states have been recognized from very early times (many centuries B.C.). Modern international law developed alongside the emergence and growth of the European nation-states beginning in the early 16th century. Other factors that influenced the development of international law included the revival of legal studies, the growth of international trade, and the practice of exchanging emissaries and establishing legations. The sources of International law are set out in Article 38-1 of the Statute of the International Court of Justice within the UN Charter.

Islamic Law - The most widespread type of religious law, it is the legal system enforced in over 30 countries, particularly in the Near East, but also in Central and South Asia, Africa, and Indonesia. In many countries Islamic law operates in tandem with a civil law system. Islamic law is embodied in the sharia, an Arabic word meaning"the right path." Sharia covers all aspects of public and private life and organizes them into five categories: obligatory, recommended, permitted, disliked, and forbidden. The primary sources of sharia law are the Qur'an, believed by Muslims to be the word of God revealed to the Prophet Muhammad by the angel Gabriel, and the Sunnah, the teachings of the Prophet and his works. In addition to these two primary sources, traditional Sunni Muslims recognize the consensus of Muhammad's companions and Islamic jurists on certain issues, called ijmas, and various forms of reasoning, including analogy by legal scholars, referred to as qiyas. Shia Muslims reject ijmas and qiyas as sources of sharia law.

Mixed Law - Also referred to as pluralistic law, mixed law consists of elements of some or all of the other main types of legal systems - civil, common, customary, and religious. The mixed legal systems of a number of countries came about when colonial powers overlaid their own legal systems upon colonized regions but retained elements of the colonies' existing legal systems.

Napoleonic Civil Code - A type of civil law, referred to as the Civil Code or *Code Civil des Francais*, forms part of the legal system of France, and underpins the legal systems of Bolivia, Egypt, Lebanon, Poland, and the US state of Louisiana. The Civil Code was established under Napoleon I, enacted in 1804, and officially designated the *Code Napoleon* in 1807. This legal system combined the Teutonic civil law tradition of the northern provinces of France with the Roman law tradition of the southern and eastern regions of the country. The Civil Code bears similarities in its arrangement to the Roman *Body of Civil Law* (see Civil Law above). As enacted in 1804, the Code addressed personal status, property, and the acquisition of property. Codes added over the following six years included civil procedures, commercial law, criminal law and procedures, and a penal code.

Religious Law - A legal system which stems from the sacred texts of religious traditions and in most cases professes to cover all aspects of life as a seamless part of devotional obligations to a transcendent, imminent, or deep philosophical reality. Implied as the basis of religious law is the concept of unalterability, because the word of God cannot be amended or legislated against by judges or governments. However, a detailed legal system generally requires human elaboration. The main types of religious law are sharia in Islam, halakha in Judaism, and canon law in some Christian groups. Sharia is the most widespread religious legal system (see Islamic Law), and is the sole system of law for countries including Iran, the Maldives, and Saudi Arabia. No country is fully governed by halakha, but Jewish people may decide to settle disputes through Jewish courts and be bound by their rulings. Canon law is not a divine law as such because it is not found in revelation. It is viewed instead as human law inspired by the word of God and applying the demands of that revelation to the actual situation of the church. Canon law regulates the internal ordering of the Roman Catholic Church, the Eastern Orthodox Church, and the Anglican Communion.

Roman Law - A type of civil law developed in ancient Rome and practiced from the time of the city's founding (traditionally 753 B.C.) until the fall of the Western Empire in the 5th century A.D. Roman law remained the legal system of the Byzantine (Eastern Empire) until the fall of Constantinople in 1453. Preserved fragments of the first legal text, known as the Law of the Twelve Tables, dating from the 5th century B.C., contained specific provisions designed to change the prevailing customary law. Early Roman law was drawn from custom and statutes; later, during the time of the empire, emperors asserted their authority as the ultimate source of law. The basis for Roman laws was the idea that the exact form - not the intention - of words or of actions produced legal consequences. It was only in the late 6th century A.D. that a comprehensive Roman code of laws was published (see Civil Law above). Roman law served as the basis of law systems developed in a number of continental European countries.

Roman-Dutch Law - A type of civil law based on Roman law as applied in the Netherlands. Roman-Dutch law serves as the basis for legal systems in seven African countries, as well as Guyana, Indonesia, and Sri Lanka. This law system, which originated in the province of Holland and expanded throughout the Netherlands (to be replaced by the French Civil Code in 1809), was instituted in a number of sub-Saharan African countries during the Dutch colonial period. The Dutch jurist/philosopher Hugo Grotius was the first to attempt to reduce Roman-Dutch civil law into a system in his *Jurisprudence of Holland* (written 1619-20, commentary published 1621). The Dutch historian/lawyer Simon van Leeuwen coined the term"Roman-Dutch law" in 1652.

Spanish Law - A type of civil law, often referred to as the Spanish Civil Code, it is the present legal system of Spain and is the basis of legal systems in 12 countries mostly in Central and South America, but also in southwestern Europe, northern and western Africa, and southeastern Asia. The Spanish Civil Code reflects a complex mixture of customary, Roman, Napoleonic, local, and modern codified law. The laws of the Visigoth invaders of Spain in the 5th to 7th centuries had the earliest major influence on Spanish legal system development. The Christian Reconquest of Spain in the 11th through 15th centuries witnessed the development of customary law, which combined canon (religious) and Roman law. During several centuries of Hapsburg and Bourbon rule, systematic recompilations of the existing national legal system were attempted, but these often conflicted with local and regional customary civil laws. Legal system development for most of the 19th century concentrated on formulating a national civil law system, which was finally enacted in 1889 as the Spanish Civil Code. Several sections of the code have been revised, the most recent of which are the penal code in 1989 and the judiciary code in 2001. The Spanish Civil Code separates public and private law. Public law includes constitutional law, administrative law, criminal law, process law, financial and tax law, and international public law. Private law includes civil law, commercial law, labor law, and international private law.

United States Law - A type of common law, which is the basis of the legal system of the United States and that of its island possessions in the Caribbean and the Pacific. This legal system has several layers, more possibly than in most other countries, and is due in part to the division between federal and state law. The United States was founded not as one nation but as a union of 13 colonies, each claiming independence from the British Crown. The US Constitution, implemented in 1789, began shifting power away from the states and toward the federal government, though the states today retain substantial legal authority. US law draws its authority from four sources: *constitutional law*, *statutory law*, *administrative regulations*, and *case law*. Constitutional law is based on the US Constitution and serves as the supreme federal law. Taken together with those of the state constitutions, these documents outline the general structure of the federal and state governments and provide the rules and limits of power. US statutory law is legislation enacted by the US Congress and is codified in the United States Code. The 50 state legislatures have similar authority to enact state statutes. Administrative law is the authority delegated to federal and state executive agencies. Case law, also referred to as common law, covers areas where constitutional or statutory law is lacking. Case law is a collection of judicial decisions, customs, and general principles that began in England centuries ago, that were adopted in America at the time of the Revolution, and that continue to develop today.

LEGISLATIVE BRANCH

This entry has three subfields. The *description* subfield provides the legislative structure (unicameral – single house; bicameral – an upper and a lower house); formal name(s); number of member seats; types of constituencies or voting districts (single seat, multi-seat, nationwide); electoral voting system(s); and member term of office. The elections subfield includes the dates of the last election and next election. The *election results* subfield lists *percent of vote by party/coalition* and *number of seats by party/coalition* in the last election (in bicameral legislatures, upper house results are listed first). In general, parties with less than four seats and less than 4 percent of the vote are aggregated and listed as "other," and non-party-affiliated seats are listed as "independent." Also, the entries for some countries include two sets of *percent of vote by party* and *seats by party*; the former reflects results following a formal election announcement, and the latter – following a mid-term or byelection – reflects changes in a legislature's political party composition.

Of the approximately 240 countries with legislative bodies, approximately two-thirds are unicameral, and the remainder, bicameral. The selection of legislative members is typically governed by a country's constitution and/or its electoral laws. In general, members are either directly elected by a country's eligible voters using a defined electoral system; indirectly elected or selected by its province, state, or department legislatures; or appointed by the country's executive body. Legislative members in many countries are selected both directly and indirectly, and the electoral laws of some countries reserve seats for women and various ethnic and minority groups.

Worldwide, the two predominant direct voting systems are plurality/majority and proportional representation. The most common of the several plurality/majority systems is simple majority vote, or first-past-the-post, in which the candidate receiving the most votes is elected. Countries' legislatures such as Bangladesh's Parliament, Malaysia's House of Representatives, and the United Kingdom's House of Commons use this system. Another common plurality/majority system – absolute majority or two-round – requires that candidates win at least 50 percent of the votes to be elected. If none of the candidates meets that vote threshold in the initial election, a second poll or"runoff" is held soon after for the two top vote getters, and the candidate receiving a simple vote majority is declared the winner. Examples of the two-round system are Haiti's Chamber of Deputies, Mali's National Assembly, and Uzbekistan's Legislative Chamber. Other plurality/majority voting systems, referred to as preferential voting and generally used in multi-seat constituencies, are block vote and single non-transferable vote, in which voters cast their ballots by ranking their candidate preferences from highest to lowest.

Proportional representation electoral systems – in contrast to plurality/majority systems – generally award legislative seats to political parties in approximate proportion to the number of votes each receives. For example, in a 100-member legislature, if Party A receives 50 percent of the total vote, Party B, 30 percent, and Party C, 20 percent, then Party A would be awarded 50 seats, Party B 30 seats, and Party C 20 seats. There are various forms of proportional representation and the degree of reaching proportionality varies. Some forms of proportional representation are focused solely on achieving the proportional representation of different political parties and voters cast ballots only for political parties, whereas in other forms, voters cast ballots for individual candidates within a political party.

Many countries - both unicameral and bicameral - use a mix of electoral methods, in which a portion of legislative seats are awarded using one system, such as plurality/majority, while the remaining seats are awarded by another system, such as proportional representation. Many countries with bicameral legislatures use different voting systems for the two chambers.

LIFE EXPECTANCY AT BIRTH

This entry contains the average number of years to be lived by a group of people born in the same year, if mortality at each age remains constant in the future. Life expectancy at birth is also a measure of overall quality of life in a country and summarizes the mortality at all ages. It can also be thought of as indicating the potential return on investment in human capital and is necessary for the calculation of various actuarial measures.

LITERACY

This entry includes a *definition* of literacy and Census Bureau percentages for the *total population*, *males*, and *females*. There are no universal definitions and standards of literacy. Unless otherwise specified, all rates are based on the most common definition - the ability to read and write at a specified age. Detailing the standards that individual countries use to assess the ability to read and write is beyond the scope of the *Factbook*. Information on literacy, while not a perfect measure of educational results, is probably the most easily available and valid for international comparisons. Low levels of literacy, and education in general, can impede the economic development of a country in the current rapidly changing, technology-driven world.

LOCATION

This entry identifies the country's regional location, neighboring countries, and adjacent bodies of water.

MAJOR INFECTIOUS DISEASES

This entry lists major infectious diseases likely to be encountered in countries where the risk of such diseases is assessed to be very high as compared to the United States. These infectious diseases represent risks to US government personnel traveling to the specified country for a period of less than three years. The **degree of risk** is assessed by considering the foreign nature of these infectious diseases, their severity, and the probability of being affected by the diseases present. The diseases listed do not necessarily represent the total disease burden experienced by the local population. The risk to an individual traveler varies considerably by the specific location, visit duration, type of activities, type of accommodations, time of year, and other factors. Consultation with a travel medicine physician is needed to evaluate individual risk and recommend appropriate preventive measures such as vaccines.

Diseases are organized into the following six exposure categories shown in italics *and listed in typical descending order of risk.* Note: The sequence of exposure categories listed in individual country entries may vary according to local conditions.

food or waterborne diseases acquired through eating or drinking on the local economy:

Hepatitis A - viral disease that interferes with the functioning of the liver; spread through consumption of food or water contaminated with fecal matter, principally in areas of poor sanitation; victims exhibit fever, jaundice, and diarrhea; 15% of victims will experience prolonged symptoms over 6-9 months; vaccine available.

Hepatitis E - water-borne viral disease that interferes with the functioning of the liver; most commonly spread through fecal contamination of drinking water; victims exhibit jaundice, fatigue, abdominal pain, and dark colored urine.

Typhoid fever - bacterial disease spread through contact with food or water contaminated by fecal matter or sewage; victims exhibit sustained high fevers; left untreated, mortality rates can reach 20%.

vectorborne diseases acquired through the bite of an infected arthropod:

Malaria - caused by single-cell parasitic protozoa *Plasmodium*; transmitted to humans via the bite of the female *Anopheles* mosquito; parasites multiply in the liver attacking red blood cells resulting in cycles of fever, chills, and sweats accompanied by anemia; death due to damage to vital organs and interruption of blood supply to the brain; endemic in 100, mostly tropical, countries with 90% of cases and the majority of 0.4-0.8 million estimated annual deaths occurring in sub-Saharan Africa.

Dengue fever - mosquito-borne (*Aedes aegypti*) viral disease associated with urban environments; manifests as sudden onset of fever and severe headache; occasionally produces shock and hemorrhage leading to death in 5% of cases.

Yellow fever - mosquito-borne (in urban areas *Aedes aegypti*) viral disease; severity ranges from influenza-like symptoms to severe hepatitis and hemorrhagic fever; occurs only in tropical South America and sub-Saharan Africa, where most cases are reported; fatality rate is less than 20%.

Japanese Encephalitis - mosquito-borne (*Culex tritaeniorhynchus*) viral disease associated with rural areas in Asia; acute encephalitis can progress to paralysis, coma, and death; fatality rates 30%.

African Trypanosomiasis - caused by the parasitic protozoa *Trypanosoma*; transmitted to humans via the bite of bloodsucking Tsetse flies; infection leads to malaise and irregular fevers and, in advanced cases when the parasites invade the central nervous system, coma and death; endemic in 36 countries of sub-Saharan Africa; cattle and wild animals act as reservoir hosts for the parasites.

Cutaneous Leishmaniasis - caused by the parasitic protozoa *leishmania*; transmitted to humans via the bite of sandflies; results in skin lesions that may become chronic; endemic in 88 countries; 90% of cases occur in Iran, Afghanistan, Syria, Saudi Arabia, Brazil, and Peru; wild and domesticated animals as well as humans can act as reservoirs of infection.

Plague - bacterial disease transmitted by fleas normally associated with rats; person-to-person airborne transmission also possible; recent plague epidemics occurred in areas of Asia, Africa, and South America associated with rural areas or small towns and villages; manifests as fever, headache, and painfully swollen lymph nodes; disease progresses rapidly and without antibiotic treatment leads to pneumonic form with a death rate in excess of 50%.

Crimean-Congo hemorrhagic fever - tick-borne viral disease; infection may also result from exposure to infected animal blood or tissue; geographic distribution includes Africa, Asia, the Middle East, and Eastern Europe; sudden onset of fever, headache, and muscle aches followed by hemorrhaging in the bowels, urine, nose, and gums; mortality rate is approximately 30%.

Rift Valley fever - viral disease affecting domesticated animals and humans; transmission is by mosquito and other biting insects; infection may also occur through handling of infected meat or contact with blood; geographic distribution includes eastern and southern Africa where cattle and sheep are raised; symptoms are generally mild with fever and some liver abnormalities, but the disease may progress to hemorrhagic fever, encephalitis, or ocular disease; fatality rates are low at about 1% of cases.

Chikungunya - mosquito-borne (*Aedes aegypti*) viral disease associated with urban environments, similar to Dengue Fever; characterized by sudden onset of fever, rash, and severe joint pain usually lasting 3-7 days, some cases result in persistent arthritis.

water contact diseases acquired through swimming or wading in freshwater lakes, streams, and rivers:

Leptospirosis - bacterial disease that affects animals and humans; infection occurs through contact with water, food, or soil contaminated by animal urine; symptoms include high fever, severe headache, vomiting, jaundice, and diarrhea; untreated, the disease can result in kidney damage, liver failure, meningitis, or respiratory distress; fatality rates are low but left untreated recovery can take months.

Schistosomiasis - caused by parasitic trematode flatworm *Schistosoma*; fresh water snails act as intermediate host and release larval form of parasite that penetrates the skin of people exposed to contaminated water; worms mature and reproduce in the blood vessels, liver, kidneys, and intestines releasing eggs, which become trapped in tissues triggering an immune response; may manifest as either urinary or intestinal disease resulting in decreased work or learning capacity; mortality, while generally low, may occur in advanced cases usually due to bladder cancer; endemic in 74 developing countries with 80% of infected people living in sub-Saharan Africa; humans act as the reservoir for this parasite.

aerosolized dust or soil contact disease acquired through inhalation of aerosols contaminated with rodent urine:

Lassa fever - viral disease carried by rats of the genus *Mastomys*; endemic in portions of West Africa; infection occurs through direct contact with or consumption of food contaminated by rodent urine or fecal matter containing virus particles; fatality rate can reach 50% in epidemic outbreaks.

respiratory disease acquired through close contact with an infectious person:

Meningococcal meningitis - bacterial disease causing an inflammation of the lining of the brain and spinal cord; one of the most important bacterial pathogens is *Neisseria meningitidis* because of its potential to cause epidemics; symptoms include stiff neck, high fever, headaches, and vomiting; bacteria are transmitted from person to person by respiratory droplets and facilitated by close and prolonged contact resulting from crowded living conditions, often with a seasonal distribution; death occurs in 5-15% of cases, typically within 24-48 hours of onset of symptoms; highest burden of meningococcal disease occurs in the hyperendemic region of sub-Saharan Africa known as the "Meningitis Belt" which stretches from Senegal east to Ethiopia.

animal contact disease acquired through direct contact with local animals:

Rabies - viral disease of mammals usually transmitted through the bite of an infected animal, most commonly dogs; virus affects the central nervous system causing brain alteration and death; symptoms initially are non-specific fever and headache progressing to neurological symptoms; death occurs within days of the onset of symptoms.

MAJOR URBAN AREAS - POPULATION

This entry provides the population of the capital and up to six major cities defined as urban agglomerations with populations of at least 750,000 people. An *urban agglomeration* is defined as comprising the city or town proper and also the suburban fringe or thickly settled territory lying outside of, but adjacent to, the boundaries of the city. For smaller countries, lacking urban centers of 750,000 or more, only the population of the capital is presented.

MANPOWER AVAILABLE FOR MILITARY SERVICE

This entry gives the number of males and females falling in the military age range for a country (defined as being ages 16-49) and assumes that every individual is fit to serve.

MANPOWER FIT FOR MILITARY SERVICE

This entry gives the number of males and females falling in the military age range for a country (defined as being ages 16-49) and who are not otherwise disqualified for health reasons; accounts for the health situation in the country and provides a more realistic estimate of the actual number fit to serve.

MANPOWER REACHING MILITARILY SIGNIFICANT AGE ANNUALLY

This entry gives the number of males and females entering the military manpower pool (i.e., reaching age 16) in any given year and is a measure of the availability of military-age young adults.

MAP REFERENCES

This entry includes the name of the *Factbook* reference map on which a country may be found. Note that boundary representations on these maps are not necessarily authoritative. The entry on **Geographic coordinates** may be helpful in finding some smaller countries.

MARITIME CLAIMS

This entry includes the following claims, the definitions of which are excerpted from the United Nations Convention on the Law of the Sea (UNCLOS), which alone contains the full and definitive descriptions:

territorial sea - the sovereignty of a coastal state

extends beyond its land territory and internal waters to an adjacent belt of sea, described as the territorial sea in the UNCLOS (Part II); this sovereignty extends to the air space over the territorial sea as well as its underlying seabed and subsoil; every state has the right to establish the breadth of its territorial sea up to a limit not exceeding 12 nautical miles; the normal baseline for measuring the breadth of the territorial sea is the mean low-water line along the coast as marked on large-scale charts officially recognized by the coastal state; where the coasts of two states are opposite or adjacent to each other, neither state is entitled to extend its territorial sea beyond the median line, every point of which is equidistant from the nearest points on the baseline from which the territorial seas of both states are measured; the UNCLOS describes specific rules for archipelagic states.

contiguous zone - according to the UNCLOS (Article 33), this is a zone contiguous to a coastal state's territorial sea, over which it may exercise the control necessary to: prevent infringement of its customs, fiscal, immigration, or sanitary laws and regulations within its territory or territorial sea; punish infringement of the above laws and regulations committed within its territory or territorial sea; the contiguous zone may not extend beyond 24 nautical miles from the baselines from which the breadth of the territorial sea is measured (e.g., the US has claimed a 12-nautical mile contiguous zone in addition to its 12-nautical mile territorial sea); where the coasts of two states are opposite or adjacent to each other, neither state is entitled to extend its contiguous zone beyond the median line, every point of which is equidistant from the nearest points on the baseline from which the contiguous zone of both states are measured.

exclusive economic zone (EEZ) - the UNCLOS (Part V) defines the EEZ as a zone beyond and adjacent to the territorial sea in which a coastal state has: sovereign rights for the purpose of exploring and exploiting, conserving and managing the natural resources, whether living or non-living, of the waters superjacent to the seabed and of the seabed and its subsoil, and with regard to other activities for the economic exploitation and exploration of the zone, such as the production of energy from the water, currents, and winds; jurisdiction with regard to the establishment and use of artificial islands, installations, and structures; marine scientific research; the protection and preservation of the marine environment; the outer limit of the exclusive economic zone shall not exceed 200 nautical miles from the baselines from which the breadth of the territorial sea is measured.

continental shelf - the UNCLOS (Article 76) defines the continental shelf of a coastal state as comprising the seabed and subsoil of the submarine areas that extend beyond its territorial sea throughout the natural prolongation of its land territory to the outer edge of the continental margin, or to a distance of 200 nautical miles from the baselines from which the breadth of the territorial sea is measured where the outer edge of the continental margin does not extend up to that distance; the continental margin comprises the submerged prolongation of the landmass of the coastal state, and consists of the seabed and subsoil of the shelf, the slope and the rise; wherever the continental margin extends beyond 200 nautical miles from the baseline, coastal states may extend their claim to a distance not to exceed 350 nautical miles from the baseline or 100 nautical miles from the 2,500-meter isobath, which is a line connecting points of 2,500 meters in depth; it does not include the deep ocean floor with its oceanic ridges or the subsoil thereof.

exclusive fishing zone - while this term is not used in the UNCLOS, some states (e.g., the United Kingdom) have chosen not to claim an EEZ, but rather to claim jurisdiction over the living resources off their coast; in such cases, the term exclusive fishing zone is often used; the breadth of this zone is normally the same as the EEZ or 200 nautical miles.

MARITIME THREATS

This entry describes the threat of piracy, as defined in Article 101, UN Convention on the Law of the Sea (UNCLOS), or armed robbery against ships, as defined in Resolution A. 1025 (26) adopted on 2 December 2009 at the 26th Assembly Session of the International Maritime Organization. The entry includes the number of ships on the high seas or in territorial waters that were boarded or attacked by pirates, and the number of crewmen abducted or killed, as compiled by the International Maritime Bureau. Information is also supplied on the geographical range of attacks.

MARKET VALUE OF PUBLICLY TRADED SHARES

This entry gives the value of shares issued by publicly traded companies at a price determined in the national stock markets on the final day of the period indicated. It is simply the latest price per share multiplied by the total number of outstanding shares, cumulated over all companies listed on the particular exchange.

MATERNAL MORTALITY RATE

The maternal mortality rate (MMR) is the annual number of female deaths per 100,000 live births from any cause related to or aggravated by pregnancy or its management (excluding accidental or incidental causes). The MMR includes deaths during pregnancy, childbirth, or within 42 days of termination of pregnancy, irrespective of the duration and site of the pregnancy, for a specified year.

MEDIAN AGE

This entry is the age that divides a population into two numerically equal groups; that is, half the people are younger than this age and half are older. It is a single index that summarizes the age distribution of a population. Currently, the median age ranges from a low of about 15 in Niger and Uganda to 40 or more in several European countries and Japan. See the entry for "Age structure" for the importance of a young versus an older age structure and, by implication, a low versus a higher median age.

MERCHANT MARINE

Merchant marine may be defined as all ships engaged in the carriage of goods; or all commercial vessels (as opposed to all nonmilitary ships), which excludes tugs, fishing vessels, offshore oil rigs, etc. This entry contains information in four fields - *total*, ships *by type*, *foreign-owned*, and *registered in other countries*.
Total includes the number of ships (1,000 GRT or over), total DWT for those ships, and total GRT for those ships. DWT or dead weight tonnage is the total weight of cargo, plus bunkers, stores, etc., that a ship can carry when immersed to the appropriate load line. GRT or gross register tonnage is a figure obtained by measuring the entire sheltered volume of a ship available for cargo and passengers and converting it to tons on the basis of 100 cubic feet per ton; there is no stable relationship between GRT and DWT.
Ships ***by type*** includes a listing of barge carriers, bulk cargo ships, cargo ships, chemical tankers, combination bulk carriers, combination ore/oil carriers, container ships, liquefied gas tankers, livestock carriers, multifunctional large-load carriers, petroleum tankers, passenger ships, passenger/cargo ships, railcar carriers, refrigerated cargo ships, roll-on/roll-off cargo ships, short-sea passenger ships, specialized tankers, and vehicle carriers.
Foreign-owned are ships that fly the flag of one country but belong to owners in another.
Registered in other countries are ships that belong to owners in one country but fly the flag of another.

MILITARY

This category includes the entries dealing with a country's military structure, manpower, and expenditures.

MILITARY - NOTE

This entry includes miscellaneous military information of significance not included elsewhere.

MILITARY BRANCHES

This entry lists the service branches subordinate to defense ministries or the equivalent (typically ground, naval, air, and marine forces).

MILITARY EXPENDITURES

This entry gives spending on defense programs for the most recent year available as a percent of gross domestic product (GDP); the GDP is calculated on an exchange rate basis, i.e., not in terms of purchasing power parity (PPP). For countries with no military forces, this figure can include expenditures on public security and police.

MILITARY SERVICE AGE AND OBLIGATION

This entry gives the required ages for voluntary or conscript military service and the length of service obligation.

MONEY FIGURES

All money figures are expressed in contemporaneous US dollars unless otherwise indicated.

MOTHER'S MEAN AGE AT FIRST BIRTH

This entry provides the mean (average) age of mothers at the birth of their first child. It is a useful indicator for gauging the success of family planning programs aiming to reduce maternal mortality, increase contraceptive use – particularly among married and unmarried adolescents – delay age at first marriage, and improve the health of newborns.

NATIONAL AIR TRANSPORT SYSTEM

This entry includes four subfields describing the air transport system of a given country in terms of both structure and performance. The first subfield, *number of registered air carriers*, indicates the total number of air carriers registered with the country's national aviation authority and issued an air operator certificate as required by the Convention on International Civil Aviation. The second subfield, *inventory of registered aircraft operated by air carriers*, lists the total number of aircraft operated by all registered air carriers in the country. The last two subfields measure the performance of the air transport system in terms of both passengers and freight. The subfield, *annual passenger traffic on registered air carriers*, includes the total number of passengers carried by air carriers registered in the country, including both domestic and international passengers, in a given year. The last subfield, *annual freight traffic on registered air carriers*, includes the volume of freight, express, and diplomatic bags carried by registered air carriers and measured in metric tons times kilometers traveled. Freight ton-kilometers equal the sum of the products obtained by multiplying the number of tons of freight, express, and diplomatic bags carried on each flight stage by the stage distance (operation of an aircraft from takeoff to its next landing). For statistical purposes, freight includes express and diplomatic bags but not passenger baggage.

NATIONAL ANTHEM

A generally patriotic musical composition - usually in the form of a song or hymn of praise - that evokes and eulogizes the history, traditions, or struggles of a nation or its people. National anthems can be officially recognized as a national song by a country's constitution or by an enacted law, or simply by tradition. Although most anthems contain lyrics, some do not.

NATIONAL HOLIDAY

This entry gives the primary national day of celebration - usually independence day.

NATIONAL SYMBOL(S)

A national symbol is a faunal, floral, or other abstract representation - or some distinctive object - that over time has come to be closely identified with a country or entity. Not all countries have national symbols; a few countries have more than one.

NATIONALITY

This entry provides the identifying terms for citizens - *noun* and *adjective*.

NATURAL GAS - CONSUMPTION

This entry is the total natural gas consumed in cubic meters (cu m). The discrepancy between the amount of natural gas produced and/or imported and the amount consumed and/or exported is due to the omission of stock changes and other complicating factors.

NATURAL GAS - EXPORTS

This entry is the total natural gas exported in cubic meters (cu m).

NATURAL GAS - IMPORTS

This entry is the total natural gas imported in cubic meters (cu m).

NATURAL GAS - PRODUCTION

This entry is the total natural gas produced in cubic meters (cu m). The discrepancy between the amount of natural gas produced and/or imported and the amount consumed and/or exported is due to the omission of stock changes and other complicating factors.

NATURAL GAS - PROVED RESERVES

This entry is the stock of proved reserves of natural gas in cubic meters (cu m). Proved reserves are those quantities of natural gas, which, by analysis of geological and engineering data, can be estimated with a high degree of confidence to be commercially recoverable from a given date forward, from known reservoirs and under current economic conditions.

NATURAL HAZARDS

This entry lists potential natural disasters. For countries where volcanic activity is common, a *volcanism* subfield highlights historically active volcanoes.

NATURAL RESOURCES

This entry lists a country's mineral, petroleum, hydropower, and other resources of commercial importance, such as rare earth elements (REEs). In general, products appear only if they make a significant contribution to the economy, or are likely to do so in the future.

NET MIGRATION RATE

This entry includes the figure for the difference between the number of persons entering and leaving a country during the year per 1,000 persons (based on midyear population). An excess of persons entering the country is referred to as net immigration (e.g., 3.56 migrants/1,000 population); an excess of persons leaving the country as net emigration (e.g., -9.26 migrants/1,000 population). The net migration rate indicates the contribution of migration to the overall level of population change. The net migration rate does not distinguish between economic migrants, refugees, and other types of migrants nor does it distinguish between lawful migrants and undocumented migrants.

OBESITY - ADULT PREVALENCE RATE

This entry gives the percent of a country's population considered to be obese. Obesity is defined as an adult having a Body Mass Index (BMI) greater to or equal to 30.0. BMI is calculated by taking a person's weight in kg and dividing it by the person's squared height in meters.

PEOPLE - NOTE

This entry includes miscellaneous demographic information of significance not included elsewhere.

PEOPLE AND SOCIETY

This category includes entries dealing with national identity (including ethnicities, languages, and religions), demography (a variety of population statistics) and societal characteristics (health and education indicators).

PERSONAL NAMES - CAPITALIZATION

The *Factbook* capitalizes the surname or family name of individuals for the convenience of our users who are faced with a world of different cultures and naming conventions. The need for capitalization, bold type, underlining, italics, or some other indicator of the individual's surname is apparent in the following examples: MAO Zedong, Fidel CASTRO Ruz, George W. BUSH, and TUNKU SALAHUDDIN Abdul Aziz Shah ibni Al-Marhum Sultan Hisammuddin Alam Shah. By knowing the surname, a short form without all capital letters can be used with confidence as in President Castro, Chairman Mao, President Bush, or Sultan Tunku Salahuddin. The same system of capitalization is extended to the names of leaders with surnames that are not commonly used such as Queen ELIZABETH II. For Vietnamese names, the given name is capitalized because officials are referred to by their given name rather than by their surname. For example, the president of Vietnam is Tran Duc LUONG. His surname is Tran, but he is referred to by his given name - President LUONG.

PERSONAL NAMES - SPELLING

The romanization of personal names in the *Factbook* normally follows the same transliteration system used by the US Board on Geographic Names for spelling place names. At times, however, a foreign leader expressly indicates a preference for, or the media or official documents regularly use, a romanized spelling that differs from the transliteration derived from the US Government standard. In such cases, the *Factbook* uses the alternative spelling.

PERSONAL NAMES - TITLES

The *Factbook* capitalizes any valid title (or short form of it) immediately preceding a person's name. A title standing alone is not capitalized. Examples: President PUTIN and President OBAMA are chiefs of state. In Russia, the president is chief of state and the premier is the head of the government, while in the US, the president is both chief of state and head of government.

PETROLEUM

See entries under **Refined petroleum products**.

PETROLEUM PRODUCTS

See entries under **Refined petroleum products**.

PHYSICIANS DENSITY

This entry gives the number of medical doctors (physicians), including generalist and specialist medical practitioners, per 1,000 of the population. Medical doctors are defined as doctors that study, diagnose, treat, and prevent illness, disease, injury, and other physical and mental impairments in humans through the application of modern medicine. They also plan, supervise, and evaluate care and treatment plans by other health care providers. The World Health Organization estimates that fewer than 2.3 health workers (physicians, nurses, and midwives only) per 1,000 would be insufficient to achieve coverage of primary healthcare needs.

PIPELINES

This entry gives the lengths and types of pipelines for transporting products like natural gas, crude oil, or petroleum products.

PIRACY

Piracy is defined by the 1982 United Nations Convention on the Law of the Sea as any illegal act of violence, detention, or depredation directed against a ship, aircraft, persons, or property in a place outside the jurisdiction of any State. Such criminal acts committed in the territorial waters of a littoral state are generally considered to be armed robbery against ships. Information on piracy may be found, where applicable, under **Maritime threats**.

POLITICAL PARTIES AND LEADERS

This entry includes a listing of significant political parties, coalitions, and electoral lists as of each country's last legislative election, unless otherwise noted.

POPULATION

This entry gives an estimate from the US Bureau of the Census based on statistics from population censuses, vital statistics registration systems, or sample surveys pertaining to the recent past and on assumptions about future trends. The total population presents one overall measure of the potential impact of the country on the world and within its region. Note: Starting with the 1993 *Factbook*, demographic estimates for some countries (mostly African) have explicitly taken into account the effects of the growing impact of the

HIV/AIDS epidemic. These countries are currently: The Bahamas, Benin, Botswana, Brazil, Burkina Faso, Burma, Burundi, Cambodia, Cameroon, Central African Republic, Democratic Republic of the Congo, Republic of the Congo, Cote d'Ivoire, Ethiopia, Gabon, Ghana, Guyana, Haiti, Honduras, Kenya, Lesotho, Malawi, Mozambique, Namibia, Nigeria, Rwanda, South Africa, Swaziland, Tanzania, Thailand, Togo, Uganda, Zambia, and Zimbabwe.

POPULATION BELOW POVERTY LINE

National estimates of the percentage of the population falling below the poverty line are based on surveys of sub-groups, with the results weighted by the number of people in each group. Definitions of poverty vary considerably among nations. For example, rich nations generally employ more generous standards of poverty than poor nations.

POPULATION DISTRIBUTION

This entry provides a summary description of the population dispersion within a country. While it may suggest population density, it does not provide density figures.

POPULATION GROWTH RATE

The average annual percent change in the population, resulting from a surplus (or deficit) of births over deaths and the balance of migrants entering and leaving a country. The rate may be positive or negative. The growth rate is a factor in determining how great a burden would be imposed on a country by the changing needs of its people for infrastructure (e.g., schools, hospitals, housing, roads), resources (e.g., food, water, electricity), and jobs. Rapid population growth can be seen as threatening by neighboring countries.

POPULATION PYRAMID

A population pyramid illustrates the age and sex structure of a country's population and may provide insights about political and social stability, as well as economic development. The population is distributed along the horizontal axis, with males shown on the left and females on the right. The male and female populations are broken down into 5-year age groups represented as horizontal bars along the vertical axis, with the youngest age groups at the bottom and the oldest at the top. The shape of the population pyramid gradually evolves over time based on fertility, mortality, and international migration trends.

Some distinctive types of population pyramids are:

A **youthful distribution** has a broad base and narrow peak and is characterized by a high proportion of children and low proportion of the elderly. This population distribution results from high fertility, high mortality, low life expectancy, and high population growth. It is typical of developing countries where female education and contraceptive use are low and health care and sanitation are poor.

A **transitional distribution** is caused by declining fertility and mortality rates, increasing life expectancy, and slowing population growth. The population has a larger proportion of working-age people relative to children and the elderly and produces a barrel-shaped pyramid, where the mid-section bulges and the base and top are narrower. The large proportion of working-age people can create a "demographic bonus" if it is educated and productively employed.

A **mature distribution** has fairly balanced proportions of the population in the child, working-age, and elderly age groups and will gradually form an inverted triangle population pyramid as population growth continues to fall or ceases and the proportion of older people increases. Low fertility, low mortality, and high life expectancy - made possible by the availability of advanced healthcare, family planning, sanitation, and education - lead to aging populations in industrialized countries.

PORTS AND TERMINALS

This entry lists major ports and terminals primarily on the basis of the amount of cargo tonnage shipped through the facilities on an annual basis. In some instances, the number of containers handled or ship visits were also considered. Most ports service multiple classes of vessels including bulk carriers (dry and liquid), break bulk cargoes (goods loaded individually in bags, boxes, crates, or drums; sometimes palletized), containers, roll-on/roll-off, and passenger ships. The listing leads off with *major seaports* handling all types of cargo. Inland *river/lake ports* are listed separately along with the river or lake name. Ports configured specifically to handle bulk cargoes are designated as *oil terminals* or *dry bulk cargo ports*. *LNG terminals* handle liquefied natural gas (LNG) and are differentiated as either export, where the gas is chilled to a liquid state to reduce its volume for transport on specialized gas carriers, or import, where the off-loaded LNG undergoes a regasification process before entering pipelines for distribution. As break bulk cargoes are largely transported by containers today, the entry also includes a listing of major *container ports* with the corresponding throughput measured in twenty-foot equivalent units (TEUs). Some ports are significant for handling passenger traffic and are listed as *cruise/ferry ports*. In addition to commercial traffic, many seaports also provide important military infrastructure such as naval bases or dockyards.

PRINCIPALITY

a sovereign state ruled by a monarch with the title of prince; principalities were common in the past, but today only three remain: Liechtenstein, Monaco, and the co-principality of Andorra.

PUBLIC DEBT

This entry records the cumulative total of all government borrowings less repayments that are denominated in a country's home currency. Public debt should not be confused with external debt, which reflects the foreign currency liabilities of both the private and public sector and must be financed out of foreign exchange earnings.

RAILWAYS

This entry states the *total* route length of the railway network and of its component parts by gauge, which is the measure of the distance between the inner sides of the load-bearing rails. The four typical types of gauges are: *broad*, *standard*, *narrow*, and *dual*. Other gauges are listed under *note*. Some 60% of the world's railways use the standard gauge of 1.4 m (4.7 ft). Gauges vary by country and sometimes within countries. The choice of gauge during initial construction was mainly in response to local conditions and the intent of the builder. Narrow-gauge railways were cheaper to build and could negotiate sharper curves, broad-gauge railways gave greater stability and permitted higher speeds. Standard-gauge railways were a compromise between narrow and broad gauges.

RARE EARTH ELEMENTS

Rare earth elements or REEs are 17 chemical elements that are critical in many of today's high-tech industries. They include lanthanum, cerium, praseodymium, neodymium, promethium, samarium, europium, gadolinium, terbium, dysprosium, holmium, erbium, thulium, ytterbium, lutetium, scandium, and yttrium. Typical applications for REEs include batteries in hybrid cars, fiber optic cables, flat panel displays, and permanent magnets, as well as some defense and medical products.

REFERENCE MAPS

This section includes world and regional maps.

REFINED PETROLEUM PRODUCTS - CONSUMPTION

This entry is the country's total consumption of refined petroleum products, in barrels per day (bbl/day). The discrepancy between the amount of refined petroleum products produced and/or imported and the amount consumed and/or exported is due to the omission of stock changes, refinery gains, and other complicating factors.

REFINED PETROLEUM PRODUCTS - EXPORTS

This entry is the country's total exports of refined petroleum products, in barrels per day (bbl/day).

REFINED PETROLEUM PRODUCTS - IMPORTS

This entry is the country's total imports of refined petroleum products, in barrels per day (bbl/day).

REFINED PETROLEUM PRODUCTS - PRODUCTION

This entry is the country's total output of refined petroleum products, in barrels per day (bbl/day). The discrepancy between the amount of refined petroleum products produced and/or imported and the amount consumed and/or exported is due to the omission of stock changes, refinery gains, and other complicating factors.

REFUGEES AND INTERNALLY DISPLACED PERSONS

This entry includes those persons residing in a country as *refugees*, *internally displaced persons (IDPs)*, or *stateless persons*. Each country's refugee entry includes only countries of origin that are the source of refugee populations of 5,000 or more. The definition of a refugee according to a UN Convention is "a person who is outside his/her country of nationality or habitual residence; has a well-founded fear of persecution because of his/her race, religion, nationality, membership in a particular social group or political opinion; and is unable or unwilling to avail himself/herself of the protection of that country, or to return there, for fear of persecution." The UN established the Office of the UN High Commissioner for Refugees (UNHCR) in 1950 to handle refugee matters worldwide. The UN Relief and Works Agency for Palestine Refugees in the Near East (UNRWA) has a different operational definition for a Palestinian refugee: "a person whose normal place of residence was Palestine during the period 1 June 1946 to 15 May 1948 and who lost both home and means of livelihood as a result of the 1948 conflict." However, UNHCR also assists some 400,000 Palestinian refugees not covered under the UNRWA definition. The term "internally displaced person" is not specifically covered in the UN Convention; it is used to describe people who have fled their homes for reasons similar to refugees, but who remain within their own national territory and are subject to the laws of that state. A stateless person is defined as someone who is not considered a national by any state under the operation of its law, according to UN convention.

RELIGIONS

This entry is an ordered listing of religions by adherents starting with the largest group and sometimes includes the percent of total population. The core characteristics and beliefs of the world's major religions are described below.

Baha'i - Founded by Mirza Husayn-Ali (known as Baha'u'llah) in Iran in 1852, Baha'i faith emphasizes monotheism and believes in one eternal transcendent God. Its guiding focus is to encourage the unity of all peoples on the earth so that justice and peace may be achieved on earth. Baha'i revelation contends the prophets of major world religions reflect some truth or element of the divine, believes all were manifestations of God given to specific communities in specific times, and that Baha'u'llah is an additional prophet meant to call all humankind. Bahais are an open community, located worldwide, with the greatest concentration of believers in South Asia.

Buddhism - Religion or philosophy inspired by the 5th century B.C. teachings of Siddhartha Gautama (also known as Gautama Buddha "the enlightened one"). Buddhism focuses on the goal of spiritual enlightenment centered on an understanding of Gautama Buddha's Four Noble Truths on the nature of suffering, and on the Eightfold Path of spiritual and moral practice, to break the cycle of suffering of which we are a part. Buddhism ascribes to a karmic system of rebirth. Several schools and sects of Buddhism exist, differing often on the nature of the Buddha, the extent to which enlightenment can be achieved - for one or for all, and by whom - religious orders or laity.

Basic Groupings

Theravada Buddhism: The oldest Buddhist school, Theravada is practiced mostly in Sri Lanka, Cambodia, Laos, Burma, and Thailand, with minority representation elsewhere in Asia and the West. Theravadans follow the Pali Canon of Buddha's teachings, and believe that one may escape the cycle of rebirth, worldly attachment, and suffering for oneself; this process may take one or several lifetimes.

Mahayana Buddhism, including subsets Zen and Tibetan (Lamaistic) Buddhism: Forms of Mahayana Buddhism are common in East Asia and Tibet, and parts of the West. Mahayanas have additional scriptures beyond the Pali Canon and believe the Buddha is eternal and still teaching. Unlike Theravada Buddhism, Mahayana schools maintain the Buddha-nature is present in all beings and all will ultimately achieve enlightenment.

Hoa Hao: a minority tradition of Buddhism practiced in Vietnam that stresses lay participation, primarily by peasant farmers; it eschews expensive ceremonies and temples and relocates the primary practices into the home.

Christianity - Descending from Judaism, Christianity's central belief maintains Jesus of Nazareth is the promised messiah of the Hebrew Scriptures, and that his life, death, and resurrection are salvific for the world. Christianity is one of the three monotheistic Abrahamic faiths, along with Islam and Judaism, which traces its spiritual lineage to Abraham of the Hebrew Scriptures. Its sacred texts include the Hebrew Bible and the New Testament (or the Christian Gospels).

Basic Groupings

Catholicism (or Roman Catholicism): This is the oldest established western Christian church and the world's largest single religious body. It is supranational, and recognizes a hierarchical structure with the Pope, or Bishop of Rome, as its head, located at the Vatican. Catholics believe the Pope is the divinely ordered head of the Church from a direct spiritual legacy of Jesus' apostle Peter. Catholicism is comprised of 23 particular Churches, or Rites - one Western (Roman or Latin-Rite) and 22 Eastern. The Latin Rite is by far the largest, making up about 98% of Catholic membership. Eastern-Rite Churches, such as the Maronite Church and the Ukrainian Catholic Church, are in communion with Rome although they preserve their own worship traditions and their immediate hierarchy consists of clergy within their own rite. The Catholic Church has a comprehensive theological and moral doctrine specified for believers in its catechism, which makes it unique among most forms of Christianity.

Mormonism (including the Church of Jesus Christ of Latter-Day Saints): Originating in 1830 in the United States under Joseph Smith, Mormonism is not characterized as a form of Protestant Christianity because it claims additional revealed Christian scriptures after the Hebrew Bible and New Testament. The Book of Mormon maintains there was an appearance of Jesus in the New World following the Christian account of his resurrection, and that the Americas are uniquely blessed continents. Mormonism believes earlier Christian traditions, such as the Roman Catholic, Orthodox, and Protestant reform faiths, are apostasies and that Joseph Smith's revelation of the Book of Mormon is a restoration of true Christianity. Mormons have a hierarchical religious leadership structure, and actively proselytize their faith; they are located primarily in the Americas and in a number of other Western countries.

Jehovah's Witnesses structure their faith on the Christian Bible, but their rejection of the Trinity is distinct from mainstream Christianity. They believe that a Kingdom of God, the Theocracy, will emerge following Armageddon and usher in a new earthly society. Adherents are required to evangelize and to follow a strict moral code.

Orthodox Christianity: The oldest established eastern form of Christianity, the Holy Orthodox Church, has a ceremonial head in the Bishop of Constantinople

(Istanbul), also known as a Patriarch, but its various regional forms (e.g., Greek Orthodox, Russian Orthodox, Serbian Orthodox, Ukrainian Orthodox) are autocephalous (independent of Constantinople's authority, and have their own Patriarchs). Orthodox churches are highly nationalist and ethnic. The Orthodox Christian faith shares many theological tenets with the Roman Catholic Church, but diverges on some key premises and does not recognize the governing authority of the Pope.

Protestant Christianity: Protestant Christianity originated in the 16th century as an attempt to reform Roman Catholicism's practices, dogma, and theology. It encompasses several forms or denominations which are extremely varied in structure, beliefs, relationship to state, clergy, and governance. Many protestant theologies emphasize the primary role of scripture in their faith, advocating individual interpretation of Christian texts without the mediation of a final religious authority such as the Roman Pope. The oldest Protestant Christianities include Lutheranism, Calvinism (Presbyterians), and Anglican Christianity (Episcopalians), which have established liturgies, governing structure, and formal clergy. Other variants on Protestant Christianity, including Pentecostal movements and independent churches, may lack one or more of these elements, and their leadership and beliefs are individualized and dynamic.

Hinduism - Originating in the Vedic civilization of India (second and first millennium B.C.), Hinduism is an extremely diverse set of beliefs and practices with no single founder or religious authority. Hinduism has many scriptures; the Vedas, the Upanishads, and the Bhagavad-Gita are among some of the most important. Hindus may worship one or many deities, usually with prayer rituals within their own home. The most common figures of devotion are the gods Vishnu, Shiva, and a mother goddess, Devi. Most Hindus believe the soul, or *atman*, is eternal, and goes through a cycle of birth, death, and rebirth (*samsara*) determined by one's positive or negative karma, or the consequences of one's actions. The goal of religious life is to learn to act so as to finally achieve liberation (*moksha*) of one's soul, escaping the rebirth cycle.

Islam - The third of the monotheistic Abrahamic faiths, Islam originated with the teachings of Muhammad in the 7th century. Muslims believe Muhammad is the final of all religious prophets (beginning with Abraham) and that the Qu'ran, which is the Islamic scripture, was revealed to him by God. Islam derives from the word submission, and obedience to God is a primary theme in this religion. In order to live an Islamic life, believers must follow the five pillars, or tenets, of Islam, which are the testimony of faith (*shahada*), daily prayer (*salah*), giving alms (*zakah*), fasting during Ramadan (*sawm*), and the pilgrimage to Mecca (*hajj*).

Basic Groupings

The two primary branches of Islam are Sunni and Shia, which split from each other over a religio-political leadership dispute about the rightful successor to Muhammad. The Shia believe Muhammad's cousin and son-in-law, Ali, was the only divinely ordained Imam (religious leader), while the Sunni maintain the first three caliphs after Muhammad were also legitimate authorities. In modern Islam, Sunnis and Shia continue to have different views of acceptable schools of Islamic jurisprudence, and who is a proper Islamic religious authority. Islam also has an active mystical branch, Sufism, with various Sunni and Shia subsets.

Sunni Islam accounts for over 75% of the world's Muslim population. It recognizes the Abu Bakr as the first caliph after Muhammad. Sunni has four schools of Islamic doctrine and law - Hanafi, Maliki, Shafi'i, and Hanbali - which uniquely interpret the *Hadith*, or recorded oral traditions of Muhammad. A Sunni Muslim may elect to follow any one of these schools, as all are considered equally valid.

Shia Islam represents 10-20% of Muslims worldwide, and its distinguishing feature is its reverence for Ali as an infallible, divinely inspired leader, and as the first Imam of the Muslim community after Muhammad. A majority of Shia are known as "Twelvers," because they believe that the 11 familial successor imams after Muhammad culminate in a 12th Imam (al-Mahdi) who is hidden in the world and will reappear at its end to redeem the righteous.

Variants

Ismaili faith: A sect of Shia Islam, its adherents are also known as "Seveners," because they believe that the rightful seventh Imam in Islamic leadership was Isma'il, the elder son of Imam Jafar al-Sadiq. Ismaili tradition awaits the return of the seventh Imam as the Mahdi, or Islamic messianic figure. Ismailis are located in various parts of the world, particularly South Asia and the Levant.

Alawi faith: Another Shia sect of Islam, the name reflects followers' devotion to the religious authority of Ali. Alawites are a closed, secretive religious group who assert they are Shia Muslims, although outside scholars speculate their beliefs may have a syncretic mix with other faiths originating in the Middle East. Alawis live mostly in Syria, Lebanon, and Turkey.

Druze faith: A highly secretive tradition and a closed community that derives from the Ismaili sect of Islam; its core beliefs are thought to emphasize a combination of Gnostic principles believing that the Fatimid caliph, al-Hakin, is the one who embodies the key aspects of goodness of the universe, which are, the intellect, the word, the soul, the preceder, and the follower. The Druze have a key presence in Syria, Lebanon, and Israel.

Jainism - Originating in India, Jain spiritual philosophy believes in an eternal human soul, the eternal universe, and a principle of "the own nature of things." It emphasizes compassion for all living things, seeks liberation of the human soul from reincarnation through enlightenment, and values personal responsibility due to the belief in the immediate consequences of one's behavior. Jain philosophy teaches non-violence and prescribes vegetarianism for monks and laity alike; its adherents are a highly influential religious minority in Indian society.

Judaism - One of the first known monotheistic religions, likely dating to between 2000-1500 B.C., Judaism is the native faith of the Jewish people, based upon the belief in a covenant of responsibility between a sole omnipotent creator God and Abraham, the patriarch of Judaism's Hebrew Bible, or *Tanakh*. Divine revelation of principles and prohibitions in the Hebrew Scriptures form the basis of Jewish law, or *halakhah*, which is a key component of the faith. While there are extensive traditions of Jewish halakhic and theological discourse, there is no final dogmatic authority in the tradition. Local communities have their own religious leadership. Modern Judaism has three basic categories of faith: Orthodox, Conservative, and Reform/Liberal. These differ in their views and observance of Jewish law, with the Orthodox representing the most traditional practice, and Reform/Liberal communities the most accommodating of individualized interpretations of Jewish identity and faith.

Shintoism - A native animist tradition of Japan, Shinto practice is based upon the premise that every being and object has its own spirit or *kami*. Shinto practitioners worship several particular *kamis*, including the *kamis* of nature, and families often have shrines to their ancestors' *kamis*. Shintoism has no fixed tradition of prayers or prescribed dogma, but is characterized by individual ritual. Respect for the *kamis* in nature is a key Shinto value. Prior to the end of World War II, Shinto was the state religion of Japan, and bolstered the cult of the Japanese emperor.

Sikhism - Founded by the Guru Nanak (born 1469), Sikhism believes in a non-anthropomorphic, supreme, eternal, creator God; centering one's devotion to God is seen as a means of escaping the cycle of rebirth. Sikhs follow the teachings of Nanak and nine subsequent gurus. Their scripture, the Guru Granth Sahib - also known as the Adi Granth - is considered the living Guru, or final authority of Sikh faith and theology. Sikhism emphasizes equality of humankind and disavows caste, class, or gender discrimination.

Taoism - Chinese philosophy or religion based upon Lao Tzu's Tao Te Ching, which centers on belief in the Tao, or the way, as the flow of the universe and the nature of things. Taoism encourages a principle of non-force, or wu-wei, as the means to live harmoniously with the Tao. Taoists believe the esoteric world is made up of a perfect harmonious balance and nature, while in the manifest world - particularly in the body - balance is distorted. The Three Jewels of the Tao - compassion, simplicity, and humility - serve as the basis for Taoist ethics.

Zoroastrianism - Originating from the teachings of Zoroaster in about the 9th or 10th century B.C., Zoroastrianism may be the oldest continuing creedal religion. Its key beliefs center on a transcendent creator God, Ahura Mazda, and the concept of free will. The key ethical tenets of Zoroastrianism expressed in its scripture, the Avesta, are based on a dualistic worldview where one may prevent chaos if one chooses to serve God and exercises good thoughts, good words, and good deeds. Zoroastrianism is generally a closed religion and members are almost always born to Zoroastrian parents. Prior to the spread of Islam, Zoroastrianism dominated greater Iran. Today, though a minority, Zoroastrians remain primarily in Iran, India (where they are known as Parsi), and Pakistan.

Traditional beliefs

Animism: the belief that non-human entities contain souls or spirits.

Badimo: a form of ancestor worship of the Tswana people of Botswana.

Confucianism: an ideology that humans are perfectible through self-cultivation and self-creation; developed from teachings of the Chinese philosopher Confucius. Confucianism has strongly influenced the culture and beliefs of East Asian countries, including China, Japan, Korea, Singapore, Taiwan, and Vietnam.

Inuit beliefs are a form of shamanism (see below) based on animistic principles of the Inuit or Eskimo peoples.

Kirant: the belief system of the Kirat, a people who live mainly in the Himalayas of Nepal. It is primarily a form of polytheistic shamanism, but includes elements of animism and ancestor worship.

Pagan is a blanket term used to describe many unconnected belief practices throughout history, usually in reference to religions outside of the Abrahamic category (monotheistic faiths like Judaism, Christianity, and Islam).

Shamanism: beliefs and practices promoting communication with the spiritual world. Shamanistic beliefs are organized around a shaman or medicine man who - as an intermediary between the human and spirit world - is believed to be able to heal the sick (by healing their souls), communicate with the spirit world, and help souls into the afterlife through the practice of entering a trance. In shaman-based religions, the shaman is also responsible for leading sacred rites.

Spiritualism: the belief that souls and spirits communicate with the living usually through intermediaries called mediums.

Syncretic (fusion of diverse religious beliefs and practices)

Cao Dai: a nationalistic Vietnamese sect, officially established in 1926, that draws practices and precepts from Confucianism, Taoism, Buddhism, and Catholicism.

Chondogyo: or the religion of the Heavenly Way, is based on Korean shamanism, Buddhism, and Korean folk traditions, with some elements drawn from

Christianity. Formulated in the 1860s, it holds that God lives in all of us and strives to convert society into a paradise on earth, populated by believers transformed into intelligent moral beings with a high social conscience.

Kimbanguist: a puritan form of the Baptist denomination founded by Simon Kimbangu in the 1920s in what is now the Democratic Republic of Congo. Adherents believe that salvation comes through Jesus' death and resurrection, like Christianity, but additionally that living a spiritually pure life following strict codes of conduct is required for salvation.

Modekngei: a hybrid of Christianity and ancient Palauan culture and oral traditions founded around 1915 on the island of Babeldaob. Adherents simultaneously worship Jesus Christ and Palauan goddesses.

Rastafarian: an afro-centrist ideology and movement based on Christianity that arose in Jamaica in the 1930s; it believes that Haile Selassie I, Emperor of Ethiopia from 1930-74, was the incarnation of the second coming of Jesus.

Santeria: practiced in Cuba, the merging of the Yoruba religion of Nigeria with Roman Catholicism and native Indian traditions. Its practitioners believe that each person has a destiny and eventually transcends to merge with the divine creator and source of all energy, Olorun.

Voodoo/Vodun: a form of spirit and ancestor worship combined with some Christian faiths, especially Catholicism. Haitian and Louisiana Voodoo, which have included more Catholic practices, are separate from West African Vodun, which has retained a focus on spirit worship.

Non-religious

Agnosticism: the belief that most things are unknowable. In regard to religion it is usually characterized as neither a belief nor non belief in a deity.

Atheism: the belief that there are no deities of any kind.

RESERVES OF FOREIGN EXCHANGE AND GOLD

This entry gives the dollar value for the stock of all financial assets that are available to the central monetary authority for use in meeting a country's balance of payments needs as of the end-date of the period specified. This category includes not only foreign currency and gold, but also a country's holdings of Special Drawing Rights in the International Monetary Fund, and its reserve position in the Fund.

ROADWAYS

This entry gives the *total* length of the road network and includes the length of the *paved* and *unpaved* portions.

SANITATION FACILITY ACCESS

This entry provides information about access to improved or unimproved sanitation facilities available to segments of the population of a country. *Improved* sanitation - use of any of the following facilities: flush or pour-flush to a piped sewer system, septic tank or pit latrine; ventilated improved pit (VIP) latrine; pit latrine with slab; or a composting toilet. *Unimproved* sanitation - use of any of the following facilities: flush or pour-flush not piped to a sewer system, septic tank or pit latrine; pit latrine without a slab or open pit; bucket; hanging toilet or hanging latrine; shared facilities of any type; no facilities; or bush or field.

SCHOOL LIFE EXPECTANCY (PRIMARY TO TERTIARY EDUCATION)

School life expectancy (SLE) is the total number of years of schooling (primary to tertiary) that a child can expect to receive, assuming that the probability of his or her being enrolled in school at any particular future age is equal to the current enrollment ratio at that age. Caution must be maintained when utilizing this indicator in international comparisons. For example, a year or grade completed in one country is not necessarily the same in terms of educational content or quality as a year or grade completed in another country. SLE represents the expected number of years of schooling that will be completed, including years spent repeating one or more grades.

SEX RATIO

This entry includes the number of males for each female in five age groups - *at birth, under 15 years, 15-64 years, 65 years and over*, and for the *total population*. Sex ratio at birth has recently emerged as an indicator of certain kinds of sex discrimination in some countries. For instance, high sex ratios at birth in some Asian countries are now attributed to sex-selective abortion and infanticide due to a strong preference for sons. This will affect future marriage patterns and fertility patterns. Eventually, it could cause unrest among young adult males who are unable to find partners.

STATELESS PERSON

Statelessness is the condition whereby an individual is not considered a national by any country. Stateless people are denied basic rights, such as access to employment, housing, education, healthcare, and pensions, and they may be unable to vote, own property, open a bank account, or legally register a marriage or birth. They may also be vulnerable to arbitrary treatment and human trafficking. In at least 30 states, women cannot pass their nationality on to their children. In these countries, if a child's father is foreign, stateless, or absent, the child usually becomes stateless. Estimates of the number of stateless people are inherently imprecise because few countries have procedures to identify them; the UN approximates that there are 12 million stateless people worldwide. Stateless people are counted in a country's overall population figure if they have lived there for a year.

STOCK OF BROAD MONEY

This entry covers all of "Narrow money," plus the total quantity of time and savings deposits, credit union deposits, institutional money market funds, short-term repurchase agreements between the central bank and commercial deposit banks, and other large liquid assets held by nonbank financial institutions, state and local governments, nonfinancial public enterprises, and the private sector of the economy. National currency units have been converted to US dollars at the closing exchange rate for the date of the information. Because of exchange rate movements, changes in money stocks measured in national currency units may vary significantly from those shown in US dollars, and caution is urged when making comparisons over time in US dollars. In addition to serving as a medium of exchange, broad money includes assets that are slightly less liquid than narrow money and the assets tend to function as a "store of value" - a means of holding wealth.

STOCK OF DIRECT FOREIGN INVESTMENT - ABROAD

This entry gives the cumulative US dollar value of all investments in foreign countries made directly by residents - primarily companies - of the home country, as of the end of the time period indicated. Direct investment excludes investment through purchase of shares.

STOCK OF DIRECT FOREIGN INVESTMENT - AT HOME

This entry gives the cumulative US dollar value of all investments in the home country made directly by residents - primarily companies - of other countries as of the end of the time period indicated. Direct investment excludes investment through purchase of shares.

STOCK OF DOMESTIC CREDIT

This entry is the total quantity of credit, denominated in the domestic currency, provided by financial institutions to the central bank, state and local governments, public non-financial corporations, and the private sector. The national currency units have been converted to US dollars at the closing exchange rate on the date of the information.

STOCK OF NARROW MONEY

This entry, also known as "M1," comprises the total quantity of currency in circulation (notes and coins) plus demand deposits denominated in the national currency held by nonbank financial institutions, state and local governments, nonfinancial public enterprises, and the private sector of the economy, measured at a specific point in time. National currency units have been converted to US dollars at the closing exchange rate for the date of the information. Because of exchange rate movements, changes in money stocks measured in national currency units may vary significantly from those shown in US dollars, and caution is urged when making comparisons over time in US dollars. Narrow money consists of more liquid assets than broad money and the assets generally function as a "medium of exchange" for an economy.

SUFFRAGE

This entry gives the age at enfranchisement and whether the right to vote is universal or restricted.

TAXES AND OTHER REVENUES

This entry records total taxes and other revenues received by the national government during the time period indicated, expressed as a percent of GDP. Taxes include personal and corporate income taxes, value added taxes, excise taxes, and tariffs. Other revenues include social contributions - such as payments for social security and hospital insurance - grants, and net revenues from public enterprises. Normalizing the data, by dividing total revenues by GDP, enables easy comparisons across countries, and provides an average rate at which all income (GDP) is paid to the national level government for the supply of public goods and services.

TELEPHONE NUMBERS

All telephone numbers in *The World Factbook* consist of the country code in brackets, the city or area code (where required) in parentheses, and the local number. The one component that is not presented is the international access code, which varies from country to country. For example, an international direct dial telephone call placed from the US to Madrid, Spain, would be as follows: 011 [34] (1) 577-xxxx, where 011 is the international access code for station-to-station calls; 01 is for calls other than station-to-station calls, [34] is the country code for Spain, (1) is the city code for Madrid, 577 is the local exchange, and xxxx is the local telephone number. An international direct dial telephone call placed from another country to the US would be as follows: international access code + [1] (202) 939-xxxx, where [1] is the country code for the US, (202) is the area code for Washington, DC, 939 is the local exchange, and xxxx is the local telephone number.

TELEPHONE SYSTEM

This entry includes a brief general assessment of the system with details on the domestic and international components. The following terms and abbreviations are used throughout the entry:

Arabsat - Arab Satellite Communications Organization (Riyadh, Saudi Arabia).

Autodin - Automatic Digital Network (US Department of Defense).

CB - citizen's band mobile radio communications.

Cellular telephone system - the telephones in this system are radio transceivers, with each instrument having its own private radio frequency and sufficient radiated power to reach the booster station in its area (cell), from which the telephone signal is fed to a telephone exchange.

Central American Microwave System - a trunk microwave radio relay system that links the countries of Central America and Mexico with each other.

Coaxial cable - a multichannel communication cable consisting of a central conducting wire, surrounded by and insulated from a cylindrical conducting shell; a large number of telephone channels can be made available within the insulated space by the use of a large number of carrier frequencies.

Comsat - Communications Satellite Corporation (US).

DSN - Defense Switched Network (formerly Automatic Voice Network or Autovon); basic general-purpose, switched voice network of the Defense Communications System (US Department of Defense).

Eutelsat - European Telecommunications Satellite Organization (Paris).

Fiber-optic cable - a multichannel communications cable using a thread of optical glass fibers as a transmission medium in which the signal (voice, video, etc.) is in the form of a coded pulse of light.

GSM - a global system for mobile (cellular) communications devised by the Groupe Special Mobile of the pan-European standardization organization, Conference Europeanne des Posts et Telecommunications (CEPT) in 1982.

HF - high frequency; any radio frequency in the 3,000- to 30,000-kHz range.

Inmarsat - International Maritime Satellite Organization (London); provider of global mobile satellite communications for commercial, distress, and safety applications at sea, in the air, and on land.

Intelsat - International Telecommunications Satellite Organization (Washington, DC).

Intersputnik - International Organization of Space Communications (Moscow); first established in the former Soviet Union and the East European countries, it is now marketing its services worldwide with earth stations in North America, Africa, and East Asia.

Landline - communication wire or cable of any sort that is installed on poles or buried in the ground.

Marecs - Maritime European Communications Satellite used in the Inmarsat system on lease from the European Space Agency.

Marisat - satellites of the Comsat Corporation that participate in the Inmarsat system.

Medarabtel - the Middle East Telecommunications Project of the International Telecommunications Union (ITU) providing a modern telecommunications network, primarily by microwave radio relay, linking Algeria, Djibouti, Egypt, Jordan, Libya, Morocco, Saudi Arabia, Somalia, Sudan, Syria, Tunisia, and Yemen; it was initially started in Morocco in 1970 by the Arab Telecommunications Union (ATU) and was known at that time as the Middle East Mediterranean Telecommunications Network.

Microwave radio relay - transmission of long distance telephone calls and television programs by highly directional radio microwaves that are received and sent on from one booster station to another on an optical path.

NMT - Nordic Mobile Telephone; an analog cellular telephone system that was developed jointly by the national telecommunications authorities of the Nordic countries (Denmark, Finland, Iceland, Norway, and Sweden).

Orbita - a Russian television service; also the trade name of a packet-switched digital telephone network.

Radiotelephone communications - the two-way transmission and reception of sounds by broadcast radio on authorized frequencies using telephone handsets.

PanAmSat - PanAmSat Corporation (Greenwich, CT).

SAFE - South African Far East Cable

Satellite communication system - a communication system consisting of two or more earth stations and at least one satellite that provide long distance transmission of voice, data, and television; the system usually serves as a trunk connection between telephone exchanges; if the earth stations are in the same country, it is a domestic system.

Satellite earth station - a communications facility with a microwave radio transmitting and receiving antenna and required receiving and transmitting equipment for communicating with satellites.

Satellite link - a radio connection between a satellite and an earth station permitting communication between them, either one-way (down link from satellite to earth station - television receive-only transmission) or two-way (telephone channels).

SHF - super high frequency; any radio frequency in the 3,000- to 30,000-MHz range.

Shortwave - radio frequencies (from 1.605 to 30 MHz) that fall above the commercial broadcast band

and are used for communication over long distances.
Solidaridad - geosynchronous satellites in Mexico's system of international telecommunications in the Western Hemisphere.
Statsionar - Russia's geostationary system for satellite telecommunications.
Submarine cable - a cable designed for service under water.
TAT - Trans-Atlantic Telephone; any of a number of high-capacity submarine coaxial telephone cables linking Europe with North America.
Telefax - facsimile service between subscriber stations via the public switched telephone network or the international Datel network.
Telegraph - a telecommunications system designed for unmodulated electric impulse transmission.
Telex - a communication service involving teletypewriters connected by wire through automatic exchanges.
Tropospheric scatter - a form of microwave radio transmission in which the troposphere is used to scatter and reflect a fraction of the incident radio waves back to earth; powerful, highly directional antennas are used to transmit and receive the microwave signals; reliable over-the-horizon communications are realized for distances up to 600 miles in a single hop; additional hops can extend the range of this system for very long distances.
Trunk network - a network of switching centers, connected by multichannel trunk lines.
UHF - ultra high frequency; any radio frequency in the 300- to 3,000-MHz range.
VHF - very high frequency; any radio frequency in the 30- to 300-MHz range.

TELEPHONES - FIXED LINES

This entry gives the *total* number of fixed telephone lines in use, as well as the number of *subscriptions per 100 inhabitants.*

TELEPHONES - MOBILE CELLULAR

This entry gives the *total* number of mobile cellular telephone subscribers, as well as the number of *subscriptions per 100 inhabitants.* Note that because of the ubiquity of mobile phone use in developed countries, the number of subscriptions per 100 inhabitants can exceed 100.

TERMINOLOGY

Due to the highly structured nature of the *Factbook* database, some collective generic terms have to be used. For example, the word **Country** in the **Country name** entry refers to a wide variety of dependencies, areas of special sovereignty, uninhabited islands, and other entities in addition to the traditional countries or independent states. **Military** is also used as an umbrella term for various civil defense, security, and defense activities in many entries. The **Independence** entry includes the usual colonial independence dates and former ruling states as well as other significant nationhood dates such as the traditional founding date or the date of unification, federation, confederation, establishment, or state succession that are not strictly independence dates. Dependent areas have the nature of their dependency status noted in this same entry.

TERRAIN

This entry contains a brief description of the topography.

TERRORIST GROUPS - FOREIGN BASED

This entry provides information on the US State Department's designated Foreign Terrorist Organizations operating in countries other than where a particular group is headquartered. Details on each organization's aim(s) and area(s) of operation are provided.

TERRORIST GROUPS - HOME BASED

This entry provides information on the US State Department's designated Foreign Terrorist Organizations headquartered in a specific country, which may or may not be a group's country of origin. Details on each organization's aim(s) and area(s) of operation are provided.

TIME DIFFERENCE

This entry is expressed in *The World Factbook* in two ways. First, it is stated as the difference in hours between the capital of an entity and **Coordinated Universal Time (UTC)** during Standard Time. Additionally, the difference in time between the capital of an entity and that observed in Washington, D.C. is also provided. Note that the time difference assumes both locations are simultaneously observing Standard Time or Daylight Saving Time.

TIME ZONES

Ten countries (Australia, Brazil, Canada, Indonesia, Kazakhstan, Mexico, New Zealand, Russia, Spain, and the United States) and the island of Greenland observe more than one official time depending on the number of designated time zones within their boundaries. An illustration of time zones throughout the world and within countries can be seen in the Standard Time Zones of the World map included in the **Reference Maps** section of *The World Factbook.*

TOTAL FERTILITY RATE

This entry gives a figure for the average number of children that would be born per woman if all women lived to the end of their childbearing years and bore children according to a given fertility rate at each age. The total fertility rate (TFR) is a more direct measure of the level of fertility than the crude birth rate, since it refers to births per woman. This indicator shows the potential for population change in the country. A rate of two children per woman is considered the replacement rate for a population, resulting in relative stability in terms of total numbers. Rates above two children indicate populations growing in size and whose median age is declining. Higher rates may also indicate difficulties for families, in some situations, to feed and educate their children and for women to enter the labor force. Rates below two children indicate populations decreasing in size and growing older. Global fertility rates are in general decline and this trend is most pronounced in industrialized countries, especially Western Europe, where populations are projected to decline dramatically over the next 50 years.

TRAFFICKING IN PERSONS

Trafficking in persons is modern-day slavery, involving victims who are forced, defrauded, or coerced into labor or sexual exploitation. The International Labor Organization (ILO), the UN agency charged with addressing labor standards, employment, and social protection issues, estimated in 2011 that 20.9 million people worldwide were victims of forced labor, bonded labor, forced child labor, sexual servitude, and involuntary servitude. Human trafficking is a multi-dimensional threat, depriving people of their human rights and freedoms, risking global health, promoting social breakdown, inhibiting development by depriving countries of their human capital, and helping fuel the growth of organized crime. In 2000, the US Congress passed the Trafficking Victims Protection Act (TVPA), reauthorized in 2003 and 2005, which provides tools for the US to combat trafficking in persons, both domestically and abroad. One of the law's key components is the creation of the US Department of State's annual *Trafficking in Persons Report*, which assesses the government response (i.e., the *current situation*) in some 150 countries with a significant number of victims trafficked across their borders who are recruited, harbored, transported, provided, or obtained for forced labor or sexual exploitation. Countries in the annual report are rated in three tiers, based on government efforts to combat trafficking. The countries identified in this entry are those listed in the *2010 Trafficking in Persons Report* as *Tier 2 Watch List* or *Tier 3* based on the following *tier rating* definitions:
Tier 2 Watch List *countries do not fully comply with the minimum standards for the elimination of trafficking but are making significant efforts to do so, and meet one of the following criteria:*
1. they display high or significantly increasing number of victims,
2. they have failed to provide evidence of increasing efforts to combat trafficking in persons, or,
3. they have committed to take action over the next year.
Tier 3 *countries neither satisfy the minimum standards for the elimination of trafficking nor demonstrate a significant effort to do so. Countries in this tier are subject to potential non-humanitarian and non-trade sanctions.*

TRANSNATIONAL ISSUES

This category includes four entries - **Disputes - international**, **Refugees and internally displaced persons**, **Trafficking in persons**, and **Illicit drugs** - that deal with current issues going beyond national boundaries.

TRANSPORTATION

This category includes the entries dealing with the means for movement of people and goods.

TRANSPORTATION - NOTE

This entry includes miscellaneous transportation information of significance not included elsewhere.

UNEMPLOYMENT RATE

This entry contains the percent of the labor force that is without jobs. Substantial underemployment might be noted.

UNEMPLOYMENT, YOUTH AGES 15-24

This entry gives the percent of the total labor force ages 15-24 unemployed during a specified year.

URBANIZATION

This entry provides two measures of the degree of urbanization of a population. The first, *urban population*, describes the percentage of the total population living in urban areas, as defined by the country. The second, *rate of urbanization*, describes the projected average rate of change of the size of the urban population over the given period of time. Additionally, the World entry includes a list of the *ten largest urban agglomerations*. An *urban agglomeration* is defined as comprising the city or town proper and also the suburban fringe or thickly settled territory lying outside of, but adjacent to, the boundaries of the city.

UTC (COORDINATED UNIVERSAL TIME)

See entry for Coordinated Universal Time.

WATERWAYS

This entry gives the total length of navigable rivers, canals, and other inland bodies of water.

WEIGHTS AND MEASURES

This information is presented in Appendix G: Weights and Measures and includes mathematical notations (mathematical powers and names), metric interrelationships (prefix; symbol; length, weight, or capacity; area; volume), and standard conversion factors.

YEARS

All year references are for the calendar year (CY) unless indicated as fiscal year (FY). The calendar year is an accounting period of 12 months from 1 January to 31 December. The fiscal year is an accounting period of 12 months other than 1 January to 31 December.

REGIONAL AND WORLD REFERENCE MAPS

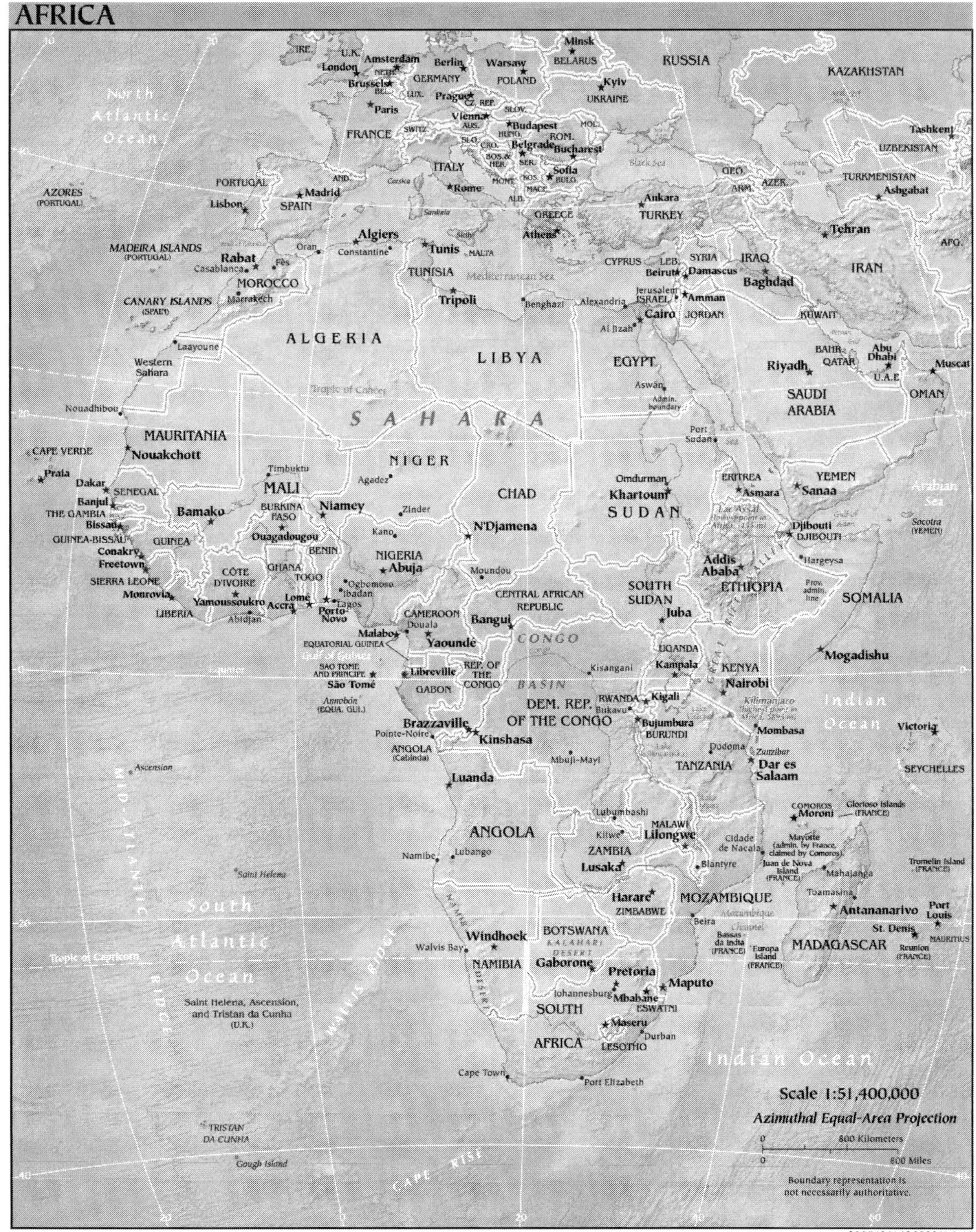
AFRICA
North Atlantic Ocean
AZORES (PORTUGAL)
MADEIRA ISLANDS (PORTUGAL)
CANARY ISLANDS (SPAIN)
CAPE VERDE
Praia
IRE.
U.K.
London
Amsterdam
NETH.
Brussels
BEL.
LUX.
Paris
FRANCE
SWITZ.
Berlin
GERMANY
Prague
CZ. REP.
Warsaw
POLAND
Minsk
BELARUS
RUSSIA
Kyiv
UKRAINE
KAZAKHSTAN
Vienna
AUS.
SLOV.
Budapest
HUNG.
MOL.
ROM.
SLO.
CRO.
BOS.& HER.
Belgrade
SER.
Bucharest
Sofia
BULG.
KOS.
MACE.
MONT.
ALB.
ITALY
Rome
Corsica
Sardinia
Sicily
MALTA
PORTUGAL
Lisbon
SPAIN
Madrid
AND.
GREECE
Athens
TURKEY
Ankara
Black Sea
Caspian Sea
GEO.
ARM.
AZER.
Tashkent
UZBEKISTAN
TURKMENISTAN
Ashgabat
Tehran
IRAN
AFG.
Algiers
Oran
Constantine
Tunis
TUNISIA
Rabat
Casablanca
Fès
MOROCCO
Marrakech
Mediterranean Sea
CYPRUS
LEB.
Beirut
SYRIA
Damascus
IRAQ
Baghdad
Jerusalem
ISRAEL
Amman
JORDAN
KUWAIT
Tripoli
Benghazi
Alexandria
Cairo
Al Jizah
ALGERIA
LIBYA
EGYPT
Laayoune
Western Sahara
Tropic of Cancer
Aswan
Admin. boundary
SAUDI ARABIA
Riyadh
BAHR.
QATAR
Abu Dhabi
U.A.E.
Muscat
OMAN
Nouadhibou
S A H A R A
MAURITANIA
Nouakchott
Port Sudan
Red Sea
Timbuktu
NIGER
Agadez
Zinder
MALI
Dakar
SENEGAL
Banjul
THE GAMBIA
Bissau
GUINEA-BISSAU
GUINEA
Conakry
Freetown
SIERRA LEONE
Monrovia
LIBERIA
Bamako
BURKINA FASO
Ouagadougou
Niamey
CHAD
N'Djamena
Omdurman
Khartoum
SUDAN
ERITREA
Asmara
YEMEN
Sanaa
Arabian Sea
Socotra (YEMEN)
Djibouti
DJIBOUTI
Hargeysa
Kano
NIGERIA
Abuja
BENIN
GHANA
TOGO
CÔTE D'IVOIRE
Yamoussoukro
Abidjan
Accra
Lomé
Porto-Novo
Lagos
Ibadan
Ogbomoso
Moundou
CENTRAL AFRICAN REPUBLIC
Bangui
SOUTH SUDAN
Juba
Addis Ababa
ETHIOPIA
Prov. admin. line
SOMALIA
Mogadishu
CAMEROON
Douala
Malabo
Yaoundé
EQUATORIAL GUINEA
Gulf of Guinea
SAO TOME AND PRINCIPE
São Tomé
Equator
Libreville
GABON
REP. OF THE CONGO
CONGO BASIN
Kisangani
UGANDA
Kampala
KENYA
Nairobi
Kilimanjaro
Indian Ocean
Annobón (EQUA. GUI.)
DEM. REP. OF THE CONGO
RWANDA
Kigali
Bukavu
Bujumbura
BURUNDI
Mombasa
Victoria
SEYCHELLES
Brazzaville
Kinshasa
Pointe-Noire
ANGOLA (Cabinda)
Mbuji-Mayi
Dodoma
Zanzibar
TANZANIA
Dar es Salaam
Ascension
Luanda
Lubumbashi
COMOROS
Moroni
Glorioso Islands (FRANCE)
ANGOLA
Namibe
Lubango
MALAWI
Lilongwe
Kitwe
ZAMBIA
Lusaka
Blantyre
Cidade de Nacala
Mayotte (admin. by France, claimed by Comoros)
Juan de Nova Island (FRANCE)
Mahajanga
Tromelin Island (FRANCE)
Saint Helena
South Atlantic Ocean
MID-ATLANTIC RIDGE
Harare
ZIMBABWE
MOZAMBIQUE
Beira
Toamasina
Antananarivo
MADAGASCAR
Port Louis
St. Denis
MAURITIUS
Reunion (FRANCE)
Bassas da India (FRANCE)
Europa Island (FRANCE)
Tropic of Capricorn
Windhoek
Walvis Bay
NAMIBIA
BOTSWANA
KALAHARI DESERT
Gaborone
Pretoria
Maputo
Johannesburg
Mbabane
ESWATINI
WALVIS RIDGE
Saint Helena, Ascension, and Tristan da Cunha (U.K.)
SOUTH AFRICA
Maseru
LESOTHO
Durban
Cape Town
Port Elizabeth
TRISTAN DA CUNHA
Gough Island
CAPE RISE
Scale 1:51,400,000
Azimuthal Equal-Area Projection
0 800 Kilometers
0 800 Miles
Boundary representation is not necessarily authoritative.
803510AI (G00392) 6-12

AFRICA

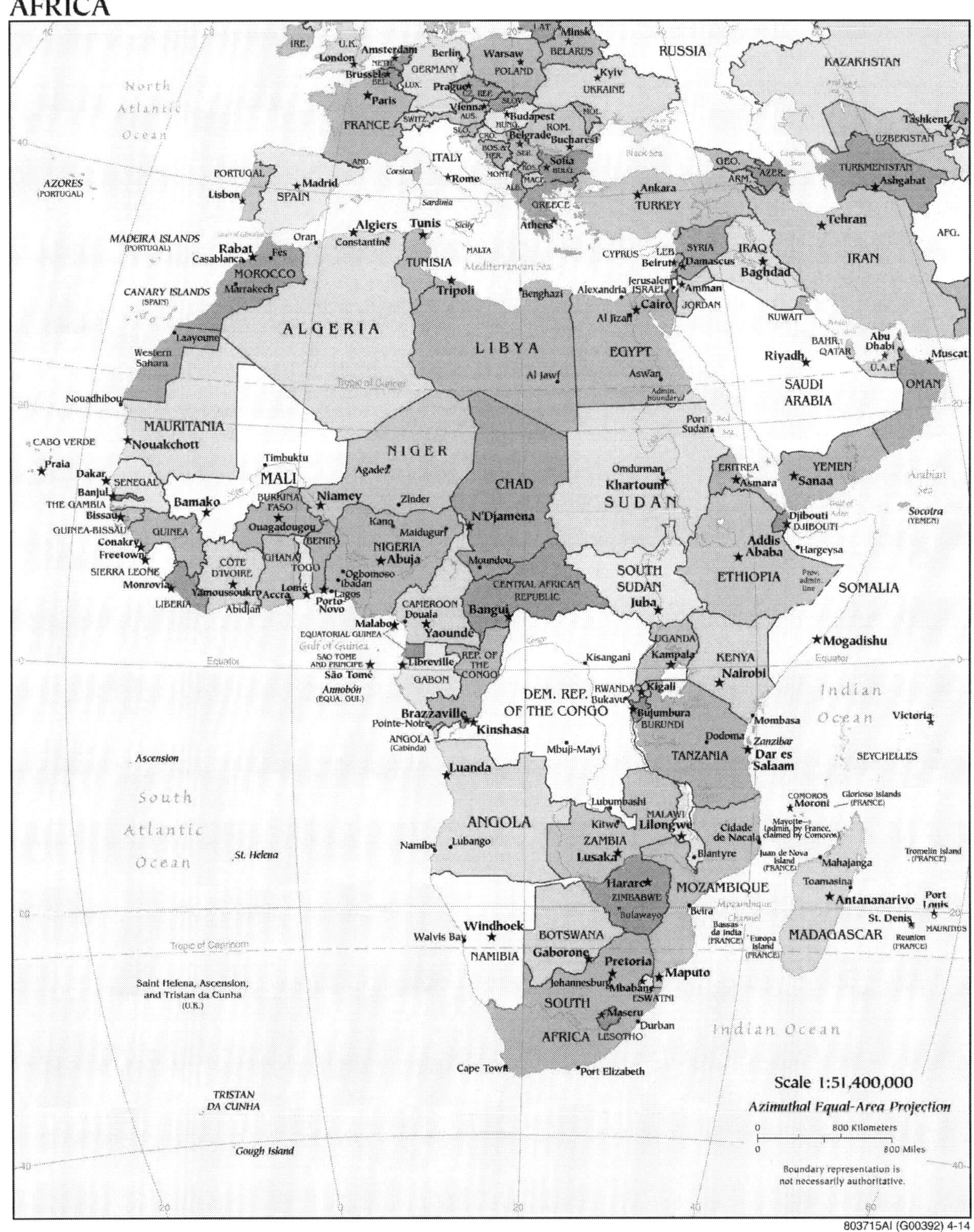
North Atlantic Ocean
AZORES (PORTUGAL)
MADEIRA ISLANDS (PORTUGAL)
CANARY ISLANDS (SPAIN)
CABO VERDE
Praia
Ascension
South Atlantic Ocean
St. Helena
Saint Helena, Ascension, and Tristan da Cunha (U.K.)
TRISTAN DA CUNHA
Gough Island
IRE.
U.K.
London
Amsterdam
NETH.
Brussels
BEL.
LUX.
Paris
FRANCE
SWITZ.
Berlin
GERMANY
Prague
Vienna
AUS.
Warsaw
POLAND
Minsk
BELARUS
Kyiv
UKRAINE
RUSSIA
KAZAKHSTAN
MOL.
Budapest
HUNG.
ROM.
Bucharest
Belgrade
Sofia
BULG.
ITALY
Rome
Corsica
Sardinia
Sicily
MALTA
AND.
PORTUGAL
Lisbon
Madrid
SPAIN
GREECE
Athens
Ankara
TURKEY
Black Sea
GEO.
ARM.
AZER.
TURKMENISTAN
Ashgabat
UZBEKISTAN
Tashkent
Tehran
IRAN
AFG.
CYPRUS
LEB.
Beirut
SYRIA
Damascus
IRAQ
Baghdad
Jerusalem
ISRAEL
Amman
JORDAN
KUWAIT
BAHR.
QATAR
Abu Dhabi
U.A.E.
Muscat
OMAN
Riyadh
SAUDI ARABIA
YEMEN
Sanaa
Arabian Sea
Socotra (YEMEN)
Mediterranean Sea
Rabat
Fès
Casablanca
MOROCCO
Marrakech
Laayoune
Western Sahara
Oran
Algiers
Constantine
Tunis
TUNISIA
Tripoli
Benghazi
ALGERIA
LIBYA
Al Jawf
Alexandria
Cairo
Al Jizah
EGYPT
Aswan
Admin. boundary
Tropic of Cancer
Nouadhibou
MAURITANIA
Nouakchott
Timbuktu
MALI
NIGER
Agadez
Zinder
Niamey
Dakar
SENEGAL
Banjul
THE GAMBIA
Bissau
GUINEA-BISSAU
GUINEA
Conakry
Freetown
SIERRA LEONE
Monrovia
LIBERIA
Bamako
BURKINA FASO
Ouagadougou
COTE D'IVOIRE
Yamoussoukro
Abidjan
GHANA
Accra
TOGO
Lomé
BENIN
Porto-Novo
Kano
Maiduguri
NIGERIA
Abuja
Ogbomoso
Ibadan
Lagos
CHAD
N'Djamena
Moundou
CENTRAL AFRICAN REPUBLIC
Bangui
CAMEROON
Douala
Yaoundé
Malabo
EQUATORIAL GUINEA
Gulf of Guinea
SAO TOME AND PRINCIPE
São Tomé
Annobón (EQUA. GUI.)
Libreville
GABON
REP. OF THE CONGO
Brazzaville
Kinshasa
Pointe-Noire
ANGOLA (Cabinda)
Equator
Port Sudan
Red Sea
Omdurman
Khartoum
SUDAN
SOUTH SUDAN
Juba
ERITREA
Asmara
Djibouti
DJIBOUTI
Gulf of Aden
Addis Ababa
Hargeysa
ETHIOPIA
Prov. admin. line
SOMALIA
Mogadishu
UGANDA
Kampala
KENYA
Nairobi
Kisangani
RWANDA
Kigali
Bukavu
Bujumbura
BURUNDI
DEM. REP. OF THE CONGO
Mbuji-Mayi
Mombasa
Dodoma
Zanzibar
Dar es Salaam
TANZANIA
Indian Ocean
Victoria
SEYCHELLES
Luanda
ANGOLA
Namibe
Lubango
Lubumbashi
Kitwe
ZAMBIA
Lusaka
MALAWI
Lilongwe
Blantyre
Cidade de Nacala
COMOROS
Moroni
Glorioso Islands (FRANCE)
Mayotte (admin. by France, claimed by Comoros)
Juan de Nova Island (FRANCE)
Mahajanga
Tromelin Island (FRANCE)
Harare
ZIMBABWE
Bulawayo
MOZAMBIQUE
Mozambique Channel
Beira
Bassas da India (FRANCE)
Europa Island (FRANCE)
Toamasina
Antananarivo
MADAGASCAR
Port Louis
MAURITIUS
St. Denis
Reunion (FRANCE)
Windhoek
Walvis Bay
NAMIBIA
BOTSWANA
Gaborone
Pretoria
Johannesburg
Mbabane
ESWATINI
Maputo
SOUTH AFRICA
Maseru
LESOTHO
Durban
Cape Town
Port Elizabeth
Tropic of Capricorn
Scale 1:51,400,000
Azimuthal Equal-Area Projection
0 800 Kilometers
0 800 Miles
Boundary representation is not necessarily authoritative.
803715AI (G00392) 4-14

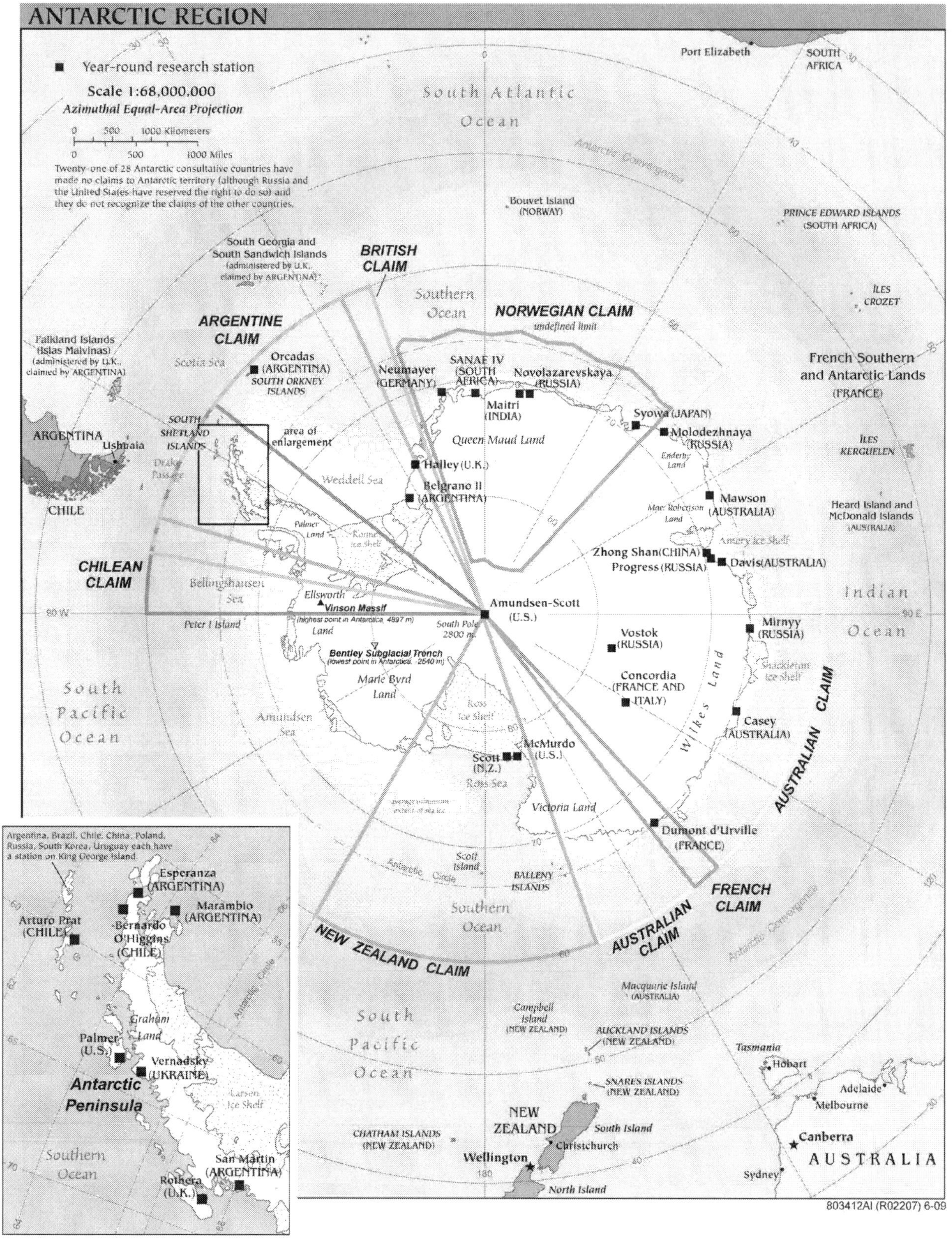
ANTARCTIC REGION
Year-round research station
Scale 1:68,000,000
Azimuthal Equal-Area Projection
Twenty-one of 28 Antarctic consultative countries have made no claims to Antarctic territory (although Russia and the United States have reserved the right to do so) and they do not recognize the claims of the other countries.
South Atlantic Ocean
Port Elizabeth
SOUTH AFRICA
Bouvet Island (NORWAY)
PRINCE EDWARD ISLANDS (SOUTH AFRICA)
ÎLES CROZET
French Southern and Antarctic Lands (FRANCE)
ÎLES KERGUELEN
Heard Island and McDonald Islands (AUSTRALIA)
South Georgia and South Sandwich Islands (administered by U.K., claimed by ARGENTINA)
BRITISH CLAIM
NORWEGIAN CLAIM
undefined limit
ARGENTINE CLAIM
CHILEAN CLAIM
AUSTRALIAN CLAIM
FRENCH CLAIM
NEW ZEALAND CLAIM
Falkland Islands (Islas Malvinas) (administered by U.K., claimed by ARGENTINA)
Orcadas (ARGENTINA)
SOUTH ORKNEY ISLANDS
Scotia Sea
ARGENTINA
Ushuaia
CHILE
SOUTH SHETLAND ISLANDS
Drake Passage
area of enlargement
Neumayer (GERMANY)
SANAE IV (SOUTH AFRICA)
Novolazarevskaya (RUSSIA)
Maitri (INDIA)
Syowa (JAPAN)
Molodezhnaya (RUSSIA)
Queen Maud Land
Enderby Land
Halley (U.K.)
Belgrano II (ARGENTINA)
Weddell Sea
Mawson (AUSTRALIA)
Mac. Robertson Land
Amery Ice Shelf
Zhong Shan (CHINA)
Progress (RUSSIA)
Davis (AUSTRALIA)
Palmer Land
Ronne Ice Shelf
Bellingshausen Sea
Ellsworth Land
Vinson Massif
(highest point in Antarctica, 4897 m)
Amundsen-Scott (U.S.)
South Pole 2800 m
Peter I Island
Bentley Subglacial Trench
(lowest point in Antarctica, -2540 m)
Mirnyy (RUSSIA)
Vostok (RUSSIA)
Indian Ocean
Concordia (FRANCE AND ITALY)
Wilkes Land
Shackleton Ice Shelf
Casey (AUSTRALIA)
Marie Byrd Land
South Pacific Ocean
Amundsen Sea
Ross Ice Shelf
McMurdo (U.S.)
Scott (N.Z.)
Ross Sea
Victoria Land
Dumont d'Urville (FRANCE)
Scott Island
Antarctic Circle
BALLENY ISLANDS
Southern Ocean
Antarctic Convergence
Macquarie Island (AUSTRALIA)
Campbell Island (NEW ZEALAND)
AUCKLAND ISLANDS (NEW ZEALAND)
SNARES ISLANDS (NEW ZEALAND)
Tasmania
Hobart
Adelaide
Melbourne
Canberra
AUSTRALIA
Sydney
NEW ZEALAND
South Island
North Island
Christchurch
Wellington
CHATHAM ISLANDS (NEW ZEALAND)
Argentina, Brazil, Chile, China, Poland, Russia, South Korea, Uruguay each have a station on King George Island
Esperanza (ARGENTINA)
Marambio (ARGENTINA)
Arturo Prat (CHILE)
Bernardo O'Higgins (CHILE)
Graham Land
Palmer (U.S.)
Vernadsky (UKRAINE)
Antarctic Peninsula
Larsen Ice Shelf
San Martín (ARGENTINA)
Rothera (U.K.)
803412AI (R02207) 6-09

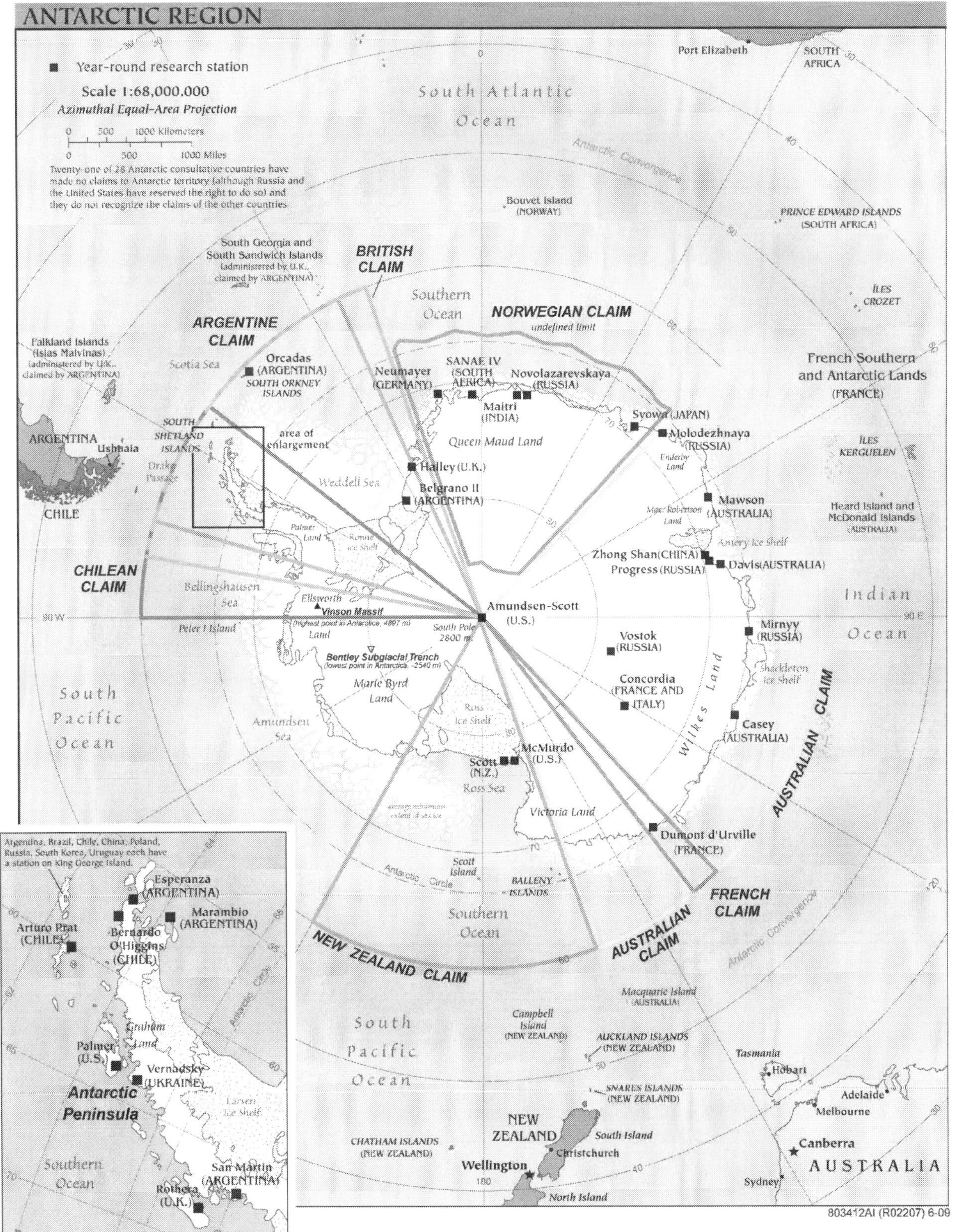
ANTARCTIC REGION
Year-round research station
Scale 1:68,000,000
Azimuthal Equal-Area Projection
Twenty-one of 28 Antarctic consultative countries have made no claims to Antarctic territory (although Russia and the United States have reserved the right to do so) and they do not recognize the claims of the other countries.
South Atlantic Ocean
Port Elizabeth
SOUTH AFRICA
Antarctic Convergence
Bouvet Island (NORWAY)
PRINCE EDWARD ISLANDS (SOUTH AFRICA)
ÎLES CROZET
French Southern and Antarctic Lands (FRANCE)
ÎLES KERGUELEN
Heard Island and McDonald Islands (AUSTRALIA)
South Georgia and South Sandwich Islands (administered by U.K., claimed by ARGENTINA)
BRITISH CLAIM
ARGENTINE CLAIM
NORWEGIAN CLAIM
undefined limit
Southern Ocean
Falkland Islands (Islas Malvinas) (administered by U.K., claimed by ARGENTINA)
Scotia Sea
Orcadas (ARGENTINA)
SOUTH ORKNEY ISLANDS
Neumayer (GERMANY)
SANAE IV (SOUTH AFRICA)
Novolazarevskaya (RUSSIA)
Maitri (INDIA)
Syowa (JAPAN)
Molodezhnaya (RUSSIA)
Enderby Land
Queen Maud Land
ARGENTINA
Ushuaia
SOUTH SHETLAND ISLANDS
area of enlargement
Drake Passage
CHILE
Halley (U.K.)
Weddell Sea
Belgrano II (ARGENTINA)
Mawson (AUSTRALIA)
Mac. Robertson Land
Palmer Land
Ronne Ice Shelf
Amery Ice Shelf
Zhong Shan (CHINA)
Progress (RUSSIA)
Davis (AUSTRALIA)
CHILEAN CLAIM
Bellingshausen Sea
Ellsworth Land
Vinson Massif
(highest point in Antarctica, 4897 m)
Amundsen-Scott (U.S.)
South Pole 2800 m
Peter I Island
Indian Ocean
Mirnyy (RUSSIA)
Vostok (RUSSIA)
Bentley Subglacial Trench
(lowest point in Antarctica, -2540 m)
Marie Byrd Land
Concordia (FRANCE AND ITALY)
Shackleton Ice Shelf
Wilkes Land
South Pacific Ocean
Amundsen Sea
Ross Ice Shelf
Casey (AUSTRALIA)
AUSTRALIAN CLAIM
McMurdo (U.S.)
Scott (N.Z.)
Ross Sea
Victoria Land
Dumont d'Urville (FRANCE)
Scott Island
BALLENY ISLANDS
Antarctic Circle
FRENCH CLAIM
Southern Ocean
NEW ZEALAND CLAIM
AUSTRALIAN CLAIM
Macquarie Island (AUSTRALIA)
Campbell Island (NEW ZEALAND)
AUCKLAND ISLANDS (NEW ZEALAND)
South Pacific Ocean
Tasmania
Hobart
SNARES ISLANDS (NEW ZEALAND)
Adelaide
Melbourne
NEW ZEALAND
South Island
CHATHAM ISLANDS (NEW ZEALAND)
Christchurch
Canberra
AUSTRALIA
Wellington
North Island
Sydney
90 W
90 E
180
Argentina, Brazil, Chile, China, Poland, Russia, South Korea, Uruguay each have a station on King George Island.
Esperanza (ARGENTINA)
Marambio (ARGENTINA)
Arturo Prat (CHILE)
Bernardo O'Higgins (CHILE)
Graham Land
Palmer (U.S.)
Vernadsky (UKRAINE)
Antarctic Peninsula
Larsen Ice Shelf
Southern Ocean
San Martin (ARGENTINA)
Rothera (U.K.)
803412AI (R02207) 6-09

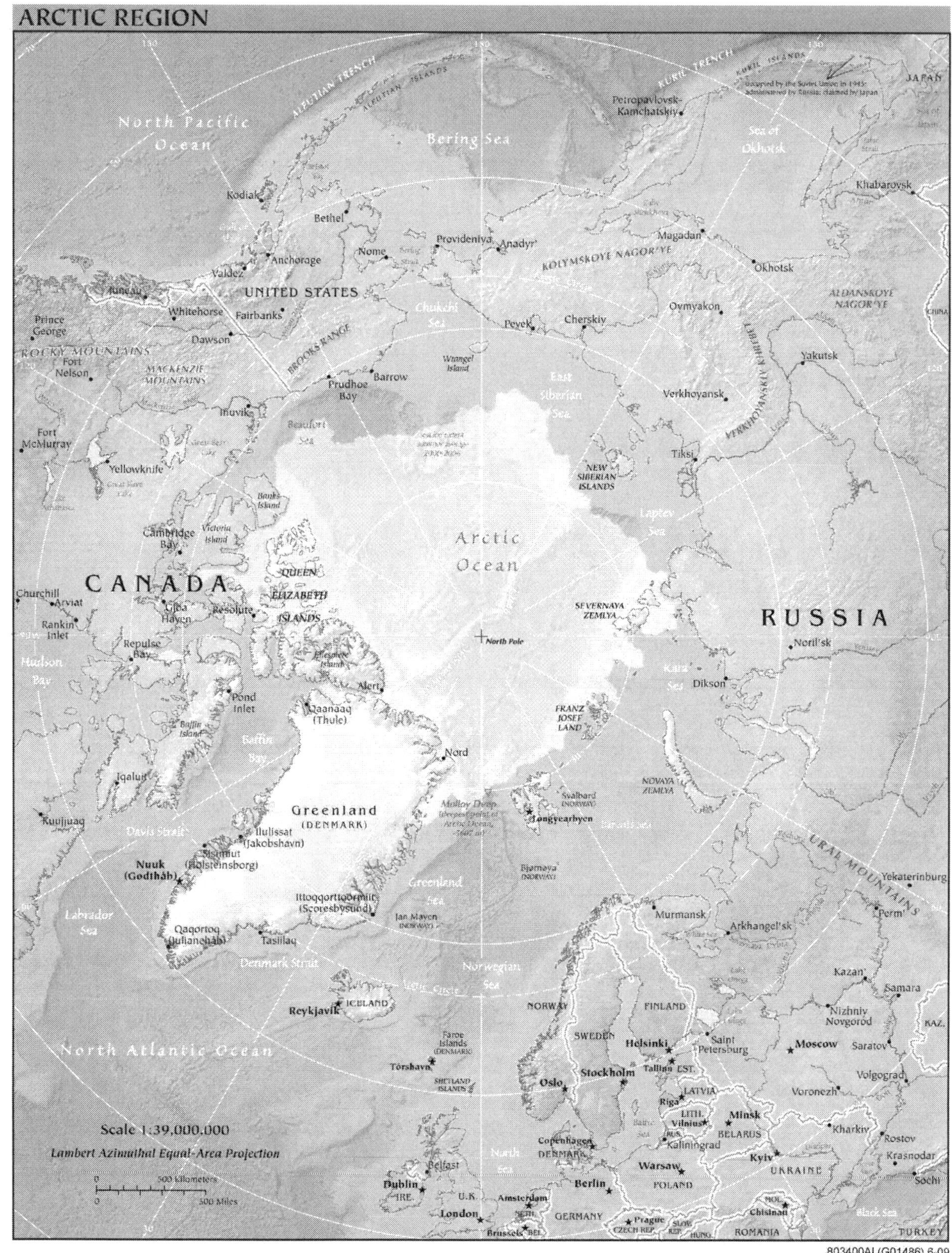

803400AI (G01486) 6-09

ARCTIC REGION

803536AI (G01486) 6-12

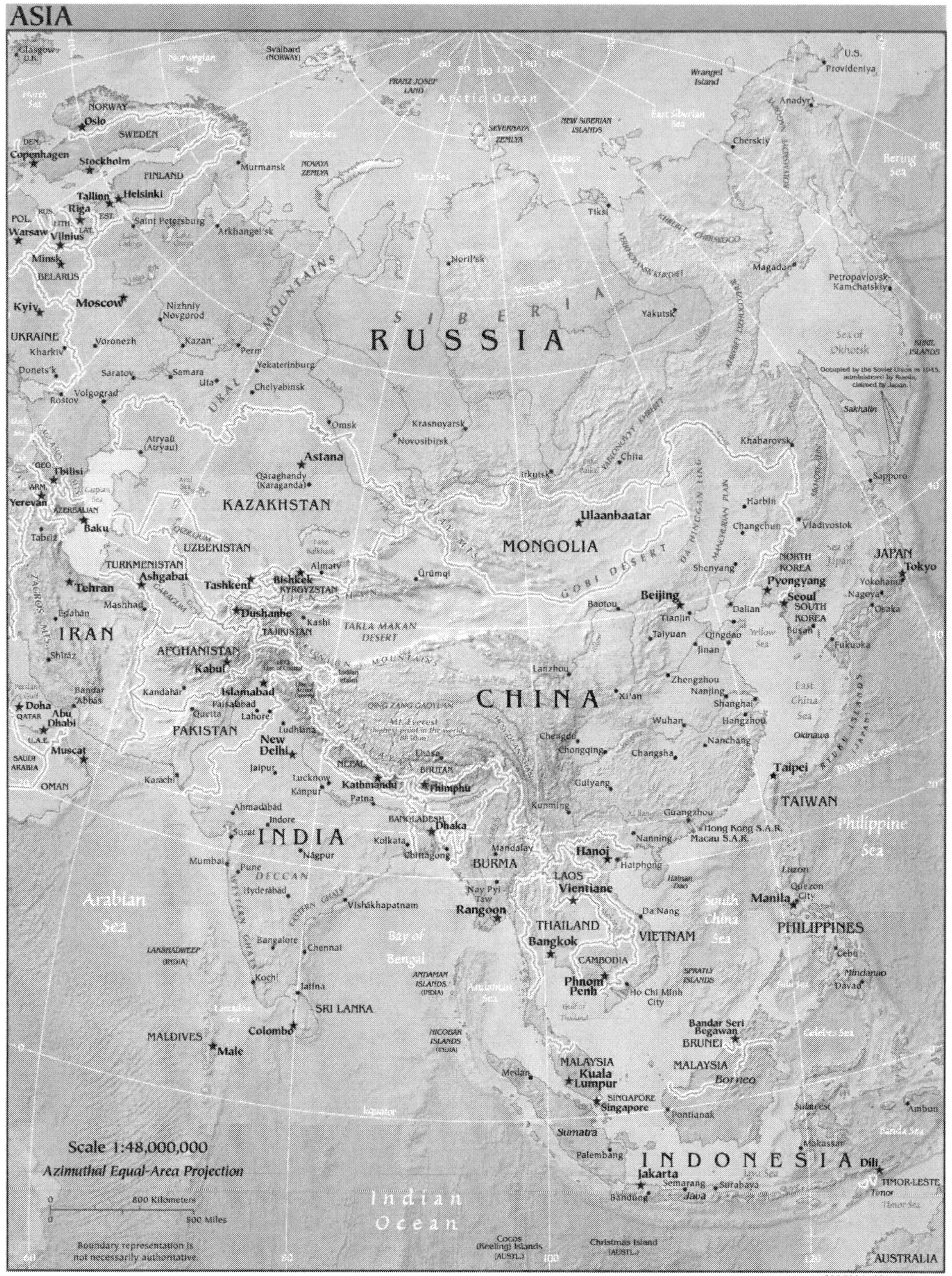

803623AI (G00543) 8-13

ASIA

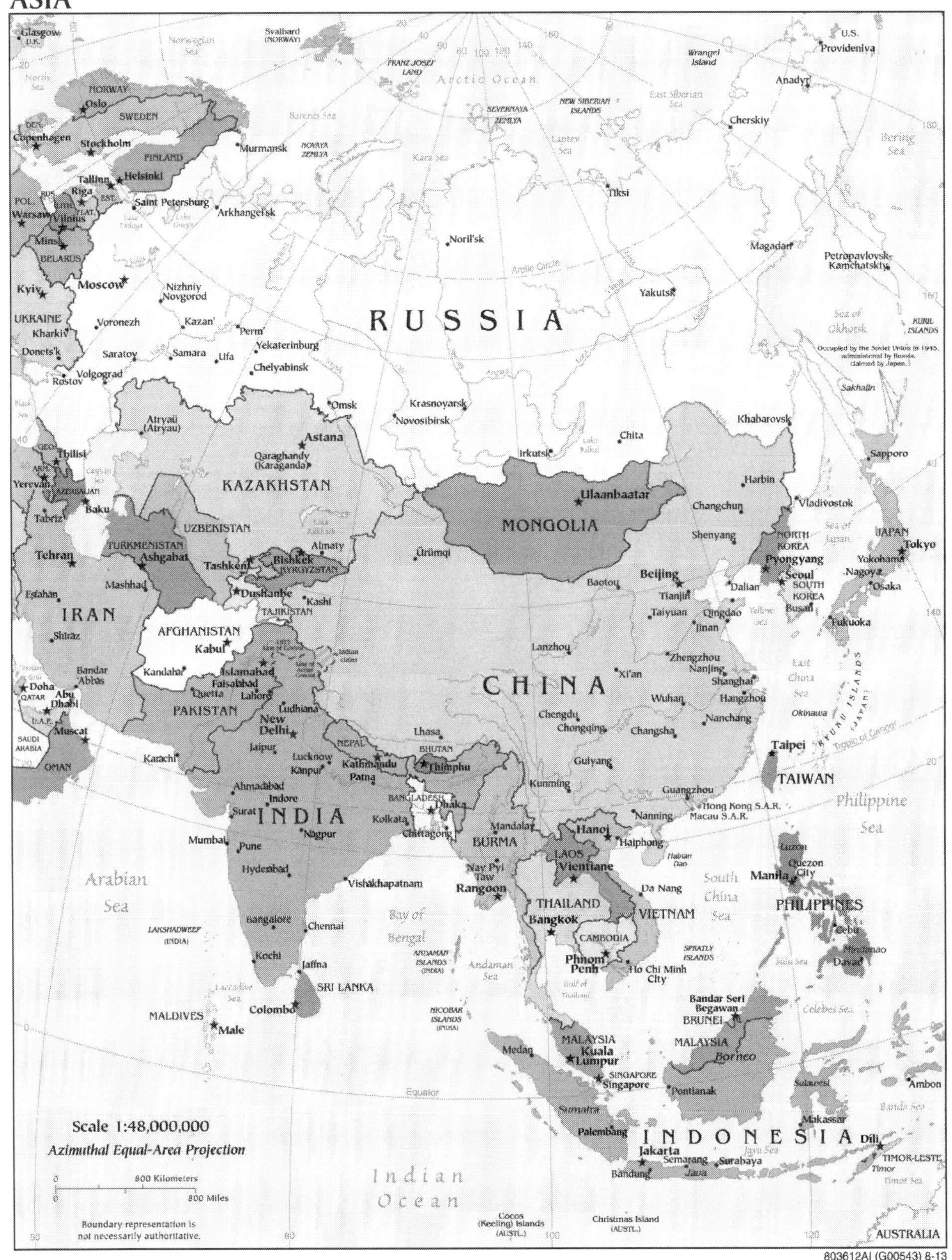

803612AI (G00543) 8-13

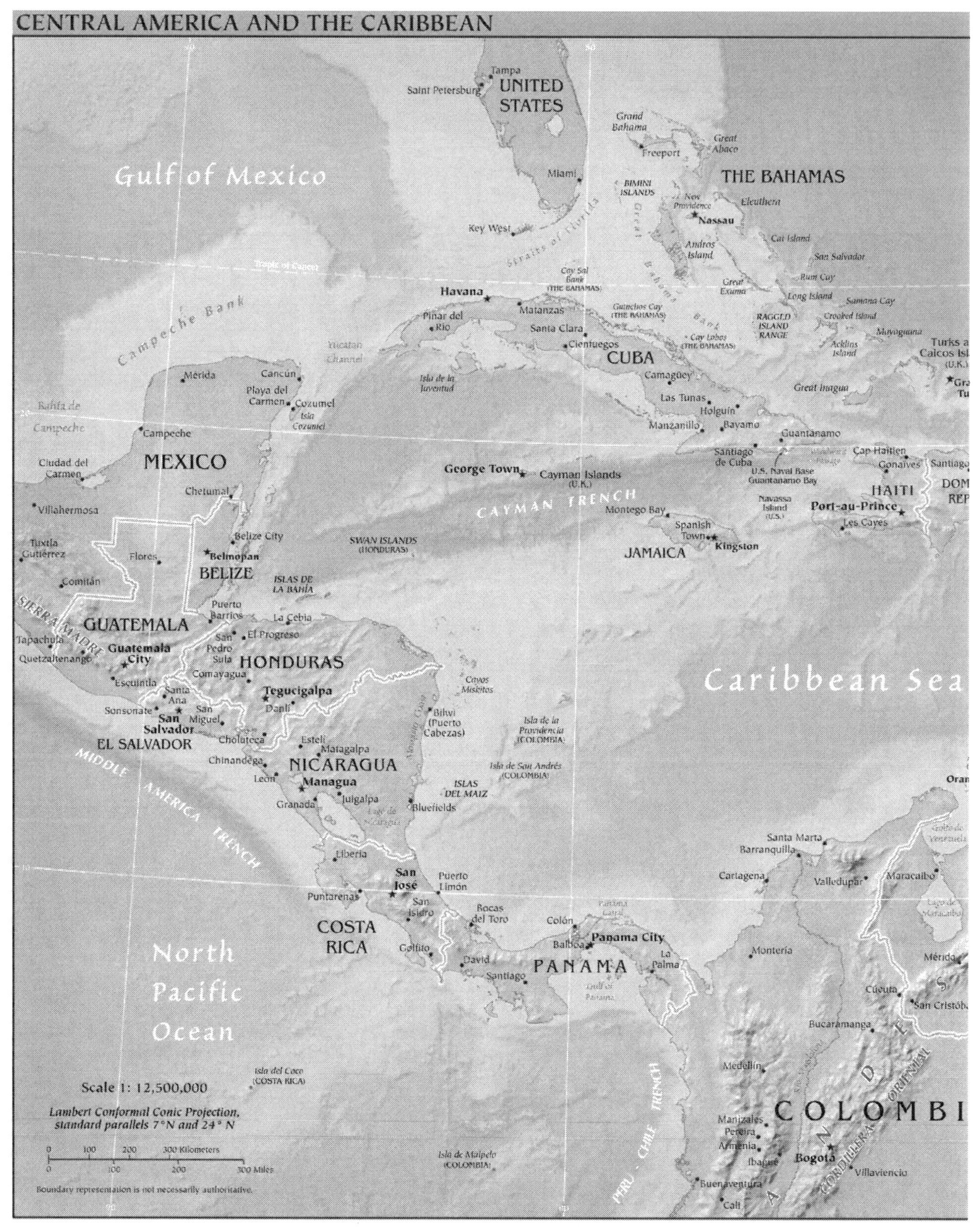
CENTRAL AMERICA AND THE CARIBBEAN
Gulf of Mexico
UNITED STATES
Tampa
Saint Petersburg
Miami
Key West
Grand Bahama
Freeport
Great Abaco
THE BAHAMAS
BIMINI ISLANDS
New Providence
Nassau
Eleuthera
Andros Island
Cat Island
San Salvador
Rum Cay
Great Exuma
Long Island
Samana Cay
Crooked Island
Mayaguana
Acklins Island
RAGGED ISLAND RANGE
Turks and Caicos Islands (U.K.)
Great Inagua
Straits of Florida
Great Bahama Bank
Cay Sal Bank (THE BAHAMAS)
Guinchos Cay (THE BAHAMAS)
Cay Lobos (THE BAHAMAS)
Tropic of Cancer
Campeche Bank
Yucatan Channel
Havana
Pinar del Rio
Matanzas
Santa Clara
Cienfuegos
CUBA
Isla de la Juventud
Camagüey
Las Tunas
Holguín
Manzanillo
Bayamo
Santiago de Cuba
Guantánamo
U.S. Naval Base Guantanamo Bay
Cap-Haïtien
Gonaïves
HAITI
Port-au-Prince
Les Cayes
Navassa Island (U.S.)
George Town
Cayman Islands (U.K.)
CAYMAN TRENCH
Montego Bay
Spanish Town
Kingston
JAMAICA
Mérida
Cancún
Playa del Carmen
Cozumel
Isla Cozumel
Bahía de Campeche
Campeche
Ciudad del Carmen
MEXICO
Chetumal
Villahermosa
Tuxtla Gutiérrez
Comitán
Flores
Belize City
Belmopan
BELIZE
SWAN ISLANDS (HONDURAS)
ISLAS DE LA BAHÍA
SIERRA MADRE
GUATEMALA
Puerto Barrios
La Ceiba
El Progreso
San Pedro Sula
Tapachula
Quetzaltenango
Guatemala City
Escuintla
HONDURAS
Comayagua
Tegucigalpa
Danlí
Santa Ana
Sonsonate
San Salvador
San Miguel
EL SALVADOR
Choluteca
Cayos Miskitos
Bilwi (Puerto Cabezas)
Isla de la Providencia (COLOMBIA)
Isla de San Andrés (COLOMBIA)
ISLAS DEL MAIZ
Caribbean Sea
MIDDLE AMERICA TRENCH
Chinandega
Estelí
Matagalpa
NICARAGUA
León
Managua
Juigalpa
Granada
Bluefields
Liberia
San José
Puerto Limón
Puntarenas
San Isidro
Bocas del Toro
COSTA RICA
Golfito
Colón
Panama City
Balboa
David
Santiago
PANAMA
La Palma
Gulf of Panama
Santa Marta
Barranquilla
Cartagena
Valledupar
Maracaibo
Montería
Mérida
Cúcuta
San Cristóbal
Bucaramanga
Medellín
Manizales
Pereira
Armenia
Ibagué
Bogotá
Villavicencio
Buenaventura
Cali
COLOMBI
ANDES
CORDILLERA ORIENTAL
PERU - CHILE TRENCH
North Pacific Ocean
Isla del Coco (COSTA RICA)
Isla de Malpelo (COLOMBIA)
Scale 1: 12,500,000
Lambert Conformal Conic Projection, standard parallels 7° N and 24° N
0 100 200 300 Kilometers
0 100 200 300 Miles
Boundary representation is not necessarily authoritative.

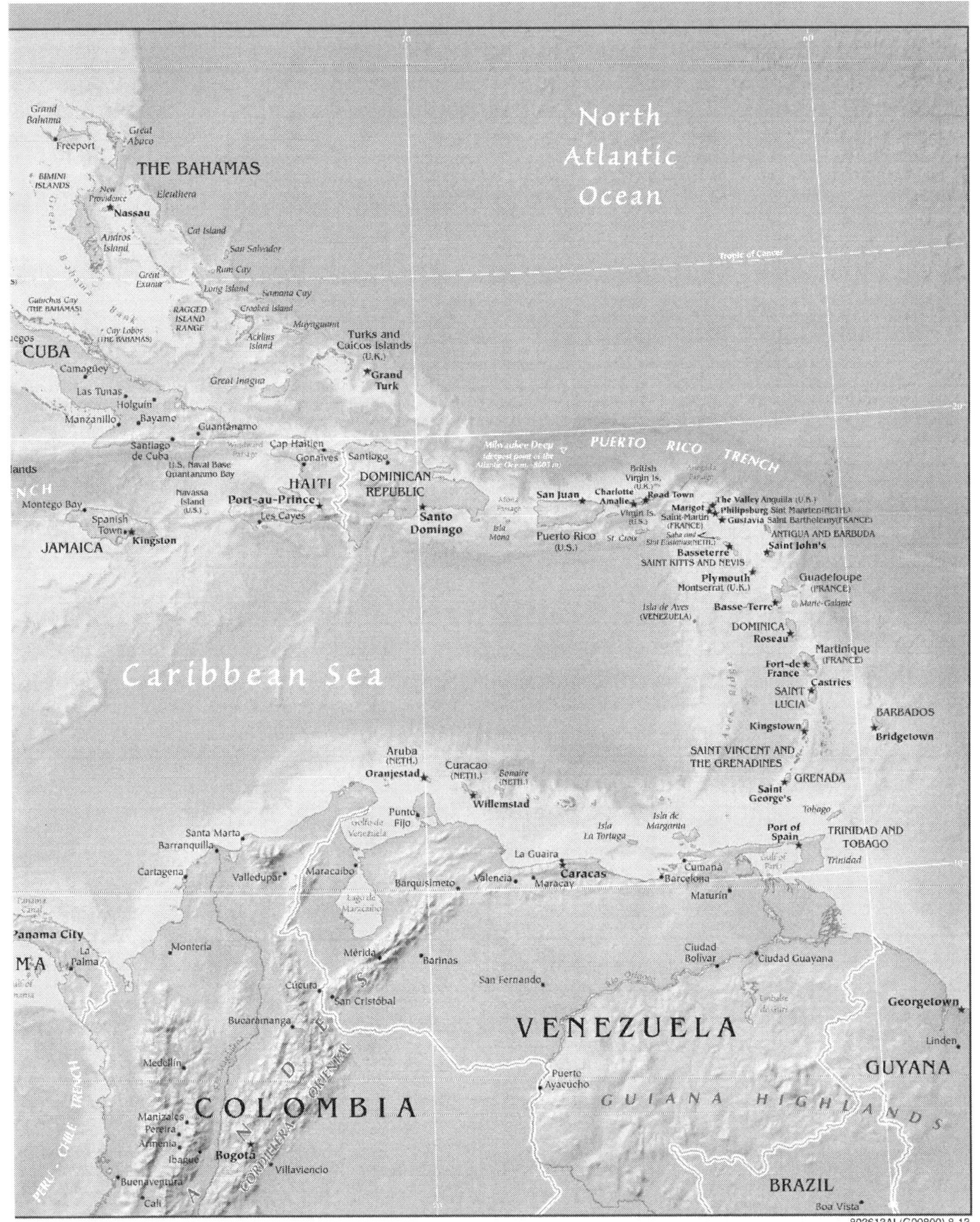

803613AI (G00800) 8-13

CENTRAL AMERICA AND THE CARIBBEAN

North Atlantic Ocean
Caribbean Sea
THE BAHAMAS
CUBA
HAITI
DOMINICAN REPUBLIC
JAMAICA
Puerto Rico (U.S.)
Turks and Caicos Islands (U.K.)
ANTIGUA AND BARBUDA
SAINT KITTS AND NEVIS
DOMINICA
SAINT LUCIA
BARBADOS
SAINT VINCENT AND THE GRENADINES
GRENADA
TRINIDAD AND TOBAGO
VENEZUELA
COLOMBIA
GUYANA
BRAZIL
Nassau
Havana
Port-au-Prince
Santo Domingo
Kingston
San Juan
Caracas
Bogotá
Georgetown
803614AI (G00800) 8-13

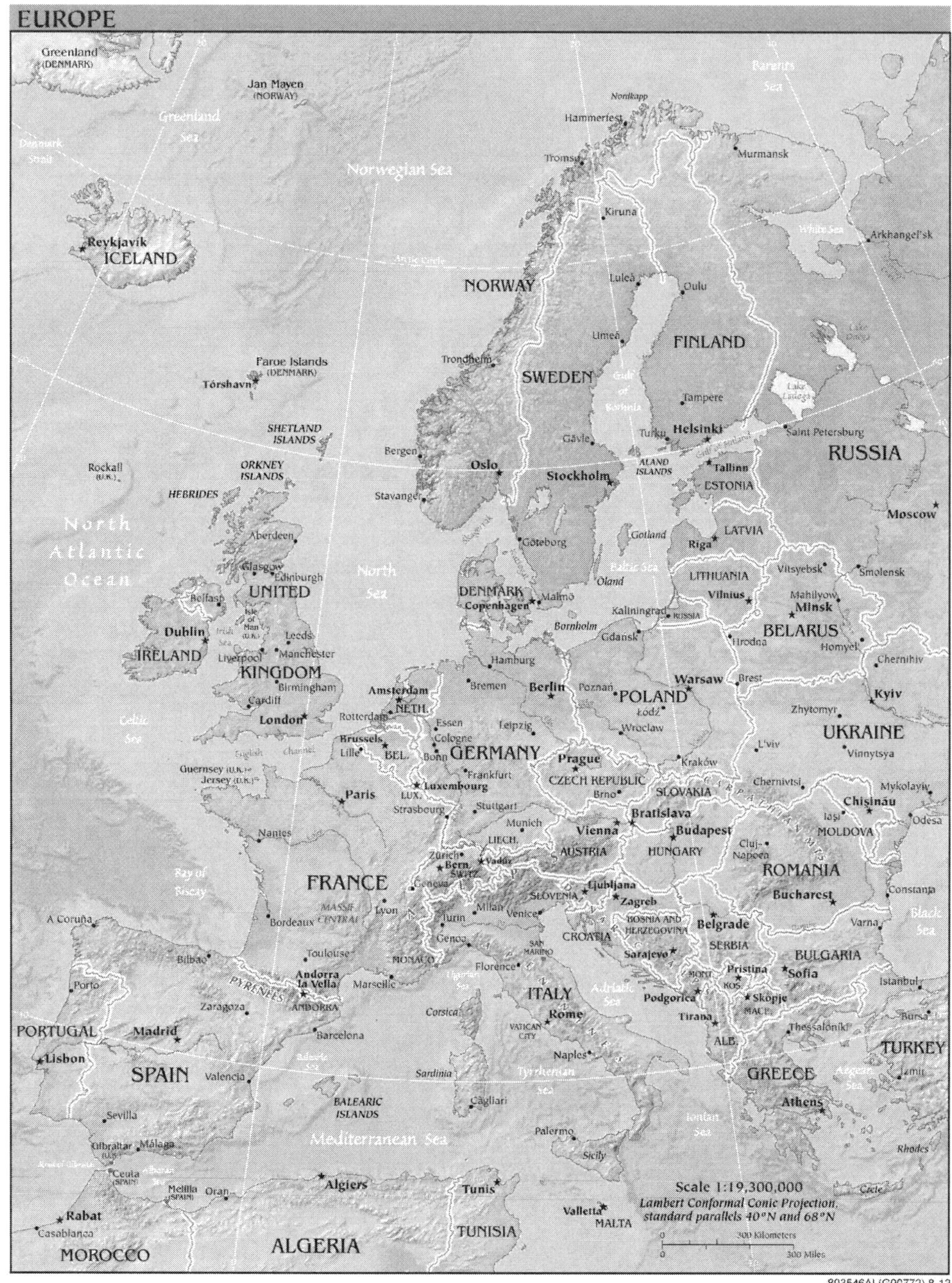

803546AI (G00772) 8-12

EUROPE

803539AI (G00772) 6-12

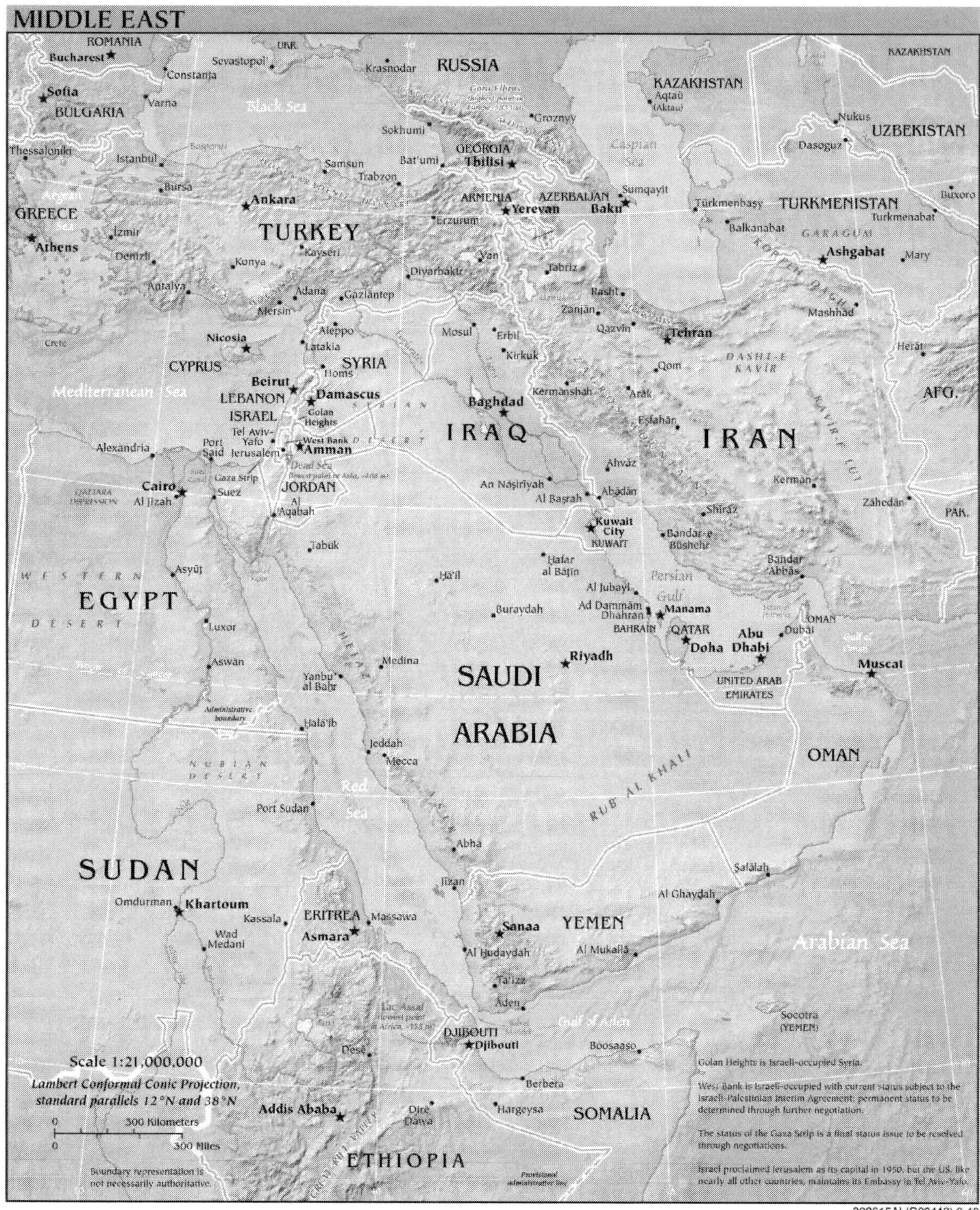

803615AI (G00412) 8-13

MIDDLE EAST

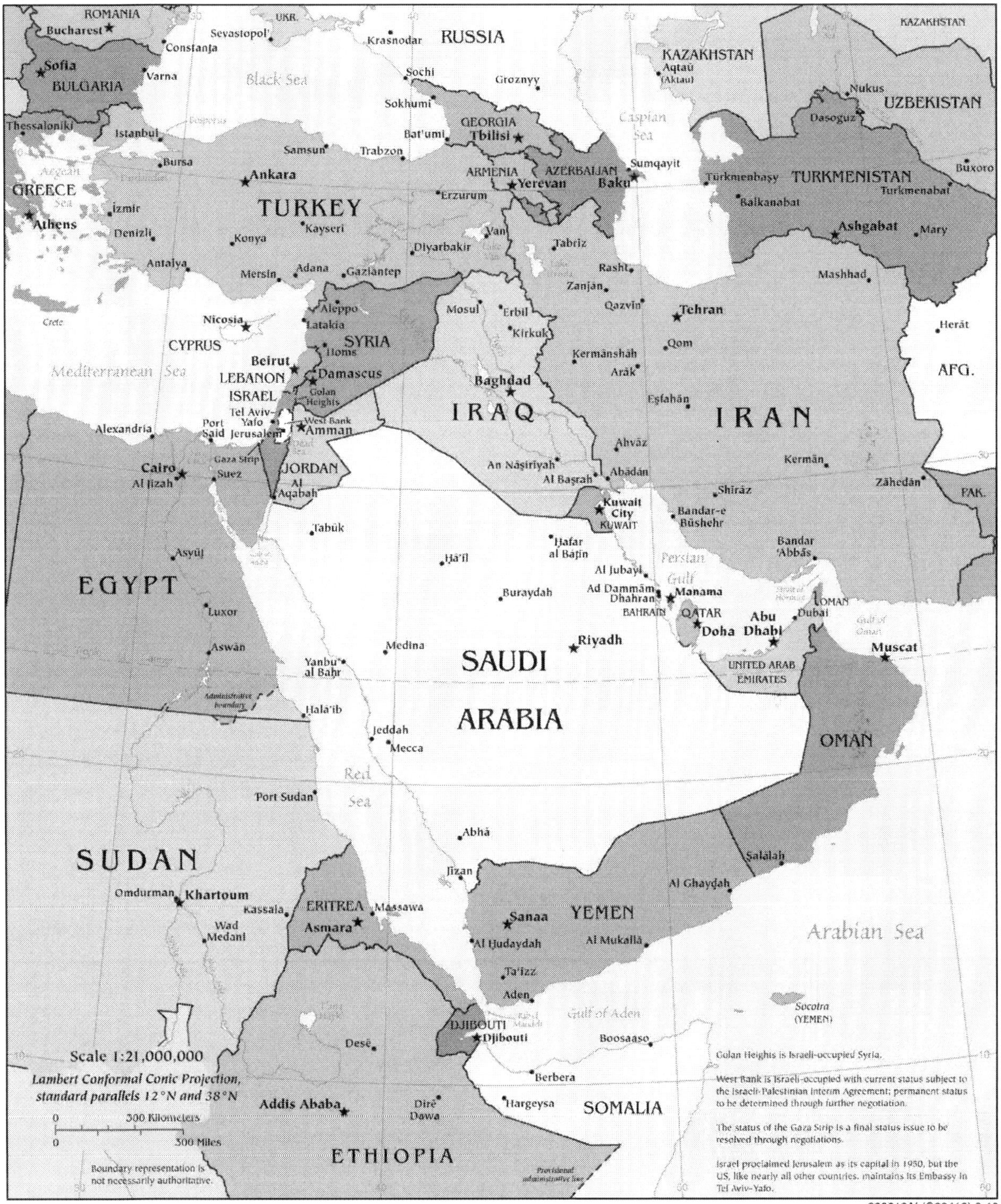

ROMANIA
Bucharest
Sevastopol'
UKR.
Krasnodar
RUSSIA
KAZAKHSTAN
Constanța
Sofia
BULGARIA
Varna
Black Sea
Sochi
Groznyy
KAZAKHSTAN
Aqtaū (Aktau)
Nukus
UZBEKISTAN
Sokhumi
Thessaloniki
Istanbul
Bosporus
GEORGIA
Bat'umi
Tbilisi
Caspian Sea
Dasoguz
Samsun
Trabzon
Bursa
Aegean Sea
Ankara
ARMENIA
Yerevan
AZERBAIJAN
Baku
Sumqayit
Türkmenbaşy
TURKMENISTAN
Türkmenabat
Buxoro
GREECE
Erzurum
Balkanabat
İzmir
TURKEY
Athens
Kayseri
Van
Ashgabat
Mary
Denizli
Konya
Diyarbakir
Tabriz
Antalya
Mersin
Adana
Gaziantep
Rasht
Mashhad
Zanjan
Aleppo
Mosul
Erbil
Qazvin
Tehran
Crete
Nicosia
Latakia
Kirkuk
Herāt
CYPRUS
SYRIA
Homs
Qom
Beirut
Kermānshāh
Mediterranean Sea
LEBANON
Damascus
Arāk
AFG.
ISRAEL
Golan Heights
Baghdad
Eşfahān
Tel Aviv-Yafo
IRAQ
IRAN
Alexandria
Port Said
Jerusalem
West Bank
Amman
Ahvāz
Gaza Strip
Dead Sea
An Nāşiriyah
Kermān
Cairo
Al Jīzah
Suez
JORDAN
Al Başrah
Abādān
Zāhedān
PAK.
Al Aqabah
Shīrāz
Kuwait City
KUWAIT
Bandar-e Būshehr
Tabūk
Ḩafar al Bāţin
Bandar 'Abbās
Asyūţ
Ḩā'il
Persian Gulf
Al Jubayl
EGYPT
Buraydah
Ad Dammām
Dhahran
Manama
BAHRAIN
OMAN
Luxor
QATAR
Dubai
Doha
Abu Dhabi
Gulf of Oman
Riyadh
Muscat
Aswān
Medina
SAUDI ARABIA
Yanbu' al Bahr
UNITED ARAB EMIRATES
Administrative boundary
Halā'ib
Jeddah
Mecca
OMAN
Red Sea
Port Sudan
Abhā
SUDAN
Şalālah
Jīzān
Al Ghayḑah
Omdurman
Khartoum
Kassala
ERITREA
Massawa
YEMEN
Asmara
Sanaa
Wad Medani
Al Ḩudaydah
Al Mukallā
Arabian Sea
Ta'izz
Aden
Gulf of Aden
Socotra (YEMEN)
DJIBOUTI
Djibouti
Boosaaso
Desē
Berbera
Hargeysa
SOMALIA
Addis Ababa
Dirē Dawa
ETHIOPIA
Provisional administrative line

Scale 1:21,000,000

Lambert Conformal Conic Projection, standard parallels 12°N and 38°N

0 — 300 Kilometers
0 — 300 Miles

Boundary representation is not necessarily authoritative.

Golan Heights is Israeli-occupied Syria.

West Bank is Israeli-occupied with current status subject to the Israeli-Palestinian Interim Agreement; permanent status to be determined through further negotiation.

The status of the Gaza Strip is a final status issue to be resolved through negotiations.

Israel proclaimed Jerusalem as its capital in 1950, but the US, like nearly all other countries, maintains its Embassy in Tel Aviv-Yafo.

803616AI (G00412) 8-13

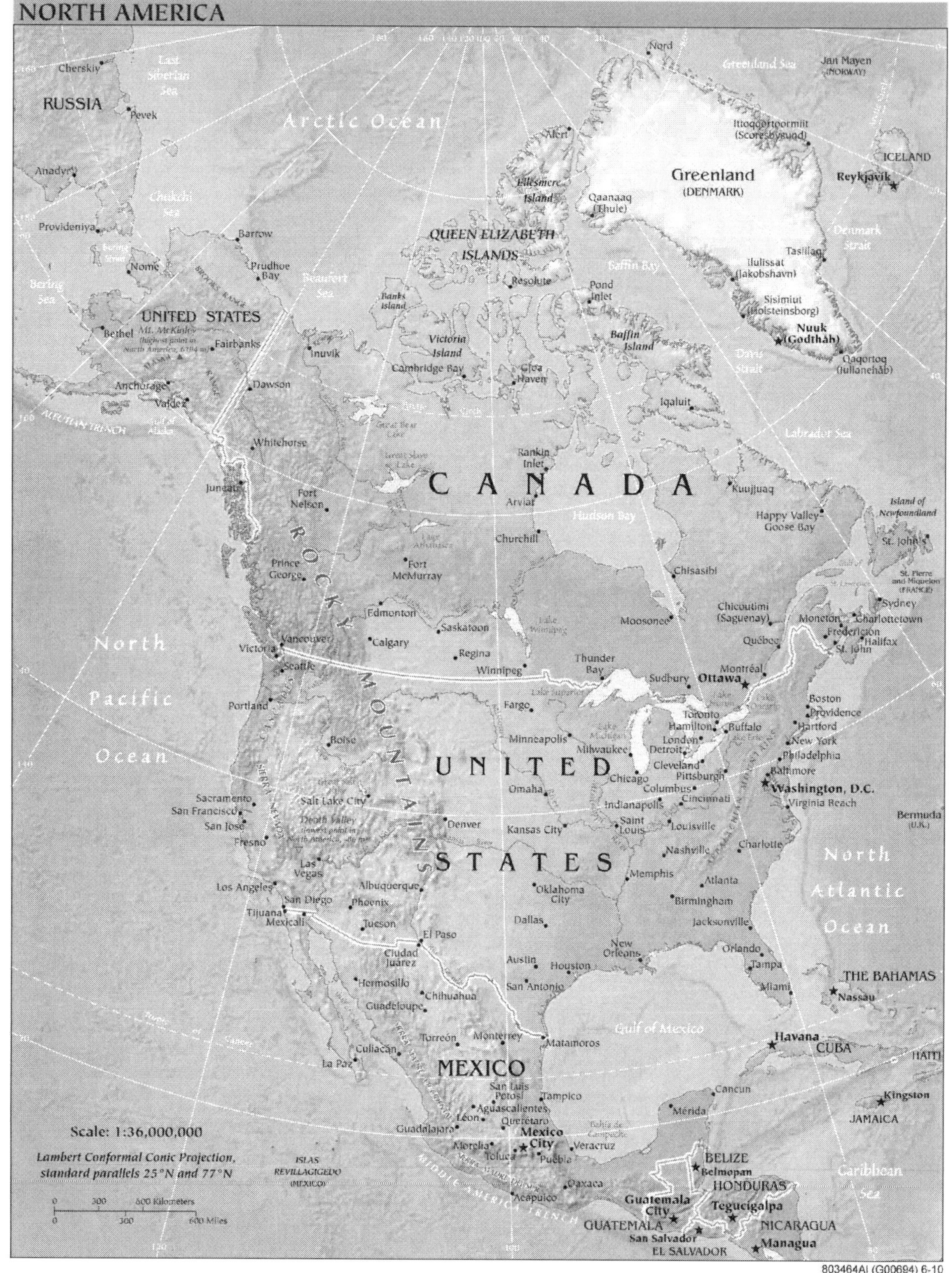
NORTH AMERICA
Arctic Ocean
RUSSIA
Greenland
(DENMARK)
ICELAND
Reykjavik
CANADA
UNITED STATES
MEXICO
ROCKY MOUNTAINS
North Pacific Ocean
North Atlantic Ocean
Hudson Bay
Gulf of Mexico
Baffin Bay
Labrador Sea
QUEEN ELIZABETH ISLANDS
Victoria Island
Baffin Island
Ellesmere Island
Ottawa
Washington, D.C.
Mexico City
THE BAHAMAS
CUBA
Havana
JAMAICA
Kingston
BELIZE
Belmopan
HONDURAS
Tegucigalpa
GUATEMALA
Guatemala City
EL SALVADOR
San Salvador
NICARAGUA
Managua
Bermuda (U.K.)
Scale: 1:36,000,000
Lambert Conformal Conic Projection, standard parallels 25°N and 77°N
0 300 600 Kilometers
0 300 600 Miles
803464AI (G00694) 6-10

NORTH AMERICA

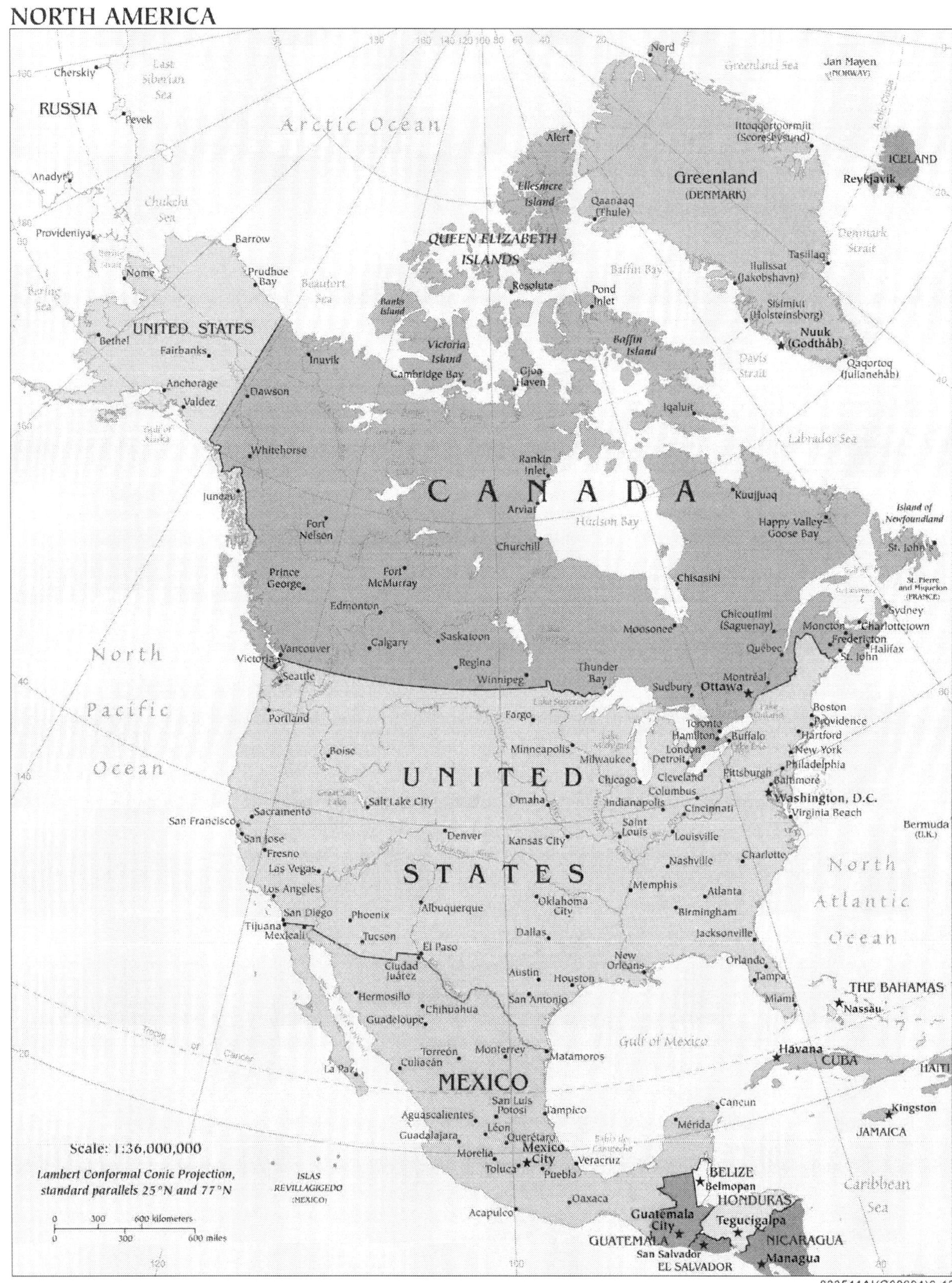

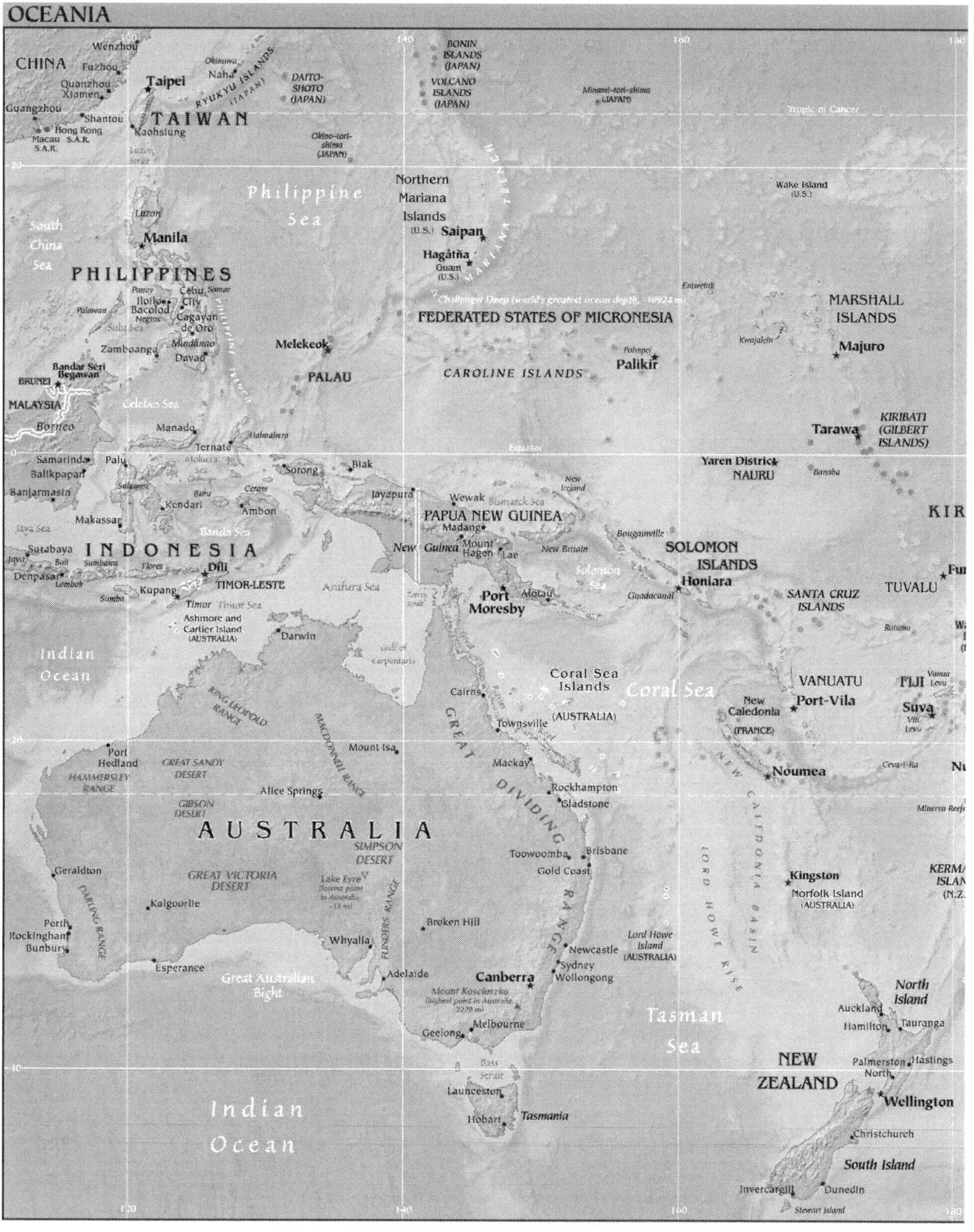
OCEANIA
CHINA
Wenzhou
Fuzhou
Quanzhou
Xiamen
Guangzhou
Shantou
Hong Kong S.A.R.
Macau S.A.R.
Taipei
TAIWAN
Kaohsiung
Okinawa
Naha
RYUKYU ISLANDS (JAPAN)
DAITO-SHOTO (JAPAN)
BONIN ISLANDS (JAPAN)
VOLCANO ISLANDS (JAPAN)
Minami-tori-shima (JAPAN)
Okino-tori-shima (JAPAN)
Tropic of Cancer
Luzon Strait
Philippine Sea
South China Sea
Luzon
Manila
Northern Mariana Islands (U.S.)
Saipan
Hagåtña
Guam (U.S.)
MARIANA TRENCH
Wake Island (U.S.)
PHILIPPINES
Panay
Cebu
Samar
Iloilo
City
Bacolod
Negros
Cagayan de Oro
Palawan
Sulu Sea
Mindanao
Zamboanga
Davao
PHILIPPINE TRENCH
Challenger Deep (world's greatest ocean depth, -10924 m)
FEDERATED STATES OF MICRONESIA
Enewetak
MARSHALL ISLANDS
Kwajalein
Majuro
Melekeok
PALAU
CAROLINE ISLANDS
Pohnpei
Palikir
Bandar Seri Begawan
BRUNEI
MALAYSIA
Celebes Sea
Borneo
Manado
Halmahera
Ternate
Tarawa
KIRIBATI (GILBERT ISLANDS)
Equator
Samarinda
Palu
Balikpapan
Molucca Sea
Sorong
Biak
Yaren District
NAURU
Banaba
Banjarmasin
Sulawesi
Buru
Ceram
Kendari
Ambon
Jayapura
Wewak
Bismarck Sea
New Ireland
Makassar
Banda Sea
PAPUA NEW GUINEA
Madang
Java Sea
Surabaya
Java
Bali
Sumbawa
Flores
INDONESIA
Dili
Denpasar
Lombok
Kupang
TIMOR-LESTE
Sumba
Timor
Timor Sea
New Guinea
Mount Hagen
Lae
New Britain
Bougainville
SOLOMON ISLANDS
Solomon Sea
Honiara
Guadalcanal
Arafura Sea
Torres Strait
Port Moresby
Alotau
SANTA CRUZ ISLANDS
TUVALU
Rotuma
Ashmore and Cartier Island (AUSTRALIA)
Darwin
Gulf of Carpentaria
Indian Ocean
KING LEOPOLD RANGE
Coral Sea Islands (AUSTRALIA)
Coral Sea
Cairns
VANUATU
Port-Vila
FIJI
Vanua Levu
Suva
Viti Levu
New Caledonia (FRANCE)
Townsville
Port Hedland
GREAT SANDY DESERT
HAMMERSLEY RANGE
MACDONNELL RANGES
Mount Isa
Mackay
Noumea
Ceva-i-Ra
Alice Springs
GIBSON DESERT
Rockhampton
Gladstone
Minerva Reefs
AUSTRALIA
SIMPSON DESERT
GREAT DIVIDING RANGE
NEW CALEDONIA BASIN
LORD HOWE RISE
Toowoomba
Brisbane
Gold Coast
Geraldton
GREAT VICTORIA DESERT
Lake Eyre
Kingston
Norfolk Island (AUSTRALIA)
Kalgoorlie
DARLING RANGE
FLINDERS RANGES
Perth
Rockingham
Bunbury
Broken Hill
Whyalla
Lord Howe Island (AUSTRALIA)
Newcastle
Sydney
Wollongong
Esperance
Adelaide
Great Australian Bight
Canberra
Mount Kosciuszko
North Island
Auckland
Hamilton
Tauranga
Tasman Sea
Melbourne
Geelong
Bass Strait
NEW ZEALAND
Palmerston North
Hastings
Launceston
Wellington
Indian Ocean
Hobart
Tasmania
Christchurch
South Island
Invercargill
Dunedin
Stewart Island

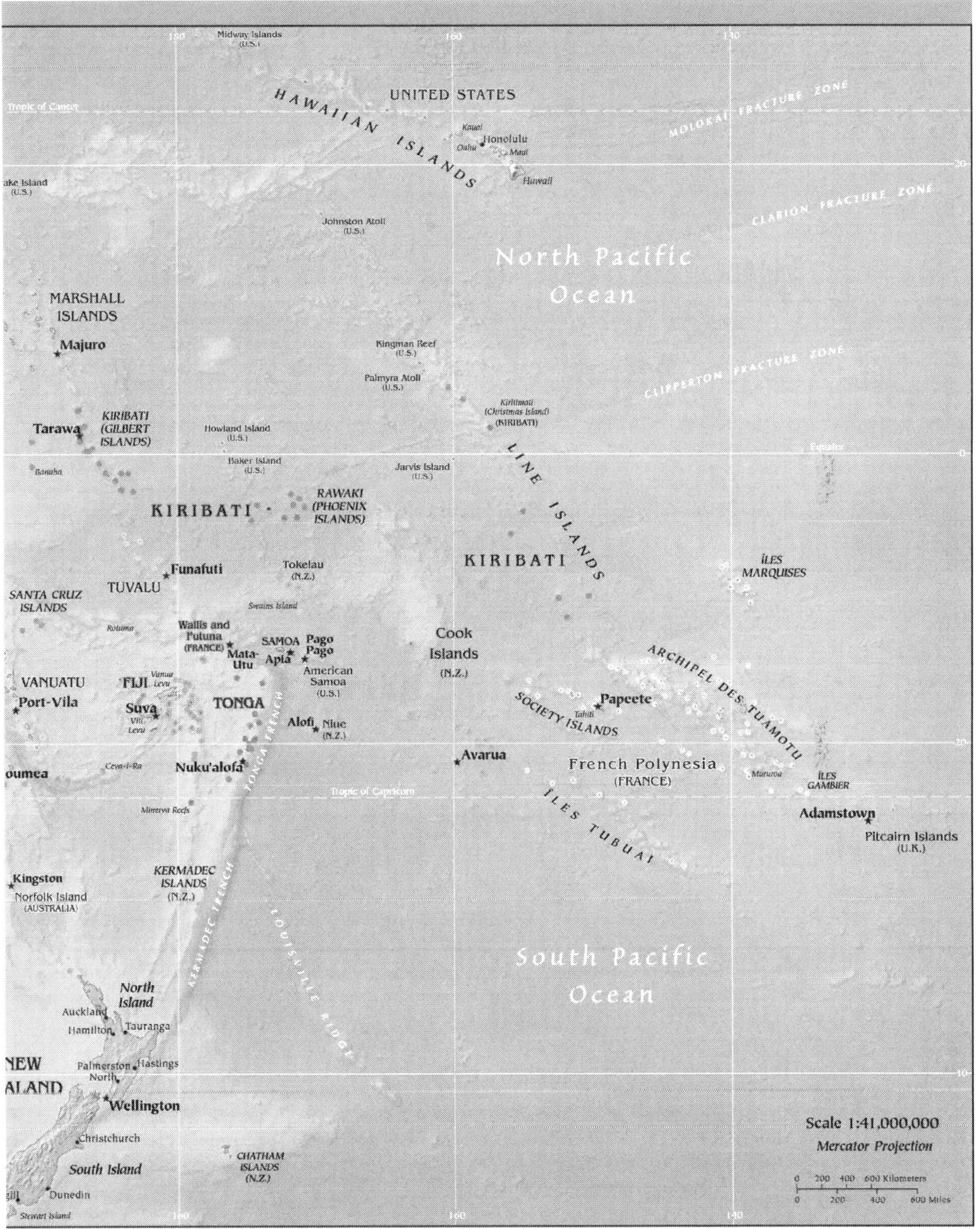

803617AI (G01512) 8-12

OCEANIA

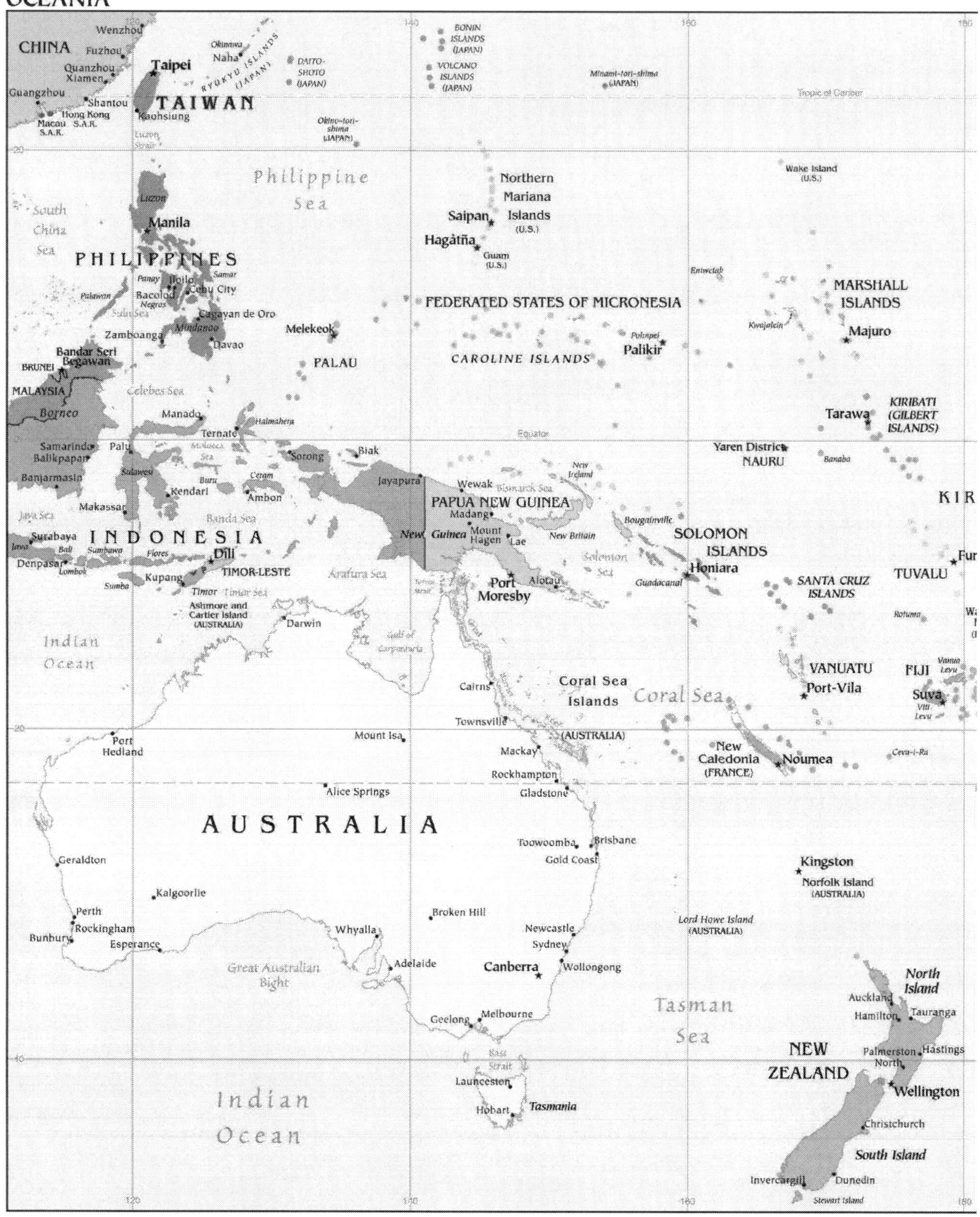
CHINA
Wenzhou
Fuzhou
Quanzhou
Xiamen
Guangzhou
Shantou
Hong Kong S.A.R.
Macau S.A.R.
Taipei
TAIWAN
Kaohsiung
Okinawa
Naha
RYUKYU ISLANDS (JAPAN)
DAITO-SHOTO (JAPAN)
BONIN ISLANDS (JAPAN)
VOLCANO ISLANDS (JAPAN)
Okino-tori-shima (JAPAN)
Minami-tori-shima (JAPAN)
Tropic of Cancer
Luzon Strait
Philippine Sea
South China Sea
Luzon
Manila
PHILIPPINES
Samar
Panay
Iloilo
Cebu City
Palawan
Bacolod
Negros
Sulu Sea
Cagayan de Oro
Mindanao
Zamboanga
Davao
Bandar Seri Begawan
BRUNEI
MALAYSIA
Borneo
Celebes Sea
Manado
Halmahera
Ternate
Northern Mariana Islands (U.S.)
Saipan
Hagåtña
Guam (U.S.)
Wake Island (U.S.)
Enewetak
MARSHALL ISLANDS
FEDERATED STATES OF MICRONESIA
Kwajalein
Majuro
Melekeok
PALAU
CAROLINE ISLANDS
Pohnpei
Palikir
Tarawa
KIRIBATI (GILBERT ISLANDS)
Equator
Yaren District
NAURU
Banaba
Samarinda
Balikpapan
Palu
Molucca Sea
Sorong
Biak
Banjarmasin
Sulawesi
Buru
Ceram
Kendari
Ambon
Jayapura
Wewak
Bismarck Sea
New Ireland
PAPUA NEW GUINEA
Madang
Makassar
Banda Sea
Java Sea
Surabaya
Java
Bali
Sumbawa
INDONESIA
Flores
Dili
New Guinea
Mount Hagen
Lae
New Britain
Bougainville
SOLOMON ISLANDS
Solomon Sea
Honiara
Guadalcanal
KIR
Funafuti
TUVALU
Denpasar
Lombok
Sumba
Kupang
TIMOR-LESTE
Timor
Timor Sea
Arafura Sea
Torres Strait
Port Moresby
Alotau
SANTA CRUZ ISLANDS
Rotuma
Ashmore and Cartier Island (AUSTRALIA)
Darwin
Gulf of Carpentaria
Indian Ocean
VANUATU
Port-Vila
FIJI
Vanua Levu
Suva
Viti Levu
Cairns
Coral Sea Islands
Coral Sea
Townsville
(AUSTRALIA)
Port Hedland
Mount Isa
Mackay
New Caledonia (FRANCE)
Noumea
Ceva-i-Ra
Rockhampton
Alice Springs
Gladstone
AUSTRALIA
Toowoomba
Brisbane
Gold Coast
Geraldton
Kingston
Norfolk Island (AUSTRALIA)
Kalgoorlie
Broken Hill
Lord Howe Island (AUSTRALIA)
Perth
Rockingham
Bunbury
Esperance
Whyalla
Newcastle
Sydney
Great Australian Bight
Adelaide
Canberra
Wollongong
North Island
Auckland
Hamilton
Tauranga
Tasman Sea
Geelong
Melbourne
NEW ZEALAND
Palmerston North
Hastings
Bass Strait
Launceston
Wellington
Indian Ocean
Hobart
Tasmania
Christchurch
South Island
Invercargill
Dunedin
Stewart Island
120
140
160
180
20
40

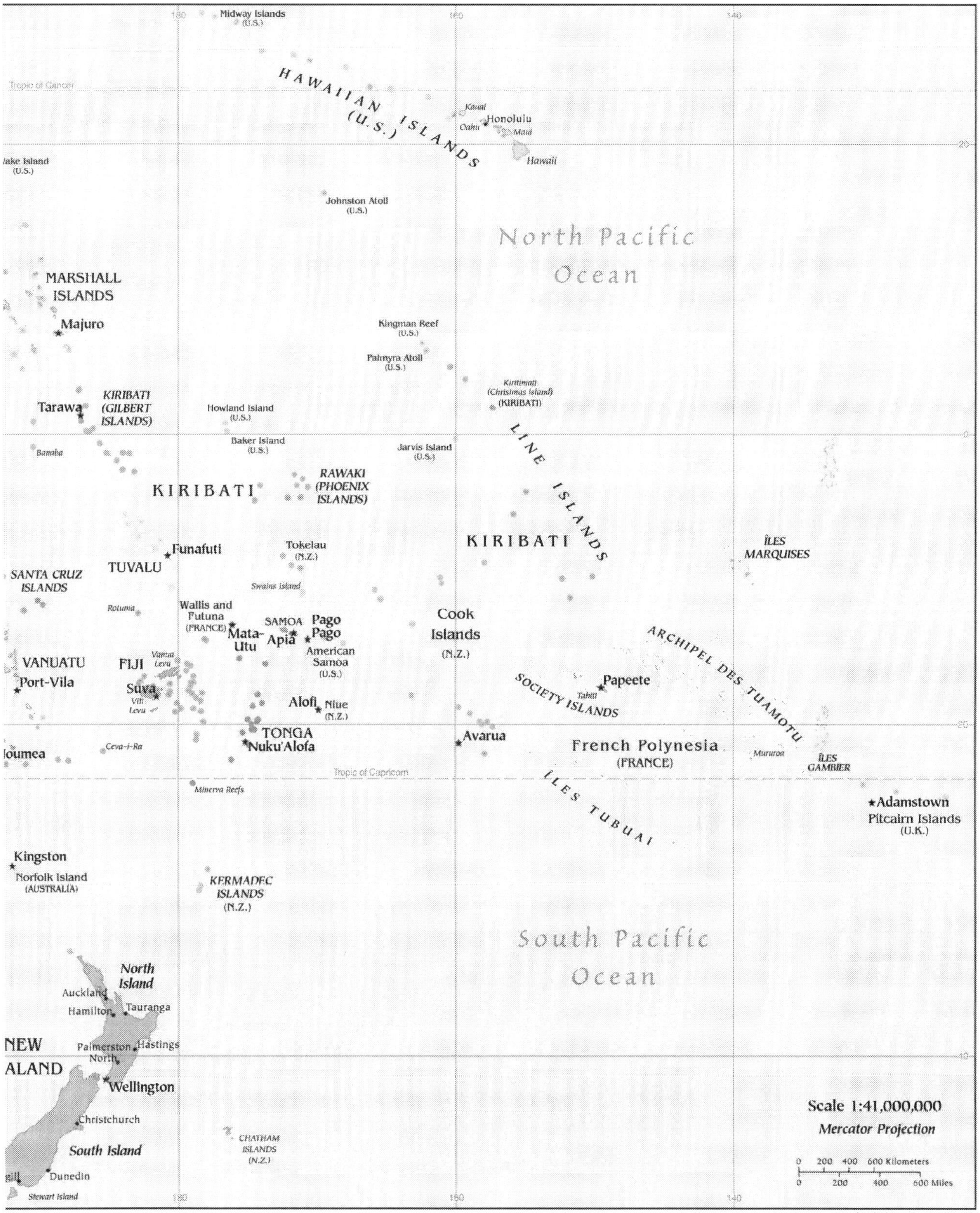

Midway Islands (U.S.)
Tropic of Cancer
HAWAIIAN ISLANDS (U.S.)
Kauai
Oahu
Honolulu
Maui
Hawaii
Wake Island (U.S.)
Johnston Atoll (U.S.)
North Pacific Ocean
MARSHALL ISLANDS
Majuro
Kingman Reef (U.S.)
Palmyra Atoll (U.S.)
Kiritimati (Christmas Island) (KIRIBATI)
Tarawa
KIRIBATI (GILBERT ISLANDS)
Howland Island (U.S.)
Baker Island (U.S.)
Jarvis Island (U.S.)
LINE ISLANDS
Banaba
KIRIBATI
RAWAKI (PHOENIX ISLANDS)
Tokelau (N.Z.)
KIRIBATI
ÎLES MARQUISES
Funafuti
TUVALU
SANTA CRUZ ISLANDS
Swains Island
Rotuma
Wallis and Futuna (FRANCE)
Mata-Utu
SAMOA
Apia
Pago Pago
American Samoa (U.S.)
Cook Islands (N.Z.)
ARCHIPEL DES TUAMOTU
VANUATU
Port-Vila
FIJI
Vanua Levu
Suva
Viti Levu
SOCIETY ISLANDS
Tahiti
Papeete
Alofi
Niue (N.Z.)
TONGA
Nuku'Alofa
Avarua
French Polynesia (FRANCE)
Mururoa
ÎLES GAMBIER
Nouméa
Ceva-i-Ra
Tropic of Capricorn
Minerva Reefs
ÎLES TUBUAI
Adamstown
Pitcairn Islands (U.K.)
Kingston
Norfolk Island (AUSTRALIA)
KERMADEC ISLANDS (N.Z.)
South Pacific Ocean
North Island
Auckland
Hamilton
Tauranga
NEW ZEALAND
Palmerston North
Hastings
Wellington
Christchurch
South Island
CHATHAM ISLANDS (N.Z.)
Invercargill
Dunedin
Stewart Island

Scale 1:41,000,000
Mercator Projection
0 200 400 600 Kilometers
0 200 400 600 Miles

180 160 140
20 0 20 40

803618AI (G01512) 8-13

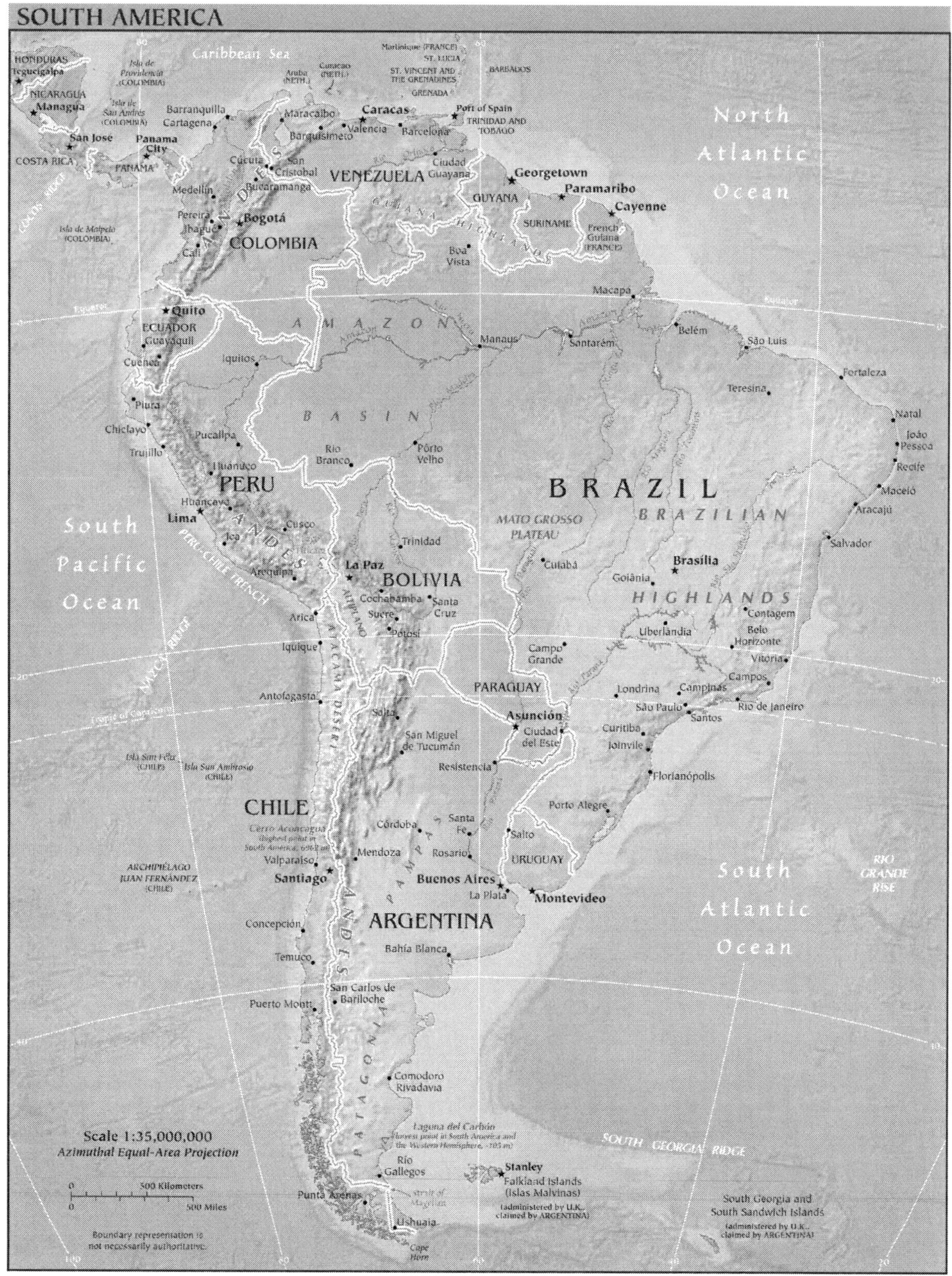

803521AI (G00186) 11-11

SOUTH AMERICA

Caribbean Sea
North Atlantic Ocean
South Pacific Ocean
South Atlantic Ocean

HONDURAS
Tegucigalpa
NICARAGUA
Managua
San José
COSTA RICA
Panama City
PANAMA
Isla de Providencia (COLOMBIA)
Isla de San Andrés (COLOMBIA)
Isla de Malpelo (COLOMBIA)
Aruba (NETH.)
Curaçao (NETH.)
Martinique (FRANCE)
ST. LUCIA
BARBADOS
ST. VINCENT AND THE GRENADINES
GRENADA
Port of Spain
TRINIDAD AND TOBAGO

Barranquilla
Cartagena
Cúcuta
Medellín
Bucaramanga
Pereira
Ibagué
Bogotá
Cali
COLOMBIA

Maracaibo
Caracas
Valencia
Barquisimeto
Barcelona
San Cristóbal
Ciudad Guayana
VENEZUELA

Georgetown
GUYANA
Paramaribo
SURINAME
Cayenne
French Guiana (FRANCE)

Quito
ECUADOR
Guayaquil
Cuenca

Iquitos
Piura
Chiclayo
Trujillo
Pucallpa
Huánuco
PERU
Huancayo
Lima
Cusco
Ica
Arequipa

La Paz
BOLIVIA
Trinidad
Cochabamba
Santa Cruz
Sucre
Potosí

Boa Vista
Macapá
Manaus
Santarém
Belém
São Luís
Fortaleza
Teresina
Natal
João Pessoa
Recife
Maceió
Aracaju
Salvador
Rio Branco
Porto Velho
BRAZIL
Cuiabá
Brasília
Goiânia
Contagem
Uberlândia
Belo Horizonte
Campo Grande
Vitória
Londrina
Campinas
São Paulo
Santos
Rio de Janeiro
Curitiba
Joinvile
Florianópolis
Porto Alegre

PARAGUAY
Asunción
Ciudad del Este

Arica
Iquique
Antofagasta
Tropic of Capricorn
Equator
Isla San Félix (CHILE)
Isla San Ambrosio (CHILE)
CHILE
ARCHIPIÉLAGO JUAN FERNÁNDEZ (CHILE)
Valparaíso
Santiago
Concepción
Temuco
Puerto Montt
Punta Arenas

Salta
San Miguel de Tucumán
Resistencia
Córdoba
Santa Fe
Mendoza
Rosario
Buenos Aires
La Plata
ARGENTINA
Bahía Blanca
Mar del Plata
San Carlos de Bariloche
Comodoro Rivadavia
Río Gallegos
Strait of Magellan
Ushuaia
Cape Horn

Salto
URUGUAY
Montevideo

Stanley
Falkland Islands (Islas Malvinas)
(administered by U.K., claimed by ARGENTINA)

South Georgia and South Sandwich Islands
(administered by U.K., claimed by ARGENTINA)

Scale 1:35,000,000
Azimuthal Equal-Area Projection

0 500 Kilometers
0 500 Miles

Boundary representation is not necessarily authoritative.

803543AI (G00186) 6-12

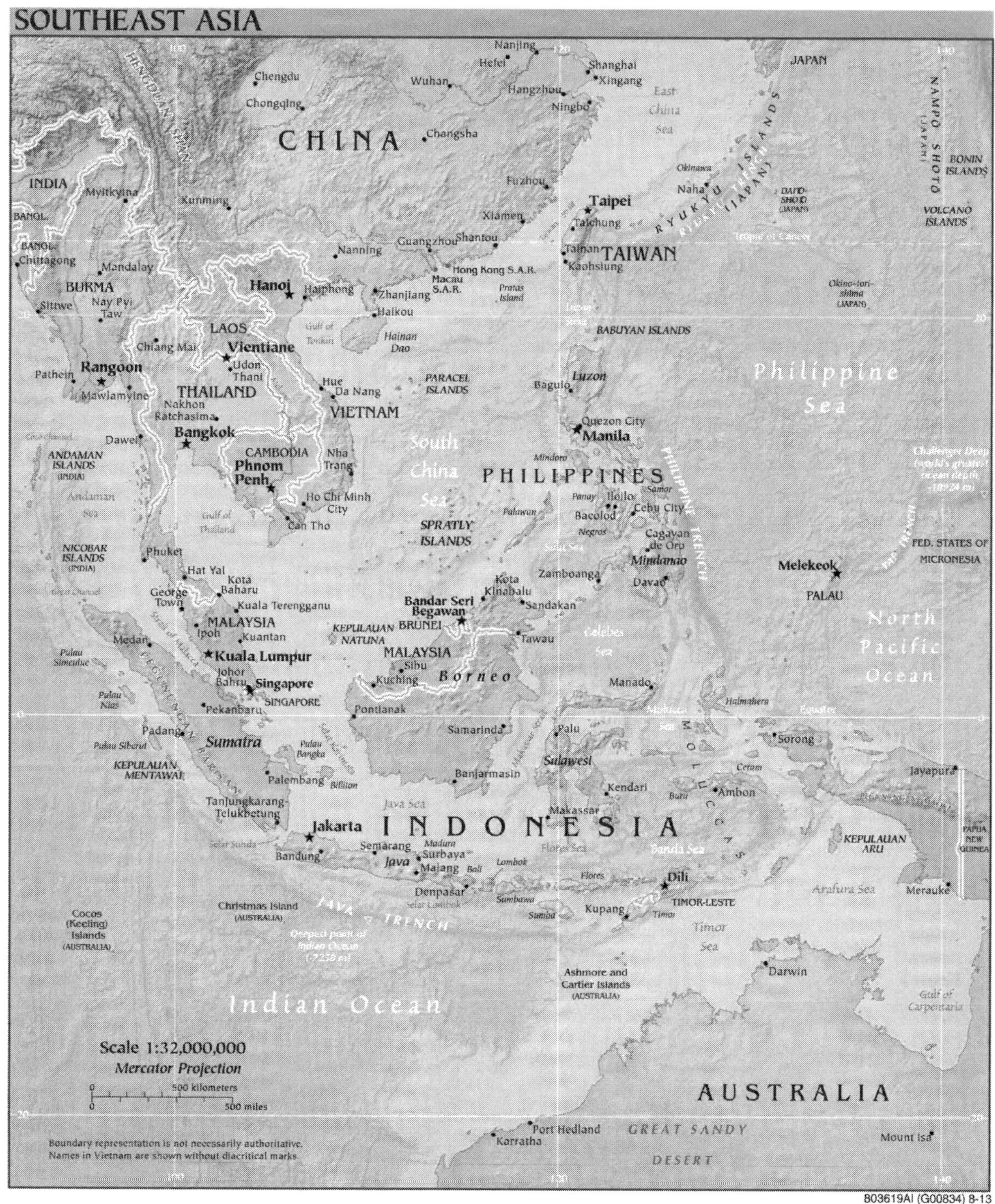

803619AI (G00834) 8-13

SOUTHEAST ASIA

Nanjing
Hefei
Shanghai
Xingang
Chengdu
Wuhan
Hangzhou
Ningbo
East China Sea
Chongqing
JAPAN
NAMPO SHOTO (JAPAN)
CHINA
Changsha
RYUKYU ISLANDS (JAPAN)
Okinawa
Naha
DAITO SHOTO (JAPAN)
BONIN ISLANDS
VOLCANO ISLANDS
INDIA
Myitkyina
Kunming
Fuzhou
Taipei
Xiamen
Taichung
Tropic of Cancer
BANGL.
Chittagong
Guangzhou
Shantou
Nanning
Tainan
TAIWAN
Kaohsiung
Mandalay
BURMA
Hanoi
Haiphong
Hong Kong S.A.R.
Macau S.A.R.
Pratas Island
Okino-tori-shima (JAPAN)
Sittwe
Nay Pyi Taw
Zhanjiang
Haikou
Luzon Strait
LAOS
Gulf of Tonkin
Hainan Dao
BABUYAN ISLANDS
Chiang Mai
Vientiane
Udon Thani
Pathein
Rangoon
Hue
Da Nang
PARACEL ISLANDS
Baguio
Luzon
Philippine Sea
Mawlamyine
THAILAND
Nakhon Ratchasima
VIETNAM
Quezon City
Manila
Dawei
Bangkok
South China Sea
Mindoro
ANDAMAN ISLANDS (INDIA)
CAMBODIA
Phnom Penh
Nha Trang
PHILIPPINES
Samar
Andaman Sea
Ho Chi Minh City
Panay
Iloilo
Cebu City
Gulf of Thailand
Can Tho
Palawan
Bacolod
Negros
SPRATLY ISLANDS
Sulu Sea
Cagayan de Oro
FED. STATES OF MICRONESIA
NICOBAR ISLANDS (INDIA)
Phuket
Mindanao
Zamboanga
Melekeok
Hat Yai
Kota Baharu
Kota Kinabalu
Davao
George Town
Kuala Terengganu
Bandar Seri Begawan
Sandakan
PALAU
MALAYSIA
Ipoh
BRUNEI
Tawau
North Pacific Ocean
Medan
Kuantan
KEPULAUAN NATUNA
Celebes Sea
Pulau Simeulue
Kuala Lumpur
MALAYSIA
Sibu
Johor Bahru
Kuching
Borneo
Manado
Singapore
SINGAPORE
Halmahera
Pulau Nias
Pekanbaru
Pontianak
Equator
Padang
Samarinda
Palu
Molucca Sea
Sorong
Sumatra
Pulau Bangka
Pulau Siberut
KEPULAUAN MENTAWAI
Palembang
Sulawesi
Ceram
Jayapura
Banjarmasin
MOLUCCAS
Kendari
Buru
Ambon
Billiton
Tanjungkarang-Telukbetung
Java Sea
Makassar
Jakarta
INDONESIA
Banda Sea
KEPULAUAN ARU
PAPUA NEW GUINEA
Selat Sunda
Semarang
Madura
Surabaya
Bandung
Java
Malang
Bali
Lombok
Flores Sea
Flores
Dili
Arafura Sea
Merauke
Denpasar
Selat Lombok
Sumbawa
EAST TIMOR
Christmas Island (AUSTRALIA)
Kupang
Sumba
Timor
Cocos (Keeling) Islands (AUSTRALIA)
Timor Sea
Ashmore and Cartier Islands (AUSTRALIA)
Darwin
Gulf of Carpentaria
Indian Ocean
AUSTRALIA
Port Hedland
Karratha
Mount Isa

Scale 1:32,000,000
Mercator Projection
0 500 kilometers
0 500 miles

Boundary representation is not necessarily authoritative.
Names in Vietnam are shown without diacritical marks.

803620AI (G00834) 8-13

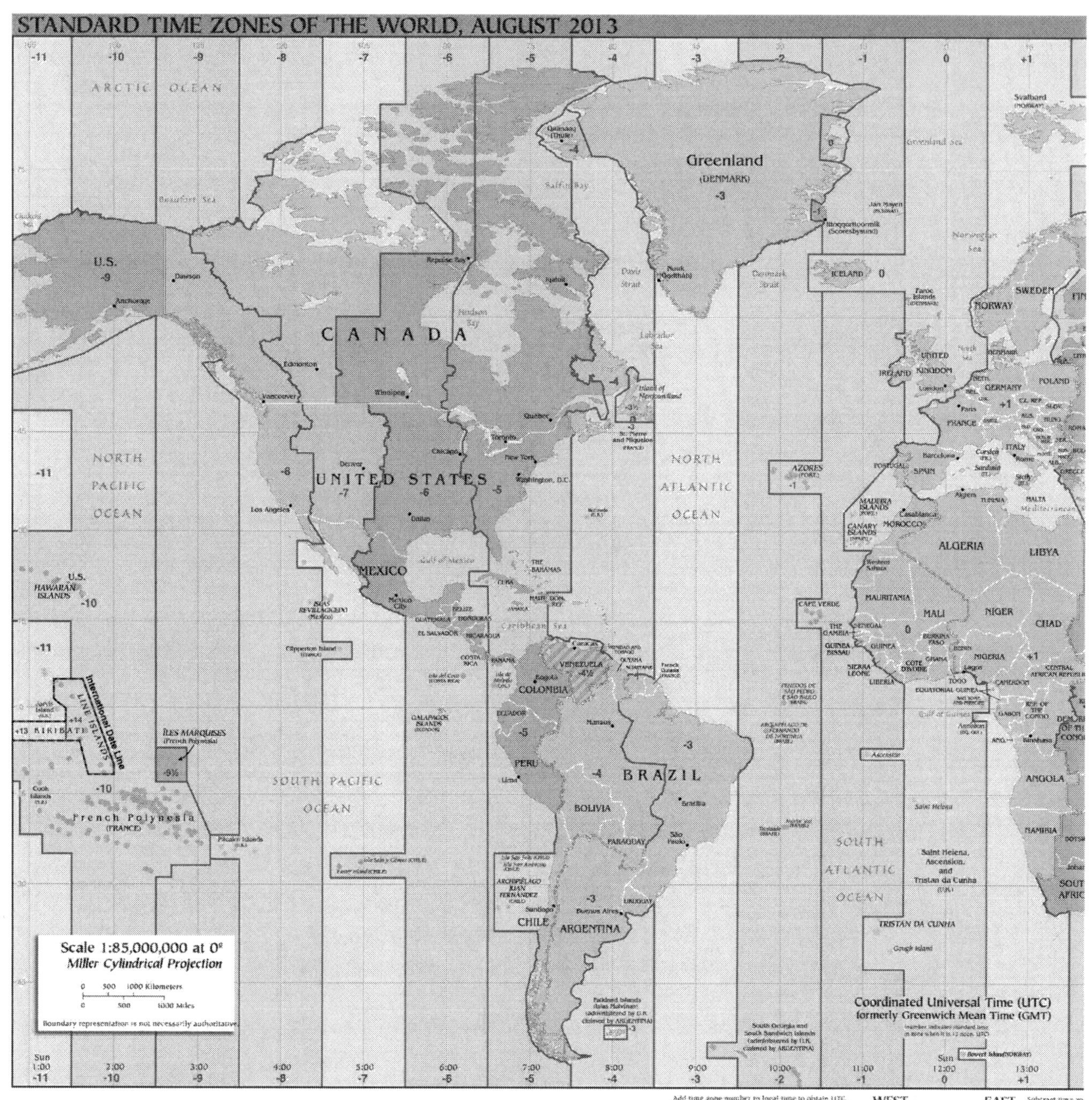

STANDARD TIME ZONES OF THE WORLD, AUGUST 2013
ARCTIC OCEAN
Greenland
(DENMARK)
CANADA
UNITED STATES
MEXICO
NORTH PACIFIC OCEAN
NORTH ATLANTIC OCEAN
SOUTH PACIFIC OCEAN
SOUTH ATLANTIC OCEAN
BRAZIL
BOLIVIA
ARGENTINA
CHILE
PERU
COLOMBIA
ALGERIA
LIBYA
MALI
NIGER
CHAD
ANGOLA
French Polynesia
International Date Line
Scale 1:85,000,000 at 0°
Miller Cylindrical Projection
Boundary representation is not necessarily authoritative
Coordinated Universal Time (UTC)
formerly Greenwich Mean Time (GMT)
WEST
EAST

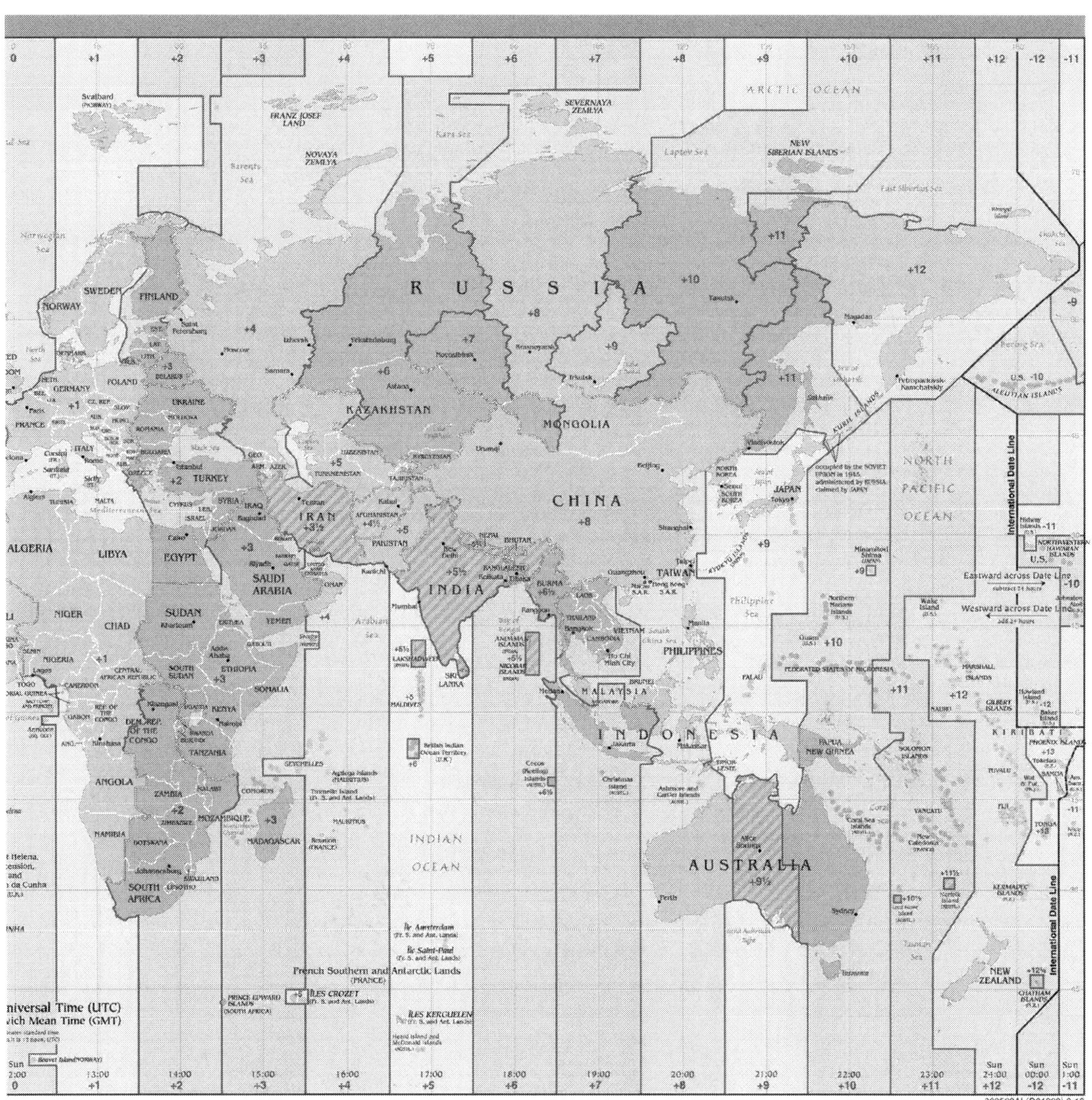

0 +1 +2 +3 +4 +5 +6 +7 +8 +9 +10 +11 +12 -12 -11
ARCTIC OCEAN
SEVERNAYA ZEMLYA
FRANZ JOSEF LAND
NOVAYA ZEMLYA
NEW SIBERIAN ISLANDS
RUSSIA
SWEDEN
FINLAND
NORWAY
POLAND
GERMANY
FRANCE
UKRAINE
ROMANIA
ITALY
TURKEY
KAZAKHSTAN
MONGOLIA
CHINA
JAPAN
NORTH PACIFIC OCEAN
International Date Line
ALGERIA
LIBYA
EGYPT
SAUDI ARABIA
IRAN
INDIA
NIGER
CHAD
SUDAN
ETHIOPIA
SOMALIA
KENYA
TANZANIA
ANGOLA
ZAMBIA
MOZAMBIQUE
NAMIBIA
SOUTH AFRICA
MADAGASCAR
INDIAN OCEAN
PHILIPPINES
MALAYSIA
INDONESIA
PAPUA NEW GUINEA
AUSTRALIA
NEW ZEALAND
TAIWAN
Eastward across Date Line
Westward across Date Line
French Southern and Antarctic Lands
Universal Time (UTC)
Greenwich Mean Time (GMT)
12:00 13:00 14:00 15:00 16:00 17:00 18:00 19:00 20:00 21:00 22:00 23:00
EAST
Subtract time zone number from local time to obtain UTC.
Add time zone number to UTC to obtain local time.
803569AI (G01802) 9-13

Map of the World Oceans, August 2013

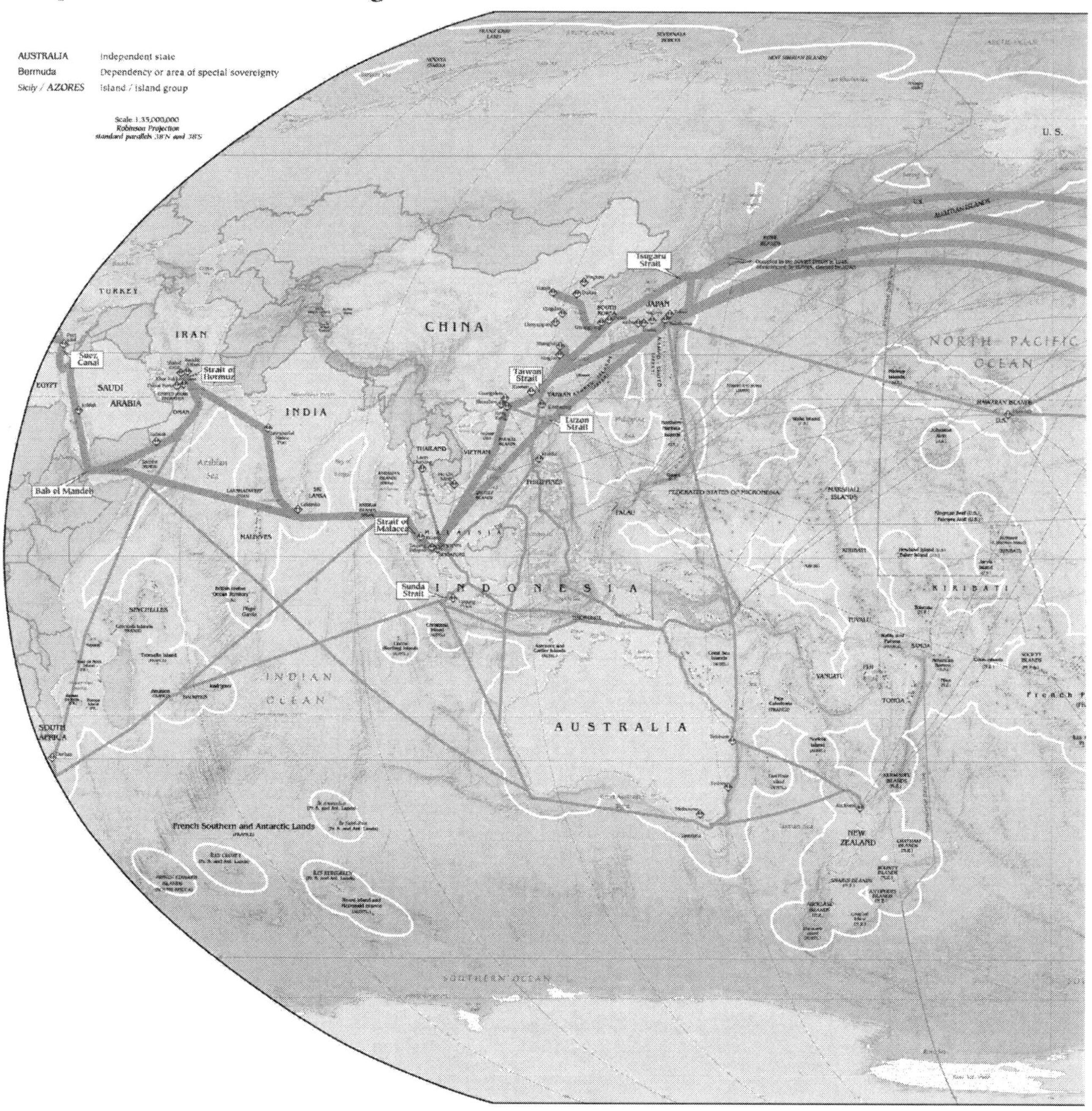

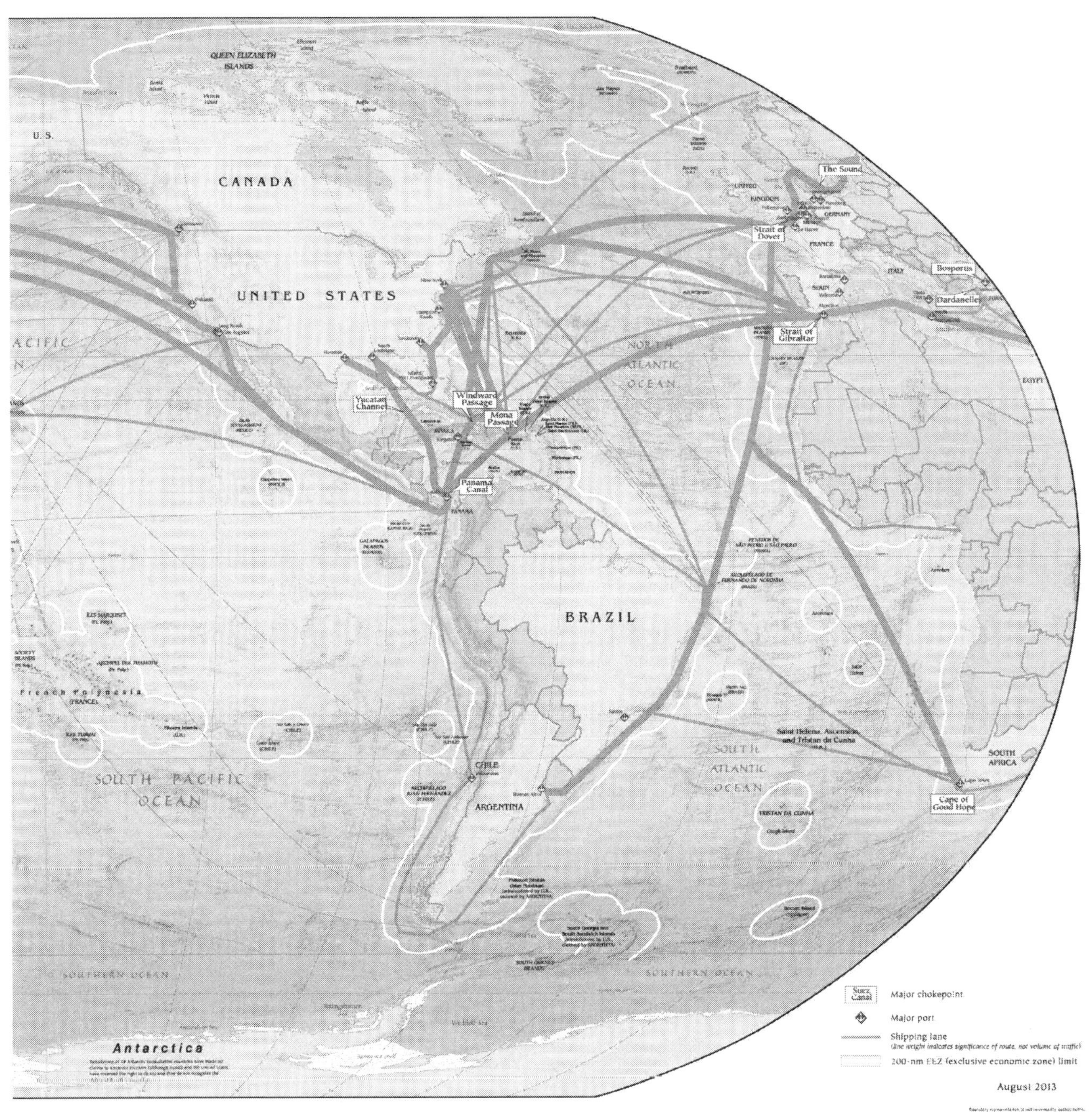
CANADA
UNITED STATES
BRAZIL
ARGENTINA
CHILE
SOUTH AFRICA
NORTH ATLANTIC OCEAN
SOUTH ATLANTIC OCEAN
SOUTH PACIFIC OCEAN
SOUTHERN OCEAN
Antarctica
The Sound
Strait of Dover
Bosporus
Dardanelles
Strait of Gibraltar
Yucatan Channel
Windward Passage
Mona Passage
Panama Canal
Cape of Good Hope
Saint Helena, Ascension, and Tristan da Cunha
French Polynesia (FRANCE)
Suez Canal Major chokepoint
Major port
Shipping lane
200-nm EEZ (exclusive economic zone) limit
August 2013

Physical Map of the World, August 2013

AUSTRALIA	Independent state
Bermuda	Dependency or area of special sovereignty
Sicily / AZORES	Island / island group
★	Capital

Scale 1:35,000,000
Robinson Projection
standard parallels 38°N and 38°S

RUSSIA
SIBERIA
KAZAKHSTAN
MONGOLIA
CHINA
JAPAN
NORTH PACIFIC OCEAN
TURKEY
IRAN
LIBYA
EGYPT
SAUDI ARABIA
INDIA
SUDAN
CHAD
NIGER
NIGERIA
SOUTH SUDAN
ETHIOPIA
SOMALIA
DEMOCRATIC REPUBLIC OF THE CONGO
TANZANIA
ANGOLA
MOZAMBIQUE
MADAGASCAR
BOTSWANA
SOUTH AFRICA
INDIAN OCEAN
INDONESIA
PAPUA NEW GUINEA
AUSTRALIA
NEW ZEALAND
THAILAND
PHILIPPINES
French Southern and Antarctic Lands
SOUTHERN OCEAN
Antarctica
August 2013

Political Map of the World, October 2016
AUSTRALIA Independent country
Bermuda Dependency or area of special sovereignty
Sicily / AZORES Island / island group
National capital
Other capital
Scale 1:35,000,000
Robinson Projection
CANADA
UNITED STATES
MEXICO
BRAZIL
PERU
BOLIVIA
PARAGUAY
CHILE
ARGENTINA
VENEZUELA
COLOMBIA
Greenland
ALGERIA
MOROCCO
MALI
NIGER
NIGERIA
MAURITANIA
NORTH PACIFIC OCEAN
NORTH ATLANTIC OCEAN
SOUTH ATLANTIC OCEAN
SOUTH PACIFIC OCEAN
SOUTHERN OCEAN
KIRIBATI
French Polynesia (FRANCE)
Gulf of Mexico
Caribbean Sea
Saint Helena, Ascension, and Tristan da Cunha (U.K.)
Antarct

RUSSIA
KAZAKHSTAN
MONGOLIA
CHINA
TURKEY
IRAN
IRAQ
AFGHANISTAN
PAKISTAN
INDIA
BURMA
THAILAND
VIETNAM
PHILIPPINES
JAPAN
TAIWAN
LIBYA
EGYPT
SAUDI
ARABIA
NIGER
CHAD
SUDAN
NIGERIA
SOUTH
SUDAN
ETHIOPIA
SOMALIA
KENYA
DEMOCRATIC
REPUBLIC
OF THE CONGO
TANZANIA
ANGOLA
ZAMBIA
MOZAMBIQUE
MADAGASCAR
NAMIBIA
SOUTH
AFRICA
INDONESIA
PAPUA NEW GUINEA
SOLOMON
ISLANDS
AUSTRALIA
NEW
ZEALAND
NORTH
PACIFIC
OCEAN
SOUTH
PACIFIC
OCEAN
INDIAN
OCEAN
Arabian
Sea
SOUTHERN OCEAN
Antarctica

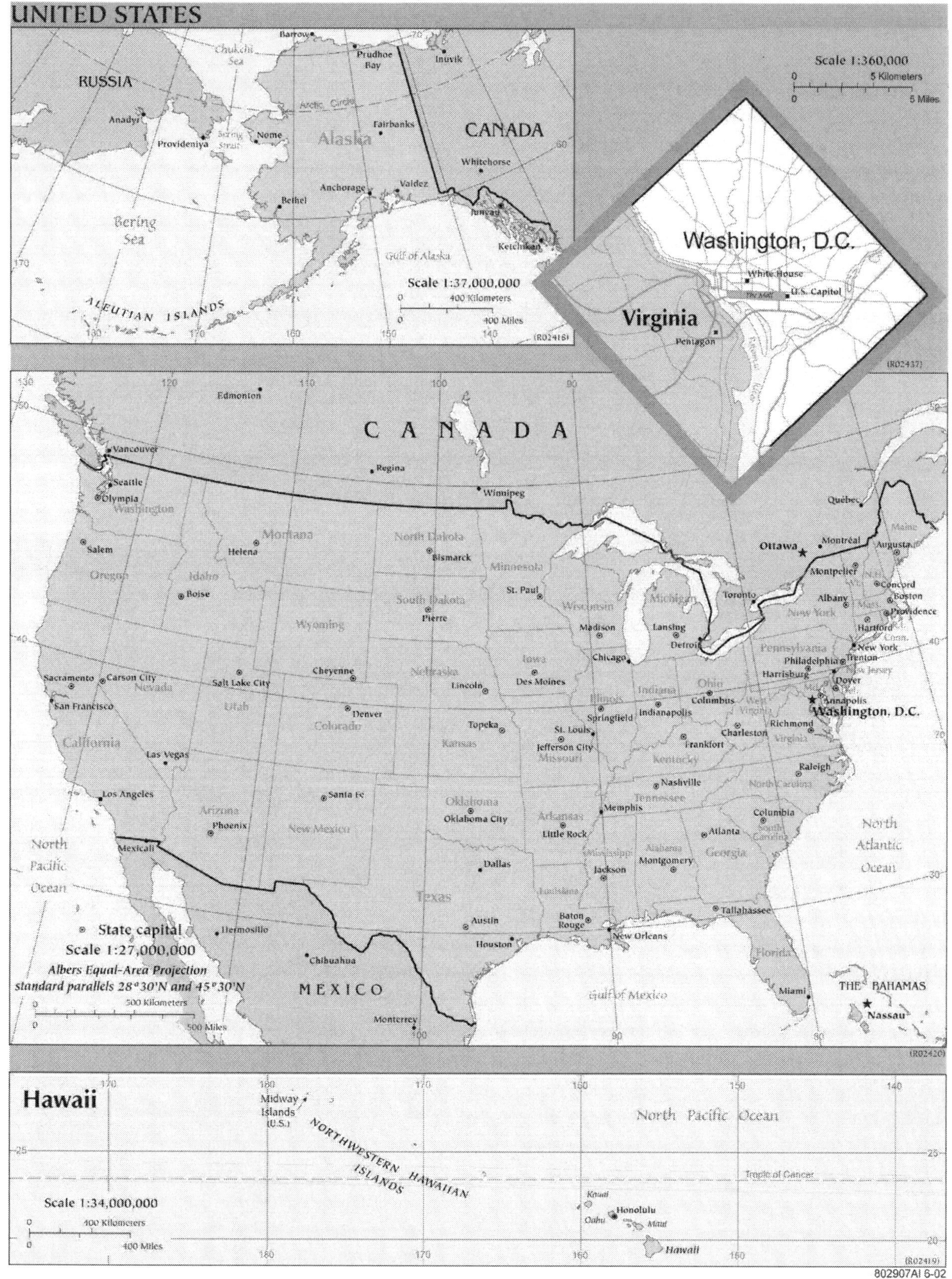
UNITED STATES
RUSSIA
CANADA
Alaska
Bering Sea
Gulf of Alaska
ALEUTIAN ISLANDS
Scale 1:37,000,000
Washington, D.C.
Virginia
White House
U.S. Capitol
Pentagon
Scale 1:360,000
C A N A D A
North Pacific Ocean
North Atlantic Ocean
Gulf of Mexico
MEXICO
THE BAHAMAS
State capital
Scale 1:27,000,000
Albers Equal-Area Projection
standard parallels 28°30'N and 45°30'N
Hawaii
North Pacific Ocean
NORTHWESTERN HAWAIIAN ISLANDS
Midway Islands (U.S.)
Tropic of Cancer
Honolulu
Scale 1:34,000,000
802907AI 6-02

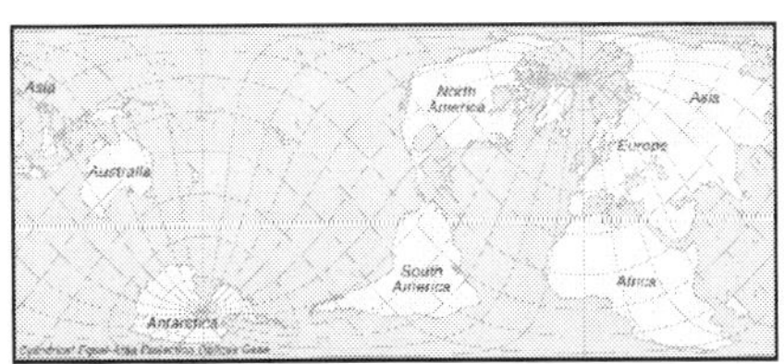

WORLD

INTRODUCTION :: WORLD

BACKGROUND:

Globally, the 20th century was marked by: (a) two devastating world wars; (b) the Great Depression of the 1930s; (c) the end of vast colonial empires; (d) rapid advances in science and technology, from the first airplane flight at Kitty Hawk, North Carolina (US) to the landing on the moon; (e) the Cold War between the Western alliance and the Warsaw Pact nations; (f) a sharp rise in living standards in North America, Europe, and Japan; (g) increased concerns about environmental degradation including deforestation, energy and water shortages, declining biological diversity, and air pollution; (h) the onset of the AIDS epidemic; and (i) the ultimate emergence of the US as the only world superpower. The planet's population continues to explode: from 1 billion in 1820 to 2 billion in 1930, 3 billion in 1960, 4 billion in 1974, 5 billion in 1987, 6 billion in 1999, and 7 billion in 2012. For the 21st century, the continued exponential growth in science and technology raises both hopes (e.g., advances in medicine and agriculture) and fears (e.g., development of even more lethal weapons of war).

GEOGRAPHY :: WORLD

GEOGRAPHIC OVERVIEW:

The surface of the earth is approximately 70.9% water and 29.1% land. The former portion is divided into large bodies termed oceans. The World Factbook recognizes and describes five oceans, which are in decreasing order of size: the Pacific Ocean, Atlantic Ocean, Indian Ocean, Southern Ocean, and Arctic Ocean. Because of their immense size, the Pacific and Atlantic Oceans are generally divided at the equator into the North and South Pacific Oceans and the North and South Atlantic Oceans, thus creating seven major water bodies - the so-called "Seven Seas."

Some 97.5% of the earth's water is saltwater. Of the 2.5% that is fresh, about two-thirds is frozen mostly locked up in the Antarctic ice sheets and mountain glaciers worldwide. If all the surface ice on earth fully melted, the sea level would rise about 70 m.

Earth's land portion is generally divided into several, large, discrete landmasses termed continents. Depending on the convention used, the number of continents can vary from five to seven. The most common classification recognizes seven, which are (from largest to smallest): Asia, Africa, North America, South America, Antarctica, Europe, and Australia. Asia and Europe are sometimes lumped together into a Eurasian continent resulting in six continents. Alternatively, North and South America are sometimes grouped as simply the Americas, resulting in a continent total of six (or five, if the Eurasia designation is used).

North America is commonly understood to include the island of Greenland, the isles of the Caribbean, and to extend south all the way to the Isthmus of Panama. The easternmost extent of Europe is generally defined as being the Ural Mountains and the Ural River; on the southeast the Caspian Sea; and on the south the Caucasus Mountains, the Black Sea, and the Mediterranean. Portions of five countries - Azerbaijan, Georgia, Kazakhstan, Russia, and Turkey - fall within both Europe and Asia, but in every instance the larger section is in Asia. These countries are considered part of both continents. Armenia and Cyprus, which lie completely in Western Asia, are geopolitically European countries.

Asia usually incorporates all the islands of the Philippines, Malaysia, and Indonesia. The islands of the Pacific are often lumped with Australia into a "land mass" termed Oceania or Australasia. Africa's northeast extremity is frequently delimited at the Isthmus of Suez, but for geopolitical purposes, the Egyptian Sinai Peninsula is often included as part of Africa.

Although the above groupings are the most common, different continental dispositions are recognized or taught in certain parts of the world, with some arrangements more heavily based on cultural spheres rather than physical geographic considerations.

Based on the seven-continent model, and grouping islands with adjacent continents, Africa has the most countries with 54. Europe contains 49 countries and Asia 48, but these two continents share five countries: Azerbaijan, Georgia, Kazakhstan, Russia, and Turkey. North America consists of 23 sovereign states, Oceania has 14, and South America 12.

countries by continent: Africa (54): Algeria, Angola, Benin, Botswana, Burkina Faso, Burundi, Cabo Verde, Cameroon, Central African Republic, Chad, Comoros, Democratic Republic of the Congo, Republic of the Congo, Cote d'Ivoire, Djibouti, Egypt, Equatorial Guinea, Eritrea, Eswatini, Ethiopia, Gabon, The Gambia, Ghana, Guinea, Guinea-Bissau, Kenya, Lesotho, Liberia, Libya, Madagascar, Malawi, Mali, Mauritania, Mauritius, Morocco, Mozambique, Namibia, Niger, Nigeria, Rwanda, Sao Tome and Principe, Senegal, Seychelles, Sierra Leone, Somalia, South Africa, South Sudan, Sudan, Tanzania, Togo, Tunisia, Uganda, Zambia, Zimbabwe;

Europe (49): Albania, Andorra, Austria, Azerbaijan*, Belarus, Belgium, Bosnia and Herzegovina, Bulgaria, Croatia, Czech Republic, Denmark, Estonia, Finland, France, Georgia*, Germany, Greece, Holy See (Vatican City), Hungary, Iceland, Ireland, Italy, Kazakhstan*, Kosovo, Latvia, Liechtenstein, Lithuania, Luxembourg, Macedonia, Malta, Moldova, Monaco, Montenegro, Netherlands, Norway, Poland, Portugal, Romania, Russia*, San Marino, Serbia, Slovakia, Slovenia, Spain, Sweden, Switzerland, Turkey*, Ukraine, United Kingdom (* indicates part of the country is also in Asia);

Asia (48): Afghanistan, Armenia, Azerbaijan*, Bahrain, Bangladesh, Bhutan, Brunei, Burma, Cambodia, China, Cyprus, Georgia*, India, Indonesia, Iran, Iraq, Israel, Japan, Jordan, Kazakhstan*, North Korea, South Korea, Kuwait, Kyrgyzstan, Laos, Lebanon, Malaysia, Maldives, Mongolia, Nepal, Oman, Pakistan, Philippines, Qatar, Russia*, Saudi Arabia, Singapore, Sri Lanka, Syria,

Tajikistan, Thailand, Timor-Leste, Turkey*, Turkmenistan, United Arab Emirates, Uzbekistan, Vietnam, Yemen (* indicates part of the country is also in Europe);

North America (23): Antigua and Barbuda, The Bahamas, Barbados, Belize, Canada, Costa Rica, Cuba, Dominica, Dominican Republic, El Salvador, Grenada, Guatemala, Haiti, Honduras, Jamaica, Mexico, Nicaragua, Panama, Saint Kitts and Nevis, Saint Lucia, Saint Vincent and the Grenadines, Trinidad and Tobago, United States;

Oceania (14): Australia, Fiji, Kiribati, Marshall Islands, Federated States of Micronesia, Nauru, New Zealand, Palau, Papua New Guinea, Samoa, Solomon Islands, Tonga, Tuvalu, Vanuatu;

South America (12): Argentina, Bolivia, Brazil, Chile, Colombia, Ecuador, Guyana, Paraguay, Peru, Suriname, Uruguay, Venezuela

MAP REFERENCES:

Physical Map of the World

AREA:

total: 510.072 million sq km

land: 148.94 million sq km

water: 361.132 million sq km

note: 70.9% of the world's surface is water, 29.1% is land

AREA - COMPARATIVE:

land area about 16 times the size of the US

top fifteen World Factbook entities ranked by size: 155,557,000 Pacific Ocean; 76,762,000 Atlantic Ocean; 68,556,000 Indian Ocean; 20,327,000 Southern Ocean; 17,098,242 Russia; 14,056,000 Arctic Ocean; 14,000,000 Antarctica; 9,984,670 Canada; 9,826,675 United States; 9,596,960 China; 8,515,770 Brazil; 7,741,220 Australia; 4,324,782 European Union; 3,287,263 India; 2,780,400 Argentina

top ten largest water bodies: 155,557,000 Pacific Ocean; 76,762,000 Atlantic Ocean; 68,556,000 Indian Ocean; 20,327,000 Southern Ocean; 14,056,000 Arctic Ocean; 4,184,100 Coral Sea; 3595900 South China Sea; 2,834,000 Caribbean Sea; 2,520,000 Bering Sea; 2,469,000 Mediterranean Sea

top ten largest landmasses: 44,568,500 Asia; 30,065,000 Africa; 24,473,000 North America; 17,819,000 South America; 14,000,000 Antarctica; 9,948,000 Europe; 7,741,220 Australia; 2,166,086 Greenland; 785,753 New Guinea; 751,929 Borneo

top ten largest islands: 2,166,086 Greenland; 785,753 New Guinea (Indonesia, Papua New Guinea); 751,929 Borneo (Brunei, Indonesia, Malaysia); 587,713 Madagascar; 507,451 Baffin Island (Canada); 472,784 Sumatra (Indonesia); 227,963 Honshu (Japan); 217,291 Victoria Island (Canada); 209,331 Great Britain (United Kingdom); 196,236 Ellesmere Island (Canada)

ten smallest independent countries: 0.44 Holy See (Vatican City); 2 Monaco; 21 Nauru; 26 Tuvalu; 61 San Marino; 160 Liechtenstein; 181 Marshall Islands; 261 Saint Kitts and Nevis; 298 Maldives; 316 Malta

LAND BOUNDARIES:

the land boundaries in the world total 251,060 km (not counting shared boundaries twice); two nations, China and Russia, each border 14 other countries

note: 46 nations and other areas are landlocked, these include: Afghanistan, Andorra, Armenia, Austria, Azerbaijan, Belarus, Bhutan, Bolivia, Botswana, Burkina Faso, Burundi, Central African Republic, Chad, Czechia, Eswatini, Ethiopia, Holy See (Vatican City), Hungary, Kazakhstan, Kosovo, Kyrgyzstan, Laos, Lesotho, Liechtenstein, Luxembourg, Macedonia, Malawi, Mali, Moldova, Mongolia, Nepal, Niger, Paraguay, Rwanda, San Marino, Serbia, Slovakia, South Sudan, Switzerland, Tajikistan, Turkmenistan, Uganda, Uzbekistan, West Bank, Zambia, Zimbabwe; two of these, Liechtenstein and Uzbekistan, are doubly landlocked

COASTLINE:

356,000 km

note: 95 nations and other entities are islands that border no other countries, they include: American Samoa, Anguilla, Antigua and Barbuda, Aruba, Ashmore and Cartier Islands, The Bahamas, Bahrain, Baker Island, Barbados, Bermuda, Bouvet Island, British Indian Ocean Territory, British Virgin Islands, Cabo Verde, Cayman Islands, Christmas Island, Clipperton Island, Cocos (Keeling) Islands, Comoros, Cook Islands, Coral Sea Islands, Cuba, Curacao, Cyprus, Dominica, Falkland Islands (Islas Malvinas), Faroe Islands, Fiji, French Polynesia, French Southern and Antarctic Lands, Greenland, Grenada, Guam, Guernsey, Heard Island and McDonald Islands, Howland Island, Iceland, Isle of Man, Jamaica, Jan Mayen, Japan, Jarvis Island, Jersey, Johnston Atoll, Kingman Reef, Kiribati, Madagascar, Maldives, Malta, Marshall Islands, Mauritius, Mayotte, Federated States of Micronesia, Midway Islands, Montserrat, Nauru, Navassa Island, New Caledonia, New Zealand, Niue, Norfolk Island, Northern Mariana Islands, Palau, Palmyra Atoll, Paracel Islands, Philippines, Pitcairn Islands, Puerto Rico, Saint Barthelemy, Saint Helena, Saint Kitts and Nevis, Saint Lucia, Saint Pierre and Miquelon, Saint Vincent and the Grenadines, Samoa, Sao Tome and Principe, Seychelles, Singapore, Sint Maarten, Solomon Islands, South Georgia and the South Sandwich Islands, Spratly Islands, Sri Lanka, Svalbard, Taiwan, Tokelau, Tonga, Trinidad and Tobago, Turks and Caicos Islands, Tuvalu, Vanuatu, Virgin Islands, Wake Island, Wallis and Futuna

MARITIME CLAIMS:

a variety of situations exist, but in general, most countries make the following claims measured from the mean low-tide baseline as described in the 1982 UN Convention on the Law of the Sea: territorial sea - 12 nm, contiguous zone - 24 nm, and exclusive economic zone - 200 nm; additional zones provide for exploitation of continental shelf resources and an exclusive fishing zone; boundary situations with neighboring states prevent many countries from extending their fishing or economic zones to a full 200 nm

CLIMATE:

a wide equatorial band of hot and humid tropical climates, bordered north and south by subtropical temperate zones that separate two large areas of cold and dry polar climates

TERRAIN:

tremendous variation of terrain on each of the continents; check the World 'Elevation' entry for a compilation of terrain extremes; the world's ocean floors are marked by mid-ocean ridges while the ocean surfaces form a dynamic, continuously changing environment; check the 'Terrain' field and its 'major surface currents' subfield under each of the five ocean (Arctic, Atlantic, Indian, Pacific, and Southern) entries for further information on oceanic environs

ELEVATION:

mean elevation: 840 m

elevation extremes: -2,555 m lowest point: Bentley Subglacial Trench (Antarctica) (in the oceanic realm, Challenger Deep in the Mariana Trench is the lowest point, lying -10,924 m below the surface of the Pacific Ocean)

highest point: Mount Everest 8,850 m

top ten highest mountains (measured from sea level): Mount Everest (China-Nepal) 8,850 m; K2 (Pakistan) 8,611 m; Kanchenjunga (India-Nepal) 8,598 m; Lhotse (Nepal) 8,516 m; Makalu (China-Nepal) 8,463 m; Cho Oyu (China-Nepal) 8,201 m; Dhaulagiri (Nepal) 8,167 m; Manaslu (Nepal) 8,163 m; Nanga Parbat (Pakistan) 8,125 m; Anapurna (Nepal) 8,091 m

note: Mauna Kea (United States) is the world's tallest mountain as measured from base to summit; the peak of this volcanic colossus lies on the island of Hawaii, but its base begins more than 70 km offshore and at a depth of about 6,000 m; total height estimates range from 9,966 m to 10,203 m

highest point on each continent: Asia - Mount Everest (China-Nepal) 8,850 m; South America - Cerro Aconcagua (Argentina) 6,960 m; North America - Denali (Mount McKinley) (United States) 6,190 m; Africa - Kilimanjaro (Tanzania) 5,895 m; Europe - El'brus (Russia) 5,633 m; Antarctica - Vinson Massif 4,897 m; Australia - Mount Kosciuszko 2,229 m

highest capital on each continent: South America - La Paz (Bolivia) 3,640 m; Africa - Addis Ababa (Ethiopia) 2,355 m; Asia - Thimphu (Bhutan) 2,334 m; North America - Mexico City (Mexico) 2,240 m; Europe - Andorra la Vella (Andorra) 1,023 m; Australia - Canberra (Australia) 605 m

lowest point on each continent: Antarctica - Bentley Subglacial Trench -2,555 m; Asia - Dead Sea (Israel-Jordan) -408 m; Africa - Lac Assal (Djibouti) -155 m; South America - Laguna del Carbon (Argentina) -105 m; North America - Death Valley (United States) -86 m; Europe - Caspian Sea (Azerbaijan-Kazakhstan-Russia) -28 m; Australia - Lake Eyre -15 m

lowest capital on each continent: Asia - Baku (Azerbaijan) -28 m; Europe - Amsterdam (Netherlands) -2 m; Africa - Banjul (Gambia); Bissau (Guinea-Bissau), Conakry (Guinea), Djibouti (Djibouti), Libreville (Gabon), Male (Maldives), Monrovia (Liberia), Tunis (Tunisia), Victoria (Seychelles) 0 m; North America - Basseterre (Saint Kitts and Nevis), Kingstown (Saint Vincent and the Grenadines), Panama City (Panama), Port of Spain (Trinidad and Tobago), Roseau (Dominica), Saint John's (Antigua and Barbuda), Santo Domingo (Dominican Republic) 0 m; South America - Georgetown (Guyana) 0 m; Australia - Canberra (Australia) 605 m

NATURAL RESOURCES:

the rapid depletion of nonrenewable mineral resources, the depletion of forest areas and wetlands, the extinction of animal and plant species, and the deterioration in air and water quality pose serious long-term problems

IRRIGATED LAND:

3,242,917 sq km (2012 est.)

POPULATION DISTRIBUTION:

six of the world's seven continents are widely and permanently inhabited; Asia is easily the most populous continent with about 60% of the world's population (China and India together account for over 35%); Africa comes in second with over 15% of the earth's populace, Europe has about 10%, North America 8%, South America almost 6%, and Oceania less than 1%; the harsh conditions on Antarctica prevent any permanent habitation

NATURAL HAZARDS:

large areas subject to severe weather (tropical cyclones); natural disasters (earthquakes, landslides, tsunamis, volcanic eruptions)

volcanism: volcanism is a fundamental driver and consequence of plate tectonics, the physical process reshaping the Earth's lithosphere; the world is home to more than 1,500 potentially active volcanoes, with over 500 of these having erupted in historical times; an estimated 500 million people live near these volcanoes; associated dangers include lava flows, lahars (mudflows), pyroclastic flows, ash clouds, ash fall, ballistic projectiles, gas emissions, landslides, earthquakes, and tsunamis; in the 1990s, the International Association of Volcanology and Chemistry of the Earth's Interior, created a list of 16 Decade Volcanoes worthy of special study because of their great potential for destruction: Avachinsky-Koryaksky (Russia), Colima (Mexico), Etna (Italy), Galeras (Colombia), Mauna Loa (United States), Merapi (Indonesia), Nyiragongo (Democratic Republic of the Congo), Rainier (United States), Sakurajima (Japan), Santa Maria (Guatemala), Santorini (Greece), Taal (Philippines), Teide (Spain), Ulawun (Papua New Guinea), Unzen (Japan), Vesuvius (Italy); see second note under "Geography - note"

ENVIRONMENT - CURRENT ISSUES:

large areas subject to overpopulation, industrial disasters, pollution (air, water, acid rain, toxic substances), loss of vegetation (overgrazing, deforestation, desertification), loss of biodiversity; soil degradation, soil depletion, erosion; ozone layer depletion; waste disposal; global warming becoming a greater concern

GEOGRAPHY - NOTE:

note: the world is now thought to be about 4.55 billion years old, just about one-third of the 13.8-billion-year age estimated for the universe

note: although earthquakes can strike anywhere at any time, the vast majority occur in three large zones of the earth; the world's greatest earthquake belt, the Circum-Pacific Belt (popularly referred to as the Ring of Fire), is the zone of active volcanoes and earthquake epicenters bordering the Pacific Ocean; about 90% of the world's earthquakes (81% of the largest earthquakes) and some 75% of the world's volcanoes occur within the Ring of Fire; the belt extends northward from Chile, along the South American coast, through Central America, Mexico, the western US, southern Alaska and the Aleutian Islands, to Japan, the Philippines, Papua New Guinea, island groups in the southwestern Pacific, and New Zealand

the second prominent belt, the Alpide, extends from Java to Sumatra, northward along the mountains of Burma, then eastward through the Himalayas, the Mediterranean, and out into the Atlantic Ocean; it accounts for about 17% of the world's largest earthquakes; the third important belt follows the long Mid-Atlantic Ridge

PEOPLE AND SOCIETY :: WORLD

POPULATION:

7,405,107,650 (2017 est.)

top ten most populous countries (in millions): China 1379.3; India 1281.93; United States 326.63; Indonesia 260.58; Brazil 207.35; Pakistan 204.92; Nigeria 190.63; Bangladesh 157.83; Russia 142.26; Japan 126.45;

ten least populous countries: Holy See (Vatican City) 1,000; Montserrat 5,292; Saint Pierre and Miquelon 5,533; Saint Barthelemy 7,184; Saint Helena, Ascension, and Tristan de Cunha 7,828; Cook Islands 9,290; Tuvalu 11,052; Nauru 11359; Wallis and Futuna 15,714; Anguilla 17,087;

ten most densely populated countries (population per sq km): Macau 21,346; Monaco 15,322; Singapore 8,572; Hong Kong 6,702; Gaza Strip 4,987; Gibraltar 4,523; Bahrain 1,857; Maldives 1,318; Malta 1,317; Bermuda 1,312;

ten least densely populated countries (population per sq km): Greenland less than 1; Mongolia 2; Western Sahara 2.3; Australia 3; Namibia 3; Iceland 3.4; Mauritania 3.6; Guyana 3.7; Libya 3.8; Suriname 3.8

LANGUAGES:

Mandarin Chinese 12.3%, Spanish 6%, English 5.1%, Arabic 5.1%, Hindi 3.5%, Bengali 3.3%, Portuguese 3%, Russian 2.1%, Japanese 1.7%, Punjabi, Western 1.3%, Javanese 1.1% (2018 est.)

note 1: percents are for "first language" speakers only; the six UN languages - Arabic, Chinese (Mandarin), English, French, Russian, and Spanish (Castilian) - are the mother tongue or second language of about 45% of the world's population, and are the official languages in more than half the states in the world; some 400 languages have more than a million first-language speakers

note 2: all told, there are an estimated 7,100 languages spoken in the world; approximately 80% of these languages are spoken by less than 100,000 people; about 150 languages are spoken by less than 10 people; communities that are isolated from each other in mountainous regions often develop multiple languages; Papua New Guinea, for example, boasts about 840 separate languages

note 3: approximately 2,300 languages are spoken in Asia, 2,140, in Africa, 1,310 in the Pacific, 1,060 in the Americas, and 290 in Europe (2018)

RELIGIONS:

Christian 31.4%, Muslim 23.2%, Hindu 15%, Buddhist 7.1%, folk religions 5.9%, Jewish 0.2%, other 0.8%, unaffiliated 16.4%

AGE STRUCTURE:

0-14 years: 25.44% (male 963,981,944/female 898,974,458) (2017 est.)

15-24 years: 16.16% (male 611,311,930/female 572,229,547) (2017 est.)

25-54 years: 41.12% (male 1,522,999,578/female 1,488,011,505) (2017 est.)

55-64 years: 8.6% (male 307,262,939/female 322,668,546) (2017 est.)

65 years and over: 8.68% (male 283,540,918/female 352,206,092) (2017 est.)

DEPENDENCY RATIOS:

total dependency ratio: 52.5 (2015 est.)

youth dependency ratio: 39.9 (2015 est.)

elderly dependency ratio: 12.6 (2015 est.)

potential support ratio: 7.9 (2015 est.)

MEDIAN AGE:

total: 30.6 years

male: 29.9 years

female: 31.4 years (2018 est.)

POPULATION GROWTH RATE:

1.06% (2017 est.)

note: this rate results in about 149 net additions to the worldwide population every minute or 2.5 every second

BIRTH RATE:

18.4 births/1,000 population (2017 est.)

note: this rate results in about 259 worldwide births per minute or 4.3 births every second

DEATH RATE:

7.7 deaths/1,000 population (2016 est.)

note: this rate results in about 108 worldwide deaths per minute or 1.8 deaths every second

POPULATION DISTRIBUTION:

six of the world's seven continents are widely and permanently inhabited; Asia is easily the most populous continent with about 60% of the world's population (China and India together account for over 35%); Africa comes in second with over 15% of the earth's populace, Europe has about 10%, North America 8%, South America almost 6%, and Oceania less than 1%; the harsh conditions on Antarctica prevent any permanent habitation

URBANIZATION:

urban population: 55.3% of total population (2017)

rate of urbanization: 1.9% annual rate of change (2017)

ten largest urban agglomerations: Tokyo (Japan) - 38,241,000; New Delhi (India) - 27,197,000; Shanghai (China) - 25,202,000; Beijing (China) - 22,063,000; Mumbai (India) - 21,690,000; Sao Paulo (Brazil) - 21,519,000; Mexico City (Mexico) - 21,321,000; Osaka (Japan) - 20,415,000; Cairo (Egypt) - 19,486,000; Dhaka (Bangladesh) - 18,898,000 (2017)

SEX RATIO:

at birth: 1.03 male(s)/female (2017 est.)

0-14 years: 1.07 male(s)/female (2017 est.)

15-24 years: 1.07 male(s)/female (2017 est.)

25-54 years: 1.02 male(s)/female (2017 est.)

55-64 years: 0.95 male(s)/female (2017 est.)

65 years and over: 0.81 male(s)/female (2017 est.)

total population: 1.02 male(s)/female (2017 est.)

MATERNAL MORTALITY RATE:

216 deaths/100,000 live births (2015 est.)

INFANT MORTALITY RATE:

total: 32.9 deaths/1,000 live births (2017 est.)

male: 34.9 deaths/1,000 live births (2017 est.)

female: 30.9 deaths/1,000 live births (2017 est.)

LIFE EXPECTANCY AT BIRTH:

total population: 69 years (2017 est.)

male: 67 years (2017 est.)

female: 71.1 years (2017 est.)

TOTAL FERTILITY RATE:

2.42 children born/woman (2017 est.)

DRINKING WATER SOURCE:

improved:

urban: 96.5% of population

rural: 84.7% of population

total: 91.1% of population

unimproved:

urban: 3.5% of population

rural: 15.3% of population

total: 8.9% of population (2015 est.)

SANITATION FACILITY ACCESS:

improved:

urban: 82.3% of population (2015 est.)

rural: 50.5% of population (2015 est.)

total: 67.7% of population (2015 est.)

unimproved:

urban: 17.7% of population (2015 est.)

rural: 49.5% of population (2015 est.)

total: 32.3% of population (2015 est.)

HIV/AIDS - ADULT PREVALENCE RATE:

0.8% (2017 est.)

HIV/AIDS - PEOPLE LIVING WITH HIV/AIDS:

36.9 million (2017 est.)

HIV/AIDS - DEATHS:

940,000 (2017 est.)

LITERACY:

definition: age 15 and over can read and write

total population: 86.2%

male: 89.8%

female: 82.6% (2016 est.)

note: more than three-quarters of the world's 750 million illiterate adults are found in South Asia and sub-Saharan Africa; of all the illiterate adults in the world, almost two-thirds are women (2016)

SCHOOL LIFE EXPECTANCY (PRIMARY TO TERTIARY EDUCATION):

total: 12 years (2014)

male: 12 years (2014)

female: 12 years (2014)

GOVERNMENT :: WORLD

CAPITAL:

there are 21 World entities (20 countries and 1 dependency) with multiple time zones: Australia, Brazil, Canada, Chile, Democratic Republic of Congo, Ecuador, France, Greenland, Indonesia, Kazakhstan, Kiribati, Mexico, Micronesia, Mongolia, Netherlands, New Zealand, Papua New Guinea, Portugal, Russia, Spain, United States

note: in some instances, the time zones pertain to portions of a country that lie overseas

ADMINISTRATIVE DIVISIONS:

195 countries, 72 dependent areas and other entities

LEGAL SYSTEM:

the legal systems of nearly all countries are generally modeled upon elements of five main types: civil law (including French law, the Napoleonic Code, Roman law, Roman-Dutch law, and Spanish law); common law (including English and US law); customary law; mixed or pluralistic law; and religious law (including Islamic law); an additional type of legal system - international law - governs the conduct of independent nations in their relationships with one another

INTERNATIONAL LAW ORGANIZATION PARTICIPATION:

all members of the UN are parties to the statute that established the International Court of Justice (ICJ) or World Court; 62 countries have accepted jurisdiction of the ICJ as compulsory with reservations and 12 countries have accepted ICJ jurisdiction as compulsory without reservations; states parties to the Rome Statute of the International Criminal Court (ICCt) are those countries that have ratified or acceded to the Rome Statute, the treaty that established the Court; a total of 123 (as of October 2017) countries have accepted jurisdiction of the ICCt (see Appendix B for a clarification on the differing mandates of the ICJ and ICCt)

LEGISLATIVE BRANCH:

there are 230 political entities with legislative bodies; of these 144 are unicameral (a single "house") and 86 are bicameral (both upper and lower houses); note - while there are 195 countries in the world, 35 territories, possessions, or other special administrative units also have their own governing bodies

FLAG DESCRIPTION:

note: the flags of 12 nations: Austria, Botswana, Georgia, Jamaica, Japan, Laos, Latvia, Macedonia, Micronesia, Nigeria, Switzerland, and Thailand have no top or bottom and may be flown with either long edge on top without any notice being taken

ECONOMY :: WORLD

ECONOMY - OVERVIEW:

The international financial crisis of 2008-09 led to the first downturn in global output since 1946 and presented the world with a major new challenge: determining what mix of fiscal and monetary policies to follow to restore growth and jobs, while keeping inflation and debt under control. Financial stabilization and stimulus programs that started in 2009-11, combined with lower tax revenues in 2009-10, required most countries to run large budget deficits. Treasuries issued new public debt - totaling $9.1 trillion since 2008 - to pay for the additional expenditures. To keep interest rates low, most central banks monetized that debt, injecting large sums of money into their economies - between December 2008 and December 2013 the global money supply increased by more than 35%. Governments are now faced with the difficult task of spurring current growth and employment without saddling their economies with so much debt that they sacrifice long-term growth and financial stability. When economic activity picks up, central banks will confront the difficult task of containing inflation without raising interest rates so high they snuff out further growth.

Fiscal and monetary data for 2013 are currently available for 180 countries, which together account for 98.5% of world GDP. Of the 180 countries, 82 pursued unequivocally expansionary policies, boosting government spending while also expanding their money supply relatively rapidly - faster than the world average of 3.1%; 28 followed restrictive fiscal and monetary policies, reducing government spending and holding money growth to less than the 3.1%

average; and the remaining 70 followed a mix of counterbalancing fiscal and monetary policies, either reducing government spending while accelerating money growth, or boosting spending while curtailing money growth.

In 2013, for many countries the drive for fiscal austerity that began in 2011 abated. While 5 out of 6 countries slowed spending in 2012, only 1 in 2 countries slowed spending in 2013. About 1 in 3 countries actually lowered the level of their expenditures. The global growth rate for government expenditures increased from 1.6% in 2012 to 5.1% in 2013, after falling from a 10.1% growth rate in 2011. On the other hand, nearly 2 out of 3 central banks tightened monetary policy in 2013, decelerating the rate of growth of their money supply, compared with only 1 out of 3 in 2012. Roughly 1 of 4 central banks actually withdrew money from circulation, an increase from 1 out of 7 in 2012. Growth of the global money supply, as measured by the narrowly defined M1, slowed from 8.7% in 2009 and 10.4% in 2010 to 5.2% in 2011, 4.6% in 2012, and 3.1% in 2013. Several notable shifts occurred in 2013. By cutting government expenditures and expanding money supplies, the US and Canada moved against the trend in the rest of the world. France reversed course completely. Rather than reducing expenditures and money as it had in 2012, it expanded both. Germany reversed its fiscal policy, sharply expanding federal spending, while continuing to grow the money supply. South Korea shifted monetary policy into high gear, while maintaining a strongly expansionary fiscal policy. Japan, however, continued to pursue austere fiscal and monetary policies.

Austere economic policies have significantly affected economic performance. The global budget deficit narrowed to roughly $2.7 trillion in 2012 and $2.1 trillion in 2013, or 3.8% and 2.5% of World GDP, respectively. But growth of the world economy slipped from 5.1% in 2010 and 3.7% in 2011, to just 3.1% in 2012, and 2.9% in 2013.

Countries with expansionary fiscal and monetary policies achieved significantly higher rates of growth, higher growth of tax revenues, and greater success reducing the public debt burden than those countries that chose contractionary policies. In 2013, the 82 countries that followed a pro-growth approach achieved a median GDP growth rate of 4.7%, compared to 1.7% for the 28 countries with restrictive fiscal and monetary policies, a difference of 3 percentage points. Among the 82, China grew 7.7%, Philippines 6.8%, Malaysia 4.7%, Pakistan and Saudi Arabia 3.6%, Argentina 3.5%, South Korea 2.8%, and Russia 1.3%, while among the 28, Brazil grew 2.3%, Japan 2.0%, South Africa 2.0%, Netherlands -0.8%, Croatia -1.0%, Iran -1.5%, Portugal -1.8%, Greece -3.8%, and Cyprus -8.7%.

Faster GDP growth and lower unemployment rates translated into increased tax revenues and a less cumbersome debt burden. Revenues for the 82 expansionary countries grew at a median rate of 10.7%, whereas tax revenues fell at a median rate of 6.8% for the 28 countries that chose austere economic policies. Budget balances improved for about three-quarters of the 28, but, for most, debt grew faster than GDP, and the median level of their public debt as a share of GDP increased 9.1 percentage points, to 59.2%. On the other hand, budget balances deteriorated for most of the 82 pro-growth countries, but GDP growth outpaced increases in debt, and the median level of public debt as a share of GDP increased just 1.9%, to 39.8%.

The world recession has suppressed inflation rates - world inflation declined 1.0 percentage point in 2012 to about 4.1% and 0.2 percentage point to 3.9% in 2013. In 2013 the median inflation rate for the 82 pro-growth countries was 1.3 percentage points higher than that for the countries that followed more austere fiscal and monetary policies. Overall, the latter countries also improved their current account balances by shedding imports; as a result, current account balances deteriorated for most of the countries that pursued pro-growth policies. Slow growth of world income continued to hold import demand in check and crude oil prices fell. Consequently, the dollar value of world trade grew just 1.3% in 2013.

Beyond the current global slowdown, the world faces several long standing economic challenges. The addition of 80 million people each year to an already overcrowded globe is exacerbating the problems of pollution, waste-disposal, epidemics, water-shortages, famine, over-fishing of oceans, deforestation, desertification, and depletion of non-renewable resources. The nation-state, as a bedrock economic-political institution, is steadily losing control over international flows of people, goods, services, funds, and technology. The introduction of the euro as the common currency of much of Western Europe in January 1999, while paving the way for an integrated economic powerhouse, has created economic risks because the participating nations have varying income levels and growth rates, and hence, require a different mix of monetary and fiscal policies. Governments, especially in Western Europe, face the difficult political problem of channeling resources away from welfare programs in order to increase investment and strengthen incentives to seek employment. Because of their own internal problems and priorities, the industrialized countries are unable to devote sufficient resources to deal effectively with the poorer areas of the world, which, at least from an economic point of view, are becoming further marginalized. The terrorist attacks on the US on 11 September 2001 accentuated a growing risk to global prosperity - the diversion of resources away from capital investments to counter-terrorism programs.

Despite these vexing problems, the world economy also shows great promise. Technology has made possible further advances in a wide range of fields, from agriculture, to medicine, alternative energy, metallurgy, and transportation. Improved global communications have greatly reduced the costs of international trade, helping the world gain from the international division of labor, raise living standards, and reduce income disparities among nations. Much of the resilience of the world economy in the aftermath of the financial crisis resulted from government and central bank leaders around the globe working in concert to stem the financial onslaught, knowing well the lessons of past economic failures.

GDP (PURCHASING POWER PARITY):

$127.8 trillion (2017 est.)

$123.3 trillion (2016 est.)

$119.5 trillion (2015 est.)

note: data are in 2017 dollars

GDP (OFFICIAL EXCHANGE RATE):

$80.27 trillion SGWP (gross world product) (2017 est.)

GDP - REAL GROWTH RATE:

3.7% (2017 est.)

3.2% (2016 est.)

3.3% (2014 est.)

GDP - PER CAPITA (PPP):

$17,500 (2017 est.)

$17,000 (2016 est.)

$16,800 (2015 est.)

note: data are in 2017 dollars

GROSS NATIONAL SAVING:

27.9% of GDP (2017 est.)

27.4% of GDP (2016 est.)

27.8% of GDP (2015 est.)

GDP - COMPOSITION, BY END USE:

household consumption: 56.4% (2017 est.)

government consumption: 16.1% (2017 est.)

investment in fixed capital: 25.7% (2017 est.)

investment in inventories: 1.4% (2017 est.)

exports of goods and services: 28.8% (2017 est.)

imports of goods and services: -28.3% (2017 est.)

GDP - COMPOSITION, BY SECTOR OF ORIGIN:

agriculture: 6.4% (2017 est.)

industry: 30% (2017 est.)

services: 63% (2017 est.)

INDUSTRIES:

dominated by the onrush of technology, especially in computers, robotics, telecommunications, and medicines and medical equipment; most of these advances take place in OECD nations; only a small portion of non-OECD countries have succeeded in rapidly adjusting to these technological forces; the accelerated development of new technologies is complicating already grim environmental problems

INDUSTRIAL PRODUCTION GROWTH RATE:

3.2% (2017 est.)

LABOR FORCE:

3.432 billion (2017 est.)

LABOR FORCE - BY OCCUPATION:

agriculture: 31%

industry: 23.5%

services: 45.5% (2014 est.)

UNEMPLOYMENT RATE:

7.7% (2017 est.)

7.5% (2016 est.)

note: combined unemployment and underemployment in many non-industrialized countries; developed countries typically 4%-12% unemployment (2007 est.)

HOUSEHOLD INCOME OR CONSUMPTION BY PERCENTAGE SHARE:

lowest 10%: 30.2% (2008 est.)

highest 10%: 30.2% (2007.75 est.)

DISTRIBUTION OF FAMILY INCOME - GINI INDEX:

37.9 (2012 est.)

37.9 (2005 est.)

BUDGET:

revenues: 21.68 trillion (2017 est.)

expenditures: 23.81 trillion (2017 est.)

TAXES AND OTHER REVENUES:

26.7% (of GDP) (2016 est.)

BUDGET SURPLUS (+) OR DEFICIT (-):

-3% (of GDP) (2016 est.)

PUBLIC DEBT:

67.2% of GDP (2017 est.)

67.2% of GDP (2016 est.)

INFLATION RATE (CONSUMER PRICES):

6.4% (2017 est.)

3.7% (2016 est.)

developed countries: 1.9% (2017 est.)
0.9% (2016 est.)
developing countries: 8.8% (2017 est.)
3.7% (2016 est.)
note: the above estimates are weighted averages; inflation in developed countries is 0% to 4% typically, in developing countries, 4% to 10% typically; national inflation rates vary widely in individual cases; inflation rates have declined for most countries for the last several years, held in check by increasing international competition from several low wage countries and by soft demand due to the world financial crisis

STOCK OF NARROW MONEY:

$34.4 trillion (31 December 2017 est.)

$30.17 trillion (31 December 2016 est.)

STOCK OF BROAD MONEY:

$86.47 trillion (31 December 2017 est.)

$77.71 trillion (31 December 2016 est.)

STOCK OF DOMESTIC CREDIT:

$111.7 trillion (31 December 2017 est.)

$100.4 trillion (31 December 2016 est.)

MARKET VALUE OF PUBLICLY TRADED SHARES:

$67.47 trillion (31 December 2015 est.)

$68.51 trillion (31 December 2014 est.)

$68.37 trillion (31 December 2013 est.)

EXPORTS:

$17.31 trillion (2017 est.)

$15.82 trillion (2016 est.)

EXPORTS - COMMODITIES:

the whole range of industrial and agricultural goods and services

top ten - share of world trade: 14.8 electrical machinery, including computers; 14.4 mineral fuels, including oil, coal, gas, and refined products; 14.2 nuclear reactors, boilers, and parts; 8.9 cars, trucks, and buses; 3.5 scientific and precision instruments; 3.4 plastics; 2.7 iron and steel; 2.6 organic chemicals; 2.6 pharmaceutical products; 1.9 diamonds, pearls, and precious stones

(2007 est.)

IMPORTS:

$20.01 trillion (2018 est.)

$16.02 trillion (2017 est.)

IMPORTS - COMMODITIES:

the whole range of industrial and agricultural goods and services

top ten - share of world trade: see listing for exports

DEBT - EXTERNAL:

$76.56 trillion (31 December 2017 est.)

$75.09 trillion (31 December 2016 est.)

note: this figure is the sum total of all countries' external debt, both public and private

STOCK OF DIRECT FOREIGN INVESTMENT - AT HOME:

$33.6 trillion (31 December 2017 est.)

$31.62 trillion (31 December 2016 est.)

STOCK OF DIRECT FOREIGN INVESTMENT - ABROAD:

$34.73 trillion (31 December 2017 est.)

$32.94 trillion (31 December 2016 est.)

ENERGY :: WORLD

ELECTRICITY ACCESS:

population without electricity: 1.201 billion (2013)

electrification - total population: 83% (2013)

electrification - urban areas: 95% (2013)

electrification - rural areas: 70% (2013)

ELECTRICITY - PRODUCTION:

23.65 trillion kWh (2015 est.)

ELECTRICITY - CONSUMPTION:

21.78 trillion kWh (2015 est.)

ELECTRICITY - EXPORTS:

696.1 billion kWh (2016)

ELECTRICITY - IMPORTS:

721.9 billion kWh (2016 est.)

ELECTRICITY - INSTALLED GENERATING CAPACITY:

6.386 billion kW (2015 est.)

ELECTRICITY - FROM FOSSIL FUELS:

63% of total installed capacity (2015 est.)

ELECTRICITY - FROM NUCLEAR FUELS:

6% of total installed capacity (2015 est.)

ELECTRICITY - FROM HYDROELECTRIC PLANTS:

18% of total installed capacity (2015 est.)

ELECTRICITY - FROM OTHER RENEWABLE SOURCES:

14% of total installed capacity (2015 est.)

CRUDE OIL - PRODUCTION:

80.77 million bbl/day (2016 est.)

CRUDE OIL - EXPORTS:

43.57 million bbl/day (2014 est.)

CRUDE OIL - IMPORTS:

44.58 million bbl/day (2014 est.)

CRUDE OIL - PROVED RESERVES:

1.665 trillion bbl (1 January 2017 est.)

REFINED PETROLEUM PRODUCTS - PRODUCTION:

88.4 million bbl/day (2014 est.)

REFINED PETROLEUM PRODUCTS - CONSUMPTION:

96.26 million bbl/day (2015 est.)

REFINED PETROLEUM PRODUCTS - EXPORTS:

29.66 million bbl/day (2014 est.)

REFINED PETROLEUM PRODUCTS - IMPORTS:

28.62 million bbl/day (2014 est.)

NATURAL GAS - PRODUCTION:

3.481 trillion cu m (2015 est.)

NATURAL GAS - CONSUMPTION:

3.477 trillion cu m (2015 est.)

NATURAL GAS - EXPORTS:

1.156 trillion cu m (2013 est.)

NATURAL GAS - IMPORTS:

1.496 trillion cu m (2013 est.)

NATURAL GAS - PROVED RESERVES:

196.1 trillion cu m (1 January 2016 est.)

CARBON DIOXIDE EMISSIONS FROM CONSUMPTION OF ENERGY:

33.62 billion Mt (2013 est.)

COMMUNICATIONS :: WORLD

TELEPHONES - FIXED LINES:

total subscriptions: 984,289,950 (2017 est.)

subscriptions per 100 inhabitants: 1 (2017 est.)

TELEPHONES - MOBILE CELLULAR:

total subscriptions: 7,806,142,681 (2017 est.)

subscriptions per 100 inhabitants: 11 (2017 est.)

INTERNET USERS:

3.174 billion (July 2016 est.)

top ten countries by Internet usage (in millions): 730.7 China; 374.3 India; 246.8 United States; 122.8 Brazil; 116.6 Japan; 108.8 Russia; 73.3 Mexico; 72.3 Germany; 65.5 Indonesia; 61 United Kingdom

BROADBAND - FIXED SUBSCRIPTIONS:

total: 1,002,793,951

subscriptions per 100 inhabitants: 1

COMMUNICATIONS - NOTE:

three major data centers - which provide colocation, telecommunications, cloud services, and content ecosystems - compete to be called the world's biggest in terms of physical space occupied:

no. 1. - a data farm in Langfang, Hebei Province, China, identified as the Range International Information Group, claims to be the largest with 585,000 sq m (6.3 million sq ft),

no. 2. - a data farm in Las Vegas, Nevada, USA, known as the Switch SuperNAP data center, comes in second with over 325,000 sq m (3.5 million sq ft); it intends to expand to over 1.615 million sq m (17.4 million sq ft) by 2020,

no. 3. - a data farm in Ashburn, Virginia, USA, referred to as the DFT Data Center, is a transit point for 70% of the world's Internet traffic; it includes 150,000 sq m (1.6 million sq ft) spread out over six separate buildings

TRANSPORTATION :: WORLD

AIRPORTS:

41,820 (2016)

top ten by passengers: Atlanta (ATL) - 104,171,935; Beijing (PEK) - 94,393,454; Dubai (DXB) - 83,654,250; Los Angeles (LAX) - 80,921,527; Tokyo (HND) - 79,699,762; Chicago (ORD) - 77,960,588; London (LHR) - 75,715,474; Hong Kong (HKG) 70,305,857; Shanghai (PVG) 66, 002,414; Paris (CDG) - 65,933,145 (2016)

top ten by cargo (metric tons): Hong Kong (HKG) - 4,615,241; Memphis, TN (MEM) - 4,322,071; Shanghai (PVG) - 3,440,280; Incheon (ICN) - 2,714,341; Dubai (DXB) - 2,592,454; Anchorage, AK (ANC) - 2,542,526; Louisville, KY (SDF) - 2,437,010; Tokyo (NRT) - 2,165427; Paris (CDG) - 2,135,172; Frankfurt (FRA) - 2,113,594 (2016)

HELIPORTS:

6,524 (2013)

RAILWAYS:

total: 1,148,186 km (2013)

ROADWAYS:

total: 64,285,009 km (2013)

WATERWAYS:

2,293,412 km (2017)

top ten longest rivers: Nile (Africa) 6,693 km; Amazon (South America) 6,436 km; Mississippi-Missouri (North America) 6,238 km; Yenisey-Angara (Asia) 5,981 km; Ob-Irtysh (Asia) 5,569 km; Yangtze (Asia) 5,525 km; Yellow (Asia) 4,671 km; Amur (Asia) 4,352 km; Lena (Asia) 4,345 km; Congo (Africa) 4,344 km

note: rivers are not necessarily navigable along the entire length; if measured by volume, the Amazon is the largest river in the world, responsible for about 20% of the Earth's freshwater entering the ocean

top ten largest natural lakes (by surface area): Caspian Sea (Azerbaijan, Iran, Kazakhstan, Russia, Turkmenistan) 372,960 sq km; Lake Superior (Canada, United States) 82,414 sq km; Lake Victoria (Kenya, Tanzania, Uganda) 69,490 sq km; Lake Huron (Canada, United States) 59,596 sq km; Lake Michigan (United States) 57,441 sq km; Lake Tanganyika (Burundi, Democratic Republic of the Congo, Tanzania, Zambia) 32,890 sq km; Great Bear Lake (Canada) 31,800 sq km; Lake Baikal (Russia) 31,494 sq km; Lake Nyasa (Malawi, Mozambique, Tanzania) 30,044 sq km; Great Slave Lake (Canada) 28,400 sq km

note: the areas of the lakes are subject to seasonal variation; only the Caspian Sea is saline, the rest are fresh water

note: Lakes Huron and Michigan are technically a single lake because the flow of water between the Straits of Mackinac that connects the two lakes keeps their water levels at near-equilibrium; combined, Lake Huron-Michigan is the largest freshwater lake by surface area in the world

MERCHANT MARINE:

total: 91,557 (2017)

by type: bulk carrier 10872, container ship 5137, general cargo 19160, oil tanker 9995, other 46396 (2017)

PORTS AND TERMINALS:

top twenty container ports as measured by Twenty-Foot Equivalent Units (TEUs) throughput: Shanghai (China) - 37,133,000; Singapore (Singapore) - 30,922,600; Shenzhen (China) - 23,979,300; Ningbo (China) - 21,560,000; Busan (South Korea) - 19,850,000; Hong Kong (China) - 19,813,000; Guangzhou (China) - 18,857,700; Qingdao (China) - 18,010,000; Dubai (UAE) - 14,772,000; - Tianjin (China) - 14,490,000; Port Kelang (Malaysia) - 13,169,577; Rotterdam (Netherlands) - 12,385,168; Kaohsiung (Taiwan) - 10,464,860; Antwerp (Belgium) - 10,037,341; Dalian (China) - 9,614,000; Xiamen (China) - 9,613,679; Hamburg (Germany) - 8,910,000; Los Angeles (US) - 8,856,783; Tanjung Pelepas (Malaysia) - 8,280,661; Laem Chabang (Thailand) - 7,227,431 (2016)

MILITARY AND SECURITY :: WORLD

MILITARY EXPENDITURES:

2.22% of GDP (2016)

2.27% of GDP (2015)

2.26% of GDP (2014)

2.3% of GDP (2013)

2.36% of GDP (2012)

MARITIME THREATS:

the International Maritime Bureau (IMB) reports that 2017 saw a continued slight decrease in global pirate activities; in 2017, pirates attacked a total of 180 ships world-wide including boarding 136 ships, hijacking six ships, and firing on 16; this activity is down from 191 incidents in 2016; in 2017, the number of hostages dropped to 91, however, the number of seafarers kidnapped for ransom increased dramatically to 75 with nearly all taken off West Africa; three mariners were killed world-wide in 2017

Operation Ocean Shield, the NATO naval task force established in 2009 to combat Somali piracy, concluded its operations in December 2016 as a result of the drop in reported incidents over the last few years; the EU naval mission, Operation ATALANTA, continues its operations in the Gulf of Aden and Indian Ocean through 2020; naval units from Japan, India, and China also operate in conjuction with EU forces; China has established a logistical base in Djibouti to support its deployed naval units in the Horn of Africa

the Horn of Africa continued to see pirate activities with 12 incidents in 2017, a slight increase over 2016; the decrease in successful pirate attacks off the Horn of Africa since the peak in 2007 was due, in part, to anti-piracy operations by international naval forces, the hardening of vessels, and the increased use of armed security teams aboard merchant ships; despite these preventative measures, the assessed risk remains high

West African piracy is a continuing threat with 33 attacks in 2017 compared to 36 in 2016; Nigerian pirates are very aggressive, operating as far as 200 nm offshore and boarding 20 ships in 2017; attacks in South Asian waters remain at low levels with an increase in Bangladesh from three incidents in 2016 to 11 in 2017; Peru reported two incidents in 2017, down from 11 in 2016; attacks in Vietnam declined from nine in 2016 to two in 2017; the majority of global attacks against shipping have occured in the offshore waters of five countries - Nigeria, Indonesia, Philippines, Venezuela, and Bangladesh

TRANSNATIONAL ISSUES :: WORLD

DISPUTES - INTERNATIONAL:

stretching over 250,000 km, the world's 325 international land boundaries separate 195 independent states and 71 dependencies, areas of special sovereignty, and other miscellaneous entitiesethnicity, culture, race, religion, and language have divided states into separate political entities as much as history, physical terrain, political fiat, or conquest, resulting in sometimes arbitrary and imposed boundariesmost maritime states have claimed limits that include territorial seas and exclusive economic zones; overlapping limits due to adjacent or opposite coasts create the potential for 430 bilateral maritime boundaries of which 209 have agreements that include contiguous and non-contiguous segmentsboundary, borderland/resource, and territorial disputes vary in intensity from managed or dormant to violent or militarizedundemarcated, indefinite, porous, and unmanaged boundaries tend to encourage illegal cross-border activities, uncontrolled migration, and confrontationterritorial disputes may evolve from historical and/or cultural claims, or they may be brought on by resource competitionethnic and cultural clashes continue to be responsible for much of the territorial fragmentation and internal displacement of the estimated 20.8 million people and cross-border displacements of approximately 12.1 million refugees and asylum seekers around the world as of mid-2013over half a million refugees were repatriated during 2012other sources of contention include access to water and mineral (especially hydrocarbon) resources, fisheries, and arable landarmed conflict prevails not so much between the uniformed armed forces of independent states as between stateless armed entities that detract from the sustenance and welfare of local populations, leaving the community of nations to cope with resultant refugees, hunger, disease, impoverishment, and environmental degradation

REFUGEES AND INTERNALLY DISPLACED PERSONS:

the UN High Commissioner for Refugees (UNHCR) estimated that as of the end of 2017 there were 68.5 million people forcibly displaced worldwide, the highest level ever recorded; this includes 25.4 million refugees, 3.1 million asylum seekers, and 40 million conflict IDPs; the UNHCR estimates there are currently at least 10 million stateless persons

TRAFFICKING IN PERSONS:

current situation: the International Labour Organization conservatively estimated that 20.9 million people in 2012 were victims of forced labor, representing the full range of human trafficking (also referred to as 'modern-day slavery') for labor and sexual exploitation; about one-third of reported cases involved crossing international borders, which is often associated with sexual exploitation; trafficking in persons is most prevalent in southeastern Europe, Eurasia, and Africa and least frequent in EU member states, Canada, the US, and other developed countries (2012)

tier rating: (2015)

Tier 2 Watch List: countries that do not fully comply with the minimum standards for the elimination of trafficking but are making significant efforts to do so; (44 countries) Antigua and Barbuda, Bolivia, Botswana, Bulgaria, Burkina Faso, Burma, Cambodia, China, Democratic Republic of the Congo, Republic of the Congo, Costa Rica, Cuba, Djibouti, Egypt, Gabon, Ghana, Guinea, Guyana, Haiti, Jamaica, Laos, Lebanon, Lesotho, Malaysia, Maldives, Mali, Mauritius, Namibia, Pakistan, Papua New Guinea, Qatar, Saudi Arabia, Saint Vincent and the Grenadines, Solomon Islands, Sri Lanka, Sudan, Suriname, Tanzania, Timor-Leste, Trinidad and Tobago, Tunisia, Turkmenistan, Ukraine, Uzbekistan

Tier 3: countries that neither satisfy the minimum standards for the elimination of trafficking nor demonstrate a significant effort to do so; (23 countries) Algeria, Belarus, Belize, Burundi, Central African Republic, Comoros, Equatorial Guinea, Eritrea, The Gambia, Guinea-Bissau, Iran, North Korea, Kuwait, Libya, Marshall Islands, Mauritania, Russia, South Sudan, Syria, Thailand, Venezuela, Yemen, Zimbabwe

ILLICIT DRUGS:

cocaine: worldwide coca leaf cultivation in 2013 likely amounted to 165,000 hectares, assuming a stable crop in Bolivia; Colombia produced slightly less than half of the worldwide crop, followed by Peru and Bolivia; potential pure cocaine production increased 7% to 640 metric tons in 2013; Colombia conducts an aggressive coca eradication campaign, Peru has increased its eradication efforts, but remains hesitant to eradicate coca in key growing areas;

opiates: worldwide illicit opium poppy cultivation increased in 2013, with potential opium production reaching 6,800 metric tons; Afghanistan is world's primary opium producer, accounting for 82% of the global supply; Southeast Asia was responsible for 12% of global opium; Pakistan produced 3% of global opium; Latin America produced 4% of global opium, and most was refined into heroin destined for the US market

(2015)

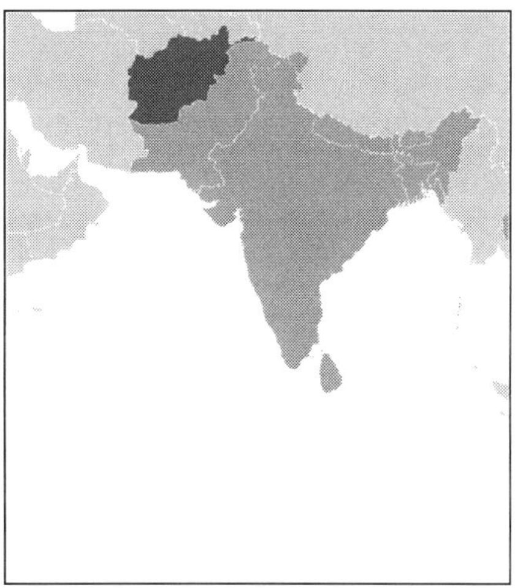

SOUTH ASIA :: AFGHANISTAN

INTRODUCTION :: AFGHANISTAN

BACKGROUND:

Ahmad Shah DURRANI unified the Pashtun tribes and founded Afghanistan in 1747. The country served as a buffer between the British and Russian Empires until it won independence from notional British control in 1919. A brief experiment in democracy ended in a 1973 coup and a 1978 communist countercoup. The Soviet Union invaded in 1979 to support the tottering Afghan communist regime, touching off a long and destructive war. The USSR withdrew in 1989 under relentless pressure by internationally supported anti-communist mujahidin rebels. A series of subsequent civil wars saw Kabul finally fall in 1996 to the Taliban, a hardline Pakistani-sponsored movement that emerged in 1994 to end the country's civil war and anarchy. Following the 11 September 2001 terrorist attacks, a US, Allied, and anti-Taliban Northern Alliance military action toppled the Taliban for sheltering Usama BIN LADIN.

A UN-sponsored Bonn Conference in 2001 established a process for political reconstruction that included the adoption of a new constitution, a presidential election in 2004, and National Assembly elections in 2005. In December 2004, Hamid KARZAI became the first democratically elected president of Afghanistan, and the National Assembly was inaugurated the following December. KARZAI was reelected in August 2009 for a second term. The 2014 presidential election was the country's first to include a runoff, which featured the top two vote-getters from the first round, Abdullah ABDULLAH and Ashraf GHANI. Throughout the summer of 2014, their campaigns disputed the results and traded accusations of fraud, leading to a US-led diplomatic intervention that included a full vote audit as well as political negotiations between the two camps. In September 2014, GHANI and ABDULLAH agreed to form the Government of National Unity, with GHANI inaugurated as president and ABDULLAH elevated to the newly-created position of chief executive officer. The day after the inauguration, the GHANI administration signed the US-Afghan Bilateral Security Agreement and NATO Status of Forces Agreement, which provide the legal basis for the post-2014 international military presence in Afghanistan.

Despite gains toward building a stable central government, the Taliban remains a serious challenge for the Afghan Government in almost every province. The Taliban still considers itself the rightful government of Afghanistan, and it remains a capable and confident insurgent force despite its last two spiritual leaders being killed; it continues to declare that it will pursue a peace deal with Kabul only after foreign military forces depart.

GEOGRAPHY :: AFGHANISTAN

LOCATION:

Southern Asia, north and west of Pakistan, east of Iran

GEOGRAPHIC COORDINATES:

33 00 N, 65 00 E

MAP REFERENCES:

Asia

AREA:

total: 652,230 sq km

land: 652,230 sq km

water: 0 sq km

country comparison to the world: 42

AREA - COMPARATIVE:

almost six times the size of Virginia; slightly smaller than Texas

LAND BOUNDARIES:

total: 5,987 km

border countries (6): China 91 km, Iran 921 km, Pakistan 2670 km, Tajikistan 1357 km, Turkmenistan 804 km, Uzbekistan 144 km

COASTLINE:

0 km (landlocked)

MARITIME CLAIMS:

none (landlocked)

CLIMATE:

arid to semiarid; cold winters and hot summers

TERRAIN:

mostly rugged mountains; plains in north and southwest

ELEVATION:

mean elevation: 1,884 m

elevation extremes: 258 m lowest point: Amu Darya

7492 highest point: Noshak

NATURAL RESOURCES:

natural gas, petroleum, coal, copper, chromite, talc, barites, sulfur, lead, zinc, iron ore, salt, precious and semiprecious stones, arable land

LAND USE:

agricultural land: 58.1% (2014 est.)

arable land: 20.5% (2014 est.) / permanent crops: 0.37% (2014 est.) / permanent pasture: 79% (2014 est.)

forest: 2.07% (2014 est.)

other: 39.9% (2014 est.)

IRRIGATED LAND:

32,080 sq km (2012)

POPULATION DISTRIBUTION:

populations tend to cluster in the foothills and periphery of the rugged Hindu Kush range; smaller groups are found in many of the country's interior valleys; in general, the east is more densely settled, while the south is sparsely populated

NATURAL HAZARDS:

damaging earthquakes occur in Hindu Kush mountains; flooding; droughts

ENVIRONMENT - CURRENT ISSUES:

limited natural freshwater resources; inadequate supplies of potable water; soil degradation; overgrazing; deforestation (much of the remaining forests are being cut down for fuel and building materials); desertification; air and water pollution in overcrowded urban areas

ENVIRONMENT - INTERNATIONAL AGREEMENTS:

party to: Biodiversity, Climate Change, Desertification, Endangered Species, Environmental Modification, Marine Dumping, Ozone Layer Protection

signed, but not ratified: Hazardous Wastes, Law of the Sea, Marine Life Conservation

GEOGRAPHY - NOTE:

landlocked; the Hindu Kush mountains that run northeast to southwest divide the northern provinces from the rest of the country; the highest peaks are in the northern Vakhan (Wakhan Corridor)

PEOPLE AND SOCIETY :: AFGHANISTAN

POPULATION:

34,940,837 (July 2018 est.)

country comparison to the world: 39

NATIONALITY:

noun: Afghan(s)

adjective: Afghan

ETHNIC GROUPS:

Pashtun, Tajik, Hazara, Uzbek, other (includes smaller numbers of Baloch, Turkmen, Nuristani, Pamiri, Arab, Gujar, Brahui, Qizilbash, Aimaq, Pashai, and Kyrghyz) (2015)

note: current statistical data on the sensitive subject of ethnicity in Afghanistan are not available, and ethnicity data from small samples of respondents to opinion polls are not a reliable alternative; Afghanistan's 2004 constitution recognizes 14 ethnic groups: Pashtun, Tajik, Hazara, Uzbek, Baloch, Turkmen, Nuristani, Pamiri, Arab, Gujar, Brahui, Qizilbash, Aimaq, and Pashai

LANGUAGES:

Afghan Persian or Dari (official) 80% (Dari functions as the lingua franca), Pashto (official) 47%, Uzbek 11%, English 5%, Turkmen 2%, Urdu 2%, Pashayi 1%, Nuristani 1%, Arabic 1%, Balochi, Shughni, Pamiri, Hindi, Russian, German, French (2017 est.)

note: data represent most widely spoken languages; shares sum to more than 100% because there is much bilingualism in the country and because respondents were allowed to select more than one language

note: the Turkic languages Uzbek and Turkmen, as well as Balochi, Pashayi, Nuristani, and Pamiri are the third official languages in areas where the majority speaks them

RELIGIONS:

Muslim 99.7% (Sunni 84.7 - 89.7%, Shia 10 - 15%), other 0.3% (2009 est.)

AGE STRUCTURE:

0-14 years: 40.92% (male 7,263,716 /female 7,033,427)

15-24 years: 21.85% (male 3,883,693 /female 3,749,760)

25-54 years: 30.68% (male 5,456,305 /female 5,263,332)

55-64 years: 3.95% (male 679,766 /female 699,308)

65 years and over: 2.61% (male 420,445 /female 491,085) (2018 est.)

DEPENDENCY RATIOS:

total dependency ratio: 88.8 (2015 est.)

youth dependency ratio: 84.1 (2015 est.)

elderly dependency ratio: 4.7 (2015 est.)

potential support ratio: 21.2 (2015 est.)

MEDIAN AGE:

total: 19 years

male: 19 years

female: 19.1 years (2018 est.)

country comparison to the world: 203

POPULATION GROWTH RATE:

2.37% (2018 est.)

country comparison to the world: 29

BIRTH RATE:

37.5 births/1,000 population (2018 est.)

country comparison to the world: 12

DEATH RATE:

13.2 deaths/1,000 population (2018 est.)

country comparison to the world: 9

NET MIGRATION RATE:

-0.9 migrant(s)/1,000 population (2017 est.)

country comparison to the world: 134

POPULATION DISTRIBUTION:

populations tend to cluster in the foothills and periphery of the rugged Hindu Kush range; smaller groups are found in many of the country's interior valleys; in general, the east is more densely settled, while the south is sparsely populated

URBANIZATION:

urban population: 25.5% of total population (2018)

rate of urbanization: 3.37% annual rate of change (2015-20 est.)

MAJOR URBAN AREAS - POPULATION:

4.012 million KABUL (capital) (2018)

SEX RATIO:

at birth: 1.04 male(s)/female (2017 est.)

0-14 years: 1.03 male(s)/female (2017 est.)

15-24 years: 1.04 male(s)/female (2017 est.)

25-54 years: 1.04 male(s)/female (2017 est.)

55-64 years: 0.97 male(s)/female (2017 est.)

65 years and over: 0.86 male(s)/female (2017 est.)

total population: 1.03 male(s)/female (2017 est.)

MOTHER'S MEAN AGE AT FIRST BIRTH:

19.9 years (2015 est.)

note: median age at first birth among women 25-29

MATERNAL MORTALITY RATE:

396 deaths/100,000 live births (2015 est.)

country comparison to the world: 28

INFANT MORTALITY RATE:

total: 108.5 deaths/1,000 live births (2018 est.)

male: 115.7 deaths/1,000 live births (2018 est.)

female: 100.9 deaths/1,000 live births (2018 est.)

country comparison to the world: 1

LIFE EXPECTANCY AT BIRTH:

total population: 52.1 years (2018 est.)

male: 50.6 years (2018 est.)

female: 53.6 years (2018 est.)

country comparison to the world: 223

TOTAL FERTILITY RATE:

5.02 children born/woman (2018 est.)

country comparison to the world: 11

CONTRACEPTIVE PREVALENCE RATE:

22.5% (2015/16)

HEALTH EXPENDITURES:

8.2% of GDP (2014)

country comparison to the world: 52

PHYSICIANS DENSITY:

0.3 physicians/1,000 population (2016)

HOSPITAL BED DENSITY:

0.5 beds/1,000 population (2014)

DRINKING WATER SOURCE:

improved:

urban: 78.2% of population

rural: 47% of population

total: 55.3% of population

unimproved:

urban: 21.8% of population

rural: 53% of population

total: 44.7% of population (2015 est.)

SANITATION FACILITY ACCESS:

improved:

urban: 45.1% of population (2015 est.)

rural: 27% of population (2015 est.)

total: 31.9% of population (2015 est.)

unimproved:

urban: 54.9% of population (2015 est.)

rural: 73% of population (2015 est.)

total: 68.1% of population (2015 est.)

HIV/AIDS - ADULT PREVALENCE RATE:

<.1% (2016 est.)

HIV/AIDS - PEOPLE LIVING WITH HIV/AIDS:

7,500 (2016 est.)

country comparison to the world: 109

HIV/AIDS - DEATHS:

<500 (2016 est.)

MAJOR INFECTIOUS DISEASES:

degree of risk: intermediate (2016)

food or waterborne diseases: bacterial diarrhea, hepatitis A, and typhoid fever (2016)

vectorborne diseases: malaria (2016)

OBESITY - ADULT PREVALENCE RATE:

5.5% (2016)

country comparison to the world: 176

CHILDREN UNDER THE AGE OF 5 YEARS UNDERWEIGHT:

25% (2013)

country comparison to the world: 16

EDUCATION EXPENDITURES:

3.2% of GDP (2015)

country comparison to the world: 138

LITERACY:

definition: age 15 and over can read and write (2015 est.)

total population: 38.2% (2015 est.)

male: 52% (2015 est.)

female: 24.2% (2015 est.)

SCHOOL LIFE EXPECTANCY (PRIMARY TO TERTIARY EDUCATION):

total: 11 years (2014)

male: 13 years (2014)

female: 8 years (2014)

GOVERNMENT :: AFGHANISTAN

COUNTRY NAME:

conventional long form: Islamic Republic of Afghanistan

conventional short form: Afghanistan

local long form: Jamhuri-ye Islami-ye Afghanistan

local short form: Afghanistan

former: Republic of Afghanistan

etymology: the name "Afghan" originally referred to the Pashtun people (today it is understood to include all the country's ethnic groups), while the suffix "-stan" means "place of" or "country"; so Afghanistan literally means the "Land of the Afghans"

GOVERNMENT TYPE:

presidential Islamic republic

CAPITAL:

name: Kabul

geographic coordinates: 34 31 N, 69 11 E

time difference: UTC+4.5 (9.5 hours ahead of Washington, DC, during Standard Time)

etymology: named for the Kabul River, but the river's name is of unknown origin

ADMINISTRATIVE DIVISIONS:

34 provinces (welayat, singular - welayat); Badakhshan, Badghis, Baghlan, Balkh, Bamyan, Daykundi, Farah, Faryab, Ghazni, Ghor, Helmand, Herat, Jowzjan, Kabul, Kandahar, Kapisa, Khost, Kunar, Kunduz, Laghman, Logar, Nangarhar, Nimroz, Nuristan, Paktika, Paktiya, Panjshir, Parwan, Samangan, Sar-e Pul, Takhar, Uruzgan, Wardak, Zabul

INDEPENDENCE:

19 August 1919 (from UK control over Afghan foreign affairs)

NATIONAL HOLIDAY:

Independence Day, 19 August (1919)

CONSTITUTION:

history: several previous; latest drafted 14 December 2003 - 4 January 2004, signed 16 January 2004, ratified 26 January 2004 (2017)

amendments: proposed by a commission formed by presidential decree followed by the convention of a Grand Council (Loya Jirga) decreed by the president; passage requires at least two-thirds majority vote of the Loya Jirga membership and endorsement by the president (2017)

LEGAL SYSTEM:

mixed legal system of civil, customary, and Islamic law

INTERNATIONAL LAW ORGANIZATION PARTICIPATION:

has not submitted an ICJ jurisdiction declaration; accepts ICCt jurisdiction

CITIZENSHIP:

citizenship by birth: no

citizenship by descent only: at least one parent must have been born in - and continuously lived in - Afghanistan

dual citizenship recognized: no

residency requirement for naturalization: 5 years

SUFFRAGE:

18 years of age; universal

EXECUTIVE BRANCH:

chief of state: President of the Islamic Republic of Afghanistan Ashraf GHANI Ahmadzai (since 29 September 2014); CEO Abdullah ABDULLAH, Dr. (since 29 September 2014); First Vice President Abdul Rashid DOSTAM (since 29 September 2014); Second Vice President Sarwar DANESH (since 29 September 2014); First Deputy CEO Khyal Mohammad KHAN; Second Deputy CEO Mohammad MOHAQQEQ; note - the president is both chief of state and head of government

head of government: President of the Islamic Republic of Afghanistan Ashraf GHANI Ahmadzai (since 29 September 2014); CEO Abdullah ABDULLAH, Dr. (since 29 September 2014); First Vice President Abdul Rashid DOSTAM (since 29 September 2014); Second Vice President Sarwar DANESH (since 29 September 2014); First Deputy CEO Khyal Mohammad KHAN; Second Deputy CEO Mohammad MOHAQQEQ

cabinet: Cabinet consists of 25 ministers appointed by the president, approved by the National Assembly

elections/appointments: president directly elected by absolute majority popular vote in 2 rounds if needed for a 5-year term (eligible for a second term); election last held in 2 rounds on 5 April and 14 June 2014 (next to be held in 2018)

election results: Ashraf GHANI elected president in the second round; percent of vote in first round - Abdullah ABDULLAH (National Coalition of Afghanistan) 45%, Ashraf GHANI (independent) 31.6%, Zalmai RASSOUL 11.4%, other 12%; percent of vote in second round - Ashraf GHANI 56.4%, Abdullah ABDULLAH 43.6%

LEGISLATIVE BRANCH:

description: bicameral National Assembly consists of:
Meshrano Jirga or House of Elders (102 seats; 34 members indirectly elected by district councils to serve 3-year terms, 34 indirectly elected by provincial councils to serve 4-year terms, and 34 nominated by the president of which 17 must be women, 2 must represent the disabled, and 2 must be Kuchi nomads; members nominated by the president serve 5-year terms)
Wolesi Jirga or House of People (249 seats; members directly elected in multi-seat constituencies by proportional representation vote to serve 5-year terms)

elections:
Meshrano Jirga - last held 10 January 2015 (next to be held in 2018)
Wolesi Jirga - last held on 20 October 2018) (next tobe held in 2023)

election results:
Meshrano Jirga - percent of vote by party - NA; seats by party - NA; composition - men 84, women 18, percent of women 17.6%
Wolesi Jirga - percent of vote by party NA; seats by party - NA; composition - men 148, women 69, percent of women 27.7%; note - total National Assembly percent of women 24.8%

note: the constitution allows the government to convene a constitutional Loya Jirga (Grand Council) on issues of independence, national sovereignty, and territorial integrity; it consists of members of the National Assembly and chairpersons of the provincial and district councils; a Loya Jirga can amend provisions of the constitution and prosecute the president; no constitutional Loya Jirga has ever been held, and district councils have never been elected; the president appointed 34 members of the Meshrano Jirga that the district councils should have indirectly elected

JUDICIAL BRANCH:

highest courts: Supreme Court or Stera Mahkama (consists of the supreme court chief and 8 justices organized into criminal, public security, civil, and commercial divisions or dewans)

judge selection and term of office: court chief and justices appointed by the president with the approval of the Wolesi Jirga; court chief and justices serve single 10-year terms

subordinate courts: Appeals Courts; Primary Courts; Special Courts for issues including narcotics, security, property, family, and juveniles

POLITICAL PARTIES AND LEADERS:

note - the Ministry of Justice licensed 57 political parties as of September 2016

INTERNATIONAL ORGANIZATION PARTICIPATION:

ADB, CICA, CP, ECO, EITI (candidate country), FAO, G-77, IAEA, IBRD, ICAO, ICC (NGOs), ICCt, ICRM, IDA, IDB, IFAD, IFC, IFRCS, ILO, IMF, Interpol, IOC, IOM, IPU, ISO (correspondent), ITSO, ITU, ITUC (NGOs), MIGA, NAM, OIC, OPCW, OSCE (partner), SAARC, SACEP, SCO (dialogue member), UN, UNAMA, UNCTAD, UNESCO, UNHCR, UNIDO, UNWTO, UPU, WCO, WFTU (NGOs), WHO, WIPO, WMO, WTO

DIPLOMATIC REPRESENTATION IN THE US:

chief of mission: Ambassador Hamdullah MOHIB (since 17 September 2015)

chancery: 2341 Wyoming Avenue NW, Washington, DC 20008

telephone: [1] (202) 483-6410

FAX: [1] (202) 483-6488

consulate(s) general: Los Angeles, New York, Washington, DC

DIPLOMATIC REPRESENTATION FROM THE US:

chief of mission: Ambassador John BASS (since December 2017)

embassy: Bibi Mahru, Kabul

mailing address: U.S. Embassy Kabul, APO, AE 09806

telephone: [00 93] 0700 108 001

FAX: [00 93] 0700 108 564

FLAG DESCRIPTION:

three equal vertical bands of black (hoist side), red, and green, with the national emblem in white centered on the red band and slightly overlapping the other 2 bands; the center of the emblem features a mosque with pulpit and flags on either side, below the mosque are numerals for the solar year 1298 (1919 in the Gregorian calendar, the year of Afghan independence from the UK); this central image is circled by a border consisting of sheaves of wheat on the left and right, in the upper-center is an Arabic inscription of the Shahada (Muslim creed) below which are rays of the rising sun over the Takbir (Arabic expression meaning "God is great"), and at bottom center is a scroll bearing the name Afghanistan; black signifies the past, red is for the blood shed for independence, and green can represent either hope for the future, agricultural prosperity, or Islam

note: Afghanistan had more changes to its national flag in the 20th century - 19 by one count - than any other country; the colors black, red, and green appeared on most of them

NATIONAL SYMBOL(S):

lion; national colors: red, green, black

NATIONAL ANTHEM:

name: "Milli Surood" (National Anthem)

lyrics/music: Abdul Bari JAHANI/Babrak WASA

note: adopted 2006; the 2004 constitution of the post-Taliban government mandated that a new national anthem should be written containing the phrase "Allahu Akbar" (God is Greatest) and mentioning the names of Afghanistan's ethnic groups

ECONOMY :: AFGHANISTAN

ECONOMY - OVERVIEW:

Despite improvements in life expectancy, incomes, and literacy since 2001, Afghanistan is extremely poor, landlocked, and highly dependent on foreign aid. Much of the population continues to suffer from shortages of housing, clean water, electricity, medical care, and jobs. Corruption, insecurity, weak governance, lack of infrastructure, and the Afghan Government's difficulty in extending rule of law to all parts of the country pose challenges to future economic growth. Afghanistan's living standards are among the lowest in the world. Since 2014, the economy has slowed, in large part because of the withdrawal of nearly 100,000 foreign troops that had artificially inflated the country's economic growth.

The international community remains committed to Afghanistan's development, pledging over $83 billion at ten donors' conferences between 2003 and 2016. In October 2016, the donors at the Brussels conference pledged an additional $3.8 billion in development aid annually from 2017 to 2020. Even with this help, Government of Afghanistan still faces number of challenges, including low revenue collection, anemic job creation, high levels of corruption, weak government capacity, and poor public infrastructure.

In 2017 Afghanistan's growth rate was only marginally above that of the 2014-2016 average. The drawdown of international security forces that started in 2012 has negatively affected economic growth, as a substantial portion of commerce, especially in the services sector, has catered to the ongoing international troop presence in the country. Afghan President Ashraf GHANI Ahmadzai is dedicated to instituting economic reforms to include improving revenue collection and fighting corruption. The government has implemented reforms to the budget process and in some other areas. However, many other reforms will take time to implement and Afghanistan will remain dependent on international donor support over the next several years.

GDP (PURCHASING POWER PARITY):

$69.45 billion (2017 est.)

$67.65 billion (2016 est.)

$66.21 billion (2015 est.)

note: data are in 2017 dollars

country comparison to the world: 101

GDP (OFFICIAL EXCHANGE RATE):

$20.24 billion (2017 est.) (2017 est.)

GDP - REAL GROWTH RATE:

2.7% (2017 est.)

2.2% (2016 est.)

1% (2015 est.)

country comparison to the world: 124

GDP - PER CAPITA (PPP):

$2,000 (2017 est.)

$2,000 (2016 est.)

$2,000 (2015 est.)

note: data are in 2017 dollars

country comparison to the world: 209

GROSS NATIONAL SAVING:

22.7% of GDP (2017 est.)

25.8% of GDP (2016 est.)

21.4% of GDP (2015 est.)

country comparison to the world: 78

GDP - COMPOSITION, BY END USE:

household consumption: 81.6% (2016 est.)

government consumption: 12% (2016 est.)

investment in fixed capital: 17.2% (2016 est.)

investment in inventories: 30% (2016 est.)

exports of goods and services: 6.7% (2016 est.)

imports of goods and services: -47.6% (2016 est.)

GDP - COMPOSITION, BY SECTOR OF ORIGIN:

agriculture: 23% (2016 est.)

industry: 21.1% (2016 est.)

services: 55.9% (2016 est.)

note: data exclude opium production

AGRICULTURE - PRODUCTS:

opium, wheat, fruits, nuts, wool, mutton, sheepskins, lambskins, poppies

INDUSTRIES:

small-scale production of bricks, textiles, soap, furniture, shoes, fertilizer, apparel, food products, non-alcoholic beverages, mineral water, cement; handwoven carpets; natural gas, coal, copper

INDUSTRIAL PRODUCTION GROWTH RATE:

-1.9% (2016 est.)

country comparison to the world: 181

LABOR FORCE:

8.478 million (2017 est.)

country comparison to the world: 61

LABOR FORCE - BY OCCUPATION:

agriculture: 44.3%

industry: 18.1%

services: 37.6% (2017 est.)

UNEMPLOYMENT RATE:

23.9% (2017 est.)

22.6% (2016 est.)

country comparison to the world: 194

POPULATION BELOW POVERTY LINE:

54.5% (2017 est.)

HOUSEHOLD INCOME OR CONSUMPTION BY PERCENTAGE SHARE:

lowest 10%: 3.8% (2008)

highest 10%: 24% (2008)

DISTRIBUTION OF FAMILY INCOME - GINI INDEX:

29.4 (2008)

country comparison to the world: 136

BUDGET:

revenues: 2.276 billion (2017 est.)

expenditures: 5.328 billion (2017 est.)

TAXES AND OTHER REVENUES:

11.2% (of GDP) (2017 est.)

country comparison to the world: 210

BUDGET SURPLUS (+) OR DEFICIT (-):

-15.1% (of GDP) (2017 est.)

country comparison to the world: 217

PUBLIC DEBT:

7% of GDP (2017 est.)

7.8% of GDP (2016 est.)

country comparison to the world: 202

FISCAL YEAR:

21 December - 20 December

INFLATION RATE (CONSUMER PRICES):

5% (2017 est.)

4.4% (2016 est.)

country comparison to the world: 171

COMMERCIAL BANK PRIME LENDING RATE:

15% (31 December 2016 est.)

15% (31 December 2015 est.)

country comparison to the world: 37

STOCK OF NARROW MONEY:

$6.644 billion (31 December 2014 est.)

$6.192 billion (31 December 2013 est.)

country comparison to the world: 94

STOCK OF BROAD MONEY:

$6.945 billion (31 December 2014 est.)

$6.544 billion (31 December 2013 est.)

country comparison to the world: 95

STOCK OF DOMESTIC CREDIT:

-$240.6 million (31 December 2016 est.)

country comparison to the world: 192

MARKET VALUE OF PUBLICLY TRADED SHARES:

NA

CURRENT ACCOUNT BALANCE:

$1.014 billion (2017 est.)

$1.409 billion (2016 est.)

country comparison to the world: 48

EXPORTS:

$784 million (2017 est.)

$614.2 million (2016 est.)

note: not including illicit exports or reexports

country comparison to the world: 171

EXPORTS - PARTNERS:

India 56.5%, Pakistan 29.6% (2017)

EXPORTS - COMMODITIES:

opium, fruits and nuts, handwoven carpets, wool, cotton, hides and pelts, precious and semi-precious gems, and medical herbs

IMPORTS:

$7.616 billion (2017 est.)

$6.16 billion (2016 est.)

country comparison to the world: 114

IMPORTS - COMMODITIES:

machinery and other capital goods, food, textiles, petroleum products

IMPORTS - PARTNERS:

China 21%, Iran 20.5%, Pakistan 11.8%, Kazakhstan 11%, Uzbekistan 6.8%, Malaysia 5.3% (2017)

RESERVES OF FOREIGN EXCHANGE AND GOLD:

$7.187 billion (31 December 2017 est.)

$6.901 billion (31 December 2015 est.)

country comparison to the world: 85

DEBT - EXTERNAL:

$2.84 billion (FY/)

country comparison to the world: 144

EXCHANGE RATES:

afghanis (AFA) per US dollar -

7.87 (2017 est.)

68.03 (2016 est.)

67.87 (2015)

61.14 (2014 est.)

57.25 (2013 est.)

ENERGY :: AFGHANISTAN

ELECTRICITY ACCESS:

population without electricity: 18,999,254 (2012)

electrification - total population: 43% (2012)

electrification - urban areas: 83% (2012)

electrification - rural areas: 32% (2012)

ELECTRICITY - PRODUCTION:

1.211 billion kWh (2016 est.)

country comparison to the world: 146

ELECTRICITY - CONSUMPTION:

5.526 billion kWh (2016 est.)

country comparison to the world: 119

ELECTRICITY - EXPORTS:

0 kWh (2016 est.)

country comparison to the world: 96

ELECTRICITY - IMPORTS:

4.4 billion kWh (2016 est.)

country comparison to the world: 42

ELECTRICITY - INSTALLED GENERATING CAPACITY:

634,100 kW (2016 est.)

country comparison to the world: 138

ELECTRICITY - FROM FOSSIL FUELS:

45% of total installed capacity (2016 est.)

country comparison to the world: 159

ELECTRICITY - FROM NUCLEAR FUELS:

0% of total installed capacity (2017 est.)

country comparison to the world: 32

ELECTRICITY - FROM HYDROELECTRIC PLANTS:

52% of total installed capacity (2017 est.)

country comparison to the world: 34

ELECTRICITY - FROM OTHER RENEWABLE SOURCES:

4% of total installed capacity (2017 est.)

country comparison to the world: 111

CRUDE OIL - PRODUCTION:

0 bbl/day (2017 est.)

country comparison to the world: 101

CRUDE OIL - EXPORTS:

0 bbl/day (2015 est.)

country comparison to the world: 82

CRUDE OIL - IMPORTS:

0 bbl/day (2015 est.)

country comparison to the world: 84

CRUDE OIL - PROVED RESERVES:

0 bbl (1 January 2018 est.)

country comparison to the world: 99

REFINED PETROLEUM PRODUCTS - PRODUCTION:

0 bbl/day (2015 est.)

country comparison to the world: 110

REFINED PETROLEUM PRODUCTS - CONSUMPTION:

35,000 bbl/day (2016 est.)

country comparison to the world: 117

REFINED PETROLEUM PRODUCTS - EXPORTS:

0 bbl/day (2015 est.)

country comparison to the world: 124

REFINED PETROLEUM PRODUCTS - IMPORTS:

34,210 bbl/day (2015 est.)

country comparison to the world: 97

NATURAL GAS - PRODUCTION:

164.2 million cu m (2017 est.)

country comparison to the world: 79

NATURAL GAS - CONSUMPTION:

164.2 million cu m (2017 est.)

country comparison to the world: 108

NATURAL GAS - EXPORTS:

0 cu m (2017 est.)

country comparison to the world: 57

NATURAL GAS - IMPORTS:

0 cu m (2017 est.)

country comparison to the world: 81

NATURAL GAS - PROVED RESERVES:

49.55 billion cu m (1 January 2018 est.)

country comparison to the world: 62

CARBON DIOXIDE EMISSIONS FROM CONSUMPTION OF ENERGY:

9.067 million Mt (2017 est.)

country comparison to the world: 111

COMMUNICATIONS :: AFGHANISTAN

TELEPHONES - FIXED LINES:

total subscriptions: 118,769 (2017 est.)

subscriptions per 100 inhabitants: less than 1 (2017 est.)

country comparison to the world: 138

TELEPHONES - MOBILE CELLULAR:

total subscriptions: 23,929,713 (2017 est.)

subscriptions per 100 inhabitants: 70 (2017 est.)

country comparison to the world: 52

TELEPHONE SYSTEM:

general assessment: progress has been made on Afghanistan's first limited fixed-line telephone service and nationwide optical fibre backbone; aided by the presence of multiple providers, mobile-cellular telephone service continues to improve swiftly; the Afghan Ministry of Communications and Information claims that more than 90% of the population live in areas with access to mobile-cellular services (2017)

domestic: less than 1 per 100 for fixed-line teledensity; 70 per 100 for mobile-cellular; an increasing number of Afghans utilize mobile-cellular phone networks (2017)

international: country code - 93; multiple VSAT's provide international and domestic voice and data connectivity (2016)

BROADCAST MEDIA:

state-owned broadcaster, Radio Television Afghanistan (RTA), operates a series of radio and television stations in Kabul and the provinces; an estimated 150 private radio stations, 50 TV stations, and about a dozen international broadcasters are available (2018)

INTERNET COUNTRY CODE:

.af

INTERNET USERS:

total: 3,531,770 (July 2016 est.)

percent of population: 10.6% (July 2016 est.)

country comparison to the world: 92

BROADBAND - FIXED SUBSCRIPTIONS:

total: 16,810 (2017 est.)

subscriptions per 100 inhabitants: less than 1 (2017 est.)

country comparison to the world: 156

TRANSPORTATION :: AFGHANISTAN

NATIONAL AIR TRANSPORT SYSTEM:

number of registered air carriers: 4 (2015)

inventory of registered aircraft operated by air carriers: 20 (2015)

annual passenger traffic on registered air carriers: 1,929,907 (2015)

annual freight traffic on registered air carriers: 33,102,038 mt-km (2015)

CIVIL AIRCRAFT REGISTRATION COUNTRY CODE PREFIX:

YA (2016)

AIRPORTS:

43 (2016)

country comparison to the world: 99

AIRPORTS - WITH PAVED RUNWAYS:

total: 25 (2017)

over 3,047 m: 4 (2017)

2,438 to 3,047 m: 4 (2017)

1,524 to 2,437 m: 14 (2017)

914 to 1,523 m: 2 (2017)

under 914 m: 1 (2017)

AIRPORTS - WITH UNPAVED RUNWAYS:

total: 18 (2016)

2,438 to 3,047 m: 1 (2016)

1,524 to 2,437 m: 8 (2016)

914 to 1,523 m: 4 (2016)

under 914 m: 5 (2016)

HELIPORTS:

9 (2013)

PIPELINES:

466 km gas (2013)

ROADWAYS:

total: 42,150 km (2006)

paved: 12,350 km (2006)

unpaved: 29,800 km (2006)

country comparison to the world: 86

WATERWAYS:

1,200 km (chiefly Amu Darya, which handles vessels up to 500 DWT) (2011)

country comparison to the world: 58

PORTS AND TERMINALS:

river port(s): Kheyrabad, Shir Khan

MILITARY AND SECURITY :: AFGHANISTAN

MILITARY EXPENDITURES:

0.89% of GDP (2016)

0.99% of GDP (2015)

1.33% of GDP (2014)

country comparison to the world: 126

MILITARY BRANCHES:

Afghan National Defense and Security Forces (ANDSF) comprised of military, police, and other security elements: Afghan National Army (includes Afghan Air Force), Afghan National Police, Afghan Local Police, and the National Directorate of Security (2017)

MILITARY SERVICE AGE AND OBLIGATION:

18 is the legal minimum age for voluntary military service; no conscription (2017)

TERRORISM :: AFGHANISTAN

TERRORIST GROUPS - HOME BASED:

al-Qa'ida (AQ):
aim(s): eject Western influence from the Islamic world, unite the worldwide Muslim community, overthrow governments perceived as un-Islamic, and ultimately, establish a pan-Islamic caliphate under a strict Salafi Muslim interpretation of sharia
area(s) of operation: maintains established networks and a longtime operational presence in Afghanistan, especially in the south, northwest, and

northeast near the Afghanistan-Pakistan border (April 2018)

Islamic Jihad Union (IJU):
aim(s): drive NATO forces out of Afghanistan and destabilize the country; overthrow the Government of Uzbekistan
area(s) of operation: conducts attacks in collaboration with other extremist groups, including the Taliban, against NATO and Afghan forces across the country, especially in the northern and eastern Paktika, Paktia, and Nangarhar provinces (April 2018)

Islamic Movement of Uzbekistan (IMU):
aim(s): enhance its networks and secure territory in Afghanistan to establish a secure presence from which it can pursue its historic goal of establishing an Islamic state in the Fergana Valley, a fertile valley spread across eastern Uzbekistan, southern Kyrgyzstan, and northern Tajikistan
area(s) of operation: operates mostly in the north along the Afghanistan-Pakistan border, with its heaviest presence in Badakhshan Province, where IMU has operated paramilitary training camps and bases
note: the IMU is fractured and mostly supports ISIS-K although some members have continued working with the Taliban (April 2018)

Islamic State of Iraq and ash-Sham-Khorasan (ISIS-K):
aim(s): establish an Islamic caliphate in Afghanistan, Pakistan, and parts of Central Asia; counter Westerners and Shia Muslims
area(s) of operation: stronghold in Nangarhar Province near the Afghanistan-Pakistan border and operating in Kunar, Laghman, Jowzjan provinces with pockets of support throughout Afghanistan
note: recruits from among the local population, Central Asian extremists in Afghanistan, and other militant groups, such as Tehrik-e Taliban Pakistan, the Afghan Taliban, and the Islamic Movement of Uzbekistan (April 2018)

Tehrik-e-Taliban Pakistan (TTP):
aim(s): drive foreign troops from Afghanistan; remove Pakistani forces from Pakistan's Federally Administered Tribal Areas (FATA) and, ultimately, overthrow the Pakistan Government to implement TTP's strict interpretation of sharia
area(s) of operation: headquartered in several eastern Afghanistan provinces near the Afghanistan-Pakistan border; operates primarily along the northeastern Afghanistan-Pakistan border, especially in Kunar and Paktika provinces, where TTP has established sanctuaries (April 2018)

TERRORIST GROUPS - FOREIGN BASED:

al-Qa'ida in the Indian Subcontinent (AQIS):
aim(s): establish an Islamic caliphate in the Indian subcontinent
area(s) of operation: heaviest presence is in Afghanistan, especially in the eastern and southern regions, where most of the Afghan-based leaders are located
note: targets primarily Afghan military and security personnel and US interests (April 2018)

Haqqani Taliban Network (HQN):
aim(s): expel US and Coalition forces and replace the Afghan Government with an Islamic state operating according to a strict Salafi Muslim interpretation of sharia under the Afghan Taliban
area(s) of operation: stages attacks from Kurram and North Waziristan Agency in Pakistan's Federally Administered Tribal Areas (FATA) across from Afghanistan's southeastern border; operational throughout the country, especially in Kabul and Paktiya and Khost provinces
note: plays a leading role in planning and executing high-profile attacks against Afghan personnel, NATO's Resolute Support Mission, US and Coalition Forces, and other US and Western interests (April 2018)

Harakat ul-Jihad-i-Islami (HUJI):
aim(s): implement sharia in Afghanistan; enhance its networks and drive foreign troops from Afghanistan
area(s) of operation: operations throughout Afghanistan, targeting primarily Afghan Government personnel and Coalition forces (April 2018)

Harakat ul-Mujahidin (HUM):
aim(s): enhance its networks and paramilitary training in Afghanistan and, ultimately, incorporate Kashmir into Pakistan; establish an Islamic state in Kashmir
area(s) of operation: maintains paramilitary training camps in eastern Afghanistan (April 2018)

Jaish-e-Mohammed (JEM):
aim(s): participate in the insurgency against Afghan and international forces to support a Taliban return to power in Afghanistan and annex the Indian state of Jammu and Kashmir to Pakistan
area(s) of operation: historically operated in Afghanistan's eastern provinces (April 2018)

Jaysh al Adl:
aim(s): enhance its operational networks and capabilities for staging cross-border attacks into Pakistan and Iran
area(s) of operation: operational in the greater Balochistan area, where fighters stage attacks targeting Shia Muslims in Iran and Pakistan
note: formerly known as Jundallah (April 2018)

Lashkar i Jhangvi (LJ):
aim(s): enhance its networks and paramilitary training in Afghanistan; exterminate Shia Muslims, rid the Afghanistan-Pakistan region of Western influence
area(s) of operation: headquartered in the east; operates paramilitary training camps near the Afghanistan-Pakistan border across from the central area of Pakistan's Federally Administered Tribal Areas (FATA) region; operatives conduct operations inside Afghanistan (April 2018)

Lashkar-e Tayyiba (LT):
aim(s): annex the Indian state of Jammu and Kashmir to Pakistan and foment Islamic insurgency in India; attack Western, Indian, and Afghan interests in Afghanistan; support the Taliban's return to power; enhance its recruitment networks and paramilitary training in Afghanistan, and, ultimately, install Islamic rule throughout South Asia
area(s) of operation: targets Coalition forces and Western interests throughout the country; maintains several facilities, such as paramilitary training camps, medical clinics serving locals, and schools for youths; targets Pashtun youth for recruitmentAdministered Tribal Areas (FATA) region; operatives conduct operations inside Afghanistan (April 2018)

TRANSNATIONAL ISSUES :: AFGHANISTAN

DISPUTES - INTERNATIONAL:

Afghan, Coalition, and Pakistan military meet periodically to clarify the alignment of the boundary on the ground and on maps and since 2014 have met to discuss collaboration on the Taliban insurgency and counterterrorism effortsAfghan and Iranian commissioners have discussed boundary monument densification and resurveyIran protests Afghanistan's restricting flow of dammed Helmand River tributaries during droughtPakistan has sent troops across and built fences along some remote tribal areas of its treaty-defined Durand Line border with Afghanistan which serve as bases for foreign terrorists and other illegal activitiesRussia remains concerned about the smuggling of poppy derivatives from Afghanistan through Central Asian countries

REFUGEES AND INTERNALLY DISPLACED PERSONS:

refugees (country of origin): 59,737 (Pakistan) (2016)

IDPs: 1.286 million (mostly Pashtuns and Kuchis displaced in the south and west due to natural disasters and political instability) (2017)

ILLICIT DRUGS:

world's largest producer of opium; poppy cultivation increased 63 percent, to 328,304 hectares in 2017; while eradication increased slightly, it still remains well below levels achieved in 2015; the 2017 crop yielded an estimated 9,000 mt of raw opium, a 88% increase over 2016; the Taliban and other antigovernment groups participate in and profit from the opiate trade, which is a key source of revenue for the Taliban inside Afghanistan; widespread corruption and instability impede counterdrug efforts; most of the heroin consumed in Europe and Eurasia is derived from Afghan opium; Afghanistan is also struggling to respond to a burgeoning domestic opiate addiction problem; a 2015 national drug use survey found that roughly 11% of the population tested positive for one or more illicit drugs; vulnerable to drug money laundering through informal financial networks; illicit cultivation of cannabis and regional source of hashish (2018)

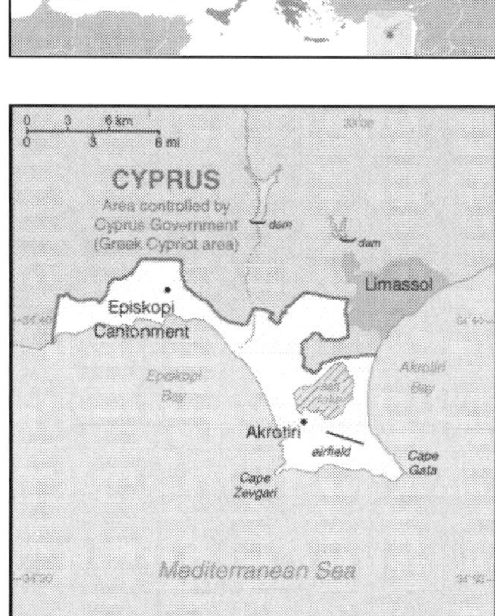

EUROPE :: AKROTIRI

INTRODUCTION :: AKROTIRI

BACKGROUND:

By terms of the 1960 Treaty of Establishment that created the independent Republic of Cyprus, the UK retained full sovereignty and jurisdiction over two areas of almost 254 square kilometers - Akrotiri and Dhekelia. The southernmost and smallest of these is the Akrotiri Sovereign Base Area, which is also referred to as the Western Sovereign Base Area.

GEOGRAPHY :: AKROTIRI

LOCATION:

Eastern Mediterranean, peninsula on the southwest coast of Cyprus

GEOGRAPHIC COORDINATES:

34 37 N, 32 58 E

MAP REFERENCES:

Middle East

AREA:

total: 123 sq km

note: includes a salt lake and wetlands

country comparison to the world: 224

AREA - COMPARATIVE:

about 0.7 times the size of Washington, DC

LAND BOUNDARIES:

total: 48 km

border countries (1): Cyprus 48 km

COASTLINE:

56.3 km

CLIMATE:

temperate; Mediterranean with hot, dry summers and cool winters

ENVIRONMENT - CURRENT ISSUES:

hunting around the salt lake; note - breeding place for loggerhead and green turtles; only remaining colony of griffon vultures is on the base

GEOGRAPHY - NOTE:

British extraterritorial rights also extended to several small off-post sites scattered across Cyprus; of the Sovereign Base Area (SBA) land, 60% is privately owned and farmed, 20% is owned by the Ministry of Defense, and 20% is SBA Crown land

PEOPLE AND SOCIETY :: AKROTIRI

POPULATION:

approximately 15,500 on the Sovereign Base Areas of Akrotiri and Dhekelia including 9,700 Cypriots and 5,800 Service and UK-based contract personnel and dependents (2011)

LANGUAGES:

English, Greek

HIV/AIDS - ADULT PREVALENCE RATE:

NA

GOVERNMENT :: AKROTIRI

COUNTRY NAME:

conventional long form: none

conventional short form: Akrotiri

etymology: named for the village that lies within the Western Sovereign Base Area on Cyprus

DEPENDENCY STATUS:

a special form of UK overseas territory; administered by an administrator who is also the Commander, British Forces Cyprus

CAPITAL:

name: Episkopi Cantonment (base administrative center for Akrotiri and Dhekelia)

geographic coordinates: 34 40 N, 32 51 E

time difference: UTC+2 (7 hours ahead of Washington, DC, during Standard Time)

daylight saving time: +1hr, begins last Sunday in March; ends last Sunday in October

etymology: "Episkopi" means "episcopal" in Greek and stems from the fact that the site previously served as the bishop's seat of an Orthodox diocese

CONSTITUTION:

presented 3 August 1960, effective 16 August 1960 (The Sovereign Base Areas of Akrotiri and Dhekelia Order in Council 1960 serves as a basic legal document); amended 1966 (2016)

LEGAL SYSTEM:

laws applicable to the Cypriot population are, as far as possible, the same as the laws of the Republic of Cyprus; note - the Sovereign Base Area Administration has its own court system to deal with civil and criminal matters

EXECUTIVE BRANCH:

chief of state: Queen ELIZABETH II (since 6 February 1952)

head of government: Administrator Major General James ILLINGWORTH (since 14 March 2017); note -

administrator reports to the British Ministry of Defense; the chief officer is responsible for the day-to-day running of the civil government of the Sovereign Bases

elections/appointments: the monarchy is hereditary; administrator appointed by the monarch on the advice of the Ministry of Defense

JUDICIAL BRANCH:

highest courts: Senior Judges' Court (consists of several visiting judges from England and Wales)

judge selection and term of office: see entry for United Kingdom

subordinate courts: Resident Judges' Court; Courts Martial

DIPLOMATIC REPRESENTATION IN THE US:

none (overseas territory of the UK)

DIPLOMATIC REPRESENTATION FROM THE US:

none (overseas territory of the UK)

FLAG DESCRIPTION:

the flag of the UK is used

NATIONAL ANTHEM:

note: as a UK area of special sovereignty, "God Save the Queen" is official (see United Kingdom)

ECONOMY :: AKROTIRI

ECONOMY - OVERVIEW:

Economic activity is limited to providing services to the military and their families located in Akrotiri. All food and manufactured goods must be imported.

EXCHANGE RATES:

note: uses the euro

COMMUNICATIONS :: AKROTIRI

BROADCAST MEDIA:

British Forces Broadcast Service (BFBS) provides multi-channel satellite TV service as well as BFBS radio broadcasts to the Akrotiri Sovereign Base Area (2009)

TRANSPORTATION :: AKROTIRI

AIRPORTS:

1 (2017)

country comparison to the world: 211

AIRPORTS - WITH PAVED RUNWAYS:

2,438 to 3,047 m: 1 (2017)

MILITARY AND SECURITY :: AKROTIRI

MILITARY - NOTE:

defense is the responsibility of the UK; Akrotiri has a full RAF base, headquarters for British Forces Cyprus, and Episkopi Support Unit

INTRODUCTION :: ALBANIA

BACKGROUND:

Albania declared its independence from the Ottoman Empire in 1912, but was conquered by Italy in 1939 and occupied by Germany in 1943. Communist partisans took over the country in 1944. Albania allied itself first with the USSR (until 1960), and then with China (to 1978). In the early 1990s, Albania ended 46 years of isolated communist rule and established a multiparty democracy. The transition has proven challenging as successive governments have tried to deal with high unemployment, widespread corruption, dilapidated infrastructure, powerful organized crime networks, and combative political opponents.

Albania has made progress in its democratic development since it first held multiparty elections in 1991, but deficiencies remain. Most of Albania's post-communist elections were marred by claims of electoral fraud; however, international observers judged elections to be largely free and fair since the restoration of political stability following the collapse of pyramid schemes in 1997. Albania joined NATO in April 2009 and in June 2014 became an EU candidate. Albania in April 2017 received a European Commission recommendation to open EU accession negotiations following the passage of historic EU-mandated justice reforms in 2016. Although Albania's economy continues to grow, it has slowed, and the country is still one of the poorest in Europe. A large informal economy and a weak energy and transportation infrastructure remain obstacles.

GEOGRAPHY :: ALBANIA

LOCATION:

Southeastern Europe, bordering the Adriatic Sea and Ionian Sea, between Greece to the south and Montenegro and Kosovo to the north

GEOGRAPHIC COORDINATES:

41 00 N, 20 00 E

MAP REFERENCES:

Europe

AREA:

total: 28,748 sq km

land: 27,398 sq km

water: 1,350 sq km

country comparison to the world: 145

AREA - COMPARATIVE:

slightly smaller than Maryland

LAND BOUNDARIES:

total: 691 km

border countries (4): Greece 212 km, Kosovo 112 km, Macedonia 181 km, Montenegro 186 km

COASTLINE:

362 km

MARITIME CLAIMS:

territorial sea: 12 nm

continental shelf: 200-m depth or to the depth of exploitation

CLIMATE:

mild temperate; cool, cloudy, wet winters; hot, clear, dry summers; interior is cooler and wetter

TERRAIN:

mostly mountains and hills; small plains along coast

ELEVATION:

mean elevation: 708 m

elevation extremes: 0 m lowest point: Adriatic Sea

2764 highest point: Maja e Korabit (Golem Korab)

NATURAL RESOURCES:

petroleum, natural gas, coal, bauxite, chromite, copper, iron ore, nickel, salt, timber, hydropower, arable land

LAND USE:

agricultural land: 42.86% (2014 est.)

arable land: 52.42% (2014 est.) / permanent crops: 6.84% (2014 est.) / permanent pasture: 40.73% (2014 est.)

forest: 28.19% (2014 est.)

other: 28.95% (2014 est.)

IRRIGATED LAND:

3,537 sq km (2014)

POPULATION DISTRIBUTION:

a fairly even distribution, with somewhat higher concentrations of people in the western and central parts of the country

NATURAL HAZARDS:

destructive earthquakes; tsunamis occur along southwestern coast; floods; drought

ENVIRONMENT - CURRENT ISSUES:

deforestation; soil erosion; water pollution from industrial and domestic effluents; air pollution from industrial and power plants; loss of biodiversity due to lack of resources for sound environmental management

ENVIRONMENT - INTERNATIONAL AGREEMENTS:

party to: Air Pollution, Biodiversity, Climate Change, Climate Change-Kyoto Protocol, Desertification, Endangered Species, Hazardous Wastes, Law of the Sea, Ozone Layer Protection, Wetlands

signed, but not ratified: none of the selected agreements

GEOGRAPHY - NOTE:

strategic location along Strait of Otranto (links Adriatic Sea to Ionian Sea and Mediterranean Sea)

PEOPLE AND SOCIETY :: ALBANIA

POPULATION:

3,057,220 (July 2018 est.)

country comparison to the world: 136

NATIONALITY:

noun: Albanian(s)

adjective: Albanian

ETHNIC GROUPS:

Albanian 82.6%, Greek 0.9%, other 1% (including Vlach, Romani, Macedonian, Montenegrin, and Egyptian), unspecified 15.5% (2011 est.)

note: data represent population by ethnic and cultural affiliation

LANGUAGES:

Albanian 98.8% (official - derived from Tosk dialect), Greek 0.5%, other 0.6% (including Macedonian, Romani, Vlach, Turkish, Italian, and Serbo-Croatian), unspecified 0.1% (2011 est.)

RELIGIONS:

Muslim 56.7%, Roman Catholic 10%, Orthodox 6.8%, atheist 2.5%, Bektashi (a Sufi order) 2.1%, other 5.7%, unspecified 16.2% (2011 est.)

note: all mosques and churches were closed in 1967 and religious observances prohibited; in November 1990, Albania began allowing private religious practice

AGE STRUCTURE:

0-14 years: 17.84% (male 287,750 /female 257,675)

15-24 years: 16.84% (male 267,695 /female 247,230)

25-54 years: 41.31% (male 604,250 /female 658,773)

55-64 years: 11.77% (male 176,420 /female 183,391)

65 years and over: 12.23% (male 174,752 /female 199,284) (2018 est.)

DEPENDENCY RATIOS:

total dependency ratio: 44 (2015 est.)

youth dependency ratio: 26 (2015 est.)

elderly dependency ratio: 18.1 (2015 est.)

potential support ratio: 5.5 (2015 est.)

MEDIAN AGE:

total: 33.4 years

male: 32 years

female: 34.7 years (2018 est.)

country comparison to the world: 93

POPULATION GROWTH RATE:

0.3% (2018 est.)

country comparison to the world: 169

BIRTH RATE:

13.2 births/1,000 population (2018 est.)

country comparison to the world: 143

DEATH RATE:

6.9 deaths/1,000 population (2018 est.)

country comparison to the world: 131

NET MIGRATION RATE:

-3.3 migrant(s)/1,000 population (2017 est.)

country comparison to the world: 179

POPULATION DISTRIBUTION:

a fairly even distribution, with somewhat higher concentrations of people in the western and central parts of the country

URBANIZATION:

urban population: 60.3% of total population (2018)

rate of urbanization: 1.69% annual rate of change (2015-20 est.)

MAJOR URBAN AREAS - POPULATION:

476,000 TIRANA (capital) (2018)

SEX RATIO:

at birth: 1.09 male(s)/female (2017 est.)

0-14 years: 1.12 male(s)/female (2017 est.)

15-24 years: 1.07 male(s)/female (2017 est.)

25-54 years: 0.91 male(s)/female (2017 est.)

55-64 years: 0.98 male(s)/female (2017 est.)

65 years and over: 0.89 male(s)/female (2017 est.)

total population: 0.98 male(s)/female (2017 est.)

MOTHER'S MEAN AGE AT FIRST BIRTH:

24.5 years (2014 est.)

MATERNAL MORTALITY RATE:

29 deaths/100,000 live births (2015 est.)

country comparison to the world: 115

INFANT MORTALITY RATE:

total: 11.6 deaths/1,000 live births (2018 est.)

male: 12.9 deaths/1,000 live births (2018 est.)

female: 10.1 deaths/1,000 live births (2018 est.)

country comparison to the world: 124

LIFE EXPECTANCY AT BIRTH:

total population: 78.6 years (2018 est.)

male: 76 years (2018 est.)

female: 81.6 years (2018 est.)

country comparison to the world: 60

TOTAL FERTILITY RATE:

1.52 children born/woman (2018 est.)

country comparison to the world: 192

CONTRACEPTIVE PREVALENCE RATE:

69.3% (2008/09)

HEALTH EXPENDITURES:

8.2% of GDP (2014)

country comparison to the world: 53

PHYSICIANS DENSITY:

1.29 physicians/1,000 population (2013)

HOSPITAL BED DENSITY:

2.9 beds/1,000 population (2013)

DRINKING WATER SOURCE:

improved:

urban: 84.3% of population

rural: 81.8% of population

total: 83.6% of population

unimproved:

urban: 15.7% of population

rural: 18.2% of population

total: 16.4% of population (2015 est.)

SANITATION FACILITY ACCESS:

improved:

urban: 95.5% of population (2015 est.)

rural: 90.2% of population (2015 est.)

total: 93.2% of population (2015 est.)

unimproved:

urban: 4.5% of population (2015 est.)

rural: 9.8% of population (2015 est.)

total: 6.8% of population (2015 est.)

HIV/AIDS - ADULT PREVALENCE RATE:

<.1 (2017 est.)

HIV/AIDS - PEOPLE LIVING WITH HIV/AIDS:

1,400 (2017 est.)

country comparison to the world: 132

HIV/AIDS - DEATHS:

<100 (2017 est.)

OBESITY - ADULT PREVALENCE RATE:

21.7% (2016)

country comparison to the world: 85

CHILDREN UNDER THE AGE OF 5 YEARS UNDERWEIGHT:

6.3% (2009)

country comparison to the world: 75

EDUCATION EXPENDITURES:

3.5% of GDP (2015)

country comparison to the world: 127

LITERACY:

definition: age 15 and over can read and write (2015 est.)

total population: 97.6% (2015 est.)

male: 98.4% (2015 est.)

female: 96.9% (2015 est.)

SCHOOL LIFE EXPECTANCY (PRIMARY TO TERTIARY EDUCATION):

total: 16 years (2015)

male: 15 years (2015)

female: 16 years (2015)

UNEMPLOYMENT, YOUTH AGES 15-24:

total: 39.8% (2015 est.)

male: 39.3% (2015 est.)

female: 40.8% (2015 est.)

country comparison to the world: 13

GOVERNMENT :: ALBANIA

COUNTRY NAME:

conventional long form: Republic of Albania

conventional short form: Albania

local long form: Republika e Shqiperise

local short form: Shqiperia

former: People's Socialist Republic of Albania

etymology: the English-language country name seems to be derived from the ancient Illyrian tribe of the Albani; the native name "Shqiperia" is derived from the Albanian word "Shqiponje" ("Eagle") and is popularly interpreted to mean "Land of the Eagles"

GOVERNMENT TYPE:

parliamentary republic

CAPITAL:

name: Tirana (Tirane)

geographic coordinates: 41 19 N, 19 49 E

time difference: UTC+1 (6 hours ahead of Washington, DC, during Standard Time)

daylight saving time: +1hr, begins last Sunday in March; ends last Sunday in October

etymology: the name Tirana first appears in a 1418 Venetian document; the origin of the name is unclear, but may derive from Tirkan fortress, whose ruins survive on the slopes of Dajti mountain and which overlooks the city

ADMINISTRATIVE DIVISIONS:

12 counties (qarqe, singular - qark); Berat, Diber, Durres, Elbasan, Fier, Gjirokaster, Korce, Kukes, Lezhe, Shkoder, Tirane, Vlore

INDEPENDENCE:

28 November 1912 (from the Ottoman Empire)

NATIONAL HOLIDAY:

Independence Day, 28 November (1912) also known as Flag Day

CONSTITUTION:

history: several previous; latest approved by the Assembly 21 October 1998, adopted by referendum 22 November 1998, promulgated 28 November 1998 (2017)

amendments: proposed by at least one-fifth of the Assembly membership; passage requires at least a two-thirds majority vote by the Assembly; referendum required only if approved by two-thirds of the Assembly; amendments approved by referendum effective upon declaration by the president of the republic; amended several times, last in 2016 (2017)

LEGAL SYSTEM:

civil law system except in the northern rural areas where customary law known as the "Code of Leke" prevails

INTERNATIONAL LAW ORGANIZATION PARTICIPATION:

has not submitted an ICJ jurisdiction declaration; accepts ICCt jurisdiction

CITIZENSHIP:

citizenship by birth: no

citizenship by descent only: at least one parent must be a citizen of Albania

dual citizenship recognized: yes

residency requirement for naturalization: 5 years

SUFFRAGE:

18 years of age; universal

EXECUTIVE BRANCH:

chief of state: President of the Republic Ilir META (since 24 July 2017)

head of government: Prime Minister Edi RAMA (since 10 September 2013); Deputy Prime Minister Senida MESI (since 13 September 2017)

cabinet: Council of Ministers proposed by the prime minister, nominated by the president, and approved by the Assembly

elections/appointments: president indirectly elected by the Assembly for a 5-year term (eligible for a second term); a candidate needs three-fifths majority vote of the Assembly in 1 of 3 rounds or a simple majority in 2 additional rounds to become president; election last held in 4 rounds on 19, 20, 27, and 28 April 2017 (next election to be held in 2022); prime minister appointed by the president on the proposal of the majority party or coalition of parties in the Assembly

election results: Ilir META elected president; Assembly vote - 87 - 2 in fourth round

LEGISLATIVE BRANCH:

description: unicameral Assembly or Kuvendi (140 seats; members directly elected in multi-seat constituencies by proportional representation vote to serve 4-year terms)

elections: last held on 25 June 2017 (next to be held in 2021)

election results: percent of vote by party - PS 48.3%, PD 28.9%, LSI 14.3%, PDIU 4.8%, PSD 1%, other 2.7%; seats by party - PS 74, PD 43, LSI 19, PDIU 3, PSD 1; composition - men 108, women 32, percent of women 22.9%

JUDICIAL BRANCH:

highest courts: Supreme Court (consists of 17 judges, including the chief justice); Constitutional Court (consists of 9 judges, including the chairman)

judge selection and term of office: Supreme Court judges, including the chairman, appointed by the president with the consent of the Assembly to serve single 9-year terms; Constitutional Court judges appointed by the president with the consent of the Assembly to serve single 9-year terms with one-third of the membership renewed every 3 years; chairman elected by the People's Assembly for a single 3-year term

subordinate courts: Courts of Appeal; Courts of First Instance

POLITICAL PARTIES AND LEADERS:

Democratic Party or PD [Lulzim BASHA]
Party for Justice, Integration and Unity or PDIU [Shpetim IDRIZI] (formerly part of APMI)
Social Democratic Party or PSD [Skender GJINUSHI]Socialist Movement for Integration or LSI [Monika KRYEMADHI]
Socialist Party or PS [Edi RAMA]

INTERNATIONAL ORGANIZATION PARTICIPATION:

BSEC, CD, CE, CEI, EAPC, EBRD, EITI (compliant country), FAO, IAEA, IBRD, ICAO, ICC (national committees), ICCt, ICRM, IDA, IDB, IFAD, IFC, IFRCS, ILO, IMF, IMO, Interpol, IOC, IOM, IPU, ISO (correspondent), ITU, ITUC (NGOs), MIGA, NATO, OAS (observer), OIC, OIF, OPCW, OSCE, PCA, SELEC, UN, UNCTAD, UNESCO, UNIDO, UNWTO, UPU, WCO, WFTU (NGOs), WHO, WIPO, WMO, WTO

DIPLOMATIC REPRESENTATION IN THE US:

chief of mission: Ambassador Floreta FABER (since 18 May 2015)

chancery: 2100 S Street NW, Washington, DC 20008

telephone: [1] (202) 223-4942

FAX: [1] (202) 628-7342

consulate(s) general: New York

DIPLOMATIC REPRESENTATION FROM THE US:

chief of mission: Ambassador Donald LU (since 13 January 2015)

embassy: Rruga e Elbasanit, 103, Tirana

mailing address: US Department of State, 9510 Tirana Place, Dulles, VA 20189-9510

telephone: [355] (4) 2247-285

FAX: [355] (4) 2232-222

FLAG DESCRIPTION:

red with a black two-headed eagle in the center; the design is claimed to be that of 15th-century hero Georgi Kastrioti SKANDERBEG, who led a successful uprising against the Ottoman Turks that resulted in a short-lived independence for some Albanian regions (1443-78); an unsubstantiated explanation for the eagle symbol is the tradition that Albanians see themselves as descendants of the eagle; they refer to themselves as "Shqiptare," which translates as "sons of the eagle"

NATIONAL SYMBOL(S):

black double-headed eagle; national colors: red, black

NATIONAL ANTHEM:

name: "Hymni i Flamurit" (Hymn to the Flag)

lyrics/music: Aleksander Stavre DRENOVA/Ciprian PORUMBESCU

note: adopted 1912

ECONOMY :: ALBANIA

ECONOMY - OVERVIEW:

Albania, a formerly closed, centrally-planned state, is a developing country with a modern open-market economy. Albania managed to weather the first waves of the global financial crisis but, the negative effects of the crisis caused a significant economic slowdown. Since 2014, Albania's economy has steadily improved and economic growth reached 3.8% in 2017. However, close trade, remittance, and banking sector ties with Greece and Italy make Albania vulnerable to spillover effects of possible debt crises and weak growth in the euro zone.

Remittances, a significant catalyst for economic growth, declined from 12-15% of GDP before the 2008 financial crisis to 5.8% of GDP in 2015, mostly from Albanians residing in Greece and Italy. The agricultural sector, which accounts for more than 40% of employment but less than one quarter of GDP, is limited primarily to small family operations and subsistence farming, because of a lack of modern equipment, unclear property rights, and the prevalence of small, inefficient plots of land. Complex tax codes and licensing requirements, a weak judicial system, endemic corruption, poor enforcement of contracts and property issues, and antiquated infrastructure contribute to Albania's poor business environment making attracting foreign investment difficult. Since 2015, Albania has launched an ambitious program to increase tax compliance and bring more businesses into the formal economy. In July 2016, Albania passed constitutional amendments reforming the judicial system in order to strengthen the rule of law and to reduce deeply entrenched corruption.

Albania's electricity supply is uneven despite upgraded transmission capacities with neighboring countries. However, the government has recently taken steps to stem non-technical losses and has begun to upgrade the distribution grid. Better enforcement of electricity contracts has improved the financial viability of the sector, decreasing its reliance on budget support. Also, with help from international donors, the government is taking steps to improve the poor road and rail networks, a long standing barrier to sustained economic growth.

Inward foreign direct investment has increased significantly in recent years as the government has embarked on an ambitious program to improve the business climate through fiscal and legislative reforms. The government is focused on the simplification of licensing requirements and tax codes, and it entered into a new arrangement with the IMF for additional financial and technical support. Albania's three-year IMF program, an extended fund facility arrangement, was successfully concluded in February 2017. The Albanian Government has strengthened tax collection amid moderate public wage and pension increases in an effort to reduce its budget deficit. The country continues to face high public debt, exceeding its former statutory limit of 60% of GDP in 2013 and reaching 72% in 2016.

GDP (PURCHASING POWER PARITY):

$36.01 billion (2017 est.)

$34.67 billion (2016 est.)

$33.55 billion (2015 est.)

note: data are in 2017 dollars; unreported output may be as large as 50% of official GDP

country comparison to the world: 125

GDP (OFFICIAL EXCHANGE RATE):

$13.07 billion (2017 est.) (2017 est.)

GDP - REAL GROWTH RATE:

3.8% (2017 est.)

3.4% (2016 est.)

2.2% (2015 est.)

country comparison to the world: 85

GDP - PER CAPITA (PPP):

$12,500 (2017 est.)

$12,100 (2016 est.)

$11,600 (2015 est.)

note: data are in 2017 dollars

country comparison to the world: 125

GROSS NATIONAL SAVING:

15.9% of GDP (2017 est.)

16.7% of GDP (2016 est.)

16.9% of GDP (2015 est.)

country comparison to the world: 130

GDP - COMPOSITION, BY END USE:

household consumption: 78.1% (2017 est.)

government consumption: 11.5% (2017 est.)

investment in fixed capital: 25.2% (2017 est.)

investment in inventories: 0.2% (2017 est.)

exports of goods and services: 31.5% (2017 est.)

imports of goods and services: -46.6% (2017 est.)

GDP - COMPOSITION, BY SECTOR OF ORIGIN:

agriculture: 21.7% (2017 est.)

industry: 24.2% (2017 est.)

services: 54.1% (2017 est.)

AGRICULTURE - PRODUCTS:

wheat, corn, potatoes, vegetables, fruits, olives and olive oil, grapes; meat, dairy products; sheep and goats

INDUSTRIES:

food; footwear, apparel and clothing; lumber, oil, cement, chemicals, mining, basic metals, hydropower

INDUSTRIAL PRODUCTION GROWTH RATE:

6.8% (2017 est.)

country comparison to the world: 31

LABOR FORCE:

1.198 million (2017 est.)

country comparison to the world: 140

LABOR FORCE - BY OCCUPATION:

agriculture: 41.4%

industry: 18.3%

services: 40.3% (2017 est.)

UNEMPLOYMENT RATE:

13.8% (2017 est.)

15.2% (2016 est.)

note: these official rates may not include those working at near-subsistence farming

country comparison to the world: 168

POPULATION BELOW POVERTY LINE:

14.3% (2012 est.)

HOUSEHOLD INCOME OR CONSUMPTION BY PERCENTAGE SHARE:

lowest 10%: 19.6% (2015 est.)

highest 10%: 19.6% (2015 est.)

DISTRIBUTION OF FAMILY INCOME - GINI INDEX:

29 (2012 est.)

30 (2008 est.)

country comparison to the world: 138

BUDGET:

revenues: 3.614 billion (2017 est.)

expenditures: 3.874 billion (2017 est.)

TAXES AND OTHER REVENUES:

27.6% (of GDP) (2017 est.)

country comparison to the world: 99

BUDGET SURPLUS (+) OR DEFICIT (-):

-2% (of GDP) (2017 est.)

country comparison to the world: 103

PUBLIC DEBT:

71.8% of GDP (2017 est.)

73.2% of GDP (2016 est.)

country comparison to the world: 45

FISCAL YEAR:

calendar year

INFLATION RATE (CONSUMER PRICES):

2% (2017 est.)

1.3% (2016 est.)

country comparison to the world: 102

CENTRAL BANK DISCOUNT RATE:

1.25% (31 December 2017)

1.25% (31 December 2016)

country comparison to the world: 130

COMMERCIAL BANK PRIME LENDING RATE:

8.22% (31 December 2017 est.)

9.78% (31 December 2016 est.)

country comparison to the world: 104

STOCK OF NARROW MONEY:

$4.155 billion (31 December 2017 est.)

$3.397 billion (31 December 2016 est.)

country comparison to the world: 111

STOCK OF BROAD MONEY:

$4.155 billion (31 December 2017 est.)

$3.397 billion (31 December 2016 est.)

country comparison to the world: 116

STOCK OF DOMESTIC CREDIT:

$8.122 billion (31 December 2017 est.)

$7.065 billion (31 December 2016 est.)

country comparison to the world: 116

MARKET VALUE OF PUBLICLY TRADED SHARES:

NA

CURRENT ACCOUNT BALANCE:

-$908 million (2017 est.)

-$899 million (2016 est.)

country comparison to the world: 139

EXPORTS:

$900.7 million (2017 est.)

$789.1 million (2016 est.)

country comparison to the world: 165

EXPORTS - PARTNERS:

Italy 53.4%, Kosovo 7.7%, Spain 5.6%, Greece 4.2% (2017)

EXPORTS - COMMODITIES:

apparel and clothing, footwear; asphalt, metals and metallic ores, crude oil; cement and construction materials, vegetables, fruits, tobacco

IMPORTS:

$4.103 billion (2017 est.)

$3.67 billion (2016 est.)

country comparison to the world: 139

IMPORTS - COMMODITIES:

machinery and equipment, foodstuffs, textiles, chemicals

IMPORTS - PARTNERS:

Italy 28.5%, Turkey 8.1%, Germany 8%, Greece 8%, China 7.9%, Serbia 4% (2017)

RESERVES OF FOREIGN EXCHANGE AND GOLD:

$3.59 billion (31 December 2017 est.)

$3.109 billion (31 December 2016 est.)

country comparison to the world: 103

DEBT - EXTERNAL:

$9.505 billion (31 December 2017 est.)

$8.421 billion (31 December 2016 est.)

country comparison to the world: 114

STOCK OF DIRECT FOREIGN INVESTMENT - AT HOME:

$6.12 billion (31 December 2016 est.)

$5.452 billion (31 December 2015 est.)

country comparison to the world: 104

EXCHANGE RATES:

leke (ALL) per US dollar -

121.9 (2017 est.)

124.14 (2016 est.)

124.14 (2015 est.)

125.96 (2014 est.)

105.48 (2013 est.)

ENERGY :: ALBANIA

ELECTRICITY ACCESS:

electrification - total population: 100% (2016)

ELECTRICITY - PRODUCTION:

7.138 billion kWh (2016 est.)

country comparison to the world: 111

ELECTRICITY - CONSUMPTION:

5.11 billion kWh (2016 est.)

country comparison to the world: 122

ELECTRICITY - EXPORTS:

1.869 billion kWh (2016 est.)

country comparison to the world: 46

ELECTRICITY - IMPORTS:

1.827 billion kWh (2016 est.)

country comparison to the world: 58

ELECTRICITY - INSTALLED GENERATING CAPACITY:

2.109 million kW (2016 est.)

country comparison to the world: 112

ELECTRICITY - FROM FOSSIL FUELS:

5% of total installed capacity (2016 est.)

country comparison to the world: 202

ELECTRICITY - FROM NUCLEAR FUELS:

0% of total installed capacity (2017 est.)

country comparison to the world: 33

ELECTRICITY - FROM HYDROELECTRIC PLANTS:

95% of total installed capacity (2017 est.)

country comparison to the world: 5

ELECTRICITY - FROM OTHER RENEWABLE SOURCES:

0% of total installed capacity (2017 est.)

country comparison to the world: 172

CRUDE OIL - PRODUCTION:

16,000 bbl/day (2017 est.)

country comparison to the world: 69

CRUDE OIL - EXPORTS:

17,290 bbl/day (2015 est.)

country comparison to the world: 51

CRUDE OIL - IMPORTS:

0 bbl/day (2015 est.)

country comparison to the world: 85

CRUDE OIL - PROVED RESERVES:

168.3 million bbl (1 January 2018 est.)

country comparison to the world: 59

REFINED PETROLEUM PRODUCTS - PRODUCTION:

5,638 bbl/day (2015 est.)

country comparison to the world: 103

REFINED PETROLEUM PRODUCTS - CONSUMPTION:

29,000 bbl/day (2016 est.)

country comparison to the world: 120

REFINED PETROLEUM PRODUCTS - EXPORTS:

3,250 bbl/day (2015 est.)

country comparison to the world: 98

REFINED PETROLEUM PRODUCTS - IMPORTS:

26,660 bbl/day (2015 est.)

country comparison to the world: 103

NATURAL GAS - PRODUCTION:

50.97 million cu m (2017 est.)

country comparison to the world: 86

NATURAL GAS - CONSUMPTION:

50.97 million cu m (2017 est.)

country comparison to the world: 112

NATURAL GAS - EXPORTS:

0 cu m (2017 est.)

country comparison to the world: 58

NATURAL GAS - IMPORTS:

0 cu m (2017 est.)

country comparison to the world: 82

NATURAL GAS - PROVED RESERVES:

821.2 million cu m (1 January 2018 est.)

country comparison to the world: 101

CARBON DIOXIDE EMISSIONS FROM CONSUMPTION OF ENERGY:

4.5 million Mt (2017 est.)

country comparison to the world: 136

COMMUNICATIONS :: ALBANIA

TELEPHONES - FIXED LINES:

total subscriptions: 247,010 (2017 est.)

subscriptions per 100 inhabitants: 8 (2017 est.)

country comparison to the world: 122

TELEPHONES - MOBILE CELLULAR:

total subscriptions: 3,497,950 (2017 est.)

subscriptions per 100 inhabitants: 115 (2017 est.)

country comparison to the world: 134

TELEPHONE SYSTEM:

general assessment: consistant with the region; offsetting the deficit of fixed-line capacity, mobile-cellular phone service has been available since 1996; four companies presently providing mobile services and mobile teledensity; Internet broadband services initiated in 2005, and the penetration rate rose to over 65% by 2016; Internet cafes are popular in major urban areas; 1.3 million use mobile broadband services (3G/4G) (2017)

domestic: fixed-line 8 per 100, teledensity continues to decline due to heavy use of mobile-cellular telephone services; mobile-cellular telephone use is widespread and generally effective, 115 per 100 for mobile-cellular (2017)

international: country code - 355; submarine cable provides connectivity to Italy, Croatia, and Greece; the Trans-Balkan Line, a combination submarine cable and land fiber-optic system, provides additional connectivity to Bulgaria, Macedonia, and Turkey; international traffic carried by fiber-optic cable and, when necessary, by microwave radio relay from the Tirana exchange to Italy and Greece (2016)

BROADCAST MEDIA:

Albania has more than 65 TV stations, including several that broadcast nationally; Albanian TV broadcasts are also available to Albanian-speaking populations in neighboring countries; many viewers have access to Italian and Greek TV broadcasts via terrestrial reception; Albania's TV stations have begun a government-mandated conversion from analog to digital broadcast; the government has pledged to provide analog-to-digital converters to low-income families affected by this decision; cable TV service is available; 2 public radio networks and roughly 78 private radio stations; several international broadcasters are available (2017)

INTERNET COUNTRY CODE:

.al

INTERNET USERS:

total: 2,016,516 (July 2016 est.)

percent of population: 66.4% (July 2016 est.)

country comparison to the world: 112

BROADBAND - FIXED SUBSCRIPTIONS:

total: 293,623 (2017 est.)

subscriptions per 100 inhabitants: 10 (2017 est.)

country comparison to the world: 96

TRANSPORTATION :: ALBANIA

NATIONAL AIR TRANSPORT SYSTEM:

number of registered air carriers: 1 (2015)

inventory of registered aircraft operated by air carriers: 1 (2015)

annual passenger traffic on registered air carriers: 151,632 (2015)

annual freight traffic on registered air carriers: 0 mt-km (2015)

CIVIL AIRCRAFT REGISTRATION COUNTRY CODE PREFIX:

ZA (2016)

AIRPORTS:

4 (2016)

country comparison to the world: 183

AIRPORTS - WITH PAVED RUNWAYS:

total: 4 (2017)

2,438 to 3,047 m: 3 (2017)

1,524 to 2,437 m: 1 (2017)

AIRPORTS - WITH UNPAVED RUNWAYS:

total: 1 (2012)

914 to 1,523 m: 1 (2012)

HELIPORTS:

1 (2013)

PIPELINES:

498 km gas (a majority of the network is in disrepair and parts of it are missing), 249 km oil (2015)

RAILWAYS:

total: 677 km (447 km of major railway lines and 230 km of secondary lines) (2015)

standard gauge: 677 km 1.435-m gauge (2015)

country comparison to the world: 103

ROADWAYS:

total: 18,000 km (2002)

paved: 7,020 km (2002)

unpaved: 10,980 km (2002)

country comparison to the world: 117

WATERWAYS:

41 km (on the Bojana River) (2011)

country comparison to the world: 103

MERCHANT MARINE:

total: 57 (2017)

by type: bulk carrier 1, general cargo 49, other 7 (2017)

country comparison to the world: 108

PORTS AND TERMINALS:

major seaport(s): Durres, Sarande, Shengjin, Vlore

MILITARY AND SECURITY :: ALBANIA

MILITARY EXPENDITURES:

1.22% of GDP (2017)

1.23% of GDP (2016)

1.16% of GDP (2015)

1.35% of GDP (2014)

1.41% of GDP (2013)

country comparison to the world: 96

MILITARY BRANCHES:

Land Forces Command, Navy Force Command, Air Forces Command (2013)

MILITARY SERVICE AGE AND OBLIGATION:

19 is the legal minimum age for voluntary military service; 18 is the legal minimum age in case of general/partial compulsory mobilization (2012)

TRANSNATIONAL ISSUES :: ALBANIA

DISPUTES - INTERNATIONAL:

none

REFUGEES AND INTERNALLY DISPLACED PERSONS:

stateless persons: 4,460 (2017)

ILLICIT DRUGS:

active transshipment point for Southwest Asian opiates, hashish, and cannabis transiting the Balkan route and - to a lesser extent - cocaine from South America destined for Western Europe; significant source country for cannabis production; ethnic Albanian narcotrafficking organizations active and expanding in Europe; vulnerable to money laundering associated with regional trafficking in narcotics, arms, contraband, and illegal aliens

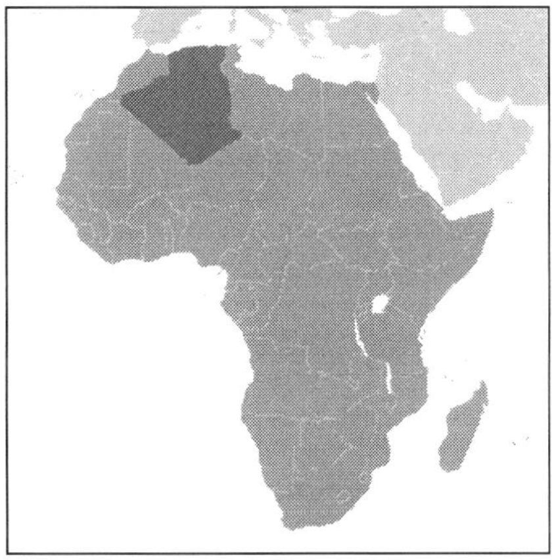

AFRICA :: ALGERIA

INTRODUCTION :: ALGERIA

BACKGROUND:

After more than a century of rule by France, Algerians fought through much of the 1950s to achieve independence in 1962. Algeria's primary political party, the National Liberation Front (FLN), was established in 1954 as part of the struggle for independence and has since largely dominated politics. The Government of Algeria in 1988 instituted a multi-party system in response to public unrest, but the surprising first round success of the Islamic Salvation Front (FIS) in the December 1991 legislative elections led the Algerian army to intervene and postpone the second round of elections to prevent what the secular elite feared would be an extremist-led government from assuming power. The army began a crackdown on the FIS that spurred FIS supporters to begin attacking government targets. Fighting escalated into an insurgency, which saw intense violence from 1992-98, resulting in over 100,000 deaths - many attributed to indiscriminate massacres of villagers by extremists. The government gained the upper hand by the late-1990s, and FIS's armed wing, the Islamic Salvation Army, disbanded in January 2000.

Abdelaziz BOUTEFLIKA, with the backing of the military, won the presidency in 1999 in an election that was boycotted by several candidates protesting alleged fraud, and won subsequent elections in 2004, 2009, and 2014. The government in 2011 introduced some political reforms in response to the Arab Spring, including lifting the 19-year-old state of emergency restrictions and increasing women's quotas for elected assemblies, while also increasing subsidies to the populace. Since 2014, Algeria's reliance on hydrocarbon revenues to fund the government and finance the large subsidies for the population has fallen under stress because of declining oil prices. As of December 2018, the country planned to hold its next presidential elections in late spring 2019.

GEOGRAPHY :: ALGERIA

LOCATION:

Northern Africa, bordering the Mediterranean Sea, between Morocco and Tunisia

GEOGRAPHIC COORDINATES:

28 00 N, 3 00 E

MAP REFERENCES:

Africa

AREA:

total: 2,381,740 sq km

land: 2,381,740 sq km

water: 0 sq km

country comparison to the world: 11

AREA - COMPARATIVE:

slightly less than 3.5 times the size of Texas

LAND BOUNDARIES:

total: 6,734 km

border countries (7): Libya 989 km, Mali 1359 km, Mauritania 460 km, Morocco 1900 km, Niger 951 km, Tunisia 1034 km, Western Sahara 41 km

COASTLINE:

998 km

MARITIME CLAIMS:

territorial sea: 12 nm

exclusive fishing zone: 32-52 nm

CLIMATE:

arid to semiarid; mild, wet winters with hot, dry summers along coast; drier with cold winters and hot summers on high plateau; sirocco is a hot, dust/sand-laden wind especially common in summer

TERRAIN:

mostly high plateau and desert; Atlas Mountains in the far north and Hoggar Mountains in the south; narrow, discontinuous coastal plain

ELEVATION:

mean elevation: 800 m

elevation extremes: -40 m lowest point: Chott Melrhir

2908 highest point: Tahat

NATURAL RESOURCES:

petroleum, natural gas, iron ore, phosphates, uranium, lead, zinc

LAND USE:

agricultural land: 17.4% (2014 est.)

arable land: 18.02% (2014 est.) / permanent crops: 2.34% (2014 est.) / permanent pasture: 79.63% (2014 est.)

forest: 0.82% (2014 est.)

other: 81.8% (2014 est.)

IRRIGATED LAND:

13,600 sq km (2014)

POPULATION DISTRIBUTION:

the vast majority of the populace is found in the extreme northern part of the country along the Mediterranean Coast

NATURAL HAZARDS:

mountainous areas subject to severe earthquakes; mudslides and floods in rainy season; droughts

ENVIRONMENT - CURRENT ISSUES:

air pollution in major cities; soil erosion from overgrazing and other poor farming practices; desertification; dumping of raw sewage, petroleum refining wastes, and other industrial effluents is leading to the pollution of rivers and coastal waters; Mediterranean Sea, in particular, becoming polluted from oil wastes, soil erosion, and fertilizer runoff; inadequate supplies of potable water

ENVIRONMENT - INTERNATIONAL AGREEMENTS:

party to: Biodiversity, Climate Change, Climate Change-Kyoto Protocol, Desertification, Endangered Species, Environmental Modification, Hazardous Wastes, Law of the Sea, Ozone Layer Protection, Ship Pollution, Wetlands

signed, but not ratified: none of the selected agreements

GEOGRAPHY - NOTE:

largest country in Africa but 80% desert; canyons and caves in the southern Hoggar Mountains and in the barren Tassili n'Ajjer area in the southeast of the country contain numerous examples of prehistoric art - rock paintings and carvings depicting human activities and wild and domestic animals (elephants, giraffes, cattle) - that date to the African Humid Period, roughly 11,000 to 5,000 years ago, when the region was completely vegetated

PEOPLE AND SOCIETY :: ALGERIA

POPULATION:

41,657,488 (July 2018 est.)

country comparison to the world: 34

NATIONALITY:

noun: Algerian(s)

adjective: Algerian

ETHNIC GROUPS:

Arab-Berber 99%, European less than 1%

note: although almost all Algerians are Berber in origin (not Arab), only a minority identify themselves as Berber, about 15% of the total population; these people live mostly in the mountainous region of Kabylie east of Algiers; the Berbers are also Muslim but identify with their Berber rather than Arab cultural heritage; Berbers have long agitated, sometimes violently, for autonomy; the government is unlikely to grant autonomy but has officially recognized Berber languages and introduced them into public schools

LANGUAGES:

Arabic (official), French (lingua franca), Berber or Tamazight (official); dialects include Kabyle Berber (Taqbaylit), Shawiya Berber (Tacawit), Mzab Berber, Tuareg Berber (Tamahaq)

RELIGIONS:

Muslim (official; predominantly Sunni) 99%, other (includes Christian and Jewish) <1% (2012 est.)

DEMOGRAPHIC PROFILE:

For the first two thirds of the 20th century, Algeria's high fertility rate caused its population to grow rapidly. However, about a decade after independence from France in 1962, the total fertility rate fell dramatically from 7 children per woman in the 1970s to about 2.4 in 2000, slowing Algeria's population growth rate by the late 1980s. The lower fertility rate was mainly the result of women's rising age at first marriage (virtually all Algerian children being born in wedlock) and to a lesser extent the wider use of contraceptives. Later marriages and a preference for smaller families are attributed to increases in women's education and participation in the labor market; higher unemployment; and a shortage of housing forcing multiple generations to live together. The average woman's age at first marriage increased from about 19 in the mid-1950s to 24 in the mid-1970s to 30.5 in the late 1990s.

Algeria's fertility rate experienced an unexpected upturn in the early 2000s, as the average woman's age at first marriage dropped slightly. The reversal in fertility could represent a temporary fluctuation in marriage age or, less likely, a decrease in the steady rate of contraceptive use.

Thousands of Algerian peasants - mainly Berber men from the Kabylia region - faced with land dispossession and economic hardship under French rule migrated temporarily to France to work in manufacturing and mining during the first half of the 20th century. This movement accelerated during World War I, when Algerians filled in for French factory workers or served as soldiers. In the years following independence, low-skilled Algerian workers and Algerians who had supported the French (known as Harkis) emigrated en masse to France. Tighter French immigration rules and Algiers' decision to cease managing labor migration to France in the 1970s limited legal emigration largely to family reunification.

Not until Algeria's civil war in the 1990s did the country again experience substantial outmigration. Many Algerians legally entered Tunisia without visas claiming to be tourists and then stayed as workers. Other Algerians headed to Europe seeking asylum, although France imposed restrictions. Sub-Saharan African migrants came to Algeria after its civil war to work in agriculture and mining. In the 2000s, a wave of educated Algerians went abroad seeking skilled jobs in a wider range of destinations, increasing their presence in North America and Spain. At the same time, legal foreign workers principally from China and Egypt came to work in Algeria's construction and oil sectors. Illegal migrants from sub-Saharan Africa, particularly Malians, Nigeriens, and Gambians, continue to come to Algeria in search of work or to use it as a stepping stone to Libya and Europe.

Since 1975, Algeria also has been the main recipient of Sahrawi refugees from the ongoing conflict in Western Sahara. More than 1000,000 Sahrawis are estimated to be living in five refugee camps in southwestern Algeria near Tindouf.

AGE STRUCTURE:

0-14 years: 29.49% (male 6,290,619 /female 5,993,733)

15-24 years: 14.72% (male 3,137,975 /female 2,994,056)

25-54 years: 42.97% (male 9,067,597 /female 8,833,238)

55-64 years: 7.01% (male 1,472,527 /female 1,446,083)

65 years and over: 5.81% (male 1,133,852 /female 1,287,808) (2018 est.)

DEPENDENCY RATIOS:

total dependency ratio: 52.7 (2015 est.)

youth dependency ratio: 43.8 (2015 est.)

elderly dependency ratio: 9 (2015 est.)

potential support ratio: 11.2 (2015 est.)

MEDIAN AGE:

total: 28.3 years

male: 28 years

female: 28.7 years (2018 est.)

country comparison to the world: 138

POPULATION GROWTH RATE:

1.63% (2018 est.)

country comparison to the world: 63

BIRTH RATE:

21.5 births/1,000 population (2018 est.)

country comparison to the world: 74

DEATH RATE:

4.3 deaths/1,000 population (2018 est.)

country comparison to the world: 205

NET MIGRATION RATE:

-0.9 migrant(s)/1,000 population (2017 est.)

country comparison to the world: 135

POPULATION DISTRIBUTION:

the vast majority of the populace is found in the extreme northern part of the country along the Mediterranean Coast

URBANIZATION:

urban population: 72.6% of total population (2018)

rate of urbanization: 2.46% annual rate of change (2015-20 est.)

MAJOR URBAN AREAS - POPULATION:

2.694 million ALGIERS (capital), 881,000 Oran (2018)

SEX RATIO:

at birth: 1.05 male(s)/female (2017 est.)

0-14 years: 1.05 male(s)/female (2017 est.)

15-24 years: 1.05 male(s)/female (2017 est.)

25-54 years: 1.02 male(s)/female (2017 est.)

55-64 years: 1.03 male(s)/female (2017 est.)

65 years and over: 0.86 male(s)/female (2017 est.)

total population: 1.03 male(s)/female (2017 est.)

MATERNAL MORTALITY RATE:

140 deaths/100,000 live births (2015 est.)

country comparison to the world: 62

INFANT MORTALITY RATE:

total: 18.9 deaths/1,000 live births (2018 est.)

male: 20.4 deaths/1,000 live births (2018 est.)

female: 17.2 deaths/1,000 live births (2018 est.)

country comparison to the world: 83

LIFE EXPECTANCY AT BIRTH:

total population: 77.2 years (2018 est.)

male: 75.8 years (2018 est.)

female: 78.7 years (2018 est.)

country comparison to the world: 76

TOTAL FERTILITY RATE:

2.66 children born/woman (2018 est.)

country comparison to the world: 64

CONTRACEPTIVE PREVALENCE RATE:

57.1% (2012/13)

HEALTH EXPENDITURES:

7.2% of GDP (2014)

country comparison to the world: 75

HOSPITAL BED DENSITY:

1.9 beds/1,000 population (2015)

DRINKING WATER SOURCE:

improved:

urban: 84.3% of population

rural: 81.8% of population

total: 83.6% of population

unimproved:

urban: 15.7% of population

rural: 18.2% of population

total: 16.4% of population (2015 est.)

SANITATION FACILITY ACCESS:

improved:

urban: 89.8% of population (2015 est.)

rural: 82.2% of population (2015 est.)

total: 87.6% of population (2015 est.)

unimproved:

urban: 10.2% of population (2015 est.)

rural: 17.8% of population (2015 est.)

total: 12.4% of population (2015 est.)

HIV/AIDS - ADULT PREVALENCE RATE:

<.1% (2017 est.)

HIV/AIDS - PEOPLE LIVING WITH HIV/AIDS:

14,000 (2017 est.)

country comparison to the world: 89

HIV/AIDS - DEATHS:

<200 (2017 est.)

OBESITY - ADULT PREVALENCE RATE:

27.4% (2016)

country comparison to the world: 38

CHILDREN UNDER THE AGE OF 5 YEARS UNDERWEIGHT:

3% (2012)

country comparison to the world: 99

EDUCATION EXPENDITURES:

4.3% of GDP (2008)

country comparison to the world: 101

LITERACY:

definition: age 15 and over can read and write (2015 est.)

total population: 80.2% (2015 est.)

male: 87.2% (2015 est.)

female: 73.1% (2015 est.)

SCHOOL LIFE EXPECTANCY (PRIMARY TO TERTIARY EDUCATION):

total: 14 years (2011)

male: 14 years (2011)

female: 15 years (2011)

UNEMPLOYMENT, YOUTH AGES 15-24:

total: 25.2% (2014 est.)

male: 22.1% (2014 est.)

female: 41.5% (2014 est.)

country comparison to the world: 45

GOVERNMENT :: ALGERIA

COUNTRY NAME:

conventional long form: People's Democratic Republic of Algeria

conventional short form: Algeria

local long form: Al Jumhuriyah al Jaza'iriyah ad Dimuqratiyah ash Sha'biyah

local short form: Al Jaza'ir

etymology: the country name derives from the capital city of Algiers

GOVERNMENT TYPE:

presidential republic

CAPITAL:

name: Algiers

geographic coordinates: 36 45 N, 3 03 E

time difference: UTC+1 (6 hours ahead of Washington, DC, during Standard Time)

etymology: name derives from the Arabic "al-Jazair" meaning "the islands" and refers to the four islands formerly off the coast but joined to the mainland since 1525

ADMINISTRATIVE DIVISIONS:

48 provinces (wilayas, singular - wilaya); Adrar, Ain Defla, Ain Temouchent, Alger, Annaba, Batna, Bechar, Bejaia, Biskra, Blida, Bordj Bou Arreridj, Bouira, Boumerdes, Chlef, Constantine, Djelfa, El Bayadh, El Oued, El Tarf, Ghardaia, Guelma, Illizi, Jijel, Khenchela, Laghouat, Mascara, Medea, Mila, Mostaganem, M'Sila, Naama, Oran, Ouargla, Oum el Bouaghi, Relizane, Saida, Setif, Sidi Bel Abbes, Skikda, Souk Ahras, Tamanrasset, Tebessa, Tiaret, Tindouf, Tipaza, Tissemsilt, Tizi Ouzou, Tlemcen

INDEPENDENCE:

5 July 1962 (from France)

NATIONAL HOLIDAY:

Revolution Day, 1 November (1954)

CONSTITUTION:

history: several previous; latest approved by referendum 23 February 1989 (2016)

amendments: proposed by the president of the republic or through the president with the support of three-fourths of the members of both houses of Parliament in joint session; passage requires approval by both houses, approval by referendum, and promulgation by the president; the president can forego a referendum if the Constitutional Council determines the proposed amendment does not conflict with basic constitutional principles; articles including the republican form of government, the integrity and unity of the country, and fundamental citizens' liberties and rights cannot be amended; amended several times, last in 2016 (2016)

LEGAL SYSTEM:

mixed legal system of French civil law and Islamic law; judicial review of legislative acts in ad hoc Constitutional Council composed of various public officials including several Supreme Court justices

INTERNATIONAL LAW ORGANIZATION PARTICIPATION:

has not submitted an ICJ jurisdiction declaration; non-party state to the ICCt

CITIZENSHIP:

citizenship by birth: no

citizenship by descent only: the mother must be a citizen of Algeria

dual citizenship recognized: no

residency requirement for naturalization: 7 years

SUFFRAGE:

18 years of age; universal

EXECUTIVE BRANCH:

chief of state: President Abdelaziz BOUTEFLIKA (since 28 April 1999)

head of government: Prime Minister Ahmed OUYAHIA (since 16 August 2017)

cabinet: Cabinet of Ministers appointed by the president

elections/appointments: president directly elected by absolute majority popular vote in two rounds if needed for a 5-year term (2-term limit reinstated by constitutional amendment in February 2016); election last held on 17 April 2014 (next to be held in April 2019); prime minister nominated by the president after consultation with the majority party in Parliament

election results: Abdelaziz BOUTEFLIKA reelected president for a fourth term; percent of vote - Abdelaziz BOUTEFLIKA (FLN) 81.5%, Ali BENFLIS (FLN) 12.2%, Abdelaziz BELAID (Future Front) 3.4%, other 2.9%

LEGISLATIVE BRANCH:

description: bicameral Parliament consists of:
Council of the Nation (upper house with 144 seats; one-third of members appointed by the president, two-thirds indirectly elected by simple majority vote by an electoral college composed of local council members; members serve 6-year terms with one-half of the membership renewed every 3 years)
National People's Assembly (lower house with 462 seats including 8 seats for Algerians living abroad); members directly elected in multi-seat constituencies by proportional representation vote to serve 5-year terms)

elections:
Council of the Nation - last held on 29 December 2015 (next to be held in December 2018)
National People's Assembly - last held on 4 May 2017 (next to be held in 2022)

election results:
Council of the Nation - percent of vote by party - NA; seats by party - NA; composition - men 133, women 10, percent of women 7%
National People's Assembly - percent of vote by party - NA; seats by party - FLN 164, RND 97, MSP-FC 33, TAJ 19, Ennahda-FJD 15, FFS 14, El Mostakbel 14, MPA 13, PT 11, RCD 9, ANR 8, MEN 4, other 33, independent 28; composition - men 343, women 119, percent of women 25.8%; note - total Parliament percent of women 21.3%

JUDICIAL BRANCH:

highest courts: Supreme Court or Cour Suprême, (consists of 150 judges organized into 8 chambers: Civil, Commercial and Maritime, Criminal, House of Offenses and Contraventions, House of Petitions, Land, Personal Status, and Social; Constitutional Council (consists of 12 members including the court chairman and deputy chairman); note - Algeria's judicial system does not include sharia courts

judge selection and term of office: Supreme Court judges appointed by the High Council of Magistracy, an administrative body presided over by the president of the republic, and includes the republic vice-president and several members; judges appointed for life; Constitutional Council members - 4 appointed by the president of the republic, 2 each by the 2 houses of Parliament, 2 by the Supreme Court, and 2 by the Council of State; Council president and members appointed for single 6-year terms with half the membership renewed every 3 years

subordinate courts: appellate or wilaya courts; first instance or daira tribunals

POLITICAL PARTIES AND LEADERS:

Algerian National Front or FNA [Moussa TOUATI]
Algerian Popular Movement or MPA [Amara BENYOUNES]
Algerian Rally or RA [Ali ZAGHDOUD]
Algeria's Hope Rally or TAJ [Amar GHOUL]
Dignity or El Karama [Mohamed BENHAMOU]
Ennour El Djazairi Party (Algerian Radiance Party) or PED [Badreddine BELBAZ]
Front for Justice and Development or El Adala [Abdallah DJABALLAH]
Future Front or El Mostakbel

[Abdelaziz BELAID]
Islamic Renaissance Movement or Ennahda Movement [Mohamed DOUIBI]
Justice and Development Front or FJD [Abdellah DJABALLAH]Movement of National Understanding or MEN
Movement for National Reform or Islah [Djilali GHOUINI]
Movement of Society for Peace or MSP [Abderrazak MOKRI]
National Democratic Rally (Rassemblement National Democratique) or RND [Ahmed OUYAHIA]
National Front for Social Justice or FNJS [Khaled BOUNEDJEMA]
National Liberation Front or FLN [Djamel OULD ABBES]
National Party for Solidarity and Development or PNSD [Dalila YALAQUI]
National Reform Movement or Islah [Djahid YOUNSI]
National Republican Alliance or ANR [Belkacem SAHLI]
New Dawn Party or PFJ [Tahar BENBAIBECHE]
New Generation or Jil Jadid [Soufiane DJILALI]
Oath of 1954 or Ahd 54 [Ali Fawzi REBAINE]
Party of Justice and Liberty [Mohammed SAID]
Rally for Culture and Democracy or RCD [Mohcine BELABBAS]
Socialist Forces Front or FFS [Mustafa BOUCHACHI]
Union of Democratic and Social Forces or UFDS [Noureddine BAHBOUH]
Vanguard of Freedoms [Ali BENFLIS]
Youth Party or PJ [Hamana BOUCHARMA]
Workers Party or PT [Louisa HANOUNE]

note: a law banning political parties based on religion was enacted in March 1997

INTERNATIONAL ORGANIZATION PARTICIPATION:

ABEDA, AfDB, AFESD, AMF, AMU, AU, BIS, CAEU, CD, FAO, G-15, G-24, G-77, IAEA, IBRD, ICAO, ICC (national committees), ICRM, IDA, IDB, IFAD, IFC, IFRCS, IHO, ILO, IMF, IMO, IMSO, Interpol, IOC, IOM, IPU, ISO, ITSO, ITU, ITUC (NGOs), LAS, MIGA, MONUSCO, NAM, OAPEC, OAS (observer), OIC, OPCW, OPEC, OSCE (partner), UN, UNCTAD, UNESCO, UNHCR, UNIDO, UNITAR, UNWTO, UPU, WCO, WHO, WIPO, WMO, WTO (observer)

DIPLOMATIC REPRESENTATION IN THE US:

chief of mission: Ambassador Madjid BOUGUERRA (since 23 February 2015)

chancery: 2118 Kalorama Road NW, Washington, DC 20008

telephone: [1] (202) 265-2800

FAX: [1] (202) 986-5906

consulate(s) general: New York

DIPLOMATIC REPRESENTATION FROM THE US:

chief of mission: Ambassador John P. DESROCHER (since 5 September 2017)

embassy: 05 Chemin Cheikh Bachir, El Ibrahimi, El-Biar 16030 Algeria

mailing address: B. P. 408, Alger-Gare, 16030 Algiers

telephone: [213] (0) 770-08-2000

FAX: [213] (0) 770-08-2064

FLAG DESCRIPTION:

two equal vertical bands of green (hoist side) and white; a red, 5-pointed star within a red crescent centered over the two-color boundary; the colors represent Islam (green), purity and peace (white), and liberty (red); the crescent and star are also Islamic symbols, but the crescent is more closed than those of other Muslim countries because Algerians believe the long crescent horns bring happiness

NATIONAL SYMBOL(S):

star and crescent, fennec fox; national colors: green, white, red

NATIONAL ANTHEM:

name: "Kassaman" (We Pledge)

lyrics/music: Mufdi ZAKARIAH/Mohamed FAWZI

note: adopted 1962; ZAKARIAH wrote "Kassaman" as a poem while imprisoned in Algiers by French colonial forces

ECONOMY :: ALGERIA

ECONOMY - OVERVIEW:

Algeria's economy remains dominated by the state, a legacy of the country's socialist post-independence development model. In recent years the Algerian Government has halted the privatization of state-owned industries and imposed restrictions on imports and foreign involvement in its economy, pursuing an explicit import substitution policy.

Hydrocarbons have long been the backbone of the economy, accounting for roughly 30% of GDP, 60% of budget revenues, and nearly 95% of export earnings. Algeria has the 10th-largest reserves of natural gas in the world - including the 3rd-largest reserves of shale gas - and is the 6th-largest gas exporter. It ranks 16th in proven oil reserves. Hydrocarbon exports enabled Algeria to maintain macroeconomic stability, amass large foreign currency reserves, and maintain low external debt while global oil prices were high. With lower oil prices since 2014, Algeria's foreign exchange reserves have declined by more than half and its oil stabilization fund has decreased from about $20 billion at the end of 2013 to about $7 billion in 2017, which is the statutory minimum.

Declining oil prices have also reduced the government's ability to use state-driven growth to distribute rents and fund generous public subsidies, and the government has been under pressure to reduce spending. Over the past three years, the government has enacted incremental increases in some taxes, resulting in modest increases in prices for gasoline, cigarettes, alcohol, and certain imported goods, but it has refrained from reducing subsidies, particularly for education, healthcare, and housing programs.

Algiers has increased protectionist measures since 2015 to limit its import bill and encourage domestic production of non-oil and gas industries. Since 2015, the government has imposed additional restrictions on access to foreign exchange for imports, and import quotas for specific products, such as cars. In January 2018 the government imposed an indefinite suspension on the importation of roughly 850 products, subject to periodic review.

President BOUTEFLIKA announced in fall 2017 that Algeria intends to develop its non-conventional energy resources. Algeria has struggled to develop non-hydrocarbon industries because of heavy regulation and an emphasis on state-driven growth. Algeria has not increased non-hydrocarbon exports, and hydrocarbon exports have declined because of field depletion and increased domestic demand.

GDP (PURCHASING POWER PARITY):

$630 billion (2017 est.)

$621.3 billion (2016 est.)

$602 billion (2015 est.)

note: data are in 2017 dollars

country comparison to the world: 36

GDP (OFFICIAL EXCHANGE RATE):

$167.6 billion (2017 est.) (2017 est.)

GDP - REAL GROWTH RATE:

1.4% (2017 est.)

3.2% (2016 est.)

3.7% (2015 est.)

country comparison to the world: 174

GDP - PER CAPITA (PPP):

$15,200 (2017 est.)

$15,200 (2016 est.)

$15,100 (2015 est.)

note: data are in 2017 dollars

country comparison to the world: 109

GROSS NATIONAL SAVING:

37.8% of GDP (2017 est.)

37.4% of GDP (2016 est.)

36.4% of GDP (2015 est.)

country comparison to the world: 13

GDP - COMPOSITION, BY END USE:

household consumption: 42.7% (2017 est.)

government consumption: 20.2% (2017 est.)

investment in fixed capital: 38.1% (2017 est.)

investment in inventories: 11.2% (2017 est.)

exports of goods and services: 23.6% (2017 est.)

imports of goods and services: -35.8% (2017 est.)

GDP - COMPOSITION, BY SECTOR OF ORIGIN:

agriculture: 13.3% (2017 est.)

industry: 39.3% (2017 est.)

services: 47.4% (2017 est.)

AGRICULTURE - PRODUCTS:

wheat, barley, oats, grapes, olives, citrus, fruits; sheep, cattle

INDUSTRIES:

petroleum, natural gas, light industries, mining, electrical, petrochemical, food processing

INDUSTRIAL PRODUCTION GROWTH RATE:

0.6% (2017 est.)

country comparison to the world: 164

LABOR FORCE:

11.82 million (2017 est.)

country comparison to the world: 50

LABOR FORCE - BY OCCUPATION:

agriculture: 10.8%

industry: 30.9%

services: 58.4% (2011 est.)

UNEMPLOYMENT RATE:

11.7% (2017 est.)

10.5% (2016 est.)

country comparison to the world: 155

POPULATION BELOW POVERTY LINE:

23% (2006 est.)

HOUSEHOLD INCOME OR CONSUMPTION BY PERCENTAGE SHARE:

lowest 10%: 26.8% (1995)

highest 10%: 26.8% (1995)

DISTRIBUTION OF FAMILY INCOME - GINI INDEX:

35.3 (1995)

country comparison to the world: 95

BUDGET:

revenues: 54.15 billion (2017 est.)

expenditures: 70.2 billion (2017 est.)

TAXES AND OTHER REVENUES:

32.3% (of GDP) (2017 est.)

country comparison to the world: 67

BUDGET SURPLUS (+) OR DEFICIT (-):

-9.6% (of GDP) (2017 est.)

country comparison to the world: 207

PUBLIC DEBT:

27.5% of GDP (2017 est.)

20.4% of GDP (2016 est.)

note: data cover central government debt as well as debt issued by subnational entities and intra-governmental debt

country comparison to the world: 170

FISCAL YEAR:

calendar year

INFLATION RATE (CONSUMER PRICES):

5.6% (2017 est.)

6.4% (2016 est.)

country comparison to the world: 179

CENTRAL BANK DISCOUNT RATE:

4% (31 December 2010)

4% (31 December 2009)

country comparison to the world: 99

COMMERCIAL BANK PRIME LENDING RATE:

8% (31 December 2017 est.)

8% (31 December 2016 est.)

country comparison to the world: 109

STOCK OF NARROW MONEY:

$84.56 billion (31 December 2017 est.)

$85.21 billion (31 December 2016 est.)

country comparison to the world: 44

STOCK OF BROAD MONEY:

$84.56 billion (31 December 2017 est.)

$85.21 billion (31 December 2016 est.)

country comparison to the world: 44

STOCK OF DOMESTIC CREDIT:

$110.2 billion (31 December 2017 est.)

$86.63 billion (31 December 2016 est.)

country comparison to the world: 54

MARKET VALUE OF PUBLICLY TRADED SHARES:

NA

CURRENT ACCOUNT BALANCE:

-$22.1 billion (2017 est.)

-$26.47 billion (2016 est.)

country comparison to the world: 199

EXPORTS:

$34.37 billion (2017 est.)

$29.06 billion (2016 est.)

country comparison to the world: 60

EXPORTS - PARTNERS:

Italy 17.4%, Spain 13%, France 11.9%, US 9.4%, Brazil 6.2%, Netherlands 5.5% (2017)

EXPORTS - COMMODITIES:

petroleum, natural gas, and petroleum products 97% (2009 est.)

IMPORTS:

$48.54 billion (2017 est.)

$49.43 billion (2016 est.)

country comparison to the world: 55

IMPORTS - COMMODITIES:

capital goods, foodstuffs, consumer goods

IMPORTS - PARTNERS:

China 18.2%, France 9.1%, Italy 8%, Germany 7%, Spain 6.9%, Turkey 4.4% (2017)

RESERVES OF FOREIGN EXCHANGE AND GOLD:

$97.89 billion (31 December 2017 est.)

$114.7 billion (31 December 2016 est.)

country comparison to the world: 26

DEBT - EXTERNAL:

$6.26 billion (31 December 2017 est.)

$5.088 billion (31 December 2016 est.)

country comparison to the world: 128

STOCK OF DIRECT FOREIGN INVESTMENT - AT HOME:

$29.05 billion (31 December 2017 est.)

$25.74 billion (31 December 2016 est.)

country comparison to the world: 72

STOCK OF DIRECT FOREIGN INVESTMENT - ABROAD:

$1.893 billion (31 December 2017 est.)

$2.025 billion (31 December 2016 est.)

country comparison to the world: 85

EXCHANGE RATES:

Algerian dinars (DZD) per US dollar -

108.9 (2017 est.)

109.443 (2016 est.)

109.443 (2015 est.)

100.691 (2014 est.)

80.579 (2013 est.)

ENERGY :: ALGERIA

ELECTRICITY ACCESS:

population without electricity: 400,000 (2016)

electrification - total population: 99% (2016)

electrification - urban areas: 100% (2016)

electrification - rural areas: 97% (2016)

ELECTRICITY - PRODUCTION:

66.89 billion kWh (2016 est.)

country comparison to the world: 42

ELECTRICITY - CONSUMPTION:

55.96 billion kWh (2016 est.)

country comparison to the world: 46

ELECTRICITY - EXPORTS:

641 million kWh (2015 est.)

country comparison to the world: 65

ELECTRICITY - IMPORTS:

257 million kWh (2016 est.)

country comparison to the world: 91

ELECTRICITY - INSTALLED GENERATING CAPACITY:

19.27 million kW (2016 est.)

country comparison to the world: 45

ELECTRICITY - FROM FOSSIL FUELS:

96% of total installed capacity (2016 est.)

country comparison to the world: 36

ELECTRICITY - FROM NUCLEAR FUELS:

0% of total installed capacity (2017 est.)

country comparison to the world: 34

ELECTRICITY - FROM HYDROELECTRIC PLANTS:

1% of total installed capacity (2017 est.)

country comparison to the world: 144

ELECTRICITY - FROM OTHER RENEWABLE SOURCES:

2% of total installed capacity (2017 est.)

country comparison to the world: 130

CRUDE OIL - PRODUCTION:

1.306 million bbl/day (2017 est.)

country comparison to the world: 18

CRUDE OIL - EXPORTS:

756,400 bbl/day (2015 est.)

country comparison to the world: 15

CRUDE OIL - IMPORTS:

5,340 bbl/day (2015 est.)

country comparison to the world: 75

CRUDE OIL - PROVED RESERVES:

12.2 billion bbl (1 January 2018 est.)

country comparison to the world: 15

REFINED PETROLEUM PRODUCTS - PRODUCTION:

627,900 bbl/day (2015 est.)

country comparison to the world: 29

REFINED PETROLEUM PRODUCTS - CONSUMPTION:

405,000 bbl/day (2016 est.)

country comparison to the world: 37

REFINED PETROLEUM PRODUCTS - EXPORTS:

578,800 bbl/day (2015 est.)

country comparison to the world: 15

REFINED PETROLEUM PRODUCTS - IMPORTS:

82,930 bbl/day (2015 est.)

country comparison to the world: 61

NATURAL GAS - PRODUCTION:

93.5 billion cu m (2017 est.)

country comparison to the world: 10

NATURAL GAS - CONSUMPTION:

41.28 billion cu m (2017 est.)

country comparison to the world: 25

NATURAL GAS - EXPORTS:

53.88 billion cu m (2017 est.)

country comparison to the world: 7

NATURAL GAS - IMPORTS:

0 cu m (2017 est.)

country comparison to the world: 83

NATURAL GAS - PROVED RESERVES:

4.504 trillion cu m (1 January 2018 est.)

country comparison to the world: 10

CARBON DIOXIDE EMISSIONS FROM CONSUMPTION OF ENERGY:

135.9 million Mt (2017 est.)

country comparison to the world: 34

COMMUNICATIONS :: ALGERIA

TELEPHONES - FIXED LINES:

total subscriptions: 3,130,090 (2017 est.)

subscriptions per 100 inhabitants: 8 (2017 est.)

country comparison to the world: 45

TELEPHONES - MOBILE CELLULAR:

total subscriptions: 49,873,389 (2017 est.)

subscriptions per 100 inhabitants: 122 (2017 est.)

country comparison to the world: 29

TELEPHONE SYSTEM:

general assessment: privatization of Algeria's telecommunications sector began in 2000; three mobile-cellular licenses have been issued; regulator permits network operators to extend LTE services to additional provinces; a consortium led by Egypt's Orascom Telecom won a 15-year license to build and operate a fixed-line network in Algeria; migration to 5G (2017)

domestic: a limited network of fixed-lines with a teledensity of less than 10 telephones per 100 persons has been offset by the rapid increase in mobile-cellular subscribership; mobile-cellular teledensity was roughly 122 telephones per 100 persons (2017)

international: country code - 213; landing point for the SEA-ME-WE-4 fiber-optic submarine cable system that provides links to Europe, the Middle East, and Asia; microwave radio relay to Italy, France, Spain, Morocco, and Tunisia; coaxial cable to Morocco and Tunisia; new submarine cables to link to the US and France; (2016)

BROADCAST MEDIA:

state-run Radio-Television Algerienne operates the broadcast media and carries programming in Arabic, Berber dialects, and French; use of satellite dishes is widespread, providing easy access to European and Arab satellite stations; state-run radio operates several national networks and roughly 40 regional radio stations (2009)

INTERNET COUNTRY CODE:

.dz

INTERNET USERS:

total: 17,291,463 (July 2016 est.)

percent of population: 42.9% (July 2016 est.)

country comparison to the world: 37

BROADBAND - FIXED SUBSCRIPTIONS:

total: 3,166,907 (2017 est.)

subscriptions per 100 inhabitants: 8 (2017 est.)

country comparison to the world: 37

TRANSPORTATION :: ALGERIA

NATIONAL AIR TRANSPORT SYSTEM:

number of registered air carriers: 4 (2015)

inventory of registered aircraft operated by air carriers: 74 (2015)

annual passenger traffic on registered air carriers: 5,910,835 (2015)

annual freight traffic on registered air carriers: 24,723,377 mt-km (2015)

CIVIL AIRCRAFT REGISTRATION COUNTRY CODE PREFIX:

7T (2016)

AIRPORTS:

157 (2016)

country comparison to the world: 36

AIRPORTS - WITH PAVED RUNWAYS:

total: 64 (2017)

over 3,047 m: 12 (2017)

2,438 to 3,047 m: 29 (2017)

1,524 to 2,437 m: 17 (2017)

914 to 1,523 m: 5 (2017)

under 914 m: 1 (2017)

AIRPORTS - WITH UNPAVED RUNWAYS:

total: 93 (2013)

2,438 to 3,047 m: 2 (2013)

1,524 to 2,437 m: 18 (2013)

914 to 1,523 m: 39 (2013)

under 914 m: 34 (2013)

HELIPORTS:

3 (2013)

PIPELINES:

2600 km condensate, 16415 km gas, 3447 km liquid petroleum gas, 7036 km oil, 144 km refined products (2013)

RAILWAYS:

total: 3,973 km (2014)

standard gauge: 2,888 km 1.432-m gauge (283 km electrified) (2014)

narrow gauge: 1,085 km 1.055-m gauge (2014)

country comparison to the world: 49

ROADWAYS:

total: 113,655 km (2010)

paved: 87,605 km (includes 645 km of expressways) (2010)

unpaved: 26,050 km (2010)

country comparison to the world: 43

MERCHANT MARINE:

total: 110 (2017)

by type: bulk carrier 3, general cargo 13, oil tanker 9, other 85 (2017)

country comparison to the world: 81

PORTS AND TERMINALS:

major seaport(s): Algiers, Annaba, Arzew, Bejaia, Djendjene, Jijel, Mostaganem, Oran, Skikda

LNG terminal(s) (export): Arzew, Bethioua, Skikda

MILITARY AND SECURITY :: ALGERIA

MILITARY EXPENDITURES:

5.81% of GDP (2017)

6.55% of GDP (2016)

6.32% of GDP (2015)

5.54% of GDP (2014)

4.84% of GDP (2013)

country comparison to the world: 5

MILITARY BRANCHES:

People's National Army (Armee Nationale Populaire, ANP): Land Forces (Forces Terrestres, FT), Navy of the Republic of Algeria (Marine de la Republique Algerienne, MRA), Air Force (Al-Quwwat al-Jawwiya al-Jaza'eriya, QJJ), Territorial Air Defense Force (2016)

MILITARY SERVICE AGE AND OBLIGATION:

18 is the legal minimum age for voluntary military service; 19-30 years of age for compulsory service; conscript service obligation is 18 months (6 months basic training, 12 months civil projects) (2018)

TERRORISM :: ALGERIA

TERRORIST GROUPS - HOME BASED:

al-Qa'ida in the Islamic Maghreb (AQIM):
aim: overthrow various African regimes and replace them with one ruled by sharia; establish a regional Islamic caliphate across all of North and West Africa
area(s) of operation: leadership headquartered in Algeria; operates in Tunisia, Libya, and northern Mali
note: al-Qa'ida's affiliate in North Africa; Tunisia-based branch known as the Uqbah bin Nafi Battalion; Mali-based cadre merged with allies to form JNIM in March 2017, which pledged allegiance to AQIM and al-Qa'ida (April 2018)

Islamic State of Iraq and ash-Sham (ISIS)-Algeria:
aim(s): replace the Algerian Government with an Islamic state and implement ISIS's strict interpretation of sharia
area(s) of operation: maintains an operational and recruitment presence mostly in the northeast
note: formerly known as Jund al-Khilafa - Algeria (JAK-A) (April 2018)

TRANSNATIONAL ISSUES :: ALGERIA

DISPUTES - INTERNATIONAL:

Algeria and many other states reject Moroccan administration of Western Sahara; the Polisario Front, exiled in Algeria, represents the Sahrawi Arab Democratic RepublicAlgeria's border with Morocco remains an irritant to bilateral relations, each nation accusing the other of harboring militants and arms smugglingdormant disputes include Libyan claims of about 32,000 sq km still reflected on its maps of southeastern Algeria and the National Liberation Front's (FLN) assertions of a claim to Chirac Pastures in southeastern Morocco

REFUGEES AND INTERNALLY DISPLACED PERSONS:

refugees (country of origin): more than 100,000 (Western Saharan Sahrawi, mostly living in Algerian-sponsored camps in the southwestern Algerian town of Tindouf) (2018)

TRAFFICKING IN PERSONS:

current situation: Algeria is a transit and, to a lesser extent, a destination and source country for women subjected to forced labor and sex trafficking and, to a lesser extent, men subjected to forced labor; criminal networks, sometimes extending to sub-Saharan Africa and to Europe, are involved in human smuggling and trafficking in Algeria; sub-Saharan adults enter Algeria voluntarily but illegally, often with the aid of smugglers, for onward travel to Europe, but some of the women are forced into prostitution, domestic service, and begging; some sub-Saharan men, mostly from Mali, are forced into domestic servitude; some Algerian women and children are also forced into prostitution domestically

tier rating: Tier 3 – Algeria does not fully comply with the minimum standards for the elimination of trafficking and is not making significant efforts to do so: some officials denied the existence of human trafficking, hindering law enforcement efforts; the government reported its first conviction under its anti-trafficking law; one potential trafficking case was investigated in 2014, but no suspected offenders were arrested; no progress was made in identifying victims among vulnerable groups or referring them to NGO-run protection service, which left trafficking victims subject to arrest and detention; no anti-trafficking public awareness or educational campaigns were conducted (2015)

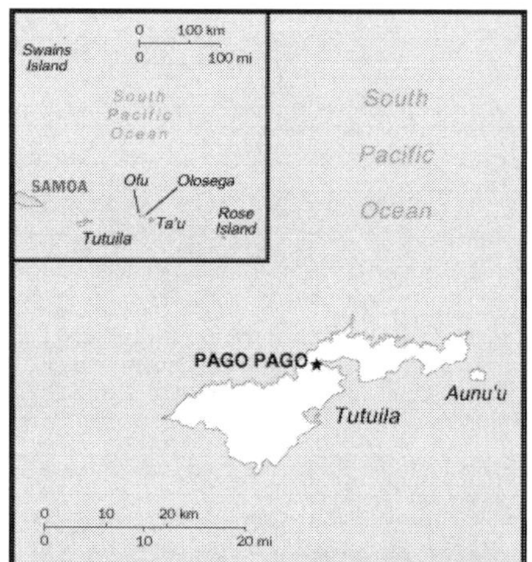

AUSTRALIA - OCEANIA :: AMERICAN SAMOA

INTRODUCTION :: AMERICAN SAMOA

BACKGROUND:

Settled as early as 1000 B.C., Samoa was not reached by European explorers until the 18th century. International rivalries in the latter half of the 19th century were settled by an 1899 treaty in which Germany and the US divided the Samoan archipelago. The US formally occupied its portion - a smaller group of eastern islands with the excellent harbor of Pago Pago - the following year.

GEOGRAPHY :: AMERICAN SAMOA

LOCATION:

Oceania, group of islands in the South Pacific Ocean, about halfway between Hawaii and New Zealand

GEOGRAPHIC COORDINATES:

14 20 S, 170 00 W

MAP REFERENCES:

Oceania

AREA:

total: 224 sq km

land: 224 sq km

water: 0 sq km

note: includes Rose Island and Swains Island

country comparison to the world: 216

AREA - COMPARATIVE:

slightly larger than Washington, DC

LAND BOUNDARIES:

0 km

COASTLINE:

116 km

MARITIME CLAIMS:

territorial sea: 12 nm

exclusive economic zone: 200 nm

CLIMATE:

tropical marine, moderated by southeast trade winds; annual rainfall averages about 3 m; rainy season (November to April), dry season (May to October); little seasonal temperature variation

TERRAIN:

five volcanic islands with rugged peaks and limited coastal plains, two coral atolls (Rose Island, Swains Island)

ELEVATION:

0 m lowest point: Pacific Ocean

964 highest point: Lata Mountain

NATURAL RESOURCES:

pumice, pumicite

LAND USE:

agricultural land: 21.8% (2014 est.)

arable land: 61.22% (2014 est.) / permanent crops: 38.78% (2014 est.) / permanent pasture: 0% (2014 est.)

forest: 78.2% (2014 est.)

other: 0% (2014 est.)

IRRIGATED LAND:

0 sq km (2012)

NATURAL HAZARDS:

cyclones common from December to March

volcanism: limited volcanic activity on the Ofu and Olosega Islands; neither has erupted since the 19th century

ENVIRONMENT - CURRENT ISSUES:

limited supply of drinking water; pollution; waste disposal; coastal and stream alteration; soil erosion

GEOGRAPHY - NOTE:

Pago Pago has one of the best natural deepwater harbors in the South Pacific Ocean, sheltered by shape from rough seas and protected by peripheral mountains from high winds; strategic location in the South Pacific Ocean

PEOPLE AND SOCIETY :: AMERICAN SAMOA

POPULATION:

50,826 (July 2018 est.)

country comparison to the world: 211

NATIONALITY:

noun: American Samoan(s) (US nationals)

adjective: American Samoan

ETHNIC GROUPS:

Pacific Islander 92.6% (includes Samoan 88.9%, Tongan 2.9%, other .8%), Asian 3.6% (includes Filipino 2.2%, other 1.4%), mixed 2.7%, other 1.2% (2010 est.)

note: data represent population by ethnic origin or race

LANGUAGES:

Samoan 88.6% (closely related to Hawaiian and other Polynesian languages), English 3.9%, Tongan 2.7%, other Pacific islander 3%, other 1.8% (2010 est.)

note: most people are bilingual

RELIGIONS:

Christian 98.3%, other 1%, unaffiliated 0.7% (2010 est.)

AGE STRUCTURE:

0-14 years: 29.59% (male 7,732 /female 7,305)

15-24 years: 18.42% (male 4,695 /female 4,669)

25-54 years: 36.79% (male 9,255 /female 9,442)

55-64 years: 8.96% (male 2,244 /female 2,310)

65 years and over: 6.24% (male 1,486 /female 1,688) (2018 est.)

MEDIAN AGE:

total: 26.1 years

male: 25.6 years

female: 26.5 years (2018 est.)

country comparison to the world: 151

POPULATION GROWTH RATE:

-1.35% (2018 est.)

country comparison to the world: 231

BIRTH RATE:

19 births/1,000 population (2018 est.)

country comparison to the world: 83

DEATH RATE:

5.9 deaths/1,000 population (2018 est.)

country comparison to the world: 166

NET MIGRATION RATE:

-26.7 migrant(s)/1,000 population (2017 est.)

country comparison to the world: 221

URBANIZATION:

urban population: 87.2% of total population (2018)

rate of urbanization: 0.07% annual rate of change (2015-20 est.)

MAJOR URBAN AREAS - POPULATION:

49,000 PAGO PAGO (capital) (2018)

SEX RATIO:

at birth: 1.06 male(s)/female (2017 est.)

0-14 years: 0.96 male(s)/female (2017 est.)

15-24 years: 0.96 male(s)/female (2017 est.)

25-54 years: 1.06 male(s)/female (2017 est.)

55-64 years: 0.96 male(s)/female (2017 est.)

65 years and over: 0.85 male(s)/female (2017 est.)

total population: 1 male(s)/female (2017 est.)

INFANT MORTALITY RATE:

total: 10.8 deaths/1,000 live births (2018 est.)

male: 12.7 deaths/1,000 live births (2018 est.)

female: 8.9 deaths/1,000 live births (2018 est.)

country comparison to the world: 128

LIFE EXPECTANCY AT BIRTH:

total population: 73.9 years (2018 est.)

male: 71.6 years (2018 est.)

female: 76.2 years (2018 est.)

country comparison to the world: 131

TOTAL FERTILITY RATE:

2.57 children born/woman (2018 est.)

country comparison to the world: 75

DRINKING WATER SOURCE:

improved:

urban: 100% of population (2015 est.)

rural: 100% of population (2015 est.)

total: 100% of population (2015 est.)

unimproved:

urban: 0% of population (2015 est.)

rural: 0% of population (2015 est.)

total: 0% of population (2015 est.)

SANITATION FACILITY ACCESS:

improved:

urban: 62.5% of population (2015 est.)

rural: 62.5% of population (2015 est.)

total: 62.5% of population (2015 est.)

unimproved:

urban: 37.5% of population (2015 est.)

rural: 37.5% of population (2015 est.)

total: 37.5% of population (2015 est.)

HIV/AIDS - ADULT PREVALENCE RATE:

NA

HIV/AIDS - PEOPLE LIVING WITH HIV/AIDS:

NA

HIV/AIDS - DEATHS:

NA

MAJOR INFECTIOUS DISEASES:

note: active local transmission of Zika virus by Aedes species mosquitoes has been identified in this country (as of August 2016); it poses an important risk (a large number of cases possible) among US citizens if bitten by an infective mosquito; other less common ways to get Zika are through sex, via blood transfusion, or during pregnancy, in which the pregnant woman passes Zika virus to her fetus

EDUCATION EXPENDITURES:

NA

GOVERNMENT :: AMERICAN SAMOA

COUNTRY NAME:

conventional long form: American Samoa

conventional short form: American Samoa

abbreviation: AS

etymology: the name Samoa is composed of two parts, "sa" meaning "sacred" and "moa" meaning "center," so the name can mean Holy Center; alternatively, it can mean "place of the sacred moa bird" of Polynesian mythology

DEPENDENCY STATUS:

unincorporated unorganized territory of the US; administered by the Office of Insular Affairs, US Department of the Interior

GOVERNMENT TYPE:

presidential democracy; a self-governing territory of the US

CAPITAL:

name: Pago Pago

geographic coordinates: 14 16 S, 170 42 W

time difference: UTC-11 (6 hours behind Washington, DC, during Standard Time)

note: pronounced "pahn-go pahn-go"

ADMINISTRATIVE DIVISIONS:

none (territory of the US); there are no first-order administrative divisions as defined by the US Government, but there are 3 districts and 2 islands* at the second order; Eastern, Manu'a, Rose Island*, Swains Island*, Western

INDEPENDENCE:

none (territory of the US)

NATIONAL HOLIDAY:

Flag Day, 17 April (1900)

CONSTITUTION:

history: adopted 17 October 1960; revised 1 July 1967 (2017)

amendments: proposed by either house of the Legislative Assembly; passage requires three-fifths majority vote by the membership of each house, approval in a referendum, and approval by the US Secretary of the Interior; amended 1971, 1977, 1979 (2017)

LEGAL SYSTEM:

mixed legal system of US common law and customary law

CITIZENSHIP:

see United States

SUFFRAGE:

18 years of age; universal

EXECUTIVE BRANCH:

chief of state: President Donald J. TRUMP (since 20 January 2017); Vice President Michael R. PENCE (since 20 January 2017)

head of government: Governor Lolo Matalasi MOLIGA (since 3 January 2013)

cabinet: Cabinet consists of 12 department directors appointed by the governor with the consent of the Legislature or Fono

elections/appointments: president and vice president indirectly elected on the same ballot by an Electoral College of 'electors' chosen from each state to serve a 4-year term (eligible for a second term); under the US Constitution, residents of unincorporated territories, such as American Samoa, do not vote in elections for US president and vice president; however, they may vote in Democratic and Republican presidential primary elections; governor and lieutenant governor directly elected on the same ballot by absolute majority popular vote in 2 rounds if needed for a 4-year term (eligible for a second term); election last held on 8 November 2016 (next to be held in November 2020)

election results: Lolo Matalasi MOLIGA reelected governor in first round; percent of vote - Lolo Matalasi MOLIGA (independent) 60.2%, Faoa Aitofele SUNIA (Democratic Party) 35.8%, Tuika TUIKA (independent) 4%

LEGISLATIVE BRANCH:

description: bicameral Legislature or Fono consists of:
Senate (18 seats; members indirectly selected by regional governing councils to serve 4-year terms)
House of Representatives (21 seats; 20 members directly elected by simple majority vote and 1 decided by public meeting on Swains Island; members serve 2-year terms)

elections:
Senate - last held on 8 November 2016 (next to be held in November 2020)
House of Representatives - last held on 8 November 2016 (next to be held in November 2018)

election results:
Senate - percent of vote by party - NA; seats by party - independent 18
House of Representatives - percent of vote by party - NA; seats by party - independent 20

note: American Samoa elects 1 member by simple majority vote to serve a 2-year term as a delegate to the US House of Representatives; the delegate can vote when serving on a committee and when the House meets as the Committee of the Whole House, but not when legislation is submitted for a "full floor" House vote; election of delegate last held on 8 November 2016 (next to be held in November 2018)

JUDICIAL BRANCH:

highest courts: High Court of American Samoa (consists of the chief justice, associate chief justice, and 6 Samoan associate judges and organized into trial, family, drug, and appellate divisions); note - American Samoa has no US federal courts

judge selection and term of office: chief justice and associate chief justice appointed by the US Secretary of the Interior to serve for life; Samoan associate judges appointed by the governor to serve for life

subordinate courts: district and village courts

POLITICAL PARTIES AND LEADERS:

Democratic Party [Fagafaga Daniel LANGKILDE]
Republican Party [Utu Abe MALAE, chairman]

INTERNATIONAL ORGANIZATION PARTICIPATION:

AOSIS (observer), Interpol (subbureau), IOC, PIF (observer), SPC

DIPLOMATIC REPRESENTATION IN THE US:

none (territory of the US)

DIPLOMATIC REPRESENTATION FROM THE US:

none (territory of the US)

FLAG DESCRIPTION:

blue, with a white triangle edged in red that is based on the fly side and extends to the hoist side; a brown and white American bald eagle flying toward the hoist side is carrying 2 traditional Samoan symbols of authority, a war club known as a "fa'alaufa'i" (upper; left talon), and a coconut-fiber fly whisk known as a "fue" (lower; right talon); the combination of symbols broadly mimics that seen on the US Great Seal and reflects the relationship between the US and American Samoa

NATIONAL SYMBOL(S):

a fue (coconut fiber fly whisk; representing wisdom) crossed with a to'oto'o (staff; representing authority); national colors: red, white, blue

NATIONAL ANTHEM:

name: "Amerika Samoa" (American Samoa)

lyrics/music: Mariota Tiumalu TUIASOSOPO/Napoleon Andrew TUITELELEAPAGA

note: local anthem adopted 1950; as a territory of the United States, "The Star-Spangled Banner" is official (see United States)

ECONOMY :: AMERICAN SAMOA

ECONOMY - OVERVIEW:

American Samoa s a traditional Polynesian economy in which more than 90% of the land is communally owned. Economic activity is strongly linked to the US with which American Samoa conducts most of its commerce. Tuna fishing and processing are the backbone of the private sector with processed fish products as the primary exports. The fish processing business accounted for 15.5% of employment in 2015.

In late September 2009, an earthquake and the resulting tsunami devastated American Samoa and nearby Samoa, disrupting transportation and power generation, and resulting in about 200 deaths. The US Federal Emergency Management Agency oversaw a relief program of nearly $25 million. Transfers from the US Government add substantially to American Samoa's economic well-being.

Attempts by the government to develop a larger and broader economy are restrained by Samoa's remote location, its limited transportation, and its devastating hurricanes. Tourism has some potential as a source of income and jobs.

GDP (PURCHASING POWER PARITY):

$658 million (2016 est.)

$674.9 million (2015 est.)

$666.9 million (2014 est.)

note: data are in 2016 US dollars

country comparison to the world: 209

GDP (OFFICIAL EXCHANGE RATE):

$658 million (2016 est.) (2016 est.)

GDP - REAL GROWTH RATE:

-2.5% (2016 est.)

1.2% (2015 est.)

1% (2014 est.)

country comparison to the world: 208

GDP - PER CAPITA (PPP):

$11,200 (2016 est.)

$11,300 (2015 est.)

$11,200 (2014 est.)

country comparison to the world: 134

GDP - COMPOSITION, BY END USE:

household consumption: 66.4% (2016 est.)

government consumption: 49.7% (2016 est.)

investment in fixed capital: 7.3% (2016 est.)

investment in inventories: 5.1% (2016 est.)

exports of goods and services: 65% (2016 est.)

imports of goods and services: -93.5% (2016 est.)

GDP - COMPOSITION, BY SECTOR OF ORIGIN:

agriculture: 27.4% (2012)

industry: 12.4% (2012)

services: 60.2% (2012)

AGRICULTURE - PRODUCTS:

bananas, coconuts, vegetables, taro, breadfruit, yams, copra, pineapples, papayas; dairy products, livestock

INDUSTRIES:

tuna canneries (largely supplied by foreign fishing vessels), handicrafts

INDUSTRIAL PRODUCTION GROWTH RATE:

NA

LABOR FORCE:

17,850 (2015 est.)

country comparison to the world: 213

LABOR FORCE - BY OCCUPATION:

agriculture: NA

industry: 15.5%

services: 46.4% (2015 est.)

UNEMPLOYMENT RATE:

29.8% (2005)

country comparison to the world: 206

POPULATION BELOW POVERTY LINE:

NA

HOUSEHOLD INCOME OR CONSUMPTION BY PERCENTAGE SHARE:

lowest 10%: NA

highest 10%: NA

BUDGET:

revenues: 249 million (2016 est.)

expenditures: 262.5 million (2016 est.)

TAXES AND OTHER REVENUES:

37.8% (of GDP) (2016 est.)

country comparison to the world: 53

BUDGET SURPLUS (+) OR DEFICIT (-):

-2.1% (of GDP) (2016 est.)

country comparison to the world: 107

PUBLIC DEBT:

12.2% of GDP (2016 est.)

country comparison to the world: 197

FISCAL YEAR:

1 October - 30 September

INFLATION RATE (CONSUMER PRICES):

-0.5% (2015 est.)

1.4% (2014 est.)

country comparison to the world: 5

EXPORTS:

$428 million (2016 est.)

$427 million (2015 est.)

country comparison to the world: 179

EXPORTS - PARTNERS:

Australia 25%, Ghana 19%, Indonesia 15.6%, Burma 10.4%, Portugal 5.1% (2017)

EXPORTS - COMMODITIES:

canned tuna 93%

IMPORTS:

$615 million (2016 est.)

$657 million (2015 est.)

country comparison to the world: 193

IMPORTS - COMMODITIES:

raw materials for canneries, food, petroleum products, machinery and parts

IMPORTS - PARTNERS:

Fiji 10.7%, Singapore 10.4%, NZ 10.4%, South Korea 9.3%, Samoa 8.2%, Kenya 6.4%, Australia 5.2% (2017)

DEBT - EXTERNAL:

NA

EXCHANGE RATES:

the US dollar is used

ENERGY :: AMERICAN SAMOA

ELECTRICITY ACCESS:

population without electricity: 22,219 (2012)

electrification - total population: 59% (2012)

electrification - urban areas: 60% (2012)

electrification - rural areas: 45% (2012)

ELECTRICITY - PRODUCTION:

169 million kWh (2016 est.)

country comparison to the world: 195

ELECTRICITY - CONSUMPTION:

157.2 million kWh (2016 est.)

country comparison to the world: 197

ELECTRICITY - EXPORTS:

0 kWh (2016 est.)

country comparison to the world: 97

ELECTRICITY - IMPORTS:

0 kWh (2016 est.)

country comparison to the world: 118

ELECTRICITY - INSTALLED GENERATING CAPACITY:

43,000 kW (2016 est.)

country comparison to the world: 195

ELECTRICITY - FROM FOSSIL FUELS:

98% of total installed capacity (2016 est.)

country comparison to the world: 27

ELECTRICITY - FROM NUCLEAR FUELS:

0% of total installed capacity (2017 est.)

country comparison to the world: 35

ELECTRICITY - FROM HYDROELECTRIC PLANTS:

0% of total installed capacity (2017 est.)

country comparison to the world: 152

ELECTRICITY - FROM OTHER RENEWABLE SOURCES:

2% of total installed capacity (2017 est.)

country comparison to the world: 131

CRUDE OIL - PRODUCTION:

0 bbl/day (2017 est.)

country comparison to the world: 102

CRUDE OIL - EXPORTS:

0 bbl/day (2015 est.)

country comparison to the world: 83

CRUDE OIL - IMPORTS:

0 bbl/day (2015 est.)

country comparison to the world: 86

CRUDE OIL - PROVED RESERVES:

0 bbl (1 January 2018 est.)

country comparison to the world: 100

REFINED PETROLEUM PRODUCTS - PRODUCTION:

0 bbl/day (2015 est.)

country comparison to the world: 111

REFINED PETROLEUM PRODUCTS - CONSUMPTION:

2,375 bbl/day (2016 est.)

country comparison to the world: 192

REFINED PETROLEUM PRODUCTS - EXPORTS:

0 bbl/day (2015 est.)

country comparison to the world: 125

REFINED PETROLEUM PRODUCTS - IMPORTS:

2,346 bbl/day (2015 est.)

country comparison to the world: 188

NATURAL GAS - PRODUCTION:

0 cu m (2017 est.)

country comparison to the world: 97

NATURAL GAS - CONSUMPTION:

0 cu m (2017 est.)

country comparison to the world: 117

NATURAL GAS - EXPORTS:

0 cu m (2017 est.)

country comparison to the world: 59

NATURAL GAS - IMPORTS:

0 cu m (2017 est.)

country comparison to the world: 84

NATURAL GAS - PROVED RESERVES:

0 cu m (1 January 2014 est.)

country comparison to the world: 103

CARBON DIOXIDE EMISSIONS FROM CONSUMPTION OF ENERGY:

361,100 Mt (2017 est.)

country comparison to the world: 189

COMMUNICATIONS :: AMERICAN SAMOA

TELEPHONES - FIXED LINES:

total subscriptions: 10,000 (July 2016 est.)

subscriptions per 100 inhabitants: 18 (July 2016 est.)

country comparison to the world: 196

TELEPHONE SYSTEM:

general assessment: good telex, telegraph, facsimile, and cellular telephone services; one of the most complete and modern telecommunications systems in the South Pacific Islands; all inhabited islands have telephone connectivity (2017)

domestic: 18 per 100 fixed-line teledensity, domestic satellite system with 1 Comsat earth station (2017)

international: country code - 1-684; satellite earth station - 1 (Intelsat-Pacific Ocean)

BROADCAST MEDIA:

3 TV stations; multi-channel pay TV services are available; about a dozen radio stations, some of which are repeater stations (2009)

INTERNET COUNTRY CODE:

.as

INTERNET USERS:

total: 17,000 (July 2016 est.)

percent of population: 31.3% (July 2016 est.)

country comparison to the world: 207

TRANSPORTATION :: AMERICAN SAMOA

AIRPORTS:

3 (2016)

country comparison to the world: 192

AIRPORTS - WITH PAVED RUNWAYS:

total: 3 (2017)

over 3,047 m: 1 (2017)

914 to 1,523 m: 1 (2017)

under 914 m: 1 (2017)

ROADWAYS:

total: 241 km (2008)

country comparison to the world: 208

PORTS AND TERMINALS:

major seaport(s): Pago Pago

MILITARY AND SECURITY :: AMERICAN SAMOA

MILITARY - NOTE:

defense is the responsibility of the US

TRANSNATIONAL ISSUES :: AMERICAN SAMOA

DISPUTES - INTERNATIONAL:

Tokelau included American Samoa's Swains Island (Olosega) in its 2006 draft independence constitution

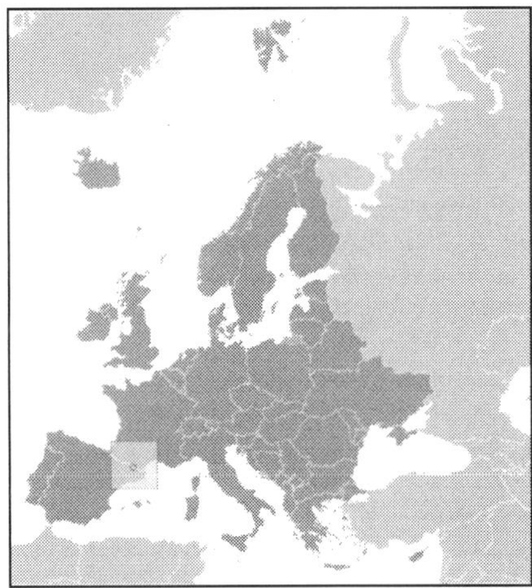

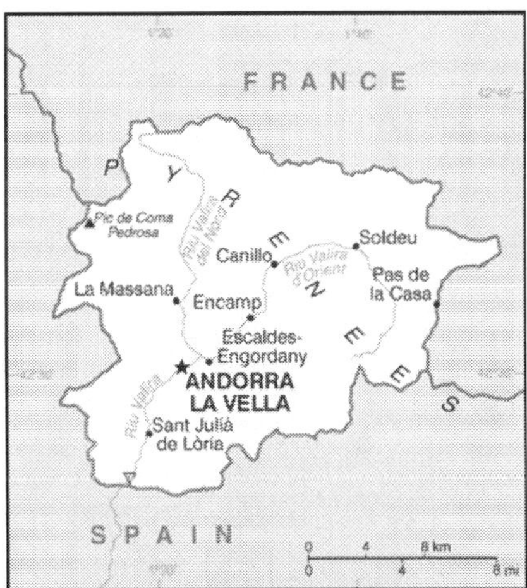

EUROPE :: ANDORRA

INTRODUCTION :: ANDORRA

BACKGROUND:

The landlocked Principality of Andorra is one of the smallest states in Europe, nestled high in the Pyrenees between the French and Spanish borders. For 715 years, from 1278 to 1993, Andorrans lived under a unique coprincipality, ruled by French and Spanish leaders (from 1607 onward, the French chief of state and the Bishop of Urgell). In 1993, this feudal system was modified with the introduction of a modern constitution; the co-princes remained as titular heads of state, but the government transformed into a parliamentary democracy.

Andorra has become a popular tourist destination visited by approximately 8 million people each year drawn by the winter sports, summer climate, and duty-free shopping. Andorra has also become a wealthy international commercial center because of its mature banking sector and low taxes. As part of its effort to modernize its economy, Andorra has opened to foreign investment, and engaged in other reforms, such as advancing tax initiatives aimed at supporting a broader infrastructure. Although not a member of the EU, Andorra enjoys a special relationship with the bloc that is governed by various customs and cooperation agreements and uses the euro as its national currency.

GEOGRAPHY :: ANDORRA

LOCATION:

Southwestern Europe, Pyrenees mountains, on the border between France and Spain

GEOGRAPHIC COORDINATES:

42 30 N, 1 30 E

MAP REFERENCES:

Europe

AREA:

total: 468 sq km

land: 468 sq km

water: 0 sq km

country comparison to the world: 196

AREA - COMPARATIVE:

2.5 times the size of Washington, DC

LAND BOUNDARIES:

total: 118 km

border countries (2): France 55 km, Spain 63 km

COASTLINE:

0 km (landlocked)

MARITIME CLAIMS:

none (landlocked)

CLIMATE:

temperate; snowy, cold winters and warm, dry summers

TERRAIN:

rugged mountains dissected by narrow valleys

ELEVATION:

mean elevation: 1,996 m

elevation extremes: 840 m lowest point: Riu Runer

2946 highest point: Pic de Coma Pedrosa

NATURAL RESOURCES:

hydropower, mineral water, timber, iron ore, lead

LAND USE:

agricultural land: 44.47% (2014 est.)

arable land: 13.4% (2014 est.) / permanent crops: 0% (2014 est.) / permanent pasture: 86.6% (2014 est.)

forest: 34% (2014 est.)

other: 21.5% (2014 est.)

IRRIGATED LAND:

0 sq km (2012)

POPULATION DISTRIBUTION:

population is unevenly distributed and is concentrated in the seven urbanized valleys that make up the country's parishes (political administrative divisions)

NATURAL HAZARDS:

avalanches

ENVIRONMENT - CURRENT ISSUES:

deforestation; overgrazing of mountain meadows contributes to soil erosion; air pollution; wastewater treatment and solid waste disposal

ENVIRONMENT - INTERNATIONAL AGREEMENTS:

party to: Biodiversity, Desertification, Hazardous Wastes, Ozone Layer Protection

signed, but not ratified: none of the selected agreements

GEOGRAPHY - NOTE:

landlocked; straddles a number of important crossroads in the Pyrenees

PEOPLE AND SOCIETY :: ANDORRA

POPULATION:

85,708 (July 2018 est.)

country comparison to the world: 200

NATIONALITY:

noun: Andorran(s)

adjective: Andorran

ETHNIC GROUPS:

Andorran 45.5%, Spanish 26.6%, Portuguese 12.9%, French 5.2%, other 9.8% (2017 est.)

note: data represent population by nationality

LANGUAGES:

Catalan (official), French, Castilian, Portuguese

RELIGIONS:

Roman Catholic (predominant)

AGE STRUCTURE:

0-14 years: 14.06% (male 6,197 /female 5,856)

15-24 years: 9.78% (male 4,344 /female 4,035)

25-54 years: 45.27% (male 19,813 /female 18,990)

55-64 years: 14.71% (male 6,674 /female 5,935)

65 years and over: 16.18% (male 7,047 /female 6,817) (2018 est.)

MEDIAN AGE:

total: 44.9 years

male: 45.1 years

female: 44.8 years (2018 est.)

country comparison to the world: 6

POPULATION GROWTH RATE:

-0.01% (2018 est.)

country comparison to the world: 195

BIRTH RATE:

7.3 births/1,000 population (2018 est.)

country comparison to the world: 224

DEATH RATE:

7.4 deaths/1,000 population (2018 est.)

country comparison to the world: 113

NET MIGRATION RATE:

0 migrant(s)/1,000 population (2017 est.)

country comparison to the world: 70

POPULATION DISTRIBUTION:

population is unevenly distributed and is concentrated in the seven urbanized valleys that make up the country's parishes (political administrative divisions)

URBANIZATION:

urban population: 88.1% of total population (2018)

rate of urbanization: -0.31% annual rate of change (2015-20 est.)

MAJOR URBAN AREAS - POPULATION:

23,000 ANDORRA LA VELLA (capital) (2018)

SEX RATIO:

at birth: 1.07 male(s)/female (2017 est.)

0-14 years: 1.05 male(s)/female (2017 est.)

15-24 years: 1.08 male(s)/female (2017 est.)

25-54 years: 1.05 male(s)/female (2017 est.)

55-64 years: 1.15 male(s)/female (2017 est.)

65 years and over: 1.02 male(s)/female (2017 est.)

total population: 1.06 male(s)/female (2017 est.)

INFANT MORTALITY RATE:

total: 3.6 deaths/1,000 live births (2018 est.)

male: 3.6 deaths/1,000 live births (2018 est.)

female: 3.5 deaths/1,000 live births (2018 est.)

country comparison to the world: 195

LIFE EXPECTANCY AT BIRTH:

total population: 82.9 years (2018 est.)

male: 80.7 years (2018 est.)

female: 85.3 years (2018 est.)

country comparison to the world: 8

TOTAL FERTILITY RATE:

1.41 children born/woman (2018 est.)

country comparison to the world: 211

HEALTH EXPENDITURES:

8.1% of GDP (2014)

country comparison to the world: 54

PHYSICIANS DENSITY:

3.69 physicians/1,000 population (2015)

HOSPITAL BED DENSITY:

2.5 beds/1,000 population (2009)

DRINKING WATER SOURCE:

improved:

urban: 100% of population

rural: 100% of population

total: 100% of population

unimproved:

urban: 0% of population

rural: 0% of population

total: 0% of population (2015 est.)

SANITATION FACILITY ACCESS:

improved:

urban: 100% of population (2015 est.)

rural: 100% of population (2015 est.)

total: 100% of population (2015 est.)

unimproved:

urban: 0% of population (2015 est.)

rural: 0% of population (2015 est.)

total: 0% of population (2015 est.)

HIV/AIDS - ADULT PREVALENCE RATE:

NA

HIV/AIDS - PEOPLE LIVING WITH HIV/AIDS:

NA

HIV/AIDS - DEATHS:

NA

OBESITY - ADULT PREVALENCE RATE:

25.6% (2016)

country comparison to the world: 49

EDUCATION EXPENDITURES:

3.3% of GDP (2016)

country comparison to the world: 135

LITERACY:

definition: age 15 and over can read and write (2016 est.)

total population: 100% (2016 est.)

male: 100% (2016 est.)

female: 100% (2016 est.)

GOVERNMENT :: ANDORRA

COUNTRY NAME:

conventional long form: Principality of Andorra

conventional short form: Andorra

local long form: Principat d'Andorra

local short form: Andorra

etymology: the origin of the country's name is obscure; the name may derive from the Arabic "ad-darra" meaning "the forest," a reference to its location as part of the Spanish March (defensive buffer zone) against the invading Moors in the 8th century

GOVERNMENT TYPE:

parliamentary democracy (since March 1993) that retains its chiefs of state in the form of a co-principality; the two princes are the President of France and Bishop of Seu d'Urgell, Spain, who delegate responsibility to other officials

CAPITAL:

name: Andorra la Vella

geographic coordinates: 42 30 N, 1 31 E

time difference: UTC+1 (6 hours ahead of Washington, DC during Standard Time)

daylight saving time: +1hr, begins last Sunday in March; ends last Sunday in October

etymology: translates as "Andorra the Old" in Catalan

ADMINISTRATIVE DIVISIONS:

7 parishes (parroquies, singular - parroquia); Andorra la Vella, Canillo, Encamp, Escaldes-Engordany, La Massana, Ordino, Sant Julia de Loria

INDEPENDENCE:

1278 (formed under the joint sovereignty of the French Count of Foix and the Spanish Bishop of Urgell)

NATIONAL HOLIDAY:

Our Lady of Meritxell Day, 8 September (1278)

CONSTITUTION:

history: drafted 1991, approved by referendum 14 March 1993, effective 28 April 1993 (2017)

amendments: proposed by the coprinces jointly or by the General Council; passage requires at least a two-thirds majority vote by the General Council, ratification in a referendum, and sanctioning by the coprinces (2017)

LEGAL SYSTEM:

mixed legal system of civil and customary law with the influence of canon law

INTERNATIONAL LAW ORGANIZATION PARTICIPATION:

has not submitted an ICJ jurisdiction declaration; accepts ICCt jurisdiction

CITIZENSHIP:

citizenship by birth: no

citizenship by descent only: the mother must be an Andorran citizen or the father must have been born in Andorra and both parents maintain permanent residence in Andorra

dual citizenship recognized: no

residency requirement for naturalization: 25 years

SUFFRAGE:

18 years of age; universal

EXECUTIVE BRANCH:

chief of state: Co-prince Emmanuel MACRON (since 14 May 2017); represented by Patrick STROZDA (since 14 May 2017); and Co-prince Archbishop Joan-Enric VIVES i Sicilia (since 12 May 2003); represented by Josep Maria MAURI (since 20 July 2012)

head of government: Head of Government (or Cap de Govern) Antoni MARTI PETIT (since 1 April 2015)

cabinet: Executive Council of ten ministers designated by the head of government

elections/appointments: head of government indirectly elected by the General Council (Andorran parliament), formally appointed by the coprinces for a 4-year term; election last held on 31 March 2015 (next to be held in March 2019); the leader of the majority party in the General Council is usually elected head of government

election results: Antoni MARTI Petit (DA) elected head of government; percent of General Council vote - 79%

LEGISLATIVE BRANCH:

description: unicameral General Council of the Valleys or Consell General de les Valls (a minimum of 28 seats; 14 members directly elected in multi-seat constituencies (parishes) by simple majority vote and 14 directly elected in a single national constituency by proportional representation vote; members serve 4-year terms); note - voters cast two separate ballots - one for a national list and one for a parish list

elections: last held on 1 March 2015 (next to be held in March 2019)

election results: percent of vote by party - DA 37%, PLA 27.7%, PS-VA-IC-independent coalition 23.5%, SDP 11.7%; seats by party - DA 15, PLA 8, PS-VA-IC-independent coalition 3, SDP 2; composition - men 18, women 10, percent of women 35.7%

JUDICIAL BRANCH:

highest courts: Supreme Court of Justice of Andorra or Tribunal Superior de la Justicia d'Andorra (consists of the court president and 8 judges organized into civil, criminal, and administrative chambers); Constitutional Court or Tribunal Constitucional (consists of 4 magistrates)

judge selection and term of office: Supreme Court president and judges appointed by the Supreme Council of Justice, a 5-member judicial policy and administrative body appointed 1 each by the coprinces, 1 by the General Council, 1 by the executive council president, and 1 by the courts; judges serve 6-year renewable terms; Constitutional magistrates appointed 2 by the coprinces and 2 by the General Council; magistrates' appointments limited to 2 consecutive 8-year terms

subordinate courts: Tribunal of Judges or Tribunal de Batlles; Tribunal of the Courts or Tribunal de Corts

POLITICAL PARTIES AND LEADERS:

Citizens' Initiative or IC [Sergi RICART] (including PS, VA, IC, and independents)
Democrats for Andorra or DA [Antoni MARTI PETIT]
Greens of Andorra or VA [Isabel LOZANO MUNOZ, Juli FERNANDEZ BLASI]
Liberal Party or PLA [Jordi GALLARDO]
Social Democratic Party or PS [Vincenc ALAY FERRER]
Social Democratic Progress Party or SDP [Victor NAUDI ZAMORA]

note: Andorra has several smaller parties at the parish level (one is Lauredian Union)

INTERNATIONAL ORGANIZATION PARTICIPATION:

CE, FAO, ICAO, ICC (NGOs), ICCt, ICRM, IFRCS, Interpol, IOC, IPU, ITU, OIF, OPCW, OSCE, UN, UNCTAD, UNESCO, Union Latina, UNWTO, WCO, WHO, WIPO, WTO (observer)

DIPLOMATIC REPRESENTATION IN THE US:

chief of mission: Ambassador Elisenda VIVES BALMANA (since 2 March 2016)

chancery: 2 United Nations Plaza, 27th Floor, New York, NY 10017

telephone: [1] (212) 750-8064

FAX: [1] (212) 750-6630

DIPLOMATIC REPRESENTATION FROM THE US:

the US does not have an embassy in Andorra; the US ambassador to Spain is accredited to Andorra; US interests in Andorra are represented by the US

Consulate General's office in Barcelona (Spain); mailing address: Paseo Reina Elisenda de Montcada, 23, 08034 Barcelona, Spain; telephone: [34] (93) 280-2227; FAX: [34] (93) 280-6175

FLAG DESCRIPTION:

three vertical bands of blue (hoist side), yellow, and red, with the national coat of arms centered in the yellow band; the latter band is slightly wider than the other 2 so that the ratio of band widths is 8:9:8; the coat of arms features a quartered shield with the emblems of (starting in the upper left and proceeding clockwise): Urgell, Foix, Bearn, and Catalonia; the motto reads VIRTUS UNITA FORTIOR (Strength United is Stronger); the flag combines the blue and red French colors with the red and yellow of Spain to show Franco-Spanish protection

note: similar to the flags of Chad and Romania, which do not have a national coat of arms in the center, and the flag of Moldova, which does bear a national emblem

NATIONAL SYMBOL(S):

red cow (breed unspecified); national colors: blue, yellow, red

NATIONAL ANTHEM:

name: "El Gran Carlemany" (The Great Charlemagne)

lyrics/music: Joan BENLLOCH i VIVO/Enric MARFANY BONS

note: adopted 1921; the anthem provides a brief history of Andorra in a first person narrative

ECONOMY :: ANDORRA

ECONOMY - OVERVIEW:

Andorra has a developed economy and a free market, with per capita income above the European average and above the level of its neighbors, Spain and France. The country has developed a sophisticated infrastructure including a one-of-a-kind micro-fiber-optic network for the entire country. Tourism, retail sales, and finance comprise more than three-quarters of GDP. Duty-free shopping for some products and the country's summer and winter resorts attract millions of visitors annually. Andorra uses the euro and is effectively subject to the monetary policy of the European Central Bank. Andorra's comparative advantage as a tax haven eroded when the borders of neighboring France and Spain opened and the government eased bank secrecy laws under pressure from the EU and OECD.

Agricultural production is limited - only about 5% of the land is arable - and most food has to be imported, making the economy vulnerable to changes in fuel and food prices. The principal livestock is sheep. Manufacturing output and exports consist mainly of perfumes and cosmetic products, products of the printing industry, electrical machinery and equipment, clothing, tobacco products, and furniture. Andorra is a member of the EU Customs Union and is treated as an EU member for trade in manufactured goods (no tariffs) and as a non-EU member for agricultural products.

To provide incentives for growth and diversification in the economy, the Andorran government began sweeping economic reforms in 2006. The Parliament approved three laws to complement the first phase of economic openness: on companies (October 2007), on business accounting (December 2007), and on foreign investment (April 2008 and June 2012). From 2011 to 2015, the Parliament also approved direct taxes in the form of taxes on corporations, on individual incomes of residents and non-residents, and on capital gains, savings, and economic activities. These regulations aim to establish a transparent, modern, and internationally comparable regulatory framework, in order to attract foreign investment and businesses that offer higher value added.

GDP (PURCHASING POWER PARITY):

$3.327 billion (2015 est.)

$3.363 billion (2014 est.)

$3.273 billion (2013 est.)

note: data are in 2012 US dollars

country comparison to the world: 186

GDP (OFFICIAL EXCHANGE RATE):

$2.712 billion (2016 est.) (2016 est.)

GDP - REAL GROWTH RATE:

-1.1% (2015 est.)

1.4% (2014 est.)

-0.1% (2013 est.)

country comparison to the world: 203

GDP - PER CAPITA (PPP):

$49,900 (2015 est.)

$51,300 (2014 est.)

$50,300 (2013 est.)

country comparison to the world: 32

GDP - COMPOSITION, BY SECTOR OF ORIGIN:

agriculture: 11.9% (2015 est.)

industry: 33.6% (2015 est.)

services: 54.5% (2015 est.)

AGRICULTURE - PRODUCTS:

small quantities of rye, wheat, barley, oats, vegetables, tobacco; sheep, cattle

INDUSTRIES:

tourism (particularly skiing), banking, timber, furniture

INDUSTRIAL PRODUCTION GROWTH RATE:

NA

LABOR FORCE:

39,750 (2016)

country comparison to the world: 196

LABOR FORCE - BY OCCUPATION:

agriculture: 0.5%

industry: 4.4%

services: 95.1% (2015)

UNEMPLOYMENT RATE:

3.7% (2016 est.)

4.1% (2015 est.)

country comparison to the world: 44

HOUSEHOLD INCOME OR CONSUMPTION BY PERCENTAGE SHARE:

lowest 10%: NA

highest 10%: NA

BUDGET:

revenues: 1.872 billion (2016)

expenditures: 2.06 billion (2016)

TAXES AND OTHER REVENUES:

69% (of GDP) (2016)

country comparison to the world: 5

BUDGET SURPLUS (+) OR DEFICIT (-):

-6.9% (of GDP) (2016)

country comparison to the world: 192

PUBLIC DEBT:

41% of GDP (2014 est.)

41.4% of GDP (2013 est.)

country comparison to the world: 122

FISCAL YEAR:

calendar year

INFLATION RATE (CONSUMER PRICES):

-0.9% (2015 est.)

-0.1% (2014 est.)

country comparison to the world: 1

EXPORTS:

$78.71 million (2015 est.)

$79.57 million (2014 est.)

country comparison to the world: 200

EXPORTS - COMMODITIES:

tobacco products, furniture

IMPORTS:

$1.257 billion (2015 est.)

$1.264 billion (2014 est.)

country comparison to the world: 177

IMPORTS - COMMODITIES:

consumer goods, food, fuel, electricity

DEBT - EXTERNAL:

$0 (2016)

country comparison to the world: 203

EXCHANGE RATES:

euros (EUR) per US dollar -

0.885 (2017 est.)

0.903 (2016 est.)

0.9214 (2015 est.)

0.885 (2014 est.)

0.7634 (2013 est.)

ENERGY :: ANDORRA

ELECTRICITY ACCESS:

electrification - total population: 100% (2016)

ELECTRICITY - PRODUCTION:

99.48 million kWh (2015 est.)

country comparison to the world: 201

ELECTRICITY - CONSUMPTION:

221.6 million kWh (2015 est.)

country comparison to the world: 190

ELECTRICITY - EXPORTS:

6,000 kWh (2015 est.)

country comparison to the world: 95

ELECTRICITY - IMPORTS:

471.3 million kWh (2015 est.)

country comparison to the world: 81

ELECTRICITY - INSTALLED GENERATING CAPACITY:

520,000 kW (2010 est.)

country comparison to the world: 147

ELECTRICITY - FROM FOSSIL FUELS:

61% of total installed capacity (2010 est.)

country comparison to the world: 126

ELECTRICITY - FROM NUCLEAR FUELS:

0% of total installed capacity (2016 est.)

country comparison to the world: 36

ELECTRICITY - FROM HYDROELECTRIC PLANTS:

23% of total installed capacity (2010 est.)

country comparison to the world: 82

ELECTRICITY - FROM OTHER RENEWABLE SOURCES:

15% of total installed capacity (2010 est.)

country comparison to the world: 56

CRUDE OIL - PRODUCTION:

0 bbl/day (2016)

country comparison to the world: 103

CRUDE OIL - EXPORTS:

0 bbl/day (2016) (2016)

country comparison to the world: 84

CRUDE OIL - IMPORTS:

0 bbl/day (2016) (2016)

country comparison to the world: 87

CRUDE OIL - PROVED RESERVES:

0 bbl (2016) (2016)

country comparison to the world: 101

REFINED PETROLEUM PRODUCTS - PRODUCTION:

0 bbl/day (2016)

country comparison to the world: 112

NATURAL GAS - PRODUCTION:

0 cu m (2016) (2016)

country comparison to the world: 98

NATURAL GAS - CONSUMPTION:

0 cu m (2016) (2016)

country comparison to the world: 118

NATURAL GAS - EXPORTS:

0 cu m (2016) (2016)

country comparison to the world: 60

NATURAL GAS - IMPORTS:

0 cu m (2016) (2016)

country comparison to the world: 85

NATURAL GAS - PROVED RESERVES:

0 cu m (2016)

country comparison to the world: 104

COMMUNICATIONS :: ANDORRA

TELEPHONES - FIXED LINES:

total subscriptions: 38,411 (2017 est.)

subscriptions per 100 inhabitants: 50 (2017 est.)

country comparison to the world: 161

TELEPHONES - MOBILE CELLULAR:

total subscriptions: 80,337 (2017 est.)

subscriptions per 100 inhabitants: 104 (2017 est.)

country comparison to the world: 193

TELEPHONE SYSTEM:

general assessment: modern automatic telephone system; broadband internet and LTE mobile lines for both consumer and enterprise customers available (2017)

domestic: 50 per 100 fixed-line, 45 per 100 mobile-cellular; modern system with microwave radio relay connections between exchanges (2017)

international: country code - 376; landline circuits to France and Spain (2016)

BROADCAST MEDIA:

1 public TV station and 2 public radio stations; about 10 commercial radio stations; good reception of radio and TV broadcasts from stations in France and Spain; upgraded to terrestrial digital TV broadcasting in 2007; roughly 25 international TV channels available (2016)

INTERNET COUNTRY CODE:

.ad

INTERNET USERS:

total: 83,887 (July 2016 est.)

percent of population: 97.9% (July 2016 est.)

country comparison to the world: 179

BROADBAND - FIXED SUBSCRIPTIONS:

total: 34,284 (2017 est.)

subscriptions per 100 inhabitants: 45 (2017 est.)

country comparison to the world: 137

TRANSPORTATION :: ANDORRA

CIVIL AIRCRAFT REGISTRATION COUNTRY CODE PREFIX:

C3 (2016)

ROADWAYS:

total: 320 km (2015)

country comparison to the world: 204

MILITARY AND SECURITY :: ANDORRA

MILITARY BRANCHES:

no regular military forces; Police Corps of Andorra

MILITARY - NOTE:

defense is the responsibility of France and Spain

TRANSNATIONAL ISSUES :: ANDORRA

DISPUTES - INTERNATIONAL:

none

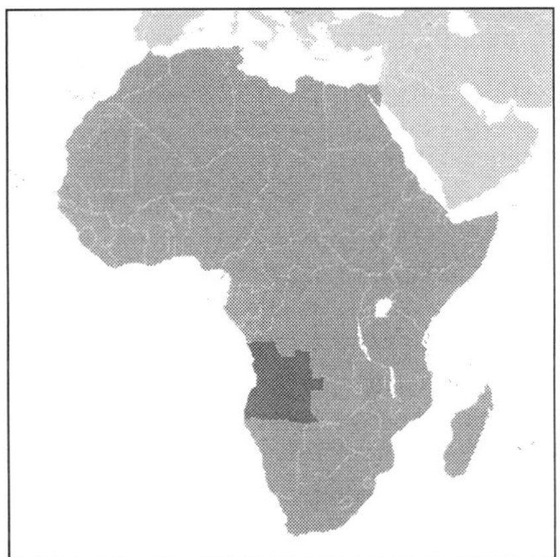

AFRICA :: ANGOLA

INTRODUCTION :: ANGOLA

BACKGROUND:

Angola scores low on human development indexes despite using its large oil reserves to rebuild since the end of a 27-year civil war in 2002. Fighting between the Popular Movement for the Liberation of Angola (MPLA), led by Jose Eduardo DOS SANTOS, and the National Union for the Total Independence of Angola (UNITA), led by Jonas SAVIMBI, followed independence from Portugal in 1975. Peace seemed imminent in 1992 when Angola held national elections, but fighting picked up again in 1993. Up to 1.5 million lives may have been lost - and 4 million people displaced - during the more than a quarter century of fighting. SAVIMBI's death in 2002 ended UNITA's insurgency and cemented the MPLA's hold on power. DOS SANTOS stepped down from the presidency in 2017, having led the country since 1979. He pushed through a new constitution in 2010.

GEOGRAPHY :: ANGOLA

LOCATION:

Southern Africa, bordering the South Atlantic Ocean, between Namibia and Democratic Republic of the Congo

GEOGRAPHIC COORDINATES:

12 30 S, 18 30 E

MAP REFERENCES:

Africa

AREA:

total: 1,246,700 sq km

land: 1,246,700 sq km

water: 0 sq km

country comparison to the world: 24

AREA - COMPARATIVE:

about eight times the size of Georgia; slightly less than twice the size of Texas

LAND BOUNDARIES:

total: 5,369 km

border countries (4): Democratic Republic of the Congo 2646 km (of which 225 km is the boundary of discontiguous Cabinda Province), Republic of the Congo 231 km, Namibia 1427 km, Zambia 1065 km

COASTLINE:

1,600 km

MARITIME CLAIMS:

territorial sea: 12 nm

exclusive economic zone: 200 nm

contiguous zone: 24 nm

CLIMATE:

semiarid in south and along coast to Luanda; north has cool, dry season (May to October) and hot, rainy season (November to April)

TERRAIN:

narrow coastal plain rises abruptly to vast interior plateau

ELEVATION:

mean elevation: 1,112 m

elevation extremes: 0 m lowest point: Atlantic Ocean

2620 highest point: Moca

NATURAL RESOURCES:

petroleum, diamonds, iron ore, phosphates, copper, feldspar, gold, bauxite, uranium

LAND USE:

agricultural land: 47.5% (2014 est.)

arable land: 8.3% (2014 est.) / permanent crops: 0.5% (2014 est.) / permanent pasture: 91.23% (2014 est.)

forest: 46.5% (2014 est.)

other: 6% (2014 est.)

IRRIGATED LAND:

860 sq km (2014)

POPULATION DISTRIBUTION:

most people live in the western half of the country; urban areas account for the highest concentrations of people, particularly Luanda

NATURAL HAZARDS:

locally heavy rainfall causes periodic flooding on the plateau

ENVIRONMENT - CURRENT ISSUES:

overuse of pastures and subsequent soil erosion attributable to population pressures; desertification; deforestation of tropical rain forest, in response to both international demand for tropical timber and to domestic use as fuel, resulting in loss of biodiversity; soil erosion contributing to water pollution and siltation of rivers and dams; inadequate supplies of potable water

ENVIRONMENT - INTERNATIONAL AGREEMENTS:

party to: Biodiversity, Climate Change, Climate Change-Kyoto Protocol, Desertification, Hazardous Wastes, Law of the Sea, Marine Dumping, Ozone Layer Protection, Ship Pollution

signed, but not ratified: none of the selected agreements

GEOGRAPHY - NOTE:

the province of Cabinda is an exclave, separated from the rest of the country by the Democratic Republic of the Congo

PEOPLE AND SOCIETY :: ANGOLA

POPULATION:

30,355,880 (July 2017 est.) (July 2018 est.)

note: Angola's national statistical agency projects the country's 2017 population to be 28.4 million

country comparison to the world: 45

NATIONALITY:

noun: Angolan(s)

adjective: Angolan

ETHNIC GROUPS:

Ovimbundu 37%, Kimbundu 25%, Bakongo 13%, mestico (mixed European and native African) 2%, European 1%, other 22%

LANGUAGES:

Portuguese 71.2% (official), Umbundu 23%, Kikongo 8.2%, Kimbundu 7.8%, Chokwe 6.5%, Nhaneca 3.4%, Nganguela 3.1%, Fiote 2.4%, Kwanhama 2.3%, Muhumbi 2.1%, Luvale 1%, other 3.6% (2014 est.)

note: most widely spoken languages; shares sum to more than 100% because some respondents gave more than one answer on the census

RELIGIONS:

Roman Catholic 41.1%, Protestant 38.1%, other 8.6%, none 12.3% (2014 est.)

DEMOGRAPHIC PROFILE:

More than a decade after the end of Angola's 27-year civil war, the country still faces a variety of socioeconomic problems, including poverty, high maternal and child mortality, and illiteracy. Despite the country's rapid post-war economic growth based on oil production, about 40 percent of Angolans live below the poverty line and unemployment is widespread, especially among the large young-adult population. Only about 70% of the population is literate, and the rate drops to around 60% for women. The youthful population - about 45% are under the age of 15 - is expected to continue growing rapidly with a fertility rate of more than 5 children per woman and a low rate of contraceptive use. Fewer than half of women deliver their babies with the assistance of trained health care personnel, which contributes to Angola's high maternal mortality rate.

Of the estimated 550,000 Angolans who fled their homeland during its civil war, most have returned home since 2002. In 2012, the UN assessed that conditions in Angola had been stable for several years and invoked a cessation of refugee status for Angolans. Following the cessation clause, some of those still in exile returned home voluntarily through UN repatriation programs, and others integrated into host countries.

AGE STRUCTURE:

0-14 years: 48.07% (male 7,257,155 /female 7,336,084)

15-24 years: 18.33% (male 2,701,123 /female 2,863,950)

25-54 years: 27.95% (male 4,044,944 /female 4,441,028)

55-64 years: 3.32% (male 466,085 /female 540,452)

65 years and over: 2.32% (male 296,411 /female 408,648) (2018 est.)

DEPENDENCY RATIOS:

total dependency ratio: 97.6 (2015 est.)

youth dependency ratio: 93 (2015 est.)

elderly dependency ratio: 4.6 (2015 est.)

potential support ratio: 21.9 (2015 est.)

MEDIAN AGE:

total: 15.9 years

male: 15.4 years

female: 16.3 years (2018 est.)

country comparison to the world: 224

POPULATION GROWTH RATE:

3.49% (2018 est.)

country comparison to the world: 2

BIRTH RATE:

43.7 births/1,000 population (2018 est.)

country comparison to the world: 1

DEATH RATE:

9 deaths/1,000 population (2018 est.)

country comparison to the world: 60

NET MIGRATION RATE:

0.2 migrant(s)/1,000 population (2017 est.)

country comparison to the world: 67

POPULATION DISTRIBUTION:

most people live in the western half of the country; urban areas account for the highest concentrations of people, particularly Luanda

URBANIZATION:

urban population: 65.5% of total population (2018)

rate of urbanization: 4.32% annual rate of change (2015-20 est.)

MAJOR URBAN AREAS - POPULATION:

7.774 million LUANDA (capital) (2018)

SEX RATIO:

at birth: 1.02 male(s)/female (2017 est.)

0-14 years: 1.04 male(s)/female (2017 est.)

15-24 years: 1.04 male(s)/female (2017 est.)

25-54 years: 1.02 male(s)/female (2017 est.)

55-64 years: 0.94 male(s)/female (2017 est.)

65 years and over: 0.86 male(s)/female (2017 est.)

total population: 1.02 male(s)/female (2017 est.)

MOTHER'S MEAN AGE AT FIRST BIRTH:

19.4 years (2015/16 est.)

note: median age at first birth among women 25-29

MATERNAL MORTALITY RATE:

477 deaths/100,000 live births (2015 est.)

country comparison to the world: 23

INFANT MORTALITY RATE:

total: 65.8 deaths/1,000 live births (2018 est.)

male: 71.4 deaths/1,000 live births (2018 est.)

female: 60.1 deaths/1,000 live births (2018 est.)

country comparison to the world: 10

LIFE EXPECTANCY AT BIRTH:

total population: 60.6 years (2018 est.)

male: 58.5 years (2018 est.)

female: 62.7 years (2018 est.)

country comparison to the world: 207

TOTAL FERTILITY RATE:

6.09 children born/woman (2018 est.)

country comparison to the world: 2

CONTRACEPTIVE PREVALENCE RATE:

13.7% (2015/16)

HEALTH EXPENDITURES:

3.3% of GDP (2014)

country comparison to the world: 177

PHYSICIANS DENSITY:

0.14 physicians/1,000 population (2009)

DRINKING WATER SOURCE:

improved:

urban: 75.4% of population

rural: 28.2% of population

total: 49% of population

unimproved:

urban: 24.6% of population

rural: 71.8% of population

total: 51% of population (2015 est.)

SANITATION FACILITY ACCESS:

improved:

urban: 88.6% of population (2015 est.)

rural: 22.5% of population (2015 est.)

total: 51.6% of population (2015 est.)

unimproved:

urban: 11.4% of population (2015 est.)

rural: 77.5% of population (2015 est.)

total: 48.4% of population (2015 est.)

HIV/AIDS - ADULT PREVALENCE RATE:

1.9% (2017 est.)

country comparison to the world: 24

HIV/AIDS - PEOPLE LIVING WITH HIV/AIDS:

310,000 (2017 est.)

country comparison to the world: 21

HIV/AIDS - DEATHS:

13,000 (2017 est.)

country comparison to the world: 19

MAJOR INFECTIOUS DISEASES:

degree of risk: very high (2016)

food or waterborne diseases: bacterial and protozoal diarrhea, hepatitis A, typhoid fever (2016)

vectorborne diseases: dengue fever, malaria (2016)

water contact diseases: schistosomiasis (2016)

animal contact diseases: rabies (2016)

OBESITY - ADULT PREVALENCE RATE:

8.2% (2016)

country comparison to the world: 154

CHILDREN UNDER THE AGE OF 5 YEARS UNDERWEIGHT:

19% (2016)

country comparison to the world: 28

EDUCATION EXPENDITURES:

3.5% of GDP (2010)

country comparison to the world: 128

LITERACY:

definition: age 15 and over can read and write (2015 est.)

total population: 71.1% (2015 est.)

male: 82% (2015 est.)

female: 60.7% (2015 est.)

SCHOOL LIFE EXPECTANCY (PRIMARY TO TERTIARY EDUCATION):

total: 10 years (2011)

male: 13 years (2011)

female: 8 years (2011)

UNEMPLOYMENT, YOUTH AGES 15-24:

total: 16.7% (2011 est.)

male: 16.8% (2011 est.)

female: 16.6% (2011 est.)

country comparison to the world: 80

GOVERNMENT :: ANGOLA

COUNTRY NAME:

conventional long form: Republic of Angola

conventional short form: Angola

local long form: Republica de Angola

local short form: Angola

former: People's Republic of Angola

etymology: name derived by the Portuguese from the title "ngola" held by kings of the Ndongo (Ndongo was a kingdom in what is now northern Angola)

GOVERNMENT TYPE:

presidential republic

CAPITAL:

name: Luanda

geographic coordinates: 8 50 S, 13 13 E

time difference: UTC+1 (6 hours ahead of Washington, DC, during Standard Time)

etymology: originally named "Sao Paulo da Assuncao de Loanda" (Saint Paul of the Assumption of Loanda), which over time was shortened and corrupted to just Luanda

ADMINISTRATIVE DIVISIONS:

18 provinces (provincias, singular - provincia); Bengo, Benguela, Bie, Cabinda, Cunene, Huambo, Huila, Kwando Kubango, Kwanza Norte, Kwanza Sul, Luanda, Lunda Norte, Lunda Sul, Malanje, Moxico, Namibe, Uige, Zaire

INDEPENDENCE:

11 November 1975 (from Portugal)

NATIONAL HOLIDAY:

Independence Day, 11 November (1975)

CONSTITUTION:

history: previous 1975, 1992; latest passed by National Assembly 21 January 2010, adopted 5 February 2010 (2017)

amendments: proposed by the president of the republic or supported by at least one-third of the National Assembly membership; passage requires at least two-thirds majority vote of the Assembly subject to prior Constitutional Court review if requested by the president of the republic (2017)

LEGAL SYSTEM:

civil legal system based on Portuguese civil law; no judicial review of legislation

INTERNATIONAL LAW ORGANIZATION PARTICIPATION:

has not submitted an ICJ jurisdiction declaration; non-party state to the ICCt

CITIZENSHIP:

citizenship by birth: no

citizenship by descent only: at least one parent must be a citizen of Angola

dual citizenship recognized: no

residency requirement for naturalization: 10 years

SUFFRAGE:

18 years of age; universal

EXECUTIVE BRANCH:

chief of state: President Joao Manuel Goncalves LOURENCO (since 26 September 2017); Vice President Bornito De Sousa Baltazar DIOGO (since 26 September 2017); note - the president is both chief of state and head of government

head of government: President Joao Manuel Goncalves LOURENCO (since 26 September 2017); Vice President

Bornito De Sousa Baltazar DIOGO (since 26 September 2017)

cabinet: Council of Ministers appointed by the president

elections/appointments: the candidate of the winning party or coalition in the last legislative election becomes the president; president serves a 5-year term (eligible for a second consecutive or discontinuous term); last held on 23 August 2017 (next to be held in 2022)

election results: Joao Manuel Goncalves LOURENCO (MPLA) elected president by the winning party following the 23 August 2017 general election

LEGISLATIVE BRANCH:

description: unicameral National Assembly or Assembleia Nacional (220 seats; members directly elected in a single national constituency and in multi-seat constituencies by closed list proportional representation vote; members serve 5-year terms)

elections: last held on 23 August 2017 (next to be held in August 2022)

election results: percent of vote by party - MPLA 61.1%, UNITA 26.7%, CASA-CE 9.5%, PRS 1.4%, FNLA 0.9%, other 0.5%; seats by party - MPLA 150, UNITA 51, CASA-CE 16, PRS 2, FNLA 1; composition - men 136, women 84, percent of women 38.2%

JUDICIAL BRANCH:

highest courts: Supreme Court or Supremo Tribunal de Justica (consists of the court president, vice president, and a minimum of 16 judges); Constitutional Court or Tribunal Constitucional (consists of 11 judges)

judge selection and term of office: Supreme Court judges appointed by the president upon recommendation of the Supreme Judicial Council, an 18-member body chaired by the president; judge tenure NA; Constitutional Court judges - 4 nominated by the president, 4 elected by National Assembly, 2 elected by Supreme National Council, 1 elected by competitive submission of curricula; judges serve single 7-year terms

subordinate courts: provincial and municipal courts

POLITICAL PARTIES AND LEADERS:

Broad Convergence for the Salvation of Angola Electoral Coalition or CASA-CE [Abel CHIVUKUVUKU]
National Front for the Liberation of Angola or FNLA; note - party has two factions; one led by Lucas NGONDA; the other by Ngola KABANGU
National Union for the Total Independence of Angola or UNITA [Isaias SAMAKUVA] (largest opposition party)
Popular Movement for the Liberation of Angola or MPLA [Joao LOURENCO]; note - Jose Eduardo DOS SANTOS stepped down 8 Sept 2018 ruling party in power since 1975
Social Renewal Party or PRS [Benedito DANIEL]

INTERNATIONAL ORGANIZATION PARTICIPATION:

ACP, AfDB, AU, CEMAC, CPLP, FAO, G-77, IAEA, IBRD, ICAO, ICRM, IDA, IFAD, IFC, IFRCS, ILO, IMF, IMO, Interpol, IOC, IOM, IPU, ISO (correspondent), ITSO, ITU, ITUC (NGOs), MIGA, NAM, OAS (observer), OPEC, SADC, UN, UNCTAD, UNESCO, UNIDO, Union Latina, UNWTO, UPU, WCO, WFTU (NGOs), WHO, WIPO, WMO, WTO

DIPLOMATIC REPRESENTATION IN THE US:

chief of mission: Ambassador Agostinho Tavares da Silva NETO (since 18 November 2014)

chancery: 2100-2108 16th Street NW, Washington, DC 20009

telephone: [1] (202) 785-1156

FAX: [1] (202) 822-9049

consulate(s) general: Houston, Los Angeles, New York

DIPLOMATIC REPRESENTATION FROM THE US:

chief of mission: Ambassador Nina Maria FITE (14 February 2018)

embassy: number 32 Rua Houari Boumedienne (in the Miramar area of Luanda), Luanda, C.P. 6468, Angola

mailing address: international mail: Caixa Postal 6468, Luanda; pouch: US Embassy Luanda, US Department of State, 2550 Luanda Place, Washington, DC 20521-2550

telephone: [244] 946440977

FAX: [244] (222) 64-1000

FLAG DESCRIPTION:

two equal horizontal bands of red (top) and black with a centered yellow emblem consisting of a 5-pointed star within half a cogwheel crossed by a machete (in the style of a hammer and sickle); red represents liberty and black the African continent; the symbols characterize workers and peasants

NATIONAL SYMBOL(S):

Palanca Negra Gigante (giant black sable antelope); national colors: red, black, yellow

NATIONAL ANTHEM:

name: "Angola Avante" (Forward Angola)

lyrics/music: Manuel Rui Alves MONTEIRO/Rui Alberto Vieira Dias MINGAO

note: adopted 1975

ECONOMY :: ANGOLA

ECONOMY - OVERVIEW:

Angola's economy is overwhelmingly driven by its oil sector. Oil production and its supporting activities contribute about 50% of GDP, more than 70% of government revenue, and more than 90% of the country's exports; Angola is an OPEC member and subject to its direction regarding oil production levels. Diamonds contribute an additional 5% to exports. Subsistence agriculture provides the main livelihood for most of the people, but half of the country's food is still imported.

Increased oil production supported growth averaging more than 17% per year from 2004 to 2008. A postwar reconstruction boom and resettlement of displaced persons led to high rates of growth in construction and agriculture as well. Some of the country's infrastructure is still damaged or undeveloped from the 27-year-long civil war (1975-2002). However, the government since 2005 has used billions of dollars in credit from China, Brazil, Portugal, Germany, Spain, and the EU to help rebuild Angola's public infrastructure. Land mines left from the war still mar the countryside, and as a result, the national military, international partners, and private Angolan firms all continue to remove them.

The global recession that started in 2008 stalled Angola's economic growth and many construction projects stopped because Luanda accrued billions in arrears to foreign construction companies when government revenue fell. Lower prices for oil and diamonds also resulted in GDP falling 0.7% in 2016. Angola formally abandoned its currency peg in 2009 but reinstituted it in April 2016 and maintains an overvalued exchange rate. In late 2016, Angola lost the last of its correspondent relationships with foreign banks, further exacerbating hard currency problems. Since 2013 the central bank has consistently spent down reserves to defend the kwanza, gradually allowing a 40% depreciation since late 2014. Consumer inflation declined from 325% in 2000 to less than 9% in 2014, before rising again to above 30% from 2015-2017.

Continued low oil prices, the depreciation of the kwanza, and slower than expected growth in non-oil GDP have reduced growth prospects, although several major international oil companies remain in Angola. Corruption, especially in the extractive sectors, is a major long-term challenge that poses an additional threat to the economy.

GDP (PURCHASING POWER PARITY):

$193.6 billion (2017 est.)

$198.6 billion (2016 est.)

$203.9 billion (2015 est.)

note: data are in 2017 dollars

country comparison to the world: 65

GDP (OFFICIAL EXCHANGE RATE):

$126.5 billion (2017 est.) (2017 est.)

GDP - REAL GROWTH RATE:

-2.5% (2017 est.)

-2.6% (2016 est.)

0.9% (2015 est.)

country comparison to the world: 209

GDP - PER CAPITA (PPP):

$6,800 (2017 est.)

$7,200 (2016 est.)

$7,600 (2015 est.)

note: data are in 2017 dollars

country comparison to the world: 160

GROSS NATIONAL SAVING:

28.6% of GDP (2017 est.)

24.5% of GDP (2016 est.)

28.5% of GDP (2015 est.)

country comparison to the world: 37

GDP - COMPOSITION, BY END USE:

household consumption: 80.6% (2017 est.)

government consumption: 15.6% (2017 est.)

investment in fixed capital: 10.3% (2017 est.)

investment in inventories: -1.2% (2017 est.)

exports of goods and services: 25.4% (2017 est.)

imports of goods and services: -30.7% (2017 est.)

GDP - COMPOSITION, BY SECTOR OF ORIGIN:

agriculture: 10.2% (2011 est.)

industry: 61.4% (2011 est.)

services: 28.4% (2011 est.)

AGRICULTURE - PRODUCTS:

bananas, sugarcane, coffee, sisal, corn, cotton, cassava (manioc, tapioca), tobacco, vegetables, plantains; livestock; forest products; fish

INDUSTRIES:

petroleum; diamonds, iron ore, phosphates, feldspar, bauxite, uranium, and gold; cement; basic metal products; fish processing; food processing, brewing, tobacco products, sugar; textiles; ship repair

INDUSTRIAL PRODUCTION GROWTH RATE:

2.5% (2017 est.)

country comparison to the world: 115

LABOR FORCE:

12.51 million (2017 est.)

country comparison to the world: 46

LABOR FORCE - BY OCCUPATION:

agriculture: 85%

industry: 15% (2015 est.)

industry and services: 15% (2003 est.)

UNEMPLOYMENT RATE:

6.6% (2016 est.)

country comparison to the world: 97

POPULATION BELOW POVERTY LINE:

36.6% (2008 est.)

HOUSEHOLD INCOME OR CONSUMPTION BY PERCENTAGE SHARE:

lowest 10%: 44.7% (2000)

highest 10%: 44.7% (2000)

DISTRIBUTION OF FAMILY INCOME - GINI INDEX:

42.7 (2008 est.)

country comparison to the world: 50

BUDGET:

revenues: 37.02 billion (2017 est.)

expenditures: 45.44 billion (2017 est.)

TAXES AND OTHER REVENUES:

29.3% (of GDP) (2017 est.)

country comparison to the world: 83

BUDGET SURPLUS (+) OR DEFICIT (-):

-6.7% (of GDP) (2017 est.)

country comparison to the world: 189

PUBLIC DEBT:

65% of GDP (2017 est.)

75.3% of GDP (2016 est.)

country comparison to the world: 59

FISCAL YEAR:

calendar year

INFLATION RATE (CONSUMER PRICES):

29.8% (2017 est.)

30.7% (2016 est.)

country comparison to the world: 222

CENTRAL BANK DISCOUNT RATE:

9% (31 December 2014)

25% (31 December 2010)

country comparison to the world: 30

COMMERCIAL BANK PRIME LENDING RATE:

15.82% (31 December 2017 est.)

15.78% (31 December 2016 est.)

country comparison to the world: 32

STOCK OF NARROW MONEY:

$32.39 billion (31 December 2017 est.)

$23.17 billion (31 December 2016 est.)

country comparison to the world: 62

STOCK OF BROAD MONEY:

$32.39 billion (31 December 2017 est.)

$23.17 billion (31 December 2016 est.)

country comparison to the world: 62

STOCK OF DOMESTIC CREDIT:

$16.02 billion (31 December 2017 est.)

$14.25 billion (31 December 2016 est.)

country comparison to the world: 97

CURRENT ACCOUNT BALANCE:

-$1.254 billion (2017 est.)

-$4.834 billion (2016 est.)

country comparison to the world: 150

EXPORTS:

$33.07 billion (2017 est.)

$31.03 billion (2016 est.)

country comparison to the world: 61

EXPORTS - PARTNERS:

China 61.2%, India 13%, US 4.2% (2017)

EXPORTS - COMMODITIES:

crude oil, diamonds, refined petroleum products, coffee, sisal, fish and fish products, timber, cotton

IMPORTS:

$19.5 billion (2017 est.)

$13.04 billion (2016 est.)

country comparison to the world: 78

IMPORTS - COMMODITIES:

machinery and electrical equipment, vehicles and spare parts; medicines, food, textiles, military goods

IMPORTS - PARTNERS:

Portugal 17.8%, China 13.5%, US 7.4%, South Africa 6.2%, Brazil 6.1%, UK 4% (2017)

RESERVES OF FOREIGN EXCHANGE AND GOLD:

$17.29 billion (31 December 2017 est.)

$23.74 billion (31 December 2016 est.)

country comparison to the world: 63

DEBT - EXTERNAL:

$42.08 billion (31 December 2017 est.)

$27.14 billion (31 December 2016 est.)

country comparison to the world: 71

STOCK OF DIRECT FOREIGN INVESTMENT - AT HOME:

$11.21 billion (31 December 2017 est.)

$9.16 billion (31 December 2016 est.)

country comparison to the world: 94

STOCK OF DIRECT FOREIGN INVESTMENT - ABROAD:

$28 billion (31 December 2017 est.)

$23.02 billion (31 December 2016 est.)

country comparison to the world: 50

EXCHANGE RATES:

kwanza (AOA) per US dollar -

172.6 (2017 est.)

163.656 (2016 est.)

163.656 (2015 est.)

120.061 (2014 est.)

98.303 (2013 est.)

ENERGY :: ANGOLA

ELECTRICITY ACCESS:

population without electricity: 15 million (2013)

electrification - total population: 30% (2013)

electrification - urban areas: 46% (2013)

electrification - rural areas: 18% (2013)

ELECTRICITY - PRODUCTION:

10.2 billion kWh (2016 est.)

country comparison to the world: 102

ELECTRICITY - CONSUMPTION:

9.036 billion kWh (2016 est.)

country comparison to the world: 101

ELECTRICITY - EXPORTS:

0 kWh (2016 est.)

country comparison to the world: 98

ELECTRICITY - IMPORTS:

0 kWh (2016 est.)

country comparison to the world: 119

ELECTRICITY - INSTALLED GENERATING CAPACITY:

2.613 million kW (2016 est.)

country comparison to the world: 103

ELECTRICITY - FROM FOSSIL FUELS:

34% of total installed capacity (2016 est.)

country comparison to the world: 180

ELECTRICITY - FROM NUCLEAR FUELS:

0% of total installed capacity (2017 est.)

country comparison to the world: 37

ELECTRICITY - FROM HYDROELECTRIC PLANTS:

64% of total installed capacity (2017 est.)

country comparison to the world: 23

ELECTRICITY - FROM OTHER RENEWABLE SOURCES:

2% of total installed capacity (2017 est.)

country comparison to the world: 132

CRUDE OIL - PRODUCTION:

1.666 million bbl/day (2017 est.)

country comparison to the world: 15

CRUDE OIL - EXPORTS:

1.782 million bbl/day (2015 est.)

country comparison to the world: 7

CRUDE OIL - IMPORTS:

0 bbl/day (2015 est.)

country comparison to the world: 88

CRUDE OIL - PROVED RESERVES:

9.523 billion bbl (1 January 2018 est.)

country comparison to the world: 16

REFINED PETROLEUM PRODUCTS - PRODUCTION:

53,480 bbl/day (2015 est.)

country comparison to the world: 80

REFINED PETROLEUM PRODUCTS - CONSUMPTION:

130,000 bbl/day (2016 est.)

country comparison to the world: 72

REFINED PETROLEUM PRODUCTS - EXPORTS:

30,340 bbl/day (2015 est.)

country comparison to the world: 62

REFINED PETROLEUM PRODUCTS - IMPORTS:

111,600 bbl/day (2015 est.)

country comparison to the world: 50

NATURAL GAS - PRODUCTION:

3.115 billion cu m (2017 est.)

country comparison to the world: 55

NATURAL GAS - CONSUMPTION:

821.2 million cu m (2017 est.)

country comparison to the world: 95

NATURAL GAS - EXPORTS:

3.993 billion cu m (2017 est.)

country comparison to the world: 33

NATURAL GAS - IMPORTS:

0 cu m (2017 est.)

country comparison to the world: 86

NATURAL GAS - PROVED RESERVES:

308.1 billion cu m (1 January 2018 est.)

country comparison to the world: 36

CARBON DIOXIDE EMISSIONS FROM CONSUMPTION OF ENERGY:

20.95 million Mt (2017 est.)

country comparison to the world: 85

COMMUNICATIONS :: ANGOLA

TELEPHONES - FIXED LINES:

total subscriptions: 161,070 (2017 est.)

subscriptions per 100 inhabitants: 1 (2017 est.)

country comparison to the world: 126

TELEPHONES - MOBILE CELLULAR:

total subscriptions: 13,323,952 (2017 est.)

subscriptions per 100 inhabitants: 45 (2017 est.)

country comparison to the world: 71

TELEPHONE SYSTEM:

general assessment:

in the process of a restructure plan and opening up the telecom sector to new competitors, while still retaining a 45% govt portion of the share; slow progress in LTE network development, with only about 10% of the country covered by network infrastructure at the end of 2017

(2017)

domestic: only about one fixed-line per 100 persons; mobile-cellular teledensity about 45 telephones per 100 persons (2017)

international: country code - 244; landing point for the SAT-3/WASC fiber-optic submarine cable that provides connectivity to Europe and Asia; satellite earth stations - 29 (2016)

BROADCAST MEDIA:

state controls all broadcast media with nationwide reach; state-owned Televisao Popular de Angola (TPA) provides terrestrial TV service on 2 channels; a third TPA channel is available via cable and satellite; TV subscription services are available; state-owned Radio Nacional de Angola (RNA) broadcasts on 5 stations; about a half-dozen private radio stations broadcast locally (2009)

INTERNET COUNTRY CODE:

.ao

INTERNET USERS:

total: 2,622,403 (July 2016 est.)

percent of population: 13% (July 2016 est.)

country comparison to the world: 104

BROADBAND - FIXED SUBSCRIPTIONS:

total: 96,919 (2017 est.)

subscriptions per 100 inhabitants: less than 1 (2017 est.)

country comparison to the world: 120

TRANSPORTATION :: ANGOLA

NATIONAL AIR TRANSPORT SYSTEM:

number of registered air carriers: 10 (2015)

inventory of registered aircraft operated by air carriers: 55 (2015)

annual passenger traffic on registered air carriers: 1,244,491 (2015)

annual freight traffic on registered air carriers: 46.043 million mt-km (2015)

CIVIL AIRCRAFT REGISTRATION COUNTRY CODE PREFIX:

D2 (2016)

AIRPORTS:

176 (2013)

country comparison to the world: 32

AIRPORTS - WITH PAVED RUNWAYS:

total: 31 (2017)

over 3,047 m: 7 (2017)

2,438 to 3,047 m: 8 (2017)

1,524 to 2,437 m: 12 (2017)

914 to 1,523 m: 4 (2017)

AIRPORTS - WITH UNPAVED RUNWAYS:

total: 145 (2013)

over 3,047 m: 2 (2013)

2,438 to 3,047 m: 3 (2013)

1,524 to 2,437 m: 31 (2013)

914 to 1,523 m: 66 (2013)

under 914 m: 43 (2013)

HELIPORTS:

1 (2013)

PIPELINES:

352 km gas, 85 km liquid petroleum gas, 1065 km oil, 5 km oil/gas/water (2013)

RAILWAYS:

total: 2,852 km (2014)

narrow gauge: 2,729 km 1.067-m gauge (2014)

123 0.600-m gauge

country comparison to the world: 63

ROADWAYS:

total: 51,429 km (2001)

paved: 5,349 km (2001)

unpaved: 46,080 km (2001)

country comparison to the world: 77

WATERWAYS:

1,300 km (2011)

country comparison to the world: 53

MERCHANT MARINE:

total: 55 (2017)

by type: general cargo 14, oil tanker 9, other 32 (2017)

country comparison to the world: 110

PORTS AND TERMINALS:

major seaport(s): Cabinda, Lobito, Luanda, Namibe

LNG terminal(s) (export): Angola Soyo

MILITARY AND SECURITY :: ANGOLA

MILITARY EXPENDITURES:

2.95% of GDP (2016)

3.52% of GDP (2015)

5.4% of GDP (2014)

4.88% of GDP (2013)

3.59% of GDP (2012)

country comparison to the world: 29

MILITARY BRANCHES:

Angolan Armed Forces (Forcas Armadas Angolanas, FAA): Army, Navy (Marinha de Guerra Angola, MGA), Angolan National Air Force (Forca Aerea Nacional Angolana, FANA; under operational control of the Army) (2012)

MILITARY SERVICE AGE AND OBLIGATION:

20-45 years of age for compulsory male and 18-45 years for voluntary male military service (registration at age 18 is mandatory); 20-45 years of age for voluntary female service; 2-year conscript service obligation; Angolan citizenship required; the Navy (MGA) is entirely staffed with volunteers (2013)

TRANSNATIONAL ISSUES :: ANGOLA

REFUGEES AND INTERNALLY DISPLACED PERSONS:

refugees (country of origin): 36,500 (Democratic Republic of the Congo) (refugees and asylum seekers), 6,448 (Cote d'Ivoire), 5,709 (Mauritania) (2018)

ILLICIT DRUGS:

used as a transshipment point for cocaine destined for Western Europe and other African states, particularly South Africa

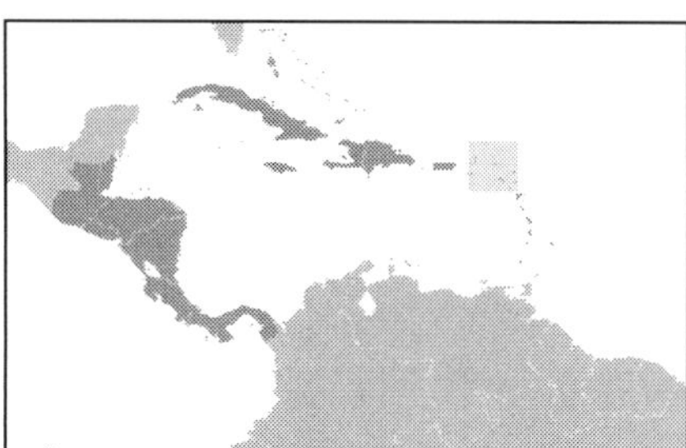

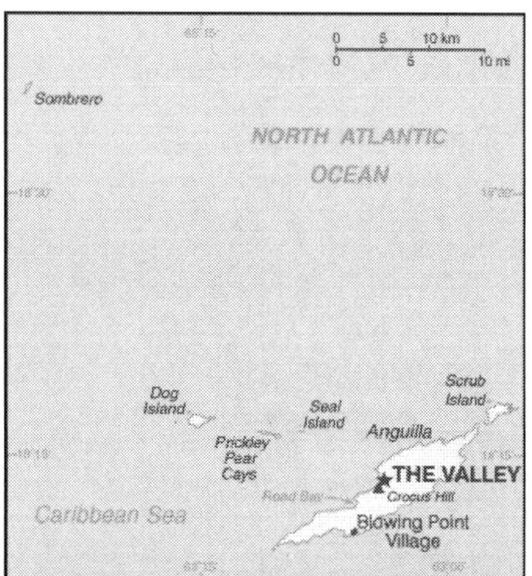

CENTRAL AMERICA :: ANGUILLA

INTRODUCTION :: ANGUILLA

BACKGROUND:

Colonized by English settlers from Saint Kitts in 1650, Anguilla was administered by Great Britain until the early 19th century, when the island - against the wishes of the inhabitants - was incorporated into a single British dependency along with Saint Kitts and Nevis. Several attempts at separation failed. In 1971, two years after a revolt, Anguilla was finally allowed to secede; this arrangement was formally recognized in 1980, with Anguilla becoming a separate British dependency. On 7 September 2017, the island suffered extensive damage from Hurricane Irma, particularly to communications and residential and business infrastructure.

GEOGRAPHY :: ANGUILLA

LOCATION:

Caribbean, islands between the Caribbean Sea and North Atlantic Ocean, east of Puerto Rico

GEOGRAPHIC COORDINATES:

18 15 N, 63 10 W

MAP REFERENCES:

Central America and the Caribbean

AREA:

total: 91 sq km

land: 91 sq km

water: 0 sq km

country comparison to the world: 227

AREA - COMPARATIVE:

about one-half the size of Washington, DC

LAND BOUNDARIES:

0 km

COASTLINE:

61 km

MARITIME CLAIMS:

territorial sea: 3 nm

exclusive fishing zone: 200 nm

CLIMATE:

tropical; moderated by northeast trade winds

TERRAIN:

flat and low-lying island of coral and limestone

ELEVATION:

0 m lowest point: Caribbean Sea

73 highest point: Crocus Hill

NATURAL RESOURCES:

salt, fish, lobster

LAND USE:

agricultural land: 0% (2014 est.)

arable land: 0% (2014 est.) / permanent crops: 0% (2014 est.) / permanent pasture: 0% (2014 est.)

forest: 61.1% (2014 est.)

other: 38.9% (2014 est.)

IRRIGATED LAND:

0 sq km (2012)

POPULATION DISTRIBUTION:

most of the population is concentrated in The Valley in the center of the island; settlmement is fairly uniform in the southwest, but rather sparce in the northeast

NATURAL HAZARDS:

frequent hurricanes and other tropical storms (July to October)

ENVIRONMENT - CURRENT ISSUES:

supplies of potable water sometimes cannot meet increasing demand largely because of poor distribution system

GEOGRAPHY - NOTE:

the most northerly of the Leeward Islands in the Lesser Antilles

PEOPLE AND SOCIETY :: ANGUILLA

POPULATION:

17,422 (July 2018 est.)

country comparison to the world: 220

NATIONALITY:

noun: Anguillan(s)

adjective: Anguillan

ETHNIC GROUPS:

African/black 85.3%, hispanic 4.9%, mixed 3.8%, white 3.2%, East Indian/Indian 1%, other 1.6%, unspecified 0.3% (2011 est.)

note: data represent population by ethnic origin

LANGUAGES:

English (official)

RELIGIONS:

Protestant 73.2% (includes Anglican 22.7%, Methodist 19.4%, Pentecostal 10.5%, Seventh Day Adventist 8.3%, Baptist 7.1%, Church of God 4.9%, Presbytarian 0.2%, Brethren 0.1%), Roman Catholic 6.8%, Jehovah's Witness 1.1%, other Christian 10.9%, other 3.2%, unspecified 0.3%, none 4.5% (2011 est.)

AGE STRUCTURE:

0-14 years: 22.01% (male 1,954 /female 1,880)

15-24 years: 14.06% (male 1,231 /female 1,219)

25-54 years: 43.27% (male 3,386 /female 4,152)

55-64 years: 11.54% (male 918 /female 1,092)

65 years and over: 9.13% (male 786 /female 804) (2018 est.)

MEDIAN AGE:

total: 35.1 years

male: 33.2 years

female: 37 years (2018 est.)

country comparison to the world: 81

POPULATION GROWTH RATE:

1.92% (2018 est.)

country comparison to the world: 51

BIRTH RATE:

12.4 births/1,000 population (2018 est.)

country comparison to the world: 156

DEATH RATE:

4.7 deaths/1,000 population (2018 est.)

country comparison to the world: 202

NET MIGRATION RATE:

11.7 migrant(s)/1,000 population (2017 est.)

country comparison to the world: 7

POPULATION DISTRIBUTION:

most of the population is concentrated in The Valley in the center of the island; settlmement is fairly uniform in the southwest, but rather sparce in the northeast

URBANIZATION:

urban population: 100% of total population (2018)

rate of urbanization: 0.9% annual rate of change (2015-20 est.)

MAJOR URBAN AREAS - POPULATION:

1,000 THE VALLEY (capital) (2018)

SEX RATIO:

at birth: 1.04 male(s)/female (2017 est.)

0-14 years: 1.04 male(s)/female (2017 est.)

15-24 years: 1 male(s)/female (2017 est.)

25-54 years: 0.82 male(s)/female (2017 est.)

55-64 years: 0.9 male(s)/female (2017 est.)

65 years and over: 0.98 male(s)/female (2017 est.)

total population: 0.91 male(s)/female (2017 est.)

INFANT MORTALITY RATE:

total: 3.3 deaths/1,000 live births (2018 est.)

male: 3.7 deaths/1,000 live births (2018 est.)

female: 2.9 deaths/1,000 live births (2018 est.)

country comparison to the world: 206

LIFE EXPECTANCY AT BIRTH:

total population: 81.6 years (2018 est.)

male: 79 years (2018 est.)

female: 84.3 years (2018 est.)

country comparison to the world: 25

TOTAL FERTILITY RATE:

1.74 children born/woman (2018 est.)

country comparison to the world: 162

DRINKING WATER SOURCE:

improved:

urban: 94.6% of population (2015 est.)

total: 94.6% of population (2015 est.)

unimproved:

urban: 5.4% of population (2015 est.)

total: 5.4% of population (2015 est.)

SANITATION FACILITY ACCESS:

improved:

urban: 97.9% of population (2015 est.)

total: 97.9% of population (2015 est.)

unimproved:

urban: 2.1% of population (2015 est.)

total: 2.1% of population (2015 est.)

HIV/AIDS - ADULT PREVALENCE RATE:

NA

HIV/AIDS - PEOPLE LIVING WITH HIV/AIDS:

NA

HIV/AIDS - DEATHS:

NA

MAJOR INFECTIOUS DISEASES:

note: active local transmission of Zika virus by Aedes species mosquitoes has been identified in this country (as of August 2016); It poses an Important risk (a large number of cases possible) among US citizens if bitten by an infective mosquito; other less common ways to get Zika are through sex, via blood transfusion, or during pregnancy, in which the pregnant woman passes Zika virus to her fetus

EDUCATION EXPENDITURES:

2.8% of GDP (2008)

country comparison to the world: 150

GOVERNMENT :: ANGUILLA

COUNTRY NAME:

conventional long form: none

conventional short form: Anguilla

etymology: the name Anguilla means "eel" in various Romance languages (Spanish, Italian, Portuguese, French) and likely derives from the island's lengthy shape

DEPENDENCY STATUS:

overseas territory of the UK

GOVERNMENT TYPE:

parliamentary democracy (House of Assembly); self-governing overseas territory of the UK

CAPITAL:

name: The Valley

geographic coordinates: 18 13 N, 63 03 W

time difference: UTC-4 (1 hour ahead of Washington, DC, during Standard Time)

etymology: name derives from the capital's location between several hills

ADMINISTRATIVE DIVISIONS:

none (overseas territory of the UK)

INDEPENDENCE:

none (overseas territory of the UK)

NATIONAL HOLIDAY:

Anguilla Day, 30 May (1967)

CONSTITUTION:

history: several previous; latest 1 April 1982 (2018)

amendments: amended 1990 (2018)

LEGAL SYSTEM:

common law based on the English model

CITIZENSHIP:

see United Kingdom

SUFFRAGE:

18 years of age; universal

EXECUTIVE BRANCH:

chief of state: Queen ELIZABETH II (since 6 February 1952); represented by Governor Tim FOY (since August 2017)

head of government: Chief Minister Victor BANKS (since 23 April 2015)

cabinet: Executive Council appointed by the governor from among elected members of the House of Assembly

elections/appointments: the monarchy is hereditary; governor appointed by the monarch; following legislative elections, the leader of the majority party or majority coalition usually appointed chief minister by the governor

LEGISLATIVE BRANCH:

description: unicameral House of Assembly (11 seats; 7 members directly elected in single-seat constituencies by simple majority vote, 2 appointed by the governor, and 2 ex officio members - the attorney general and deputy governor; members serve five-year terms)

elections: last held on 22 April 2015 (next to be held in 2020)

election results: percent of vote by party - AUF 54.4%, AUM 38.3%, DOVE 1.4%, independent 5.9%; seats by party - AUF 6, independent 1; composition - men 8, women 3, percent of women 27.3%

JUDICIAL BRANCH:

highest courts: the Eastern Caribbean Supreme Court (ECSC) is the superior court of the Organization of Eastern Caribbean States; the ECSC - headquartered on St. Lucia - consists of the Court of Appeal - headed by the chief justice and 4 judges - and the High Court with 18 judges; the Court of Appeal is itinerant, travelling to member states on a schedule to hear appeals from the High Court and subordinate courts; High Court judges reside in the member states, though none on Anguilla

judge selection and term of office: Eastern Caribbean Supreme Court chief justice appointed by Her Majesty, Queen ELIZABETH II; other justices and judges appointed by the Judicial and Legal Services Commission; Court of Appeal justices appointed for life with mandatory retirement at age 65; High Court judges appointed for life with mandatory retirement at age 62

subordinate courts: Magistrate's Court; Juvenile Court

POLITICAL PARTIES AND LEADERS:

Anguilla Democratic Party or ADP
Anguilla National Alliance or ANA
Anguilla United Front or AUF [Victor BANKS] (alliance includes ADP, ANA)
Anguilla United Movement or AUM [Dr. Ellis WEBSTER]
Democracy, Opportunity, Vision, and Empowerment Party or DOVE [Sutcliffe HODGE]

INTERNATIONAL ORGANIZATION PARTICIPATION:

Caricom (associate), CDB, Interpol (subbureau), OECS, UNESCO (associate), UPU

DIPLOMATIC REPRESENTATION IN THE US:

none (overseas territory of the UK)

DIPLOMATIC REPRESENTATION FROM THE US:

none (overseas territory of the UK)

FLAG DESCRIPTION:

blue, with the flag of the UK in the upper hoist-side quadrant and the Anguillan coat of arms centered in the outer half of the flag; the coat of arms depicts three orange dolphins in an interlocking circular design on a white background with a turquoise-blue field below; the white in the background represents peace; the blue base symbolizes the surrounding sea, as well as faith, youth, and hope; the three dolphins stand for endurance, unity, and strength

NATIONAL SYMBOL(S):

dolphin

NATIONAL ANTHEM:

name: God Bless Anguilla

lyrics/music: Alex RICHARDSON

note: local anthem adopted 1981; as a territory of the United Kingdom, "God Save the Queen" is official (see United Kingdom)

ECONOMY :: ANGUILLA

ECONOMY - OVERVIEW:

Anguilla has few natural resources, is unsuited for agriculture, and the economy depends heavily on luxury tourism, offshore banking, lobster fishing, and remittances from emigrants. Increased activity in the tourism industry has spurred the growth of the construction sector contributing to economic growth. Anguillan officials have put substantial effort into developing the offshore financial sector, which is small but growing. In the medium term, prospects for the economy will depend largely on the recovery of the tourism sector and, therefore, on revived income growth in the industrialized nations as well as on favorable weather conditions.

GDP (PURCHASING POWER PARITY):

$175.4 million (2009 est.)

$191.7 million (2008 est.)

$108.9 million (2004 est.)

country comparison to the world: 222

GDP (OFFICIAL EXCHANGE RATE):

$175.4 million (2009 est.) (2009 est.)

GDP - REAL GROWTH RATE:

-8.5% (2009 est.)

country comparison to the world: 220

GDP - PER CAPITA (PPP):

$12,200 (2008 est.)

country comparison to the world: 130

GDP - COMPOSITION, BY END USE:

household consumption: 74.1% (2017 est.)

government consumption: 18.3% (2017 est.)

investment in fixed capital: 26.8% (2017 est.)

investment in inventories: 0% (2017 est.)

exports of goods and services: 48.2% (2017 est.)

imports of goods and services: -67.4% (2017 est.)

GDP - COMPOSITION, BY SECTOR OF ORIGIN:

agriculture: 3% (2017 est.)

industry: 10.5% (2017 est.)

services: 86.4% (2017 est.)

AGRICULTURE - PRODUCTS:

small quantities of tobacco, vegetables; cattle raising

INDUSTRIES:

tourism, boat building, offshore financial services

INDUSTRIAL PRODUCTION GROWTH RATE:

4% (2017 est.)

country comparison to the world: 75

LABOR FORCE:

6,049 (2001)

country comparison to the world: 219

LABOR FORCE - BY OCCUPATION:

agriculture: 74.1%

industry: 3%

services: 18%

agriculture/fishing/forestry/mining: 4% (2000 est.)

manufacturing: 3% (2000 est.)

construction: 18% (2000 est.)

transportation and utilities: 10% (2000 est.)

commerce: 36% (2000 est.)

UNEMPLOYMENT RATE:

8% (2002)

country comparison to the world: 115

POPULATION BELOW POVERTY LINE:

23% (2002 est.)

HOUSEHOLD INCOME OR CONSUMPTION BY PERCENTAGE SHARE:

lowest 10%: NA

highest 10%: NA

BUDGET:

revenues: 81.92 million (2017 est.)

expenditures: 80.32 million (2017 est.)

TAXES AND OTHER REVENUES:

46.7% (of GDP) (2017 est.)

country comparison to the world: 19

BUDGET SURPLUS (+) OR DEFICIT (-):

0.9% (of GDP) (2017 est.)

country comparison to the world: 34

PUBLIC DEBT:

20.1% of GDP (2015 est.)

20.8% of GDP (2014 est.)

country comparison to the world: 189

FISCAL YEAR:

1 April - 31 March

INFLATION RATE (CONSUMER PRICES):

1.3% (2017 est.)

-0.6% (2016 est.)

country comparison to the world: 67

CENTRAL BANK DISCOUNT RATE:

6.5% (31 December 2010)

6.5% (31 December 2009)

country comparison to the world: 55

COMMERCIAL BANK PRIME LENDING RATE:

9.48% (31 December 2017 est.)

9.01% (31 December 2016 est.)

country comparison to the world: 90

STOCK OF NARROW MONEY:

$25.37 million (31 December 2017 est.)

$23.74 million (31 December 2016 est.)

country comparison to the world: 193

STOCK OF BROAD MONEY:

$25.37 million (31 December 2017 est.)

$23.74 million (31 December 2016 est.)

country comparison to the world: 196

STOCK OF DOMESTIC CREDIT:

$218.5 million (31 December 2017 est.)

$209.1 million (31 December 2016 est.)

country comparison to the world: 183

CURRENT ACCOUNT BALANCE:

-$23.2 million (2017 est.)

-$25.3 million (2016 est.)

country comparison to the world: 73

EXPORTS:

$7.9 million (2017 est.)

$3.9 million (2016 est.)

country comparison to the world: 216

EXPORTS - COMMODITIES:

lobster, fish, livestock, salt, concrete blocks, rum

IMPORTS:

$186.2 million (2017 est.)

$170.1 million (2016 est.)

country comparison to the world: 210

IMPORTS - COMMODITIES:

fuels, foodstuffs, manufactures, chemicals, trucks, textiles

RESERVES OF FOREIGN EXCHANGE AND GOLD:

$76.38 million (31 December 2017 est.)

$48.14 million (31 December 2015 est.)

country comparison to the world: 183

DEBT - EXTERNAL:

$41.04 million (31 December 2013)

$8.8 million (1998)

country comparison to the world: 195

EXCHANGE RATES:

East Caribbean dollars (XCD) per US dollar -

2.7 (2017 est.)

2.7 (2016 est.)

2.7 (2015 est.)

2.7 (2014 est.)

2.7 (2013 est.)

COMMUNICATIONS :: ANGUILLA

TELEPHONES - FIXED LINES:

total subscriptions: 6,000 (July 2016 est.)

subscriptions per 100 inhabitants: 37 (July 2016 est.)

country comparison to the world: 203

TELEPHONES - MOBILE CELLULAR:

total subscriptions: 26,000 (July 2016 est.)

subscriptions per 100 inhabitants: 158 (July 2016 est.)

country comparison to the world: 207

TELEPHONE SYSTEM:

general assessment: modern internal telephone system with fiber-optic trunk lines; telecome sector provides a realatively high contribution to overall GDP; numberous competitors licensed, but small and localized (2017)

domestic: fixed-line teledensity is about 37 per 100 persons; mobile-cellular teledensity is roughly 158 per 100 persons (2017)

international: country code - 1-264; landing point for the East Caribbean Fiber System submarine cable with links to 13 other islands in the eastern Caribbean extending from the British Virgin Islands to Trinidad; microwave radio relay to island of Saint Martin/Sint Maarten

BROADCAST MEDIA:

1 private TV station; multi-channel cable TV subscription services are available; about 10 radio stations, one of which is government-owned (2009)

INTERNET COUNTRY CODE:

.ai

INTERNET USERS:

total: 13,665 (July 2016 est.)

percent of population: 81.6% (July 2016 est.)

country comparison to the world: 211

TRANSPORTATION :: ANGUILLA

NATIONAL AIR TRANSPORT SYSTEM:

number of registered air carriers: 2 (2015)

inventory of registered aircraft operated by air carriers: 3 (2015)

CIVIL AIRCRAFT REGISTRATION COUNTRY CODE PREFIX:

VP-A (2016)

AIRPORTS:

2 (2013)

country comparison to the world: 197

AIRPORTS - WITH PAVED RUNWAYS:

total: 1 (2017)

1,524 to 2,437 m: 1 (2017)

AIRPORTS - WITH UNPAVED RUNWAYS:

total: 1 (2013)

under 914 m: 1 (2013)

ROADWAYS:

total: 175 km (2004)

paved: 82 km (2004)

unpaved: 93 km (2004)

country comparison to the world: 212

MERCHANT MARINE:

total: 1 (2017)

by type: other 1 (2017)

country comparison to the world: 171

PORTS AND TERMINALS:

major seaport(s): Blowing Point, Road Bay

MILITARY AND SECURITY :: ANGUILLA

MILITARY - NOTE:

defense is the responsibility of the UK

TRANSNATIONAL ISSUES :: ANGUILLA

DISPUTES - INTERNATIONAL:

none

ILLICIT DRUGS:

transshipment point for South American narcotics destined for the US and Europe

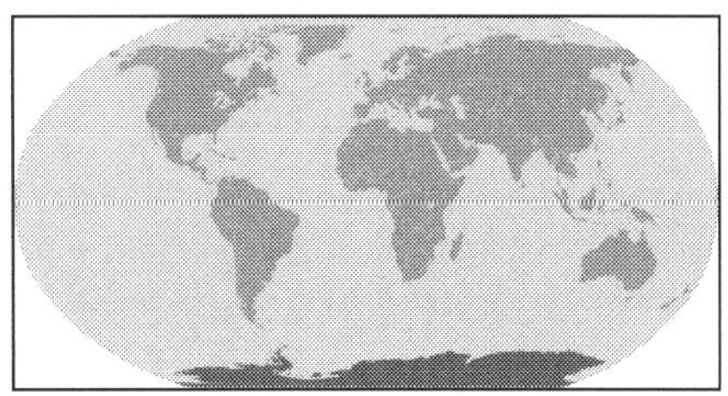

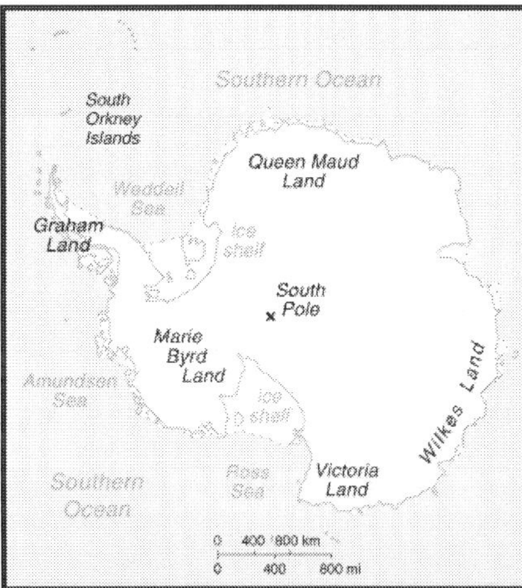

ANTARCTICA :: ANTARCTICA

INTRODUCTION :: ANTARCTICA

BACKGROUND:

Speculation over the existence of a "southern land" was not confirmed until the early 1820s when British and American commercial operators and British and Russian national expeditions began exploring the Antarctic Peninsula region and other areas south of the Antarctic Circle. Not until 1840 was it established that Antarctica was indeed a continent and not merely a group of islands or an area of ocean. Several exploration "firsts" were achieved in the early 20th century, but generally the area saw little human activity. Following World War II, however, the continent experienced an upsurge in scientific research. A number of countries have set up a range of year-round and seasonal stations, camps, and refuges to support scientific research in Antarctica. Seven have made territorial claims, but not all countries recognize these claims. In order to form a legal framework for the activities of nations on the continent, an Antarctic Treaty was negotiated that neither denies nor gives recognition to existing territorial claims; signed in 1959, it entered into force in 1961.

GEOGRAPHY :: ANTARCTICA

LOCATION:

continent mostly south of the Antarctic Circle

GEOGRAPHIC COORDINATES:

90 00 S, 0 00 E

MAP REFERENCES:

Antarctic Region

AREA:

total: 14 million sq km

land: 14 million sq km (280,000 sq km ice-free, 13.72 million sq km ice-covered) (est.)

note: fifth-largest continent, following Asia, Africa, North America, and South America, but larger than Australia and the subcontinent of Europe

country comparison to the world: 2

AREA - COMPARATIVE:

slightly less than 1.5 times the size of the US

LAND BOUNDARIES:

0

note: see entry on Disputes - international

COASTLINE:

17,968 km

MARITIME CLAIMS:

Australia, Chile, and Argentina claim Exclusive Economic Zone (EEZ) rights or similar over 200 nm extensions seaward from their continental claims, but like the claims themselves, these zones are not accepted by other countries; 22 of 29 Antarctic consultative nations have made no claims to Antarctic territory (although Russia and the US have reserved the right to do so) and do not recognize the claims of the other nations; also see the Disputes - international entry

CLIMATE:

the coldest, windiest, and driest continent on Earth; severe low temperatures vary with latitude, elevation, and distance from the ocean; East Antarctica is colder than West Antarctica because of its higher elevation; Antarctic Peninsula has the most moderate climate; higher temperatures occur in January along the coast and average slightly below freezing; summers characterized by continuous daylight, while winters bring continous darkness; persistent high pressure over the interior brings dry, subsiding air that results in very little cloud cover

TERRAIN:

about 98% thick continental ice sheet and 2% barren rock, with average elevations between 2,000 and 4,000 m; mountain ranges up to nearly 5,000 m; ice-free coastal areas include parts of southern Victoria Land, Wilkes Land, the Antarctic Peninsula area, and parts of Ross Island on McMurdo Sound; glaciers form ice shelves along about half of the coastline, and floating ice shelves constitute 11% of the area of the continent

ELEVATION:

mean elevation: 2,300 m

elevation extremes: -2,540 m lowest point: Bentley Subglacial Trench

4892 highest point: Vinson Massif

note: the lowest known land point in Antarctica is hidden in the Bentley Subglacial Trench; at its surface is the deepest ice yet discovered and the world's lowest elevation not under seawater

NATURAL RESOURCES:

iron ore, chromium, copper, gold, nickel, platinum and other minerals, and coal and hydrocarbons have been found in small noncommercial quantities; none presently exploited; krill, finfish, and crab have been taken by commercial fisheries

LAND USE:

0% (2015 est.)

NATURAL HAZARDS:

katabatic (gravity-driven) winds blow coastward from the high interior; frequent blizzards form near the foot of the plateau; cyclonic storms form over the ocean and move clockwise along the coast; volcanism on Deception Island and isolated areas of West Antarctica; other seismic activity rare and weak; large icebergs may calve from ice shelf

ENVIRONMENT - CURRENT ISSUES:

the discovery of a large Antarctic ozone hole in the earth's stratosphere (the ozone layer) - first announced in 1985 - spurred the signing of the Montreal Protocol in 1987, an international agreement phasing out the use of ozone-depleting chemicals; the ozone layer prevents most harmful wavelengths of ultra-violet (UV) light from passing through the earth's atmosphere; ozone depletion has been shown to harm a variety of Antarctic marine plants and animals (plankton); in 2002, significant areas of ice shelves disintegrated in response to regional warming; in 2016, a gradual trend toward "healing" of the ozone hole was reported

GEOGRAPHY - NOTE:

the coldest, windiest, highest (on average), and driest continent; during summer, more solar radiation reaches the surface at the South Pole than is received at the Equator in an equivalent period

mostly uninhabitable, 98% of the land area is covered by the Antarctic ice sheet, the largest single mass of ice on earth covering an area of 14 million sq km (5.4 million sq mi) and containing 26.5 million cu km (6.4 million cu mi) of ice (this is almost 62% of all of the world's fresh water); if all this ice were converted to liquid water, one estimate is that it would be sufficient to raise the height of the world's oceans by 58 m (190 ft)

PEOPLE AND SOCIETY :: ANTARCTICA

POPULATION:

no indigenous inhabitants, but there are both permanent and summer-only staffed research stations

note: 53 countries have signed the 1959 Antarctic Treaty; 30 of those operate through their National Antarctic Program a number of seasonal-only (summer) and year-round research stations on the continent and its nearby islands south of 60 degrees south latitude (the region covered by the Antarctic Treaty); the population engaging in and supporting science or managing and protecting the Antarctic region varies from approximately 4,400 in summer to 1,100 in winter; in addition, approximately 1,000 personnel, including ship's crew and scientists doing onboard research, are present in the waters of the treaty region
peak summer (December-February) population - 4,490 total; Argentina 667, Australia 200, Australia and Romania jointly 13, Belgium 20, Brazil 40, Bulgaria 18, Chile 359, China 90, Czechia 20, Ecuador 26, Finland 20, France 125, France and Italy jointly 60, Germany 90, India 65, Italy 102, Japan 125, South Korea 70, NZ 85, Norway 44, Peru 28, Poland 40, Russia 429, South Africa 80, Spain 50, Sweden 20, Ukraine 24, UK 217, US 1,293, Uruguay 70 (2008-09)
winter (June-August) station population - 1,106 total; Argentina 176, Australia 62, Brazil 12, Chile 114, China 29, France 26, France and Italy jointly 13, Germany 9, India 25, Japan 40, South Korea 18, NZ 10, Norway 7, Poland 12, Russia 148, South Africa 10, Ukraine 12, UK 37, US 337, Uruguay 9 (2009); research stations operated within the Antarctic Treaty area (south of 60 degrees south latitude) by National Antarctic Programs
year-round stations - approximately 40 total; Argentina 6, Australia 3, Brazil 1, Chile 6, China 2, France 1, France and Italy jointly 1, Germany 1, India 1, Japan 1, South Korea 1, NZ 1, Norway 1, Poland 1, Russia 5, South Africa 1, Ukraine 1, UK 2, US 3, Uruguay 1 (2009)
a range of seasonal-only (summer) stations, camps, and refuges - Argentina, Australia, Belarus, Belgium, Bulgaria, Brazil, Chile, China, Czechia, Ecuador, Finland, France, Germany, India, Italy, Japan, South Korea, New Zealand, Norway, Peru, Poland, Russia, South Africa, Spain, Sweden, Ukraine, UK, US, and Uruguay (2008-09)

in addition, during the austral summer some nations have numerous occupied locations such as tent camps, summer-long temporary facilities, and mobile traverses in support of research (May 2009 est.)

GOVERNMENT :: ANTARCTICA

COUNTRY NAME:

conventional long form: none

conventional short form: Antarctica

etymology: name derived from two Greek words meaning "opposite to the Arctic" or "opposite to the north"

GOVERNMENT TYPE:

Antarctic Treaty Summary - the Antarctic region is governed by a system known as the Antarctic Treaty System; the system includes: 1. the Antarctic Treaty, signed on 1 December 1959 and entered into force on 23 June 1961, which establishes the legal framework for the management of Antarctica, 2. Recommendations and Measures adopted at meetings of Antarctic Treaty countries, 3. The Convention for the Conservation of Antarctic Seals (1972), 4. The Convention for the Conservation of Antarctic Marine Living Resources (1980), and 5. The Protocol on Environmental Protection to the Antarctic Treaty (1991); the 40th Antarctic Treaty Consultative Meeting was held 22 May-1 June 2017 in Beijing, China; at these annual meetings, decisions are made by consensus (not by vote) of all consultative member nations; by January 2016, there were 53 treaty member nations: 29 consultative and 24 non-consultative; consultative (decision-making) members include the seven nations that claim portions of Antarctica as national territory (some claims overlap) and 46 non-claimant nations; the US and Russia have reserved the right to make claims; the US does not recognize the claims of others;

Antarctica is administered through meetings of the consultative member nations; decisions from these meetings are carried out by these member nations (with respect to their own nationals and operations) in accordance with their own national laws; the years in parentheses indicate when a consultative member-nation acceded to the Treaty and when it was accepted as a consultative member, while no date indicates the country was an original 1959 treaty signatory; claimant nations are - Argentina, Australia, Chile, France, NZ, Norway, and the UK; nonclaimant consultative nations are - Belgium, Brazil (1975/1983), Bulgaria (1978/1998), China (1983/1985), Czech Republic (1962/2017), Ecuador (1987/1990), Finland (1984/1989), Germany (1979/1981), India (1983/1983), Italy (1981/1987), Japan, South Korea (1986/1989), Netherlands (1967/1990), Peru (1981/1989), Poland (1961/1977), Russia, South Africa, Spain (1982/1988), Sweden (1984/1988), Ukraine (1992/2004), Uruguay (1980/1985), and the US; non-consultative members, with year of accession in parentheses, are - Austria (1987), Belarus (2006), Canada (1988), Colombia (1989), Cuba (1984), Denmark (1965), Estonia (2001), Greece (1987),

Guatemala (1991), Hungary (1984), Iceland (2015), Kazakhstan (2015), North Korea (1987), Malaysia (2011), Monaco (2008), Mongolia (2015), Pakistan (2012), Papua New Guinea (1981), Portugal (2010), Romania (1971), Slovakia (1962/1993), Switzerland (1990), Turkey (1996), and Venezuela (1999); note - Czechoslovakia acceded to the Treaty in 1962 and separated into the Czech Republic and Slovakia in 1993;

Article 1 - area to be used for peaceful purposes only; military activity, such as weapons testing, is prohibited, but military personnel and equipment may be used for scientific research or any other peaceful purpose;Article 2 - freedom of scientific investigation and cooperation shall continue;Article 3 - free exchange of information and personnel, cooperation with the UN and other international agencies;Article 4 - does not recognize, dispute, or establish territorial claims and no new claims shall be asserted while the treaty is in force;Article 5 - prohibits nuclear explosions or disposal of radioactive wastes;Article 6 - includes under the treaty all land and ice shelves south of 60 degrees 00 minutes south and reserves high seas rights;

Article 7 - treaty-state observers have free access, including aerial observation, to any area and may inspect all stations, installations, and equipment; advance notice of all expeditions and of the introduction of military personnel must be given;Article 8 - allows for jurisdiction over observers and scientists by their own states;Article 9 - frequent consultative meetings take place among member nations;Article 10 - treaty states will discourage activities by any country in Antarctica that are contrary to the treaty;Article 11 - disputes to be settled peacefully by the parties concerned or, ultimately, by the ICJ;Articles 12, 13, 14 - deal with upholding, interpreting, and amending the treaty among involved nations;

other agreements - some 200 recommendations adopted at treaty consultative meetings and ratified by governments; a mineral resources agreement was signed in 1988 but remains unratified; the Protocol on Environmental Protection to the Antarctic Treaty was signed 4 October 1991 and entered into force 14 January 1998; this agreement provides for the protection of the Antarctic environment through six specific annexes: 1) environmental impact assessment, 2) conservation of Antarctic fauna and flora, 3) waste disposal and waste management, 4) prevention of marine pollution, 5) area protection and management and 6) liability arising from environmental emergencies; it prohibits all activities relating to mineral resources except scientific research; a permanent Antarctic Treaty Secretariat was established in 2004 in Buenos Aires, Argentina

LEGAL SYSTEM:

Antarctica is administered through annual meetings - known as Antarctic Treaty Consultative Meetings - which include consultative member nations, non-consultative member nations, observer organizations, and expert organizations; decisions from these meetings are carried out by these member nations (with respect to their own nationals and operations) in accordance with their own national laws; more generally, access to the Antarctic Treaty area, that is to all areas between 60 and 90 degrees south latitude, is subject to a number of relevant legal instruments and authorization procedures adopted by the states party to the Antarctic Treaty; note - US law, including certain criminal offenses by or against US nationals, such as murder, may apply extraterritorially; some US laws directly apply to Antarctica; for example, the Antarctic Conservation Act, 16 U.S.C. section 2401 et seq., provides civil and criminal penalties for the following activities unless authorized by regulation of statute: the taking of native mammals or birds; the introduction of nonindigenous plants and animals; entry into specially protected areas; the discharge or disposal of pollutants; and the importation into the US of certain items from Antarctica; violation of the Antarctic Conservation Act carries penalties of up to $10,000 in fines and one year in prison; the National Science Foundation and Department of Justice share enforcement responsibilities; Public Law 95-541, the US Antarctic Conservation Act of 1978, as amended in 1996, requires expeditions from the US to Antarctica to notify, in advance, the Office of Oceans, Room 5805, Department of State, Washington, DC 20520, which reports such plans to other nations as required by the Antarctic Treaty; for more information, contact Permit Office, Office of Polar Programs, National Science Foundation, Arlington, Virginia 22230; telephone: (703) 292-8030, or visit its website at www.nsf.gov

ECONOMY :: ANTARCTICA

ECONOMY - OVERVIEW:

Scientific undertakings rather than commercial pursuits are the predominant human activity in Antarctica. Offshore fishing and tourism, both based abroad, account for Antarctica's limited economic activity.

Antarctic fisheries, targeting three main species – Chilean sea bass, mackerel, and krill– reported landing 295,000 metric tons in 2013-14. Unregulated fishing is an ongoing problem. The Convention on the Conservation of Antarctic Marine Living Resources determines the recommended catch limits for marine species.

A total of 36,702 tourists visited the Antarctic Treaty area in the 2014-15 Antarctic summer, slightly lower than the 37,405 visitors in 2013-14. These estimates were provided to the Antarctic Treaty by the International Association of Antarctica Tour Operators and do not include passengers on overflights. Nearly all of the tourists were passengers on commercial ships and several yachts that make trips during the summer.

COMMUNICATIONS :: ANTARCTICA

TELEPHONE SYSTEM:

general assessment: local systems at some research stations (2015)

domestic: commercial cellular networks operating in a small number of locations (2015)

international: country code - none allocated; via satellite (including mobile Inmarsat and Iridium systems) to and from all research stations, ships, aircraft, and most field parties (2015)

INTERNET COUNTRY CODE:

.aq

INTERNET USERS:

total: 4,400 (July 2016 est.)

percent of population: 100% (July 2016 est.)

country comparison to the world: 217

TRANSPORTATION :: ANTARCTICA

AIRPORTS:

23 (2013)

country comparison to the world: 133

AIRPORTS - WITH UNPAVED RUNWAYS:

total: 23 (2013)

over 3,047 m: 3 (2013)

2,438 to 3,047 m: 5 (2013)

1,524 to 2,437 m: 1 (2013)

914 to 1,523 m: 8 (2013)

under 914 m: 6 (2013)

HELIPORTS:

53 (2012)

note: all year-round and seasonal stations operated by National Antarctic Programs stations have some kind of helicopter landing facilities, prepared (helipads) or unprepared

PORTS AND TERMINALS:

McMurdo Station; most coastal stations have sparse and intermittent offshore anchorages; a few stations have basic wharf facilities

TRANSPORTATION - NOTE:

US coastal stations include McMurdo (77 51 S, 166 40 E) and Palmer (64 43 S, 64 03 W); government use only except by permit (see Permit Office under "Legal System"); all ships at port are subject to inspection in accordance with Article 7, Antarctic Treaty; relevant legal instruments and authorization procedures adopted by the states parties to the Antarctic Treaty regulating access to the Antarctic Treaty area to all areas between 60 and 90 degrees of latitude south have to be complied with (see "Legal System"); The Hydrographic Commission on Antarctica (HCA), a commission of the International Hydrographic Organization (IHO), is responsible for hydrographic surveying and nautical charting matters in Antarctic Treaty area; it coordinates and facilitates provision of accurate and appropriate charts and other aids to navigation in support of safety of navigation in region; membership of HCA is open to any IHO Member State whose government has acceded to the Antarctic Treaty and which contributes resources or data to IHO Chart coverage of the area

MILITARY AND SECURITY :: ANTARCTICA

MILITARY - NOTE:

the Antarctic Treaty prohibits any measures of a military nature, such as the establishment of military bases and fortifications, the carrying out of military maneuvers, or the testing of any type of weapon; it permits the use of military personnel or equipment for scientific research or for any other peaceful purposes

TRANSNATIONAL ISSUES :: ANTARCTICA

DISPUTES - INTERNATIONAL:

the Antarctic Treaty freezes, and most states do not recognize, the land and maritime territorial claims made by Argentina, Australia, Chile, France, New Zealand, Norway, and the UK (some overlapping) for three-fourths of the continentthe US and Russia reserve the right to make claimsno formal claims have been made in the sector between 90 degrees west and 150 degrees westthe International Whaling Commission created a sanctuary around the entire continent to deter catches by countries claiming to conduct scientific whalingAustralia has established a similar preserve in the waters around its territorial claim

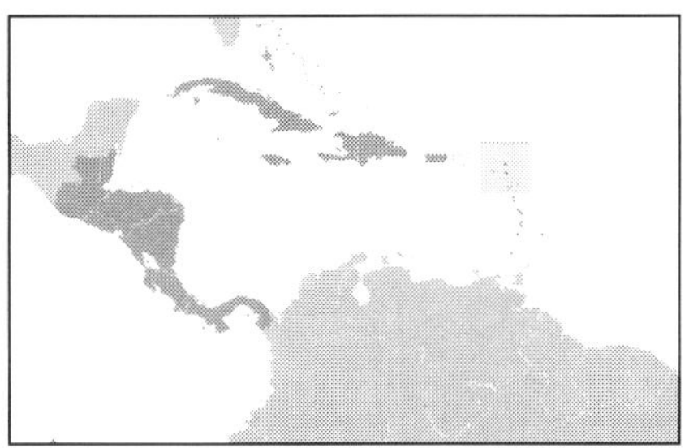

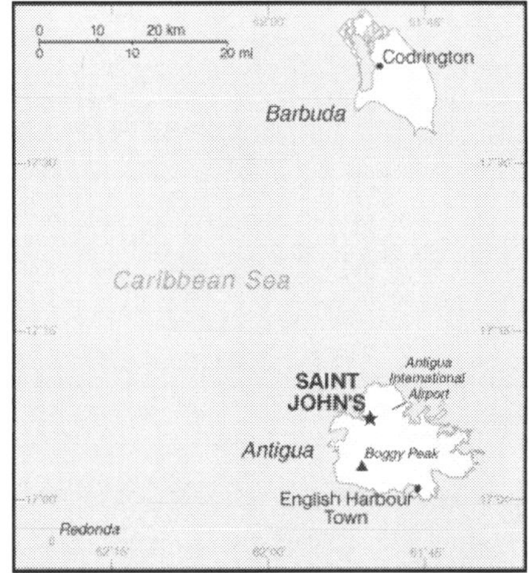

CENTRAL AMERICA :: ANTIGUA AND BARBUDA

INTRODUCTION :: ANTIGUA AND BARBUDA

BACKGROUND:

The Siboney were the first people to inhabit the islands of Antigua and Barbuda in 2400 B.C., but Arawak Indians populated the islands when COLUMBUS landed on his second voyage in 1493. Early Spanish and French settlements were succeeded by an English colony in 1667. Slavery, established to run the sugar plantations on Antigua, was abolished in 1834. The islands became an independent state within the British Commonwealth of Nations in 1981. On 6 September 2017, Hurricane Irma passed over the island of Barbuda devastating the island and forcing the evacuation of the population to Antigua. Almost all the structures on Barbuda were destroyed and the vegetation stripped, but Antigua was spared the worst.

GEOGRAPHY :: ANTIGUA AND BARBUDA

LOCATION:

Caribbean, islands between the Caribbean Sea and the North Atlantic Ocean, east-southeast of Puerto Rico

GEOGRAPHIC COORDINATES:

17 03 N, 61 48 W

MAP REFERENCES:

Central America and the Caribbean

AREA:

total: 442.6 sq km (Antigua 280 sq km; Barbuda 161 sq km)

land: 442.6 sq km

water: 0 sq km

note: includes Redonda, 1.6 sq km

country comparison to the world: 201

AREA - COMPARATIVE:

2.5 times the size of Washington, DC

LAND BOUNDARIES:

0 km

COASTLINE:

153 km

MARITIME CLAIMS:

territorial sea: 12 nm

exclusive economic zone: 200 nm

contiguous zone: 24 nm

continental shelf: 200 nm or to the edge of the continental margin

CLIMATE:

tropical maritime; little seasonal temperature variation

TERRAIN:

mostly low-lying limestone and coral islands, with some higher volcanic areas

ELEVATION:

0 m lowest point: Caribbean Sea

402 highest point: Mount Obama

NATURAL RESOURCES:

NEGL; pleasant climate fosters tourism

LAND USE:

agricultural land: 20.5% (2014 est.)

arable land: 9.1% (2014 est.) / permanent crops: 2.3% (2014 est.) / permanent pasture: 9.1% (2014 est.)

forest: 22.3% (2014 est.)

other: 57.2% (2014 est.)

IRRIGATED LAND:

1.3 sq km (2012)

POPULATION DISTRIBUTION:

the island of Antigua is home to approximately 97% of the population; nearly the entire population of Barbuda lives in Codrington

NATURAL HAZARDS:

hurricanes and tropical storms (July to October); periodic droughts

ENVIRONMENT - CURRENT ISSUES:

water management - a major concern because of limited natural freshwater resources - is further hampered by the clearing of trees to increase crop production, causing rainfall to run off quickly

ENVIRONMENT - INTERNATIONAL AGREEMENTS:

party to: Biodiversity, Climate Change, Climate Change-Kyoto Protocol, Desertification, Endangered Species, Environmental Modification, Hazardous Wastes, Law of the Sea, Marine Dumping, Ozone Layer Protection, Ship Pollution, Wetlands, Whaling

signed, but not ratified: none of the selected agreements

GEOGRAPHY - NOTE:

Antigua has a deeply indented shoreline with many natural harbors and beaches; Barbuda has a large western harbor

PEOPLE AND SOCIETY :: ANTIGUA AND BARBUDA

POPULATION:

95,882 (July 2018 est.)

country comparison to the world: 197

NATIONALITY:

noun: Antiguan(s), Barbudan(s)

adjective: Antiguan, Barbudan

ETHNIC GROUPS:

black 87.3%, mixed 4.7%, hispanic 2.7%, white 1.6%, other 2.7%, unspecified 0.9% (2011 est.)

note: data represent population by ethnic group

LANGUAGES:

English (official), Antiguan creole

RELIGIONS:

Protestant 68.3% (Anglican 17.6%, Seventh Day Adventist 12.4%, Pentecostal 12.2%, Moravian 8.3%, Methodist 5.6%, Wesleyan Holiness 4.5%, Church of God 4.1%, Baptist 3.6%), Roman Catholic 8.2%, other 12.2%, unspecified 5.5%, none 5.9% (2011 est.)

AGE STRUCTURE:

0-14 years: 22.91% (male 11,165 /female 10,800)

15-24 years: 16.6% (male 7,924 /female 7,997)

25-54 years: 42.03% (male 18,438 /female 21,861)

55-64 years: 10.13% (male 4,346 /female 5,370)

65 years and over: 8.32% (male 3,422 /female 4,559) (2018 est.)

DEPENDENCY RATIOS:

total dependency ratio: 45.2 (2015 est.)

youth dependency ratio: 35.7 (2015 est.)

elderly dependency ratio: 9.6 (2015 est.)

potential support ratio: 10.5 (2015 est.)

MEDIAN AGE:

total: 32.2 years

male: 30.2 years

female: 33.8 years (2018 est.)

country comparison to the world: 104

POPULATION GROWTH RATE:

1.2% (2018 est.)

country comparison to the world: 91

BIRTH RATE:

15.6 births/1,000 population (2018 est.)

country comparison to the world: 115

DEATH RATE:

5.8 deaths/1,000 population (2018 est.)

country comparison to the world: 172

NET MIGRATION RATE:

2.2 migrant(s)/1,000 population (2017 est.)

country comparison to the world: 42

POPULATION DISTRIBUTION:

the island of Antigua is home to approximately 97% of the population; nearly the entire population of Barbuda lives in Codrington

URBANIZATION:

urban population: 24.6% of total population (2018)

rate of urbanization: 0.55% annual rate of change (2015-20 est.)

MAJOR URBAN AREAS - POPULATION:

21,000 SAINT JOHN'S (capital) (2018)

SEX RATIO:

at birth: 1.05 male(s)/female (2017 est.)

0-14 years: 1.03 male(s)/female (2017 est.)

15-24 years: 0.99 male(s)/female (2017 est.)

25-54 years: 0.84 male(s)/female (2017 est.)

55-64 years: 0.82 male(s)/female (2017 est.)

65 years and over: 0.76 male(s)/female (2017 est.)

total population: 0.9 male(s)/female (2017 est.)

INFANT MORTALITY RATE:

total: 11.7 deaths/1,000 live births (2018 est.)

male: 13.5 deaths/1,000 live births (2018 est.)

female: 9.9 deaths/1,000 live births (2018 est.)

country comparison to the world: 119

LIFE EXPECTANCY AT BIRTH:

total population: 76.9 years (2018 est.)

male: 74.8 years (2018 est.)

female: 79.2 years (2018 est.)

country comparison to the world: 82

TOTAL FERTILITY RATE:

1.99 children born/woman (2018 est.)

country comparison to the world: 119

HEALTH EXPENDITURES:

5.5% of GDP (2014)

country comparison to the world: 124

HOSPITAL BED DENSITY:

3.8 beds/1,000 population (2014)

DRINKING WATER SOURCE:

improved:

urban: 97.9% of population (2015 est.)

rural: 97.9% of population (2015 est.)

total: 97.9% of population (2015 est.)

unimproved:

urban: 2.1% of population (2015 est.)

rural: 2.1% of population (2015 est.)

total: 2.1% of population (2015 est.)

SANITATION FACILITY ACCESS:

improved:

urban: 91.4% of population (2011 est.)

rural: 91.4% of population (2011 est.)

total: 91.4% of population (2011 est.)

unimproved:

urban: 8.6% of population (2011 est.)

rural: 8.6% of population (2011 est.)

total: 8.6% of population (2011 est.)

HIV/AIDS - ADULT PREVALENCE RATE:

NA

HIV/AIDS - PEOPLE LIVING WITH HIV/AIDS:

NA

HIV/AIDS - DEATHS:

NA

MAJOR INFECTIOUS DISEASES:

note: active local transmission of Zika virus by Aedes species mosquitoes has been identified in this country (as of August 2016); it poses an important risk (a large number of cases possible) among US citizens if bitten by an infective mosquito; other less common ways to get Zika are through sex, via blood transfusion, or during pregnancy, in which the pregnant woman passes Zika virus to her fetus

OBESITY - ADULT PREVALENCE RATE:

18.9% (2016)

country comparison to the world: 113

EDUCATION EXPENDITURES:

2.5% of GDP (2009)

country comparison to the world: 163

LITERACY:

definition: age 15 and over has completed five or more years of schooling (2012 est.)

total population: 99% (2012 est.)

male: 98.4% (2012 est.)

female: 99.4% (2012 est.)

SCHOOL LIFE EXPECTANCY (PRIMARY TO TERTIARY EDUCATION):

total: 14 years (2012)

male: 13 years (2012)

female: 15 years (2012)

GOVERNMENT :: ANTIGUA AND BARBUDA

COUNTRY NAME:

conventional long form: none

conventional short form: Antigua and Barbuda

etymology: "antiguo" is Spanish for "ancient" or "old"; the island was discovered by Christopher COLUMBUS in 1493 and, according to tradition, named by him after the church of Santa Maria la Antigua (Old Saint Mary's) in Seville; "barbuda" is Spanish for "bearded" and the adjective may refer to the alleged beards of the indigenous people or to the island's bearded fig trees

GOVERNMENT TYPE:

parliamentary democracy (Parliament) under a constitutional monarchy; a Commonwealth realm

CAPITAL:

name: Saint John's

geographic coordinates: 17 07 N, 61 51 W

time difference: UTC-4 (1 hour ahead of Washington, DC, during Standard Time)

ADMINISTRATIVE DIVISIONS:

6 parishes and 2 dependencies*; Barbuda*, Redonda*, Saint George, Saint John, Saint Mary, Saint Paul, Saint Peter, Saint Philip

INDEPENDENCE:

1 November 1981 (from the UK)

NATIONAL HOLIDAY:

Independence Day, 1 November (1981)

CONSTITUTION:

history: several previous; latest presented 31 July 1981, effective 31 October 1981 (The Antigua and Barbuda Constitution Order 1981) (2018)

amendments: proposed by either house of Parliament; passage of amendments to constitutional sections such as citizenship, fundamental rights and freedoms, the establishment, power, and authority of the executive and legislative branches, the Supreme Court Order, and the procedure for amending the constitution requires approval by at least two-thirds majority vote of the membership of both houses, approval by at least two-thirds majority in a referendum, and assent to by the governor general; passage of other amendments requires only two-thirds majority vote by both houses; amended 2009, 2011 (2018)

LEGAL SYSTEM:

common law based on the English model

INTERNATIONAL LAW ORGANIZATION PARTICIPATION:

has not submitted an ICJ jurisdiction declaration; accepts ICCt jurisdiction

CITIZENSHIP:

citizenship by birth: yes

citizenship by descent only: yes

dual citizenship recognized: yes

residency requirement for naturalization: 7 years

SUFFRAGE:

18 years of age; universal

EXECUTIVE BRANCH:

chief of state: Queen ELIZABETH II (since 6 February 1952); represented by Governor General Rodney WILLIAMS (since 14 August 2014)

head of government: Prime Minister Gaston BROWNE (since 13 June 2014)

cabinet: Council of Ministers appointed by the governor general on the advice of the prime minister

elections/appointments: the monarchy is hereditary; governor general appointed by the monarch on the advice of the prime minister; following legislative elections, the leader of the majority party or majority coalition usually appointed prime minister by the governor general

LEGISLATIVE BRANCH:

description: bicameral Parliament consists of:
Senate (17 seats; members appointed by the governor general)
House of Representatives (17 seats; members directly elected in single-seat constituencies by simple majority vote to serve 5-year terms)

elections:
Senate - last appointed on 26 March 2018 (next NA)
House of Representatives - last held on 21 March 2018 (next to be held in March 2023)

election results:
Senate - composition - men 8, women 9, percent of women 52.9%
House of Representatives - percent of vote by party - ABLP 59.4%, UPP 37.2%, BPM 1.4%, other 1.9% ; seats by party - ABLP 15, UPP 1, BPM 1; composition - men 17, women 2, percent of women 10.5%; note - total Parliament percent of women 30.6%

JUDICIAL BRANCH:

highest courts: the Eastern Caribbean Supreme Court (ECSC) is the superior court of the Organization of Eastern Caribbean States; the ECSC - headquartered on St. Lucia - consists of the Court of Appeal - headed by the chief justice and 4 judges - and the High Court with 18 judges; the Court of Appeal is itinerant, travelling to member states on a schedule to hear appeals from the High Court and subordinate courts; High Court judges reside at the member states with 2 assigned to Antigua and Barbuda

judge selection and term of office: chief justice of Eastern Caribbean Supreme Court appointed by the Her Majesty, Queen ELIZABETH II; other justices and judges appointed by the Judicial and Legal Services Commission; Court of Appeal justices appointed for life with mandatory retirement at age 65; High Court judges appointed for life with mandatory retirement at age 62

subordinate courts: Industrial Court; Magistrates' Courts

POLITICAL PARTIES AND LEADERS:

Antigua Caribbean Liberation Movement or ACLM
Antigua Labor Party or ABLP [Gaston BROWNE]
Antigua Barbuda True Labor Party or ABTLP [Sharlene SAMUEL]
Barbuda People's Movement or BPM [Trevor WALKER]
Barbuda People's Movement for Change [Arthur NIBBS]
Barbudans for a Better Barbuda [Ordrick SAMUEL]
Democratic National Alliance or DNA [Joanne MASSIAH]
Go Green for Life [Owen GEORGE]
Progressive Labor Movement or PLM

United National Democratic Party or UNDP
United Progressive Party or UPP [Harold LOVELL] (a coalition of ACLM, PLM, UNDP)

INTERNATIONAL ORGANIZATION PARTICIPATION:

ACP, AOSIS, C, Caricom, CDB, CELAC, FAO, G-77, IBRD, ICAO, ICC (NGOs), ICCt, ICRM, IDA, IFAD, IFC, IFRCS, ILO, IMF, IMO, IMSO, Interpol, IOC, IOM, ISO (subscriber), ITU, ITUC (NGOs), MIGA, NAM (observer), OAS, OECS, OPANAL, OPCW, Petrocaribe, UN, UNCTAD, UNESCO, UPU, WFTU (NGOs), WHO, WIPO, WMO, WTO

DIPLOMATIC REPRESENTATION IN THE US:

chief of mission: Ambassador Sir Ronald SANDERS (since 17 September 2015)

chancery: 3216 New Mexico Avenue NW, Washington, DC 20016

telephone: [1] (202) 362-5122

FAX: [1] (202) 362-5525

consulate(s) general: Miami, New York

DIPLOMATIC REPRESENTATION FROM THE US:

the US does not have an embassy in Antigua and Barbuda; the US Ambassador to Barbados is accredited to Antigua and Barbuda

FLAG DESCRIPTION:

red, with an inverted isosceles triangle based on the top edge of the flag; the triangle contains three horizontal bands of black (top), light blue, and white, with a yellow rising sun in the black band; the sun symbolizes the dawn of a new era, black represents the African heritage of most of the population, blue is for hope, and red is for the dynamism of the people; the "V" stands for victory; the successive yellow, blue, and white coloring is also meant to evoke the country's tourist attractions of sun, sea, and sand

NATIONAL SYMBOL(S):

fallow deer; national colors: red, white, blue, black, yellow

NATIONAL ANTHEM:

name: Fair Antigua, We Salute Thee

lyrics/music: Novelle Hamilton RICHARDS/Walter Garnet Picart CHAMBERS

note: adopted 1967; as a Commonwealth country, in addition to the national anthem, "God Save the Queen" serves as the royal anthem (see United Kingdom)

ECONOMY :: ANTIGUA AND BARBUDA

ECONOMY - OVERVIEW:

Tourism continues to dominate Antigua and Barbuda's economy, accounting for nearly 60% of GDP and 40% of investment. The dual-island nation's agricultural production is focused on the domestic market and constrained by a limited water supply and a labor shortage stemming from the lure of higher wages in tourism and construction. Manufacturing comprises enclave-type assembly for export with major products being bedding, handicrafts, and electronic components.

Like other countries in the region, Antigua's economy was severely hit by effects of the global economic recession in 2009. The country suffered from the collapse of its largest private sector employer, a steep decline in tourism, a rise in debt, and a sharp economic contraction between 2009 and 2011. Antigua has not yet returned to its pre-crisis growth levels. Barbuda suffered significant damages after hurricanes Irma and Maria passed through the Caribbean in 2017.

Prospects for economic growth in the medium term will continue to depend on tourist arrivals from the US, Canada, and Europe and could be disrupted by potential damage from natural disasters. The new government, elected in 2014 and led by Prime Minister Gaston Browne, continues to face significant fiscal challenges. The government places some hope in a new Citizenship by Investment Program, to both reduce public debt levels and spur growth, and a resolution of a WTO dispute with the US.

GDP (PURCHASING POWER PARITY):

$2.398 billion (2017 est.)

$2.334 billion (2016 est.)

$2.215 billion (2015 est.)

note: data are in 2017 dollars

country comparison to the world: 194

GDP (OFFICIAL EXCHANGE RATE):

$1.524 billion (2017 est.) (2017 est.)

GDP - REAL GROWTH RATE:

2.8% (2017 est.)

5.3% (2016 est.)

4.1% (2015 est.)

country comparison to the world: 120

GDP - PER CAPITA (PPP):

$26,400 (2017 est.)

$25,900 (2016 est.)

$24,900 (2015 est.)

note: data are in 2017 dollars

country comparison to the world: 78

GROSS NATIONAL SAVING:

17.3% of GDP (2017 est.)

24.5% of GDP (2016 est.)

30.7% of GDP (2015 est.)

country comparison to the world: 115

GDP - COMPOSITION, BY END USE:

household consumption: 53.5% (2017 est.)

government consumption: 15.2% (2017 est.)

investment in fixed capital: 23.9% (2017 est.)

investment in inventories: 0.1% (2017 est.)

exports of goods and services: 73.9% (2017 est.)

imports of goods and services: -66.5% (2017 est.)

GDP - COMPOSITION, BY SECTOR OF ORIGIN:

agriculture: 1.8% (2017 est.)

industry: 20.8% (2017 est.)

services: 77.3% (2017 est.)

AGRICULTURE - PRODUCTS:

cotton, fruits, vegetables, bananas, coconuts, cucumbers, mangoes, sugarcane; livestock

INDUSTRIES:

tourism, construction, light manufacturing (clothing, alcohol, household appliances)

INDUSTRIAL PRODUCTION GROWTH RATE:

6.8% (2017 est.)

country comparison to the world: 32

LABOR FORCE:

30,000 (1991)

country comparison to the world: 204

LABOR FORCE - BY OCCUPATION:

agriculture: 7%

industry: 11%

services: 82% (1983 est.)

UNEMPLOYMENT RATE:

11% (2014 est.)

country comparison to the world: 148

POPULATION BELOW POVERTY LINE:

NA

HOUSEHOLD INCOME OR CONSUMPTION BY PERCENTAGE SHARE:

lowest 10%: NA

highest 10%: NA

BUDGET:

revenues: 298.2 million (2017 est.)

expenditures: 334 million (2017 est.)

TAXES AND OTHER REVENUES:

19.6% (of GDP) (2017 est.)

country comparison to the world: 154

BUDGET SURPLUS (+) OR DEFICIT (-):

-2.4% (of GDP) (2017 est.)

country comparison to the world: 112

PUBLIC DEBT:

86.8% of GDP (2017 est.)

86.2% of GDP (2016 est.)

country comparison to the world: 30

FISCAL YEAR:

1 April - 31 March

INFLATION RATE (CONSUMER PRICES):

2.5% (2017 est.)

-0.5% (2016 est.)

country comparison to the world: 122

CENTRAL BANK DISCOUNT RATE:

6.5% (31 December 2010)

6.5% (31 December 2009)

country comparison to the world: 56

COMMERCIAL BANK PRIME LENDING RATE:

9.31% (31 December 2017 est.)

9.58% (31 December 2016 est.)

country comparison to the world: 92

STOCK OF NARROW MONEY:

$349.2 million (31 December 2017 est.)

$293 million (31 December 2016 est.)

country comparison to the world: 178

STOCK OF BROAD MONEY:

$349.2 million (31 December 2017 est.)

$293 million (31 December 2016 est.)

country comparison to the world: 182

STOCK OF DOMESTIC CREDIT:

$909.6 million (31 December 2017 est.)

$913 million (31 December 2016 est.)

country comparison to the world: 169

CURRENT ACCOUNT BALANCE:

-$112 million (2017 est.)

$2 million (2016 est.)

country comparison to the world: 88

EXPORTS:

$86.7 million (2017 est.)

$56.5 million (2016 est.)

country comparison to the world: 198

EXPORTS - PARTNERS:

Poland 62.2%, Cameroon 9.5%, US 5.1%, UK 4.5% (2017)

EXPORTS - COMMODITIES:

petroleum products, bedding, handicrafts, electronic components, transport equipment, food and live animals

IMPORTS:

$560 million (2017 est.)

$503.4 million (2016 est.)

country comparison to the world: 197

IMPORTS - COMMODITIES:

food and live animals, machinery and transport equipment, manufactures, chemicals, oil

IMPORTS - PARTNERS:

US 48%, Spain 4.2% (2017)

DEBT - EXTERNAL:

$441.2 million (31 December 2012)

$458 million (June 2010)

country comparison to the world: 181

EXCHANGE RATES:

East Caribbean dollars (XCD) per US dollar -

2.7 (2017 est.)

2.7 (2016 est.)

2.7 (2015 est.)

2.7 (2014 est.)

2.7 (2013 est.)

ENERGY :: ANTIGUA AND BARBUDA

ELECTRICITY ACCESS:

population without electricity: 9,358 (2012)

electrification - total population: 91% (2012)

electrification - urban areas: 100% (2012)

electrification - rural areas: 80% (2012)

ELECTRICITY - PRODUCTION:

331 million kWh (2016 est.)

country comparison to the world: 179

ELECTRICITY - CONSUMPTION:

307.8 million kWh (2016 est.)

country comparison to the world: 184

ELECTRICITY - EXPORTS:

0 kWh (2016 est.)

country comparison to the world: 99

ELECTRICITY - IMPORTS:

0 kWh (2016 est.)

country comparison to the world: 120

ELECTRICITY - INSTALLED GENERATING CAPACITY:

124,000 kW (2016 est.)

country comparison to the world: 177

ELECTRICITY - FROM FOSSIL FUELS:

97% of total installed capacity (2016 est.)

country comparison to the world: 31

ELECTRICITY - FROM NUCLEAR FUELS:

0% of total installed capacity (2017 est.)

country comparison to the world: 38

ELECTRICITY - FROM HYDROELECTRIC PLANTS:

0% of total installed capacity (2017 est.)

country comparison to the world: 153

ELECTRICITY - FROM OTHER RENEWABLE SOURCES:

3% of total installed capacity (2017 est.)

country comparison to the world: 119

CRUDE OIL - PRODUCTION:

0 bbl/day (2017 est.)

country comparison to the world: 104

CRUDE OIL - EXPORTS:

0 bbl/day (2015 est.)

country comparison to the world: 85

CRUDE OIL - IMPORTS:

0 bbl/day (2015 est.)

country comparison to the world: 89

CRUDE OIL - PROVED RESERVES:

0 bbl (1 January 2018 est.)

country comparison to the world: 102

REFINED PETROLEUM PRODUCTS - PRODUCTION:

0 bbl/day (2015 est.)

country comparison to the world: 113

REFINED PETROLEUM PRODUCTS - CONSUMPTION:

5,000 bbl/day (2016 est.)

country comparison to the world: 177

REFINED PETROLEUM PRODUCTS - EXPORTS:

91 bbl/day (2015 est.)

country comparison to the world: 119

REFINED PETROLEUM PRODUCTS - IMPORTS:

5,065 bbl/day (2015 est.)

country comparison to the world: 172

NATURAL GAS - PRODUCTION:

0 cu m (2017 est.)

country comparison to the world: 99

NATURAL GAS - CONSUMPTION:

0 cu m (2017 est.)

country comparison to the world: 119

NATURAL GAS - EXPORTS:

0 cu m (2017 est.)

country comparison to the world: 61

NATURAL GAS - IMPORTS:

0 cu m (2017 est.)

country comparison to the world: 87

NATURAL GAS - PROVED RESERVES:

0 cu m (1 January 2014 est.)

country comparison to the world: 105

CARBON DIOXIDE EMISSIONS FROM CONSUMPTION OF ENERGY:

740,300 Mt (2017 est.)

country comparison to the world: 175

COMMUNICATIONS :: ANTIGUA AND BARBUDA

TELEPHONES - FIXED LINES:

total subscriptions: 22,504 (July 2016 est.)

subscriptions per 100 inhabitants: 24 (July 2016 est.)

country comparison to the world: 172

TELEPHONES - MOBILE CELLULAR:

total subscriptions: 180,000 (July 2016 est.)

subscriptions per 100 inhabitants: 190 (July 2016 est.)

country comparison to the world: 183

TELEPHONE SYSTEM:

general assessment: good automatic telephone system with fiber-optic lines; telecom sector contributes heavily to GDP; numerous mobile network competitors licensed, but small and local (2017)

domestic: fixed-line teledensity roughly 24 per 100 persons; mobile-cellular teledensity is about 190 per 100 persons (2017)

international: country code - 1-268; landing points for the East Caribbean Fiber System (ECFS) and the Global Caribbean Network (GCN) submarine cable systems with links to other islands in the eastern Caribbean extending from the British Virgin Islands to Trinidad; satellite earth stations - 2; tropospheric scatter to Saba (Netherlands) and Guadeloupe (France); *international:* 3 fiber optic submarine cables (2 to Saint Kitts and 1 to Guadeloupe); satellite earth station - 1 Intelsat (Atlantic Ocean) (2017)

BROADCAST MEDIA:

state-controlled Antigua and Barbuda Broadcasting Service (ABS) operates 1 TV station; multi-channel cable TV subscription services are available; ABS operates 1 radio station; roughly 15 radio stations, some broadcasting on multiple frequencies (2009)

INTERNET COUNTRY CODE:

.ag

INTERNET USERS:

total: 60,000 (July 2016 est.)

percent of population: 65.2% (July 2016 est.)

country comparison to the world: 187

BROADBAND - FIXED SUBSCRIPTIONS:

total: 9,261 (2017 est.)

subscriptions per 100 inhabitants: 10 (2017 est.)

country comparison to the world: 169

TRANSPORTATION :: ANTIGUA AND BARBUDA

NATIONAL AIR TRANSPORT SYSTEM:

number of registered air carriers: 1 (2015)

inventory of registered aircraft operated by air carriers: 9 (2015)

annual passenger traffic on registered air carriers: 1,039,809 (2015)

annual freight traffic on registered air carriers: 526,545 mt-km (2015)

CIVIL AIRCRAFT REGISTRATION COUNTRY CODE PREFIX:

V2 (2016)

AIRPORTS:

3 (2013)

country comparison to the world: 193

AIRPORTS - WITH PAVED RUNWAYS:

total: 2 (2017)

2,438 to 3,047 m: 1 (2017)

under 914 m: 1 (2017)

AIRPORTS - WITH UNPAVED RUNWAYS:

total: 1 (2013)

under 914 m: 1 (2013)

ROADWAYS:

total: 1,170 km (2011)

paved: 386 km (2011)

unpaved: 784 km (2011)

country comparison to the world: 183

MERCHANT MARINE:

total: 964 (2017)

by type: bulk carrier 36, container ship 238, general cargo 615, oil tanker 2, other 73 (2017)

country comparison to the world: 25

PORTS AND TERMINALS:

major seaport(s): Saint John's

MILITARY AND SECURITY :: ANTIGUA AND BARBUDA

MILITARY BRANCHES:

Ministry of National Security, Royal Antigua and Barbuda Defense Force (includes Antigua and Barbuda Coast Guard) (2012)

MILITARY SERVICE AGE AND OBLIGATION:

18 years of age for voluntary military service; no conscription; Governor-General has powers to call up men for national service and set the age at which they could be called up (2012)

TRANSNATIONAL ISSUES :: ANTIGUA AND BARBUDA

DISPUTES - INTERNATIONAL:

none

TRAFFICKING IN PERSONS:

current situation: Antigua and Barbuda is a destination and transit country for adults and children subjected to sex trafficking and forced labor; forced prostitution has been reported in bars, taverns, and brothels, while forced labor occurs in domestic service and the retail sector

tier rating: Tier 2 Watch List – Antigua and Barbuda does not fully comply with the minimum standards for the elimination of trafficking; however, it is making significant efforts to do so; the government made no discernible progress in convicting traffickers in 2014 but charged two individuals in separate cases; efforts to convict traffickers have been impeded by a 2014 ruling that found the 2010 anti-trafficking act was unconstitutional because jurisdiction rests with the Magistrate's Court rather than the High Court; no new prosecutions, convictions, or punishments were recorded in 2014; credible sources have raised concerns about trafficking-related complicity among some off-duty police officers, which could hinder investigations or victims willingness to report offenses; prevention efforts were sustained, but progress in protecting victims was uneven; seven victims were assisted, which was an increase over 2013 (2015)

ILLICIT DRUGS:

considered a minor transshipment point for narcotics bound for the US and Europe; more significant as an offshore financial center

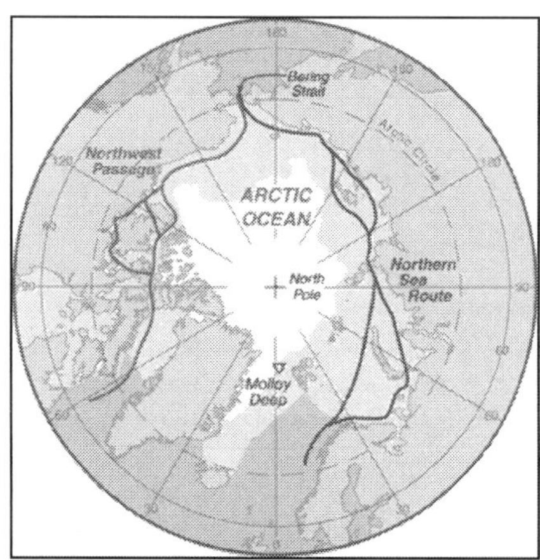

OCEANS :: ARCTIC OCEAN

INTRODUCTION :: ARCTIC OCEAN

BACKGROUND:

The Arctic Ocean is the smallest of the world's five oceans (after the Pacific Ocean, Atlantic Ocean, Indian Ocean, and the Southern Ocean). The Northwest Passage (US and Canada) and Northern Sea Route (Norway and Russia) are two important seasonal waterways. In recent years the polar ice pack has receded in the summer allowing for increased navigation and raising the possibility of future sovereignty and shipping disputes among the six countries bordering the Arctic Ocean (Canada, Denmark (Greenland), Iceland, Norway, Russia, US).

GEOGRAPHY :: ARCTIC OCEAN

LOCATION:

body of water between Europe, Asia, and North America, mostly north of the Arctic Circle

GEOGRAPHIC COORDINATES:

90 00 N, 0 00 E

MAP REFERENCES:

Arctic Region

AREA:

total: 14.056 million sq km

note: includes Baffin Bay, Barents Sea, Beaufort Sea, Chukchi Sea, East Siberian Sea, Greenland Sea, Hudson Bay, Hudson Strait, Kara Sea, Laptev Sea, Northwest Passage, and other tributary water bodies

AREA - COMPARATIVE:

slightly less than 1.5 times the size of the US

COASTLINE:

45,389 km

CLIMATE:

polar climate characterized by persistent cold and relatively narrow annual temperature range; winters characterized by continuous darkness, cold and stable weather conditions, and clear skies; summers characterized by continuous daylight, damp and foggy weather, and weak cyclones with rain or snow

TERRAIN:

central surface covered by a perennial drifting polar icepack that, on average, is about 3 m thick, although pressure ridges may be three times that thickness; the icepack is surrounded by open seas during the summer, but more than doubles in size during the winter and extends to the encircling landmasses; the ocean floor is about 50% continental shelf (highest percentage of any ocean) with the remainder a central basin interrupted by three submarine ridges (Alpha Cordillera, Nansen Cordillera, and Lomonosov Ridge)

major surface currents: two major, slow-moving, wind-driven currents (drift streams) dominate: a clockwise drift pattern in the Beaufort Gyre in the western part of the Arctic Ocean and a nearly straight line Transpolar Drift Stream that moves across the ocean from the New Siberian Islands (Russia) to the Fram Strait (between Greenland and Svalbard); sea ice that lies close to the center of the gyre can complete a 360 degree circle in about 2 years, while ice on the gyre periphery will complete the same circle in about 7-8 years; sea ice in the Transpolar Drift crosses the ocean in about 3 years

ELEVATION:

elevation extremes: -5,607 m lowest point: Molloy Deep

mean depth: -1,205 m

0 highest point: sea level

NATURAL RESOURCES:

sand and gravel aggregates, placer deposits, polymetallic nodules, oil and gas fields, fish, marine mammals (seals and whales)

NATURAL HAZARDS:

ice islands occasionally break away from northern Ellesmere Island; icebergs calved from glaciers in western Greenland and extreme northeastern Canada; permafrost in islands; virtually ice locked from October to June; ships subject to superstructure icing from October to May

ENVIRONMENT - CURRENT ISSUES:

climate change; changes in biodiversity; use of toxic chemicals; endangered marine species include walruses and whales; fragile ecosystem slow to change and slow to recover from disruptions or damage; thinning polar icepack

GEOGRAPHY - NOTE:

major chokepoint is the southern Chukchi Sea (northern access to the Pacific Ocean via the Bering Strait); strategic location between North America and Russia; shortest marine link between the extremes of eastern and western Russia; floating research stations operated by the US and Russia; maximum snow cover in March or April about 20 to 50 centimeters over the frozen ocean; snow cover lasts about 10 months

GOVERNMENT :: ARCTIC OCEAN

COUNTRY NAME:

etymology: the name Arctic comes from the Greek word "arktikos" meaning "near the bear" or "northern," and that word derives from "arktos," meaning "bear"; the name refers either to the constellation Ursa Major, the "Great Bear," which is prominent in the northern celestial sphere, or to the constellation Ursa Minor, the "Little Bear," which contains Polaris, the North (Pole) Star

ECONOMY :: ARCTIC OCEAN

ECONOMY - OVERVIEW:

Economic activity is limited to the exploitation of natural resources, including petroleum, natural gas, fish, and seals.

TRANSPORTATION :: ARCTIC OCEAN

PORTS AND TERMINALS:

major seaport(s): Churchill (Canada), Murmansk (Russia), Prudhoe Bay (US)

TRANSPORTATION - NOTE:

sparse network of air, ocean, river, and land routes; the Northwest Passage (North America) and Northern Sea Route (Eurasia) are important seasonal waterways

TRANSNATIONAL ISSUES :: ARCTIC OCEAN

DISPUTES - INTERNATIONAL:

Canada and the US dispute how to divide the Beaufort Sea and the status of the Northwest Passage but continue to work cooperatively to survey the Arctic continental shelfDenmark (Greenland) and Norway have made submissions to the Commission on the Limits of the Continental shelf (CLCS) and Russia is collecting additional data to augment its 2001 CLCS submissionrecord summer melting of sea ice in the Arctic has renewed interest in maritime shipping lanes and sea floor explorationNorway and Russia signed a comprehensive maritime boundary agreement in 2010

SOUTH AMERICA :: ARGENTINA

INTRODUCTION :: ARGENTINA

BACKGROUND:

In 1816, the United Provinces of the Rio Plata declared their independence from Spain. After Bolivia, Paraguay, and Uruguay went their separate ways, the area that remained became Argentina. The country's population and culture were heavily shaped by immigrants from throughout Europe, with Italy and Spain providing the largest percentage of newcomers from 1860 to 1930. Up until about the mid-20th century, much of Argentina's history was dominated by periods of internal political unrest and conflict between civilian and military factions.

After World War II, an era of Peronist populism and direct and indirect military interference in subsequent governments was followed by a military junta that took power in 1976. Democracy returned in 1983 after a failed bid to seize the Falkland Islands (Islas Malvinas) by force, and has persisted despite numerous challenges, the most formidable of which was a severe economic crisis in 2001-02 that led to violent public protests and the successive resignations of several presidents. The years 2003-15 saw Peronist rule by Nestor and Cristina FERNANDEZ de KIRCHNER, whose policies isolated Argentina and caused economic stagnation. With the election of Mauricio MACRI in November 2015, Argentina began a period of reform and international reintegration.

GEOGRAPHY :: ARGENTINA

LOCATION:

Southern South America, bordering the South Atlantic Ocean, between Chile and Uruguay

GEOGRAPHIC COORDINATES:

34 00 S, 64 00 W

MAP REFERENCES:

South America

AREA:

total: 2,780,400 sq km

land: 2,736,690 sq km

water: 43,710 sq km

country comparison to the world: 9

AREA - COMPARATIVE:

slightly less than three-tenths the size of the US

LAND BOUNDARIES:

total: 11,968 km

border countries (5): Bolivia 942 km, Brazil 1263 km, Chile 6691 km, Paraguay 2531 km, Uruguay 541 km

COASTLINE:

4,989 km

MARITIME CLAIMS:

territorial sea: 12 nm

exclusive economic zone: 200 nm

contiguous zone: 24 nm

continental shelf: 200 nm or to the edge of the continental margin

CLIMATE:

mostly temperate; arid in southeast; subantarctic in southwest

TERRAIN:

rich plains of the Pampas in northern half, flat to rolling plateau of Patagonia in south, rugged Andes along western border

ELEVATION:

mean elevation: 595 m

elevation extremes: -105 m lowest point: Laguna del Carbon (located between Puerto San Julian and Comandante Luis Piedra Buena in the province of Santa Cruz)

6962 highest point: Cerro Aconcagua (located in the northwestern corner of the province of Mendoza; highest point in South America)

NATURAL RESOURCES:

fertile plains of the pampas, lead, zinc, tin, copper, iron ore, manganese, petroleum, uranium, arable land

LAND USE:

agricultural land: 53.9% (2014 est.)

arable land: 13.9% (2014 est.) / permanent crops: 0.4% (2014 est.) / permanent pasture: 39.6% (2014 est.)

forest: 10.7% (2014 est.)

other: 35.4% (2014 est.)

IRRIGATED LAND:

23,600 sq km (2012)

POPULATION DISTRIBUTION:

one-third of the population lives in Buenos Aires; pockets of agglomeration occur throughout the northern and central parts of the country; Patagonia to the south remains sparsely populated

NATURAL HAZARDS:

San Miguel de Tucuman and Mendoza areas in the Andes subject to earthquakes; pamperos are violent windstorms that can strike the pampas and northeast; heavy flooding in some areas

volcanism: volcanic activity in the Andes Mountains along the Chilean border; Copahue (2,997 m) last erupted in 2000; other historically active volcanoes include Llullaillaco, Maipo, Planchon-Peteroa, San Jose, Tromen, Tupungatito, and Viedma

ENVIRONMENT - CURRENT ISSUES:

environmental problems (urban and rural) typical of an industrializing economy such as deforestation, soil degradation (erosion, salinization), desertification, air pollution, and water pollution

note: Argentina is a world leader in setting voluntary greenhouse gas targets

ENVIRONMENT - INTERNATIONAL AGREEMENTS:

party to: Antarctic-Environmental Protocol, Antarctic-Marine Living Resources, Antarctic Seals, Antarctic Treaty, Biodiversity, Climate Change, Climate Change-Kyoto Protocol, Desertification, Endangered Species, Environmental Modification, Hazardous Wastes, Law of the Sea, Marine Dumping, Ozone Layer Protection, Ship Pollution, Wetlands, Whaling

signed, but not ratified: Marine Life Conservation

GEOGRAPHY - NOTE:

second-largest country in South America (after Brazil); strategic location relative to sea lanes between the South Atlantic and the South Pacific Oceans (Strait of Magellan, Beagle Channel, Drake Passage); diverse geophysical landscapes range from tropical climates in the north to tundra in the far south; Cerro Aconcagua is the Western Hemisphere's tallest mountain, while Laguna del Carbon is the lowest point in the Western Hemisphere; shares Iguazu Falls, the world's largest waterfalls system, with Brazil

PEOPLE AND SOCIETY :: ARGENTINA

POPULATION:

44,694,198 (July 2018 est.)

country comparison to the world: 31

NATIONALITY:

noun: Argentine(s)

adjective: Argentine

ETHNIC GROUPS:

European (mostly Spanish and Italian descent) and mestizo (mixed European and Amerindian ancestry) 97.2%, Amerindian 2.4%, African 0.4% (2010 est.)

LANGUAGES:

Spanish (official), Italian, English, German, French, indigenous (Mapudungun, Quechua)

RELIGIONS:

nominally Roman Catholic 92% (less than 20% practicing), Protestant 2%, Jewish 2%, other 4%

DEMOGRAPHIC PROFILE:

Argentina's population continues to grow but at a slower rate because of its steadily declining birth rate. Argentina's fertility decline began earlier than in the rest of Latin America, occurring most rapidly between the early 20th century and the 1950s, and then becoming more gradual. Life expectancy has been improving, most notably among the young and the poor. While the population under age 15 is shrinking, the youth cohort - ages 15-24 - is the largest in Argentina's history and will continue to bolster the working-age population. If this large working-age population is well-educated and gainfully employed, Argentina is likely to experience an economic boost and possibly higher per capita savings and investment. Although literacy and primary school enrollment are nearly universal, grade repetition is problematic and secondary school completion is low. Both of these issues vary widely by region and socioeconomic group.

Argentina has been primarily a country of immigration for most of its history, welcoming European immigrants (often providing needed low-skilled labor) after its independence in the 19th century and attracting especially large numbers from Spain and Italy. More than 7 million European immigrants are estimated to have arrived in Argentina between 1880 and 1930, when it adopted a more restrictive immigration policy. European immigration also began to wane in the 1930s because of the global depression. The inflow rebounded temporarily following WWII and resumed its decline in the 1950s when Argentina's military dictators tightened immigration rules and European economies rebounded. Regional migration increased, however, supplying low-skilled workers escaping economic and political instability in their home countries. As of 2015, immigrants made up almost 5% of Argentina's population, the largest share in South America. Migration from neighboring countries accounted for approximately 80% of Argentina's immigrant population in 2015.

The first waves of highly skilled Argentine emigrant workers headed mainly to the United States and Spain in the 1960s and 1970s, driven by economic decline and repressive military dictatorships. The 2008 European economic crisis drove the return migration of some Argentinean and other Latin American nationals, as well as the immigration of Europeans to South America, where Argentina was a key recipient. In 2015, Argentina received the highest number of legal migrants in Latin America and the Caribbean. The majority of its migrant inflow came from Paraguay and Bolivia.

AGE STRUCTURE:

0-14 years: 24.44% (male 5,629,345 /female 5,293,680)

15-24 years: 15.2% (male 3,476,344 /female 3,317,151)

25-54 years: 39.46% (male 8,808,591 /female 8,826,379)

55-64 years: 9.12% (male 1,977,421 /female 2,096,665)

65 years and over: 11.79% (male 2,216,487 /female 3,052,135) (2018 est.)

DEPENDENCY RATIOS:

total dependency ratio: 56.5 (2015 est.)

youth dependency ratio: 39.4 (2015 est.)

elderly dependency ratio: 17.1 (2015 est.)

potential support ratio: 5.8 (2015 est.)

MEDIAN AGE:

total: 31.9 years

male: 30.7 years

female: 33.1 years (2018 est.)

country comparison to the world: 107

POPULATION GROWTH RATE:

0.89% (2018 est.)

country comparison to the world: 121

BIRTH RATE:

16.5 births/1,000 population (2018 est.)

country comparison to the world: 109

DEATH RATE:

7.5 deaths/1,000 population (2018 est.)

country comparison to the world: 108

NET MIGRATION RATE:

-0.1 migrant(s)/1,000 population (2017 est.)

country comparison to the world: 102

POPULATION DISTRIBUTION:

one-third of the population lives in Buenos Aires; pockets of agglomeration occur throughout the northern and central parts of the country; Patagonia to the south remains sparsely populated

URBANIZATION:

urban population: 91.9% of total population (2018)

rate of urbanization: 1.07% annual rate of change (2015-20 est.)

MAJOR URBAN AREAS - POPULATION:

14.967 million BUENOS AIRES (capital), 1.548 million Cordoba, 1.488 million Rosario, 1.133 million Mendoza, 956,000 San Miguel de Tucuman, 864,000 La Plata (2018)

SEX RATIO:

at birth: 1.06 male(s)/female (2017 est.)

0-14 years: 1.06 male(s)/female (2017 est.)

15-24 years: 1.05 male(s)/female (2017 est.)

25-54 years: 1 male(s)/female (2017 est.)

55-64 years: 0.94 male(s)/female (2017 est.)

65 years and over: 0.71 male(s)/female (2017 est.)

total population: 0.98 male(s)/female (2017 est.)

MATERNAL MORTALITY RATE:

52 deaths/100,000 live births (2015 est.)

country comparison to the world: 94

INFANT MORTALITY RATE:

total: 9.5 deaths/1,000 live births (2018 est.)

male: 10.4 deaths/1,000 live births (2018 est.)

female: 8.5 deaths/1,000 live births (2018 est.)

country comparison to the world: 138

LIFE EXPECTANCY AT BIRTH:

total population: 77.5 years (2018 est.)

male: 74.4 years (2018 est.)

female: 80.8 years (2018 est.)

country comparison to the world: 70

TOTAL FERTILITY RATE:

2.25 children born/woman (2018 est.)

country comparison to the world: 92

CONTRACEPTIVE PREVALENCE RATE:

81.3% (2013)

HEALTH EXPENDITURES:

4.8% of GDP (2014)

country comparison to the world: 146

PHYSICIANS DENSITY:

3.91 physicians/1,000 population (2013)

HOSPITAL BED DENSITY:

5 beds/1,000 population (2014)

DRINKING WATER SOURCE:

improved:

urban: 99% of population

rural: 100% of population

total: 99.1% of population

unimproved:

urban: 1% of population

rural: 0% of population

total: 0.9% of population (2015 est.)

SANITATION FACILITY ACCESS:

improved:

urban: 96.2% of population (2015 est.)

rural: 98.3% of population (2015 est.)

total: 96.4% of population (2015 est.)

unimproved:

urban: 3.8% of population (2015 est.)

rural: 1.7% of population (2015 est.)

total: 3.6% of population (2015 est.)

HIV/AIDS - ADULT PREVALENCE RATE:

0.4% (2017 est.)

country comparison to the world: 68

HIV/AIDS - PEOPLE LIVING WITH HIV/AIDS:

120,000 (2017 est.)

country comparison to the world: 38

HIV/AIDS - DEATHS:

2,000 (2017 est.)

country comparison to the world: 50

MAJOR INFECTIOUS DISEASES:

note: active local transmission of Zika virus by Aedes species mosquitoes has been identified in this country (as of August 2016); it poses an important risk (a large number of cases possible) among US citizens if bitten by an infective mosquito; other less common ways to get Zika are through sex, via blood transfusion, or during pregnancy, in which the pregnant woman passes Zika virus to her fetus

OBESITY - ADULT PREVALENCE RATE:

28.3% (2016)

country comparison to the world: 30

EDUCATION EXPENDITURES:

5.9% of GDP (2015)

country comparison to the world: 37

LITERACY:

definition: age 15 and over can read and write (2015 est.)

total population: 98.1% (2015 est.)

male: 98% (2015 est.)

female: 98.1% (2015 est.)

SCHOOL LIFE EXPECTANCY (PRIMARY TO TERTIARY EDUCATION):

total: 17 years (2014)

male: 16 years (2014)

female: 18 years (2014)

UNEMPLOYMENT, YOUTH AGES 15-24:

total: 18.3% (2014 est.)

male: 15.6% (2014 est.)

female: 22.8% (2014 est.)

country comparison to the world: 71

GOVERNMENT :: ARGENTINA

COUNTRY NAME:

conventional long form: Argentine Republic

conventional short form: Argentina

local long form: Republica Argentina

local short form: Argentina

etymology: originally the area was referred to as Tierra Argentina, i.e., "Land beside the Silvery River" or "silvery land," which referred to the massive estuary in the east of the country, the Rio de la Plata (River of Silver); over time the name shortened to simply Argentina or "silvery"

GOVERNMENT TYPE:

presidential republic

CAPITAL:

name: Buenos Aires

geographic coordinates: 34 36 S, 58 22 W

time difference: UTC-3 (2 hours ahead of Washington, DC, during Standard Time)

etymology: the name translates as "fair winds" in Spanish and derives from the original designation of the settlement that would become the present-day city, "Santa Maria del Buen Aire" (Saint Mary of the Fair Winds)

ADMINISTRATIVE DIVISIONS:

23 provinces (provincias, singular - provincia) and 1 autonomous city*; Buenos Aires, Catamarca, Chaco, Chubut, Ciudad Autonoma de Buenos Aires*, Cordoba, Corrientes, Entre Rios, Formosa, Jujuy, La Pampa, La Rioja, Mendoza, Misiones, Neuquen, Rio Negro, Salta, San Juan, San Luis, Santa Cruz, Santa Fe, Santiago del Estero, Tierra del Fuego - Antartida e Islas del Atlantico Sur (Tierra del Fuego - Antarctica and the South Atlantic Islands), Tucuman

note: the US does not recognize any claims to Antarctica

INDEPENDENCE:

9 July 1816 (from Spain)

NATIONAL HOLIDAY:

Revolution Day (May Revolution Day), 25 May (1810)

CONSTITUTION:

history: several previous; latest effective 11 May 1853 (2018)

amendments: a declaration of proposed amendments requires two-thirds majority vote by both houses of the National Congress followed by approval by an ad hoc, multi-member constitutional convention; amended many times, last significantly in 1994 (2018)

LEGAL SYSTEM:

civil law system based on West European legal systems; note - in mid-2015, Argentina adopted a new civil code, replacing the old one in force since 1871

INTERNATIONAL LAW ORGANIZATION PARTICIPATION:

has not submitted an ICJ jurisdiction declaration; accepts ICCt jurisdiction

CITIZENSHIP:

citizenship by birth: yes

citizenship by descent only: yes

dual citizenship recognized: yes

residency requirement for naturalization: 2 years

SUFFRAGE:

18-70 years of age; universal and compulsory; 16-17 years of age - optional for national elections

EXECUTIVE BRANCH:

chief of state: President Mauricio MACRI (since 10 December 2015); Vice President Gabriela MICHETTI (since 10 December 2015); note - the president is both chief of state and head of government

head of government: President Mauricio MACRI (since 10 December 2015); Vice President Gabriela MICHETTI (since 10 December 2015)

cabinet: Cabinet appointed by the president

elections/appointments: president and vice president directly elected on the same ballot by qualified majority popular vote for a 4-year term (eligible for a second consecutive term); election last held in 2 rounds on 25 October and 22 November 2015 (next to be held on 27 October 2019)

election results: Mauricio MACRI elected president in second round; percent of vote in first round - Daniel SCIOLI (PJ) 37.1%, Mauricio MACRI (PRO) 34.2%, Sergio MASSA (FR/PJ) 21.4%, other 7.3%; percent of vote in second round - Mauricio MACRI (PRO) 51.4%, Daniel SCIOLI (PJ) 48.6%

LEGISLATIVE BRANCH:

description: bicameral National Congress or Congreso Nacional consists of:
Senate (72 seats; members directly elected in multi-seat constituencies by simple majority vote to serve 6-year terms with one-third of the membership elected every 2 years)
Chamber of Deputies (257 seats; members directly elected in multi-seat constituencies by proportional representation vote; members serve 4-year terms with one-half of the membership renewed every 2 years)

elections:
Senate - last held on 22 October 2017 (next to be held in October 2019)
Chamber of Deputies - last held on 22 October 2017 (next to be held in October 2019)

election results: Senate - percent of vote by bloc or party - NA; seats by bloc or party - Cambiemos 12, UC 6, PJ 4, FRC 2; composition - men 42, women 30, percent of women 41.7%
Chamber of Deputies - percent of vote by bloc or party - NA; seats by bloc or party - Cambiemos 61, UC 28, PJ 18, FR 7, FCS 3, FRC 2, other 8; composition - men 159, women 98, percent of women 38.1%; note - total National Congress percent of women 38.9%

JUDICIAL BRANCH:

highest courts: Supreme Court or Corte Suprema (consists of the court president, vice-president, and 5 judges)

judge selection and term of office: judges nominated by the president and approved by the Senate; judges can serve until mandatory retirement at age 75

subordinate courts: federal level appellate, district, and territorial courts; provincial level supreme, appellate, and first instance courts

POLITICAL PARTIES AND LEADERS:

Cambiemos [Mauricio MACRI] (coalition of CC-ARI, PRO, and UCR)
Citizen's Unity or UC [Cristina FERNANDEZ DE KIRCHNER]
Civic Coalition ARI or CC-ARI [Elisa CARRIO]
Civic Front for Santiago or FCS [Gerardo ZAMORA]
Dissident Peronists (PJ Disidente) or Federal Peronism [Eduardo DUHALDE] (a right-wing faction of PJ opposed to the Kirchners)
Front for the Renewal of Concord or FRC
Front for Victory or FpV [Cristina FERNANDEZ DE KIRCHNER] (left-wing faction of PJ)
Justicialist Party or PJ [Jose Luis GIOJA]
Progresistas [Margarita STOLBIZER]
Radical Civic Union or UCR [Lilia PUIG DE STUBRIN]
Renewal Front (Frente Renovador) or FR [Sergio MASSA]
Republican Proposal or PRO [Mauricio MACRI]
Socialist Party or PS [Antonio BONFATTI]
United for a New Alternative or UNA (includes FR)
numerous provincial parties

INTERNATIONAL ORGANIZATION PARTICIPATION:

AfDB (nonregional member), Australia Group, BCIE, BIS, CAN (associate), CD, CELAC, FAO, FATF, G-15, G-20, G-24, G-77, IADB, IAEA, IBRD, ICAO, ICC (national committees), ICCt, ICRM, IDA, IFAD, IFC, IFRCS, IHO, ILO, IMF, IMO, IMSO, Interpol, IOC, IOM, IPU, ISO, ITSO, ITU, ITUC (NGOs), LAES, LAIA, Mercosur, MIGA, MINURSO, MINUSTAH, NAM (observer), NSG, OAS, OPANAL, OPCW, Paris Club (associate), PCA, SICA (observer), UN, UNASUR, UNCTAD, UNESCO, UNFICYP, UNHCR, UNIDO, Union Latina (observer), UNTSO, UNWTO, UPU, WCO, WFTU (NGOs), WHO, WIPO, WMO, WTO, ZC

DIPLOMATIC REPRESENTATION IN THE US:

chief of mission: Ambassador Fernando ORIS DE ROA (since 24 January 2018)

chancery: 1600 New Hampshire Avenue NW, Washington, DC 20009

telephone: [1] (202) 238-6400

FAX: [1] (202) 332-3171

consulate(s) general: Atlanta, Chicago, Houston, Los Angeles, Miami, New York, Washington, DC

DIPLOMATIC REPRESENTATION FROM THE US:

chief of mission: Ambassador Edward Charles PRADO (since 16 May 2018)

embassy: Avenida Colombia 4300, C1425GMN Buenos Aires

mailing address: international mail: use embassy street address; APO address: US Embassy Buenos Aires, Unit 4334, APO AA 34034

telephone: [54] (11) 5777-4533

FAX: [54] (11) 5777-4240

FLAG DESCRIPTION:

three equal horizontal bands of sky blue (top), white, and sky blue; centered in the white band is a radiant yellow sun with a human face (delineated in brown) known as the Sun of May; the colors represent the clear skies and snow of the Andes; the sun symbol commemorates the appearance of the sun through cloudy skies on 25 May 1810 during the first mass demonstration in favor of independence; the sun features are those of Inti, the Inca god of the sun

NATIONAL SYMBOL(S):

Sun of May (a sun-with-face symbol); national colors: sky blue, white

NATIONAL ANTHEM:

name: "Himno Nacional Argentino" (Argentine National Anthem)

lyrics/music: Vicente LOPEZ y PLANES/Jose Blas PARERA

note: adopted 1813; Vicente LOPEZ was inspired to write the anthem after watching a play about the 1810 May Revolution against Spain

ECONOMY :: ARGENTINA

ECONOMY - OVERVIEW:

Argentina benefits from rich natural resources, a highly literate population, an export-oriented agricultural sector, and a diversified industrial base. Although one of the world's wealthiest countries 100 years ago, Argentina suffered during most of the 20th century from recurring economic crises, persistent fiscal and current account deficits, high inflation, mounting external debt, and capital flight.

Cristina FERNANDEZ DE KIRCHNER succeeded her husband as president in late 2007, and in 2008 the rapid economic growth of previous years slowed sharply as government policies held back exports and the world economy fell into recession. In 2010 the economy rebounded strongly, but slowed in late 2011 even as the government continued to rely on expansionary fiscal and monetary policies, which kept inflation in the double digits.

In order to deal with these problems, the government expanded state intervention in the economy: it nationalized the oil company YPF from Spain's Repsol, expanded measures to restrict imports, and further tightened currency controls in an effort to bolster foreign reserves and stem capital flight. Between 2011 and 2013, Central Bank foreign reserves dropped $21.3 billion from a high of $52.7 billion. In July 2014, Argentina and China agreed on an $11 billion currency swap; the Argentine Central Bank has received the equivalent of $3.2 billion in Chinese yuan, which it counts as international reserves.

With the election of President Mauricio MACRI in November 2015, Argentina began a historic political and economic transformation, as his administration took steps to liberalize the Argentine economy, lifting capital controls, floating the peso, removing export controls on some commodities, cutting some energy subsidies, and reforming the country's official statistics. Argentina negotiated debt payments with holdout bond creditors, continued working with the IMF to shore up its finances, and returned to international capital markets in April 2016.

In 2017, Argentina's economy emerged from recession with GDP growth of nearly 3.0%. The government passed important pension, tax, and fiscal reforms. And after years of international isolation, Argentina took on several international leadership roles, including hosting the World Economic Forum on Latin America and the World Trade Organization Ministerial Conference, and is set to assume the presidency of the G-20 in 2018.

GDP (PURCHASING POWER PARITY):

$922.1 billion (2017 est.)

$896.5 billion (2016 est.)

$913.2 billion (2015 est.)

note: data are in 2017 dollars

country comparison to the world: 28

GDP (OFFICIAL EXCHANGE RATE):

$637.6 billion (2017 est.) (2017 est.)

GDP - REAL GROWTH RATE:

2.9% (2017 est.)

-1.8% (2016 est.)

2.7% (2015 est.)

country comparison to the world: 117

GDP - PER CAPITA (PPP):

$20,900 (2017 est.)

$20,600 (2016 est.)

$21,200 (2015 est.)

note: data are in 2017 dollars

country comparison to the world: 88

GROSS NATIONAL SAVING:

17.6% of GDP (2017 est.)

16.8% of GDP (2016 est.)

15.8% of GDP (2015 est.)

country comparison to the world: 114

GDP - COMPOSITION, BY END USE:

household consumption: 65.9% (2017 est.)

government consumption: 18.2% (2017 est.)

investment in fixed capital: 14.8% (2017 est.)

investment in inventories: 3.7% (2017 est.)

exports of goods and services: 11.2% (2017 est.)

imports of goods and services: -13.8% (2017 est.)

GDP - COMPOSITION, BY SECTOR OF ORIGIN:

agriculture: 10.8% (2017 est.)

industry: 28.1% (2017 est.)

services: 61.1% (2017 est.)

AGRICULTURE - PRODUCTS:

sunflower seeds, lemons, soybeans, grapes, corn, tobacco, peanuts, tea, wheat; livestock

INDUSTRIES:

food processing, motor vehicles, consumer durables, textiles, chemicals and petrochemicals, printing, metallurgy, steel

INDUSTRIAL PRODUCTION GROWTH RATE:

2.7% (2017 est.)

note: based on private sector estimates

country comparison to the world: 111

LABOR FORCE:

18 million (2017 est.)

note: urban areas only

country comparison to the world: 33

LABOR FORCE - BY OCCUPATION:

agriculture: 5.3%

industry: 28.6%

services: 66.1% (2017 est.)

UNEMPLOYMENT RATE:

8.4% (2017 est.)

8.5% (2016 est.)

country comparison to the world: 120

POPULATION BELOW POVERTY LINE:

25.7% (2017 est.)

note: data are based on private estimates

HOUSEHOLD INCOME OR CONSUMPTION BY PERCENTAGE SHARE:

lowest 10%: 31% (2017 est.)

highest 10%: 31% (2017 est.)

DISTRIBUTION OF FAMILY INCOME - GINI INDEX:

41.7 (2017 est.)

45.8 (2009)

country comparison to the world: 54

BUDGET:

revenues: 120.6 billion (2017 est.)

expenditures: 158.6 billion (2017 est.)

TAXES AND OTHER REVENUES:

18.9% (of GDP) (2017 est.)

country comparison to the world: 157

BUDGET SURPLUS (+) OR DEFICIT (-):

-6% (of GDP) (2017 est.)

country comparison to the world: 182

PUBLIC DEBT:

57.6% of GDP (2017 est.)

55% of GDP (2016 est.)

country comparison to the world: 77

FISCAL YEAR:

calendar year

INFLATION RATE (CONSUMER PRICES):

25.7% (2017 est.)

26.5% (2016 est.)

note: data are derived from private estimates

country comparison to the world: 219

CENTRAL BANK DISCOUNT RATE:

NA

COMMERCIAL BANK PRIME LENDING RATE:

26.58% (31 December 2017 est.)

31.23% (31 December 2016 est.)

country comparison to the world: 9

STOCK OF NARROW MONEY:

$62.61 billion (31 December 2017 est.)

$59 billion (31 December 2016 est.)

country comparison to the world: 48

STOCK OF BROAD MONEY:

$62.61 billion (31 December 2017 est.)

$59 billion (31 December 2016 est.)

country comparison to the world: 48

STOCK OF DOMESTIC CREDIT:

$219.4 billion (31 December 2017 est.)

$194 billion (31 December 2016 est.)

country comparison to the world: 44

MARKET VALUE OF PUBLICLY TRADED SHARES:

$56.13 billion (31 December 2015 est.)

$60.14 billion (31 December 2014 est.)

$53.1 billion (31 December 2013 est.)

country comparison to the world: 50

CURRENT ACCOUNT BALANCE:

-$31.32 billion (2017 est.)

-$14.69 billion (2016 est.)

country comparison to the world: 200

EXPORTS:

$58.45 billion (2017 est.)

$57.78 billion (2016 est.)

country comparison to the world: 49

EXPORTS - PARTNERS:

Brazil 16.1%, US 7.9%, China 7.5%, Chile 4.4% (2017)

EXPORTS - COMMODITIES:

soybeans and derivatives, petroleum and gas, vehicles, corn, wheat

IMPORTS:

$63.97 billion (2017 est.)

$53.5 billion (2016 est.)

country comparison to the world: 48

IMPORTS - COMMODITIES:

machinery, motor vehicles, petroleum and natural gas, organic chemicals, plastics

IMPORTS - PARTNERS:

Brazil 26.9%, China 18.5%, US 11.3%, Germany 4.9% (2017)

RESERVES OF FOREIGN EXCHANGE AND GOLD:

$55.33 billion (31 December 2017 est.)

$38.43 billion (31 December 2016 est.)

country comparison to the world: 38

DEBT - EXTERNAL:

$214.9 billion (31 December 2017 est.)

$190.2 billion (31 December 2016 est.)

country comparison to the world: 34

STOCK OF DIRECT FOREIGN INVESTMENT - AT HOME:

$76.58 billion (31 December 2017 est.)

$72.11 billion (31 December 2016 est.)

country comparison to the world: 52

STOCK OF DIRECT FOREIGN INVESTMENT - ABROAD:

$40.94 billion (31 December 2017 est.)

$39.74 billion (31 December 2016 est.)

country comparison to the world: 46

EXCHANGE RATES:

Argentine pesos (ARS) per US dollar -

16.92 (2017 est.)

14.76 (2016 est.)

14.76 (2015 est.)

9.23 (2014 est.)

8.08 (2013 est.)

ENERGY :: ARGENTINA

ELECTRICITY ACCESS:

population without electricity: 1.5 million (2013)

electrification - total population: 96.4% (2013)

electrification - urban areas: 99.2% (2013)

electrification - rural areas: 96% (2013)

ELECTRICITY - PRODUCTION:

131.9 billion kWh (2016 est.)

country comparison to the world: 30

ELECTRICITY - CONSUMPTION:

121 billion kWh (2016 est.)

country comparison to the world: 30

ELECTRICITY - EXPORTS:

55 million kWh (2015 est.)

country comparison to the world: 85

ELECTRICITY - IMPORTS:

9.851 billion kWh (2016 est.)

country comparison to the world: 26

ELECTRICITY - INSTALLED GENERATING CAPACITY:

38.35 million kW (2016 est.)

country comparison to the world: 27

ELECTRICITY - FROM FOSSIL FUELS:

69% of total installed capacity (2016 est.)

country comparison to the world: 112

ELECTRICITY - FROM NUCLEAR FUELS:

4% of total installed capacity (2017 est.)

country comparison to the world: 23

ELECTRICITY - FROM HYDROELECTRIC PLANTS:

24% of total installed capacity (2017 est.)

country comparison to the world: 79

ELECTRICITY - FROM OTHER RENEWABLE SOURCES:

3% of total installed capacity (2017 est.)

country comparison to the world: 120

CRUDE OIL - PRODUCTION:

479,400 bbl/day (2017 est.)

country comparison to the world: 29

CRUDE OIL - EXPORTS:

36,630 bbl/day (2015 est.)

country comparison to the world: 43

CRUDE OIL - IMPORTS:

16,740 bbl/day (2015 est.)

country comparison to the world: 68

CRUDE OIL - PROVED RESERVES:

2.162 billion bbl (1 January 2018 est.)

country comparison to the world: 32

REFINED PETROLEUM PRODUCTS - PRODUCTION:

669,800 bbl/day (2015 est.)

country comparison to the world: 26

REFINED PETROLEUM PRODUCTS - CONSUMPTION:

806,000 bbl/day (2016 est.)

country comparison to the world: 27

REFINED PETROLEUM PRODUCTS - EXPORTS:

58,360 bbl/day (2015 est.)

country comparison to the world: 51

REFINED PETROLEUM PRODUCTS - IMPORTS:

121,400 bbl/day (2015 est.)

country comparison to the world: 49

NATURAL GAS - PRODUCTION:

40.92 billion cu m (2017 est.)

country comparison to the world: 20

NATURAL GAS - CONSUMPTION:

49.04 billion cu m (2017 est.)

country comparison to the world: 17

NATURAL GAS - EXPORTS:

76.45 million cu m (2017 est.)

country comparison to the world: 49

NATURAL GAS - IMPORTS:

9.826 billion cu m (2017 est.)

country comparison to the world: 27

NATURAL GAS - PROVED RESERVES:

336.6 billion cu m (1 January 2018 est.)

country comparison to the world: 35

CARBON DIOXIDE EMISSIONS FROM CONSUMPTION OF ENERGY:

203.7 million Mt (2017 est.)

country comparison to the world: 32

COMMUNICATIONS :: ARGENTINA

TELEPHONES - FIXED LINES:

total subscriptions: 9,530,349 (2017 est.)

subscriptions per 100 inhabitants: 22 (2017 est.)

country comparison to the world: 19

TELEPHONES - MOBILE CELLULAR:

total subscriptions: 61,897,379 (2017 est.)

subscriptions per 100 inhabitants: 140 (2017 est.)

country comparison to the world: 26

TELEPHONE SYSTEM:

general assessment: Argentina opened its telecommunications market to competition and foreign investment encouraging the growth of modern telecommunications technology in 1998; major networks are entirely digital and the availability of telephone service continues to improve to rural areas; even with numerous providers there is a lack of competition; still Argentina is the 3rd largest in the region after Brazil and Mexico (2017)

domestic: microwave radio relay, fiber-optic cable, and a domestic satellite system with 40 earth stations serve the trunk network; 22 per 100 fixed-line, 144 per 100 mobile-cellular (2017)

international: country code - 54; landing point for the Atlantis-2, UNISUR, South America-1, and South American Crossing/Latin American Nautilus submarine cable systems that provide links to Europe, Africa, South and Central America, and US; satellite earth stations - 112; 2 international gateways near Buenos Aires; building started on the ARBR submarine cable between Argentina and Brazil (2017)

BROADCAST MEDIA:

government owns a TV station and radio network; more than 2 dozen TV stations and hundreds of privately owned radio stations; high rate of cable TV subscription usage (2009)

INTERNET COUNTRY CODE:

.ar

INTERNET USERS:

total: 30,786,889 (July 2016 est.)

percent of population: 70.2% (July 2016 est.)

country comparison to the world: 24

BROADBAND - FIXED SUBSCRIPTIONS:

total: 7,870,222 (2017 est.)

subscriptions per 100 inhabitants: 18 (2017 est.)

country comparison to the world: 20

TRANSPORTATION :: ARGENTINA

NATIONAL AIR TRANSPORT SYSTEM:

number of registered air carriers: 6 (2015)

inventory of registered aircraft operated by air carriers: 107 (2015)

annual passenger traffic on registered air carriers: 14,245,183 (2015)

annual freight traffic on registered air carriers: 243,772,567 mt-km (2015)

CIVIL AIRCRAFT REGISTRATION COUNTRY CODE PREFIX:

LV (2016)

AIRPORTS:

1,138 (2013)

country comparison to the world: 6

AIRPORTS - WITH PAVED RUNWAYS:

total: 161 (2017)

over 3,047 m: 4 (2017)

2,438 to 3,047 m: 29 (2017)

1,524 to 2,437 m: 65 (2017)

914 to 1,523 m: 53 (2017)

under 914 m: 10 (2017)

AIRPORTS - WITH UNPAVED RUNWAYS:

total: 977 (2013)

over 3,047 m: 1 (2013)

2,438 to 3,047 m: 1 (2013)

1,524 to 2,437 m: 43 (2013)

914 to 1,523 m: 484 (2013)

under 914 m: 448 (2013)

HELIPORTS:

2 (2013)

PIPELINES:

29930 km gas, 41 km liquid petroleum gas, 6248 km oil, 3631 km refined products (2013)

RAILWAYS:

total: 36,917 km (2014)

standard gauge: 2,745.1 km 1.435-m gauge (41.1 km electrified) (2014)

narrow gauge: 7,523.3 km 1.000-m gauge (2014)

broad gauge: 26,391 km 1.676-m gauge (149 km electrified) (2014)

258 0.750-m gauge

country comparison to the world: 6

ROADWAYS:

total: 231,374 km (2004)

paved: 69,412 km (includes 734 km of expressways) (2004)

unpaved: 161,962 km (2004)

country comparison to the world: 22

WATERWAYS:

11,000 km (2012)

country comparison to the world: 11

MERCHANT MARINE:

total: 161 (2017)

by type: container ship 1, general cargo 9, oil tanker 27, other 124 (2017)

country comparison to the world: 69

PORTS AND TERMINALS:

major seaport(s): Bahia Blanca, Buenos Aires, La Plata, Punta Colorada, Ushuaia

container port(s) (TEUs): Buenos Aires (1,851,701)

LNG terminal(s) (import): Bahia Blanca

river port(s): Arroyo Seco, Rosario, San Lorenzo-San Martin (Parana)

MILITARY AND SECURITY :: ARGENTINA

MILITARY EXPENDITURES:

0.95% of GDP (2016)

0.86% of GDP (2015)

0.88% of GDP (2014)

country comparison to the world: 118

MILITARY BRANCHES:

Argentine Army (Ejercito Argentino), Navy of the Argentine Republic (Armada Republica; includes naval aviation and naval infantry), Argentine Air Force (Fuerza Aerea Argentina, FAA) (2013)

MILITARY SERVICE AGE AND OBLIGATION:

18-24 years of age for voluntary military service (18-21 requires parental consent); no conscription; if the number of volunteers fails to meet the quota of recruits for a particular year, Congress can authorize the conscription of citizens turning 18 that year for a period not exceeding one year (2012)

MILITARY - NOTE:

the Argentine military is a well-organized force constrained by the country's prolonged economic hardship; the country has recently experienced a strong recovery, and the military is implementing a modernization plan aimed at making the ground forces lighter and more responsive (2008)

TERRORISM :: ARGENTINA

TERRORIST GROUPS - FOREIGN BASED:

Hizballah:
aim(s): largely limited to generating political and financial support from the Lebanese diaspora
area(s) of operation: conducted operations in the 1990s; maintains a limited presence (April 2018)

TRANSNATIONAL ISSUES :: ARGENTINA

DISPUTES - INTERNATIONAL:

Argentina continues to assert its claims to the UK-administered Falkland Islands (Islas Malvinas), South Georgia, and the South

Sandwich Islands in its constitution, forcibly occupying the Falklands in 1982, but in 1995 agreed to no longer seek settlement by forceUK continues to reject Argentine requests for sovereignty talksterritorial claim in Antarctica partially overlaps UK and Chilean claimsuncontested dispute between Brazil and Uruguay over Braziliera/Brasiliera Island in the Quarai/Cuareim River leaves the tripoint with Argentina in questionin 2010, the ICJ ruled in favor of Uruguay's operation of two paper mills on the Uruguay River, which forms the border with Argentinathe two countries formed a joint pollution monitoring regimethe joint boundary commission, established by Chile and Argentina in 2001 has yet to map and demarcate the delimited boundary in the inhospitable Andean Southern Ice Field (Campo de Hielo Sur)contraband smuggling, human trafficking, and illegal narcotic trafficking are problems in the porous areas of the border with Bolivia

REFUGEES AND INTERNALLY DISPLACED PERSONS:

refugees (country of origin): 94,632 (Venezuela) (economic and political crisis; includes Venezuelans who have claimed asylum or have received alternative legal stay) (2018)

ILLICIT DRUGS:

a transshipment country for cocaine headed for Europe, heroin headed for the US, and ephedrine and pseudoephedrine headed for Mexico; some money-laundering activity, especially in the Tri-Border Area; law enforcement corruption; a source for precursor chemicals; increasing domestic consumption of drugs in urban centers, especially cocaine base and synthetic drugs

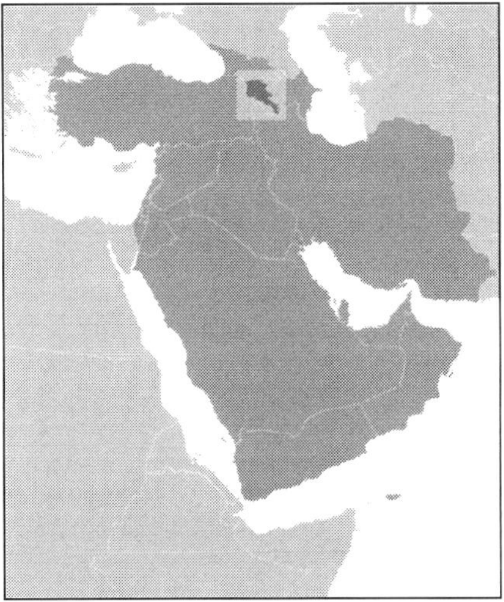

INTRODUCTION :: ARMENIA

BACKGROUND:

Armenia prides itself on being the first nation to formally adopt Christianity (early 4th century). Despite periods of autonomy, over the centuries Armenia came under the sway of various empires including the Roman, Byzantine, Arab, Persian, and Ottoman. During World War I in the western portion of Armenia, the Ottoman Empire instituted a policy of forced resettlement coupled with other harsh practices that resulted in at least 1 million Armenian deaths. The eastern area of Armenia was ceded by the Ottomans to Russia in 1828; this portion declared its independence in 1918, but was conquered by the Soviet Red Army in 1920.

Armenian leaders remain preoccupied by the long conflict with Azerbaijan over Nagorno-Karabakh, a primarily Armenian-populated region, assigned to Soviet Azerbaijan in the 1920s by Moscow. Armenia and Azerbaijan began fighting over the area in 1988; the struggle escalated after both countries attained independence from the Soviet Union in 1991. By May 1994, when a trilateral cease-fire between Armenia, Azerbaijan, and Nagorno-Karabakh took hold, ethnic Armenian forces held not only Nagorno-Karabakh but also seven surrounding regions - approximately 14 percent of Azerbaijan's territory. The economies of both sides have been hurt by their inability to make substantial progress toward a peaceful resolution.

Turkey closed the common border with Armenia in 1993 in support of Azerbaijan in its conflict with Armenia over control of Nagorno-Karabakh and surrounding areas, further hampering Armenian economic growth. In 2009, Armenia and Turkey signed Protocols normalizing relations between the two countries, but neither country ratified the Protocols, and Armenia officially withdrew from the Protocols in March 2018. In January 2015, Armenia joined Russia, Belarus, and Kazakhstan as a member of the Eurasian Economic Union. In November 2017, Armenia signed a Comprehensive and Enhanced Partnership Agreement (CEPA) with the EU.

GEOGRAPHY :: ARMENIA

LOCATION:

Southwestern Asia, between Turkey (to the west) and Azerbaijan; note - Armenia views itself as part of Europe; geopolitically, it can be classified as falling within Europe, the Middle East, or both

GEOGRAPHIC COORDINATES:

40 00 N, 45 00 E

MAP REFERENCES:

Asia

AREA:

total: 29,743 sq km

land: 28,203 sq km

water: 1,540 sq km

country comparison to the world: 143

AREA - COMPARATIVE:

slightly smaller than Maryland

LAND BOUNDARIES:

total: 1,570 km

border countries (4): Azerbaijan 996 km, Georgia 219 km, Iran 44 km, Turkey 311 km

COASTLINE:

0 km (landlocked)

MARITIME CLAIMS:

none (landlocked)

CLIMATE:

highland continental, hot summers, cold winters

TERRAIN:

Armenian Highland with mountains; little forest land; fast flowing rivers; good soil in Aras River valley

ELEVATION:

mean elevation: 1,792 m

elevation extremes: 400 m lowest point: Debed River

4090 highest point: Aragats Lerrnagagat'

NATURAL RESOURCES:

small deposits of gold, copper, molybdenum, zinc, bauxite

LAND USE:

agricultural land: 59.7% (2014 est.)

arable land: 15.8% (2014 est.) / permanent crops: 1.9% (2014 est.) / permanent pasture: 42% (2014 est.)

forest: 9.1% (2014 est.)

other: 31.2% (2014 est.)

IRRIGATED LAND:

2,740 sq km (2012)

POPULATION DISTRIBUTION:

most of the population is located in the northern half of the country; the capital of Yerevan is home to more than five times as many people as Gyumri, the second largest city in the country

NATURAL HAZARDS:

occasionally severe earthquakes; droughts

ENVIRONMENT - CURRENT ISSUES:

soil pollution from toxic chemicals such as DDT; deforestation; pollution of Hrazdan and Aras Rivers; the draining of Sevana Lich (Lake Sevan), a result of its use as a source for hydropower, threatens drinking water supplies; restart of Metsamor nuclear power plant in spite of its location in a seismically active zone

ENVIRONMENT - INTERNATIONAL AGREEMENTS:

party to: Air Pollution, Biodiversity, Climate Change, Climate Change-Kyoto Protocol, Desertification, Environmental Modification, Hazardous Wastes, Law of the Sea, Ozone Layer Protection, Wetlands

signed, but not ratified: Air Pollution-Persistent Organic Pollutants

GEOGRAPHY - NOTE:

landlocked in the Lesser Caucasus Mountains; Sevana Lich (Lake Sevan) is the largest lake in this mountain range

PEOPLE AND SOCIETY :: ARMENIA

POPULATION:

3,038,217 (July 2018 est.)

country comparison to the world: 137

NATIONALITY:

noun: Armenian(s)

adjective: Armenian

ETHNIC GROUPS:

Armenian 98.1%, Yezidi (Kurd) 1.2%, other 0.7% (2011 est.)

LANGUAGES:

Armenian (official) 97.9%, Kurdish (spoken by Yezidi minority) 1%, other 1% (2011 est.)

note: Russian is widely spoken

RELIGIONS:

Armenian Apostolic 92.6%, Evangelical 1%, other 2.4%, none 1.1%, unspecified 2.9% (2011 est.)

AGE STRUCTURE:

0-14 years: 18.86% (male 303,712 /female 269,279)

15-24 years: 12.37% (male 195,722 /female 179,970)

25-54 years: 43.31% (male 640,089 /female 675,643)

55-64 years: 13.77% (male 192,515 /female 225,882)

65 years and over: 11.7% (male 142,835 /female 212,570) (2018 est.)

DEPENDENCY RATIOS:

total dependency ratio: 44.4 (2015 est.)

youth dependency ratio: 28.7 (2015 est.)

elderly dependency ratio: 15.8 (2015 est.)

potential support ratio: 6.3 (2015 est.)

MEDIAN AGE:

total: 35.6 years

male: 33.9 years

female: 37.4 years (2018 est.)

country comparison to the world: 78

POPULATION GROWTH RATE:

-0.25% (2018 est.)

country comparison to the world: 213

BIRTH RATE:

12.6 births/1,000 population (2018 est.)

country comparison to the world: 153

DEATH RATE:

9.5 deaths/1,000 population (2018 est.)

country comparison to the world: 47

NET MIGRATION RATE:

-5.7 migrant(s)/1,000 population (2017 est.)

country comparison to the world: 194

POPULATION DISTRIBUTION:

most of the population is located in the northern half of the country; the capital of Yerevan is home to more than five times as many people as Gyumri, the second largest city in the country

URBANIZATION:

urban population: 63.1% of total population (2018)

rate of urbanization: 0.22% annual rate of change (2015-20 est.)

MAJOR URBAN AREAS - POPULATION:

1.08 million YEREVAN (capital) (2018)

SEX RATIO:

at birth: 1.12 male(s)/female (2017 est.)

0-14 years: 1.14 male(s)/female (2017 est.)

15-24 years: 1.06 male(s)/female (2017 est.)

25-54 years: 0.93 male(s)/female (2017 est.)

55-64 years: 0.84 male(s)/female (2017 est.)

65 years and over: 0.67 male(s)/female (2017 est.)

total population: 0.94 male(s)/female (2017 est.)

MOTHER'S MEAN AGE AT FIRST BIRTH:

24.4 years (2015/16 est.)

MATERNAL MORTALITY RATE:

25 deaths/100,000 live births (2015 est.)

country comparison to the world: 120

INFANT MORTALITY RATE:

total: 12.3 deaths/1,000 live births (2018 est.)

male: 13.7 deaths/1,000 live births (2018 est.)

female: 10.7 deaths/1,000 live births (2018 est.)

country comparison to the world: 110

LIFE EXPECTANCY AT BIRTH:

total population: 75.1 years (2018 est.)

male: 71.8 years (2018 est.)

female: 78.7 years (2018 est.)

country comparison to the world: 113

TOTAL FERTILITY RATE:

1.64 children born/woman (2018 est.)

country comparison to the world: 177

CONTRACEPTIVE PREVALENCE RATE:

57.1% (2015/16)

HEALTH EXPENDITURES:

4.5% of GDP (2014)

country comparison to the world: 155

PHYSICIANS DENSITY:

2.8 physicians/1,000 population (2014)

HOSPITAL BED DENSITY:

4.2 beds/1,000 population (2015)

DRINKING WATER SOURCE:

improved:

urban: 100% of population

rural: 100% of population

total: 100% of population

unimproved:

urban: 0% of population

rural: 0% of population

total: 0% of population (2015 est.)

SANITATION FACILITY ACCESS:

improved:

urban: 96.2% of population (2015 est.)

rural: 78.2% of population (2015 est.)

total: 89.5% of population (2015 est.)

unimproved:

urban: 3.8% of population (2015 est.)

rural: 21.8% of population (2015 est.)

total: 10.5% of population (2015 est.)

HIV/AIDS - ADULT PREVALENCE RATE:

0.2% (2017 est.)

country comparison to the world: 91

HIV/AIDS - PEOPLE LIVING WITH HIV/AIDS:

3,400 (2017 est.)

country comparison to the world: 121

HIV/AIDS - DEATHS:

<200 (2017 est.)

OBESITY - ADULT PREVALENCE RATE:

20.2% (2016)

country comparison to the world: 101

CHILDREN UNDER THE AGE OF 5 YEARS UNDERWEIGHT:

2.6% (2016)

country comparison to the world: 106

EDUCATION EXPENDITURES:

2.8% of GDP (2016)

country comparison to the world: 151

LITERACY:

definition: age 15 and over can read and write (2015 est.)

total population: 99.7% (2015 est.)

male: 99.7% (2015 est.)

female: 99.6% (2015 est.)

SCHOOL LIFE EXPECTANCY (PRIMARY TO TERTIARY EDUCATION):

total: 13 years (2015)

male: 13 years (2015)

female: 13 years (2015)

UNEMPLOYMENT, YOUTH AGES 15-24:

total: 36.3% (2016 est.)

male: 29.5% (2016 est.)

female: 45.7% (2016 est.)

country comparison to the world: 18

GOVERNMENT :: ARMENIA

COUNTRY NAME:

conventional long form: Republic of Armenia

conventional short form: Armenia

local long form: Hayastani Hanrapetut'yun

local short form: Hayastan

former: Armenian Soviet Socialist Republic, Armenian Republic

etymology: the etymology of the country's name remains obscure; according to tradition, the country is named after Hayk, the legendary patriarch of the Armenians and the great-great-grandson of Noah; Hayk's descendant, Aram, purportedly is the source of the name Armenia

GOVERNMENT TYPE:

parliamentary democracy; note - constitutional changes adopted in December 2015 transformed the government to a parliamentary system

CAPITAL:

name: Yerevan

geographic coordinates: 40 10 N, 44 30 E

time difference: UTC+4 (9 hours ahead of Washington, DC, during Standard Time)

etymology: name likely derives from the ancient Urartian fortress of Erebuni established on the current site of Yerevan in 782 B.C. and whose impresive ruins still survive

ADMINISTRATIVE DIVISIONS:

11 provinces (marzer, singular - marz); Aragatsotn, Ararat, Armavir, Geghark'unik', Kotayk', Lorri, Shirak, Syunik', Tavush, Vayots' Dzor, Yerevan

INDEPENDENCE:

21 September 1991 (from the Soviet Union)

NATIONAL HOLIDAY:

Independence Day, 21 September (1991)

CONSTITUTION:

history: previous 1915, 1978; latest adopted 5 July 1995 (2017)

amendments: proposed by the president of the republic or by the National Assembly; passage requires approval by the president, by the National Assembly, and by a referendum with at least 25% registered voter participation and more than 50% of votes; constitutional articles on the form of government and democratic procedures are not amendable; amended 2005, 2007, 2008, last in 2015 (2017)

note: a 2015 amendment, approved in December 2015 by a public referendum and effective for the 2017-18 electoral cycle, changes the government type from the current semi-presidential system to a parliamentary system

LEGAL SYSTEM:

civil law system

INTERNATIONAL LAW ORGANIZATION PARTICIPATION:

has not submitted an ICJ jurisdiction declaration; non-party state to the ICCt

CITIZENSHIP:

citizenship by birth: no

citizenship by descent only: at least one parent must be a citizen of Armenia

dual citizenship recognized: yes

residency requirement for naturalization: 3 years

SUFFRAGE:

18 years of age; universal

EXECUTIVE BRANCH:

chief of state: President Armen SARKISSIAN (since 9 April 2018)

head of government: Prime Minister Nikol PASHINYAN (since 8 May 2018); First Deputy Prime Minister Ararat MIRZOYAN (since 11 May 2018)

cabinet: Council of Ministers appointed by the prime minister

elections/appointments: president indirectly elected by the National Assembly in 3 rounds if needed for a single 7-year term; election last held on 2 March 2018; prime minister elected by majority vote in 2 rounds if needed by the National Assembly; election last held on 8 May 2018

election results: Armen SARKISSIAN elected president in first round; note - Armen SARKISSIAN ran unopposed and won the Assembly vote 90-10; Nikol PASHINYAN elected prime minister in second round; note - Nikol PASHINYAN ran unopposed and won the Assembly vote 59-42

note: Nikol PASHINYAN resigned his post on 16 October 2018 but remains on as Acting Prime Minister until new elections are held on 9 December 2018

LEGISLATIVE BRANCH:

description: unicameral National Assembly (Parliament) or Azgayin Zhoghov (minimum 101 seats, currently 132; members directly elected in single-seat constituencies by proportional representation vote; members serve 5-year terms)

elections: last held on 9 December 2018 (next elections to be held December 2023)

election results: percent of vote by party - My Step Alliance 70.4%, BHK 8.3%, Bright Armenia 6.4%, other 14.9%; seats by party - My Step Alliance 88, BHK 26, Bright Armenia 18; composition - men 112, women 20, percent of women 15.2%

JUDICIAL BRANCH:

highest courts: Court of Cassation (consists of the Criminal Chamber with a chairman and 5 judges and the Civil and Administrative Chamber with a chairman and 10 judges – with both civil and administrative specializations); Constitutional Court (consists of 9 judges)

judge selection and term of office: Court of Cassation judges nominated by the Supreme Judicial Council, a 10-member body of selected judges and legal scholars; judges appointed by the president; judges can serve until age 65; Constitutional Court judges - 4 appointed by the president, and 5 elected by the National Assembly; judges can serve until age 70

subordinate courts: criminal and civil appellate courts; administrative appellate court; first instance courts; specialized administrative and bankruptcy courts

POLITICAL PARTIES AND LEADERS:

Armenian National Congress or ANC (bloc of independent and opposition parties) [Levon TER-PETROSSIAN]
Armenian National Movement or ANM [Ararat ZURABIAN]
Armenian Revolutionary Federation or ARF ("Dashnak" Party) [Hrant MARKARIAN]
Bright Armenia [Edmon MARUKYAN]
Christian Democratic Rebirth Party [Levon SHIRINYAN]
Citizen's Decision [Suren SAHAKYAN]
Civil Contract [Nikol PASHINYAN]
Heritage Party [Raffi HOVHANNISIAN]
Mission Party [Manuk SUKIASYAN]
My Step Alliance (Civil Contract Party and Mission Party) [Nikol PASHINYAN]
National Progress Party [Lusine HAROYAN]
People's Party of Armenia [Stepan DEMIRCHIAN]
Prosperous Armenia or BHK [Gagik TSARUKYAN]
Republic [Aram SARGSYAN]
Republican Party of Armenia or RPA [Serzh SARGSIAN]
Rule of Law Party (Orinats Yerkir) or OEK [Artur BAGHDASARIAN]
Sasna Tser [Varuzhan AVETISYAN]
We Alliance or FD-H [Aram SARGSIAN]

INTERNATIONAL ORGANIZATION PARTICIPATION:

ADB, BSEC, CD, CE, CIS, CSTO, EAEC (observer), EAEU, EAPC, EBRD, FAO, GCTU, IAEA, IBRD, ICAO, ICC (NGOs), ICRM, IDA, IFAD, IFC, IFRCS, ILO, IMF, Interpol, IOC, IOM, IPU, ISO, ITSO, ITU, MIGA, NAM (observer), OAS (observer), OIF, OPCW, OSCE, PFP, UN, UNCTAD, UNESCO, UNIDO, UNIFIL, UNWTO, UPU, WCO, WFTU (NGOs), WHO, WIPO, WMO, WTO

DIPLOMATIC REPRESENTATION IN THE US:

chief of mission: Ambassador Grigor HOVHANNISSIAN (since 28 January 2016)

chancery: 2225 R Street NW, Washington, DC 20008

telephone: [1] (202) 319-1976

FAX: [1] (202) 319-2982

consulate(s) general: Glendale (CA)

DIPLOMATIC REPRESENTATION FROM THE US:

chief of mission: Ambassador Richard MILLS (since 13 February 2015)

embassy: 1 American Ave., Yerevan 0082

mailing address: American Embassy Yerevan, US Department of State, 7020 Yerevan Place, Washington, DC 20521-7020

telephone: [374](10) 464-700

FAX: [374](10) 464-742

FLAG DESCRIPTION:

three equal horizontal bands of red (top), blue, and orange; the color red recalls the blood shed for liberty, blue the Armenian skies as well as hope, and orange the land and the courage of the workers who farm it

NATIONAL SYMBOL(S):

Mount Ararat, eagle, lion; national colors: red, blue, orange

NATIONAL ANTHEM:

name: "Mer Hayrenik" (Our Fatherland)

lyrics/music: Mikael NALBANDIAN/Barsegh KANACHYAN

note: adopted 1991; based on the anthem of the Democratic Republic of Armenia (1918-1922) but with different lyrics

ECONOMY :: ARMENIA

ECONOMY - OVERVIEW:

Under the old Soviet central planning system, Armenia developed a modern industrial sector, supplying machine tools, textiles, and other manufactured goods to sister republics, in exchange for raw materials and energy. Armenia has since switched to small-scale agriculture and away from the large agro industrial complexes of the Soviet era. Armenia has only two open trade borders - Iran and Georgia - because its borders with Azerbaijan and Turkey have been closed since 1991 and 1993, respectively, as a result of Armenia's ongoing conflict with Azerbaijan over the separatist Nagorno-Karabakh region.

Armenia joined the World Trade Organization in January 2003. The government has made some improvements in tax and customs administration in recent years, but anti-corruption measures have been largely ineffective. Armenia will need to pursue additional economic reforms and strengthen the rule of law in order to raise its economic growth and improve economic competitiveness and employment opportunities, especially given its economic isolation from Turkey and Azerbaijan.

Armenia's geographic isolation, a narrow export base, and pervasive monopolies in important business sectors have made it particularly vulnerable to volatility in the global commodity markets and the economic challenges in Russia. Armenia is particularly dependent on Russian commercial and governmental support, as most key Armenian infrastructure is Russian-owned and/or managed, especially in the energy sector.

Remittances from expatriates working in Russia are equivalent to about 12-14% of GDP. Armenia joined the Russia-led Eurasian Economic Union in January 2015, but has remained interested in pursuing closer ties with the EU as well, signing a Comprehensive and Enhanced Partnership Agreement with the EU in November 2017. Armenia's rising government debt is leading Yerevan to tighten its fiscal policies – the amount is approaching the debt to GDP ratio threshold set by national legislation.

GDP (PURCHASING POWER PARITY):

$28.34 billion (2017 est.)

$26.37 billion (2016 est.)

$26.3 billion (2015 est.)

note: data are in 2017 dollars

country comparison to the world: 136

GDP (OFFICIAL EXCHANGE RATE):

$11.54 billion (2017 est.) (2017 est.)

GDP - REAL GROWTH RATE:

7.5% (2017 est.)

0.3% (2016 est.)

3.3% (2015 est.)

country comparison to the world: 12

GDP - PER CAPITA (PPP):

$9,500 (2017 est.)

$8,800 (2016 est.)

$8,800 (2015 est.)

note: data are in 2017 dollars

country comparison to the world: 142

GROSS NATIONAL SAVING:

17.8% of GDP (2017 est.)

16.6% of GDP (2016 est.)

18.4% of GDP (2015 est.)

country comparison to the world: 112

GDP - COMPOSITION, BY END USE:

household consumption: 76.7% (2017 est.)

government consumption: 14.2% (2017 est.)

investment in fixed capital: 17.3% (2017 est.)

investment in inventories: 4.1% (2017 est.)

exports of goods and services: 38.1% (2017 est.)

imports of goods and services: -50.4% (2017 est.)

GDP - COMPOSITION, BY SECTOR OF ORIGIN:

agriculture: 16.7% (2017 est.)

industry: 28.2% (2017 est.)

services: 54.8% (2017 est.)

AGRICULTURE - PRODUCTS:

fruit (especially grapes and apricots), vegetables; livestock

INDUSTRIES:

brandy, mining, diamond processing, metal-cutting machine tools, forging and pressing machines, electric motors, knitted wear, hosiery, shoes, silk fabric, chemicals, trucks, instruments, microelectronics, jewelry, software, food processing

INDUSTRIAL PRODUCTION GROWTH RATE:

5.4% (2017 est.)

country comparison to the world: 51

LABOR FORCE:

1.507 million (2017 est.)

country comparison to the world: 131

LABOR FORCE - BY OCCUPATION:

agriculture: 36.3%

industry: 17%

services: 46.7% (2013 est.)

UNEMPLOYMENT RATE:

18.9% (2017 est.)

18.8% (2016 est.)

country comparison to the world: 183

POPULATION BELOW POVERTY LINE:

32% (2013 est.)

HOUSEHOLD INCOME OR CONSUMPTION BY PERCENTAGE SHARE:

lowest 10%: 25.7% (2014)

highest 10%: 25.7% (2014)

DISTRIBUTION OF FAMILY INCOME - GINI INDEX:

31.5 (2014)

31.5 (2013 est.)

country comparison to the world: 125

BUDGET:

revenues: 2.644 billion (2017 est.)

expenditures: 3.192 billion (2017 est.)

TAXES AND OTHER REVENUES:

22.9% (of GDP) (2017 est.)

country comparison to the world: 130

BUDGET SURPLUS (+) OR DEFICIT (-):

-4.8% (of GDP) (2017 est.)

country comparison to the world: 167

PUBLIC DEBT:

53.5% of GDP (2017 est.)

51.9% of GDP (2016 est.)

country comparison to the world: 89

FISCAL YEAR:

calendar year

INFLATION RATE (CONSUMER PRICES):

0.9% (2017 est.)

-1.4% (2016 est.)

country comparison to the world: 44

CENTRAL BANK DISCOUNT RATE:

6.5% (14 December 2016)

10.5% (10 February 2015)

note: this is the Refinancing Rate, the key monetary policy instrument of the Armenian National Bank

country comparison to the world: 57

COMMERCIAL BANK PRIME LENDING RATE:

14.41% (31 December 2017 est.)

17.36% (31 December 2016 est.)

note: average lending rate on loans up to one year

country comparison to the world: 47

STOCK OF NARROW MONEY:

$1.629 billion (31 December 2017 est.)

$1.355 billion (31 December 2016 est.)

country comparison to the world: 141

STOCK OF BROAD MONEY:

$1.629 billion (31 December 2017 est.)

$1.355 billion (31 December 2016 est.)

country comparison to the world: 149

STOCK OF DOMESTIC CREDIT:

$6.712 billion (31 December 2017 est.)

$5.689 billion (31 December 2016 est.)

country comparison to the world: 120

MARKET VALUE OF PUBLICLY TRADED SHARES:

$132.1 million (31 December 2012 est.)

$139.6 million (31 December 2011 est.)

$144.8 million (31 December 2010 est.)

country comparison to the world: 121

CURRENT ACCOUNT BALANCE:

-$328 million (2017 est.)

-$238 million (2016 est.)

country comparison to the world: 107

EXPORTS:

$2.361 billion (2017 est.)

$1.891 billion (2016 est.)

country comparison to the world: 135

EXPORTS - PARTNERS:

Russia 24.2%, Bulgaria 12.8%, Switzerland 12%, Georgia 6.9%, Germany 5.9%, China 5.5%, Iraq 5.4%, UAE 4.6%, Netherlands 4.1% (2017)

EXPORTS - COMMODITIES:

unwrought copper, pig iron, nonferrous metals, gold, diamonds, mineral products, foodstuffs, brandy, cigarettes, energy

IMPORTS:

$3.771 billion (2017 est.)

$2.835 billion (2016 est.)

country comparison to the world: 142

IMPORTS - COMMODITIES:

natural gas, petroleum, tobacco products, foodstuffs, diamonds, pharmaceuticals, cars

IMPORTS - PARTNERS:

Russia 28%, China 11.5%, Turkey 5.5%, Germany 4.9%, Iran 4.3% (2017)

RESERVES OF FOREIGN EXCHANGE AND GOLD:

$2.314 billion (31 December 2017 est.)

$2.204 billion (31 December 2016 est.)

country comparison to the world: 119

DEBT - EXTERNAL:

$10.41 billion (31 December 2017 est.)

$8.987 billion (31 December 2016 est.)

country comparison to the world: 113

STOCK OF DIRECT FOREIGN INVESTMENT - AT HOME:

$4.169 billion (2015 est.)

$4.087 billion (31 December 2014 est.)

country comparison to the world: 109

STOCK OF DIRECT FOREIGN INVESTMENT - ABROAD:

$228 million (2015 est.)

$215 million (2014 est.)

country comparison to the world: 107

EXCHANGE RATES:

drams (AMD) per US dollar -

487.9 (2017 est.)

480.49 (2016 est.)

480.49 (2015 est.)

477.92 (2014 est.)

415.92 (2013 est.)

ENERGY :: ARMENIA

ELECTRICITY ACCESS:

electrification - total population: 100% (2016)

ELECTRICITY - PRODUCTION:

6.951 billion kWh (2016 est.)

country comparison to the world: 112

ELECTRICITY - CONSUMPTION:

5.291 billion kWh (2016 est.)

country comparison to the world: 121

ELECTRICITY - EXPORTS:

1.424 billion kWh (2015 est.)

country comparison to the world: 50

ELECTRICITY - IMPORTS:

275 million kWh (2016 est.)

country comparison to the world: 90

ELECTRICITY - INSTALLED GENERATING CAPACITY:

4.08 million kW (2016 est.)

country comparison to the world: 86

ELECTRICITY - FROM FOSSIL FUELS:

58% of total installed capacity (2016 est.)

country comparison to the world: 134

ELECTRICITY - FROM NUCLEAR FUELS:

9% of total installed capacity (2017 est.)

country comparison to the world: 15

ELECTRICITY - FROM HYDROELECTRIC PLANTS:

32% of total installed capacity (2017 est.)

country comparison to the world: 65

ELECTRICITY - FROM OTHER RENEWABLE SOURCES:

0% of total installed capacity (2017 est.)

country comparison to the world: 173

CRUDE OIL - PRODUCTION:

0 bbl/day (2017 est.)

country comparison to the world: 105

CRUDE OIL - EXPORTS:

0 bbl/day (2015 est.)

country comparison to the world: 86

CRUDE OIL - IMPORTS:

0 bbl/day (2015 est.)

country comparison to the world: 90

CRUDE OIL - PROVED RESERVES:

0 bbl (1 January 2018 est.)

country comparison to the world: 103

REFINED PETROLEUM PRODUCTS - PRODUCTION:

0 bbl/day (2015 est.)

country comparison to the world: 114

REFINED PETROLEUM PRODUCTS - CONSUMPTION:

8,000 bbl/day (2016 est.)

country comparison to the world: 162

REFINED PETROLEUM PRODUCTS - EXPORTS:

0 bbl/day (2015 est.)

country comparison to the world: 126

REFINED PETROLEUM PRODUCTS - IMPORTS:

7,145 bbl/day (2015 est.)

country comparison to the world: 158

NATURAL GAS - PRODUCTION:

0 cu m (2017 est.)

country comparison to the world: 100

NATURAL GAS - CONSUMPTION:

2.35 billion cu m (2017 est.)

country comparison to the world: 80

NATURAL GAS - EXPORTS:

0 cu m (2017 est.)

country comparison to the world: 62

NATURAL GAS - IMPORTS:

2.35 billion cu m (2017 est.)

country comparison to the world: 48

NATURAL GAS - PROVED RESERVES:

0 cu m (1 January 2014 est.)

country comparison to the world: 106

CARBON DIOXIDE EMISSIONS FROM CONSUMPTION OF ENERGY:

5.501 million Mt (2017 est.)

country comparison to the world: 131

COMMUNICATIONS :: ARMENIA

TELEPHONES - FIXED LINES:

total subscriptions: 505,190 (2017 est.)

subscriptions per 100 inhabitants: 17 (2017 est.)

country comparison to the world: 94

TELEPHONES - MOBILE CELLULAR:

total subscriptions: 3,488,524 (2017 est.)

subscriptions per 100 inhabitants: 115 (2017 est.)

country comparison to the world: 135

TELEPHONE SYSTEM:

general assessment: telecommunications investments have made major inroads in modernizing and upgrading the outdated telecommunications network inherited from the Soviet era; now 100% privately owned and undergoing modernization and expansion; with a small populaton and low GDP - moderate growth in mobile market;

mobile operators promise mobile broadband to be faster (2017)

domestic: 17 per 100 fixed-line, 115 per 100 mobile-cellular; reliable fixed-line and mobile-cellular services are available across Yerevan and in major cities and towns; mobile-cellular coverage available in most rural areas (2017)

international: country code - 374; Yerevan is connected to the Trans-Asia-Europe fiber-optic cable through Iran; additional international service is available by microwave radio relay and landline connections to the other countries of the Commonwealth of Independent States, through the Moscow international switch, and by satellite to the rest of the world; satellite earth stations - 3 (2015)

BROADCAST MEDIA:

2 public TV networks operating alongside about 40 privately owned TV stations that provide local to near nationwide coverage; major Russian broadcast stations are widely available; subscription cable TV services are available in most regions; Armenian TV completed conversion from analog to digital broadcasting in late 2016; Public Radio of Armenia is a national, state-run broadcast network that operates alongside 21 privately owned radio stations; several major international broadcasters are available (2017)

INTERNET COUNTRY CODE:

.am

INTERNET USERS:

total: 1,891,775 (July 2016 est.)

percent of population: 62% (July 2016 est.)

country comparison to the world: 116

BROADBAND - FIXED SUBSCRIPTIONS:

total: 315,319 (2017 est.)

subscriptions per 100 inhabitants: 10 (2017 est.)

country comparison to the world: 94

TRANSPORTATION :: ARMENIA

NATIONAL AIR TRANSPORT SYSTEM:

number of registered air carriers: 3 (2015)

inventory of registered aircraft operated by air carriers: 5 (2015)

CIVIL AIRCRAFT REGISTRATION COUNTRY CODE PREFIX:

EK (2016)

AIRPORTS:

11 (2013)

country comparison to the world: 153

AIRPORTS - WITH PAVED RUNWAYS:

total: 10 (2017)

over 3,047 m: 2 (2017)

2,438 to 3,047 m: 2 (2017)

1,524 to 2,437 m: 4 (2017)

914 to 1,523 m: 2 (2017)

AIRPORTS - WITH UNPAVED RUNWAYS:

total: 1 (2013)

914 to 1,523 m: 1 (2013)

PIPELINES:

3838 km gas (high and medium pressure) (2017)

RAILWAYS:

total: 780 km (2014)

broad gauge: 780 km 1.520-m gauge (780 km electrified) (2014)

note: 726 km operational

country comparison to the world: 98

ROADWAYS:

total: 7,792 km (2013)

country comparison to the world: 142

MILITARY AND SECURITY :: ARMENIA

MILITARY EXPENDITURES:

4.09% of GDP (2016)

4.25% of GDP (2015)

3.94% of GDP (2014)

4% of GDP (2013)

3.58% of GDP (2012)

country comparison to the world: 13

MILITARY BRANCHES:

Armenian Armed Forces: Ground Forces, Air Force and Air Defense; "Nagorno-Karabakh Republic": Nagorno-Karabakh Self-Defense Force (NKSDF) (2011)

MILITARY SERVICE AGE AND OBLIGATION:

18-27 years of age for voluntary or compulsory military service; 2-year conscript service obligation; 17 year olds are eligible to become cadets at military higher education institutes, where they are classified as military personnel (2012)

TRANSNATIONAL ISSUES :: ARMENIA

DISPUTES - INTERNATIONAL:

the dispute over the break-away Nagorno-Karabakh region and the Armenian military occupation of surrounding lands in Azerbaijan remains the primary focus of regional instabilityresidents have evacuated the former Soviet-era small ethnic enclaves in Armenia and AzerbaijanTurkish authorities have complained that blasting from quarries in Armenia might be damaging the medieval ruins of Ani, on the other side of the Arpacay valleyin 2009, Swiss mediators facilitated an accord reestablishing diplomatic ties between Armenia and Turkey, but neither side has ratified the agreement and the rapprochement effort has falteredlocal border forces struggle to control the illegal transit of goods and people across the porous, undemarcated Armenian, Azerbaijani, and Georgian bordersethnic Armenian groups in the Javakheti region of Georgia seek greater autonomy from the Georgian Government

REFUGEES AND INTERNALLY DISPLACED PERSONS:

refugees (country of origin): 14,626 (Syria - ethnic Armenians) (2016)

IDPs: 8,400 (conflict with Azerbaijan over Nagorno-Karabakh) (2016)

stateless persons: 773 (2017)

ILLICIT DRUGS:

illicit cultivation of small amount of cannabis for domestic consumption; minor transit point for illicit drugs - mostly opium and hashish - moving from Southwest Asia to Russia and to a lesser extent the rest of Europe

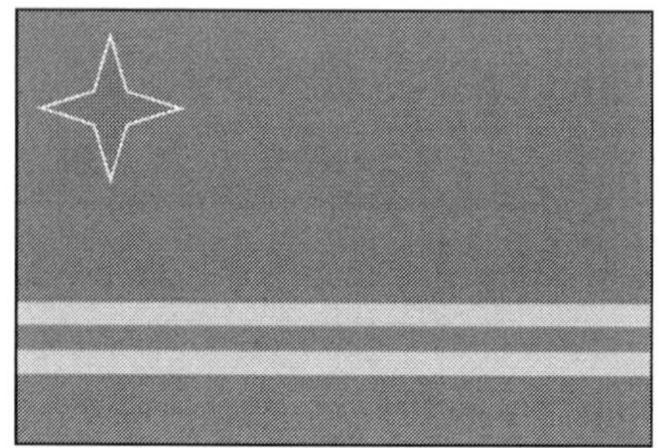

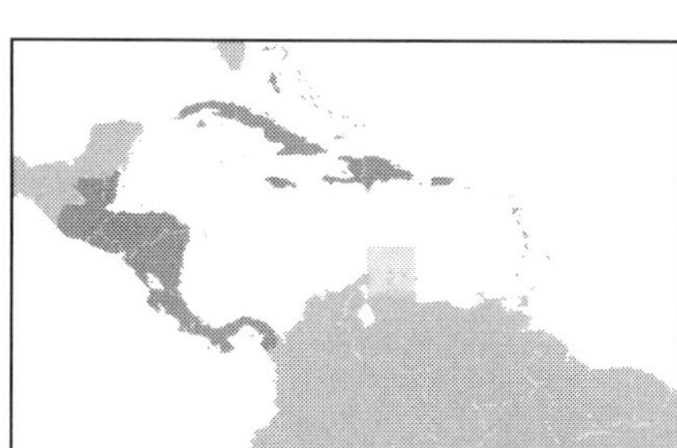

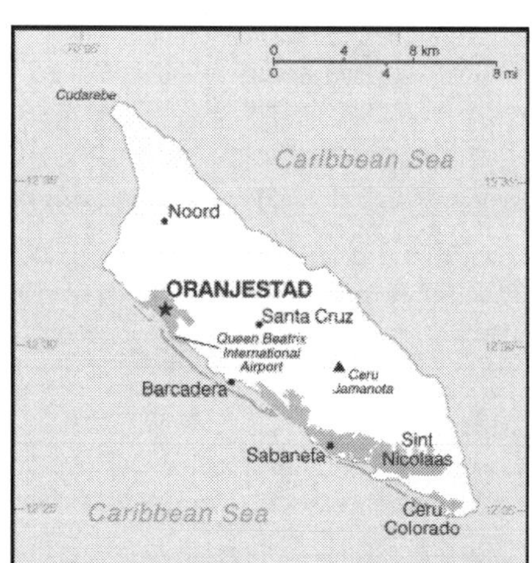

CENTRAL AMERICA :: ARUBA

INTRODUCTION :: ARUBA

BACKGROUND:

Discovered and claimed for Spain in 1499, Aruba was acquired by the Dutch in 1636. The island's economy has been dominated by three main industries. A 19th century gold rush was followed by prosperity brought on by the opening in 1924 of an oil refinery. The last decades of the 20th century saw a boom in the tourism industry. Aruba seceded from the Netherlands Antilles in 1986 and became a separate, autonomous member of the Kingdom of the Netherlands. Movement toward full independence was halted at Aruba's request in 1990.

GEOGRAPHY :: ARUBA

LOCATION:

Caribbean, island in the Caribbean Sea, north of Venezuela

GEOGRAPHIC COORDINATES:

12 30 N, 69 58 W

MAP REFERENCES:

Central America and the Caribbean

AREA:

total: 180 sq km

land: 180 sq km

water: 0 sq km

country comparison to the world: 218

AREA - COMPARATIVE:

slightly larger than Washington, DC

LAND BOUNDARIES:

0 km

COASTLINE:

68.5 km

MARITIME CLAIMS:

territorial sea: 12 nm

exclusive economic zone: 200 nm

CLIMATE:

tropical marine; little seasonal temperature variation

TERRAIN:

flat with a few hills; scant vegetation

ELEVATION:

0 m lowest point: Caribbean Sea

188 highest point: Ceru Jamanota

NATURAL RESOURCES:

NEGL; white sandy beaches foster tourism

LAND USE:

agricultural land: 11.1% (2014 est.)

arable land: 11.1% (2014 est.) / permanent crops: 0% (2014 est.) / permanent pasture: 0% (2014 est.)

forest: 2.3% (2014 est.)

other: 86.6% (2014 est.)

IRRIGATED LAND:

NA

POPULATION DISTRIBUTION:

most residents live in or around Oranjestad and San Nicolaas; most settlments tend to be located on the less mountainous western side of the island

NATURAL HAZARDS:

hurricanes; lies outside the Caribbean hurricane belt and is rarely threatened

ENVIRONMENT - CURRENT ISSUES:

difficulty in properly disposing of waste produced by large numbers of tourists; waste burning that occurs in the landfill causes air pollution and poses an environmental and health risk; ocean environmental damage due to plastic pollution

GEOGRAPHY - NOTE:

a flat, riverless island renowned for its white sand beaches; its tropical climate is moderated by constant trade winds from the Atlantic Ocean; the temperature is almost constant at about 27 degrees Celsius (81 degrees Fahrenheit)

PEOPLE AND SOCIETY :: ARUBA

POPULATION:

116,576 (July 2018 est.)

country comparison to the world: 189

NATIONALITY:

noun: Aruban(s)

adjective: Aruban; Dutch

ETHNIC GROUPS:

Aruban 66%, Colombian 9.1%, Dutch 4.3%, Dominican 4.1%, Venezuelan 3.2%, Cuacaoan 2.2%, Haitian 1.5%, Peruvian 1.1%, Chinese 1.1%, other 6.2% (2010 est.)

note: data represent population by country of birth

LANGUAGES:

Papiamento (official) (a creole language that is a mixture of Portuguese, Spanish, Dutch, English, and, to a lesser extent, French, as well as elements of African languages and the language of the Arawak) 69.4%, Spanish 13.7%, English (widely spoken) 7.1%, Dutch (official) 6.1%, Chinese 1.5%, other 1.7%, unspecified 0.4% (2010 est.)

RELIGIONS:

Roman Catholic 75.3%, Protestant 4.9% (includes Methodist 0.9%,

Adventist 0.9%, Anglican 0.4%, other Protestant 2.7%), Jehovah's Witness 1.7%, other 12%, none 5.5%, unspecified 0.5% (2010 est.)

AGE STRUCTURE:

0-14 years: 17.61% (male 10,304 /female 10,227)

15-24 years: 12.53% (male 7,355 /female 7,253)

25-54 years: 41.29% (male 23,187 /female 24,946)

55-64 years: 14.51% (male 7,910 /female 9,005)

65 years and over: 14.06% (male 6,422 /female 9,967) (2018 est.)

DEPENDENCY RATIOS:

total dependency ratio: 44.6 (2015 est.)

youth dependency ratio: 27 (2015 est.)

elderly dependency ratio: 17.5 (2015 est.)

potential support ratio: 5.7 (2015 est.)

MEDIAN AGE:

total: 39.5 years

male: 37.8 years

female: 41.2 years (2018 est.)

country comparison to the world: 53

POPULATION GROWTH RATE:

1.24% (2018 est.)

country comparison to the world: 88

BIRTH RATE:

12.3 births/1,000 population (2018 est.)

country comparison to the world: 158

DEATH RATE:

8.5 deaths/1,000 population (2018 est.)

country comparison to the world: 76

NET MIGRATION RATE:

8.7 migrant(s)/1,000 population (2017 est.)

country comparison to the world: 11

POPULATION DISTRIBUTION:

most residents live in or around Oranjestad and San Nicolaas; most settlments tend to be located on the less mountainous western side of the island

URBANIZATION:

urban population: 43.4% of total population (2018)

rate of urbanization: 0.67% annual rate of change (2015-20 est.)

MAJOR URBAN AREAS - POPULATION:

30,000 ORANJESTAD (capital) (2018)

SEX RATIO:

at birth: 1.01 male(s)/female (2017 est.)

0-14 years: 1.01 male(s)/female (2017 est.)

15-24 years: 1.01 male(s)/female (2017 est.)

25-54 years: 0.93 male(s)/female (2017 est.)

55-64 years: 0.87 male(s)/female (2017 est.)

65 years and over: 0.64 male(s)/female (2017 est.)

total population: 0.9 male(s)/female (2017 est.)

INFANT MORTALITY RATE:

total: 10.4 deaths/1,000 live births (2018 est.)

male: 13.6 deaths/1,000 live births (2018 est.)

female: 7.2 deaths/1,000 live births (2018 est.)

country comparison to the world: 131

LIFE EXPECTANCY AT BIRTH:

total population: 77.1 years (2018 est.)

male: 74.1 years (2018 est.)

female: 80.3 years (2018 est.)

country comparison to the world: 77

TOTAL FERTILITY RATE:

1.83 children born/woman (2018 est.)

country comparison to the world: 147

DRINKING WATER SOURCE:

improved:

urban: 98.1% of population (2015 est.)

rural: 98.1% of population (2015 est.)

total: 98.1% of population (2015 est.)

unimproved:

urban: 1.9% of population (2015 est.)

rural: 1.9% of population (2015 est.)

total: 1.9% of population (2015 est.)

SANITATION FACILITY ACCESS:

improved:

urban: 97.7% of population (2015 est.)

rural: 97.7% of population (2015 est.)

total: 97.7% of population (2015 est.)

unimproved:

urban: 2.3% of population (2015 est.)

rural: 2.3% of population (2015 est.)

total: 2.3% of population (2015 est.)

HIV/AIDS - ADULT PREVALENCE RATE:

NA

HIV/AIDS - PEOPLE LIVING WITH HIV/AIDS:

NA

HIV/AIDS - DEATHS:

NA

MAJOR INFECTIOUS DISEASES:

note: active local transmission of Zika virus by Aedes species mosquitoes has been identified in this country (as of August 2016); it poses an important risk (a large number of cases possible) among US citizens if bitten by an infective mosquito; other less common ways to get Zika are through sex, via blood transfusion, or during pregnancy, in which the pregnant woman passes Zika virus to her fetus

EDUCATION EXPENDITURES:

6.5% of GDP (2015)

country comparison to the world: 26

LITERACY:

definition: age 15 and over can read and write (2015 est.)

total population: 97.5% (2015 est.)

male: 97.5% (2015 est.)

female: 97.5% (2015 est.)

SCHOOL LIFE EXPECTANCY (PRIMARY TO TERTIARY EDUCATION):

total: 14 years (2012)

male: 13 years (2012)

female: 14 years (2012)

UNEMPLOYMENT, YOUTH AGES 15-24:

total: 28.9% (2010 est.)

male: 29.9% (2010 est.)

female: 27.5% (2010 est.)

country comparison to the world: 39

GOVERNMENT :: ARUBA

COUNTRY NAME:

conventional long form: none

conventional short form: Aruba

etymology: the origin of the island's name is unclear; according to tradition, the name comes from the Spanish phrase "oro huba" (there was gold), but in fact no gold was ever found on the island; another possibility is the native word "oruba," which means "well-situated"

DEPENDENCY STATUS:

constituent country of the Kingdom of the Netherlands; full autonomy in internal affairs obtained in 1986 upon separation from the Netherlands Antilles; Dutch Government responsible for defense and foreign affairs

GOVERNMENT TYPE:

parliamentary democracy (Legislature); part of the Kingdom of the Netherlands

CAPITAL:

name: Oranjestad

geographic coordinates: 12 31 N, 70 02 W

time difference: UTC-4 (1 hour ahead of Washington, DC, during Standard Time)

etymology: translates as "orange town" in Dutch; the city is named after William I, Prince of Orange, the first king of the Netherlands

ADMINISTRATIVE DIVISIONS:

none (part of the Kingdom of the Netherlands)

note: Aruba is one of four constituent countries of the Kingdom of the Netherlands; the other three are the Netherlands, Curacao, and Sint Maarten

INDEPENDENCE:

none (part of the Kingdom of the Netherlands)

NATIONAL HOLIDAY:

National Anthem and Flag Day, 18 March (1976)

CONSTITUTION:

previous 1947, 1955; latest drafted and approved August 1985, enacted 1 January 1986 (regulates governance of Aruba, but is subordinate to the Charter for the Kingdom of the Netherlands); note - in October 2010, following dissolution of the Netherlands Antilles, Aruba became a constituent country within the Kingdom of the Netherlands (2018)

LEGAL SYSTEM:

civil law system based on the Dutch civil code

CITIZENSHIP:

see the Netherlands

SUFFRAGE:

18 years of age; universal

EXECUTIVE BRANCH:

chief of state: King WILLEM-ALEXANDER of the Netherlands (since 30 April 2013); represented by Governor General Alfonso BOEKHOUDT (since 1 January 2017)

head of government: Prime Minister Evelyn WEVER-CROES (since 17 November 2017)

cabinet: Council of Ministers elected by the Legislature (Staten)

elections/appointments: the monarchy is hereditary; governor general appointed by the monarch for a 6-year term; prime minister and deputy prime minister indirectly elected by the Staten for 4-year term; election last held on 27 September 2013 (next to be held by September 2017)

election results: Evelyn WEVER-CROES (MEP) elected prime minister; percent of legislative vote - NA

LEGISLATIVE BRANCH:

description: unicameral Legislature or Staten (21 seats; members directly elected in a single nationwide constituency by proportional representation vote; members serve 4-year terms)

elections: last held on 22 September 2017 (next to be held in September 2021)

election results: percent of vote by party AVP 39.8%, MEP 37.6%, POR 9.4%, RED 7.1%, other 6.1%; seats by party - AVP 9, MEP 9, POR 2, RED 1; composition as of October 2018 - men 14, women 7, percent of women 33.3%

JUDICIAL BRANCH:

highest courts: Joint Court of Justice of Aruba, Curacao, Sint Maarten, and of Bonaire, Sint Eustatitus and Saba or "Joint Court of Justice" (sits as a 3-judge panel); final appeals heard by the Supreme Court, in The Hague, Netherlands

judge selection and term of office: Joint Court judges appointed by the monarch for life

subordinate courts: Courts in First Instance

POLITICAL PARTIES AND LEADERS:

Aruban People's Party or AVP [Michiel "Mike" EMAN]
Democratic Electoral Network or RED [L.R. CROES]
People's Electoral Movement Party or MEP [Evelyn WEVER-CROES]
Pueblo Orguyoso y Respeta or POR [O.E. ODUBER]
Real Democracy or PDR [Andin BIKKER]

INTERNATIONAL ORGANIZATION PARTICIPATION:

Caricom (observer), FATF, ILO, IMF, Interpol, IOC, ITUC (NGOs), UNESCO (associate), UNWTO (associate), UPU

DIPLOMATIC REPRESENTATION IN THE US:

none (represented by the Kingdom of the Netherlands) note - there is a Minister Plenipotentiary for Aruba, Rendolf "Andy" LEE, at the Embassy of the Kingdom of the Netherlands

DIPLOMATIC REPRESENTATION FROM THE US:

the US does not have an embassy in Aruba; the Consul General to Curacao is accredited to Aruba

FLAG DESCRIPTION:

blue, with two narrow, horizontal, yellow stripes across the lower portion and a red, four-pointed star outlined in white in the upper hoist-side corner; the star represents Aruba and its red soil and white beaches, its four points the four major languages (Papiamento, Dutch, Spanish, English) as well as the four points of a compass, to indicate that its inhabitants come from all over the world; the blue symbolizes Caribbean waters and skies; the stripes represent the island's two main "industries": the flow of tourists to the sun-drenched beaches and the flow of minerals from the earth

NATIONAL SYMBOL(S):

Hooiberg (Haystack) Hill; national colors: blue, yellow, red, white

NATIONAL ANTHEM:

name: "Aruba Deshi Tera" (Aruba Precious Country)

lyrics/music: Juan Chabaya 'Padu' LAMPE/Rufo Inocencio WEVER

note: local anthem adopted 1986; as part of the Kingdom of the Netherlands, "Het Wilhelmus" is official (see Netherlands)

ECONOMY :: ARUBA

ECONOMY - OVERVIEW:

Tourism, petroleum bunkering, hospitality, and financial and business services are the mainstays of the small open Aruban economy.

Tourism accounts for a majority of economic activity; as of 2017, over 2 million tourists visited Aruba annually, with the large majority (80-85%) of those from the US. The rapid growth of the tourism sector has resulted in a substantial expansion of other activities. Construction continues to boom, especially in the hospitality sector.

Aruba is heavily dependent on imports and is making efforts to expand exports to improve its trade balance. Almost all consumer and capital goods are imported, with the US, the Netherlands, and Panama being the major suppliers.

In 2016, Citgo Petroleum Corporation, an indirect wholly owned subsidiary of Petroleos de Venezuela SA, and the Government of Aruba signed an agreement to restart Valero Energy Corp.'s former 235,000-b/d refinery. Tourism and related industries have continued to grow, and the Aruban Government is working to attract more diverse industries. Aruba's banking sector continues to be a strong sector; unemployment has significantly decreased.

GDP (PURCHASING POWER PARITY):

$4.158 billion (2017 est.)

$4.107 billion (2016 est.)

$4.112 billion (2015 est.)

country comparison to the world: 180

GDP (OFFICIAL EXCHANGE RATE):

$2.7 billion (2009 est.) (2017 est.)

GDP - REAL GROWTH RATE:

1.2% (2017 est.)

-0.1% (2016 est.)

-0.4% (2015 est.)

country comparison to the world: 180

GDP - PER CAPITA (PPP):

$37,500 (2017 est.)

$37,300 (2016 est.)

$37,700 (2015 est.)

country comparison to the world: 51

GROSS NATIONAL SAVING:

17% of GDP (2017 est.)

17.2% of GDP (2016 est.)

15.5% of GDP (2015 est.)

country comparison to the world: 120

GDP - COMPOSITION, BY END USE:

household consumption: 60.3% (2014 est.)

government consumption: 25.3% (2015 est.)

investment in fixed capital: 22.3% (2014 est.)

investment in inventories: 0% (2015 est.)

exports of goods and services: 70.5% (2015 est.)

imports of goods and services: -76.6% (2015 est.)

GDP - COMPOSITION, BY SECTOR OF ORIGIN:

agriculture: 0.4% (2002 est.)

industry: 33.3% (2002 est.)

services: 66.3% (2002 est.)

AGRICULTURE - PRODUCTS:

aloes; livestock; fish

INDUSTRIES:

tourism, petroleum transshipment facilities, banking

INDUSTRIAL PRODUCTION GROWTH RATE:

NA

LABOR FORCE:

51,610 (2007 est.)

note: of the 51,610 workers aged 15 and over in the labor force, 32,252 were born in Aruba and 19,353 came from abroad; foreign workers are 38% of the employed population

country comparison to the world: 191

LABOR FORCE - BY OCCUPATION:

agriculture: NA

industry: NA

services: NA

note: most employment is in wholesale and retail trade, followed by hotels and restaurants

UNEMPLOYMENT RATE:

7.7% (2016 est.)

country comparison to the world: 113

POPULATION BELOW POVERTY LINE:

NA

HOUSEHOLD INCOME OR CONSUMPTION BY PERCENTAGE SHARE:

lowest 10%: NA

highest 10%: NA

BUDGET:

revenues: 681.6 million (2017 est.)

expenditures: 755.5 million (2017 est.)

TAXES AND OTHER REVENUES:

25.2% (of GDP) (2017 est.)

country comparison to the world: 118

BUDGET SURPLUS (+) OR DEFICIT (-):

-2.7% (of GDP) (2017 est.)

country comparison to the world: 118

PUBLIC DEBT:

86% of GDP (2017 est.)

84.7% of GDP (2016 est.)

country comparison to the world: 31

FISCAL YEAR:

calendar year

INFLATION RATE (CONSUMER PRICES):

-0.5% (2017 est.)

-0.9% (2016 est.)

country comparison to the world: 6

CENTRAL BANK DISCOUNT RATE:

1% (31 December 2010)

3% (31 December 2009)

country comparison to the world: 132

COMMERCIAL BANK PRIME LENDING RATE:

7% (31 December 2017 est.)

7.83% (31 December 2016 est.)

country comparison to the world: 118

STOCK OF NARROW MONEY:

$0 (31 December 2017 est.)

$1.257 billion (31 December 2016 est.)

country comparison to the world: 194

STOCK OF BROAD MONEY:

$0 (31 December 2017 est.)

$1.257 billion (31 December 2016 est.)

country comparison to the world: 197

STOCK OF DOMESTIC CREDIT:

$1.848 billion (31 December 2017 est.)

$1.848 billion (31 December 2016 est.)

country comparison to the world: 156

CURRENT ACCOUNT BALANCE:

$22 million (2017 est.)

$133 million (2016 est.)

country comparison to the world: 60

EXPORTS:

$137.1 million (2017 est.)

$283.1 million (2016 est.)

country comparison to the world: 193

EXPORTS - PARTNERS:

US 20.2%, Colombia 17.6%, Venezuela 13%, Netherlands 9.1%, Thailand 8.4%, Panama 4.8% (2017)

EXPORTS - COMMODITIES:

live animals and animal products, art and collectibles, machinery and electrical equipment, transport equipment

IMPORTS:

$1.122 billion (2017 est.)

$1.142 billion (2016 est.)

country comparison to the world: 181

IMPORTS - COMMODITIES:

machinery and electrical equipment, refined oil for bunkering and reexport, chemicals; foodstuffs

IMPORTS - PARTNERS:

US 53.7%, Netherlands 13.1% (2017)

RESERVES OF FOREIGN EXCHANGE AND GOLD:

$921.8 million (31 December 2017 est.)

$828 million (31 December 2015 est.)

country comparison to the world: 134

DEBT - EXTERNAL:

$693.2 million (31 December 2014 est.)

$666.4 million (31 December 2013 est.)

country comparison to the world: 173

EXCHANGE RATES:

Aruban guilders/florins per US dollar -

1.79 (2017 est.)

1.79 (2016 est.)

1.79 (2015 est.)

1.79 (2014 est.)

1.79 (2013 est.)

ENERGY :: ARUBA

ELECTRICITY ACCESS:

population without electricity: 11,364 (2012)

electrification - total population: 91% (2012)

electrification - urban areas: 100% (2012)

electrification - rural areas: 80% (2012)

ELECTRICITY - PRODUCTION:

939 million kWh (2016 est.)

country comparison to the world: 153

ELECTRICITY - CONSUMPTION:

873.3 million kWh (2016 est.)

country comparison to the world: 158

ELECTRICITY - EXPORTS:

0 kWh (2016 est.)

country comparison to the world: 100

ELECTRICITY - IMPORTS:

0 kWh (2016 est.)

country comparison to the world: 121

ELECTRICITY - INSTALLED GENERATING CAPACITY:

296,000 kW (2016 est.)

country comparison to the world: 159

ELECTRICITY - FROM FOSSIL FUELS:

87% of total installed capacity (2016 est.)

country comparison to the world: 61

ELECTRICITY - FROM NUCLEAR FUELS:

0% of total installed capacity (2017 est.)

country comparison to the world: 39

ELECTRICITY - FROM HYDROELECTRIC PLANTS:

0% of total installed capacity (2017 est.)

country comparison to the world: 154

ELECTRICITY - FROM OTHER RENEWABLE SOURCES:

13% of total installed capacity (2017 est.)

country comparison to the world: 66

CRUDE OIL - PRODUCTION:

0 bbl/day (2017 est.)

country comparison to the world: 106

CRUDE OIL - EXPORTS:

0 bbl/day (2015 est.)

country comparison to the world: 87

CRUDE OIL - IMPORTS:

0 bbl/day (2015 est.)

country comparison to the world: 91

CRUDE OIL - PROVED RESERVES:

0 bbl (1 January 2018 est.)

country comparison to the world: 104

REFINED PETROLEUM PRODUCTS - PRODUCTION:

0 bbl/day (2015 est.)

country comparison to the world: 115

REFINED PETROLEUM PRODUCTS - CONSUMPTION:

8,000 bbl/day (2016 est.)

country comparison to the world: 163

REFINED PETROLEUM PRODUCTS - EXPORTS:

0 bbl/day (2015 est.)

country comparison to the world: 127

REFINED PETROLEUM PRODUCTS - IMPORTS:

7,891 bbl/day (2015 est.)

country comparison to the world: 153

NATURAL GAS - PRODUCTION:

1 cu m (2017 est.)

country comparison to the world: 96

NATURAL GAS - CONSUMPTION:

1 cu m (2017 est.)

country comparison to the world: 116

NATURAL GAS - EXPORTS:

1 cu m (2017 est.)

country comparison to the world: 56

NATURAL GAS - IMPORTS:

1 cu m (2017 est.)

country comparison to the world: 80

NATURAL GAS - PROVED RESERVES:

0 cu m (1 January 2014 est.)

country comparison to the world: 107

CARBON DIOXIDE EMISSIONS FROM CONSUMPTION OF ENERGY:

1.266 million Mt (2017 est.)

country comparison to the world: 162

COMMUNICATIONS :: ARUBA

TELEPHONES - FIXED LINES:

total subscriptions: 35,000 (July 2016 est.)

subscriptions per 100 inhabitants: 31 (July 2016 est.)

country comparison to the world: 167

TELEPHONES - MOBILE CELLULAR:

total subscriptions: 141,000 (July 2016 est.)

subscriptions per 100 inhabitants: 126 (July 2016 est.)

country comparison to the world: 187

TELEPHONE SYSTEM:

general assessment: modern fully automatic telecommunications system; increased competition through privatization has increased mobile-cellular teledensity; three mobile-cellular service providers are now licensed; MNO (mobile network operator) launches island-wide LTE services; introduction of MNP (mobile number potability) (2017)

domestic: ongoing changes in regulations and competion improve teledensity; 31 per 100 fixed-line, 126 per 100 mobile-cellular (2017)

international: country code - 297; landing site for the PAN-AM submarine telecommunications cable system that extends from the US Virgin Islands through Aruba to Venezuela, Colombia, Panama, and the west coast of South America; extensive interisland microwave radio relay links (2016)

BROADCAST MEDIA:

2 commercial TV stations; cable TV subscription service provides access to foreign channels; about 19 commercial radio stations broadcast (2017)

INTERNET COUNTRY CODE:

.aw

INTERNET USERS:

total: 106,309 (July 2016 est.)

percent of population: 93.5% (July 2016 est.)

country comparison to the world: 177

TRANSPORTATION :: ARUBA

NATIONAL AIR TRANSPORT SYSTEM:

number of registered air carriers: 3 (2015)

inventory of registered aircraft operated by air carriers: 19 (2015)

annual passenger traffic on registered air carriers: 2,120,578 (2015)

annual freight traffic on registered air carriers: 0 mt-km (2015)

CIVIL AIRCRAFT REGISTRATION COUNTRY CODE PREFIX:

P4 (2016)

AIRPORTS:

1 (2013)

country comparison to the world: 212

AIRPORTS - WITH PAVED RUNWAYS:

total: 1 (2017)

2,438 to 3,047 m: 1 (2017)

PORTS AND TERMINALS:

major seaport(s): Barcadera, Oranjestad

oil terminal(s): Sint Nicolaas

cruise port(s): Oranjestad

MILITARY AND SECURITY :: ARUBA

MILITARY BRANCHES:

no regular military forces (2011)

MILITARY - NOTE:

defense is the responsibility of the Netherlands; the Aruba security services focus on organized crime and terrorism

TRANSNATIONAL ISSUES :: ARUBA

DISPUTES - INTERNATIONAL:

none

ILLICIT DRUGS:

transit point for US- and Europe-bound narcotics with some accompanying money-laundering activity; relatively high percentage of population consumes cocaine

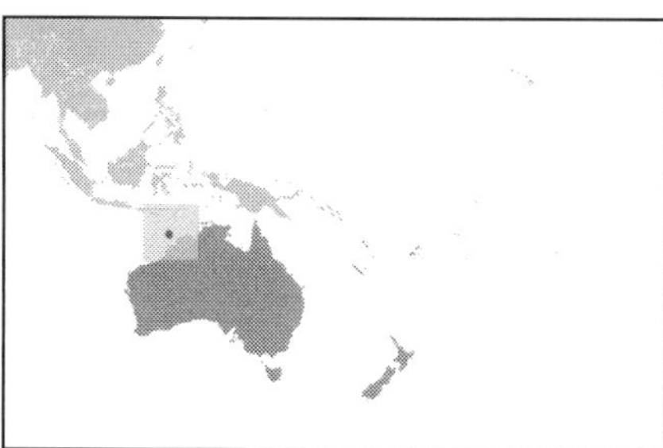

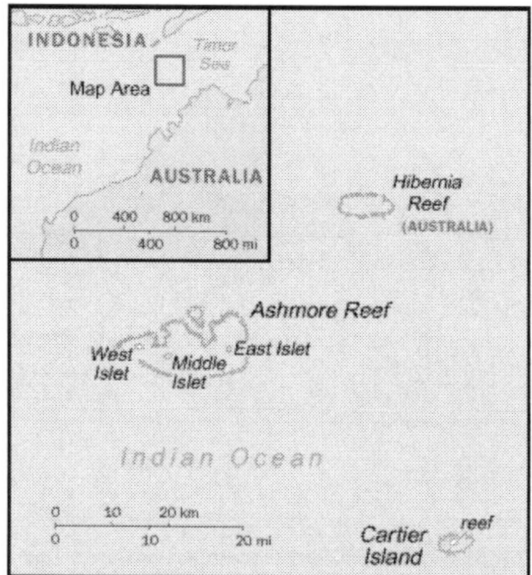

AUSTRALIA - OCEANIA :: ASHMORE AND CARTIER ISLANDS

INTRODUCTION :: ASHMORE AND CARTIER ISLANDS

BACKGROUND:

These uninhabited islands came under Australian authority in 1931; formal administration began two years later. Ashmore Reef supports a rich and diverse avian and marine habitat; in 1983, it became a National Nature Reserve. Cartier Island, a former bombing range, became a marine reserve in 2000.

GEOGRAPHY :: ASHMORE AND CARTIER ISLANDS

LOCATION:

Southeastern Asia, islands in the Indian Ocean, midway between northwestern Australia and Timor island

GEOGRAPHIC COORDINATES:

12 14 S, 123 05 E

MAP REFERENCES:

Southeast Asia

AREA:

total: 5 sq km

land: 5 sq km

water: 0 sq km

note: includes Ashmore Reef (West, Middle, and East Islets) and Cartier Island

country comparison to the world: 250

AREA - COMPARATIVE:

about eight times the size of the National Mall in Washington, DC

LAND BOUNDARIES:

0 km

COASTLINE:

74.1 km

MARITIME CLAIMS:

territorial sea: 12 nm

contiguous zone: 12 nm

continental shelf: 200-m depth or to the depth of exploitation

exclusive fishing zone: 200 nm

CLIMATE:

tropical

TERRAIN:

low with sand and coral

ELEVATION:

0 m lowest point: Indian Ocean

5 highest point: Cartier Island

NATURAL RESOURCES:

fish

LAND USE:

0% (2014 est.)

NATURAL HAZARDS:

surrounded by shoals and reefs that can pose maritime hazards

ENVIRONMENT - CURRENT ISSUES:

illegal killing of protected wildlife by traditional Indonesian fisherman, as well as fishing by non-traditional Indonesian vessels, are ongoing problems; sea level rise, changes in sea temperature, and ocean acidification are concerns; marine debris

GEOGRAPHY - NOTE:

Ashmore Reef National Nature Reserve established in August 1983; Cartier Island Marine Reserve established in 2000

PEOPLE AND SOCIETY :: ASHMORE AND CARTIER ISLANDS

POPULATION:

no indigenous inhabitants

note: Indonesian fishermen are allowed access to the lagoon and fresh water at Ashmore Reef's West Island; access to East and Middle Islands is by permit only

GOVERNMENT :: ASHMORE AND CARTIER ISLANDS

COUNTRY NAME:

conventional long form: Territory of Ashmore and Cartier Islands

conventional short form: Ashmore and Cartier Islands

etymology: named after British Captain Samuel ASHMORE, who first sighted his namesake island in 1811, and after the ship Cartier, from which the second island was discovered in 1800

DEPENDENCY STATUS:

territory of Australia; administered from Canberra by the Department of Regional Australia, Local Government, Arts and Sport

LEGAL SYSTEM:

the laws of the Commonwealth of Australia and the laws of the Northern

Territory of Australia, where applicable, apply

CITIZENSHIP:

see Australia

DIPLOMATIC REPRESENTATION IN THE US:

none (territory of Australia)

DIPLOMATIC REPRESENTATION FROM THE US:

none (territory of Australia)

FLAG DESCRIPTION:

the flag of Australia is used

ECONOMY :: ASHMORE AND CARTIER ISLANDS

ECONOMY - OVERVIEW:

no economic activity

TRANSPORTATION :: ASHMORE AND CARTIER ISLANDS

PORTS AND TERMINALS:

none; offshore anchorage only

MILITARY AND SECURITY :: ASHMORE AND CARTIER ISLANDS

MILITARY - NOTE:

defense is the responsibility of Australia; periodic visits by the Royal Australian Navy and Royal Australian Air Force

TRANSNATIONAL ISSUES :: ASHMORE AND CARTIER ISLANDS

DISPUTES - INTERNATIONAL:

Australia has closed parts of the Ashmore and Cartier reserve to Indonesian traditional fishingIndonesian groups challenge Australia's claim to Ashmore Reef

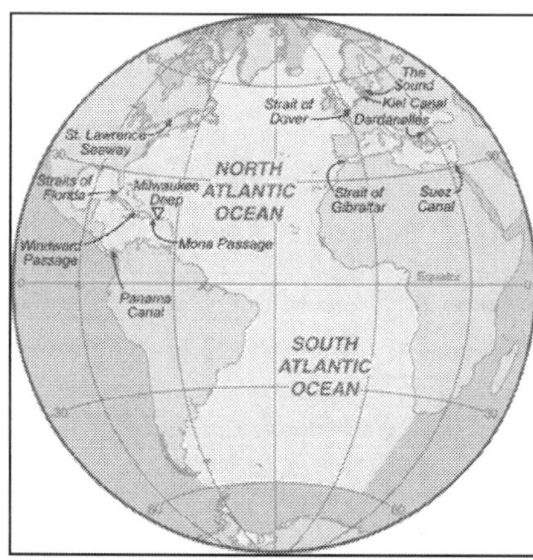

OCEANS :: ATLANTIC OCEAN

INTRODUCTION :: ATLANTIC OCEAN

BACKGROUND:

The Atlantic Ocean is the second largest of the world's five oceans (after the Pacific Ocean, but larger than the Indian Ocean, Southern Ocean, and Arctic Ocean). The Kiel Canal (Germany), Oresund (Denmark-Sweden), Bosporus (Turkey), Strait of Gibraltar (Morocco-Spain), and the Saint Lawrence Seaway (Canada-US) are important strategic access waterways.The decision by the International Hydrographic Organization in the spring of 2000 to delimit a fifth world ocean, the Southern Ocean, removed the portion of the Atlantic Ocean south of 60 degrees south latitude.

GEOGRAPHY :: ATLANTIC OCEAN

LOCATION:

body of water between Africa, Europe, the Arctic Ocean, the Americas, and the Southern Ocean

GEOGRAPHIC COORDINATES:

0 00 N, 25 00 W

MAP REFERENCES:

Political Map of the World

AREA:

total: 76.762 million sq km

note: includes Baltic Sea, Black Sea, Caribbean Sea, Davis Strait, Denmark Strait, part of the Drake Passage, Gulf of Mexico, Labrador Sea, Mediterranean Sea, North Sea, Norwegian Sea, almost all of the Scotia Sea, and other tributary water bodies

AREA - COMPARATIVE:

about 7.5 times the size of the US

COASTLINE:

111,866 km

CLIMATE:

tropical cyclones (hurricanes) develop off the coast of Africa near Cabo Verde and move westward into the Caribbean Sea; hurricanes can occur from May to December but are most frequent from August to November

TERRAIN:

surface usually covered with sea ice in Labrador Sea, Denmark Strait, and coastal portions of the Baltic Sea from October to June; surface dominated by two large gyres (broad, circular systems of currents), one in the northern Atlantic and another in the southern Atlantic; the ocean floor is dominated by the Mid-Atlantic Ridge, a rugged north-south centerline for the entire Atlantic basin

major surface currents: clockwise North Atlantic Gyre consists of the warm Gulf Stream in the west, the North Atlantic Current in the north, the cold Canary Current in the east, and the North Equatorial Current in the south; the counterclockwise South Atlantic Gyre composed of the warm Brazil Current in the west, the South Atlantic Current in the south, the cold Benguela Current in the east, and the South Equatorial Current in the north

ELEVATION:

elevation extremes: -8,605 m lowest point: Milwaukee Deep in the Puerto Rico Trench

mean depth: -3,646 m

0 highest point: sea level

NATURAL RESOURCES:

oil and gas fields, fish, marine mammals (seals and whales), sand and gravel aggregates, placer deposits, polymetallic nodules, precious stones

NATURAL HAZARDS:

icebergs common in Davis Strait, Denmark Strait, and the northwestern Atlantic Ocean from February to August and have been spotted as far south as Bermuda and the Madeira Islands; ships subject to superstructure icing in extreme northern Atlantic from October to May; persistent fog can be a maritime hazard from May to September; hurricanes (May to December)

ENVIRONMENT - CURRENT ISSUES:

endangered marine species include the manatee, seals, sea lions, turtles, and whales; unsustainable exploitation of fisheries (over fishing, bottom trawling, drift net fishing, discards, catch of non-target species); pollution (maritime transport, discharges, offshore drilling, oil spills); municipal sludge pollution off eastern US, southern Brazil, and eastern Argentina; oil pollution in Caribbean Sea, Gulf of Mexico, Lake Maracaibo, Mediterranean Sea, and North Sea; industrial waste and municipal sewage pollution in Baltic Sea, North Sea, and Mediterranean Sea

GEOGRAPHY - NOTE:

major chokepoints include the Dardanelles, Strait of Gibraltar, access to the Panama and Suez Canals; strategic straits include the Strait of Dover, Straits of Florida, Mona Passage, The Sound (Oresund), and Windward Passage; the Equator divides the Atlantic Ocean into the North Atlantic Ocean and South Atlantic Ocean

GOVERNMENT :: ATLANTIC OCEAN

COUNTRY NAME:

etymology: name derives from the Greek description of the waters beyond the Strait of Gibraltar, Atlantis thalassa, meaning "Sea of Atlas"

ECONOMY :: ATLANTIC OCEAN

ECONOMY - OVERVIEW:

The Atlantic Ocean provides some of the world's most heavily trafficked sea routes, between and within the Eastern and Western Hemispheres. Other economic activity includes the exploitation of natural resources, e.g., fishing, dredging of aragonite sands (The Bahamas), and production of crude oil and natural gas (Caribbean Sea, Gulf of Mexico, and North Sea).

TRANSPORTATION :: ATLANTIC OCEAN

PORTS AND TERMINALS:

major seaport(s): Alexandria (Egypt), Algiers (Algeria), Antwerp (Belgium), Barcelona (Spain), Buenos Aires (Argentina), Casablanca (Morocco), Colon (Panama), Copenhagen (Denmark), Dakar (Senegal), Gdansk (Poland), Hamburg (Germany), Helsinki (Finland), Las Palmas (Canary Islands, Spain), Le Havre (France), Lisbon (Portugal), London (UK), Marseille (France), Montevideo (Uruguay), Montreal (Canada), Naples (Italy), New Orleans (US), New York (US), Oran (Algeria), Oslo (Norway), Peiraiefs or Piraeus (Greece), Rio de Janeiro (Brazil), Rotterdam (Netherlands), Saint Petersburg (Russia), Stockholm (Sweden)

TRANSPORTATION - NOTE:

Kiel Canal and Saint Lawrence Seaway are two important waterways; significant domestic commercial and recreational use of Intracoastal Waterway on central and south Atlantic seaboard and Gulf of Mexico coast of US; the International Maritime Bureau reports the territorial waters of littoral states and offshore Atlantic waters as high risk for piracy and armed robbery against ships, particularly in the Gulf of Guinea off West Africa; in 2014, 41 commercial vessels were attacked in the Gulf of Guinea with 5 hijacked and 144 crew members taken hostage; hijacked vessels are often disguised and cargoes stolen; crews have been robbed and stores or cargoes stolen

MILITARY AND SECURITY :: ATLANTIC OCEAN

MARITIME THREATS:

West African piracy is a continuing threat with 33 attacks in 2017 compared to 36 in 2016; Nigerian pirates are very aggresive, operating as far as 200 nm offshore and boarding 20 ships in 2017

TRANSNATIONAL ISSUES :: ATLANTIC OCEAN

DISPUTES - INTERNATIONAL:

some maritime disputes (see littoral states)

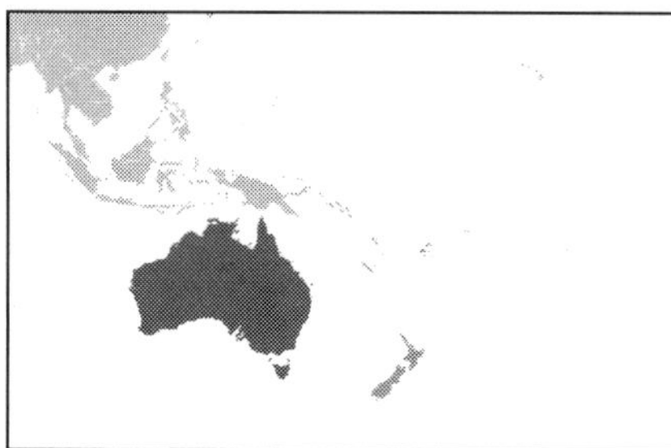

AUSTRALIA - OCEANIA :: AUSTRALIA

INTRODUCTION :: AUSTRALIA

BACKGROUND:

Prehistoric settlers arrived on the continent from Southeast Asia at least 40,000 years before the first Europeans began exploration in the 17th century. No formal territorial claims were made until 1770, when Capt. James COOK took possession of the east coast in the name of Great Britain (all of Australia was claimed as British territory in 1829 with the creation of the colony of Western Australia). Six colonies were created in the late 18th and 19th centuries; they federated and became the Commonwealth of Australia in 1901. The new country took advantage of its natural resources to rapidly develop agricultural and manufacturing industries and to make a major contribution to the Allied effort in World Wars I and II.

In recent decades, Australia has become an internationally competitive, advanced market economy due in large part to economic reforms adopted in the 1980s and its location in one of the fastest growing regions of the world economy. Long-term concerns include an aging population, pressure on infrastructure, and environmental issues such as floods, droughts, and bushfires. Australia is the driest inhabited continent on earth, making it particularly vulnerable to the challenges of climate change. Australia is home to 10% of the world's biodiversity, and a great number of its flora and fauna exist nowhere else in the world.

GEOGRAPHY :: AUSTRALIA

LOCATION:

Oceania, continent between the Indian Ocean and the South Pacific Ocean

GEOGRAPHIC COORDINATES:

27 00 S, 133 00 E

MAP REFERENCES:

Oceania

AREA:

total: 7,741,220 sq km

land: 7,682,300 sq km

water: 58,920 sq km

note: includes Lord Howe Island and Macquarie Island

country comparison to the world: 7

AREA - COMPARATIVE:

slightly smaller than the US contiguous 48 states

LAND BOUNDARIES:

0 km

COASTLINE:

25,760 km

MARITIME CLAIMS:

territorial sea: 12 nm

exclusive economic zone: 200 nm

contiguous zone: 24 nm

continental shelf: 200 nm or to the edge of the continental margin

CLIMATE:

generally arid to semiarid; temperate in south and east; tropical in north

TERRAIN:

mostly low plateau with deserts; fertile plain in southeast

ELEVATION:

mean elevation: 330 m

elevation extremes: -15 m lowest point: Lake Eyre

2228 highest point: Mount Kosciuszko

NATURAL RESOURCES:

alumina, coal, iron ore, copper, tin, gold, silver, uranium, nickel, tungsten, rare earth elements, mineral sands, lead, zinc, diamonds, natural gas, petroleum; note - Australia is the world's largest net exporter of coal accounting for 29% of global coal exports

LAND USE:

agricultural land: 52.9% (2014 est.)

arable land: 11.6% (2014 est.) / permanent crops: 0.09% (2014 est.) / permanent pasture: 88.4% (2014 est.)

forest: 16.2% (2014 est.)

other: 30.9% (2014 est.)

IRRIGATED LAND:

25,460 sq km (2014)

POPULATION DISTRIBUTION:

population is primarily located on the periphery, with the highest concentration of people residing in the southeast; a secondary population center is located in and around Perth in the west; of the States and Territories, New South Wales has, by far, the largest population; the interior, or "outback", has a very sparse population

NATURAL HAZARDS:

cyclones along the coast; severe droughts; forest fires

volcanism: volcanic activity on Heard and McDonald Islands

ENVIRONMENT - CURRENT ISSUES:

soil erosion from overgrazing, deforestation, industrial development, urbanization, and poor farming practices; soil salinity rising due to the use of poor quality water; desertification; clearing for agricultural purposes threatens the natural habitat of many unique animal and plant species; the Great Barrier Reef off the northeast coast, the largest coral reef in the world, is threatened by increased shipping and its popularity as a tourist site; limited natural freshwater resources; drought, overfishing, pollution, and invasive species are also problems

ENVIRONMENT - INTERNATIONAL AGREEMENTS:

party to: Antarctic-Environmental Protocol, Antarctic-Marine Living Resources, Antarctic Seals, Antarctic Treaty, Biodiversity, Climate Change, Climate Change-Kyoto Protocol, Desertification, Endangered Species, Environmental Modification, Hazardous Wastes, Law of the Sea, Marine Dumping, Marine Life Conservation, Ozone Layer Protection, Ship Pollution, Tropical Timber 83, Tropical Timber 94, Wetlands, Whaling

signed, but not ratified: none of the selected agreements

GEOGRAPHY - NOTE:

world's smallest continent but sixth-largest country; the largest country in Oceania, the largest country entirely in the Southern Hemisphere, and the largest country without land borders; the only continent without glaciers; population concentrated along the eastern and southeastern coasts; the invigorating sea breeze known as the "Fremantle Doctor" affects the city of Perth on the west coast and is one of the most consistent winds in the world

PEOPLE AND SOCIETY :: AUSTRALIA

POPULATION:

23,470,145 (July 2018 est.)

country comparison to the world: 56

NATIONALITY:

noun: Australian(s)

adjective: Australian

ETHNIC GROUPS:

English 25.9%, Australian 25.4%, Irish 7.5%, Scottish 6.4%, Italian 3.3%, German 3.2%, Chinese 3.1%, Indian 1.4%, Greek 1.4%, Dutch 1.2%, other 15.8% (includes Australian aboriginal .5%), unspecified 5.4% (2011 est.)

note: data represent self-identified ancestry, over a third of respondents reported two ancestries

LANGUAGES:

English 72.7%, Mandarin 2.5%, Arabic 1.4%, Cantonese 1.2%, Vietnamese 1.2%, Italian 1.2%, Greek 1%, other 14.8%, unspecified 6.5% (2016 est.)

note: data represent language spoken at home

RELIGIONS:

Protestant 23.1% (Anglican 13.3%, Uniting Church 3.7%, Presbyterian and Reformed 2.3%, Baptist 1.5%, Pentecostal 1.1%, Lutheran .7%, other Protestant .5%), Roman Catholic 22.6%, other Christian 4.2%, Muslim 2.6%, Buddhist 2.4%, Orthodox 2.3% (Eastern Orthodox 2.1%, Oriental Orthodox .2%), Hindu 1.9%, other 1.3%, none 30.1%, unspecified 9.6% (2016 est.)

AGE STRUCTURE:

0-14 years: 17.75% (male 2,138,080 /female 2,027,583)

15-24 years: 12.62% (male 1,520,528 /female 1,442,461)

25-54 years: 41.35% (male 4,944,587 /female 4,760,752)

55-64 years: 11.84% (male 1,379,681 /female 1,398,177)

65 years and over: 16.44% (male 1,786,595 /female 2,071,701) (2018 est.)

DEPENDENCY RATIOS:

total dependency ratio: 51.1 (2015 est.)

youth dependency ratio: 28.5 (2015 est.)

elderly dependency ratio: 22.6 (2015 est.)

potential support ratio: 4.4 (2015 est.)

MEDIAN AGE:

total: 38.8 years

male: 38.1 years

female: 39.7 years (2018 est.)

country comparison to the world: 58

POPULATION GROWTH RATE:

1.01% (2018 est.)

country comparison to the world: 107

BIRTH RATE:

12 births/1,000 population (2018 est.)

country comparison to the world: 165

DEATH RATE:

7.3 deaths/1,000 population (2018 est.)

country comparison to the world: 118

NET MIGRATION RATE:

5.5 migrant(s)/1,000 population (2017 est.)

country comparison to the world: 21

POPULATION DISTRIBUTION:

population is primarily located on the periphery, with the highest concentration of people residing in the southeast; a secondary population center is located in and around Perth in the west; of the States and Territories, New South Wales has, by far, the largest population; the interior, or "outback", has a very sparse population

URBANIZATION:

urban population: 86% of total population (2018)

rate of urbanization: 1.43% annual rate of change (2015-20 est.)

note: data include Christmas Island, Cocos Islands, and Norfolk Island

MAJOR URBAN AREAS - POPULATION:

4.792 million Sydney, 4.771 million Melbourne, 2.338 million Brisbane, 1.991 million Perth, 1.32 million Adelaide, 423,000 CANBERRA (capital) (2018)

SEX RATIO:

at birth: 1.05 male(s)/female (2017 est.)

0-14 years: 1.05 male(s)/female (2017 est.)

15-24 years: 1.05 male(s)/female (2017 est.)

25-54 years: 1.04 male(s)/female (2017 est.)

55-64 years: 0.98 male(s)/female (2017 est.)

65 years and over: 0.86 male(s)/female (2017 est.)

total population: 1.01 male(s)/female (2017 est.)

MOTHER'S MEAN AGE AT FIRST BIRTH:

28.7 years (2014 est.)

MATERNAL MORTALITY RATE:

6 deaths/100,000 live births (2015 est.)

country comparison to the world: 165

INFANT MORTALITY RATE:

total: 4.2 deaths/1,000 live births (2018 est.)

male: 4.5 deaths/1,000 live births (2018 est.)

female: 3.9 deaths/1,000 live births (2018 est.)

country comparison to the world: 188

LIFE EXPECTANCY AT BIRTH:

total population: 82.4 years (2018 est.)

male: 79.9 years (2018 est.)

female: 85 years (2018 est.)

country comparison to the world: 14

TOTAL FERTILITY RATE:

1.77 children born/woman (2018 est.)

country comparison to the world: 155

CONTRACEPTIVE PREVALENCE RATE:

66.9% (2015/16)

note: percent of women aged 18-45

HEALTH EXPENDITURES:

9.4% of GDP (2014)

country comparison to the world: 32

PHYSICIANS DENSITY:

3.5 physicians/1,000 population (2015)

HOSPITAL BED DENSITY:

3.8 beds/1,000 population (2014)

DRINKING WATER SOURCE:

improved:

urban: 100% of population

rural: 100% of population

total: 100% of population

unimproved:

urban: 0% of population

rural: 0% of population

total: 0% of population (2015 est.)

SANITATION FACILITY ACCESS:

improved:

urban: 100% of population (2015 est.)

rural: 100% of population (2015 est.)

total: 100% of population (2015 est.)

unimproved:

urban: 0% of population (2015 est.)

rural: 0% of population (2015 est.)

total: 0% of population (2015 est.)

HIV/AIDS - ADULT PREVALENCE RATE:

0.1% (2017 est.)

country comparison to the world: 106

HIV/AIDS - PEOPLE LIVING WITH HIV/AIDS:

26,000 (2017 est.)

country comparison to the world: 75

HIV/AIDS - DEATHS:

<200 (2017 est.)

OBESITY - ADULT PREVALENCE RATE:

29% (2016)

country comparison to the world: 27

EDUCATION EXPENDITURES:

5.2% of GDP (2014)

country comparison to the world: 63

SCHOOL LIFE EXPECTANCY (PRIMARY TO TERTIARY EDUCATION):

total: 20 years (2014)

male: 20 years (2014)

female: 21 years (2014)

UNEMPLOYMENT, YOUTH AGES 15-24:

total: 12.6% (2017 est.)

male: 13.7% (2017 est.)

female: 11.5% (2017 est.)

country comparison to the world: 105

GOVERNMENT :: AUSTRALIA

COUNTRY NAME:

conventional long form: Commonwealth of Australia

conventional short form: Australia

etymology: the name Australia derives from the Latin "australis" meaning "southern"; the Australian landmass was long referred to as "Terra Australis" or the Southern Land

GOVERNMENT TYPE:

parliamentary democracy (Federal Parliament) under a constitutional monarchy; a Commonwealth realm

CAPITAL:

name: Canberra

geographic coordinates: 35 16 S, 149 08 E

time difference: UTC+10 (15 hours ahead of Washington, DC, during Standard Time)

daylight saving time: +1hr, begins first Sunday in October; ends first Sunday in April

etymolgy: the name is claimed to derive from either Kambera or Camberry, which are names corrupted from the original native designation for the area "Nganbra" or "Nganbira"

note: Australia has four time zones, including Lord Howe Island (UTC+10:30)

ADMINISTRATIVE DIVISIONS:

6 states and 2 territories*; Australian Capital Territory*, New South Wales, Northern Territory*, Queensland, South Australia, Tasmania, Victoria, Western Australia

DEPENDENT AREAS:

Ashmore and Cartier Islands, Christmas Island, Cocos (Keeling) Islands, Coral Sea Islands, Heard Island and McDonald Islands, Norfolk Island

INDEPENDENCE:

1 January 1901 (from the federation of UK colonies)

NATIONAL HOLIDAY:

Australia Day (commemorates the arrival of the First Fleet of Australian settlers), 26 January (1788)ANZAC Day (commemorates the anniversary of the landing of troops of the Australian and New Zealand Army Corps during World War I at Gallipoli, Turkey), 25 April (1915)

CONSTITUTION:

history: approved in a series of referenda 1898 through 1900, became law 9 July 1900, effective 1 January 1901 (2017)

amendments: proposed by Parliament; passage requires approval of a referendum bill by absolute majority vote in both houses of Parliament, approval in a referendum by a majority of voters in at least four states and in the territories, and Royal Assent; proposals that would reduce a state's representation in either house or change a state's boundaries require that state's approval prior to Royal Assent; amended several times, last in 1977 (2017)

LEGAL SYSTEM:

common law system based on the English model

INTERNATIONAL LAW ORGANIZATION PARTICIPATION:

accepts compulsory ICJ jurisdiction with reservations; accepts ICCt jurisdiction

CITIZENSHIP:

citizenship by birth: no

citizenship by descent only: at least one parent must be a citizen or permanent resident of Australia

dual citizenship recognized: yes

residency requirement for naturalization: 4 years

SUFFRAGE:

18 years of age; universal and compulsory

EXECUTIVE BRANCH:

chief of state: Queen of Australia ELIZABETH II (since 6 February 1952); represented by Governor Gen. Sir Peter COSGROVE (since 28 March 2014)

head of government: Prime Minister Scott MORRISON (since 24 August 2018)

cabinet: Cabinet nominated by the prime minister from among members of Parliament and sworn in by the governor general

elections/appointments: the monarchy is hereditary; governor general appointed by the monarch on the recommendation of the prime minister; following legislative elections, the leader of the majority party or majority coalition is sworn in as prime minister by the governor general

LEGISLATIVE BRANCH:

description: bicameral Federal Parliament consists of:
Senate (76 seats; 12 members from each of the 6 states and 2 each from the 2 mainland territories; members directly elected in multi-seat constituencies by proportional representation vote; members serve 6-year terms with one-half of state membership renewed every 3 years and territory membership renewed every 3 years)
House of Representatives (150 seats; members directly elected in single-seat constituencies by majority preferential vote; members serve terms of up to 3 years)

elections:
Senate - last held on 2 July 2016 (next to be held in 2019)
House of Representatives - last held on 2 July 2016; this election represented a rare double dissolution where all 226 seats in both the Senate and House of Representatives were up for reelection

election results:
Senate - percent of vote by party - Liberal/National Coalition 35.2%, ALP 29.8%, the Greens 8.7%, Pauline Hanson's One Nation 4.3%, Nick Xenophon Team 3.3%, other 18.7%; seats by party - Liberal/National Coalition 30, ALP 26, The Greens 9, Pauline Hanson's One Nation 4, Nick Xenophon Team 3, other 4; composition - men 48, women 28, percent of women 36.8%

House of Representatives - percent of vote by party - Liberal/National Coalition 42%, ALP 34.7%, The Greens 10.2%, Nick Xenophon Team 1.9%. Katter's Australian Party 0.5%, other 7.8%, independent 2.8%; seats by party - Liberal/National Coalition 76, ALP 69, The Greens 1, Katter's Australian Party 1, Nick Xenophon Team 1, independent 2; composition - men 107, women 43, percent of women 28.7%; note - total Federal Parliament percent of women 31.4%

JUDICIAL BRANCH:

highest courts: High Court of Australia (consists of 7 justices, including the chief justice); note - each of the 6 states, 2 territories, and Norfolk Island has a Supreme Court; the High Court is the final appellate court beyond the state and territory supreme courts

judge selection and term of office: justices appointed by the governor-general in council for life with mandatory retirement at age 70

subordinate courts: subordinate courts: subordinate courts at the federal level: Federal Court; Federal Magistrates' Courts of Australia; Family Court; subordinate courts at the state and territory level: Local Court - New South Wales; Magistrates' Courts – Victoria, Queensland, South Australia, Western Australia, Tasmania, Northern Territory, Australian Capital Territory; District Courts – New South Wales, Queensland, South Australia, Western Australia; County Court – Victoria; Family Court – Western Australia; Court of Petty Sessions – Norfolk Island

POLITICAL PARTIES AND LEADERS:

Australian Greens Party [Richard DI NATALE]
Australian Labor Party or ALP [Bill SHORTEN]
Country Liberal Party or CLP [Gary HIGGINS]
Liberal National Party of Queensland or LNP [Deborah FRECKLINGTON]
Liberal Party of Australia [Scott MORRISON]
The Nationals [Michael MCCORMACK]
Nick Xenophon Team [Nick XENOPHON]Pauline Hanson's One Nation [Pauline HANSON]

INTERNATIONAL ORGANIZATION PARTICIPATION:

ADB, ANZUS, APEC, ARF, ASEAN (dialogue partner), Australia Group, BIS, C, CD, CP, EAS, EBRD, EITI (implementing country), FAO, FATF, G-20, IAEA, IBRD, ICAO, ICC (national committees), ICCt, ICRM, IDA, IEA, IFC, IFRCS, IHO, ILO, IMF, IMO, IMSO, Interpol, IOC, IOM, IPU, ISO, ITSO, ITU, ITUC (NGOs), MIGA, NEA, NSG, OECD, OPCW, OSCE (partner), Pacific Alliance (observer), Paris Club, PCA, PIF, SAARC (observer), SICA (observer), Sparteca, SPC, UN, UNCTAD, UNESCO, UNHCR, UNMISS, UNMIT, UNRWA, UNTSO, UNWTO, UPU, WCO, WFTU (NGOs), WHO, WIPO, WMO, WTO, ZC

DIPLOMATIC REPRESENTATION IN THE US:

chief of mission: Ambassador Joseph Benedict HOCKEY (since 28 January 2016)

chancery: 1601 Massachusetts Avenue NW, Washington, DC 20036

telephone: [1] (202) 797-3000

FAX: [1] (202) 797-3168

consulate(s) general: Atlanta, Chicago, Honolulu, Houston, Los Angeles, New York, San Francisco

DIPLOMATIC REPRESENTATION FROM THE US:

chief of mission: Ambassador (vacant); Charge d'Affaires James CAROUSO (since September 2016)

embassy: Moonah Place, Yarralumla, Canberra, Australian Capital Territory 2600

mailing address: APO AP 96549

telephone: [61] (02) 6214-5600

FAX: [61] (02) 6214-5970

consulate(s) general: Melbourne, Perth, Sydney

FLAG DESCRIPTION:

blue with the flag of the UK in the upper hoist side quadrant and a large seven-pointed star in the lower hoist-side quadrant known as the Commonwealth or Federation Star, representing the federation of the colonies of Australia in 1901; the star depicts one point for each of the six original states and one representing all of Australia's internal and external territories; on the fly half is a representation of the Southern Cross constellation in white with one small, five-pointed star and four larger, seven-pointed stars

NATIONAL SYMBOL(S):

Commonwealth Star (seven-pointed Star of Federation), golden wattle tree; national colors: green, gold

NATIONAL ANTHEM:

name: Advance Australia Fair

lyrics/music: Peter Dodds McCORMICK

note: adopted 1984; although originally written in the late 19th century, the anthem was not used for all official occasions until 1984; as a Commonwealth country, in addition to the national anthem, "God Save the Queen" serves as the royal anthem (see United Kingdom)

ECONOMY :: AUSTRALIA

ECONOMY - OVERVIEW:

Australia is an open market with minimal restrictions on imports of goods and services. The process of opening up has increased productivity, stimulated growth, and made the economy more flexible and dynamic. Australia plays an active role in the WTO, APEC, the G20, and other trade forums. Australia's free trade agreement (FTA) with China entered into force in 2015, adding to existing FTAs with the Republic of Korea, Japan, Chile, Malaysia, New Zealand, Singapore, Thailand, and the US, and a regional FTA with ASEAN and New Zealand. Australia continues to negotiate bilateral agreements with Indonesia, as well as larger agreements with its Pacific neighbors and the Gulf Cooperation Council countries, and an Asia-wide Regional Comprehensive Economic Partnership that includes the 10 ASEAN countries and China, Japan, Korea, New Zealand, and India.

Australia is a significant exporter of natural resources, energy, and food. Australia's abundant and diverse natural resources attract high levels of foreign investment and include extensive reserves of coal, iron, copper, gold, natural gas, uranium, and renewable energy sources. A series of major investments, such as the US$40 billion Gorgon Liquid Natural Gas Project, will significantly expand the resources sector.

For nearly two decades up till 2017, Australia had benefited from a dramatic surge in its terms of trade. As export prices increased faster than import prices, the economy experienced continuous growth, low unemployment, contained inflation, very low public debt, and a strong and stable financial system. Australia entered 2018 facing a range of growth constraints, principally driven by the sharp fall in global prices of key export commodities. Demand for resources and energy from Asia and especially China is growing at a slower pace and sharp drops in export prices have impacted growth.

GDP (PURCHASING POWER PARITY):

$1.248 trillion (2017 est.)

$1.221 trillion (2016 est.)

$1.19 trillion (2015 est.)

note: data are in 2017 dollars

country comparison to the world: 19

GDP (OFFICIAL EXCHANGE RATE):

$1.38 trillion (2017 est.) (2017 est.)

GDP - REAL GROWTH RATE:

2.2% (2017 est.)

2.6% (2016 est.)

2.5% (2015 est.)

country comparison to the world: 144

GDP - PER CAPITA (PPP):

$50,400 (2017 est.)

$50,100 (2016 est.)

$49,600 (2015 est.)

note: data are in 2017 dollars

country comparison to the world: 29

GROSS NATIONAL SAVING:

21% of GDP (2017 est.)

20.5% of GDP (2016 est.)

21.5% of GDP (2015 est.)

country comparison to the world: 88

GDP - COMPOSITION, BY END USE:

household consumption: 56.9% (2017 est.)

government consumption: 18.4% (2017 est.)

investment in fixed capital: 24.1% (2017 est.)

investment in inventories: 0.1% (2017 est.)

exports of goods and services: 21.5% (2017 est.)

imports of goods and services: -21% (2017 est.)

GDP - COMPOSITION, BY SECTOR OF ORIGIN:

agriculture: 3.6% (2017 est.)

industry: 25.3% (2017 est.)

services: 71.2% (2017 est.)

AGRICULTURE - PRODUCTS:

wheat, barley, sugarcane, fruits; cattle, sheep, poultry

INDUSTRIES:

mining, industrial and transportation equipment, food processing, chemicals, steel

INDUSTRIAL PRODUCTION GROWTH RATE:

1.4% (2017 est.)

country comparison to the world: 144

LABOR FORCE:

12.91 million (2017 est.)

country comparison to the world: 44

LABOR FORCE - BY OCCUPATION:

agriculture: 3.6%

industry: 21.1%

services: 75.3% (2009 est.)

UNEMPLOYMENT RATE:

5.6% (2017 est.)

5.7% (2016 est.)

country comparison to the world: 81

POPULATION BELOW POVERTY LINE:

NA

HOUSEHOLD INCOME OR CONSUMPTION BY PERCENTAGE SHARE:

lowest 10%: 25.4% (1994)

highest 10%: 25.4% (1994)

DISTRIBUTION OF FAMILY INCOME - GINI INDEX:

30.3 (2008)

35.2 (1994)

country comparison to the world: 133

BUDGET:

revenues: 490 billion (2017 est.)

expenditures: 496.9 billion (2017 est.)

TAXES AND OTHER REVENUES:

35.5% (of GDP) (2017 est.)

country comparison to the world: 61

BUDGET SURPLUS (+) OR DEFICIT (-):

-0.5% (of GDP) (2017 est.)

country comparison to the world: 60

PUBLIC DEBT:

40.8% of GDP (2017 est.)

40.6% of GDP (2016 est.)

country comparison to the world: 123

FISCAL YEAR:

1 July - 30 June

INFLATION RATE (CONSUMER PRICES):

2% (2017 est.)

1.3% (2016 est.)

country comparison to the world: 103

CENTRAL BANK DISCOUNT RATE:

3% (28 February 2013)

4.35% (31 December 2010)

note: this is the Reserve Bank of Australia's "cash rate target," or policy rate

country comparison to the world: 108

COMMERCIAL BANK PRIME LENDING RATE:

5.24% (31 December 2017 est.)

5.42% (31 December 2016 est.)

country comparison to the world: 146

STOCK OF NARROW MONEY:

$277.7 billion (31 December 2017 est.)

$243.6 billion (31 December 2016 est.)

country comparison to the world: 17

STOCK OF BROAD MONEY:

$277.7 billion (31 December 2017 est.)

$243.6 billion (31 December 2016 est.)

country comparison to the world: 17

STOCK OF DOMESTIC CREDIT:

$2.384 trillion (31 December 2017 est.)

$2.097 trillion (31 December 2016 est.)

country comparison to the world: 11

MARKET VALUE OF PUBLICLY TRADED SHARES:

$1.187 trillion (31 December 2015 est.)

$1.289 trillion (31 December 2014 est.)

$1.366 trillion (31 December 2013 est.)

country comparison to the world: 12

CURRENT ACCOUNT BALANCE:

-$36.01 billion (2017 est.)

-$41.45 billion (2016 est.)

country comparison to the world: 201

EXPORTS:

$231.6 billion (2017 est.)

$191.7 billion (2016 est.)

country comparison to the world: 22

EXPORTS - PARTNERS:

China 33.5%, Japan 14.6%, South Korea 6.6%, India 5%, Hong Kong 4% (2017)

EXPORTS - COMMODITIES:

iron ore, coal, gold, natural gas, beef, aluminum ores and conc, wheat, meat (excluding beef), wool, alumina, alcohol

IMPORTS:

$221 billion (2017 est.)

$198.7 billion (2016 est.)

country comparison to the world: 24

IMPORTS - COMMODITIES:

motor vehicles, refined petroleum, telecommunication equipment and parts; crude petroleum, medicaments, goods vehicles, gold, computers

IMPORTS - PARTNERS:

China 22.9%, US 10.8%, Japan 7.5%, Thailand 5.1%, Germany 4.9%, South Korea 4.5% (2017)

RESERVES OF FOREIGN EXCHANGE AND GOLD:

$66.58 billion (31 December 2017 est.)

$55.07 billion (31 December 2016 est.)

country comparison to the world: 33

DEBT - EXTERNAL:

$1.714 trillion (31 December 2017 est.)

$1.547 trillion (31 December 2016 est.)

country comparison to the world: 11

STOCK OF DIRECT FOREIGN INVESTMENT - AT HOME:

$700.6 billion (31 December 2017 est.)

$617.7 billion (31 December 2016 est.)

country comparison to the world: 15

STOCK OF DIRECT FOREIGN INVESTMENT - ABROAD:

$509.7 billion (31 December 2017 est.)

$441.4 billion (31 December 2016 est.)

country comparison to the world: 17

EXCHANGE RATES:

Australian dollars (AUD) per US dollar -

1.311 (2017 est.)

1.3442 (2016 est.)

1.3442 (2015 est.)

1.3291 (2014 est.)

1.1094 (2013 est.)

ENERGY :: AUSTRALIA

ELECTRICITY ACCESS:

electrification - total population: 100% (2016)

ELECTRICITY - PRODUCTION:

243 billion kWh (2016 est.)

country comparison to the world: 19

ELECTRICITY - CONSUMPTION:

229.4 billion kWh (2016 est.)

country comparison to the world: 19

ELECTRICITY - EXPORTS:

0 kWh (2016 est.)

country comparison to the world: 101

ELECTRICITY - IMPORTS:

0 kWh (2016 est.)

country comparison to the world: 122

ELECTRICITY - INSTALLED GENERATING CAPACITY:

65.56 million kW (2016 est.)

country comparison to the world: 18

ELECTRICITY - FROM FOSSIL FUELS:

72% of total installed capacity (2016 est.)

country comparison to the world: 101

ELECTRICITY - FROM NUCLEAR FUELS:

0% of total installed capacity (2017 est.)

country comparison to the world: 40

ELECTRICITY - FROM HYDROELECTRIC PLANTS:

11% of total installed capacity (2017 est.)

country comparison to the world: 113

ELECTRICITY - FROM OTHER RENEWABLE SOURCES:

17% of total installed capacity (2017 est.)

country comparison to the world: 49

CRUDE OIL - PRODUCTION:

263,000 bbl/day (2017 est.)

country comparison to the world: 31

CRUDE OIL - EXPORTS:

192,500 bbl/day (2017 est.)

country comparison to the world: 31

CRUDE OIL - IMPORTS:

341,700 bbl/day (2017 est.)

country comparison to the world: 24

CRUDE OIL - PROVED RESERVES:

1.821 billion bbl (1 January 2018 est.)

country comparison to the world: 35

REFINED PETROLEUM PRODUCTS - PRODUCTION:

462,500 bbl/day (2017 est.)

country comparison to the world: 35

REFINED PETROLEUM PRODUCTS - CONSUMPTION:

1.175 million bbl/day (2017 est.)

country comparison to the world: 20

REFINED PETROLEUM PRODUCTS - EXPORTS:

64,120 bbl/day (2017 est.)

country comparison to the world: 48

REFINED PETROLEUM PRODUCTS - IMPORTS:

619,600 bbl/day (2017 est.)

country comparison to the world: 12

NATURAL GAS - PRODUCTION:

105.2 billion cu m (2017 est.)

country comparison to the world: 9

NATURAL GAS - CONSUMPTION:

45.25 billion cu m (2017 est.)

country comparison to the world: 19

NATURAL GAS - EXPORTS:

67.96 billion cu m (2017 est.)

country comparison to the world: 6

NATURAL GAS - IMPORTS:

5.776 billion cu m (2017 est.)

country comparison to the world: 33

NATURAL GAS - PROVED RESERVES:

1.989 trillion cu m (1 January 2018 est.)

country comparison to the world: 17

CARBON DIOXIDE EMISSIONS FROM CONSUMPTION OF ENERGY:

439.1 million Mt (2017 est.)

country comparison to the world: 15

COMMUNICATIONS :: AUSTRALIA

TELEPHONES - FIXED LINES:

total subscriptions: 8.46 million (2017 est.)

subscriptions per 100 inhabitants: 36 (2017 est.)

country comparison to the world: 20

TELEPHONES - MOBILE CELLULAR:

total subscriptions: 27.553 million (2017 est.)

subscriptions per 100 inhabitants: 119 (2017 est.)

country comparison to the world: 47

TELEPHONE SYSTEM:

general assessment: excellent domestic and international service; domestic satellite system; significant use of radiotelephone in areas of low population density; rapid growth of mobile telephones; 5G technologies in preparation and anticipation for 2020 (2017)

domestic: more subscribers to mobile services than there are people; 90% of all mobile device sales are now smartphones, growth in mobile traffic brisk; 36 per 100 fixed-line, 119 per 100 mobile-cellular (2017)

international: country code - 61; landing point for the SEA-ME-WE-3 optical telecommunications submarine cable with links to Asia, the Middle East, and Europe; the Southern Cross fiber-optic submarine cable provides links to NZ and the US; satellite earth stations - 10 Intelsat (4 Indian Ocean and 6 Pacific Ocean), 2 Inmarsat, 2 Globalstar, 5 other (2015)

BROADCAST MEDIA:

the Australian Broadcasting Corporation (ABC) runs multiple national and local radio networks and TV stations, as well as Australia Network, a TV service that broadcasts throughout the Asia-Pacific region and is the main public broadcaster; Special Broadcasting Service (SBS), a second large public broadcaster, operates radio and TV networks broadcasting in multiple languages; several large national commercial TV networks, a large number of local commercial TV stations, and hundreds of commercial radio stations are accessible; cable and satellite systems are available (2009)

INTERNET COUNTRY CODE:

.au

INTERNET USERS:

total: 20,288,409 (July 2016 est.)

percent of population: 88.2% (July 2016 est.)

country comparison to the world: 33

BROADBAND - FIXED SUBSCRIPTIONS:

total: 7.923 million (2017 est.)

subscriptions per 100 inhabitants: 34 (2017 est.)

country comparison to the world: 19

TRANSPORTATION :: AUSTRALIA

NATIONAL AIR TRANSPORT SYSTEM:

number of registered air carriers: 25 (2018)

inventory of registered aircraft operated by air carriers: 583 (2018)

annual passenger traffic on registered air carriers: 69,294,187 (2018)

annual freight traffic on registered air carriers: 1,887,295,820 mt-km (2018)

CIVIL AIRCRAFT REGISTRATION COUNTRY CODE PREFIX:

VH (2016)

AIRPORTS:

480 (2013)

country comparison to the world: 16

AIRPORTS - WITH PAVED RUNWAYS:

total: 349 (2017)

over 3,047 m: 11 (2017)

2,438 to 3,047 m: 14 (2017)

1,524 to 2,437 m: 155 (2017)

914 to 1,523 m: 155 (2017)

under 914 m: 14 (2017)

AIRPORTS - WITH UNPAVED RUNWAYS:

total: 131 (2013)

1,524 to 2,437 m: 16 (2013)

914 to 1,523 m: 101 (2013)

under 914 m: 14 (2013)

HELIPORTS:

1 (2013)

PIPELINES:

637 km condensate/gas, 30054 km gas, 240 km liquid petroleum gas, 3609 km oil, 110 km oil/gas/water, 72 km refined products (2013)

RAILWAYS:

total: 33,343 km (2015)

standard gauge: 17,446 km 1.435-m gauge (650 km electrified) (2015)

narrow gauge: 12,318 km 1.067-m gauge (2,075.5 km electrified) (2015)

broad gauge: 3,247 km 1.600-m gauge (372 km electrified) (2015)

country comparison to the world: 8

ROADWAYS:

total: 873,573 km (2015)

urban: 145,928 km (2015)

non-urban: 727,645 km (2015)

country comparison to the world: 9

WATERWAYS:

2,000 km (mainly used for recreation on Murray and Murray-Darling River systems) (2011)

country comparison to the world: 42

MERCHANT MARINE:

total: 549 (2017)

by type: bulk carrier 4, general cargo 83, oil tanker 10, other 452 (2017)

country comparison to the world: 39

PORTS AND TERMINALS:

major seaport(s): Brisbane, Cairns, Darwin, Fremantle, Geelong, Gladstone, Hobart, Melbourne, Newcastle, Port Adelaide, Port Kembla, Sydney

container port(s) (TEUs): Melbourne (2,640,000), Sydney (2,363,780) (2016)

LNG terminal(s) (export): Darwin, Karratha, Burrup, Curtis Island

dry bulk cargo port(s): Dampier (iron ore), Dalrymple Bay (coal), Hay Point (coal), Port Hedland (iron ore), Port Walcott (iron ore)

MILITARY AND SECURITY :: AUSTRALIA

MILITARY EXPENDITURES:

2% of GDP (2016)

1.98% of GDP (2015)

1.8% of GDP (2014)

country comparison to the world: 50

MILITARY BRANCHES:

Australian Defense Force (ADF): Australian Army (includes Special Operations Command), Royal Australian Navy (includes Naval Aviation Force), Royal Australian Air Force, Joint Operations Command (JOC) (2016)

MILITARY SERVICE AGE AND OBLIGATION:

17 years of age for voluntary military service (with parental consent); no conscription; women allowed to serve in most combat roles (2018)

TRANSNATIONAL ISSUES :: AUSTRALIA

DISPUTES - INTERNATIONAL:

in 2018, Australia and Timor-Leste signed a permanent maritime border treaty, scrapping a 2007 development zone and revenue sharing arrangement between the countriesAustralia asserts land and maritime claims to AntarcticaAustralia's 2004 submission to the Commission on the Limits of the Continental Shelf extends its continental margins over 3.37 million square kilometers, expanding its seabed roughly 30 percent beyond its claimed EEZall borders between Indonesia and Australia have been agreed upon bilaterally, but a 1997 treaty that would settle the last of their maritime and EEZ boundary has yet to be ratified by Indonesia's legislatureIndonesian groups challenge Australia's claim to Ashmore Reef, Australia closed parts of the Ashmore and Cartier reserve to Indonesian traditional fishing

REFUGEES AND INTERNALLY DISPLACED PERSONS:

refugees (country of origin): 9,217 (Afghanistan), 6,128 (Iran) (2016)

stateless persons: 52 (2017)

ILLICIT DRUGS:

Tasmania is one of the world's major suppliers of licit opiate products; government maintains strict controls over areas of opium poppy cultivation and output of poppy straw concentrate; major consumer of cocaine and amphetamines

INTRODUCTION :: AUSTRIA

BACKGROUND:

Once the center of power for the large Austro-Hungarian Empire, Austria was reduced to a small republic after its defeat in World War I. Following annexation by Nazi Germany in 1938 and subsequent occupation by the victorious Allies in 1945, Austria's status remained unclear for a decade. A State Treaty signed in 1955 ended the occupation, recognized Austria's independence, and forbade unification with Germany. A constitutional law that same year declared the country's "perpetual neutrality" as a condition for Soviet military withdrawal. The Soviet Union's collapse in 1991 and Austria's entry into the EU in 1995 have altered the meaning of this neutrality. A prosperous, democratic country, Austria entered the EU Economic and Monetary Union in 1999.

GEOGRAPHY :: AUSTRIA

LOCATION:

Central Europe, north of Italy and Slovenia

GEOGRAPHIC COORDINATES:

47 20 N, 13 20 E

MAP REFERENCES:

Europe

AREA:

total: 83,871 sq km

land: 82,445 sq km

water: 1,426 sq km

country comparison to the world: 115

AREA - COMPARATIVE:

about the size of South Carolina; slightly more than two-thirds the size of Pennsylvania

LAND BOUNDARIES:

total: 2,524 km

border countries (8): Czech Republic 402 km, Germany 801 km, Hungary 321 km, Italy 404 km, Liechtenstein 34 km, Slovakia 105 km, Slovenia 299 km, Switzerland 158 km

COASTLINE:

0 km (landlocked)

MARITIME CLAIMS:

none (landlocked)

CLIMATE:

temperate; continental, cloudy; cold winters with frequent rain and some snow in lowlands and snow in mountains; moderate summers with occasional showers

TERRAIN:

mostly mountains (Alps) in the west and south; mostly flat or gently sloping along the eastern and northern margins

ELEVATION:

mean elevation: 910 m

elevation extremes: 115 m lowest point: Neusiedler See

3798 highest point: Grossglockner

NATURAL RESOURCES:

oil, coal, lignite, timber, iron ore, copper, zinc, antimony, magnesite, tungsten, graphite, salt, hydropower

LAND USE:

agricultural land: 38.4% (2014 est.)

arable land: 16.5% (2014 est.) / permanent crops: 0.8% (2014 est.) / permanent pasture: 21.1% (2014 est.)

forest: 47.2% (2014 est.)

other: 14.4% (2014 est.)

IRRIGATED LAND:

1,170 sq km (2012)

POPULATION DISTRIBUTION:

the northern and eastern portions of the country are more densely populated; nearly two-thirds of the populace lives in urban areas

NATURAL HAZARDS:

landslides; avalanches; earthquakes

ENVIRONMENT - CURRENT ISSUES:

some forest degradation caused by air and soil pollution; soil pollution results from the use of agricultural chemicals; air pollution results from emissions by coal- and oil-fired power stations and industrial plants and from trucks transiting Austria between northern and southern Europe; water pollution; the Danube, as well as some of Austria's other rivers and lakes, are threatened by pollution

ENVIRONMENT - INTERNATIONAL AGREEMENTS:

party to: Air Pollution, Air Pollution-Nitrogen Oxides, Air Pollution-Persistent Organic Pollutants, Air Pollution-Sulfur 85, Air Pollution-Sulphur 94, Air Pollution-Volatile Organic Compounds, Antarctic Treaty, Biodiversity, Climate Change, Climate Change-Kyoto Protocol, Desertification, Endangered Species, Environmental Modification, Hazardous Wastes, Law of the Sea, Ozone Layer Protection, Ship Pollution, Tropical Timber 83, Tropical Timber 94, Wetlands, Whaling

signed, but not ratified: none of the selected agreements

GEOGRAPHY - NOTE:

landlocked; strategic location at the crossroads of central Europe with many easily traversable Alpine passes and valleys; major river is the Danube; population is concentrated on eastern lowlands because of steep slopes, poor soils, and low temperatures elsewhere

PEOPLE AND SOCIETY :: AUSTRIA

POPULATION:

8,793,370 (July 2018 est.)

country comparison to the world: 96

NATIONALITY:

noun: Austrian(s)

adjective: Austrian

ETHNIC GROUPS:

Austrian 84.2%, German 2.1% (includes Croatians, Slovenes, Serbs, and Bosniaks), Serbian 1.4%, Turkish 1.3%, Romanian 1.2%, Bosnian or Herzegovinian 1.1%, other 10.8% (2018 est.)

note: data represent population by nationality

LANGUAGES:

German (official nationwide) 88.6%, Turkish 2.3%, Serbian 2.2%, Croatian (official in Burgenland) 1.6%, other (includes Slovene, official in South Carinthia, and Hungarian, official in Burgenland) 5.3% (2001 est.)

RELIGIONS:

Catholic 73.8% (includes Roman Catholic 73.6%, other Catholic 0.2%), Protestant 4.9%, Muslim 4.2%, Orthodox 2.2%, other 0.8% (includes other Christian), none 12%, unspecified 2% (2001 est.)

AGE STRUCTURE:

0-14 years: 14% (male 630,739 /female 600,663)

15-24 years: 10.82% (male 484,515 /female 467,064)

25-54 years: 42.1% (male 1,851,209 /female 1,851,100)

55-64 years: 13.63% (male 595,146 /female 603,249)

65 years and over: 19.44% (male 743,174 /female 966,511) (2018 est.)

DEPENDENCY RATIOS:

total dependency ratio: 49.2 (2015 est.)

youth dependency ratio: 21.1 (2015 est.)

elderly dependency ratio: 28.1 (2015 est.)

potential support ratio: 3.6 (2015 est.)

MEDIAN AGE:

total: 44.2 years

male: 42.9 years

female: 45.4 years (2018 est.)

country comparison to the world: 12

POPULATION GROWTH RATE:

0.42% (2018 est.)

country comparison to the world: 160

BIRTH RATE:

9.5 births/1,000 population (2018 est.)

country comparison to the world: 199

DEATH RATE:

9.7 deaths/1,000 population (2018 est.)

country comparison to the world: 42

NET MIGRATION RATE:

4.8 migrant(s)/1,000 population (2017 est.)

country comparison to the world: 25

POPULATION DISTRIBUTION:

the northern and eastern portions of the country are more densely populated; nearly two-thirds of the populace lives in urban areas

URBANIZATION:

urban population: 58.3% of total population (2018)

rate of urbanization: 0.59% annual rate of change (2015-20 est.)

MAJOR URBAN AREAS - POPULATION:

1.901 million VIENNA (capital) (2018)

SEX RATIO:

at birth: 1.05 male(s)/female (2017 est.)

0-14 years: 1.05 male(s)/female (2017 est.)

15-24 years: 1.04 male(s)/female (2017 est.)

25-54 years: 1 male(s)/female (2017 est.)

55-64 years: 0.98 male(s)/female (2017 est.)

65 years and over: 0.76 male(s)/female (2017 est.)

total population: 0.96 male(s)/female (2017 est.)

MOTHER'S MEAN AGE AT FIRST BIRTH:

29 years (2014 est.)

MATERNAL MORTALITY RATE:

4 deaths/100,000 live births (2015 est.)

country comparison to the world: 175

INFANT MORTALITY RATE:

total: 3.4 deaths/1,000 live births (2018 est.)

male: 3.7 deaths/1,000 live births (2018 est.)

female: 3 deaths/1,000 live births (2018 est.)

country comparison to the world: 200

LIFE EXPECTANCY AT BIRTH:

total population: 81.7 years (2018 est.)

male: 79 years (2018 est.)

female: 84.5 years (2018 est.)

country comparison to the world: 24

TOTAL FERTILITY RATE:

1.48 children born/woman (2018 est.)

country comparison to the world: 199

CONTRACEPTIVE PREVALENCE RATE:

65.7% (2012/13)

note: percent of women aged 18-49

HEALTH EXPENDITURES:

11.2% of GDP (2014)

country comparison to the world: 11

PHYSICIANS DENSITY:

5.23 physicians/1,000 population (2016)

HOSPITAL BED DENSITY:

7.6 beds/1,000 population (2013)

DRINKING WATER SOURCE:

improved:

urban: 100% of population (2015 est.)

rural: 100% of population (2015 est.)

total: 100% of population (2015 est.)

unimproved:

urban: 0% of population (2015 est.)

rural: 0% of population (2015 est.)

total: 0% of population (2015 est.)

SANITATION FACILITY ACCESS:

improved:

urban: 100% of population (2015 est.)

rural: 100% of population (2015 est.)

total: 100% of population (2015 est.)

unimproved:

urban: 0% of population (2015 est.)

rural: 0% of population (2015 est.)

total: 0% of population (2015 est.)

HIV/AIDS - ADULT PREVALENCE RATE:

0.1% (2017 est.)

country comparison to the world: 107

HIV/AIDS - PEOPLE LIVING WITH HIV/AIDS:

7,400 (2017 est.)

country comparison to the world: 110

HIV/AIDS - DEATHS:

<100 (2017 est.)

OBESITY - ADULT PREVALENCE RATE:

20.1% (2016)

country comparison to the world: 105

EDUCATION EXPENDITURES:

5.4% of GDP (2014)

country comparison to the world: 53

SCHOOL LIFE EXPECTANCY (PRIMARY TO TERTIARY EDUCATION):

total: 16 years (2015)

male: 16 years (2015)

female: 16 years (2015)

UNEMPLOYMENT, YOUTH AGES 15-24:

total: 11.3% (2016 est.)

male: 12.1% (2016 est.)

female: 10.2% (2016 est.)

country comparison to the world: 113

GOVERNMENT :: AUSTRIA

COUNTRY NAME:

conventional long form: Republic of Austria

conventional short form: Austria

local long form: Republik Oesterreich

local short form: Oesterreich

etymology: the name Oesterreich means "eastern realm" or "eastern march" and dates to the 10th century; the designation refers to the fact that Austria was the easternmost extension of Bavaria, and, in fact, of all the Germans; the word Austria is a Latinization of the German name

GOVERNMENT TYPE:

federal parliamentary republic

CAPITAL:

name: Vienna

geographic coordinates: 48 12 N, 16 22 E

time difference: UTC+1 (6 hours ahead of Washington, DC, during Standard Time)

daylight saving time: +1hr, begins last Sunday in March; ends last Sunday in October

etymology: the origin of the name is disputed but may derive from earlier settlements of the area; a Celtic town of Vedunia, established about 500 B.C., came under Roman dominance aound 15 B.C. and became known as Vindobona; archeological remains of the latter survive at many sites in the center of Vienna

ADMINISTRATIVE DIVISIONS:

9 states (Bundeslaender, singular - Bundesland); Burgenland, Kaernten (Carinthia), Niederoesterreich (Lower Austria), Oberoesterreich (Upper Austria), Salzburg, Steiermark (Styria), Tirol (Tyrol), Vorarlberg, Wien (Vienna)

INDEPENDENCE:

no official date of independence: 976 (Margravate of Austria established);17 September 1156 (Duchy of Austria founded);6 January 1453 (Archduchy of Austria acknowledged);11 August 1804 (Austrian Empire proclaimed);30 March 1867 (Austro-Hungarian dual monarchy established);12 November 1918 (First Republic proclaimed);27 April 1945 (Second Republic proclaimed)

NATIONAL HOLIDAY:

National Day (commemorates passage of the law on permanent neutrality), 26 October (1955)

CONSTITUTION:

history: several previous; latest adopted 1 October 1920, revised 1929, replaced May 1934, replaced by German Weimar constitution in 1938 following German annexation, reinstated 1 May 1945 (2016)

amendments: proposed through laws designated "constitutional laws" or through the constitutional process if the amendment is part of another law; approval required by at least a two-thirds majority vote by the National Assembly if one-half of the members are present; a referendum is required only if requested by one-third of the National Council or Federal Council membership; passage by referendum requires absolute majority vote; amended many times, last in 2014 (2016)

LEGAL SYSTEM:

civil law system; judicial review of legislative acts by the Constitutional Court

INTERNATIONAL LAW ORGANIZATION PARTICIPATION:

accepts compulsory ICJ jurisdiction; accepts ICCt jurisdiction

CITIZENSHIP:

citizenship by birth: no

citizenship by descent only: at least one parent must be a citizen of Austria

dual citizenship recognized: no

residency requirement for naturalization: 10 years

SUFFRAGE:

16 years of age; universal

EXECUTIVE BRANCH:

chief of state: President Alexander VAN DER BELLEN (since 26 January 2017)

head of government: Chancellor Sebastian KURZ (since 18 December 2017); Vice Chancellor Heinz-Christian STRACHE (since 18 December 2017)

cabinet: Council of Ministers chosen by the president on the advice of the chancellor

elections/appointments: president directly elected by absolute majority popular vote in 2 rounds if needed for a 6-year term (eligible for a second term); elections last held on 24 April 2016 (first round), 22 May 2016 (second round, which was annulled), and 4 December 2016 (second round re-vote) (next election to be held in April 2022); chancellor appointed by the president but determined by the majority coalition parties in the Federal Assembly; vice chancellor appointed by the president on the advice of the chancellor

election results: Alexander VAN DER BELLEN elected in second round; percent of vote in first round - Norbet HOFER (FPOe) 35.1%, Alexander VAN DER BELLEN (independent, allied with the Greens) 21.3%, Irmgard GRISS (independent) 18.9%, Rudolf HUNDSTORFER (SPOe) 11.3%, Andreas KHOL (OeVP) 11.1%, Richard LUGNER (independent) 2.3%; percent of vote in second round - Alexander VAN DER BELLEN 53.8%, Norbet HOFER 46.2%

LEGISLATIVE BRANCH:

description: bicameral Federal Assembly or Bundesversammlung

consists of:
Federal Council or Bundesrat (61 seats; members appointed by state parliaments with each state receiving 3 to 12 seats in proportion to its population; members serve 5- or 6-year terms)
National Council or Nationalrat (183 seats; members directly elected in single-seat constituencies by proportional representation vote; members serve 5-year terms)

elections:
Federal Council - appointed
National Council - last held on 15 October 2017 (next to be held in 2022)

election results:
Federal Council - percent of vote by party - NA; seats by party - NA; composition - men 42, women 19, percent of women 30.6%
National Council - percent of vote by party - OeVP 31.5%, SPOe 26.9%, FPOe 26%, NEOS 5.3%, PILZ 4.4%, other 5.9%; seats by party - OeVP 62, SPOe 52, FPOe 51, NEOS 10, PILZ 8; composition - men 122, women 61, percent of women 33.3%; note - total Federal Assembly percent of women 32.7%

JUDICIAL BRANCH:

highest courts: Supreme Court of Justice or Oberster Gerichtshof (consists of 85 judges organized into 17 senates or panels of 5 judges each); Constitutional Court or Verfassungsgerichtshof (consists of 20 judges including 6 substitutes; Administrative Court or Verwaltungsgerichtshof - 2 judges plus other members depending on the importance of the case)

judge selection and term of office: Supreme Court judges nominated by executive branch departments and appointed by the president; judges serve for life; Constitutional Court judges nominated by several executive branch departments and approved by the president; judges serve for life; Administrative Court judges recommended by executive branch departments and appointed by the president; terms of judges and members determined by the president

subordinate courts: Courts of Appeal (4); Regional Courts (20); district courts (120); county courts

POLITICAL PARTIES AND LEADERS:

Austrian People's Party or OeVP [Sebastian KURZ]
Communist Party of Austria or KPOe [Mirko MESSNER]
Freedom Party of Austria or FPOe [Heinz-Christian STRACHE]
The Greens [Werner KOGLER]
NEOS - The New Austria [Matthias STROLZ]
Pilz List or PILZ [Bruno ROSSMANN and Wolfgang ZINGGL]
Social Democratic Party of Austria or SPOe [Christian KERN]

INTERNATIONAL ORGANIZATION PARTICIPATION:

ADB (nonregional member), AfDB (nonregional member), Australia Group, BIS, BSEC (observer), CD, CE, CEI, CERN, EAPC, EBRD, ECB, EIB, EMU, ESA, EU, FAO, FATF, G-9, IADB, IAEA, IBRD, ICAO, ICC (national committees), ICCt, ICRM, IDA, IEA, IFAD, IFC, IFRCS, IGAD (partners), ILO, IMF, IMO, Interpol, IOC, IOM, IPU, ISO, ITSO, ITU, ITUC (NGOs), MIGA, MINURSO, NEA, NSG, OAS (observer), OECD, OIF (observer), OPCW, OSCE, Paris Club, PCA, PFP, Schengen Convention, SELEC (observer), UN, UNCTAD, UNESCO, UNFICYP, UNHCR, UNIDO, UNIFIL, UNTSO, UNWTO, UPU, WCO, WFTU (NGOs), WHO, WIPO, WMO, WTO, ZC

DIPLOMATIC REPRESENTATION IN THE US:

chief of mission: Ambassador Wolfgang WALDNER (since 28 January 2016)

chancery: 3524 International Court NW, Washington, DC 20008-3035

telephone: [1] (202) 895-6700

FAX: [1] (202) 895-6750

consulate(s) general: Los Angeles, New York

consulate(s): Chicago

DIPLOMATIC REPRESENTATION FROM THE US:

chief of mission: Ambassador Trevor TRAINA (since 24 May 2018)

embassy: Boltzmanngasse 16, A-1090, Vienna

mailing address: Boltzmanngasse 16, 1090 Vienna, Austria

telephone: [43] (1) 31339-0

FAX: [43] (1) 3100682

FLAG DESCRIPTION:

three equal horizontal bands of red (top), white, and red; the flag design is certainly one of the oldest - if not the oldest - national banners in the world; according to tradition, in 1191, following a fierce battle in the Third Crusade, Duke Leopold V of Austria's white tunic became completely blood-spattered; upon removal of his wide belt or sash, a white band was revealed; the red-white-red color combination was subsequently adopted as his banner

NATIONAL SYMBOL(S):

eagle, edelweiss, Alpine gentian; national colors: red, white

NATIONAL ANTHEM:

name: "Bundeshymne" (Federal Hymn)

lyrics/music: Paula von PRERADOVIC/Wolfgang Amadeus MOZART or Johann HOLZER (disputed)

note: adopted 1947; the anthem is also known as "Land der Berge, Land am Strome" (Land of the Mountains, Land by the River); Austria adopted a new national anthem after World War II to replace the former imperial anthem composed by Franz Josef HAYDN, which had been appropriated by Germany in 1922 and was thereafter associated with the Nazi regime; a gendered version of the lyrics was adopted by the Austrian Federal Assembly in fall 2011 and became effective 1 January 2012

ECONOMY :: AUSTRIA

ECONOMY - OVERVIEW:

Austria is a well-developed market economy with skilled labor force and high standard of living. It is closely tied to other EU economies, especially Germany's, but also the US', its third-largest trade partner. Its economy features a large service sector, a sound industrial sector, and a small, but highly developed agricultural sector.

Austrian economic growth strengthen in 2017, with a 2.9% increase in GDP. Austrian exports, accounting for around 60% of the GDP, were up 8.2% in 2017. Austria's unemployment rate fell by 0.3% to 5.5%, which is low by European standards, but still at its second highest rate since the end of World War II, driven by an increased number of refugees and EU migrants entering the labor market.

Austria's fiscal position compares favorably with other euro-zone countries. The budget deficit stood at a low 0.7% of GDP in 2017 and public debt declined again to 78.4% of GDP in 2017, after reaching a post-war high 84.6% in 2015. The Austrian government has announced it plans to balance the fiscal budget in 2019. Several external risks, such as Austrian banks' exposure to Central and Eastern Europe, the refugee crisis, and continued unrest in Russia/Ukraine, eased in 2017, but are still a factor for the Austrian economy. Exposure to the Russian banking sector and a deep energy relationship with Russia present additional risks.

Austria elected a new pro-business government in October 2017 that campaigned on promises to reduce bureaucracy, improve public sector efficiency, reduce labor market protections, and provide positive investment incentives.

GDP (PURCHASING POWER PARITY):

$441 billion (2017 est.)

$428.1 billion (2016 est.)

$422 billion (2015 est.)

note: data are in 2017 dollars

country comparison to the world: 45

GDP (OFFICIAL EXCHANGE RATE):

$417.4 billion (2017 est.) (2017 est.)

GDP - REAL GROWTH RATE:

3% (2017 est.)

1.5% (2016 est.)

1.1% (2015 est.)

country comparison to the world: 110

GDP - PER CAPITA (PPP):

$50,000 (2017 est.)

$49,000 (2016 est.)

$48,900 (2015 est.)

note: data are in 2017 dollars

country comparison to the world: 31

GROSS NATIONAL SAVING:

27% of GDP (2017 est.)

26.2% of GDP (2016 est.)

25.5% of GDP (2015 est.)

country comparison to the world: 43

GDP - COMPOSITION, BY END USE:

household consumption: 52.1% (2017 est.)

government consumption: 19.5% (2017 est.)

investment in fixed capital: 23.5% (2017 est.)

investment in inventories: 1.6% (2017 est.)

exports of goods and services: 54.2% (2017 est.)

imports of goods and services: -50.7% (2017 est.)

GDP - COMPOSITION, BY SECTOR OF ORIGIN:

agriculture: 1.3% (2017 est.)

industry: 28.4% (2017 est.)

services: 70.3% (2017 est.)

AGRICULTURE - PRODUCTS:

grains, potatoes, wine, fruit; dairy products, cattle, pigs, poultry; lumber and other forestry products

INDUSTRIES:

construction, machinery, vehicles and parts, food, metals, chemicals, lumber and paper, electronics, tourism

INDUSTRIAL PRODUCTION GROWTH RATE:

6.5% (2017 est.)

country comparison to the world: 35

LABOR FORCE:

4.26 million (2017 est.)

country comparison to the world: 90

LABOR FORCE - BY OCCUPATION:

agriculture: 0.7%

industry: 25.2%

services: 74.1% (2017 est.)

UNEMPLOYMENT RATE:

5.5% (2017 est.)

6% (2016 est.)

country comparison to the world: 80

POPULATION BELOW POVERTY LINE:

3% (2017 est.)

HOUSEHOLD INCOME OR CONSUMPTION BY PERCENTAGE SHARE:

lowest 10%: 23.5% (2012 est.)

highest 10%: 23.5% (2012 est.)

DISTRIBUTION OF FAMILY INCOME - GINI INDEX:

30.5 (2015)

30.5 (2014)

country comparison to the world: 131

BUDGET:

revenues: 201.7 billion (2017 est.)

expenditures: 204.6 billion (2017 est.)

TAXES AND OTHER REVENUES:

48.3% (of GDP) (2017 est.)

country comparison to the world: 18

BUDGET SURPLUS (+) OR DEFICIT (-):

-0.7% (of GDP) (2017 est.)

country comparison to the world: 67

PUBLIC DEBT:

78.6% of GDP (2017 est.)

83.6% of GDP (2016 est.)

note: this is general government gross debt, defined in the Maastricht Treaty as consolidated general government gross debt at nominal value, outstanding at the end of the year; it covers the following categories of government liabilities (as defined in ESA95): currency and deposits (AF.2), securities other than shares excluding financial derivatives (AF.3, excluding AF.34), and loans (AF.4); the general government sector comprises the sub-sectors of central government, state government, local government and social security funds; as a percentage of GDP, the GDP used as a denominator is the gross domestic product in current year prices

country comparison to the world: 37

FISCAL YEAR:

calendar year

INFLATION RATE (CONSUMER PRICES):

2.2% (2017 est.)

1% (2016 est.)

country comparison to the world: 111

CENTRAL BANK DISCOUNT RATE:

0% (31 December 2017)

0% (31 December 2010)

note: this is the European Central Bank's rate on the marginal lending facility, which offers overnight credit to banks in the euro area

country comparison to the world: 147

COMMERCIAL BANK PRIME LENDING RATE:

1.57% (31 December 2017 est.)

1.86% (31 December 2016 est.)

country comparison to the world: 189

STOCK OF NARROW MONEY:

$271.4 billion (31 December 2017 est.)

$214 billion (31 December 2016 est.)

note: see entry for the European Union for money supply for the entire euro area; the European Central Bank (ECB) controls monetary policy for the 18 members of the Economic and Monetary Union (EMU); individual members of the EMU do not control the quantity of money circulating within their own borders

country comparison to the world: 19

STOCK OF BROAD MONEY:

$271.4 billion (31 December 2017 est.)

$214 billion (31 December 2016 est.)

country comparison to the world: 19

STOCK OF DOMESTIC CREDIT:

$555.4 billion (31 December 2017 est.)

$483.7 billion (31 December 2016 est.)

country comparison to the world: 25

MARKET VALUE OF PUBLICLY TRADED SHARES:

$96.08 billion (31 December 2015 est.)

$96.79 billion (31 December 2014 est.)

$117.7 billion (31 December 2013 est.)

country comparison to the world: 40

CURRENT ACCOUNT BALANCE:

$7.859 billion (2017 est.)

$8.313 billion (2016 est.)

country comparison to the world: 25

EXPORTS:

$156.7 billion (2017 est.)

$149.5 billion (2016 est.)

country comparison to the world: 32

EXPORTS - PARTNERS:

Germany 29.4%, US 6.3%, Italy 6.2%, Switzerland 5.1%, France 4.8%, Slovakia 4.8% (2017)

EXPORTS - COMMODITIES:

machinery and equipment, motor vehicles and parts, manufactured goods, chemicals, iron and steel, foodstuffs

IMPORTS:

$158.1 billion (2017 est.)

$142.3 billion (2016 est.)

country comparison to the world: 28

IMPORTS - COMMODITIES:

machinery and equipment, motor vehicles, chemicals, metal goods, oil and oil products, natural gas; foodstuffs

IMPORTS - PARTNERS:

Germany 41.8%, Italy 5.8%, Switzerland 5.5%, Czech Republic 4.4%, Netherlands 4.2% (2017)

RESERVES OF FOREIGN EXCHANGE AND GOLD:

$21.57 billion (31 December 2017 est.)

$23.36 billion (31 December 2016 est.)

country comparison to the world: 57

DEBT - EXTERNAL:

$630.8 billion (31 December 2017 est.)

$679.3 billion (31 March 2015 est.)

country comparison to the world: 19

STOCK OF DIRECT FOREIGN INVESTMENT - AT HOME:

$294.1 billion (31 December 2017 est.)

$158.9 billion (31 December 2016 est.)

country comparison to the world: 21

STOCK OF DIRECT FOREIGN INVESTMENT - ABROAD:

$339.7 billion (31 December 2017 est.)

$214.7 billion (31 December 2016 est.)

country comparison to the world: 21

EXCHANGE RATES:

euros (EUR) per US dollar -

0.885 (2017 est.)

0.903 (2016 est.)

0.9214 (2015 est.)

0.885 (2014 est.)

0.7634 (2013 est.)

ENERGY :: AUSTRIA

ELECTRICITY ACCESS:

electrification - total population: 100% (2016)

ELECTRICITY - PRODUCTION:

60.78 billion kWh (2016 est.)

country comparison to the world: 48

ELECTRICITY - CONSUMPTION:

64.6 billion kWh (2016 est.)

country comparison to the world: 41

ELECTRICITY - EXPORTS:

19.21 billion kWh (2016 est.)

country comparison to the world: 9

ELECTRICITY - IMPORTS:

26.37 billion kWh (2016 est.)

country comparison to the world: 6

ELECTRICITY - INSTALLED GENERATING CAPACITY:

24.79 million kW (2016 est.)

country comparison to the world: 36

ELECTRICITY - FROM FOSSIL FUELS:

25% of total installed capacity (2016 est.)

country comparison to the world: 188

ELECTRICITY - FROM NUCLEAR FUELS:

0% of total installed capacity (2017 est.)

country comparison to the world: 41

ELECTRICITY - FROM HYDROELECTRIC PLANTS:

43% of total installed capacity (2017 est.)

country comparison to the world: 45

ELECTRICITY - FROM OTHER RENEWABLE SOURCES:

31% of total installed capacity (2017 est.)

country comparison to the world: 17

CRUDE OIL - PRODUCTION:

14,260 bbl/day (2017 est.)

country comparison to the world: 72

CRUDE OIL - EXPORTS:

0 bbl/day (2017 est.)

country comparison to the world: 88

CRUDE OIL - IMPORTS:

146,600 bbl/day (2017 est.)

country comparison to the world: 37

CRUDE OIL - PROVED RESERVES:

41.2 million bbl (1 January 2018 est.)

country comparison to the world: 78

REFINED PETROLEUM PRODUCTS - PRODUCTION:

186,500 bbl/day (2017 est.)

country comparison to the world: 54

REFINED PETROLEUM PRODUCTS - CONSUMPTION:

268,000 bbl/day (2017 est.)

country comparison to the world: 47

REFINED PETROLEUM PRODUCTS - EXPORTS:

49,960 bbl/day (2017 est.)

country comparison to the world: 55

REFINED PETROLEUM PRODUCTS - IMPORTS:

135,500 bbl/day (2017 est.)

country comparison to the world: 42

NATURAL GAS - PRODUCTION:

1.274 billion cu m (2017 est.)

country comparison to the world: 62

NATURAL GAS - CONSUMPTION:

9.486 billion cu m (2017 est.)

country comparison to the world: 50

NATURAL GAS - EXPORTS:

5.437 billion cu m (2017 est.)

country comparison to the world: 29

NATURAL GAS - IMPORTS:

14.02 billion cu m (2017 est.)

country comparison to the world: 22

NATURAL GAS - PROVED RESERVES:

6.513 billion cu m (1 January 2018 est.)

country comparison to the world: 84

CARBON DIOXIDE EMISSIONS FROM CONSUMPTION OF ENERGY:

63.93 million Mt (2017 est.)

country comparison to the world: 53

COMMUNICATIONS :: AUSTRIA

TELEPHONES - FIXED LINES:

total subscriptions: 3,762,801 (2017 est.)

subscriptions per 100 inhabitants: 43 (2017 est.)

country comparison to the world: 36

TELEPHONES - MOBILE CELLULAR:

total subscriptions: 14,924,340 (2017 est.)

subscriptions per 100 inhabitants: 170 (2017 est.)

country comparison to the world: 66

TELEPHONE SYSTEM:

general assessment: mobile-cellular subscribership is everywhere; cable networks are very extensive, the fiber-optic net is being developed; all telephone applications and Internet services are accessible; broadband is available in all large municipalities; regulatory measures have pomoted the reality of 5G use for 2020 (2017)

domestic: highly developed and efficient; 43 per 100 fixed-line, 170 per 100 mobile-cellular; (2017)

international: country code - 43; earth stations available in the Astra, Intelsat, Eutelsat satellite systems (2018)

BROADCAST MEDIA:

worldwide cable and satellite TV are available; the public incumbent ORF competes with three other major, several regional domestic, and up to 400 international TV stations; TV coverage is in principle 100%, but only 90% use broadcast media; Internet streaming not only complements, but increasingly replaces regular TV stations (2018)

INTERNET COUNTRY CODE:

.at

INTERNET USERS:

total: 7,346,055 (July 2016 est.)

percent of population: 84.3% (July 2016 est.)

country comparison to the world: 58

BROADBAND - FIXED SUBSCRIPTIONS:

total: 2,511,200 (2017 est.)

subscriptions per 100 inhabitants: 29 (2017 est.)

country comparison to the world: 46

COMMUNICATIONS - NOTE:

the Austrian National Library contains important collections of the Imperial Library of the Holy Roman Empire and of the Austrian Empire, as well as of the Austrian Republic; among its more than 12 million items are outstanding holdings of rare books, maps, globes, papyrus, and music; its Globe Museum is the only one in the world

TRANSPORTATION :: AUSTRIA

NATIONAL AIR TRANSPORT SYSTEM:

number of registered air carriers: 11 (2015)

inventory of registered aircraft operated by air carriers: 130 (2015)

annual passenger traffic on registered air carriers: 14,718,641 (2015)

annual freight traffic on registered air carriers: 351.379 million mt-km (2015)

CIVIL AIRCRAFT REGISTRATION COUNTRY CODE PREFIX:

OE (2016)

AIRPORTS:

52 (2013)

country comparison to the world: 90

AIRPORTS - WITH PAVED RUNWAYS:

total: 24 (2017)

over 3,047 m: 1 (2017)

2,438 to 3,047 m: 5 (2017)

1,524 to 2,437 m: 1 (2017)

914 to 1,523 m: 4 (2017)

under 914 m: 13 (2017)

AIRPORTS - WITH UNPAVED RUNWAYS:

total: 28 (2013)

1,524 to 2,437 m: 1 (2013)

914 to 1,523 m: 3 (2013)

under 914 m: 24 (2013)

HELIPORTS:

1 (2013)

PIPELINES:

1888 km gas, 594 km oil, 157 km refined products (2017)

RAILWAYS:

total: 5,800 km (2017)

standard gauge: 5,300 km 1.435-m gauge (3,826 km electrified) (2016)

country comparison to the world: 33

ROADWAYS:

total: 138,696 km (2016)

paved: 138,696 km (includes 2,208 km of expressways) (2016)

country comparison to the world: 38

WATERWAYS:

358 km (2011)

country comparison to the world: 89

PORTS AND TERMINALS:

river port(s): Enns, Krems, Linz, Vienna (Danube)

MILITARY AND SECURITY :: AUSTRIA

MILITARY EXPENDITURES:

0.58% of GDP (2018)

0.6% of GDP (2017)

0.68% of GDP (2016)

country comparison to the world: 140

MILITARY BRANCHES:

Land Forces (KdoLdSK), Air Forces (KdoLuSK) (2014)

MILITARY SERVICE AGE AND OBLIGATION:

registration requirement at age 17, the legal minimum age for voluntary military service; 18 is the legal minimum age for compulsory military service (6 months), or optionally, alternative civil/community service (9 months); males 18 to 50 years old in the militia or inactive reserve are subject to compulsory service; in a January 2012 referendum, a majority of Austrians voted in favor of retaining the system of compulsory military service (with the option of alternative/non-military service) instead of switching to a professional army system (2015)

TRANSNATIONAL ISSUES :: AUSTRIA

DISPUTES - INTERNATIONAL:

none

REFUGEES AND INTERNALLY DISPLACED PERSONS:

refugees (country of origin): 30,958 (Syria), 20,220 (Afghanistan), 13,773 (Russia), 5,555 (Iraq) (2016)

stateless persons: 1,003 (2017)

ILLICIT DRUGS:

transshipment point for Southwest Asian heroin and South American cocaine destined for Western Europe; increasing consumption of European-produced synthetic drugs

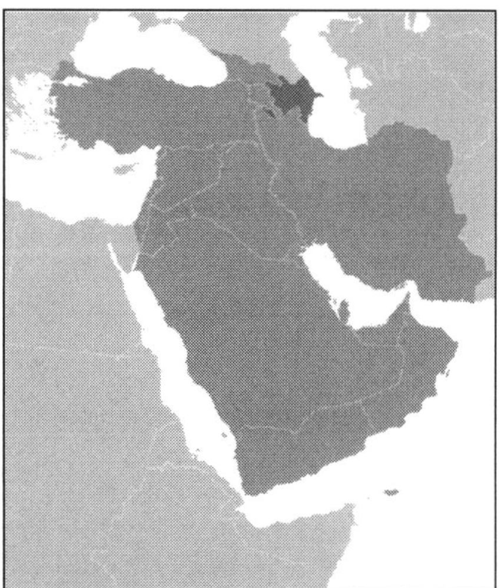

INTRODUCTION :: AZERBAIJAN

BACKGROUND:

Azerbaijan - a nation with a majority-Turkic and majority-Shia Muslim population - was briefly independent (from 1918 to 1920) following the collapse of the Russian Empire; it was subsequently incorporated into the Soviet Union for seven decades. Azerbaijan has yet to resolve its conflict with Armenia over Nagorno-Karabakh, a primarily ethnic Armenian-populated region that Moscow recognized in 1923 as an autonomous republic within Soviet Azerbaijan after Armenia and Azerbaijan disputed the territory's status. Armenia and Azerbaijan reignited their dispute over the area in 1988; the struggle escalated militarily after both countries attained independence from the Soviet Union in 1991. By May 1994, when a cease-fire took hold, ethnic Armenian forces held not only Nagorno-Karabakh but also seven surrounding provinces in the territory of Azerbaijan. The OSCE Minsk Group, co-chaired by the US, France, and Russia, is the framework established to mediate a peaceful resolution of the conflict.

In the 25 years following its independence, Azerbaijan succeeded in significantly reducing the poverty rate and has directed revenues from its oil and gas production to significant development of the country's infrastructure. However, corruption in the country is widespread, and the government has been accused of authoritarianism. The country's leadership has remained in the Aliyev family since Heydar ALIYEV became president in 1993 and was succeeded by his son, President Ilham ALIYEV in 2003. Following two national referendums in the past several years that eliminated presidential term limits and extended presidential terms from 5 to 7 years, President ALIYEV secured a fourth term as president in April 2018 in elections that international observers noted had serious shortcomings. Reforms to diversify the country's non-oil economy remain dependent on subsidies from oil and gas revenues, while other reforms have not adequately addressed weaknesses in most government institutions, particularly in the education and health sectors, as well as the court system.

GEOGRAPHY :: AZERBAIJAN

LOCATION:

Southwestern Asia, bordering the Caspian Sea, between Iran and Russia, with a small European portion north of the Caucasus range

GEOGRAPHIC COORDINATES:

40 30 N, 47 30 E

MAP REFERENCES:

Asia

AREA:

total: 86,600 sq km

land: 82,629 sq km

water: 3,971 sq km

note: includes the exclave of Naxcivan Autonomous Republic and the Nagorno-Karabakh region; the region's autonomy was abolished by Azerbaijani Supreme Soviet on 26 November 1991

country comparison to the world: 114

AREA - COMPARATIVE:

about three-quarters the size of Pennsylvania; slightly smaller than Maine

LAND BOUNDARIES:

total: 2,468 km

border countries (5): Armenia 996 km, Georgia 428 km, Iran 689 km, Russia 338 km, Turkey 17 km

COASTLINE:

0 km (landlocked); note - Azerbaijan borders the Caspian Sea (713 km)

MARITIME CLAIMS:

none (landlocked)

CLIMATE:

dry, semiarid steppe

TERRAIN:

large, flat Kur-Araz Ovaligi (Kura-Araks Lowland, much of it below sea level) with Great Caucasus Mountains to the north, Qarabag Yaylasi (Karabakh Upland) to the west; Baku lies on Abseron Yasaqligi (Apsheron Peninsula) that juts into Caspian Sea

ELEVATION:

mean elevation: 384 m

elevation extremes: -28 m lowest point: Caspian Sea

4466 highest point: Bazarduzu Dagi

NATURAL RESOURCES:

petroleum, natural gas, iron ore, nonferrous metals, bauxite

LAND USE:

agricultural land: 57.6% (2014 est.)

arable land: 22.8% (2014 est.) / permanent crops: 2.7% (2014 est.) / permanent pasture: 32.1% (2014 est.)

forest: 11.3% (2014 est.)

other: 31.1% (2014 est.)

IRRIGATED LAND:

14,277 sq km (2012)

POPULATION DISTRIBUTION:

highest population density is found in the far eastern area of the county, in and around Baku; apart from smaller urbanized areas, the rest of the country has a fairly light and evenly distributed population

NATURAL HAZARDS:

droughts

ENVIRONMENT - CURRENT ISSUES:

local scientists consider the Abseron Yasaqligi (Apsheron Peninsula) (including Baku and Sumqayit) and the Caspian Sea to be the ecologically most devastated area in the world because of severe air, soil, and water pollution; soil pollution results from oil spills, from the use of DDT pesticide, and from toxic defoliants used in the production of cotton; surface and underground water are polluted by untreated municipal and industrial wastewater and agricultural run-off

ENVIRONMENT - INTERNATIONAL AGREEMENTS:

party to: Air Pollution, Biodiversity, Climate Change, Climate Change-Kyoto Protocol, Desertification, Endangered Species, Hazardous Wastes, Marine Dumping, Ozone Layer Protection, Ship Pollution, Wetlands

signed, but not ratified: none of the selected agreements

GEOGRAPHY - NOTE:

both the main area of the country and the Naxcivan exclave are landlocked

PEOPLE AND SOCIETY :: AZERBAIJAN

POPULATION:

10,046,516 (July 2018 est.)

country comparison to the world: 90

NATIONALITY:

noun: Azerbaijani(s)

adjective: Azerbaijani

ETHNIC GROUPS:

Azerbaijani 91.6%, Lezghin 2%, Russian 1.3%, Armenian 1.3%, Talysh 1.3%, other 2.4% (2009 est.)

note: the separatist Nagorno-Karabakh region is populated almost entirely by ethnic Armenians

LANGUAGES:

Azerbaijani (Azeri) (official) 92.5%, Russian 1.4%, Armenian 1.4%, other 4.7% (2009 est.)

RELIGIONS:

Muslim 96.9% (predominantly Shia), Christian 3%, other <0.1, unaffiliated <0.1 (2010 est.)

note: religious affiliation is still nominal in Azerbaijan; percentages for actual practicing adherents are much lower

AGE STRUCTURE:

0-14 years: 23.05% (male 1,233,424 /female 1,082,007)

15-24 years: 14.03% (male 743,142 /female 666,550)

25-54 years: 45.44% (male 2,247,545 /female 2,317,630)

55-64 years: 10.67% (male 493,555 /female 578,440)

65 years and over: 6.81% (male 262,989 /female 421,234) (2018 est.)

DEPENDENCY RATIOS:

total dependency ratio: 40.2 (2015 est.)

youth dependency ratio: 32.1 (2015 est.)

elderly dependency ratio: 8 (2015 est.)

potential support ratio: 12.4 (2015 est.)

MEDIAN AGE:

total: 31.7 years

male: 30.2 years

female: 33.4 years (2018 est.)

country comparison to the world: 108

POPULATION GROWTH RATE:

0.83% (2018 est.)

country comparison to the world: 126

BIRTH RATE:

15.3 births/1,000 population (2018 est.)

country comparison to the world: 120

DEATH RATE:

7 deaths/1,000 population (2018 est.)

country comparison to the world: 128

NET MIGRATION RATE:

0 migrant(s)/1,000 population (2017 est.)

country comparison to the world: 71

POPULATION DISTRIBUTION:

highest population density is found in the far eastern area of the county, in and around Baku; apart from smaller urbanized areas, the rest of the country has a fairly light and evenly distributed population

URBANIZATION:

urban population: 55.7% of total population (2018)

rate of urbanization: 1.58% annual rate of change (2015-20 est.)

MAJOR URBAN AREAS - POPULATION:

2.286 million BAKU (capital) (2018)

SEX RATIO:

at birth: 1.09 male(s)/female (2017 est.)

0-14 years: 1.15 male(s)/female (2017 est.)

15-24 years: 1.09 male(s)/female (2017 est.)

25-54 years: 0.96 male(s)/female (2017 est.)

55-64 years: 0.86 male(s)/female (2017 est.)

65 years and over: 0.62 male(s)/female (2017 est.)

total population: 0.98 male(s)/female (2017 est.)

MOTHER'S MEAN AGE AT FIRST BIRTH:

23.2 years (2014 est.)

MATERNAL MORTALITY RATE:

25 deaths/100,000 live births (2015 est.)

country comparison to the world: 121

INFANT MORTALITY RATE:

total: 23 deaths/1,000 live births (2018 est.)

male: 23.9 deaths/1,000 live births (2018 est.)

female: 22 deaths/1,000 live births (2018 est.)

country comparison to the world: 71

LIFE EXPECTANCY AT BIRTH:

total population: 73 years (2018 est.)

male: 70 years (2018 est.)

female: 76.4 years (2018 est.)

country comparison to the world: 143

TOTAL FERTILITY RATE:

1.89 children born/woman (2018 est.)

country comparison to the world: 134

HEALTH EXPENDITURES:

6% of GDP (2014)

country comparison to the world: 105

PHYSICIANS DENSITY:

3.4 physicians/1,000 population (2014)

HOSPITAL BED DENSITY:

4.7 beds/1,000 population (2013)

DRINKING WATER SOURCE:

improved:

urban: 94.7% of population (2015 est.)

rural: 77.8% of population (2015 est.)

total: 87% of population (2015 est.)

unimproved:

urban: 5.3% of population (2015 est.)

rural: 22.2% of population (2015 est.)

total: 13% of population (2015 est.)

SANITATION FACILITY ACCESS:

improved:

urban: 91.6% of population (2015 est.)

rural: 86.6% of population (2015 est.)

total: 89.3% of population (2015 est.)

unimproved:

urban: 8.4% of population (2015 est.)

rural: 13.4% of population (2015 est.)

total: 10.7% of population (2015 est.)

HIV/AIDS - ADULT PREVALENCE RATE:

0.1% (2017 est.)

country comparison to the world: 108

HIV/AIDS - PEOPLE LIVING WITH HIV/AIDS:

8,000 (2017 est.)

country comparison to the world: 106

HIV/AIDS - DEATHS:

<500 (2017 est.)

OBESITY - ADULT PREVALENCE RATE:

19.9% (2016)

country comparison to the world: 106

CHILDREN UNDER THE AGE OF 5 YEARS UNDERWEIGHT:

4.9% (2013)

country comparison to the world: 83

EDUCATION EXPENDITURES:

3% of GDP (2015)

country comparison to the world: 142

LITERACY:

definition: age 15 and over can read and write (2016 est.)

total population: 99.8% (2016 est.)

male: 99.9% (2016 est.)

female: 99.7% (2016 est.)

SCHOOL LIFE EXPECTANCY (PRIMARY TO TERTIARY EDUCATION):

total: 13 years (2014)

male: 13 years (2014)

female: 13 years (2014)

UNEMPLOYMENT, YOUTH AGES 15-24:

total: 13.4% (2015 est.)

male: 11.4% (2015 est.)

female: 15.8% (2015 est.)

country comparison to the world: 96

GOVERNMENT :: AZERBAIJAN

COUNTRY NAME:

conventional long form: Republic of Azerbaijan

conventional short form: Azerbaijan

local long form: Azarbaycan Respublikasi

local short form: Azarbaycan

former: Azerbaijan Soviet Socialist Republic

etymology: the name translates as "Land of Fire" and refers to naturally occurring surface fires on ancient oil pools or from natural gas discharges

GOVERNMENT TYPE:

presidential republic

CAPITAL:

name: Baku (Baki, Baky)

geographic coordinates: 40 23 N, 49 52 E

time difference: UTC+4 (9 hours ahead of Washington, DC, during Standard Time)

etymology: the name derives from the Persian designation of the city "bad-kube" meaning "wind-pounded city" and refers to the harsh winds and severe snow storms that can hit the city

note: at approximately 28 m below sea level, Baku's elevation makes it the lowest capital city in the world

ADMINISTRATIVE DIVISIONS:

66 rayons (rayonlar; rayon - singular), 11 cities (saharlar; sahar - singular);

rayons: Abseron, Agcabadi, Agdam, Agdas, Agstafa, Agsu, Astara, Babak, Balakan, Barda, Beylaqan, Bilasuvar, Cabrayil, Calilabad, Culfa, Daskasan, Fuzuli, Gadabay, Goranboy, Goycay, Goygol, Haciqabul, Imisli, Ismayilli, Kalbacar, Kangarli, Kurdamir, Lacin, Lankaran, Lerik, Masalli, Neftcala, Oguz, Ordubad, Qabala, Qax, Qazax, Qobustan, Quba, Qubadli, Qusar, Saatli, Sabirabad, Sabran, Sadarak, Sahbuz, Saki, Salyan, Samaxi, Samkir, Samux, Sarur, Siyazan, Susa, Tartar, Tovuz, Ucar, Xacmaz, Xizi, Xocali, Xocavand, Yardimli, Yevlax, Zangilan, Zaqatala, Zardab;

cities: Baku, Ganca, Lankaran, Mingacevir, Naftalan, Naxcivan (Nakhichevan), Saki, Sirvan, Sumqayit, Xankandi, Yevlax

INDEPENDENCE:

30 August 1991 (declared from the Soviet Union);18 October 1991 (adopted by the Supreme Council of Azerbaijan)

NATIONAL HOLIDAY:

Republic Day (founding of the Democratic Republic of Azerbaijan), 28 May (1918)

CONSTITUTION:

history: several previous; latest adopted 12 November 1995 (2017)

amendments: proposed by the president of the republic or by at least 63 members of the National Assembly; passage requires at least 95 votes of Assembly members in two separate readings of the draft amendment six months apart and requires presidential approval after each of the two Assembly votes, followed by presidential signature; constitutional articles on the authority, sovereignty, and unity of the people cannot be amended; amended 2002, 2009, 2016 (2017)

LEGAL SYSTEM:

civil law system

INTERNATIONAL LAW ORGANIZATION PARTICIPATION:

has not submitted an ICJ jurisdiction declaration; non-party state to the ICCt

CITIZENSHIP:

citizenship by birth: yes

citizenship by descent only: yes

dual citizenship recognized: no

residency requirement for naturalization: 5 years

SUFFRAGE:

18 years of age; universal

EXECUTIVE BRANCH:

chief of state: President Ilham ALIYEV (since 31 October 2003); First Vice President Mehriban ALIYEVA (since 21 February 2017)

head of government: Prime Minister Novruz MAMMADOV (since 21 April 2018); First Deputy Prime Minister Yaqub EYYUBOV (since June 2006)

cabinet: Council of Ministers appointed by the president and confirmed by the National Assembly

elections/appointments: president directly elected by absolute majority popular vote in 2 rounds if needed for a 7-year term (eligible for unlimited terms); election last held on 11 April 2018 (next to be held in 2025); prime minister and first deputy prime minister appointed by the president and confirmed by the National Assembly; note - a constitutional amendment approved in a September 2016 referendum expanded presidential terms from 5 to 7 years; a separate constitutional amendment approved in the same referendum also introduced the post of first vice-president and additional vice-presidents, who are directly appointed by the president

election results: Ilham ALIYEV reelected president in first round; percent of vote - Ilham ALIYEV (YAP) 86%, Zahid ORUJ (independent) 3.1%, other 10.9%

note: OSCE observers noted shortcomings in the election, including a restrictive political environment, limits on fundamental freedoms, a lack of genuine competition, and ballot box stuffing

LEGISLATIVE BRANCH:

description: unicameral National Assembly or Milli Mejlis (125 seats; members directly elected in single-seat constituencies by simple majority vote to serve 5-year terms)

elections: last held on 1 November 2015 (next to be held in November 2020)

election results: percent of vote by party - NA; seats by party - YAP 69, CSP 2, AVP 1, Civil Unity 1, CUP 1, Democratic Enlightenment 1, Democratic Reforms 1, Great Undertaking Party 1, National Renaissance Party 1, Social Democratic Party 1, Social Prosperity Party 1, Whole Azerbaijan Popular Front 1, independent 43, invalid 1; composition - men 104, women 21, percent of women 16.8%

JUDICIAL BRANCH:

highest courts: Supreme Court (consists of the chairman, vice chairman, and 23 judges in plenum sessions and organized into civil, economic affairs, criminal, and rights violations chambers); Constitutional Court (consists of 9 judges)

judge selection and term of office: Supreme Court judges nominated by the president and appointed by the Milli Majlis; judges appointed for 10 years; Constitutional Court chairman and deputy chairman appointed by the president; other court judges nominated by the president and appointed by the Milli Majlis to serve single 15-year terms

subordinate courts: Courts of Appeal (replaced the Economic Court in 2002); district and municipal courts;

POLITICAL PARTIES AND LEADERS:

Civil Solidarity Party or CSP [Sabir RUSTAMKHANLI]Civil Unity Party or CUP [Sabir HAJIYEV]
Democratic Enlightenment [Elshan MUSAYEV]
Democratic Reforms Party [Asim MOLLAZADE]
Great Undertaking [Fazil MUSTAFA]
Musavat [Arif HAJILI]
Popular Front Party [Ali KARIMLI]
Motherland Party or AVP [Fazail AGAMALI]
National Renaissance Party
Social Democratic Party [Ayaz MUTALIBOV]
Social Prosperity Party [Khanhusein KAZIMLI]
Unity Party [Tahir KARIMLI]
Whole Azerbaijan Popular Front Party [Gudrat HASANGULIYEV]
Yeni (New) Azerbaijan Party or YAP [President Ilham ALIYEV]

INTERNATIONAL ORGANIZATION PARTICIPATION:

ADB, BSEC, CD, CE, CICA, CIS, EAPC, EBRD, ECO, EITI (compliant country), FAO, GCTU, GUAM, IAEA, IBRD, ICAO, ICC (NGOs), ICRM, IDA, IDB, IFAD, IFC, IFRCS, ILO, IMF, IMO, Interpol, IOC, IOM, IPU, ISO, ITSO, ITU, ITUC (NGOs), MIGA, NAM, OAS (observer), OIC, OPCW, OSCE, PFP, SELEC (observer), UN, UNCTAD, UNESCO, UNHCR, UNIDO, UNWTO, UPU, WCO, WFTU (NGOs), WHO, WIPO, WMO, WTO (observer)

DIPLOMATIC REPRESENTATION IN THE US:

chief of mission: Ambassador Elin SULEYMANOV (since 5 December 2011)

chancery: 2741 34th Street NW, Washington, DC 20008

telephone: [1] (202) 337-3500

FAX: [1] (202) 337-5911

consulate(s) general: Los Angeles

DIPLOMATIC REPRESENTATION FROM THE US:

chief of mission: Ambassador (vacant); Charge d'Affaires William GILL (since August 2016)

embassy: 111 Azadlig Prospekti, Baku AZ1007

mailing address: American Embassy Baku, US Department of State, 7050 Baku Place, Washington, DC 20521-7050

telephone: [994] (12) 488-3300

FAX: [994] (12) 488-3330

FLAG DESCRIPTION:

three equal horizontal bands of sky blue (top), red, and green; a crescent and eight-pointed star in white are centered in the red band; the blue band recalls Azerbaijan's Turkic heritage, red stands for modernization and progress, and green refers to Islam; the crescent moon and star are a Turkic insignia; the eight star points represent the eight Turkic peoples of the world

NATIONAL SYMBOL(S):

flames of fire; national colors: blue, red, green

NATIONAL ANTHEM:

name: "Azerbaijan Marsi" (March of Azerbaijan)

lyrics/music: Ahmed JAVAD/Uzeyir HAJIBEYOV

note: adopted 1992; although originally written in 1919 during a brief period of independence, "Azerbaijan Marsi" did not become the official anthem until after the dissolution of the Soviet Union

ECONOMY :: AZERBAIJAN

ECONOMY - OVERVIEW:

Prior to the decline in global oil prices since 2014, Azerbaijan's high economic growth was attributable to rising energy exports and to some non-export sectors. Oil exports through the Baku-Tbilisi-Ceyhan Pipeline, the Baku-Novorossiysk, and the Baku-Supsa Pipelines remain the main economic driver, but efforts to boost

Azerbaijan's gas production are underway. The expected completion of the geopolitically important Southern Gas Corridor (SGC) between Azerbaijan and Europe will open up another source of revenue from gas exports. First gas to Turkey through the SGC is expected in 2018 with project completion expected by 2020-21.

Declining oil prices caused a 3.1% contraction in GDP in 2016, and a 0.8% decline in 2017, highlighted by a sharp reduction in the construction sector. The economic decline was accompanied by higher inflation, a weakened banking sector, and two sharp currency devaluations in 2015. Azerbaijan's financial sector continued to struggle. In May 2017, Baku allowed the majority state-owed International Bank of Azerbaijan (IBA), the nation's largest bank, to default on some of its outstanding debt and file for restructuring in Azerbaijani courts; IBA also filed in US and UK bankruptcy courts to have its restructuring recognized in their respective jurisdictions.

Azerbaijan has made limited progress with market-based economic reforms. Pervasive public and private sector corruption and structural economic inefficiencies remain a drag on long-term growth, particularly in non-energy sectors. The government has, however, made efforts to combat corruption, particularly in customs and government services. Several other obstacles impede Azerbaijan's economic progress, including the need for more foreign investment in the non-energy sector and the continuing conflict with Armenia over the Nagorno-Karabakh region. While trade with Russia and the other former Soviet republics remains important, Azerbaijan has expanded trade with Turkey and Europe and is seeking new markets for non-oil/gas exports - mainly in the agricultural sector - with Gulf Cooperation Council member countries, the US, and others. It is also improving Baku airport and the Caspian Sea port of Alat for use as a regional transportation and logistics hub.

Long-term prospects depend on world oil prices, Azerbaijan's ability to develop export routes for its growing gas production, and its ability to improve the business environment and diversify the economy. In late 2016, the president approved a strategic roadmap for economic reforms that identified key non-energy segments of the economy for development, such as agriculture, logistics, information technology, and tourism. In October 2017, the long-awaited Baku-Tbilisi-Kars railway, stretching from the Azerbaijani capital to Kars in north-eastern Turkey, began limited service.

GDP (PURCHASING POWER PARITY):

$172.2 billion (2017 est.)

$172.1 billion (2016 est.)

$177.6 billion (2015 est.)

note: data are in 2017 dollars

country comparison to the world: 73

GDP (OFFICIAL EXCHANGE RATE):

$40.67 billion (2017 est.) (2017 est.)

GDP - REAL GROWTH RATE:

0.1% (2017 est.)

-3.1% (2016 est.)

0.6% (2015 est.)

country comparison to the world: 194

GDP - PER CAPITA (PPP):

$17,500 (2017 est.)

$17,700 (2016 est.)

$18,500 (2015 est.)

note: data are in 2017 dollars

country comparison to the world: 100

GROSS NATIONAL SAVING:

24.6% of GDP (2017 est.)

22.7% of GDP (2016 est.)

27.3% of GDP (2015 est.)

country comparison to the world: 63

GDP - COMPOSITION, BY END USE:

household consumption: 57.6% (2017 est.)

government consumption: 11.5% (2017 est.)

investment in fixed capital: 23.6% (2017 est.)

investment in inventories: 0.5% (2017 est.)

exports of goods and services: 48.7% (2017 est.)

imports of goods and services: -42% (2017 est.)

GDP - COMPOSITION, BY SECTOR OF ORIGIN:

agriculture: 6.1% (2017 est.)

industry: 53.5% (2017 est.)

services: 40.4% (2017 est.)

AGRICULTURE - PRODUCTS:

fruit, vegetables, grain, rice, grapes, tea, cotton, tobacco; cattle, pigs, sheep, goats

INDUSTRIES:

petroleum and petroleum products, natural gas, oilfield equipment; steel, iron ore; cement; chemicals and petrochemicals; textiles

INDUSTRIAL PRODUCTION GROWTH RATE:

-3.8% (2017 est.)

country comparison to the world: 191

LABOR FORCE:

5.118 million (2017 est.)

country comparison to the world: 82

LABOR FORCE - BY OCCUPATION:

agriculture: 37%

industry: 14.3%

services: 48.9% (2014)

UNEMPLOYMENT RATE:

5% (2017 est.)

5% (2016 est.)

country comparison to the world: 73

POPULATION BELOW POVERTY LINE:

4.9% (2015 est.)

HOUSEHOLD INCOME OR CONSUMPTION BY PERCENTAGE SHARE:

lowest 10%: 27.4% (2008)

highest 10%: 27.4% (2008)

DISTRIBUTION OF FAMILY INCOME - GINI INDEX:

33.7 (2008)

36.5 (2001)

country comparison to the world: 110

BUDGET:

revenues: 9.556 billion (2017 est.)

expenditures: 10.22 billion (2017 est.)

TAXES AND OTHER REVENUES:

23.5% (of GDP) (2017 est.)

country comparison to the world: 126

BUDGET SURPLUS (+) OR DEFICIT (-):

-1.6% (of GDP) (2017 est.)

country comparison to the world: 93

PUBLIC DEBT:

54.1% of GDP (2017 est.)

50.7% of GDP (2016 est.)

country comparison to the world: 85

FISCAL YEAR:

calendar year

INFLATION RATE (CONSUMER PRICES):

13% (2017 est.)

12.6% (2016 est.)

country comparison to the world: 209

CENTRAL BANK DISCOUNT RATE:

15% (10 March 2017)

15% (14 September 2016)

note: this is the Refinancing Rate, the key policy rate for the National Bank of Azerbaijan

country comparison to the world: 13

COMMERCIAL BANK PRIME LENDING RATE:

12.7% (31 December 2017 est.)

12.56% (31 December 2016 est.)

country comparison to the world: 64

STOCK OF NARROW MONEY:

$6.202 billion (31 December 2017 est.)

$5.06 billion (31 December 2016 est.)

country comparison to the world: 96

STOCK OF BROAD MONEY:

$6.202 billion (31 December 2017 est.)

$5.06 billion (31 December 2016 est.)

country comparison to the world: 98

STOCK OF DOMESTIC CREDIT:

$13.31 billion (31 December 2017 est.)

$13.44 billion (31 December 2016 est.)

country comparison to the world: 102

MARKET VALUE OF PUBLICLY TRADED SHARES:

NA

CURRENT ACCOUNT BALANCE:

$1.685 billion (2017 est.)

-$1.363 billion (2016 est.)

country comparison to the world: 45

EXPORTS:

$15.15 billion (2017 est.)

$13.21 billion (2016 est.)

country comparison to the world: 78

EXPORTS - PARTNERS:

Italy 23.2%, Turkey 13.6%, Israel 6.1%, Russia 5.4%, Germany 5%, Czech Republic 4.6%, Georgia 4.3% (2017)

EXPORTS - COMMODITIES:

oil and gas roughly 90%, machinery, foodstuffs, cotton

IMPORTS:

$9.037 billion (2017 est.)

$9.004 billion (2016 est.)

country comparison to the world: 106

IMPORTS - COMMODITIES:

machinery and equipment, foodstuffs, metals, chemicals

IMPORTS - PARTNERS:

Russia 17.7%, Turkey 14.8%, China 9.9%, US 8.3%, Ukraine 5.3%, Germany 5.1% (2017)

RESERVES OF FOREIGN EXCHANGE AND GOLD:

$6.681 billion (31 December 2017 est.)

$7.142 billion (31 December 2016 est.)

country comparison to the world: 88

DEBT - EXTERNAL:

$17.41 billion (31 December 2017 est.)

$13.83 billion (31 December 2016 est.)

country comparison to the world: 99

STOCK OF DIRECT FOREIGN INVESTMENT - AT HOME:

$79.53 billion (31 December 2017 est.)

$73.83 billion (31 December 2016 est.)

country comparison to the world: 49

STOCK OF DIRECT FOREIGN INVESTMENT - ABROAD:

$19.6 billion (31 December 2017 est.)

$17.05 billion (31 December 2016 est.)

country comparison to the world: 56

EXCHANGE RATES:

Azerbaijani manats (AZN) per US dollar -

1.723 (2017 est.)

1.5957 (2016 est.)

1.5957 (2015 est.)

1.0246 (2014 est.)

0.7844 (2013 est.)

ENERGY :: AZERBAIJAN

ELECTRICITY ACCESS:

electrification - total population: 100% (2016)

ELECTRICITY - PRODUCTION:

23.57 billion kWh (2016 est.)

country comparison to the world: 73

ELECTRICITY - CONSUMPTION:

20.24 billion kWh (2016 est.)

country comparison to the world: 71

ELECTRICITY - EXPORTS:

265 million kWh (2015 est.)

country comparison to the world: 71

ELECTRICITY - IMPORTS:

114 million kWh (2016 est.)

country comparison to the world: 97

ELECTRICITY - INSTALLED GENERATING CAPACITY:

7.876 million kW (2016 est.)

country comparison to the world: 71

ELECTRICITY - FROM FOSSIL FUELS:

84% of total installed capacity (2016 est.)

country comparison to the world: 74

ELECTRICITY - FROM NUCLEAR FUELS:

0% of total installed capacity (2017 est.)

country comparison to the world: 42

ELECTRICITY - FROM HYDROELECTRIC PLANTS:

14% of total installed capacity (2017 est.)

country comparison to the world: 104

ELECTRICITY - FROM OTHER RENEWABLE SOURCES:

2% of total installed capacity (2017 est.)

country comparison to the world: 133

CRUDE OIL - PRODUCTION:

789,300 bbl/day (2017 est.)

country comparison to the world: 24

CRUDE OIL - EXPORTS:

718,800 bbl/day (2015 est.)

country comparison to the world: 19

CRUDE OIL - IMPORTS:

0 bbl/day (2015 est.)

country comparison to the world: 92

CRUDE OIL - PROVED RESERVES:

7 billion bbl (1 January 2018 est.)

country comparison to the world: 18

REFINED PETROLEUM PRODUCTS - PRODUCTION:

138,900 bbl/day (2015 est.)

country comparison to the world: 61

REFINED PETROLEUM PRODUCTS - CONSUMPTION:

100,000 bbl/day (2016 est.)

country comparison to the world: 80

REFINED PETROLEUM PRODUCTS - EXPORTS:

46,480 bbl/day (2015 est.)

country comparison to the world: 57

REFINED PETROLEUM PRODUCTS - IMPORTS:

5,576 bbl/day (2015 est.)

country comparison to the world: 168

NATURAL GAS - PRODUCTION:

16.96 billion cu m (2017 est.)

country comparison to the world: 35

NATURAL GAS - CONSUMPTION:

10.34 billion cu m (2017 est.)

country comparison to the world: 47

NATURAL GAS - EXPORTS:

8.042 billion cu m (2017 est.)

country comparison to the world: 24

NATURAL GAS - IMPORTS:

2.095 billion cu m (2017 est.)

country comparison to the world: 51

NATURAL GAS - PROVED RESERVES:

991.1 billion cu m (1 January 2018 est.)

country comparison to the world: 25

CARBON DIOXIDE EMISSIONS FROM CONSUMPTION OF ENERGY:

35.6 million Mt (2017 est.)

country comparison to the world: 72

COMMUNICATIONS :: AZERBAIJAN

TELEPHONES - FIXED LINES:

total subscriptions: 1,688,325 (2017 est.)

subscriptions per 100 inhabitants: 17 (2017 est.)

country comparison to the world: 61

TELEPHONES - MOBILE CELLULAR:

total subscriptions: 10.127 million (2017 est.)

subscriptions per 100 inhabitants: 102 (2017 est.)

country comparison to the world: 83

TELEPHONE SYSTEM:

general assessment: more competition exists in the mobile-cellular market; Azerbaijan has moderate mobile, mobile broadband and fixed broadband penetration compared to other Asian nations; Pre-5G network operating on the TD-LTE standard (2017)

domestic: teledensity of some 17 fixed-lines per 100 persons; mobile-cellular teledensity has increased to 102 telephones per 100 persons; satellite service connects Baku to a modern switch in its exclave of Naxcivan (Nakhchivan) (2017)

international: country code - 994; the Trans-Asia-Europe (TAE) fiber-optic link transits Azerbaijan providing international connectivity to neighboring countries; the old Soviet system of cable and microwave is still serviceable; satellite earth stations - 2 (2017)

BROADCAST MEDIA:

3 state-run and 1 public TV channels; 4 domestic commercial TV stations and about 15 regional TV stations; cable TV services are available in Baku; 1 state-run and 1 public radio network operating; a small number of private commercial radio stations broadcasting; local FM relays of Baku commercial stations are available in many localities; note - all broadcast media is pro-government, and most private broadcast media outlets are owned by entities directly linked to the government (2018)

INTERNET COUNTRY CODE:

.az

INTERNET USERS:

total: 7,720,502 (July 2016 est.)

percent of population: 78.2% (July 2016 est.)

country comparison to the world: 55

BROADBAND - FIXED SUBSCRIPTIONS:

total: 1,805,214 (2017 est.)

subscriptions per 100 inhabitants: 18 (2017 est.)

country comparison to the world: 54

TRANSPORTATION :: AZERBAIJAN

NATIONAL AIR TRANSPORT SYSTEM:

number of registered air carriers: 2 (2015)

inventory of registered aircraft operated by air carriers: 35 (2015)

annual passenger traffic on registered air carriers: 1,803,112 (2015)

annual freight traffic on registered air carriers: 41,954,600 mt-km (2015)

CIVIL AIRCRAFT REGISTRATION COUNTRY CODE PREFIX:

4K (2016)

AIRPORTS:

37 (2013)

country comparison to the world: 107

AIRPORTS - WITH PAVED RUNWAYS:

total: 30 (2017)

over 3,047 m: 5 (2017)

2,438 to 3,047 m: 5 (2017)

1,524 to 2,437 m: 13 (2017)

914 to 1,523 m: 4 (2017)

under 914 m: 3 (2017)

AIRPORTS - WITH UNPAVED RUNWAYS:

total: 7 (2013)

under 914 m: 7 (2013)

HELIPORTS:

1 (2012)

PIPELINES:

89 km condensate, 3890 km gas, 2446 km oil (2013)

RAILWAYS:

total: 2,944 km (2017)

broad gauge: 2,944.3 km 1.520-m gauge (approx. 1,767 km electrified) (2017)

country comparison to the world: 62

ROADWAYS:

total: 52,942 km (2006)

paved: 26,789 km (2006)

unpaved: 26,153 km (2006)

country comparison to the world: 76

MERCHANT MARINE:

total: 311 (2017)

by type: general cargo 48, oil tanker 48, other 215 (2017)

country comparison to the world: 50

PORTS AND TERMINALS:

major seaport(s): Baku (Baki) located on the Caspian Sea

MILITARY AND SECURITY :: AZERBAIJAN

MILITARY EXPENDITURES:

3.64% of GDP (2016)

5.61% of GDP (2015)

4.56% of GDP (2014)

country comparison to the world: 17

MILITARY BRANCHES:

Army, Navy, Air, and Air Defense Forces (2010)

MILITARY SERVICE AGE AND OBLIGATION:

18-35 years of age for compulsory military service; service obligation 18 months or 12 months for university graduates; 17 years of age for voluntary service; 17 year olds are considered to be on active service at cadet military schools (2012)

TRANSNATIONAL ISSUES :: AZERBAIJAN

DISPUTES - INTERNATIONAL:

Azerbaijan, Kazakhstan, and Russia ratified the Caspian seabed delimitation treaties based on equidistance, while Iran continues to insist on a one-fifth slice of the seathe dispute over the break-away Nagorno-Karabakh region and the Armenian military occupation of surrounding lands in Azerbaijan remains the primary focus of regional instabilityresidents have evacuated the former Soviet-era small ethnic enclaves in Armenia and Azerbaijanlocal border forces struggle to control the illegal transit of goods and people across the porous, undemarcated Armenian, Azerbaijani, and Georgian bordersbilateral talks continue with Turkmenistan on dividing the seabed and contested oilfields in the middle of the Caspian

REFUGEES AND INTERNALLY DISPLACED PERSONS:

IDPs: 393,000 (conflict with Armenia over Nagorno-Karabakh; IDPs are mainly ethnic Azerbaijanis but also include ethnic Kurds, Russians, and Turks predominantly from occupied territories around Nagorno-Karabakh; includes IDPs' descendants, returned IDPs, and people living in insecure areas and excludes people displaced by natural disasters; around half the IDPs live in the capital Baku) (2017)

stateless persons: 3,585 (2017)

ILLICIT DRUGS:

limited illicit cultivation of cannabis and opium poppy, mostly for CIS consumption; small government eradication program; transit point for Southwest Asian opiates bound for Russia and to a lesser extent the rest of Europe

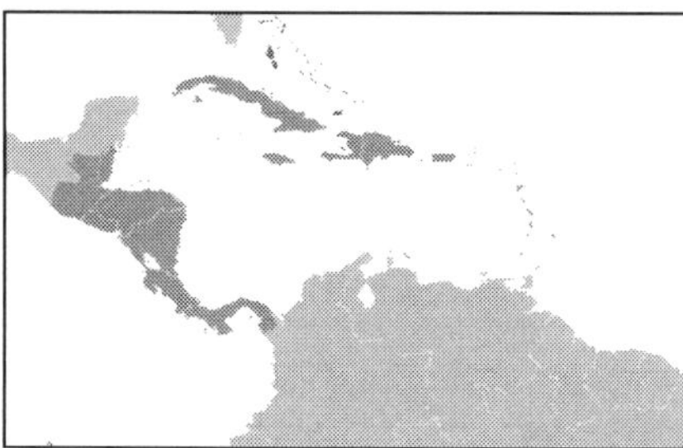

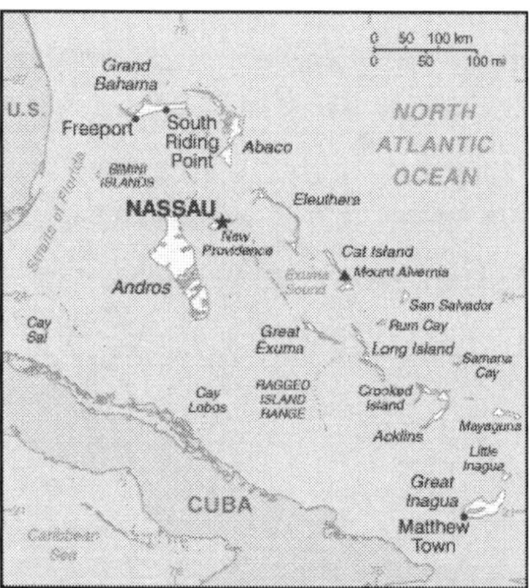

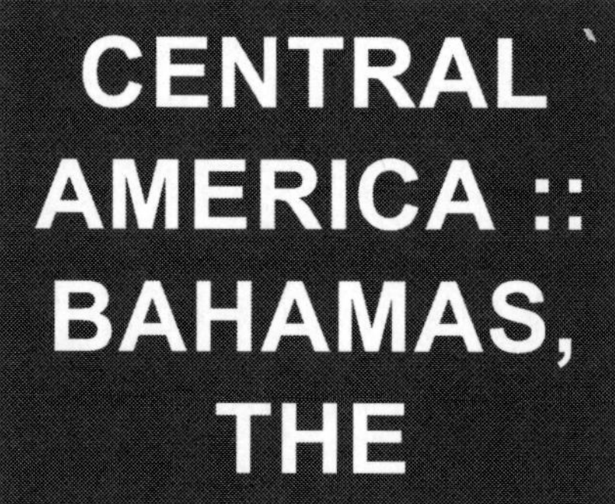

CENTRAL AMERICA :: BAHAMAS, THE

INTRODUCTION :: BAHAMAS, THE

BACKGROUND:

Lucayan Indians inhabited the islands when Christopher COLUMBUS first set foot in the New World on San Salvador in 1492. British settlement of the islands began in 1647; the islands became a colony in 1783. Piracy thrived in the 17th and 18th centuries because of The Bahamas close proximity to shipping lanes. Since attaining independence from the UK in 1973, The Bahamas has prospered through tourism, international banking, and investment management. Because of its location, the country is a major transshipment point for illegal drugs, particularly shipments to the US and Europe, and its territory is used for smuggling illegal migrants into the US. Current Prime Minister Hubert MINNIS is only the fourth prime minister in Bahamian history following its independence from the UK; he is also the first prime minister in 25 years besides Perry CHRISTIE and Hubert INGRAHAM, who repeatedly traded the premiership from 1992 to 2017.

GEOGRAPHY :: BAHAMAS, THE

LOCATION:

chain of islands in the North Atlantic Ocean, southeast of Florida, northeast of Cuba

GEOGRAPHIC COORDINATES:

24 15 N, 76 00 W

MAP REFERENCES:

Central America and the Caribbean

AREA:

total: 13,880 sq km

land: 10,010 sq km

water: 3,870 sq km

country comparison to the world: 161

AREA - COMPARATIVE:

slightly smaller than Connecticut

LAND BOUNDARIES:

0 km

COASTLINE:

3,542 km

MARITIME CLAIMS:

territorial sea: 12 nm

exclusive economic zone: 200 nm

CLIMATE:

tropical marine; moderated by warm waters of Gulf Stream

TERRAIN:

long, flat coral formations with some low rounded hills

ELEVATION:

0 m lowest point: Atlantic Ocean 64 highest point: Mount Alvernia on Cat Island

NATURAL RESOURCES:

salt, aragonite, timber, arable land

LAND USE:

agricultural land: 1.4% (2014 est.)

arable land: 0.8% (2014 est.) / permanent crops: 0.4% (2014 est.) / permanent pasture: 0.2% (2014 est.)

forest: 51.4% (2014 est.)

other: 47.2% (2014 est.)

IRRIGATED LAND:

10 sq km (2012)

POPULATION DISTRIBUTION:

most of the population lives in urban areas, with two-thirds living on New Providence Island where Nassau is located

NATURAL HAZARDS:

hurricanes and other tropical storms cause extensive flood and wind damage

ENVIRONMENT - CURRENT ISSUES:

coral reef decay; solid waste disposal

ENVIRONMENT - INTERNATIONAL AGREEMENTS:

party to: Biodiversity, Climate Change, Climate Change-Kyoto Protocol, Desertification, Endangered Species, Hazardous Wastes, Law of the Sea, Ozone Layer Protection, Ship Pollution, Wetlands

signed, but not ratified: none of the selected agreements

GEOGRAPHY - NOTE:

strategic location adjacent to US and Cuba; extensive island chain of which 30 are inhabited

PEOPLE AND SOCIETY :: BAHAMAS, THE

POPULATION:

332,634 (July 2018 est.)

note: estimates for this country explicitly take into account the effects of excess mortality due to AIDS; this can result in lower life expectancy, higher infant mortality, higher death rates, lower population growth rates, and changes in the distribution of population by age and sex than would otherwise be expected

country comparison to the world: 179

NATIONALITY:

noun: Bahamian(s)

adjective: Bahamian

ETHNIC GROUPS:

black 90.6%, white 4.7%, black and white 2.1%, other 1.9%, unspecified 0.7% (2010 est.)

note: data represent population by racial group

LANGUAGES:

English (official), Creole (among Haitian immigrants)

RELIGIONS:

Protestant 69.9% (includes Baptist 34.9%, Anglican 13.7%, Pentecostal 8.9% Seventh Day Adventist 4.4%, Methodist 3.6%, Church of God 1.9%, Brethren 1.6%), Roman Catholic 12%, other Christian 13% (includes Jehovah's Witness 1.1%), other 0.6%, none 1.9%, unspecified 2.6% (2010 est.)

AGE STRUCTURE:

0-14 years: 22.39% (male 37,777 /female 36,686)

15-24 years: 16.01% (male 26,984 /female 26,281)

25-54 years: 44.1% (male 73,627 /female 73,068)

55-64 years: 9.45% (male 14,298 /female 17,140)

65 years and over: 8.05% (male 10,318 /female 16,455) (2018 est.)

DEPENDENCY RATIOS:

total dependency ratio: 40.8 (2015 est.)

youth dependency ratio: 29.1 (2015 est.)

elderly dependency ratio: 11.7 (2015 est.)

potential support ratio: 8.5 (2015 est.)

MEDIAN AGE:

total: 32.3 years

male: 31.1 years

female: 33.5 years (2018 est.)

country comparison to the world: 102

POPULATION GROWTH RATE:

0.79% (2018 est.)

country comparison to the world: 131

BIRTH RATE:

15.1 births/1,000 population (2018 est.)

country comparison to the world: 124

DEATH RATE:

7.3 deaths/1,000 population (2018 est.)

country comparison to the world: 119

NET MIGRATION RATE:

0 migrant(s)/1,000 population (2017 est.)

country comparison to the world: 72

POPULATION DISTRIBUTION:

most of the population lives in urban areas, with two-thirds living on New Providence Island where Nassau is located

URBANIZATION:

urban population: 83% of total population (2018)

rate of urbanization: 1.13% annual rate of change (2015-20 est.)

MAJOR URBAN AREAS - POPULATION:

280,000 NASSAU (capital) (2018)

SEX RATIO:

at birth: 1.03 male(s)/female (2017 est.)

0-14 years: 1.03 male(s)/female (2017 est.)

15-24 years: 1.03 male(s)/female (2017 est.)

25-54 years: 1 male(s)/female (2017 est.)

55-64 years: 0.81 male(s)/female (2017 est.)

65 years and over: 0.62 male(s)/female (2017 est.)

total population: 0.96 male(s)/female (2017 est.)

MATERNAL MORTALITY RATE:

80 deaths/100,000 live births (2015 est.)

country comparison to the world: 80

INFANT MORTALITY RATE:

total: 11.1 deaths/1,000 live births (2018 est.)

male: 11.4 deaths/1,000 live births (2018 est.)

female: 10.9 deaths/1,000 live births (2018 est.)

country comparison to the world: 126

LIFE EXPECTANCY AT BIRTH:

total population: 72.9 years (2018 est.)

male: 70.4 years (2018 est.)

female: 75.4 years (2018 est.)

country comparison to the world: 144

TOTAL FERTILITY RATE:

1.94 children born/woman (2018 est.)

country comparison to the world: 126

HEALTH EXPENDITURES:

7.7% of GDP (2014)

country comparison to the world: 62

PHYSICIANS DENSITY:

2.26 physicians/1,000 population (2011)

HOSPITAL BED DENSITY:

2.9 beds/1,000 population (2013)

DRINKING WATER SOURCE:

improved:

urban: 98.4% of population (2015 est.)

rural: 98.4% of population (2015 est.)

total: 98.4% of population (2015 est.)

unimproved:

urban: 1.6% of population (2015 est.)

rural: 1.6% of population (2015 est.)

total: 1.6% of population (2015 est.)

SANITATION FACILITY ACCESS:

improved:

urban: 92% of population (2015 est.)

rural: 92% of population (2015 est.)

total: 92% of population (2015 est.)

unimproved:

urban: 8% of population (2015 est.)

rural: 8% of population (2015 est.)

total: 8% of population (2015 est.)

HIV/AIDS - ADULT PREVALENCE RATE:

1.9% (2017 est.)

country comparison to the world: 25

HIV/AIDS - PEOPLE LIVING WITH HIV/AIDS:

5,300 (2017 est.)

country comparison to the world: 115

HIV/AIDS - DEATHS:

NA

OBESITY - ADULT PREVALENCE RATE:

31.6% (2016)

country comparison to the world: 21

EDUCATION EXPENDITURES:

NA

UNEMPLOYMENT, YOUTH AGES 15-24:

total: 30.8% (2012 est.)

male: 29.6% (2012 est.)

female: 32.2% (2012 est.)

country comparison to the world: 27

GOVERNMENT :: BAHAMAS, THE

COUNTRY NAME:

conventional long form: Commonwealth of The Bahamas

conventional short form: The Bahamas

etymology: name derives from the Spanish "baha mar," meaning "shallow sea," which describes the shallow waters of the Bahama Banks

GOVERNMENT TYPE:

parliamentary democracy (Parliament) under a constitutional monarchy; a Commonwealth realm

CAPITAL:

name: Nassau

geographic coordinates: 25 05 N, 77 21 W

time difference: UTC-5 (same time as Washington, DC, during Standard Time)

daylight saving time: +1hr, begins second Sunday in March; ends first Sunday in November

etymology: named after William III, king of England, Scotland, and Ireland, who was a member of the House of Nassau

ADMINISTRATIVE DIVISIONS:

31 districts; Acklins Islands, Berry Islands, Bimini, Black Point, Cat Island, Central Abaco, Central Andros, Central Eleuthera, City of Freeport, Crooked Island and Long Cay, East Grand Bahama, Exuma, Grand Cay, Harbour Island, Hope Town, Inagua, Long Island, Mangrove Cay, Mayaguana, Moore's Island, North Abaco, North Andros, North Eleuthera, Ragged Island, Rum Cay, San Salvador, South Abaco, South Andros, South Eleuthera, Spanish Wells, West Grand Bahama

INDEPENDENCE:

10 July 1973 (from the UK)

NATIONAL HOLIDAY:

Independence Day, 10 July (1973)

CONSTITUTION:

history: previous 1964 (preindependence); latest adopted 20 June 1973, effective 10 July 1973 (2018)

amendments: proposed as an "Act" by Parliament; passage of amendments to articles such as the organization and composition of the branches of government requires approval by at least two-thirds majority of the membership of both houses of Parliament and majority approval in a referendum; passage of amendments to constitutional articles such as fundamental rights and individual freedoms, the powers, authorities, and procedures of the branches of government, or changes to the Bahamas Independence Act 1973 requires approval by at least three-fourths majority of the membership of both houses and majority approval in a referendum; amended many times, last in 2016 (2018)

LEGAL SYSTEM:

common law system based on the English model

INTERNATIONAL LAW ORGANIZATION PARTICIPATION:

has not submitted an ICJ jurisdiction declaration; non-party state to the ICCt

CITIZENSHIP:

citizenship by birth: no

citizenship by descent only: at least one parent must be a citizen of The Bahamas

dual citizenship recognized: no

residency requirement for naturalization: 6-9 years

SUFFRAGE:

18 years of age; universal

EXECUTIVE BRANCH:

chief of state: Queen ELIZABETH II (since 6 February 1952); represented by Governor General Dame Marguerite PINDLING (since 8 July 2014)

head of government: Prime Minister Hubert MINNIS (since 11 May 2017)

cabinet: Cabinet appointed by governor general on recommendation of prime minister

elections/appointments: the monarchy is hereditary; governor general appointed by the monarch on the advice of the prime minister; following legislative elections, the leader of the majority party or majority coalition usually appointed prime minister by the governor general; the prime minister recommends the deputy prime minister

note: Prime Minister Hubert MINNIS is only the fourth prime minister in Bahamian history following its independence from the UK; he is also the first prime minister in 25 years besides Perry CHRISTIE and Hubert INGRAHAM, who repeatedly traded the premiership from 1992 to 2017

LEGISLATIVE BRANCH:

description: bicameral Parliament consists of:
Senate (16 seats; members appointed by the governor general upon the advice of the prime minister and the opposition leader to serve 5-year terms)
House of Assembly (39 seats; members directly elected in single-seat constituencies by simple majority vote to serve 5-year terms)

elections:
last held on 10 May 2017 (next to be held by May 2022)

election results:
House of Assembly - percent of vote by party - FNM 57%, PLP 36.9%, other 6.1%; seats by party - FNM 35, PLP 4

note: the government may dissolve the parliament and call elections at any time

JUDICIAL BRANCH:

highest courts: Court of Appeal (consists of the court president and 4 justices, organized in 3-member panels); Supreme Court (consists of the chief justice and a maximum of 11 and a minimum of 2 justices)

judge selection and term of office: Court of Appeal president and Supreme Court chief justice appointed by the governor-general on the advice of the prime minister after consultation with the leader of the opposition party; other Court of Appeal and Supreme Court justices appointed by the governor general upon recommendation of the Judicial and Legal Services Commission, a 5-member body headed by the chief justice; Court of Appeal justices appointed for life with mandatory retirement normally at age 68 but can be extended until age 70; Supreme Court justices appointed for life with mandatory retirement normally at age 65 but can be extended until age 67

subordinate courts: Industrial Tribunal; Stipendiary and Magistrates' Courts; Family Island Administrators

note: as of 2008, the Bahamas was not a party to the agreement establishing the Caribbean Court of Justice as the highest appellate court for the 15-member Caribbean Community (CARICOM); the Judicial Committee of the Privy Council (in London) serves as the final court of appeal for The Bahamas

POLITICAL PARTIES AND LEADERS:

Democratic National Alliance or DNA [Christopher MORTIMER]
Free National Movement or FNM [Hubert MINNIS]
Progressive Liberal Party or PLP [Philip "Brave" DAVIS]

INTERNATIONAL ORGANIZATION PARTICIPATION:

ACP, AOSIS, C, Caricom, CDB, CELAC, FAO, G-77, IADB, IAEA, IBRD, ICAO, ICC (NGOs), ICRM, IDA, IFAD, IFC, IFRCS, ILO, IMF, IMO, IMSO, Interpol, IOC, IOM, ISO (correspondent), ITSO, ITU, LAES, MIGA, NAM, OAS, OPANAL, OPCW, Petrocaribe, UN, UNCTAD, UNESCO, UNIDO, UNWTO, UPU, WCO, WHO, WIPO, WMO, WTO (observer)

DIPLOMATIC REPRESENTATION IN THE US:

chief of mission: Ambassador Sidney Stanley COLLIE (since 20 November 2017)

chancery: 2220 Massachusetts Avenue NW, Washington, DC 20008

telephone: [1] (202) 319-2660

FAX: [1] (202) 319-2668

consulate(s) general: Atlanta, Miami, New York

DIPLOMATIC REPRESENTATION FROM THE US:

chief of mission: Ambassador (vacant); Charge d' Affaires Stephanie BOWERS (since 1 March 2018)

embassy: 42 Queen Street, Nassau, New Providence

mailing address: local or express mail address: P. O. Box N-8197, Nassau; US Department of State, 3370 Nassau Place, Washington, DC 20521-3370

telephone: [1] (242) 322-1181, 328-2206 (after hours)

FAX: [1] (242) 356-7174

FLAG DESCRIPTION:

three equal horizontal bands of aquamarine (top), gold, and aquamarine, with a black equilateral triangle based on the hoist side; the band colors represent the golden beaches of the islands surrounded by the aquamarine sea; black represents the vigor and force of a united people, while the pointing triangle indicates the enterprise and determination of the Bahamian people to develop the rich resources of land and sea

NATIONAL SYMBOL(S):

blue marlin, flamingo, Yellow Elder flower; national colors: aquamarine, yellow, black

NATIONAL ANTHEM:

name: March On, Bahamaland!

lyrics/music: Timothy GIBSON

note: adopted 1973; as a Commonwealth country, in addition to the national anthem, "God Save the Queen" serves as the royal anthem (see United Kingdom)

ECONOMY :: BAHAMAS, THE

ECONOMY - OVERVIEW:

The Bahamas has the second highest per capita GDP in the English-speaking Caribbean with an economy heavily dependent on tourism and financial services. Tourism accounts for approximately 50% of GDP and directly or indirectly employs half of the archipelago's labor force. Financial services constitute the second-most important sector of the Bahamian economy, accounting for about 15% of GDP. Manufacturing and agriculture combined contribute less than 7% of GDP and show little growth, despite government incentives aimed at those sectors. The new government led by Prime Minister Hubert MINNIS has prioritized addressing fiscal imbalances and rising debt, which stood at 75% of GDP in 2016. Large capital projects like the Baha Mar Casino and Hotel are driving growth. Public debt increased in 2017 in large part due to hurricane reconstruction and relief financing. The primary fiscal balance was a deficit of 0.4% of GDP in 2016. The Bahamas is the only country in the Western Hemisphere that is not a member of the World Trade Organization.

GDP (PURCHASING POWER PARITY):

$12.06 billion (2017 est.)

$11.89 billion (2016 est.)

$12.09 billion (2015 est.)

note: data are in 2017 dollars

country comparison to the world: 156

GDP (OFFICIAL EXCHANGE RATE):

$12.16 billion (2017 est.) (2017 est.)

GDP - REAL GROWTH RATE:

1.4% (2017 est.)

-1.7% (2016 est.)

1% (2015 est.)

country comparison to the world: 175

GDP - PER CAPITA (PPP):

$32,400 (2017 est.)

$32,300 (2016 est.)

$33,200 (2015 est.)

note: data are in 2017 dollars

country comparison to the world: 62

GROSS NATIONAL SAVING:

11.4% of GDP (2017 est.)

18.2% of GDP (2016 est.)

12.3% of GDP (2015 est.)

country comparison to the world: 155

GDP - COMPOSITION, BY END USE:

household consumption: 68% (2017 est.)

government consumption: 13% (2017 est.)

investment in fixed capital: 26.3% (2017 est.)

investment in inventories: 0.7% (2017 est.)

exports of goods and services: 33.7% (2017 est.)

imports of goods and services: -41.8% (2017 est.)

GDP - COMPOSITION, BY SECTOR OF ORIGIN:

agriculture: 2.3% (2017 est.)

industry: 7.7% (2017 est.)

services: 90% (2017 est.)

AGRICULTURE - PRODUCTS:

citrus, vegetables; poultry; seafood

INDUSTRIES:

tourism, banking, oil bunkering, maritime industries, transshipment and logistics, salt, aragonite, pharmaceuticals

INDUSTRIAL PRODUCTION GROWTH RATE:

5.8% (2017 est.)

country comparison to the world: 44

LABOR FORCE:

196,900 (2013 est.)

country comparison to the world: 173

LABOR FORCE - BY OCCUPATION:

agriculture: 3%

industry: 11%

services: 49%

tourism: 37% (2011 est.)

UNEMPLOYMENT RATE:

10.1% (2017 est.)

12.2% (2016 est.)

country comparison to the world: 140

POPULATION BELOW POVERTY LINE:

9.3% (2010 est.)

HOUSEHOLD INCOME OR CONSUMPTION BY PERCENTAGE SHARE:

lowest 10%: 22% (2007 est.)

highest 10%: 22% (2007)

BUDGET:

revenues: 2.139 billion (2017 est.)

expenditures: 2.46 billion (2017 est.)

TAXES AND OTHER REVENUES:

17.6% (of GDP) (2017 est.)

country comparison to the world: 166

BUDGET SURPLUS (+) OR DEFICIT (-):

-2.6% (of GDP) (2017 est.)

country comparison to the world: 115

PUBLIC DEBT:

54.6% of GDP (2017 est.)

50.5% of GDP (2016 est.)

country comparison to the world: 80

FISCAL YEAR:

1 July - 30 June

INFLATION RATE (CONSUMER PRICES):

1.4% (2017 est.)

-0.3% (2016 est.)

country comparison to the world: 75

CENTRAL BANK DISCOUNT RATE:

4.5% (1 January 2014)

4.5% (31 December 2012)

country comparison to the world: 85

COMMERCIAL BANK PRIME LENDING RATE:

4.25% (31 December 2017 est.)

4.75% (31 December 2016 est.)

country comparison to the world: 161

STOCK OF NARROW MONEY:

$2.654 billion (31 December 2017 est.)

$2.461 billion (31 December 2016 est.)

country comparison to the world: 124

STOCK OF BROAD MONEY:

$2.654 billion (31 December 2017 est.)

$2.461 billion (31 December 2016 est.)

country comparison to the world: 131

STOCK OF DOMESTIC CREDIT:

$8.805 billion (31 December 2017 est.)

$9.09 billion (31 December 2016 est.)

country comparison to the world: 113

MARKET VALUE OF PUBLICLY TRADED SHARES:

$2.78 billion (31 December 2012 est.)

country comparison to the world: 95

CURRENT ACCOUNT BALANCE:

-$1.909 billion (2017 est.)

-$868 million (2016 est.)

country comparison to the world: 163

EXPORTS:

$550 million (2017 est.)

$444.3 million (2016 est.)

country comparison to the world: 175

EXPORTS - PARTNERS:

US 63.9%, Namibia 19.3% (2017)

EXPORTS - COMMODITIES:

Rock lobster, aragonite, crude salt, polystyrene products

IMPORTS:

$3.18 billion (2017 est.)

$2.594 billion (2016 est.)

country comparison to the world: 147

IMPORTS - COMMODITIES:

machinery and transport equipment, manufactures, chemicals, mineral fuels; food and live animals

IMPORTS - PARTNERS:

US 83.2% (2017)

RESERVES OF FOREIGN EXCHANGE AND GOLD:

$1.522 billion (31 December 2017 est.)

$1.002 billion (31 December 2016 est.)

country comparison to the world: 125

DEBT - EXTERNAL:

$17.56 billion (31 December 2013 est.)

$16.35 billion (31 December 2012 est.)

country comparison to the world: 98

EXCHANGE RATES:

Bahamian dollars (BSD) per US dollar

-

1 (2017 est.)

1 (2016 est.)

1 (2015 est.)

1 (2014 est.)

1 (2013 est.)

ENERGY :: BAHAMAS, THE

ELECTRICITY ACCESS:

electrification - total population: 100% (2016)

ELECTRICITY - PRODUCTION:

1.778 billion kWh (2016 est.)

country comparison to the world: 140

ELECTRICITY - CONSUMPTION:

1.654 billion kWh (2016 est.)

country comparison to the world: 145

ELECTRICITY - EXPORTS:

0 kWh (2016 est.)

country comparison to the world: 102

ELECTRICITY - IMPORTS:

0 kWh (2016 est.)

country comparison to the world: 123

ELECTRICITY - INSTALLED GENERATING CAPACITY:

577,000 kW (2016 est.)

country comparison to the world: 141

ELECTRICITY - FROM FOSSIL FUELS:

100% of total installed capacity (2016 est.)

country comparison to the world: 1

ELECTRICITY - FROM NUCLEAR FUELS:

0% of total installed capacity (2017 est.)

country comparison to the world: 43

ELECTRICITY - FROM HYDROELECTRIC PLANTS:

0% of total installed capacity (2017 est.)

country comparison to the world: 155

ELECTRICITY - FROM OTHER RENEWABLE SOURCES:

0% of total installed capacity (2017 est.)

country comparison to the world: 174

CRUDE OIL - PRODUCTION:

0 bbl/day (2017 est.)

country comparison to the world: 107

CRUDE OIL - EXPORTS:

0 bbl/day (2015 est.)

country comparison to the world: 89

CRUDE OIL - IMPORTS:

0 bbl/day (2015 est.)

country comparison to the world: 93

CRUDE OIL - PROVED RESERVES:

0 bbl (1 January 2018 est.)

country comparison to the world: 105

REFINED PETROLEUM PRODUCTS - PRODUCTION:

0 bbl/day (2015 est.)

country comparison to the world: 116

REFINED PETROLEUM PRODUCTS - CONSUMPTION:

20,040 bbl/day (2016 est.)

country comparison to the world: 140

REFINED PETROLEUM PRODUCTS - EXPORTS:

0 bbl/day (2015 est.)

country comparison to the world: 128

REFINED PETROLEUM PRODUCTS - IMPORTS:

19,150 bbl/day (2015 est.)

country comparison to the world: 123

NATURAL GAS - PRODUCTION:

0 cu m (2017 est.)

country comparison to the world: 101

NATURAL GAS - CONSUMPTION:

48,020 cu m (2017 est.)

country comparison to the world: 115

NATURAL GAS - EXPORTS:

0 cu m (2017 est.)

country comparison to the world: 63

NATURAL GAS - IMPORTS:

48,020 cu m (2017 est.)

country comparison to the world: 79

NATURAL GAS - PROVED RESERVES:

0 cu m (1 January 2009 est.)

country comparison to the world: 108

CARBON DIOXIDE EMISSIONS FROM CONSUMPTION OF ENERGY:

3.089 million Mt (2017 est.)

country comparison to the world: 147

COMMUNICATIONS :: BAHAMAS, THE

TELEPHONES - FIXED LINES:

total subscriptions: 113,852 (2017 est.)

subscriptions per 100 inhabitants: 35 (2017 est.)

country comparison to the world: 140

TELEPHONES - MOBILE CELLULAR:

total subscriptions: 353,540 (2017 est.)

subscriptions per 100 inhabitants: 107 (2017 est.)

country comparison to the world: 176

TELEPHONE SYSTEM:

general assessment: modern facilities; the telecom sector provides a relatively high contribution to overall GDP; activation of Mobile Number Portability (MNP) in April 2017, allowing mobile subscribers to port their numbers between competing MNO (mobile network operators) (2017)

domestic: totally automatic system; highly developed; operators focus investment on mobile networks; 35 per 100 fixed-line, 107 per 100 mobile-cellular (2017)

international: country code - 1-242; landing point for the Americas Region Caribbean Ring System (ARCOS-1) and two additional fiber-optic submarine cables that provide links to South and Central America, parts of the Caribbean, and the US; satellite earth stations - 2; the Bahamas Domestic Submarine Network links all of the major islands; (2017)

BROADCAST MEDIA:

The Bahamas has 4 major TV providers that provide service to all major islands in the archipelago; 1 TV station is operated by government-owned, commercially run Broadcasting Corporation of the Bahamas (BCB) and competes freely with 3 privately owned TV stations; multi-channel cable TV subscription service is widely available; there are 31 licensed broadcast (radio) service providers, 28 are privately owned FM radio stations operating on New Providence, Grand Bahama Island, Abaco Island, and on smaller islands in the country; the BCB operates a multi-channel radio broadcasting network that has national coverage; the sector is regulated by the Utilities Regulation and Competition Authority (2017)

INTERNET COUNTRY CODE:

.bs

INTERNET USERS:

total: 261,853 (July 2016 est.)

percent of population: 80% (July 2016 est.)

country comparison to the world: 165

BROADBAND - FIXED SUBSCRIPTIONS:

total: 86,868 (2017 est.)

subscriptions per 100 inhabitants: 26 (2017 est.)

country comparison to the world: 123

TRANSPORTATION :: BAHAMAS, THE

NATIONAL AIR TRANSPORT SYSTEM:

number of registered air carriers: 4 (2015)

inventory of registered aircraft operated by air carriers: 16 (2015)

annual passenger traffic on registered air carriers: 587,516 (2015)

annual freight traffic on registered air carriers: 172,730 mt-km (2015)

CIVIL AIRCRAFT REGISTRATION COUNTRY CODE PREFIX:

C6 (2016)

AIRPORTS:

61 (2013)

country comparison to the world: 79

AIRPORTS - WITH PAVED RUNWAYS:

total: 24 (2017)

over 3,047 m: 2 (2017)

2,438 to 3,047 m: 2 (2017)

1,524 to 2,437 m: 13 (2017)

914 to 1,523 m: 7 (2017)

AIRPORTS - WITH UNPAVED RUNWAYS:

total: 37 (2013)

1,524 to 2,437 m: 4 (2013)

914 to 1,523 m: 16 (2013)

under 914 m: 17 (2013)

HELIPORTS:

1 (2013)

ROADWAYS:

total: 2,700 km (2011)

paved: 1,620 km (2011)

unpaved: 1,080 km (2011)

country comparison to the world: 170

MERCHANT MARINE:

total: 1,440 (2017)

by type: bulk carrier 335, container ship 53, general cargo 98, oil tanker 284, other 670 (2017)

country comparison to the world: 19

PORTS AND TERMINALS:

major seaport(s): Freeport, Nassau, South Riding Point

cruise port(s): Nassau

container port(s) (TEUs): Freeport (1,116,272)(2011)

MILITARY AND SECURITY :: BAHAMAS, THE

MILITARY BRANCHES:

Royal Bahamas Defense Force: Land Force, Navy, Air Wing (2011)

MILITARY SERVICE AGE AND OBLIGATION:

18 years of age for voluntary male and female service; no conscription (2012)

TRANSNATIONAL ISSUES :: BAHAMAS, THE

DISPUTES - INTERNATIONAL:

disagrees with the US on the alignment of the northern axis of a potential maritime boundary

ILLICIT DRUGS:

transshipment point for cocaine and marijuana bound for US and Europe; offshore financial center

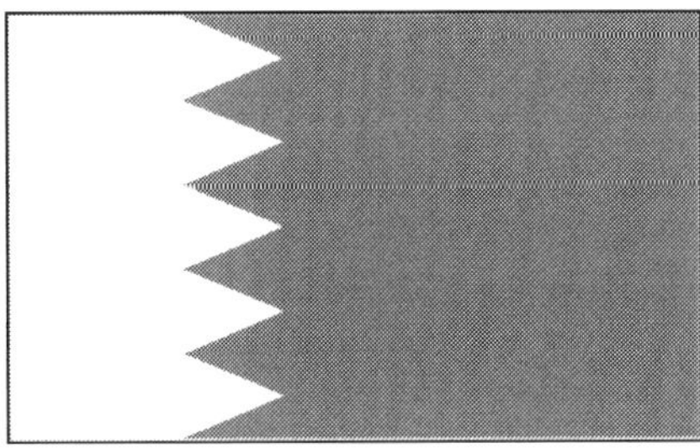

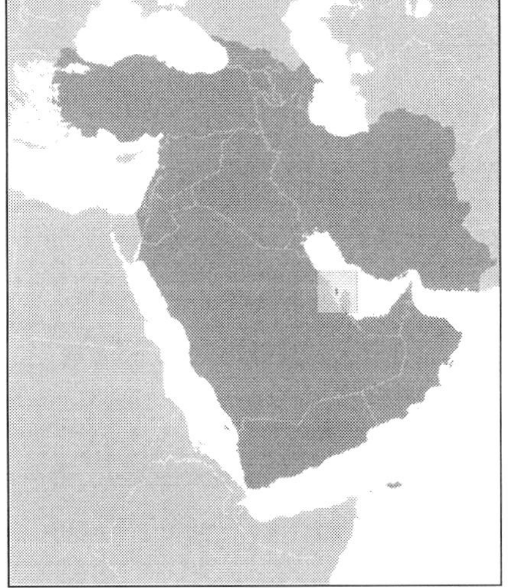

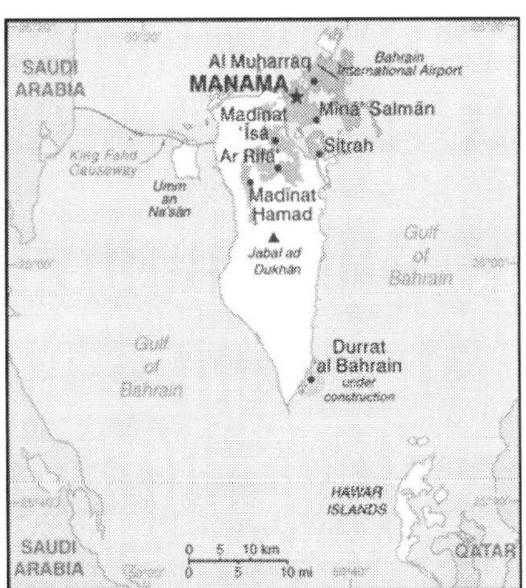

MIDDLE EAST :: BAHRAIN

INTRODUCTION :: BAHRAIN

BACKGROUND:

In 1783, the Sunni Al-Khalifa family took power in Bahrain. In order to secure these holdings, it entered into a series of treaties with the UK during the 19th century that made Bahrain a British protectorate. The archipelago attained its independence in 1971. A steady decline in oil production and reserves since 1970 prompted Bahrain to take steps to diversify its economy, in the process developing petroleum processing and refining, aluminum production, and hospitality and retail sectors. It has also endeavored to become a leading regional banking center, especially with respect to Islamic finance. Bahrain's small size, central location among Gulf countries, economic dependence on Saudi Arabia, and proximity to Iran require it to play a delicate balancing act in foreign affairs among its larger neighbors. Its foreign policy activities usually fall in line with Saudi Arabia and the UAE.

The Sunni royal family has long struggled to manage relations with its large Shia-majority population. In early 2011, amid Arab uprisings elsewhere in the region, the Bahraini Government confronted similar pro-democracy and reform protests at home with police and military action, including deploying Gulf Cooperation Council security forces to Bahrain. Political talks throughout 2014 between the government and opposition and loyalist political groups failed to reach an agreement, prompting opposition political societies to boycott legislative and municipal council elections in late 2014. Ongoing dissatisfaction with the political status quo continues to factor into sporadic clashes between demonstrators and security forces.

GEOGRAPHY :: BAHRAIN

LOCATION:

Middle East, archipelago in the Persian Gulf, east of Saudi Arabia

GEOGRAPHIC COORDINATES:

26 00 N, 50 33 E

MAP REFERENCES:

Middle East

AREA:

total: 760 sq km

land: 760 sq km

water: 0 sq km

country comparison to the world: 188

AREA - COMPARATIVE:

3.5 times the size of Washington, DC

LAND BOUNDARIES:

0 km

COASTLINE:

161 km

MARITIME CLAIMS:

territorial sea: 12 nm

contiguous zone: 24 nm

continental shelf: extending to boundaries to be determined

CLIMATE:

arid; mild, pleasant winters; very hot, humid summers

TERRAIN:

mostly low desert plain rising gently to low central escarpment

ELEVATION:

0 m lowest point: Persian Gulf

135 highest point: Jabal ad Dukhan

NATURAL RESOURCES:

oil, associated and nonassociated natural gas, fish, pearls

LAND USE:

agricultural land: 11.3% (2014 est.)

arable land: 2.1% (2014 est.) / permanent crops: 3.9% (2014 est.) / permanent pasture: 5.3% (2014 est.)

forest: 0.7% (2014 est.)

other: 88% (2014 est.)

IRRIGATED LAND:

40 sq km (2012)

POPULATION DISTRIBUTION:

smallest population of the Gulf States, but urbanization rate exceeds 90%; largest settlement concentration is found on the far northern end of the island in and around Manamah and Al Muharraq

NATURAL HAZARDS:

periodic droughts; dust storms

ENVIRONMENT - CURRENT ISSUES:

desertification resulting from the degradation of limited arable land, periods of drought, and dust storms; coastal degradation (damage to coastlines, coral reefs, and sea vegetation) resulting from oil spills and other discharges from large tankers, oil refineries, and distribution stations; lack of freshwater resources (groundwater and seawater are the only sources for all water needs); lowered water table leaves aquifers vulnerable to saline contamination; desalinization provides some 90% of the country's freshwater

ENVIRONMENT - INTERNATIONAL AGREEMENTS:

party to: Biodiversity, Climate Change, Climate Change-Kyoto Protocol, Desertification, Hazardous Wastes, Law of the Sea, Ozone Layer Protection, Wetlands

signed, but not ratified: none of the selected agreements

GEOGRAPHY - NOTE:

close to primary Middle Eastern petroleum sources; strategic location in Persian Gulf, through which much of the Western world's petroleum must transit to reach open ocean

PEOPLE AND SOCIETY :: BAHRAIN

POPULATION:

1,442,659 (July 2017 est.) (July 2018 est.)

note: immigrants make up approximately 48% of the total population, according to UN data (2017)

country comparison to the world: 154

NATIONALITY:

noun: Bahraini(s)

adjective: Bahraini

ETHNIC GROUPS:

Bahraini 46%, Asian 45.5%, other Arab 4.7%, African 1.6%, European 1%, other 1.2% (includes Gulf Co-operative country nationals, North and South Americans, and Oceanians) (2010 est.)

LANGUAGES:

Arabic (official), English, Farsi, Urdu

RELIGIONS:

Muslim 73.7%, Christian 9.3%, Jewish 0.1%, other 16.9% (2017 est.)

AGE STRUCTURE:

0-14 years: 18.88% (male 138,309 /female 134,067)

15-24 years: 15.49% (male 126,564 /female 96,834)

25-54 years: 56.06% (male 527,417 /female 281,391)

55-64 years: 6.49% (male 59,404 /female 34,284)

65 years and over: 3.08% (male 22,258 /female 22,131) (2018 est.)

DEPENDENCY RATIOS:

total dependency ratio: 30.2 (2015 est.)

youth dependency ratio: 27.1 (2015 est.)

elderly dependency ratio: 3 (2015 est.)

potential support ratio: 33.1 (2015 est.)

MEDIAN AGE:

total: 32.5 years

male: 34 years

female: 29.8 years (2018 est.)

country comparison to the world: 99

POPULATION GROWTH RATE:

2.19% (2018 est.)

country comparison to the world: 37

BIRTH RATE:

13.1 births/1,000 population (2018 est.)

country comparison to the world: 144

DEATH RATE:

2.8 deaths/1,000 population (2018 est.)

country comparison to the world: 223

NET MIGRATION RATE:

12.1 migrant(s)/1,000 population (2017 est.)

country comparison to the world: 6

POPULATION DISTRIBUTION:

smallest population of the Gulf States, but urbanization rate exceeds 90%; largest settlement concentration is found on the far northern end of the island in and around Manamah and Al Muharraq

URBANIZATION:

urban population: 89.3% of total population (2018)

rate of urbanization: 4.38% annual rate of change (2015-20 est.)

MAJOR URBAN AREAS - POPULATION:

565,000 MANAMA (capital) (2018)

SEX RATIO:

at birth: 1.03 male(s)/female (2017 est.)

0-14 years: 1.03 male(s)/female (2017 est.)

15-24 years: 1.3 male(s)/female (2017 est.)

25-54 years: 1.88 male(s)/female (2017 est.)

55-64 years: 1.81 male(s)/female (2017 est.)

65 years and over: 0.95 male(s)/female (2017 est.)

total population: 1.54 male(s)/female (2017 est.)

MATERNAL MORTALITY RATE:

15 deaths/100,000 live births (2015 est.)

country comparison to the world: 135

INFANT MORTALITY RATE:

total: 8.8 deaths/1,000 live births (2018 est.)

male: 9.7 deaths/1,000 live births (2018 est.)

female: 7.7 deaths/1,000 live births (2018 est.)

country comparison to the world: 146

LIFE EXPECTANCY AT BIRTH:

total population: 79.1 years (2018 est.)

male: 76.9 years (2018 est.)

female: 81.5 years (2018 est.)

country comparison to the world: 50

TOTAL FERTILITY RATE:

1.73 children born/woman (2018 est.)

country comparison to the world: 165

HEALTH EXPENDITURES:

5% of GDP (2014)

country comparison to the world: 139

PHYSICIANS DENSITY:

0.92 physicians/1,000 population (2015)

HOSPITAL BED DENSITY:

2 beds/1,000 population (2014)

DRINKING WATER SOURCE:

improved:

urban: 100% of population (2015 est.)

rural: 100% of population (2015 est.)

total: 100% of population (2015 est.)

unimproved:

urban: 0% of population (2015 est.)

rural: 0% of population (2015 est.)

total: 0% of population (2015 est.)

SANITATION FACILITY ACCESS:

improved:

urban: 99.2% of population (2015 est.)

rural: 99.2% of population (2015 est.)

total: 99.2% of population (2015 est.)

unimproved:

urban: 0.8% of population (2015 est.)

rural: 0.8% of population (2015 est.)

total: 0.8% of population (2015 est.)

HIV/AIDS - ADULT PREVALENCE RATE:

<.1% (2017 est.)

HIV/AIDS - PEOPLE LIVING WITH HIV/AIDS:

<500 (2017 est.)

HIV/AIDS - DEATHS:

<100 (2017 est.)

OBESITY - ADULT PREVALENCE RATE:

29.8% (2016)

country comparison to the world: 25

EDUCATION EXPENDITURES:

2.7% of GDP (2016)

country comparison to the world: 158

LITERACY:

definition: age 15 and over can read and write (2015 est.)

total population: 95.7% (2015 est.)

male: 96.9% (2015 est.)

female: 93.5% (2015 est.)

UNEMPLOYMENT, YOUTH AGES 15-24:

total: 5.3% (2012 est.)

male: 2.6% (2012 est.)

female: 12.2% (2012 est.)

country comparison to the world: 153

GOVERNMENT :: BAHRAIN

COUNTRY NAME:

conventional long form: Kingdom of Bahrain

conventional short form: Bahrain

local long form: Mamlakat al Bahrayn

local short form: Al Bahrayn

former: Dilmun, Tylos, Awal, Mishmahig, Bahrayn, State of Bahrain

etymology: the name means "the two seas" in Arabic and refers to the water bodies surrounding the archipelago

GOVERNMENT TYPE:

constitutional monarchy

CAPITAL:

name: Manama

geographic coordinates: 26 14 N, 50 34 E

time difference: UTC+3 (8 hours ahead of Washington, DC, during Standard Time)

etymology: name derives from the Arabic "al manama" meaning "place of rest" or "place of dreams"

ADMINISTRATIVE DIVISIONS:

4 governorates (muhafazat, singular - muhafazah); Asimah (Capital), Janubiyah (Southern), Muharraq, Shamaliyah (Northern)

note: each governorate administered by an appointed governor

INDEPENDENCE:

15 August 1971 (from the UK)

NATIONAL HOLIDAY:

National Day, 16 December (1971); note - 15 August 1971 was the date of independence from the UK, 16 December 1971 was the date of independence from British protection

CONSTITUTION:

history: adopted 14 February 2002 (2017)

amendments: proposed by the king or by at least 15 members of either chamber of the National Assembly followed by submission to an Assembly committee for review and, if approved, submitted to the government for restatement as drafts; passage requires a two-thirds majority vote by the membership of both chambers and validation by the king; constitutional articles on the state religion (Islam), state language (Arabic), and the monarchy and "inherited rule" cannot be amended; amended 2012, 2017 (2017)

LEGAL SYSTEM:

mixed legal system of Islamic law, English common law, Egyptian civil, criminal, and commercial codes; customary law

INTERNATIONAL LAW ORGANIZATION PARTICIPATION:

has not submitted an ICJ jurisdiction declaration; non-party state to the ICCt

CITIZENSHIP:

citizenship by birth: no

citizenship by descent only: the father must be a citizen of Bahrain

dual citizenship recognized: no

residency requirement for naturalization: 25 years; 15 years for Arab nationals

SUFFRAGE:

20 years of age; universal

EXECUTIVE BRANCH:

chief of state: King HAMAD bin Isa Al-Khalifa (since 6 March 1999); Crown Prince SALMAN bin Hamad Al-Khalifa (son of the monarch, born 21 October 1969)

head of government: Prime Minister KHALIFA bin Salman Al-Khalifa (since 1971); First Deputy Prime Minister SALMAN bin Hamad Al Khalifa (since 11 March 2013); Deputy Prime Ministers MUHAMMAD bin Mubarak Al-Khalifa (since September 2005), Jawad bin Salim al-ARAIDH, ALI bin Khalifa bin Salman Al-Khalifa (since 11 December 2006), KHALID bin Abdallah Al Khalifa (since November 2010)

cabinet: Cabinet appointed by the monarch

elections/appointments: the monarchy is hereditary; prime minister appointed by the monarch

LEGISLATIVE BRANCH:

description: bicameral National Assembly consists of:
Consultative Council or Majlis al Shura (40 seats; members appointed by the king)
Council of Representatives or Majlis al Nuwab (40 seats; members directly elected in single-seat constituencies by absolute majority vote in 2 rounds if needed; members serve 4-year renewable terms)

elections:
Consultative Council - last appointments on 7 December 2014 (next NA)
Council of Representatives - first round for 9 members held on 24 November 2018; second round for remaining 31 members held on 1 December 2018 (next to be held in 2022)

election results:
Consultative Council - composition - men 31, women 9, percent of women 22.5%
Council of Representatives (for 2014 election) - percent of vote by society (Bahrain has societies rather than parties) - NA; seats by society - Islamic Al-Asalah (Sunni Salafi) 2, National Islamic Minbar (Sunni Muslim Brotherhood) 1, independent 37; composition - men 37, women 3, percent of women 7.5%; note - total National Assembly percent of women 15%

JUDICIAL BRANCH:

highest courts: Court of Cassation or Supreme Court of Appeal (consists of the chairman and 3 judges); Constitutional Court (consists of the president and 6 members); High Sharia Court of Appeal (court sittings include the president and at least one judge); appeals beyond the High Sharia Court of Appeal are heard by the Supreme Court of Appeal

judge selection and term of office: Court of Cassation judges appointed by royal decree and serve for a specified tenure; Constitutional Court president and members appointed by the Higher Judicial Council, a body chaired by the monarch and includes judges from the Court of Cassation, sharia law courts, and Civil High Courts of Appeal; members serve 9-year terms; High Sharia Court of Appeal member appointment and tenure NA

subordinate courts: Civil High Courts of Appeal; middle and lower civil courts; High Sharia Court of Appeal; Senior Sharia Court; Administrative Courts of Appeal; military courts

note: the judiciary of Bahrain is divided into civil law courts and sharia law courts; sharia courts(involving personal status and family law) are further divided into Sunni Muslim and Shia Muslim

POLITICAL PARTIES AND LEADERS:

note: political parties are prohibited, but political societies were legalized under a July 2005 law

INTERNATIONAL ORGANIZATION PARTICIPATION:

ABEDA, AFESD, AMF, CAEU, CICA, FAO, G-77, GCC, IAEA, IBRD, ICAO, ICC (national committees), ICRM, IDA, IDB, IFC, IFRCS, IHO, ILO, IMF, IMO, IMSO, Interpol, IOC, IOM (observer), IPU, ISO, ITSO, ITU, ITUC (NGOs), LAS, MIGA, NAM, OAPEC, OIC, OPCW, PCA, UN, UNCTAD, UNESCO, UNIDO, UNWTO, UPU, WCO, WFTU (NGOs), WHO, WIPO, WMO, WTO

DIPLOMATIC REPRESENTATION IN THE US:

chief of mission: Ambassador Abdulla bin Rashid AL KHALIFA (since 21 July 2017)

chancery: 3502 International Drive NW, Washington, DC 20008

telephone: [1] (202) 342-1111

FAX: [1] (202) 362-2192

consulate(s) general: New York

DIPLOMATIC REPRESENTATION FROM THE US:

chief of mission: Ambassador Justin H. SIBERELL (since November 2017)

embassy: Building #979, Road 3119 (next to Al-Ahli Sports Club), Block 331, Zinj District, Manama

mailing address: PSC 451, Box 660, FPO AE 09834-5100; international mail: American Embassy, Box 26431, Manama

telephone: [973] 1724-2700

FAX: [973] 1727-2594

FLAG DESCRIPTION:

red, the traditional color for flags of Persian Gulf states, with a white serrated band (five white points) on the hoist side; the five points represent the five pillars of Islam

note: until 2002, the flag had eight white points, but this was reduced to five to avoid confusion with the Qatari flag

NATIONAL SYMBOL(S):

a red field surmounted by a white serrated band with five white points; national colors: red, white

NATIONAL ANTHEM:

name: "Bahrainona" (Our Bahrain)

lyrics/music: unknown

note: adopted 1971; although Mohamed Sudqi AYYASH wrote the original lyrics, they were changed in 2002 following the transformation of Bahrain from an emirate to a kingdom

ECONOMY :: BAHRAIN

ECONOMY - OVERVIEW:

Oil and natural gas play a dominant role in Bahrain's economy. Despite the Government's past efforts to diversify the economy, oil still comprises 85% of Bahraini budget revenues. In the last few years lower world energy prices have generated sizable budget deficits - about 10% of GDP in 2017 alone. Bahrain has few options for covering these deficits, with low foreign assets and fewer oil resources compared to its GCC neighbors. The three major US credit agencies downgraded Bahrain's sovereign debt rating to "junk" status in 2016, citing persistently low oil prices and the government's high debt levels. Nevertheless, Bahrain was able to raise about $4 billion by issuing foreign currency denominated debt in 2017. Other major economic activities are production of aluminum - Bahrain's second biggest export after oil and gas –finance, and construction. Bahrain continues to seek new natural gas supplies as feedstock to support its expanding petrochemical and aluminum industries. In April 2018 Bahrain announced it had found a significant oil field off the country's west coast, but is still assessing how much of the oil can be extracted profitably.

In addition to addressing its current fiscal woes, Bahraini authorities face the long-term challenge of boosting Bahrain's regional competitiveness — especially regarding industry, finance, and tourism — and reconciling revenue constraints with popular pressure to maintain generous state subsidies and a large public sector. Since 2015, the government lifted subsidies on meat, diesel, kerosene, and gasoline and has begun to phase in higher prices for electricity and water. As part of its diversification plans, Bahrain implemented a Free Trade Agreement (FTA) with the US in August 2006, the first FTA between the US and a Gulf state. It plans to introduce a Value Added Tax (VAT) by the end of 2018.

GDP (PURCHASING POWER PARITY):

$71.17 billion (2017 est.)

$68.59 billion (2016 est.)

$66.3 billion (2015 est.)

note: data are in 2017 dollars

country comparison to the world: 100

GDP (OFFICIAL EXCHANGE RATE):

$35.33 billion (2017 est.) (2017 est.)

GDP - REAL GROWTH RATE:

3.8% (2017 est.)

3.5% (2016 est.)

2.9% (2015 est.)

country comparison to the world: 86

GDP - PER CAPITA (PPP):

$49,000 (2017 est.)

$48,200 (2016 est.)

$48,400 (2015 est.)

note: data are in 2017 dollars

country comparison to the world: 33

GROSS NATIONAL SAVING:

19.8% of GDP (2017 est.)

21.2% of GDP (2016 est.)

22% of GDP (2015 est.)

country comparison to the world: 99

GDP - COMPOSITION, BY END USE:

household consumption: 45.8% (2017 est.)

government consumption: 15.5% (2017 est.)

investment in fixed capital: 26.1% (2017 est.)

investment in inventories: 0.4% (2017 est.)

exports of goods and services: 80.2% (2017 est.)

imports of goods and services: -67.9% (2017 est.)

GDP - COMPOSITION, BY SECTOR OF ORIGIN:

agriculture: 0.3% (2017 est.)

industry: 39.3% (2017 est.)

services: 60.4% (2017 est.)

AGRICULTURE - PRODUCTS:

fruit, vegetables; poultry, dairy products; shrimp, fish

INDUSTRIES:

petroleum processing and refining, aluminum smelting, iron pelletization, fertilizers, Islamic and offshore banking, insurance, ship repairing, tourism

INDUSTRIAL PRODUCTION GROWTH RATE:

0.6% (2017 est.)

country comparison to the world: 165

LABOR FORCE:

831,600 (2017 est.)

note: excludes unemployed; 44% of the population in the 15-64 age group is non-national

country comparison to the world: 149

LABOR FORCE - BY OCCUPATION:

agriculture: 1%

industry: 32%

services: 67% (2004 est.)

UNEMPLOYMENT RATE:

3.6% (2017 est.)

3.7% (2016 est.)

note: official estimate; actual rate is higher

country comparison to the world: 43

POPULATION BELOW POVERTY LINE:

NA

HOUSEHOLD INCOME OR CONSUMPTION BY PERCENTAGE SHARE:

lowest 10%: NA

highest 10%: NA

BUDGET:

revenues: 5.854 billion (2017 est.)

expenditures: 9.407 billion (2017 est.)

TAXES AND OTHER REVENUES:

16.6% (of GDP) (2017 est.)

country comparison to the world: 176

BUDGET SURPLUS (+) OR DEFICIT (-):

-10.1% (of GDP) (2017 est.)

country comparison to the world: 211

PUBLIC DEBT:

88.5% of GDP (2017 est.)

81.4% of GDP (2016 est.)

country comparison to the world: 26

FISCAL YEAR:

calendar year

INFLATION RATE (CONSUMER PRICES):

1.4% (2017 est.)

2.8% (2016 est.)

country comparison to the world: 76

CENTRAL BANK DISCOUNT RATE:

1.75% (18 December 2017)

0.5% (31 December 2010)

country comparison to the world: 121

COMMERCIAL BANK PRIME LENDING RATE:

5.33% (31 December 2017 est.)

5.18% (31 December 2016 est.)

country comparison to the world: 139

STOCK OF NARROW MONEY:

$9.185 billion (31 December 2017 est.)

$9.078 billion (31 December 2016 est.)

country comparison to the world: 84

STOCK OF BROAD MONEY:

$9.185 billion (31 December 2017 est.)

$9.078 billion (31 December 2016 est.)

country comparison to the world: 86

STOCK OF DOMESTIC CREDIT:

$29.72 billion (31 December 2017 est.)

$29.08 billion (31 December 2016 est.)

country comparison to the world: 80

MARKET VALUE OF PUBLICLY TRADED SHARES:

$19.25 billion (31 December 2015 est.)

$22.07 billion (31 December 2014 est.)

$18.57 billion (31 December 2013 est.)

country comparison to the world: 64

CURRENT ACCOUNT BALANCE:

-$1.6 billion (2017 est.)

-$1.493 billion (2016 est.)

country comparison to the world: 159

EXPORTS:

$15.38 billion (2017 est.)

$12.78 billion (2016 est.)

country comparison to the world: 77

EXPORTS - PARTNERS:

UAE 19.6%, Saudi Arabia 11.7%, US 10.8%, Oman 8.1%, China 6.5%, Qatar 5.7%, Japan 4.2% (2017)

EXPORTS - COMMODITIES:

petroleum and petroleum products, aluminum, textiles

IMPORTS:

$16.08 billion (2017 est.)

$13.59 billion (2016 est.)

country comparison to the world: 85

IMPORTS - COMMODITIES:

crude oil, machinery, chemicals

IMPORTS - PARTNERS:

China 8.8%, UAE 7.2%, US 7.1%, Australia 5.3%, Japan 4.8% (2017)

RESERVES OF FOREIGN EXCHANGE AND GOLD:

$2.349 billion (31 December 2017 est.)

$3.094 billion (31 December 2016 est.)

country comparison to the world: 118

DEBT - EXTERNAL:

$52.15 billion (31 December 2017 est.)

$42.55 billion (31 December 2016 est.)

country comparison to the world: 63

STOCK OF DIRECT FOREIGN INVESTMENT - AT HOME:

$22.08 billion (31 December 2017 est.)

$21.56 billion (31 December 2016 est.)

country comparison to the world: 76

STOCK OF DIRECT FOREIGN INVESTMENT - ABROAD:

$10.66 billion (31 December 2017 est.)

$10.5 billion (31 December 2016 est.)

country comparison to the world: 65

EXCHANGE RATES:

Bahraini dinars (BHD) per US dollar -

0.376 (2017 est.)

0.376 (2016 est.)

0.376 (2015 est.)

0.376 (2014 est.)

0.376 (2013 est.)

ENERGY :: BAHRAIN

ELECTRICITY ACCESS:

population without electricity: 41,317 (2012)

electrification - total population: 98% (2012)

electrification - urban areas: 98% (2012)

electrification - rural areas: 93% (2012)

ELECTRICITY - PRODUCTION:

26.81 billion kWh (2016 est.)

country comparison to the world: 70

ELECTRICITY - CONSUMPTION:

26.11 billion kWh (2016 est.)

country comparison to the world: 67

ELECTRICITY - EXPORTS:

213 million kWh (2015 est.)

country comparison to the world: 74

ELECTRICITY - IMPORTS:

276 million kWh (2016 est.)

country comparison to the world: 89

ELECTRICITY - INSTALLED GENERATING CAPACITY:

3.928 million kW (2016 est.)

country comparison to the world: 90

ELECTRICITY - FROM FOSSIL FUELS:

100% of total installed capacity (2016 est.)

country comparison to the world: 2

ELECTRICITY - FROM NUCLEAR FUELS:

0% of total installed capacity (2017 est.)

country comparison to the world: 44

ELECTRICITY - FROM HYDROELECTRIC PLANTS:

0% of total installed capacity (2017 est.)

country comparison to the world: 156

ELECTRICITY - FROM OTHER RENEWABLE SOURCES:

0% of total installed capacity (2017 est.)

country comparison to the world: 175

CRUDE OIL - PRODUCTION:

45,000 bbl/day (2017 est.)

country comparison to the world: 55

CRUDE OIL - EXPORTS:

0 bbl/day (2015 est.)

country comparison to the world: 90

CRUDE OIL - IMPORTS:

226,200 bbl/day (2015 est.)

country comparison to the world: 29

CRUDE OIL - PROVED RESERVES:

124.6 million bbl (1 January 2018 est.)

country comparison to the world: 67

REFINED PETROLEUM PRODUCTS - PRODUCTION:

274,500 bbl/day (2015 est.)

country comparison to the world: 45

REFINED PETROLEUM PRODUCTS - CONSUMPTION:

61,000 bbl/day (2016 est.)

country comparison to the world: 94

REFINED PETROLEUM PRODUCTS - EXPORTS:

245,300 bbl/day (2015 est.)

country comparison to the world: 30

REFINED PETROLEUM PRODUCTS - IMPORTS:

14,530 bbl/day (2015 est.)

country comparison to the world: 136

NATURAL GAS - PRODUCTION:

15.89 billion cu m (2017 est.)

country comparison to the world: 36

NATURAL GAS - CONSUMPTION:

15.89 billion cu m (2017 est.)

country comparison to the world: 42

NATURAL GAS - EXPORTS:

0 cu m (2017 est.)

country comparison to the world: 64

NATURAL GAS - IMPORTS:

0 cu m (2017 est.)

country comparison to the world: 88

NATURAL GAS - PROVED RESERVES:

92.03 billion cu m (1 January 2018 est.)

country comparison to the world: 53

CARBON DIOXIDE EMISSIONS FROM CONSUMPTION OF ENERGY:

37.98 million Mt (2017 est.)

country comparison to the world: 67

COMMUNICATIONS :: BAHRAIN

TELEPHONES - FIXED LINES:

total subscriptions: 285,318 (2017 est.)

subscriptions per 100 inhabitants: 20 (2017 est.)

country comparison to the world: 117

TELEPHONES - MOBILE CELLULAR:

total subscriptions: 2,364,477 (2017 est.)

subscriptions per 100 inhabitants: 168 (2017 est.)

country comparison to the world: 147

TELEPHONE SYSTEM:

general assessment: modern system; well developed LTE networks, 5G trials tested and deployment in near future; mobile penetration is high compared to the region; development of it own National Broadband Network (NBN); competion is good and telecos are regulated (2017)

domestic: modern fiber-optic integrated services; digital network with rapidly growing use of mobile-cellular telephones; 20 per 100 fixed-line, 168 per 100 mobile-cellular; (2017)

international: country code - 973; landing point for the Fiber-Optic Link Around the Globe (FLAG) submarine cable network that provides links to Asia, Middle East, Europe, and US; tropospheric scatter to Qatar and UAE; microwave radio relay to Saudi Arabia; satellite earth station - 1 (2016)

BROADCAST MEDIA:

state-run Bahrain Radio and Television Corporation (BRTC) operates 5 terrestrial TV networks and several radio stations; satellite TV systems provide access to international broadcasts; 1 private FM station directs broadcasts to Indian listeners; radio and TV broadcasts from countries in the region are available (2009)

INTERNET COUNTRY CODE:

.bh

INTERNET USERS:

total: 1,351,326 (July 2016 est.)

percent of population: 98% (July 2016 est.)

country comparison to the world: 124

BROADBAND - FIXED SUBSCRIPTIONS:

total: 213,633 (2017 est.)

subscriptions per 100 inhabitants: 15 (2017 est.)

country comparison to the world: 106

TRANSPORTATION :: BAHRAIN

NATIONAL AIR TRANSPORT SYSTEM:

number of registered air carriers: 6 (2015)

inventory of registered aircraft operated by air carriers: 42 (2015)

annual passenger traffic on registered air carriers: 5,313,756 (2015)

annual freight traffic on registered air carriers: 240,107,004 mt-km (2015)

CIVIL AIRCRAFT REGISTRATION COUNTRY CODE PREFIX:

A9C (2016)

AIRPORTS:

4 (2013)

country comparison to the world: 184

AIRPORTS - WITH PAVED RUNWAYS:

total: 4 (2017)

over 3,047 m: 3 (2017)

914 to 1,523 m: 1 (2017)

HELIPORTS:

1 (2013)

PIPELINES:

20 km gas, 54 km oil (2013)

ROADWAYS:

total: 4,122 km (2010)

paved: 3,392 km (2010)

unpaved: 730 km (2010)

country comparison to the world: 156

MERCHANT MARINE:

total: 260 (2017)

by type: container ship 3, general cargo 11, oil tanker 4, other 242 (2017)

country comparison to the world: 60

PORTS AND TERMINALS:

major seaport(s): Mina' Salman, Sitrah

MILITARY AND SECURITY :: BAHRAIN

MILITARY EXPENDITURES:

4.59% of GDP (2015)

4.42% of GDP (2014)

4.14% of GDP (2013)

country comparison to the world: 11

MILITARY BRANCHES:

Bahrain Defense Force (BDF): Royal Bahraini Army (RBA), Royal Bahraini Navy (RBN), Royal Bahraini Air Force (RBAF), Royal Bahraini Air Defense Force (RBADF) (2013)

MILITARY SERVICE AGE AND OBLIGATION:

18 years of age for voluntary military service; 15 years of age for NCOs, technicians, and cadets; no conscription (2012)

TRANSNATIONAL ISSUES :: BAHRAIN

DISPUTES - INTERNATIONAL:

none

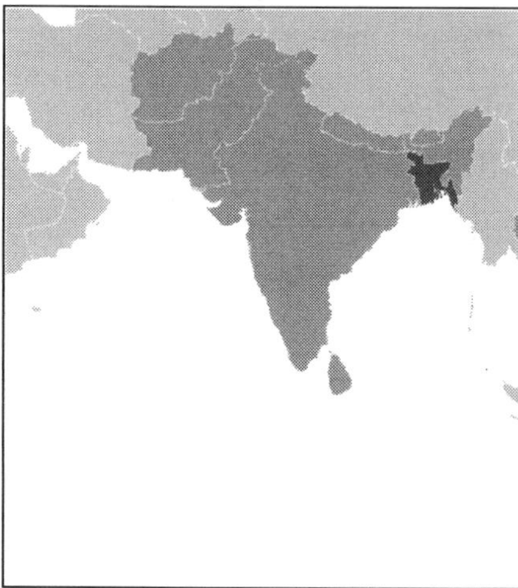

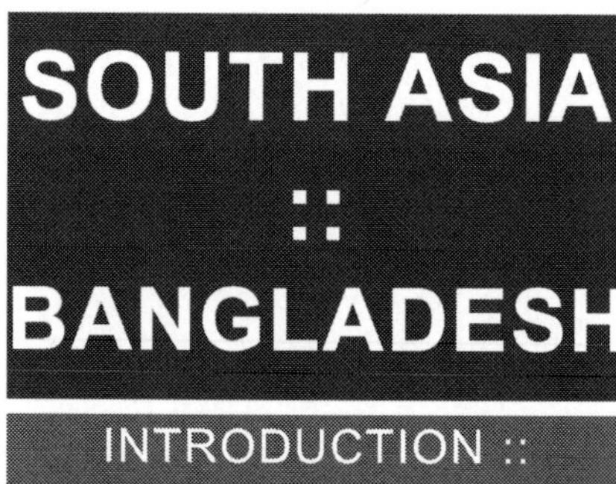

SOUTH ASIA :: BANGLADESH

INTRODUCTION :: BANGLADESH

BACKGROUND:

The huge delta region formed at the confluence of the Ganges and Brahmaputra River systems - now referred to as Bangladesh - was a loosely incorporated outpost of various empires centered on the Gangetic plain for much of the first millennium A.D. Muslim conversions and settlement in the region began in the 10th century, primarily from Arab and Persian traders and preachers. Europeans established trading posts in the area in the 16th century. Eventually the area known as Bengal, primarily Hindu in the western section and mostly Muslim in the eastern half, became part of British India. Partition in 1947 resulted in an eastern wing of Pakistan in the Muslim-majority area, which became East Pakistan. Calls for greater autonomy and animosity between the eastern and western wings of Pakistan led to a Bengali independence movement. That movement, led by the Awami League (AL) and supported by India, won the independence war for Bangladesh in 1971.

The post-independence AL government faced daunting challenges and in 1975 was overthrown by the military, triggering a series of military coups that resulted in a military-backed government and subsequent creation of the Bangladesh Nationalist Party (BNP) in 1978. That government also ended in a coup in 1981, followed by military-backed rule until democratic elections occurred in 1991. The BNP and AL alternated in power between 1991 and 2013, with the exception of a military-backed, emergency caretaker regime that suspended parliamentary elections planned for January 2007 in an effort to reform the political system and root out corruption. That government returned the country to fully democratic rule in December 2008 with the election of the AL and Prime Minister Sheikh HASINA. In January 2014, the incumbent AL won the national election by an overwhelming majority after the BNP boycotted, extending HASINA's term as prime minister. With the help of international development assistance, Bangladesh has reduced the poverty rate from over half of the population to less than a third, achieved Millennium Development Goals for maternal and child health, and made great progress in food security since independence. The economy has grown at an annual average of about 6% over the last two decades and the country reached World Bank lower-middle income status in 2014.

GEOGRAPHY :: BANGLADESH

LOCATION:

Southern Asia, bordering the Bay of Bengal, between Burma and India

GEOGRAPHIC COORDINATES:

24 00 N, 90 00 E

MAP REFERENCES:

Asia

AREA:

total: 148,460 sq km

land: 130,170 sq km

water: 18,290 sq km

country comparison to the world: 95

AREA - COMPARATIVE:

slightly larger than Pennsylvania and New Jersey combined; slightly smaller than Iowa

LAND BOUNDARIES:

total: 4,413 km

border countries (2): Burma 271 km, India 4142 km

COASTLINE:

580 km

MARITIME CLAIMS:

territorial sea: 12 nm

exclusive economic zone: 200 nm

contiguous zone: 18 nm

continental shelf: to the outer limits of the continental margin

CLIMATE:

tropical; mild winter (October to March); hot, humid summer (March to June); humid, warm rainy monsoon (June to October)

TERRAIN:

mostly flat alluvial plain; hilly in southeast

ELEVATION:

mean elevation: 85 m

elevation extremes: 0 m lowest point: Indian Ocean

1230 highest point: Keokradong

NATURAL RESOURCES:

natural gas, arable land, timber, coal

LAND USE:

agricultural land: 70.1% (2014 est.)

arable land: 59% (2014 est.) / permanent crops: 6.5% (2014 est.) / permanent pasture: 4.6% (2014 est.)

forest: 11.1% (2014 est.)

other: 18.8% (2014 est.)

IRRIGATED LAND:

53,000 sq km (2012)

NATURAL HAZARDS:

droughts; cyclones; much of the country routinely inundated during the summer monsoon season

ENVIRONMENT - CURRENT ISSUES:

many people are landless and forced to live on and cultivate flood-prone land; waterborne diseases prevalent in surface water; water pollution, especially of fishing areas, results from the use of commercial pesticides; ground water contaminated by naturally occurring arsenic; intermittent water shortages because of falling water tables in the northern and central parts of the country; soil degradation and erosion; deforestation; destruction of wetlands; severe overpopulation with noise pollution

ENVIRONMENT - INTERNATIONAL AGREEMENTS:

party to: Biodiversity, Climate Change, Climate Change-Kyoto Protocol, Desertification, Endangered Species, Environmental Modification, Hazardous Wastes, Law of the Sea, Ozone Layer Protection, Ship Pollution, Wetlands

signed, but not ratified: none of the selected agreements

GEOGRAPHY - NOTE:

most of the country is situated on deltas of large rivers flowing from the Himalayas: the Ganges unites with the Jamuna (main channel of the Brahmaputra) and later joins the Meghna to eventually empty into the Bay of Bengal

PEOPLE AND SOCIETY :: BANGLADESH

POPULATION:

159,453,001 (July 2018 est.)

country comparison to the world: 8

NATIONALITY:

noun: Bangladeshi(s)

adjective: Bangladeshi

ETHNIC GROUPS:

Bengali at least 98%, indigenous ethnic groups 1.1% (2011 est.)

note: Bangladesh's government recognizes 27 indigenous ethnic groups under the 2010 Cultural Institution for Small Anthropological Groups Act; other sources estimate there are about 75 ethnic groups; critics of the 2011 census claim that it underestimates the size of Bangladesh's ethnic population

LANGUAGES:

Bangla 98.8% (official, also known as Bengali), other 1.2% (2011 est.)

RELIGIONS:

Muslim 89.1%, Hindu 10%, other 0.9% (includes Buddhist, Christian) (2013 est.)

AGE STRUCTURE:

0-14 years: 27.29% (male 22,135,349 /female 21,373,470)

15-24 years: 19.14% (male 15,313,674 /female 15,200,861)

25-54 years: 40.07% (male 30,626,005 /female 33,267,339)

55-64 years: 7.09% (male 5,582,450 /female 5,716,763)

65 years and over: 6.42% (male 4,844,612 /female 5,392,478) (2018 est.)

DEPENDENCY RATIOS:

total dependency ratio: 52.6 (2015 est.)

youth dependency ratio: 44.9 (2015 est.)

elderly dependency ratio: 7.7 (2015 est.)

potential support ratio: 13 (2015 est.)

MEDIAN AGE:

total: 27.1 years

male: 26.3 years

female: 27.8 years (2018 est.)

country comparison to the world: 146

POPULATION GROWTH RATE:

1.02% (2018 est.)

country comparison to the world: 105

BIRTH RATE:

18.6 births/1,000 population (2018 est.)

country comparison to the world: 89

DEATH RATE:

5.4 deaths/1,000 population (2018 est.)

country comparison to the world: 179

NET MIGRATION RATE:

-3.1 migrant(s)/1,000 population (2017 est.)

country comparison to the world: 175

URBANIZATION:

urban population: 36.6% of total population (2018)

rate of urbanization: 3.17% annual rate of change (2015-20 est.)

MAJOR URBAN AREAS - POPULATION:

19.578 million DHAKA (capital), 4.816 million Chittagong, 975,000 Khulna, 880,000 Rajshahi, 776,000 Sylhet (2018)

SEX RATIO:

at birth: 1.04 male(s)/female (2017 est.)

0-14 years: 1.04 male(s)/female (2017 est.)

15-24 years: 1 male(s)/female (2017 est.)

25-54 years: 0.93 male(s)/female (2017 est.)

55-64 years: 0.98 male(s)/female (2017 est.)

65 years and over: 0.97 male(s)/female (2017 est.)

total population: 0.97 male(s)/female (2017 est.)

MOTHER'S MEAN AGE AT FIRST BIRTH:

18.5 years (2014 est.)

note: median age at first birth among women 25-29

MATERNAL MORTALITY RATE:

176 deaths/100,000 live births (2015 est.)

country comparison to the world: 55

INFANT MORTALITY RATE:

total: 30.5 deaths/1,000 live births (2018 est.)

male: 32.8 deaths/1,000 live births (2018 est.)

female: 28.1 deaths/1,000 live births (2018 est.)

country comparison to the world: 60

LIFE EXPECTANCY AT BIRTH:

total population: 73.7 years (2018 est.)

male: 71.5 years (2018 est.)

female: 75.9 years (2018 est.)

country comparison to the world: 133

TOTAL FERTILITY RATE:

2.15 children born/woman (2018 est.)

country comparison to the world: 98

CONTRACEPTIVE PREVALENCE RATE:

62.3% (2014)

HEALTH EXPENDITURES:

2.8% of GDP (2014)

country comparison to the world: 183

PHYSICIANS DENSITY:

0.47 physicians/1,000 population (2015)

HOSPITAL BED DENSITY:

0.8 beds/1,000 population (2015)

DRINKING WATER SOURCE:

improved:

urban: 86.5% of population (2015 est.)

rural: 87% of population (2015 est.)

total: 86.9% of population (2015 est.)

unimproved:

urban: 13.5% of population (2015 est.)

rural: 13% of population (2015 est.)

total: 13.1% of population (2015 est.)

SANITATION FACILITY ACCESS:

improved:

urban: 57.7% of population (2015 est.)

rural: 62.1% of population (2015 est.)

total: 60.6% of population (2015 est.)

unimproved:

urban: 42.3% of population (2015 est.)

rural: 37.9% of population (2015 est.)

total: 39.4% of population (2015 est.)

HIV/AIDS - ADULT PREVALENCE RATE:

<.1% (2017 est.)

HIV/AIDS - PEOPLE LIVING WITH HIV/AIDS:

13,000 (2017 est.)

country comparison to the world: 92

HIV/AIDS - DEATHS:

1,100 (2017 est.)

country comparison to the world: 62

MAJOR INFECTIOUS DISEASES:

degree of risk: high (2016)

food or waterborne diseases: bacterial and protozoal diarrhea, hepatitis A and E, and typhoid fever (2016)

vectorborne diseases: dengue fever and malaria are high risks in some locations (2016)

water contact diseases: leptospirosis (2016)

animal contact diseases: rabies (2016)

OBESITY - ADULT PREVALENCE RATE:

3.6% (2016)

country comparison to the world: 191

CHILDREN UNDER THE AGE OF 5 YEARS UNDERWEIGHT:

32.6% (2014)

country comparison to the world: 5

EDUCATION EXPENDITURES:

2.5% of GDP (2016)

country comparison to the world: 164

LITERACY:

definition: age 15 and over can read and write (2016 est.)

total population: 72.8% (2016 est.)

male: 75.6% (2016 est.)

female: 69.9% (2016 est.)

SCHOOL LIFE EXPECTANCY (PRIMARY TO TERTIARY EDUCATION):

total: 10 years (2011)

male: 10 years (2011)

female: 10 years (2011)

UNEMPLOYMENT, YOUTH AGES 15-24:

total: 11.4% (2016 est.)

male: 10.1% (2016 est.)

female: 14.1% (2016 est.)

country comparison to the world: 112

GOVERNMENT :: BANGLADESH

COUNTRY NAME:

conventional long form: People's Republic of Bangladesh

conventional short form: Bangladesh

local long form: Gana Prajatantri Bangladesh

local short form: Bangladesh

former: East Bengal, East Pakistan

etymology: the name - a compound of the Bengali words "Bangla" (Bengal) and "desh" (country) - means "Country of Bengal"

GOVERNMENT TYPE:

parliamentary republic

CAPITAL:

name: Dhaka

geographic coordinates: 23 43 N, 90 24 E

time difference: UTC+6 (11 hours ahead of Washington, DC, during Standard Time)

etymology: the origins of the name are unclear, but some sources state that the city's site was originally called "dhakka," meaning "watchtower," and that the area served as a watch-station for Bengal rulers

ADMINISTRATIVE DIVISIONS:

8 divisions; Barisal, Chittagong, Dhaka, Khulna, Mymensingh, Rajshahi, Rangpur, Sylhet

INDEPENDENCE:

16 December 1971 (from West Pakistan)

NATIONAL HOLIDAY:

Independence Day, 26 March (1971); Victory Day, 16 December (1971); note - 26 March 1971 is the date of the Awami League's declaration of an independent Bangladesh, and 16 December (Victory Day) memorializes the military victory over Pakistan and the official creation of the state of Bangladesh

CONSTITUTION:

history: previous 1935, 1956, 1962 (preindependence); latest enacted 4 November 1972, effective 16 December 1972, suspended March 1982, restored November 1986 (2017)

amendments: proposed by the House of the Nation; approval requires at least two-thirds majority vote by the House membership and assent to by the president of the republic; amended many times, last in 2014 (2017)

LEGAL SYSTEM:

mixed legal system of mostly English common law and Islamic law

INTERNATIONAL LAW ORGANIZATION PARTICIPATION:

has not submitted an ICJ jurisdiction declaration; accepts ICCt jurisdiction

CITIZENSHIP:

citizenship by birth: no

citizenship by descent only: at least one parent must be a citizen of Bangladesh

dual citizenship recognized: yes, but limited to select countries

residency requirement for naturalization: 5 years

SUFFRAGE:

18 years of age; universal

EXECUTIVE BRANCH:

chief of state: President Abdul HAMID (since 24 April 2013); note - Abdul HAMID served as acting president following the death of Zillur RAHMAN in March 2013; HAMID was subsequently indirectly elected by the National Parliament and sworn in 24 April 2013

head of government: Prime Minister Sheikh HASINA (since 6 January 2009)

cabinet: Cabinet selected by the prime minister, appointed by the president

elections/appointments: president indirectly elected by the National Parliament for a 5-year term (eligible for a second term); election last held on 7 February 2018 (next to be held by 2023); the president appoints as prime minister the majority party leader in the National Parliament

election results: President Abdul HAMID (AL) reelected by the National Parliament unopposed for a second term; Sheikh HASINA reappointed prime minister as leader of the majority AL party following parliamentary elections in 2014

LEGISLATIVE BRANCH:

description: unicameral House of the Nation or Jatiya Sangsad (350 seats; 300 members in single-seat territorial constituencies directly elected by simple majority popular vote; 50 members - reserved for women only - indirectly elected by the elected members by proportional representation vote using single transferable vote; all members serve 5-year terms)

elections: last held on 5 January 2014 (next to be held by January 2019); note - the 5 January 2014 poll was marred by widespread violence, boycotts, general strikes, and low voter turnout

election results: percent of vote by party - AL 79.1%, JP (Ershad) 11.3%, WP 2.1%, JSD 1.8%, other 1%, independent 4.8%; seats by party - AL 234, JP 34, WP 6, JSD 5, other 5, independent 15; 1 seat repolled; composition - men 281, women 69, percent of women 19.7%

JUDICIAL BRANCH:

highest courts: Supreme Court of Bangladesh (organized into the Appellate Division with 7 justices and the High Court Division with 99 justices)

judge selection and term of office: chief justice and justices appointed by the president; justices serve until retirement at age 67

subordinate courts: subordinate courts: civil courts include: Assistant Judge's Court; Joint District Judge's Court; Additional District Judge's Court; District Judge's Court; criminal courts include: Court of Sessions; Court of Metropolitan Sessions; Metropolitan Magistrate Courts; Magistrate Court; special courts/tribunals

POLITICAL PARTIES AND LEADERS:

Awami League or AL [Sheikh HASINA]
Bangladesh Nationalist Front or BNF [Abdul Kalam AZADI]Bangladesh Nationalist Party or BNP [Khaleda ZIA]
Bangladesh Tariqat Federation or BTF [Syed Nozibul Bashar MAIZBHANDARI]
Jamaat-i-Islami Bangladesh or JIB (Makbul AHMAD)
Jatiya Party or JP (Ershad faction) [Hussain Mohammad ERSHAD]
Jatiya Party or JP (Manju faction) [Anwar Hossain MANJU]Liberal Democratic Party or LDP [Oli AHMED]
National Socialist Party or JSD [KHALEQUZZAMAN]
Workers Party or WP [Rashed Khan MENON]

INTERNATIONAL ORGANIZATION PARTICIPATION:

ADB, ARF, BIMSTEC, C, CD, CICA (observer), CP, D-8, FAO, G-77, IAEA, IBRD, ICAO, ICC (national committees), ICRM, IDA, IDB, IFAD, IFC, IFRCS, IHO, ILO, IMF, IMO, IMSO, Interpol, IOC, IOM, IPU, ISO, ITSO, ITU, ITUC (NGOs), MIGA, MINURSO, MINUSMA, MONUSCO, NAM, OIC, OPCW, PCA, SAARC, SACEP, UN, UNAMID, UNCTAD, UNESCO, UNHCR, UNIDO, UNIFIL, UNMIL, UNMISS, UNOCI, UNWTO, UPU, WCO, WFTU (NGOs), WHO, WIPO, WMO, WTO

DIPLOMATIC REPRESENTATION IN THE US:

chief of mission: Ambassador Mohammad ZIAUDDIN (since 18 September 2014)

chancery: 3510 International Drive NW, Washington, DC 20008

telephone: [1] (202) 244-0183

FAX: [1] (202) 244-2771

consulate(s) general: Los Angeles, New York

DIPLOMATIC REPRESENTATION FROM THE US:

chief of mission: Ambassador Earl Robert MILLER (since 29 November 2018)

embassy: Madani Avenue, Baridhara, Dhaka 1212

mailing address: G. P. O. Box 323, Dhaka 1000

telephone: [880] (2) 5566-2000

FAX: [880] (2) 5566-2915

FLAG DESCRIPTION:

green field with a large red disk shifted slightly to the hoist side of center; the red disk represents the rising sun and the sacrifice to achieve independence; the green field symbolizes the lush vegetation of Bangladesh

NATIONAL SYMBOL(S):

Bengal tiger, water lily; national colors: green, red

NATIONAL ANTHEM:

name: "Amar Shonar Bangla" (My Golden Bengal)

lyrics/music: Rabindranath TAGORE

note: adopted 1971; Rabindranath TAGORE, a Nobel laureate, also wrote India's national anthem

ECONOMY :: BANGLADESH

ECONOMY - OVERVIEW:

Bangladesh's economy has grown roughly 6% per year since 2005 despite prolonged periods of political instability, poor infrastructure, endemic corruption, insufficient power supplies, and slow implementation of economic reforms. Although more than half of GDP is generated through the services sector, almost half of Bangladeshis are employed in the agriculture sector, with rice as the single-most-important product.

Garments, the backbone of Bangladesh's industrial sector, accounted for more than 80% of total exports in FY 2016-17. The industrial sector continues to grow, despite the need for improvements in factory safety conditions. Steady export growth in the garment sector, combined with $13 billion in remittances from overseas Bangladeshis, contributed to

Bangladesh's rising foreign exchange reserves in FY 2016-17.

The recent influx of over 700,000 additional refugees from Burma will place pressure on the Bangladeshi government's budget and the country's rice supplies, which declined in 2017 in part because of record flooding. Recent improvements to energy infrastructure, including the start of liquefied natural gas imports in 2018, represent a major step forward in resolving a key growth bottleneck.

GDP (PURCHASING POWER PARITY):

$690.3 billion (2017 est.)

$642.7 billion (2016 est.)

$599.5 billion (2015 est.)

note: data are in 2017 dollars

country comparison to the world: 33

GDP (OFFICIAL EXCHANGE RATE):

$261.5 billion (2017 est.) (2017 est.)

GDP - REAL GROWTH RATE:

7.4% (2017 est.)

7.2% (2016 est.)

6.8% (2015 est.)

country comparison to the world: 13

GDP - PER CAPITA (PPP):

$4,200 (2017 est.)

$4,000 (2016 est.)

$3,800 (2015 est.)

note: data are in 2017 dollars

country comparison to the world: 176

GROSS NATIONAL SAVING:

30.2% of GDP (2017 est.)

30.6% of GDP (2016 est.)

30.3% of GDP (2015 est.)

country comparison to the world: 30

GDP - COMPOSITION, BY END USE:

household consumption: 68.7% (2017 est.)

government consumption: 6% (2017 est.)

investment in fixed capital: 30.5% (2017 est.)

investment in inventories: 1% (2017 est.)

exports of goods and services: 15% (2017 est.)

imports of goods and services: -20.3% (2017 est.)

GDP - COMPOSITION, BY SECTOR OF ORIGIN:

agriculture: 14.2% (2017 est.)

industry: 29.3% (2017 est.)

services: 56.5% (2017 est.)

AGRICULTURE - PRODUCTS:

rice, jute, tea, wheat, sugarcane, potatoes, tobacco, pulses, oilseeds, spices, fruit; beef, milk, poultry

INDUSTRIES:

jute, cotton, garments, paper, leather, fertilizer, iron and steel, cement, petroleum products, tobacco, pharmaceuticals, ceramics, tea, salt, sugar, edible oils, soap and detergent, fabricated metal products, electricity, natural gas

INDUSTRIAL PRODUCTION GROWTH RATE:

10.2% (2017 est.)

country comparison to the world: 15

LABOR FORCE:

66.64 million (2017 est.)

note: extensive migration of labor to Saudi Arabia, Kuwait, UAE, Oman, Qatar, and Malaysia

country comparison to the world: 7

LABOR FORCE - BY OCCUPATION:

agriculture: 42.7%

industry: 20.5%

services: 36.9% (2016 est.)

UNEMPLOYMENT RATE:

4.4% (2017 est.)

4.4% (2016 est.)

note: about 40% of the population is underemployed; many persons counted as employed work only a few hours a week and at low wages

country comparison to the world: 58

POPULATION BELOW POVERTY LINE:

24.3% (2016 est.)

HOUSEHOLD INCOME OR CONSUMPTION BY PERCENTAGE SHARE:

lowest 10%: 27% (2010 est.)

highest 10%: 27% (2010 est.)

DISTRIBUTION OF FAMILY INCOME - GINI INDEX:

32.1 (2010)

33.2 (2005)

country comparison to the world: 118

BUDGET:

revenues: 25.1 billion (2017 est.)

expenditures: 33.5 billion (2017 est.)

TAXES AND OTHER REVENUES:

9.6% (of GDP) (2017 est.)

country comparison to the world: 214

BUDGET SURPLUS (+) OR DEFICIT (-):

-3.2% (of GDP) (2017 est.)

country comparison to the world: 137

PUBLIC DEBT:

33.1% of GDP (2017 est.)

33.3% of GDP (2016 est.)

country comparison to the world: 159

FISCAL YEAR:

1 July - 30 June

INFLATION RATE (CONSUMER PRICES):

5.6% (2017 est.)

5.7% (2016 est.)

country comparison to the world: 180

CENTRAL BANK DISCOUNT RATE:

5% (11 December 2017)

5% (30 October 2015)

country comparison to the world: 80

COMMERCIAL BANK PRIME LENDING RATE:

9.54% (31 December 2017 est.)

10.41% (31 December 2016 est.)

country comparison to the world: 87

STOCK OF NARROW MONEY:

$28.68 billion (31 December 2017 est.)

$25.98 billion (31 December 2016 est.)

country comparison to the world: 64

STOCK OF BROAD MONEY:

$28.68 billion (31 December 2017 est.)

$25.98 billion (31 December 2016 est.)

country comparison to the world: 64

STOCK OF DOMESTIC CREDIT:

$152.1 billion (31 December 2017 est.)

$135.3 billion (31 December 2016 est.)

country comparison to the world: 49

MARKET VALUE OF PUBLICLY TRADED SHARES:

$92.33 billion (30 September 2017 est.)

$77.99 billion (31 December 2016 est.)

$71.73 billion (31 December 2015 est.)

country comparison to the world: 41

CURRENT ACCOUNT BALANCE:

-$5.322 billion (2017 est.)

$1.391 billion (2016 est.)

country comparison to the world: 184

EXPORTS:

$35.3 billion (2017 est.)

$34.14 billion (2016 est.)

country comparison to the world: 59

EXPORTS - PARTNERS:

Germany 12.9%, US 12.2%, UK 8.7%, Spain 5.3%, France 5.1%, Italy 4.1% (2017)

EXPORTS - COMMODITIES:

garments, knitwear, agricultural products, frozen food (fish and seafood), jute and jute goods, leather

IMPORTS:

$47.56 billion (2017 est.)

$40.28 billion (2016 est.)

country comparison to the world: 56

IMPORTS - COMMODITIES:

cotton, machinery and equipment, chemicals, iron and steel, foodstuffs

IMPORTS - PARTNERS:

China 21.9%, India 15.3%, Singapore 5.7% (2017)

RESERVES OF FOREIGN EXCHANGE AND GOLD:

$33.42 billion (31 December 2017 est.)

$32.28 billion (31 December 2016 est.)

country comparison to the world: 49

DEBT - EXTERNAL:

$50.26 billion (31 December 2017 est.)

$41.85 billion (31 December 2016 est.)

country comparison to the world: 66

STOCK OF DIRECT FOREIGN INVESTMENT - AT HOME:

$14.62 billion (31 December 2017 est.)

$13.24 billion (31 December 2016 est.)

country comparison to the world: 91

STOCK OF DIRECT FOREIGN INVESTMENT - ABROAD:

$369.6 million (31 December 2017 est.)

$228.5 million (31 December 2016 est.)

country comparison to the world: 100

EXCHANGE RATES:

taka (BDT) per US dollar -

80.69 (2017 est.)

78.468 (2016 est.)

78.468 (2015 est.)

77.947 (2014 est.)

77.614 (2013 est.)

ENERGY :: BANGLADESH

ELECTRICITY ACCESS:

population without electricity: 60.3 million (2013)

electrification - total population: 60% (2013)

electrification - urban areas: 90% (2013)

electrification - rural areas: 49% (2013)

ELECTRICITY - PRODUCTION:

60.51 billion kWh (2016 est.)

country comparison to the world: 49

ELECTRICITY - CONSUMPTION:

53.65 billion kWh (2016 est.)

country comparison to the world: 48

ELECTRICITY - EXPORTS:

0 kWh (2016 est.)

country comparison to the world: 103

ELECTRICITY - IMPORTS:

0 kWh (2016 est.)

country comparison to the world: 124

ELECTRICITY - INSTALLED GENERATING CAPACITY:

11.9 million kW (2016 est.)

country comparison to the world: 56

ELECTRICITY - FROM FOSSIL FUELS:

97% of total installed capacity (2016 est.)

country comparison to the world: 32

ELECTRICITY - FROM NUCLEAR FUELS:

0% of total installed capacity (2017 est.)

country comparison to the world: 45

ELECTRICITY - FROM HYDROELECTRIC PLANTS:

2% of total installed capacity (2017 est.)

country comparison to the world: 136

ELECTRICITY - FROM OTHER RENEWABLE SOURCES:

2% of total installed capacity (2017 est.)

country comparison to the world: 134

CRUDE OIL - PRODUCTION:

3,666 bbl/day (2017 est.)

country comparison to the world: 82

CRUDE OIL - EXPORTS:

0 bbl/day (2015 est.)

country comparison to the world: 91

CRUDE OIL - IMPORTS:

21,860 bbl/day (2015 est.)

country comparison to the world: 63

CRUDE OIL - PROVED RESERVES:

28 million bbl (1 January 2018 est.)

country comparison to the world: 81

REFINED PETROLEUM PRODUCTS - PRODUCTION:

26,280 bbl/day (2015 est.)

country comparison to the world: 86

REFINED PETROLEUM PRODUCTS - CONSUMPTION:

106,000 bbl/day (2016 est.)

country comparison to the world: 77

REFINED PETROLEUM PRODUCTS - EXPORTS:

901 bbl/day (2015 est.)

country comparison to the world: 108

REFINED PETROLEUM PRODUCTS - IMPORTS:

81,570 bbl/day (2015 est.)

country comparison to the world: 63

NATURAL GAS - PRODUCTION:

29.53 billion cu m (2017 est.)

country comparison to the world: 27

NATURAL GAS - CONSUMPTION:

29.53 billion cu m (2017 est.)

country comparison to the world: 32

NATURAL GAS - EXPORTS:

0 cu m (2017 est.)

country comparison to the world: 65

NATURAL GAS - IMPORTS:

0 cu m (2017 est.)

country comparison to the world: 89

NATURAL GAS - PROVED RESERVES:

185.8 billion cu m (1 January 2018 est.)

country comparison to the world: 44

CARBON DIOXIDE EMISSIONS FROM CONSUMPTION OF ENERGY:

79.97 million Mt (2017 est.)

country comparison to the world: 48

COMMUNICATIONS :: BANGLADESH

TELEPHONES - FIXED LINES:

total subscriptions: 710,189 (2017 est.)

subscriptions per 100 inhabitants: less than 1 (2017 est.)

country comparison to the world: 87

TELEPHONES - MOBILE CELLULAR:

total subscriptions: 145,113,669 (2017 est.)

subscriptions per 100 inhabitants: 92 (2017 est.)

country comparison to the world: 8

TELEPHONE SYSTEM:

general assessment: inadequate for a modern country; introducing digital systems; trunk systems include VHF and UHF microwave radio relay links, and some fiber-optic cable in cities; fixed broadband penetration in Bangladesh remains very low mainly due to the dominance of the mobile platform; in July 2018 first test run of 5G technology in Bangladesh took place in Dhaka (2017)

domestic: fixed-line teledensity remains less than 1 per 100 persons; mobile-cellular telephone subscribership has been increasing rapidly and now exceeds 92 telephones per 100 persons; slow to moderate mobile subscriber growth is anticipated over the next five years to 2023; strong local competition (2017)

international: country code - 880; landing point for the SEA-ME-WE-4 fiber-optic submarine cable system that provides links to Europe, the Middle East, and Asia; satellite earth stations - 6; international radiotelephone communications and landline service to neighboring countries (2016)

BROADCAST MEDIA:

state-owned Bangladesh Television (BTV) broadcasts throughout the country. Some channels, such as BTV World, operate via satellite. The government also owns a medium wave radio channel and some private FM radio broadcast news channels. Of the 41 Bangladesh approved TV stations, 26 are currently being used to broadcast. Of those, 23 operate under private management via cable distribution. Collectively, TV channels can reach more than 50 million people across the country. (2018)

INTERNET COUNTRY CODE:

.bd

INTERNET USERS:

total: 28,499,324 (July 2016 est.)

percent of population: 18.2% (July 2016 est.)

country comparison to the world: 26

BROADBAND - FIXED SUBSCRIPTIONS:

total: 7.296 million (2017 est.)

subscriptions per 100 inhabitants: 5 (2017 est.)

country comparison to the world: 21

TRANSPORTATION :: BANGLADESH

NATIONAL AIR TRANSPORT SYSTEM:

number of registered air carriers: 6 (2015)

inventory of registered aircraft operated by air carriers: 30 (2015)

annual passenger traffic on registered air carriers: 2,906,799 (2015)

annual freight traffic on registered air carriers: 182,692,553 mt-km (2015)

CIVIL AIRCRAFT REGISTRATION COUNTRY CODE PREFIX:

S2 (2016)

AIRPORTS:

18 (2013)

country comparison to the world: 139

AIRPORTS - WITH PAVED RUNWAYS:

total: 16 (2017)

over 3,047 m: 2 (2017)

2,438 to 3,047 m: 2 (2017)

1,524 to 2,437 m: 6 (2017)

914 to 1,523 m: 1 (2017)

under 914 m: 5 (2017)

AIRPORTS - WITH UNPAVED RUNWAYS:

total: 2 (2013)

1,524 to 2,437 m: 1 (2013)

under 914 m: 1 (2013)

HELIPORTS:

3 (2013)

PIPELINES:

2950 km gas (2013)

RAILWAYS:

total: 2,460 km (2014)

narrow gauge: 1,801 km 1.000-m gauge (2014)

broad gauge: 659 km 1.676-m gauge (2014)

country comparison to the world: 68

ROADWAYS:

total: 21,269 km (2010)

paved: 2,021 km (2010)

unpaved: 19,248 km (2010)

country comparison to the world: 107

WATERWAYS:

8,370 km (includes up to 3,060 km of main cargo routes; network reduced to 5,200 km in the dry season) (2011)

country comparison to the world: 16

MERCHANT MARINE:

total: 306 (2017)

by type: bulk carrier 28, container ship 4, general cargo 75, oil tanker 110, other 89 (2017)

country comparison to the world: 52

PORTS AND TERMINALS:

major seaport(s): Chittagong

container port(s) (TEUs): Chittagong (2,346,909) (2016)

river port(s): Mongla Port (Sela River)

MILITARY AND SECURITY :: BANGLADESH

MILITARY EXPENDITURES:

1.44% of GDP (2017)

1.44% of GDP (2016)

1.46% of GDP (2015)

country comparison to the world: 79

MILITARY BRANCHES:

Bangladesh Defense Force: Bangladesh Army (Sena Bahini), Bangladesh Navy (Noh Bahini, BN), Bangladesh Air Force (Biman Bahini, BAF) (2013)

MILITARY SERVICE AGE AND OBLIGATION:

16-21 years of age for voluntary military service; Bangladeshi nationality and 10th grade education required; officers: 17-21 years of age, Bangladeshi nationality, and 12th grade education required (2018)

MARITIME THREATS:

the International Maritime Bureau reports the territorial waters of Bangladesh remain a risk for armed robbery against ships; in 2017, the number of attacks against commercial vessels increased to 11 over three such incidents in 2016

TERRORISM :: BANGLADESH

TERRORIST GROUPS - HOME BASED:

Harakat ul-Jihad-i-Islami/Bangladesh (HUJI-B):
aim(s): install an Islamic state in Bangladesh
area(s) of operation: headquartered in Bangladesh and mostly active in the southeast; maintains a network of madrassas in Bangladesh (April 2018)

Islamic State of Iraq and ash-Sham (ISIS) networks in Bangladesh:
aim(s): replace the Bangladesh Government with an Islamic state and implement ISIS's strict interpretation of Sharia; ISIS operates in Bangladesh under the name Islamic State in Bangladesh (ISB)
area(s) of operation: operates primarily in Dhaka
note: targets foreigners, foreign aid workers, university professors, students, and secular bloggers for assassination; core ISIS refers to its Bangladesh branch as Bengal (April 2018)

TERRORIST GROUPS - FOREIGN BASED:

al-Qa'ida (AQ):
aim(s): overthrow the Bangladesh Government and, ultimately, establish a pan-Islamic caliphate under a strict Salafi Muslim interpretation of sharia
area(s) of operation: operates in collaboration with its al-Qa'ida in the Indian Subcontinent affiliate (April 2018)

al-Qa'ida in the Indian Subcontinent (AQIS):
aim(s): protect Muslims in Bangladesh from perceived injustices and, ultimately, establish an Islamic caliphate in the Indian subcontinent
area(s) of operation: active throughout the country, targeting primarily military and security personnel and US interests (April 2018)

TRANSNATIONAL ISSUES :: BANGLADESH

DISPUTES - INTERNATIONAL:

Bangladesh referred its maritime boundary claims with Burma and India to the International Tribunal on the Law of the SeaIndian Prime Minister Singh's September 2011 visit to Bangladesh resulted in the signing of a Protocol to the 1974 Land Boundary Agreement between India and Bangladesh, which had called for the settlement of longstanding boundary disputes over undemarcated areas and the exchange of territorial enclaves, but which had never been implementedBangladesh is struggling to accommodate more than 700,000 newly arrived Rohingya, a Burmese Muslim minority from Arakan State, who fled violence in Rakhine State, Burma, since 2017, joining a Rohingya refugee population of 200,000-300,000 living in Cox's Bazar District that arrived after bouts of violence in the 1990s and 2000sthe Bangladesh-Burma border remains tense, with a Burmese military build-up along the border and a 200 km (124 mi) wire fence the Burmese border authorities are constructing designed to deter illegal cross-border transit

REFUGEES AND INTERNALLY DISPLACED PERSONS:

refugees (country of origin): 923,000 (Burma) (2018) (includes an estimated 710,000 Rohingya refugees who have fled conflict since 25 August 2017)

IDPs: 432,000 (conflict, development, human rights violations, religious persecution, natural disasters) (2017)

ILLICIT DRUGS:

transit country for illegal drugs produced in neighboring countries

CENTRAL AMERICA :: BARBADOS

INTRODUCTION :: BARBADOS

BACKGROUND:

The island was uninhabited when first settled by the British in 1627. African slaves worked the sugar plantations established on the island until 1834 when slavery was abolished. The economy remained heavily dependent on sugar, rum, and molasses production through most of the 20th century. The gradual introduction of social and political reforms in the 1940s and 1950s led to complete independence from the UK in 1966. In the 1990s, tourism and manufacturing surpassed the sugar industry in economic importance.

GEOGRAPHY :: BARBADOS

LOCATION:

Caribbean, island in the North Atlantic Ocean, northeast of Venezuela

GEOGRAPHIC COORDINATES:

13 10 N, 59 32 W

MAP REFERENCES:

Central America and the Caribbean

AREA:

total: 430 sq km

land: 430 sq km

water: 0 sq km

country comparison to the world: 202

AREA - COMPARATIVE:

2.5 times the size of Washington, DC

LAND BOUNDARIES:

0 km

COASTLINE:

97 km

MARITIME CLAIMS:

territorial sea: 12 nm

exclusive economic zone: 200 nm

CLIMATE:

tropical; rainy season (June to October)

TERRAIN:

relatively flat; rises gently to central highland region

ELEVATION:

0 m lowest point: Atlantic Ocean

336 highest point: Mount Hillaby

NATURAL RESOURCES:

petroleum, fish, natural gas

LAND USE:

agricultural land: 32.6% (2011 est.)

arable land: 25.6% (2011 est.) / permanent crops: 2.3% (2011 est.) / permanent pasture: 4.7% (2011 est.)

forest: 19.4% (2011 est.)

other: 48% (2011 est.)

IRRIGATED LAND:

50 sq km (2012)

POPULATION DISTRIBUTION:

most densely populated country in the eastern Caribbean; approximately one-third live in urban areas

NATURAL HAZARDS:

infrequent hurricanes; periodic landslides

ENVIRONMENT - CURRENT ISSUES:

pollution of coastal waters from waste disposal by ships; soil erosion; illegal solid waste disposal threatens contamination of aquifers

ENVIRONMENT - INTERNATIONAL AGREEMENTS:

party to: Biodiversity, Climate Change, Climate Change-Kyoto Protocol, Desertification, Endangered Species, Hazardous Wastes, Law of the Sea, Marine Dumping, Ozone Layer Protection, Ship Pollution, Wetlands

signed, but not ratified: none of the selected agreements

GEOGRAPHY - NOTE:

easternmost Caribbean island

PEOPLE AND SOCIETY :: BARBADOS

POPULATION:

293,131 (July 2018 est.)

country comparison to the world: 180

NATIONALITY:

noun: Barbadian(s) or Bajan (colloquial)

adjective: Barbadian or Bajan (colloquial)

ETHNIC GROUPS:

black 92.4%, mixed 3.1%, white 2.7%, East Indian 1.3%, other 0.2%, unspecified 0.3% (2010 est.)

LANGUAGES:

English (official), Bajan (English-based creole language, widely spoken in informal settings)

RELIGIONS:

Protestant 66.4% (includes Anglican 23.9%, other Pentecostal 19.5%, Adventist 5.9%, Methodist 4.2%, Wesleyan 3.4%, Nazarene 3.2%, Church of God 2.4%, Baptist 1.8%, Moravian 1.2%, other Protestant 0.9%), Roman Catholic 3.8%, other Christian 5.4% (includes Jehovah's Witness 2.0%, other 3.4%), Rastafarian

1%, other 1.5%, none 20.6%, unspecified 1.2% (2010 est.)

AGE STRUCTURE:

0-14 years: 17.8% (male 26,084 /female 26,090)

15-24 years: 12.53% (male 18,236 /female 18,479)

25-54 years: 43.69% (male 63,829 /female 64,249)

55-64 years: 13.62% (male 18,888 /female 21,043)

65 years and over: 12.36% (male 14,705 /female 21,528) (2018 est.)

DEPENDENCY RATIOS:

total dependency ratio: 50.4 (2015 est.)

youth dependency ratio: 29.1 (2015 est.)

elderly dependency ratio: 21.3 (2015 est.)

potential support ratio: 4.7 (2015 est.)

MEDIAN AGE:

total: 38.9 years

male: 37.8 years

female: 40.1 years (2018 est.)

country comparison to the world: 56

POPULATION GROWTH RATE:

0.26% (2018 est.)

country comparison to the world: 176

BIRTH RATE:

11.6 births/1,000 population (2018 est.)

country comparison to the world: 169

DEATH RATE:

8.6 deaths/1,000 population (2018 est.)

country comparison to the world: 73

NET MIGRATION RATE:

-0.3 migrant(s)/1,000 population (2017 est.)

country comparison to the world: 113

POPULATION DISTRIBUTION:

most densely populated country in the eastern Caribbean; approximately one-third live in urban areas

URBANIZATION:

urban population: 31.1% of total population (2018)

rate of urbanization: 0.2% annual rate of change (2015-20 est.)

MAJOR URBAN AREAS - POPULATION:

89,000 BRIDGETOWN (capital) (2018)

SEX RATIO:

at birth: 1.01 male(s)/female (2017 est.)

0-14 years: 1 male(s)/female (2017 est.)

15-24 years: 0.99 male(s)/female (2017 est.)

25-54 years: 0.99 male(s)/female (2017 est.)

55-64 years: 0.88 male(s)/female (2017 est.)

65 years and over: 0.66 male(s)/female (2017 est.)

total population: 0.94 male(s)/female (2017 est.)

MATERNAL MORTALITY RATE:

27 deaths/100,000 live births (2015 est.)

country comparison to the world: 117

INFANT MORTALITY RATE:

total: 10 deaths/1,000 live births (2018 est.)

male: 11.1 deaths/1,000 live births (2018 est.)

female: 8.9 deaths/1,000 live births (2018 est.)

country comparison to the world: 134

LIFE EXPECTANCY AT BIRTH:

total population: 75.7 years (2018 est.)

male: 73.3 years (2018 est.)

female: 78.1 years (2018 est.)

country comparison to the world: 103

TOTAL FERTILITY RATE:

1.68 children born/woman (2018 est.)

country comparison to the world: 175

CONTRACEPTIVE PREVALENCE RATE:

59.2% (2012)

HEALTH EXPENDITURES:

7.5% of GDP (2014)

country comparison to the world: 64

HOSPITAL BED DENSITY:

5.8 beds/1,000 population (2014)

DRINKING WATER SOURCE:

improved:

urban: 99.7% of population (2015 est.)

rural: 99.7% of population (2015 est.)

total: 99.7% of population (2015 est.)

unimproved:

urban: 0.3% of population (2015 est.)

rural: 0.3% of population (2015 est.)

total: 0.3% of population (2015 est.)

SANITATION FACILITY ACCESS:

improved:

urban: 96.2% of population (2015 est.)

rural: 96.2% of population (2015 est.)

total: 96.2% of population (2015 est.)

unimproved:

urban: 3.8% of population (2015 est.)

rural: 3.8% of population (2015 est.)

total: 3.8% of population (2015 est.)

HIV/AIDS - ADULT PREVALENCE RATE:

1.6% (2017 est.)

country comparison to the world: 31

HIV/AIDS - PEOPLE LIVING WITH HIV/AIDS:

2,700 (2017 est.)

country comparison to the world: 127

HIV/AIDS - DEATHS:

<100 (2017 est.)

MAJOR INFECTIOUS DISEASES:

note: active local transmission of Zika virus by Aedes species mosquitoes has been identified in this country (as of August 2016); it poses an important risk (a large number of cases possible) among US citizens if bitten by an infective mosquito; other less common ways to get Zika are through sex, via blood transfusion, or during pregnancy, in which the pregnant woman passes Zika virus to her fetus

OBESITY - ADULT PREVALENCE RATE:

23.1% (2016)

country comparison to the world: 67

CHILDREN UNDER THE AGE OF 5 YEARS UNDERWEIGHT:

3.5% (2012)

country comparison to the world: 92

EDUCATION EXPENDITURES:

5.1% of GDP (2016)

country comparison to the world: 66

SCHOOL LIFE EXPECTANCY (PRIMARY TO TERTIARY EDUCATION):

total: 15 years (2011)

male: 14 years (2011)

female: 17 years (2011)

UNEMPLOYMENT, YOUTH AGES 15-24:

total: 29.6% (2016 est.)

male: 27.9% (2016 est.)

female: 31.5% (2016 est.)

country comparison to the world: 33

GOVERNMENT :: BARBADOS

COUNTRY NAME:

conventional long form: none

conventional short form: Barbados

etymology: the name derives from the Portuguese "as barbadas," which means "the bearded ones" and can refer either to the long, hanging roots of the island's bearded fig trees or to the alleged beards of the native Carib inhabitants

GOVERNMENT TYPE:

parliamentary democracy (Parliament) under a constitutional monarchy; a Commonwealth realm

CAPITAL:

name: Bridgetown

geographic coordinates: 13 06 N, 59 37 W

time difference: UTC-4 (1 hour ahead of Washington, DC, during Standard Time)

etymology: named after a bridge constructed over the swampy area (known as the Careenage) around the Constitution River that flows through the center of Bridgetown

ADMINISTRATIVE DIVISIONS:

11 parishes and 1 city*; Bridgetown*, Christ Church, Saint Andrew, Saint George, Saint James, Saint John, Saint Joseph, Saint Lucy, Saint Michael, Saint Peter, Saint Philip, Saint Thomas

INDEPENDENCE:

30 November 1966 (from the UK)

NATIONAL HOLIDAY:

Independence Day, 30 November (1966)

CONSTITUTION:

history: adopted 22 November 1966, effective 30 November 1966 (2018)

amendments: proposed by Parliament; passage of amendments to constitutional sections such as citizenship, fundamental rights and freedoms, and the organization and authorities of the branches of government requires two-thirds majority vote by the membership of both houses of Parliament; passage of other amendments only requires a majority vote of both houses; amended several times, last in 2010 (2018)

LEGAL SYSTEM:

English common law; no judicial review of legislative acts

INTERNATIONAL LAW ORGANIZATION PARTICIPATION:

accepts compulsory ICJ jurisdiction with reservations; accepts ICCt jurisdiction

CITIZENSHIP:

citizenship by birth: yes

citizenship by descent only: yes

dual citizenship recognized: yes

residency requirement for naturalization: 5 years

SUFFRAGE:

18 years of age; universal

EXECUTIVE BRANCH:

chief of state: Queen ELIZABETH II (since 6 February 1952); represented by Governor General Sandra MASON (since 8 January 2018)

head of government: Prime Minister Mia MOTTLEY (since 25 May 2018)

cabinet: Cabinet appointed by the governor general on the advice of the prime minister

elections/appointments: the monarchy is hereditary; governor general appointed by the monarch; following legislative elections, the leader of the majority party or leader of the majority coalition usually appointed prime minister by the governor general; the prime minister recommends the deputy prime minister

LEGISLATIVE BRANCH:

description: bicameral Parliament consists of:
Senate (21 seats; members appointed by the governor general - 12 on the advice of the Prime Minister, 2 on the advice of the opposition leader, and 7 at the discretion of the governor general)
House of Assembly (30 seats; members directly elected in single-seat constituencies by simple majority vote to serve 5-year terms)

elections:
House of Assembly - last held on 24 May 2018 (next to be held in 2023)

election results:
House of Assembly - percent of vote by party - BLP 74.6%, DLP 22.6%, other 2.8%; seats by party - BLP 30

note: tradition dictates that the election is held within 5 years of the last election, but constitutionally it is 5 years from the first seating of Parliament plus a 90-day grace period

JUDICIAL BRANCH:

highest courts: Supreme Court (consists of the High Court with 8 justices) and the Court of Appeal (consists of the High Court chief justice and president of the court and 4 justices; note - in 2005, Barbados acceded to the Caribbean Court of Justice as the final court of appeal, replacing that of the Judicial Committee of the Privy Council in London

judge selection and term of office: Supreme Court chief justice appointed by the governor-general on the recommendation of the prime minister and opposition leader of Parliament; other justices appointed by the governor-general on the recommendation of the Judicial and Legal Service Commission, a 5-member independent body consisting of the Supreme Court chief justice, the commission head, and governor-general appointees recommended by the prime minister; justices serve until mandatory retirement at age 65

subordinate courts: Magistrates' Courts

POLITICAL PARTIES AND LEADERS:

Bajan Free Party [Alex MITCHELL]
Barbados Integrity Movement [Neil HOLDER]
Barbados Labor Party or BLP [Mia MOTTLEY]
Democratic Labor Party or DLP [Freundel STUART]
People's Democratic Congress [Mark ADAMSON]
People's Empowerment Party or PEP [David COMISSIONG]
Solutions Barbados [Grenville PHILLIPS II]
United Progressive Party or UPP [Lynette EASTMOND]

INTERNATIONAL ORGANIZATION PARTICIPATION:

ACP, AOSIS, C, Caricom, CDB, CELAC, FAO, G-77, IADB, IBRD, ICAO, ICCt, ICRM, IDA, IFAD, IFC, IFRCS, ILO, IMF, IMO, Interpol, IOC, ISO, ITSO, ITU, ITUC (NGOs), LAES, MIGA, NAM, OAS, OPANAL, OPCW, UN, UNCTAD, UNESCO, UNHCR, UNIDO, UPU, WCO, WFTU (NGOs), WHO, WIPO, WMO, WTO

DIPLOMATIC REPRESENTATION IN THE US:

chief of mission: Ambassador Selwin Charles HART (since 18 January

2017)

chancery: 2144 Wyoming Avenue NW, Washington, DC 20008

telephone: [1] (202) 939-9200

FAX: [1] (202) 332-7467

consulate(s) general: Miami, New York

DIPLOMATIC REPRESENTATION FROM THE US:

chief of mission: Ambassador Linda S. TAGLIALATELA (since 1 February 2016) note - also accredited to Antigua and Barbuda, Dominica, Grenada, Saint Kitts and Nevis, Saint Lucia, and Saint Vincent and the Grenadines

embassy: Wildey Business Park, Wildey, St. Michael BB 14006, Barbados

mailing address: P. O. Box 302, Bridgetown BB 11000; (Department Name) Unit 3120, DPO AA 34055

telephone: [1] (246) 227-4000

FAX: [1] (246) 431-0179

FLAG DESCRIPTION:

three equal vertical bands of ultramarine blue (hoist side), gold, and ultramarine blue with the head of a black trident centered on the gold band; the band colors represent the blue of the sea and sky and the gold of the beaches; the trident head represents independence and a break with the past (the colonial coat of arms contained a complete trident)

NATIONAL SYMBOL(S):

Neptune's trident, pelican, Red Bird of Paradise flower (also known as Pride of Barbados); national colors: blue, yellow, black

NATIONAL ANTHEM:

name: The National Anthem of Barbados

lyrics/music: Irving BURGIE/C. Van Roland EDWARDS

note: adopted 1966; the anthem is also known as "In Plenty and In Time of Need"

ECONOMY :: BARBADOS

ECONOMY - OVERVIEW:

Barbados is the wealthiest and one of the most developed countries in the Eastern Caribbean and enjoys one of the highest per capita incomes in the region. Historically, the Barbadian economy was dependent on sugarcane cultivation and related activities. However, in recent years the economy has diversified into light industry and tourism. Offshore finance and information services are important foreign exchange earners, boosted by being in the same time zone as eastern US financial centers and by a relatively highly educated workforce. Following the 2008-09 recession, external vulnerabilities such as fluctuations in international oil prices have hurt economic growth, raised Barbados' already high public debt to GDP ratio - which stood at 105% of GDP in 2016 - and cut into its international reserves.

GDP (PURCHASING POWER PARITY):

$5.218 billion (2017 est.)

$5.227 billion (2016 est.)

$5.111 billion (2015 est.)

note: data are in 2017 dollars

country comparison to the world: 178

GDP (OFFICIAL EXCHANGE RATE):

$4.99 billion (2017 est.) (2017 est.)

GDP - REAL GROWTH RATE:

-0.2% (2017 est.)

2.3% (2016 est.)

2.2% (2015 est.)

country comparison to the world: 199

GDP - PER CAPITA (PPP):

$18,600 (2017 est.)

$18,700 (2016 est.)

$18,300 (2015 est.)

note: data are in 2017 dollars

country comparison to the world: 95

GROSS NATIONAL SAVING:

7.2% of GDP (2017 est.)

11.8% of GDP (2016 est.)

10.8% of GDP (2015 est.)

country comparison to the world: 171

GDP - COMPOSITION, BY END USE:

household consumption: 84.2% (2017 est.)

government consumption: 13.4% (2017 est.)

investment in fixed capital: 17.6% (2017 est.)

investment in inventories: 0.2% (2017 est.)

exports of goods and services: 31.6% (2017 est.)

imports of goods and services: -47% (2017 est.)

GDP - COMPOSITION, BY SECTOR OF ORIGIN:

agriculture: 1.5% (2017 est.)

industry: 9.8% (2017 est.)

services: 88.7% (2017 est.)

AGRICULTURE - PRODUCTS:

sugarcane, vegetables, cotton

INDUSTRIES:

tourism, sugar, light manufacturing, component assembly for export

INDUSTRIAL PRODUCTION GROWTH RATE:

2.4% (2017 est.)

country comparison to the world: 119

LABOR FORCE:

144,000 (2017 est.)

country comparison to the world: 176

LABOR FORCE - BY OCCUPATION:

agriculture: 10%

industry: 15%

services: 75% (1996 est.)

UNEMPLOYMENT RATE:

10.1% (2017 est.)

9.9% (2016 est.)

country comparison to the world: 141

POPULATION BELOW POVERTY LINE:

NA

HOUSEHOLD INCOME OR CONSUMPTION BY PERCENTAGE SHARE:

lowest 10%: NA

highest 10%: NA

BUDGET:

revenues: 1.466 billion (2013 est.) (2017 est.)

expenditures: 1.664 billion (2017 est.)

TAXES AND OTHER REVENUES:

29.4% (of GDP) (2017 est.)

country comparison to the world: 82

BUDGET SURPLUS (+) OR DEFICIT (-):

-4% (of GDP) (2017 est.)

country comparison to the world: 155

PUBLIC DEBT:

157.3% of GDP (2017 est.)

149.1% of GDP (2016 est.)

country comparison to the world: 3

FISCAL YEAR:

1 April - 31 March

INFLATION RATE (CONSUMER PRICES):

4.4% (2017 est.)

1.5% (2016 est.)

country comparison to the world: 164

CENTRAL BANK DISCOUNT RATE:

7% (2017)

7% (31 December 2016)

country comparison to the world: 47

COMMERCIAL BANK PRIME LENDING RATE:

8.1% (31 December 2017 est.)

8.05% (31 December 2016 est.)

country comparison to the world: 107

STOCK OF NARROW MONEY:

$2.47 billion (31 December 2017 est.)

$2.381 billion (31 December 2016 est.)

country comparison to the world: 128

STOCK OF BROAD MONEY:

$2.47 billion (31 December 2017 est.)

$2.381 billion (31 December 2016 est.)

country comparison to the world: 135

STOCK OF DOMESTIC CREDIT:

$6.184 billion (31 December 2017 est.)

$5.871 billion (31 December 2016 est.)

country comparison to the world: 124

MARKET VALUE OF PUBLICLY TRADED SHARES:

$4.495 billion (31 December 2012 est.)

$4.571 billion (31 December 2011 est.)

$4.366 billion (31 December 2010 est.)

country comparison to the world: 87

CURRENT ACCOUNT BALANCE:

-$189 million (2017 est.)

-$206 million (2016 est.)

country comparison to the world: 96

EXPORTS:

$485.4 million (2017 est.)

$516.9 million (2016 est.)

country comparison to the world: 176

EXPORTS - PARTNERS:

US 38%, Trinidad and Tobago 10.2%, Guyana 5.5%, Jamaica 5%, China 4.8%, St. Lucia 4.6% (2017)

EXPORTS - COMMODITIES:

manufactures, sugar, molasses, rum, other foodstuffs and beverages, chemicals, electrical components

IMPORTS:

$1.52 billion (2017 est.)

$1.541 billion (2016 est.)

country comparison to the world: 173

IMPORTS - COMMODITIES:

consumer goods, machinery, foodstuffs, construction materials, chemicals, fuel, electrical components

IMPORTS - PARTNERS:

US 38.5%, Trinidad and Tobago 14.6%, China 7.1%, UK 4.7% (2017)

RESERVES OF FOREIGN EXCHANGE AND GOLD:

$264.5 million (31 December 2017 est.)

$341.8 million (31 December 2016 est.)

country comparison to the world: 169

DEBT - EXTERNAL:

$4.49 billion (2010 est.)

$668 million (2003 est.)

country comparison to the world: 136

EXCHANGE RATES:

Barbadian dollars (BBD) per US dollar -

2 (2017 est.)

2 (2016 est.)

2 (2015 est.)

2 (2014 est.)

2 (2013 est.)

note: the Barbadian dollar is pegged to the US dollar

ENERGY :: BARBADOS

ELECTRICITY ACCESS:

population without electricity: 29,149 (2012)

electrification - total population: 91% (2012)

electrification - urban areas: 100% (2012)

electrification - rural areas: 80% (2012)

ELECTRICITY - PRODUCTION:

1.01 billion kWh (2016 est.)

country comparison to the world: 150

ELECTRICITY - CONSUMPTION:

990 million kWh (2016 est.)

country comparison to the world: 155

ELECTRICITY - EXPORTS:

0 kWh (2017 est.)

country comparison to the world: 104

ELECTRICITY - IMPORTS:

0 kWh (2016 est.)

country comparison to the world: 125

ELECTRICITY - INSTALLED GENERATING CAPACITY:

269,000 kW (2016 est.)

country comparison to the world: 162

ELECTRICITY - FROM FOSSIL FUELS:

93% of total installed capacity (2016 est.)

country comparison to the world: 50

ELECTRICITY - FROM NUCLEAR FUELS:

0% of total installed capacity (2017 est.)

country comparison to the world: 46

ELECTRICITY - FROM HYDROELECTRIC PLANTS:

0% of total installed capacity (2017 est.)

country comparison to the world: 157

ELECTRICITY - FROM OTHER RENEWABLE SOURCES:

7% of total installed capacity (2017 est.)

country comparison to the world: 91

CRUDE OIL - PRODUCTION:

1,000 bbl/day (2017 est.)

country comparison to the world: 90

CRUDE OIL - EXPORTS:

674 bbl/day (2015 est.)

country comparison to the world: 77

CRUDE OIL - IMPORTS:

0 bbl/day (2015 est.)

country comparison to the world: 94

CRUDE OIL - PROVED RESERVES:

2.534 million bbl (1 January 2018 est.)

country comparison to the world: 94

REFINED PETROLEUM PRODUCTS - PRODUCTION:

0 bbl/day (2015 est.)

country comparison to the world: 117

REFINED PETROLEUM PRODUCTS - CONSUMPTION:

11,000 bbl/day (2016 est.)

country comparison to the world: 159

REFINED PETROLEUM PRODUCTS - EXPORTS:

0 bbl/day (2015 est.)

country comparison to the world: 129

REFINED PETROLEUM PRODUCTS - IMPORTS:

10,630 bbl/day (2015 est.)

country comparison to the world: 147

NATURAL GAS - PRODUCTION:

14.16 million cu m (2017 est.)

country comparison to the world: 91

NATURAL GAS - CONSUMPTION:

19.82 million cu m (2017 est.)

country comparison to the world: 113

NATURAL GAS - EXPORTS:

0 cu m (2017 est.)

country comparison to the world: 66

NATURAL GAS - IMPORTS:

5.653 million cu m (2017 est.)

country comparison to the world: 78

NATURAL GAS - PROVED RESERVES:

141.6 million cu m (1 January 2018 est.)

country comparison to the world: 102

CARBON DIOXIDE EMISSIONS FROM CONSUMPTION OF ENERGY:

1.76 million Mt (2017 est.)

country comparison to the world: 160

COMMUNICATIONS :: BARBADOS

TELEPHONES - FIXED LINES:

total subscriptions: 139,645 (2017 est.)

subscriptions per 100 inhabitants: 48 (2017 est.)

country comparison to the world: 133

TELEPHONES - MOBILE CELLULAR:

total subscriptions: 337,791 (2017 est.)

subscriptions per 100 inhabitants: 116 (2017 est.)

country comparison to the world: 177

TELEPHONE SYSTEM:

general assessment: island-wide automatic telephone system; telecom sector across the Caribbean region remains one of the key growth areas; numerous competitors licensed, but small and localized (2017)

domestic: fixed-line teledensity of roughly 48 per 100 persons; mobile-cellular telephone density about 116 per 100 persons (2017)

international: country code - 1-246; landing point for the East Caribbean Fiber System (ECFS) submarine cable with links to 13 other islands in the eastern Caribbean extending from the British Virgin Islands to Trinidad; satellite earth stations - 1 (Intelsat - Atlantic Ocean); tropospheric scatter to Trinidad and Saint Lucia (2016)

BROADCAST MEDIA:

government-owned Caribbean Broadcasting Corporation (CBC) operates the lone terrestrial TV station; CBC also operates a multi-channel cable TV subscription service; roughly a dozen radio stations, consisting of a CBC-operated network operating alongside privately owned radio stations (2009)

INTERNET COUNTRY CODE:

.bb

INTERNET USERS:

total: 231,883 (July 2016 est.)

percent of population: 79.5% (July 2016 est.)

country comparison to the world: 168

BROADBAND - FIXED SUBSCRIPTIONS:

total: 89,340 (2017 est.)

subscriptions per 100 inhabitants: 31 (2017 est.)

country comparison to the world: 122

TRANSPORTATION :: BARBADOS

CIVIL AIRCRAFT REGISTRATION COUNTRY CODE PREFIX:

8P (2016)

AIRPORTS:

1 (2013)

country comparison to the world: 213

AIRPORTS - WITH PAVED RUNWAYS:

total: 1 (2017)

over 3,047 m: 1 (2017)

PIPELINES:

33 km gas, 64 km oil, 6 km refined products (2013)

ROADWAYS:

total: 1,700 km (2015)

paved: 1,700 km (2015)

country comparison to the world: 176

MERCHANT MARINE:

total: 112 (2017)

by type: bulk carrier 18, general cargo 71, oil tanker 2, other 21 (2017)

country comparison to the world: 80

PORTS AND TERMINALS:

major seaport(s): Bridgetown

MILITARY AND SECURITY :: BARBADOS

MILITARY BRANCHES:

Royal Barbados Defense Force: Troops Command, Barbados Coast Guard (2011)

MILITARY SERVICE AGE AND OBLIGATION:

18 years of age for voluntary military service, or earlier with parental consent; no conscription (2013)

MILITARY - NOTE:

the Royal Barbados Defense Force includes a land-based Troop Command and a small Coast Guard; the primary role of the land element is island defense against external aggression; the Command consists of a single, part-time battalion with a small regular cadre deployed throughout the island; the cadre increasingly supports the police in patrolling the coastline for smuggling and other illicit activities

TRANSNATIONAL ISSUES :: BARBADOS

DISPUTES - INTERNATIONAL:

Barbados and Trinidad and Tobago abide by the April 2006 Permanent Court of Arbitration decision delimiting a maritime boundary and limiting catches of flying fish in Trinidad and Tobago's exclusive economic zonejoins other Caribbean states to counter Venezuela's claim that Aves Island sustains human habitation, a criterion under the UN Convention on the Law of the Sea, which permits Venezuela to extend its Economic Exclusion Zone/continental shelf over a large portion of the eastern Caribbean Sea

ILLICIT DRUGS:

one of many Caribbean transshipment points for narcotics bound for Europe and the US; offshore financial center

EUROPE :: BELARUS

INTRODUCTION :: BELARUS

BACKGROUND:

After seven decades as a constituent republic of the USSR, Belarus attained its independence in 1991. It has retained closer political and economic ties to Russia than have any of the other former Soviet republics. Belarus and Russia signed a treaty on a two-state union on 8 December 1999 envisioning greater political and economic integration. Although Belarus agreed to a framework to carry out the accord, serious implementation has yet to take place. Since his election in July 1994 as the country's first and only directly elected president, Aleksandr LUKASHENKO has steadily consolidated his power through authoritarian means and a centralized economic system. Government restrictions on political and civil freedoms, freedom of speech and the press, peaceful assembly, and religion have remained in place.

GEOGRAPHY :: BELARUS

LOCATION:

Eastern Europe, east of Poland

GEOGRAPHIC COORDINATES:

53 00 N, 28 00 E

MAP REFERENCES:

Europe

AREA:

total: 207,600 sq km

land: 202,900 sq km

water: 4,700 sq km

country comparison to the world: 87

AREA - COMPARATIVE:

slightly less than twice the size of Kentucky; slightly smaller than Kansas

LAND BOUNDARIES:

total: 3,642 km

border countries (5): Latvia 161 km, Lithuania 640 km, Poland 418 km, Russia 1312 km, Ukraine 1111 km

COASTLINE:

0 km (landlocked)

MARITIME CLAIMS:

none (landlocked)

CLIMATE:

cold winters, cool and moist summers; transitional between continental and maritime

TERRAIN:

generally flat with much marshland

ELEVATION:

mean elevation: 160 m

elevation extremes: 90 m lowest point: Nyoman River 346 highest point: Dzyarzhynskaya Hara

NATURAL RESOURCES:

timber, peat deposits, small quantities of oil and natural gas, granite, dolomitic limestone, marl, chalk, sand, gravel, clay

LAND USE:

agricultural land: 43.7% (2011 est.)

arable land: 27.2% (2011 est.) / permanent crops: 0.6% (2011 est.) / permanent pasture: 15.9% (2011 est.)

forest: 42.7% (2011 est.)

other: 13.6% (2011 est.)

IRRIGATED LAND:

1,140 sq km (2012)

POPULATION DISTRIBUTION:

a fairly even distribution throughout most of the country, with urban areas attracting larger and denser populations

NATURAL HAZARDS:

large tracts of marshy land

ENVIRONMENT - CURRENT ISSUES:

soil pollution from pesticide use; southern part of the country contaminated with fallout from 1986 nuclear reactor accident at Chornobyl' in northern Ukraine

ENVIRONMENT - INTERNATIONAL AGREEMENTS:

party to: Air Pollution, Air Pollution-Nitrogen Oxides, Air Pollution-Sulfur 85, Biodiversity, Climate Change, Climate Change-Kyoto Protocol, Desertification, Endangered Species, Environmental Modification, Hazardous Wastes, Law of the Sea, Marine Dumping, Ozone Layer Protection, Ship Pollution, Wetlands

signed, but not ratified: none of the selected agreements

GEOGRAPHY - NOTE:

landlocked; glacial scouring accounts for the flatness of Belarusian terrain and for its 11,000 lakes

PEOPLE AND SOCIETY :: BELARUS

POPULATION:

9,527,543 (July 2018 est.)

country comparison to the world: 94

NATIONALITY:

noun: Belarusian(s)

adjective: Belarusian

ETHNIC GROUPS:

Belarusian 83.7%, Russian 8.3%, Polish 3.1%, Ukrainian 1.7%, other 2.4%, unspecified 0.9% (2009 est.)

LANGUAGES:

Russian (official) 70.2%, Belarusian (official) 23.4%, other 3.1% (includes small Polish- and Ukrainian-speaking minorities), unspecified 3.3% (2009 est.)

RELIGIONS:

Orthodox 48.3%, Catholic 7.1%, other 3.5%, non-believers 41.1% (2011 est.)

AGE STRUCTURE:

0-14 years: 15.91% (male 779,577 /female 736,481)

15-24 years: 9.96% (male 488,240 /female 460,673)

25-54 years: 44.49% (male 2,089,202 /female 2,149,486)

55-64 years: 14.42% (male 607,368 /female 766,238)

65 years and over: 15.22% (male 467,299 /female 982,979) (2018 est.)

DEPENDENCY RATIOS:

total dependency ratio: 43.8 (2015 est.)

youth dependency ratio: 23.2 (2015 est.)

elderly dependency ratio: 20.6 (2015 est.)

potential support ratio: 4.9 (2015 est.)

MEDIAN AGE:

total: 40.3 years

male: 37.4 years

female: 43.3 years (2018 est.)

country comparison to the world: 49

POPULATION GROWTH RATE:

-0.24% (2018 est.)

country comparison to the world: 211

BIRTH RATE:

10 births/1,000 population (2018 est.)

country comparison to the world: 191

DEATH RATE:

13.2 deaths/1,000 population (2018 est.)

country comparison to the world: 10

NET MIGRATION RATE:

0.7 migrant(s)/1,000 population (2017 est.)

country comparison to the world: 61

POPULATION DISTRIBUTION:

a fairly even distribution throughout most of the country, with urban areas attracting larger and denser populations

URBANIZATION:

urban population: 78.6% of total population (2018)

rate of urbanization: 0.44% annual rate of change (2015-20 est.)

MAJOR URBAN AREAS - POPULATION:

2.005 million MINSK (capital) (2018)

SEX RATIO:

at birth: 1.06 male(s)/female (2017 est.)

0-14 years: 1.06 male(s)/female (2017 est.)

15-24 years: 1.06 male(s)/female (2017 est.)

25-54 years: 0.97 male(s)/female (2017 est.)

55-64 years: 0.79 male(s)/female (2017 est.)

65 years and over: 0.46 male(s)/female (2017 est.)

total population: 0.87 male(s)/female (2017 est.)

MOTHER'S MEAN AGE AT FIRST BIRTH:

25.7 years (2014 est.)

MATERNAL MORTALITY RATE:

4 deaths/100,000 live births (2015 est.)

country comparison to the world: 176

INFANT MORTALITY RATE:

total: 3.6 deaths/1,000 live births (2018 est.)

male: 4 deaths/1,000 live births (2018 est.)

female: 3.1 deaths/1,000 live births (2018 est.)

country comparison to the world: 196

LIFE EXPECTANCY AT BIRTH:

total population: 73.2 years (2018 est.)

male: 67.8 years (2018 est.)

female: 79 years (2018 est.)

country comparison to the world: 139

TOTAL FERTILITY RATE:

1.49 children born/woman (2018 est.)

country comparison to the world: 197

CONTRACEPTIVE PREVALENCE RATE:

63.1% (2012)

HEALTH EXPENDITURES:

5.7% of GDP (2014)

country comparison to the world: 113

PHYSICIANS DENSITY:

4.07 physicians/1,000 population (2014)

HOSPITAL BED DENSITY:

11 beds/1,000 population (2013)

DRINKING WATER SOURCE:

improved:

urban: 99.9% of population

rural: 99.1% of population

total: 99.7% of population

unimproved:

urban: 0.1% of population

rural: 0.9% of population

total: 0.3% of population (2015 est.)

SANITATION FACILITY ACCESS:

improved:

urban: 94.1% of population (2015 est.)

rural: 95.2% of population (2015 est.)

total: 94.3% of population (2015 est.)

unimproved:

urban: 5.9% of population (2015 est.)

rural: 4.8% of population (2015 est.)

total: 5.7% of population (2015 est.)

HIV/AIDS - ADULT PREVALENCE RATE:

0.4% (2017 est.)

country comparison to the world: 69

HIV/AIDS - PEOPLE LIVING WITH HIV/AIDS:

24,000 (2017 est.)

country comparison to the world: 78

HIV/AIDS - DEATHS:

<500 (2017 est.)

OBESITY - ADULT PREVALENCE RATE:

24.5% (2016)

country comparison to the world: 58

EDUCATION EXPENDITURES:

5% of GDP (2016)

country comparison to the world: 75

LITERACY:

definition: age 15 and over can read and write (2015 est.)

total population: 99.7% (2015 est.)

male: 99.8% (2015 est.)

female: 99.7% (2015 est.)

SCHOOL LIFE EXPECTANCY (PRIMARY TO TERTIARY EDUCATION):

total: 16 years (2015)

male: 15 years (2015)

female: 16 years (2015)

UNEMPLOYMENT, YOUTH AGES 15-24:

total: 10.7% (2016 est.)

male: 12.6% (2016 est.)

female: 8.5% (2016 est.)

country comparison to the world: 118

GOVERNMENT :: BELARUS

COUNTRY NAME:

conventional long form: Republic of Belarus

conventional short form: Belarus

local long form: Respublika Byelarus'/Respublika Belarus'

local short form: Byelarus'/Belarus'

former: Belorussian (Byelorussian) Soviet Socialist Republic

etymology: the name is a compound of the Belarusian words "bel" (white) and "Rus" (the Old East Slavic ethnic designation) to form the meaning White Rusian or White Ruthenian

GOVERNMENT TYPE:

presidential republic in name, although in fact a dictatorship

CAPITAL:

name: Minsk

geographic coordinates: 53 54 N, 27 34 E

time difference: UTC+2 (7 hours ahead of Washington, DC, during Standard Time)

ADMINISTRATIVE DIVISIONS:

6 provinces (voblastsi, singular - voblasts') and 1 municipality* (horad); Brest, Homyel' (Gomel'), Horad Minsk* (Minsk City), Hrodna (Grodno), Mahilyow (Mogilev), Minsk, Vitsyebsk (Vitebsk)

note: administrative divisions have the same names as their administrative centers; Russian spelling provided for reference when different from Belarusian

INDEPENDENCE:

25 August 1991 (from the Soviet Union)

NATIONAL HOLIDAY:

Independence Day, 3 July (1944); note - 3 July 1944 was the date Minsk was liberated from German troops, 25 August 1991 was the date of independence from the Soviet Union

CONSTITUTION:

history: several previous; latest drafted between late 1991 and early 1994, signed 15 March 1994 (2016)

amendments: proposed by the president of the republic through petition to the National Assembly or by petition of least 150,000 eligible voters; approval required by at least two-thirds majority vote in both chambers or by simple majority of votes cast in a referendum (2016)

LEGAL SYSTEM:

civil law system; note - nearly all major codes (civil, civil procedure, criminal, criminal procedure, family, and labor) were revised and came into force in 1999 and 2000

INTERNATIONAL LAW ORGANIZATION PARTICIPATION:

has not submitted an ICJ jurisdiction declaration; non-party state to the ICCt

CITIZENSHIP:

citizenship by birth: no

citizenship by descent only: at least one parent must be a citizen of Belarus

dual citizenship recognized: no

residency requirement for naturalization: 7 years

SUFFRAGE:

18 years of age; universal

EXECUTIVE BRANCH:

chief of state: President Aleksandr LUKASHENKO (since 20 July 1994)

head of government: Prime Minister Sergey RUMAS (since 18 August 2018); First Deputy Prime Minister Aleksandr TURCHIN (since 18 August 2018); Deputy Prime Ministers Igor LYASHENKO, Vladimir KUKHAREV, Igor PETRISHENKO (since 18 August 2018), Mikhail RUSYY (since 2012)

cabinet: Council of Ministers appointed by the president

elections/appointments: president directly elected by absolute majority popular vote in 2 rounds if needed for a 5-year term (no term limits); first election took place on 23 June and 10 July 1994; according to the 1994 constitution, the next election should have been held in 1999; however, Aleksandr LUKASHENKO extended his term to 2001 via a November 1996 referendum; subsequent election held on 9 September 2001; an October 2004 referendum ended presidential term limits and allowed the president to run and win in a third (19 March 2006), fourth (19 December 2010), and fifth election (11 October 2015); next election in 2020; prime minister and deputy prime ministers appointed by the president and approved by the National Assembly

election results: Aleksandr LUKASHENKO reelected president; percent of vote - Aleksandr LUKASHENKO (independent) 83.5%, Tatstyana KARATKEVICH (Tell the Truth) 4.4%, Sergey GAYDUKEVICH (LDP) 3.3%, other 8.8%; note - election marred by electoral fraud

LEGISLATIVE BRANCH:

description: bicameral National Assembly or Natsionalnoye Sobraniye consists of:
Council of the Republic or Sovet Respubliki (64 seats; 56 members indirectly elected by regional and Minsk city councils and 8 members appointed by the president; members serve 4-year terms)
House of Representatives or Palata Predstaviteley (110 seats; members directly elected in single-seat constituencies by absolute majority vote in 2 rounds if needed; members serve 4-year terms)

elections:
Council of the Republic - NA
House of Representatives - last held on 11 September 2016 (next to be held in 2020); OSCE observers determined that the election was neither free nor impartial and that vote counting was problematic in a number of polling stations; pro-LUKASHENKO candidates won virtually every seat, with only the UCP member and one independent forming alternative representation in the House; international observers determined that the previous elections, on 28 September 2008 and 23 September 2012, also fell short of democratic standards, with pro-LUKASHENKO candidates winning every seat

election results:
Council of the Republic - percent of vote by party - NA; seats by party - NA; composition - men 39, women 17, percent of women 26.6%
House of Representatives - percent of vote by party - NA; seats by party - KPB 8, Belarusian Patriotic Party 3, Republican Party of Labor and Justice 3, LDP 1, UCP 1, independent 94; composition - men 72, women 38, percent of women 34.5%; note - total

National Assembly percent of women 31.6%

note: the US does not recognize the legitimacy of the National Assembly

JUDICIAL BRANCH:

highest courts: Supreme Court (consists of the chairman and deputy chairman and organized into several specialized panels, including economic and military; number of judges set by the president of the republic and the court chairman); Constitutional Court (consists of 12 judges including a chairman and deputy chairman)

judge selection and term of office: Supreme Court judges appointed by the president with the consent of the Council of the Republic; judges initially appointed for 5 years and evaluated for life appointment; Constitutional Court judges - 6 appointed by the president and 6 elected by the Council of the Republic; the presiding judge directly elected by the president and approved by the Council of the Republic; judges can serve for 11 years with an age limit of 70

subordinate courts: oblast courts; Minsk City Court; town courts; Minsk city and oblast economic courts

POLITICAL PARTIES AND LEADERS:

pro-government parties:
Belarusian Agrarian Party or AP [Mikhail SHIMANSKIY];
Belarusian Patriotic Party [Nikolai ULAKHOVICH];
Belarusian Social Sport Party [Vladimir ALEKSANDROVICH];
Communist Party of Belarus or KPB [Aleksei SOKOL];
Liberal Democratic Party or LDP [Sergey GAYDUKEVICH];
Republican Party [Vladimir BELOZOR];
Republican Party of Labor and Justice [Vasiliy ZADNEPRYANIY];
opposition parties:
Belarusian Christian Democracy Party [Paval SEVIARYNETS] (unregistered);
Belarusian Party of the Green [Anastasiya DOROFEYEVA];
Belarusian Party of the Left "Just World" [Sergey KALYAKIN];
Belarusian Popular Front or BPF [Ryhor KASTUSEU];
Belarusian Social-Democratic Assembly [Stanislav SHUSHKEVICH];
Belarusian Social Democratic Party ("Assembly") or BSDPH [Ihar BARYSAU];
Belarusian Social Democratic Party (People's Assembly) [Mikalay STATKEVICH] (unregistered);
Christian Conservative Party or BPF [Zyanon PAZNYAK];
United Civic Party or UCP [Anatoliy LEBEDKO]

INTERNATIONAL ORGANIZATION PARTICIPATION:

BSEC (observer), CBSS (observer), CEI, CIS, CSTO, EAEC, EAEU, EAPC, EBRD, FAO, GCTU, IAEA, IBRD, ICAO, ICC (NGOs), ICRM, IDA, IFC, IFRCS, ILO, IMF, IMSO, Interpol, IOC, IOM, IPU, ISO, ITU, ITUC (NGOs), MIGA, NAM, NSG, OPCW, OSCE, PCA, PFP, SCO (dialogue member), UN, UNCTAD, UNESCO, UNIDO, UNIFIL, UNWTO, UPU, WCO, WFTU (NGOs), WHO, WIPO, WMO, WTO (observer), ZC

DIPLOMATIC REPRESENTATION IN THE US:

chief of mission: Ambassador (vacant; recalled by Belarus in 2008); Charge d'Affaires Pavel SHIDLOVSKIY (since 23 April 2014)

chancery: 1619 New Hampshire Avenue NW, Washington, DC 20009

telephone: [1] (202) 986-1606

FAX: [1] (202) 986-1805

consulate(s) general: New York

DIPLOMATIC REPRESENTATION FROM THE US:

chief of mission: Ambassador (vacant; left in 2008 upon insistence of Belarusian Government); Charge d'Affaires Jenifer MOORE(since August 2018)

embassy: 46 Starovilenskaya Street, Minsk 220002

mailing address: Unit 7010 Box 100, DPO AE 09769

telephone: [375] (17) 210-1283

FAX: [375] (17) 234-7853

FLAG DESCRIPTION:

red horizontal band (top) and green horizontal band one-half the width of the red band; a white vertical stripe on the hoist side bears Belarusian national ornamentation in red; the red band color recalls past struggles from oppression, the green band represents hope and the many forests of the country

NATIONAL SYMBOL(S):

no clearly defined current national symbol, the mounted knight known as Pahonia (the Chaser) is the traditional Belarusian symbol; national colors: green, red, white

NATIONAL ANTHEM:

name: "My, Bielarusy" (We Belarusians)

lyrics/music: Mikhas KLIMKOVICH and Uladzimir KARYZNA/Nester SAKALOUSKI

note: music adopted 1955, lyrics adopted 2002; after the fall of the Soviet Union, Belarus kept the music of its Soviet-era anthem but adopted new lyrics; also known as "Dziarzauny himn Respubliki Bielarus" (State Anthem of the Republic of Belarus)

ECONOMY :: BELARUS

ECONOMY - OVERVIEW:

As part of the former Soviet Union, Belarus had a relatively well-developed industrial base, but it is now outdated, inefficient, and dependent on subsidized Russian energy and preferential access to Russian markets. The country's agricultural base is largely dependent on government subsidies. Following the collapse of the Soviet Union, an initial burst of economic reforms included privatization of state enterprises, creation of private property rights, and the acceptance of private entrepreneurship, but by 1994 the reform effort dissipated. About 80% of industry remains in state hands, and foreign investment has virtually disappeared. Several businesses have been renationalized. State-owned entities account for 70-75% of GDP, and state banks make up 75% of the banking sector.

Economic output declined for several years following the break-up of the Soviet Union, but revived in the mid-2000s. Belarus has only small reserves of crude oil and imports crude oil and natural gas from Russia at subsidized, below market, prices. Belarus derives export revenue by refining Russian crude and selling it at market prices. Russia and Belarus have had serious disagreements over prices and quantities for Russian energy. Beginning in early 2016, Russia claimed Belarus began accumulating debt – reaching $740 million by April 2017 – for paying below the agreed price for Russian natural gas and Russia cut back its export of crude oil as a result of the debt. In April 2017, Belarus agreed to pay its gas debt and Russia restored the flow of crude.

New non-Russian foreign investment has been limited in recent years, largely because of an unfavorable financial climate. In 2011, a financial crisis lead to a nearly three-fold devaluation of the Belarusian ruble. The Belarusian economy has continued to struggle under the weight of high external debt servicing payments and a trade deficit. In mid-December 2014, the devaluation of the Russian ruble triggered a near 40% devaluation of the Belarusian ruble.

Belarus's economy stagnated between 2012 and 2016, widening productivity and income gaps between Belarus and neighboring countries. Budget revenues dropped because of falling global prices on key Belarusian export commodities. Since 2015, the Belarusian government has tightened its macro-economic policies, allowed more flexibility to its exchange rate, taken some steps towards price liberalization, and reduced subsidized government lending to state-owned enterprises. Belarus returned to modest growth in 2017, largely driven by improvement of external conditions and Belarus issued sovereign debt for the first time since 2011, which provided the country with badly-needed liquidity, and issued $600 million worth of Eurobonds in February 2018, predominantly to US and British investors.

GDP (PURCHASING POWER PARITY):

$179.4 billion (2017 est.)

$175.1 billion (2016 est.)

$179.7 billion (2015 est.)

note: data are in 2017 dollars

country comparison to the world: 70

GDP (OFFICIAL EXCHANGE RATE):

$54.44 billion (2017 est.) (2017 est.)

GDP - REAL GROWTH RATE:

2.4% (2017 est.)

-2.5% (2016 est.)

-3.8% (2015 est.)

country comparison to the world: 136

GDP - PER CAPITA (PPP):

$18,900 (2017 est.)

$18,400 (2016 est.)

$19,000 (2015 est.)

note: data are in 2017 dollars

country comparison to the world: 94

GROSS NATIONAL SAVING:

24.5% of GDP (2017 est.)

23% of GDP (2016 est.)

25.8% of GDP (2015 est.)

country comparison to the world: 64

GDP - COMPOSITION, BY END USE:

household consumption: 54.8% (2017 est.)

government consumption: 14.6% (2017 est.)

investment in fixed capital: 24.9% (2017 est.)

investment in inventories: 5.7% (2017 est.)

exports of goods and services: 67% (2017 est.)

imports of goods and services: -67% (2017 est.)

GDP - COMPOSITION, BY SECTOR OF ORIGIN:

agriculture: 8.1% (2017 est.)

industry: 40.8% (2017 est.)

services: 51.1% (2017 est.)

AGRICULTURE - PRODUCTS:

grain, potatoes, vegetables, sugar beets, flax; beef, milk

INDUSTRIES:

metal-cutting machine tools, tractors, trucks, earthmovers, motorcycles, synthetic fibers, fertilizer, textiles, refrigerators, washing machines and other household appliances

INDUSTRIAL PRODUCTION GROWTH RATE:

5.6% (2017 est.)

country comparison to the world: 47

LABOR FORCE:

4.381 million (2016 est.)

country comparison to the world: 89

LABOR FORCE - BY OCCUPATION:

agriculture: 9.7%

industry: 23.4%

services: 66.8% (2015 est.)

UNEMPLOYMENT RATE:

0.8% (2017 est.)

1% (2016 est.)

note: official registered unemployed; large number of underemployed workers

country comparison to the world: 6

POPULATION BELOW POVERTY LINE:

5.7% (2016 est.)

HOUSEHOLD INCOME OR CONSUMPTION BY PERCENTAGE SHARE:

lowest 10%: 21.9% (2008)

highest 10%: 21.9% (2008)

DISTRIBUTION OF FAMILY INCOME - GINI INDEX:

26.5 (2011)

21.7 (1998)

country comparison to the world: 148

BUDGET:

revenues: 22.15 billion (2017 est.)

expenditures: 20.57 billion (2017 est.)

TAXES AND OTHER REVENUES:

40.7% (of GDP) (2017 est.)

country comparison to the world: 35

BUDGET SURPLUS (+) OR DEFICIT (-):

2.9% (of GDP) (2017 est.)

country comparison to the world: 14

PUBLIC DEBT:

53.4% of GDP (2017 est.)

53.5% of GDP (2016 est.)

country comparison to the world: 90

FISCAL YEAR:

calendar year

INFLATION RATE (CONSUMER PRICES):

6% (2017 est.)

11.8% (2016 est.)

country comparison to the world: 184

CENTRAL BANK DISCOUNT RATE:

14% (19 April 2017)

15% (15 March 2017)

country comparison to the world: 14

COMMERCIAL BANK PRIME LENDING RATE:

9.66% (31 December 2017 est.)

14.4% (31 December 2016 est.)

country comparison to the world: 86

STOCK OF NARROW MONEY:

$3.702 billion (31 December 2017 est.)

$2.719 billion (31 December 2016 est.)

country comparison to the world: 113

STOCK OF BROAD MONEY:

$3.702 billion (31 December 2017 est.)

$2.719 billion (31 December 2016 est.)

country comparison to the world: 119

STOCK OF DOMESTIC CREDIT:

$19.81 billion (31 December 2017 est.)

$20.65 billion (31 December 2016 est.)

country comparison to the world: 92

MARKET VALUE OF PUBLICLY TRADED SHARES:

NA

CURRENT ACCOUNT BALANCE:

-$931 million (2017 est.)

-$1.669 billion (2016 est.)

country comparison to the world: 140

EXPORTS:

$28.65 billion (2017 est.)

$22.98 billion (2016 est.)

country comparison to the world: 68

EXPORTS - PARTNERS:

Russia 43.9%, Ukraine 11.5%, UK 8.2% (2017)

EXPORTS - COMMODITIES:

machinery and equipment, mineral products, chemicals, metals, textiles, foodstuffs

IMPORTS:

$31.58 billion (2017 est.)

$25.61 billion (2016 est.)

country comparison to the world: 65

IMPORTS - COMMODITIES:

mineral products, machinery and equipment, chemicals, foodstuffs, metals

IMPORTS - PARTNERS:

Russia 57.2%, China 8%, Germany 5.1% (2017)

RESERVES OF FOREIGN EXCHANGE AND GOLD:

$7.315 billion (31 December 2017 est.)

$4.927 billion (31 December 2016 est.)

country comparison to the world: 84

DEBT - EXTERNAL:

$39.92 billion (31 December 2017 est.)

$37.74 billion (31 December 2016 est.)

country comparison to the world: 75

STOCK OF DIRECT FOREIGN INVESTMENT - AT HOME:

$6.929 billion (31 December 2016 est.)

$7.241 billion (31 December 2015)

country comparison to the world: 100

STOCK OF DIRECT FOREIGN INVESTMENT - ABROAD:

$3.547 billion (31 December 2016 est.)

$4.649 billion (31 December 2015)

country comparison to the world: 79

EXCHANGE RATES:

Belarusian rubles (BYB/BYR) per US dollar -

1.9 (2017 est.)

2 (2016 est.)

2 (2015 est.)

15,926 (2014 est.)

10,224.1 (2013 est.)

ENERGY :: BELARUS

ELECTRICITY ACCESS:

electrification - total population: 100% (2016)

ELECTRICITY - PRODUCTION:

31.58 billion kWh (2016 est.)

country comparison to the world: 63

ELECTRICITY - CONSUMPTION:

31.72 billion kWh (2016 est.)

country comparison to the world: 61

ELECTRICITY - EXPORTS:

3.482 billion kWh (2015 est.)

country comparison to the world: 40

ELECTRICITY - IMPORTS:

6.319 billion kWh (2016 est.)

country comparison to the world: 32

ELECTRICITY - INSTALLED GENERATING CAPACITY:

10.04 million kW (2016 est.)

country comparison to the world: 59

ELECTRICITY - FROM FOSSIL FUELS:

96% of total installed capacity (2016 est.)

country comparison to the world: 37

ELECTRICITY - FROM NUCLEAR FUELS:

0% of total installed capacity (2017 est.)

country comparison to the world: 47

ELECTRICITY - FROM HYDROELECTRIC PLANTS:

1% of total installed capacity (2017 est.)

country comparison to the world: 145

ELECTRICITY - FROM OTHER RENEWABLE SOURCES:

3% of total installed capacity (2017 est.)

country comparison to the world: 121

CRUDE OIL - PRODUCTION:

32,000 bbl/day (2017 est.)

country comparison to the world: 60

CRUDE OIL - EXPORTS:

31,730 bbl/day (2015 est.)

country comparison to the world: 44

CRUDE OIL - IMPORTS:

468,400 bbl/day (2015 est.)

country comparison to the world: 21

CRUDE OIL - PROVED RESERVES:

198 million bbl (1 January 2018 est.)

country comparison to the world: 56

REFINED PETROLEUM PRODUCTS - PRODUCTION:

477,200 bbl/day (2015 est.)

country comparison to the world: 34

REFINED PETROLEUM PRODUCTS - CONSUMPTION:

141,000 bbl/day (2016 est.)

country comparison to the world: 68

REFINED PETROLEUM PRODUCTS - EXPORTS:

351,200 bbl/day (2015 est.)

country comparison to the world: 25

REFINED PETROLEUM PRODUCTS - IMPORTS:

14,630 bbl/day (2015 est.)

country comparison to the world: 135

NATURAL GAS - PRODUCTION:

59.46 million cu m (2017 est.)

country comparison to the world: 84

NATURAL GAS - CONSUMPTION:

17.7 billion cu m (2017 est.)

country comparison to the world: 39

NATURAL GAS - EXPORTS:

0 cu m (2017 est.)

country comparison to the world: 67

NATURAL GAS - IMPORTS:

17.53 billion cu m (2017 est.)

country comparison to the world: 18

NATURAL GAS - PROVED RESERVES:

2.832 billion cu m (1 January 2018 est.)

country comparison to the world: 95

CARBON DIOXIDE EMISSIONS FROM CONSUMPTION OF ENERGY:

56.07 million Mt (2017 est.)

country comparison to the world: 54

COMMUNICATIONS :: BELARUS

TELEPHONES - FIXED LINES:

total subscriptions: 4,499,821 (2017 est.)

subscriptions per 100 inhabitants: 47 (2017 est.)

country comparison to the world: 31

TELEPHONES - MOBILE CELLULAR:

total subscriptions: 10,963,224 (2017 est.)

subscriptions per 100 inhabitants: 115 (2017 est.)

country comparison to the world: 80

TELEPHONE SYSTEM:

general assessment: fibre network reaches two million establishments; trial 5G services during the first half of 2019; 10,000km of fibre cabling laid; August 2018 almost two million GPON connections (Gigabit Passive Optical Network, point-to-multi point acess mechanism); 5 year plan is on track; Belarus launches its first telecoms satellite; LTE use reaches 75% of mobile subscribers (2018)

domestic: fixed-line teledensity is improving although rural areas continue to be underserved, 47 per 100 fixed-line; mobile-cellular teledensity now approaches 120 telephones per 100 persons (2017)

international: country code - 375; Belarus is a member of the Trans-European Line (TEL), Trans-Asia-Europe (TAE) fiber-optic line, and has access to the Trans-Siberia Line (TSL); 3 fiber-optic segments provide connectivity to Latvia, Poland, Russia, and Ukraine; worldwide service is available to Belarus through this infrastructure; additional analog lines to Russia; Intelsat, Eutelsat, and Intersputnik earth stations (2017)

BROADCAST MEDIA:

7 state-controlled national TV channels; Polish and Russian TV broadcasts are available in some areas; state-run Belarusian Radio operates 5 national networks and an external service; Russian and Polish radio broadcasts are available (2017)

INTERNET COUNTRY CODE:

.by

INTERNET USERS:

total: 6,805,786 (July 2016 est.)

percent of population: 71.1% (July 2016 est.)

country comparison to the world: 62

BROADBAND - FIXED SUBSCRIPTIONS:

total: 3,163,286 (2017 est.)

subscriptions per 100 inhabitants: 33 (2017 est.)

country comparison to the world: 38

TRANSPORTATION :: BELARUS

NATIONAL AIR TRANSPORT SYSTEM:

number of registered air carriers: 2 (2015)

inventory of registered aircraft operated by air carriers: 30 (2015)

annual passenger traffic on registered air carriers: 1,489,035 (2015)

annual freight traffic on registered air carriers: 1.807 million mt-km (2015)

CIVIL AIRCRAFT REGISTRATION COUNTRY CODE PREFIX:

EW (2016)

AIRPORTS:

65 (2013)

country comparison to the world: 75

AIRPORTS - WITH PAVED RUNWAYS:

total: 33 (2017)

over 3,047 m: 1 (2017)

2,438 to 3,047 m: 20 (2017)

1,524 to 2,437 m: 4 (2017)

914 to 1,523 m: 1 (2017)

under 914 m: 7 (2017)

AIRPORTS - WITH UNPAVED RUNWAYS:

total: 32 (2013)

over 3,047 m: 1 (2013)

1,524 to 2,437 m: 1 (2013)

914 to 1,523 m: 2 (2013)

under 914 m: 28 (2013)

HELIPORTS:

1 (2013)

PIPELINES:

5386 km gas, 1589 km oil, 1730 km refined products (2013)

RAILWAYS:

total: 5,528 km (2014)

standard gauge: 25 km 1.435-m gauge (2014)

broad gauge: 5,503 km 1.520-m gauge (874 km electrified) (2014)

country comparison to the world: 35

ROADWAYS:

total: 86,392 km (2010)

paved: 74,651 km (2010)

unpaved: 11,741 km (2010)

country comparison to the world: 57

WATERWAYS:

2,500 km (major rivers are the west-flowing Western Dvina and Neman Rivers and the south-flowing Dnepr River and its tributaries, the Berezina, Sozh, and Pripyat Rivers) (2011)

country comparison to the world: 35

MERCHANT MARINE:

total: 4 (2017)

by type: other 4 (2017)

country comparison to the world: 164

PORTS AND TERMINALS:

river port(s): Mazyr (Prypyats')

MILITARY AND SECURITY :: BELARUS

MILITARY EXPENDITURES:

0.93% of GDP (2017)

1.2% of GDP (2016)

1.33% of GDP (2015)

1.33% of GDP (2014)

1.33% of GDP (2013)

country comparison to the world: 119

MILITARY BRANCHES:

Belarus Armed Forces: Land Force, Air and Air Defense Force, Special Operations Force (2013)

MILITARY SERVICE AGE AND OBLIGATION:

18-27 years of age for compulsory military or alternative service; conscript service obligation is 12-18 months, depending on academic qualifications, and 24-36 months for alternative service, depending on academic qualifications; 17 year olds are eligible to become cadets at military higher education institutes, where they are classified as military personnel (2016)

TRANSNATIONAL ISSUES :: BELARUS

DISPUTES - INTERNATIONAL:

boundary demarcated with Latvia and Lithuaniaas a member state that forms part of the EU's external border, Poland has implemented strict Schengen border rules to restrict illegal immigration and trade along its border with Belarus

REFUGEES AND INTERNALLY DISPLACED PERSONS:

refugees (country of origin): 244,621 applicants for forms of legal stay other than asylum (Ukraine) (2017)

stateless persons: 6,007 (2017)

TRAFFICKING IN PERSONS:

current situation: Belarus is a source, transit, and destination country for women, men, and children subjected to sex trafficking and forced labor; more victims are exploited within Belarus than abroad; Belarusians exploited abroad are primarily trafficked to Germany, Poland,

Russian, and Turkey but also other European countries, the Middle East, Japan, Kazakhstan, and Mexico; Moldovans, Russians, Ukrainians, and Vietnamese are exploited in Belarus; state sponsored forced labor is a continuing problem; students are forced to do farm labor without pay and military conscripts are forced to perform unpaid non-military work; the government has retained a decree forbidding workers in state-owned wood processing factories from leaving their jobs without their employers' permission

tier rating: Tier 3 – Belarus does not fully comply with the minimum standards for the elimination of trafficking and was placed on Tier 3 after being on the Tier 2 Watch List for two consecutive years without making progress; government efforts to repeal state-sponsored forced labor policies and domestic trafficking were inadequate; no trafficking offenders were convicted in 2014, and the number of investigations progressively declined from 2005-14; efforts to protect trafficking victims remain insufficient, with no identification and referral mechanism in place; care facilities were not trafficking-specific and were poorly equipped, leading most victims to seek assistance from private shelters (2015)

ILLICIT DRUGS:

limited cultivation of opium poppy and cannabis, mostly for the domestic market; transshipment point for illicit drugs to and via Russia, and to the Baltics and Western Europe; a small and lightly regulated financial center; anti-money-laundering legislation does not meet international standards and was weakened further when know-your-customer requirements were curtailed in 2008; few investigations or prosecutions of money-laundering activities

EUROPE :: BELGIUM

INTRODUCTION :: BELGIUM

BACKGROUND:

Belgium became independent from the Netherlands in 1830; it was occupied by Germany during World Wars I and II. The country prospered in the past half century as a modern, technologically advanced European state and member of NATO and the EU. In recent years, political divisions between the Dutch-speaking Flemish of the north and the French-speaking Walloons of the south have led to constitutional amendments granting these regions formal recognition and autonomy. The capital city of Brussels is home to numerous international organizations including the EU and NATO.

GEOGRAPHY :: BELGIUM

LOCATION:

Western Europe, bordering the North Sea, between France and the Netherlands

GEOGRAPHIC COORDINATES:

50 50 N, 4 00 E

MAP REFERENCES:

Europe

AREA:

total: 30,528 sq km

land: 30,278 sq km

water: 250 sq km

country comparison to the world: 141

AREA - COMPARATIVE:

about the size of Maryland

LAND BOUNDARIES:

total: 1,297 km

border countries (4): France 556 km, Germany 133 km, Luxembourg 130 km, Netherlands 478 km

COASTLINE:

66.5 km

MARITIME CLAIMS:

territorial sea: 12 nm

exclusive economic zone: geographic coordinates define outer limit

contiguous zone: 24 nm

continental shelf: median line with neighbors

CLIMATE:

temperate; mild winters, cool summers; rainy, humid, cloudy

TERRAIN:

flat coastal plains in northwest, central rolling hills, rugged mountains of Ardennes Forest in southeast

ELEVATION:

mean elevation: 181 m

elevation extremes: 0 m lowest point: North Sea

694 highest point: Botrange

NATURAL RESOURCES:

construction materials, silica sand, carbonates, arable land

LAND USE:

agricultural land: 44.1% (2011 est.)

arable land: 27.2% (2011 est.) / permanent crops: 0.8% (2011 est.) / permanent pasture: 16.1% (2011 est.)

forest: 22.4% (2011 est.)

other: 33.5% (2011 est.)

IRRIGATED LAND:

230 sq km (2012)

POPULATION DISTRIBUTION:

most of the population concentrated in the northern two-thirds of the country; the southeast is more thinly populated; considered to have one of the highest population densities in the world; approximately 97% live in urban areas

NATURAL HAZARDS:

flooding is a threat along rivers and in areas of reclaimed coastal land, protected from the sea by concrete dikes

ENVIRONMENT - CURRENT ISSUES:

intense pressures from human activities: urbanization, dense transportation network, industry, extensive animal breeding and crop cultivation; air and water pollution also have repercussions for neighboring countries

ENVIRONMENT - INTERNATIONAL AGREEMENTS:

party to: Air Pollution, Air Pollution-Nitrogen Oxides, Air Pollution-Persistent Organic Pollutants, Air Pollution-Sulfur 85, Air Pollution-Sulfur 94, Air Pollution-Volatile Organic Compounds, Antarctic-Environmental Protocol, Antarctic-Marine Living Resources, Antarctic Seals, Antarctic Treaty, Biodiversity, Climate Change, Climate Change-Kyoto Protocol, Desertification, Endangered Species, Environmental Modification, Hazardous Wastes, Law of the Sea, Marine Dumping, Marine Life Conservation, Ozone Layer

Protection, Ship Pollution, Tropical Timber 83, Tropical Timber 94, Wetlands, Whaling

signed, but not ratified: none of the selected agreements

GEOGRAPHY - NOTE:

crossroads of Western Europe; most West European capitals are within 1,000 km of Brussels, the seat of both the European Union and NATO

PEOPLE AND SOCIETY :: BELGIUM

POPULATION:

11,570,762 (July 2018 est.)

country comparison to the world: 77

NATIONALITY:

noun: Belgian(s)

adjective: Belgian

ETHNIC GROUPS:

Belgian 75%, Italian 4.1%, Moroccan 3.7%, French 2.4%, Turkish 2%, Dutch 2%, other 12.8% (2011 est.)

LANGUAGES:

Dutch (official) 60%, French (official) 40%, German (official) less than 1%

RELIGIONS:

Roman Catholic 50%, Protestant and other Christian 2.5%, Muslim 5%, Jewish 0.4%, Buddhist 0.3%, atheist 9.2%, none 32.6% (2009 est.)

AGE STRUCTURE:

0-14 years: 17.2% (male 1,019,427 /female 970,845)

15-24 years: 11.25% (male 664,789 /female 636,452)

25-54 years: 39.82% (male 2,323,488 /female 2,283,533)

55-64 years: 12.96% (male 742,842 /female 756,509)

65 years and over: 18.78% (male 948,956 /female 1,223,921) (2018 est.)

DEPENDENCY RATIOS:

total dependency ratio: 54.2 (2015 est.)

youth dependency ratio: 26.2 (2015 est.)

elderly dependency ratio: 28 (2015 est.)

potential support ratio: 3.6 (2015 est.)

MEDIAN AGE:

total: 41.5 years

male: 40.3 years

female: 42.7 years (2018 est.)

country comparison to the world: 39

POPULATION GROWTH RATE:

0.67% (2018 est.)

country comparison to the world: 145

BIRTH RATE:

11.3 births/1,000 population (2018 est.)

country comparison to the world: 171

DEATH RATE:

9.7 deaths/1,000 population (2018 est.)

country comparison to the world: 43

NET MIGRATION RATE:

5.4 migrant(s)/1,000 population (2017 est.)

country comparison to the world: 22

POPULATION DISTRIBUTION:

most of the population concentrated in the northern two-thirds of the country; the southeast is more thinly populated; considered to have one of the highest population densities in the world; approximately 97% live in urban areas

URBANIZATION:

urban population: 98% of total population (2018)

rate of urbanization: 0.62% annual rate of change (2015-20 est.)

MAJOR URBAN AREAS - POPULATION:

2.05 million BRUSSELS (capital), 1.032 million Antwerp (2018)

SEX RATIO:

at birth: 1.05 male(s)/female (2017 est.)

0-14 years: 1.05 male(s)/female (2017 est.)

15-24 years: 1.04 male(s)/female (2017 est.)

25-54 years: 1.02 male(s)/female (2017 est.)

55-64 years: 0.98 male(s)/female (2017 est.)

65 years and over: 0.76 male(s)/female (2017 est.)

total population: 0.97 male(s)/female (2017 est.)

MOTHER'S MEAN AGE AT FIRST BIRTH:

28.6 years (2013 est.)

MATERNAL MORTALITY RATE:

7 deaths/100,000 live births (2015 est.)

country comparison to the world: 160

INFANT MORTALITY RATE:

total: 3.4 deaths/1,000 live births (2018 est.)

male: 3.7 deaths/1,000 live births (2018 est.)

female: 3 deaths/1,000 live births (2018 est.)

country comparison to the world: 201

LIFE EXPECTANCY AT BIRTH:

total population: 81.2 years (2018 est.)

male: 78.6 years (2018 est.)

female: 83.9 years (2018 est.)

country comparison to the world: 31

TOTAL FERTILITY RATE:

1.78 children born/woman (2018 est.)

country comparison to the world: 151

CONTRACEPTIVE PREVALENCE RATE:

66.8% (2013)

note: percent of women aged 15-54

HEALTH EXPENDITURES:

10.6% of GDP (2014)

country comparison to the world: 17

PHYSICIANS DENSITY:

3.01 physicians/1,000 population (2015)

HOSPITAL BED DENSITY:

6.2 beds/1,000 population (2014)

DRINKING WATER SOURCE:

improved:

urban: 100% of population

rural: 100% of population

total: 100% of population

unimproved:

urban: 0% of population

rural: 0% of population

total: 0% of population (2015 est.)

SANITATION FACILITY ACCESS:

improved:

urban: 99.5% of population (2015 est.)

rural: 99.4% of population (2015 est.)

total: 99.5% of population (2015 est.)

unimproved:

urban: 0.5% of population (2015 est.)

rural: 0.6% of population (2015 est.)

total: 0.5% of population (2015 est.)

HIV/AIDS - ADULT PREVALENCE RATE:

NA

HIV/AIDS - PEOPLE LIVING WITH HIV/AIDS:

NA

HIV/AIDS - DEATHS:

NA

OBESITY - ADULT PREVALENCE RATE:

22.1% (2016)

country comparison to the world: 81

EDUCATION EXPENDITURES:

6.6% of GDP (2014)

country comparison to the world: 24

SCHOOL LIFE EXPECTANCY (PRIMARY TO TERTIARY EDUCATION):

total: 20 years (2014)

male: 19 years (2014)

female: 21 years (2014)

UNEMPLOYMENT, YOUTH AGES 15-24:

total: 20.1% (2016 est.)

male: 21.8% (2016 est.)

female: 18.2% (2016 est.)

country comparison to the world: 64

GOVERNMENT :: BELGIUM

COUNTRY NAME:

conventional long form: Kingdom of Belgium

conventional short form: Belgium

local long form: Royaume de Belgique (French)/Koninkrijk Belgie (Dutch)/Koenigreich Belgien (German)

local short form: Belgique/Belgie/Belgien

etymology: the name derives from the Belgae, an ancient Celtic tribal confederation that inhabited an area between the English Channel and the west bank of the Rhine in the first centuries B.C.

GOVERNMENT TYPE:

federal parliamentary democracy under a constitutional monarchy

CAPITAL:

name: Brussels

geographic coordinates: 50 50 N, 4 20 E

time difference: UTC+1 (6 hours ahead of Washington, DC, during Standard Time)

daylight saving time: +1hr, begins last Sunday in March; ends last Sunday in October

ADMINISTRATIVE DIVISIONS:

3 regions (French: regions, singular - region; Dutch: gewesten, singular - gewest); Brussels-Capital Region, also known as Brussels Hoofdstedelijk Gewest (Dutch), Region de Bruxelles-Capitale (French long form), Bruxelles-Capitale (French short form); Flemish Region (Flanders), also known as Vlaams Gewest (Dutch long form), Vlaanderen (Dutch short form), Region Flamande (French long form), Flandre (French short form); Walloon Region (Wallonia), also known as Region Wallone (French long form), Wallonie (French short form), Waals Gewest (Dutch long form), Wallonie (Dutch short form)

note: as a result of the 1993 constitutional revision that furthered devolution into a federal state, there are now three levels of government (federal, regional, and linguistic community) with a complex division of responsibilities; the 2012 sixth state reform transferred additional competencies from the federal state to the regions and linguistic communities

INDEPENDENCE:

4 October 1830 (a provisional government declared independence from the Netherlands);21 July 1831 (King LEOPOLD I ascended to the throne)

NATIONAL HOLIDAY:

Belgian National Day (ascension to the throne of King LEOPOLD I), 21 July (1831)

CONSTITUTION:

history: drafted 25 November 1830, approved 7 February 1831, entered into force 26 July 1831, revised 14 July 1993 (creating a federal state) (2016)

amendments: "revisions" proposed as declarations by the federal government in accord with the king or by Parliament followed by dissolution of Parliament and new elections; adoption requires two-thirds majority vote of a two-thirds quorum in both houses of the next elected Parliament; amended many times, last in 2014 (2016)

LEGAL SYSTEM:

civil law system based on the French Civil Code; note - Belgian law continues to be modified in conformance with the legislative norms mandated by the European Union; judicial review of legislative acts

INTERNATIONAL LAW ORGANIZATION PARTICIPATION:

accepts compulsory ICJ jurisdiction with reservations; accepts ICCt jurisdiction

CITIZENSHIP:

citizenship by birth: no

citizenship by descent only: at least one parent must be a citizen of Belgium

dual citizenship recognized: yes

residency requirement for naturalization: 5 years

SUFFRAGE:

18 years of age; universal and compulsory

EXECUTIVE BRANCH:

chief of state: King PHILIPPE (since 21 July 2013); Heir Apparent Princess ELISABETH (daughter of the monarch, born 25 October 2001)

head of government: Prime Minister (vacant); Deputy Prime Ministers Alexander DE CROO (since 22 October 2012), Kris PEETERS (since 11 October 2014), Didier REYNDERS (since 30 December 2008); note - Prime Minister Charles MICHEL (since 11 October 2014) resigned on 19 December 2018; an interim prime minister has not been designated

cabinet: Council of Ministers formally appointed by the monarch

elections/appointments: the monarchy is hereditary and constitutional; following legislative elections, the leader of the majority party or majority coalition usually appointed prime minister by the monarch and approved by Parliament

LEGISLATIVE BRANCH:

description: bicameral Parliament consists of:
Senate or Senaat (in Dutch), Senat (in French) (60 seats; 50 members indirectly elected by the community and regional parliaments based on their election results, and 10 elected by the 50 other senators; members serve 5-year terms
Chamber of Representatives or Kamer van Volksvertegenwoordigers (in Dutch), Chambre des Representants (in French) (150 seats; members directly elected in multi-seat constituencies by proportional representation vote; members serve 5-year terms)

elections:

Senate - last held 3 July 2014 (next to be held in 2019)
Chamber of Representatives - last held on 25 May 2014 (next to be held in May 2019); note - elections will coincide with the EU's elections

election results: Senate - percent of vote by party - NA; seats by party - NA; composition men 30, women 30, percent of women 50%

Chamber of Representatives - percent of vote by party - N-VA 20.3%, PS 11.7%, CD&V 11.6%, Open VLD 9.8%, MR 9.6%, SP.A 8.8%, Groen 5.3%, CDH 5% PTB 3.7%, VB 3.7%, Ecolo 3.3%, Defi 1.8%, PP 1.5%, other 3.9%; seats by party - N-VA 33, PS 23, MR 20, CD&V 18, Open VLD 14, SP.A 13, CDH 9, Ecolo 6, Groen 6, VB 3, Defi 2, PTB 2, PP 1; composition - men 91, women 59, percent of women 39.3%; note - total Parliament percent of women 42.4%

note: the 1993 constitutional revision that further devolved Belgium into a federal state created three levels of government (federal, regional, and linguistic community) with a complex division of responsibilities; this reality leaves six governments, each with its own legislative assembly; changes above occurred since the sixth state reform

JUDICIAL BRANCH:

highest courts: Constitutional Court or Grondwettelijk Hof (in Dutch) and Cour constitutionelle (in French) (consists of 12 judges - 6 Dutch-speaking and 6 French-speaking); Supreme Court of Justice or Hof van Cassatie (in Dutch) and Cour de Cassation (in French) (court organized into 3 chambers: civil and commercial; criminal; social, fiscal, and armed forces; each chamber includes a Dutch division and a French division, each with a chairperson and 5-6 judges)

judge selection and term of office: Constitutional Court judges appointed by the monarch from candidates submitted by Parliament; judges appointed for life with mandatory retirement at age 70; Supreme Court judges appointed by the monarch from candidates submitted by the High Council of Justice, a 44-member independent body of judicial and non-judicial members; judges appointed for life

subordinate courts: Courts of Appeal; regional courts; specialized courts for administrative, commercial, labor, immigration, and audit issues; magistrate's courts; justices of the peace

POLITICAL PARTIES AND LEADERS:

Flemish parties:
Christian Democratic and Flemish or CD&V [Wouter BEKE];
Flemish Liberals and Democrats or Open VLD [Gwendolyn RUTTEN];
Groen [Meyrem ALMACI] (formerly AGALEV, Flemish Greens);
New Flemish Alliance or N-VA [Bart DE WEVER];
Social Progressive Alternative or SP.A [John CROMBEZ, Stephanie VAN HOUTVEN];
Vlaams Belang (Flemish Interest) or VB [Tom VAN GRIEKEN];
Francophone parties:
Ecolo (Francophone Greens) [Patrick DUPRIEZ, Zakia KHATTABI];
Francophone Federalist Democrats or Defi [Olivier MAINGAIN];
Humanist and Democratic Center or CDH [Benoit LUTGEN];
People's Party or PP [Mischael MODRIKAMEN];
Reform Movement or MR [Olivier CHASTEL];
Socialist Party or PS [Elio DI RUPO];
Workers' Party or PTB [Peter MERTENS];
other minor parties

INTERNATIONAL ORGANIZATION PARTICIPATION:

ADB (nonregional members), AfDB (nonregional members), Australia Group, Benelux, BIS, CD, CE, CERN, EAPC, EBRD, ECB, EIB, EITI (implementing country), EMU, ESA, EU, FAO, FATF, G-9, G-10, IADB, IAEA, IBRD, ICAO, ICC (national committees), ICCt, ICRM, IDA, IEA, IFAD, IFC, IFRCS, IGAD (partners), IHO, ILO, IMF, IMO, IMSO, Interpol, IOC, IOM, IPU, ISO, ITSO, ITU, ITUC (NGOs), MIGA, MONUSCO, NATO, NEA, NSG, OAS (observer), OECD, OIF, OPCW, OSCE, Pacific Alliance (observer), Paris Club, PCA, Schengen Convention, SELEC (observer), UN, UNCTAD, UNESCO, UNHCR, UNIDO, UNIFIL, UNRWA, UNTSO, UPU, WCO, WHO, WIPO, WMO, WTO, ZC

DIPLOMATIC REPRESENTATION IN THE US:

chief of mission: Ambassador Dirk Jozef M. WOUTERS (since 16 September 2016)

chancery: 3330 Garfield Street NW, Washington, DC 20008

telephone: [1] (202) 333-6900

FAX: [1] (202) 333-3079

consulate(s) general: Atlanta, Los Angeles, New York

DIPLOMATIC REPRESENTATION FROM THE US:

chief of mission: Ambassador (vacant); Charge d'Affaires Matthew LUSSENHOP (since 21 January 2017)

embassy: 27 Boulevard du Regent [Regentlaan], B-1000 Brussels

mailing address: PSC 82, Box 002, APO AE 09710

telephone: [32] (2) 811-4000

FAX: [32] (2) 811-4500

FLAG DESCRIPTION:

three equal vertical bands of black (hoist side), yellow, and red; the vertical design was based on the flag of France; the colors are those of the arms of the duchy of Brabant (yellow lion with red claws and tongue on a black field)

NATIONAL SYMBOL(S):

golden rampant lion; national colors: red, black, yellow

NATIONAL ANTHEM:

name: "La Brabanconne" (The Song of Brabant)

lyrics/music: Louis-Alexandre DECHET[French] Victor CEULEMANS [Dutch]/Francois VAN CAMPENHOUT

note: adopted 1830; according to legend, Louis-Alexandre DECHET, an actor at the theater in which the revolution against the Netherlands began, wrote the lyrics with a group of young people in a Brussels cafe

ECONOMY :: BELGIUM

ECONOMY - OVERVIEW:

Belgium's central geographic location and highly developed transport network have helped develop a well-diversified economy, with a broad mix of transport, services, manufacturing, and high tech. Service and high-tech industries are concentrated in the northern Flanders region while the southern region of Wallonia is home to industries like coal and steel manufacturing. Belgium is completely reliant on foreign sources of fossil fuels, and the planned closure of its seven nuclear plants by 2025 should increase its dependence on foreign energy. Its role as a regional logistical hub makes its economy vulnerable to shifts in foreign demand, particularly with EU trading partners. Roughly three-quarters of Belgium's trade is with other EU countries, and the port of Zeebrugge conducts almost half its trade with the United Kingdom alone, leaving Belgium's economy vulnerable to the outcome of negotiations on the UK's exit from the EU.

Belgium's GDP grew by 1.7% in 2017 and the budget deficit was 1.5% of GDP. Unemployment stood at 7.3%, however the unemployment rate is lower in Flanders than Wallonia, 4.4% compared to 9.4%, because of industrial differences between the regions. The economy largely recovered from the March 2016 terrorist attacks that mainly impacted the Brussels region tourist and hospitality industry. Prime Minister Charles MICHEL's center-right government has pledged to further reduce the deficit in response to EU pressure to decrease Belgium's high public debt of about 104% of GDP, but such efforts would also dampen economic growth. In addition to restrained public spending, low wage growth and higher inflation promise to curtail a more robust recovery in private consumption.

The government has pledged to pursue a reform program to improve Belgium's competitiveness, including changes to labor market rules and welfare benefits. These changes have generally made Belgian wages more competitive regionally, but have raised tensions with trade unions, which have called for extended strikes. In 2017, Belgium approved a tax reform plan to ease corporate rates from 33% to 29% by 2018 and down to 25% by 2020. The tax plan also included benefits for innovation and SMEs, intended to spur competitiveness and private investment.

GDP (PURCHASING POWER PARITY):

$529.2 billion (2017 est.)

$520.2 billion (2016 est.)

$513 billion (2015 est.)

note: data are in 2017 dollars

country comparison to the world: 37

GDP (OFFICIAL EXCHANGE RATE):

$493.7 billion (2017 est.) (2017 est.)

GDP - REAL GROWTH RATE:

1.7% (2017 est.)

1.4% (2016 est.)

1.4% (2015 est.)

country comparison to the world: 162

GDP - PER CAPITA (PPP):

$46,600 (2017 est.)

$46,000 (2016 est.)

$45,700 (2015 est.)

note: data are in 2017 dollars

country comparison to the world: 35

GROSS NATIONAL SAVING:

24.5% of GDP (2017 est.)

24% of GDP (2016 est.)

23.4% of GDP (2015 est.)

country comparison to the world: 65

GDP - COMPOSITION, BY END USE:

household consumption: 51.2% (2017 est.)

government consumption: 23.4% (2017 est.)

investment in fixed capital: 23.3% (2017 est.)

investment in inventories: 1.3% (2017 est.)

exports of goods and services: 85.1% (2017 est.)

imports of goods and services: -84.4% (2017 est.)

GDP - COMPOSITION, BY SECTOR OF ORIGIN:

agriculture: 0.7% (2017 est.)

industry: 22.1% (2017 est.)

services: 77.2% (2017 est.)

AGRICULTURE - PRODUCTS:

sugar beets, fresh vegetables, fruits, grain, tobacco; beef, veal, pork, milk

INDUSTRIES:

engineering and metal products, motor vehicle assembly, transportation equipment, scientific instruments, processed food and beverages, chemicals, pharmaceuticals, base metals, textiles, glass, petroleum

INDUSTRIAL PRODUCTION GROWTH RATE:

0.2% (2017 est.)

country comparison to the world: 168

LABOR FORCE:

5.324 million (2017 est.)

country comparison to the world: 79

LABOR FORCE - BY OCCUPATION:

agriculture: 1.3%

industry: 18.6%

services: 80.1% (2013 est.)

UNEMPLOYMENT RATE:

7.1% (2017 est.)

7.9% (2016 est.)

country comparison to the world: 108

POPULATION BELOW POVERTY LINE:

15.1% (2013 est.)

HOUSEHOLD INCOME OR CONSUMPTION BY PERCENTAGE SHARE:

lowest 10%: 28.4% (2006)

highest 10%: 28.4% (2006)

DISTRIBUTION OF FAMILY INCOME - GINI INDEX:

25.9 (2013 est.)

28.7 (1996)

country comparison to the world: 150

BUDGET:

revenues: 253.5 billion (2017 est.)

expenditures: 258.6 billion (2017 est.)

TAXES AND OTHER REVENUES:

51.3% (of GDP) (2017 est.)

country comparison to the world: 15

BUDGET SURPLUS (+) OR DEFICIT (-):

-1% (of GDP) (2017 est.)

country comparison to the world: 74

PUBLIC DEBT:

103.4% of GDP (2017 est.)

106% of GDP (2016 est.)

note: data cover general government debt and includes debt instruments issued (or owned) by government entities other than the treasury; the data include treasury debt held by foreign entities; the data include debt issued by subnational entities, as well as intra-governmental debt; intra-governmental debt consists of treasury borrowings from surpluses in the social funds, such as for retirement, medical care, and unemployment; debt instruments for the social funds are not sold at public auctions; general government debt is defined by the Maastricht definition and calculated by the National Bank of Belgium as consolidated gross debt; the debt is defined in European Regulation EC479/2009 concerning the implementation of the protocol on the excessive deficit procedure annexed to the Treaty on European Union (Treaty of Maastricht) of 7 February 1992; the sub-sectors of consolidated gross debt are: federal government, communities and regions, local government, and social security funds

country comparison to the world: 13

FISCAL YEAR:

calendar year

INFLATION RATE (CONSUMER PRICES):

2.2% (2017 est.)

1.8% (2016 est.)

country comparison to the world: 112

CENTRAL BANK DISCOUNT RATE:

0% (31 December 2017)

0% (31 December 2010)

note: this is the European Central Bank's rate on the marginal lending facility, which offers overnight credit to banks in the euro area

country comparison to the world: 148

COMMERCIAL BANK PRIME LENDING RATE:

2.08% (31 December 2017 est.)

2.02% (31 December 2016 est.)

country comparison to the world: 183

STOCK OF NARROW MONEY:

$240.5 billion (31 December 2017 est.)

$198 billion (31 December 2016 est.)

note: see entry for the European Union for money supply for the entire euro area; the European Central Bank (ECB) controls monetary policy for the 18 members of the Economic and Monetary Union (EMU); individual members of the EMU do not control the quantity of money circulating within their own borders

country comparison to the world: 22

STOCK OF BROAD MONEY:

$240.5 billion (31 December 2017 est.)

$198 billion (31 December 2016 est.)

country comparison to the world: 22

STOCK OF DOMESTIC CREDIT:

$711.3 billion (31 December 2017 est.)

$684.8 billion (31 December 2016 est.)

country comparison to the world: 20

MARKET VALUE OF PUBLICLY TRADED SHARES:

$414.6 billion (31 December 2015 est.)

$378.5 billion (31 December 2014 est.)

$374.3 billion (31 December 2013 est.)

country comparison to the world: 24

CURRENT ACCOUNT BALANCE:

-$807 million (2017 est.)

$451 million (2016 est.)

country comparison to the world: 134

EXPORTS:

$300.8 billion (2017 est.)

$277.7 billion (2016 est.)

country comparison to the world: 20

EXPORTS - PARTNERS:

Germany 16.6%, France 14.9%, Netherlands 12%, UK 8.4%, Italy 4.9%, US 4.8% (2017)

EXPORTS - COMMODITIES:

chemicals, machinery and equipment, finished diamonds, metals and metal products, foodstuffs

IMPORTS:

$300.4 billion (2017 est.)

$273.4 billion (2016 est.)

country comparison to the world: 17

IMPORTS - COMMODITIES:

raw materials, machinery and equipment, chemicals, raw diamonds, pharmaceuticals, foodstuffs, transportation equipment, oil products

IMPORTS - PARTNERS:

Netherlands 17.3%, Germany 13.8%, France 9.5%, US 7.1%, UK 4.9%, Ireland 4.2%, China 4.1% (2017)

RESERVES OF FOREIGN EXCHANGE AND GOLD:

$26.16 billion (31 December 2017 est.)

$24.1 billion (31 December 2015 est.)

country comparison to the world: 54

DEBT - EXTERNAL:

$1.281 trillion (31 March 2016 est.)

$1.214 trillion (31 March 2015 est.)

country comparison to the world: 15

STOCK OF DIRECT FOREIGN INVESTMENT - AT HOME:

$1.035 trillion (31 December 2017 est.)

$1.054 trillion (31 December 2016 est.)

country comparison to the world: 11

STOCK OF DIRECT FOREIGN INVESTMENT - ABROAD:

$1.159 trillion (31 December 2017 est.)

$1.016 trillion (31 December 2016 est.)

country comparison to the world: 12

EXCHANGE RATES:

euros (EUR) per US dollar -

0.885 (2017 est.)

0.903 (2016 est.)

0.9214 (2015 est.)

0.885 (2014 est.)

0.7634 (2013 est.)

ENERGY :: BELGIUM

ELECTRICITY ACCESS:

electrification - total population: 100% (2016)

ELECTRICITY - PRODUCTION:

79.83 billion kWh (2016 est.)

country comparison to the world: 37

ELECTRICITY - CONSUMPTION:

82.16 billion kWh (2016 est.)

country comparison to the world: 36

ELECTRICITY - EXPORTS:

8.465 billion kWh (2016 est.)

country comparison to the world: 25

ELECTRICITY - IMPORTS:

14.65 billion kWh (2016 est.)

country comparison to the world: 15

ELECTRICITY - INSTALLED GENERATING CAPACITY:

21.56 million kW (2016 est.)

country comparison to the world: 41

ELECTRICITY - FROM FOSSIL FUELS:

35% of total installed capacity (2016 est.)

country comparison to the world: 177

ELECTRICITY - FROM NUCLEAR FUELS:

28% of total installed capacity (2017 est.)

country comparison to the world: 2

ELECTRICITY - FROM HYDROELECTRIC PLANTS:

1% of total installed capacity (2017 est.)

country comparison to the world: 146

ELECTRICITY - FROM OTHER RENEWABLE SOURCES:

36% of total installed capacity (2017 est.)

country comparison to the world: 8

CRUDE OIL - PRODUCTION:

0 bbl/day (2017 est.)

country comparison to the world: 108

CRUDE OIL - EXPORTS:

0 bbl/day (2017 est.)

country comparison to the world: 92

CRUDE OIL - IMPORTS:

687,600 bbl/day (2017 est.)

country comparison to the world: 16

CRUDE OIL - PROVED RESERVES:

0 bbl (1 January 2018 est.)

country comparison to the world: 106

REFINED PETROLEUM PRODUCTS - PRODUCTION:

731,700 bbl/day (2017 est.)

country comparison to the world: 25

REFINED PETROLEUM PRODUCTS - CONSUMPTION:

648,600 bbl/day (2017 est.)

country comparison to the world: 31

REFINED PETROLEUM PRODUCTS - EXPORTS:

680,800 bbl/day (2017 est.)

country comparison to the world: 12

REFINED PETROLEUM PRODUCTS - IMPORTS:

601,400 bbl/day (2017 est.)

country comparison to the world: 14

NATURAL GAS - PRODUCTION:

0 cu m (2017 est.)

country comparison to the world: 102

NATURAL GAS - CONSUMPTION:

17.61 billion cu m (2017 est.)

country comparison to the world: 40

NATURAL GAS - EXPORTS:

736.2 million cu m (2017 est.)

country comparison to the world: 40

NATURAL GAS - IMPORTS:

18.09 billion cu m (2017 est.)

country comparison to the world: 17

NATURAL GAS - PROVED RESERVES:

0 cu m (1 January 2014 est.)

country comparison to the world: 109

CARBON DIOXIDE EMISSIONS FROM CONSUMPTION OF ENERGY:

134.7 million Mt (2017 est.)

country comparison to the world: 35

COMMUNICATIONS :: BELGIUM

TELEPHONES - FIXED LINES:

total subscriptions: 4,251,564 (2017 est.)

subscriptions per 100 inhabitants: 37 (2017 est.)

country comparison to the world: 33

TELEPHONES - MOBILE CELLULAR:

total subscriptions: 11,961,089 (2017 est.)

subscriptions per 100 inhabitants: 104 (2017 est.)

country comparison to the world: 76

TELEPHONE SYSTEM:

general assessment: highly developed, technologically advanced, and completely automated domestic and international telephone and telegraph facilities; LTE availability is nearly universal in mobile sector; ongoing investments in developing applications and services for 5G; consumer are interested in quad-play services (broadband +television +telephone +wireless services) which will mean MNOs (mobile network operators) are enhancing their fixed-line offerings (2017)

domestic: nationwide mobile-cellular telephone system; extensive cable network; limited microwave radio relay network; 37 per 100 fixed-line, 104 per 100 mobile-cellular (2017)

international: country code - 32; landing point for a number of submarine cables that provide links to Europe, the Middle East, and Asia; satellite earth stations - 7 (Intelsat - 3) (2015)

BROADCAST MEDIA:

a segmented market with the three major communities (Flemish, French, and German-speaking) each having responsibility for their own broadcast media; multiple TV channels exist for each community; additionally, in excess of 90% of households are connected to cable and can access broadcasts of TV stations from neighboring countries; each community has a public radio network coexisting with private broadcasters (2009)

INTERNET COUNTRY CODE:

.be

INTERNET USERS:

total: 9,870,734 (July 2016 est.)

percent of population: 86.5% (July 2016 est.)

country comparison to the world: 48

BROADBAND - FIXED SUBSCRIPTIONS:

total: 4,378,973 (2017 est.)

subscriptions per 100 inhabitants: 38 (2017 est.)

country comparison to the world: 30

TRANSPORTATION :: BELGIUM

NATIONAL AIR TRANSPORT SYSTEM:

number of registered air carriers: 7 (2015)

inventory of registered aircraft operated by air carriers: 117 (2015)

annual passenger traffic on registered air carriers: 11,193,023 (2015)

annual freight traffic on registered air carriers: 1,464,316,900 mt-km (2015)

CIVIL AIRCRAFT REGISTRATION COUNTRY CODE PREFIX:

OO (2016)

AIRPORTS:

41 (2013)

country comparison to the world: 102

AIRPORTS - WITH PAVED RUNWAYS:

total: 26 (2017)

over 3,047 m: 6 (2017)

2,438 to 3,047 m: 9 (2017)

1,524 to 2,437 m: 2 (2017)

914 to 1,523 m: 1 (2017)

under 914 m: 8 (2017)

AIRPORTS - WITH UNPAVED RUNWAYS:

total: 15 (2013)

under 914 m: 15 (2013)

HELIPORTS:

1 (2013)

PIPELINES:

3139 km gas, 154 km oil, 535 km refined products (2013)

RAILWAYS:

total: 3,592 km (2014)

standard gauge: 3,592 km 1.435-m gauge (2,960 km electrified) (2014)

country comparison to the world: 53

ROADWAYS:

total: 154,012 km (2010)

paved: 120,514 km (includes 1,756 km of expressways) (2010)

unpaved: 33,498 km (2010)

country comparison to the world: 33

WATERWAYS:

2,043 km (1,528 km in regular commercial use) (2012)

country comparison to the world: 41

MERCHANT MARINE:

total: 185 (2017)

by type: bulk carrier 15, general cargo 15, oil tanker 20, other 135 (2017)

country comparison to the world: 66

PORTS AND TERMINALS:

major seaport(s): Oostende, Zeebrugge

container port(s) (TEUs): Antwerp (10,037,341) (2016)

LNG terminal(s) (import): Zeebrugge

river port(s): Antwerp, Gent (Schelde River)

Brussels (Senne River) Liege (Meuse River)

MILITARY AND SECURITY :: BELGIUM

MILITARY EXPENDITURES:

0.93% of GDP (2018)

0.91% of GDP (2017)

0.92% of GDP (2016)

0.92% of GDP (2015)

0.97% of GDP (2014)

country comparison to the world: 120

MILITARY BRANCHES:

Belgian Armed Forces: Land Component, Naval Component, Air Component, Medical Component (2018)

MILITARY SERVICE AGE AND OBLIGATION:

18 years of age for male and female voluntary military service; conscription abolished in 1994 (2012)

TRANSNATIONAL ISSUES :: BELGIUM

DISPUTES - INTERNATIONAL:

none

REFUGEES AND INTERNALLY DISPLACED PERSONS:

refugees (country of origin): 9,080 (Syria) (2016)

stateless persons: 7,695 (2017)

ILLICIT DRUGS:

growing producer of synthetic drugs and cannabis; transit point for US-bound ecstasy; source of precursor chemicals for South American cocaine processors; transshipment point for cocaine, heroin, hashish, and marijuana entering Western Europe; despite a strengthening of legislation, the country remains vulnerable to money laundering related to narcotics, automobiles, alcohol, and tobacco; significant domestic consumption of ecstasy

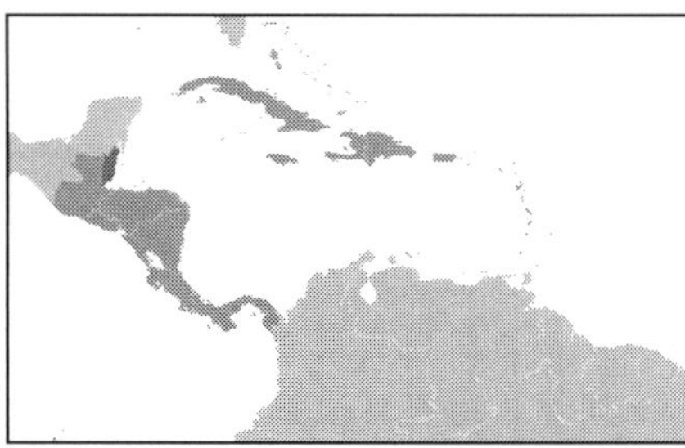

CENTRAL AMERICA :: BELIZE

INTRODUCTION :: BELIZE

BACKGROUND:

Belize was the site of several Mayan city states until their decline at the end of the first millennium A.D. The British and Spanish disputed the region in the 17th and 18th centuries; it formally became the colony of British Honduras in 1862. Territorial disputes between the UK and Guatemala delayed the independence of Belize until 1981. Guatemala refused to recognize the new nation until 1992 and the two countries are involved in an ongoing border dispute. Tourism has become the mainstay of the economy. Current concerns include the country's heavy foreign debt burden, high unemployment, growing involvement in the Mexican and South American drug trade, high crime rates, and one of the highest HIV/AIDS prevalence rates in Central America.

GEOGRAPHY :: BELIZE

LOCATION:

Central America, bordering the Caribbean Sea, between Guatemala and Mexico

GEOGRAPHIC COORDINATES:

17 15 N, 88 45 W

MAP REFERENCES:

Central America and the Caribbean

AREA:

total: 22,966 sq km

land: 22,806 sq km

water: 160 sq km

country comparison to the world: 152

AREA - COMPARATIVE:

slightly smaller than Massachusetts

LAND BOUNDARIES:

total: 542 km

border countries (2): Guatemala 266 km, Mexico 276 km

COASTLINE:

386 km

MARITIME CLAIMS:

territorial sea: 12 nm in the north, 3 nm in the south; note - from the mouth of the Sarstoon River to Ranguana Cay, Belize's territorial sea is 3 nm; according to Belize's Maritime Areas Act, 1992, the purpose of this limitation is to provide a framework for negotiating a definitive agreement on territorial differences with Guatemala

exclusive economic zone: 200 nm

CLIMATE:

tropical; very hot and humid; rainy season (May to November); dry season (February to May)

TERRAIN:

flat, swampy coastal plain; low mountains in south

ELEVATION:

mean elevation: 173 m

elevation extremes: 0 m lowest point: Caribbean Sea

1124 highest point: Doyle's Delight

NATURAL RESOURCES:

arable land potential, timber, fish, hydropower

LAND USE:

agricultural land: 6.9% (2011 est.)

arable land: 3.3% (2011 est.) / permanent crops: 1.4% (2011 est.) / permanent pasture: 2.2% (2011 est.)

forest: 60.6% (2011 est.)

other: 32.5% (2011 est.)

IRRIGATED LAND:

35 sq km (2012)

POPULATION DISTRIBUTION:

approximately 25% to 30% of the population lives in the former capital, Belize City; over half of the overall population is rural; population density is slightly higher in the north and east

NATURAL HAZARDS:

frequent, devastating hurricanes (June to November) and coastal flooding (especially in south)

ENVIRONMENT - CURRENT ISSUES:

deforestation; water pollution, including pollution of Belize's Barrier Reef System, from sewage, industrial effluents, agricultural runoff; inability to properly dispose of solid waste

ENVIRONMENT - INTERNATIONAL AGREEMENTS:

party to: Biodiversity, Climate Change, Climate Change-Kyoto Protocol, Desertification, Endangered Species, Hazardous Wastes, Law of the Sea, Ozone Layer Protection, Ship Pollution, Wetlands, Whaling

signed, but not ratified: none of the selected agreements

GEOGRAPHY - NOTE:

only country in Central America without a coastline on the North Pacific Ocean

PEOPLE AND SOCIETY :: BELIZE

POPULATION:

385,854 (July 2018 est.)

country comparison to the world: 177

NATIONALITY:

noun: Belizean(s)

adjective: Belizean

ETHNIC GROUPS:

mestizo 52.9%, Creole 25.9%, Maya 11.3%, Garifuna 6.1%, East Indian 3.9%, Mennonite 3.6%, white 1.2%, Asian 1%, other 1.2%, unknown 0.3% (2010 est.)

note: percentages add up to more than 100% because respondents were able to identify more than one ethnic origin

LANGUAGES:

English 62.9% (official), Spanish 56.6%, Creole 44.6%, Maya 10.5%, German 3.2%, Garifuna 2.9%, other 1.8%, unknown 0.3%, none 0.2% (cannot speak) (2010 est.)

note: shares sum to more than 100% because some respondents gave more than one answer on the census

RELIGIONS:

Roman Catholic 40.1%, Protestant 31.5% (includes Pentecostal 8.4%, Seventh Day Adventist 5.4%, Anglican 4.7%, Mennonite 3.7%, Baptist 3.6%, Methodist 2.9%, Nazarene 2.8%), Jehovah's Witness 1.7%, other 10.5% (includes Baha'i, Buddhist, Hindu, Mormon, Muslim, Rastafarian, Salvation Army), unspecified 0.6%, none 15.5% (2010 est.)

DEMOGRAPHIC PROFILE:

Migration continues to transform Belize's population. About 16% of Belizeans live abroad, while immigrants constitute approximately 15% of Belize's population. Belizeans seeking job and educational opportunities have preferred to emigrate to the United States rather than former colonizer Great Britain because of the United States' closer proximity and stronger trade ties with Belize. Belizeans also emigrate to Canada, Mexico, and English-speaking Caribbean countries. The emigration of a large share of Creoles (Afro-Belizeans) and the influx of Central American immigrants, mainly Guatemalans, Salvadorans, and Hondurans, has changed Belize's ethnic composition. Mestizos have become the largest ethnic group, and Belize now has more native Spanish speakers than English or Creole speakers, despite English being the official language. In addition, Central American immigrants are establishing new communities in rural areas, which contrasts with the urbanization trend seen in neighboring countries. Recently, Chinese, European, and North American immigrants have become more frequent.

Immigration accounts for an increasing share of Belize's population growth rate, which is steadily falling due to fertility decline. Belize's declining birth rate and its increased life expectancy are creating an aging population. As the elderly population grows and nuclear families replace extended households, Belize's government will be challenged to balance a rising demand for pensions, social services, and healthcare for its senior citizens with the need to reduce poverty and social inequality and to improve sanitation.

AGE STRUCTURE:

0-14 years: 33.61% (male 66,207 /female 63,466)

15-24 years: 18.74% (male 37,184 /female 35,127)

25-54 years: 37.43% (male 70,222 /female 74,187)

55-64 years: 5.88% (male 11,397 /female 11,284)

65 years and over: 4.35% (male 8,293 /female 8,487) (2018 est.)

DEPENDENCY RATIOS:

total dependency ratio: 56.8 (2015 est.)

youth dependency ratio: 50.9 (2015 est.)

elderly dependency ratio: 5.9 (2015 est.)

potential support ratio: 17 (2015 est.)

MEDIAN AGE:

total: 23.7 years

male: 23.2 years

female: 24.4 years (2018 est.)

country comparison to the world: 168

POPULATION GROWTH RATE:

1.8% (2018 est.)

country comparison to the world: 57

BIRTH RATE:

22.9 births/1,000 population (2018 est.)

country comparison to the world: 63

DEATH RATE:

4.2 deaths/1,000 population (2018 est.)

country comparison to the world: 206

NET MIGRATION RATE:

0 migrant(s)/1,000 population (2017 est.)

country comparison to the world: 73

POPULATION DISTRIBUTION:

approximately 25% to 30% of the population lives in the former capital, Belize City; over half of the overall population is rural; population density is slightly higher in the north and east

URBANIZATION:

urban population: 45.7% of total population (2018)

rate of urbanization: 2.32% annual rate of change (2015-20 est.)

MAJOR URBAN AREAS - POPULATION:

23,000 BELMOPAN (capital) (2018)

SEX RATIO:

at birth: 1.05 male(s)/female (2017 est.)

0-14 years: 1.04 male(s)/female (2017 est.)

15-24 years: 1.04 male(s)/female (2017 est.)

25-54 years: 1.03 male(s)/female (2017 est.)

55-64 years: 0.97 male(s)/female (2017 est.)

65 years and over: 0.89 male(s)/female (2017 est.)

total population: 1.03 male(s)/female (2017 est.)

MATERNAL MORTALITY RATE:

28 deaths/100,000 live births (2015 est.)

country comparison to the world: 116

INFANT MORTALITY RATE:

total: 12 deaths/1,000 live births (2018 est.)

male: 13.3 deaths/1,000 live births (2018 est.)

female: 10.7 deaths/1,000 live births (2018 est.)

country comparison to the world: 114

LIFE EXPECTANCY AT BIRTH:

total population: 74.7 years (2018 est.)

male: 73.1 years (2018 est.)

female: 76.3 years (2018 est.)

country comparison to the world: 122

TOTAL FERTILITY RATE:

2.8 children born/woman (2018 est.)

country comparison to the world: 60

CONTRACEPTIVE PREVALENCE RATE:

51.4% (2015/16)

HEALTH EXPENDITURES:

5.8% of GDP (2014)

country comparison to the world: 109

PHYSICIANS DENSITY:

0.77 physicians/1,000 population (2009)

HOSPITAL BED DENSITY:

1.3 beds/1,000 population (2014)

DRINKING WATER SOURCE:

improved:

urban: 98.9% of population

rural: 100% of population

total: 99.5% of population

unimproved:

urban: 1.1% of population

rural: 0% of population

total: 0.5% of population (2015 est.)

SANITATION FACILITY ACCESS:

improved:

urban: 93.5% of population (2015 est.)

rural: 88.2% of population (2015 est.)

total: 90.5% of population (2015 est.)

unimproved:

urban: 6.5% of population (2015 est.)

rural: 11.8% of population (2015 est.)

total: 9.5% of population (2015 est.)

HIV/AIDS - ADULT PREVALENCE RATE:

1.9% (2017 est.)

country comparison to the world: 26

HIV/AIDS - PEOPLE LIVING WITH HIV/AIDS:

4,500 (2017 est.)

country comparison to the world: 118

HIV/AIDS - DEATHS:

<200 (2017 est.)

MAJOR INFECTIOUS DISEASES:

degree of risk: high (2016)

food or waterborne diseases: bacterial diarrhea, hepatitis A, and typhoid fever (2016)

vectorborne diseases: dengue fever and malaria (2016)

note: active local transmission of Zika virus by Aedes species mosquitoes has been identified in this country (as of August 2016); it poses an important risk (a large number of cases possible) among US citizens if bitten by an infective mosquito; other less common ways to get Zika are through sex, via blood transfusion, or during pregnancy, in which the pregnant woman passes Zika virus to her fetus

OBESITY - ADULT PREVALENCE RATE:

24.1% (2016)

country comparison to the world: 60

CHILDREN UNDER THE AGE OF 5 YEARS UNDERWEIGHT:

4.6% (2015)

country comparison to the world: 84

EDUCATION EXPENDITURES:

7.4% of GDP (2017)

country comparison to the world: 14

SCHOOL LIFE EXPECTANCY (PRIMARY TO TERTIARY EDUCATION):

total: 13 years (2015)

male: 13 years (2015)

female: 13 years (2015)

UNEMPLOYMENT, YOUTH AGES 15-24:

total: 17.7% (2016 est.)

male: 11% (2016 est.)

female: 28.4% (2016 est.)

country comparison to the world: 73

GOVERNMENT :: BELIZE

COUNTRY NAME:

conventional long form: none

conventional short form: Belize

former: British Honduras

etymology: may be named for the Belize River, whose name possibly derives from the Maya word "belix," meaning "muddy-watered"

GOVERNMENT TYPE:

parliamentary democracy (National Assembly) under a constitutional monarchy; a Commonwealth realm

CAPITAL:

name: Belmopan

geographic coordinates: 17 15 N, 88 46 W

time difference: UTC-6 (1 hour behind Washington, DC, during Standard Time)

ADMINISTRATIVE DIVISIONS:

6 districts; Belize, Cayo, Corozal, Orange Walk, Stann Creek, Toledo

INDEPENDENCE:

21 September 1981 (from the UK)

NATIONAL HOLIDAY:

Battle of St. George's Caye Day (National Day), 10 September (1798); Independence Day, 21 September (1981)

CONSTITUTION:

history: previous 1954, 1963 (preindependence); latest signed and entered into force 21 September 1981 (2018)

amendments: proposed and adopted by two-thirds majority vote by the National Assembly House of Representatives except for amendments relating to rights and freedoms, changes to the Assembly, and to elections and judiciary matters, which require at least three-quarters majority vote by the House; both types of amendments require assent by the governor general; amended several times, last in 2018 (2018)

LEGAL SYSTEM:

English common law

INTERNATIONAL LAW ORGANIZATION PARTICIPATION:

has not submitted an ICJ jurisdiction declaration; accepts ICCt jurisdiction

CITIZENSHIP:

citizenship by birth: yes

citizenship by descent only: yes

dual citizenship recognized: yes

residency requirement for naturalization: 5 years

SUFFRAGE:

18 years of age; universal

EXECUTIVE BRANCH:

chief of state: Queen ELIZABETH II (since 6 February 1952); represented by Governor General Sir Colville Norbert YOUNG, Sr. (since 17 November 1993)

head of government: Prime Minister Dean Oliver BARROW (since 8 February 2008); Deputy Prime Minister Patrick FABER (since 7 June 2016)

cabinet: Cabinet appointed by the governor general on the advice of the prime minister from among members of the National Assembly

elections/appointments: the monarchy is hereditary; governor general appointed by the monarch; following legislative elections, the leader of the majority party or majority coalition usually appointed prime minister by the governor general; prime minister recommends the deputy prime minister

LEGISLATIVE BRANCH:

description: bicameral National Assembly consists of:

elections:
Senate (12 seats; members appointed by the governor general - 6 on the advice of the prime minister, 3 on the advice of the leader of the opposition, and 1 each on the advice of the Belize Council of Churches and Evangelical Association of Churches, the Belize Chamber of Commerce and Industry and the Belize Better Business Bureau, and the National Trade Union Congress
House of Representatives (31 seats; members directly elected in single-seat constituencies by simple majority vote to serve 5-year terms)

election results:
percent of vote by party - UDP 50%, PUP 47.3%, other 2.7%; seats by party - UDP 19, PUP 12

note: House of Representatives - last held on 4 November 2015 (next to be held in November 2020)

JUDICIAL BRANCH:

highest courts: Supreme Court of Judicature (consists of the Court of Appeal with the court president and 3 justices, and the Supreme Court with the chief justice and 2 judges); note - in 2010, Belize acceded to the Caribbean Court of Justice as the final court of appeal, replacing that of the Judicial Committee of the Privy Council in London

judge selection and term of office:
Court of Appeal president and justices appointed by the governor general upon advice of the prime minister after consultation with the National Assembly opposition leader; justices' tenures vary by terms of appointment; Supreme Court chief justice appointed by the governor-general upon the advice of the prime minister and the National Assembly opposition leader; other judges appointed by the governor-general upon the advice of the Judicial and Legal Services Section of the Public Services Commission and with the concurrence of the prime minister after consultation with the National Assembly opposition leader; judges can be appointed beyond age 65 but must retire by age 75; in 2013, the Supreme Court chief justice overturned a constitutional amendment that had restricted Court of Appeal judge appointments to as short as 1 year

subordinate courts: Magistrate Courts; Family Court

POLITICAL PARTIES AND LEADERS:

Belize Progressive Party or BPP [Patrick ROGERS] (formed in 2015 from a merger of the People's National Party, elements of the Vision Inspired by the People, and other smaller political groups)
People's United Party or PUP [Johnny BRICENO]
United Democratic Party or UDP [Dean Oliver BARROW]

INTERNATIONAL ORGANIZATION PARTICIPATION:

ACP, AOSIS, C, Caricom, CD, CDB, CELAC, FAO, G-77, IADB, IAEA, IBRD, ICAO, ICC (NGOs), ICRM, IDA, IFAD, IFC, IFRCS, ILO, IMF, IMO, Interpol, IOC, IOM, ITU, LAES, MIGA, NAM, OAS, OPANAL, OPCW, PCA, Petrocaribe, SICA, UN, UNCTAD, UNESCO, UNIDO, UPU, WCO, WHO, WIPO, WMO, WTO

DIPLOMATIC REPRESENTATION IN THE US:

chief of mission: Ambassador Francisco Daniel GUTIEREZ (since 21 July 2017)

chancery: 2535 Massachusetts Avenue NW, Washington, DC 20008

telephone: [1] (202) 332-9636

FAX: [1] (202) 332-6888

consulate(s) general: Los Angeles

DIPLOMATIC REPRESENTATION FROM THE US:

chief of mission: Ambassador (vacant); Charge d'Affaires Adrienne GALANEK (since 20 January 2017)

embassy: Floral Park Road, Belmopan City, Cayo District

mailing address: P.O. Box 497, Belmopan City, Cayo District, Belize

telephone: [011] (501) 822-4011

FAX: [011] (501) 822-4012

FLAG DESCRIPTION:

royal blue with a narrow red stripe along the top and the bottom edges; centered is a large white disk bearing the coat of arms; the coat of arms features a shield flanked by two workers in front of a mahogany tree with the related motto SUB UMBRA FLOREO (I Flourish in the Shade) on a scroll at the bottom, all encircled by a green garland of 50 mahogany leaves; the colors are those of the two main political parties: blue for the PUP and red for the UDP; various elements of the coat of arms - the figures, the tools, the mahogany tree, and the garland of leaves - recall the logging industry that led to British settlement of Belize

note: Belize's flag is the only national flag that depicts human beings; two British overseas territories, Montserrat and the British Virgin Islands, also depict humans

NATIONAL SYMBOL(S):

Baird's tapir (a large, browsing, forest-dwelling mammal), keel-billed toucan, Black Orchid; national colors: red, blue

NATIONAL ANTHEM:

name: Land of the Free

lyrics/music: Samuel Alfred HAYNES/Selwyn Walford YOUNG

note: adopted 1981; as a Commonwealth country, in addition to the national anthem, "God Save the Queen" serves as the royal anthem (see United Kingdom)

ECONOMY :: BELIZE

ECONOMY - OVERVIEW:

Tourism is the number one foreign exchange earner in this small economy, followed by exports of sugar, bananas, citrus, marine products, and crude oil.

The government's expansionary monetary and fiscal policies, initiated in September 1998, led to GDP growth averaging nearly 4% in 1999-2007, but GPD growth has averaged only 2.1% from 2007-2016, with 2.5% growth estimated for 2017. Belize's dependence on energy imports makes it susceptible to energy price shocks.

Although Belize has the third highest per capita income in Central America, the average income figure masks a huge income disparity between rich and poor, and a key government objective remains reducing poverty and inequality with the help of international donors. High unemployment, a growing trade deficit and heavy foreign debt burden continue to be major concerns. Belize faces continued pressure from rising sovereign debt, and a growing trade imbalance

GDP (PURCHASING POWER PARITY):

$3.218 billion (2017 est.)

$3.194 billion (2016 est.)

$3.21 billion (2015 est.)

note: data are in 2017 dollars

country comparison to the world: 187

GDP (OFFICIAL EXCHANGE RATE):

$1.854 billion (2017 est.) (2017 est.)

GDP - REAL GROWTH RATE:

0.8% (2017 est.)

-0.5% (2016 est.)

3.8% (2015 est.)

country comparison to the world: 186

GDP - PER CAPITA (PPP):

$8,300 (2017 est.)

$8,500 (2016 est.)

$8,800 (2015 est.)

note: data are in 2017 dollars

country comparison to the world: 149

GROSS NATIONAL SAVING:

11.3% of GDP (2017 est.)

13.3% of GDP (2016 est.)

14.2% of GDP (2015 est.)

country comparison to the world: 157

GDP - COMPOSITION, BY END USE:

household consumption: 75.1% (2017 est.)

government consumption: 15.2% (2017 est.)

investment in fixed capital: 22.5% (2017 est.)

investment in inventories: 1.2% (2017 est.)

exports of goods and services: 49.1% (2017 est.)

imports of goods and services: -63.2% (2017 est.)

GDP - COMPOSITION, BY SECTOR OF ORIGIN:

agriculture: 10.3% (2017 est.)

industry: 21.6% (2017 est.)

services: 68% (2017 est.)

AGRICULTURE - PRODUCTS:

bananas, cacao, citrus, sugar; fish, cultured shrimp; lumber

INDUSTRIES:

garment production, food processing, tourism, construction, oil

INDUSTRIAL PRODUCTION GROWTH RATE:

-0.6% (2017 est.)

country comparison to the world: 172

LABOR FORCE:

120,500 (2008 est.)

note: shortage of skilled labor and all types of technical personnel

country comparison to the world: 180

LABOR FORCE - BY OCCUPATION:

agriculture: 10.2%

industry: 18.1%

services: 71.7% (2007 est.)

UNEMPLOYMENT RATE:

9% (2017 est.)

8% (2016 est.)

country comparison to the world: 130

POPULATION BELOW POVERTY LINE:

41% (2013 est.)

HOUSEHOLD INCOME OR CONSUMPTION BY PERCENTAGE SHARE:

lowest 10%: NA

highest 10%: NA

BUDGET:

revenues: 553.5 million (2017 est.)

expenditures: 572 million (2017 est.)

TAXES AND OTHER REVENUES:

29.9% (of GDP) (2017 est.)

country comparison to the world: 78

BUDGET SURPLUS (+) OR DEFICIT (-):

-1% (of GDP) (2017 est.)

country comparison to the world: 75

PUBLIC DEBT:

99% of GDP (2017 est.)

95.9% of GDP (2016 est.)

country comparison to the world: 17

FISCAL YEAR:

1 April - 31 March

INFLATION RATE (CONSUMER PRICES):

1.1% (2017 est.)

0.7% (2016 est.)

country comparison to the world: 55

CENTRAL BANK DISCOUNT RATE:

9.58% (1 November 2017)

9.14% (1 November 2016)

country comparison to the world: 26

COMMERCIAL BANK PRIME LENDING RATE:

9.46% (31 December 2017 est.)

9.84% (31 December 2016 est.)

country comparison to the world: 91

STOCK OF NARROW MONEY:

$768.8 million (31 December 2017 est.)

$735.9 million (31 December 2016 est.)

country comparison to the world: 162

STOCK OF BROAD MONEY:

$768.8 million (31 December 2017 est.)

$735.9 million (31 December 2016 est.)

country comparison to the world: 166

STOCK OF DOMESTIC CREDIT:

$1.323 billion (31 December 2017 est.)

$1.278 billion (31 December 2016 est.)

country comparison to the world: 163

MARKET VALUE OF PUBLICLY TRADED SHARES:

NA

CURRENT ACCOUNT BALANCE:

-$143 million (2017 est.)

-$163 million (2016 est.)

country comparison to the world: 91

EXPORTS:

$457.5 million (2017 est.)

$442.7 million (2016 est.)

country comparison to the world: 178

EXPORTS - PARTNERS:

UK 33.9%, US 22%, Jamaica 6.7%, Italy 6.4%, Barbados 5.9%, Ireland 5.5%, Netherlands 4.3% (2017)

EXPORTS - COMMODITIES:

sugar, bananas, citrus, clothing, fish products, molasses, wood, crude oil

IMPORTS:

$845.9 million (2017 est.)

$916.2 million (2016 est.)

country comparison to the world: 187

IMPORTS - COMMODITIES:

machinery and transport equipment, manufactured goods; fuels, chemicals, pharmaceuticals; food, beverages, tobacco

IMPORTS - PARTNERS:

US 35.6%, China 11.2%, Mexico 11.2%, Guatemala 6.9% (2017)

RESERVES OF FOREIGN EXCHANGE AND GOLD:

$312.1 million (31 December 2017 est.)

$376.7 million (31 December 2016 est.)

country comparison to the world: 167

DEBT - EXTERNAL:

$1.315 billion (31 December 2017 est.)

$1.338 billion (31 December 2016 est.)

country comparison to the world: 162

STOCK OF DIRECT FOREIGN INVESTMENT - AT HOME:

NA

EXCHANGE RATES:

Belizean dollars (BZD) per US dollar -

2 (2017 est.)

2 (2016 est.)

2 (2015 est.)

2 (2014 est.)

2 (2013 est.)

ENERGY :: BELIZE

ELECTRICITY ACCESS:

electrification - total population: 100% (2016)

ELECTRICITY - PRODUCTION:

280 million kWh (2016 est.)

country comparison to the world: 186

ELECTRICITY - CONSUMPTION:

453 million kWh (2016 est.)

country comparison to the world: 172

ELECTRICITY - EXPORTS:

0 kWh (2016 est.)

country comparison to the world: 105

ELECTRICITY - IMPORTS:

243 million kWh (2016 est.)

country comparison to the world: 92

ELECTRICITY - INSTALLED GENERATING CAPACITY:

198,000 kW (2016 est.)

country comparison to the world: 165

ELECTRICITY - FROM FOSSIL FUELS:

51% of total installed capacity (2016 est.)

country comparison to the world: 147

ELECTRICITY - FROM NUCLEAR FUELS:

0% of total installed capacity (2017 est.)

country comparison to the world: 48

ELECTRICITY - FROM HYDROELECTRIC PLANTS:

27% of total installed capacity (2017 est.)

country comparison to the world: 73

ELECTRICITY - FROM OTHER RENEWABLE SOURCES:

22% of total installed capacity (2017 est.)

country comparison to the world: 33

CRUDE OIL - PRODUCTION:

2,000 bbl/day (2017 est.)

country comparison to the world: 86

CRUDE OIL - EXPORTS:

1,220 bbl/day (2015 est.)

country comparison to the world: 73

CRUDE OIL - IMPORTS:

0 bbl/day (2015 est.)

country comparison to the world: 95

CRUDE OIL - PROVED RESERVES:

6.7 million bbl (1 January 2018 est.)

country comparison to the world: 93

REFINED PETROLEUM PRODUCTS - PRODUCTION:

36 bbl/day (2015 est.)

country comparison to the world: 109

REFINED PETROLEUM PRODUCTS - CONSUMPTION:

4,000 bbl/day (2016 est.)

country comparison to the world: 182

REFINED PETROLEUM PRODUCTS - EXPORTS:

0 bbl/day (2015 est.)

country comparison to the world: 130

REFINED PETROLEUM PRODUCTS - IMPORTS:

4,161 bbl/day (2015 est.)

country comparison to the world: 176

NATURAL GAS - PRODUCTION:

0 cu m (2017 est.)

country comparison to the world: 103

NATURAL GAS - CONSUMPTION:

0 cu m (2017 est.)

country comparison to the world: 120

NATURAL GAS - EXPORTS:

0 cu m (2017 est.)

country comparison to the world: 68

NATURAL GAS - IMPORTS:

0 cu m (2017 est.)

country comparison to the world: 90

NATURAL GAS - PROVED RESERVES:

0 cu m (1 January 2014 est.)

country comparison to the world: 110

CARBON DIOXIDE EMISSIONS FROM CONSUMPTION OF ENERGY:

556,700 Mt (2017 est.)

country comparison to the world: 183

COMMUNICATIONS :: BELIZE

TELEPHONES - FIXED LINES:

total subscriptions: 23,000 (July 2016 est.)

subscriptions per 100 inhabitants: 6 (July 2016 est.)

country comparison to the world: 171

TELEPHONES - MOBILE CELLULAR:

total subscriptions: 227,000 (July 2016 est.)

subscriptions per 100 inhabitants: 63 (July 2016 est.)

country comparison to the world: 181

TELEPHONE SYSTEM:

general assessment: govt telecome company, BTL, continues to hold a monopoly in fixed-line services and mobile and broadband fixed-line teledensity; small market, underinvestment with lack of competion, yet BTL reports stable telecome revenue for fiscal 2017 (2017)

domestic: mobile sector accounting for over 90% of all phone subscriptions; 6 per 100 fixed-line; mobile-cellular teledensity approaching 65 per 100 persons (2017)

international: country code - 501; landing point for the Americas Region Caribbean Ring System (ARCOS-1) fiber-optic telecommunications submarine cable that provides links to South and Central America, parts of the Caribbean, and the US; satellite earth station - 8 (Intelsat - 2, unknown - 6); mid-2017 completing a submarine cable to Ambergris Caye; SEUL submarine cable connecting the mainland with Ambergris Caye completed (2017)

BROADCAST MEDIA:

8 privately owned TV stations; multi-channel cable TV provides access to foreign stations; about 25 radio stations broadcasting on roughly 50 different frequencies; state-run radio was privatized in 1998 (2009)

INTERNET COUNTRY CODE:

.bz

INTERNET USERS:

total: 157,735 (July 2016 est.)

percent of population: 44.6% (July 2016 est.)

country comparison to the world: 173

BROADBAND - FIXED SUBSCRIPTIONS:

total: 22,000 (2017 est.)

subscriptions per 100 inhabitants: 6 (2017 est.)

country comparison to the world: 149

TRANSPORTATION :: BELIZE

NATIONAL AIR TRANSPORT SYSTEM:

number of registered air carriers: 2 (2015)

inventory of registered aircraft operated by air carriers: 28 (2015)

annual passenger traffic on registered air carriers: 935,603 (2015)

annual freight traffic on registered air carriers: 2,463,420 mt-km (2015)

CIVIL AIRCRAFT REGISTRATION COUNTRY CODE PREFIX:

V3 (2016)

AIRPORTS:

47 (2013)

country comparison to the world: 91

AIRPORTS - WITH PAVED RUNWAYS:

total: 6 (2017)

2,438 to 3,047 m: 1 (2017)

914 to 1,523 m: 2 (2017)

under 914 m: 3 (2017)

AIRPORTS - WITH UNPAVED RUNWAYS:

total: 41 (2013)

2,438 to 3,047 m: 1 (2013)

914 to 1,523 m: 11 (2013)

under 914 m: 29 (2013)

ROADWAYS:

total: 2,870 km (2011)

paved: 488 km (2011)

unpaved: 2,382 km (2011)

country comparison to the world: 169

WATERWAYS:

825 km (navigable only by small craft) (2011)

country comparison to the world: 70

MERCHANT MARINE:

total: 756 (2017)

by type: bulk carrier 53, container ship 3, general cargo 373, oil tanker 55, other 272 (2017)

country comparison to the world: 29

PORTS AND TERMINALS:

major seaport(s): Belize City, Big Creek

MILITARY AND SECURITY :: BELIZE

MILITARY EXPENDITURES:

1.17% of GDP (2016)

1.09% of GDP (2015)

1.06% of GDP (2014)

1.1% of GDP (2013)

0.97% of GDP (2012)

country comparison to the world: 101

MILITARY BRANCHES:

Belize Defense Force (BDF): Army, BDF Air Wing; Belize Coast Guard; Belize Police Department (2017)

MILITARY SERVICE AGE AND OBLIGATION:

18 years of age for voluntary military service; laws allow for conscription only if volunteers are insufficient; conscription has never been implemented; volunteers typically outnumber available positions by 3:1; initial service obligation 12 years (2012)

TRANSNATIONAL ISSUES :: BELIZE

DISPUTES - INTERNATIONAL:

Guatemala persists in its territorial claim to approximately half of Belize, but agrees to the Line of Adjacency to keep Guatemalan squatters out of Belize's forested interiorboth countries agreed in April 2012 to hold simultaneous referenda, scheduled for 6 October 2013, to decide whether to refer the dispute to the ICJ for binding resolution, but this vote was suspended indefinitelyBelize and Mexico are working to solve minor border demarcation discrepancies arising from inaccuracies in the 1898 border treaty

TRAFFICKING IN PERSONS:

current situation: Belize is a source, destination, and transit country for men, women, and children subjected to forced labor and sex trafficking; the coerced prostitution of women and children by family members has not led to arrests; child sex tourism, involving primarily US citizens, is on the rise; sex trafficking and forced labor of Belizean and foreign women and LGBT individuals occurs in bars, nightclubs, brothels, and domestic service; workers from Central America, Mexico, and Asia may fall victim to forced labor in restaurants, shops, agriculture, and fishing

tier rating: Tier 3 – Belize does not comply fully with the minimum standards for the elimination of human trafficking and is not making significant efforts to do so; authorities did not initiate any new trafficking investigations of prosecutions, and cases from previous years remain pending; law enforcement efforts to use informal means to identify and refer victims were ineffective and draft procedures for referring victims to services are still not finalized; trafficking victims were more commonly arrested, detained, or deported based on immigration violations than provided with assistance; the government did not make progress in implementing the 2012-14 anti-trafficking national strategic plan (2015)

ILLICIT DRUGS:

major transshipment point for cocaine; small-scale illicit producer of cannabis, primarily for local consumption; offshore sector money-laundering activity related to narcotics trafficking and other crimes

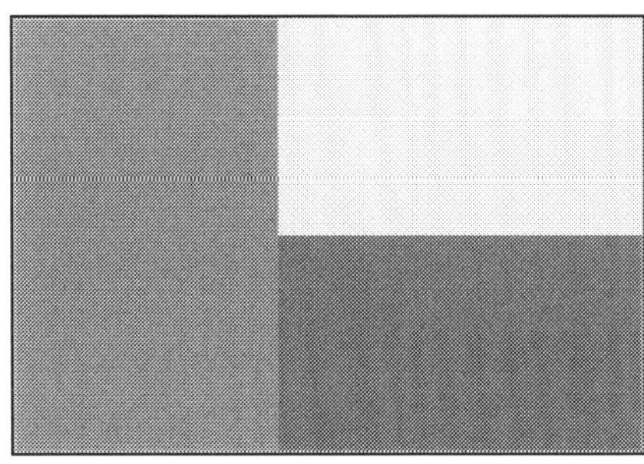

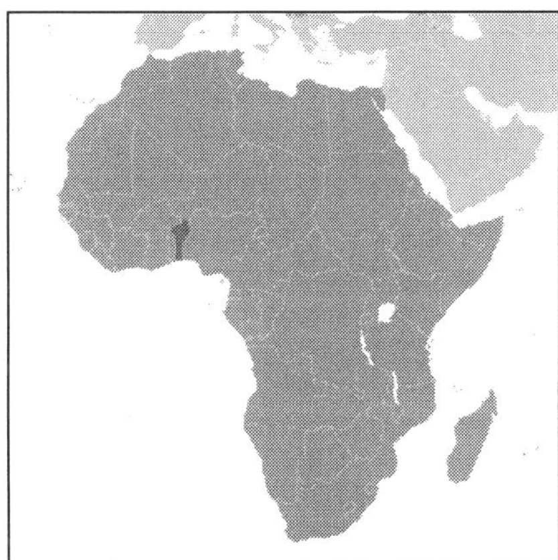

AFRICA :: BENIN

INTRODUCTION :: BENIN

BACKGROUND:

Present day Benin was the site of Dahomey, a West African kingdom that rose to prominence in about 1600 and over the next two and a half centuries became a regional power, largely based on its slave trade. Coastal areas of Dahomey began to be controlled by the French in the second half of the 19th century; the entire kingdom was conquered by 1894. French Dahomey achieved independence in 1960; it changed its name to the Republic of Benin in 1975.

A succession of military governments ended in 1972 with the rise to power of Mathieu KEREKOU and the establishment of a government based on Marxist-Leninist principles. A move to representative government began in 1989. Two years later, free elections ushered in former Prime Minister Nicephore SOGLO as president, marking the first successful transfer of power in Africa from a dictatorship to a democracy. KEREKOU was returned to power by elections held in 1996 and 2001, though some irregularities were alleged. KEREKOU stepped down at the end of his second term in 2006 and was succeeded by Thomas YAYI Boni, a political outsider and independent, who won a second five-year term in March 2011. Patrice TALON, a wealthy businessman, took office in 2016 after campaigning to restore public confidence in the government.

GEOGRAPHY :: BENIN

LOCATION:

Western Africa, bordering the Bight of Benin, between Nigeria and Togo

GEOGRAPHIC COORDINATES:

9 30 N, 2 15 E

MAP REFERENCES:

Africa

AREA:

total: 112,622 sq km

land: 110,622 sq km

water: 2,000 sq km

country comparison to the world: 103

AREA - COMPARATIVE:

slightly smaller than Pennsylvania

LAND BOUNDARIES:

total: 2,123 km

border countries (4): Burkina Faso 386 km, Niger 277 km, Nigeria 809 km, Togo 651 km

COASTLINE:

121 km

MARITIME CLAIMS:

territorial sea: 200 nm

continental shelf: 200 nm

exclusive fishing zone: 200 nm

CLIMATE:

tropical; hot, humid in south; semiarid in north

TERRAIN:

mostly flat to undulating plain; some hills and low mountains

ELEVATION:

mean elevation: 273 m

elevation extremes: 0 m lowest point: Atlantic Ocean

658 highest point: Mont Sokbaro

NATURAL RESOURCES:

small offshore oil deposits, limestone, marble, timber

LAND USE:

agricultural land: 31.3% (2011 est.)

arable land: 22.9% (2011 est.) / permanent crops: 3.5% (2011 est.) / permanent pasture: 4.9% (2011 est.)

forest: 40% (2011 est.)

other: 28.7% (2011 est.)

IRRIGATED LAND:

230 sq km (2012)

POPULATION DISTRIBUTION:

the population is primarily located in the south, with the highest concentration of people residing in and around the cities on the Atlantic coast; most of the north remains sparsely populated with higher concentrations of residents in the west

NATURAL HAZARDS:

hot, dry, dusty harmattan wind may affect north from December to March

ENVIRONMENT - CURRENT ISSUES:

inadequate supplies of potable water; water pollution; poaching threatens wildlife populations; deforestation; desertification (the spread of the desert into agricultural lands in the north is accelerated by regular droughts)

ENVIRONMENT - INTERNATIONAL AGREEMENTS:

party to: Biodiversity, Climate Change, Climate Change-Kyoto Protocol, Desertification, Endangered Species, Environmental Modification, Hazardous Wastes, Law of the Sea, Ozone Layer Protection, Ship Pollution, Wetlands, Whaling

signed, but not ratified: none of the selected agreements

GEOGRAPHY - NOTE:

sandbanks create difficult access to a coast with no natural harbors, river mouths, or islands

PEOPLE AND SOCIETY :: BENIN

POPULATION:

11,340,504 (July 2018 est.)

note: estimates for this country explicitly take into account the effects of excess mortality due to AIDS; this can result in lower life expectancy, higher infant mortality, higher death rates, lower population growth rates, and changes in the distribution of population by age and sex than would otherwise be expected

country comparison to the world: 79

NATIONALITY:

noun: Beninese (singular and plural)

adjective: Beninese

ETHNIC GROUPS:

Fon and related 38.4%, Adja and related 15.1%, Yoruba and related 12%, Bariba and related 9.6%, Fulani and related 8.6%, Ottamari and related 6.1%, Yoa-Lokpa and related 4.3%, Dendi and related 2.9%, other 0.9%, foreigner 1.9% (2013 est.)

LANGUAGES:

French (official), Fon and Yoruba (most common vernaculars in south), tribal languages (at least six major ones in north)

RELIGIONS:

Muslim 27.7%, Roman Catholic 25.5%, Protestant 13.5% (Celestial 6.7%, Methodist 3.4%, other Protestant 3.4%), Vodoun 11.6%, other Christian 9.5%, other traditional religions 2.6%, other 2.6%, none 5.8% (2013 est.)

DEMOGRAPHIC PROFILE:

Benin has a youthful age structure – almost 65% of the population is under the age of 25 – which is bolstered by high fertility and population growth rates. Benin's total fertility has been falling over time but remains high, declining from almost 7 children per women in 1990 to 4.8 in 2016. Benin's low contraceptive use and high unmet need for contraception contribute to the sustained high fertility rate. Although the majority of Beninese women use skilled health care personnel for antenatal care and delivery, the high rate of maternal mortality indicates the need for more access to high quality obstetric care.

Poverty, unemployment, increased living costs, and dwindling resources increasingly drive the Beninese to migrate. An estimated 4.4 million, more than 40%, of Beninese live abroad. Virtually all Beninese emigrants move to West African countries, particularly Nigeria and Cote d'Ivoire. Of the less than 1% of Beninese emigrants who settle in Europe, the vast majority live in France, Benin's former colonial ruler.

With about 40% of the population living below the poverty line, many desperate parents resort to sending their children to work in wealthy households as domestic servants (a common practice known as vidomegon), mines, quarries, or agriculture domestically or in Nigeria and other neighboring countries, often under brutal conditions. Unlike in other West African countries, where rural people move to the coast, farmers from Benin's densely populated southern and northwestern regions move to the historically sparsely populated central region to pursue agriculture. Immigrants from West African countries came to Benin in increasing numbers between 1992 and 2002 because of its political stability and porous borders.

AGE STRUCTURE:

0-14 years: 42.26% (male 2,445,265 /female 2,347,091)

15-24 years: 20.53% (male 1,184,977 /female 1,143,605)

25-54 years: 30.66% (male 1,759,834 /female 1,717,467)

55-64 years: 3.65% (male 184,453 /female 229,945)

65 years and over: 2.89% (male 128,920 /female 198,947) (2018 est.)

DEPENDENCY RATIOS:

total dependency ratio: 86.1 (2015 est.)

youth dependency ratio: 80.1 (2015 est.)

elderly dependency ratio: 6 (2015 est.)

potential support ratio: 16.6 (2015 est.)

MEDIAN AGE:

total: 18.4 years

male: 18.1 years

female: 18.7 years (2018 est.)

country comparison to the world: 209

POPULATION GROWTH RATE:

2.68% (2018 est.)

country comparison to the world: 16

BIRTH RATE:

34.5 births/1,000 population (2018 est.)

country comparison to the world: 22

DEATH RATE:

7.7 deaths/1,000 population (2018 est.)

country comparison to the world: 99

NET MIGRATION RATE:

0 migrant(s)/1,000 population (2017 est.)

country comparison to the world: 74

POPULATION DISTRIBUTION:

the population is primarily located in the south, with the highest concentration of people residing in and around the cities on the Atlantic coast; most of the north remains sparsely populated with higher concentrations of residents in the west

URBANIZATION:

urban population: 47.3% of total population (2018)

rate of urbanization: 3.89% annual rate of change (2015-20 est.)

MAJOR URBAN AREAS - POPULATION:

285,000 PORTO-NOVO (capital), 685,000 COTONOU (seat of government), 928,000 Abomey-Calavi (2018)

SEX RATIO:

at birth: 1.05 male(s)/female (2017 est.)

0-14 years: 1.04 male(s)/female (2017 est.)

15-24 years: 1.04 male(s)/female (2017 est.)

25-54 years: 1.02 male(s)/female (2017 est.)

55-64 years: 0.76 male(s)/female (2017 est.)

65 years and over: 0.66 male(s)/female (2017 est.)

total population: 1.01 male(s)/female (2017 est.)

MOTHER'S MEAN AGE AT FIRST BIRTH:

20.3 years (2011/12 est.)

note: median age at first birth among women 25-29

MATERNAL MORTALITY RATE:

405 deaths/100,000 live births (2015 est.)

country comparison to the world: 26

INFANT MORTALITY RATE:

total: 51.5 deaths/1,000 live births (2018 est.)

male: 54.5 deaths/1,000 live births (2018 est.)

female: 48.3 deaths/1,000 live births (2018 est.)

country comparison to the world: 24

LIFE EXPECTANCY AT BIRTH:

total population: 62.7 years (2018 est.)

male: 61.2 years (2018 est.)

female: 64.2 years (2018 est.)

country comparison to the world: 198

TOTAL FERTILITY RATE:

4.67 children born/woman (2018 est.)

country comparison to the world: 22

CONTRACEPTIVE PREVALENCE RATE:

17.9% (2014)

HEALTH EXPENDITURES:

4.6% of GDP (2014)

country comparison to the world: 154

PHYSICIANS DENSITY:

0.15 physicians/1,000 population (2016)

HOSPITAL BED DENSITY:

0.5 beds/1,000 population (2010)

DRINKING WATER SOURCE:

improved:

urban: 85.2% of population

rural: 72.1% of population

total: 77.9% of population

unimproved:

urban: 14.8% of population

rural: 27.9% of population

total: 22.1% of population (2015 est.)

SANITATION FACILITY ACCESS:

improved:

urban: 35.6% of population (2015 est.)

rural: 7.3% of population (2015 est.)

total: 19.7% of population (2015 est.)

unimproved:

urban: 64.4% of population (2015 est.)

rural: 92.7% of population (2015 est.)

total: 80.3% of population (2015 est.)

HIV/AIDS - ADULT PREVALENCE RATE:

1% (2017 est.)

country comparison to the world: 44

HIV/AIDS - PEOPLE LIVING WITH HIV/AIDS:

70,000 (2017 est.)

country comparison to the world: 50

HIV/AIDS - DEATHS:

2,500 (2017 est.)

country comparison to the world: 45

MAJOR INFECTIOUS DISEASES:

degree of risk: very high (2016)

food or waterborne diseases: bacterial and protozoal diarrhea, hepatitis A, and typhoid fever (2016)

vectorborne diseases: dengue fever, malaria, and yellow fever (2016)

animal contact diseases: rabies (2016)

respiratory diseases: meningococcal meningitis (2016)

OBESITY - ADULT PREVALENCE RATE:

9.6% (2016)

country comparison to the world: 142

CHILDREN UNDER THE AGE OF 5 YEARS UNDERWEIGHT:

18% (2014)

country comparison to the world: 32

EDUCATION EXPENDITURES:

4.4% of GDP (2015)

country comparison to the world: 97

LITERACY:

definition: age 15 and over can read and write (2015 est.)

total population: 38.4% (2015 est.)

male: 49.9% (2015 est.)

female: 27.3% (2015 est.)

SCHOOL LIFE EXPECTANCY (PRIMARY TO TERTIARY EDUCATION):

total: 12 years (2013)

male: 14 years (2013)

female: 11 years (2013)

UNEMPLOYMENT, YOUTH AGES 15-24:

total: 5.6% (2011 est.)

male: 5.2% (2011 est.)

female: 5.9% (2011 est.)

country comparison to the world: 152

GOVERNMENT :: BENIN

COUNTRY NAME:

conventional long form: Republic of Benin

conventional short form: Benin

local long form: Republique du Benin

local short form: Benin

former: Dahomey, People's Republic of Benin

etymology: named for the Bight of Benin, the body of water on which the country lies

GOVERNMENT TYPE:

presidential republic

CAPITAL:

name: Porto-Novo (constitutional capital); Cotonou (seat of government)

geographic coordinates: 6 29 N, 2 37 E

time difference: UTC+1 (6 hours ahead of Washington, DC, during Standard Time)

ADMINISTRATIVE DIVISIONS:

12 departments; Alibori, Atacora, Atlantique, Borgou, Collines, Couffo, Donga, Littoral, Mono, Oueme, Plateau, Zou

INDEPENDENCE:

1 August 1960 (from France)

NATIONAL HOLIDAY:

Independence Day, 1 August (1960)

CONSTITUTION:

history: previous 1946, 1958 (preindependence); latest adopted by referendum 2 December 1990, promulgated 11 December 1990 (2017)

amendments: proposed concurrently by the president of the republic (after a decision in the Council of Ministers) and the National Assembly;

consideration of drafts or proposals requires at least three-fourths majority vote of the Assembly membership; passage requires approval in a referendum unless approved by at least four-fifths majority vote of the Assembly membership; constitutional articles affecting territorial sovereignty, the republican form of government, and secularity of Benin cannot be amended (2017)

LEGAL SYSTEM:

civil law system modeled largely on the French system and some customary law

INTERNATIONAL LAW ORGANIZATION PARTICIPATION:

has not submitted an ICJ jurisdiction declaration; accepts ICCt jurisdiction

CITIZENSHIP:

citizenship by birth: no

citizenship by descent only: at least one parent must be a citizen of Benin

dual citizenship recognized: yes

residency requirement for naturalization: 10 years

SUFFRAGE:

18 years of age; universal

EXECUTIVE BRANCH:

chief of state: President Patrice TALON (since 6 April 2016); note - the president is both chief of state and head of government

head of government: President Patrice TALON (since 6 April 2016); prime minister position abolished

cabinet: Council of Ministers appointed by the president

elections/appointments: president directly elected by absolute majority popular vote in 2 rounds if needed for a 5-year term (eligible for a second term); last held on 6 March and 20 March 2016 (next to be held in 2021)

election results: Patrice TALON elected president in second round; percent of vote in first round - Lionel ZINSOU (FCBE) 28.4%, Patrice TALON (independent) 24.8%, Sebastien AJAVON (independent) 23.%, Abdoulaye Bio TCHANE (ABT) 8.8%, Pascal KOUPAKI (NC) 5.9%, other 9.1%; percent of vote in second round - Patrice TALON 65.4%, Lionel ZINSOU 34.6%

LEGISLATIVE BRANCH:

description: unicameral National Assembly or Assemblee Nationale (83 seats; members directly elected in multi-seat constituencies by proportional representation vote; members serve 4-year terms)

elections: last held on 26 April 2015 (next to be held in April 2019)

election results: percent of vote by party - FCBE 30.2%, UN 14.4%, PRD 10.6%, AND 7.6%, RB-RP 7.1%, other 30.1%; seats by party - FCBE 33, UN 13, PRD 10, RB-RP 7, AND 5, other 15; composition - men 77, women 6, percent of women 7.2%

JUDICIAL BRANCH:

highest courts: Supreme Court or Cour Supreme (consists of the court president and 3 chamber presidents organized into an administrative division, judicial chamber, and chamber of accounts); Constitutional Court or Cour Constitutionnelle (consists of 7 members including the court president); High Court of Justice (consists of the Constitutional Court members, 6 members appointed by the National Assembly, and the Supreme Court president); note - jurisdiction of the High Court of Justice is limited to cases of high treason by the national president or members of the government while in office

judge selection and term of office: Supreme Court president and judges appointed by the national president upon the advice of the National Assembly; judges appointed for single renewable 5-year terms; Constitutional Court members - 4 appointed by the National Assembly and 3 by the national president; members appointed for single renewable 5-year terms; High Court of Justice "other" members elected by the National Assembly; member tenure NA

subordinate courts: Court of Appeal or Cour d'Appel; district courts; village courts; Assize courts

POLITICAL PARTIES AND LEADERS:

Alliance for a Triumphant Benin or ABT [Abdoulaye BIO TCHANE]
African Movement for Development and Progress or MADEP [Sefou FAGBOHOUN]
Benin Renaissance or RB [Lehady SOGLO]
Cowrie Force for an Emerging Benin or FCBE [Yayi BONI]
Democratic Renewal Party or PRD [Adrien HOUNGBEDJI]
National Alliance for Development and Democracy or AND [Valentin Aditi HOUDE]
New Consciousness Rally or NC [Pascal KOUPAKI]
Patriotic Awakening or RP [Janvier YAHOUEDEOU]
Social Democrat Party or PSD [Emmanuel GOLOU]
Sun Alliance or AS [Sacca LAFIA]
Union Makes the Nation or UN [Adrien HOUNGBEDJI] (includes PRD, MADEP)
United Democratic Forces or FDU [Mathurin NAGO]

note: approximately 20 additional minor parties

INTERNATIONAL ORGANIZATION PARTICIPATION:

ACP, AfDB, AU, CD, ECOWAS, Entente, FAO, FZ, G-77, IAEA, IBRD, ICAO, ICCt, ICRM, IDA, IDB, IFAD, IFC, IFRCS, ILO, IMF, IMO, Interpol, IOC, IOM, IPU, ISO, ITSO, ITU, ITUC (NGOs), MIGA, MINUSMA, MONUSCO, NAM, OAS (observer), OIC, OIF, OPCW, PCA, UN, UNAMID, UNCTAD, UNESCO, UNHCR, UNIDO, UNMIL, UNMISS, UNOCI, UNWTO, UPU, WADB (regional), WAEMU, WCO, WFTU (NGOs), WHO, WIPO, WMO, WTO

DIPLOMATIC REPRESENTATION IN THE US:

chief of mission: Ambassador Hector POSSET (since 18 January 2017)

chancery: 2124 Kalorama Road NW, Washington, DC 20008

telephone: [1] (202) 232-6656

FAX: [1] (202) 265-1996

DIPLOMATIC REPRESENTATION FROM THE US:

chief of mission: Ambassador Lucy TAMLYN (since 8 November 2015)

embassy: Caporal Bernard Anani, 01 BP 2012, Cotonou

mailing address: 01 B. P. 2012, Cotonou

telephone: [229] 21-30-06-50

FAX: [229] 21-30-03-84

FLAG DESCRIPTION:

two equal horizontal bands of yellow (top) and red (bottom) with a vertical green band on the hoist side; green symbolizes hope and revival, yellow wealth, and red courage

note: uses the popular Pan-African colors of Ethiopia

NATIONAL SYMBOL(S):

leopard; national colors: green, yellow, red

NATIONAL ANTHEM:

name: "L'Aube Nouvelle" (The Dawn of a New Day)

lyrics/music: Gilbert Jean DAGNON

note: adopted 1960

ECONOMY :: BENIN

ECONOMY - OVERVIEW:

The free market economy of Benin has grown consecutively for four years, though growth slowed in 2017, as its close trade links to Nigeria expose Benin to risks from volatile commodity prices. Cotton is a key export commodity, with export earnings significantly impacted by the price of cotton in the broader market. The economy began deflating in 2017, with the consumer price index falling 0.8%.

During the first two years of President TALON's administration, which began in April 2016, the government has followed an ambitious action plan to kickstart development through investments in infrastructure, education, agriculture, and governance. Electricity generation, which has constrained Benin's economic growth, has increased and blackouts have been considerably reduced. Private foreign direct investment is small, and foreign aid accounts for a large proportion of investment in infrastructure projects.

Benin has appealed for international assistance to mitigate piracy against commercial shipping in its territory, and has used equipment from donors effectively against such piracy. Pilferage has significantly dropped at the Port of Cotonou, though the port is still struggling with effective implementation of the International Ship and Port Facility Security (ISPS) Code. Projects included in Benin's $307 million Millennium Challenge Corporation (MCC) first compact (2006-11) were designed to increase investment and private sector activity by improving key institutional and physical infrastructure. The four projects focused on access to land, access to financial services, access to justice, and access to markets (including modernization of the port). The Port of Cotonou is a major contributor to Benin's economy, with revenues projected to account for more than 40% of Benin's national budget.

Benin will need further efforts to upgrade infrastructure, stem corruption, and expand access to foreign markets to achieve its potential. In September 2015, Benin signed a second MCC Compact for $375 million that entered into force in June 2017 and is designed to strengthen the national utility service provider, attract private sector investment, fund infrastructure investments in electricity generation and distribution, and develop off-grid electrification for poor and unserved households. As part of the Government of Benin's action plan to spur growth, Benin passed public private partnership legislation in 2017 to attract more foreign investment, place more emphasis on tourism, facilitate the development of new food processing systems and agricultural products, encourage new information and communication technology, and establish Independent Power Producers. In April 2017, the IMF approved a three year $150.4 million Extended Credit Facility agreement to maintain debt sustainability and boost donor confidence.

GDP (PURCHASING POWER PARITY):

$25.39 billion (2017 est.)

$24.04 billion (2016 est.)

$23.12 billion (2015 est.)

note: data are in 2017 dollars

country comparison to the world: 141

GDP (OFFICIAL EXCHANGE RATE):

$9.246 billion (2017 est.) (2017 est.)

GDP - REAL GROWTH RATE:

5.6% (2017 est.)

4% (2016 est.)

2.1% (2015 est.)

country comparison to the world: 38

GDP - PER CAPITA (PPP):

$2,300 (2017 est.)

$2,200 (2016 est.)

$2,200 (2015 est.)

note: data are in 2017 dollars

country comparison to the world: 201

GROSS NATIONAL SAVING:

17.3% of GDP (2017 est.)

15.2% of GDP (2016 est.)

16.6% of GDP (2015 est.)

country comparison to the world: 116

GDP - COMPOSITION, BY END USE:

household consumption: 70.5% (2017 est.)

government consumption: 13.1% (2017 est.)

investment in fixed capital: 27.6% (2017 est.)

investment in inventories: 0% (2017 est.)

exports of goods and services: 31.6% (2017 est.)

imports of goods and services: -43% (2017 est.)

GDP - COMPOSITION, BY SECTOR OF ORIGIN:

agriculture: 26.1% (2017 est.)

industry: 22.8% (2017 est.)

services: 51.1% (2017 est.)

AGRICULTURE - PRODUCTS:

cotton, corn, cassava (manioc, tapioca), yams, beans, palm oil, peanuts, cashews; livestock

INDUSTRIES:

textiles, food processing, construction materials, cement

INDUSTRIAL PRODUCTION GROWTH RATE:

3% (2017 est.)

country comparison to the world: 101

LABOR FORCE:

3.662 million (2007 est.)

country comparison to the world: 98

UNEMPLOYMENT RATE:

1% (2014 est.)

country comparison to the world: 7

POPULATION BELOW POVERTY LINE:

36.2% (2011 est.)

HOUSEHOLD INCOME OR CONSUMPTION BY PERCENTAGE SHARE:

lowest 10%: 29% (2003)

highest 10%: 29% (2003)

DISTRIBUTION OF FAMILY INCOME - GINI INDEX:

36.5 (2003)

country comparison to the world: 88

BUDGET:

revenues: 1.578 billion (2017 est.)

expenditures: 2.152 billion (2017 est.)

TAXES AND OTHER REVENUES:

17.1% (of GDP) (2017 est.)

country comparison to the world: 171

BUDGET SURPLUS (+) OR DEFICIT (-):

-6.2% (of GDP) (2017 est.)

country comparison to the world: 186

PUBLIC DEBT:

54.6% of GDP (2017 est.)

49.7% of GDP (2016 est.)

country comparison to the world: 81

FISCAL YEAR:

calendar year

INFLATION RATE (CONSUMER PRICES):

0.1% (2017 est.)

-0.8% (2016 est.)

country comparison to the world: 13

CENTRAL BANK DISCOUNT RATE:

4.25% (31 December 2010)

4.25% (31 December 2009)

country comparison to the world: 87

COMMERCIAL BANK PRIME LENDING RATE:

5.3% (31 December 2017 est.)

5.3% (31 December 2016 est.)

country comparison to the world: 140

STOCK OF NARROW MONEY:

$2.644 billion (31 December 2017 est.)

$2.189 billion (31 December 2016 est.)

country comparison to the world: 125

STOCK OF BROAD MONEY:

$2.644 billion (31 December 2017 est.)

$2.189 billion (31 December 2016 est.)

country comparison to the world: 132

STOCK OF DOMESTIC CREDIT:

$1.963 billion (31 December 2017 est.)

$1.553 billion (31 December 2016 est.)

country comparison to the world: 151

MARKET VALUE OF PUBLICLY TRADED SHARES:

NA

CURRENT ACCOUNT BALANCE:

-$1.024 billion (2017 est.)

-$808 million (2016 est.)

country comparison to the world: 144

EXPORTS:

$1.974 billion (2017 est.)

$1.588 billion (2016 est.)

country comparison to the world: 141

EXPORTS - PARTNERS:

Bangladesh 18.1%, India 10.7%, Ukraine 9%, Niger 8.1%, China 7.7%, Nigeria 7.2%, Turkey 4% (2017)

EXPORTS - COMMODITIES:

cotton, cashews, shea butter, textiles, palm products, seafood

IMPORTS:

$2.787 billion (2017 est.)

$2.443 billion (2016 est.)

country comparison to the world: 152

IMPORTS - COMMODITIES:

foodstuffs, capital goods, petroleum products

IMPORTS - PARTNERS:

Thailand 18.1%, India 15.9%, France 8.5%, China 7.5%, Togo 5.9%, Netherlands 4.3%, Belgium 4.3% (2017)

RESERVES OF FOREIGN EXCHANGE AND GOLD:

$698.9 million (31 December 2017 est.)

$57.5 million (31 December 2016 est.)

country comparison to the world: 141

DEBT - EXTERNAL:

$2.804 billion (31 December 2017 est.)

$2.476 billion (31 December 2016 est.)

country comparison to the world: 145

EXCHANGE RATES:

Communaute Financiere Africaine francs (XOF) per US dollar -

605.3 (2017 est.)

593.01 (2016 est.)

593.01 (2015 est.)

591.45 (2014 est.)

494.42 (2013 est.)

ENERGY :: BENIN

ELECTRICITY ACCESS:

population without electricity: 7.3 million (2013)

electrification - total population: 29% (2013)

electrification - urban areas: 57% (2013)

electrification - rural areas: 9% (2013)

ELECTRICITY - PRODUCTION:

335 million kWh (2016 est.)

country comparison to the world: 177

ELECTRICITY - CONSUMPTION:

1.143 billion kWh (2016 est.)

country comparison to the world: 152

ELECTRICITY - EXPORTS:

0 kWh (2016 est.)

country comparison to the world: 106

ELECTRICITY - IMPORTS:

1.088 billion kWh (2016 est.)

country comparison to the world: 68

ELECTRICITY - INSTALLED GENERATING CAPACITY:

321,000 kW (2016 est.)

country comparison to the world: 158

ELECTRICITY - FROM FOSSIL FUELS:

88% of total installed capacity (2016 est.)

country comparison to the world: 58

ELECTRICITY - FROM NUCLEAR FUELS:

0% of total installed capacity (2017 est.)

country comparison to the world: 49

ELECTRICITY - FROM HYDROELECTRIC PLANTS:

9% of total installed capacity (2017 est.)

country comparison to the world: 116

ELECTRICITY - FROM OTHER RENEWABLE SOURCES:

2% of total installed capacity (2017 est.)

country comparison to the world: 135

CRUDE OIL - PRODUCTION:

0 bbl/day (2017 est.)

country comparison to the world: 109

CRUDE OIL - EXPORTS:

0 bbl/day (2015 est.)

country comparison to the world: 93

CRUDE OIL - IMPORTS:

0 bbl/day (2015 est.)

country comparison to the world: 96

CRUDE OIL - PROVED RESERVES:

8 million bbl (1 January 2018 est.)

country comparison to the world: 92

REFINED PETROLEUM PRODUCTS - PRODUCTION:

0 bbl/day (2015 est.)

country comparison to the world: 118

REFINED PETROLEUM PRODUCTS - CONSUMPTION:

38,000 bbl/day (2016 est.)

country comparison to the world: 113

REFINED PETROLEUM PRODUCTS - EXPORTS:

1,514 bbl/day (2015 est.)

country comparison to the world: 107

REFINED PETROLEUM PRODUCTS - IMPORTS:

38,040 bbl/day (2015 est.)

country comparison to the world: 93

NATURAL GAS - PRODUCTION:

0 cu m (2017 est.)

country comparison to the world: 104

NATURAL GAS - CONSUMPTION:

0 cu m (2017 est.)

country comparison to the world: 121

NATURAL GAS - EXPORTS:

0 cu m (2017 est.)

country comparison to the world: 69

NATURAL GAS - IMPORTS:

0 cu m (2017 est.)

country comparison to the world: 91

NATURAL GAS - PROVED RESERVES:

1.133 billion cu m (1 January 2018 est.)

country comparison to the world: 98

CARBON DIOXIDE EMISSIONS FROM CONSUMPTION OF ENERGY:

5.664 million Mt (2017 est.)

country comparison to the world: 130

COMMUNICATIONS :: BENIN

TELEPHONES - FIXED LINES:

total subscriptions: 56,787 (2017 est.)

subscriptions per 100 inhabitants: 1 (2017 est.)

country comparison to the world: 156

TELEPHONES - MOBILE CELLULAR:

total subscriptions: 8,773,044 (2017 est.)

subscriptions per 100 inhabitants: 79 (2017 est.)

country comparison to the world: 91

TELEPHONE SYSTEM:

general assessment: fixed-line network characterized by aging, deteriorating equipment; mobile networks account for almost all internet connections; govt. aims to provide telecoms services to 80% of the country, mostly via mobile infrastructure; govt. restructures state-owned telcos; Mobile Number Portability (MNP) becomes available; Benin joins free roaming scheme (2017)

domestic: fixed-line teledensity only about 1 per 100 persons; spurred by the presence of multiple mobile-cellular providers, cellular telephone subscribership has increased rapidly, exceeding 79 per 100 persons in 2017 (2017)

international: country code - 229; landing point for the SAT-3/WASC fiber-optic submarine cable that provides connectivity to Europe and Asia; long distance fiber-optic links with Togo, Burkina Faso, Niger, and Nigeria; satellite earth stations - 7 (Intelsat-Atlantic Ocean);Orange commissions new connection from the ACE submarine cable, connecting Benin with Tenerife (2017)

BROADCAST MEDIA:

state-run Office de Radiodiffusion et de Television du Benin (ORTB) operates a TV station providing a wide broadcast reach; several privately owned TV stations broadcast from Cotonou; satellite TV subscription service is available; state-owned radio, under ORTB control, includes a national station supplemented by a number of regional stations; substantial number of privately owned radio broadcast stations; transmissions of a few international broadcasters are available on FM in Cotonou (2016)

INTERNET COUNTRY CODE:

.bj

INTERNET USERS:

total: 1,288,336 (July 2016 est.)

percent of population: 12% (July 2016 est.)

country comparison to the world: 127

BROADBAND - FIXED SUBSCRIPTIONS:

total: 28,833 (2017 est.)

subscriptions per 100 inhabitants: less than 1 (2017 est.)

country comparison to the world: 142

TRANSPORTATION :: BENIN

NATIONAL AIR TRANSPORT SYSTEM:

number of registered air carriers: 1 (2015)

inventory of registered aircraft operated by air carriers: 1 (2015)

annual passenger traffic on registered air carriers: 112,392 (2015)

annual freight traffic on registered air carriers: 805,347 mt-km (2015)

CIVIL AIRCRAFT REGISTRATION COUNTRY CODE PREFIX:

TY (2016)

AIRPORTS:

6 (2013)

country comparison to the world: 171

AIRPORTS - WITH PAVED RUNWAYS:

total: 1 (2017)

1,524 to 2,437 m: 1 (2017)

AIRPORTS - WITH UNPAVED RUNWAYS:

total: 5 (2013)

2,438 to 3,047 m: 2 (2013)

1,524 to 2,437 m: 1 (2013)

914 to 1,523 m: 2 (2013)

PIPELINES:

134 km gas

RAILWAYS:

total: 438 km (2014)

narrow gauge: 438 km 1.000-m gauge (2014)

country comparison to the world: 116

ROADWAYS:

total: 16,000 km (2006)

paved: 1,400 km (2006)

unpaved: 14,600 km (2006)

country comparison to the world: 122

WATERWAYS:

150 km (seasonal navigation on River Niger along northern border) (2011)

country comparison to the world: 101

MERCHANT MARINE:

total: 6 (2017)

by type: other 6 (2017)

country comparison to the world: 159

PORTS AND TERMINALS:

major seaport(s): Cotonou

LNG terminal(s) (import): Cotonou

MILITARY AND SECURITY :: BENIN

MILITARY EXPENDITURES:

1.14% of GDP (2016)

1.1% of GDP (2015)

0.96% of GDP (2014)

0.94% of GDP (2013)

0.96% of GDP (2012)

country comparison to the world: 104

MILITARY BRANCHES:

Benin Armed Forces (Forces Armees Beninoises, FAB): Army (l'Arme de Terre), Benin Navy (Forces Navales Beninois, FNB), Benin Air Force (Force Aerienne du Benin, FAB) (2013)

MILITARY SERVICE AGE AND OBLIGATION:

18-35 years of age for selective compulsory and voluntary military service; a higher education diploma is required; both sexes are eligible for military service; conscript tour of duty - 18 months (2013)

TRANSNATIONAL ISSUES :: BENIN

DISPUTES - INTERNATIONAL:

talks continue between Benin and Togo on funding the Adjrala hydroelectric dam on the Mona RiverBenin retains a border dispute with Burkina Faso near the town of Koualoulocation of Benin-Niger-Nigeria tripoint is unresolved

ILLICIT DRUGS:

transshipment point used by traffickers for cocaine destined for Western Europe; vulnerable to money laundering due to poorly enforced financial regulations

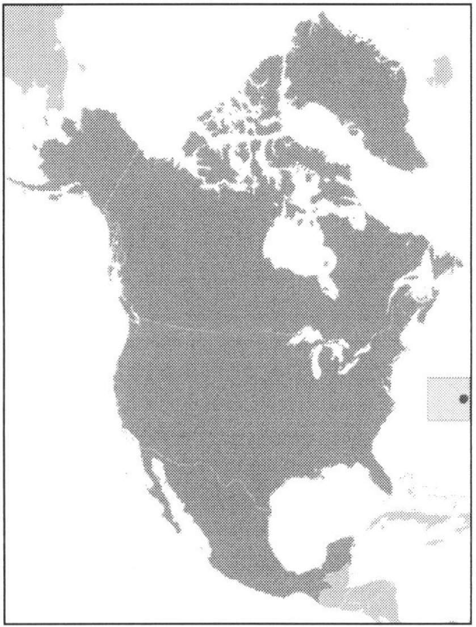

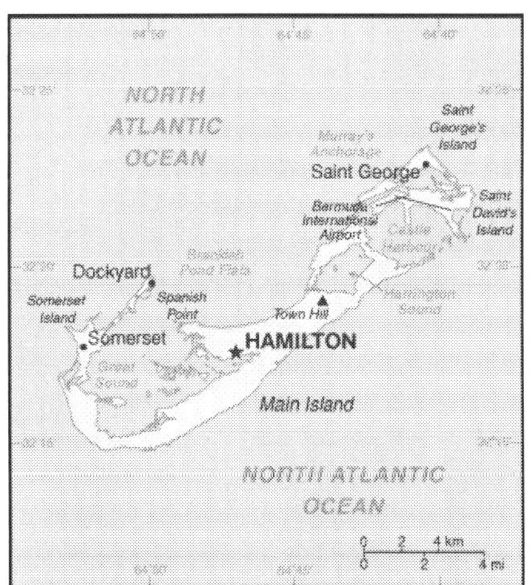

NORTH AMERICA :: BERMUDA

INTRODUCTION :: BERMUDA

BACKGROUND:

Bermuda was first settled in 1609 by shipwrecked English colonists heading for Virginia. Self-governing since 1620, Bermuda is the oldest and most populous of the British overseas territories. Vacationing to the island to escape North American winters first developed in Victorian times. Tourism continues to be important to the island's economy, although international business has overtaken it in recent years. Bermuda has also developed into a highly successful offshore financial center. A referendum on independence from the UK was soundly defeated in 1995.

GEOGRAPHY :: BERMUDA

LOCATION:

North America, group of islands in the North Atlantic Ocean, east of South Carolina (US)

GEOGRAPHIC COORDINATES:

32 20 N, 64 45 W

MAP REFERENCES:

North America

AREA:

total: 54 sq km

land: 54 sq km

water: 0 sq km

country comparison to the world: 232

AREA - COMPARATIVE:

about one-third the size of Washington, DC

LAND BOUNDARIES:

0 km

COASTLINE:

103 km

MARITIME CLAIMS:

territorial sea: 12 nm

exclusive fishing zone: 200 nm

CLIMATE:

subtropical; mild, humid; gales, strong winds common in winter

TERRAIN:

low hills separated by fertile depressions

ELEVATION:

0 m lowest point: Atlantic Ocean

79 highest point: Town Hill

NATURAL RESOURCES:

limestone, pleasant climate fostering tourism

LAND USE:

agricultural land: 14.8% (2011 est.)

arable land: 14.8% (2011 est.) / permanent crops: 0% (2011 est.) / permanent pasture: 0% (2011 est.)

forest: 20% (2011 est.)

other: 65.2% (2011 est.)

IRRIGATED LAND:

NA

POPULATION DISTRIBUTION:

relatively even population distribution throughout

NATURAL HAZARDS:

hurricanes (June to November)

ENVIRONMENT - CURRENT ISSUES:

dense population and heavy vehicle traffic create serious congestion and air pollution problems; water resources scarce (most obtained as rainwater or from wells); solid waste disposal; hazardous waste disposal; sewage disposal; overfishing; oil spills

GEOGRAPHY - NOTE:

consists of about 138 coral islands and islets with ample rainfall, but no rivers or freshwater lakes; some land was leased by the US Government from 1941 to 1995

PEOPLE AND SOCIETY :: BERMUDA

POPULATION:

71,176 (July 2018 est.)

country comparison to the world: 203

NATIONALITY:

noun: Bermudian(s)

adjective: Bermudian

ETHNIC GROUPS:

black 53.8%, white 31%, mixed 7.5%, other 7.1%, unspecified 0.6% (2010 est.)

LANGUAGES:

English (official), Portuguese

RELIGIONS:

Protestant 46.2% (includes Anglican 15.8%, African Methodist Episcopal 8.6%, Seventh Day Adventist 6.7, Pentecostal 3.5%, Methodist 2.7%, Presbyterian 2.0%, Church of God 1.6%, Baptist 1.2%, Salvation Army 1.1%, Brethren 1.0%, other Protestant 2.0%), Roman Catholic 14.5%,

Jehovah's Witness 1.3%, other Christian 9.1%, Muslim 1%, other 3.9%, none 17.8%, unspecified 6.2% (2010 est.)

AGE STRUCTURE:

0-14 years: 16.92% (male 6,088 /female 5,957)

15-24 years: 11.95% (male 4,306 /female 4,197)

25-54 years: 36.56% (male 13,049 /female 12,972)

55-64 years: 16.04% (male 5,383 /female 6,034)

65 years and over: 18.53% (male 5,596 /female 7,594) (2018 est.)

MEDIAN AGE:

total: 43.5 years

male: 41.5 years

female: 45.4 years (2018 est.)

country comparison to the world: 18

POPULATION GROWTH RATE:

0.43% (2018 est.)

country comparison to the world: 158

BIRTH RATE:

11.3 births/1,000 population (2018 est.)

country comparison to the world: 172

DEATH RATE:

8.7 deaths/1,000 population (2018 est.)

country comparison to the world: 71

NET MIGRATION RATE:

1.8 migrant(s)/1,000 population (2017 est.)

country comparison to the world: 50

POPULATION DISTRIBUTION:

relatively even population distribution throughout

URBANIZATION:

urban population: 100% of total population (2018)

rate of urbanization: -0.44% annual rate of change (2015-20 est.)

MAJOR URBAN AREAS - POPULATION:

10,000 HAMILTON (capital) (2018)

SEX RATIO:

at birth: 1.02 male(s)/female (2017 est.)

0-14 years: 1.02 male(s)/female (2017 est.)

15-24 years: 1.01 male(s)/female (2017 est.)

25-54 years: 1 male(s)/female (2017 est.)

55-64 years: 0.89 male(s)/female (2017 est.)

65 years and over: 0.73 male(s)/female (2017 est.)

total population: 0.94 male(s)/female (2017 est.)

INFANT MORTALITY RATE:

total: 2.5 deaths/1,000 live births (2018 est.)

male: 2.6 deaths/1,000 live births (2018 est.)

female: 2.4 deaths/1,000 live births (2018 est.)

country comparison to the world: 217

LIFE EXPECTANCY AT BIRTH:

total population: 81.5 years (2018 est.)

male: 78.3 years (2018 est.)

female: 84.7 years (2018 est.)

country comparison to the world: 26

TOTAL FERTILITY RATE:

1.92 children born/woman (2018 est.)

country comparison to the world: 128

HIV/AIDS - ADULT PREVALENCE RATE:

NA

HIV/AIDS - PEOPLE LIVING WITH HIV/AIDS:

NA

HIV/AIDS - DEATHS:

NA

EDUCATION EXPENDITURES:

1.5% of GDP (2017)

country comparison to the world: 175

SCHOOL LIFE EXPECTANCY (PRIMARY TO TERTIARY EDUCATION):

total: 12 years (2015)

male: 11 years (2015)

female: 12 years (2015)

UNEMPLOYMENT, YOUTH AGES 15-24:

total: 29.3% (2014 est.)

male: 29.7% (2014 est.)

female: 29% (2014 est.)

country comparison to the world: 35

GOVERNMENT :: BERMUDA

COUNTRY NAME:

conventional long form: none

conventional short form: Bermuda

former: Somers Islands

etymology: the islands making up Bermuda are named after Juan de BERMUDEZ, an early 16th century Spanish sea captain and the first European explorer of the archipelago

DEPENDENCY STATUS:

overseas territory of the UK

GOVERNMENT TYPE:

parliamentary democracy (Parliament); self-governing overseas territory of the UK

CAPITAL:

name: Hamilton

geographic coordinates: 32 17 N, 64 47 W

time difference: UTC-4 (1 hour ahead of Washington, DC, during Standard Time)

daylight saving time: +1hr, begins second Sunday in March; ends first Sunday in November

ADMINISTRATIVE DIVISIONS:

9 parishes and 2 municipalities*; Devonshire, Hamilton, Hamilton*, Paget, Pembroke, Saint George*, Saint George's, Sandys, Smith's, Southampton, Warwick

INDEPENDENCE:

none (overseas territory of the UK)

NATIONAL HOLIDAY:

Bermuda Day, 24 May; note - formerly known as Victoria Day, Empire Day, and Commonwealth Day

CONSTITUTION:

history: several previous (dating to 1684); latest entered into force 8 June 1968 (Bermuda Constitution Order 1968) (2018)

amendments: proposal procedure - NA; passage by an Order in Council in the UK; amended several times, last in 2012 (2018)

LEGAL SYSTEM:

English common law

INTERNATIONAL LAW ORGANIZATION PARTICIPATION:

has not submitted an ICJ jurisdiction declaration; non-party state to the ICCt

CITIZENSHIP:

citizenship by birth: no

citizenship by descent only: at least one parent must be a citizen of the UK

dual citizenship recognized: yes

residency requirement for naturalization: 10 years

SUFFRAGE:

18 years of age; universal

EXECUTIVE BRANCH:

chief of state: Queen ELIZABETH II (since 6 February 1952), represented by Governor John RANKIN (since 5 December 2016)

head of government: Premier David BURT (since 19 July 2017)

cabinet: Cabinet nominated by the premier, appointed by the governor

elections/appointments: the monarchy is hereditary; governor appointed by the monarch; following legislative elections, the leader of the majority party or majority coalition usually appointed premier by the governor

LEGISLATIVE BRANCH:

description: bicameral Parliament consists of:
Senate (11 seats; 3 members appointed by the governor, 5 by the premier, and 3 by the opposition party; members serve 5-year terms) and the House of Assembly (36 seats; members directly elected in single-seat constituencies by simple majority vote to serve up to 5-year terms)
House of Assembly (36 seats; members directly elected in single-seat constituencies by simple majority vote to serve up to 5-year terms)

elections:
House of Assembly - last held on 18 July 2017 (next to be held not later than 2022)

election results:
percent of vote by party - PLP 58.9%, OBA 40.6%, other 0.5%; seats by party - PLP 24, OBA 12

JUDICIAL BRANCH:

highest courts: Court of Appeal (consists of the court president and at least 2 justices); Supreme Court (consists of the chief justice, 4 puisne judges, and 1 associate justice); note - the Judicial Committee of the Privy Council in London is the court of final appeal

judge selection and term of office: Court of Appeal justice appointed by the governor; justice tenure by individual appointment; Supreme Court judges nominated by the Judicial and Legal Services Commission and appointed by the governor; judge tenure based on terms of appointment

subordinate courts: commercial court (began in 2006); magistrates' courts

POLITICAL PARTIES AND LEADERS:

One Bermuda Alliance or OBA (vacant)
Progressive Labor Party or PLP [E. David BURT]

INTERNATIONAL ORGANIZATION PARTICIPATION:

Caricom (associate), ICC (NGOs), Interpol (subbureau), IOC, ITUC (NGOs), UPU, WCO

DIPLOMATIC REPRESENTATION IN THE US:

none (overseas territory of the UK)

DIPLOMATIC REPRESENTATION FROM THE US:

chief of mission: Consul General Mary Ellen KOENIG (since 28 November 2015)

mailing address: P. O. Box HM325, Hamilton HMBX; American Consulate General Hamilton, US Department of State, 5300 Hamilton Place, Washington, DC 20520-5300

telephone: [1] (441) 295-1342

FAX: [1] (441) 295-1592, 296-9233

consulate(s) general: Crown Hill, 16 Middle Road, Devonshire DVO3

FLAG DESCRIPTION:

red, with the flag of the UK in the upper hoist-side quadrant and the Bermudian coat of arms (a white shield with a red lion standing on a green grassy field holding a scrolled shield showing the sinking of the ship Sea Venture off Bermuda in 1609) centered on the outer half of the flag; it was the shipwreck of the vessel, filled with English colonists originally bound for Virginia, that led to the settling of Bermuda

note: the flag is unusual in that it is only British overseas territory that uses a red ensign, all others use blue

NATIONAL SYMBOL(S):

red lion

NATIONAL ANTHEM:

name: Hail to Bermuda

lyrics/music: Bette JOHNS

note: serves as a local anthem; as a territory of the United Kingdom, "God Save the Queen" is official (see United Kingdom)

ECONOMY :: BERMUDA

ECONOMY - OVERVIEW:

International business, which consists primarily of insurance and other financial services, is the real bedrock of Bermuda's economy, consistently accounting for about 85% of the island's GDP. Tourism is the country's second largest industry, accounting for about 5% of Bermuda's GDP but a much larger share of employment. Over 80% of visitors come from the US and the sector struggled in the wake of the global recession of 2008-09. Even the financial sector has lost roughly 5,000 high-paying expatriate jobs since 2008, weighing heavily on household consumption and retail sales. Bermuda must import almost everything. Agriculture and industry are limited due to the small size of the island.

Bermuda's economy returned to negative growth in 2016, reporting a contraction of 0.1% GDP, after growing by 0.6% in 2015. Unemployment reached 7% in 2016 and 2017, public debt is growing and exceeds $2.4 billion, and the government continues to work on attracting foreign investment. Still, Bermuda enjoys one of the highest per capita incomes in the world.

GDP (PURCHASING POWER PARITY):

$6.127 billion (2016 est.)

$6.133 billion (2015 est.)

$6.097 billion (2014 est.)

country comparison to the world: 172

GDP (OFFICIAL EXCHANGE RATE):

$6.127 billion (2016 est.) (2016 est.)

GDP - REAL GROWTH RATE:

-0.1% (2016 est.)

0.6% (2015 est.)

-0.3% (2014 est.)

country comparison to the world: 198

GDP - PER CAPITA (PPP):

$99,400 (2016 est.)

$95,500 (2015 est.)

$87,500 (2014 est.)

country comparison to the world: 6

GDP - COMPOSITION, BY END USE:

household consumption: 51.3% (2017 est.)

government consumption: 15.7% (2017 est.)

investment in fixed capital: 13.7% (2017 est.)

investment in inventories: 0% (2017 est.)

exports of goods and services: 49.8% (2017 est.)

imports of goods and services: -30.4% (2017 est.)

GDP - COMPOSITION, BY SECTOR OF ORIGIN:

agriculture: 0.9% (2017 est.)

industry: 5.3% (2017 est.)

services: 93.8% (2017 est.)

AGRICULTURE - PRODUCTS:

bananas, vegetables, citrus, flowers; dairy products, honey

INDUSTRIES:

international business, tourism, light manufacturing

INDUSTRIAL PRODUCTION GROWTH RATE:

2% (2017 est.)

country comparison to the world: 129

LABOR FORCE:

33,480 (2016 est.)

country comparison to the world: 202

LABOR FORCE - BY OCCUPATION:

agriculture: 2%

industry: 13%

services: 85% (2016 est.)

UNEMPLOYMENT RATE:

7% (2017 est.)

7% (2016 est.)

country comparison to the world: 106

POPULATION BELOW POVERTY LINE:

11% (2008 est.)

HOUSEHOLD INCOME OR CONSUMPTION BY PERCENTAGE SHARE:

lowest 10%: NA

highest 10%: NA

BUDGET:

revenues: 999.2 million (2017 est.)

expenditures: 1.176 billion (2017 est.)

TAXES AND OTHER REVENUES:

16.3% (of GDP) (2017 est.)

country comparison to the world: 183

BUDGET SURPLUS (+) OR DEFICIT (-):

-2.9% (of GDP) (2017 est.)

country comparison to the world: 127

PUBLIC DEBT:

43% of GDP (FY14/15)

country comparison to the world: 117

FISCAL YEAR:

1 April - 31 March

INFLATION RATE (CONSUMER PRICES):

1.9% (2017 est.)

1.4% (2016 est.)

country comparison to the world: 96

STOCK OF NARROW MONEY:

$3.374 billion (30 September 2014 est.)

$3.422 billion (31 December 2013 est.)

note: figures do not include US dollars, which also circulate freely

country comparison to the world: 118

STOCK OF BROAD MONEY:

$22.1 billion (30 September 2014 est.)

$25.1 billion (31 December 2013 est.)

country comparison to the world: 67

STOCK OF DOMESTIC CREDIT:

NA

MARKET VALUE OF PUBLICLY TRADED SHARES:

$1.85 billion (31 December 2015 est.)

$1.601 billion (31 December 2014 est.)

$1.467 billion (31 December 2013 est.)

country comparison to the world: 100

CURRENT ACCOUNT BALANCE:

$818.6 million (2017 est.)

$763 million (2016 est.)

country comparison to the world: 53

EXPORTS:

$19 million (2017 est.)

$19 million (2016 est.)

country comparison to the world: 210

EXPORTS - PARTNERS:

Jamaica 49.1%, Luxembourg 36.1%, US 4.9% (2017)

EXPORTS - COMMODITIES:

reexports of pharmaceuticals

IMPORTS:

$1.094 billion (2017 est.)

$980 million (2016 est.)

country comparison to the world: 183

IMPORTS - COMMODITIES:

clothing, fuels, machinery and transport equipment, construction materials, chemicals, food and live animals

IMPORTS - PARTNERS:

US 72.1%, South Korea 9.7%, Canada 4.2% (2017)

DEBT - EXTERNAL:

$2.515 billion (2017 est.)

$2.435 billion (2015 est.)

country comparison to the world: 150

STOCK OF DIRECT FOREIGN INVESTMENT - AT HOME:

$2.641 billion (2014 est.)

$2.664 billion (2013 est.)

country comparison to the world: 116

STOCK OF DIRECT FOREIGN INVESTMENT - ABROAD:

$889 million (2014 est.)

$835 million (2013 est.)

country comparison to the world: 90

EXCHANGE RATES:

Bermudian dollars (BMD) per US dollar -

1 (2017 est.)

1 (2016 est.)

1 (2015 est.)

1 (2014 est.)

1 (2013 est.)

ENERGY :: BERMUDA

ELECTRICITY ACCESS:

electrification - total population: 100% (2016)

ELECTRICITY - PRODUCTION:

650 million kWh (2016 est.)

country comparison to the world: 159

ELECTRICITY - CONSUMPTION:

604.5 million kWh (2016 est.)

country comparison to the world: 166

ELECTRICITY - EXPORTS:

0 kWh (2016 est.)

country comparison to the world: 107

ELECTRICITY - IMPORTS:

0 kWh (2016 est.)

country comparison to the world: 126

ELECTRICITY - INSTALLED GENERATING CAPACITY:

171,000 kW (2016 est.)

country comparison to the world: 169

ELECTRICITY - FROM FOSSIL FUELS:

100% of total installed capacity (2016 est.)

country comparison to the world: 3

ELECTRICITY - FROM NUCLEAR FUELS:

0% of total installed capacity (2017 est.)

country comparison to the world: 50

ELECTRICITY - FROM HYDROELECTRIC PLANTS:

0% of total installed capacity (2017 est.)

country comparison to the world: 158

ELECTRICITY - FROM OTHER RENEWABLE SOURCES:

0% of total installed capacity (2017 est.)

note: the Tynes Bay Waste Treatment Facility turns waste to electric energy

country comparison to the world: 176

CRUDE OIL - PRODUCTION:

0 bbl/day (2017 est.)

country comparison to the world: 110

CRUDE OIL - EXPORTS:

0 bbl/day (2015 est.)

country comparison to the world: 94

CRUDE OIL - IMPORTS:

0 bbl/day (2015 est.)

country comparison to the world: 97

CRUDE OIL - PROVED RESERVES:

0 bbl (1 January 2018 est.)

country comparison to the world: 107

REFINED PETROLEUM PRODUCTS - PRODUCTION:

0 bbl/day (2017 est.)

country comparison to the world: 119

REFINED PETROLEUM PRODUCTS - CONSUMPTION:

5,000 bbl/day (2016 est.)

country comparison to the world: 178

REFINED PETROLEUM PRODUCTS - EXPORTS:

0 bbl/day (2015 est.)

country comparison to the world: 131

REFINED PETROLEUM PRODUCTS - IMPORTS:

3,939 bbl/day (2015 est.)

country comparison to the world: 178

NATURAL GAS - PRODUCTION:

0 cu m (2017 est.)

country comparison to the world: 105

NATURAL GAS - CONSUMPTION:

0 cu m (2017 est.)

country comparison to the world: 122

NATURAL GAS - EXPORTS:

0 cu m (2017 est.)

country comparison to the world: 70

NATURAL GAS - IMPORTS:

0 cu m (2017 est.)

country comparison to the world: 92

NATURAL GAS - PROVED RESERVES:

0 cu m (1 January 2014 est.)

country comparison to the world: 111

CARBON DIOXIDE EMISSIONS FROM CONSUMPTION OF ENERGY:

793,700 Mt (2017 est.)

country comparison to the world: 174

COMMUNICATIONS :: BERMUDA

TELEPHONES - FIXED LINES:

total subscriptions: 21,883 (2017 est.)

subscriptions per 100 inhabitants: 31 (2017 est.)

country comparison to the world: 173

TELEPHONES - MOBILE CELLULAR:

total subscriptions: 64,997 (2017 est.)

subscriptions per 100 inhabitants: 92 (2017 est.)

country comparison to the world: 198

TELEPHONE SYSTEM:

general assessment: a good, fully automatic digital telephone system with fiber-optic trunk lines; telecom sector provides a relatively high contribution to overall GDP; numerous competitors licensed, but small and localized (2017)

domestic: the system has a high fixed-line teledensity 31 per 100, coupled with a mobile-cellular teledensity of roughly 92 per 100 persons (2017)

international: country code - 1-441; landing points for the GlobeNet, Gemini Bermuda, CBUS, and the Challenger Bermuda-1 (CB-1) submarine cables; satellite earth stations - 3 (2015)

BROADCAST MEDIA:

3 TV stations; cable and satellite TV subscription services are available; roughly 13 radio stations operating (2012)

INTERNET COUNTRY CODE:

.bm

INTERNET USERS:

total: 69,126 (July 2016 est.)

percent of population: 98% (July 2016 est.)

country comparison to the world: 181

TRANSPORTATION :: BERMUDA

CIVIL AIRCRAFT REGISTRATION COUNTRY CODE PREFIX:

VP-B (2016)

AIRPORTS:

1 (2013)

country comparison to the world: 214

AIRPORTS - WITH PAVED RUNWAYS:

total: 1 (2017)

2,438 to 3,047 m: 1 (2017)

ROADWAYS:

total: 447 km (2010)

paved: 447 km (2010)

note: 225 km public roads; 222 km private roads

country comparison to the world: 198

MERCHANT MARINE:

total: 160 (2017)

by type: bulk carrier 10, container ship 8, general cargo 1, oil tanker 18, other 123 (2017)

country comparison to the world: 72

PORTS AND TERMINALS:

major seaport(s): Hamilton, Ireland Island, Saint George

MILITARY AND SECURITY :: BERMUDA

MILITARY BRANCHES:

Bermuda Regiment (2012)

MILITARY SERVICE AGE AND OBLIGATION:

18-45 years of age for voluntary male or female enlistment in the Bermuda Regiment; males must register at age 18 and may be subject to conscription; term of service is 38 months for volunteers or conscripts (2012)

MILITARY - NOTE:

defense is the responsibility of the UK

TRANSNATIONAL ISSUES :: BERMUDA

DISPUTES - INTERNATIONAL:

none

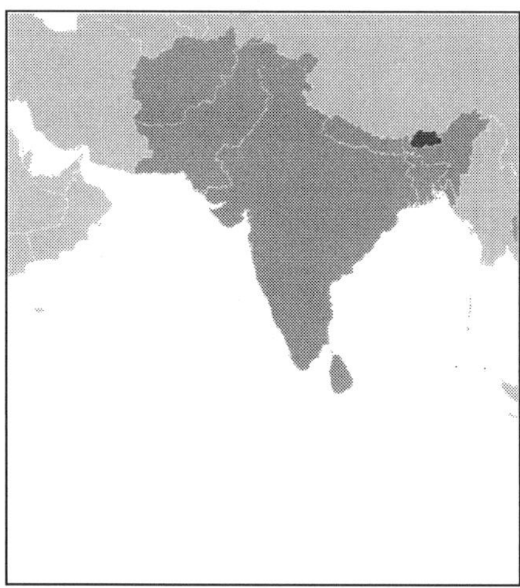

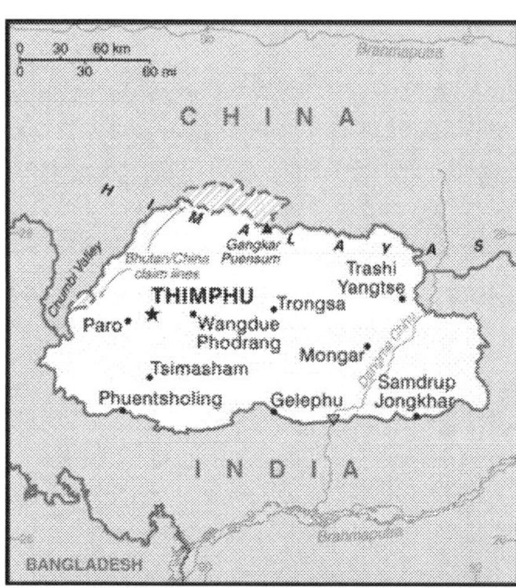

SOUTH ASIA :: BHUTAN

INTRODUCTION :: BHUTAN

BACKGROUND:

Following Britain's victory in the 1865 Duar War, Britain and Bhutan signed the Treaty of Sinchulu, under which Bhutan would receive an annual subsidy in exchange for ceding land to British India. Ugyen WANGCHUCK - who had served as the de facto ruler of an increasingly unified Bhutan and had improved relations with the British toward the end of the 19th century - was named king in 1907. Three years later, a treaty was signed whereby the British agreed not to interfere in Bhutanese internal affairs, and Bhutan allowed Britain to direct its foreign affairs. Bhutan negotiated a similar arrangement with independent India after 1947. Two years later, a formal Indo-Bhutanese accord returned to Bhutan a small piece of the territory annexed by the British, formalized the annual subsidies the country received, and defined India's responsibilities in defense and foreign relations. Under a succession of modernizing monarchs beginning in the 1950s, Bhutan joined the UN in 1971 and slowly continued its engagement beyond its borders.

In March 2005, King Jigme Singye WANGCHUCK unveiled the government's draft constitution - which introduced major democratic reforms - and held a national referendum for its approval. In December 2006, the King abdicated the throne in favor of his son, Jigme Khesar Namgyel WANGCHUCK. In early 2007, India and Bhutan renegotiated their treaty, eliminating the clause that stated that Bhutan would be "guided by" India in conducting its foreign policy, although Thimphu continues to coordinate closely with New Delhi. Elections for seating the country's first parliament were completed in March 2008; the king ratified the country's first constitution in July 2008. Bhutan experienced a peaceful turnover of power following parliamentary elections in 2013, which resulted in the defeat of the incumbent party. The disposition of some 8,500 refugees of the more than 100,000 who fled or were forced out of Bhutan in the 1990s - and who are housed in two UN refugee camps in Nepal - remains unresolved.

GEOGRAPHY :: BHUTAN

LOCATION:

Southern Asia, between China and India

GEOGRAPHIC COORDINATES:

27 30 N, 90 30 E

MAP REFERENCES:

Asia

AREA:

total: 38,394 sq km

land: 38,394 sq km

water: 0 sq km

country comparison to the world: 137

AREA - COMPARATIVE:

slightly larger than Maryland; about one-half the size of Indiana

LAND BOUNDARIES:

total: 1,136 km

border countries (2): China 477 km, India 659 km

COASTLINE:

0 km (landlocked)

MARITIME CLAIMS:

none (landlocked)

CLIMATE:

varies; tropical in southern plains; cool winters and hot summers in central valleys; severe winters and cool summers in Himalayas

TERRAIN:

mostly mountainous with some fertile valleys and savanna

ELEVATION:

mean elevation: 2,220 m

elevation extremes: 97 m lowest point: Drangeme Chhu

7570 highest point: Gangkar Puensum

NATURAL RESOURCES:

timber, hydropower, gypsum, calcium carbonate

LAND USE:

agricultural land: 13.6% (2011 est.)

arable land: 2.6% (2011 est.) / permanent crops: 0.3% (2011 est.) / permanent pasture: 10.7% (2011 est.)

forest: 85.5% (2011 est.)

other: 0.9% (2011 est.)

IRRIGATED LAND:

320 sq km (2012)

NATURAL HAZARDS:

violent storms from the Himalayas are the source of the country's Bhutanese name, which translates as Land of the Thunder Dragon; frequent landslides during the rainy season

ENVIRONMENT - CURRENT ISSUES:

soil erosion; limited access to potable water; wildlife conservation; industrial pollution; waste disposal

ENVIRONMENT - INTERNATIONAL AGREEMENTS:

party to: Biodiversity, Climate Change, Climate Change-Kyoto Protocol, Desertification, Endangered Species, Hazardous Wastes, Ozone Layer Protection

signed, but not ratified: Law of the Sea

GEOGRAPHY - NOTE:

landlocked; strategic location between China and India; controls several key Himalayan mountain passes

PEOPLE AND SOCIETY :: BHUTAN

POPULATION:

766,397 (July 2018 est.)

country comparison to the world: 165

NATIONALITY:

noun: Bhutanese (singular and plural)

adjective: Bhutanese

ETHNIC GROUPS:

Ngalop (also known as Bhote) 50%, ethnic Nepalese 35% (includes Lhotsampas - one of several Nepalese ethnic groups), indigenous or migrant tribes 15%

LANGUAGES:

Sharchhopka 28%, Dzongkha (official) 24%, Lhotshamkha 22%, other 26% (includes foreign languages) (2005 est.)

RELIGIONS:

Lamaistic Buddhist 75.3%, Indian- and Nepalese-influenced Hinduism 22.1%, other 2.6% (2005 est.)

AGE STRUCTURE:

0-14 years: 25.35% (male 99,325 /female 94,985)

15-24 years: 18.4% (male 71,790 /female 69,205)

25-54 years: 43.73% (male 177,436 /female 157,729)

55-64 years: 6.13% (male 25,160 /female 21,817)

65 years and over: 6.39% (male 25,492 /female 23,458) (2018 est.)

DEPENDENCY RATIOS:

total dependency ratio: 47.3 (2015 est.)

youth dependency ratio: 40.4 (2015 est.)

elderly dependency ratio: 6.9 (2015 est.)

potential support ratio: 14.5 (2015 est.)

MEDIAN AGE:

total: 28.1 years

male: 28.6 years

female: 27.6 years (2018 est.)

country comparison to the world: 140

POPULATION GROWTH RATE:

1.05% (2018 est.)

country comparison to the world: 104

BIRTH RATE:

17 births/1,000 population (2018 est.)

country comparison to the world: 105

DEATH RATE:

6.4 deaths/1,000 population (2018 est.)

country comparison to the world: 144

NET MIGRATION RATE:

0 migrant(s)/1,000 population (2017 est.)

country comparison to the world: 75

URBANIZATION:

urban population: 40.9% of total population (2018)

rate of urbanization: 2.98% annual rate of change (2015-20 est.)

MAJOR URBAN AREAS - POPULATION:

203,000 THIMPHU (capital) (2018)

SEX RATIO:

at birth: 1.05 male(s)/female (2017 est.)

0-14 years: 1.04 male(s)/female (2017 est.)

15-24 years: 1.04 male(s)/female (2017 est.)

25-54 years: 1.14 male(s)/female (2017 est.)

55-64 years: 1.16 male(s)/female (2017 est.)

65 years and over: 1.1 male(s)/female (2017 est.)

total population: 1.09 male(s)/female (2017 est.)

MATERNAL MORTALITY RATE:

148 deaths/100,000 live births (2015 est.)

country comparison to the world: 61

INFANT MORTALITY RATE:

total: 30.3 deaths/1,000 live births (2018 est.)

male: 30.4 deaths/1,000 live births (2018 est.)

female: 30.1 deaths/1,000 live births (2018 est.)

country comparison to the world: 61

LIFE EXPECTANCY AT BIRTH:

total population: 71.1 years (2018 est.)

male: 70.1 years (2018 est.)

female: 72.2 years (2018 est.)

country comparison to the world: 157

TOTAL FERTILITY RATE:

1.87 children born/woman (2018 est.)

country comparison to the world: 138

CONTRACEPTIVE PREVALENCE RATE:

65.6% (2010)

HEALTH EXPENDITURES:

3.6% of GDP (2014)

country comparison to the world: 168

PHYSICIANS DENSITY:

0.38 physicians/1,000 population (2016)

HOSPITAL BED DENSITY:

1.7 beds/1,000 population (2012)

DRINKING WATER SOURCE:

improved:

urban: 100% of population (2015 est.)

rural: 100% of population (2015 est.)

total: 100% of population (2015 est.)

unimproved:

urban: 0% of population (2015 est.)

rural: 0% of population (2015 est.)

total: 0% of population (2015 est.)

SANITATION FACILITY ACCESS:

improved:

urban: 77.9% of population (2015 est.)

rural: 33.1% of population (2015 est.)

total: 50.4% of population (2015 est.)

unimproved:

urban: 22.1% of population (2015 est.)

rural: 66.9% of population (2015 est.)

total: 49.6% of population (2015 est.)

HIV/AIDS - ADULT PREVALENCE RATE:

NA

HIV/AIDS - PEOPLE LIVING WITH HIV/AIDS:

NA

HIV/AIDS - DEATHS:

NA

MAJOR INFECTIOUS DISEASES:

degree of risk: high (2016)

food or waterborne diseases: bacterial and protozoal diarrhea, hepatitis A, and typhoid fever (2016)

vectorborne diseases: dengue fever (2016)

OBESITY - ADULT PREVALENCE RATE:

6.4% (2016)

country comparison to the world: 167

CHILDREN UNDER THE AGE OF 5 YEARS UNDERWEIGHT:

12.8% (2010)

country comparison to the world: 52

EDUCATION EXPENDITURES:

7.4% of GDP (2015)

country comparison to the world: 15

LITERACY:

definition: age 15 and over can read and write (2015 est.)

total population: 64.9% (2015 est.)

male: 73.1% (2015 est.)

female: 55% (2015 est.)

SCHOOL LIFE EXPECTANCY (PRIMARY TO TERTIARY EDUCATION):

total: 13 years (2013)

male: 12 years (2013)

female: 13 years (2013)

UNEMPLOYMENT, YOUTH AGES 15-24:

total: 10.7% (2015 est.)

male: 8.2% (2015 est.)

female: 12.7% (2015 est.)

country comparison to the world: 119

GOVERNMENT :: BHUTAN

COUNTRY NAME:

conventional long form: Kingdom of Bhutan

conventional short form: Bhutan

local long form: Druk Gyalkhap

local short form: Druk Yul

etymology: named after the Bhotia, the ethnic Tibetans who migrated from Tibet to Bhutan; "Bod" is the Tibetan name for their land; the Bhutanese name "Druk Yul" means "Land of the Thunder Dragon"

GOVERNMENT TYPE:

constitutional monarchy

CAPITAL:

name: Thimphu

geographic coordinates: 27 28 N, 89 38 E

time difference: UTC+6 (11 hours ahead of Washington, DC, during Standard Time)

ADMINISTRATIVE DIVISIONS:

20 districts (dzongkhag, singular and plural); Bumthang, Chhukha, Dagana, Gasa, Haa, Lhuentse, Mongar, Paro, Pemagatshel, Punakha, Samdrup Jongkhar, Samtse, Sarpang, Thimphu, Trashigang, Trashi Yangtse, Trongsa, Tsirang, Wangdue Phodrang, Zhemgang

INDEPENDENCE:

17 December 1907 (became a unified kingdom under its first hereditary king); 8 August 1949 (Treaty of Friendship with India maintains Bhutanese independence)

NATIONAL HOLIDAY:

National Day (Ugyen WANGCHUCK became first hereditary king), 17 December (1907)

CONSTITUTION:

history: previous governing documents were various royal decrees; first constitution drafted November 2001 to March 2005, ratified 18 July 2008 (2017)

amendments: proposed as a motion by simple majority vote in a joint session of Parliament; passage requires at least a three-fourths majority vote in a joint session of the next Parliament and assented to by the king; amended 2011 (2017)

LEGAL SYSTEM:

civil law based on Buddhist religious law

INTERNATIONAL LAW ORGANIZATION PARTICIPATION:

has not submitted an ICJ jurisdiction declaration; non-party state to the ICCt

CITIZENSHIP:

citizenship by birth: no

citizenship by descent only: the father must be a citizen of Bhutan

dual citizenship recognized: no

residency requirement for naturalization: 10 years

SUFFRAGE:

18 years of age; universal

EXECUTIVE BRANCH:

chief of state: King Jigme Khesar Namgyel WANGCHUCK (since 14 December 2006); note - King Jigme Singye WANGCHUCK abdicated the throne on 14 December 2006 to his son

head of government: Prime Minister Tshering TOBGAY (since 27 July 2013)

cabinet: Council of Ministers or Lhengye Zhungtshog members nominated by the monarch in consultation with the prime minister and approved by the National Assembly; members serve 5-year terms

elections/appointments: the monarchy is hereditary but can be removed by a two-third vote of Parliament; leader of the majority party in Parliament is nominated as the prime minister, appointed by the monarch

LEGISLATIVE BRANCH:

description: bicameral Parliament or Chi Tshog consists of:
non-partisan National Council or Gyelyong Tshogde (25 seats; 20 members directly elected in single-seat constituencies by simple majority vote and 5 members appointed by the king; members serve 5-year terms)
National Assembly or Tshogdu (47 seats; members directly elected in single-seat constituencies by proportional representation vote to serve 5-year terms)

elections:
National Council election last held on 20 April 2018 (next to be held in 2023)
National Assembly - first round held on 15 September 2018 and second round held on 18 October 2018 (next to be held in 2023)

election results:
National Council - seats by party - independent 20 (all candidates ran as independents); composition - men 23, women 2, percent of women 8%
National Assembly - first round - percent of vote by party - DNT 31.9%, DPT 30.9%, PDP 27.4%, BKP 9.8%; second round - percent of vote by party - NA; seats by party - DNT 30, DPT 17; composition - men 40, women 7, percent of women 14.9%; note - total Parliament percent of women 12.5%

JUDICIAL BRANCH:

highest courts: Supreme Court (consists of 5 justices including the chief justice); note - the Supreme Court has sole jurisdiction in constitutional matters

judge selection and term of office: Supreme Court chief justice appointed by the monarch upon the advice of the National Judicial Commission, a 4-member body to include the Legislative Committee of the National Assembly, the attorney general, the Chief Justice of Bhutan and the senior Associate Justice of the Supreme Court; other judges (drangpons) appointed by the monarch from among the High Court judges selected by the National Judicial Commission; chief justice serves a 5-year term or until reaching age 65 years, whichever is earlier; the 4 other judges serve 10-year terms or until age 65, whichever is earlier

subordinate courts: High Court (first appellate court); District or Dzongkhag Courts; sub-district or Dungkhag Courts

POLITICAL PARTIES AND LEADERS:

Bhutan Kuen-Nyam Party or BKP [Dasho Neten ZANGMO]
Bhutan Peace and Prosperity Party (Druk Phuensum Tshogpa) or DPT [Pema GYAMTSHO]
Druk Chirwang Tshogpa or DCT [Lily WANGCHUK]
Druk Nymarup Tshogpa or DNT [Tandin DORJI]
People's Democratic Party or PDP [Tshering TOBGAY]

INTERNATIONAL ORGANIZATION PARTICIPATION:

ADB, BIMSTEC, CP, FAO, G-77, IBRD, ICAO, IDA, IFAD, IFC, IMF, Interpol, IOC, IOM (observer), IPU, ISO (correspondent), ITSO, ITU, MIGA, NAM, OPCW, SAARC, SACEP, UN, UNCTAD, UNESCO, UNIDO, UNTSO, UNWTO, UPU, WCO, WHO, WIPO, WMO, WTO (observer)

DIPLOMATIC REPRESENTATION IN THE US:

New York

none; note - the Permanent Mission to the UN for Bhutan has consular jurisdiction in the US; the permanent representative to the UN is Donna TSHERING (since 13 September 2017); address: 343 East 43rd Street, New York, NY 10017; telephone [1] (212) 682-2268; FAX [1] (212) 661-0551

DIPLOMATIC REPRESENTATION FROM THE US:

the US and Bhutan have no formal diplomatic relations, although frequent informal contact is maintained via the US embassy in New Delhi (India) and Bhutan's Permanent Mission to the UN

FLAG DESCRIPTION:

divided diagonally from the lower hoist-side corner; the upper triangle is yellow and the lower triangle is orange; centered along the dividing line is a large black and white dragon facing away from the hoist side; the dragon, called the Druk (Thunder Dragon), is the emblem of the nation; its white color stands for purity and the jewels in its claws symbolize wealth; the background colors represent spiritual and secular powers within Bhutan: the orange is associated with Buddhism, while the yellow denotes the ruling dynasty

NATIONAL SYMBOL(S):

thunder dragon known as Druk Gyalpo; national colors: orange, yellow

NATIONAL ANTHEM:

name: "Druk tsendhen" (The Thunder Dragon Kingdom)

lyrics/music: Gyaldun Dasho Thinley DORJI/Aku TONGMI

note: adopted 1953

ECONOMY :: BHUTAN

ECONOMY - OVERVIEW:

Bhutan's small economy is based largely on hydropower, agriculture, and forestry, which provide the main livelihood for more than half the population. Because rugged mountains dominate the terrain and make the building of roads and other infrastructure difficult and expensive, industrial production is primarily of the cottage industry type. The economy is closely aligned with India's through strong trade and monetary links and is dependent on India for financial assistance and migrant laborers for development projects, especially for road construction. Bhutan signed a pact in December 2014 to expand duty-free trade with Bangladesh.

Multilateral development organizations administer most educational, social, and environment programs, and take into account the government's desire to protect the country's environment and cultural traditions. For example, the government is cautious in its expansion of the tourist sector, restricing visits to environmentally conscientious tourists. Complicated controls and uncertain policies in areas such as industrial licensing, trade, labor, and finance continue to hamper foreign investment.

Bhutan's largest export - hydropower to India - could spur sustainable growth in the coming years if Bhutan resolves chronic delays in construction. Bhutan's hydropower exports comprise 40% of total exports and 25% of the government's total revenue. Bhutan currently taps only 6.5% of its 24,000-megawatt hydropower potential and is behind schedule in building 12 new hydropower dams with a combined capacity of 10,000 megawatts by 2020 in accordance with a deal signed in 2008 with India. The high volume of imported materials to build hydropower plants has expanded Bhutan's trade and current account deficits. Bhutan also signed a memorandum of understanding with Bangladesh and India in July 2017 to jointly construct a new hydropower plant for exporting electricity to Bangladesh.

GDP (PURCHASING POWER PARITY):

$7.205 billion (2017 est.)

$6.71 billion (2016 est.)

$6.252 billion (2015 est.)

note: data are in 2017 dollars

country comparison to the world: 167

GDP (OFFICIAL EXCHANGE RATE):

$2.405 billion (2017 est.) (2017 est.)

GDP - REAL GROWTH RATE:

7.4% (2017 est.)

7.3% (2016 est.)

6.2% (2015 est.)

country comparison to the world: 14

GDP - PER CAPITA (PPP):

$9,000 (2017 est.)

$8,500 (2016 est.)

$8,000 (2015 est.)

note: data are in 2017 dollars

country comparison to the world: 145

GROSS NATIONAL SAVING:

40.4% of GDP (2017 est.)

33.3% of GDP (2016 est.)

32% of GDP (2015 est.)

country comparison to the world: 8

GDP - COMPOSITION, BY END USE:

household consumption: 58% (2017 est.)

government consumption: 16.8% (2017 est.)

investment in fixed capital: 47.2% (2017 est.)

investment in inventories: 0% (2017 est.)

exports of goods and services: 26% (2017 est.)

imports of goods and services: -48% (2017 est.)

GDP - COMPOSITION, BY SECTOR OF ORIGIN:

agriculture: 16.2% (2017 est.)

industry: 41.8% (2017 est.)

services: 42% (2017 est.)

AGRICULTURE - PRODUCTS:

rice, corn, root crops, citrus; dairy products, eggs

INDUSTRIES:

cement, wood products, processed fruits, alcoholic beverages, calcium carbide, tourism

INDUSTRIAL PRODUCTION GROWTH RATE:

6.3% (2017 est.)

country comparison to the world: 36

LABOR FORCE:

397,900 (2017 est.)

note: major shortage of skilled labor

country comparison to the world: 160

LABOR FORCE - BY OCCUPATION:

agriculture: 58%

industry: 20%

services: 22% (2015 est.)

UNEMPLOYMENT RATE:

3.2% (2017 est.)

3.2% (2016 est.)

country comparison to the world: 39

POPULATION BELOW POVERTY LINE:

12% (2012 est.)

HOUSEHOLD INCOME OR CONSUMPTION BY PERCENTAGE SHARE:

lowest 10%: 30.6% (2012)

highest 10%: 30.6% (2012)

DISTRIBUTION OF FAMILY INCOME - GINI INDEX:

38.8 (2012)

38.1 (2007)

country comparison to the world: 75

BUDGET:

revenues: 655.3 million (2017 est.)

expenditures: 737.4 million (2017 est.)

note: the Government of India finances nearly one-quarter of Bhutan's budget expenditures

TAXES AND OTHER REVENUES:

27.2% (of GDP) (2017 est.)

country comparison to the world: 101

BUDGET SURPLUS (+) OR DEFICIT (-):

-3.4% (of GDP) (2017 est.)

country comparison to the world: 142

PUBLIC DEBT:

106.3% of GDP (2017 est.)

114.2% of GDP (2016 est.)

country comparison to the world: 12

FISCAL YEAR:

1 July - 30 June

INFLATION RATE (CONSUMER PRICES):

5.8% (2017 est.)

7.6% (2016 est.)

country comparison to the world: 183

CENTRAL BANK DISCOUNT RATE:

6% (2017 est.)

note: this is the policy rate of Bhutan's central bank

country comparison to the world: 68

COMMERCIAL BANK PRIME LENDING RATE:

15% (31 December 2017 est.)

14.15% (31 December 2016 est.)

country comparison to the world: 38

STOCK OF NARROW MONEY:

$993.5 million (31 December 2017 est.)

$769 million (31 December 2016 est.)

country comparison to the world: 158

STOCK OF BROAD MONEY:

$993.5 million (31 December 2017 est.)

$769 million (31 December 2016 est.)

country comparison to the world: 163

STOCK OF DOMESTIC CREDIT:

$1.535 billion (31 December 2017 est.)

$1.17 billion (31 December 2016 est.)

country comparison to the world: 161

MARKET VALUE OF PUBLICLY TRADED SHARES:

$401.4 million (31 December 2017 est.)

$340.5 million (31 December 2016 est.)

$359.3 million (31 December 2015 est.)

country comparison to the world: 114

CURRENT ACCOUNT BALANCE:

-$547 million (2017 est.)

-$621 million (2016 est.)

country comparison to the world: 120

EXPORTS:

$554.6 million (2017 est.)

$495.3 million (2016 est.)

country comparison to the world: 174

EXPORTS - PARTNERS:

India 95.3% (2017)

EXPORTS - COMMODITIES:

electricity (to India), ferrosilicon, cement, cardamom, calcium carbide, steel rods/bars, dolomite, gypsum

IMPORTS:

$1.025 billion (2017 est.)

$1.03 billion (2016 est.)

country comparison to the world: 184

IMPORTS - COMMODITIES:

fuel and lubricants, airplanes, machinery and parts, rice, motor vehicles

IMPORTS - PARTNERS:

India 89.5% (2017)

RESERVES OF FOREIGN EXCHANGE AND GOLD:

$1.206 billion (31 December 2017 est.)

$1.127 billion (31 December 2016 est.)

country comparison to the world: 129

DEBT - EXTERNAL:

$2.671 billion (31 December 2017 est.)

$2.355 billion (31 December 2016 est.)

country comparison to the world: 147

STOCK OF DIRECT FOREIGN INVESTMENT - AT HOME:

$160.4 million (31 December 2017 est.)

$168.4 million (31 December 2016 est.)

country comparison to the world: 135

EXCHANGE RATES:

ngultrum (BTN) per US dollar -

64.97 (2017 est.)

67.2 (2016 est.)

67.2 (2015 est.)

64.15 (2014 est.)

61.03 (2013 est.)

ENERGY :: BHUTAN

ELECTRICITY ACCESS:

population without electricity: 187,531 (2012)

electrification - total population: 76% (2012)

electrification - urban areas: 100% (2012)

electrification - rural areas: 53% (2012)

ELECTRICITY - PRODUCTION:

7.883 billion kWh (2016 est.)

country comparison to the world: 110

ELECTRICITY - CONSUMPTION:

2.184 billion kWh (2016 est.)

country comparison to the world: 141

ELECTRICITY - EXPORTS:

5.763 billion kWh (2016 est.)

country comparison to the world: 32

ELECTRICITY - IMPORTS:

84 million kWh (2016 est.)

country comparison to the world: 101

ELECTRICITY - INSTALLED GENERATING CAPACITY:

1.632 million kW (2016 est.)

country comparison to the world: 120

ELECTRICITY - FROM FOSSIL FUELS:

1% of total installed capacity (2016 est.)

country comparison to the world: 211

ELECTRICITY - FROM NUCLEAR FUELS:

0% of total installed capacity (2017 est.)

country comparison to the world: 51

ELECTRICITY - FROM HYDROELECTRIC PLANTS:

99% of total installed capacity (2017 est.)

country comparison to the world: 2

ELECTRICITY - FROM OTHER RENEWABLE SOURCES:

0% of total installed capacity (2017 est.)

country comparison to the world: 177

CRUDE OIL - PRODUCTION:

0 bbl/day (2017 est.)

country comparison to the world: 111

CRUDE OIL - EXPORTS:

0 bbl/day (2015 est.)

country comparison to the world: 95

CRUDE OIL - IMPORTS:

0 bbl/day (2015 est.)

country comparison to the world: 98

CRUDE OIL - PROVED RESERVES:

0 bbl (1 January 2018 est.)

country comparison to the world: 108

REFINED PETROLEUM PRODUCTS - PRODUCTION:

0 bbl/day (2017 est.)

country comparison to the world: 120

REFINED PETROLEUM PRODUCTS - CONSUMPTION:

3,000 bbl/day (2016 est.)

country comparison to the world: 188

REFINED PETROLEUM PRODUCTS - EXPORTS:

0 bbl/day (2015 est.)

country comparison to the world: 132

REFINED PETROLEUM PRODUCTS - IMPORTS:

3,120 bbl/day (2015 est.)

country comparison to the world: 183

NATURAL GAS - PRODUCTION:

0 cu m (2017 est.)

country comparison to the world: 106

NATURAL GAS - CONSUMPTION:

0 cu m (2017 est.)

country comparison to the world: 123

NATURAL GAS - EXPORTS:

0 cu m (2017 est.)

country comparison to the world: 71

NATURAL GAS - IMPORTS:

0 cu m (2017 est.)

country comparison to the world: 93

NATURAL GAS - PROVED RESERVES:

0 cu m (2016 est.)

country comparison to the world: 112

CARBON DIOXIDE EMISSIONS FROM CONSUMPTION OF ENERGY:

604,900 Mt (2017 est.)

country comparison to the world: 181

COMMUNICATIONS :: BHUTAN

TELEPHONES - FIXED LINES:

total subscriptions: 21,364 (2017 est.)

subscriptions per 100 inhabitants: 3 (2017 est.)

country comparison to the world: 174

TELEPHONES - MOBILE CELLULAR:

total subscriptions: 730,623 (2017 est.)

subscriptions per 100 inhabitants: 96 (2017 est.)

country comparison to the world: 164

TELEPHONE SYSTEM:

general assessment: urban towns and district headquarters have telecommunications services; telecom sector has been continuing on a steady development path; fixed broadband penetration remains very low, due to the preeminence of the mobile platform; next five years to 2023 low to moderate growth is expected from this small base (2017)

domestic: domestic service inadequate, notably in rural areas; mobile-cellular service, begun in 2003, is now widely available; 3 to 100 fixed-line, 96 to 100 mobile cellular (2017)

international: country code - 975; international telephone and telegraph service via landline and microwave relay through India; satellite earth station - 1 Intelsat (2016)

BROADCAST MEDIA:

state-owned TV station established in 1999; cable TV service offers dozens of Indian and other international channels; first radio station, privately launched in 1973, is now state-owned; 5 private radio stations are currently broadcasting (2012)

INTERNET COUNTRY CODE:

.bt

INTERNET USERS:

total: 313,347 (July 2016 est.)

percent of population: 41.8% (July 2016 est.)

country comparison to the world: 160

BROADBAND - FIXED SUBSCRIPTIONS:

total: 16,707 (2017 est.)

subscriptions per 100 inhabitants: 2 (2017 est.)

country comparison to the world: 157

TRANSPORTATION :: BHUTAN

NATIONAL AIR TRANSPORT SYSTEM:

number of registered air carriers: 2 (2015)

inventory of registered aircraft operated by air carriers: 6 (2015)

annual passenger traffic on registered air carriers: 162,864 (2015)

annual freight traffic on registered air carriers: 538,041 mt-km (2015)

CIVIL AIRCRAFT REGISTRATION COUNTRY CODE PREFIX:

A5 (2016)

AIRPORTS:

2 (2013)

country comparison to the world: 198

AIRPORTS - WITH PAVED RUNWAYS:

total: 2 (2017)

1,524 to 2,437 m: 1 (2017)

914 to 1,523 m: 1 (2017)

AIRPORTS - WITH UNPAVED RUNWAYS:

total: 1 (2012)

914 to 1,523 m: 1 (2012)

ROADWAYS:

total: 10,578 km

paved: 2,975 km (includes 2,180 km of national highways)

unpaved: 7,603 km (2013)

note: a more recent figure for 2015 lists 11,177 km for total roadway length, but no breakdown of paved or unpaved

country comparison to the world: 135

MILITARY AND SECURITY :: BHUTAN

MILITARY BRANCHES:

Royal Bhutan Army (includes Royal Bodyguard and Royal Bhutan Police) (2009)

MILITARY SERVICE AGE AND OBLIGATION:

18 years of age for voluntary military service; no conscription; militia training is compulsory for males aged 20-25, over a 3-year period (2012)

TRANSNATIONAL ISSUES :: BHUTAN

DISPUTES - INTERNATIONAL:

lacking any treaty describing the boundary, Bhutan and China continue negotiations to establish a common boundary alignment to resolve territorial disputes arising from substantial cartographic discrepancies, the most contentious of which lie in Bhutan's west along China's Chumbi salient

INTRODUCTION :: BOLIVIA

BACKGROUND:

Bolivia, named after independence fighter Simon BOLIVAR, broke away from Spanish rule in 1825; much of its subsequent history has consisted of a series of coups and countercoups, with the last coup occurring in 1978. Democratic civilian rule was established in 1982, but leaders have faced difficult problems of deep-seated poverty, social unrest, and illegal drug production.

In December 2005, Bolivians elected Movement Toward Socialism leader Evo MORALES president - by the widest margin of any leader since the restoration of civilian rule in 1982 - after he ran on a promise to change the country's traditional political class and empower the nation's poor, indigenous majority. In December 2009 and October 2014, President MORALES easily won reelection. His party maintained control of the legislative branch of the government, which has allowed him to continue his process of change. In February 2016, MORALES narrowly lost a referendum to approve a constitutional amendment that would have allowed him to compete in the 2019 presidential election. Despite the loss, MORALES has already been chosen by his party to run again in 2019, via a still-undetermined method for him to appear on the ballot.

GEOGRAPHY :: BOLIVIA

LOCATION:

Central South America, southwest of Brazil

GEOGRAPHIC COORDINATES:

17 00 S, 65 00 W

MAP REFERENCES:

South America

AREA:

total: 1,098,581 sq km

land: 1,083,301 sq km

water: 15,280 sq km

country comparison to the world: 29

AREA - COMPARATIVE:

slightly less than three times the size of Montana

LAND BOUNDARIES:

total: 7,252 km

border countries (5): Argentina 942 km, Brazil 3403 km, Chile 942 km, Paraguay 753 km, Peru 1212 km

COASTLINE:

0 km (landlocked)

MARITIME CLAIMS:

none (landlocked)

CLIMATE:

varies with altitude; humid and tropical to cold and semiarid

TERRAIN:

rugged Andes Mountains with a highland plateau (Altiplano), hills, lowland plains of the Amazon Basin

ELEVATION:

mean elevation: 1,192 m

elevation extremes: 90 m lowest point: Rio Paraguay

6542 highest point: Nevado Sajama

NATURAL RESOURCES:

tin, natural gas, petroleum, zinc, tungsten, antimony, silver, iron, lead, gold, timber, hydropower

LAND USE:

agricultural land: 34.3% (2011 est.)

arable land: 3.6% (2011 est.) / permanent crops: 0.2% (2011 est.) / permanent pasture: 30.5% (2011 est.)

forest: 52.5% (2011 est.)

other: 13.2% (2011 est.)

IRRIGATED LAND:

3,000 sq km (2012)

POPULATION DISTRIBUTION:

a high altitude plain in the west between two cordillera of the Andes, known as the Altiplano, is the focal area for most of the population; a dense settlement pattern is also found in and around the city of Santa Cruz, located on the eastern side of the Andes

NATURAL HAZARDS:

flooding in the northeast (March to April)

volcanism: volcanic activity in Andes Mountains on the border with Chile; historically active volcanoes in this region are Irruputuncu (5,163 m), which last erupted in 1995, and the Olca-Paruma volcanic complex (5,762 m to 5,167 m)

ENVIRONMENT - CURRENT ISSUES:

the clearing of land for agricultural purposes and the international demand for tropical timber are contributing to deforestation; soil erosion from overgrazing and poor cultivation methods (including slash-and-burn agriculture); desertification; loss of biodiversity; industrial pollution of water supplies used for drinking and irrigation

ENVIRONMENT - INTERNATIONAL AGREEMENTS:

party to: Biodiversity, Climate Change, Climate Change-Kyoto Protocol, Desertification, Endangered Species, Hazardous Wastes, Law of the Sea, Marine Dumping, Ozone Layer Protection, Ship Pollution, Tropical Timber 83, Tropical Timber 94, Wetlands

signed, but not ratified: Environmental Modification, Marine Life Conservation

GEOGRAPHY - NOTE:

landlocked; shares control of Lago Titicaca, world's highest navigable lake (elevation 3,805 m), with Peru

PEOPLE AND SOCIETY :: BOLIVIA

POPULATION:

11,306,341 (July 2018 est.)

country comparison to the world: 80

NATIONALITY:

noun: Bolivian(s)

adjective: Bolivian

ETHNIC GROUPS:

mestizo (mixed white and Amerindian ancestry) 68%, indigenous 20%, white 5%, cholo/chola 2%, black 1%, other 1%, unspecified 3% ; 44% of respondents indicated feeling part of some indigenous group, predominantly Quechua or Aymara (2009 est.)

note: results among surveys vary based on the wording of the ethnicity question and the available response choices; the 2001 national census did not provide "mestizo" as a response choice, resulting in a much higher proportion of respondents identifying themselves as belonging to one of the available indigenous ethnicity choices; the use of "mestizo" and "cholo" varies among response choices in surveys, with surveys using the terms interchangeably, providing one or the other as a response choice, or providing the two as separate response choices

LANGUAGES:

Spanish (official) 60.7%, Quechua (official) 21.2%, Aymara (official) 14.6%, foreign languages 2.4%, Guarani (official) 0.6%, other native languages 0.4%, none 0.1% (2001 est.)

note: Bolivia's 2009 constitution designates Spanish and all indigenous languages as official; 36 indigenous languages are specified, including a few that are extinct

RELIGIONS:

Roman Catholic 76.8%, Evangelical and Pentecostal 8.1%, Protestant 7.9%, other 1.7%, none 5.5% (2012 est.)

DEMOGRAPHIC PROFILE:

Bolivia ranks at or near the bottom among Latin American countries in several areas of health and development, including poverty, education, fertility, malnutrition, mortality, and life expectancy. On the positive side, more children are being vaccinated and more pregnant women are getting prenatal care and having skilled health practitioners attend their births.

Bolivia's income inequality is the highest in Latin America and one of the highest in the world. Public education is of poor quality, and educational opportunities are among the most unevenly distributed in Latin America, with girls and indigenous and rural children less likely to be literate or to complete primary school. The lack of access to education and family planning services helps to sustain Bolivia's high fertility rate—approximately three children per woman. Bolivia's lack of clean water and basic sanitation, especially in rural areas, contributes to health problems.

Between 7% and 16% of Bolivia's population lives abroad (estimates vary in part because of illegal migration). Emigrants primarily seek jobs and better wages in Argentina (the principal destination), the US, and Spain. In recent years, more restrictive immigration policies in Europe and the US have increased the flow of Bolivian emigrants to neighboring countries. Fewer Bolivians migrated to Brazil in 2015 and 2016 because of its recession; increasing numbers have been going to Chile, mainly to work as miners.

AGE STRUCTURE:

0-14 years: 31.34% (male 1,805,765 /female 1,737,647)

15-24 years: 19.37% (male 1,109,388 /female 1,080,662)

25-54 years: 37.9% (male 2,098,847 /female 2,185,890)

55-64 years: 5.96% (male 310,250 /female 363,403)

65 years and over: 5.43% (male 270,435 /female 344,054) (2018 est.)

DEPENDENCY RATIOS:

total dependency ratio: 63.7 (2015 est.)

youth dependency ratio: 53.1 (2015 est.)

elderly dependency ratio: 10.6 (2015 est.)

potential support ratio: 9.4 (2015 est.)

MEDIAN AGE:

total: 24.6 years

male: 23.9 years

female: 25.4 years (2018 est.)

country comparison to the world: 161

POPULATION GROWTH RATE:

1.48% (2018 est.)

country comparison to the world: 74

BIRTH RATE:

21.6 births/1,000 population (2018 est.)

country comparison to the world: 71

DEATH RATE:

6.3 deaths/1,000 population (2018 est.)

country comparison to the world: 149

NET MIGRATION RATE:

-0.5 migrant(s)/1,000 population (2017 est.)

country comparison to the world: 122

POPULATION DISTRIBUTION:

a high altitude plain in the west between two cordillera of the Andes, known as the Altiplano, is the focal area for most of the population; a dense settlement pattern is also found in and around the city of Santa Cruz, located on the eastern side of the Andes

URBANIZATION:

urban population: 69.4% of total population (2018)

rate of urbanization: 1.97% annual rate of change (2015-20 est.)

MAJOR URBAN AREAS - POPULATION:

1.814 million LA PAZ (capital), 1.641 million Santa Cruz, 1.24 million Cochabamba, 278,000 Sucre (constitutional capital) (2018)

SEX RATIO:

at birth: 1.04 male(s)/female (2017 est.)

0-14 years: 1.04 male(s)/female (2017 est.)

15-24 years: 1.03 male(s)/female (2017 est.)

25-54 years: 0.95 male(s)/female (2017 est.)

55-64 years: 0.86 male(s)/female (2017 est.)

65 years and over: 0.79 male(s)/female (2017 est.)

total population: 0.98 male(s)/female (2017 est.)

MOTHER'S MEAN AGE AT FIRST BIRTH:

21.2 years (2008 est.)

note: median age at first birth among women 25-29

MATERNAL MORTALITY RATE:

206 deaths/100,000 live births (2015 est.)

country comparison to the world: 51

INFANT MORTALITY RATE:

total: 34.2 deaths/1,000 live births (2018 est.)

male: 37.6 deaths/1,000 live births (2018 est.)

female: 30.7 deaths/1,000 live births (2018 est.)

country comparison to the world: 51

LIFE EXPECTANCY AT BIRTH:

total population: 69.8 years (2018 est.)

male: 67 years (2018 est.)

female: 72.8 years (2018 est.)

country comparison to the world: 161

TOTAL FERTILITY RATE:

2.58 children born/woman (2018 est.)

country comparison to the world: 74

CONTRACEPTIVE PREVALENCE RATE:

66.5% (2016)

HEALTH EXPENDITURES:

6.3% of GDP (2014)

country comparison to the world: 100

PHYSICIANS DENSITY:

0.47 physicians/1,000 population (2011)

HOSPITAL BED DENSITY:

1.1 beds/1,000 population (2014)

DRINKING WATER SOURCE:

improved:

urban: 96.7% of population (2015 est.)

rural: 75.6% of population (2015 est.)

total: 90% of population (2015 est.)

unimproved:

urban: 3.3% of population (2015 est.)

rural: 24.4% of population (2015 est.)

total: 10% of population (2015 est.)

SANITATION FACILITY ACCESS:

improved:

urban: 60.8% of population (2015 est.)

rural: 27.5% of population (2015 est.)

total: 50.3% of population (2015 est.)

unimproved:

urban: 39.2% of population (2015 est.)

rural: 72.5% of population (2015 est.)

total: 49.7% of population (2015 est.)

HIV/AIDS - ADULT PREVALENCE RATE:

0.3% (2017 est.)

country comparison to the world: 78

HIV/AIDS - PEOPLE LIVING WITH HIV/AIDS:

21,000 (2017 est.)

country comparison to the world: 81

HIV/AIDS - DEATHS:

<1000 (2017 est.)

MAJOR INFECTIOUS DISEASES:

degree of risk: very high (2016)

food or waterborne diseases: bacterial diarrhea and hepatitis A (2016)

vectorborne diseases: dengue fever, malaria, and yellow fever (2016)

note: active local transmission of Zika virus by Aedes species mosquitoes has been identified in this country (as of August 2016); it poses an important risk (a large number of cases possible) among US citizens if bitten by an infective mosquito; other less common ways to get Zika are through sex, via blood transfusion, or during pregnancy, in which the pregnant woman passes Zika virus to her fetus

OBESITY - ADULT PREVALENCE RATE:

20.2% (2016)

country comparison to the world: 102

CHILDREN UNDER THE AGE OF 5 YEARS UNDERWEIGHT:

3.4% (2016)

country comparison to the world: 93

EDUCATION EXPENDITURES:

7.3% of GDP (2014)

country comparison to the world: 16

LITERACY:

definition: age 15 and over can read and write (2015 est.)

total population: 92.5% (2015 est.)

male: 96.5% (2015 est.)

female: 88.6% (2015 est.)

UNEMPLOYMENT, YOUTH AGES 15-24:

total: 6.9% (2015 est.)

male: 5.8% (2015 est.)

female: 8.6% (2015 est.)

country comparison to the world: 146

GOVERNMENT :: BOLIVIA

COUNTRY NAME:

conventional long form: Plurinational State of Bolivia

conventional short form: Bolivia

local long form: Estado Plurinacional de Bolivia

local short form: Bolivia

etymology: the country is named after Simon BOLIVAR, a 19th-century leader in the South American wars for independence

GOVERNMENT TYPE:

presidential republic

CAPITAL:

name: La Paz (administrative capital); Sucre (constitutional [legislative and judicial] capital)

geographic coordinates: 16 30 S, 68 09 W

time difference: UTC-4 (1 hour ahead of Washington, DC, during Standard Time)

note: at approximately 3,630 m above sea level, La Paz's elevation makes it the highest capital city in the world

ADMINISTRATIVE DIVISIONS:

9 departments (departamentos, singular - departamento); Beni, Chuquisaca, Cochabamba, La Paz, Oruro, Pando, Potosi, Santa Cruz, Tarija

INDEPENDENCE:

6 August 1825 (from Spain)

NATIONAL HOLIDAY:

Independence Day, 6 August (1825)

CONSTITUTION:

history: many previous; latest drafted 6 August 2006 to 9 December 2008, approved by referendum 25 January 2009, effective 7 February 2009; note - in late 2017, the Constitutional Tribunal declared inapplicable provisions of the constitution that prohibit elected officials, including the president, from serving more than 2 consecutive terms (2018)

amendments: proposed through public petition by at least 20% of voters or by the Plurinational Legislative Assembly; passage requires approval by at least two-thirds majority vote of the total membership of the Assembly and approval in a referendum; amended 2013 (2018)

LEGAL SYSTEM:

civil law system with influences from Roman, Spanish, canon (religious), French, and indigenous law

INTERNATIONAL LAW ORGANIZATION PARTICIPATION:

has not submitted an ICJ jurisdiction declaration; accepts ICCt jurisdiction

CITIZENSHIP:

citizenship by birth: yes

citizenship by descent only: yes

dual citizenship recognized: yes

residency requirement for naturalization: 3 years

SUFFRAGE:

18 years of age; universal and compulsory

EXECUTIVE BRANCH:

chief of state: President Juan Evo MORALES Ayma (since 22 January 2006); Vice President Alvaro GARCIA Linera (since 22 January 2006); note - the president is both chief of state and head of government

head of government: President Juan Evo MORALES Ayma (since 22 January 2006); Vice President Alvaro GARCIA Linera (since 22 January 2006)

cabinet: Cabinet appointed by the president

elections/appointments: president and vice president directly elected on the same ballot one of 3 ways: candidate wins at least 50% of the vote, or at least 40% of the vote and 10% more than the next highest candidate; otherwise a second round is held and the winner determined by simple majority vote; no term limits (changed from two consecutive term limit by Constitutional Court in late 2017); election last held on 12 October 2014 (next to be held in 2019)

election results: Juan Evo MORALES Ayma reelected president; percent of vote - Juan Evo MORALES Ayma (MAS) 61%; Samuel DORIA MEDINA Arana (UN) 24.5%; Jorge QUIROGA Ramirez (POC) 9.1%; other 5.4%

LEGISLATIVE BRANCH:

description: bicameral Plurinational Legislative Assembly or Asamblea Legislativa Plurinacional consists of:
Chamber of Senators or Camara de Senadores (36 seats; members directly elected in multi-seat constituencies by proportional representation vote; members serve 5-year terms)
Chamber of Deputies or Camara de Diputados (130 seats; 70 members directly elected in single-seat constituencies by simple majority vote, 53 directly elected in single-seat constituencies by proportional representation vote, and 7 - apportioned to non-contiguous, rural areas in 7 of the 9 states - directly elected in single-seat constituencies by simple majority vote; members serve 5-year terms)

elections:
Chamber of Senators - last held on 12 October 2014 (next to be held in 2019)
Chamber of Deputies - last held on 12 October 2014 (next to be held in 2019)

election results:
Chamber of Senators - percent of vote by party - NA; seats by party - MAS 25, UD 9, PDC 2;
Chamber of Deputies - percent of vote by party - NA; seats by party - MAS 88, UD 32, PDC 10

JUDICIAL BRANCH:

highest courts: Supreme Court or Tribunal Supremo de Justicia (consists of 12 judges or ministros organized into civil, penal, social, and administrative chambers); Plurinational Constitutional Tribunal (consists of 7 primary and 7 alternate magistrates); Plurinational Electoral Organ (consists of 7 members and 6 alternates); National Agro-Environment Court (consists of 5 primary and 5 alternate judges; Council of the Judiciary (consists of 3 primary and 3 alternate judges)

judge selection and term of office: Supreme Court, Plurinational Constitutional Tribunal, National Agro-Environmental Court, and Council of the Judiciary candidates pre-selected by the Plurinational Legislative Assembly and elected by direct popular vote; judges elected for 6-year terms; Plurinational Electoral Organ judges appointed - 6 by the Legislative Assembly and 1 by the president of the republic; members serve single 6-year terms

subordinate courts: National Electoral Court; District Courts (in each of the 9 administrative departments); agro-environmental lower courts

POLITICAL PARTIES AND LEADERS:

Christian Democratic Party or PDC [Jorge Fernando QUIROGA Ramirez]
Movement Toward Socialism or MAS [Juan Evo MORALES Ayma]
National Unity or UN [Samuel DORIA MEDINA Arana]

INTERNATIONAL ORGANIZATION PARTICIPATION:

CAN, CD, CELAC, FAO, G-77, IADB, IAEA, IBRD, ICAO, ICC (national committees), ICCt, ICRM, IDA, IFAD, IFC, IFRCS, ILO, IMF, IMO, Interpol, IOC, IOM, IPU, ISO (correspondent), ITSO, ITU, LAES, LAIA, Mercosur (associate), MIGA, MINUSTAH, MONUSCO, NAM, OAS, OPANAL, OPCW, PCA, UN, UN Security Council (temporary), UNAMID, UNASUR, UNCTAD, UNESCO, UNIDO, Union Latina, UNMIL, UNMISS, UNOCI, UNWTO, UPU, WCO, WFTU (NGOs), WHO, WIPO, WMO, WTO

DIPLOMATIC REPRESENTATION IN THE US:

chief of mission: Ambassador (vacant); Charge d'Affaires Rafael Pablo CANEDO Daroca (since July 2017)

chancery: 3014 Massachusetts Avenue NW, Washington, DC 20008

telephone: [1] (202) 328-4155

FAX: [1] (202) 328-3712

consulate(s) general: Houston, Los Angeles, Miami, New York, Washington, DC

note: in September 2008, the US expelled the Bolivian ambassador to the US in reciprocity for Bolivia expelling the US ambassador to Bolivia

DIPLOMATIC REPRESENTATION FROM THE US:

chief of mission: Ambassador (vacant); Charge d'Affaires Bruce WILLIAMSON (since December 2017)

embassy: Avenida Arce 2780, Casilla 425, La Paz

mailing address: 3220 La Paz Place, Dulles, VA, 20189-3220

telephone: [591] (2) 216-8000

FAX: [591] (2) 216-8111

note: in September 2008, the Bolivian Government expelled the US Ambassador to Bolivia, Philip GOLDBERG, and both countries have yet to reinstate their ambassadors

FLAG DESCRIPTION:

three equal horizontal bands of red (top), yellow, and green with the coat of arms centered on the yellow band; red stands for bravery and the blood of national heroes, yellow for the nation's mineral resources, and green for the fertility of the land

note: similar to the flag of Ghana, which has a large black five-pointed star centered in the yellow band; in 2009, a presidential decree made it mandatory for a so-called wiphala - a square, multi-colored flag representing the country's indigenous peoples - to be used alongside the traditional flag

NATIONAL SYMBOL(S):

llama, Andean condor; national colors: red, yellow, green

NATIONAL ANTHEM:

name: "Cancion Patriotica" (Patriotic Song)

lyrics/music: Jose Ignacio de SANJINES/Leopoldo Benedetto VINCENTI

note: adopted 1852

ECONOMY :: BOLIVIA

ECONOMY - OVERVIEW:

Bolivia is a resource rich country with strong growth attributed to captive markets for natural gas exports – to Brazil and Argentina. However, the country remains one of the least developed countries in Latin America because of state-oriented policies that deter investment.

Following an economic crisis during the early 1980s, reforms in the 1990s spurred private investment, stimulated economic growth, and cut poverty rates. The period 2003-05 was characterized by political instability, racial tensions, and violent protests against plans - subsequently abandoned - to export Bolivia's newly discovered natural gas reserves to large Northern Hemisphere markets. In 2005-06, the government passed hydrocarbon laws that imposed significantly higher royalties and required foreign firms then operating under risk-sharing contracts to surrender all production to the state energy company in exchange for a predetermined service fee; the laws engendered much public debate. High commodity prices between 2010 and 2014 sustained rapid growth and large trade surpluses with GDP growing 6.8% in 2013 and 5.4% in 2014. The global decline in oil prices that began in late 2014 exerted downward pressure on the price Bolivia receives for exported gas and resulted in lower GDP growth rates - 4.9% in 2015 and 4.3% in 2016 - and losses in government revenue as well as fiscal and trade deficits.

A lack of foreign investment in the key sectors of mining and hydrocarbons, along with conflict among social groups, pose challenges for the Bolivian economy. In 2015, President Evo MORALES expanded efforts to court international investment and boost Bolivia's energy production capacity. MORALES passed an investment law and promised not to nationalize additional industries in an effort to improve the investment climate. In early 2016, the Government of Bolivia approved the 2016-2020 National Economic and Social Development Plan aimed at maintaining growth of 5% and reducing poverty.

GDP (PURCHASING POWER PARITY):

$83.72 billion (2017 est.)

$80.35 billion (2016 est.)

$77.07 billion (2015 est.)

note: data are in 2017 dollars

country comparison to the world: 94

GDP (OFFICIAL EXCHANGE RATE):

$37.78 billion (2017 est.) (2017 est.)

GDP - REAL GROWTH RATE:

4.2% (2017 est.)

4.3% (2016 est.)

4.9% (2015 est.)

country comparison to the world: 70

GDP - PER CAPITA (PPP):

$7,600 (2017 est.)

$7,400 (2016 est.)

$7,200 (2015 est.)

note: data are in 2017 dollars

country comparison to the world: 154

GROSS NATIONAL SAVING:

15.7% of GDP (2017 est.)

15.3% of GDP (2016 est.)

14.2% of GDP (2015 est.)

country comparison to the world: 132

GDP - COMPOSITION, BY END USE:

household consumption: 67.7% (2017 est.)

government consumption: 17% (2017 est.)

investment in fixed capital: 21.3% (2017 est.)

investment in inventories: 3.8% (2017 est.)

exports of goods and services: 21.7% (2017 est.)

imports of goods and services: -31.3% (2017 est.)

GDP - COMPOSITION, BY SECTOR OF ORIGIN:

agriculture: 13.8% (2017 est.)

industry: 37.8% (2017 est.)

services: 48.2% (2017 est.)

AGRICULTURE - PRODUCTS:

soybeans, quinoa, Brazil nuts, sugarcane, coffee, corn, rice, potatoes, chia, coca

INDUSTRIES:

mining, smelting, electricity, petroleum, food and beverages, handicrafts, clothing, jewelry

INDUSTRIAL PRODUCTION GROWTH RATE:

2.2% (2017 est.)

country comparison to the world: 123

LABOR FORCE:

5.719 million (2016 est.)

country comparison to the world: 73

LABOR FORCE - BY OCCUPATION:

agriculture: 29.4%

industry: 22%

services: 48.6% (2015 est.)

UNEMPLOYMENT RATE:

4% (2017 est.)

4% (2016 est.)

note: data are for urban areas; widespread underemployment

country comparison to the world: 49

POPULATION BELOW POVERTY LINE:

38.6% (2015 est.)

note: based on percent of population living on less than the international standard of $2/day

HOUSEHOLD INCOME OR CONSUMPTION BY PERCENTAGE SHARE:

lowest 10%: 36.1% (2014 est.)

highest 10%: 36.1% (2014 est.)

DISTRIBUTION OF FAMILY INCOME - GINI INDEX:

47 (2016 est.)

57.9 (1999)

country comparison to the world: 28

BUDGET:

revenues: 15.09 billion (2017 est.)

expenditures: 18.02 billion (2017 est.)

TAXES AND OTHER REVENUES:

39.9% (of GDP) (2017 est.)

country comparison to the world: 39

BUDGET SURPLUS (+) OR DEFICIT (-):

-7.8% (of GDP) (2017 est.)

country comparison to the world: 196

PUBLIC DEBT:

49% of GDP (2017 est.)

44.9% of GDP (2016 est.)

note: data cover general government debt and includes debt instruments issued by government entities other than the treasury; the data include treasury debt held by foreign entities; the data include debt issued by subnational entities

country comparison to the world: 104

FISCAL YEAR:

calendar year

INFLATION RATE (CONSUMER PRICES):

2.8% (2017 est.)

3.6% (2016 est.)

country comparison to the world: 127

CENTRAL BANK DISCOUNT RATE:

2.5% (31 December 2017 est.)

2.5% (31 December 2016 est.)

country comparison to the world: 114

COMMERCIAL BANK PRIME LENDING RATE:

8.11% (31 December 2017 est.)

7.95% (31 December 2016 est.)

country comparison to the world: 106

STOCK OF NARROW MONEY:

$9.616 billion (31 December 2017 est.)

$9.09 billion (31 December 2016 est.)

country comparison to the world: 82

STOCK OF BROAD MONEY:

$9.616 billion (31 December 2017 est.)

$9.09 billion (31 December 2016 est.)

country comparison to the world: 84

STOCK OF DOMESTIC CREDIT:

$25.61 billion (31 December 2017 est.)

$22.39 billion (31 December 2016 est.)

country comparison to the world: 85

MARKET VALUE OF PUBLICLY TRADED SHARES:

$12.8 billion (31 December 2017 est.)

$12.3 billion (31 December 2016 est.)

$11.11 billion (31 December 2015 est.)

country comparison to the world: 70

CURRENT ACCOUNT BALANCE:

-$2.375 billion (2017 est.)

-$1.932 billion (2016 est.)

country comparison to the world: 171

EXPORTS:

$7.746 billion (2017 est.)

$7.214 billion (2016 est.)

country comparison to the world: 99

EXPORTS - PARTNERS:

Brazil 17.9%, Argentina 16%, US 7.8%, Japan 7.3%, India 6.6%, South Korea 6.3%, Colombia 5.8%, China 5.1%, UAE 4.7% (2017)

EXPORTS - COMMODITIES:

natural gas, silver, zinc, lead, tin, gold, quinoa, soybeans and soy products

IMPORTS:

$8.601 billion (2017 est.)

$7.888 billion (2016 est.)

country comparison to the world: 108

IMPORTS - COMMODITIES:

machinery, petroleum products, vehicles, iron and steel, plastics

IMPORTS - PARTNERS:

China 21.7%, Brazil 16.8%, Argentina 12.6%, US 8.4%, Peru 6.5% (2017)

RESERVES OF FOREIGN EXCHANGE AND GOLD:

$10.26 billion (31 December 2017 est.)

$10.08 billion (31 December 2016 est.)

country comparison to the world: 74

DEBT - EXTERNAL:

$12.81 billion (31 December 2017 est.)

$7.268 billion (31 December 2016 est.)

country comparison to the world: 106

STOCK OF DIRECT FOREIGN INVESTMENT - AT HOME:

$12.31 billion (31 December 2017 est.)

$11.6 billion (31 December 2016 est.)

country comparison to the world: 93

STOCK OF DIRECT FOREIGN INVESTMENT - ABROAD:

$0 (31 December 2017 est.)

$0 (31 December 2016 est.)

country comparison to the world: 120

EXCHANGE RATES:

bolivianos (BOB) per US dollar -

6.86 (2017 est.)

6.86 (2016 est.)

6.91 (2015 est.)

6.91 (2014 est.)

6.91 (2013 est.)

ENERGY :: BOLIVIA

ELECTRICITY ACCESS:

population without electricity: 1.2 million (2013)

electrification - total population: 90% (2013)

electrification - urban areas: 99% (2013)

electrification - rural areas: 72% (2013)

ELECTRICITY - PRODUCTION:

8.951 billion kWh (2016 est.)

country comparison to the world: 107

ELECTRICITY - CONSUMPTION:

7.785 billion kWh (2016 est.)

country comparison to the world: 105

ELECTRICITY - EXPORTS:

0 kWh (2017 est.)

country comparison to the world: 108

ELECTRICITY - IMPORTS:

0 kWh (2016 est.)

country comparison to the world: 127

ELECTRICITY - INSTALLED GENERATING CAPACITY:

2.764 million kW (2016 est.)

country comparison to the world: 101

ELECTRICITY - FROM FOSSIL FUELS:

76% of total installed capacity (2016 est.)

country comparison to the world: 93

ELECTRICITY - FROM NUCLEAR FUELS:

0% of total installed capacity (2017 est.)

country comparison to the world: 52

ELECTRICITY - FROM HYDROELECTRIC PLANTS:

18% of total installed capacity (2017 est.)

country comparison to the world: 92

ELECTRICITY - FROM OTHER RENEWABLE SOURCES:

7% of total installed capacity (2017 est.)

country comparison to the world: 92

CRUDE OIL - PRODUCTION:

59,330 bbl/day (2017 est.)

country comparison to the world: 49

CRUDE OIL - EXPORTS:

1,274 bbl/day (2015 est.)

country comparison to the world: 72

CRUDE OIL - IMPORTS:

0 bbl/day (2015 est.)

country comparison to the world: 99

CRUDE OIL - PROVED RESERVES:

211.5 million bbl (1 January 2018 est.)

country comparison to the world: 54

REFINED PETROLEUM PRODUCTS - PRODUCTION:

65,960 bbl/day (2015 est.)

country comparison to the world: 75

REFINED PETROLEUM PRODUCTS - CONSUMPTION:

83,000 bbl/day (2016 est.)

country comparison to the world: 86

REFINED PETROLEUM PRODUCTS - EXPORTS:

9,686 bbl/day (2015 est.)

country comparison to the world: 82

REFINED PETROLEUM PRODUCTS - IMPORTS:

20,620 bbl/day (2015 est.)

country comparison to the world: 118

NATURAL GAS - PRODUCTION:

18.69 billion cu m (2017 est.)

country comparison to the world: 32

NATURAL GAS - CONSUMPTION:

3.171 billion cu m (2017 est.)

country comparison to the world: 71

NATURAL GAS - EXPORTS:

15.46 billion cu m (2017 est.)

country comparison to the world: 15

NATURAL GAS - IMPORTS:

0 cu m (2017 est.)

country comparison to the world: 94

NATURAL GAS - PROVED RESERVES:

295.9 billion cu m (1 January 2018 est.)

country comparison to the world: 37

CARBON DIOXIDE EMISSIONS FROM CONSUMPTION OF ENERGY:

17.66 million Mt (2017 est.)

country comparison to the world: 90

COMMUNICATIONS :: BOLIVIA

TELEPHONES - FIXED LINES:

total subscriptions: 851,110 (2017 est.)

subscriptions per 100 inhabitants: 8 (2017 est.)

country comparison to the world: 78

TELEPHONES - MOBILE CELLULAR:

total subscriptions: 10,106,216 (July 2016 est.)

subscriptions per 100 inhabitants: 91 (July 2016 est.)

country comparison to the world: 84

TELEPHONE SYSTEM:

general assessment: state-owned Empresa Nacional de Telecomunicaciones (Entel) is the country's incumbent long-distance operator, and offers local telephone service, DSL, and satellite TV; its subsidiary Entel Movil is Bolivia's largest mobile network provider, reliability, and coverage have steadily improved, but some remote areas are still underserved; Entel plans to extend fibre to all 339 municipal capital cities by 2022; MNP (mobile number potability) launched in October 2018; Bolivian Space Agency planning to launch a second telecom satellite after 2020 (2018)

domestic: most telephones are concentrated in La Paz, Santa Cruz, and other capital cities; 8 per 100 fixed-line, mobile-cellular telephone use expanding rapidly and teledensity stood at 91 per 100 persons (2017)

international: country code - 591; satellite earth station - 1 Intelsat (Atlantic Ocean); Bolivia has no direct access to submarine cable networks and must therefore connect to the rest of the world either via satellite or through terrestrial links across neighbouring countries (2017)

BROADCAST MEDIA:

large number of radio and TV stations broadcasting with private media outlets dominating; state-owned and private radio and TV stations generally operating freely, although both pro-government and anti-government groups have attacked media outlets in response to their reporting (2010)

INTERNET COUNTRY CODE:

.bo

INTERNET USERS:

total: 4,354,678 (July 2016 est.)

percent of population: 39.7% (July 2016 est.)

country comparison to the world: 83

BROADBAND - FIXED SUBSCRIPTIONS:

total: 358,680 (2017 est.)

subscriptions per 100 inhabitants: 3 (2017 est.)

country comparison to the world: 90

TRANSPORTATION :: BOLIVIA

NATIONAL AIR TRANSPORT SYSTEM:

number of registered air carriers: 7 (2015)

inventory of registered aircraft operated by air carriers: 39 (2015)

annual passenger traffic on registered air carriers: 2,578,959 (2015)

annual freight traffic on registered air carriers: 9,456,548 mt-km (2015)

CIVIL AIRCRAFT REGISTRATION COUNTRY CODE PREFIX:

CP (2016)

AIRPORTS:

855 (2013)

country comparison to the world: 7

AIRPORTS - WITH PAVED RUNWAYS:

total: 21 (2017)

over 3,047 m: 5 (2017)

2,438 to 3,047 m: 4 (2017)

1,524 to 2,437 m: 6 (2017)

914 to 1,523 m: 6 (2017)

AIRPORTS - WITH UNPAVED RUNWAYS:

total: 834 (2013)

over 3,047 m: 1 (2013)

2,438 to 3,047 m: 4 (2013)

1,524 to 2,437 m: 47 (2013)

914 to 1,523 m: 151 (2013)

under 914 m: 631 (2013)

PIPELINES:

5457 km gas, 51 km liquid petroleum gas, 2511 km oil, 1627 km refined products (2013)

RAILWAYS:

total: 3,504 km (2014)

narrow gauge: 3,504 km 1.000-m gauge (2014)

country comparison to the world: 55

ROADWAYS:

total: 90,568 km (2017)

paved: 9,792 km (2017)

unpaved: 80,776 km (2017)

country comparison to the world: 54

WATERWAYS:

10,000 km (commercially navigable almost exclusively in the northern and eastern parts of the country) (2012)

country comparison to the world: 13

MERCHANT MARINE:

total: 55 (2017)

by type: general cargo 41, oil tanker 3, other 11 (2017)

country comparison to the world: 111

PORTS AND TERMINALS:

river port(s): Puerto Aguirre (Paraguay/Parana)

note: Bolivia has free port privileges in maritime ports in Argentina, Brazil, Chile, and Paraguay

MILITARY AND SECURITY :: BOLIVIA

MILITARY EXPENDITURES:

1.5% of GDP (2017 est.)

1.68% of GDP (2016)

1.74% of GDP (2015)

country comparison to the world: 76

MILITARY BRANCHES:

Bolivian Armed Forces: Bolivian Army (Ejercito Boliviano, EB), Bolivian Naval Force (Fuerza Naval Boliviana, FNB, includes Marines), Bolivian Air Force (Fuerza Aerea Boliviana, FAB) (2017)

MILITARY SERVICE AGE AND OBLIGATION:

16-49 years of age for 12-month voluntary male and female military service; Bolivian citizenship required; minimum age of combat is 18; when annual number of volunteers falls short of goal, compulsory recruitment is effected, including conscription of boys as young as 14; 15-19 years of age for voluntary premilitary service, provides exemption from further military service (2017)

TRANSNATIONAL ISSUES :: BOLIVIA

DISPUTES - INTERNATIONAL:

Chile and Peru rebuff Bolivia's reactivated claim to restore the Atacama corridor, ceded to Chile in 1884, but Chile offers instead unrestricted but not sovereign maritime access through Chile for Bolivian productscontraband smuggling, human trafficking, and illegal narcotic trafficking are problems in the porous areas of its border regions with all of its neighbors (Argentina, Brazil, Chile, Paraguay, and Peru)

TRAFFICKING IN PERSONS:

current situation: Bolivia is a source country for men, women, and children subjected to forced labor and sex trafficking domestically and abroad; rural and poor Bolivians, most of whom are indigenous, and LGBT youth are particularly vulnerable; Bolivians perform forced labor domestically in mining, ranching, agriculture, and domestic service, and a significant number are in forced labor abroad in sweatshops, agriculture, domestic service, and the informal sector; women and girls are sex trafficked within Bolivia and in neighboring countries, such as Argentina, Peru, and Chile; a limited number of women from nearby countries are sex trafficked in Bolivia

tier rating: Tier 2 Watch List – Bolivia does not comply fully with the minimum standards for the elimination of human trafficking; however, it is making significant efforts to do so; the government did not demonstrate overall increasing anti-trafficking efforts, and poor data collection made it difficult to assess the number of investigations, prosecutions, and victim identifications and referrals to care services; authorities did not adequately differentiate between human trafficking and other crimes, such as domestic violence and child abuse; law enforcement failed to implement an early detection protocol for identifying trafficking cases and lacked a formal process for identifying trafficking victims among vulnerable populations; specialized victim services were inadequately funded and virtually non-existent for adult women and male victims (2015)

ILLICIT DRUGS:

world's third-largest cultivator of coca (after Colombia and Peru) with an estimated 37,500 hectares under cultivation in 2016, a 3 percent increase over 2015; third largest producer of cocaine, estimated at 275 metric tons potential pure cocaine in 2016; transit country for Peruvian and Colombian cocaine destined for Brazil, Argentina, Chile, Paraguay, and Europe; weak border controls; some money-laundering activity related to narcotics trade; major cocaine consumption

EUROPE :: BOSNIA AND HERZEGOVINA

INTRODUCTION :: BOSNIA AND HERZEGOVINA

BACKGROUND:

Bosnia and Herzegovina declared sovereignty in October 1991 and independence from the former Yugoslavia on 3 March 1992 after a referendum boycotted by ethnic Serbs. The Bosnian Serbs - supported by neighboring Serbia and Montenegro - responded with armed resistance aimed at partitioning the republic along ethnic lines and joining Serb-held areas to form a "Greater Serbia." In March 1994, Bosniaks and Croats reduced the number of warring factions from three to two by signing an agreement creating a joint Bosniak-Croat Federation of Bosnia and Herzegovina. On 21 November 1995, in Dayton, Ohio, the warring parties initialed a peace agreement that ended three years of interethnic civil strife (the final agreement was signed in Paris on 14 December 1995).

The Dayton Peace Accords retained Bosnia and Herzegovina's international boundaries and created a multiethnic and democratic government charged with conducting foreign, diplomatic, and fiscal policy. Also recognized was a second tier of government composed of two entities roughly equal in size: the predominantly Bosniak-Bosnian Croat Federation of Bosnia and Herzegovina and the predominantly Bosnian Serb-led Republika Srpska (RS). The Federation and RS governments are responsible for overseeing most government functions. Additionally, the Dayton Accords established the Office of the High Representative to oversee the implementation of the civilian aspects of the agreement. The Peace Implementation Council at its conference in Bonn in 1997 also gave the High Representative the authority to impose legislation and remove officials, the so-called "Bonn Powers." An original NATO-led international peacekeeping force (IFOR) of 60,000 troops assembled in 1995 was succeeded over time by a smaller, NATO-led Stabilization Force (SFOR). In 2004, European Union peacekeeping troops (EUFOR) replaced SFOR. Currently, EUFOR deploys around 600 troops in theater in a security assistance and training capacity.

GEOGRAPHY :: BOSNIA AND HERZEGOVINA

LOCATION:

Southeastern Europe, bordering the Adriatic Sea and Croatia

GEOGRAPHIC COORDINATES:

44 00 N, 18 00 E

MAP REFERENCES:

Europe

AREA:

total: 51,197 sq km

land: 51,187 sq km

water: 10 sq km

country comparison to the world: 129

AREA - COMPARATIVE:

slightly smaller than West Virginia

LAND BOUNDARIES:

total: 1,543 km

border countries (3): Croatia 956 km, Montenegro 242 km, Serbia 345 km

COASTLINE:

20 km

MARITIME CLAIMS:

NA

CLIMATE:

hot summers and cold winters; areas of high elevation have short, cool summers and long, severe winters; mild, rainy winters along coast

TERRAIN:

mountains and valleys

ELEVATION:

mean elevation: 500 m

elevation extremes: 0 m lowest point: Adriatic Sea

2386 highest point: Maglic

NATURAL RESOURCES:

coal, iron ore, antimony, bauxite, copper, lead, zinc, chromite, cobalt, manganese, nickel, clay, gypsum, salt, sand, timber, hydropower

LAND USE:

agricultural land: 42.2% (2011 est.)

arable land: 19.7% (2011 est.) / permanent crops: 2% (2011 est.) / permanent pasture: 20.5% (2011 est.)

forest: 42.8% (2011 est.)

other: 15% (2011 est.)

IRRIGATED LAND:

30 sq km (2012)

POPULATION DISTRIBUTION:

the northern and central areas of the country are the most densely populated

NATURAL HAZARDS:

destructive earthquakes

ENVIRONMENT - CURRENT ISSUES:

air pollution; deforestation and illegal logging; inadequate wastewater treatment and flood management facilities; sites for disposing of urban waste are limited; land mines left over from the 1992-95 civil strife are a hazard in some areas

ENVIRONMENT - INTERNATIONAL AGREEMENTS:

party to: Air Pollution, Biodiversity, Climate Change, Climate Change-Kyoto Protocol, Desertification, Hazardous Wastes, Law of the Sea, Marine Life Conservation, Ozone Layer Protection, Wetlands

signed, but not ratified: none of the selected agreements

GEOGRAPHY - NOTE:

within Bosnia and Herzegovina's recognized borders, the country is divided into a joint Bosniak/Croat Federation (about 51% of the territory) and the Bosnian Serb-led Republika Srpska or RS (about 49% of the territory); the region called Herzegovina is contiguous to Croatia and Montenegro, and traditionally has been settled by an ethnic Croat majority in the west and an ethnic Serb majority in the east

PEOPLE AND SOCIETY :: BOSNIA AND HERZEGOVINA

POPULATION:

3,849,891 (July 2018 est.)

country comparison to the world: 128

NATIONALITY:

noun: Bosnian(s), Herzegovinian(s)

adjective: Bosnian, Herzegovinian

ETHNIC GROUPS:

Bosniak 50.1%, Serb 30.8%, Croat 15.4%, other 2.7%, not declared/no answer 1% (2013 est.)

note: the methodology remains disputed and Republika Srspka authorities refuse to recognize the results; Bosniak has replaced Muslim as an ethnic term in part to avoid confusion with the religious term Muslim - an adherent of Islam

LANGUAGES:

Bosnian (official) 52.9%, Serbian (official) 30.8%, Croatian (official) 14.6%, other 1.6%, no answer 0.2% (2013 est.)

RELIGIONS:

Muslim 50.7%, Orthodox 30.7%, Roman Catholic 15.2%, atheist 0.8%, agnostic 0.3%, other 1.2%, undeclared/no answer 1.1% (2013 est.)

AGE STRUCTURE:

0-14 years: 13.24% (male 263,338 /female 246,220)

15-24 years: 11.26% (male 223,824 /female 209,829)

25-54 years: 45.51% (male 881,331 /female 870,601)

55-64 years: 14.95% (male 278,460 /female 297,231)

65 years and over: 15.04% (male 229,282 /female 349,775) (2018 est.)

DEPENDENCY RATIOS:

total dependency ratio: 43.3 (2015 est.)

youth dependency ratio: 20.7 (2015 est.)

elderly dependency ratio: 22.5 (2015 est.)

potential support ratio: 4.4 (2015 est.)

MEDIAN AGE:

total: 42.5 years

male: 40.9 years

female: 43.9 years (2018 est.)

country comparison to the world: 28

POPULATION GROWTH RATE:

-0.17% (2018 est.)

country comparison to the world: 207

BIRTH RATE:

8.7 births/1,000 population (2018 est.)

country comparison to the world: 210

DEATH RATE:

10.1 deaths/1,000 population (2018 est.)

country comparison to the world: 34

NET MIGRATION RATE:

-0.4 migrant(s)/1,000 population (2017 est.)

country comparison to the world: 118

POPULATION DISTRIBUTION:

the northern and central areas of the country are the most densely populated

URBANIZATION:

urban population: 48.2% of total population (2018)

rate of urbanization: 0.55% annual rate of change (2015-20 est.)

MAJOR URBAN AREAS - POPULATION:

343,000 SARAJEVO (capital) (2018)

SEX RATIO:

at birth: 1.07 male(s)/female (2017 est.)

0-14 years: 1.07 male(s)/female (2017 est.)

15-24 years: 1.07 male(s)/female (2017 est.)

25-54 years: 1.01 male(s)/female (2017 est.)

55-64 years: 0.92 male(s)/female (2017 est.)

65 years and over: 0.64 male(s)/female (2017 est.)

total population: 0.95 male(s)/female (2017 est.)

MOTHER'S MEAN AGE AT FIRST BIRTH:

27 years (2014 est.)

MATERNAL MORTALITY RATE:

11 deaths/100,000 live births (2015 est.)

country comparison to the world: 143

INFANT MORTALITY RATE:

total: 5.4 deaths/1,000 live births (2018 est.)

male: 5.5 deaths/1,000 live births (2018 est.)

female: 5.3 deaths/1,000 live births (2018 est.)

country comparison to the world: 172

LIFE EXPECTANCY AT BIRTH:

total population: 77.1 years (2018 est.)

male: 74.1 years (2018 est.)

female: 80.3 years (2018 est.)

country comparison to the world: 78

TOTAL FERTILITY RATE:

1.31 children born/woman (2018 est.)

country comparison to the world: 217

CONTRACEPTIVE PREVALENCE RATE:

45.8% (2011/12)

HEALTH EXPENDITURES:

9.6% of GDP (2014)

country comparison to the world: 30

PHYSICIANS DENSITY:

1.89 physicians/1,000 population (2013)

HOSPITAL BED DENSITY:

3.5 beds/1,000 population (2013)

DRINKING WATER SOURCE:

improved:

urban: 99.7% of population (2015 est.)

rural: 100% of population (2015 est.)

total: 99.9% of population (2015 est.)

unimproved:

urban: 0.3% of population (2015 est.)

rural: 0% of population (2015 est.)

total: 0.1% of population (2015 est.)

SANITATION FACILITY ACCESS:

improved:

urban: 98.9% of population (2015 est.)

rural: 92% of population (2015 est.)

total: 94.8% of population (2015 est.)

unimproved:

urban: 1.1% of population (2015 est.)

rural: 8% of population (2015 est.)

total: 5.2% of population (2015 est.)

HIV/AIDS - ADULT PREVALENCE RATE:

NA

HIV/AIDS - PEOPLE LIVING WITH HIV/AIDS:

NA

HIV/AIDS - DEATHS:

NA

OBESITY - ADULT PREVALENCE RATE:

17.9% (2016)

country comparison to the world: 118

CHILDREN UNDER THE AGE OF 5 YEARS UNDERWEIGHT:

1.5% (2012)

country comparison to the world: 116

EDUCATION EXPENDITURES:

NA

LITERACY:

definition: age 15 and over can read and write (2015 est.)

total population: 98.5% (2015 est.)

male: 99.5% (2015 est.)

female: 97.5% (2015 est.)

SCHOOL LIFE EXPECTANCY (PRIMARY TO TERTIARY EDUCATION):

total: 14 years (2014)

male: 14 years (2014)

female: 15 years (2014)

UNEMPLOYMENT, YOUTH AGES 15-24:

total: 62.3% (2015 est.)

male: 43.5% (2015 est.)

female: 62.3% (2015 est.)

country comparison to the world: 1

GOVERNMENT :: BOSNIA AND HERZEGOVINA

COUNTRY NAME:

conventional long form: none

conventional short form: Bosnia and Herzegovina

local long form: none

local short form: Bosna i Hercegovina

former: People's Republic of Bosnia and Herzegovina, Socialist Republic of Bosnia and Herzegovina

abbreviation: BiH

etymology: the larger northern territory is named for the Bosna River; the smaller southern section takes its name from the German word "herzog," meaning "duke," and the ending "-ovina," meaning "land," forming the combination denoting "dukedom"

GOVERNMENT TYPE:

parliamentary republic

CAPITAL:

name: Sarajevo

geographic coordinates: 43 52 N, 18 25 E

time difference: UTC+1 (6 hours ahead of Washington, DC, during Standard Time)

daylight saving time: +1hr, begins last Sunday in March; ends last Sunday in October

ADMINISTRATIVE DIVISIONS:

3 first-order administrative divisions - Brcko District (Brcko Distrikt) (ethnically mixed), Federation of Bosnia and Herzegovina (Federacija Bosne i Hercegovine) (predominantly Bosniak-Croat), Republika Srpska (predominantly Serb)

INDEPENDENCE:

1 March 1992 (from Yugoslavia); note - referendum for independence completed on 1 March 1992; independence declared on 3 March 1992

NATIONAL HOLIDAY:

Independence Day, 1 March (1992) and Statehood Day, 25 November (1943) - both observed in the Federation of Bosnia and Herzegovina entityVictory Day, 9 May (1945) and Dayton Agreement Day, 21 November (1995) - both observed in the Republika Srpska entity

note: there is no national-level holiday

CONSTITUTION:

history: 14 December 1995 (constitution included as part of the Dayton Peace Accords); note - each of the political entities has its own constitution

amendments: decided by the Parliamentary Assembly, including a two-thirds majority vote of members present in the House of Representatives; the constitutional article on human rights and fundamental freedoms cannot be amended; amended several times, last in 2009 (2016)

LEGAL SYSTEM:

civil law system; Constitutional Court review of legislative acts

INTERNATIONAL LAW ORGANIZATION PARTICIPATION:

has not submitted an ICJ jurisdiction declaration; accepts ICCt jurisdiction

CITIZENSHIP:

citizenship by birth: no

citizenship by descent only: at least one parent must be a citizen of Bosnia and Herzegovina

dual citizenship recognized: yes, provided there is a bilateral agreement with the other state

residency requirement for naturalization: 8 years

SUFFRAGE:

18 years of age, 16 if employed; universal

EXECUTIVE BRANCH:

chief of state: Chairman of the Presidency Milorad DODIK (chairman since 20 November 2018, presidency member since 20 November 2018 - Serb seat); Zeljko KOMSIC (presidency member since 20 November 2018 - Croat seat); Sefik DZAFEROVIC (presidency member since 20 November 2018 Bosniak seat)

head of government: Chairman of the Council of Ministers Denis ZVIZDIC (since 11 February 2015)

cabinet: Council of Ministers nominated by the council chairman, approved by the state-level House of Representatives

elections/appointments: 3-member presidency (1 Bosniak and 1 Croat elected from the Federation of Bosnia and Herzegovina and 1 Serb elected from the Republika Srpska) directly elected by simple majority popular vote for a 4-year term (eligible for a second term, but then ineligible for 4 years); the presidency chairpersonship rotates every 8 months and resumes where it left off following each general election; election last held on 7 October 2018 (next to be held in October 2022); the chairman of the Council of Ministers appointed by the presidency and confirmed by the state-level House of Representatives

election results: percent of vote - Milorad DODIK (SNSD) 53.9% - Serb seat; Zeljko KOMSIC (DF) 52.6% - Croat seat; Sefik DZAFEROVIC (SDA) 36.6% - Bosniak seat

note: President of the Federation of Bosnia and Herzegovina Marinko CAVARA (since 11 February 2015); Vice Presidents Melika MAHMUTBEGOVIC (since 11 February 2015), Milan DUNOVIC (since 11 February 2015); President of the Republika Srpska Milorad DODIK (since 15 November 2010); Vice Presidents Ramiz SALKIC (since 24 November 2014), Josip JERKOVIC (since 24 November 2014)

LEGISLATIVE BRANCH:

description: bicameral Parliamentary Assembly or Skupstina consists of:
House of Peoples or Dom Naroda (15 seats - 5 Bosniak, 5 Croat, 5 Serb; members designated by the Federation of Bosnia and Herzegovina's House of Peoples and the Republika Srpska's National Assembly to serve 4-year terms)
House of Representatives or Predstavnicki Dom (42 seats to include 28 seats allocated to the Federation of Bosnia and Herzegovina and 14 to the Republika Srpska; members directly elected by proportional representation vote to serve 4-year terms); note - the Federation of Bosnia and Herzegovina has a bicameral legislature that consists of the House of Peoples (58 seats - 17 Bosniak, 17 Croat, 17 Serb, 7 other) and the House of Representatives (98 seats; members directly elected by proportional representation vote to serve 4-year terms); Republika Srpska's unicameral legislature is the National Assembly (83 directly elected delegates serve 4-year terms)

elections: House of Peoples - last constituted in 11 February 2015 (next likely to be constituted in 2019)
House of Representatives - last held on 7 October 2018 (next to be held in October 2022)

election results: House of Peoples - percent of vote by coalition/party - NA; seats by coalition/party - NA; composition - men 13, women 2, percent of women 13.3%
House of Representatives - percent of vote by coalition/party - SDA 17%, SNSD 16%, SDS/NDP/NS/SRS-VS 9.8%, HDZ-BiH/HSS/HKDU/HSP-AS BiH/HDU BiH 9.1%, DF, 5.8%, PDP 5.1%, DNS 4.2%, SBB BiH 4.2%, NS/HC 2.9%, NB 2.5%, PDA 2.3%, SP 1.9%, A-SDA 1.8%, other 17.4%; seats by coalition/party - SDA 9, SNSD 6, SDP 5, HDZ-BiH/HSS/HKDU/HSP-AS BiH/HDU BiH 5, SDS/NDP/NS/SRS-VS 3, DF 3, PDP 2, SBB BiH 2, NS/HC 2, DNS 1, NB 1 PDA 1, SP 1, A-SDA 1; composition - men 33, women 9, percent of women 21.4%; note - total Parliamentary Assembly percent of women 19.3%

JUDICIAL BRANCH:

highest courts: Bosnia and Herzegovina (BiH) Constitutional Court (consists of 9 members); Court of BiH (consists of 44 national judges and 7 international judges organized into 3 divisions - Administrative, Appellate, and Criminal, which includes a War Crimes Chamber)

judge selection and term of office: BiH Constitutional Court judges - 4 selected by the Federation of Bosnia and Herzegovina House of Representatives, 2 selected by the Republika Srpska's National Assembly, and 3 non-Bosnian judges selected by the president of the European Court of Human Rights; Court of BiH president and national judges appointed by the High Judicial and Prosecutorial Council; Court of BiH president appointed for renewable 6-year term; other national judges appointed to serve until age 70; international judges recommended by the president of the Court of BiH and appointed by the High Representative for Bosnia and Herzegovina; international judges appointed to serve until age 70

subordinate courts: the Federation has 10 cantonal courts plus a number of municipal courts; the Republika Srpska has a supreme court, 5 district courts, and a number of municipal courts

POLITICAL PARTIES AND LEADERS:

Alliance for a Better Future of BiH or SBB BiH [Fahrudin RADONCIC]
Alliance of Independent Social Democrats or SNSD [Milorad DODIK]
Alternative Party for Democratic Activity or A-SDA [Nermin OGREŠEVIC]
Croat Peasants' Party or HSS [Mario KARAMATIC]
Croatian Christian Democratic Union of Bosnia and Herzegovina or HKDU [Ivan MUSA]
Croatian Democratic Union of Bosnia and Herzegovina or HDU-BiH [Miro GRABOVAC-TITAN]
Croatian Democratic Union of Bosnia and Herzegovina or HDZ-BiH [Dragan COVIC]
Croatian Democratic Union 1990 or HDZ-1990 [Ilija CVITANOVIC]
Croatian Party of Rights dr. Ante Starcevic or HSP-AS Bih [Karlo STARCEVIC]
Democratic Front of DF [Zeljko KOMSIC]
Democratic Peoples' Alliance or DNS [Marko PAVIC]
Independent Bloc or NB [Senad SEPIC]
Movement for Democratic Action or PDA [Mirsad KUKIC]
Progressive Srpska or NS [Goran DORDIC]
Our Party or NS/HC [Predrag KOJOVIC]
Party for Democratic Action or SDA [Bakir IZETBEGOVIC]
Party of Democratic Progress or PDP [Branislav BORENOVIC]
People's Democratic Movement or NDP [Dragan CAVIC]
Serb Democratic Party or SDS [Vukota GOVEDARICA]
Serb Radical Party-Dr. Vojislav Seselj or SRS-VS [Vojislav SESELJ]
Social Democratic Party or SDP [Nermin NIKSIC]
Socialist Party or SP [Petar DOKIC]

INTERNATIONAL ORGANIZATION PARTICIPATION:

BIS, CD, CE, CEI, EAPC, EBRD, FAO, G-77, IAEA, IBRD, ICAO, ICC (NGOs), ICCt, ICRM, IDA, IFAD, IFC, IFRCS, ILO, IMF, IMO, IMSO, Interpol, IOC, IOM, IPU, ISO, ITSO, ITU, ITUC (NGOs), MIGA, MINUSMA, MONUSCO, NAM (observer), OAS (observer), OIC (observer), OIF (observer), OPCW, OSCE, PFP, SELEC, UN, UNCTAD, UNESCO, UNIDO, UNWTO, UPU, WCO, WHO, WIPO, WMO, WTO (observer)

DIPLOMATIC REPRESENTATION IN THE US:

chief of mission: Ambassador Haris HRLE (since 23 October 2015)

chancery: 2109 E Street NW, Washington, DC 20037

telephone: [1] (202) 337-1500

FAX: [1] (202) 337-1502

consulate(s) general: Chicago, New York

DIPLOMATIC REPRESENTATION FROM THE US:

chief of mission: Ambassador Maureen CORMACK (since 16 January 2015)

embassy: 1 Robert C. Frasure Street, 71000 Sarajevo

mailing address: use embassy street address

telephone: [387] (33) 704-000

FAX: [387] (33) 659-722

branch office(s): Banja Luka, Mostar

FLAG DESCRIPTION:

a wide blue vertical band on the fly side with a yellow isosceles triangle abutting the band and the top of the flag; the remainder of the flag is blue with seven full five-pointed white stars and two half stars top and bottom along the hypotenuse of the triangle; the triangle approximates the shape of the country and its three points stand for the constituent peoples - Bosniaks, Croats, and Serbs; the stars represent Europe and are meant to be continuous (thus the half stars at top and bottom); the colors (white, blue, and yellow) are often associated with neutrality and peace, and traditionally are linked with Bosnia

note: one of several flags where a prominent component of the design reflects the shape of the country; other such flags are those of Brazil, Eritrea, and Vanuatu

NATIONAL SYMBOL(S):

golden lily; national colors: blue, yellow, white

NATIONAL ANTHEM:

name: "Drzavna himna Bosne i Hercegovine" (The National Anthem of Bosnia and Herzegovina)

lyrics/music: none officially; Dusan SESTIC and Benjamin ISOVIC/Dusan SESTIC

note: music adopted 1999; lyrics proposed in 2009 and others in 2016 were not approved; a parliamentary committee launched a new initiative for lyrics in February 2018

ECONOMY :: BOSNIA AND HERZEGOVINA

ECONOMY - OVERVIEW:

Bosnia and Herzegovina has a transitional economy with limited market reforms. The economy relies heavily on the export of metals, energy, textiles, and furniture as well as on remittances and foreign aid. A highly decentralized government hampers economic policy coordination and reform, while excessive bureaucracy and a segmented market discourage foreign investment. The economy is among the least competitive in the region. Foreign banks, primarily from Austria and Italy, control much of the banking sector, though the largest bank is a private domestic one. The konvertibilna marka (convertible mark) - the national currency introduced in 1998 - is pegged to the euro through a currency board arrangement, which has maintained confidence in the currency and has facilitated reliable trade links with European partners. Bosnia and Herzegovina became a full member of the Central European Free Trade Agreement in September 2007. In 2016, Bosnia began a three-year IMF loan program, but it has struggled to meet the economic reform benchmarks required to receive all funding installments.

Bosnia and Herzegovina's private sector is growing slowly, but foreign investment dropped sharply after 2007 and remains low. High unemployment remains the most serious macroeconomic problem. Successful implementation of a value-added tax in 2006 provided a steady source of revenue for the government and helped rein in gray-market activity, though public perceptions of government corruption and misuse of taxpayer money has encouraged a large informal economy to persist. National-level statistics have improved over time, but a large share of economic activity remains unofficial and unrecorded.

Bosnia and Herzegovina's top economic priorities are: acceleration of integration into the EU; strengthening the fiscal system; public administration reform; World Trade Organization membership; and securing economic growth by fostering a dynamic, competitive private sector.

GDP (PURCHASING POWER PARITY):

$44.83 billion (2017 est.)

$43.54 billion (2016 est.)

$42.19 billion (2015 est.)

note: data are in 2017 dollars

country comparison to the world: 113

GDP (OFFICIAL EXCHANGE RATE):

$18.17 billion (2017 est.) (2017 est.)

GDP - REAL GROWTH RATE:

3% (2017 est.)

3.2% (2016 est.)

3.1% (2015 est.)

country comparison to the world: 111

GDP - PER CAPITA (PPP):

$12,800 (2017 est.)

$12,400 (2016 est.)

$11,900 (2015 est.)

note: data are in 2017 dollars

country comparison to the world: 122

GROSS NATIONAL SAVING:

11% of GDP (2017 est.)

11.1% of GDP (2016 est.)

10.5% of GDP (2015 est.)

country comparison to the world: 158

GDP - COMPOSITION, BY END USE:

household consumption: 77.4% (2017 est.)

government consumption: 20% (2017 est.)

investment in fixed capital: 16.6% (2017 est.)

investment in inventories: 2.3% (2017 est.)

exports of goods and services: 38.7% (2017 est.)

imports of goods and services: -55.1% (2017 est.)

GDP - COMPOSITION, BY SECTOR OF ORIGIN:

agriculture: 6.8% (2017 est.)

industry: 28.9% (2017 est.)

services: 64.3% (2017 est.)

AGRICULTURE - PRODUCTS:

wheat, corn, fruits, vegetables; livestock

INDUSTRIES:

steel, coal, iron ore, lead, zinc, manganese, bauxite, aluminum, motor vehicle assembly, textiles, tobacco products, wooden furniture, ammunition, domestic appliances, oil refining

INDUSTRIAL PRODUCTION GROWTH RATE:

3% (2017 est.)

country comparison to the world: 102

LABOR FORCE:

1.38 million (2017 est.)

country comparison to the world: 134

LABOR FORCE - BY OCCUPATION:

agriculture: 18%

industry: 30.4%

services: 51.7% (2017 est.)

UNEMPLOYMENT RATE:

20.5% (2017 est.)

25.4% (2016 est.)

note: official rate; actual rate is lower as many technically unemployed persons work in the gray economy

country comparison to the world: 188

POPULATION BELOW POVERTY LINE:

16.9% (2015 est.)

HOUSEHOLD INCOME OR CONSUMPTION BY PERCENTAGE SHARE:

lowest 10%: 25.8% (2011 est.)

highest 10%: 25.8% (2011 est.)

DISTRIBUTION OF FAMILY INCOME - GINI INDEX:

33.8 (2011)

33.1 (2007)

country comparison to the world: 109

BUDGET:

revenues: 7.993 billion (2017 est.)

expenditures: 7.607 billion (2017 est.)

TAXES AND OTHER REVENUES:

44% (of GDP) (2017 est.)

country comparison to the world: 26

BUDGET SURPLUS (+) OR DEFICIT (-):

2.1% (of GDP) (2017 est.)

country comparison to the world: 15

PUBLIC DEBT:

39.5% of GDP (2017 est.)

44.1% of GDP (2016 est.)

note: data cover general government debt and includes debt instruments issued (or owned) by government entities other than the treasury; the data include treasury debt held by foreign entities; the data include debt issued by subnational entities, as well as intra-governmental debt; intra-governmental debt consists of treasury borrowings from surpluses in the social funds, such as for retirement, medical care, and unemployment; debt instruments for the social funds are not sold at public auctions.

country comparison to the world: 130

FISCAL YEAR:

calendar year

INFLATION RATE (CONSUMER PRICES):

1.2% (2017 est.)

-1.1% (2016 est.)

country comparison to the world: 62

COMMERCIAL BANK PRIME LENDING RATE:

4.38% (31 December 2017 est.)

5.24% (31 December 2016 est.)

country comparison to the world: 158

STOCK OF NARROW MONEY:

$6.483 billion (31 December 2017 est.)

$5.013 billion (31 December 2016 est.)

country comparison to the world: 95

STOCK OF BROAD MONEY:

$6.483 billion (31 December 2017 est.)

$5.013 billion (31 December 2016 est.)

country comparison to the world: 97

STOCK OF DOMESTIC CREDIT:

$11.3 billion (31 December 2017 est.)

$9.27 billion (31 December 2016 est.)

country comparison to the world: 105

MARKET VALUE OF PUBLICLY TRADED SHARES:

NA

CURRENT ACCOUNT BALANCE:

-$873 million (2017 est.)

-$821 million (2016 est.)

country comparison to the world: 135

EXPORTS:

$5.205 billion (2017 est.)

$4.288 billion (2016 est.)

country comparison to the world: 108

EXPORTS - PARTNERS:

Germany 14.7%, Croatia 11.8%, Italy 11.1%, Serbia 10%, Slovenia 9%, Austria 8.3% (2017)

EXPORTS - COMMODITIES:

metals, clothing, wood products

IMPORTS:

$9.547 billion (2017 est.)

$8.337 billion (2016 est.)

country comparison to the world: 103

IMPORTS - COMMODITIES:

machinery and equipment, chemicals, fuels, foodstuffs

IMPORTS - PARTNERS:

Germany 11.6%, Italy 11.3%, Serbia 11.1%, Croatia 10.1%, China 6.5%, Slovenia 5%, Russia 4.7%, Turkey 4.2% (2017)

RESERVES OF FOREIGN EXCHANGE AND GOLD:

$6.474 billion (31 December 2017 est.)

$5.137 billion (31 December 2016 est.)

country comparison to the world: 90

DEBT - EXTERNAL:

$10.87 billion (31 December 2017 est.)

$10.64 billion (31 December 2016 est.)

country comparison to the world: 111

STOCK OF DIRECT FOREIGN INVESTMENT - AT HOME:

$7.332 billion (31 December 2016 est.)

$7.071 billion (31 December 2015 est.)

country comparison to the world: 98

STOCK OF DIRECT FOREIGN INVESTMENT - ABROAD:

$0 (2014)

country comparison to the world: 121

EXCHANGE RATES:

konvertibilna markas (BAM) per US dollar -

1.729 (2017 est.)

1.7674 (2016 est.)

1.7674 (2015 est.)

1.7626 (2014 est.)

1.4718 (2013 est.)

ENERGY :: BOSNIA AND HERZEGOVINA

ELECTRICITY ACCESS:

electrification - total population: 100% (2016)

ELECTRICITY - PRODUCTION:

16.99 billion kWh (2016 est.)

country comparison to the world: 86

ELECTRICITY - CONSUMPTION:

11.87 billion kWh (2016 est.)

country comparison to the world: 89

ELECTRICITY - EXPORTS:

6.007 billion kWh (2015 est.)

country comparison to the world: 31

ELECTRICITY - IMPORTS:

3.084 billion kWh (2016 est.)

country comparison to the world: 49

ELECTRICITY - INSTALLED GENERATING CAPACITY:

4.676 million kW (2016 est.)

country comparison to the world: 83

ELECTRICITY - FROM FOSSIL FUELS:

49% of total installed capacity (2016 est.)

country comparison to the world: 153

ELECTRICITY - FROM NUCLEAR FUELS:

0% of total installed capacity (2017 est.)

country comparison to the world: 53

ELECTRICITY - FROM HYDROELECTRIC PLANTS:

51% of total installed capacity (2017 est.)

country comparison to the world: 35

ELECTRICITY - FROM OTHER RENEWABLE SOURCES:

1% of total installed capacity (2017 est.)

country comparison to the world: 148

CRUDE OIL - PRODUCTION:

0 bbl/day (2017 est.)

country comparison to the world: 112

CRUDE OIL - EXPORTS:

0 bbl/day (2015 est.)

country comparison to the world: 96

CRUDE OIL - IMPORTS:

18,480 bbl/day (2015 est.)

country comparison to the world: 64

CRUDE OIL - PROVED RESERVES:

0 bbl (1 January 2018 est.)

country comparison to the world: 109

REFINED PETROLEUM PRODUCTS - PRODUCTION:

0 bbl/day (2015 est.)

country comparison to the world: 121

REFINED PETROLEUM PRODUCTS - CONSUMPTION:

32,000 bbl/day (2016 est.)

country comparison to the world: 118

REFINED PETROLEUM PRODUCTS - EXPORTS:

4,603 bbl/day (2015 est.)

country comparison to the world: 92

REFINED PETROLEUM PRODUCTS - IMPORTS:

18,280 bbl/day (2015 est.)

country comparison to the world: 129

NATURAL GAS - PRODUCTION:

0 cu m (2017 est.)

country comparison to the world: 107

NATURAL GAS - CONSUMPTION:

226.5 million cu m (2017 est.)

country comparison to the world: 103

NATURAL GAS - EXPORTS:

0 cu m (2017 est.)

country comparison to the world: 72

NATURAL GAS - IMPORTS:

226.5 million cu m (2017 est.)

country comparison to the world: 70

NATURAL GAS - PROVED RESERVES:

0 cu m (1 January 2014 est.)

country comparison to the world: 113

CARBON DIOXIDE EMISSIONS FROM CONSUMPTION OF ENERGY:

22.07 million Mt (2017 est.)

country comparison to the world: 84

COMMUNICATIONS :: BOSNIA AND HERZEGOVINA

TELEPHONES - FIXED LINES:

total subscriptions: 759,344 (2017 est.)

subscriptions per 100 inhabitants: 20 (2017 est.)

country comparison to the world: 82

TELEPHONES - MOBILE CELLULAR:

total subscriptions: 3,440,085 (2017 est.)

subscriptions per 100 inhabitants: 89 (2017 est.)

country comparison to the world: 136

TELEPHONE SYSTEM:

general assessment: post-war reconstruction of the telecommunications network, aided by an internationally sponsored program, resulted in sharp increases in fixed-line telephone availability; integration with the EU has given stability to the present economy, added a regulatory framework and the market has been liberalised; DSL and cable are the chief platforms for fixed-line connectivity, there is a small market presence of fibre broadband; new mobile roaming fees come into effect similar to other EU countries; rural areas still suffer from insufficient connectivity (2017)

domestic: fixed-line teledensity roughly 20 per 100 persons; mobile-cellular subscribership has been increasing rapidly and stands at roughly 90 telephones per 100 persons (2017)

international: country code - 387; no satellite earth stations (2016)

BROADCAST MEDIA:

3 public TV broadcasters: Radio and TV of Bosnia and Herzegovina, Federation TV (operating 2 networks), and Republika Srpska Radio-TV; a local commercial network of 5 TV stations; 3 private, near-national TV stations and dozens of small independent TV broadcasting stations; 3 large public radio broadcasters and many private radio stations (2010)

INTERNET COUNTRY CODE:

.ba

INTERNET USERS:

total: 2,677,502 (July 2016 est.)

percent of population: 69.3% (July 2016 est.)

country comparison to the world: 100

BROADBAND - FIXED SUBSCRIPTIONS:

total: 663,670 (2017 est.)

subscriptions per 100 inhabitants: 17 (2017 est.)

country comparison to the world: 75

TRANSPORTATION :: BOSNIA AND HERZEGOVINA

NATIONAL AIR TRANSPORT SYSTEM:

number of registered air carriers: 1 (2015)

inventory of registered aircraft operated by air carriers: 1 (2015)

annual passenger traffic on registered air carriers: 7,070 (2015)

annual freight traffic on registered air carriers: 87 mt-km (2015)

CIVIL AIRCRAFT REGISTRATION COUNTRY CODE PREFIX:

T9 (2016)

AIRPORTS:

24 (2013)

country comparison to the world: 130

AIRPORTS - WITH PAVED RUNWAYS:

total: 7 (2017)

2,438 to 3,047 m: 4 (2017)

1,524 to 2,437 m: 1 (2017)

under 914 m: 2 (2017)

AIRPORTS - WITH UNPAVED RUNWAYS:

total: 17 (2013)

1,524 to 2,437 m: 1 (2013)

914 to 1,523 m: 5 (2013)

under 914 m: 11 (2013)

HELIPORTS:

6 (2013)

PIPELINES:

147 km gas, 9 km oil (2013)

RAILWAYS:

total: 965 km (2014)

standard gauge: 965 km 1.435-m gauge (565 km electrified) (2014)

country comparison to the world: 90

ROADWAYS:

total: 22,926 km (2010)

paved: 19,426 km (4,652 km of interurban roads) (2010)

unpaved: 3,500 km (2010)

country comparison to the world: 103

WATERWAYS:

(Sava River on northern border; open to shipping but use limited) (2011)

PORTS AND TERMINALS:

river port(s): Bosanska Gradiska, Bosanski Brod, Bosanski Samac, Brcko, Orasje (Sava River)

MILITARY AND SECURITY :: BOSNIA AND HERZEGOVINA

MILITARY EXPENDITURES:

0.99% of GDP (2016)

1% of GDP (2015)

1.03% of GDP (2014)

country comparison to the world: 113

MILITARY BRANCHES:

Armed Forces of Bosnia and Herzegovina (Oruzanih Snaga Bosne i Hercegovine, OSBiH): Army of Bosnia and Herzegovina, Air Force and Air Defense (Brigada Zracnih Snaga i Protuzracne Odbrane, br ZSiPZO), Tactical Support Brigade (Brigada Takticke Podrske, br TP) (2015)

MILITARY SERVICE AGE AND OBLIGATION:

18 years of age for voluntary military service; mandatory retirement at age 35 or after 15 years of service for E-1 through E-4, mandatory retirement at age 50 and 30 years of service for E-5 through E-9, mandatory retirement at age 55 and 30 years of service for all officers (2014)

TRANSNATIONAL ISSUES :: BOSNIA AND HERZEGOVINA

DISPUTES - INTERNATIONAL:

Serbia delimited about half of the boundary with Bosnia and Herzegovina, but sections along the Drina River remain in dispute

REFUGEES AND INTERNALLY DISPLACED PERSONS:

refugees (country of origin): 5,164 (Croatia) (2016)

IDPs: 99,000 (Bosnian Croats, Serbs, and Bosniaks displaced by inter-ethnic violence, human rights violations, and armed conflict during the 1992-95 war) (2017)

stateless persons: 65 (2017)

ILLICIT DRUGS:

increasingly a transit point for heroin being trafficked to Western Europe; minor transit point for marijuana; remains highly vulnerable to money-laundering activity given a primarily cash-based and unregulated economy, weak law enforcement, and instances of corruption

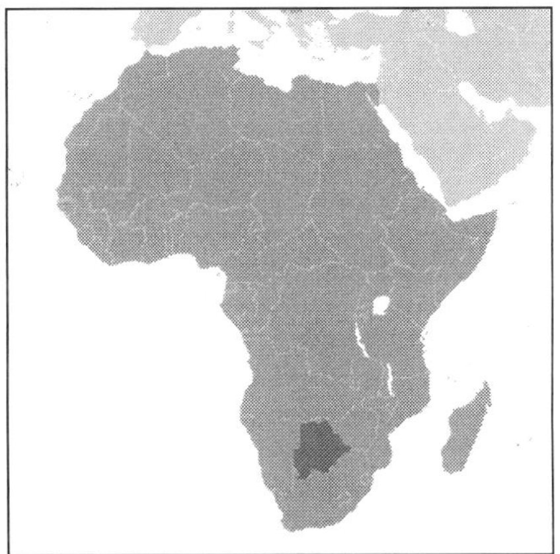

AFRICA :: BOTSWANA

INTRODUCTION :: BOTSWANA

BACKGROUND:

Formerly the British protectorate of Bechuanaland, Botswana adopted its new name at independence in 1966. More than five decades of uninterrupted civilian leadership, progressive social policies, and significant capital investment have created one of the most stable economies in Africa. The ruling Botswana Democratic Party has won every election since independence; President Mokgweetsi Eric MASISI assumed the presidency in April 2018 following the retirement of former President Ian KHAMA due to constitutional term limits. MASISI is Botswana's fifth president since independence. Mineral extraction, principally diamond mining, dominates economic activity, though tourism is a growing sector due to the country's conservation practices and extensive nature preserves. Botswana has one of the world's highest known rates of HIV/AIDS infection, but also one of Africa's most progressive and comprehensive programs for dealing with the disease.

GEOGRAPHY :: BOTSWANA

LOCATION:

Southern Africa, north of South Africa

GEOGRAPHIC COORDINATES:

22 00 S, 24 00 E

MAP REFERENCES:

Africa

AREA:

total: 581,730 sq km

land: 566,730 sq km

water: 15,000 sq km

country comparison to the world: 49

AREA - COMPARATIVE:

slightly smaller than Texas

LAND BOUNDARIES:

total: 4,347.15 km

border countries (4): Namibia 1544 km, South Africa 1969 km, Zambia 0.15 km, Zimbabwe 834 km

COASTLINE:

0 km (landlocked)

MARITIME CLAIMS:

none (landlocked)

CLIMATE:

semiarid; warm winters and hot summers

TERRAIN:

predominantly flat to gently rolling tableland; Kalahari Desert in southwest

ELEVATION:

mean elevation: 1,013 m

elevation extremes: 513 m lowest point: junction of the Limpopo and Shashe Rivers

1489 highest point: Tsodilo Hills

NATURAL RESOURCES:

diamonds, copper, nickel, salt, soda ash, potash, coal, iron ore, silver

LAND USE:

agricultural land: 45.8% (2011 est.)

arable land: 0.6% (2011 est.) / permanent crops: 0% (2011 est.) / permanent pasture: 45.2% (2011 est.)

forest: 19.8% (2011 est.)

other: 34.4% (2011 est.)

IRRIGATED LAND:

20 sq km (2012)

POPULATION DISTRIBUTION:

the population is primarily concentrated in the east with a focus in and around the captial of Gaborone, and the far central-eastern city of Francistown; population density remains low in other areas in the country, especially in the Kalahari to the west

NATURAL HAZARDS:

periodic droughts; seasonal August winds blow from the west, carrying sand and dust across the country, which can obscure visibility

ENVIRONMENT - CURRENT ISSUES:

overgrazing; desertification; limited freshwater resources; air pollution

ENVIRONMENT - INTERNATIONAL AGREEMENTS:

party to: Biodiversity, Climate Change, Climate Change-Kyoto Protocol, Desertification, Endangered Species, Hazardous Wastes, Law of the Sea, Ozone Layer Protection, Wetlands

signed, but not ratified: none of the selected agreements

GEOGRAPHY - NOTE:

landlocked; population concentrated in eastern part of the country

PEOPLE AND SOCIETY :: BOTSWANA

POPULATION:

2,249,104 (July 2018 est.)

note: estimates for this country explicitly take into account the effects of excess mortality due to AIDS; this can result in lower life expectancy, higher infant mortality, higher death rates, lower population growth rates, and changes in the distribution of population by age and sex than would otherwise be expected

country comparison to the world: 144

NATIONALITY:

noun: Motswana (singular), Batswana (plural)

adjective: Motswana (singular), Batswana (plural)

ETHNIC GROUPS:

Tswana (or Setswana) 79%, Kalanga 11%, Basarwa 3%, other, including Kgalagadi and white 7%

LANGUAGES:

Setswana 77.3%, Sekalanga 7.4%, Shekgalagadi 3.4%, English (official) 2.8%, Zezuru/Shona 2%, Sesarwa 1.7%, Sembukushu 1.6%, Ndebele 1%, other 2.8% (2011 est.)

RELIGIONS:

Christian 79.1%, Badimo 4.1%, other 1.4% (includes Baha'i, Hindu, Muslim, Rastafarian), none 15.2%, unspecified 0.3% (2011 est.)

DEMOGRAPHIC PROFILE:

Botswana has experienced one of the most rapid declines in fertility in sub-Saharan Africa. The total fertility rate has fallen from more than 5 children per woman in the mid 1980s to approximately 2.4 in 2013. The fertility reduction has been attributed to a host of factors, including higher educational attainment among women, greater participation of women in the workforce, increased contraceptive use, later first births, and a strong national family planning program. Botswana was making significant progress in several health indicators, including life expectancy and infant and child mortality rates, until being devastated by the HIV/AIDs epidemic in the 1990s.

Today Botswana has the third highest HIV/AIDS prevalence rate in the world at approximately 22%, however comprehensive and effective treatment programs have reduced HIV/AIDS-related deaths. The combination of declining fertility and increasing mortality rates because of HIV/AIDS is slowing the population aging process, with a narrowing of the youngest age groups and little expansion of the oldest age groups. Nevertheless, having the bulk of its population (about 60%) of working age will only yield economic benefits if the labor force is healthy, educated, and productively employed.

Batswana have been working as contract miners in South Africa since the 19th century. Although Botswana's economy improved shortly after independence in 1966 with the discovery of diamonds and other minerals, its lingering high poverty rate and lack of job opportunities continued to push workers to seek mining work in southern African countries. In the early 1970s, about a third of Botswana's male labor force worked in South Africa (lesser numbers went to Namibia and Zimbabwe). Not until the 1980s and 1990s, when South African mining companies had reduced their recruitment of foreign workers and Botswana's economic prospects had improved, were Batswana increasingly able to find job opportunities at home.

Most Batswana prefer life in their home country and choose cross-border migration on a temporary basis only for work, shopping, visiting family, or tourism. Since the 1970s, Botswana has pursued an open migration policy enabling it to recruit thousands of foreign workers to fill skilled labor shortages. In the late 1990s, Botswana's prosperity and political stability attracted not only skilled workers but small numbers of refugees from neighboring Angola, Namibia, and Zimbabwe.

AGE STRUCTURE:

0-14 years: 31.48% (male 357,175 /female 350,775)

15-24 years: 18.7% (male 207,611 /female 212,874)

25-54 years: 38.88% (male 412,475 /female 462,013)

55-64 years: 5.61% (male 53,653 /female 72,617)

65 years and over: 5.33% (male 51,304 /female 68,607) (2018 est.)

DEPENDENCY RATIOS:

total dependency ratio: 55.1 (2015 est.)

youth dependency ratio: 49.3 (2015 est.)

elderly dependency ratio: 5.8 (2015 est.)

potential support ratio: 17.3 (2015 est.)

MEDIAN AGE:

total: 24.9 years

male: 23.8 years

female: 26 years (2018 est.)

country comparison to the world: 158

POPULATION GROWTH RATE:

1.52% (2018 est.)

country comparison to the world: 71

BIRTH RATE:

21.7 births/1,000 population (2018 est.)

country comparison to the world: 70

DEATH RATE:

9.5 deaths/1,000 population (2018 est.)

country comparison to the world: 48

NET MIGRATION RATE:

3 migrant(s)/1,000 population (2017 est.)

country comparison to the world: 34

POPULATION DISTRIBUTION:

the population is primarily concentrated in the east with a focus in and around the captial of Gaborone, and the far central-eastern city of Francistown; population density remains low in other areas in the country, especially in the Kalahari to the west

URBANIZATION:

urban population: 69.4% of total population (2018)

rate of urbanization: 2.87% annual rate of change (2015-20 est.)

MAJOR URBAN AREAS - POPULATION:

269,000 GABORONE (capital) (2018)

SEX RATIO:

at birth: 1.03 male(s)/female (2017 est.)

0-14 years: 1.04 male(s)/female (2017 est.)

15-24 years: 0.99 male(s)/female (2017 est.)

25-54 years: 1.15 male(s)/female (2017 est.)

55-64 years: 0.82 male(s)/female (2017 est.)

65 years and over: 0.66 male(s)/female (2017 est.)

total population: 1.04 male(s)/female (2017 est.)

MATERNAL MORTALITY RATE:

129 deaths/100,000 live births (2015 est.)

country comparison to the world: 65

INFANT MORTALITY RATE:

total: 28.6 deaths/1,000 live births (2018 est.)

male: 31.2 deaths/1,000 live births (2018 est.)

female: 26 deaths/1,000 live births (2018 est.)

country comparison to the world: 65

LIFE EXPECTANCY AT BIRTH:

total population: 63.8 years (2018 est.)

male: 61.8 years (2018 est.)

female: 66 years (2018 est.)

country comparison to the world: 192

TOTAL FERTILITY RATE:

2.53 children born/woman (2018 est.)

country comparison to the world: 77

HEALTH EXPENDITURES:

5.4% of GDP (2014)

country comparison to the world: 129

PHYSICIANS DENSITY:

0.38 physicians/1,000 population (2012)

HOSPITAL BED DENSITY:

1.8 beds/1,000 population (2010)

DRINKING WATER SOURCE:

improved:

urban: 99.2% of population

rural: 92.3% of population

total: 96.2% of population

unimproved:

urban: 0.8% of population

rural: 7.7% of population

total: 3.8% of population (2015 est.)

SANITATION FACILITY ACCESS:

improved:

urban: 78.5% of population (2015 est.)

rural: 43.1% of population (2015 est.)

total: 63.4% of population (2015 est.)

unimproved:

urban: 21.5% of population (2015 est.)

rural: 56.9% of population (2015 est.)

total: 36.6% of population (2015 est.)

HIV/AIDS - ADULT PREVALENCE RATE:

22.8% (2017 est.)

country comparison to the world: 3

HIV/AIDS - PEOPLE LIVING WITH HIV/AIDS:

380,000 (2017 est.)

country comparison to the world: 19

HIV/AIDS - DEATHS:

4,100 (2017 est.)

country comparison to the world: 34

MAJOR INFECTIOUS DISEASES:

degree of risk: high (2016)

food or waterborne diseases: bacterial diarrhea, hepatitis A, and typhoid fever (2016)

vectorborne diseases: malaria (2016)

OBESITY - ADULT PREVALENCE RATE:

18.9% (2016)

country comparison to the world: 114

EDUCATION EXPENDITURES:

9.6% of GDP (2009)

country comparison to the world: 6

LITERACY:

definition: age 15 and over can read and write (2015 est.)

total population: 88.5% (2015 est.)

male: 88% (2015 est.)

female: 88.9% (2015 est.)

SCHOOL LIFE EXPECTANCY (PRIMARY TO TERTIARY EDUCATION):

total: 13 years (2013)

male: 13 years (2013)

female: 13 years (2013)

UNEMPLOYMENT, YOUTH AGES 15-24:

total: 36% (2010 est.)

male: 29.6% (2010 est.)

female: 43.5% (2010 est.)

country comparison to the world: 19

GOVERNMENT :: BOTSWANA

COUNTRY NAME:

conventional long form: Republic of Botswana

conventional short form: Botswana

local long form: Republic of Botswana

local short form: Botswana

former: Bechuanaland

etymology: the name Botswana means "Land of the Tswana" - referring to the country's major ethnic group

GOVERNMENT TYPE:

parliamentary republic

CAPITAL:

name: Gaborone

geographic coordinates: 24 38 S, 25 54 E

time difference: UTC+2 (7 hours ahead of Washington, DC, during Standard Time)

ADMINISTRATIVE DIVISIONS:

10 districts and 6 town councils*; Central, Chobe, Francistown*, Gaborone*, Ghanzi, Jwaneng*, Kgalagadi, Kgatleng, Kweneng, Lobatse*, North East, North West, Selebi-Phikwe*, South East, Southern, Sowa Town*

INDEPENDENCE:

30 September 1966 (from the UK)

NATIONAL HOLIDAY:

Independence Day (Botswana Day), 30 September (1966)

CONSTITUTION:

history: previous 1960 (preindependence); latest adopted March 1965, effective 30 September 1966 (2017)

amendments: proposed by the National Assembly; passage requires approval in two successive Assembly votes with at least two-thirds majority in the final vote; proposals to amend constitutional provisions on fundamental rights and freedoms, the structure and branches of government, and public services also requires approval by majority vote in a referendum and assent by the president of the republic; amended several times, last in 2006 (2017)

LEGAL SYSTEM:

mixed legal system of civil law influenced by the Roman-Dutch model and also customary and common law

INTERNATIONAL LAW ORGANIZATION PARTICIPATION:

accepts compulsory ICJ jurisdiction with reservations; accepts ICCt jurisdiction

CITIZENSHIP:

citizenship by birth: no

citizenship by descent only: at least one parent must be a citizen of Botswana

dual citizenship recognized: no

residency requirement for naturalization: 10 years

SUFFRAGE:

18 years of age; universal

EXECUTIVE BRANCH:

chief of state: President Mokgweetse Eric MASISI (since 1 April 2018); Vice President Slumber TSOGWANE (since 4 April 2018); note - the president is both chief of state and head of government

head of government: President Mokgweetse Eric MASISI (since 1 April 2018); Vice President Slumber TSOGWANE (since 4 April 2018); note - the president is both chief of state and head of government

cabinet: Cabinet appointed by the president

elections/appointments: president indirectly elected by the National Assembly for a 5-year term (eligible for a second term); election last held on 24 October 2014 (next to be held in October 2019); vice president appointed by the president

election results: President Seretse Khama Ian KHAMA (since 1 April 2008) stepped down on 1 April 2018 having completed the constitutionally mandated 10-year term limit; upon his retirement, then Vice President MASISI became president

LEGISLATIVE BRANCH:

description: unicameral Parliament consists of the National Assembly (63 seats; 57 members directly elected in single-seat constituencies by simple majority vote, 4 nominated by the president and indirectly elected by simple majority vote by the rest of the National Assembly, and 2 ex-officio members - the president and attorney general; elected members serve 5-year terms); note - the House of Chiefs (Ntlo ya Dikgosi), an advisory body to the National Assembly, consists of 35 members - 8 hereditary chiefs from Botswana's principal tribes, 22 indirectly elected by the chiefs, and 5 appointed by the president; the House of Chiefs consults on issues including powers of chiefs, customary courts, customary law, tribal property, and constitutional amendments

elections: last held on 24 October 2014 (next to be held in October 2019)

election results: percent of vote by party - BDP 46.5%, UDC 30.0%, BCP 20.4%, independent 3.1%; seats by party - BDP 37, UDC 17, BCP 3; composition - men 57, women 6, percent of women 9.5%

JUDICIAL BRANCH:

highest courts: Court of Appeal, High Court (each consists of a chief justice and a number of other judges as prescribed by the Parliament)

judge selection and term of office: Court of Appeal and High Court chief justices appointed by the president and other judges appointed by the president upon the advice of the Judicial Service Commission; all judges appointed to serve until age 70

subordinate courts: Industrial Court (with circuits scheduled monthly in the capital city and in 3 districts); Magistrates Courts (1 in each district); Customary Court of Appeal; Paramount Chief's Court/Urban Customary Court; Senior Chief's Representative Court; Chief's Representative's Court; Headman's Court

POLITICAL PARTIES AND LEADERS:

Botswana Alliance Movement or BAM [Ephraim Lepetu SETSHWAELO]
Botswana Congress Party or BCP [Dumelang SALESHANDO]
Botswana Democratic Party or BDP [Ian KHAMA]
Botswana Movement for Democracy or BMD [Sidney PILANE]
Botswana National Front or BNF [Duma BOKO]
Botswana Peoples Party or BPP [Motlatsi MOLAPISI]
Real Alternative Party or RAP [Gaontebale MOKGOSI]
Umbrella for Democratic Change or UDC [Duma BOKO] (coalition includes BMD, BPP, BCP and BNF)

INTERNATIONAL ORGANIZATION PARTICIPATION:

ACP, AfDB, AU, C, CD, FAO, G-77, IAEA, IBRD, ICAO, ICCt, ICRM, IDA, IFAD, IFC, IFRCS, ILO, IMF, Interpol, IOC, IOM, IPU, ISO, ITSO, ITU, ITUC (NGOs), MIGA, NAM, OPCW, SACU, SADC, UN, UNCTAD, UNESCO, UNIDO, UNWTO, UPU, WCO, WFTU (NGOs), WHO, WIPO, WMO, WTO

DIPLOMATIC REPRESENTATION IN THE US:

chief of mission: Ambassador David John NEWMAN (since 3 August 2015)

chancery: 1531-1533 New Hampshire Avenue NW, Washington, DC 20036

telephone: [1] (202) 244-4990

FAX: [1] (202) 244-4164

consulate(s) general: Atlanta

DIPLOMATIC REPRESENTATION FROM THE US:

chief of mission: Ambassador Earl R. MILLER (since 30 January 2015)

embassy: Embassy Drive, Government Enclave (off Khama Crescent), Gaborone

mailing address: Embassy Enclave, P. O. Box 90, Gaborone

telephone: [267] 395-3982

FAX: [267] 318-0232

FLAG DESCRIPTION:

light blue with a horizontal white-edged black stripe in the center; the blue symbolizes water in the form of rain, while the black and white bands represent racial harmony

NATIONAL SYMBOL(S):

zebra; national colors: blue, white, black

NATIONAL ANTHEM:

name: "Fatshe leno la rona" (Our Land)

lyrics/music: Kgalemang Tumedisco MOTSETE

note: adopted 1966

ECONOMY :: BOTSWANA

ECONOMY - OVERVIEW:

Until the beginning of the global recession in 2008, Botswana maintained one of the world's highest economic growth rates since its independence in 1966. Botswana recovered from the global recession in 2010, but only grew modestly until 2017, primarily due to a downturn in the global diamond market, though water and power shortages also played a role. Through fiscal discipline and sound management, Botswana has transformed itself from one of the poorest countries in the world five decades ago into a middle-income country with a per capita GDP of approximately $18,100 in 2017. Botswana also ranks as one of the least corrupt and best places to do business in sub-Saharan Africa.

Because of its heavy reliance on diamond exports, Botswana's economy closely follows global price trends for that one commodity. Diamond mining fueled much of Botswana's past economic expansion and currently accounts for one-quarter of GDP, approximately 85% of export earnings, and about one-third of the government's revenues. In 2017, Diamond exports increased to the highest levels since 2013 at about 22 million carats of output, driving Botswana's economic growth to about 4.5% and increasing foreign exchange reserves to about 45% of GDP. De Beers, a major international diamond company, signed a 10-year deal with Botswana in 2012 and moved its rough stone sorting and trading division from London to Gaborone in 2013. The move was geared to support the development of Botswana's nascent downstream diamond industry.

Tourism is a secondary earner of foreign exchange and many Batswana engage in tourism-related services, subsistence farming, and cattle rearing. According to official government statistics, unemployment is around 20%, but unofficial estimates run much higher. The prevalence of HIV/AIDS is second highest in the world and threatens the country's impressive economic gains.

GDP (PURCHASING POWER PARITY):

$39.01 billion (2017 est.)

$38.11 billion (2016 est.)

$36.54 billion (2015 est.)

note: data are in 2017 dollars

country comparison to the world: 121

GDP (OFFICIAL EXCHANGE RATE):

$17.38 billion (2017 est.) (2017 est.)

GDP - REAL GROWTH RATE:

2.4% (2017 est.)

4.3% (2016 est.)

-1.7% (2015 est.)

country comparison to the world: 137

GDP - PER CAPITA (PPP):

$17,000 (2017 est.)

$16,900 (2016 est.)

$16,500 (2015 est.)

note: data are in 2017 dollars

country comparison to the world: 101

GROSS NATIONAL SAVING:

40.3% of GDP (2017 est.)

38.8% of GDP (2016 est.)

41.2% of GDP (2015 est.)

country comparison to the world: 9

GDP - COMPOSITION, BY END USE:

household consumption: 48.5% (2017 est.)

government consumption: 18.4% (2017 est.)

investment in fixed capital: 29% (2017 est.)

investment in inventories: -1.8% (2017 est.)

exports of goods and services: 39.8% (2017 est.)

imports of goods and services: -33.9% (2017 est.)

GDP - COMPOSITION, BY SECTOR OF ORIGIN:

agriculture: 1.8% (2017 est.)

industry: 27.5% (2017 est.)

services: 70.6% (2017 est.)

AGRICULTURE - PRODUCTS:

livestock, sorghum, maize, millet, beans, sunflowers, groundnuts

INDUSTRIES:

diamonds, copper, nickel, salt, soda ash, potash, coal, iron ore, silver; beef processing; textiles

INDUSTRIAL PRODUCTION GROWTH RATE:

-4.2% (2017 est.)

country comparison to the world: 193

LABOR FORCE:

1.177 million (2017 est.)

country comparison to the world: 141

LABOR FORCE - BY OCCUPATION:

agriculture: NA

industry: NA

services: NA

UNEMPLOYMENT RATE:

20% (2013 est.)

17.8% (2009 est.)

country comparison to the world: 185

POPULATION BELOW POVERTY LINE:

19.3% (2009 est.)

HOUSEHOLD INCOME OR CONSUMPTION BY PERCENTAGE SHARE:

lowest 10%: NA

highest 10%: NA

DISTRIBUTION OF FAMILY INCOME - GINI INDEX:

60.5 (2009)

63 (1993)

country comparison to the world: 5

BUDGET:

revenues: 5.305 billion (2017 est.)

expenditures: 5.478 billion (2017 est.)

TAXES AND OTHER REVENUES:

30.5% (of GDP) (2017 est.)

country comparison to the world: 75

BUDGET SURPLUS (+) OR DEFICIT (-):

-1% (of GDP) (2017 est.)

country comparison to the world: 76

PUBLIC DEBT:

14% of GDP (2017 est.)

15.6% of GDP (2016 est.)

country comparison to the world: 195

FISCAL YEAR:

1 April - 31 March

INFLATION RATE (CONSUMER PRICES):

3.3% (2017 est.)

2.8% (2016 est.)

country comparison to the world: 136

CENTRAL BANK DISCOUNT RATE:

5.5% (31 December 2016)

6% (31 December 2015)

country comparison to the world: 74

COMMERCIAL BANK PRIME LENDING RATE:

6.88% (31 December 2017 est.)

7.3% (31 December 2016 est.)

country comparison to the world: 121

STOCK OF NARROW MONEY:

$1.645 billion (31 December 2017 est.)

$1.494 billion (31 December 2016 est.)

country comparison to the world: 140

STOCK OF BROAD MONEY:

$1.645 billion (31 December 2017 est.)

$1.494 billion (31 December 2016 est.)

country comparison to the world: 148

STOCK OF DOMESTIC CREDIT:

$3.002 billion (31 December 2017 est.)

$2.579 billion (31 December 2016 est.)

country comparison to the world: 140

MARKET VALUE OF PUBLICLY TRADED SHARES:

$4.588 billion (31 December 2012 est.)

$4.107 billion (31 December 2011 est.)

$4.076 billion (31 December 2010 est.)

country comparison to the world: 85

CURRENT ACCOUNT BALANCE:

$2.146 billion (2017 est.)

$2.147 billion (2016 est.)

country comparison to the world: 40

EXPORTS:

$5.934 billion (2017 est.)

$7.226 billion (2016 est.)

country comparison to the world: 103

EXPORTS - PARTNERS:

Belgium 20.3%, India 12.6%, UAE 12.4%, South Africa 11.9%, Singapore

8.7%, Israel 7%, Hong Kong 4.1%, Namibia 4.1% (2017)

EXPORTS - COMMODITIES:

diamonds, copper, nickel, soda ash, beef, textiles

IMPORTS:

$5.005 billion (2017 est.)

$5.871 billion (2016 est.)

country comparison to the world: 128

IMPORTS - COMMODITIES:

foodstuffs, machinery, electrical goods, transport equipment, textiles, fuel and petroleum products, wood and paper products, metal and metal products

IMPORTS - PARTNERS:

South Africa 66.1%, Canada 8.3%, Israel 5.3% (2017)

RESERVES OF FOREIGN EXCHANGE AND GOLD:

$7.491 billion (31 December 2017 est.)

$7.189 billion (31 December 2016 est.)

country comparison to the world: 82

DEBT - EXTERNAL:

$2.187 billion (31 December 2017 est.)

$2.421 billion (31 December 2016 est.)

country comparison to the world: 151

STOCK OF DIRECT FOREIGN INVESTMENT - AT HOME:

$5.319 billion (31 December 2017 est.)

$5.699 billion (31 December 2016 est.)

country comparison to the world: 106

STOCK OF DIRECT FOREIGN INVESTMENT - ABROAD:

$1.973 billion (31 December 2017 est.)

$1.312 billion (31 December 2016 est.)

country comparison to the world: 84

EXCHANGE RATES:

pulas (BWP) per US dollar -

10.19 (2017 est.)

10.9022 (2016 est.)

10.9022 (2015 est.)

10.1263 (2014 est.)

8.9761 (2013 est.)

ENERGY :: BOTSWANA

ELECTRICITY ACCESS:

population without electricity: 700,000 (2013)

electrification - total population: 66% (2013)

electrification - urban areas: 75% (2013)

electrification - rural areas: 54% (2013)

ELECTRICITY - PRODUCTION:

2.527 billion kWh (2016 est.)

country comparison to the world: 135

ELECTRICITY - CONSUMPTION:

3.636 billion kWh (2016 est.)

country comparison to the world: 131

ELECTRICITY - EXPORTS:

0 kWh (2016 est.)

country comparison to the world: 109

ELECTRICITY - IMPORTS:

1.673 billion kWh (2016 est.)

country comparison to the world: 59

ELECTRICITY - INSTALLED GENERATING CAPACITY:

735,000 kW (2016 est.)

country comparison to the world: 135

ELECTRICITY - FROM FOSSIL FUELS:

100% of total installed capacity (2016 est.)

country comparison to the world: 4

ELECTRICITY - FROM NUCLEAR FUELS:

0% of total installed capacity (2017 est.)

country comparison to the world: 54

ELECTRICITY - FROM HYDROELECTRIC PLANTS:

0% of total installed capacity (2017 est.)

country comparison to the world: 159

ELECTRICITY - FROM OTHER RENEWABLE SOURCES:

0% of total installed capacity (2017 est.)

country comparison to the world: 178

CRUDE OIL - PRODUCTION:

0 bbl/day (2017 est.)

country comparison to the world: 113

CRUDE OIL - EXPORTS:

0 bbl/day (2015 est.)

country comparison to the world: 97

CRUDE OIL - IMPORTS:

0 bbl/day (2015 est.)

country comparison to the world: 100

CRUDE OIL - PROVED RESERVES:

0 bbl (1 January 2018 est.)

country comparison to the world: 110

REFINED PETROLEUM PRODUCTS - PRODUCTION:

0 bbl/day (2015 est.)

country comparison to the world: 122

REFINED PETROLEUM PRODUCTS - CONSUMPTION:

21,000 bbl/day (2016 est.)

country comparison to the world: 135

REFINED PETROLEUM PRODUCTS - EXPORTS:

0 bbl/day (2015 est.)

country comparison to the world: 133

REFINED PETROLEUM PRODUCTS - IMPORTS:

21,090 bbl/day (2015 est.)

country comparison to the world: 116

NATURAL GAS - PRODUCTION:

0 cu m (2017 est.)

country comparison to the world: 108

NATURAL GAS - CONSUMPTION:

0 cu m (2017 est.)

country comparison to the world: 124

NATURAL GAS - EXPORTS:

0 cu m (2017 est.)

country comparison to the world: 73

NATURAL GAS - IMPORTS:

0 cu m (2017 est.)

country comparison to the world: 95

NATURAL GAS - PROVED RESERVES:

0 cu m (1 January 2014 est.)

country comparison to the world: 114

CARBON DIOXIDE EMISSIONS FROM CONSUMPTION OF ENERGY:

6.235 million Mt (2017 est.)

country comparison to the world: 127

COMMUNICATIONS :: BOTSWANA

TELEPHONES - FIXED LINES:

total subscriptions: 141,207 (2017 est.)

subscriptions per 100 inhabitants: 6 (2017 est.)

country comparison to the world: 132

TELEPHONES - MOBILE CELLULAR:

total subscriptions: 3,240,589 (2017 est.)

subscriptions per 100 inhabitants: 146 (2017 est.)

country comparison to the world: 138

TELEPHONE SYSTEM:

general assessment:

effective regulatory reform has turned the Botswana's telecom market into one of the most liberalised in the region; Botswana has one of the highest mobile penetration rates in Africa; 3 MNOs have entered the underdeveloped broadband sector with the adoption of 3G, LTE and WiMAX technologies; mobile internet remains the preferred choice

(2017)

domestic: fixed-line teledensity has declined in recent years and now stands at roughly 6 telephones per 100 persons; mobile-cellular teledensity has advanced to 150 telephones per 100 persons (2017)

international: country code - 267; international calls are made via satellite, using international direct dialing; 2 international exchanges; digital microwave radio relay links to Namibia, Zambia, Zimbabwe, and South Africa; satellite earth station - 1 Intelsat (Indian Ocean) (2016)

Botswana is participating in regional development efforts; expanding fully digital system with fiber-optic cables linking the major population centers in the east as well as a system of open-wire lines, microwave radio relays links, and radiotelephone communication stations; the Botswana Telecommunications Corporation is rolling out 4G service to over 95 sites in the country that will improve network connectivity

BROADCAST MEDIA:

2 TV stations - 1 state-owned and 1 privately owned; privately owned satellite TV subscription service is available; 2 state-owned national radio stations; 3 privately owned radio stations broadcast locally (2007)

INTERNET COUNTRY CODE:

.bw

INTERNET USERS:

total: 869,610 (July 2016 est.)

percent of population: 39.4% (July 2016 est.)

country comparison to the world: 136

BROADBAND - FIXED SUBSCRIPTIONS:

total: 48,901 (2017 est.)

subscriptions per 100 inhabitants: 2 (2017 est.)

country comparison to the world: 130

TRANSPORTATION :: BOTSWANA

NATIONAL AIR TRANSPORT SYSTEM:

number of registered air carriers: 1 (2015)

inventory of registered aircraft operated by air carriers: 6 (2015)

annual passenger traffic on registered air carriers: 194,005 (2015)

annual freight traffic on registered air carriers: 94,729 mt-km (2015)

CIVIL AIRCRAFT REGISTRATION COUNTRY CODE PREFIX:

A2 (2016)

AIRPORTS:

74 (2013)

country comparison to the world: 70

AIRPORTS - WITH PAVED RUNWAYS:

total: 10 (2017)

over 3,047 m: 2 (2017)

2,438 to 3,047 m: 1 (2017)

1,524 to 2,437 m: 6 (2017)

914 to 1,523 m: 1 (2017)

AIRPORTS - WITH UNPAVED RUNWAYS:

total: 64 (2013)

1,524 to 2,437 m: 5 (2013)

914 to 1,523 m: 46 (2013)

under 914 m: 13 (2013)

RAILWAYS:

total: 888 km (2014)

narrow gauge: 888 km 1.067-m gauge (2014)

country comparison to the world: 95

ROADWAYS:

total: 17,916 km (2011)

note: includes 8,916 km of Public Highway Network roads (6,116 km paved and 2,800 km unpaved) and 9,000 km of District Council roads

country comparison to the world: 118

MILITARY AND SECURITY :: BOTSWANA

MILITARY EXPENDITURES:

3.37% of GDP (2016)

2.66% of GDP (2015)

2.13% of GDP (2014)

country comparison to the world: 23

MILITARY BRANCHES:

Botswana Defence Force (BDF): Ground Forces Command, Air Arm Command, Defense Logistics Command (2017)

MILITARY SERVICE AGE AND OBLIGATION:

18 is the legal minimum age for voluntary military service; no conscription (2012)

TRANSNATIONAL ISSUES :: BOTSWANA

DISPUTES - INTERNATIONAL:

none

TRAFFICKING IN PERSONS:

current situation: Botswana is a source, transit, and destination country for women and children subjected to sex trafficking and forced labor; young Batswana serving as domestic workers, sometimes sent by their parents, may be denied education and basic necessities or experience confinement and abuse indicative of forced labor; Batswana girls and women also are forced into prostitution domestically; adults and children of San ethnicity were reported to be in forced labor on farms and at cattle posts in the country's rural west

tier rating: Tier 2 Watch List – Botswana does not fully comply with the minimum standards for the elimination of trafficking; however, it is making significant efforts to do so; an anti-trafficking act was passed at the beginning of 2014, but authorities did not investigate, prosecute, or convict any offenders or government officials complicit in trafficking or operationalize victim identification and referral procedures based on the new law; the government sponsored a radio campaign to familiarize the public with the issue of human trafficking (2015)

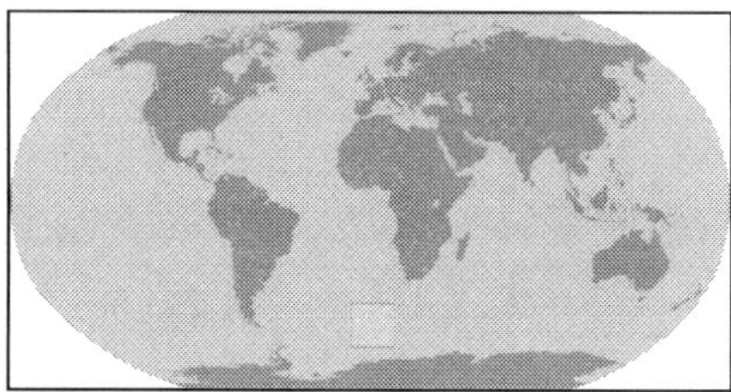

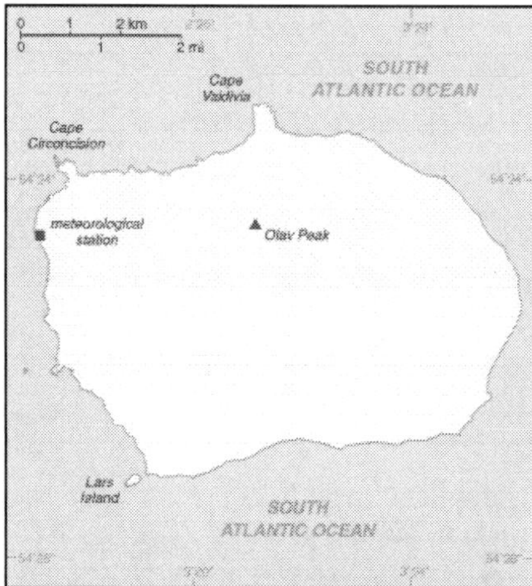

ANTARCTICA :: BOUVET ISLAND

INTRODUCTION :: BOUVET ISLAND

BACKGROUND:

This uninhabited, volcanic, Antarctic island is almost entirely covered by glaciers making it difficult to approach; it is recognized as the most remote island on Earth. (It is furthest in distance from any other point of land, 1,639 km from Antarctica.) Bouvet Island was discovered in 1739 by a French naval officer after whom it is named. No claim was made until 1825, when the British flag was raised. A few expeditions visited the island in the late 19th century. In 1929, the UK waived its claim in favor of Norway, which had occupied the island two years previously. In 1971, Norway designated Bouvet Island and the adjacent territorial waters a nature reserve. Since 1977, Norway has run an automated meteorological station and studied foraging strategies and distribution of fur seals and penguins on the island. In February 2006, an earthquake weakened the station's foundation causing it to be blown out to sea in a winter storm. Norway erected a new research station in 2014 that can hold six people for periods of two to four months.

GEOGRAPHY :: BOUVET ISLAND

LOCATION:

island in the South Atlantic Ocean, southwest of the Cape of Good Hope (South Africa)

GEOGRAPHIC COORDINATES:

54 26 S, 3 24 E

MAP REFERENCES:

Antarctic Region

AREA:

total: 49 sq km

land: 49 sq km

water: 0 sq km

country comparison to the world: 233

AREA - COMPARATIVE:

about 0.3 times the size of Washington, DC

LAND BOUNDARIES:

0 km

COASTLINE:

29.6 km

MARITIME CLAIMS:

territorial sea: 4 nm

CLIMATE:

antarctic

TERRAIN:

volcanic; coast is mostly inaccessible

ELEVATION:

0 m lowest point: South Atlantic Ocean

780 highest point: Olavtoppen (Olav Peak)

NATURAL RESOURCES:

none

LAND USE:

agricultural land: 0% (2011 est.)

arable land: 0% (2011 est.) / permanent crops: 0% (2011 est.) / permanent pasture: 0% (2011 est.)

forest: 0% (2011 est.)

other: 100% (2011 est.)

NATURAL HAZARDS:

occasional volcanism, rock slides; harsh climate, surrounded by pack ice in winter

ENVIRONMENT - CURRENT ISSUES:

none; almost entirely ice covered

GEOGRAPHY - NOTE:

almost entirely covered by glacial ice (93%); declared a nature reserve by Norway; the distance from Bouvet Island to Norway is 12,776 km, which is almost one-third the circumference of the earth

PEOPLE AND SOCIETY :: BOUVET ISLAND

POPULATION:

uninhabited

GOVERNMENT :: BOUVET ISLAND

COUNTRY NAME:

conventional long form: none

conventional short form: Bouvet Island

etymology: named after the French naval officer Jean-Baptiste Charles BOUVET who discovered the island in 1739

note: pronounced boo-vay i-land

DEPENDENCY STATUS:

territory of Norway; administered by the Polar Department of the Ministry of Justice and Oslo Police

LEGAL SYSTEM:

the laws of Norway, where applicable, apply

FLAG DESCRIPTION:

the flag of Norway is used

ECONOMY :: BOUVET ISLAND

ECONOMY - OVERVIEW:

no economic activity; declared a nature reserve

COMMUNICATIONS :: BOUVET ISLAND

INTERNET COUNTRY CODE:

.bv

COMMUNICATIONS - NOTE:

has an automated meteorological station

TRANSPORTATION :: BOUVET ISLAND

PORTS AND TERMINALS:

none; offshore anchorage only

MILITARY AND SECURITY :: BOUVET ISLAND

MILITARY - NOTE:

defense is the responsibility of Norway

TRANSNATIONAL ISSUES :: BOUVET ISLAND

DISPUTES - INTERNATIONAL:

none

INTRODUCTION :: BRAZIL

BACKGROUND:

Following more than three centuries under Portuguese rule, Brazil gained its independence in 1822, maintaining a monarchical system of government until the abolition of slavery in 1888 and the subsequent proclamation of a republic by the military in 1889. Brazilian coffee exporters politically dominated the country until populist leader Getulio VARGAS rose to power in 1930. By far the largest and most populous country in South America, Brazil underwent more than a half century of populist and military government until 1985, when the military regime peacefully ceded power to civilian rulers. Brazil continues to pursue industrial and agricultural growth and development of its interior. Having successfully weathered a period of global financial difficulty in the late 20th century, Brazil was seen as one of the world's strongest emerging markets and a contributor to global growth. The awarding of the 2014 FIFA World Cup and 2016 Summer Olympic Games, the first ever to be held in South America, was seen as symbolic of the country's rise. However, from about 2013 to 2016, Brazil was plagued by a sagging economy, high unemployment, and high inflation, only emerging from recession in 2017. Political scandal resulted in the impeachment of President Dilma ROUSSEFF in May 2016, a conviction that was upheld by the Senate in August 2016; her vice president, Michel TEMER, will serve as president until 1 January 2019, completing her second term.

GEOGRAPHY :: BRAZIL

LOCATION:

Eastern South America, bordering the Atlantic Ocean

GEOGRAPHIC COORDINATES:

10 00 S, 55 00 W

MAP REFERENCES:

South America

AREA:

total: 8,515,770 sq km

land: 8,358,140 sq km

water: 157,630 sq km

note: includes Arquipelago de Fernando de Noronha, Atol das Rocas, Ilha da Trindade, Ilhas Martin Vaz, and Penedos de Sao Pedro e Sao Paulo

country comparison to the world: 6

AREA - COMPARATIVE:

slightly smaller than the US

LAND BOUNDARIES:

total: 16,145 km

border countries (10): Argentina 1263 km, Bolivia 3403 km, Colombia 1790 km, French Guiana 649 km, Guyana 1308 km, Paraguay 1371 km, Peru 2659 km, Suriname 515 km, Uruguay 1050 km, Venezuela 2137 km

COASTLINE:

7,491 km

MARITIME CLAIMS:

territorial sea: 12 nm

exclusive economic zone: 200 nm

contiguous zone: 24 nm

continental shelf: 200 nm or to edge of the continental margin

CLIMATE:

mostly tropical, but temperate in south

TERRAIN:

mostly flat to rolling lowlands in north; some plains, hills, mountains, and narrow coastal belt

ELEVATION:

mean elevation: 320 m

elevation extremes: 0 m lowest point: Atlantic Ocean

2994 highest point: Pico da Neblina

NATURAL RESOURCES:

bauxite, gold, iron ore, manganese, nickel, phosphates, platinum, tin, rare earth elements, uranium, petroleum, hydropower, timber

LAND USE:

agricultural land: 32.9% (2011 est.)

arable land: 8.6% (2011 est.) / permanent crops: 0.8% (2011 est.) / permanent pasture: 23.5% (2011 est.)

forest: 61.9% (2011 est.)

other: 5.2% (2011 est.)

IRRIGATED LAND:

54,000 sq km (2012)

POPULATION DISTRIBUTION:

the vast majority of people live along, or relatively near, the Atlantic coast in the east; the population core is in the southeast, anchored by the cities of Sao Paolo, Brasilia, and Rio de Janeiro

NATURAL HAZARDS:

recurring droughts in northeast; floods and occasional frost in south

ENVIRONMENT - CURRENT ISSUES:

deforestation in Amazon Basin destroys the habitat and endangers a multitude of plant and animal species indigenous to the area; illegal wildlife trade; illegal poaching; air and water pollution in Rio de Janeiro, Sao Paulo, and several other large cities; land degradation and water pollution caused by improper mining activities; wetland degradation; severe oil spills

ENVIRONMENT - INTERNATIONAL AGREEMENTS:

party to: Antarctic-Environmental Protocol, Antarctic-Marine Living Resources, Antarctic Seals, Antarctic Treaty, Biodiversity, Climate Change, Climate Change-Kyoto Protocol, Desertification, Endangered Species, Environmental Modification, Hazardous Wastes, Law of the Sea, Marine Dumping, Ozone Layer Protection, Ship Pollution, Tropical Timber 83, Tropical Timber 94, Wetlands, Whaling

signed, but not ratified: none of the selected agreements

GEOGRAPHY - NOTE:

largest country in South America and in the Southern Hemisphere; shares common boundaries with every South American country except Chile and Ecuador; most of the Pantanal, the world's largest tropical wetland, extends through the west central part of the country; shares Iguazu Falls, the world's largest waterfalls system, with Argentina

PEOPLE AND SOCIETY :: BRAZIL

POPULATION:

208,846,892 (July 2018 est.)

country comparison to the world: 5

NATIONALITY:

noun: Brazilian(s)

adjective: Brazilian

ETHNIC GROUPS:

white 47.7%, mulatto (mixed white and black) 43.1%, black 7.6%, Asian 1.1%, indigenous 0.4% (2010 est.)

LANGUAGES:

Portuguese (official and most widely spoken language)

note: less common languages include Spanish (border areas and schools), German, Italian, Japanese, English, and a large number of minor Amerindian languages

RELIGIONS:

Roman Catholic 64.6%, other Catholic 0.4%, Protestant 22.2% (includes Adventist 6.5%, Assembly of God 2.0%, Christian Congregation of Brazil 1.2%, Universal Kingdom of God 1.0%, other Protestant 11.5%), other Christian 0.7%, Spiritist 2.2%, other 1.4%, none 8%, unspecified 0.4% (2010 est.)

DEMOGRAPHIC PROFILE:

Brazil's rapid fertility decline since the 1960s is the main factor behind the country's slowing population growth rate, aging population, and fast-paced demographic transition. Brasilia has not taken full advantage of its large working-age population to develop its human capital and strengthen its social and economic institutions but is funding a study abroad program to bring advanced skills back to the country. The current favorable age structure will begin to shift around 2025, with the labor force shrinking and the elderly starting to compose an increasing share of the total population. Well-funded public pensions have nearly wiped out poverty among the elderly, and Bolsa Familia and other social programs have lifted tens of millions out of poverty. More than half of Brazil's population is considered middle class, but poverty and income inequality levels remain high; the Northeast, North, and Center-West, women, and black, mixed race, and indigenous populations are disproportionately affected. Disparities in opportunities foster social exclusion and contribute to Brazil's high crime rate, particularly violent crime in cities and favelas (slums).

Brazil has traditionally been a net recipient of immigrants, with its southeast being the prime destination. After the importation of African slaves was outlawed in the mid-19th century, Brazil sought Europeans (Italians, Portuguese, Spaniards, and Germans) and later Asians (Japanese) to work in agriculture, especially coffee cultivation. Recent immigrants come mainly from Argentina, Chile, and Andean countries (many are unskilled illegal migrants) or are returning Brazilian nationals. Since Brazil's economic downturn in the 1980s, emigration to the United States, Europe, and Japan has been rising but is negligible relative to Brazil's total population. The majority of these emigrants are well-educated and middle-class. Fewer Brazilian peasants are emigrating to neighboring countries to take up agricultural work.

AGE STRUCTURE:

0-14 years: 21.89% (male 23,310,437 /female 22,414,551)

15-24 years: 16.29% (male 17,254,084 /female 16,758,140)

25-54 years: 43.86% (male 45,449,158 /female 46,151,759)

55-64 years: 9.35% (male 9,229,665 /female 10,296,824)

65 years and over: 8.61% (male 7,666,845 /female 10,315,429) (2018 est.)

DEPENDENCY RATIOS:

total dependency ratio: 43.8 (2015 est.)

youth dependency ratio: 32.4 (2015 est.)

elderly dependency ratio: 11.4 (2015 est.)

potential support ratio: 8.7 (2015 est.)

MEDIAN AGE:

total: 32.4 years

male: 31.5 years

female: 33.3 years (2018 est.)

country comparison to the world: 100

POPULATION GROWTH RATE:

0.71% (2018 est.)

country comparison to the world: 140

BIRTH RATE:

13.9 births/1,000 population (2018 est.)

country comparison to the world: 135

DEATH RATE:

6.7 deaths/1,000 population (2018 est.)

country comparison to the world: 136

NET MIGRATION RATE:

-0.1 migrant(s)/1,000 population (2017 est.)

country comparison to the world: 103

POPULATION DISTRIBUTION:

the vast majority of people live along, or relatively near, the Atlantic coast in the east; the population core is in the southeast, anchored by the cities of Sao Paolo, Brasilia, and Rio de Janeiro

URBANIZATION:

urban population: 86.6% of total population (2018)

rate of urbanization: 1.05% annual rate of change (2015-20 est.)

MAJOR URBAN AREAS - POPULATION:

21.65 million Sao Paulo, 13.293 million Rio de Janeiro, 5.972 million Belo Horizonte, 4.47 million BRASILIA (capital), 4.094 million Porto Alegre, 4.028 million Recife (2018)

SEX RATIO:

at birth: 1.04 male(s)/female (2017 est.)

0-14 years: 1.04 male(s)/female (2017 est.)

15-24 years: 1.03 male(s)/female (2017 est.)

25-54 years: 0.98 male(s)/female (2017 est.)

55-64 years: 0.89 male(s)/female (2017 est.)

65 years and over: 0.74 male(s)/female (2017 est.)

total population: 0.97 male(s)/female (2017 est.)

MATERNAL MORTALITY RATE:

44 deaths/100,000 live births (2015 est.)

country comparison to the world: 101

INFANT MORTALITY RATE:

total: 16.9 deaths/1,000 live births (2018 est.)

male: 19.9 deaths/1,000 live births (2018 est.)

female: 13.8 deaths/1,000 live births (2018 est.)

country comparison to the world: 91

LIFE EXPECTANCY AT BIRTH:

total population: 74.3 years (2018 est.)

male: 70.7 years (2018 est.)

female: 78 years (2018 est.)

country comparison to the world: 125

TOTAL FERTILITY RATE:

1.75 children born/woman (2018 est.)

country comparison to the world: 159

CONTRACEPTIVE PREVALENCE RATE:

80.2% (2013)

HEALTH EXPENDITURES:

8.3% of GDP (2014)

country comparison to the world: 51

PHYSICIANS DENSITY:

1.85 physicians/1,000 population (2013)

HOSPITAL BED DENSITY:

2.2 beds/1,000 population (2014)

DRINKING WATER SOURCE:

improved:

urban: 100% of population (2015 est.)

rural: 87% of population (2015 est.)

total: 98.1% of population (2015 est.)

unimproved:

urban: 0% of population (2015 est.)

rural: 13% of population (2015 est.)

total: 1.9% of population (2015 est.)

SANITATION FACILITY ACCESS:

improved:

urban: 88% of population (2015 est.)

rural: 51.5% of population (2015 est.)

total: 82.8% of population (2015 est.)

unimproved:

urban: 12% of population (2015 est.)

rural: 48.5% of population (2015 est.)

total: 17.2% of population (2015 est.)

HIV/AIDS - ADULT PREVALENCE RATE:

0.6% (2017 est.)

country comparison to the world: 55

HIV/AIDS - PEOPLE LIVING WITH HIV/AIDS:

860,000 (2017 est.)

country comparison to the world: 12

HIV/AIDS - DEATHS:

14,000 (2017 est.)

country comparison to the world: 18

MAJOR INFECTIOUS DISEASES:

degree of risk: very high (2016)

food or waterborne diseases: bacterial diarrhea and hepatitis A (2016)

vectorborne diseases: dengue fever and malaria (2016)

water contact diseases: schistosomiasis (2016)

note: active local transmission of Zika virus by Aedes species mosquitoes has been identified in this country (as of August 2016); it poses an important risk (a large number of cases possible) among US citizens if bitten by an infective mosquito; other less common ways to get Zika are through sex, via blood transfusion, or during pregnancy, in which the pregnant woman passes Zika virus to her fetus

OBESITY - ADULT PREVALENCE RATE:

22.1% (2016)

country comparison to the world: 82

EDUCATION EXPENDITURES:

5.9% of GDP (2014)

country comparison to the world: 38

LITERACY:

definition: age 15 and over can read and write (2015 est.)

total population: 92.6% (2015 est.)

male: 92.2% (2015 est.)

female: 92.9% (2015 est.)

SCHOOL LIFE EXPECTANCY (PRIMARY TO TERTIARY EDUCATION):

total: 15 years (2014)

male: 15 years (2014)

female: 16 years (2014)

UNEMPLOYMENT, YOUTH AGES 15-24:

total: 30.2% (2017 est.)

male: 26.5% (2017 est.)

female: 35% (2017 est.)

country comparison to the world: 31

GOVERNMENT :: BRAZIL

COUNTRY NAME:

conventional long form: Federative Republic of Brazil

conventional short form: Brazil

local long form: Republica Federativa do Brasil

local short form: Brasil

etymology: the country name derives from the brazilwood tree that used to grow plentifully along the coast of Brazil and that was used to produce a deep red dye

GOVERNMENT TYPE:

federal presidential republic

CAPITAL:

name: Brasilia

geographic coordinates: 15 47 S, 47 55 W

time difference: UTC-3 (2 hours ahead of Washington, DC, during Standard Time)

daylight saving time: +1hr, begins third Sunday in October; ends third Sunday in February

note: Brazil has four time zones, including one for the Fernando de

Noronha Islands

ADMINISTRATIVE DIVISIONS:

26 states (estados, singular - estado) and 1 federal district* (distrito federal); Acre, Alagoas, Amapa, Amazonas, Bahia, Ceara, Distrito Federal*, Espirito Santo, Goias, Maranhao, Mato Grosso, Mato Grosso do Sul, Minas Gerais, Para, Paraiba, Parana, Pernambuco, Piaui, Rio de Janeiro, Rio Grande do Norte, Rio Grande do Sul, Rondonia, Roraima, Santa Catarina, Sao Paulo, Sergipe, Tocantins

INDEPENDENCE:

7 September 1822 (from Portugal)

NATIONAL HOLIDAY:

Independence Day, 7 September (1822)

CONSTITUTION:

history: several previous; latest ratified 5 October 1988 (2018)

amendments: proposed by at least one-third of either house of the National Congress, by the president of the republic, or by simple majority vote by more than half of the state legislative assemblies; passage requires at least three-fifths majority vote by both houses in each of 2 readings; constitutional provisions affecting the federal form of government, separation of powers, suffrage, or individual rights and guarantees cannot be amended; amended many times, last in 2017 (2018)

LEGAL SYSTEM:

civil law; note - a new civil law code was enacted in 2002 replacing the 1916 code

INTERNATIONAL LAW ORGANIZATION PARTICIPATION:

has not submitted an ICJ jurisdiction declaration; accepts ICCt jurisdiction

CITIZENSHIP:

citizenship by birth: yes

citizenship by descent only: yes

dual citizenship recognized: yes

residency requirement for naturalization: 4 years

SUFFRAGE:

voluntary between 16 to 18 years of age, over 70, and if illiterate; compulsory between 18 to 70 years of age; note - military conscripts by law cannot vote

EXECUTIVE BRANCH:

chief of state: President Michel Miguel Elias TEMER Lulia (since 31 August 2016); Vice President (vacant); note - the president is both chief of state and head of government

head of government: President Michel Miguel Elias TEMER Lulia (since 31 August 2016); Vice President (vacant)

cabinet: Cabinet appointed by the president

elections/appointments: president and vice president directly elected on the same ballot by absolute majority popular vote in 2 rounds if needed for a single 4-year term (eligible for a second term); election last held on 7 October 2018 with runoff on 28 October 2018 (next to be held in October 2022)

election results: Jair BOLSONARO elected president in second round; percent of vote in first round - Jair BOLSONARO (PSL) 46%, Fernando HADDAD (PT) 29.3%, Ciro GOMEZ (PDT) 12.5%, Geraldo ALCKMIN (PSDB) 4.8%, other 7.4%; percent of vote in second round - Jair BOLSONARO (PSL) 55.1%, Fernando HADDAD (PT) 44.9%; note - BOLSONARO will take office 1 January 2019

note: on 12 May 2016, Brazil's Senate voted to hold an impeachment trial of President Dilma ROUSSEFF, who was then suspended from her executive duties; Vice President Michel TEMER took over as acting president; on 31 August 2016 the Senate voted 61-20 in favor of conviction and her removal from office; TEMER is serving as president for the remainder of ROUSSEFF's term, which ends 1 January 2019

LEGISLATIVE BRANCH:

description: bicameral National Congress or Congresso Nacional consists of:
Federal Senate or Senado Federal (81 seats; 3 members each from 26 states and 3 from the federal district directly elected in multi-seat constituencies by simple majority vote to serve 8-year terms, with one-third and two-thirds of the membership elected alternately every 4 years)
Chamber of Deputies or Camara dos Deputados (513 seats; members directly elected in multi-seat constituencies by proportional representation vote to serve 4-year terms)

elections:
Federal Senate - last held on 7 October 2018 for two-thirds of the Senate (next to be held in October 2022 for one-third of the Senate)
Chamber of Deputies - last held on 7 October 2018 (next to be held in October 2022)

election results:
Federal Senate - percent of vote by party - NA; seats by party - PMDB 7, PP 5, REDE 5, DEM 4, PSDB 4, PSDC 4, PSL 4, PT 4, PDT 2, PHS 2, PPS 2, PSB 2, PTB 2, Podemos 1, PR 1, PRB 1, PROS 1, PRP 1, PSC 1, SD 1
Chamber of Deputies - percent of vote by party - NA; seats by party - PT 56, PSL 52, PP 37, PMDB 34, PSDC 34, PR 33, PSB 32, PRB 30, DEM 29, PSDB 29, PDT 28, SD 13, Podemos 11, PSOL 10, PTB 10, PCdoB 9, NOVO 8, PPS 8, PROS 8, PSC 8, Avante 7, PHS 6, Patriota 5, PRP 4, PV 4, PMN 3, PTC 2, DC 1, PPL 1, REDE 1

JUDICIAL BRANCH:

highest courts: Supreme Federal Court or Supremo Tribunal Federal (consists of 11 justices)

judge selection and term of office: justices appointed by the president and approved by the Federal Senate; justices appointed to serve until mandatory retirement at age 75

subordinate courts: Tribunal of the Union, Federal Appeals Court, Superior Court of Justice, Superior Electoral Court, regional federal courts; state court system

POLITICAL PARTIES AND LEADERS:

Avante [Luis TIBE] (formerly Labor Party of Brazil or PTdoB)
Brazilian Communist Party or PCB [Ivan Martins PINHEIRO]
Brazilian Democratic Movement Party or PMDB [Michel TEMER]
Brazilian Labor Party or PTB [Cristiane BRASIL]
Brazilian Renewal Labor Party or PRTB [Jose Levy FIDELIX da Cruz]
Brazilian Republican Party or PRB [Marcos Antonio PEREIRA]
Brazilian Social Democracy Party or PSDB [Aecio NEVES]
Brazilian Socialist Party or PSB [Carlos Roberto SIQUEIRA de Barros]
Christian Democracy or DC [Jose Maria EYMAEL] (formerly Christian Social Democratic Party or PSDC)
Christian Labor Party or PTC [Daniel TOURINHO]
Communist Party of Brazil or PCdoB [Jose Renato RABELO]
Democratic Labor Party or PDT [Carlos Roberto LUPI]
The Democrats or DEM [Jose AGRIPINO] (formerly Liberal Front Party or PFL)

Free Homeland Party or PPL [Sergio RUBENS]
Green Party or PV [Jose Luiz PENNA]
Humanist Party of Solidarity or PHS [Eduardo MACHADO]
National Mobilization Party or PMN [Telma RIBEIRO dos Santos]
New Party or NOVO [Moises JARDIM]
Party of the Republic or PR [Alfredo NASCIMENTO]
Patriota [Adilson BARROSO Oliveira] (formerly National Ecologic Party or PEN)
Podemos [Renata ABREU] (formerly National Labor Party or PTN)
Popular Socialist Party or PPS [Roberto Joao Pereira FREIRE]
Progressive Party or PP [Ciro NOGUEIRA]
Progressive Republican Party or PRP [Ovasco Roma Altimari RESENDE]
Republican Social Order Party or PROS [Euripedes JUNIOR]
Social Christian Party or PSC [Vitor Jorge Abdala NOSSEIS]
Social Democratic Party or PSD [Guilherme CAMPOS]
Social Liberal Party or PSL [Luciano Caldas BIVAR]
Socialism and Freedom Party or PSOL [Luiz ARAUJO]
Solidarity or SD [Paulo PEREIRA DA SILVA]
Sustainability Network or REDE [Marina SILVA]
United Socialist Workers' Party or PSTU [Jose Maria DE ALMEIDA]
Workers' Cause Party or PCO [Rui Costa PIMENTA]
Workers' Party or PT [Rui FALCAO]

INTERNATIONAL ORGANIZATION PARTICIPATION:

AfDB (nonregional member), BIS, BRICS, CAN (associate), CD, CELAC, CPLP, FAO, FATF, G-15, G-20, G-24, G-5, G-77, IADB, IAEA, IBRD, ICAO, ICC (national committees), ICCt, ICRM, IDA, IFAD, IFC, IFRCS, IHO, ILO, IMF, IMO, IMSO, Interpol, IOC, IOM, IPU, ISO, ITSO, ITU, ITUC (NGOs), LAES, LAIA, LAS (observer), Mercosur, MIGA, MINURSO, MINUSTAH, MONUSCO, NAM (observer), NSG, OAS, OECD (enhanced engagement), OPANAL, OPCW, Paris Club (associate), PCA, SICA (observer), UN, UNASUR, UNCTAD, UNESCO, UNFICYP, UNHCR, UNIDO, UNIFIL, Union Latina, UNISFA, UNITAR, UNMIL, UNMISS, UNOCI, UNRWA, UNWTO, UPU, WCO, WFTU (NGOs), WHO, WIPO, WMO, WTO

DIPLOMATIC REPRESENTATION IN THE US:

chief of mission: Ambassador Sergio Silva do AMARAL (since 16 September 2016)

chancery: 3006 Massachusetts Avenue NW, Washington, DC 20008

telephone: [1] (202) 238-2700

FAX: [1] (202) 238-2827

consulate(s) general: Atlanta, Boston, Chicago, Hartford (CT), Houston, Los Angeles, Miami, New York, San Francisco, Washington, DC

DIPLOMATIC REPRESENTATION FROM THE US:

chief of mission: Ambassador Michael MCKINLEY (since 19 December 2016)

embassy: Avenida das Nacoes, Quadra 801, Lote 3, Distrito Federal Cep 70403-900, Brasilia

mailing address: Unit 7500, DPO, AA 34030

telephone: [55] (61) 3312-7000

FAX: [55] (61) 3225-9136

consulate(s) general: Recife, Rio de Janeiro, Sao Paulo

FLAG DESCRIPTION:

green with a large yellow diamond in the center bearing a blue celestial globe with 27 white five-pointed stars; the globe has a white equatorial band with the motto ORDEM E PROGRESSO (Order and Progress); the current flag was inspired by the banner of the former Empire of Brazil (1822-1889); on the imperial flag, the green represented the House of Braganza of Pedro I, the first Emperor of Brazil, while the yellow stood for the Habsburg Family of his wife; on the modern flag the green represents the forests of the country and the yellow rhombus its mineral wealth (the diamond shape roughly mirrors that of the country); the blue circle and stars, which replaced the coat of arms of the original flag, depict the sky over Rio de Janeiro on the morning of 15 November 1889 - the day the Republic of Brazil was declared; the number of stars has changed with the creation of new states and has risen from an original 21 to the current 27 (one for each state and the Federal District)

note: one of several flags where a prominent component of the design reflects the shape of the country; other such flags are those of Bosnia and Herzegovina, Eritrea, and Vanuatu

NATIONAL SYMBOL(S):

Southern Cross constellation; national colors: green, yellow, blue

NATIONAL ANTHEM:

name: "Hino Nacional Brasileiro" (Brazilian National Anthem)

lyrics/music: Joaquim Osorio Duque ESTRADA/Francisco Manoel DA SILVA

note: music adopted 1890, lyrics adopted 1922; the anthem's music, composed in 1822, was used unofficially for many years before it was adopted

ECONOMY :: BRAZIL

ECONOMY - OVERVIEW:

Brazil is the eighth-largest economy in the world, but is recovering from a recession in 2015 and 2016 that ranks as the worst in the country's history. In 2017, Brazil's GDP grew 1%, inflation fell to historic lows of 2.9%, and the Central Bank lowered benchmark interest rates from 13.75% in 2016 to 7%.

The economy has been negatively affected by multiple corruption scandals involving private companies and government officials, including the impeachment and conviction of Former President Dilma ROUSSEFF in August 2016. Sanctions against the firms involved — some of the largest in Brazil — have limited their business opportunities, producing a ripple effect on associated businesses and contractors but creating opportunities for foreign companies to step into what had been a closed market.

The succeeding TEMER administration has implemented a series of fiscal and structural reforms to restore credibility to government finances. Congress approved legislation in December 2016 to cap public spending. Government spending growth had pushed public debt to 73.7% of GDP at the end of 2017, up from over 50% in 2012. The government also boosted infrastructure projects, such as oil and natural gas auctions, in part to raise revenues. Other economic reforms, proposed in 2016, aim to reduce barriers to foreign investment, and to improve labor conditions. Policies to strengthen Brazil's workforce and industrial sector, such as local content requirements, have boosted employment, but at the expense of investment.

Brazil is a member of the Common Market of the South (Mercosur), a trade bloc that includes Argentina, Paraguay and Uruguay - Venezuela's membership in the organization was suspended In August 2017. After the Asian and Russian financial crises, Mercosur adopted a protectionist stance to guard against exposure to volatile foreign markets and it currently is negotiating Free Trade Agreements with the European Union and Canada.

GDP (PURCHASING POWER PARITY):

$3.248 trillion (2017 est.)

$3.216 trillion (2016 est.)

$3.332 trillion (2015 est.)

note: data are in 2017 dollars

country comparison to the world: 8

GDP (OFFICIAL EXCHANGE RATE):

$2.055 trillion (2017 est.) (2017 est.)

GDP - REAL GROWTH RATE:

1% (2017 est.)

-3.5% (2016 est.)

-3.5% (2015 est.)

country comparison to the world: 182

GDP - PER CAPITA (PPP):

$15,600 (2017 est.)

$15,600 (2016 est.)

$16,300 (2015 est.)

note: data are in 2017 dollars

country comparison to the world: 108

GROSS NATIONAL SAVING:

15% of GDP (2017 est.)

14.1% of GDP (2016 est.)

14.1% of GDP (2015 est.)

country comparison to the world: 136

GDP - COMPOSITION, BY END USE:

household consumption: 63.4% (2017 est.)

government consumption: 20% (2017 est.)

investment in fixed capital: 15.6% (2017 est.)

investment in inventories: -0.1% (2017 est.)

exports of goods and services: 12.6% (2017 est.)

imports of goods and services: -11.6% (2017 est.)

GDP - COMPOSITION, BY SECTOR OF ORIGIN:

agriculture: 6.6% (2017 est.)

industry: 20.7% (2017 est.)

services: 72.7% (2017 est.)

AGRICULTURE - PRODUCTS:

coffee, soybeans, wheat, rice, corn, sugarcane, cocoa, citrus; beef

INDUSTRIES:

textiles, shoes, chemicals, cement, lumber, iron ore, tin, steel, aircraft, motor vehicles and parts, other machinery and equipment

INDUSTRIAL PRODUCTION GROWTH RATE:

0% (2017 est.)

country comparison to the world: 169

LABOR FORCE:

104.2 million (2017)

country comparison to the world: 5

LABOR FORCE - BY OCCUPATION:

agriculture: 9.4%

industry: 32.1%

services: 58.5% (2017 est.)

UNEMPLOYMENT RATE:

12.8% (2017 est.)

11.3% (2016 est.)

country comparison to the world: 165

POPULATION BELOW POVERTY LINE:

4.2% (2016 est.)

note: approximately 4% of the population are below the "extreme" poverty line

HOUSEHOLD INCOME OR CONSUMPTION BY PERCENTAGE SHARE:

lowest 10%: 43.4% (2016 est.)

highest 10%: 43.4% (2016 est.)

DISTRIBUTION OF FAMILY INCOME - GINI INDEX:

49 (2014)

54 (2004)

country comparison to the world: 19

BUDGET:

revenues: 733.7 billion (2017 est.)

expenditures: 756.3 billion (2017 est.)

TAXES AND OTHER REVENUES:

35.7% (of GDP) (2017 est.)

country comparison to the world: 57

BUDGET SURPLUS (+) OR DEFICIT (-):

-1.1% (of GDP) (2017 est.)

country comparison to the world: 82

PUBLIC DEBT:

84% of GDP (2017 est.)

78.4% of GDP (2016 est.)

country comparison to the world: 32

FISCAL YEAR:

calendar year

INFLATION RATE (CONSUMER PRICES):

3.4% (2017 est.)

8.7% (2016 est.)

country comparison to the world: 139

CENTRAL BANK DISCOUNT RATE:

7% (31 December 2017 est.)

13.75% (31 December 2016)

country comparison to the world: 48

COMMERCIAL BANK PRIME LENDING RATE:

46.92% (31 December 2017 est.)

52.1% (31 December 2016 est.)

country comparison to the world: 2

STOCK OF NARROW MONEY:

$110.3 billion (31 December 2017 est.)

$106.7 billion (31 December 2016 est.)

country comparison to the world: 35

STOCK OF BROAD MONEY:

$110.3 billion (31 December 2017 est.)

$106.7 billion (31 December 2016 est.)

country comparison to the world: 35

STOCK OF DOMESTIC CREDIT:

$2.206 trillion (31 December 2017 est.)

$2.138 trillion (31 December 2016 est.)

country comparison to the world: 12

MARKET VALUE OF PUBLICLY TRADED SHARES:

$642.5 billion (31 December 2017 est.)

$561.1 billion (31 December 2014 est.)

$420 billion (31 December 2013 est.)

country comparison to the world: 18

CURRENT ACCOUNT BALANCE:

-$9.762 billion (2017 est.)

-$23.55 billion (2016 est.)

country comparison to the world: 190

EXPORTS:

$217.2 billion (2017 est.)

$184.5 billion (2016 est.)

country comparison to the world: 26

EXPORTS - PARTNERS:

China 21.8%, US 12.5%, Argentina 8.1%, Netherlands 4.3% (2017)

EXPORTS - COMMODITIES:

transport equipment, iron ore, soybeans, footwear, coffee, automobiles

IMPORTS:

$153.2 billion (2017 est.)

$139.4 billion (2016 est.)

country comparison to the world: 29

IMPORTS - COMMODITIES:

machinery, electrical and transport equipment, chemical products, oil, automotive parts, electronics

IMPORTS - PARTNERS:

China 18.1%, US 16.7%, Argentina 6.3%, Germany 6.1% (2017)

RESERVES OF FOREIGN EXCHANGE AND GOLD:

$374 billion (31 December 2017 est.)

$367.5 billion (31 December 2016 est.)

country comparison to the world: 10

DEBT - EXTERNAL:

$547.4 billion (31 December 2017 est.)

$548.6 billion (31 December 2016 est.)

country comparison to the world: 21

STOCK OF DIRECT FOREIGN INVESTMENT - AT HOME:

$778.3 billion (31 December 2017 est.)

$703.3 billion (31 December 2016 est.)

country comparison to the world: 14

STOCK OF DIRECT FOREIGN INVESTMENT - ABROAD:

$358.9 billion (31 December 2017 est.)

$341.5 billion (31 December 2016 est.)

country comparison to the world: 19

EXCHANGE RATES:

reals (BRL) per US dollar -

3.19 (2017 est.)

3.48 (2016 est.)

3.4901 (2015 est.)

3.3315 (2014 est.)

2.3535 (2013 est.)

ENERGY :: BRAZIL

ELECTRICITY ACCESS:

population without electricity: 800,000 (2013)

electrification - total population: 99.5% (2013)

electrification - urban areas: 100% (2013)

electrification - rural areas: 97% (2013)

ELECTRICITY - PRODUCTION:

567.9 billion kWh (2016 est.)

country comparison to the world: 8

ELECTRICITY - CONSUMPTION:

509.1 billion kWh (2016 est.)

country comparison to the world: 8

ELECTRICITY - EXPORTS:

219 million kWh (2015 est.)

country comparison to the world: 73

ELECTRICITY - IMPORTS:

41.31 billion kWh (2016 est.)

country comparison to the world: 3

ELECTRICITY - INSTALLED GENERATING CAPACITY:

150.8 million kW (2016 est.)

country comparison to the world: 7

ELECTRICITY - FROM FOSSIL FUELS:

17% of total installed capacity (2016 est.)

country comparison to the world: 197

ELECTRICITY - FROM NUCLEAR FUELS:

1% of total installed capacity (2017 est.)

country comparison to the world: 28

ELECTRICITY - FROM HYDROELECTRIC PLANTS:

64% of total installed capacity (2017 est.)

country comparison to the world: 24

ELECTRICITY - FROM OTHER RENEWABLE SOURCES:

18% of total installed capacity (2017 est.)

country comparison to the world: 46

CRUDE OIL - PRODUCTION:

2.622 million bbl/day (2017 est.)

country comparison to the world: 10

CRUDE OIL - EXPORTS:

736,600 bbl/day (2015 est.)

country comparison to the world: 17

CRUDE OIL - IMPORTS:

297,700 bbl/day (2015 est.)

country comparison to the world: 25

CRUDE OIL - PROVED RESERVES:

12.63 billion bbl (1 January 2018 est.)

country comparison to the world: 14

REFINED PETROLEUM PRODUCTS - PRODUCTION:

2.811 million bbl/day (2015 est.)

country comparison to the world: 7

REFINED PETROLEUM PRODUCTS - CONSUMPTION:

2.956 million bbl/day (2016 est.)

country comparison to the world: 7

REFINED PETROLEUM PRODUCTS - EXPORTS:

279,000 bbl/day (2015 est.)

country comparison to the world: 28

REFINED PETROLEUM PRODUCTS - IMPORTS:

490,400 bbl/day (2015 est.)

country comparison to the world: 17

NATURAL GAS - PRODUCTION:

23.96 billion cu m (2017 est.)

country comparison to the world: 29

NATURAL GAS - CONSUMPTION:

34.35 billion cu m (2017 est.)

country comparison to the world: 28

NATURAL GAS - EXPORTS:

134.5 million cu m (2017 est.)

country comparison to the world: 48

NATURAL GAS - IMPORTS:

10.51 billion cu m (2017 est.)

country comparison to the world: 26

NATURAL GAS - PROVED RESERVES:

377.4 billion cu m (1 January 2018 est.)

country comparison to the world: 34

CARBON DIOXIDE EMISSIONS FROM CONSUMPTION OF ENERGY:

513.8 million Mt (2017 est.)

country comparison to the world: 13

COMMUNICATIONS :: BRAZIL

TELEPHONES - FIXED LINES:

total subscriptions: 40,878,018 (2017 est.)

subscriptions per 100 inhabitants: 20 (2017 est.)

country comparison to the world: 5

TELEPHONES - MOBILE CELLULAR:

total subscriptions: 236,488,548 (2017 est.)

subscriptions per 100 inhabitants: 114 (2017 est.)

country comparison to the world: 5

TELEPHONE SYSTEM:

general assessment: good working system including an extensive microwave radio relay system and a domestic satellite system with 64 earth stations; four major mobile operators offering a range of voice and data services; one of the largest broadband markets in Latin America, broadband penetration only behind Chile, Argentina, and Uruguay; country is a pioneer in the region for m-commerce (electronic commerce conducted on mobile phones) (2017)

domestic: fixed-line connections have remained relatively stable in recent years and stand at about 20 per 100 persons; less-expensive mobile-cellular technology has been a major impetus broadening telephone service to the lower-income segments of the population with mobile-cellular teledensity roughly 114 per 100 persons (2017)

international: country code - 55; landing point for a number of submarine cables, including Americas-1, Americas-2, Atlantis-2, GlobeNet, South America-1, South American Crossing/Latin American Nautilus, and UNISUR that provide direct connectivity to South and Central America, the Caribbean, the US, Africa, and Europe; satellite earth stations - 3 Intelsat (Atlantic Ocean), 1 Inmarsat (Atlantic Ocean region east), connected by microwave relay system to Mercosur Brazilsat B3 satellite earth station; Brazil is connected through submarine cables to the USA, Central and South America, and the Caribbean; satellites is a major communication platform, as it is almost impossible to lay fibre optic cable in the thick vegetation (2017)

BROADCAST MEDIA:

state-run Radiobras operates a radio and a TV network; more than 1,000 radio stations and more than 100 TV channels operating - mostly privately owned; private media ownership highly concentrated (2007)

INTERNET COUNTRY CODE:

.br

INTERNET USERS:

total: 122,841,218 (July 2016 est.)

percent of population: 59.7% (July 2016 est.)

country comparison to the world: 4

BROADBAND - FIXED SUBSCRIPTIONS:

total: 28,670,016 (2017 est.)

subscriptions per 100 inhabitants: 14 (2017 est.)

country comparison to the world: 6

TRANSPORTATION :: BRAZIL

NATIONAL AIR TRANSPORT SYSTEM:

number of registered air carriers: 9 (2015)

inventory of registered aircraft operated by air carriers: 443 (2015)

annual passenger traffic on registered air carriers: 102,039,359 (2015)

annual freight traffic on registered air carriers: 149.393 million mt-km (2015)

CIVIL AIRCRAFT REGISTRATION COUNTRY CODE PREFIX:

PP (2016)

AIRPORTS:

4,093 (2013)

country comparison to the world: 2

AIRPORTS - WITH PAVED RUNWAYS:

total: 698 (2017)

over 3,047 m: 7 (2017)

2,438 to 3,047 m: 27 (2017)

1,524 to 2,437 m: 179 (2017)

914 to 1,523 m: 436 (2017)

under 914 m: 49 (2017)

AIRPORTS - WITH UNPAVED RUNWAYS:

total: 3,395 (2013)

1,524 to 2,437 m: 92 (2013)

914 to 1,523 m: 1,619 (2013)

under 914 m: 1,684 (2013)

HELIPORTS:

13 (2013)

PIPELINES:

5959 km refined petroleum product (1,165 km distribution, 4,794 km transport), 11696 km natural gas (2,274 km distribution, 9,422 km transport), 1985 km crude oil (distribution), 77 km ethanol/petrochemical (37 km distribution, 40 km transport) (2016)

RAILWAYS:

total: 29,850 km (2014)

standard gauge: 194 km 1.435-m gauge (2014)

narrow gauge: 23,341.6 km 1.000-m gauge (24 km electrified) (2014)

broad gauge: 5,822.3 km 1.600-m gauge (498.3 km electrified) (2014)

dual gauge: 492 km 1.600-1.000-m gauge (2014)

country comparison to the world: 9

ROADWAYS:

total: 1,580,964 km (2010)

paved: 212,798 km (2010)

unpaved: 1,368,166 km (2010)

note: does not include urban roads

country comparison to the world: 4

WATERWAYS:

50,000 km (most in areas remote from industry and population) (2012)

country comparison to the world: 3

MERCHANT MARINE:

total: 775 (2017)

by type: bulk carrier 20, container ship 18, general cargo 48, oil tanker 38, other 651 (2017)

country comparison to the world: 28

PORTS AND TERMINALS:

major seaport(s): Belem, Paranagua, Rio Grande, Rio de Janeiro, Santos, Sao Sebastiao, Tubarao

oil terminal(s): DTSE/Gegua oil terminal, Ilha Grande (Gebig), Guaiba Island terminal, Guamare oil terminal

container port(s) (TEUs): Santos (3,393,593) (2016)

LNG terminal(s) (import): Pecem, Rio de Janiero

river port(s): Manaus (Amazon)

dry bulk cargo port(s): Sepetiba ore terminal, Tubarao

MILITARY AND SECURITY :: BRAZIL

MILITARY EXPENDITURES:

1.32% of GDP (2016)

1.36% of GDP (2015)

1.33% of GDP (2014)

country comparison to the world: 87

MILITARY BRANCHES:

Brazilian Army (Exercito Brasileiro, EB), Brazilian Navy (Marinha do Brasil, MB, includes Naval Air and Marine Corps (Corpo de Fuzileiros Navais)), Brazilian Air Force (Forca Aerea Brasileira, FAB) (2011)

MILITARY SERVICE AGE AND OBLIGATION:

18-45 years of age for compulsory military service; conscript service obligation is 10-12 months; 17-45 years of age for voluntary service; an increasing percentage of the ranks are "long-service" volunteer professionals; women were allowed to serve in the armed forces beginning in early 1980s, when the Brazilian Army became the first army in South America to accept women into career ranks; women serve in Navy and Air Force only in Women's Reserve Corps (2012)

TRANSNATIONAL ISSUES :: BRAZIL

DISPUTES - INTERNATIONAL:

uncontested boundary dispute between Brazil and Uruguay over Braziliera/Brasiliera Island in the Quarai/Cuareim River leaves the tripoint with Argentina in questionsmuggling of firearms and narcotics continues to be an issue along the Uruguay-Brazil borderColombian-organized illegal narcotics and paramilitary activities penetrate Brazil's border region with Venezuela

REFUGEES AND INTERNALLY DISPLACED PERSONS:

refugees (country of origin): 84,746 (Venezuela) (economic and political crisis; includes Venezuelans who have claimed asylum or have received alternative legal stay) (2018)

stateless persons: 294 (2017)

ILLICIT DRUGS:

second-largest consumer of cocaine in the world; illicit producer of cannabis; trace amounts of coca cultivation in the Amazon region, used for domestic consumption; government has a large-scale eradication program to control cannabis; important transshipment country for Bolivian, Colombian, and Peruvian cocaine headed for Europe; also used by traffickers as a way station for narcotics air transshipments between Peru and Colombia; upsurge in drug-related violence and weapons smuggling; important market for Colombian, Bolivian, and Peruvian cocaine; illicit narcotics proceeds are often laundered through the financial system; significant illicit financial activity in the Tri-Border Area

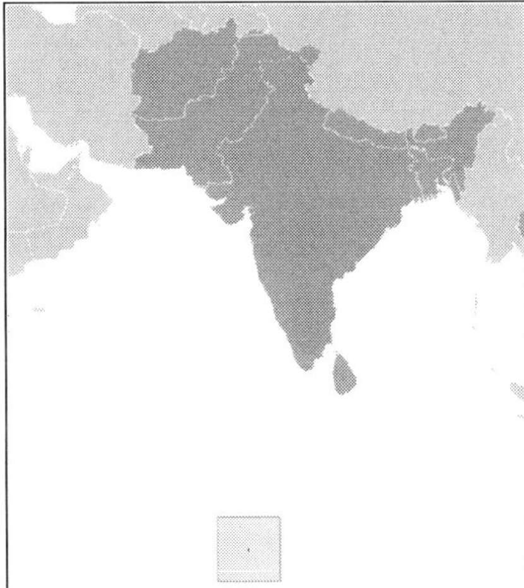

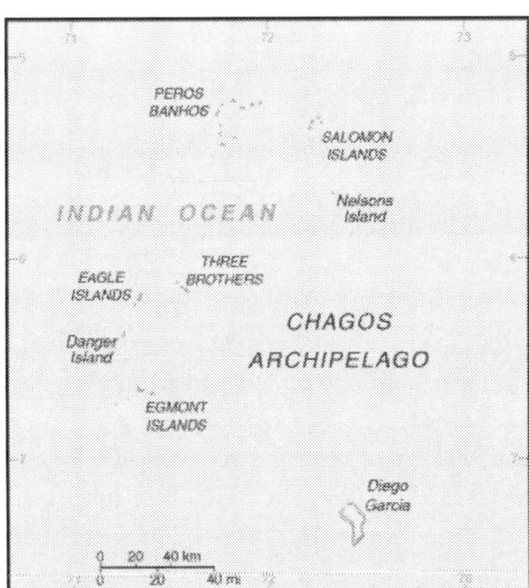

INTRODUCTION :: BRITISH INDIAN OCEAN TERRITORY

BACKGROUND:

Formerly administered as part of the British Crown Colony of Mauritius, the British Indian Ocean Territory (BIOT) was established as an overseas territory of the UK in 1965. A number of the islands of the territory were later transferred to the Seychelles when it attained independence in 1976. Subsequently, BIOT has consisted only of the six main island groups comprising the Chagos Archipelago. Only Diego Garcia, the largest and most southerly of the islands, is inhabited. It contains a joint UK-US naval support facility and hosts one of four dedicated ground antennas that assist in the operation of the Global Positioning System (GPS) navigation system (the others are on Kwajalein (Marshall Islands), at Cape Canaveral, Florida (US), and on Ascension Island (Saint Helena, Ascension, and Tristan da Cunha)). The US Air Force also operates a telescope array on Diego Garcia as part of the Ground-Based Electro-Optical Deep Space Surveillance System (GEODSS) for tracking orbital debris, which can be a hazard to spacecraft and astronauts.

Between 1967 and 1973, former agricultural workers, earlier residents in the islands, were relocated primarily to Mauritius, but also to the Seychelles. Negotiations between 1971 and 1982 resulted in the establishment of a trust fund by the British Government as compensation for the displaced islanders, known as Chagossians. Beginning in 1998, the islanders pursued a series of lawsuits against the British Government seeking further compensation and the right to return to the territory. In 2006 and 2007, British court rulings invalidated the immigration policies contained in the 2004 BIOT Constitution Order that had excluded the islanders from the archipelago, but upheld the special military status of Diego Garcia. In 2008, the House of Lords, as the final court of appeal in the UK, ruled in favor of the British Government by overturning the lower court rulings and finding no right of return for the Chagossians. In March 2015, the Permanent Court of Arbitration unanimously held that the marine protected area (MPA) that the UK declared around the Chagos Archipelago in April 2010 was in violation of the UN Convention on the Law of the Sea

GEOGRAPHY :: BRITISH INDIAN OCEAN TERRITORY

LOCATION:

archipelago in the Indian Ocean, south of India, about halfway between Africa and Indonesia

GEOGRAPHIC COORDINATES:

6 00 S, 71 30 E;note - Diego Garcia 7 20 S, 72 25 E

MAP REFERENCES:

Political Map of the World

AREA:

total: 60 sq km

land: 60 sq km (44 Diego Garcia)

water: 54,340 sq km

note: includes the entire Chagos Archipelago of 55 islands

country comparison to the world: 230

AREA - COMPARATIVE:

land area is about one-third the size of Washington, DC

LAND BOUNDARIES:

0 km

COASTLINE:

698 km

MARITIME CLAIMS:

territorial sea: 12 nm

Environment (Protection and Preservation) Zone: 200 nm

CLIMATE:

tropical marine; hot, humid, moderated by trade winds

TERRAIN:

flat and low (most areas do not exceed two m in elevation)

ELEVATION:

0 m lowest point: Indian Ocean

9 highest point: ocean-side dunes on Diego Garcia

NATURAL RESOURCES:

coconuts, fish, sugarcane

LAND USE:

agricultural land: 0% (2011 est.)

arable land: 0% (2011 est.) / permanent crops: 0% (2011 est.) / permanent pasture: 0% (2011 est.)

forest: 0% (2011 est.)

other: 100% (2011 est.)

NATURAL HAZARDS:

none; located outside routes of Indian Ocean cyclones

ENVIRONMENT - CURRENT ISSUES:

wastewater discharge into the lagoon on Diego Garcia

GEOGRAPHY - NOTE:

note 1: archipelago of 55 islands; Diego Garcia, the largest and southernmost island, occupies a strategic location in the central Indian Ocean; the island is the site of a joint US-UK military facility

note 2: Diego Garcia is the only inhabited island of the BIOT and one of only two British territories where traffic drives on the right, the other being Gibraltar

PEOPLE AND SOCIETY :: BRITISH INDIAN OCEAN TERRITORY

POPULATION:

no indigenous inhabitants

note: approximately 1,200 former agricultural workers resident in the Chagos Archipelago, often referred to as Chagossians or Ilois, were relocated to Mauritius and the Seychelles in the 1960s and 1970s; approximately 3,000 UK and US military personnel and civilian contractors living on the island of Diego Garcia (2018)

GOVERNMENT :: BRITISH INDIAN OCEAN TERRITORY

COUNTRY NAME:

conventional long form: British Indian Ocean Territory

conventional short form: none

abbreviation: BIOT

etymology: self-descriptive name specifying the territory's affiliation and location

DEPENDENCY STATUS:

overseas territory of the UK; administered by a commissioner, resident in the Foreign and Commonwealth Office in London

LEGAL SYSTEM:

the laws of the UK, where applicable, apply

EXECUTIVE BRANCH:

chief of state: Queen ELIZABETH II (since 6 February 1952)

head of government: Commissioner Dr. Peter HAYES (since 17 October 2012); Administrator John MCMANUS (since April 2011); note - both reside in the UK and are represented by the officer commanding British Forces on Diego Garcia

cabinet: NA

elections/appointments: the monarchy is hereditary; commissioner and administrator appointed by the monarch

INTERNATIONAL ORGANIZATION PARTICIPATION:

UPU

DIPLOMATIC REPRESENTATION IN THE US:

none (overseas territory of the UK)

DIPLOMATIC REPRESENTATION FROM THE US:

none (overseas territory of the UK)

FLAG DESCRIPTION:

white with six blue wavy horizontal stripes; the flag of the UK is in the upper hoist-side quadrant; the striped section bears a palm tree and yellow crown (the symbols of the territory) centered on the outer half of the flag; the wavy stripes represent the Indian Ocean; although not officially described, the six blue stripes may stand for the six main atolls of the archipelago

ECONOMY :: BRITISH INDIAN OCEAN TERRITORY

ECONOMY - OVERVIEW:

All economic activity is concentrated on the largest island of Diego Garcia, where a joint UK-US military facility is located. Construction projects and various services needed to support the military installation are performed by military and contract employees from the UK, Mauritius, the Philippines, and the US. Some of the natural resources found in this territory include coconuts, fish, and sugarcane.

EXCHANGE RATES:

the US dollar is used

COMMUNICATIONS :: BRITISH INDIAN OCEAN TERRITORY

TELEPHONE SYSTEM:

general assessment: separate facilities for military and public needs are available (2015)

domestic: all commercial telephone services are available, including connection to the Internet (2015)

international: country code (Diego Garcia) - 246; international telephone service is carried by satellite (2015)

BROADCAST MEDIA:

Armed Forces Radio and Television Service (AFRTS) broadcasts over 3 separate frequencies for US and UK military personnel stationed on the islands (2009)

INTERNET COUNTRY CODE:

.io

COMMUNICATIONS - NOTE:

Diego Garcia hosts one of four dedicated ground antennas that assist in the operation of the Global Positioning System (GPS) navigation system (the others are on Kwajalein (Marshall Islands), at Cape Canaveral, Florida (US), and on Ascension Island (Saint Helena, Ascension, and Tristan da Cunha))

TRANSPORTATION :: BRITISH INDIAN OCEAN TERRITORY

AIRPORTS:

1 (2013)

country comparison to the world: 215

AIRPORTS - WITH PAVED RUNWAYS:

total: 1 (2017)

over 3,047 m: 1 (2017)

ROADWAYS:

note: short section of paved road between port and airfield on Diego Garcia

PORTS AND TERMINALS:

major seaport(s): Diego Garcia

MILITARY AND SECURITY :: BRITISH INDIAN OCEAN TERRITORY

MILITARY BRANCHES:

no regular military forces (2014)

MILITARY - NOTE:

defense is the responsibility of the UK; in November 2016, the UK extended the US lease on Diego Garcia for 20 years; the lease now expires in December 2036

TRANSNATIONAL ISSUES :: BRITISH INDIAN OCEAN TERRITORY

DISPUTES - INTERNATIONAL:

Mauritius and Seychelles claim the Chagos Islandsnegotiations between 1971 and 1982 resulted in the establishment of a trust fund by the British Government as compensation for the displaced islanders, known as Chagossians, who were evicted between 1967-73; in 2001, the former inhabitants of the archipelago were granted UK citizenship and the right of return; in 2006 and 2007, British court rulings invalidated the immigration policies contained in the 2004 BIOT Constitution Order that had excluded the islanders from the archipelago; in 2008 a House of Lords' decision overturned lower court rulings, once again denying the right of return to Chagossiansin addition, the UK created the world's largest marine protection area around the Chagos islands prohibiting the extraction of any natural resources therein

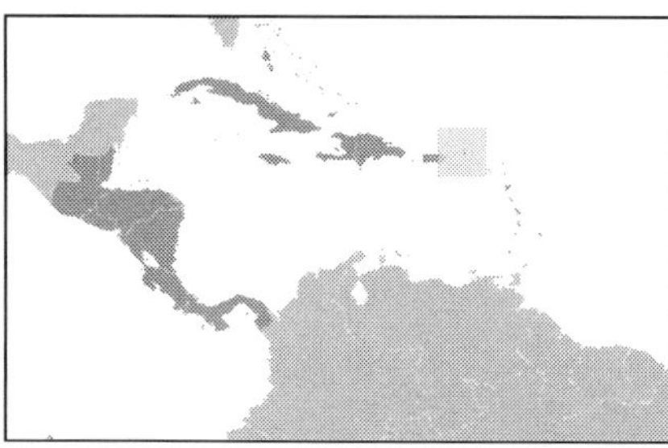

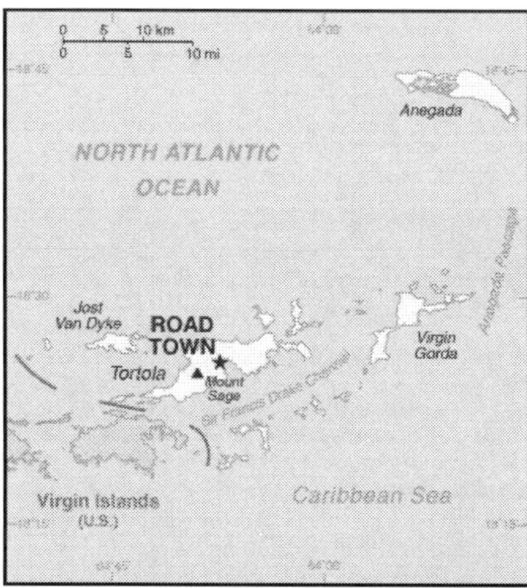

CENTRAL AMERICA :: BRITISH VIRGIN ISLANDS

INTRODUCTION :: BRITISH VIRGIN ISLANDS

BACKGROUND:

First inhabited by Arawak and later by Carib Indians, the Virgin Islands were settled by the Dutch in 1648 and then annexed by the English in 1672. The islands were part of the British colony of the Leeward Islands from 1872-1960; they were granted autonomy in 1967. The economy is closely tied to the larger and more populous US Virgin Islands to the west; the US dollar is the legal currency. On 6 September 2017, Hurricane Irma devastated the island of Tortola. An estimated 80% of residential and business structures were destroyed or damaged, communications disrupted, and local roads rendered impassable.

GEOGRAPHY :: BRITISH VIRGIN ISLANDS

LOCATION:

Caribbean, between the Caribbean Sea and the North Atlantic Ocean, east of Puerto Rico

GEOGRAPHIC COORDINATES:

18 30 N, 64 30 W

MAP REFERENCES:

Central America and the Caribbean

AREA:

total: 151 sq km

land: 151 sq km

water: 0 sq km

note: comprised of 16 inhabited and more than 20 uninhabited islands; includes the islands of Tortola, Anegada, Virgin Gorda, Jost van Dyke

country comparison to the world: 220

AREA - COMPARATIVE:

about 0.9 times the size of Washington, DC

LAND BOUNDARIES:

0 km

COASTLINE:

80 km

MARITIME CLAIMS:

territorial sea: 3 nm

exclusive fishing zone: 200 nm

CLIMATE:

subtropical; humid; temperatures moderated by trade winds

TERRAIN:

coral islands relatively flat; volcanic islands steep, hilly

ELEVATION:

0 m lowest point: Caribbean Sea

521 highest point: Mount Sage

NATURAL RESOURCES:

NEGL; pleasant climate, beaches foster tourism

LAND USE:

agricultural land: 46.7% (2011 est.)

arable land: 6.7% (2011 est.) / permanent crops: 6.7% (2011 est.) / permanent pasture: 33.3% (2011 est.)

forest: 24.3% (2011 est.)

other: 29% (2011 est.)

IRRIGATED LAND:

NA

POPULATION DISTRIBUTION:

a fairly even distribution throughout the inhabited islands, with the largest islands of Tortola, Anegada, Virgin Gorda, and Jost Van Dyke having the largest populations

NATURAL HAZARDS:

hurricanes and tropical storms (July to October)

ENVIRONMENT - CURRENT ISSUES:

limited natural freshwater resources except for a few seasonal streams and springs on Tortola; most of the islands' water supply comes from desalination plants; sewage and mining/industry waste contribute to water pollution, threatening coral reefs

GEOGRAPHY - NOTE:

strong ties to nearby US Virgin Islands and Puerto Rico

PEOPLE AND SOCIETY :: BRITISH VIRGIN ISLANDS

POPULATION:

35,802 (July 2018 est.)

country comparison to the world: 214

NATIONALITY:

noun: British Virgin Islander(s)

adjective: British Virgin Islander

ETHNIC GROUPS:

African/black 76.3%, Latino 5.5%, white 5.4%, mixed 5.3%, Indian 2.1%, East Indian 1.6%, other 3%, unspecified 0.8% (2010 est.)

LANGUAGES:

English (official)

RELIGIONS:

Protestant 70.2% (Methodist 17.6%, Church of God 10.4%, Anglican 9.5%, Seventh Day Adventist 9.0%,

Pentecostal 8.2%, Baptist 7.4%, New Testament Church of God 6.9%, other Protestant 1.2%), Roman Catholic 8.9%, Jehovah's Witness 2.5%, Hindu 1.9%, other 6.2%, none 7.9%, unspecified 2.4% (2010 est.)

AGE STRUCTURE:

0-14 years: 16.72% (male 2,949 /female 3,036)

15-24 years: 12.98% (male 2,223 /female 2,425)

25-54 years: 49.05% (male 8,230 /female 9,330)

55-64 years: 11.93% (male 2,073 /female 2,199)

65 years and over: 9.32% (male 1,611 /female 1,726) (2018 est.)

MEDIAN AGE:

total: 36.7 years

male: 36.5 years

female: 36.9 years (2018 est.)

country comparison to the world: 72

POPULATION GROWTH RATE:

2.2% (2018 est.)

country comparison to the world: 36

BIRTH RATE:

11.1 births/1,000 population (2018 est.)

country comparison to the world: 176

DEATH RATE:

5.2 deaths/1,000 population (2018 est.)

country comparison to the world: 188

NET MIGRATION RATE:

16.5 migrant(s)/1,000 population (2017 est.)

country comparison to the world: 1

POPULATION DISTRIBUTION:

a fairly even distribution throughout the inhabited islands, with the largest islands of Tortola, Anegada, Virgin Gorda, and Jost Van Dyke having the largest populations

URBANIZATION:

urban population: 47.7% of total population (2018)

rate of urbanization: 2.42% annual rate of change (2015-20 est.)

MAJOR URBAN AREAS - POPULATION:

15,000 ROAD TOWN (capital) (2018)

SEX RATIO:

at birth: 1.03 male(s)/female (2017 est.)

0-14 years: 0.97 male(s)/female (2017 est.)

15-24 years: 0.92 male(s)/female (2017 est.)

25-54 years: 0.89 male(s)/female (2017 est.)

55-64 years: 0.95 male(s)/female (2017 est.)

65 years and over: 0.95 male(s)/female (2017 est.)

total population: 0.92 male(s)/female (2017 est.)

INFANT MORTALITY RATE:

total: 11.7 deaths/1,000 live births (2018 est.)

male: 13.4 deaths/1,000 live births (2018 est.)

female: 10 deaths/1,000 live births (2018 est.)

country comparison to the world: 120

LIFE EXPECTANCY AT BIRTH:

total population: 78.9 years (2018 est.)

male: 77.5 years (2018 est.)

female: 80.4 years (2018 est.)

country comparison to the world: 54

TOTAL FERTILITY RATE:

1.3 children born/woman (2018 est.)

country comparison to the world: 218

DRINKING WATER SOURCE:

improved:

urban: 98% of population (2010 est.)

rural: 98% of population (2010 est.)

total: 98% of population (2010 est.)

unimproved:

urban: 2% of population (2010 est.)

rural: 2% of population (2010 est.)

total: 2% of population (2010 est.)

SANITATION FACILITY ACCESS:

improved:

urban: 97.5% of population (2015 est.)

rural: 97.5% of population (2015 est.)

total: 97.5% of population (2015 est.)

unimproved:

urban: 2.5% of population (2015 est.)

rural: 2.5% of population (2015 est.)

total: 2.5% of population (2015 est.)

HIV/AIDS - ADULT PREVALENCE RATE:

NA

HIV/AIDS - PEOPLE LIVING WITH HIV/AIDS:

NA

HIV/AIDS - DEATHS:

NA

EDUCATION EXPENDITURES:

6.3% of GDP (2015)

country comparison to the world: 28

SCHOOL LIFE EXPECTANCY (PRIMARY TO TERTIARY EDUCATION):

total: 14 years (2015)

male: NA (2015)

female: NA (2015)

GOVERNMENT :: BRITISH VIRGIN ISLANDS

COUNTRY NAME:

conventional long form: none

conventional short form: British Virgin Islands

abbreviation: BVI

etymology: the myriad islets, cays, and rocks surrounding the major islands reminded explorer Christopher COLUMBUS in 1493 of Saint Ursula and her 11,000 virgin followers (Santa Ursula y las Once Mil Virgenes), which over time shortened to the Virgins (las Virgenes)

DEPENDENCY STATUS:

overseas territory of the UK; internal self-governing

GOVERNMENT TYPE:

parliamentary democracy (House of Assembly); self-governing overseas territory of the UK

CAPITAL:

name: Road Town

geographic coordinates: 18 25 N, 64 37 W

time difference: UTC-4 (1 hour ahead of Washington, DC, during Standard Time)

ADMINISTRATIVE DIVISIONS:

none (overseas territory of the UK)

INDEPENDENCE:

none (overseas territory of the UK)

NATIONAL HOLIDAY:

Territory Day, 1 July (1956)

CONSTITUTION:

several previous; latest effective 15 June 2007 (The Virgin Islands Constitution Order 2007) (2018)

LEGAL SYSTEM:

English common law

CITIZENSHIP:

see United Kingdom

SUFFRAGE:

18 years of age; universal

EXECUTIVE BRANCH:

chief of state: Queen ELIZABETH II (since 6 February 1952); represented by Governor Gus JASPERT (since 22 August 2017)

head of government: Premier Orlando SMITH (since 9 November 2011)

cabinet: Executive Council appointed by the governor from members of the House of Assembly

elections/appointments: the monarchy is hereditary; governor appointed by the monarch; following legislative elections, the leader of the majority party or majority coalition usually appointed premier by the governor

LEGISLATIVE BRANCH:

description: unicameral House of Assembly (13 seats; 9 members directly elected in single-seat constituencies and 4 at-large seats by simple majority vote to serve 4-year terms); note - the Assembly includes the attorney general, a non-voting ex officio member

elections: last held on 8 June 2015 (next to be held in 2019)

election results: percent of vote by party - NDP 60.2%, VIP 30.2%, PEP 4%, other 5.6%; seats by party - NDP 11, VIP 2

JUDICIAL BRANCH:

highest courts: the Eastern Caribbean Supreme Court (ECSC) is the superior court of the Organization of Eastern Caribbean States; the ECSC - headquartered on St. Lucia - consists of the Court of Appeal - headed by the chief justice and 4 judges - and the High Court with 18 judges; the Court of Appeal is itinerant, travelling to member states on a schedule to hear appeals from the High Court and subordinate courts; High Court judges reside at the member states with 3 on the British Virgin Islands

judge selection and term of office: Eastern Caribbean Supreme Court chief justice appointed by Her Majesty, Queen ELIZABETH II; other justices and judges appointed by the Judicial and Legal Services Commission; Court of Appeal justices appointed for life with mandatory retirement at age 65; High Court judges appointed for life with mandatory retirement at age 62

subordinate courts: Magistrates' Courts

POLITICAL PARTIES AND LEADERS:

National Democratic Party or NDP [Myron WALWYN]
People's Empowerment Party or PEP [Alvin CHRISTOPHER]
Virgin Islands Party or VIP [Julian FRASER]

INTERNATIONAL ORGANIZATION PARTICIPATION:

Caricom (associate), CDB, Interpol (subbureau), IOC, OECS, UNESCO (associate), UPU

DIPLOMATIC REPRESENTATION IN THE US:

none (overseas territory of the UK)

DIPLOMATIC REPRESENTATION FROM THE US:

none (overseas territory of the UK)

FLAG DESCRIPTION:

blue with the flag of the UK in the upper hoist-side quadrant and the Virgin Islander coat of arms centered in the outer half of the flag; the coat of arms depicts a woman flanked on either side by a vertical column of six oil lamps above a scroll bearing the Latin word VIGILATE (Be Watchful); the islands were named by COLUMBUS in 1493 in honor of Saint Ursula and her 11 virgin followers (some sources say 11,000) who reputedly were martyred by the Huns in the 4th or 5th century; the figure on the banner holding a lamp represents the saint; the other lamps symbolize her followers

NATIONAL SYMBOL(S):

zenaida dove, white cedar flower; national colors: yellow, green, red, white, blue

NATIONAL ANTHEM:

note: as a territory of the United Kingdom, "God Save the Queen" is official (see United Kingdom)

ECONOMY :: BRITISH VIRGIN ISLANDS

ECONOMY - OVERVIEW:

The economy, one of the most stable and prosperous in the Caribbean, is highly dependent on tourism, which generates an estimated 45% of the national income. More than 934,000 tourists, mainly from the US, visited the islands in 2008. Because of traditionally close links with the US Virgin Islands, the British Virgin Islands has used the US dollar as its currency since 1959.

Livestock raising is the most important agricultural activity; poor soils limit the islands' ability to meet domestic food requirements.

In the mid-1980s, the government began offering offshore registration to companies wishing to incorporate in the islands, and incorporation fees now generate substantial revenues. Roughly 400,000 companies were on the offshore registry by yearend 2000. The adoption of a comprehensive insurance law in late 1994, which provides a blanket of confidentiality with regulated statutory gateways for investigation of criminal offenses, made the British Virgin Islands even more attractive to international business.

GDP (PURCHASING POWER PARITY):

$500 million (2017 est.)

$490.2 million (2016 est.)

$481.1 million (2015 est.)

country comparison to the world: 213

GDP (OFFICIAL EXCHANGE RATE):

$1.028 billion (2017 est.) (2017 est.)

GDP - REAL GROWTH RATE:

2% (2017 est.)

1.9% (2016 est.)

1.8% (2015 est.)

country comparison to the world: 149

GDP - PER CAPITA (PPP):

$34,200 (2017 est.)

country comparison to the world: 59

GDP - COMPOSITION, BY END USE:

household consumption: 25.1% (2017 est.)

government consumption: 7.5% (2017 est.)

investment in fixed capital: 21.7% (2017 est.)

investment in inventories: 20.4% (2017 est.)

exports of goods and services: 94.7% (2017 est.)

imports of goods and services: -69.4% (2017 est.)

GDP - COMPOSITION, BY SECTOR OF ORIGIN:

agriculture: 0.2% (2017 est.)

industry: 6.8% (2017 est.)

services: 93.1% (2017 est.)

AGRICULTURE - PRODUCTS:

fruits, vegetables; livestock, poultry; fish

INDUSTRIES:

tourism, light industry, construction, rum, concrete block, offshore banking center

INDUSTRIAL PRODUCTION GROWTH RATE:

1.1% (2017 est.)

country comparison to the world: 152

LABOR FORCE:

12,770 (2004)

country comparison to the world: 215

LABOR FORCE - BY OCCUPATION:

agriculture: 0.6%

industry: 40%

services: 59.4% (2005)

UNEMPLOYMENT RATE:

2.9% (2015 est.)

country comparison to the world: 32

POPULATION BELOW POVERTY LINE:

NA

HOUSEHOLD INCOME OR CONSUMPTION BY PERCENTAGE SHARE:

lowest 10%: NA

highest 10%: NA

BUDGET:

revenues: 400 million (2017 est.)

expenditures: 400 million (2017 est.)

TAXES AND OTHER REVENUES:

38.9% (of GDP) (2017 est.)

country comparison to the world: 50

BUDGET SURPLUS (+) OR DEFICIT (-):

0% (of GDP) (2017 est.)

country comparison to the world: 44

FISCAL YEAR:

1 April - 31 March

INFLATION RATE (CONSUMER PRICES):

1.1% (2017 est.)

1.1% (2016 est.)

country comparison to the world: 56

CURRENT ACCOUNT BALANCE:

$362.6 million (2011 est.)

$279.8 million (2010 est.)

country comparison to the world: 57

EXPORTS:

$23 million (2017 est.)

$23 million (2015 est.)

country comparison to the world: 209

EXPORTS - COMMODITIES:

rum, fresh fish, fruits, animals; gravel, sand

IMPORTS:

$300 million NA (2017 est.)

$210 million (2016 est.)

country comparison to the world: 203

IMPORTS - COMMODITIES:

building materials, automobiles, foodstuffs, machinery

DEBT - EXTERNAL:

$36.1 million (1997)

country comparison to the world: 198

EXCHANGE RATES:

the US dollar is used

ENERGY :: BRITISH VIRGIN ISLANDS

ELECTRICITY - PRODUCTION:

126.3 million kWh (2016 est.)

country comparison to the world: 198

ELECTRICITY - CONSUMPTION:

117.5 million kWh (2016 est.)

country comparison to the world: 200

ELECTRICITY - EXPORTS:

0 kWh (2016 est.)

country comparison to the world: 110

ELECTRICITY - IMPORTS:

0 kWh (2016 est.)

country comparison to the world: 128

ELECTRICITY - INSTALLED GENERATING CAPACITY:

45,200 kW (2016 est.)

country comparison to the world: 193

ELECTRICITY - FROM FOSSIL FUELS:

97% of total installed capacity (2016 est.)

country comparison to the world: 33

ELECTRICITY - FROM NUCLEAR FUELS:

0% of total installed capacity (2017 est.)

country comparison to the world: 55

ELECTRICITY - FROM HYDROELECTRIC PLANTS:

0% of total installed capacity (2017 est.)

country comparison to the world: 160

ELECTRICITY - FROM OTHER RENEWABLE SOURCES:

3% of total installed capacity (2017 est.)

country comparison to the world: 122

CRUDE OIL - PRODUCTION:

0 bbl/day (2017 est.)

country comparison to the world: 114

CRUDE OIL - EXPORTS:

0 bbl/day (2015 est.)

country comparison to the world: 98

CRUDE OIL - IMPORTS:

0 bbl/day (2015 est.)

country comparison to the world: 101

CRUDE OIL - PROVED RESERVES:

0 bbl (1 January 2018 est.)

country comparison to the world: 111

REFINED PETROLEUM PRODUCTS - PRODUCTION:

0 bbl/day (2015 est.)

country comparison to the world: 123

REFINED PETROLEUM PRODUCTS - CONSUMPTION:

20,000 bbl/day (2016 est.)

country comparison to the world: 141

REFINED PETROLEUM PRODUCTS - EXPORTS:

0 bbl/day (2015 est.)

country comparison to the world: 134

REFINED PETROLEUM PRODUCTS - IMPORTS:

1,227 bbl/day (2015 est.)

country comparison to the world: 200

NATURAL GAS - PRODUCTION:

0 cu m (2017 est.)

country comparison to the world: 109

NATURAL GAS - CONSUMPTION:

0 cu m (2017 est.)

country comparison to the world: 125

NATURAL GAS - EXPORTS:

0 cu m (2017 est.)

country comparison to the world: 74

NATURAL GAS - IMPORTS:

0 cu m (2017 est.)

country comparison to the world: 96

NATURAL GAS - PROVED RESERVES:

0 cu m (1 January 2014 est.)

country comparison to the world: 115

CARBON DIOXIDE EMISSIONS FROM CONSUMPTION OF ENERGY:

183,300 Mt (2017 est.)

country comparison to the world: 202

COMMUNICATIONS :: BRITISH VIRGIN ISLANDS

TELEPHONES - FIXED LINES:

total subscriptions: 10,004 (2017 est.)

subscriptions per 100 inhabitants: 29 (2017 est.)

country comparison to the world: 195

TELEPHONES - MOBILE CELLULAR:

total subscriptions: 42,000 (July 2016 est.)

subscriptions per 100 inhabitants: 126 (July 2016 est.)

country comparison to the world: 203

TELEPHONE SYSTEM:

general assessment: good overall telephone service; major expansion sectors include the mobile telephony and data segments, which continue to appeal to operator investment; several operators licensed to provide services within individual markets, most of them are small and localised (2017)

domestic: fixed-line connections exceed 29 per 100 persons and mobile cellular subscribership is roughly 125 per 100 persons (2017)

international: country code - 1-284; connected via submarine cable to Bermuda; the East Caribbean Fiber System (ECFS) submarine cable provides connectivity to 13 other islands in the eastern Caribbean

BROADCAST MEDIA:

1 private TV station; multi-channel TV is available from cable and satellite subscription services; about a half-dozen private radio stations (2007)

INTERNET COUNTRY CODE:

.vg

INTERNET USERS:

total: 14,600 (July 2016 est.)

percent of population: 43.6% (July 2016 est.)

country comparison to the world: 210

TRANSPORTATION :: BRITISH VIRGIN ISLANDS

NATIONAL AIR TRANSPORT SYSTEM:

number of registered air carriers: 1 (2015)

inventory of registered aircraft operated by air carriers: 3 (2015)

CIVIL AIRCRAFT REGISTRATION COUNTRY CODE PREFIX:

VP-L (2016)

AIRPORTS:

4 (2013)

country comparison to the world: 185

AIRPORTS - WITH PAVED RUNWAYS:

total: 2 (2017)

914 to 1,523 m: 1 (2017)

under 914 m: 1 (2017)

AIRPORTS - WITH UNPAVED RUNWAYS:

total: 2 (2013)

914 to 1,523 m: 2 (2013)

ROADWAYS:

total: 200 km (2007)

paved: 200 km (2007)

country comparison to the world: 210

MERCHANT MARINE:

total: 20 (2017)

by type: general cargo 4, other 16 (2017)

country comparison to the world: 138

PORTS AND TERMINALS:

major seaport(s): Road Harbor

MILITARY AND SECURITY :: BRITISH VIRGIN ISLANDS

MILITARY - NOTE:

defense is the responsibility of the UK

TRANSNATIONAL ISSUES :: BRITISH VIRGIN ISLANDS

DISPUTES - INTERNATIONAL:

none

ILLICIT DRUGS:

transshipment point for South American narcotics destined for the US and Europe; large offshore financial center makes it vulnerable to money laundering

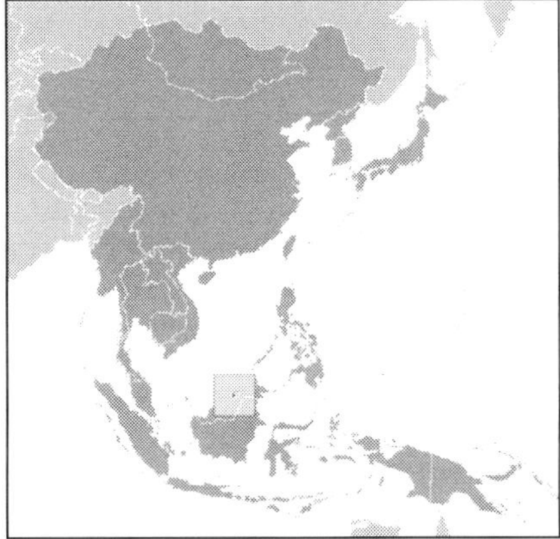

EAST ASIA / SOUTHEAST ASIA :: BRUNEI

INTRODUCTION :: BRUNEI

BACKGROUND:

The Sultanate of Brunei's influence peaked between the 15th and 17th centuries when its control extended over coastal areas of northwest Borneo and the southern Philippines. Brunei subsequently entered a period of decline brought on by internal strife over royal succession, colonial expansion of European powers, and piracy. In 1888, Brunei became a British protectorate; independence was achieved in 1984. The same family has ruled Brunei for over six centuries. Brunei benefits from extensive petroleum and natural gas fields, the source of one of the highest per capita GDPs in the world. In 2017, Brunei celebrated the 50th anniversary of the Sultan Hassanal BOLKIAH's accession to the throne.

GEOGRAPHY :: BRUNEI

LOCATION:

Southeastern Asia, along the northern coast of the island of Borneo, bordering the South China Sea and Malaysia

GEOGRAPHIC COORDINATES:

4 30 N, 114 40 E

MAP REFERENCES:

Southeast Asia

AREA:

total: 5,765 sq km

land: 5,265 sq km

water: 500 sq km

country comparison to the world: 173

AREA - COMPARATIVE:

slightly smaller than Delaware

LAND BOUNDARIES:

total: 266 km

border countries (1): Malaysia 266 km

COASTLINE:

161 km

MARITIME CLAIMS:

territorial sea: 12 nm

exclusive economic zone: 200 nm or to median line

CLIMATE:

tropical; hot, humid, rainy

TERRAIN:

flat coastal plain rises to mountains in east; hilly lowland in west

ELEVATION:

mean elevation: 478 m

elevation extremes: 0 m lowest point: South China Sea

1850 highest point: Bukit Pagon

NATURAL RESOURCES:

petroleum, natural gas, timber

LAND USE:

agricultural land: 2.5% (2011 est.)

arable land: 0.8% (2011 est.) / permanent crops: 1.1% (2011 est.) / permanent pasture: 0.6% (2011 est.)

forest: 71.8% (2011 est.)

other: 25.7% (2011 est.)

IRRIGATED LAND:

10 sq km (2012)

NATURAL HAZARDS:

typhoons, earthquakes, and severe flooding are rare

ENVIRONMENT - CURRENT ISSUES:

no major environmental problems, but air pollution control is becoming a concern; seasonal trans-boundary haze from forest fires in Indonesia

ENVIRONMENT - INTERNATIONAL AGREEMENTS:

party to: Biodiversity, Climate Change, Desertification, Endangered Species, Hazardous Wastes, Law of the Sea, Ozone Layer Protection, Ship Pollution

signed, but not ratified: none of the selected agreements

GEOGRAPHY - NOTE:

close to vital sea lanes through South China Sea linking Indian and Pacific Oceans; two parts physically separated by Malaysia; the eastern part, the Temburong district, is an exclave and is almost an enclave within Malaysia

PEOPLE AND SOCIETY :: BRUNEI

POPULATION:

450,565 (July 2018 est.)

country comparison to the world: 174

NATIONALITY:

noun: Bruneian(s)

adjective: Bruneian

ETHNIC GROUPS:

Malay 65.7%, Chinese 10.3%, other 24% (2016 est.)

LANGUAGES:

Malay (Bahasa Melayu) (official), English, Chinese dialects

RELIGIONS:

Muslim (official) 78.8%, Christian 8.7%, Buddhist 7.8%, other (includes indigenous beliefs) 4.7% (2011 est.)

AGE STRUCTURE:

0-14 years: 22.82% (male 52,995 /female 49,836)

15-24 years: 16.8% (male 37,707 /female 37,985)

25-54 years: 46.9% (male 100,740 /female 110,596)

55-64 years: 8.3% (male 18,859 /female 18,551)

65 years and over: 5.17% (male 11,336 /female 11,960) (2018 est.)

DEPENDENCY RATIOS:

total dependency ratio: 38.4 (2015 est.)

youth dependency ratio: 32.8 (2015 est.)

elderly dependency ratio: 5.7 (2015 est.)

potential support ratio: 17.6 (2015 est.)

MEDIAN AGE:

total: 30.5 years

male: 30 years

female: 31 years (2018 est.)

country comparison to the world: 115

POPULATION GROWTH RATE:

1.55% (2018 est.)

country comparison to the world: 69

BIRTH RATE:

16.9 births/1,000 population (2018 est.)

country comparison to the world: 106

DEATH RATE:

3.7 deaths/1,000 population (2018 est.)

country comparison to the world: 214

NET MIGRATION RATE:

2.4 migrant(s)/1,000 population (2017 est.)

country comparison to the world: 39

URBANIZATION:

urban population: 77.6% of total population (2018)

rate of urbanization: 1.66% annual rate of change (2015-20 est.)

MAJOR URBAN AREAS - POPULATION:

241,000 BANDAR SERI BEGAWAN (capital) (2011)

note: the boundaries of the capital city were expanded in 2007, greatly increasing the city area; the population of the capital increased tenfold

SEX RATIO:

at birth: 1.05 male(s)/female (2017 est.)

0-14 years: 1.06 male(s)/female (2017 est.)

15-24 years: 0.99 male(s)/female (2017 est.)

25-54 years: 0.92 male(s)/female (2017 est.)

55-64 years: 1.04 male(s)/female (2017 est.)

65 years and over: 0.95 male(s)/female (2017 est.)

total population: 0.98 male(s)/female (2017 est.)

MATERNAL MORTALITY RATE:

23 deaths/100,000 live births (2015 est.)

country comparison to the world: 126

INFANT MORTALITY RATE:

total: 9.3 deaths/1,000 live births (2018 est.)

male: 11.1 deaths/1,000 live births (2018 est.)

female: 7.5 deaths/1,000 live births (2018 est.)

country comparison to the world: 141

LIFE EXPECTANCY AT BIRTH:

total population: 77.5 years (2018 est.)

male: 75.2 years (2018 est.)

female: 80 years (2018 est.)

country comparison to the world: 71

TOTAL FERTILITY RATE:

1.77 children born/woman (2018 est.)

country comparison to the world: 156

HEALTH EXPENDITURES:

2.6% of GDP (2014)

country comparison to the world: 186

PHYSICIANS DENSITY:

1.75 physicians/1,000 population (2015)

HOSPITAL BED DENSITY:

2.7 beds/1,000 population (2015)

HIV/AIDS - ADULT PREVALENCE RATE:

NA

HIV/AIDS - PEOPLE LIVING WITH HIV/AIDS:

NA

HIV/AIDS - DEATHS:

NA

OBESITY - ADULT PREVALENCE RATE:

14.1% (2016)

country comparison to the world: 129

CHILDREN UNDER THE AGE OF 5 YEARS UNDERWEIGHT:

9.6% (2009)

country comparison to the world: 65

EDUCATION EXPENDITURES:

4.4% of GDP (2016)

country comparison to the world: 98

LITERACY:

definition: age 15 and over can read and write (2015 est.)

total population: 96% (2015 est.)

male: 97.5% (2015 est.)

female: 94.5% (2015 est.)

SCHOOL LIFE EXPECTANCY (PRIMARY TO TERTIARY EDUCATION):

total: 15 years (2015)

male: 14 years (2015)

female: 15 years (2015)

UNEMPLOYMENT, YOUTH AGES 15-24:

total: 25.4% (2014 est.)

male: 23.5% (2014 est.)

female: 28.1% (2014 est.)

country comparison to the world: 44

GOVERNMENT :: BRUNEI

COUNTRY NAME:

conventional long form: Brunei Darussalam

conventional short form: Brunei

local long form: Negara Brunei Darussalam

local short form: Brunei

etymology: derivation of the name is unclear; according to legend, MUHAMMAD SHAH, who would become the first sultan of Brunei, upon discovering what would become Brunei exclaimed "Baru nah," which roughly translates as "there" or "that's it"

GOVERNMENT TYPE:

absolute monarchy or sultanate

CAPITAL:

name: Bandar Seri Begawan

geographic coordinates: 4 53 N, 114 56 E

time difference: UTC+8 (13 hours ahead of Washington, DC, during Standard Time)

ADMINISTRATIVE DIVISIONS:

4 districts (daerah-daerah, singular - daerah); Belait, Brunei and Muara, Temburong, Tutong

INDEPENDENCE:

1 January 1984 (from the UK)

NATIONAL HOLIDAY:

National Day, 23 February (1984); note - 1 January 1984 was the date of independence from the UK, 23 February 1984 was the date of independence from British protectionthe Sultan's birthday, 15 June

CONSTITUTION:

history: drafted 1954 to 1959, signed 29 September 1959; note - some constitutional provisions suspended since 1962 under a State of Emergency, others suspended since independence in 1984 (2017)

amendments: proposed by the monarch; passage requires submission to the Privy Council for Legislative Council review and finalization takes place by proclamation; the monarch can accept or reject changes to the original proposal provided by the Legislative Council; amended 1984, 2004, 2011 (2017)

LEGAL SYSTEM:

mixed legal system based on English common law and Islamic law; note - in May 2014, the first of three phases of sharia-based penal codes was instituted, which applies to Muslims and non-Muslims and exists in parallel to the existing common law-based code

INTERNATIONAL LAW ORGANIZATION PARTICIPATION:

has not submitted an ICJ jurisdiction declaration; non-party state to the ICCt

CITIZENSHIP:

citizenship by birth: no

citizenship by descent only: the father must be a citizen of Brunei

dual citizenship recognized: no

residency requirement for naturalization: 12 years

SUFFRAGE:

18 years of age for village elections; universal

EXECUTIVE BRANCH:

chief of state: Sultan and Prime Minister Sir HASSANAL Bolkiah (since 5 October 1967); note - the monarch is both chief of state and head of government

head of government: Sultan and Prime Minister Sir HASSANAL Bolkiah (since 5 October 1967)

cabinet: Council of Ministers appointed and presided over by the monarch; note - 4 additional advisory councils appointed by the monarch are the Religious Council, Privy Council for constitutional issues, Council of Succession, and Legislative Council

elections/appointments: none; the monarchy is hereditary

LEGISLATIVE BRANCH:

description: unicameral Legislative Council or Majlis Mesyuarat Negara Brunei (36 seats; members appointed by the sultan including 3 ex-officio members - the speaker and first and second secretaries; members appointed for 5-year terms)

elections: appointed by the sultan

JUDICIAL BRANCH:

highest courts: Supreme Court (consists of Court of Appeal and High Court, each with a chief justice and 2 judges); Sharia Court of Appeal (consists of judges appointed by the monarch); note - Brunei has a dual judicial system of secular and sharia (religious) courts; the Judicial Committee of Privy Council in London serves as the final appellate court for civil cases only

judge selection and term of office: Supreme Court judges appointed by the monarch to serve until age 65, and older if approved by the monarch; Sharia Court of Appeal judges appointed by the monarch for life

subordinate courts: Intermediate Court; Magistrate's Courts; Juvenile Court; small claims courts; lower sharia courts

POLITICAL PARTIES AND LEADERS:

National Development Party or NDP [YASSIN Affendi]

note: Brunei National Solidarity Party or PPKB [Abdul LATIF bin Chuchu] and People's Awareness Party or PAKAR [Awang Haji MAIDIN bin Haji Ahmad] were deregistered in 2007; parties are small and have limited activity

INTERNATIONAL ORGANIZATION PARTICIPATION:

ADB, APEC, ARF, ASEAN, C, CP, EAS, FAO, G-77, IAEA, IBRD, ICAO, ICC (NGOs), ICRM, IDA, IFRCS, ILO, IMF, IMO, IMSO, Interpol, IOC, ISO (correspondent), ITSO, ITU, NAM, OIC, OPCW, UN, UNCTAD, UNESCO, UNIFIL, UNWTO, UPU, WCO, WHO, WIPO, WMO, WTO

DIPLOMATIC REPRESENTATION IN THE US:

chief of mission: Ambassador Serbini ALI (since 28 January 2016)

chancery: 3520 International Court NW, Washington, DC 20008

telephone: [1] (202) 237-1838

FAX: [1] (202) 885-0560

consulate(s): New York

DIPLOMATIC REPRESENTATION FROM THE US:

chief of mission: Ambassador Craig B. ALLEN (since 9 March 2015)

embassy: Simpang 336-52-16-9, Jalan Datu, Bandar Seri Begawan, BC4115

mailing address: Unit 4280, Box 40, FPO AP 96507; P.O. Box 2991, Bandar Seri Begawan BS8675, Negara Brunei Darussalam

telephone: [673] 238-4616

FAX: [673] 238-4604

FLAG DESCRIPTION:

yellow with two diagonal bands of white (top, almost double width) and black starting from the upper hoist side; the national emblem in red is superimposed at the center; yellow is the color of royalty and symbolizes the sultanate; the white and black bands denote Brunei's chief ministers; the emblem includes five main components: a swallow-tailed flag, the royal umbrella representing the monarchy, the wings of four feathers symbolizing justice, tranquility, prosperity, and peace, the two upraised hands signifying the government's pledge to preserve and promote the welfare of the people, and the crescent moon denoting Islam, the state religion; the state motto "Always render service with God's guidance" appears in yellow Arabic script on the crescent; a ribbon below the crescent reads "Brunei, the Abode of Peace"

NATIONAL SYMBOL(S):

royal parasol; national colors: yellow, white, black

NATIONAL ANTHEM:

name: "Allah Peliharakan Sultan" (God Bless His Majesty)

lyrics/music: Pengiran Haji Mohamed YUSUF bin Pengiran Abdul

Rahim/Awang Haji BESAR bin Sagap

note: adopted 1951

ECONOMY :: BRUNEI

ECONOMY - OVERVIEW:

Brunei is an energy-rich sultanate on the northern coast of Borneo in Southeast Asia. Brunei boasts a well-educated, largely English-speaking population; excellent infrastructure; and a stable government intent on attracting foreign investment. Crude oil and natural gas production account for approximately 65% of GDP and 95% of exports, with Japan as the primary export market.

Per capita GDP is among the highest in the world, and substantial income from overseas investment supplements income from domestic hydrocarbon production. Bruneian citizens pay no personal income taxes, and the government provides free medical services and free education through the university level.

The Bruneian Government wants to diversify its economy away from hydrocarbon exports to other industries such as information and communications technology and halal manufacturing, permissible under Islamic law. Brunei's trade increased in 2016 and 2017, following its regional economic integration in the ASEAN Economic Community, and the expected ratification of the Trans-Pacific Partnership trade agreement.

GDP (PURCHASING POWER PARITY):

$33.87 billion (2017 est.)

$33.42 billion (2016 est.)

$34.27 billion (2015 est.)

note: data are in 2017 dollars

country comparison to the world: 128

GDP (OFFICIAL EXCHANGE RATE):

$12.13 billion (2017 est.) (2017 est.)

GDP - REAL GROWTH RATE:

1.3% (2017 est.)

-2.5% (2016 est.)

-0.4% (2015 est.)

country comparison to the world: 178

GDP - PER CAPITA (PPP):

$78,900 (2017 est.)

$79,000 (2016 est.)

$82,200 (2015 est.)

note: data are in 2017 dollars

country comparison to the world: 9

GROSS NATIONAL SAVING:

47.5% of GDP (2017 est.)

50.1% of GDP (2016 est.)

51.9% of GDP (2015 est.)

country comparison to the world: 3

GDP - COMPOSITION, BY END USE:

household consumption: 25% (2017 est.)

government consumption: 24.8% (2017 est.)

investment in fixed capital: 32.6% (2017 est.)

investment in inventories: 8.5% (2017 est.)

exports of goods and services: 45.9% (2017 est.)

imports of goods and services: -36.8% (2017 est.)

GDP - COMPOSITION, BY SECTOR OF ORIGIN:

agriculture: 1.2% (2017 est.)

industry: 56.6% (2017 est.)

services: 42.3% (2017 est.)

AGRICULTURE - PRODUCTS:

rice, vegetables, fruits; chickens, water buffalo, cattle, goats, eggs

INDUSTRIES:

petroleum, petroleum refining, liquefied natural gas, construction, agriculture, aquaculture, transportation

INDUSTRIAL PRODUCTION GROWTH RATE:

1.5% (2017 est.)

country comparison to the world: 142

LABOR FORCE:

203,600 (2014 est.)

country comparison to the world: 170

LABOR FORCE - BY OCCUPATION:

agriculture: 4.2%

industry: 62.8%

services: 33% (2008 est.)

UNEMPLOYMENT RATE:

6.9% (2017 est.)

6.9% (2016 est.)

country comparison to the world: 102

POPULATION BELOW POVERTY LINE:

NA

HOUSEHOLD INCOME OR CONSUMPTION BY PERCENTAGE SHARE:

lowest 10%: NA

highest 10%: NA

BUDGET:

revenues: 2.245 billion (2017 est.)

expenditures: 4.345 billion (2017 est.)

TAXES AND OTHER REVENUES:

18.5% (of GDP) (2017 est.)

country comparison to the world: 158

BUDGET SURPLUS (+) OR DEFICIT (-):

-17.3% (of GDP) (2017 est.)

country comparison to the world: 218

PUBLIC DEBT:

2.8% of GDP (2017 est.)

3% of GDP (2016 est.)

country comparison to the world: 207

FISCAL YEAR:

1 April - 31 March

INFLATION RATE (CONSUMER PRICES):

-0.2% (2017 est.)

-0.7% (2016 est.)

country comparison to the world: 9

COMMERCIAL BANK PRIME LENDING RATE:

5.5% (31 December 2017 est.)

5.5% (31 December 2016 est.)

country comparison to the world: 133

STOCK OF NARROW MONEY:

$3.387 billion (31 December 2017 est.)

$3.232 billion (31 December 2016 est.)

country comparison to the world: 117

STOCK OF BROAD MONEY:

$3.387 billion (31 December 2017 est.)

$3.232 billion (31 December 2016 est.)

country comparison to the world: 123

STOCK OF DOMESTIC CREDIT:

$3.665 billion (31 December 2017 est.)

$4.066 billion (31 December 2016 est.)

country comparison to the world: 134

MARKET VALUE OF PUBLICLY TRADED SHARES:

NA

CURRENT ACCOUNT BALANCE:

$2.021 billion (2017 est.)

$1.47 billion (2016 est.)

country comparison to the world: 41

EXPORTS:

$5.885 billion (2017 est.)

$5.023 billion (2016 est.)

country comparison to the world: 104

EXPORTS - PARTNERS:

Japan 27.8%, South Korea 12.4%, Thailand 11.5%, Malaysia 11.3%, India 9.3%, Singapore 7.7%, Switzerland 5%, China 4.7% (2017)

EXPORTS - COMMODITIES:

mineral fuels, organic chemicals

IMPORTS:

$2.998 billion (2017 est.)

$2.658 billion (2016 est.)

country comparison to the world: 148

IMPORTS - COMMODITIES:

machinery and mechanical appliance parts, mineral fuels, motor vehicles, electric machinery

IMPORTS - PARTNERS:

China 19.6%, Singapore 19%, Malaysia 18.8%, US 9.2%, Germany 5.9%, Japan 4.1%, UK 4% (2017)

RESERVES OF FOREIGN EXCHANGE AND GOLD:

$3.488 billion (31 December 2017 est.)

$3.366 billion (31 December 2015 est.)

country comparison to the world: 105

DEBT - EXTERNAL:

$0 (2014)

$0 (2013)

note: public external debt only; private external debt unavailable

country comparison to the world: 204

EXCHANGE RATES:

Bruneian dollars (BND) per US dollar -

1.394 (2017 est.)

1.3814 (2016 est.)

1.3814 (2015 est.)

1.3749 (2014 est.)

1.267 (2013 est.)

ENERGY :: BRUNEI

ELECTRICITY ACCESS:

population without electricity: 104,788 (2012)

electrification - total population: 76% (2012)

electrification - urban areas: 79% (2012)

electrification - rural areas: 67% (2012)

ELECTRICITY - PRODUCTION:

4.014 billion kWh (2016 est.)

country comparison to the world: 127

ELECTRICITY - CONSUMPTION:

3.771 billion kWh (2016 est.)

country comparison to the world: 129

ELECTRICITY - EXPORTS:

0 kWh (2016 est.)

country comparison to the world: 111

ELECTRICITY - IMPORTS:

0 kWh (2016 est.)

country comparison to the world: 129

ELECTRICITY - INSTALLED GENERATING CAPACITY:

821,000 kW (2016 est.)

country comparison to the world: 134

ELECTRICITY - FROM FOSSIL FUELS:

100% of total installed capacity (2016 est.)

country comparison to the world: 5

ELECTRICITY - FROM NUCLEAR FUELS:

0% of total installed capacity (2017 est.)

country comparison to the world: 56

ELECTRICITY - FROM HYDROELECTRIC PLANTS:

0% of total installed capacity (2017 est.)

country comparison to the world: 161

ELECTRICITY - FROM OTHER RENEWABLE SOURCES:

0% of total installed capacity (2017 est.)

country comparison to the world: 179

CRUDE OIL - PRODUCTION:

100,600 bbl/day (2017 est.)

country comparison to the world: 43

CRUDE OIL - EXPORTS:

127,400 bbl/day (2015 est.)

country comparison to the world: 33

CRUDE OIL - IMPORTS:

160 bbl/day (2015 est.)

country comparison to the world: 82

CRUDE OIL - PROVED RESERVES:

1.1 billion bbl (1 January 2018 est.)

country comparison to the world: 39

REFINED PETROLEUM PRODUCTS - PRODUCTION:

10,310 bbl/day (2015 est.)

country comparison to the world: 100

REFINED PETROLEUM PRODUCTS - CONSUMPTION:

18,000 bbl/day (2016 est.)

country comparison to the world: 144

REFINED PETROLEUM PRODUCTS - EXPORTS:

0 bbl/day (2015 est.)

country comparison to the world: 135

REFINED PETROLEUM PRODUCTS - IMPORTS:

6,948 bbl/day (2015 est.)

country comparison to the world: 159

NATURAL GAS - PRODUCTION:

12.74 billion cu m (2017 est.)

country comparison to the world: 38

NATURAL GAS - CONSUMPTION:

3.936 billion cu m (2017 est.)

country comparison to the world: 66

NATURAL GAS - EXPORTS:

8.268 billion cu m (2017 est.)

country comparison to the world: 23

NATURAL GAS - IMPORTS:

0 cu m (2017 est.)

country comparison to the world: 97

NATURAL GAS - PROVED RESERVES:

260.5 billion cu m (1 January 2018 est.)

country comparison to the world: 39

CARBON DIOXIDE EMISSIONS FROM CONSUMPTION OF ENERGY:

10.04 million Mt (2017 est.)

country comparison to the world: 107

COMMUNICATIONS :: BRUNEI

TELEPHONES - FIXED LINES:

total subscriptions: 74,213 (July 2016 est.)

subscriptions per 100 inhabitants: 17 (July 2016 est.)

country comparison to the world: 148

TELEPHONES - MOBILE CELLULAR:

total subscriptions: 544,732 (2017 est.)

subscriptions per 100 inhabitants: 123 (2017 est.)

country comparison to the world: 170

TELEPHONE SYSTEM:

general assessment: service throughout the country is good; international service is good to Southeast Asia, Middle East, Western Europe, and the US; while fixed-line is slowing down, mobile broadband has taken over in the advancement in the telecoms access market; broadband penetration slow to moderate growth predicted over the next five years to 2023 (2017)

domestic: every service available; 17 per 100 fixed-line, 123 per 100 mobile-cellular (2017)

international: country code - 673; landing point for the SEA-ME-WE-3 optical telecommunications submarine cable that provides links to Asia, the Middle East, and Europe; the Asia-America Gateway submarine cable network provides new links to Asia and the US; the South-East Asia Japan Cable System linking Brunei, China, Hong Kong, Japan, Singapore, Philipines and Thailand; satellite earth stations - 2 Intelsat (1 Indian Ocean and 1 Pacific Ocean) (2017)

BROADCAST MEDIA:

state-controlled Radio Television Brunei (RTB) operates 5 channels; 3 Malaysian TV stations are available; foreign TV broadcasts are available via satellite systems; RTB operates 5 radio networks and broadcasts on multiple frequencies; British Forces Broadcast Service (BFBS) provides radio broadcasts on 2 FM stations; some radio broadcast stations from Malaysia are available via repeaters (2017)

INTERNET COUNTRY CODE:

.bn

INTERNET USERS:

total: 306,000 (July 2016 est.)

percent of population: 71.2% (July 2016 est.)

country comparison to the world: 161

BROADBAND - FIXED SUBSCRIPTIONS:

total: 41,209 (2017 est.)

subscriptions per 100 inhabitants: 9 (2017 est.)

country comparison to the world: 134

TRANSPORTATION :: BRUNEI

NATIONAL AIR TRANSPORT SYSTEM:

number of registered air carriers: 1 (2015)

inventory of registered aircraft operated by air carriers: 10 (2015)

annual passenger traffic on registered air carriers: 1,150,003 (2015)

annual freight traffic on registered air carriers: 115.147 million mt-km (2015)

CIVIL AIRCRAFT REGISTRATION COUNTRY CODE PREFIX:

V8 (2016)

AIRPORTS:

1 (2013)

country comparison to the world: 216

AIRPORTS - WITH PAVED RUNWAYS:

total: 1 (2017)

over 3,047 m: 1 (2017)

HELIPORTS:

3 (2013)

PIPELINES:

33 km condensate, 86 km condensate/gas, 628 km gas, 492 km oil (2013)

ROADWAYS:

total: 2,976 km (2014)

paved: 2,559 km (2014)

unpaved: 417 km (2014)

country comparison to the world: 166

WATERWAYS:

209 km (navigable by craft drawing less than 1.2 m; the Belait, Brunei, and Tutong Rivers are major transport links) (2012)

country comparison to the world: 96

MERCHANT MARINE:

total: 106 (2018)

by type: general cargo 20, LNG tanker 5, other 81 (2018)

country comparison to the world: 82

PORTS AND TERMINALS:

major seaport(s): Muara

oil terminal(s): Lumut, Seria

LNG terminal(s) (export): Lumut

MILITARY AND SECURITY :: BRUNEI

MILITARY EXPENDITURES:

2.87% of GDP (2017)

3.54% of GDP (2016)

3.28% of GDP (2015)

3.08% of GDP (2014)

2.28% of GDP (2013)

country comparison to the world: 31

MILITARY BRANCHES:

Royal Brunei Armed Forces: Royal Brunei Land Forces, Royal Brunei Navy, Royal Brunei Air Force (Tentera Udara Diraja Brunei) (2013)

MILITARY SERVICE AGE AND OBLIGATION:

17 years of age for voluntary military service; non-Malays are ineligible to serve; recruits from the army, navy, and air force all undergo 43-week initial training (2013)

TRANSNATIONAL ISSUES :: BRUNEI

DISPUTES - INTERNATIONAL:

per Letters of Exchange signed in 2009, Malaysia in 2010 ceded two hydrocarbon concession blocks to Brunei in exchange for Brunei's sultan dropping claims to the Limbang corridor, which divides Bruneinonetheless, Brunei claims a maritime boundary extending as far as a median with Vietnam, thus asserting an implicit claim to Louisa Reef

REFUGEES AND INTERNALLY DISPLACED PERSONS:

stateless persons: 20,524 (2017); note - thousands of stateless persons, often ethnic Chinese, are permanent residents and their families have lived in Brunei for generations; obtaining citizenship is difficult and requires individuals to pass rigorous tests on Malay culture, customs, and language; stateless residents receive an International Certificate of Identity, which enables them to travel overseas; the government is considering changing the law prohibiting non-Bruneians, including stateless permanent residents, from owning land

ILLICIT DRUGS:

drug trafficking and illegally importing controlled substances are serious offenses in Brunei and carry a mandatory death penalty

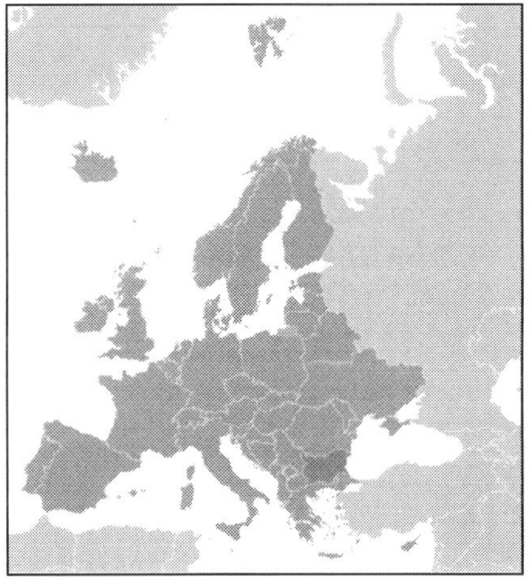

EUROPE :: BULGARIA

INTRODUCTION :: BULGARIA

BACKGROUND:

The Bulgars, a Central Asian Turkic tribe, merged with the local Slavic inhabitants in the late 7th century to form the first Bulgarian state. In succeeding centuries, Bulgaria struggled with the Byzantine Empire to assert its place in the Balkans, but by the end of the 14th century the country was overrun by the Ottoman Turks. Northern Bulgaria attained autonomy in 1878 and all of Bulgaria became independent from the Ottoman Empire in 1908. Having fought on the losing side in both World Wars, Bulgaria fell within the Soviet sphere of influence and became a People's Republic in 1946. Communist domination ended in 1990, when Bulgaria held its first multiparty election since World War II and began the contentious process of moving toward political democracy and a market economy while combating inflation, unemployment, corruption, and crime. The country joined NATO in 2004 and the EU in 2007.

GEOGRAPHY :: BULGARIA

LOCATION:

Southeastern Europe, bordering the Black Sea, between Romania and Turkey

GEOGRAPHIC COORDINATES:

43 00 N, 25 00 E

MAP REFERENCES:

Europe

AREA:

total: 110,879 sq km

land: 108,489 sq km

water: 2,390 sq km

country comparison to the world: 106

AREA - COMPARATIVE:

almost identical in size to Virginia; slightly larger than Tennessee

LAND BOUNDARIES:

total: 1,806 km

border countries (5): Greece 472 km, Macedonia 162 km, Romania 605 km, Serbia 344 km, Turkey 223 km

COASTLINE:

354 km

MARITIME CLAIMS:

territorial sea: 12 nm

exclusive economic zone: 200 nm

contiguous zone: 24 nm

CLIMATE:

temperate; cold, damp winters; hot, dry summers

TERRAIN:

mostly mountains with lowlands in north and southeast

ELEVATION:

mean elevation: 472 m

elevation extremes: 0 m lowest point: Black Sea

2925 highest point: Musala

NATURAL RESOURCES:

bauxite, copper, lead, zinc, coal, timber, arable land

LAND USE:

agricultural land: 46.9% (2011 est.)

arable land: 29.9% (2011 est.) / permanent crops: 1.5% (2011 est.) / permanent pasture: 15.5% (2011 est.)

forest: 36.7% (2011 est.)

other: 16.4% (2011 est.)

IRRIGATED LAND:

1,020 sq km (2012)

POPULATION DISTRIBUTION:

a fairly even distribution throughout most of the country, with urban areas attracting larger populations

NATURAL HAZARDS:

earthquakes; landslides

ENVIRONMENT - CURRENT ISSUES:

air pollution from industrial emissions; rivers polluted from raw sewage, heavy metals, detergents; deforestation; forest damage from air pollution and resulting acid rain; soil contamination from heavy metals from metallurgical plants and industrial wastes

ENVIRONMENT - INTERNATIONAL AGREEMENTS:

party to: Air Pollution, Air Pollution-Nitrogen Oxides, Air Pollution-Persistent Organic Pollutants, Air Pollution-Sulfur 85, Air Pollution-Sulfur 94, Air Pollution-Volatile Organic Compounds, Antarctic-Environmental Protocol, Antarctic-Marine Living Resources, Antarctic Treaty, Biodiversity, Climate Change, Climate Change-Kyoto Protocol, Desertification, Endangered Species, Environmental Modification, Hazardous Wastes, Law of the Sea, Marine Dumping, Ozone Layer Protection, Ship Pollution, Wetlands

signed, but not ratified: none of the selected agreements

GEOGRAPHY - NOTE:

strategic location near Turkish Straits; controls key land routes from Europe to Middle East and Asia

PEOPLE AND SOCIETY :: BULGARIA

POPULATION:

7,057,504 (July 2018 est.)

country comparison to the world: 104

NATIONALITY:

noun: Bulgarian(s)

adjective: Bulgarian

ETHNIC GROUPS:

Bulgarian 76.9%, Turkish 8%, Romani 4.4%, other 0.7% (including Russian, Armenian, and Vlach), other (unknown) 10% (2011 est.)

note: Romani populations are usually underestimated in official statistics and may represent 9–11% of Bulgaria's population

LANGUAGES:

Bulgarian (official) 76.8%, Turkish 8.2%, Romani 3.8%, other 0.7%, unspecified 10.5% (2011 est.)

RELIGIONS:

Eastern Orthodox 59.4%, Muslim 7.8%, other (including Catholic, Protestant, Armenian Apostolic Orthodox, and Jewish) 1.7%, none 3.7%, unspecified 27.4% (2011 est.)

AGE STRUCTURE:

0-14 years: 14.6% (male 530,219 /female 500,398)

15-24 years: 9.43% (male 346,588 /female 318,645)

25-54 years: 43.12% (male 1,565,770 /female 1,477,719)

55-64 years: 13.3% (male 442,083 /female 496,888)

65 years and over: 19.54% (male 557,237 /female 821,957) (2018 est.)

DEPENDENCY RATIOS:

total dependency ratio: 51.7 (2015 est.)

youth dependency ratio: 21.2 (2015 est.)

elderly dependency ratio: 30.5 (2015 est.)

potential support ratio: 3.3 (2015 est.)

MEDIAN AGE:

total: 43 years

male: 41.2 years

female: 44.9 years (2018 est.)

country comparison to the world: 22

POPULATION GROWTH RATE:

-0.63% (2018 est.)

country comparison to the world: 225

BIRTH RATE:

8.5 births/1,000 population (2018 est.)

country comparison to the world: 215

DEATH RATE:

14.5 deaths/1,000 population (2018 est.)

country comparison to the world: 4

NET MIGRATION RATE:

-0.3 migrant(s)/1,000 population (2017 est.)

country comparison to the world: 114

POPULATION DISTRIBUTION:

a fairly even distribution throughout most of the country, with urban areas attracting larger populations

URBANIZATION:

urban population: 75% of total population (2018)

rate of urbanization: -0.22% annual rate of change (2015-20 est.)

MAJOR URBAN AREAS - POPULATION:

1.272 million SOFIA (capital) (2018)

SEX RATIO:

at birth: 1.06 male(s)/female (2017 est.)

0-14 years: 1.06 male(s)/female (2017 est.)

15-24 years: 1.09 male(s)/female (2017 est.)

25-54 years: 1.06 male(s)/female (2017 est.)

55-64 years: 0.88 male(s)/female (2017 est.)

65 years and over: 0.69 male(s)/female (2017 est.)

total population: 0.95 male(s)/female (2017 est.)

MOTHER'S MEAN AGE AT FIRST BIRTH:

26.7 years (2014 est.)

MATERNAL MORTALITY RATE:

11 deaths/100,000 live births (2015 est.)

country comparison to the world: 144

INFANT MORTALITY RATE:

total: 8.3 deaths/1,000 live births (2018 est.)

male: 9.3 deaths/1,000 live births (2018 est.)

female: 7.2 deaths/1,000 live births (2018 est.)

country comparison to the world: 148

LIFE EXPECTANCY AT BIRTH:

total population: 74.8 years (2018 est.)

male: 71.5 years (2018 est.)

female: 78.3 years (2018 est.)

country comparison to the world: 119

TOTAL FERTILITY RATE:

1.47 children born/woman (2018 est.)

country comparison to the world: 201

HEALTH EXPENDITURES:

8.4% of GDP (2014)

country comparison to the world: 48

PHYSICIANS DENSITY:

4 physicians/1,000 population (2014)

HOSPITAL BED DENSITY:

6.8 beds/1,000 population (2013)

DRINKING WATER SOURCE:

improved:

urban: 99.6% of population

rural: 99% of population

total: 99.4% of population

unimproved:

urban: 0.4% of population

rural: 1% of population

total: 0.6% of population (2015 est.)

SANITATION FACILITY ACCESS:

improved:

urban: 86.8% of population (2015 est.)

rural: 83.7% of population (2015 est.)

total: 86% of population (2015 est.)

unimproved:

urban: 13.2% of population (2015 est.)

rural: 16.3% of population (2015 est.)

total: 14% of population (2015 est.)

HIV/AIDS - ADULT PREVALENCE RATE:

<.1% (2017 est.)

HIV/AIDS - PEOPLE LIVING WITH HIV/AIDS:

2,800 (2017 est.)

country comparison to the world: 124

HIV/AIDS - DEATHS:

<100 (2017 est.)

OBESITY - ADULT PREVALENCE RATE:

25% (2016)

country comparison to the world: 53

EDUCATION EXPENDITURES:

4.1% of GDP (2013)

country comparison to the world: 106

LITERACY:

definition: age 15 and over can read and write (2015 est.)

total population: 98.4% (2015 est.)

male: 98.7% (2015 est.)

female: 98.1% (2015 est.)

SCHOOL LIFE EXPECTANCY (PRIMARY TO TERTIARY EDUCATION):

total: 15 years (2015)

male: 15 years (2015)

female: 15 years (2015)

UNEMPLOYMENT, YOUTH AGES 15-24:

total: 17.2% (2016 est.)

male: 17.4% (2016 est.)

female: 16.9% (2016 est.)

country comparison to the world: 77

GOVERNMENT :: BULGARIA

COUNTRY NAME:

conventional long form: Republic of Bulgaria

conventional short form: Bulgaria

local long form: Republika Bulgaria

local short form: Bulgaria

former: Kingdom of Bulgaria, People's Repulic of Bulgaria

etymology: named after the Bulgar tribes who settled the lower Balkan region in the 7th century A.D.

GOVERNMENT TYPE:

parliamentary republic

CAPITAL:

name: Sofia

geographic coordinates: 42 41 N, 23 19 E

time difference: UTC+2 (7 hours ahead of Washington, DC, during Standard Time)

daylight saving time: +1hr, begins last Sunday in March; ends last Sunday in October

ADMINISTRATIVE DIVISIONS:

28 provinces (oblasti, singular - oblast); Blagoevgrad, Burgas, Dobrich, Gabrovo, Haskovo, Kardzhali, Kyustendil, Lovech, Montana, Pazardzhik, Pernik, Pleven, Plovdiv, Razgrad, Ruse, Shumen, Silistra, Sliven, Smolyan, Sofia, Sofia-Grad (Sofia City), Stara Zagora, Targovishte, Varna, Veliko Tarnovo, Vidin, Vratsa, Yambol

INDEPENDENCE:

3 March 1878 (as an autonomous principality within the Ottoman Empire); 22 September 1908 (complete independence from the Ottoman Empire)

NATIONAL HOLIDAY:

Liberation Day, 3 March (1878)

CONSTITUTION:

history: several previous; latest drafted between late 1990 and early 1991, adopted 13 July 1991 (2016)

amendments: proposed by the National Assembly or by the president of the republic; passage requires three-fourths majority vote of National Assembly members in three ballots; signed by the National Assembly chairperson; note - under special circumstances, a "Grand National Assembly" is elected with the authority to write a new constitution and amend certain articles of the constitution, including those affecting basic civil rights and national sovereignty; passage requires at least two-thirds majority vote in each of several readings; amended several times, last in 2015 (2016)

LEGAL SYSTEM:

civil law

INTERNATIONAL LAW ORGANIZATION PARTICIPATION:

accepts compulsory ICJ jurisdiction with reservations; accepts ICCt jurisdiction

CITIZENSHIP:

citizenship by birth: no

citizenship by descent only: at least one parent must be a citizen of Bulgaria

dual citizenship recognized: yes

residency requirement for naturalization: 5 years

SUFFRAGE:

18 years of age; universal

EXECUTIVE BRANCH:

chief of state: President Rumen RADEV (since 22 January 2017); Vice President Iliana IOTOVA (since 22 January 2017)

head of government: Prime Minister Boyko BORISSOV (since 4 May 2017); note - BORISSOV served 2 previous terms as prime minister (27 July 2009-13 March 2013 and 7 November 2014-27 January 2017)

cabinet: Council of Ministers nominated by the prime minister, elected by the National Assembly

elections/appointments: president and vice president elected on the same ballot by absolute majority popular vote in 2 rounds if needed for a 5-year term (eligible for a second term); election last held on 6 and 13 November 2016 (next to be held in fall 2021); chairman of the Council of Ministers (prime minister) elected by the National Assembly; deputy prime ministers nominated by the prime minister, elected by the National Assembly

election results: Rumen RADEV elected president in second round; percent of vote - Rumen RADEV (independent, supported by Bulgarian Socialist Party) 59.4%, Tsetska TSACHEVA (GERB) 36.2%, neither 4.5%; Boyko BORISSOV (GERB) elected prime minister; National Assembly vote - 133 to 100

LEGISLATIVE BRANCH:

description: unicameral National Assembly or Narodno Sabranie (240 seats; members directly elected in multi-seat constituencies by proportional representation vote to serve 4-year terms)

elections: last held on 26 March 2017 (next to be held spring 2021)

election results: percent of vote by party/coalition - GERB 32.7%, BSP 27.2%, United Patriots 9.1%, DPS 9%, Volya 4.2%, other 17.8%; seats by party/coalition - GERB 95, BSP 80, United Patriots 27, DPS 26, Volya 12; composition - men 183, women 57, percent of women 23.8%

JUDICIAL BRANCH:

highest courts: Supreme Court of Cassation (consists of a chairman and approximately 72 judges organized into penal, civil, and commercial colleges); Supreme Administrative Court (organized in 2 colleges with various panels of 5 judges each); Constitutional Court (consists of 12 justices); note - Constitutional Court resides outside the judiciary

judge selection and term of office: Supreme Court of Cassation and Supreme Administrative judges elected by the Supreme Judicial Council or SJC (consists of 25 members with extensive legal experience) and appointed by the president; judges can serve until mandatory retirement at age 65; Constitutional Court justices elected by the National Assembly and appointed by the president and the SJC; justices appointed for 9-year terms with renewal of 4 justices every 3 years

subordinate courts: appeals courts; regional and district courts; administrative courts; courts martial

POLITICAL PARTIES AND LEADERS:

Alternative for Bulgarian Revival or ABV [Rumen PETKOV]
Attack (Ataka) [Volen Nikolov SIDEROV]
Bulgarian Agrarian People's Union [Nikolay NENCHEV]
Bulgarian Socialist Party or BSP [Korneliya NINOVA]
Bulgaria of the Citizens or DBG [Dimiter DELCHEV]]
Citizens for the European Development of Bulgaria or GERB [Boyko BORISSOV]
Democrats for a Strong Bulgaria or DSB [Atanas ATANASOV]
Democrats for Responsibility, Solidarity, and Tolerance or DOST [Lyutvi MESTAN]
IMRO - Bulgarian National Movement or IMRO-BNM [Krasimir KARAKACHANOV]
Movement for Rights and Freedoms or DPS [Mustafa KARADAYI]
National Front for the Salvation of Bulgaria or NFSB [Valeri SIMEONOV]
Reformist Bloc or RB (a four-party alliance including DBG and SDS)
United Patriots (alliance of IMRO-BNM, NFSB, and Attack)
Union of Democratic Forces or SDS [Bozhidar LUKARSKI]
Yes! Bulgaria [Hristo IVANOV]
Volya [Veselin MARESHKI]

INTERNATIONAL ORGANIZATION PARTICIPATION:

Australia Group, BIS, BSEC, CD, CE, CEI, CERN, EAPC, EBRD, ECB, EIB, EU, FAO, G- 9, IAEA, IBRD, ICAO, ICC (national committees), ICCt, ICRM, IDA, IFC, IFRCS, IHO (pending member), ILO, IMF, IMO, IMSO, Interpol, IOC, IOM, IPU, ISO, ITU, ITUC (NGOs), MIGA, NATO, NSG, OAS (observer), OIF, OPCW, OSCE, PCA, SELEC, UN, UNCTAD, UNESCO, UNHCR, UNIDO, UNMIL, UNWTO, UPU, WCO, WFTU (NGOs), WHO, WIPO, WMO, WTO, ZC

DIPLOMATIC REPRESENTATION IN THE US:

chief of mission: Ambassador Tihomir Anguelov STOYTCHEV (since 27 June 2016)

chancery: 1621 22nd Street NW, Washington, DC 20008

telephone: [1] (202) 387-0174

FAX: [1] (202) 234-7973

consulate(s) general: Chicago, Los Angeles, New York

DIPLOMATIC REPRESENTATION FROM THE US:

chief of mission: Ambassador Eric Seth RUBIN (since 24 February 2016)

embassy: 16 Kozyak Street, Sofia 1408

mailing address: American Embassy Sofia, US Department of State, 5740 Sofia Place, Washington, DC 20521-5740

telephone: [359] (2) 937-5100

FAX: [359] (2) 937-5320

FLAG DESCRIPTION:

three equal horizontal bands of white (top), green, and red; the pan-Slavic white-blue-red colors were modified by substituting a green band (representing freedom) for the blue

note: the national emblem, formerly on the hoist side of the white stripe, has been removed

NATIONAL SYMBOL(S):

lion; national colors: white, green, red

NATIONAL ANTHEM:

name: "Mila Rodino" (Dear Homeland)

lyrics/music: Tsvetan Tsvetkov RADOSLAVOV

note: adopted 1964; composed in 1885 by a student en route to fight in the Serbo-Bulgarian War

ECONOMY :: BULGARIA

ECONOMY - OVERVIEW:

Bulgaria, a former communist country that entered the EU in 2007, has an open economy that historically has demonstrated strong growth, but its per-capita income remains the lowest among EU members and its reliance on energy imports and foreign demand for its exports makes its growth sensitive to external market conditions.

The government undertook significant structural economic reforms in the 1990s to move the economy from a centralized, planned economy to a more liberal, market-driven economy. These reforms included privatization of state-owned enterprises, liberalization of trade, and strengthening of the tax system - changes that initially caused some economic hardships but later helped to attract investment, spur growth, and make gradual improvements to living conditions. From 2000 through 2008, Bulgaria maintained robust, average annual real GDP growth in excess of 6%, which was followed by a deep recession in 2009 as the financial crisis caused domestic demand, exports, capital inflows and industrial production to contract, prompting the government to rein in spending. Real GDP growth remained slow - less than 2% annually - until 2015, when demand from EU countries for Bulgarian exports, plus an inflow of EU development funds, boosted growth to more than 3%. In recent years, strong domestic demand combined with low international energy prices have contributed to Bulgaria's economic growth approaching 4% and have also helped to ease inflation. Bulgaria's prudent public financial management contributed to budget surpluses both in 2016 and 2017.

Bulgaria is heavily reliant on energy imports from Russia, a potential vulnerability, and is a participant in EU-backed efforts to diversify regional natural gas supplies. In late 2016, the Bulgarian Government provided funding to Bulgaria's National Electric Company to cover the $695 million compensation owed to Russian nuclear equipment manufacturer Atomstroyexport for the cancellation of the Belene Nuclear Power Plant project, which the Bulgarian Government terminated in 2012. As of early 2018, the government was floating the possibility of resurrecting the Belene project. The natural gas market, dominated by state-owned Bulgargaz, is also almost entirely supplied by Russia. Infrastructure projects such as the Inter-Connector Greece-Bulgaria and Inter-Connector Bulgaria-Serbia, which would enable Bulgaria to have access to non-Russian gas, have either stalled or made limited progress. In 2016, the Bulgarian Government established the State eGovernment Agency. This new agency is responsible for the electronic governance, coordinating national policies with the EU, and strengthening cybersecurity.

Despite a favorable investment regime, including low, flat corporate income taxes, significant challenges remain. Corruption in public administration, a weak judiciary, low productivity, lack of transparency in public procurements, and the presence of organized crime continue to hamper the country's investment climate and economic prospects.

GDP (PURCHASING POWER PARITY):

$153.5 billion (2017 est.)

$148.2 billion (2016 est.)

$142.6 billion (2015 est.)

note: data are in 2017 dollars

country comparison to the world: 76

GDP (OFFICIAL EXCHANGE RATE):

$56.94 billion (2017 est.) (2017 est.)

GDP - REAL GROWTH RATE:

3.6% (2017 est.)

3.9% (2016 est.)

3.6% (2015 est.)

country comparison to the world: 94

GDP - PER CAPITA (PPP):

$21,800 (2017 est.)

$20,900 (2016 est.)

$19,900 (2015 est.)

note: data are in 2017 dollars

country comparison to the world: 87

GROSS NATIONAL SAVING:

25.4% of GDP (2017 est.)

21.4% of GDP (2016 est.)

21.2% of GDP (2015 est.)

country comparison to the world: 58

GDP - COMPOSITION, BY END USE:

household consumption: 61.6% (2017 est.)

government consumption: 16% (2017 est.)

investment in fixed capital: 19.2% (2017 est.)

investment in inventories: 1.7% (2017 est.)

exports of goods and services: 66.3% (2017 est.)

imports of goods and services: -64.8% (2017 est.)

GDP - COMPOSITION, BY SECTOR OF ORIGIN:

agriculture: 4.3% (2017 est.)

industry: 28% (2017 est.)

services: 67.4% (2017 est.)

AGRICULTURE - PRODUCTS:

vegetables, fruits, tobacco, wine, wheat, barley, sunflowers, sugar beets; livestock

INDUSTRIES:

electricity, gas, water; food, beverages, tobacco; machinery and equipment, automotive parts, base metals, chemical products, coke, refined petroleum, nuclear fuel; outsourcing centers

INDUSTRIAL PRODUCTION GROWTH RATE:

3.6% (2017 est.)

country comparison to the world: 80

LABOR FORCE:

3.357 million (2017 est.)

note: number of employed persons

country comparison to the world: 102

LABOR FORCE - BY OCCUPATION:

agriculture: 6.8%

industry: 26.6%

services: 66.6% (2016 est.)

UNEMPLOYMENT RATE:

6.2% (2017 est.)

7.7% (2016 est.)

country comparison to the world: 93

POPULATION BELOW POVERTY LINE:

23.4% (2016 est.)

HOUSEHOLD INCOME OR CONSUMPTION BY PERCENTAGE SHARE:

lowest 10%: 31.2% (2017)

highest 10%: 31.2% (2017)

DISTRIBUTION OF FAMILY INCOME - GINI INDEX:

40.2 (2017)

38.3 (2016)

country comparison to the world: 64

BUDGET:

revenues: 20.35 billion (2017 est.)

expenditures: 19.35 billion (2017 est.)

TAXES AND OTHER REVENUES:

35.7% (of GDP) (2017 est.)

country comparison to the world: 58

BUDGET SURPLUS (+) OR DEFICIT (-):

1.8% (of GDP) (2017 est.)

country comparison to the world: 16

PUBLIC DEBT:

23.9% of GDP (2017 est.)

27.4% of GDP (2016 est.)

note: defined by the EU's Maastricht Treaty as consolidated general government gross debt at nominal value, outstanding at the end of the year in the following categories of government liabilities: currency and deposits, securities other than shares excluding financial derivatives, and loans; general government sector comprises the subsectors: central government, state government, local government, and social security funds

country comparison to the world: 181

FISCAL YEAR:

calendar year

INFLATION RATE (CONSUMER PRICES):

1.2% (2017 est.)

-1.3% (2016 est.)

country comparison to the world: 63

CENTRAL BANK DISCOUNT RATE:

0% (31 December 2017)

0.01% (31 December 2015)

note: Bulgarian National Bank (BNB) has had no independent monetary policy since the introduction of the Currency Board regime in 1997; this is BNB's base interest rate

country comparison to the world: 149

COMMERCIAL BANK PRIME LENDING RATE:

5.41% (31 December 2017 est.)

6.39% (31 December 2016 est.)

country comparison to the world: 135

STOCK OF NARROW MONEY:

$29.27 billion (31 December 2017 est.)

$22.01 billion (31 December 2016 est.)

country comparison to the world: 63

STOCK OF BROAD MONEY:

$29.27 billion (31 December 2017 est.)

$22.01 billion (31 December 2016 est.)

country comparison to the world: 63

STOCK OF DOMESTIC CREDIT:

$33.44 billion (31 December 2017 est.)

$27.57 billion (31 December 2016 est.)

country comparison to the world: 77

MARKET VALUE OF PUBLICLY TRADED SHARES:

$14.49 billion (31 December 2017 est.)

$5.205 billion (31 December 2016 est.)

$4.797 billion (31 December 2015 est.)

country comparison to the world: 68

CURRENT ACCOUNT BALANCE:

$2.562 billion (2017 est.)

$1.207 billion (2016 est.)

country comparison to the world: 36

EXPORTS:

$29.08 billion (2017 est.)

$25.37 billion (2016 est.)

country comparison to the world: 67

EXPORTS - PARTNERS:

Germany 13.5%, Italy 8.3%, Romania 8.2%, Turkey 7.7%, Greece 6.5%, Belgium 4.2%, France 4.1% (2017)

EXPORTS - COMMODITIES:

clothing, footwear, iron and steel, machinery and equipment, fuels, agriculture, tobacco, IT components

IMPORTS:

$31.43 billion (2017 est.)

$26.66 billion (2016 est.)

country comparison to the world: 67

IMPORTS - COMMODITIES:

machinery and equipment; metals and ores; chemicals and plastics; fuels, minerals, and raw materials

IMPORTS - PARTNERS:

Germany 12.3%, Russia 10.3%, Italy 7.3%, Romania 7.1%, Turkey 6.2%, Spain 5.3%, Greece 4.4% (2017)

RESERVES OF FOREIGN EXCHANGE AND GOLD:

$28.38 billion (31 December 2017 est.)

$25.13 billion (31 December 2016 est.)

country comparison to the world: 51

DEBT - EXTERNAL:

$42.06 billion (31 December 2017 est.)

$35.98 billion (31 December 2016 est.)

country comparison to the world: 72

STOCK OF DIRECT FOREIGN INVESTMENT - AT HOME:

$46.92 billion (31 December 2017 est.)

$45.26 billion (31 December 2016 est.)

country comparison to the world: 59

STOCK OF DIRECT FOREIGN INVESTMENT - ABROAD:

$5.868 billion (31 December 2017 est.)

$4.988 billion (31 December 2016 est.)

country comparison to the world: 73

EXCHANGE RATES:

leva (BGN) per US dollar -

1.63 (2017 est.)

1.86 (2016 est.)

1.768 (2015 est.)

1.7644 (2014 est.)

1.4742 (2013 est.)

ENERGY :: BULGARIA

ELECTRICITY ACCESS:

electrification - total population: 100% (2016)

ELECTRICITY - PRODUCTION:

42.29 billion kWh (2016 est.)

country comparison to the world: 57

ELECTRICITY - CONSUMPTION:

32.34 billion kWh (2016 est.)

country comparison to the world: 60

ELECTRICITY - EXPORTS:

9.187 billion kWh (2017 est.)

country comparison to the world: 23

ELECTRICITY - IMPORTS:

4.568 billion kWh (2016 est.)

country comparison to the world: 41

ELECTRICITY - INSTALLED GENERATING CAPACITY:

10.75 million kW (2016 est.)

country comparison to the world: 57

ELECTRICITY - FROM FOSSIL FUELS:

39% of total installed capacity (2016 est.)

country comparison to the world: 170

ELECTRICITY - FROM NUCLEAR FUELS:

20% of total installed capacity (2017 est.)

country comparison to the world: 8

ELECTRICITY - FROM HYDROELECTRIC PLANTS:

23% of total installed capacity (2017 est.)

country comparison to the world: 83

ELECTRICITY - FROM OTHER RENEWABLE SOURCES:

19% of total installed capacity (2017 est.)

country comparison to the world: 41

CRUDE OIL - PRODUCTION:

1,000 bbl/day (2017 est.)

country comparison to the world: 91

CRUDE OIL - EXPORTS:

0 bbl/day (2015 est.)

country comparison to the world: 99

CRUDE OIL - IMPORTS:

133,900 bbl/day (2015 est.)

country comparison to the world: 39

CRUDE OIL - PROVED RESERVES:

15 million bbl (1 January 2018 est.)

country comparison to the world: 84

REFINED PETROLEUM PRODUCTS - PRODUCTION:

144,300 bbl/day (2015 est.)

country comparison to the world: 60

REFINED PETROLEUM PRODUCTS - CONSUMPTION:

97,000 bbl/day (2016 est.)

country comparison to the world: 82

REFINED PETROLEUM PRODUCTS - EXPORTS:

92,720 bbl/day (2015 est.)

country comparison to the world: 45

REFINED PETROLEUM PRODUCTS - IMPORTS:

49,260 bbl/day (2015 est.)

country comparison to the world: 83

NATURAL GAS - PRODUCTION:

79.28 million cu m (2017 est.)

country comparison to the world: 83

NATURAL GAS - CONSUMPTION:

3.313 billion cu m (2017 est.)

country comparison to the world: 70

NATURAL GAS - EXPORTS:

31.15 million cu m (2017 est.)

country comparison to the world: 52

NATURAL GAS - IMPORTS:

3.256 billion cu m (2017 est.)

country comparison to the world: 44

NATURAL GAS - PROVED RESERVES:

5.663 billion cu m (1 January 2018 est.)

country comparison to the world: 88

CARBON DIOXIDE EMISSIONS FROM CONSUMPTION OF ENERGY:

46.31 million Mt (2017 est.)

country comparison to the world: 63

COMMUNICATIONS :: BULGARIA

TELEPHONES - FIXED LINES:

total subscriptions: 1,302,316 (2017 est.)

subscriptions per 100 inhabitants: 18 (2017 est.)

country comparison to the world: 69

TELEPHONES - MOBILE CELLULAR:

total subscriptions: 8,532,908 (2017 est.)

subscriptions per 100 inhabitants: 120 (2017 est.)

country comparison to the world: 96

TELEPHONE SYSTEM:

general assessment: inherited an extensive but antiquated telecommunications network from the Soviet era; quality has improved with a modern digital trunk line now connecting switching centers in most of the regions; remaining areas are connected by digital microwave radio relay; Bulgaria has a mature mobile market with active competition (2017)

domestic: fixed-line 18 per 100 persons, mobile-cellular teledensity, fostered by multiple service providers, is over 120 telephones per 100 persons (2017)

international: country code - 359; submarine cable provides connectivity to Ukraine and Russia; a combination submarine cable and land fiber-optic system provides connectivity to Italy, Albania, and Macedonia; satellite earth stations - 3 (1 Intersputnik in the Atlantic Ocean region, 2 Intelsat in the Atlantic and Indian Ocean regions) (2016)

BROADCAST MEDIA:

4 national terrestrial TV stations with 1 state-owned and 3 privately owned; a vast array of TV stations are available from cable and satellite TV providers; state-owned national radio broadcasts over 3 networks; large number of private radio stations broadcasting, especially in urban areas (2010)

INTERNET COUNTRY CODE:

.bg

INTERNET USERS:

total: 4,274,328 (July 2016 est.)

percent of population: 59.8% (July 2016 est.)

country comparison to the world: 85

BROADBAND - FIXED SUBSCRIPTIONS:

total: 1,764,782 (2017 est.)

subscriptions per 100 inhabitants: 25 (2017 est.)

country comparison to the world: 55

TRANSPORTATION :: BULGARIA

NATIONAL AIR TRANSPORT SYSTEM:

number of registered air carriers: 8 (2015)

inventory of registered aircraft operated by air carriers: 44 (2015)

annual passenger traffic on registered air carriers: 1,118,689 (2015)

annual freight traffic on registered air carriers: 1,583,340 mt-km (2015)

CIVIL AIRCRAFT REGISTRATION COUNTRY CODE PREFIX:

LZ (2016)

AIRPORTS:

68 (2013)

country comparison to the world: 73

AIRPORTS - WITH PAVED RUNWAYS:

total: 57 (2017)

over 3,047 m: 2 (2017)

2,438 to 3,047 m: 17 (2017)

1,524 to 2,437 m: 12 (2017)

under 914 m: 26 (2017)

AIRPORTS - WITH UNPAVED RUNWAYS:

total: 11 (2013)

914 to 1,523 m: 2 (2013)

under 914 m: 9 (2013)

HELIPORTS:

1 (2013)

PIPELINES:

2765 km gas, 346 km oil, 378 km refined products (2017)

RAILWAYS:

total: 5,114 km (2014)

standard gauge: 4,989 km 1.435-m gauge (2,880 km electrified) (2014)

narrow gauge: 125 km 0.760-m gauge (2014)

country comparison to the world: 37

ROADWAYS:

total: 19,512 km (2011)

paved: 19,235 km (includes 458 km of expressways) (2011)

unpaved: 277 km (2011)

note: does not include Category IV local roads

country comparison to the world: 112

WATERWAYS:

470 km (2009)

country comparison to the world: 83

MERCHANT MARINE:

total: 80 (2017)

by type: bulk carrier 2, general cargo 18, oil tanker 8, other 52 (2017)

country comparison to the world: 97

PORTS AND TERMINALS:

major seaport(s): Burgas, Varna (Black Sea)

MILITARY AND SECURITY :: BULGARIA

MILITARY EXPENDITURES:

1.53% of GDP (2017)

1.44% of GDP (2016)

1.32% of GDP (2015)

country comparison to the world: 73

MILITARY BRANCHES:

Bulgarian Armed Forces: Land Forces (aka Army), Naval Forces, Bulgarian Air Forces (Voennovazdushni Sili, VVS) (2018)

MILITARY SERVICE AGE AND OBLIGATION:

18-27 years of age for voluntary military service; conscription ended in January 2008; service obligation 6-9 months (2012)

TRANSNATIONAL ISSUES :: BULGARIA

DISPUTES - INTERNATIONAL:

none

REFUGEES AND INTERNALLY DISPLACED PERSONS:

refugees (country of origin): 15,027 (Syria) (2016)

stateless persons: 48 (2017)

note: 53,371 estimated refugee and migrant arrivals (January 2015-December 2018); Bulgaria is predominantly a transit country and hosts approximately 992 migrants and asylum seekers as of the end of September 2018; 2,562 migrant arrivals in 2017

TRAFFICKING IN PERSONS:

current situation: Bulgaria is a source and, to a lesser extent, a transit and destination country for men, women, and children subjected to sex trafficking and forced labor; Bulgaria is one of the main sources of human trafficking in the EU; women and children are increasingly sex trafficked domestically, as well as in Europe, Russia, the Middle East, and the US, adults and children become forced laborers in agriculture, construction, and the service sector in Europe, Israel, and Zambia; Romanian girls are also subjected to sex trafficking in Bulgaria

tier rating: Tier 2 Watch List – Bulgaria does not fully comply with the minimum standards for the elimination of trafficking; however, it is making significant efforts to do so; in 2014, authorities prosecuted and convicted fewer traffickers and issued suspended sentences for the majority of those convicted; victim protection efforts declined and were minimal relative to the number of victims identified; funding for the state's two NGO-operated shelters was significantly cut, forcing them to close; specialized services for child and adult male victims were non-existent; the government took action to combat trafficking-related complicity among public officials and police officers (2015)

ILLICIT DRUGS:

major European transshipment point for Southwest Asian heroin and, to a lesser degree, South American cocaine for the European market; limited producer of precursor chemicals; vulnerable to money laundering because of corruption, organized crime; some money laundering of drug-related proceeds through financial institutions

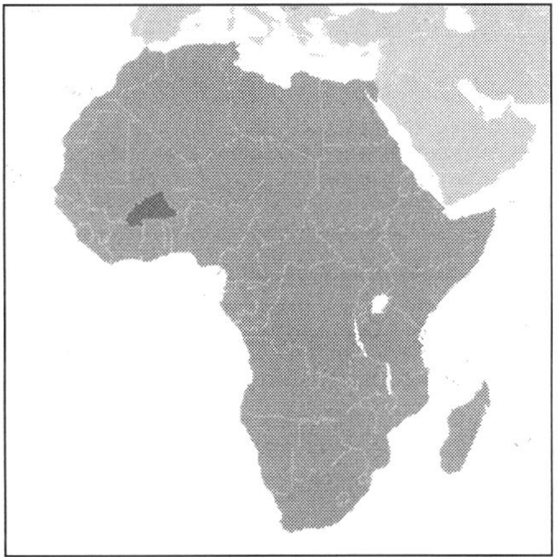

AFRICA :: BURKINA FASO

INTRODUCTION :: BURKINA FASO

BACKGROUND:

Burkina Faso (formerly Upper Volta) achieved independence from France in 1960. Repeated military coups during the 1970s and 1980s were followed by multiparty elections in the early 1990s. Former President Blaise COMPAORE (1987-2014) resigned in late October 2014 following popular protests against his efforts to amend the constitution's two-term presidential limit. An interim administration organized presidential and legislative elections - finally held in November 2015 - where Roch Marc Christian KABORE was elected president. The country experienced terrorist attacks in its capital in 2016, 2017, and 2018 and continues to mobilize resources to counter terrorist threats. Burkina Faso's high population growth, recurring drought, pervasive and perennial food insecurity, and limited natural resources result in poor economic prospects for the majority of its citizens.

GEOGRAPHY :: BURKINA FASO

LOCATION:

Western Africa, north of Ghana

GEOGRAPHIC COORDINATES:

13 00 N, 2 00 W

MAP REFERENCES:

Africa

AREA:

total: 274,200 sq km

land: 273,800 sq km

water: 400 sq km

country comparison to the world: 76

AREA - COMPARATIVE:

slightly larger than Colorado

LAND BOUNDARIES:

total: 3,611 km

border countries (6): Benin 386 km, Cote d'Ivoire 545 km, Ghana 602 km, Mali 1325 km, Niger 622 km, Togo 131 km

COASTLINE:

0 km (landlocked)

MARITIME CLAIMS:

none (landlocked)

CLIMATE:

tropical; warm, dry winters; hot, wet summers

TERRAIN:

mostly flat to dissected, undulating plains; hills in west and southeast

ELEVATION:

mean elevation: 297 m

elevation extremes: 200 m lowest point: Mouhoun (Black Volta) River

749 highest point: Tena Kourou

NATURAL RESOURCES:

manganese, limestone, marble; small deposits of gold, phosphates, pumice, salt

LAND USE:

agricultural land: 43% (2011 est.)

arable land: 20.8% (2011 est.) / permanent crops: 0.3% (2011 est.) / permanent pasture: 21.9% (2011 est.)

forest: 20.4% (2011 est.)

other: 36.6% (2011 est.)

IRRIGATED LAND:

550 sq km (2012)

POPULATION DISTRIBUTION:

the population is concentrated in the central and southern parts of the country; the east, north, and southwest are less populated

NATURAL HAZARDS:

recurring droughts

ENVIRONMENT - CURRENT ISSUES:

recent droughts and desertification severely affecting agricultural activities, population distribution, and the economy; overgrazing; soil degradation; deforestation

ENVIRONMENT - INTERNATIONAL AGREEMENTS:

party to: Biodiversity, Climate Change, Climate Change-Kyoto Protocol, Desertification, Endangered Species, Hazardous Wastes, Law of the Sea, Marine Life Conservation, Ozone Layer Protection, Wetlands

signed, but not ratified: none of the selected agreements

GEOGRAPHY - NOTE:

landlocked savanna cut by the three principal rivers of the Black, Red, and White Voltas

PEOPLE AND SOCIETY :: BURKINA FASO

POPULATION:

19,742,715 (July 2018 est.)

note: estimates for this country explicitly take into account the effects of excess mortality due to AIDS; this can result in lower life expectancy, higher infant mortality, higher death rates, lower population growth rates, and changes in the distribution of population by age and sex than would otherwise be expected

country comparison to the world: 61

NATIONALITY:

noun: Burkinabe (singular and plural)

adjective: Burkinabe

ETHNIC GROUPS:

Mossi 52%, Fulani 8.4%, Gurma 7%, Bobo 4.9%, Gurunsi 4.6%, Senufo 4.5%, Bissa 3.7%, Lobi 2.4%, Dagara 2.4%, Tuareg/Bella 1.9%, Dioula 0.8%, unspecified/no answer 0.3%, other 7.2% (2010 est.)

LANGUAGES:

French (official), French native African languages belonging to Sudanic family spoken by 90% of the population

RELIGIONS:

Muslim 61.5%, Roman Catholic 23.3%, traditional/animist 7.8%, Protestant 6.5%, other/no answer 0.2%, none 0.7% (2010 est.)

DEMOGRAPHIC PROFILE:

Burkina Faso has a young age structure – the result of declining mortality combined with steady high fertility – and continues to experience rapid population growth, which is putting increasing pressure on the country's limited arable land. More than 65% of the population is under the age of 25, and the population is growing at 3% annually. Mortality rates, especially those of infants and children, have decreased because of improved health care, hygiene, and sanitation, but women continue to have an average of almost 6 children. Even if fertility were substantially reduced, today's large cohort entering their reproductive years would sustain high population growth for the foreseeable future. Only about a third of the population is literate and unemployment is widespread, dampening the economic prospects of Burkina Faso's large working-age population.

Migration has traditionally been a way of life for Burkinabe, with seasonal migration being replaced by stints of up to two years abroad. Cote d'Ivoire remains the top destination, although it has experienced periods of internal conflict. Under French colonization, Burkina Faso became a main labor source for agricultural and factory work in Cote d'Ivoire. Burkinabe also migrated to Ghana, Mali, and Senegal for work between the world wars. Burkina Faso attracts migrants from Cote d'Ivoire, Ghana, and Mali, who often share common ethnic backgrounds with the Burkinabe. Despite its food shortages and high poverty rate, Burkina Faso has become a destination for refugees in recent years and hosts about 33,500 Malians as of May 2017.

AGE STRUCTURE:

0-14 years: 44.28% (male 4,434,908 /female 4,307,438)

15-24 years: 20.19% (male 1,980,755 /female 2,004,763)

25-54 years: 28.82% (male 2,639,235 /female 3,051,333)

55-64 years: 3.55% (male 304,642 /female 396,072)

65 years and over: 3.16% (male 273,031 /female 350,538) (2018 est.)

DEPENDENCY RATIOS:

total dependency ratio: 92.2 (2015 est.)

youth dependency ratio: 87.6 (2015 est.)

elderly dependency ratio: 4.6 (2015 est.)

potential support ratio: 21.6 (2015 est.)

MEDIAN AGE:

total: 17.4 years

male: 16.6 years

female: 18.2 years (2018 est.)

country comparison to the world: 218

POPULATION GROWTH RATE:

2.76% (2018 est.)

country comparison to the world: 12

BIRTH RATE:

36.9 births/1,000 population (2018 est.)

country comparison to the world: 14

DEATH RATE:

8.7 deaths/1,000 population (2018 est.)

country comparison to the world: 72

NET MIGRATION RATE:

0 migrant(s)/1,000 population (2017 est.)

country comparison to the world: 76

POPULATION DISTRIBUTION:

the population is concentrated in the central and southern parts of the country; the east, north, and southwest are less populated

URBANIZATION:

urban population: 29.4% of total population (2018)

rate of urbanization: 4.99% annual rate of change (2015-20 est.)

MAJOR URBAN AREAS - POPULATION:

2.531 million OUAGADOUGOU (capital), 879,000 Bobo-Dioulasso (2018)

SEX RATIO:

at birth: 1.02 male(s)/female (2017 est.)

0-14 years: 1 male(s)/female (2017 est.)

15-24 years: 1.01 male(s)/female (2017 est.)

25-54 years: 1.03 male(s)/female (2017 est.)

55-64 years: 0.77 male(s)/female (2017 est.)

65 years and over: 0.6 male(s)/female (2017 est.)

total population: 0.99 male(s)/female (2017 est.)

MOTHER'S MEAN AGE AT FIRST BIRTH:

19.4 years (2010 est.)

note: median age at first birth among women 25-29

MATERNAL MORTALITY RATE:

371 deaths/100,000 live births (2015 est.)

country comparison to the world: 31

INFANT MORTALITY RATE:

total: 54.7 deaths/1,000 live births (2018 est.)

male: 59.2 deaths/1,000 live births (2018 est.)

female: 50 deaths/1,000 live births (2018 est.)

country comparison to the world: 21

LIFE EXPECTANCY AT BIRTH:

total population: 61.8 years (2018 est.)

male: 60.1 years (2018 est.)

female: 63.6 years (2018 est.)

country comparison to the world: 202

TOTAL FERTILITY RATE:

4.77 children born/woman (2018 est.)

country comparison to the world: 19

CONTRACEPTIVE PREVALENCE RATE:

25.4% (2016/17)

HEALTH EXPENDITURES:

5% of GDP (2014)

country comparison to the world: 140

PHYSICIANS DENSITY:

0.05 physicians/1,000 population (2012)

HOSPITAL BED DENSITY:

0.4 beds/1,000 population (2010)

DRINKING WATER SOURCE:

improved:

urban: 97.5% of population

rural: 75.8% of population

total: 82.3% of population

unimproved:

urban: 2.5% of population

rural: 24.2% of population

total: 17.7% of population (2015 est.)

SANITATION FACILITY ACCESS:

improved:

urban: 50.4% of population (2015 est.)

rural: 6.7% of population (2015 est.)

total: 19.7% of population (2015 est.)

unimproved:

urban: 49.6% of population (2015 est.)

rural: 93.3% of population (2015 est.)

total: 80.3% of population (2015 est.)

HIV/AIDS - ADULT PREVALENCE RATE:

0.8% (2017 est.)

country comparison to the world: 50

HIV/AIDS - PEOPLE LIVING WITH HIV/AIDS:

94,000 (2017 est.)

country comparison to the world: 45

HIV/AIDS - DEATHS:

2,900 (2017 est.)

country comparison to the world: 40

MAJOR INFECTIOUS DISEASES:

degree of risk: very high (2016)

food or waterborne diseases: bacterial and protozoal diarrhea, hepatitis A, and typhoid fever (2016)

vectorborne diseases: dengue fever, malaria, and yellow fever (2016)

water contact diseases: schistosomiasis (2016)

animal contact diseases: rabies (2016)

respiratory diseases: meningococcal meningitis (2016)

OBESITY - ADULT PREVALENCE RATE:

5.6% (2016)

country comparison to the world: 175

CHILDREN UNDER THE AGE OF 5 YEARS UNDERWEIGHT:

19.2% (2016)

country comparison to the world: 27

EDUCATION EXPENDITURES:

4.2% of GDP (2015)

country comparison to the world: 105

LITERACY:

definition: age 15 and over can read and write (2015 est.)

total population: 36% (2015 est.)

male: 43% (2015 est.)

female: 29.3% (2015 est.)

SCHOOL LIFE EXPECTANCY (PRIMARY TO TERTIARY EDUCATION):

total: 8 years (2013)

male: 8 years (2013)

female: 7 years (2013)

UNEMPLOYMENT, YOUTH AGES 15-24:

total: 8.7%

male: 5.3%

female: 12.6%

country comparison to the world: 133

GOVERNMENT :: BURKINA FASO

COUNTRY NAME:

conventional long form: none

conventional short form: Burkina Faso

local long form: none

local short form: Burkina Faso

former: Upper Volta, Republic of Upper Volta

etymology: name translates as "Land of the Honest (Incorruptible) Men"

GOVERNMENT TYPE:

presidential republic

CAPITAL:

name: Ouagadougou

geographic coordinates: 12 22 N, 1 31 W

time difference: UTC 0 (5 hours ahead of Washington, DC, during Standard Time)

ADMINISTRATIVE DIVISIONS:

13 regions; Boucle du Mouhoun, Cascades, Centre, Centre-Est, Centre-Nord, Centre-Ouest, Centre-Sud, Est, Hauts-Bassins, Nord, Plateau-Central, Sahel, Sud-Ouest

INDEPENDENCE:

5 August 1960 (from France)

NATIONAL HOLIDAY:

Republic Day, 11 December (1958); note - commemorates the day that Upper Volta became an autonomous republic in the French Community

CONSTITUTION:

history: several previous; latest approved by referendum 2 June 1991, adopted 11 June 1991, temporarily suspended late October to mid-November 2014 (2017)

amendments: proposed by the president, by a majority of National Assembly membership, or by petition of at least 30,000 eligible voters submitted to the Assembly; passage requires at least three-fourths majority vote in the Assembly; failure to meet that threshold requires majority voter approval in a referendum; constitutional provisions on the form of government, the multiparty system, and national sovereignty cannot be amended; amended several times, last in 2012 (2017)

LEGAL SYSTEM:

civil law based on the French model and customary law

INTERNATIONAL LAW ORGANIZATION PARTICIPATION:

has not submitted an ICJ jurisdiction declaration; accepts ICCt jurisdiction

CITIZENSHIP:

citizenship by birth: no

citizenship by descent only: at least one parent must be a citizen of Burkina Faso

dual citizenship recognized: yes

residency requirement for naturalization: 10 years

SUFFRAGE:

18 years of age; universal

EXECUTIVE BRANCH:

chief of state: President Roch Marc Christian KABORE (since 29 December 2015)

head of government: Prime Minister Paul Kaba THIEBA (since 6 January 2016)

cabinet: Council of Ministers appointed by the president on the recommendation of the prime minister

elections/appointments: president elected by absolute majority popular vote in 2 rounds if needed for a 5-year term (eligible for a second); election last held on 29 November 2015 (next to be held November 2020); prime minister appointed by the president with consent of the National Assembly

election results: Roch Marc Christian KABORE elected president in first round; percent of vote - Roch Marc Christian KABORE (MPP) 53.5%, Zephirin DIABRE (UPC) 29.6%, Tahirou BARRY (PAREN) 3.1%. Benewende Stanislas SANKARA (UNIR-MS) 2.8%, other 10.9%

LEGISLATIVE BRANCH:

description: unicameral National Assembly (127 seats; members directly elected in multi-seat constituencies by party-list proportional representation vote to serve 5-year terms)

elections: last held on 29 November 2015 (next to be held in 2020)

election results: percent of vote by party - NA; seats by party - MPP 55, UPC 33, CDP 18, Union for Rebirth-Sankarist Party 5, ADF/RDA 3, NTD 3, other 10; composition - men 115, women 12, percent of women 9.4%

JUDICIAL BRANCH:

highest courts: Supreme Court of Appeals or Cour de Cassation (consists of NA judges); Council of State (consists of NA judges); Constitutional Council or Conseil Constitutionnel (consists of the council president and 9 members)

judge selection and term of office: Supreme Court judge appointments mostly controlled by the president of Burkina Faso; judges have no term limits; Council of State judge appointment and tenure NA; Constitutional Council judges appointed by the president of Burkina Faso upon the proposal of the minister of justice and the president of the National Assembly; judges appointed for 9-year terms with one-third of membership renewed every 3 years

subordinate courts: Appeals Court; High Court; first instance tribunals; district courts; specialized courts relating to issues of labor, children, and juveniles; village (customary) courts

POLITICAL PARTIES AND LEADERS:

African Democratic Rally/Alliance for Democracy and Federation or ADF/RDA [Gilbert Noel OUEDRAOGO]
African People's Movement or MAP [Victorien TOUGOUMA]
Congress for Democracy and Progress or CDP [Eddie KOMBOIGO]
Le Faso Autrement [Ablasse OUEDRAOGO]
New Alliance of the Faso or NAFA [Mahamoudou DICKO]
New Time for Democracy or NTD [Vincent DABILGOU]
Organization for Democracy and Work or ODT [Anatole BONKOUNGOU]
Party for Development and Change or PDC [Aziz SEREME]
Party for Democracy and Progress-Socialist Party or PDP-PS [Drabo TORO]
Party for Democracy and Socialism/Metba or PDS/Metba [Philippe OUEDRAOGO]
Party for National Renaissance or PAREN [Michel BERE]
People's Movement for Progress or MPP [Simon COMPAORE]
Rally for Democracy and Socialism or RDS [Francois OUEDRAOGO]
Rally for the Development of Burkina or RDB [Celestin Saidou COMPAORE]
Rally of Ecologists of Burkina Faso or RDEB [Adama SERE]
Union for a New Burkina or UBN [Diemdioda DICKO]
Union for Progress and Change or UPC [Zephirin DIABRE]
Union for Rebirth - Sankarist Party or UNIR-MS [Benewende Stanislas SANKARA]
Union for the Republic or UPR [Toussaint Abel COULIBALY]
Youth Alliance for the Republic and Independence or AJIR [Adama KANAZOE]

INTERNATIONAL ORGANIZATION PARTICIPATION:

ACP, AfDB, AU, CD, ECOWAS, EITI (compliant country), Entente, FAO, FZ, G-77, IAEA, IBRD, ICAO, ICC (NGOs), ICCt, ICRM, IDA, IDB, IFAD, IFC, IFRCS, ILO, IMF, Interpol, IOC, IOM, IPU, ISO, ITSO, ITU, ITUC (NGOs), MIGA, MINUSMA, MONUSCO, NAM, OIC, OIF, OPCW, PCA, UN, UNAMID, UNCTAD, UNESCO, UNIDO, UNISFA, UNITAR, UNWTO, UPU, WADB (regional), WAEMU, WCO, WFTU (NGOs), WHO, WIPO, WMO, WTO

DIPLOMATIC REPRESENTATION IN THE US:

chief of mission: Ambassador Seydou KABORE (since 18 January 2017)

chancery: 2340 Massachusetts Avenue NW, Washington, DC 20008

telephone: [1] (202) 332-5577

FAX: [1] (202) 667-1882

DIPLOMATIC REPRESENTATION FROM THE US:

chief of mission: Ambassador Andrew YOUNG (since 1 December 2016)

embassy: Rue 15.873, Avenue Sembene Ousmane, Ouaga 2000, Secteur 15

mailing address: 01 B. P. 35, Ouagadougou 01; pouch mail - US Department of State, 2440 Ouagadougou Place, Washington, DC 20521-2440

telephone: [226] 25-49-53-00

FAX: [226] 25-49-56-28

FLAG DESCRIPTION:

two equal horizontal bands of red (top) and green with a yellow five-pointed star in the center; red recalls the country's struggle for independence, green is for hope and abundance, and yellow represents the country's mineral wealth

note: uses the popular Pan-African colors of Ethiopia

NATIONAL SYMBOL(S):

white stallion; national colors: red, yellow, green

NATIONAL ANTHEM:

name: "Le Ditanye" (Anthem of Victory)

lyrics/music: Thomas SANKARA

note: adopted 1974; also known as "Une Seule Nuit" (One Single Night); written by the country's former president, an avid guitar player

ECONOMY :: BURKINA FASO

ECONOMY - OVERVIEW:

Burkina Faso is a poor, landlocked country that depends on adequate rainfall. Irregular patterns of rainfall, poor soil, and the lack of adequate communications and other infrastructure contribute to the economy's vulnerability to external shocks. About 80% of the population is engaged in subsistence farming and cotton is the main cash crop. The country has few natural resources and a weak industrial base.

Cotton and gold are Burkina Faso's key exports - gold has accounted for about three-quarters of the country's total export revenues. Burkina Faso's economic growth and revenue depends largely on production levels and global prices for the two commodities. The country has seen an upswing in gold exploration, production, and exports.

In 2016, the government adopted a new development strategy, set forth in the 2016-2020 National Plan for Economic and Social Development, that aims to reduce poverty, build human capital, and to satisfy basic needs. A new three-year IMF program (2018-2020), approved in 2018, will allow the government to reduce the budget deficit and preserve critical spending on social services and priority public investments.

While the end of the political crisis has allowed Burkina Faso's economy to resume positive growth, the country's fragile security situation could put these gains at risk. Political insecurity in neighboring Mali, unreliable energy supplies, and poor transportation links pose long-term challenges.

GDP (PURCHASING POWER PARITY):

$35.85 billion (2017 est.)

$33.69 billion (2016 est.)

$31.81 billion (2015 est.)

note: data are in 2017 dollars

country comparison to the world: 126

GDP (OFFICIAL EXCHANGE RATE):

$12.57 billion (2017 est.) (2017 est.)

GDP - REAL GROWTH RATE:

6.4% (2017 est.)

5.9% (2016 est.)

3.9% (2015 est.)

country comparison to the world: 31

GDP - PER CAPITA (PPP):

$1,900 (2017 est.)

$1,800 (2016 est.)

$1,800 (2015 est.)

note: data are in 2017 dollars

country comparison to the world: 211

GROSS NATIONAL SAVING:

9.3% of GDP (2017 est.)

8.5% of GDP (2016 est.)

5.3% of GDP (2015 est.)

country comparison to the world: 164

GDP - COMPOSITION, BY END USE:

household consumption: 56.5% (2017 est.)

government consumption: 23.9% (2017 est.)

investment in fixed capital: 24.6% (2017 est.)

investment in inventories: 1% (2017 est.)

exports of goods and services: 28.4% (2017 est.)

imports of goods and services: -34.4% (2017 est.)

GDP - COMPOSITION, BY SECTOR OF ORIGIN:

agriculture: 31% (2017 est.)

industry: 23.9% (2017 est.)

services: 44.9% (2017 est.)

AGRICULTURE - PRODUCTS:

cotton, peanuts, shea nuts, sesame, sorghum, millet, corn, rice; livestock

INDUSTRIES:

cotton lint, beverages, agricultural processing, soap, cigarettes, textiles, gold

INDUSTRIAL PRODUCTION GROWTH RATE:

10.4% (2017 est.)

country comparison to the world: 14

LABOR FORCE:

8.501 million (2016 est.)

note: a large part of the male labor force migrates annually to neighboring countries for seasonal employment

country comparison to the world: 60

LABOR FORCE - BY OCCUPATION:

agriculture: 90%

industry and services: 10% (2000 est.)

UNEMPLOYMENT RATE:

77% (2004)

country comparison to the world: 218

POPULATION BELOW POVERTY LINE:

40.1% (2009 est.)

HOUSEHOLD INCOME OR CONSUMPTION BY PERCENTAGE SHARE:

lowest 10%: 32.2% (2009 est.)

highest 10%: 32.2% (2009 est.)

DISTRIBUTION OF FAMILY INCOME - GINI INDEX:

39.5 (2007)

48.2 (1994)

country comparison to the world: 70

BUDGET:

revenues: 2.666 billion (2017 est.)

expenditures: 3.655 billion (2017 est.)

TAXES AND OTHER REVENUES:

21.2% (of GDP) (2017 est.)

country comparison to the world: 143

BUDGET SURPLUS (+) OR DEFICIT (-):

-7.9% (of GDP) (2017 est.)

country comparison to the world: 198

PUBLIC DEBT:

38.1% of GDP (2017 est.)

38.3% of GDP (2016 est.)

country comparison to the world: 136

FISCAL YEAR:

calendar year

INFLATION RATE (CONSUMER PRICES):

0.4% (2017 est.)

-0.2% (2016 est.)

country comparison to the world: 22

CENTRAL BANK DISCOUNT RATE:

4.25% (31 December 2010)

4.25% (31 December 2009)

country comparison to the world: 88

COMMERCIAL BANK PRIME LENDING RATE:

5.3% (31 December 2017 est.)

5.3% (31 December 2016 est.)

country comparison to the world: 141

STOCK OF NARROW MONEY:

$3.357 billion (31 December 2017 est.)

$2.602 billion (31 December 2016 est.)

country comparison to the world: 119

STOCK OF BROAD MONEY:

$3.357 billion (31 December 2017 est.)

$2.602 billion (31 December 2016 est.)

country comparison to the world: 124

STOCK OF DOMESTIC CREDIT:

$4.409 billion (31 December 2017 est.)

$3.301 billion (31 December 2016 est.)

country comparison to the world: 130

MARKET VALUE OF PUBLICLY TRADED SHARES:

NA

CURRENT ACCOUNT BALANCE:

-$1.019 billion (2017 est.)

-$820 million (2016 est.)

country comparison to the world: 143

EXPORTS:

$3.14 billion (2017 est.)

$2.641 billion (2016 est.)

country comparison to the world: 129

EXPORTS - PARTNERS:

Switzerland 44.9%, India 15.6%, South Africa 11.3%, Cote dIvoire 4.9%

(2017)

EXPORTS - COMMODITIES:

gold, cotton, livestock

IMPORTS:

$3.305 billion (2017 est.)

$2.827 billion (2016 est.)

country comparison to the world: 145

IMPORTS - COMMODITIES:

capital goods, foodstuffs, petroleum

IMPORTS - PARTNERS:

China 13.2%, Cote dIvoire 9.5%, US 8.2%, Thailand 8.1%, France 6.5%, Ghana 4.4%, Togo 4.4%, India 4.3% (2017)

RESERVES OF FOREIGN EXCHANGE AND GOLD:

$49 million (31 December 2017 est.)

$50.9 million (31 December 2016 est.)

country comparison to the world: 186

DEBT - EXTERNAL:

$3.056 billion (31 December 2017 est.)

$2.88 billion (31 December 2016 est.)

country comparison to the world: 142

EXCHANGE RATES:

Communaute Financiere Africaine francs (XOF) per US dollar -

605.3 (2017 est.)

593.01 (2016 est.)

593.01 (2015 est.)

591.45 (2014 est.)

494.42 (2013 est.)

ENERGY :: BURKINA FASO

ELECTRICITY ACCESS:

population without electricity: 14.1 million (2013)

electrification - total population: 17% (2013)

electrification - urban areas: 56% (2013)

electrification - rural areas: 1% (2013)

ELECTRICITY - PRODUCTION:

990 million kWh (2016 est.)

country comparison to the world: 152

ELECTRICITY - CONSUMPTION:

1.551 billion kWh (2016 est.)

country comparison to the world: 148

ELECTRICITY - EXPORTS:

0 kWh (2016 est.)

country comparison to the world: 112

ELECTRICITY - IMPORTS:

630 million kWh (2016 est.)

country comparison to the world: 77

ELECTRICITY - INSTALLED GENERATING CAPACITY:

342,400 kW (2016 est.)

country comparison to the world: 153

ELECTRICITY - FROM FOSSIL FUELS:

80% of total installed capacity (2016 est.)

country comparison to the world: 82

ELECTRICITY - FROM NUCLEAR FUELS:

0% of total installed capacity (2017 est.)

country comparison to the world: 57

ELECTRICITY - FROM HYDROELECTRIC PLANTS:

9% of total installed capacity (2017 est.)

country comparison to the world: 117

ELECTRICITY - FROM OTHER RENEWABLE SOURCES:

12% of total installed capacity (2017 est.)

country comparison to the world: 72

CRUDE OIL - PRODUCTION:

0 bbl/day (2017 est.)

country comparison to the world: 115

CRUDE OIL - EXPORTS:

0 bbl/day (2015 est.)

country comparison to the world: 100

CRUDE OIL - IMPORTS:

0 bbl/day (2015 est.)

country comparison to the world: 102

CRUDE OIL - PROVED RESERVES:

0 bbl (1 January 2018 est.)

country comparison to the world: 112

REFINED PETROLEUM PRODUCTS - PRODUCTION:

0 bbl/day (2015 est.)

country comparison to the world: 124

REFINED PETROLEUM PRODUCTS - CONSUMPTION:

23,000 bbl/day (2016 est.)

country comparison to the world: 132

REFINED PETROLEUM PRODUCTS - EXPORTS:

0 bbl/day (2015 est.)

country comparison to the world: 136

REFINED PETROLEUM PRODUCTS - IMPORTS:

23,580 bbl/day (2015 est.)

country comparison to the world: 110

NATURAL GAS - PRODUCTION:

0 cu m (2017 est.)

country comparison to the world: 110

NATURAL GAS - CONSUMPTION:

0 cu m (2017 est.)

country comparison to the world: 126

NATURAL GAS - EXPORTS:

0 cu m (2017 est.)

country comparison to the world: 75

NATURAL GAS - IMPORTS:

0 cu m (2017 est.)

country comparison to the world: 98

NATURAL GAS - PROVED RESERVES:

0 cu m (1 January 2014 est.)

country comparison to the world: 116

CARBON DIOXIDE EMISSIONS FROM CONSUMPTION OF ENERGY:

3.421 million Mt (2017 est.)

country comparison to the world: 142

COMMUNICATIONS :: BURKINA FASO

TELEPHONES - FIXED LINES:

total subscriptions: 76,000 (2017 est.)

subscriptions per 100 inhabitants: less than 1 (2017 est.)

country comparison to the world: 145

TELEPHONES - MOBILE CELLULAR:

total subscriptions: 17,946,375 (2017 est.)

subscriptions per 100 inhabitants: 89 (2017 est.)

country comparison to the world: 62

TELEPHONE SYSTEM:

general assessment: system includes microwave radio relay, open-wire, and radiotelephone communication stations; with slow regulatory procedures, insufficient mobile spectrum, and poor condition of fixed-line networks the development of fixed-line internet services leave Burkina Faso with some of the most expensive telecommunications globally; mobile telephony has experienced growth, but below the African average; Burkina Faso joins G5 Sahel countries to stop roaming fees by 2019; govt. proposes technology-neutral licences to boost mobile broadband connectivity (2017)

domestic: fixed-line connections stand at less than 1 per 100 persons; mobile-cellular usage 89 per 100, with multiple providers there is competion and the hope for growth from a low base; internet penetration is 11% countrywide, but higher in urban areas (2017)

international: country code - 226; satellite earth station - 1 Intelsat (Atlantic Ocean) (2016)

BROADCAST MEDIA:

since the official inauguration of Terrestrial Digital Television (TNT) in December 2017, Burkina Faso now has 14 digital TV channels among which 2 are state-owned; there are more than 140 radio stations (commercial, religious, community) available throughout the country including a national and regional state-owned network; the state-owned Radio Burkina and the private Radio Omega are among the most widespread stations and both include broadcasts in French and local languages (2018)

INTERNET COUNTRY CODE:

.bf

INTERNET USERS:

total: 2,723,950 (July 2016 est.)

percent of population: 14% (July 2016 est.)

country comparison to the world: 99

BROADBAND - FIXED SUBSCRIPTIONS:

total: 14,067 (2017 est.)

subscriptions per 100 inhabitants: less than 1 (2017 est.)

country comparison to the world: 164

TRANSPORTATION :: BURKINA FASO

NATIONAL AIR TRANSPORT SYSTEM:

number of registered air carriers: 1 (2015)

inventory of registered aircraft operated by air carriers: 3 (2015)

annual passenger traffic on registered air carriers: 122,589 (2015)

annual freight traffic on registered air carriers: 55,868 mt-km (2015)

CIVIL AIRCRAFT REGISTRATION COUNTRY CODE PREFIX:

XT (2016)

AIRPORTS:

23 (2013)

country comparison to the world: 134

AIRPORTS - WITH PAVED RUNWAYS:

total: 2 (2017)

over 3,047 m: 1 (2017)

2,438 to 3,047 m: 1 (2017)

AIRPORTS - WITH UNPAVED RUNWAYS:

total: 21 (2013)

1,524 to 2,437 m: 3 (2013)

914 to 1,523 m: 13 (2013)

under 914 m: 5 (2013)

RAILWAYS:

total: 622 km (2014)

narrow gauge: 622 km 1.000-m gauge (2014)

note: another 660 km of this railway extends into Cote d'Ivoire

country comparison to the world: 108

ROADWAYS:

total: 15,272 km (2010)

note: does not include urban roads

country comparison to the world: 124

MILITARY AND SECURITY :: BURKINA FASO

MILITARY EXPENDITURES:

1.23% of GDP (2016)

1.33% of GDP (2015)

1.43% of GDP (2014)

1.39% of GDP (2013)

1.32% of GDP (2012)

country comparison to the world: 94

MILITARY BRANCHES:

Army, Central Army Group (joint logistics command), Air Force of Burkina Faso (Force Aerienne de Burkina Faso, FABF), National Gendarmerie, National Fire Brigade (Brigade Nationale des Sapeurs-Pompiers, BNSP) (2018)

MILITARY SERVICE AGE AND OBLIGATION:

18 years of age for voluntary military service; no conscription; women may serve in supporting roles (2013)

TERRORISM :: BURKINA FASO

TERRORIST GROUPS - HOME BASED:

Ansarul Islam:
aim(s): to end government control in parts of the north of the country and enforce sharia in the area of the ancient Fulani Empire of Djeelgodji
area(s) of operation: targets Burkinabe security forces and civilians primarily in the country's northern Sahel Region (April 2018)

Islamic State of Iraq and ash-sham networks in the Greater Sahara (ISGS):
aim(s): replace regional governments with an Islamic state
area(s) of operation: mostly concentrated in the Mali-Burkina Faso-Niger tri-border region; targets primarily security forces (December 2018)

TERRORIST GROUPS - FOREIGN BASED:

al-Mulathamun Battalion:
aim(s): replace several African governments, including Burkina Faso's government, with an Islamic state
area(s) of operation: engages in kidnappings for ransom and violent activities across the country, including in the capital Ouagadougou (November 2018)

al-Qa'ida-affiliated Jama'at Nusrat al-Islam wal-Muslimin (JNIM):
aim(s): establish an Islamic state centered in Mali
area(s) of operation: primarily based in northern and central Mali; targets Western and local interests in West Africa and Sahel; has claimed responsibility for attacks in Mali, Niger, and Burkina Faso
note: pledged allegiance to al-Qa'ida and AQIM; holds Western hostages; wages attacks against security and peacekeeping forces in Mali (April 2018)

TRANSNATIONAL ISSUES :: BURKINA FASO

DISPUTES - INTERNATIONAL:

adding to illicit cross-border activities, Burkina Faso has issues concerning unresolved boundary alignments with its neighborsdemarcation is currently underway with Mali; the dispute with Niger was referred to the ICJ in 2010, and a dispute over several villages with Benin persistsBenin retains a border dispute with Burkina Faso around the town of Koualou

REFUGEES AND INTERNALLY DISPLACED PERSONS:

refugees (country of origin): 24,586 (Mali) (2018)

IDPs: 39,731 (2018)

TRAFFICKING IN PERSONS:

current situation: Burkina Faso is a source, transit, and destination country for women and children subjected to forced labor and sex trafficking; Burkinabe children are forced to work as farm hands, gold panners and washers, street vendors, domestic servants, and beggars or in the commercial sex trade, with some transported to nearby countries; to a lesser extent, Burkinabe women are recruited for legitimate jobs in the Middle East or Europe and subsequently forced into prostitution; women from other West African countries are also lured to Burkina Faso for work and subjected to forced prostitution, forced labor in restaurants, or domestic servitude

tier rating: Tier 2 Watch List – Burkina Faso does not fully comply with the minimum standards for the elimination of trafficking; however, it is making significant efforts to do so; law enforcement efforts decreased in 2014, with a significant decline in trafficking prosecutions (none for forced begging involving Koranic school teachers – a prevalent form of trafficking) and no convictions, a 2014 law criminalizing the sale of children, child prostitution, and child pornography is undermined by a provision allowing offenders to pay a fine in lieu of serving prison time proportionate to the crime; the government sustained efforts to identify and protect a large number of child victims, relying on support from NGOs and international organizations; nationwide awareness-raising activities were sustained, but little was done to stop forced begging (2015)

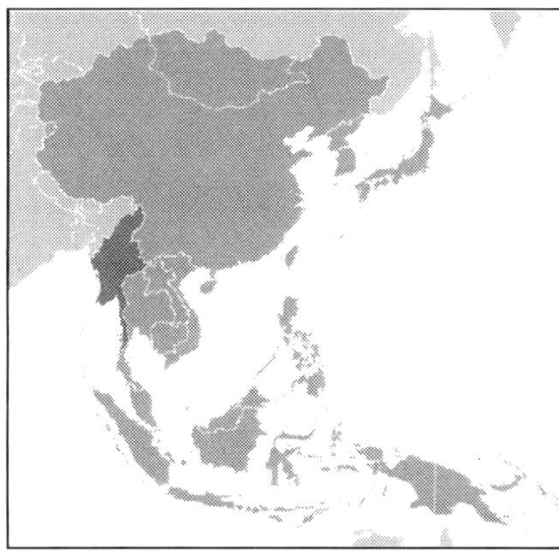

EAST ASIA / SOUTHEAST ASIA :: BURMA

INTRODUCTION :: BURMA

BACKGROUND:

Various ethnic Burmese and ethnic minority city-states or kingdoms occupied the present borders through the 19th century. Over a period of 62 years (1824-1886), Britain conquered Burma and incorporated the country into its Indian Empire. Burma was administered as a province of India until 1937 when it became a separate, self-governing colony; in 1948, Burma attained independence from the British Commonwealth. Gen. NE WIN dominated the government from 1962 to 1988, first as military ruler, then as self-appointed president, and later as political kingpin. In response to widespread civil unrest, NE WIN resigned in 1988, but within months the military crushed student-led protests and took power.

Multiparty legislative elections in 1990 resulted in the main opposition party - the National League for Democracy (NLD) - winning a landslide victory. Instead of handing over power, the junta placed NLD leader (and 1991 Nobel Peace Prize recipient) AUNG SAN SUU KYI under house arrest from 1989 to 1995, 2000 to 2002, and from May 2003 to November 2010. In late September 2007, the ruling junta brutally suppressed protests over increased fuel prices led by prodemocracy activists and Buddhist monks, killing an unknown number of people and arresting thousands for participating in the demonstrations. In early May 2008, Cyclone Nargis struck Burma, which left over 138,000 dead and tens of thousands injured and homeless. Despite this tragedy, the junta proceeded with its May constitutional referendum, the first vote in Burma since 1990. Legislative elections held in November 2010, which the NLD boycotted and many in the international community considered flawed, saw the ruling Union Solidarity and Development Party garner over 75% of the contested seats.

The national legislature convened in January 2011 and selected former Prime Minister THEIN SEIN as president. Although the vast majority of national-level appointees named by THEIN SEIN were former or current military officers, the government initiated a series of political and economic reforms leading to a substantial opening of the long-isolated country. These reforms included releasing hundreds of political prisoners, signing a nationwide cease-fire with several of the country's ethnic armed groups, pursuing legal reform, and gradually reducing restrictions on freedom of the press, association, and civil society. At least due in part to these reforms, AUNG SAN SUU KYI was elected to the national legislature in April 2012 and became chair of the Committee for Rule of Law and Tranquility. Burma served as chair of the Association of Southeast Asian Nations (ASEAN) for 2014. In a flawed but largely credible national legislative election in November 2015 featuring more than 90 political parties, the NLD again won a landslide victory. Using its overwhelming majority in both houses of parliament, the NLD elected HTIN KYAW, AUNG SAN SUU KYI's confidant and long-time NLD supporter, as president. Burma's first credibly elected civilian government after more than five decades of military dictatorship was sworn into office on 30 March 2016.

In August 2017, members of the Arakan Rohingya Salvation Army (ARSA), a Rohingya militant group, attacked security forces in northern Rakhine State, leading to a disproportionate response by Burmese security forces and local vigilantes that resulted in an unknown number of deaths and over 700,000 Rohingya fleeing to neighboring Bangladesh as refugees. This refugee outflow followed a smaller scale displacement of Rohingya to Bangladesh after similar ARSA attacks in October 2016. The UN has called for Burma to allow access to a Fact Finding Mission to investigate reports of human rights violations and abuses and to work with Bangladesh to facilitate repatriation of Rohingya refugees. Burma rejected charges of ethnic cleansing and has chosen not to work with the UN Fact Finding Mission. In March 2018, President HTIN KYAW announced his voluntary retirement; parliamentarian WIN MYINT won a snap election to become president.

GEOGRAPHY :: BURMA

LOCATION:

Southeastern Asia, bordering the Andaman Sea and the Bay of Bengal, between Bangladesh and Thailand

GEOGRAPHIC COORDINATES:

22 00 N, 98 00 E

MAP REFERENCES:

Southeast Asia

AREA:

total: 676,578 sq km

land: 653,508 sq km

water: 23,070 sq km

country comparison to the world: 41

AREA - COMPARATIVE:

slightly smaller than Texas

LAND BOUNDARIES:

total: 6,522 km

border countries (5): Bangladesh 271 km, China 2129 km, India 1468 km, Laos 238 km, Thailand 2416 km

COASTLINE:

1,930 km

MARITIME CLAIMS:

territorial sea: 12 nm

exclusive economic zone: 200 nm

contiguous zone: 24 nm

continental shelf: 200 nm or to the edge of the continental margin

CLIMATE:

tropical monsoon; cloudy, rainy, hot, humid summers (southwest monsoon, June to September); less cloudy, scant rainfall, mild temperatures, lower humidity during winter (northeast monsoon, December to April)

TERRAIN:

central lowlands ringed by steep, rugged highlands

ELEVATION:

mean elevation: 702 m

elevation extremes: 0 m lowest point: Andaman Sea/Bay of Bengal

5870 highest point: Gamlang Razi

NATURAL RESOURCES:

petroleum, timber, tin, antimony, zinc, copper, tungsten, lead, coal, marble, limestone, precious stones, natural gas, hydropower, arable land

LAND USE:

agricultural land: 19.2% (2011 est.)

arable land: 16.5% (2011 est.) / permanent crops: 2.2% (2011 est.) / permanent pasture: 0.5% (2011 est.)

forest: 48.2% (2011 est.)

other: 32.6% (2011 est.)

IRRIGATED LAND:

22,950 sq km (2012)

POPULATION DISTRIBUTION:

population concentrated along coastal areas and in general proximity to the shores of the Irrawaddy River; the extreme north is relatively underpopulated

NATURAL HAZARDS:

destructive earthquakes and cyclones; flooding and landslides common during rainy season (June to September); periodic droughts

ENVIRONMENT - CURRENT ISSUES:

deforestation; industrial pollution of air, soil, and water; inadequate sanitation and water treatment contribute to disease; rapid depletion of the country's natural resources

ENVIRONMENT - INTERNATIONAL AGREEMENTS:

party to: Biodiversity, Climate Change, Climate Change-Kyoto Protocol, Desertification, Endangered Species, Hazardous Wastes, Law of the Sea, Ozone Layer Protection, Ship Pollution, Tropical Timber 83, Tropical Timber 94

signed, but not ratified: none of the selected agreements

GEOGRAPHY - NOTE:

strategic location near major Indian Ocean shipping lanes; the north-south flowing Irrawaddy River is the country's largest and most important commercial waterway

PEOPLE AND SOCIETY :: BURMA

POPULATION:

55,622,506 (July 2018 est.)

country comparison to the world: 24

NATIONALITY:

noun: Burmese (singular and plural)

adjective: Burmese

ETHNIC GROUPS:

Burman (Bamar) 68%, Shan 9%, Karen 7%, Rakhine 4%, Chinese 3%, Indian 2%, Mon 2%, other 5%

note: government recognizes 135 indigenous ethnic groups

LANGUAGES:

Burmese (official)

note: minority ethnic groups use their own languages

RELIGIONS:

Buddhist 87.9%, Christian 6.2%, Muslim 4.3%, Animist 0.8%, Hindu 0.5%, other 0.2%, none 0.1% (2014 est.)

note: religion estimate is based on the 2014 national census, including an estimate for the non-enumerated population of Rakhine State, which is assumed to mainly affiliate with the Islamic faith

AGE STRUCTURE:

0-14 years: 26.56% (male 7,556,848 /female 7,216,374)

15-24 years: 17.51% (male 4,900,092 /female 4,837,726)

25-54 years: 42.51% (male 11,577,883 /female 12,068,190)

55-64 years: 7.75% (male 2,011,057 /female 2,301,983)

65 years and over: 5.67% (male 1,373,892 /female 1,778,461) (2018 est.)

DEPENDENCY RATIOS:

total dependency ratio: 49.7 (2015 est.)

youth dependency ratio: 41.7 (2015 est.)

elderly dependency ratio: 8 (2015 est.)

potential support ratio: 12.6 (2015 est.)

MEDIAN AGE:

total: 28.5 years

male: 27.7 years

female: 29.4 years (2018 est.)

country comparison to the world: 136

POPULATION GROWTH RATE:

0.89% (2018 est.)

country comparison to the world: 122

BIRTH RATE:

17.7 births/1,000 population (2018 est.)

country comparison to the world: 95

DEATH RATE:

7.3 deaths/1,000 population (2018 est.)

country comparison to the world: 120

NET MIGRATION RATE:

-1.5 migrant(s)/1,000 population (2017 est.)

country comparison to the world: 148

POPULATION DISTRIBUTION:

population concentrated along coastal areas and in general proximity to the shores of the Irrawaddy River; the extreme north is relatively underpopulated

URBANIZATION:

urban population: 30.6% of total population (2018)

rate of urbanization: 1.74% annual rate of change (2015-20 est.)

MAJOR URBAN AREAS - POPULATION:

5.157 million RANGOON (Yangon) (capital), 1.374 million Mandalay (2018)

SEX RATIO:

at birth: 1.06 male(s)/female (2017 est.)

0-14 years: 1.04 male(s)/female (2017 est.)

15-24 years: 1.03 male(s)/female (2017 est.)

25-54 years: 0.99 male(s)/female (2017 est.)

55-64 years: 0.89 male(s)/female (2017 est.)

65 years and over: 0.77 male(s)/female (2017 est.)

total population: 0.99 male(s)/female (2017 est.)

MOTHER'S MEAN AGE AT FIRST BIRTH:

25 years (2015/16 est.)

note: median age at first birth among women 25-29

MATERNAL MORTALITY RATE:

178 deaths/100,000 live births (2015 est.)

country comparison to the world: 53

INFANT MORTALITY RATE:

total: 34.4 deaths/1,000 live births (2018 est.)

male: 37.3 deaths/1,000 live births (2018 est.)

female: 31.3 deaths/1,000 live births (2018 est.)

country comparison to the world: 50

LIFE EXPECTANCY AT BIRTH:

total population: 68.6 years (2018 est.)

male: 67 years (2018 est.)

female: 70.3 years (2018 est.)

country comparison to the world: 166

TOTAL FERTILITY RATE:

2.13 children born/woman (2018 est.)

country comparison to the world: 100

CONTRACEPTIVE PREVALENCE RATE:

52.2% (2015/16)

HEALTH EXPENDITURES:

2.3% of GDP (2014)

country comparison to the world: 188

PHYSICIANS DENSITY:

0.57 physicians/1,000 population (2012)

HOSPITAL BED DENSITY:

0.9 beds/1,000 population (2012)

DRINKING WATER SOURCE:

improved:

urban: 92.7% of population

rural: 74.4% of population

total: 80.6% of population

unimproved:

urban: 7.3% of population

rural: 25.6% of population

total: 19.4% of population (2015 est.)

SANITATION FACILITY ACCESS:

improved:

urban: 84.3% of population (2012 est.)

rural: 73.9% of population (2012 est.)

total: 77.4% of population (2012 est.)

unimproved:

urban: 15.7% of population (2012 est.)

rural: 26.1% of population (2012 est.)

total: 22.6% of population (2012 est.)

HIV/AIDS - ADULT PREVALENCE RATE:

0.7% (2017 est.)

country comparison to the world: 51

HIV/AIDS - PEOPLE LIVING WITH HIV/AIDS:

220,000 (2017 est.)

country comparison to the world: 26

HIV/AIDS - DEATHS:

6,700 (2017 est.)

country comparison to the world: 23

MAJOR INFECTIOUS DISEASES:

degree of risk: very high (2016)

food or waterborne diseases: bacterial and protozoal diarrhea, hepatitis A, and typhoid fever (2016)

vectorborne diseases: dengue fever, malaria, and Japanese encephalitis (2016)

water contact diseases: leptospirosis (2016)

animal contact diseases: rabies (2016)

OBESITY - ADULT PREVALENCE RATE:

5.8% (2016)

country comparison to the world: 172

CHILDREN UNDER THE AGE OF 5 YEARS UNDERWEIGHT:

18.9% (2016)

country comparison to the world: 29

EDUCATION EXPENDITURES:

0.8% of GDP (2011)

country comparison to the world: 179

LITERACY:

definition: age 15 and over can read and write (2016 est.)

total population: 75.6% (2016 est.)

male: 80% (2016 est.)

female: 71.8% (2016 est.)

SCHOOL LIFE EXPECTANCY (PRIMARY TO TERTIARY EDUCATION):

total: 10 years (2017)

male: 10 years (2017)

female: 10 years (2017)

UNEMPLOYMENT, YOUTH AGES 15-24:

total: 1.6% (2015 est.)

male: 1.4% (2015 est.)

female: 1.8% (2015 est.)

country comparison to the world: 169

GOVERNMENT :: BURMA

COUNTRY NAME:

conventional long form: Union of Burma

conventional short form: Burma

local long form: Pyidaungzu Thammada Myanma Naingngandaw (translated as the Republic of the Union of Myanmar)

local short form: Myanma Naingngandaw

former: Socialist Republic of the Union of Burma, Union of Myanmar

etymology: both "Burma" and "Myanmar" derive from the name of the majority Burmese Bamar ethnic group

note: since 1989 the military authorities in Burma and the current parliamentary government have promoted the name Myanmar as a conventional name for their state; the US Government has not adopted the name

GOVERNMENT TYPE:

parliamentary republic

CAPITAL:

name: Rangoon (Yangon); note - Nay Pyi Taw is the administrative capital

geographic coordinates: 16 48 N, 96 09 E

time difference: UTC+6.5 (11.5 hours ahead of Washington, DC, during Standard Time)

ADMINISTRATIVE DIVISIONS:

7 regions (taing-myar, singular - taing), 7 states (pyi ne-myar, singular - pyi ne), 1 union territory

regions: Ayeyarwady (Irrawaddy), Bago, Magway, Mandalay, Sagaing, Tanintharyi, Yangon (Rangoon);

states: Chin, Kachin, Kayah, Kayin, Mon, Rakhine, Shan;

union territory: Nay Pyi Taw

INDEPENDENCE:

4 January 1948 (from the UK)

NATIONAL HOLIDAY:

Independence Day, 4 January (1948)Union Day, 12 February (1947)

CONSTITUTION:

history: previous 1947, 1974 (suspended until 2008); latest drafted 9 April 2008, approved by referendum 29 May 2008 (2017)

amendments: proposals require at least 20% approval by the Assembly of the Union membership; passage of amendments to sections of the constitution on basic principles, government structure, branches of government, state emergencies, and amendment procedures requires 75% approval by the Assembly and approval in a referendum by absolute majority of registered voters; passage of amendments to other sections requires only 75% Assembly approval; amended 2015 (2017)

LEGAL SYSTEM:

mixed legal system of English common law (as introduced in codifications designed for colonial India) and customary law

INTERNATIONAL LAW ORGANIZATION PARTICIPATION:

has not submitted an ICJ jurisdiction declaration; non-party state to the ICCt

CITIZENSHIP:

citizenship by birth: no

citizenship by descent only: both parents must be citizens of Burma

dual citizenship recognized: no

residency requirement for naturalization: none

note: an applicant for naturalization must be the child or spouse of a citizen

SUFFRAGE:

18 years of age; universal

EXECUTIVE BRANCH:

chief of state: President WIN MYINT (since 30 March 2018); Vice Presidents MYINT SWE (since 16 March 2016) and HENRY VAN THIO (since 30 March 2016); note - President HTIN KYAW (since 30 March 2016) resigned on 21 March 2018; the president is both chief of state and head of government

head of government: President WIN MYINT (since 30 March 2018); Vice Presidents MYINT SWE (since 16 March 2016) and HENRY VAN THIO (since 30 March 2016

cabinet: Cabinet appointments shared by the president and the commander-in-chief

elections/appointments: president indirectly elected by simple majority vote by the full Assembly of the Union from among 3 vice-presidential candidates nominated by the Presidential Electoral College (consists of members of the lower and upper houses and military members); the other 2 candidates become vice-presidents (president elected for a 5-year term); election last held on 28 March 2018 (next election to be held in 2023)

election results: WIN MYINT elected president; Assembly of the Union vote - WIN MYINT (NLD) 403, MYINT SWE (USDP) 211, HENRY VAN THIO (NLD) 18, 4 votes canceled (636 votes cast)

state counsellor: State Counselor AUNG SAN SUU KYI (since 6 April 2016); she concurrently serves as minister of foreign affairs and minister for the office of the president

note: a parliamentary bill creating the position of "state counsellor" was signed into law by former President HTIN KYAW on 6 April 2016; a state counsellor serves the equivalent term of the president and is similar to a prime minister in that the holder acts as a link between the parliament and the executive branch

LEGISLATIVE BRANCH:

description: bicameral Assembly of the Union or Pyidaungsu consists of:
House of Nationalities or Amyotha Hluttaw, (224 seats; 168 members directly elected in single-seat constituencies by absolute majority vote with a second round if needed and 56 appointed by the military; members serve 5-year terms)
House of Representatives or Pyithu Hluttaw, (440 seats; 330 members directly elected in single-seat constituencies by simple majority vote and 110 appointed by the military; members serve 5-year terms)

elections:
House of Nationalities - last held on 8 November 2015 (next to be held in 2020)
House of Representatives - last held on 8 November 2015 (next to be held in 2020)

election results:
House of Nationalities - percent of vote by party - NLD 60.3%, USDP 4.9%, ANP 4.5%, SNLD 1.3%, other 4%, military appointees 25%; seats by party - NLD 135, USDP 11, ANP 10, SNLD 3, TNP 2, ZCD 2, other 3, independent 2, military appointees 56
House of Representatives - percent of vote by party - NLD 58%, USDP 6.8%, ANP 2.7%, SNLD 2.7%, military 25%, other 4.8%; seats by party - NLD 255, USDP 30, ANP 12, SNLD 12, PNO 3, TNP 3, LNDP 2, ZCD 2, other 3, independent 1, canceled due to insurgence 7, military appointees 110

JUDICIAL BRANCH:

highest courts: Supreme Court of the Union (consists of the chief justice and 7-11 judges)

judge selection and term of office: chief justice and judges nominated by the president, with approval of the Lower House, and appointed by the president; judges normally serve until mandatory retirement at age 70

subordinate courts: High Courts of the Region; High Courts of the State; Court of the Self-Administered

Division; Court of the Self-Administered Zone; district and township courts; special courts (for juvenile, municipal, and traffic offenses); courts martial

POLITICAL PARTIES AND LEADERS:

All Mon Region Democracy Party or AMRDP
Arakan National Party or ANP (formed from the 2013 merger of the Rakhine Nationalities Development Party and the Arakan League for Democracy)
National Democratic Force or NDF [KHIN MAUNG SWE]
National League for Democracy or NLD [AUNG SAN SUU KYI]
National Unity Party or NUP [THAN TIN]
Pa-O National Organization or PNO [AUNG KHAM HTI]
Shan Nationalities Democratic Party or SNDP [SAI AIK PAUNG]
Shan Nationalities League for Democracy or SNLD [KHUN HTUN OO]
Ta'ang National Party or TNP [AIK MONE]
Union Solidarity and Development Party or USDP [THAN HTAY]
Zomi Congress for Democracy or ZCD [PU CIN SIAN THANG]
numerous smaller parties

INTERNATIONAL ORGANIZATION PARTICIPATION:

ADB, ARF, ASEAN, BIMSTEC, CP, EAS, EITI (candidate country), FAO, G-77, IAEA, IBRD, ICAO, ICRM, IDA, IFAD, IFC, IFRCS, IHO, ILO, IMF, IMO, Interpol, IOC, IOM, IPU, ISO (correspondent), ITU, ITUC (NGOs), NAM, OPCW (signatory), SAARC (observer), UN, UNCTAD, UNESCO, UNIDO, UNWTO, UPU, WCO, WHO, WIPO, WMO, WTO

DIPLOMATIC REPRESENTATION IN THE US:

chief of mission: Ambassador AUNG LYNN (since 16 September 2016)

chancery: 2300 S Street NW, Washington, DC 20008

telephone: [1] (202) 332-3344

FAX: [1] (202) 332-4351

consulate(s) general: Los Angeles, New York

DIPLOMATIC REPRESENTATION FROM THE US:

chief of mission: Ambassador Scot MARCIEL (since 27 April 2016)

embassy: 110 University Avenue, Kamayut Township, Rangoon

mailing address: Box B, APO AP 96546

telephone: [95] (1) 536-509, 535-756, 538-038

FAX: [95] (1) 511-069

FLAG DESCRIPTION:

design consists of three equal horizontal stripes of yellow (top), green, and red; centered on the green band is a large white five-pointed star that partially overlaps onto the adjacent colored stripes; the design revives the triband colors used by Burma from 1943-45, during the Japanese occupation

NATIONAL SYMBOL(S):

chinthe (mythical lion); national colors: yellow, green, red, white

NATIONAL ANTHEM:

name: "Kaba Ma Kyei" (Till the End of the World, Myanmar)

lyrics/music: SAYA TIN

note: adopted 1948; Burma is among a handful of non-European nations that have anthems rooted in indigenous traditions; the beginning portion of the anthem is a traditional Burmese anthem before transitioning into a Western-style orchestrated work

ECONOMY :: BURMA

ECONOMY - OVERVIEW:

Since Burma began the transition to a civilian-led government in 2011, the country initiated economic reforms aimed at attracting foreign investment and reintegrating into the global economy. Burma established a managed float of the Burmese kyat in 2012, granted the Central Bank operational independence in July 2013, enacted a new anti-corruption law in September 2013, and granted licenses to 13 foreign banks in 2014-16. State Counsellor AUNG SAN SUU KYI and the ruling National League for Democracy, who took power in March 2016, have sought to improve Burma's investment climate following the US sanctions lift in October 2016 and reinstatement of Generalized System of Preferences trade benefits in November 2016. In October 2016, Burma passed a foreign investment law that consolidates investment regulations and eases rules on foreign ownership of businesses.

Burma's economic growth rate recovered from a low growth under 6% in 2011 but has been volatile between 6% and 7.2% during the past few years. Burma's abundant natural resources and young labor force have the potential to attract foreign investment in the energy, garment, information technology, and food and beverage sectors. The government is focusing on accelerating agricultural productivity and land reforms, modernizing and opening the financial sector, and developing transportation and electricity infrastructure. The government has also taken steps to improve transparency in the mining and oil sectors through publication of reports under the Extractive Industries Transparency Initiative (EITI) in 2016 and 2018.

Despite these improvements, living standards have not improved for the majority of the people residing in rural areas. Burma remains one of the poorest countries in Asia – approximately 26% of the country's 51 million people live in poverty. The isolationist policies and economic mismanagement of previous governments have left Burma with poor infrastructure, endemic corruption, underdeveloped human resources, and inadequate access to capital, which will require a major commitment to reverse. The Burmese Government has been slow to address impediments to economic development such as unclear land rights, a restrictive trade licensing system, an opaque revenue collection system, and an antiquated banking system.

GDP (PURCHASING POWER PARITY):

$329.8 billion (2017 est.)

$308.7 billion (2016 est.)

$291.5 billion (2015 est.)

note: data are in 2017 dollars

country comparison to the world: 53

GDP (OFFICIAL EXCHANGE RATE):

$67.28 billion (2017 est.) (2017 est.)

GDP - REAL GROWTH RATE:

6.8% (2017 est.)

5.9% (2016 est.)

7% (2015 est.)

country comparison to the world: 24

GDP - PER CAPITA (PPP):

$6,300 (2017 est.)

$5,900 (2016 est.)

$5,600 (2015 est.)

note: data are in 2017 dollars

country comparison to the world: 163

GROSS NATIONAL SAVING:

17.7% of GDP (2017 est.)

17.6% of GDP (2016 est.)

18.1% of GDP (2015 est.)

country comparison to the world: 113

GDP - COMPOSITION, BY END USE:

household consumption: 59.2% (2017 est.)

government consumption: 13.8% (2017 est.)

investment in fixed capital: 33.5% (2017 est.)

investment in inventories: 1.5% (2017 est.)

exports of goods and services: 21.4% (2017 est.)

imports of goods and services: -28.6% (2017 est.)

GDP - COMPOSITION, BY SECTOR OF ORIGIN:

agriculture: 24.1% (2017 est.)

industry: 35.6% (2017 est.)

services: 40.3% (2017 est.)

AGRICULTURE - PRODUCTS:

rice, pulses, beans, sesame, groundnuts; sugarcane; fish and fish products; hardwood

INDUSTRIES:

agricultural processing; wood and wood products; copper, tin, tungsten, iron; cement, construction materials; pharmaceuticals; fertilizer; oil and natural gas; garments; jade and gems

INDUSTRIAL PRODUCTION GROWTH RATE:

8.9% (2017 est.)

country comparison to the world: 20

LABOR FORCE:

22.3 million (2017 est.)

country comparison to the world: 28

LABOR FORCE - BY OCCUPATION:

agriculture: 70%

industry: 7%

services: 23% (2001 est.)

UNEMPLOYMENT RATE:

4% (2017 est.)

4% (2016 est.)

country comparison to the world: 50

POPULATION BELOW POVERTY LINE:

25.6% (2016 est.)

HOUSEHOLD INCOME OR CONSUMPTION BY PERCENTAGE SHARE:

lowest 10%: 32.4% (1998)

highest 10%: 32.4% (1998)

BUDGET:

revenues: 9.108 billion (2017 est.)

expenditures: 11.23 billion (2017 est.)

TAXES AND OTHER REVENUES:

13.5% (of GDP) (2017 est.)

country comparison to the world: 205

BUDGET SURPLUS (+) OR DEFICIT (-):

-3.2% (of GDP) (2017 est.)

country comparison to the world: 138

PUBLIC DEBT:

33.6% of GDP (2017 est.)

35.7% of GDP (2016 est.)

country comparison to the world: 156

FISCAL YEAR:

1 April - 31 March

INFLATION RATE (CONSUMER PRICES):

4% (2017 est.)

6.8% (2016 est.)

country comparison to the world: 154

CENTRAL BANK DISCOUNT RATE:

9.95% (31 December 2010)

12% (31 December 2009)

country comparison to the world: 25

COMMERCIAL BANK PRIME LENDING RATE:

13% (31 December 2017 est.)

13% (31 December 2016 est.)

country comparison to the world: 60

STOCK OF NARROW MONEY:

$18.78 billion (31 December 2017 est.)

$15.84 billion (31 December 2016 est.)

country comparison to the world: 70

STOCK OF BROAD MONEY:

$18.78 billion (31 December 2017 est.)

$15.84 billion (31 December 2016 est.)

country comparison to the world: 71

STOCK OF DOMESTIC CREDIT:

$28.24 billion (31 December 2017 est.)

$23.08 billion (31 December 2016 est.)

country comparison to the world: 83

MARKET VALUE OF PUBLICLY TRADED SHARES:

NA

CURRENT ACCOUNT BALANCE:

-$2.9 billion (2017 est.)

-$2.475 billion (2016 est.)

country comparison to the world: 175

EXPORTS:

$9.832 billion (2017 est.)

$9.085 billion (2016 est.)

note: official export figures are grossly underestimated due to the value of timber, gems, narcotics, rice, and other products smuggled to Thailand, China, and Bangladesh

country comparison to the world: 95

EXPORTS - PARTNERS:

China 36.5%, Thailand 21.8%, Japan 6.6%, Singapore 6.4%, India 5.9% (2017)

EXPORTS - COMMODITIES:

natural gas; wood products; pulses and beans; fish; rice; clothing; minerals, including jade and gems

IMPORTS:

$15.78 billion (2017 est.)

$12.81 billion (2016 est.)

note: import figures are grossly underestimated due to the value of consumer goods, diesel fuel, and other products smuggled in from Thailand, China, Malaysia, and India

country comparison to the world: 88

IMPORTS - COMMODITIES:

fabric; petroleum products; fertilizer; plastics; machinery; transport equipment; cement, construction materials; food products‘ edible oil

IMPORTS - PARTNERS:

China 31.4%, Singapore 15%, Thailand 11.1%, Saudi Arabia 7.5%, Malaysia 6.2%, Japan 6%, India 5.5%, Indonesia 4.5% (2017)

RESERVES OF FOREIGN EXCHANGE AND GOLD:

$4.924 billion (31 December 2017 est.)

$4.63 billion (31 December 2016 est.)

country comparison to the world: 95

DEBT - EXTERNAL:

$6.594 billion (31 December 2017 est.)

$8.2 billion (31 December 2016 est.)

country comparison to the world: 125

EXCHANGE RATES:

kyats (MMK) per US dollar -

1,361.9 (2017 est.)

1,234.87 (2016 est.)

1,234.87 (2015 est.)

1,162.62 (2014 est.)

984.35 (2013 est.)

ENERGY :: BURMA

ELECTRICITY ACCESS:

population without electricity: 36.3 million (2013)

electrification - total population: 52% (2013)

electrification - urban areas: 95% (2013)

electrification - rural areas: 31% (2013)

ELECTRICITY - PRODUCTION:

17.32 billion kWh (2016 est.)

country comparison to the world: 83

ELECTRICITY - CONSUMPTION:

14.93 billion kWh (2016 est.)

country comparison to the world: 81

ELECTRICITY - EXPORTS:

0 kWh (2016 est.)

country comparison to the world: 113

ELECTRICITY - IMPORTS:

0 kWh (2016 est.)

country comparison to the world: 130

ELECTRICITY - INSTALLED GENERATING CAPACITY:

5.205 million kW (2016 est.)

country comparison to the world: 79

ELECTRICITY - FROM FOSSIL FUELS:

39% of total installed capacity (2016 est.)

country comparison to the world: 171

ELECTRICITY - FROM NUCLEAR FUELS:

0% of total installed capacity (2017 est.)

country comparison to the world: 58

ELECTRICITY - FROM HYDROELECTRIC PLANTS:

61% of total installed capacity (2017 est.)

country comparison to the world: 28

ELECTRICITY - FROM OTHER RENEWABLE SOURCES:

1% of total installed capacity (2017 est.)

country comparison to the world: 149

CRUDE OIL - PRODUCTION:

12,000 bbl/day (2017 est.)

country comparison to the world: 77

CRUDE OIL - EXPORTS:

1,824 bbl/day (2015 est.)

country comparison to the world: 71

CRUDE OIL - IMPORTS:

0 bbl/day (2015 est.)

country comparison to the world: 103

CRUDE OIL - PROVED RESERVES:

139 million bbl (1 January 2018 est.)

country comparison to the world: 63

REFINED PETROLEUM PRODUCTS - PRODUCTION:

13,330 bbl/day (2017 est.)

country comparison to the world: 97

REFINED PETROLEUM PRODUCTS - CONSUMPTION:

123,000 bbl/day (2016 est.)

country comparison to the world: 73

REFINED PETROLEUM PRODUCTS - EXPORTS:

0 bbl/day (2015 est.)

country comparison to the world: 137

REFINED PETROLEUM PRODUCTS - IMPORTS:

102,600 bbl/day (2015 est.)

country comparison to the world: 53

NATURAL GAS - PRODUCTION:

18.41 billion cu m (2017 est.)

country comparison to the world: 33

NATURAL GAS - CONSUMPTION:

4.502 billion cu m (2017 est.)

country comparison to the world: 63

NATURAL GAS - EXPORTS:

14.07 billion cu m (2017 est.)

country comparison to the world: 16

NATURAL GAS - IMPORTS:

0 cu m (2017 est.)

country comparison to the world: 99

NATURAL GAS - PROVED RESERVES:

637.1 billion cu m (1 January 2018 est.)

country comparison to the world: 29

CARBON DIOXIDE EMISSIONS FROM CONSUMPTION OF ENERGY:

27.01 million Mt (2017 est.)

country comparison to the world: 77

COMMUNICATIONS :: BURMA

TELEPHONES - FIXED LINES:

total subscriptions: 556,112 (2017 est.)

subscriptions per 100 inhabitants: 1 (2017 est.)

country comparison to the world: 92

TELEPHONES - MOBILE CELLULAR:

total subscriptions: 47,951,228 (2017 est.)

subscriptions per 100 inhabitants: 87 (2017 est.)

country comparison to the world: 31

TELEPHONE SYSTEM:

general assessment: remains one of the last underdeveloped telecoms markets in Asia; the mobile market has experienced rapid growth from 2013 to 2017, in 2014 foreign competion was allowed to compete in the market (2017)

domestic: fixed-line is less than 1 per 100, while moblie-cellular is 87 per 100 and shows great potential for the future (2017)

international: country code - 95; landing point for the SEA-ME-WE-3 optical telecommunications submarine cable that provides links to Asia, the Middle East, and Europe; satellite earth stations - 2, Intelsat (Indian Ocean) and ShinSat (2016)

BROADCAST MEDIA:

government controls all domestic broadcast media; 2 state-controlled TV stations with 1 of the stations controlled by the armed forces; 2 pay-TV stations are joint state-private ventures; access to satellite TV is limited; 1 state-controlled domestic radio station and 9 FM stations that are joint state-private ventures; transmissions of several international broadcasters are available in parts of Burma; the Voice of America (VOA), Radio Free Asia (RFA), BBC Burmese service, the Democratic Voice of Burma (DVB), and Radio Australia use shortwave to broadcast in Burma; VOA, RFA, and DVB produce daily TV news programs that are transmitted by satellite to audiences in Burma; in March 2017, the government granted licenses to 5 private broadcasters, allowing them digital free-to-air TV channels to be operated in partnership with government-owned Myanmar Radio and Television (MRTV) and will rely upon MRTV's transmission infrastructure; the new channels are expected to begin airing programming early in 2018 (2017)

INTERNET COUNTRY CODE:

.mm

INTERNET USERS:

total: 14,264,308 (July 2016 est.)

percent of population: 25.1% (July 2016 est.)

country comparison to the world: 40

BROADBAND - FIXED SUBSCRIPTIONS:

total: 404,932 (2017 est.)

subscriptions per 100 inhabitants: less than 1 (2017 est.)

country comparison to the world: 86

TRANSPORTATION :: BURMA

NATIONAL AIR TRANSPORT SYSTEM:

number of registered air carriers: 11 (2015)

inventory of registered aircraft operated by air carriers: 45 (2015)

annual passenger traffic on registered air carriers: 2,029,139 (2015)

annual freight traffic on registered air carriers: 3,365,967 mt-km (2015)

CIVIL AIRCRAFT REGISTRATION COUNTRY CODE PREFIX:

XY (2016)

AIRPORTS:

64 (2013)

country comparison to the world: 76

AIRPORTS - WITH PAVED RUNWAYS:

total: 36 (2017)

over 3,047 m: 12 (2017)

2,438 to 3,047 m: 11 (2017)

1,524 to 2,437 m: 12 (2017)

under 914 m: 1 (2017)

AIRPORTS - WITH UNPAVED RUNWAYS:

total: 28 (2013)

over 3,047 m: 1 (2013)

1,524 to 2,437 m: 4 (2013)

914 to 1,523 m: 10 (2013)

under 914 m: 13 (2013)

HELIPORTS:

11 (2013)

PIPELINES:

3739 km gas, 1321 km oil (2017)

RAILWAYS:

total: 5,031 km (2008)

narrow gauge: 5,031 km 1.000-m gauge (2008)

country comparison to the world: 40

ROADWAYS:

total: 34,377 km (includes 358 km of expressways) (2010)

country comparison to the world: 93

WATERWAYS:

12,800 km (2011)

country comparison to the world: 10

MERCHANT MARINE:

total: 97 (2017)

by type: bulk carrier 1, general cargo 43, oil tanker 5, other 48 (2017)

country comparison to the world: 87

PORTS AND TERMINALS:

major seaport(s): Mawlamyine (Moulmein), Sittwe

river port(s): Rangoon (Yangon) (Rangoon River)

MILITARY AND SECURITY :: BURMA

MILITARY EXPENDITURES:

4.08% of GDP (2015)

3.58% of GDP (2014)

3.81% of GDP (2013)

3.71% of GDP (2012)

country comparison to the world: 14

MILITARY BRANCHES:

Burmese Defense Service (Tatmadaw): Army (Tatmadaw Kyi), Navy (Tatmadaw Yay), Air Force (Tatmadaw Lay) (2013)

MILITARY SERVICE AGE AND OBLIGATION:

18-35 years of age (men) and 18-27 years of age (women) for voluntary military service; no conscription (a 2010 law reintroducing conscription has not yet entered into force); 2-year service obligation; male (ages 18-45) and female (ages 18-35) professionals (including doctors, engineers, mechanics) serve up to 3 years; service terms may be stretched to 5 years in an officially declared emergency; Burma signed the Convention on the Rights of the Child on 15 August 1991; on 27 June 2012, the regime signed a Joint Action Plan on prevention of child recruitment; in February 2013, the military formed a new task force to address forced child conscription; since that time, approximately 880 children have been released from military service (2015)

TRANSNATIONAL ISSUES :: BURMA

DISPUTES - INTERNATIONAL:

over half of Burma's population consists of diverse ethnic groups who have substantial numbers of kin in neighboring countriesthe Naf River on the border with Bangladesh serves as a smuggling and illegal transit routeBangladesh struggles to accommodate 29,000 Rohingya, Burmese Muslim minority from Arakan State, living as refugees in Cox's BazarBurmese border authorities are constructing a 200 km (124 mi) wire fence designed to deter illegal cross-border transit and tensions from the military build-up along border with Bangladesh in 2010Bangladesh referred its maritime boundary claims with Burma and India to the International Tribunal on the Law of the SeaBurmese forces attempting to dig in to the largely autonomous Shan State to rout local militias tied to the drug trade, prompts local residents to periodically flee into neighboring Yunnan Province in Chinafencing along the India-Burma international border at Manipur's Moreh town is in progress to check illegal drug trafficking and movement of militantsover 100,000 mostly Karen refugees and asylum seekers fleeing civil strife, political upheaval, and economic stagnation in Burma were living in remote camps in Thailand near the border as of May 2017

REFUGEES AND INTERNALLY DISPLACED PERSONS:

IDPs: 635,000 (government offensives against armed ethnic minority groups near its borders with China and Thailand, natural disasters, forced land evictions) (2017)

stateless persons: 495,939 (2017); note - Rohingya Muslims, living predominantly in Rakhine State, are Burma's main group of stateless people; the Burmese Government does not recognize the Rohingya as a "national race" and stripped them of their citizenship under the 1982 Citizenship Law, categorizing them as "non-nationals" or "foreign residents"; under the Rakhine State Action Plan drafted in October 2014, the Rohingya must demonstrate their family has lived in Burma for at least 60 years to qualify for a lesser naturalized citizenship and the classification of Bengali or be put in detention camps and face deportation; native-born but non-indigenous people, such as Indians, are also stateless; the Burmese Government does not grant citizenship to children born outside of the country to Burmese parents who left the country illegally or fled persecution, such as those born in Thailand; the number of stateless persons has decreased dramatically since late 2017 because hundreds of thousands of Rohingya have fled to

Bangladesh since 25 August 2017 to escape violence

note: estimate does not include stateless IDPs or stateless persons in IDP like situations because they are included in estimates of IDPs (2017)

TRAFFICKING IN PERSONS:

current situation: Burma is a source country for men, women, and children trafficked for the purpose of forced labor and for women and children subjected to sex trafficking; Burmese adult and child labor migrants travel to East Asia, the Middle East, South Asia, and the US, where men are forced to work in the fishing, manufacturing, forestry, and construction industries and women and girls are forced into prostitution, domestic servitude, or forced labor in the garment sector; some Burmese economic migrants and Rohingya asylum seekers have become forced laborers on Thai fishing boats; some military personnel and armed ethnic groups unlawfully conscript child soldiers or coerce adults and children into forced labor; domestically, adults and children from ethnic areas are vulnerable to forced labor on plantations and in mines, while children may also be subject to forced prostitution, domestic service, and begging

tier rating: Tier 2 Watch List – Burma does not fully comply with the minimum standards for the elimination of trafficking, but it is making significant efforts to do so; the government has a written plan that, if implemented, would constitute making a significant effort toward meeting the minimum standard for eliminating human trafficking; in 2014, law enforcement continued to investigate and prosecute cross-border trafficking offenses but did little to address domestic trafficking; no civilians or government officials were prosecuted or convicted for the recruitment of child soldiers, a serious problem that is hampered by corruption and the influence of the military; victim referral and protection services remained inadequate, especially for men, and left victims vulnerable to being re-trafficked; the government coordinated anti-trafficking programs as part of its five-year national action plan (2015)

ILLICIT DRUGS:

world's second largest producer of illicit opium with an estimated poppy cultivation totaling 55,500 hectares in 2015 and an estimated potential production of 647 mt of raw opium; Shan state is the source of 91% of Burma's poppy cultivation; lack of government will to take on major narcotrafficking groups and lack of serious commitment against money laundering continues to hinder the overall antidrug effort; major source of methamphetamine and heroin for regional consumption

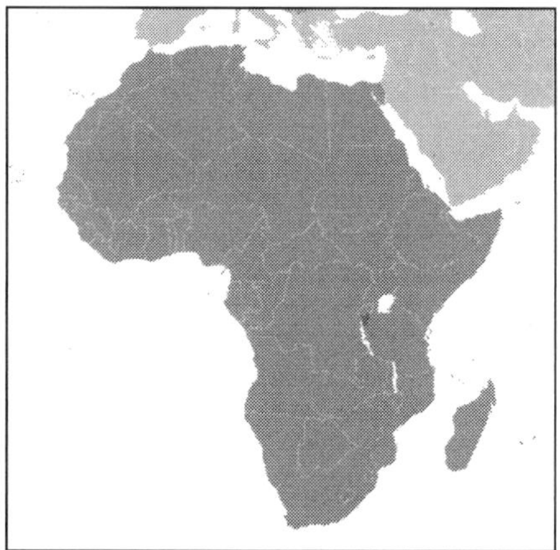

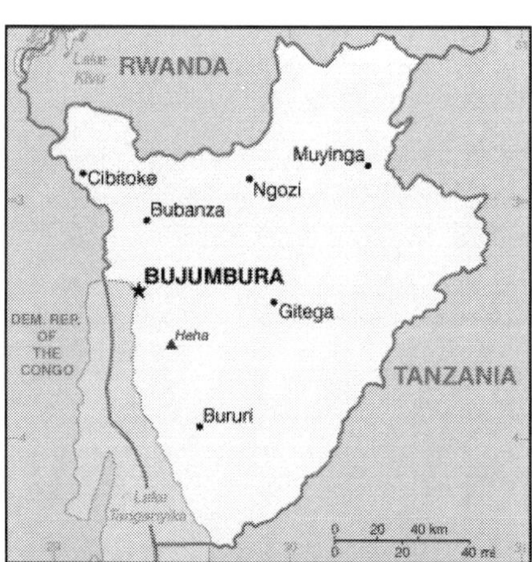
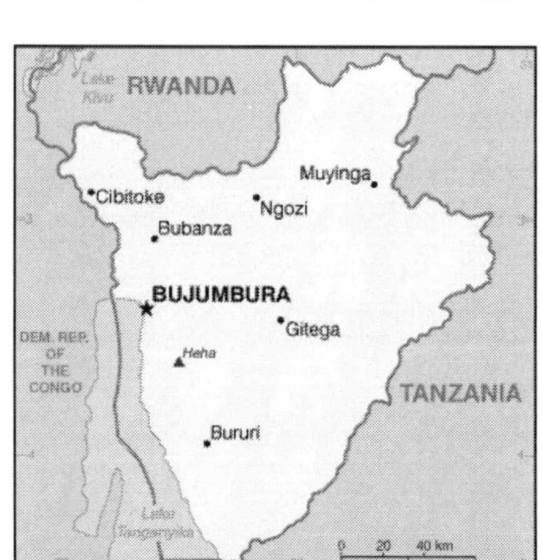

AFRICA :: BURUNDI

INTRODUCTION :: BURUNDI

BACKGROUND:

Burundi is a small country in Central-East Africa bordered by Tanzania, Rwanda, the Democratic Republic of Congo, and Lake Tanganyika. Burundi gained its independence from Belgium in 1962. Much of its history has been marked by political violence and non-democratic transfers of power; Burundi's first democratically elected president, a Hutu, was assassinated in October 1993 after only 100 days in office. The internationally brokered Arusha Agreement, signed in 2000, and subsequent ceasefire agreements with armed movements ended the 1993-2005 civil war. Burundi's second democratic elections were held in 2005. Pierre NKURUNZIZA was elected president in 2005 and 2010, and again in a controversial election in 2015. Burundi continues to face many economic and political challenges.

GEOGRAPHY :: BURUNDI

LOCATION:

Central Africa, east of the Democratic Republic of the Congo, west of Tanzania

GEOGRAPHIC COORDINATES:

3 30 S, 30 00 E

MAP REFERENCES:

Africa

AREA:

total: 27,830 sq km

land: 25,680 sq km

water: 2,150 sq km

country comparison to the world: 147

AREA - COMPARATIVE:

slightly smaller than Maryland

LAND BOUNDARIES:

total: 1,140 km

border countries (3): Democratic Republic of the Congo 236 km, Rwanda 315 km, Tanzania 589 km

COASTLINE:

0 km (landlocked)

MARITIME CLAIMS:

none (landlocked)

CLIMATE:

equatorial; high plateau with considerable altitude variation (772 m to 2,670 m above sea level); average annual temperature varies with altitude from 23 to 17 degrees Celsius but is generally moderate as the average altitude is about 1,700 m; average annual rainfall is about 150 cm; two wet seasons (February to May and September to November), and two dry seasons (June to August and December to January)

TERRAIN:

hilly and mountainous, dropping to a plateau in east, some plains

ELEVATION:

mean elevation: 1,504 m

elevation extremes: 772 m lowest point: Lake Tanganyika

2670 highest point: Heha

NATURAL RESOURCES:

nickel, uranium, rare earth oxides, peat, cobalt, copper, platinum, vanadium, arable land, hydropower, niobium, tantalum, gold, tin, tungsten, kaolin, limestone

LAND USE:

agricultural land: 73.3% (2011 est.)

arable land: 38.9% (2011 est.) / permanent crops: 15.6% (2011 est.) / permanent pasture: 18.8% (2011 est.)

forest: 6.6% (2011 est.)

other: 20.1% (2011 est.)

IRRIGATED LAND:

230 sq km (2012)

POPULATION DISTRIBUTION:

one of Africa's most densely populated countries; concentrations tend to be in the north and along the northern shore of Lake Tanganyika in the west; most people live on farms near areas of fertile volcanic soil

NATURAL HAZARDS:

flooding; landslides; drought

ENVIRONMENT - CURRENT ISSUES:

soil erosion as a result of overgrazing and the expansion of agriculture into marginal lands; deforestation (little forested land remains because of uncontrolled cutting of trees for fuel); habitat loss threatens wildlife populations

ENVIRONMENT - INTERNATIONAL AGREEMENTS:

party to: Biodiversity, Climate Change, Climate Change-Kyoto Protocol, Desertification, Endangered Species, Hazardous Wastes, Ozone Layer Protection, Wetlands

signed, but not ratified: Law of the Sea

GEOGRAPHY - NOTE:

landlocked; straddles crest of the Nile-Congo watershed; the Kagera, which drains into Lake Victoria, is the most remote headstream of the White Nile

PEOPLE AND SOCIETY :: BURUNDI

POPULATION:

11,844,520 (July 2018 est.)

note: estimates for this country explicitly take into account the effects of excess mortality due to AIDS; this can result in lower life expectancy, higher infant mortality, higher death rates, lower population growth rates, and changes in the distribution of population by age and sex than would otherwise be expected

country comparison to the world: 76

NATIONALITY:

noun: Burundian(s)

adjective: Burundian

ETHNIC GROUPS:

Hutu 85%, Tutsi 14%, Twa (Pygmy) 1%, Europeans 3,000, South Asians 2,000

LANGUAGES:

Kirundi 29.7% (official), Kirundi and other language 9.1%, French (official); French and other language 0.3%, Swahili; Swahili and other language 0.2% (along Lake Tanganyika and in the Bujumbura area), English (official); English and other language 0.06%, more than 2 languages 3.7%, unspecified 56.9% (2008 est.)

note: data represent language read and written by people 10 years of age or older; spoken Kirundi is nearly universal

RELIGIONS:

Roman Catholic 62.1%, Protestant 23.9% (includes Adventist 2.3% and other Protestant 21.6%), Muslim 2.5%, other 3.6%, unspecified 7.9% (2008 est.)

DEMOGRAPHIC PROFILE:

Burundi is a densely populated country with a high population growth rate, factors that combined with land scarcity and poverty place a large share of its population at risk of food insecurity. About 90% of the population relies on subsistence agriculture. Subdivision of land to sons, and redistribution to returning refugees, results in smaller, overworked, and less productive plots. Food shortages, poverty, and a lack of clean water contribute to a 60% chronic malnutrition rate among children. A lack of reproductive health services has prevented a significant reduction in Burundi's maternal mortality and fertility rates, which are both among the world's highest. With two-thirds of its population under the age of 25 and a birth rate of about 6 children per woman, Burundi's population will continue to expand rapidly for decades to come, putting additional strain on a poor country.

Historically, migration flows into and out of Burundi have consisted overwhelmingly of refugees from violent conflicts. In the last decade, more than a half million Burundian refugees returned home from neighboring countries, mainly Tanzania. Reintegrating the returnees has been problematic due to their prolonged time in exile, land scarcity, poor infrastructure, poverty, and unemployment. Repatriates and existing residents (including internally displaced persons) compete for limited land and other resources. To further complicate matters, international aid organizations reduced their assistance because they no longer classified Burundi as a post-conflict country. Conditions have deteriorated since renewed violence erupted in April 2015, causing another outpouring of refugees. In addition to refugee out-migration, Burundi has hosted thousands of refugees from neighboring countries, mostly from the Democratic Republic of the Congo and lesser numbers from Rwanda.

AGE STRUCTURE:

0-14 years: 45.52% (male 2,712,836 /female 2,678,223)

15-24 years: 19.21% (male 1,135,145 /female 1,139,717)

25-54 years: 28.7% (male 1,694,547 /female 1,704,369)

55-64 years: 3.89% (male 218,272 /female 242,855)

65 years and over: 2.69% (male 137,590 /female 180,966) (2018 est.)

DEPENDENCY RATIOS:

total dependency ratio: 89.6 (2015 est.)

youth dependency ratio: 84.8 (2015 est.)

elderly dependency ratio: 4.7 (2015 est.)

potential support ratio: 21.1 (2015 est.)

MEDIAN AGE:

total: 17.1 years

male: 16.8 years

female: 17.3 years (2018 est.)

country comparison to the world: 221

POPULATION GROWTH RATE:

3.23% (2018 est.)

country comparison to the world: 4

BIRTH RATE:

40.9 births/1,000 population (2018 est.)

country comparison to the world: 7

DEATH RATE:

8.6 deaths/1,000 population (2018 est.)

country comparison to the world: 74

NET MIGRATION RATE:

0 migrant(s)/1,000 population (2017 est.)

country comparison to the world: 77

POPULATION DISTRIBUTION:

one of Africa's most densely populated countries; concentrations tend to be in the north and along the northern shore of Lake Tanganyika in the west; most people live on farms near areas of fertile volcanic soil

URBANIZATION:

urban population: 13% of total population (2018)

rate of urbanization: 5.68% annual rate of change (2015-20 est.)

MAJOR URBAN AREAS - POPULATION:

899,000 BUJUMBURA (capital) (2018)

SEX RATIO:

at birth: 1.02 male(s)/female (2017 est.)

0-14 years: 1.01 male(s)/female (2017 est.)

15-24 years: 1 male(s)/female (2017 est.)

25-54 years: 1 male(s)/female (2017 est.)

55-64 years: 0.89 male(s)/female (2017 est.)

65 years and over: 0.74 male(s)/female (2017 est.)

total population: 0.99 male(s)/female (2017 est.)

MOTHER'S MEAN AGE AT FIRST BIRTH:

21.3 years (2010 est.)

note: median age at first birth among women 25-29

MATERNAL MORTALITY RATE:

712 deaths/100,000 live births (2015 est.)

country comparison to the world: 8

INFANT MORTALITY RATE:

total: 57.4 deaths/1,000 live births (2018 est.)

male: 63.7 deaths/1,000 live births (2018 est.)

female: 50.9 deaths/1,000 live births (2018 est.)

country comparison to the world: 18

LIFE EXPECTANCY AT BIRTH:

total population: 61.4 years (2018 est.)

male: 59.6 years (2018 est.)

female: 63.2 years (2018 est.)

country comparison to the world: 203

TOTAL FERTILITY RATE:

5.93 children born/woman (2018 est.)

country comparison to the world: 3

CONTRACEPTIVE PREVALENCE RATE:

28.5% (2016/17)

HEALTH EXPENDITURES:

7.5% of GDP (2014)

country comparison to the world: 65

HOSPITAL BED DENSITY:

0.8 beds/1,000 population (2014)

DRINKING WATER SOURCE:

improved:

urban: 91.1% of population

rural: 73.8% of population

total: 75.9% of population

unimproved:

urban: 8.9% of population

rural: 26.2% of population

total: 24.1% of population (2015 est.)

SANITATION FACILITY ACCESS:

improved:

urban: 43.8% of population (2015 est.)

rural: 48.6% of population (2015 est.)

total: 48% of population (2015 est.)

unimproved:

urban: 56.2% of population (2015 est.)

rural: 51.4% of population (2015 est.)

total: 52% of population (2015 est.)

HIV/AIDS - ADULT PREVALENCE RATE:

1.1% (2017 est.)

country comparison to the world: 41

HIV/AIDS - PEOPLE LIVING WITH HIV/AIDS:

78,000 (2017 est.)

country comparison to the world: 48

HIV/AIDS - DEATHS:

1,700 (2017 est.)

country comparison to the world: 56

MAJOR INFECTIOUS DISEASES:

degree of risk: very high (2016)

food or waterborne diseases: bacterial and protozoal diarrhea, hepatitis A, and typhoid fever (2016)

vectorborne diseases: malaria and dengue fever (2016)

water contact diseases: schistosomiasis (2016)

animal contact diseases: rabies (2016)

OBESITY - ADULT PREVALENCE RATE:

5.4% (2016)

country comparison to the world: 178

CHILDREN UNDER THE AGE OF 5 YEARS UNDERWEIGHT:

29.3% (2016)

country comparison to the world: 10

EDUCATION EXPENDITURES:

5.4% of GDP (2013)

country comparison to the world: 54

LITERACY:

definition: age 15 and over can read and write (2015 est.)

total population: 85.6% (2015 est.)

male: 88.2% (2015 est.)

female: 83.1% (2015 est.)

SCHOOL LIFE EXPECTANCY (PRIMARY TO TERTIARY EDUCATION):

total: 11 years (2013)

male: 11 years (2013)

female: 10 years (2013)

UNEMPLOYMENT, YOUTH AGES 15-24:

total: 2.9% (2014 est.)

male: 4.4% (2014 est.)

female: 2% (2014 est.)

country comparison to the world: 164

GOVERNMENT :: BURUNDI

COUNTRY NAME:

conventional long form: Republic of Burundi

conventional short form: Burundi

local long form: Republique du Burundi/Republika y'u Burundi

local short form: Burundi

former: Urundi, German East Africa, Kingdom of Burundi

etymology: name derived from the pre-colonial Kingdom of Burundi (17th-19th century)

GOVERNMENT TYPE:

presidential republic

CAPITAL:

name: Bujumbura

geographic coordinates: 3 22 S, 29 21 E

time difference: UTC+2 (7 hours ahead of Washington, DC, during Standard Time)

ADMINISTRATIVE DIVISIONS:

18 provinces; Bubanza, Bujumbura Mairie, Bujumbura Rural, Bururi, Cankuzo, Cibitoke, Gitega, Karuzi, Kayanza, Kirundo, Makamba, Muramvya, Muyinga, Mwaro, Ngozi, Rumonge, Rutana, Ruyigi

INDEPENDENCE:

1 July 1962 (from UN trusteeship under Belgian administration)

NATIONAL HOLIDAY:

Independence Day, 1 July (1962)

CONSTITUTION:

history: several previous; latest ratified by referendum 28 February 2005 (2018)

amendments: proposed by the president of the republic after consultation with the government or by absolute majority support of the membership in both houses of Parliament; passage requires at least two-thirds majority vote by the Senate membership and at least four-fifths majority vote by the National Assembly; the president can opt to submit amendment bills to a referendum; constitutional articles including those on national unity, the secularity of Burundi, its democratic form of government, and its sovereignty cannot be amended; amended 2018 (2018)

LEGAL SYSTEM:

mixed legal system of Belgian civil law and customary law

INTERNATIONAL LAW ORGANIZATION PARTICIPATION:

has not submitted an ICJ jurisdiction declaration; withdrew from ICCt in October 2017

CITIZENSHIP:

citizenship by birth: no

citizenship by descent only: the father must be a citizen of Burundi

dual citizenship recognized: no

residency requirement for naturalization: 10 years

SUFFRAGE:

18 years of age; universal

EXECUTIVE BRANCH:

chief of state: President Pierre NKURUNZIZA (since 26 August 2005); First Vice President Gaston SINDIMWO (since 20 August 2015); Second Vice President Joseph BUTORE (since 20 August 2015); note - the president is both chief of state and head of government

head of government: President Pierre NKURUNZIZA (since 26 August 2005); First Vice President Gaston SINDIMWO (since 20 August 2015); Second Vice President Joseph BUTORE (since 20 August 2015)

cabinet: Council of Ministers appointed by president

elections/appointments: president directly elected by absolute majority popular vote in 2 rounds if needed for a 5-year term (eligible for a second term); election last held on 21 July 2015 (next to be held in 2020); vice presidents nominated by the president, endorsed by Parliament; note - a 2018 constitutional referendum effective for the 2020 election, approved reinstatement of the prime minister position, reduced the number of vice presidents from 2 to 1, and increased the presidential term from 5 to 7 years with a 2-consecutive-term limit

election results: Pierre NKURUNZIZA reelected president; percent of vote - Pierre NKURUNZIZA (CNDD-FDD) 69.4%, Agathon RWASA (Hope of Burundians - Amizerio y'ABARUNDI) 19%, other 11.6%

LEGISLATIVE BRANCH:

description: bicameral Parliament or Parlement consists of:
Senate or Inama Nkenguzamateka (43 seats in the July 2015 election; 36 members indirectly elected by an electoral college of provincial councils using a three-round voting system, which requires a two-thirds majority vote in the first two rounds and simple majority vote for the two leading candidates in the final round; 4 seats reserved for former heads of state, 3 seats reserved for Twas, and 30% of all votes reserved for women; members serve 5-year terms)
National Assembly or Inama Nshingamateka (121 seats in the June 2015 election; 100 members directly elected in multi-seat constituencies by proportional representation vote and 21 co-opted members; 60% of seats allocated to Hutu and 40% to Tutsi; 3 seats reserved for Twas; 30% of total seats reserved for women; members serve 5-year terms)

elections:
Senate - last held on 24 July 2015 (next to be held in 2019)
National Assembly - last held on 29 June 2015 (next to be held in 2020)

election results:
Senate - percent of vote by party - NA; seats by party - CNDD-FDD 33, FRODEBU 2, CNDD 1, former heads of state 4, Twas 3, women 8; composition - men 25, women 18, percent of women 41.9%;
National Assembly - percent of vote by party - CNDD-FDD 60.3%, Independents of Hope 11.2%, UPRONA 2.5%, other 26%; seats by party - CNDD-FDD 77, Independents of Hope 21, UPRONA 2, women 18, Twas 3; composition - men 77, women 44, percent of women 36.4%; note - total Parliament percent of women 37.8%

JUDICIAL BRANCH:

highest courts: Supreme Court (consists of 9 judges and organized into judicial, administrative, and cassation chambers); Constitutional Court (consists of 7 members)

judge selection and term of office: Supreme Court judges nominated by the Judicial Service Commission, a 15-member independent body of judicial and legal profession officials), appointed by the president and confirmed by the Senate; judge tenure NA; Constitutional Court judges appointed by the president and confirmed by the Senate and serve 6-year nonrenewable terms

subordinate courts: Courts of Appeal; County Courts; Courts of Residence; Martial Court; Court Against Corruption; Commercial Court; Commerce Court

POLITICAL PARTIES AND LEADERS:

Front for Democracy in Burundi or FRODEBU [Keffa NIBIZI]
Hope of Burundians (Amizero y'Abarundi) [Agathon RWASA, Charles NDITIJE]
Movement for Solidarity and Development or MSD [Alexis SINDUHIJE]
National Council for the Defense of Democracy or CNDD [Leonard NYANGOMA]
National Council for the Defense of Democracy - Front for the Defense of Democracy or CNDD-FDD [Evariste NDAYISHIMIYE]
National Liberation Forces or FNL [Jacques BIGITIMANA]
Union for National Progress (Union pour le Progress Nationale) or UPRONA [Abel GASHATSI]

INTERNATIONAL ORGANIZATION PARTICIPATION:

ACP, AfDB, AU, CEMAC, CEPGL, CICA, COMESA, EAC, FAO, G-77, IBRD, ICAO, ICCt, ICRM, IDA, IFAD, IFC, IFRCS, ILO, IMF, Interpol, IOC, IOM, IPU, ISO (correspondent), ITU, ITUC (NGOs), MIGA, NAM, OIF, OPCW, UN, UNAMID, UNCTAD, UNESCO, UNIDO, UNISFA, UNWTO, UPU, WCO, WHO, WIPO, WMO, WTO

DIPLOMATIC REPRESENTATION IN THE US:

chief of mission: Ambassador (vacant); Charge D'Affaires Benjamin MANIRAKIZA (since 7 December 2017)

chancery: 2233 Wisconsin Avenue NW, Suite 408, Washington, DC 20007

telephone: [1] (202) 342-2574

FAX: [1] (202) 342-2578

DIPLOMATIC REPRESENTATION FROM THE US:

chief of mission: Ambassador Anne S. CASPER (since 20 October 2016)

embassy: Avenue Des Etats-Unis, Bujumbura

mailing address: B.P. 1720, Bujumbura

telephone: [257] 22-207-000

FAX: [257] 22-222-926

FLAG DESCRIPTION:

divided by a white diagonal cross into red panels (top and bottom) and green panels (hoist side and fly side) with a white disk superimposed at the center bearing three red six-pointed stars outlined in green arranged in a triangular design (one star above, two stars below); green symbolizes hope and optimism, white purity and peace, and red the blood shed in the struggle for independence; the three stars in the disk represent the three major ethnic groups: Hutu, Twa, Tutsi, as well as the three elements in the national motto: unity, work, progress

NATIONAL SYMBOL(S):

lion; national colors: red, white, green

NATIONAL ANTHEM:

name: "Burundi Bwacu" (Our Beloved Burundi)

lyrics/music: Jean-Baptiste NTAHOKAJA/Marc BARENGAYABO

note: adopted 1962

ECONOMY :: BURUNDI

ECONOMY - OVERVIEW:

Burundi is a landlocked, resource-poor country with an underdeveloped manufacturing sector. Agriculture accounts for over 40% of GDP and employs more than 90% of the population. Burundi's primary exports are coffee and tea, which account for more than half of foreign exchange earnings, but these earnings are subject to fluctuations in weather and international coffee and tea prices, Burundi is heavily dependent on aid from bilateral and multilateral donors, as well as foreign exchange earnings from participation in the African Union Mission to Somalia (AMISOM). Foreign aid represented 48% of Burundi's national income in 2015, one of the highest percentages in Sub-Saharan Africa, but this figure decreased to 33.5% in 2016 due to political turmoil surrounding President NKURUNZIZA's bid for a third term. Burundi joined the East African Community (EAC) in 2009.

Burundi faces several underlying weaknesses – low governmental capacity, corruption, a high poverty rate, poor educational levels, a weak legal system, a poor transportation network, and overburdened utilities – that have prevented the implementation of planned economic reforms. The purchasing power of most Burundians has decreased as wage increases have not kept pace with inflation, which reached approximately 18% in 2017.

Real GDP growth dropped precipitously following political events in 2015 and has yet to recover to pre-conflict levels. Continued resistance by donors and the international community will restrict Burundi's economic growth as the country deals with a large current account deficit.

GDP (PURCHASING POWER PARITY):

$8.007 billion (2017 est.)

$8.007 billion (2016 est.)

$8.091 billion (2015 est.)

note: data are in 2017 dollars

country comparison to the world: 164

GDP (OFFICIAL EXCHANGE RATE):

$3.396 billion (2017 est.) (2017 est.)

GDP - REAL GROWTH RATE:

0% (2017 est.)

-1% (2016 est.)

-4% (2015 est.)

country comparison to the world: 196

GDP - PER CAPITA (PPP):

$700 (2017 est.)

$800 (2016 est.)

$800 (2015 est.)

note: data are in 2017 dollars

country comparison to the world: 227

GROSS NATIONAL SAVING:

-5.3% of GDP (2017 est.)

-4.1% of GDP (2016 est.)

-6.7% of GDP (2015 est.)

country comparison to the world: 183

GDP - COMPOSITION, BY END USE:

household consumption: 83% (2017 est.)

government consumption: 20.8% (2017 est.)

investment in fixed capital: 16% (2017 est.)

investment in inventories: 0% (2017 est.)

exports of goods and services: 5.5% (2017 est.)

imports of goods and services: -25.3% (2017 est.)

GDP - COMPOSITION, BY SECTOR OF ORIGIN:

agriculture: 39.5% (2017 est.)

industry: 16.4% (2017 est.)

services: 44.2% (2017 est.)

AGRICULTURE - PRODUCTS:

coffee, cotton, tea, corn, beans, sorghum, sweet potatoes, bananas, cassava (manioc, tapioca); beef, milk, hides

INDUSTRIES:

light consumer goods (sugar, shoes, soap, beer); cement, assembly of imported components; public works construction; food processing (fruits)

INDUSTRIAL PRODUCTION GROWTH RATE:

-2% (2017 est.)

country comparison to the world: 182

LABOR FORCE:

5.012 million (2017 est.)

country comparison to the world: 83

LABOR FORCE - BY OCCUPATION:

agriculture: 93.6%

industry: 2.3%

services: 4.1% (2002 est.)

UNEMPLOYMENT RATE:

NA

POPULATION BELOW POVERTY LINE:

64.6% (2014 est.)

HOUSEHOLD INCOME OR CONSUMPTION BY PERCENTAGE SHARE:

lowest 10%: 28% (2006)

highest 10%: 28% (2006)

DISTRIBUTION OF FAMILY INCOME - GINI INDEX:

42.4 (1998)

country comparison to the world: 51

BUDGET:

revenues: 536.7 million (2017 est.)

expenditures: 729.6 million (2017 est.)

TAXES AND OTHER REVENUES:

15.8% (of GDP) (2017 est.)

country comparison to the world: 186

BUDGET SURPLUS (+) OR DEFICIT (-):

-5.7% (of GDP) (2017 est.)

country comparison to the world: 177

PUBLIC DEBT:

51.7% of GDP (2017 est.)

48.4% of GDP (2016 est.)

country comparison to the world: 96

FISCAL YEAR:

calendar year

INFLATION RATE (CONSUMER PRICES):

16.6% (2017 est.)

5.5% (2016 est.)

country comparison to the world: 214

CENTRAL BANK DISCOUNT RATE:

11.25% (31 December 2010)

10% (31 December 2009)

country comparison to the world: 16

COMMERCIAL BANK PRIME LENDING RATE:

14.8% (31 December 2017 est.)

14.24% (31 December 2016 est.)

country comparison to the world: 43

STOCK OF NARROW MONEY:

$540 million (31 December 2017 est.)

$476.7 million (31 December 2016 est.)

country comparison to the world: 169

STOCK OF BROAD MONEY:

$540 million (31 December 2017 est.)

$476.7 million (31 December 2016 est.)

country comparison to the world: 174

STOCK OF DOMESTIC CREDIT:

$1.116 billion (31 December 2017 est.)

$1.03 billion (31 December 2016 est.)

country comparison to the world: 167

MARKET VALUE OF PUBLICLY TRADED SHARES:

NA

CURRENT ACCOUNT BALANCE:

-$418 million (2017 est.)

-$411 million (2016 est.)

country comparison to the world: 114

EXPORTS:

$119 million (2017 est.)

$109.7 million (2016 est.)

country comparison to the world: 195

EXPORTS - PARTNERS:

Democratic Republic of the Congo 25.5%, Switzerland 18.4%, UAE 14.9%, Belgium 6% (2017)

EXPORTS - COMMODITIES:

coffee, tea, sugar, cotton, hides

IMPORTS:

$603.8 million (2017 est.)

$527.2 million (2016 est.)

country comparison to the world: 194

IMPORTS - COMMODITIES:

capital goods, petroleum products, foodstuffs

IMPORTS - PARTNERS:

India 18.5%, China 13%, Kenya 7.9%, UAE 6.8%, Saudi Arabia 6.8%, Uganda 6%, Tanzania 5.4%, Zambia 4.6% (2017)

RESERVES OF FOREIGN EXCHANGE AND GOLD:

$97.4 million (31 December 2017 est.)

$95.17 million (31 December 2016 est.)

country comparison to the world: 181

DEBT - EXTERNAL:

$610.9 million (31 December 2017 est.)

$622.4 million (31 December 2016 est.)

country comparison to the world: 174

EXCHANGE RATES:

Burundi francs (BIF) per US dollar -

1,731 (2017 est.)

1,654.63 (2016 est.)

1,654.63 (2015 est.)

1,571.9 (2014 est.)

1,546.7 (2013 est.)

ENERGY :: BURUNDI

ELECTRICITY ACCESS:

population without electricity: 9.7 million (2013)

electrification - total population: 5% (2013)

electrification - urban areas: 28% (2013)

electrification - rural areas: 2% (2013)

ELECTRICITY - PRODUCTION:

304 million kWh (2016 est.)

country comparison to the world: 183

ELECTRICITY - CONSUMPTION:

382.7 million kWh (2016 est.)

country comparison to the world: 176

ELECTRICITY - EXPORTS:

0 kWh (2016 est.)

country comparison to the world: 114

ELECTRICITY - IMPORTS:

100 million kWh (2016 est.)

country comparison to the world: 100

ELECTRICITY - INSTALLED GENERATING CAPACITY:

68,000 kW (2016 est.)

country comparison to the world: 186

ELECTRICITY - FROM FOSSIL FUELS:

14% of total installed capacity (2016 est.)

country comparison to the world: 200

ELECTRICITY - FROM NUCLEAR FUELS:

0% of total installed capacity (2017 est.)

country comparison to the world: 59

ELECTRICITY - FROM HYDROELECTRIC PLANTS:

73% of total installed capacity (2017 est.)

country comparison to the world: 14

ELECTRICITY - FROM OTHER RENEWABLE SOURCES:

14% of total installed capacity (2017 est.)

country comparison to the world: 61

CRUDE OIL - PRODUCTION:

0 bbl/day (2017 est.)

country comparison to the world: 116

CRUDE OIL - EXPORTS:

0 bbl/day (2015 est.)

country comparison to the world: 101

CRUDE OIL - IMPORTS:

0 bbl/day (2015 est.)

country comparison to the world: 104

CRUDE OIL - PROVED RESERVES:

0 bbl (1 January 2018 est.)

country comparison to the world: 113

REFINED PETROLEUM PRODUCTS - PRODUCTION:

0 bbl/day (2015 est.)

country comparison to the world: 125

REFINED PETROLEUM PRODUCTS - CONSUMPTION:

1,500 bbl/day (2016 est.)

country comparison to the world: 200

REFINED PETROLEUM PRODUCTS - EXPORTS:

0 bbl/day (2015 est.)

country comparison to the world: 138

REFINED PETROLEUM PRODUCTS - IMPORTS:

1,374 bbl/day (2015 est.)

country comparison to the world: 196

NATURAL GAS - PRODUCTION:

0 cu m (2017 est.)

country comparison to the world: 111

NATURAL GAS - CONSUMPTION:

0 cu m (2017 est.)

country comparison to the world: 127

NATURAL GAS - EXPORTS:

0 cu m (2017 est.)

country comparison to the world: 76

NATURAL GAS - IMPORTS:

0 cu m (2017 est.)

country comparison to the world: 100

NATURAL GAS - PROVED RESERVES:

0 cu m (1 January 2014 est.)

country comparison to the world: 117

CARBON DIOXIDE EMISSIONS FROM CONSUMPTION OF ENERGY:

217,000 Mt (2017 est.)

country comparison to the world: 199

COMMUNICATIONS :: BURUNDI

TELEPHONES - FIXED LINES:

total subscriptions: 23,409 (2017 est.)

subscriptions per 100 inhabitants: less than 1 (2017 est.)

country comparison to the world: 170

TELEPHONES - MOBILE CELLULAR:

total subscriptions: 5,920,612 (2017 est.)

subscriptions per 100 inhabitants: 52 (2017 est.)

country comparison to the world: 115

TELEPHONE SYSTEM:

general assessment: with the great population density Burundi remains one of the most alluring telecom markets in Africa for investors; the government in early 2018 began the Burundi Broadband project, which plans to deliver nationwide connectivity by 2025; mobile operators have launched 3G and LTE mobile services to capitalise on the expanding demand for Internet access (2018)

domestic: telephone density one of the lowest in the world; fixed-line connections stand at well less than 1 per 100 persons; mobile-cellular usage is approaching 52 per 100 persons (2017)

international: country code - 257; satellite earth station - 1 Intelsat (Indian Ocean); the government, supported by the Word Bank, has backed a joint venture with a number of prominent telcos to build a national fibre backbone network, offering onward connectivity to submarine cable infrastructure landings in Kenya and Tanzania (2017)

BROADCAST MEDIA:

state-controlled Radio Television Nationale de Burundi (RTNB) operates a TV station and a national radio network; 3 private TV stations and about 10 privately owned radio stations; transmissions of several international broadcasters are available in Bujumbura (2017)

INTERNET COUNTRY CODE:

.bi

INTERNET USERS:

total: 574,236 (July 2016 est.)

percent of population: 5.2% (July 2016 est.)

country comparison to the world: 147

BROADBAND - FIXED SUBSCRIPTIONS:

total: 3,914 (2017 est.)

subscriptions per 100 inhabitants: less than 1 (2017 est.)

country comparison to the world: 178

TRANSPORTATION :: BURUNDI

CIVIL AIRCRAFT REGISTRATION COUNTRY CODE PREFIX:

9U (2016)

AIRPORTS:

7 (2013)

country comparison to the world: 165

AIRPORTS - WITH PAVED RUNWAYS:

total: 1 (2017)

over 3,047 m: 1 (2017)

AIRPORTS - WITH UNPAVED RUNWAYS:

total: 6 (2013)

914 to 1,523 m: 4 (2013)

under 914 m: 2 (2013)

HELIPORTS:

1 (2012)

ROADWAYS:

total: 12,322 km (2016)

paved: 1,500 km (2016)

unpaved: 10,822 km (2016)

country comparison to the world: 129

WATERWAYS:

(mainly on Lake Tanganyika between Bujumbura, Burundi's principal port, and lake ports in Tanzania, Zambia, and the Democratic Republic of the Congo) (2011)

PORTS AND TERMINALS:

lake port(s): Bujumbura (Lake Tanganyika)

MILITARY AND SECURITY :: BURUNDI

MILITARY EXPENDITURES:

2.21% of GDP (2016)

2.14% of GDP (2015)

2.01% of GDP (2014)

2.24% of GDP (2013)

2.39% of GDP (2012)

country comparison to the world: 45

MILITARY BRANCHES:

National Defense Forces (Forces de Defense Nationale, FDN): Army (includes maritime wing, air wing), National Police (Police Nationale du Burundi) (2017)

MILITARY SERVICE AGE AND OBLIGATION:

18 years of age for voluntary military service; the armed forces law of 31 December 2004 did not specify a minimum age for enlistment, but the government claimed that no one younger than 18 was being recruited; mandatory retirement ages: 45 (enlisted), 50 (NCOs), 55 (officers), and 60 (officers with the rank of general) (2017)

TRANSNATIONAL ISSUES :: BURUNDI

DISPUTES - INTERNATIONAL:

Burundi and Rwanda dispute two sq km (0.8 sq mi) of Sabanerwa, a farmed area in the Rukurazi Valley where the Akanyaru/Kanyaru River shifted its course southward after heavy rains in 1965cross-border conflicts persist among Tutsi, Hutu, other ethnic groups, associated political rebels, armed gangs, and various government forces in the Great Lakes region

REFUGEES AND INTERNALLY DISPLACED PERSONS:

refugees (country of origin): 75,297 (Democratic Republic of the Congo) (refugees and asylum seekers) (2018)

IDPs: 147,086 (some ethnic Tutsis remain displaced from intercommunal violence that broke out after the 1,993 coup and fighting between government forces and rebel groups; violence since April 2015) (2018)

stateless persons: 974 (2017)

TRAFFICKING IN PERSONS:

current situation: Burundi is a source country for children and possibly women subjected to forced labor and sex trafficking; business people recruit Burundian girls for prostitution domestically, as well as in Rwanda, Kenya, Uganda, and the Middle East, and recruit boys and girls for forced labor in Burundi and Tanzania; children and young adults are coerced into forced labor in farming, mining, informal commerce, fishing, or collecting river stones for construction; sometimes family, friends, and neighbors are complicit in exploiting children, at times luring them in with offers of educational or job opportunities

tier rating: Tier 3 – Burundi does not comply fully with the minimum standards for the elimination of human trafficking and is not making significant efforts to do so; corruption, a lack of political will, and limited resources continue to hamper efforts to combat human trafficking; in 2014, the government did not inform judicial and law enforcement officials of the enactment of an anti-trafficking law or how to implement it and approved – but did not fund – its national anti-trafficking action plan; authorities again failed to identify trafficking victims or to provide them with adequate protective services; the government has focused on transnational child trafficking but gave little attention to its domestic child trafficking problem and adult trafficking victims (2015)

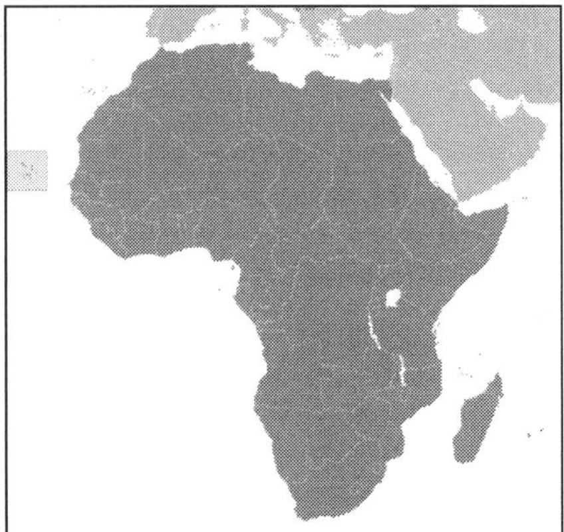

AFRICA :: CABO VERDE

INTRODUCTION :: CABO VERDE

BACKGROUND:

The uninhabited islands were discovered and colonized by the Portuguese in the 15th century; Cabo Verde subsequently became a trading center for African slaves and later an important coaling and resupply stop for whaling and transatlantic shipping. The fusing of European and various African cultural traditions is reflected in Cabo Verde's Crioulo language, music, and pano textiles. Following independence in 1975, and a tentative interest in unification with Guinea-Bissau, a one-party system was established and maintained until multi-party elections were held in 1990. Cabo Verde continues to sustain one of Africa's most stable democratic governments. Repeated droughts during the second half of the 20th century caused significant hardship and prompted heavy emigration. As a result, Cabo Verde's expatriate population is greater than its domestic one. Most Cabo Verdeans have both African and Portuguese antecedents. Cabo Verde's population descends from its first permanent inhabitants in the late 15th-century – a preponderance of West African slaves, a small share of Portuguese colonists, and even fewer Italians, Spaniards, and Portuguese Jews. Among the nine inhabited islands, population distribution is variable. Islands in the east are very dry and are only sparsely settled to exploit their extensive salt deposits. The more southerly islands receive more precipitation and support larger populations, but agriculture and livestock grazing have damaged their soil fertility and vegetation. For centuries, the country's overall population size has fluctuated significantly, as recurring periods of famine and epidemics have caused high death tolls and emigration.

GEOGRAPHY :: CABO VERDE

LOCATION:

Western Africa, group of islands in the North Atlantic Ocean, west of Senegal

GEOGRAPHIC COORDINATES:

16 00 N, 24 00 W

MAP REFERENCES:

Africa

AREA:

total: 4,033 sq km

land: 4,033 sq km

water: 0 sq km

country comparison to the world: 176

AREA - COMPARATIVE:

slightly larger than Rhode Island

LAND BOUNDARIES:

0 km

COASTLINE:

965 km

MARITIME CLAIMS:

territorial sea: 12 nm

exclusive economic zone: 200 nm

contiguous zone: 24 nm

measured from claimed archipelagic baselines

CLIMATE:

temperate; warm, dry summer; precipitation meager and erratic

TERRAIN:

steep, rugged, rocky, volcanic

ELEVATION:

0 m lowest point: Atlantic Ocean

2829 highest point: Mt. Fogo (a volcano on Fogo Island)

NATURAL RESOURCES:

salt, basalt rock, limestone, kaolin, fish, clay, gypsum

LAND USE:

agricultural land: 18.6% (2011 est.)

arable land: 11.7% (2011 est.) / permanent crops: 0.7% (2011 est.) / permanent pasture: 6.2% (2011 est.)

forest: 21% (2011 est.)

other: 60.4% (2011 est.)

IRRIGATED LAND:

35 sq km (2012)

POPULATION DISTRIBUTION:

among the nine inhabited islands, population distribution is variable; islands in the east are very dry and are only sparsely settled to exploit their extensive salt deposits; the more southerly islands receive more precipitation and support larger populations, but agriculture and livestock grazing have damaged the soil fertility and vegetation; approximately half of the population lives on Sao Tiago Island, which is the location of the capital of Praia; Mindelo, on the northern island of Sao Vicente, also has a large urban population

NATURAL HAZARDS:

prolonged droughts; seasonal harmattan wind produces obscuring dust; volcanically and seismically active

volcanism: Fogo (2,829 m), which last erupted in 1995, is Cabo Verde's only active volcano

ENVIRONMENT - CURRENT ISSUES:

deforestation due to demand for firewood; water shortages; prolonged droughts and improper use of land (overgrazing, crop cultivation on hillsides lead to desertification and erosion); environmental damage has threatened several species of birds and reptiles; illegal beach sand extraction; overfishing

ENVIRONMENT - INTERNATIONAL AGREEMENTS:

party to: Biodiversity, Climate Change, Climate Change-Kyoto Protocol, Desertification, Endangered Species, Environmental Modification, Hazardous Wastes, Law of the Sea, Marine Dumping, Ozone Layer Protection, Ship Pollution, Wetlands

signed, but not ratified: none of the selected agreements

GEOGRAPHY - NOTE:

strategic location 500 km from west coast of Africa near major north-south sea routes; important communications station; important sea and air refueling site

PEOPLE AND SOCIETY :: CABO VERDE

POPULATION:

568,373 (July 2018 est.)

country comparison to the world: 173

NATIONALITY:

noun: Cabo Verdean(s)

adjective: Cabo Verdean

ETHNIC GROUPS:

Creole (mulatto) 71%, African 28%, European 1%

LANGUAGES:

Portuguese (official), Crioulo (a blend of Portuguese and West African words)

RELIGIONS:

Roman Catholic 77.3%, Protestant 4.6% (includes Church of the Nazarene 1.7%, Adventist 1.5%, Assembly of God 0.9%, Universal Kingdom of God 0.4%, and God and Love 0.1%), other Christian 3.4% (includes Christian Rationalism 1.9%, Jehovah's Witness 1%, and New Apostolic 0.5%), Muslim 1.8%, other 1.3%, none 10.8%, unspecified 0.7% (2010 est.)

DEMOGRAPHIC PROFILE:

Cabo Verde's population descends from its first permanent inhabitants in the late 15th-century – a preponderance of West African slaves, a small share of Portuguese colonists, and even fewer Italians, Spaniards, and Portuguese Jews. Over the centuries, the country's overall population size has fluctuated significantly, as recurring periods of famine and epidemics have caused high death tolls and emigration.

Labor migration historically reduced Cabo Verde's population growth and still provides a key source of income through remittances. Expatriates probably outnumber Cabo Verde's resident population, with most families having a member abroad. Cabo Verdeans have settled in the US, Europe, Africa, and South America. The largest diaspora community in New Bedford, Massachusetts, dating to the early 1800s, is a byproduct of the transatlantic whaling industry. Cabo Verdean men fleeing poverty at home joined the crews of US whaling ships that stopped in the islands. Many settled in New Bedford and stayed in the whaling or shipping trade, worked in the textile or cranberry industries, or operated their own transatlantic packet ships that transported compatriots to the US. Increased Cabo Verdean emigration to the US coincided with the gradual and eventually complete abolition of slavery in the archipelago in 1878.

During the same period, Portuguese authorities coerced Cabo Verdeans to go to Sao Tome and Principe and other Portuguese colonies in Africa to work as indentured laborers on plantations. In the 1920s, when the US implemented immigration quotas, Cabo Verdean emigration shifted toward Portugal, West Africa (Senegal), and South America (Argentina). Growing numbers of Cabo Verdean labor migrants headed to Western Europe in the 1960s and 1970s. They filled unskilled jobs in Portugal, as many Portuguese sought out work opportunities in the more prosperous economies of northwest Europe. Cabo Verdeans eventually expanded their emigration to the Netherlands, where they worked in the shipping industry. Migration to the US resumed under relaxed migration laws. Cabo Verdean women also began migrating to southern Europe to become domestic workers, a trend that continues today and has shifted the gender balance of Cabo Verdean emigration.

Emigration has declined in more recent decades due to the adoption of more restrictive migration policies in destination countries. Reduced emigration along with a large youth population, decreased mortality rates, and increased life expectancies, has boosted population growth, putting further pressure on domestic employment and resources. In addition, Cabo Verde has attracted increasing numbers of migrants in recent decades, consisting primarily of people from West Africa, Portuguese-speaking African countries, Portugal, and China. Since the 1990s, some West African migrants have used Cabo Verde as a stepping stone for illegal migration to Europe.

AGE STRUCTURE:

0-14 years: 28.7% (male 82,035 /female 81,082)

15-24 years: 19.64% (male 55,811 /female 55,798)

25-54 years: 40.02% (male 110,646 /female 116,804)

55-64 years: 6.4% (male 16,154 /female 20,245)

65 years and over: 5.24% (male 11,272 /female 18,526) (2018 est.)

DEPENDENCY RATIOS:

total dependency ratio: 55.4 (2015 est.)

youth dependency ratio: 48.4 (2015 est.)

elderly dependency ratio: 6.9 (2015 est.)

potential support ratio: 14.4 (2015 est.)

MEDIAN AGE:

total: 25.8 years

male: 25 years

female: 26.7 years (2018 est.)

country comparison to the world: 153

POPULATION GROWTH RATE:

1.32% (2018 est.)

country comparison to the world: 83

BIRTH RATE:

19.7 births/1,000 population (2018 est.)

country comparison to the world: 79

DEATH RATE:

6 deaths/1,000 population (2018 est.)

country comparison to the world: 163

NET MIGRATION RATE:

-0.6 migrant(s)/1,000 population (2017 est.)

country comparison to the world: 128

POPULATION DISTRIBUTION:

among the nine inhabited islands, population distribution is variable; islands in the east are very dry and are only sparsely settled to exploit their extensive salt deposits; the more southerly islands receive more precipitation and support larger populations, but agriculture and livestock grazing have damaged the soil fertility and vegetation; approximately half of the population lives on Sao Tiago Island, which is the location of the capital of Praia; Mindelo, on the northern island of Sao Vicente, also has a large urban population

URBANIZATION:

urban population: 65.7% of total population (2018)

rate of urbanization: 1.97% annual rate of change (2015-20 est.)

MAJOR URBAN AREAS - POPULATION:

168,000 PRAIA (capital) (2018)

SEX RATIO:

at birth: 1.02 male(s)/female (2017 est.)

0-14 years: 1.01 male(s)/female (2017 est.)

15-24 years: 1 male(s)/female (2017 est.)

25-54 years: 0.94 male(s)/female (2017 est.)

55-64 years: 0.75 male(s)/female (2017 est.)

65 years and over: 0.61 male(s)/female (2017 est.)

total population: 0.94 male(s)/female (2017 est.)

MATERNAL MORTALITY RATE:

42 deaths/100,000 live births (2015 est.)

country comparison to the world: 103

INFANT MORTALITY RATE:

total: 21.1 deaths/1,000 live births (2018 est.)

male: 24.3 deaths/1,000 live births (2018 est.)

female: 17.9 deaths/1,000 live births (2018 est.)

country comparison to the world: 77

LIFE EXPECTANCY AT BIRTH:

total population: 72.7 years (2018 est.)

male: 70.3 years (2018 est.)

female: 75.1 years (2018 est.)

country comparison to the world: 147

TOTAL FERTILITY RATE:

2.21 children born/woman (2018 est.)

country comparison to the world: 95

HEALTH EXPENDITURES:

4.8% of GDP (2014)

country comparison to the world: 147

PHYSICIANS DENSITY:

0.79 physicians/1,000 population (2015)

HOSPITAL BED DENSITY:

2.1 beds/1,000 population (2010)

DRINKING WATER SOURCE:

improved:

urban: 94% of population

rural: 87.3% of population

total: 91.7% of population

unimproved:

urban: 6% of population

rural: 12.7% of population

total: 8.3% of population (2015 est.)

SANITATION FACILITY ACCESS:

improved:

urban: 81.6% of population (2015 est.)

rural: 54.3% of population (2015 est.)

total: 72.2% of population (2015 est.)

unimproved:

urban: 1.4% of population (2015 est.)

rural: 45.7% of population (2015 est.)

total: 27.8% of population (2015 est.)

HIV/AIDS - ADULT PREVALENCE RATE:

0.6% (2017 est.)

country comparison to the world: 56

HIV/AIDS - PEOPLE LIVING WITH HIV/AIDS:

2,400 (2017 est.)

country comparison to the world: 129

HIV/AIDS - DEATHS:

<100 (2017 est.)

MAJOR INFECTIOUS DISEASES:

note: active local transmission of Zika virus by Aedes species mosquitoes has been identified in this country (as of August 2016); it poses an important risk (a large number of cases possible) among US citizens if bitten by an infective mosquito; other less common ways to get Zika are through sex, via blood transfusion, or during pregnancy, in which the pregnant woman passes Zika virus to her fetus

OBESITY - ADULT PREVALENCE RATE:

11.8% (2016)

country comparison to the world: 134

EDUCATION EXPENDITURES:

5.4% of GDP (2016)

country comparison to the world: 55

LITERACY:

definition: age 15 and over can read and write (2015 est.)

total population: 86.8% (2015 est.)

male: 91.7% (2015 est.)

female: 82% (2015 est.)

SCHOOL LIFE EXPECTANCY (PRIMARY TO TERTIARY EDUCATION):

total: 13 years (2015)

male: 13 years (2015)

female: 13 years (2015)

GOVERNMENT :: CABO VERDE

COUNTRY NAME:

conventional long form: Republic of Cabo Verde

conventional short form: Cabo Verde

local long form: Republica de Cabo Verde

local short form: Cabo Verde

etymology: the name derives from Cap-Vert (Green Cape) on the Senegalese coast, the westernmost point of Africa and the nearest mainland to the islands

GOVERNMENT TYPE:

parliamentary republic

CAPITAL:

name: Praia

geographic coordinates: 14 55 N, 23 31 W

time difference: UTC-1 (4 hours ahead of Washington, DC, during Standard Time)

ADMINISTRATIVE DIVISIONS:

22 municipalities (concelhos, singular - concelho); Boa Vista, Brava, Maio, Mosteiros, Paul, Porto Novo, Praia, Ribeira Brava, Ribeira Grande, Ribeira Grande de Santiago, Sal, Santa

Catarina, Santa Catarina do Fogo, Santa Cruz, Sao Domingos, Sao Filipe, Sao Lourenco dos Orgaos, Sao Miguel, Sao Salvador do Mundo, Sao Vicente, Tarrafal, Tarrafal de Sao Nicolau

INDEPENDENCE:

5 July 1975 (from Portugal)

NATIONAL HOLIDAY:

Independence Day, 5 July (1975)

CONSTITUTION:

history: previous 1981; latest effective 25 September 1992 (2017)

amendments: proposals require support of at least four-fifths of the active National Assembly membership; amendment drafts require sponsorship of at least one-third of the active Assembly membership; passage requires at least two-thirds majority vote by the Assembly membership; constitutional sections including those on national independence, form of government, political pluralism, suffrage, and human rights and liberties cannot be amended; revised 1995, 1999, 2010 (2017)

LEGAL SYSTEM:

civil law system of Portugal

INTERNATIONAL LAW ORGANIZATION PARTICIPATION:

has not submitted an ICJ jurisdiction declaration; accepts ICCt jurisdiction

CITIZENSHIP:

citizenship by birth: no

citizenship by descent only: at least one parent must be a citizen of Cabo Verde

dual citizenship recognized: yes

residency requirement for naturalization: 5 years

SUFFRAGE:

18 years of age; universal

EXECUTIVE BRANCH:

chief of state: President Jorge Carlos FONSECA (since 9 September 2011)

head of government: Prime Minister Ulisses CORREIA E. SILVA (since 22 April 2016)

cabinet: Council of Ministers appointed by the president on the recommendation of the prime minister

elections/appointments: president directly elected by absolute majority popular vote in 2 rounds if needed for a 5-year term (eligible for a second term); election last held on 2 October 2016 (next to be held in 2021); prime minister nominated by the National Assembly and appointed by the president

election results: Jorge Carlos FONSECA reelected president; percent of vote - Jorge Carlos FONSECA (MPD) 74%, Albertino GRACA (independent) 23%, other 3%

LEGISLATIVE BRANCH:

description: unicameral National Assembly or Assembleia Nacional (72 seats; members directly elected in multi-seat constituencies by proportional representation vote; members serve 5-year terms)

elections: last held on 20 March 2016 (next to be held in 2021)

election results: percent of vote by party MPD 54.5%, PAICV 38.2%, UCID 7%, other 0.3%; seats by party - MPD 40, PAICV 29, UCID 3; composition - men 57, women 15, percent of women 20.8%

JUDICIAL BRANCH:

highest courts: Supreme Court of Justice (consists of the chief justice and at least 7 judges and organized into civil, criminal, and administrative sections)

judge selection and term of office: judge appointments - 1 by the president of the republic, 1 elected by the National Assembly, and 3 by the Superior Judicial Council (SJC), a 16-member independent body chaired by the chief justice and includes the attorney general, 8 private citizens, 2 judges, 2 prosecutors, the senior legal inspector of the Attorney General's office, and a representative of the Ministry of Justice; chief justice appointed by the president of the republic from among peers of the Supreme Court of Justice and in consultation with the SJC; judges appointed for life

subordinate courts: appeals courts, first instance (municipal) courts; audit, military, and fiscal and customs courts

POLITICAL PARTIES AND LEADERS:

rz African Party for Independence of Cabo Verde or PAICV [Janira Hopffer ALMADA]
Democratic and Independent Cabo Verdean Union or UCID [Antonio MONTEIRO]
Democratic Christian Party or PDC [Manuel RODRIGUES]
Democratic Renovation Party or PRD [Victor FIDALGO]
Movement for Democracy or MPD [Ulisses CORREIA E SILVA]
Party for Democratic Convergence or PCD [Dr. Eurico MONTEIRO]
Party of Work and Solidarity or PTS [Anibal MEDINA]
Social Democratic Party or PSD [Joao ALEM]

INTERNATIONAL ORGANIZATION PARTICIPATION:

ACP, AfDB, AOSIS, AU, CD, CPLP, ECOWAS, FAO, G-77, IAEA, IBRD, ICAO, ICCt (signatory), ICRM, IDA, IFAD, IFC, IFRCS, ILO, IMF, IMO, Interpol, IOC, IOM, IPU, ITSO, ITU, ITUC (NGOs), MIGA, NAM, OIF, OPCW, UN, UNCTAD, UNESCO, UNIDO, Union Latina, UNWTO, UPU, WCO, WHO, WIPO, WMO, WTO

DIPLOMATIC REPRESENTATION IN THE US:

chief of mission: Ambassador Carlos VEIGA (since 18 January 2017)

chancery: 3415 Massachusetts Avenue NW, Washington, DC 20007

telephone: [1] (202) 965-6820

FAX: [1] (202) 965-1207

consulate(s) general: Boston

DIPLOMATIC REPRESENTATION FROM THE US:

chief of mission: Ambassador Donald L. HEFLIN (since 5 February 2015)

embassy: Rua Abilio Macedo 6, Praia

mailing address: C. P. 201, Praia

telephone: [238] 260-89-00

FAX: [238] 261-13-55

FLAG DESCRIPTION:

five unequal horizontal bands; the top-most band of blue - equal to one half the width of the flag - is followed by three bands of white, red, and white, each equal to 1/12 of the width, and a bottom stripe of blue equal to one quarter of the flag width; a circle of 10 yellow, five-pointed stars is centered on the red stripe and positioned 3/8 of the length of the flag from the hoist side; blue stands for the sea and the sky, the circle of stars represents the 10 major islands united into a nation, the stripes symbolize the road to formation of the country through peace (white) and effort (red)

NATIONAL SYMBOL(S):

ten, five-pointed, yellow stars; national colors: blue, white, red, yellow

NATIONAL ANTHEM:

name: "Cantico da Liberdade" (Song of Freedom)

lyrics/music: Amilcar Spencer LOPES/Adalberto Higino Tavares SILVA

note: adopted 1996

ECONOMY :: CABO VERDE

ECONOMY - OVERVIEW:

Cabo Verde's economy depends on development aid, foreign investment, remittances, and tourism. The economy is service-oriented with commerce, transport, tourism, and public services accounting for about three-fourths of GDP. Tourism is the mainstay of the economy and depends on conditions in the euro-zone countries. Cabo Verde annually runs a high trade deficit financed by foreign aid and remittances from its large pool of emigrants; remittances as a share of GDP are one of the highest in Sub-Saharan Africa.

Although about 40% of the population lives in rural areas, the share of food production in GDP is low. The island economy suffers from a poor natural resource base, including serious water shortages, exacerbated by cycles of long-term drought, and poor soil for growing food on several of the islands, requiring it to import most of what it consumes. The fishing potential, mostly lobster and tuna, is not fully exploited.

Economic reforms are aimed at developing the private sector and attracting foreign investment to diversify the economy and mitigate high unemployment. The government's elevated debt levels have limited its capacity to finance any shortfalls.

GDP (PURCHASING POWER PARITY):

$3.777 billion (2017 est.)

$3.631 billion (2016 est.)

$3.468 billion (2015 est.)

note: data are in 2017 dollars

country comparison to the world: 182

GDP (OFFICIAL EXCHANGE RATE):

$1.776 billion (2017 est.) (2017 est.)

GDP - REAL GROWTH RATE:

4% (2017 est.)

4.7% (2016 est.)

1% (2015 est.)

country comparison to the world: 75

GDP - PER CAPITA (PPP):

$7,000 (2017 est.)

$6,800 (2016 est.)

$6,600 (2015 est.)

note: data are in 2017 dollars

country comparison to the world: 157

GROSS NATIONAL SAVING:

32.4% of GDP (2017 est.)

34.8% of GDP (2016 est.)

35.6% of GDP (2015 est.)

country comparison to the world: 25

GDP - COMPOSITION, BY END USE:

household consumption: 50.1% (2017 est.)

government consumption: 18.3% (2017 est.)

investment in fixed capital: 32.2% (2017 est.)

investment in inventories: 1.9% (2017 est.)

exports of goods and services: 48.6% (2017 est.)

imports of goods and services: -51.1% (2017 est.)

GDP - COMPOSITION, BY SECTOR OF ORIGIN:

agriculture: 8.9% (2017 est.)

industry: 17.5% (2017 est.)

services: 73.7% (2017 est.)

AGRICULTURE - PRODUCTS:

bananas, corn, beans, sweet potatoes, sugarcane, coffee, peanuts; fish

INDUSTRIES:

food and beverages, fish processing, shoes and garments, salt mining, ship repair

INDUSTRIAL PRODUCTION GROWTH RATE:

2.9% (2017 est.)

country comparison to the world: 107

LABOR FORCE:

196,100 (2007 est.)

country comparison to the world: 174

UNEMPLOYMENT RATE:

9% (2017 est.)

9% (2016 est.)

country comparison to the world: 131

POPULATION BELOW POVERTY LINE:

30% (2000 est.)

HOUSEHOLD INCOME OR CONSUMPTION BY PERCENTAGE SHARE:

lowest 10%: 40.6% (2000)

highest 10%: 40.6% (2001)

BUDGET:

revenues: 493.5 million (2017 est.)

expenditures: 546.7 million (2017 est.)

TAXES AND OTHER REVENUES:

27.8% (of GDP) (2017 est.)

country comparison to the world: 98

BUDGET SURPLUS (+) OR DEFICIT (-):

-3% (of GDP) (2017 est.)

country comparison to the world: 131

PUBLIC DEBT:

125.8% of GDP (2017 est.)

127.6% of GDP (2016 est.)

country comparison to the world: 8

FISCAL YEAR:

calendar year

INFLATION RATE (CONSUMER PRICES):

0.8% (2017 est.)

-1.4% (2016 est.)

country comparison to the world: 39

CENTRAL BANK DISCOUNT RATE:

7.5% (31 December 2010)

7.5% (31 December 2009)

country comparison to the world: 42

COMMERCIAL BANK PRIME LENDING RATE:

9.5% (31 December 2017 est.)

9.61% (31 December 2016 est.)

country comparison to the world: 89

STOCK OF NARROW MONEY:

$774 million (31 December 2017 est.)

$602.1 million (31 December 2016 est.)

country comparison to the world: 161

STOCK OF BROAD MONEY:

$774 million (31 December 2017 est.)

$602.1 million (31 December 2016 est.)

country comparison to the world: 165

STOCK OF DOMESTIC CREDIT:

$1.61 billion (31 December 2017 est.)

$1.316 billion (31 December 2016 est.)

country comparison to the world: 158

CURRENT ACCOUNT BALANCE:

-$109 million (2017 est.)

-$40 million (2016 est.)

country comparison to the world: 87

EXPORTS:

$189 million (2017 est.)

$148.4 million (2016 est.)

country comparison to the world: 190

EXPORTS - PARTNERS:

Spain 45.3%, Portugal 40.3%, Netherlands 8.1% (2017)

EXPORTS - COMMODITIES:

fuel (re-exports), shoes, garments, fish, hides

IMPORTS:

$836.1 million (2017 est.)

$687.3 million (2016 est.)

country comparison to the world: 188

IMPORTS - COMMODITIES:

foodstuffs, industrial products, transport equipment, fuels

IMPORTS - PARTNERS:

Portugal 43.9%, Spain 11.6%, Netherlands 6.1%, China 6.1% (2017)

RESERVES OF FOREIGN EXCHANGE AND GOLD:

$617.4 million (31 December 2017 est.)

$572.7 million (31 December 2016 est.)

country comparison to the world: 145

DEBT - EXTERNAL:

$1.713 billion (31 December 2017 est.)

$1.688 billion (31 December 2016 est.)

country comparison to the world: 155

STOCK OF DIRECT FOREIGN INVESTMENT - AT HOME:

$2.088 billion (31 December 2017 est.)

$1.735 billion (31 December 2016 est.)

country comparison to the world: 119

STOCK OF DIRECT FOREIGN INVESTMENT - ABROAD:

$64.6 million (31 December 2017 est.)

$39.9 million (31 December 2016 est.)

country comparison to the world: 113

EXCHANGE RATES:

Cabo Verdean escudos (CVE) per US dollar -

101.8 (2017 est.)

99.688 (2016 est.)

99.688 (2015 est.)

99.426 (2014 est.)

83.114 (2013 est.)

ENERGY :: CABO VERDE

ELECTRICITY ACCESS:

population without electricity: 153,027 (2012)

electrification - total population: 70.6% (2012)

electrification - urban areas: 84.4% (2012)

electrification - rural areas: 46.8% (2012)

ELECTRICITY - PRODUCTION:

395 million kWh (2016 est.)

country comparison to the world: 172

ELECTRICITY - CONSUMPTION:

367.4 million kWh (2016 est.)

country comparison to the world: 179

ELECTRICITY - EXPORTS:

0 kWh (2016 est.)

country comparison to the world: 115

ELECTRICITY - IMPORTS:

0 kWh (2016 est.)

country comparison to the world: 131

ELECTRICITY - INSTALLED GENERATING CAPACITY:

162,500 kW (2016 est.)

country comparison to the world: 171

ELECTRICITY - FROM FOSSIL FUELS:

79% of total installed capacity (2016 est.)

country comparison to the world: 84

ELECTRICITY - FROM NUCLEAR FUELS:

0% of total installed capacity (2017 est.)

country comparison to the world: 60

ELECTRICITY - FROM HYDROELECTRIC PLANTS:

0% of total installed capacity (2017 est.)

country comparison to the world: 162

ELECTRICITY - FROM OTHER RENEWABLE SOURCES:

21% of total installed capacity (2017 est.)

country comparison to the world: 35

CRUDE OIL - PRODUCTION:

0 bbl/day (2017 est.)

country comparison to the world: 117

CRUDE OIL - EXPORTS:

0 bbl/day (2015 est.)

country comparison to the world: 102

CRUDE OIL - IMPORTS:

0 bbl/day (2015 est.)

country comparison to the world: 105

CRUDE OIL - PROVED RESERVES:

0 bbl (1 January 2018 est.)

country comparison to the world: 114

REFINED PETROLEUM PRODUCTS - PRODUCTION:

0 bbl/day (2015 est.)

country comparison to the world: 126

REFINED PETROLEUM PRODUCTS - CONSUMPTION:

5,600 bbl/day (2016 est.)

country comparison to the world: 173

REFINED PETROLEUM PRODUCTS - EXPORTS:

0 bbl/day (2015 est.)

country comparison to the world: 139

REFINED PETROLEUM PRODUCTS - IMPORTS:

5,607 bbl/day (2015 est.)

country comparison to the world: 166

NATURAL GAS - PRODUCTION:

0 cu m (2017 est.)

country comparison to the world: 112

NATURAL GAS - CONSUMPTION:

0 cu m (2017 est.)

country comparison to the world: 128

NATURAL GAS - EXPORTS:

0 cu m (2017 est.)

country comparison to the world: 77

NATURAL GAS - IMPORTS:

0 cu m (2017 est.)

country comparison to the world: 101

NATURAL GAS - PROVED RESERVES:

0 cu m (1 January 2016 est.)

country comparison to the world: 118

CARBON DIOXIDE EMISSIONS FROM CONSUMPTION OF ENERGY:

867,800 Mt (2017 est.)

country comparison to the world: 172

COMMUNICATIONS :: CABO VERDE

TELEPHONES - FIXED LINES:

total subscriptions: 64,970 (2017 est.)

subscriptions per 100 inhabitants: 12 (2017 est.)

country comparison to the world: 153

TELEPHONES - MOBILE CELLULAR:

total subscriptions: 612,259 (2017 est.)

subscriptions per 100 inhabitants: 109 (2017 est.)

country comparison to the world: 166

TELEPHONE SYSTEM:

general assessment: good system, extensive modernization from 1996-2000 following partial privatization in 1995; major service provider is Cabo Verde Telecom (CVT) (2017)

domestic: 12 per 100 fixed-line and 109 per 100 mobile-cellular; fiber-optic ring, completed in 2001, links all islands providing Internet access and ISDN services; cellular service introduced in 1998; broadband services launched early in the decade (2017)

international: country code - 238; landing point for the Atlantis-2 fiber-optic transatlantic telephone cable that provides links to South America, Senegal, and Europe; HF radiotelephone to Senegal and Guinea-Bissau; satellite earth station - 1 Intelsat (Atlantic Ocean); new agreement between CVT and private company and subsea fibre connectivity in 2020
will promote growth in Internet, cloud computing and 5G services to the region, reaching Europe and Latin America (2017)

BROADCAST MEDIA:

state-run TV and radio broadcast network plus a growing number of private broadcasters; Portuguese public TV and radio services for Africa are available; transmissions of a few international broadcasters are available (2007)

INTERNET COUNTRY CODE:

.cv

INTERNET USERS:

total: 266,562 (July 2016 est.)

percent of population: 48.2% (July 2016 est.)

country comparison to the world: 162

BROADBAND - FIXED SUBSCRIPTIONS:

total: 14,493 (2017 est.)

subscriptions per 100 inhabitants: 3 (2017 est.)

country comparison to the world: 163

TRANSPORTATION :: CABO VERDE

NATIONAL AIR TRANSPORT SYSTEM:

number of registered air carriers: 2 (2015)

inventory of registered aircraft operated by air carriers: 5 (2015)

annual passenger traffic on registered air carriers: 567,182 (2015)

annual freight traffic on registered air carriers: 1,728,152 mt-km (2015)

CIVIL AIRCRAFT REGISTRATION COUNTRY CODE PREFIX:

D4 (2016)

AIRPORTS:

9 (2013)

country comparison to the world: 157

AIRPORTS - WITH PAVED RUNWAYS:

total: 9 (2017)

over 3,047 m: 1 (2017)

1,524 to 2,437 m: 3 (2017)

914 to 1,523 m: 3 (2017)

under 914 m: 2 (2017)

ROADWAYS:

total: 1,350 km (2013)

paved: 932 km (2013)

unpaved: 418 km (2013)

country comparison to the world: 179

MERCHANT MARINE:

total: 42 (2017)

by type: general cargo 19, oil tanker 2, other 21 (2017)

country comparison to the world: 119

PORTS AND TERMINALS:

major seaport(s): Porto Grande

MILITARY AND SECURITY :: CABO VERDE

MILITARY EXPENDITURES:

0.63% of GDP (2016)

0.57% of GDP (2015)

0.54% of GDP (2014)

country comparison to the world: 137

MILITARY BRANCHES:

Armed Forces: Army (also called the National Guard, GN), Cabo Verde Coast Guard (Guardia Costeira de Cabo Verde, GCCV, includes naval infantry) (2013)

MILITARY SERVICE AGE AND OBLIGATION:

18-35 years of age for male and female selective compulsory military service; 2-years conscript service obligation; 17 years of age for voluntary service (with parental consent) (2013)

TRANSNATIONAL ISSUES :: CABO VERDE

DISPUTES - INTERNATIONAL:

none

REFUGEES AND INTERNALLY DISPLACED PERSONS:

stateless persons: 115 (2017)

ILLICIT DRUGS:

used as a transshipment point for Latin American cocaine destined for Western Europe, particularly because of Lusophone links to Brazil, Portugal, and Guinea-Bissau; has taken steps to deter drug money laundering, including a 2002 anti-money laundering reform that criminalizes laundering the proceeds of narcotics trafficking and other crimes and the establishment in 2008 of a Financial Intelligence Unit

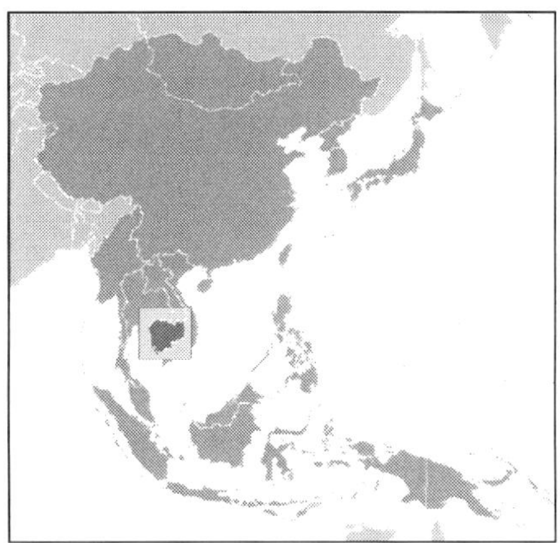

INTRODUCTION :: CAMBODIA

BACKGROUND:

Most Cambodians consider themselves to be Khmers, descendants of the Angkor Empire that extended over much of Southeast Asia and reached its zenith between the 10th and 13th centuries. Attacks by the Thai and Cham (from present-day Vietnam) weakened the empire, ushering in a long period of decline. The king placed the country under French protection in 1863, and it became part of French Indochina in 1887. Following Japanese occupation in World War II, Cambodia gained full independence from France in 1953. In April 1975, after a seven-year struggle, communist Khmer Rouge forces captured Phnom Penh and evacuated all cities and towns. At least 1.5 million Cambodians died from execution, forced hardships, or starvation during the Khmer Rouge regime under POL POT. A December 1978 Vietnamese invasion drove the Khmer Rouge into the countryside, began a 10-year Vietnamese occupation, and touched off almost 13 years of civil war.

The 1991 Paris Peace Accords mandated democratic elections and a cease-fire, which was not fully respected by the Khmer Rouge. UN-sponsored elections in 1993 helped restore some semblance of normalcy under a coalition government. Factional fighting in 1997 ended the first coalition government, but a second round of national elections in 1998 led to the formation of another coalition government and renewed political stability. The remaining elements of the Khmer Rouge surrendered in early 1999. Some of the surviving Khmer Rouge leaders have been tried or are awaiting trial for crimes against humanity by a hybrid UN-Cambodian tribunal supported by international assistance. Elections in July 2003 were relatively peaceful, but it took one year of negotiations between contending political parties before a coalition government was formed. In October 2004, King Norodom SIHANOUK abdicated the throne and his son, Prince Norodom SIHAMONI, was selected to succeed him. The most recent local (Commune Council) elections were held in Cambodia in 2012, with little of the preelection violence that preceded prior elections. National elections in July 2013 were disputed, with the opposition - the Cambodian National Rescue Party (CNRP) - boycotting the National Assembly. The political impasse was ended nearly a year later, with the CNRP agreeing to enter parliament in exchange for ruling party commitments to electoral and legislative reforms. The CNRP made further gains in local commune elections in June 2017, accelerating sitting Prime Minister Hun SEN's efforts to marginalize the CNRP before national elections in 2018. Hun Sen arrested CNRP's President Kem Sokha in September 2017 and subsequently dissolved the CNRP in November 2017 and banned its leaders from participating in politics for at least five years. CNRP's seats in the National Assembly were redistributed to smaller, more pliant opposition parties.

GEOGRAPHY :: CAMBODIA

LOCATION:

Southeastern Asia, bordering the Gulf of Thailand, between Thailand, Vietnam, and Laos

GEOGRAPHIC COORDINATES:

13 00 N, 105 00 E

MAP REFERENCES:

Southeast Asia

AREA:

total: 181,035 sq km

land: 176,515 sq km

water: 4,520 sq km

country comparison to the world: 91

AREA - COMPARATIVE:

one and a half times the size of Pennsylvania; slightly smaller than Oklahoma

LAND BOUNDARIES:

total: 2,530 km

border countries (3): Laos 555 km, Thailand 817 km, Vietnam 1158 km

COASTLINE:

443 km

MARITIME CLAIMS:

territorial sea: 12 nm

exclusive economic zone: 200 nm

contiguous zone: 24 nm

continental shelf: 200 nm

CLIMATE:

tropical; rainy, monsoon season (May to November); dry season (December to April); little seasonal temperature variation

TERRAIN:

mostly low, flat plains; mountains in southwest and north

ELEVATION:

mean elevation: 126 m

elevation extremes: 0 m lowest point: Gulf of Thailand

1810 highest point: Phnum Aoral

NATURAL RESOURCES:

oil and gas, timber, gemstones, iron ore, manganese, phosphates, hydropower potential, arable land

LAND USE:

agricultural land: 32.1% (2011 est.)

arable land: 22.7% (2011 est.) / permanent crops: 0.9% (2011 est.) / permanent pasture: 8.5% (2011 est.)

forest: 56.5% (2011 est.)

other: 11.4% (2011 est.)

IRRIGATED LAND:

3,540 sq km (2012)

POPULATION DISTRIBUTION:

population concentrated in the southeast, particularly in and around the capital of Phnom Penh; further distribution is linked closely to the Tonle Sap and Mekong Rivers

NATURAL HAZARDS:

monsoonal rains (June to November); flooding; occasional droughts

ENVIRONMENT - CURRENT ISSUES:

illegal logging activities throughout the country and strip mining for gems in the western region along the border with Thailand have resulted in habitat loss and declining biodiversity (in particular, destruction of mangrove swamps threatens natural fisheries); soil erosion; in rural areas, most of the population does not have access to potable water; declining fish stocks because of illegal fishing and overfishing; coastal ecosystems choked by sediment washed loose from deforested areas inland

ENVIRONMENT - INTERNATIONAL AGREEMENTS:

party to: Biodiversity, Climate Change, Climate Change-Kyoto Protocol, Desertification, Endangered Species, Hazardous Wastes, Marine Life Conservation, Ozone Layer Protection, Ship Pollution, Tropical Timber 94, Wetlands, Whaling

signed, but not ratified: Law of the Sea

GEOGRAPHY - NOTE:

a land of paddies and forests dominated by the Mekong River and Tonle Sap (Southeast Asia's largest freshwater lake)

PEOPLE AND SOCIETY :: CAMBODIA

POPULATION:

16,449,519 (July 2018 est.)

country comparison to the world: 69

NATIONALITY:

noun: Cambodian(s)

adjective: Cambodian

ETHNIC GROUPS:

Khmer 97.6%, Cham 1.2%, Chinese 0.1%, Vietnamese 0.1%, other 0.9% (2013 est.)

LANGUAGES:

Khmer (official) 96.3%, other 3.7% (2008 est.)

RELIGIONS:

Buddhist (official) 96.9%, Muslim 1.9%, Christian 0.4%, other 0.8% (2008 est.)

AGE STRUCTURE:

0-14 years: 30.76% (male 2,556,733 /female 2,503,796)

15-24 years: 17.84% (male 1,452,795 /female 1,482,065)

25-54 years: 41.09% (male 3,312,036 /female 3,446,962)

55-64 years: 5.94% (male 406,970 /female 569,383)

65 years and over: 4.37% (male 269,159 /female 449,620) (2018 est.)

DEPENDENCY RATIOS:

total dependency ratio: 55.6 (2015 est.)

youth dependency ratio: 49.2 (2015 est.)

elderly dependency ratio: 6.4 (2015 est.)

potential support ratio: 15.6 (2015 est.)

MEDIAN AGE:

total: 25.7 years

male: 24.9 years

female: 26.4 years (2018 est.)

country comparison to the world: 155

POPULATION GROWTH RATE:

1.48% (2018 est.)

country comparison to the world: 75

BIRTH RATE:

22.5 births/1,000 population (2018 est.)

country comparison to the world: 67

DEATH RATE:

7.4 deaths/1,000 population (2018 est.)

country comparison to the world: 114

NET MIGRATION RATE:

-0.3 migrant(s)/1,000 population (2017 est.)

country comparison to the world: 115

POPULATION DISTRIBUTION:

population concentrated in the southeast, particularly in and around the capital of Phnom Penh; further distribution is linked closely to the Tonle Sap and Mekong Rivers

URBANIZATION:

urban population: 23.4% of total population (2018)

rate of urbanization: 3.25% annual rate of change (2015-20 est.)

MAJOR URBAN AREAS - POPULATION:

1.952 million PHNOM PENH (capital) (2018)

SEX RATIO:

at birth: 1.04 male(s)/female (2017 est.)

0-14 years: 1.02 male(s)/female (2017 est.)

15-24 years: 0.98 male(s)/female (2017 est.)

25-54 years: 0.96 male(s)/female (2017 est.)

55-64 years: 0.65 male(s)/female (2017 est.)

65 years and over: 0.6 male(s)/female (2017 est.)

total population: 0.94 male(s)/female (2017 est.)

MOTHER'S MEAN AGE AT FIRST BIRTH:

22.9 years (2014 est.)

note: median age at first birth among women 25-29

MATERNAL MORTALITY RATE:

161 deaths/100,000 live births (2015 est.)

country comparison to the world: 57

INFANT MORTALITY RATE:

total: 46.1 deaths/1,000 live births (2018 est.)

male: 52.5 deaths/1,000 live births (2018 est.)

female: 39.5 deaths/1,000 live births (2018 est.)

country comparison to the world: 34

LIFE EXPECTANCY AT BIRTH:

total population: 65.2 years (2018 est.)

male: 62.7 years (2018 est.)

female: 67.9 years (2018 est.)

country comparison to the world: 182

TOTAL FERTILITY RATE:

2.47 children born/woman (2018 est.)

country comparison to the world: 79

CONTRACEPTIVE PREVALENCE RATE:

56.3% (2014)

HEALTH EXPENDITURES:

5.7% of GDP (2014)

country comparison to the world: 114

PHYSICIANS DENSITY:

0.14 physicians/1,000 population (2014)

HOSPITAL BED DENSITY:

0.8 beds/1,000 population (2015)

DRINKING WATER SOURCE:

improved:

urban: 100% of population

rural: 69.1% of population

total: 75.5% of population

unimproved:

urban: 0% of population

rural: 30.9% of population

total: 24.5% of population (2015 est.)

SANITATION FACILITY ACCESS:

improved:

urban: 88.1% of population (2015 est.)

rural: 30.5% of population (2015 est.)

total: 42.4% of population (2015 est.)

unimproved:

urban: 11.9% of population (2015 est.)

rural: 69.5% of population (2015 est.)

total: 57.6% of population (2015 est.)

HIV/AIDS - ADULT PREVALENCE RATE:

0.5% (2017 est.)

country comparison to the world: 64

HIV/AIDS - PEOPLE LIVING WITH HIV/AIDS:

67,000 (2017 est.)

country comparison to the world: 52

HIV/AIDS - DEATHS:

1,300 (2017 est.)

country comparison to the world: 59

MAJOR INFECTIOUS DISEASES:

degree of risk: very high (2016)

food or waterborne diseases: bacterial diarrhea, hepatitis A, and typhoid fever (2016)

vectorborne diseases: dengue fever, Japanese encephalitis, and malaria (2016)

OBESITY - ADULT PREVALENCE RATE:

3.9% (2016)

country comparison to the world: 188

CHILDREN UNDER THE AGE OF 5 YEARS UNDERWEIGHT:

23.9% (2014)

country comparison to the world: 19

EDUCATION EXPENDITURES:

1.9% of GDP (2014)

country comparison to the world: 173

LITERACY:

definition: age 15 and over can read and write (2015 est.)

total population: 77.2% (2015 est.)

male: 84.5% (2015 est.)

female: 70.5% (2015 est.)

SCHOOL LIFE EXPECTANCY (PRIMARY TO TERTIARY EDUCATION):

total: 11 years (2008)

male: 11 years (2008)

female: 10 years (2008)

UNEMPLOYMENT, YOUTH AGES 15-24:

total: 1.6% (2012 est.)

male: 1.8% (2012 est.)

female: 1.4% (2012 est.)

country comparison to the world: 170

GOVERNMENT :: CAMBODIA

COUNTRY NAME:

conventional long form: Kingdom of Cambodia

conventional short form: Cambodia

local long form: Preahreacheanachakr Kampuchea (phonetic transliteration)

local short form: Kampuchea

former: Khmer Republic, Democratic Kampuchea, People's Republic of Kampuchea, State of Cambodia

etymology: the English name Cambodia is an anglicization of the French Cambodge, which is the French transliteration of the native name Kampuchea

GOVERNMENT TYPE:

parliamentary constitutional monarchy

CAPITAL:

name: Phnom Penh

geographic coordinates: 11 33 N, 104 55 E

time difference: UTC+7 (12 hours ahead of Washington, DC, during Standard Time)

ADMINISTRATIVE DIVISIONS:

24 provinces (khett, singular and plural) and 1 municipality (krong, singular and plural)

provinces: Banteay Meanchey, Battambang, Kampong Cham, Kampong Chhnang, Kampong Speu, Kampong Thom, Kampot, Kandal, Kep, Koh Kong, Kratie, Mondolkiri, Oddar Meanchey, Pailin, Preah Sihanouk, Preah Vihear, Prey Veng, Pursat, Ratanakiri, Siem Reap, Stung Treng, Svay Rieng, Takeo, Tbong Khmum;

municipalities: Phnom Penh (Phnum Penh)

INDEPENDENCE:

9 November 1953 (from France)

NATIONAL HOLIDAY:

Independence Day, 9 November (1953)

CONSTITUTION:

history: previous 1947; latest promulgated 21 September 1993 (2017)

amendments: proposed by the monarch, by the prime minister, or by the president of the National Assembly if supported by one-fourth of the Assembly membership; passage requires two-thirds majority of the Assembly membership; constitutional articles on the multiparty democratic form of government and the monarchy cannot be amended; amended 1999, 2008, 2014 (2017)

LEGAL SYSTEM:

civil law system (influenced by the UN Transitional Authority in Cambodia) customary law, Communist legal theory, and common law

INTERNATIONAL LAW ORGANIZATION PARTICIPATION:

accepts compulsory ICJ jurisdiction with reservations; accepts ICCt jurisdiction

CITIZENSHIP:

citizenship by birth: no

citizenship by descent only: at least one parent must be a citizen of Cambodia

dual citizenship recognized: yes

residency requirement for naturalization: 7 years

SUFFRAGE:

18 years of age; universal

EXECUTIVE BRANCH:

chief of state: King Norodom SIHAMONI (since 29 October 2004)

head of government: Prime Minister HUN SEN (since 14 January 1985); Permanent Deputy Prime Minister MEN SAM AN (since 25 September 2008); Deputy Prime Ministers SAR KHENG (since 3 February 1992), TEA BANH, Gen., HOR NAMHONG, NHEK BUNCHHAY (all since 16 July 2004), BIN CHHIN (since 5 September 2007), KEAT CHHON, YIM CHHAI LY (since 24 September 2008), KE KIMYAN (since 12 March 2009)

cabinet: Council of Ministers named by the prime minister and appointed by the monarch

elections/appointments: monarch chosen by the 9-member Royal Council of the Throne from among all eligible males of royal descent; following legislative elections, a member of the majority party or majority coalition named prime minister by the Chairman of the National Assembly and appointed by the monarch

LEGISLATIVE BRANCH:

description: bicameral Parliament of Cambodia consists of:
Senate (62 seats; 58 indirectly elected by parliamentarians and commune councils, 2 indirectly elected by the National Assembly, and 2 appointed by the monarch; members serve 6-year terms)
National Assembly (125 seats; members directly elected in multi-seat constituencies by proportional representation vote; members serve 5-year terms)

elections:
Senate - last held on 25 February 2018 (next to be held in 2024); National Assembly - last held on 29 July 2018 (next to be held in 2023)

election results:
Senate - percent of vote by party - CPP 96%, FUNCINPEC 2.4%, KNUP 1.6%; seats by party - CPP 58; composition - men 53, women 9, percent of women 14.5%
National Assembly - percent of vote by party - CPP 76.9%, FUNCINPEC 5.9%, LDP 4.9%, Khmer Will Party 3.4%, other 8.9%; seats by party - CPP 125; composition - men 100, women 25, percent of women 20%; note - total Parliament of Cambodia percent of women 18.2%

JUDICIAL BRANCH:

highest courts: Supreme Council (organized into 5- and 9-judge panels and includes a court chief and deputy chief); Constitutional Court (consists of 9 members); note - in 1997, the Cambodian Government requested UN assistance in establishing trials to prosecute former Khmer Rouge senior leaders for crimes against humanity committed during the 1975-1979 Khmer Rouge regime; the Extraordinary Chambers of the Courts in Cambodia (also called the Khmer Rouge Tribunal) were established and began hearings for the first case in 2009; court proceeding were ongoing in 2016

judge selection and term of office: Supreme Court and Constitutional Council judge candidates recommended by the Supreme Council of Magistracy, a 17-member body chaired by the monarch and includes other high-level judicial officers; judges of both courts appointed by the monarch; Supreme Court judges appointed for life; Constitutional Council judges appointed for 9-year terms with one-third of the court renewed every 3 years

subordinate courts: Appellate Court; provincial and municipal courts; Military Court

POLITICAL PARTIES AND LEADERS:

Cambodia National Rescue Party or CNRP [KHEM SOKHA] (dissolved by the government in November 2017; formed from a 2012 merger of the Sam Rangsi Party or SRP and the former Human Rights Party or HRP [KHEM SOKHA, also spelled KEM SOKHA])
Cambodian Nationality Party or CNP [SENG SOKHENG]
Cambodian People's Party or CPP [HUN SEN]
Khmer Economic Development Party or KEDP [HUON REACH CHAMROEUN]
Khmer National Unity Party or KNUP [NHEK Bun Chhay]
Khmer Will Party [KONG MONIKA]
League for Democracy Party or LDP [KHEM Veasna]
National United Front for an Independent, Neutral, Peaceful, and Cooperative Cambodia or FUNCINPEC [Prince NORODOM RANARIDDH]

INTERNATIONAL ORGANIZATION PARTICIPATION:

ADB, ARF, ASEAN, CICA, EAS, FAO, G-77, IAEA, IBRD, ICAO, ICRM, IDA, IFAD, IFC, IFRCS, ILO, IMF, IMO, Interpol, IOC, IOM, IPU, ISO (correspondent), ITU, MINUSMA, MIGA, NAM, OIF, OPCW, PCA, UN, UNAMID, UNCTAD, UNESCO, UNIDO, UNIFIL, UNISFA, UNMISS, UNWTO, UPU, WCO, WFTU (NGOs), WHO, WIPO, WMO, WTO

DIPLOMATIC REPRESENTATION IN THE US:

chief of mission: Ambassador CHUM SOUNRY (since 17 September 2018)

chancery: 4530 16th Street NW, Washington, DC 20011

telephone: [1] (202) 726-7742

FAX: [1] (202) 726-8381

DIPLOMATIC REPRESENTATION FROM THE US:

chief of mission: Ambassador William A. HEIDT (since 2 December 2015)

embassy: #1, Street 96, Sangkat Wat Phnom, Khan Daun Penh, Phnom Penh

mailing address: Unit 8166, Box P, APO AP 96546

telephone: [855] (23) 728-000

FAX: [855] (23) 728-600

FLAG DESCRIPTION:

three horizontal bands of blue (top), red (double width), and blue with a white, three-towered temple, representing Angkor Wat, outlined in black in the center of the red band; red and blue are traditional Cambodian colors

note: only national flag to incorporate an actual building into its design

NATIONAL SYMBOL(S):

Angkor Wat temple, kouprey (wild ox); national colors: red, blue

NATIONAL ANTHEM:

name: "Nokoreach" (Royal Kingdom)

lyrics/music: CHUON NAT/F. PERRUCHOT and J. JEKYLL

note: adopted 1941, restored 1993; the anthem, based on a Cambodian folk tune, was restored after the defeat of the Communist regime

ECONOMY :: CAMBODIA

ECONOMY - OVERVIEW:

Cambodia has experienced strong economic growth over the last decade; GDP grew at an average annual rate of over 8% between 2000 and 2010 and about 7% since 2011. The tourism, garment, construction and real estate, and agriculture sectors accounted for the bulk of growth. Around 700,000 people, the majority of whom are women, are employed in the garment and footwear sector. An additional 500,000 Cambodians are employed in the tourism sector, and a further 200,000 people in construction. Tourism has continued to grow rapidly with foreign arrivals exceeding 2 million per year in 2007 and reaching 5.6 million visitors in 2017. Mining also is attracting some investor interest and the government has touted opportunities for mining bauxite, gold, iron and gems.

Still, Cambodia remains one of the poorest countries in Asia and long-term economic development remains a daunting challenge, inhibited by corruption, limited human resources, high income inequality, and poor job prospects. According to the Asian Development Bank (ADB), the percentage of the population living in poverty decreased to 13.5% in 2016. More than 50% of the population is less than 25 years old. The population lacks education and productive skills, particularly in the impoverished countryside, which also lacks basic infrastructure.

The World Bank in 2016 formally reclassified Cambodia as a lower middle-income country as a result of continued rapid economic growth over the past several years. Cambodia's graduation from a low-income country will reduce its eligibility for foreign assistance and will challenge the government to seek new sources of financing. The Cambodian Government has been working with bilateral and multilateral donors, including the Asian Development Bank, the World Bank and IMF, to address the country's many pressing needs; more than 20% of the government budget will come from donor assistance in 2018. A major economic challenge for Cambodia over the next decade will be fashioning an economic environment in which the private sector can create enough jobs to handle Cambodia's demographic imbalance.

Textile exports, which accounted for 68% of total exports in 2017, have driven much of Cambodia's growth over the past several years. The textile sector relies on exports to the United States and European Union, and Cambodia's dependence on its comparative advantage in textile production is a key vulnerability for the economy, especially because Cambodia has continued to run a current account deficit above 9% of GDP since 2014.

GDP (PURCHASING POWER PARITY):

$64.21 billion (2017 est.)

$60.09 billion (2016 est.)

$56.18 billion (2015 est.)

note: data are in 2017 dollars

country comparison to the world: 104

GDP (OFFICIAL EXCHANGE RATE):

$22.09 billion (2017 est.) (2017 est.)

GDP - REAL GROWTH RATE:

6.9% (2017 est.)

7% (2016 est.)

7% (2015 est.)

country comparison to the world: 20

GDP - PER CAPITA (PPP):

$4,000 (2017 est.)

$3,800 (2016 est.)

$3,600 (2015 est.)

note: data are in 2017 dollars

country comparison to the world: 177

GROSS NATIONAL SAVING:

13.7% of GDP (2017 est.)

14.3% of GDP (2016 est.)

13.4% of GDP (2015 est.)

country comparison to the world: 139

GDP - COMPOSITION, BY END USE:

household consumption: 76% (2017 est.)

government consumption: 5.4% (2017 est.)

investment in fixed capital: 21.8% (2017 est.)

investment in inventories: 1.2% (2017 est.)

exports of goods and services: 68.6% (2017 est.)

imports of goods and services: -73% (2017 est.)

GDP - COMPOSITION, BY SECTOR OF ORIGIN:

agriculture: 25.3% (2017 est.)

industry: 32.8% (2017 est.)

services: 41.9% (2017 est.)

AGRICULTURE - PRODUCTS:

rice, rubber, corn, vegetables, cashews, cassava (manioc, tapioca), silk

INDUSTRIES:

tourism, garments, construction, rice milling, fishing, wood and wood products, rubber, cement, gem mining, textiles

INDUSTRIAL PRODUCTION GROWTH RATE:

10.6% (2017 est.)

country comparison to the world: 11

LABOR FORCE:

8.913 million (2017 est.)

country comparison to the world: 56

LABOR FORCE - BY OCCUPATION:

agriculture: 48.7%

industry: 19.9%

services: 31.5% (2013 est.)

UNEMPLOYMENT RATE:

0.3% (2017 est.)

0.2% (2016 est.)

note: high underemployment, according to official statistics

country comparison to the world: 2

POPULATION BELOW POVERTY LINE:

16.5% (2016 est.)

HOUSEHOLD INCOME OR CONSUMPTION BY PERCENTAGE SHARE:

lowest 10%: 28% (2013 est.)

highest 10%: 28% (2013 est.)

DISTRIBUTION OF FAMILY INCOME - GINI INDEX:

37.9 (2008 est.)

41.9 (2004 est.)

country comparison to the world: 78

BUDGET:

revenues: 3.947 billion (2017 est.)

expenditures: 4.354 billion (2017 est.)

TAXES AND OTHER REVENUES:

17.9% (of GDP) (2017 est.)

country comparison to the world: 164

BUDGET SURPLUS (+) OR DEFICIT (-):

-1.8% (of GDP) (2017 est.)

country comparison to the world: 97

PUBLIC DEBT:

30.4% of GDP (2017 est.)

29.1% of GDP (2016 est.)

country comparison to the world: 165

FISCAL YEAR:

calendar year

INFLATION RATE (CONSUMER PRICES):

2.9% (2017 est.)

3% (2016 est.)

country comparison to the world: 129

CENTRAL BANK DISCOUNT RATE:

NA% (31 December 2012)

5.25% (31 December 2007)

country comparison to the world: 78

COMMERCIAL BANK PRIME LENDING RATE:

10.92% (31 December 2017 est.)

11.36% (31 December 2016 est.)

country comparison to the world: 75

STOCK OF NARROW MONEY:

$2.202 billion (31 December 2017 est.)

$1.748 billion (31 December 2016 est.)

country comparison to the world: 133

STOCK OF BROAD MONEY:

$2.202 billion (31 December 2017 est.)

$1.748 billion (31 December 2016 est.)

country comparison to the world: 141

STOCK OF DOMESTIC CREDIT:

$16.53 billion (31 December 2017 est.)

$14.27 billion (31 December 2016 est.)

country comparison to the world: 96

MARKET VALUE OF PUBLICLY TRADED SHARES:

NA

CURRENT ACCOUNT BALANCE:

-$1.871 billion (2017 est.)

-$1.731 billion (2016 est.)

country comparison to the world: 162

EXPORTS:

$11.42 billion (2017 est.)

$10.07 billion (2016 est.)

country comparison to the world: 87

EXPORTS - PARTNERS:

US 21.5%, UK 9%, Germany 8.6%, Japan 7.6%, China 6.9%, Canada 6.7%, Spain 4.7%, Belgium 4.5% (2017)

EXPORTS - COMMODITIES:

clothing, timber, rubber, rice, fish, tobacco, footwear

IMPORTS:

$14.37 billion (2017 est.)

$12.65 billion (2016 est.)

country comparison to the world: 92

IMPORTS - COMMODITIES:

petroleum products, cigarettes, gold, construction materials, machinery, motor vehicles, pharmaceutical products

IMPORTS - PARTNERS:

China 34.1%, Singapore 12.8%, Thailand 12.4%, Vietnam 10.1% (2017)

RESERVES OF FOREIGN EXCHANGE AND GOLD:

$12.2 billion (31 December 2017 est.)

$9.122 billion (31 December 2016 est.)

country comparison to the world: 69

DEBT - EXTERNAL:

$11.87 billion (31 December 2017 est.)

$10.3 billion (31 December 2016 est.)

country comparison to the world: 107

STOCK OF DIRECT FOREIGN INVESTMENT - AT HOME:

$29.17 billion (2014 est.)

country comparison to the world: 71

EXCHANGE RATES:

riels (KHR) per US dollar -

4,055 (2017 est.)

4,058.7 (2016 est.)

4,058.7 (2015 est.)

4,067.8 (2014 est.)

4,037.5 (2013 est.)

ENERGY :: CAMBODIA

ELECTRICITY ACCESS:

population without electricity: 9.9 million (2013)

electrification - total population: 34% (2013)

electrification - urban areas: 97% (2013)

electrification - rural areas: 18% (2013)

ELECTRICITY - PRODUCTION:

5.21 billion kWh (2016 est.)

country comparison to the world: 121

ELECTRICITY - CONSUMPTION:

5.857 billion kWh (2016 est.)

country comparison to the world: 117

ELECTRICITY - EXPORTS:

0 kWh (2016 est.)

country comparison to the world: 116

ELECTRICITY - IMPORTS:

1.583 billion kWh (2016 est.)

country comparison to the world: 60

ELECTRICITY - INSTALLED GENERATING CAPACITY:

1.697 million kW (2016 est.)

country comparison to the world: 119

ELECTRICITY - FROM FOSSIL FUELS:

35% of total installed capacity (2016 est.)

country comparison to the world: 178

ELECTRICITY - FROM NUCLEAR FUELS:

0% of total installed capacity (2017 est.)

country comparison to the world: 61

ELECTRICITY - FROM HYDROELECTRIC PLANTS:

63% of total installed capacity (2017 est.)

country comparison to the world: 27

ELECTRICITY - FROM OTHER RENEWABLE SOURCES:

2% of total installed capacity (2017 est.)

country comparison to the world: 136

CRUDE OIL - PRODUCTION:

0 bbl/day (2017 est.)

country comparison to the world: 118

CRUDE OIL - EXPORTS:

0 bbl/day (2015 est.)

country comparison to the world: 103

CRUDE OIL - IMPORTS:

0 bbl/day (2015 est.)

country comparison to the world: 106

CRUDE OIL - PROVED RESERVES:

0 bbl (1 January 2018 est.)

country comparison to the world: 115

REFINED PETROLEUM PRODUCTS - PRODUCTION:

0 bbl/day (2015 est.)

country comparison to the world: 127

REFINED PETROLEUM PRODUCTS - CONSUMPTION:

45,000 bbl/day (2016 est.)

country comparison to the world: 108

REFINED PETROLEUM PRODUCTS - EXPORTS:

0 bbl/day (2015 est.)

country comparison to the world: 140

REFINED PETROLEUM PRODUCTS - IMPORTS:

43,030 bbl/day (2015 est.)

country comparison to the world: 86

NATURAL GAS - PRODUCTION:

0 cu m (2017 est.)

country comparison to the world: 113

NATURAL GAS - CONSUMPTION:

0 cu m (2017 est.)

country comparison to the world: 129

NATURAL GAS - EXPORTS:

0 cu m (2017 est.)

country comparison to the world: 78

NATURAL GAS - IMPORTS:

0 cu m (2017 est.)

country comparison to the world: 102

NATURAL GAS - PROVED RESERVES:

0 cu m (1 January 2014 est.)

country comparison to the world: 119

CARBON DIOXIDE EMISSIONS FROM CONSUMPTION OF ENERGY:

10.55 million Mt (2017 est.)

country comparison to the world: 104

COMMUNICATIONS :: CAMBODIA

TELEPHONES - FIXED LINES:

total subscriptions: 132,911 (2017 est.)

subscriptions per 100 inhabitants: 1 (2017 est.)

country comparison to the world: 136

TELEPHONES - MOBILE CELLULAR:

total subscriptions: 18,572,973 (2017 est.)

subscriptions per 100 inhabitants: 115 (2017 est.)

country comparison to the world: 60

TELEPHONE SYSTEM:

general assessment: adequate fixed-line and/or cellular service in Phnom Penh and other provincial cities; mobile-cellular phone systems are widely used in urban areas to bypass deficiencies in the fixed-line network; mobile-phone coverage is rapidly spreading in rural areas; about 50% of Cambodians own at least one smart phone; in 2018 the MPTC began a free Wi-Fi service for visitors and residents of Phnom Penh, in selected parks around the city customers can access free Wi-Fi services (2017)

domestic: fixed-line connections stand at about 1 per 100 persons and declining; mobile-cellular usage, aided by competition among service providers, has increased to about 115 per 100 persons; in 2021 Camboidia hopes to launch it first communications satellite into orbit; fixed broadband penetration is predicted to reach over 2% by 2023 (2017)

international: country code - 855; adequate but expensive landline and cellular service available to all countries from Phnom Penh and major provincial cities; satellite earth station - 1 Intersputnik (Indian Ocean region) (2016)

BROADCAST MEDIA:

mixture of state-owned, joint public-private, and privately owned broadcast media; 14 TV broadcast stations with most operating on multiple channels, including 1 state-operated station broadcasting from multiple locations, 11 stations either jointly operated or privately owned with some broadcasting from several locations, and 2 TV relay stations - one relaying a French TV station and the other relaying a Vietnamese TV station; multi-channel cable and satellite systems are available (2018); roughly 50 radio broadcast stations - 1 state-owned broadcaster with multiple stations and a large mixture of public and private broadcasters; several international broadcasters are available (2009)

INTERNET COUNTRY CODE:

.kh

INTERNET USERS:

total: 4,080,372 (July 2016 est.)

percent of population: 25.6% (July 2016 est.)

country comparison to the world: 86

BROADBAND - FIXED SUBSCRIPTIONS:

total: 129,650 (2017 est.)

subscriptions per 100 inhabitants: 1 (2017 est.)

country comparison to the world: 117

TRANSPORTATION :: CAMBODIA

NATIONAL AIR TRANSPORT SYSTEM:

number of registered air carriers: 4 (2015)

inventory of registered aircraft operated by air carriers: 10 (2015)

annual passenger traffic on registered air carriers: 1,103,880 (2015)

annual freight traffic on registered air carriers: 2,301,260 mt-km (2015)

CIVIL AIRCRAFT REGISTRATION COUNTRY CODE PREFIX:

XU (2016)

AIRPORTS:

16 (2013)

country comparison to the world: 142

AIRPORTS - WITH PAVED RUNWAYS:

total: 6 (2017)

2,438 to 3,047 m: 3 (2017)

1,524 to 2,437 m: 2 (2017)

914 to 1,523 m: 1 (2017)

AIRPORTS - WITH UNPAVED RUNWAYS:

total: 10 (2013)

1,524 to 2,437 m: 2 (2013)

914 to 1,523 m: 7 (2013)

under 914 m: 1 (2013)

HELIPORTS:

1 (2013)

RAILWAYS:

total: 642 km (2014)

narrow gauge: 642 km 1.000-m gauge (2014)

note: under restoration

country comparison to the world: 107

ROADWAYS:

total: 44,709 km (2010)

paved: 3,607 km (2010)

unpaved: 41,102 km (2010)

country comparison to the world: 80

WATERWAYS:

3,700 km (mainly on Mekong River) (2012)

country comparison to the world: 28

MERCHANT MARINE:

total: 442 (2017)

by type: container ship 3, general cargo 328, oil tanker 26, other 85 (2017)

country comparison to the world: 43

PORTS AND TERMINALS:

major seaport(s): Sihanoukville (Kampong Saom)

river port(s): Phnom Penh (Mekong)

MILITARY AND SECURITY :: CAMBODIA

MILITARY EXPENDITURES:

1.85% of GDP (2016)

2.11% of GDP (2015)

1.66% of GDP (2014)

country comparison to the world: 57

MILITARY BRANCHES:

Royal Cambodian Armed Forces: Royal Cambodian Army, Royal Khmer Navy, Royal Cambodian Air Force; the Royal Cambodian Gendarmerie is the military police force responsible for internal security; the National Committee for Maritime Security performs Coast Guard functions and has representation from military and civilian agencies (2016)

MILITARY SERVICE AGE AND OBLIGATION:

18 is the legal minimum age for compulsory and voluntary military service (2012)

TRANSNATIONAL ISSUES :: CAMBODIA

DISPUTES - INTERNATIONAL:

Cambodia is concerned about Laos' extensive upstream dam constructionCambodia and Thailand dispute sections of boundaryin 2011 Thailand and Cambodia resorted to arms in the dispute over the location of the boundary on the precipice surmounted by Preah Vihear Temple ruins, awarded to Cambodia by ICJ decision in 1962 and part of a UN World Heritage siteCambodia accuses Vietnam of a wide variety of illicit cross-border activitiesprogress on a joint development area with Vietnam is hampered by an unresolved dispute over sovereignty of offshore islands

TRAFFICKING IN PERSONS:

current situation: Cambodia is a source, transit, and destination country for men, women, and children subjected to forced labor and sex trafficking; Cambodian men, women, and children migrate to countries within the region and, increasingly, the Middle East for legitimate work but are subjected to sex trafficking, domestic servitude, or forced labor in fishing, agriculture, construction, and factories; Cambodian men recruited to work on Thai-owned fishing vessels are subsequently subjected to forced labor in international waters and are kept at sea for years; poor Cambodian children are vulnerable and, often with the families' complicity, are subject to forced labor, including domestic servitude and forced begging, in Thailand and Vietnam; Cambodian and ethnic Vietnamese women and girls are trafficked from rural areas to urban centers and tourist spots for sexual exploitation; Cambodian men are the main exploiters of child prostitutes, but men from other Asian countries, and the West travel to Cambodia for child sex tourism

tier rating: Tier 2 Watch List – Cambodia does not fully comply with the minimum standards for the elimination of trafficking; however, it is making significant efforts to do so; the government has a written plan that, if implemented, would constitute making significant efforts to meet the minimum standards for the elimination of trafficking; authorities made modest progress in prosecutions and convictions of traffickers in 2014 but did not provide comprehensive data; endemic corruption continued to impede law enforcement efforts, and no complicit officials were prosecuted or convicted; the government sustained efforts to identify victims and refer them to NGOs for care, but victim protection remained inadequate, particularly for assisting male victims and victims identified abroad; a new national action plan was adopted, but guidelines for victim identification and guidance on undercover investigation techniques are still pending after several years (2015)

ILLICIT DRUGS:

narcotics-related corruption reportedly involving some in the government, military, and police; limited methamphetamine production; vulnerable to money laundering due to its cash-based economy and porous borders

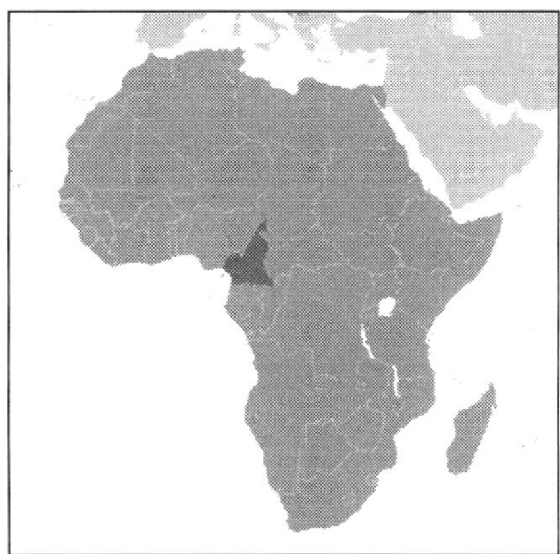

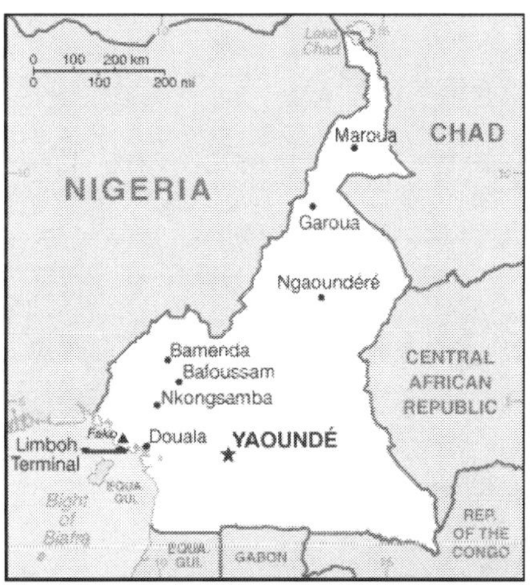

AFRICA :: CAMEROON

INTRODUCTION :: CAMEROON

BACKGROUND:

French Cameroon became independent in 1960 as the Republic of Cameroon. The following year the southern portion of neighboring British Cameroon voted to merge with the new country to form the Federal Republic of Cameroon. In 1972, a new constitution replaced the federation with a unitary state, the United Republic of Cameroon. The country has generally enjoyed stability, which has enabled the development of agriculture, roads, and railways, as well as a petroleum industry. Despite slow movement toward democratic reform, political power remains firmly in the hands of President Paul BIYA.

GEOGRAPHY :: CAMEROON

LOCATION:

Central Africa, bordering the Bight of Biafra, between Equatorial Guinea and Nigeria

GEOGRAPHIC COORDINATES:

6 00 N, 12 00 E

MAP REFERENCES:

Africa

AREA:

total: 475,440 sq km

land: 472,710 sq km

water: 2,730 sq km

country comparison to the world: 55

AREA - COMPARATIVE:

slightly larger than California

LAND BOUNDARIES:

total: 5,018 km

border countries (6): Central African Republic 901 km, Chad 1116 km, Republic of the Congo 494 km, Equatorial Guinea 183 km, Gabon 349 km, Nigeria 1975 km

COASTLINE:

402 km

MARITIME CLAIMS:

territorial sea: 12 nm

contiguous zone: 24 nm

CLIMATE:

varies with terrain, from tropical along coast to semiarid and hot in north

TERRAIN:

diverse, with coastal plain in southwest, dissected plateau in center, mountains in west, plains in north

ELEVATION:

mean elevation: 667 m

elevation extremes: 0 m lowest point: Atlantic Ocean 4045 highest point: Fako on Mont Cameroun

NATURAL RESOURCES:

petroleum, bauxite, iron ore, timber, hydropower

LAND USE:

agricultural land: 20.6% (2011 est.)

arable land: 13.1% (2011 est.) / permanent crops: 3.3% (2011 est.) / permanent pasture: 4.2% (2011 est.)

forest: 41.7% (2011 est.)

other: 37.7% (2011 est.)

IRRIGATED LAND:

290 sq km (2012)

POPULATION DISTRIBUTION:

population concentrated in the west and north, with the interior of the country sparsely populated

NATURAL HAZARDS:

volcanic activity with periodic releases of poisonous gases from Lake Nyos and Lake Monoun volcanoes

volcanism: Mt. Cameroon (4,095 m), which last erupted in 2000, is the most frequently active volcano in West Africa; lakes in Oku volcanic field have released fatal levels of gas on occasion, killing some 1,700 people in 1986

ENVIRONMENT - CURRENT ISSUES:

waterborne diseases are prevalent; deforestation and overgrazing result in erosion, desertification, and reduced quality of pastureland; poaching; overfishing; overhunting

ENVIRONMENT - INTERNATIONAL AGREEMENTS:

party to: Biodiversity, Climate Change, Climate Change-Kyoto Protocol, Desertification, Endangered Species, Hazardous Wastes, Law of the Sea, Ozone Layer Protection, Tropical Timber 83, Tropical Timber 94, Wetlands, Whaling

signed, but not ratified: none of the selected agreements

GEOGRAPHY - NOTE:

sometimes referred to as the hinge of Africa because of its central location on the continent and its position at the west-south juncture of the Gulf of Guinea; throughout the country there are areas of thermal springs and indications of current or prior volcanic activity; Mount Cameroon, the highest mountain in Sub-Saharan west Africa, is an active volcano

PEOPLE AND SOCIETY :: CAMEROON

POPULATION:

25,640,965 (July 2018 est.)

note: estimates for this country explicitly take into account the effects of excess mortality due to AIDS; this can result in lower life expectancy, higher infant mortality, higher death rates, lower population growth rates, and changes in the distribution of population by age and sex than would otherwise be expected

country comparison to the world: 53

NATIONALITY:

noun: Cameroonian(s)

adjective: Cameroonian

ETHNIC GROUPS:

Cameroon Highlanders 31%, Equatorial Bantu 19%, Kirdi 11%, Fulani 10%, Northwestern Bantu 8%, Eastern Nigritic 7%, other African 13%, non-African less than 1%

LANGUAGES:

24 major African language groups, English (official), French (official)

RELIGIONS:

Roman Catholic 38.4%, Protestant 26.3%, other Christian 4.5%, Muslim 20.9%, animist 5.6%, other 1%, non-believer 3.2% (2005 est.)

DEMOGRAPHIC PROFILE:

Cameroon has a large youth population, with more than 60% of the populace under the age of 25. Fertility is falling but remains at a high level, especially among poor, rural, and uneducated women, in part because of inadequate access to contraception. Life expectancy remains low at about 55 years due to the prevalence of HIV and AIDs and an elevated maternal mortality rate, which has remained high since 1990. Cameroon, particularly the northern region, is vulnerable to food insecurity largely because of government mismanagement, corruption, high production costs, inadequate infrastructure, and natural disasters. Despite economic growth in some regions, poverty is on the rise, and is most prevalent in rural areas, which are especially affected by a shortage of jobs, declining incomes, poor school and health care infrastructure, and a lack of clean water and sanitation. Underinvestment in social safety nets and ineffective public financial management also contribute to Cameroon's high rate of poverty.

International migration has been driven by unemployment (including fewer government jobs), poverty, the search for educational opportunities, and corruption. The US and Europe are preferred destinations, but, with tighter immigration restrictions in these countries, young Cameroonians are increasingly turning to neighboring states, such as Gabon and Nigeria, South Africa, other parts of Africa, and the Near and Far East. Cameroon's limited resources make it dependent on UN support to host more than 320,000 refugees and asylum seekers as of September 2017. These refugees and asylum seekers are primarily from the Central African Republic and more recently Nigeria.

AGE STRUCTURE:

0-14 years: 42.15% (male 5,445,142 /female 5,362,166)

15-24 years: 19.6% (male 2,524,031 /female 2,502,072)

25-54 years: 31.03% (male 4,001,963 /female 3,954,258)

55-64 years: 3.99% (male 499,101 /female 524,288)

65 years and over: 3.23% (male 384,845 /female 443,099) (2018 est.)

DEPENDENCY RATIOS:

total dependency ratio: 85.9 (2015 est.)

youth dependency ratio: 80 (2015 est.)

elderly dependency ratio: 5.9 (2015 est.)

potential support ratio: 17 (2015 est.)

MEDIAN AGE:

total: 18.6 years

male: 18.5 years

female: 18.7 years (2018 est.)

country comparison to the world: 208

POPULATION GROWTH RATE:

2.54% (2018 est.)

country comparison to the world: 20

BIRTH RATE:

35 births/1,000 population (2018 est.)

country comparison to the world: 21

DEATH RATE:

9.4 deaths/1,000 population (2018 est.)

country comparison to the world: 49

NET MIGRATION RATE:

-0.1 migrant(s)/1,000 population (2017 est.)

country comparison to the world: 104

POPULATION DISTRIBUTION:

population concentrated in the west and north, with the interior of the country sparsely populated

URBANIZATION:

urban population: 56.4% of total population (2018)

rate of urbanization: 3.63% annual rate of change (2015-20 est.)

MAJOR URBAN AREAS - POPULATION:

3.656 million Douala, 3.412 million YAOUNDE (capital) (2018)

SEX RATIO:

at birth: 1.02 male(s)/female (2017 est.)

0-14 years: 1.02 male(s)/female (2017 est.)

15-24 years: 1.01 male(s)/female (2017 est.)

25-54 years: 1.01 male(s)/female (2017 est.)

55-64 years: 0.95 male(s)/female (2017 est.)

65 years and over: 0.87 male(s)/female (2017 est.)

total population: 1.01 male(s)/female (2017 est.)

MOTHER'S MEAN AGE AT FIRST BIRTH:

19.7 years (2011 est.)

note: median age at first birth among women 25-29

MATERNAL MORTALITY RATE:

596 deaths/100,000 live births (2015 est.)

country comparison to the world: 15

INFANT MORTALITY RATE:

total: 49.8 deaths/1,000 live births (2018 est.)

male: 53.4 deaths/1,000 live births (2018 est.)

female: 46.2 deaths/1,000 live births (2018 est.)

country comparison to the world: 29

LIFE EXPECTANCY AT BIRTH:

total population: 59.4 years (2018 est.)

male: 58 years (2018 est.)

female: 60.9 years (2018 est.)

country comparison to the world: 210

TOTAL FERTILITY RATE:

4.58 children born/woman (2018 est.)

country comparison to the world: 24

CONTRACEPTIVE PREVALENCE RATE:

34.4% (2014)

HEALTH EXPENDITURES:

4.1% of GDP (2014)

country comparison to the world: 164

PHYSICIANS DENSITY:

0.08 physicians/1,000 population (2010)

HOSPITAL BED DENSITY:

1.3 beds/1,000 population (2010)

DRINKING WATER SOURCE:

improved:

urban: 94.8% of population (2015 est.)

rural: 52.7% of population (2015 est.)

total: 75.6% of population (2015 est.)

unimproved:

urban: 5.2% of population (2015 est.)

rural: 47.3% of population (2015 est.)

total: 24.4% of population (2015 est.)

SANITATION FACILITY ACCESS:

improved:

urban: 61.8% of population (2015 est.)

rural: 26.8% of population (2015 est.)

total: 45.8% of population (2015 est.)

unimproved:

urban: 38.2% of population (2015 est.)

rural: 73.2% of population (2015 est.)

total: 54.2% of population (2015 est.)

HIV/AIDS - ADULT PREVALENCE RATE:

3.7% (2017 est.)

country comparison to the world: 16

HIV/AIDS - PEOPLE LIVING WITH HIV/AIDS:

510,000 (2017 est.)

country comparison to the world: 15

HIV/AIDS - DEATHS:

24,000 (2017 est.)

country comparison to the world: 9

MAJOR INFECTIOUS DISEASES:

degree of risk: very high (2016)

food or waterborne diseases: bacterial and protozoal diarrhea, hepatitis A, and typhoid fever (2016)

vectorborne diseases: malaria, dengue fever, and yellow fever (2016)

water contact diseases: schistosomiasis (2016)

animal contact diseases: rabies (2016)

respiratory diseases: meningococcal meningitis (2016)

OBESITY - ADULT PREVALENCE RATE:

11.4% (2016)

country comparison to the world: 135

CHILDREN UNDER THE AGE OF 5 YEARS UNDERWEIGHT:

14.8% (2014)

country comparison to the world: 44

EDUCATION EXPENDITURES:

2.8% of GDP (2013)

country comparison to the world: 152

LITERACY:

definition: age 15 and over can read and write (2015 est.)

total population: 75% (2015 est.)

male: 81.2% (2015 est.)

female: 68.9% (2015 est.)

SCHOOL LIFE EXPECTANCY (PRIMARY TO TERTIARY EDUCATION):

total: 12 years (2015)

male: 13 years (2015)

female: 11 years (2015)

UNEMPLOYMENT, YOUTH AGES 15-24:

total: 10.6% (2014 est.)

male: 9% (2014 est.)

female: 12.7% (2014 est.)

country comparison to the world: 120

GOVERNMENT :: CAMEROON

COUNTRY NAME:

conventional long form: Republic of Cameroon

conventional short form: Cameroon

local long form: Republique du Cameroun/Republic of Cameroon

local short form: Cameroun/Cameroon

former: Kamerun, French Cameroon, British Cameroon, Federal Republic of Cameroon, United Republic of Cameroon

etymology: in the 15th century, Portuguese explorers named the area near the mouth of the Wouri River the Rio dos Camaroes (River of Prawns) after the abundant shrimp in the water; over time the designation became Cameroon in English; this is the only instance where a country is named after a crustacean

GOVERNMENT TYPE:

presidential republic

CAPITAL:

name: Yaounde

geographic coordinates: 3 52 N, 11 31 E

time difference: UTC+1 (6 hours ahead of Washington, DC, during Standard Time)

ADMINISTRATIVE DIVISIONS:

10 regions (regions, singular - region); Adamaoua, Centre, East (Est), Far North (Extreme-Nord), Littoral, North (Nord), North-West (Nord-Ouest), West (Ouest), South (Sud), South-West (Sud-Ouest)

INDEPENDENCE:

1 January 1960 (from French-administered UN trusteeship)

NATIONAL HOLIDAY:

State Unification Day (National Day), 20 May (1972)

CONSTITUTION:

history: several previous; latest effective 18 January 1996 (2017)

amendments: proposed by the president of the republic or by Parliament; amendment drafts require approval of at least one-third of the membership in either house of Parliament; passage requires absolute majority vote of the Parliament membership; passage of drafts requested by the president for a second reading in Parliament requires two-thirds majority vote of its membership; the president can opt to submit drafts to a referendum, in which case passage requires a simple majority; constitutional articles on Cameroon's unity and territorial integrity and its democratic principles cannot be amended; amended 2008 (2017)

LEGAL SYSTEM:

mixed legal system of English common law, French civil law, and customary law

INTERNATIONAL LAW ORGANIZATION PARTICIPATION:

accepts compulsory ICJ jurisdiction; non-party state to the ICCt

CITIZENSHIP:

citizenship by birth: no

citizenship by descent only: at least one parent must be a citizen of Cameroon

dual citizenship recognized: no

residency requirement for naturalization: 5 years

SUFFRAGE:

20 years of age; universal

EXECUTIVE BRANCH:

chief of state: President Paul BIYA (since 6 November 1982)

head of government: Prime Minister Philemon YANG (since 30 June 2009); Deputy Prime Minister Amadou ALI (since 2014)

cabinet: Cabinet proposed by the prime minister, appointed by the president

elections/appointments: president directly elected by simple majority popular vote for a 7-year term (no term limits); election last held on 7 October 2018 (next to be held in October 2025); prime minister appointed by the president

election results: Paul BIYA reelected president; percent of vote - Paul BIYA (CPDM) 71.3%, Maurice KAMTO (MRC) 14.2%, Cabral LIBII (Univers) 6.3%, other 8.2%

LEGISLATIVE BRANCH:

description: bicameral Parliament or Parlement consists of:
Senate or Senat (100 seats; 70 members indirectly elected by regional councils and 30 appointed by the president; members serve 5-year terms)
National Assembly or Assemblee Nationale (180 seats; members directly elected in multi-seat constituencies by simple majority vote to serve 5-year terms)

elections:
Senate - last held on 25 March 2018 (next to be held in 2023)
National Assembly - last held on 30 September 2013 (next delayed until October 2019)

election results:
Senate - percent of vote by party - NA; seats by party - CPDM 63, SDF 7;
National Assembly - percent of vote by party - NA; seats by party - CPDM 148, SDF 18, UNDP 5, UDC 4, UPC 3, other 2
National Assembly - last held on 30 September 2013 (next delayed until October 2019)

JUDICIAL BRANCH:

highest courts: Supreme Court of Cameroon (consists of 9 titular and 6 surrogate judges and organized into judicial, administrative, and audit chambers); Constitutional Council (consists of 11 members)

judge selection and term of office: Supreme Court judges appointed by the president with the advice of the Higher Judicial Council of Cameroon, a body chaired by the president and includes the minister of justice, selected magistrates, and representatives of the National Assembly; judge term NA; Constitutional Council members appointed by the president for single 9-year terms

subordinate courts: Parliamentary Court of Justice (jurisdiction limited to cases involving the president and prime minister); appellate and first instance courts; circuit and magistrate's courts

POLITICAL PARTIES AND LEADERS:

Alliance for Democracy and DevelopmentCameroon People's Democratic Movement or CPDM [Paul BIYA]
Cameroon People's Party or CPP [Edith Kah WALLA]
Cameroon Renaissance Movement or MRC [Maurice KAMTO]
Cameroonian Democratic Union or UDC [Adamou Ndam NJOYA]
Movement for the Defense of the Republic or MDR [Dakole DAISSALA]
Movement for the Liberation and Development of Cameroon or MLDC [Marcel YONDO]
National Union for Democracy and Progress or UNDP [Maigari BELLO BOUBA]
Progressive Movement or MP [Jean-Jacques EKINDI]
Social Democratic Front or SDF [John FRU NDI]
Union of Peoples of Cameroon or UPC [Provisionary Management Bureau]

INTERNATIONAL ORGANIZATION PARTICIPATION:

ACP, AfDB, AU, BDEAC, C, CEMAC, EITI (compliant country), FAO, FZ, G-77, IAEA, IBRD, ICAO, ICRM, IDA, IDB, IFAD, IFC, IFRCS, IHO, ILO, IMF, IMO, IMSO, Interpol, IOC, IOM, IPU, ISO, ITSO, ITU, ITUC (NGOs), MIGA, MONUSCO, NAM, OIC, OIF, OPCW, PCA, UN, UNCTAD, UNESCO, UNHCR, UNIDO, UNOCI, UNWTO, UPU, WCO, WFTU (NGOs), WHO, WIPO, WMO, WTO

DIPLOMATIC REPRESENTATION IN THE US:

chief of mission: Ambassador Essomba ETOUNDI (since 27 June 2016)

chancery:

3007 Tilden Street NW, Washington, DC, 20008

telephone: [1] (202) 265-8790

FAX: [1] (202) 387-3826

DIPLOMATIC REPRESENTATION FROM THE US:

chief of mission: Ambassador Peter Henry BARLERIN (since 20 December 2017)

embassy: Avenue Rosa Parks, Yaounde

mailing address: P.O. Box 817, Yaounde; pouch: American Embassy, US Department of State, Washington, DC 20521-2520

telephone: [237] 22220 1500; Consular: [237] 22220 1603

FAX: [237] 22220 1500 Ext. 4531; Consular FAX: [237] 22220 1752

branch office(s): Douala

FLAG DESCRIPTION:

three equal vertical bands of green (hoist side), red, and yellow, with a yellow five-pointed star centered in the red band; the vertical tricolor recalls the flag of France; red symbolizes unity, yellow the sun, happiness, and the savannahs in the north, and green hope and the forests in the south; the star is referred to as the "star of unity"

note: uses the popular Pan-African colors of Ethiopia

NATIONAL SYMBOL(S):

lion; national colors: green, red, yellow

NATIONAL ANTHEM:

name: "O Cameroun, Berceau de nos Ancetres" (O Cameroon, Cradle of Our Forefathers)

lyrics/music: Rene Djam AFAME, Samuel Minkio BAMBA, Moise Nyatte NKO'O [French], Benard Nsokika FONLON [English]/Rene Djam AFAME

note: adopted 1957; Cameroon's anthem, also known as "Chant de Ralliement" (The Rallying Song), has been used unofficially since 1948 and officially adopted in 1957; the anthem has French and English versions whose lyrics differ

ECONOMY :: CAMEROON

ECONOMY - OVERVIEW:

Cameroon's market-based, diversified economy features oil and gas, timber, aluminum, agriculture, mining and the service sector. Oil remains Cameroon's main export commodity, and despite falling global oil prices, still accounts for nearly 40% of exports. Cameroon's economy suffers from factors that often impact underdeveloped countries, such as stagnant per capita income, a relatively inequitable distribution of income, a top-heavy civil service, endemic corruption, continuing inefficiencies of a large parastatal system in key sectors, and a generally unfavorable climate for business enterprise.

Since 1990, the government has embarked on various IMF and World Bank programs designed to spur business investment, increase efficiency in agriculture, improve trade, and recapitalize the nation's banks. The IMF continues to press for economic reforms, including increased budget transparency, privatization, and poverty reduction programs. The Government of Cameroon provides subsidies for electricity, food, and fuel that have strained the federal budget and diverted funds from education, healthcare, and infrastructure projects, as low oil prices have led to lower revenues.

Cameroon devotes significant resources to several large infrastructure projects currently under construction, including a deep seaport in Kribi and the Lom Pangar Hydropower Project. Cameroon's energy sector continues to diversify, recently opening a natural gas-powered electricity generating plant. Cameroon continues to seek foreign investment to improve its inadequate infrastructure, create jobs, and improve its economic footprint, but its unfavorable business environment remains a significant deterrent to foreign investment.

GDP (PURCHASING POWER PARITY):

$89.54 billion (2017 est.)

$86.47 billion (2016 est.)

$82.63 billion (2015 est.)

note: data are in 2017 dollars

country comparison to the world: 88

GDP (OFFICIAL EXCHANGE RATE):

$34.99 billion (2017 est.) (2017 est.)

GDP - REAL GROWTH RATE:

3.5% (2017 est.)

4.6% (2016 est.)

5.7% (2015 est.)

country comparison to the world: 98

GDP - PER CAPITA (PPP):

$3,700 (2017 est.)

$3,700 (2016 est.)

$3,600 (2015 est.)

note: data are in 2017 dollars

country comparison to the world: 182

GROSS NATIONAL SAVING:

25.5% of GDP (2017 est.)

25.2% of GDP (2016 est.)

23.9% of GDP (2015 est.)

country comparison to the world: 56

GDP - COMPOSITION, BY END USE:

household consumption: 66.3% (2017 est.)

government consumption: 11.8% (2017 est.)

investment in fixed capital: 21.6% (2017 est.)

investment in inventories: -0.3% (2017 est.)

exports of goods and services: 21.6% (2017 est.)

imports of goods and services: -20.9% (2017 est.)

GDP - COMPOSITION, BY SECTOR OF ORIGIN:

agriculture: 16.7% (2017 est.)

industry: 26.5% (2017 est.)

services: 56.8% (2017 est.)

AGRICULTURE - PRODUCTS:

coffee, cocoa, cotton, rubber, bananas, oilseed, grains, cassava (manioc, tapioca); livestock; timber

INDUSTRIES:

petroleum production and refining, aluminum production, food processing, light consumer goods, textiles, lumber, ship repair

INDUSTRIAL PRODUCTION GROWTH RATE:

3.3% (2017 est.)

country comparison to the world: 94

LABOR FORCE:

9.912 million (2017 est.)

country comparison to the world: 52

LABOR FORCE - BY OCCUPATION:

agriculture: 70%

industry: 13%

services: 17% (2001 est.)

UNEMPLOYMENT RATE:

4.3% (2014 est.)

30% (2001 est.)

country comparison to the world: 57

POPULATION BELOW POVERTY LINE:

30% (2001 est.)

HOUSEHOLD INCOME OR CONSUMPTION BY PERCENTAGE SHARE:

lowest 10%: 35.4% (2001)

highest 10%: 35.4% (2014 est.)

DISTRIBUTION OF FAMILY INCOME - GINI INDEX:

46.5 (2014 est.)

44.6 (2001)

country comparison to the world: 30

BUDGET:

revenues: 5.363 billion (2017 est.)

expenditures: 6.556 billion (2017 est.)

TAXES AND OTHER REVENUES:

15.3% (of GDP) (2017 est.)

country comparison to the world: 191

BUDGET SURPLUS (+) OR DEFICIT (-):

-3.4% (of GDP) (2017 est.)

country comparison to the world: 143

PUBLIC DEBT:

36.9% of GDP (2017 est.)

32.5% of GDP (2016 est.)

country comparison to the world: 143

FISCAL YEAR:

1 July - 30 June

INFLATION RATE (CONSUMER PRICES):

0.6% (2017 est.)

0.9% (2016 est.)

country comparison to the world: 31

CENTRAL BANK DISCOUNT RATE:

4.25% (31 December 2009)

country comparison to the world: 89

COMMERCIAL BANK PRIME LENDING RATE:

13% (31 December 2017 est.)

12.5% (31 December 2016 est.)

country comparison to the world: 61

STOCK OF NARROW MONEY:

$4.857 billion (31 December 2017 est.)

$3.86 billion (31 December 2016 est.)

country comparison to the world: 107

STOCK OF BROAD MONEY:

$4.857 billion (31 December 2017 est.)

$3.86 billion (31 December 2016 est.)

country comparison to the world: 111

STOCK OF DOMESTIC CREDIT:

$6.154 billion (31 December 2017 est.)

$5.714 billion (31 December 2016 est.)

country comparison to the world: 125

MARKET VALUE OF PUBLICLY TRADED SHARES:

$230 million (31 December 2012 est.)

country comparison to the world: 116

CURRENT ACCOUNT BALANCE:

-$932 million (2017 est.)

-$1.034 billion (2016 est.)

country comparison to the world: 141

EXPORTS:

$4.732 billion (2017 est.)

$4.561 billion (2016 est.)

country comparison to the world: 111

EXPORTS - PARTNERS:

Netherlands 15.6%, France 12.6%, China 11.7%, Belgium 6.8%, Italy 6.3%, Algeria 4.8%, Malaysia 4.4% (2017)

EXPORTS - COMMODITIES:

crude oil and petroleum products, lumber, cocoa beans, aluminum, coffee, cotton

IMPORTS:

$4.812 billion (2017 est.)

$4.827 billion (2016 est.)

country comparison to the world: 132

IMPORTS - COMMODITIES:

machinery, electrical equipment, transport equipment, fuel, food

IMPORTS - PARTNERS:

China 19%, France 10.3%, Thailand 7.9%, Nigeria 4.1% (2017)

RESERVES OF FOREIGN EXCHANGE AND GOLD:

$3.235 billion (31 December 2017 est.)

$2.26 billion (31 December 2016 est.)

country comparison to the world: 107

DEBT - EXTERNAL:

$9.375 billion (31 December 2017 est.)

$7.364 billion (31 December 2016 est.)

country comparison to the world: 115

EXCHANGE RATES:

Cooperation Financiere en Afrique Centrale francs (XAF) per US dollar -

605.3 (2017 est.)

593.01 (2016 est.)

593.01 (2015 est.)

591.45 (2014 est.)

494.42 (2013 est.)

ENERGY :: CAMEROON

ELECTRICITY ACCESS:

population without electricity: 10.1 million (2013)

electrification - total population: 55% (2013)

electrification - urban areas: 88% (2013)

electrification - rural areas: 17% (2013)

ELECTRICITY - PRODUCTION:

8.108 billion kWh (2016 est.)

country comparison to the world: 109

ELECTRICITY - CONSUMPTION:

6.411 billion kWh (2016 est.)

country comparison to the world: 113

ELECTRICITY - EXPORTS:

0 kWh (2016 est.)

country comparison to the world: 117

ELECTRICITY - IMPORTS:

55 million kWh (2016 est.)

country comparison to the world: 105

ELECTRICITY - INSTALLED GENERATING CAPACITY:

1.558 million kW (2016 est.)

country comparison to the world: 122

ELECTRICITY - FROM FOSSIL FUELS:

52% of total installed capacity (2016 est.)

country comparison to the world: 145

ELECTRICITY - FROM NUCLEAR FUELS:

0% of total installed capacity (2017 est.)

country comparison to the world: 62

ELECTRICITY - FROM HYDROELECTRIC PLANTS:

47% of total installed capacity (2017 est.)

country comparison to the world: 44

ELECTRICITY - FROM OTHER RENEWABLE SOURCES:

1% of total installed capacity (2017 est.)

country comparison to the world: 150

CRUDE OIL - PRODUCTION:

75,720 bbl/day (2017 est.)

country comparison to the world: 46

CRUDE OIL - EXPORTS:

96,370 bbl/day (2015 est.)

country comparison to the world: 35

CRUDE OIL - IMPORTS:

36,480 bbl/day (2015 est.)

country comparison to the world: 59

CRUDE OIL - PROVED RESERVES:

200 million bbl (1 January 2018 est.)

country comparison to the world: 55

REFINED PETROLEUM PRODUCTS - PRODUCTION:

39,080 bbl/day (2015 est.)

country comparison to the world: 82

REFINED PETROLEUM PRODUCTS - CONSUMPTION:

45,000 bbl/day (2016 est.)

country comparison to the world: 109

REFINED PETROLEUM PRODUCTS - EXPORTS:

8,545 bbl/day (2015 est.)

country comparison to the world: 84

REFINED PETROLEUM PRODUCTS - IMPORTS:

14,090 bbl/day (2015 est.)

country comparison to the world: 138

NATURAL GAS - PRODUCTION:

910.4 million cu m (2017 est.)

country comparison to the world: 69

NATURAL GAS - CONSUMPTION:

906.1 million cu m (2017 est.)

country comparison to the world: 93

NATURAL GAS - EXPORTS:

0 cu m (2017 est.)

country comparison to the world: 79

NATURAL GAS - IMPORTS:

0 cu m (2017 est.)

country comparison to the world: 103

NATURAL GAS - PROVED RESERVES:

135.1 billion cu m (1 January 2018 est.)

country comparison to the world: 48

CARBON DIOXIDE EMISSIONS FROM CONSUMPTION OF ENERGY:

7.672 million Mt (2017 est.)

country comparison to the world: 119

COMMUNICATIONS :: CAMEROON

TELEPHONES - FIXED LINES:

total subscriptions: 699,055 (2017 est.)

subscriptions per 100 inhabitants: 3 (2017 est.)

country comparison to the world: 88

TELEPHONES - MOBILE CELLULAR:

total subscriptions: 19,706,027 (2017 est.)

subscriptions per 100 inhabitants: 79 (2017 est.)

country comparison to the world: 59

TELEPHONE SYSTEM:

general assessment: equipment is old and outdated, and connections with many parts of the country are unreliable; 3G service and LTE service both developing given growing competition, along with a fast-developing mobile broadband sector (2017)

domestic: only about 3 per 100 persons for fixed-line subscriptions; mobile-cellular usage has increased sharply, reaching a subscribership base of over 79 per 100 persons (2017)

international: country code - 237; landing point for the SAT-3/WASC fiber-optic submarine cable that provides connectivity to Europe and Asia; satellite earth stations - 2 Intelsat (Atlantic Ocean); by September 2018 the country is expected to be connected to the SAIL submarine cable, providing a direct link to Brazil and with onward connectivity to other countries in the Americas; the cable will considerably improve international bandwidth and lead to better prices for consumers (2017)

BROADCAST MEDIA:

government maintains tight control over broadcast media; state-owned Cameroon Radio Television (CRTV), broadcasting on both a TV and radio network, was the only officially recognized and fully licensed broadcaster until August 2007, when the government finally issued licenses to 2 private TV broadcasters and 1 private radio broadcaster; about 70 privately owned, unlicensed radio stations operating but are subject to closure at any time; foreign news services required to partner with state-owned national station (2007)

INTERNET COUNTRY CODE:

.cm

INTERNET USERS:

total: 6,090,201 (July 2016 est.)

percent of population: 25% (July 2016 est.)

country comparison to the world: 67

BROADBAND - FIXED SUBSCRIPTIONS:

total: 42,117 (2017 est.)

subscriptions per 100 inhabitants: less than 1 (2017 est.)

country comparison to the world: 132

TRANSPORTATION :: CAMEROON

NATIONAL AIR TRANSPORT SYSTEM:

number of registered air carriers: 1 (2015)

inventory of registered aircraft operated by air carriers: 3 (2015)

annual passenger traffic on registered air carriers: 267,208 (2015)

annual freight traffic on registered air carriers: 0 mt-km (2015)

CIVIL AIRCRAFT REGISTRATION COUNTRY CODE PREFIX:

TJ (2016)

AIRPORTS:

33 (2013)

country comparison to the world: 112

AIRPORTS - WITH PAVED RUNWAYS:

total: 11 (2017)

over 3,047 m: 2 (2017)

2,438 to 3,047 m: 5 (2017)

1,524 to 2,437 m: 3 (2017)

914 to 1,523 m: 1 (2017)

AIRPORTS - WITH UNPAVED RUNWAYS:

total: 22 (2013)

1,524 to 2,437 m: 4 (2013)

914 to 1,523 m: 10 (2013)

under 914 m: 8 (2013)

PIPELINES:

53 km gas, 5 km liquid petroleum gas, 1107 km oil, 35 km water (2013)

RAILWAYS:

total: 987 km (2014)

narrow gauge: 987 km 1.000-m gauge (2014)

note: railway connections generally efficient but limited; rail lines connect major cities of Douala, Yaounde, Ngaoundere, and Garoua; passenger and freight service provided by CAMRAIL

country comparison to the world: 89

ROADWAYS:

total: 51,350 km (2011)

paved: 4,108 km (2011)

unpaved: 47,242 km (2011)

note: there are 28,857 km of national roads

country comparison to the world: 78

WATERWAYS:

(major rivers in the south, such as the Wouri and the Sanaga, are largely non-navigable; in the north, the Benue, which connects through Nigeria to the Niger River, is navigable in the rainy season only to the port of Garoua) (2010)

MERCHANT MARINE:

total: 19 (2017)

by type: general cargo 4, other 15 (2017)

country comparison to the world: 140

PORTS AND TERMINALS:

oil terminal(s): Limboh Terminal

river port(s): Douala (Wouri)

Garoua (Benoue)

MILITARY AND SECURITY :: CAMEROON

MILITARY EXPENDITURES:

1.6% of GDP (2016)

1.25% of GDP (2015)

1.25% of GDP (2014)

country comparison to the world: 70

MILITARY BRANCHES:

Cameroon Armed Forces (Forces Armees Camerounaises, FAC): Army (L'Armee de Terre), Navy (Marine Nationale Republique, MNR, includes naval infantry), Air Force (Armee de l'Air du Cameroun, AAC), Rapid Intervention Brigade, Fire Fighter Corps, Gendarmerie (2015)

MILITARY SERVICE AGE AND OBLIGATION:

18-23 years of age for male and female voluntary military service; no conscription; high school graduation required; service obligation 4 years; periodic government calls for volunteers (2012)

TERRORISM :: CAMEROON

TERRORIST GROUPS - FOREIGN BASED:

Boko Haram:
aim(s): establish an Islamic caliphate across Africa
area(s) of operation: conducts lethal bombing attacks and assaults, displacing thousands of people, especially in the Far North Region
note: violently opposes any political or social activity associated with Western society, including voting, attending secular schools, and wearing Western dress (April 2018)

Islamic State of Iraq and ash-Sham (ISIS)-West Africa:
aim(s): implement ISIS's strict interpretation of Sharia; replace the Nigerian Government with an Islamic state
area(s) of operation: based primarily in Northeast Nigeria along the border with Niger, with its largest presence in northeast Nigeria and the Lake Chad region; targets primarily regional military installations (April 2018)

TRANSNATIONAL ISSUES :: CAMEROON

DISPUTES - INTERNATIONAL:

Joint Border Commission with Nigeria reviewed 2002 ICJ ruling on the entire boundary and bilaterally resolved differences, including June 2006 Greentree Agreement that immediately ceded sovereignty of the Bakassi Peninsula to Cameroon with a full phase-out of Nigerian control and patriation of residents in 2008Cameroon and Nigeria agreed on maritime delimitation in March 2008sovereignty dispute between Equatorial Guinea and Cameroon over an island at the mouth of the Ntem Riveronly Nigeria and Cameroon have heeded the Lake Chad Commission's admonition to ratify the delimitation treaty, which also includes the Chad-Niger and Niger-Nigeria boundaries

REFUGEES AND INTERNALLY DISPLACED PERSONS:

refugees (country of origin): 267,813 (Central African Republic), 101,404 (Nigeria) (2018)

IDPs: 238,099 (2018)

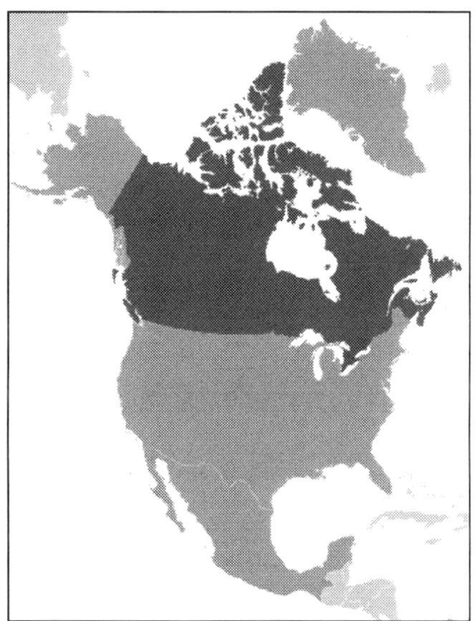

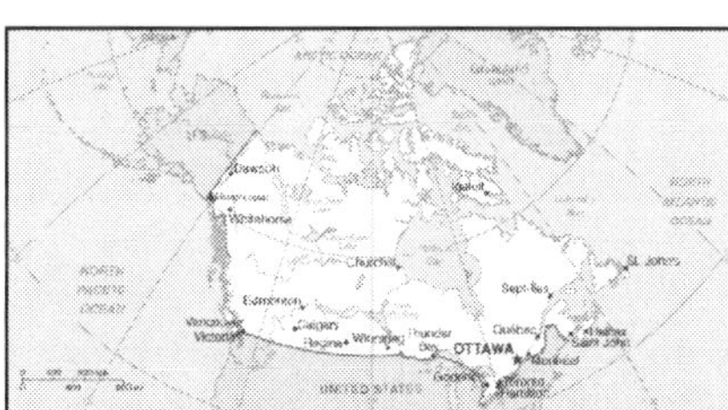

NORTH AMERICA :: CANADA

INTRODUCTION :: CANADA

BACKGROUND:

A land of vast distances and rich natural resources, Canada became a self-governing dominion in 1867, while retaining ties to the British crown. Canada repatriated its constitution from the UK in 1982, severing a final colonial tie. Economically and technologically, the nation has developed in parallel with the US, its neighbor to the south across the world's longest international border. Canada faces the political challenges of meeting public demands for quality improvements in health care, education, social services, and economic competitiveness, as well as responding to the particular concerns of predominantly francophone Quebec. Canada also aims to develop its diverse energy resources while maintaining its commitment to the environment.

GEOGRAPHY :: CANADA

LOCATION:

Northern North America, bordering the North Atlantic Ocean on the east, North Pacific Ocean on the west, and the Arctic Ocean on the north, north of the conterminous US

GEOGRAPHIC COORDINATES:

60 00 N, 95 00 W

MAP REFERENCES:

North America

AREA:

total: 9,984,670 sq km

land: 9,093,507 sq km

water: 891,163 sq km

country comparison to the world: 3

AREA - COMPARATIVE:

slightly larger than the US

LAND BOUNDARIES:

total: 8,893 km

border countries (1): US 8893 km (includes 2477 km with Alaska)

note: Canada is the world's largest country that borders only one country

COASTLINE:

202,080 km

note: the Canadian Arctic Archipelago - consisting of 36,563 islands, several of them some of the world's largest - contributes to Canada easily having the longest coastline in the world

MARITIME CLAIMS:

territorial sea: 12 nm

exclusive economic zone: 200 nm

contiguous zone: 24 nm

continental shelf: 200 nm or to the edge of the continental margin

CLIMATE:

varies from temperate in south to subarctic and arctic in north

TERRAIN:

mostly plains with mountains in west, lowlands in southeast

ELEVATION:

mean elevation: 487 m

elevation extremes: 0 m lowest point: Atlantic Ocean

5959 highest point: Mount Logan

NATURAL RESOURCES:

bauxite, iron ore, nickel, zinc, copper, gold, lead, rare earth elements, molybdenum, potash, diamonds, silver, fish, timber, wildlife, coal, petroleum, natural gas, hydropower

LAND USE:

agricultural land: 6.8% (2011 est.)

arable land: 4.7% (2011 est.) / permanent crops: 0.5% (2011 est.) / permanent pasture: 1.6% (2011 est.)

forest: 34.1% (2011 est.)

other: 59.1% (2011 est.)

IRRIGATED LAND:

8,700 sq km (2012)

POPULATION DISTRIBUTION:

vast majority of Canadians are positioned in a discontinuous band within approximately 300 km of the southern border with the United States; the most populated province is Ontario, followed by Quebec and British Columbia

NATURAL HAZARDS:

continuous permafrost in north is a serious obstacle to development; cyclonic storms form east of the Rocky Mountains, a result of the mixing of air masses from the Arctic, Pacific, and North American interior, and produce most of the country's rain and snow east of the mountains

volcanism: the vast majority of volcanoes in Western Canada's Coast Mountains remain dormant

ENVIRONMENT - CURRENT ISSUES:

metal smelting, coal-burning utilities, and vehicle emissions impacting agricultural and forest productivity; air pollution and resulting acid rain severely affecting lakes and damaging forests; ocean waters becoming contaminated due to agricultural, industrial, mining, and forestry activities

ENVIRONMENT - INTERNATIONAL AGREEMENTS:

party to: Air Pollution, Air Pollution-Nitrogen Oxides, Air Pollution-Persistent Organic Pollutants, Air Pollution-Sulfur 85, Air Pollution-Sulfur 94, Antarctic-Environmental Protocol, Antarctic-Marine Living Resources, Antarctic Seals, Antarctic Treaty, Biodiversity, Climate Change, Desertification, Endangered Species, Environmental Modification, Hazardous Wastes, Law of the Sea, Marine Dumping, Ozone Layer Protection, Ship Pollution, Tropical Timber 83, Tropical Timber 94, Wetlands

signed, but not ratified: Air Pollution-Volatile Organic Compounds, Marine Life Conservation

GEOGRAPHY - NOTE:

note 1: second-largest country in world (after Russia) and largest in the Americas; strategic location between Russia and US via north polar route; approximately 90% of the population is concentrated within 160 km (100 mi) of the US border

note 2: Canada has more fresh water than any other country and almost 9% of Canadian territory is water; Canada has at least 2 million and possibly over 3 million lakes - that is more than all other countries combined

PEOPLE AND SOCIETY :: CANADA

POPULATION:

35,881,659 (July 2018 est.)

country comparison to the world: 38

NATIONALITY:

noun: Canadian(s)

adjective: Canadian

ETHNIC GROUPS:

Canadian 32.3%, English 18.3%, Scottish 13.9%, French 13.6%, Irish 13.4%, German 9.6%, Chinese 5.1%, Italian 4.6%, North American Indian 4.4%, East Indian 4%, other 51.6% (2016 est.)

note: percentages add up to more than 100% because respondents were able to identify more than one ethnic origin

LANGUAGES:

English (official) 58.7%, French (official) 22%, Punjabi 1.4%, Italian 1.3%, Spanish 1.3%, German 1.3%, Cantonese 1.2%, Tagalog 1.2%, Arabic 1.1%, other 10.5% (2011 est.)

RELIGIONS:

Catholic 39% (includes Roman Catholic 38.8%, other Catholic .2%), Protestant 20.3% (includes United Church 6.1%, Anglican 5%, Baptist 1.9%, Lutheran 1.5%, Pentecostal 1.5%, Presbyterian 1.4%, other Protestant 2.9%), Orthodox 1.6%, other Christian 6.3%, Muslim 3.2%, Hindu 1.5%, Sikh 1.4%, Buddhist 1.1%, Jewish 1%, other 0.6%, none 23.9% (2011 est.)

AGE STRUCTURE:

0-14 years: 15.43% (male 2,839,236 /female 2,698,592)

15-24 years: 11.62% (male 2,145,626 /female 2,023,369)

25-54 years: 39.62% (male 7,215,261 /female 7,002,546)

55-64 years: 14.24% (male 2,538,820 /female 2,570,709)

65 years and over: 19.08% (male 3,055,560 /female 3,791,940) (2018 est.)

DEPENDENCY RATIOS:

total dependency ratio: 47.3 (2015 est.)

youth dependency ratio: 23.5 (2015 est.)

elderly dependency ratio: 23.8 (2015 est.)

potential support ratio: 4.2 (2015 est.)

MEDIAN AGE:

total: 42.4 years

male: 41.1 years

female: 43.7 years (2018 est.)

country comparison to the world: 31

POPULATION GROWTH RATE:

0.72% (2018 est.)

country comparison to the world: 139

BIRTH RATE:

10.2 births/1,000 population (2018 est.)

country comparison to the world: 189

DEATH RATE:

8.8 deaths/1,000 population (2018 est.)

country comparison to the world: 67

NET MIGRATION RATE:

5.7 migrant(s)/1,000 population (2017 est.)

country comparison to the world: 18

POPULATION DISTRIBUTION:

vast majority of Canadians are positioned in a discontinuous band within approximately 300 km of the southern border with the United States; the most populated province is Ontario, followed by Quebec and British Columbia

URBANIZATION:

urban population: 81.4% of total population (2018)

rate of urbanization: 0.97% annual rate of change (2015-20 est.)

MAJOR URBAN AREAS - POPULATION:

6.082 million Toronto, 4.172 million Montreal, 2.531 million Vancouver, 1.477 million Calgary, 1.397 million Edmonton, 1.363 million OTTAWA (capital) (2018)

SEX RATIO:

at birth: 1.06 male(s)/female (2017 est.)

0-14 years: 1.05 male(s)/female (2017 est.)

15-24 years: 1.06 male(s)/female (2017 est.)

25-54 years: 1.03 male(s)/female (2017 est.)

55-64 years: 0.98 male(s)/female (2017 est.)

65 years and over: 0.8 male(s)/female (2017 est.)

total population: 0.98 male(s)/female (2017 est.)

MOTHER'S MEAN AGE AT FIRST BIRTH:

28.1 years (2012 est.)

MATERNAL MORTALITY RATE:

7 deaths/100,000 live births (2015 est.)

country comparison to the world: 161

INFANT MORTALITY RATE:

total: 4.5 deaths/1,000 live births (2018 est.)

male: 4.8 deaths/1,000 live births (2018 est.)

female: 4.1 deaths/1,000 live births (2018 est.)

country comparison to the world: 180

LIFE EXPECTANCY AT BIRTH:

total population: 82 years (2018 est.)

male: 79.4 years (2018 est.)

female: 84.8 years (2018 est.)

country comparison to the world: 18

TOTAL FERTILITY RATE:

1.6 children born/woman (2018 est.)

country comparison to the world: 180

HEALTH EXPENDITURES:

10.4% of GDP (2014)

country comparison to the world: 20

PHYSICIANS DENSITY:

2.54 physicians/1,000 population (2015)

HOSPITAL BED DENSITY:

2.7 beds/1,000 population (2012)

DRINKING WATER SOURCE:

improved:

urban: 100% of population

rural: 99% of population

total: 99.8% of population

unimproved:

urban: 0% of population

rural: 1% of population

total: 0.2% of population (2015 est.)

SANITATION FACILITY ACCESS:

improved:

urban: 100% of population (2015 est.)

rural: 99% of population (2015 est.)

total: 99.8% of population (2015 est.)

unimproved:

urban: 0% of population (2015 est.)

rural: 1% of population (2015 est.)

total: 0.2% of population (2015 est.)

HIV/AIDS - ADULT PREVALENCE RATE:

NA

HIV/AIDS - PEOPLE LIVING WITH HIV/AIDS:

NA

HIV/AIDS - DEATHS:

NA

OBESITY - ADULT PREVALENCE RATE:

29.4% (2016)

country comparison to the world: 26

EDUCATION EXPENDITURES:

5.3% of GDP (2011)

country comparison to the world: 57

UNEMPLOYMENT, YOUTH AGES 15-24:

total: 11.6% (2017 est.)

male: 13.3% (2017 est.)

female: 9.9% (2017 est.)

country comparison to the world: 110

GOVERNMENT :: CANADA

COUNTRY NAME:

conventional long form: none

conventional short form: Canada

etymology: the country name likely derives from the St. Lawrence Iroquoian word "kanata" meaning village or settlement

GOVERNMENT TYPE:

federal parliamentary democracy (Parliament of Canada) under a constitutional monarchy; a Commonwealth realm; federal and state authorities and responsibilities regulated in constitution

CAPITAL:

name: Ottawa

geographic coordinates: 45 25 N, 75 42 W

time difference: UTC-5 (same time as Washington, DC, during Standard Time)

daylight saving time: +1hr, begins second Sunday in March; ends first Sunday in November

note: Canada has six time zones

ADMINISTRATIVE DIVISIONS:

10 provinces and 3 territories*; Alberta, British Columbia, Manitoba, New Brunswick, Newfoundland and Labrador, Northwest Territories*, Nova Scotia, Nunavut*, Ontario, Prince Edward Island, Quebec, Saskatchewan, Yukon*

INDEPENDENCE:

1 July 1867 (union of British North American colonies);11 December 1931 (recognized by UK per Statute of Westminster)

NATIONAL HOLIDAY:

Canada Day, 1 July (1867)

CONSTITUTION:

history: consists of unwritten and written acts, customs, judicial decisions, and traditions dating from 1763; the written part of the constitution consists of the Constitution Act of 29 March 1867, which created a federation of four provinces, and the Constitution Act of 17 April 1982 (2018)

amendments: proposed by either house of Parliament or by the provincial legislative assemblies; there are 5 methods for passage though most require approval by both houses of Parliament, approval of at least two-thirds of the provincial legislative assemblies and assent to and formalization as a proclamation by the governor general in council; the most restrictive method is reserved for amendments affecting fundamental sections of the constitution such as the office of the monarch or the governor general, and the constitutional amendment procedures, which require the unanimous approval by both houses and by all the provincial assemblies, and assent to by the governor general in council; amended 11 times, last in 2011 (Fair Representation Act, 2011) (2018)

LEGAL SYSTEM:

common law system except in Quebec, where civil law based on the French civil code prevails

INTERNATIONAL LAW ORGANIZATION PARTICIPATION:

accepts compulsory ICJ jurisdiction with reservations; accepts ICCt jurisdiction

CITIZENSHIP:

citizenship by birth: yes

citizenship by descent only: yes

dual citizenship recognized: yes

residency requirement for naturalization: minimum of 3 of last 5 years resident in Canada

SUFFRAGE:

18 years of age; universal

EXECUTIVE BRANCH:

chief of state: Queen ELIZABETH II (since 6 February 1952); represented by Governor General Julie PAYETTE (since 2 October 2017)

head of government: Prime Minister Justin Pierre James TRUDEAU (Liberal Party) (since 4 November 2015)

cabinet: Federal Ministry chosen by the prime minister usually from among members of his/her own party sitting in Parliament

elections/appointments: the monarchy is hereditary; governor general appointed by the monarch on the advice of the prime minister for a 5-year term; following legislative elections, the leader of the majority party or majority coalition in the House of Commons generally designated prime minister by the governor general

note: the governor general position is largely ceremonial; Julie PAYETTE, a former space shuttle astronaut, is Canada's fourth female governor general but the first to have flown in space

LEGISLATIVE BRANCH:

description: bicameral Parliament or Parlement consists of:
Senate or Senat (105 seats; members appointed by the governor general on the advice of the prime minister and can serve until age 75)
House of Commons or Chambre des Communes (338 seats; members directly elected in single-seat constituencies by simple majority vote with terms up to 4 years)

elections:
House of Commons - last held on 19 October 2015 (next to be held in 2019)

election results:
House of Commons - percent of vote by party - Liberal Party 39.5%, CPC 31.9%, NDP 19.7%, Bloc Quebecois 4.7%, Greens 3.4%, other 0.8%; seats by party - Liberal Party 184, CPC 99, NDP 44, Bloc Quebecois 3, Greens 1, independent 7; seats by party as of December 2018 - Liberal Party 181, CPC 96, NDP 41, Bloc Quebecois 10, Greens 1, People's Party of Canada 1, independent 4

JUDICIAL BRANCH:

highest courts: Supreme Court of Canada (consists of the chief justice and 8 judges); note - in 1949, Canada abolished all appeals beyond its Supreme Court, which prior to that time, were heard by the Judicial Committee of the Privy Council (in London)

judge selection and term of office: chief justice and judges appointed by the prime minister in council; all judges appointed for life with mandatory retirement at age 75

subordinate courts: federal level: Federal Court of Appeal; Federal Court; Tax Court; federal administrative tribunals; Courts Martial; provincial/territorial level: provincial superior, appeals, first instance, and specialized courts; in 1999, the Nunavut Court - a circuit court with the power of a provincial superior court, as well as a territorial court - was established to serve isolated settlements

POLITICAL PARTIES AND LEADERS:

Bloc Quebecois [Mario BEAULIEU]
Conservative Party of Canada or CPC [Andrew SCHEER]
Green Party [Elizabeth MAY]
Liberal Party [Justin TRUDEAU]
New Democratic Party or NDP [Jagmeet SINGH]
People's Party of Canada [Maxime BERNIER]

INTERNATIONAL ORGANIZATION PARTICIPATION:

ADB (nonregional member), AfDB (nonregional member), APEC, Arctic Council, ARF, ASEAN (dialogue partner), Australia Group, BIS, C, CD, CDB, CE (observer), EAPC, EBRD, EITI (implementing country), FAO, FATF, G-7, G-8, G-10, G-20, IADB, IAEA, IBRD, ICAO, ICC (national committees), ICCt, ICRM, IDA, IEA, IFAD, IFC, IFRCS, IGAD (partners), IHO, ILO, IMF, IMO, IMSO, Interpol, IOC, IOM, IPU, ISO, ITSO, ITU, ITUC (NGOs), MIGA, MINUSTAH, MONUSCO, NAFTA, NATO, NEA, NSG, OAS, OECD, OIF, OPCW, OSCE, Pacific Alliance (observer), Paris Club, PCA, PIF (partner), UN, UNCTAD, UNESCO, UNFICYP, UNHCR, UNMISS, UNRWA, UNTSO, UPU, WCO, WFTU (NGOs), WHO, WIPO, WMO, WTO, ZC

DIPLOMATIC REPRESENTATION IN THE US:

chief of mission: Ambassador David Brookes MACNAUGHTON (since 2 March 2016)

chancery: 501 Pennsylvania Avenue NW, Washington, DC 20001

telephone: [1] (202) 682-1740

FAX: [1] (202) 682-7726

consulate(s) general: Atlanta, Boston, Chicago, Dallas, Denver, Detroit, Los Angeles, Miami, Minneapolis, New York, San Francisco/Silicon Valley, Seattle

trade office(s): Houston, Palo Alto (CA), San Diego; note - there are trade offices in the Consulates General

DIPLOMATIC REPRESENTATION FROM THE US:

chief of mission: Ambassador Kelly CRAFT (since 23 October 2017)

embassy: 490 Sussex Drive, Ottawa, Ontario K1N 1G8

mailing address: P. O. Box 5000, Ogdensburg, NY 13669-0430; P.O. Box 866, Station B, Ottawa, Ontario K1P 5T1

telephone: [1] (613) 688-5335

FAX: [1] (613) 688-3082

consulate(s) general: Calgary, Halifax, Montreal, Quebec City, Toronto, Vancouver

consulate(s): Winnipeg

FLAG DESCRIPTION:

two vertical bands of red (hoist and fly side, half width) with white square between them; an 11-pointed red maple leaf is centered in the white square; the maple leaf has long been a Canadian symbol

NATIONAL SYMBOL(S):

maple leaf, beaver; national colors: red, white

NATIONAL ANTHEM:

name: O Canada

lyrics/music: Adolphe-Basile ROUTHIER [French], Robert Stanley WEIR [English]/Calixa LAVALLEE

note: adopted 1980; originally written in 1880, "O Canada" served as an unofficial anthem many years before its official adoption; the anthem has French and English versions whose lyrics differ; as a Commonwealth realm, in addition to the national anthem, "God Save the Queen" serves as the royal anthem (see United Kingdom)

ECONOMY :: CANADA

ECONOMY - OVERVIEW:

Canada resembles the US in its market-oriented economic system, pattern of production, and high living standards. Since World War II, the impressive growth of the manufacturing, mining, and service sectors has transformed the nation from a largely rural economy into one primarily industrial and urban. Canada has a large oil and natural gas sector with the majority of crude oil production derived from oil sands in the western provinces, especially Alberta. Canada now ranks third in the world in proved oil reserves behind Venezuela and Saudi Arabia and is the world's seventh-largest oil producer.

TThe 1989 Canada-US Free Trade Agreement and the 1994 North American Free Trade Agreement (which includes Mexico) dramatically increased trade and economic integration between the US and Canada. Canada and the US enjoy the world's most comprehensive bilateral trade and investment relationship, with goods and services trade totaling more than $680 billion in 2017, and two-way investment stocks of more than $800 billion. Over three-fourths of Canada's merchandise exports are destined for the US each year. Canada is the largest foreign supplier of energy to the US, including oil, natural gas, and electric power, and a top source of US uranium imports.

Given its abundant natural resources, highly skilled labor force, and modern capital stock, Canada enjoyed solid economic growth from 1993 through 2007. The global economic crisis of 2007-08 moved the Canadian economy into sharp recession by late 2008, and Ottawa posted its first fiscal deficit in 2009 after 12 years of surplus. Canada's major banks emerged from the financial crisis of 2008-09 among the strongest in the world, owing to the financial sector's tradition of conservative lending practices and strong capitalization. Canada's economy posted strong growth in 2017 at 3%, but most analysts are projecting Canada's economic growth will drop back closer to 2% in 2018.

GDP (PURCHASING POWER PARITY):

$1.774 trillion (2017 est.)

$1.721 trillion (2016 est.)

$1.697 trillion (2015 est.)

note: data are in 2017 dollars

country comparison to the world: 17

GDP (OFFICIAL EXCHANGE RATE):

$1.653 trillion (2017 est.) (2017 est.)

GDP - REAL GROWTH RATE:

3% (2017 est.)

1.4% (2016 est.)

1% (2015 est.)

country comparison to the world: 112

GDP - PER CAPITA (PPP):

$48,400 (2017 est.)

$47,500 (2016 est.)

$47,400 (2015 est.)

note: data are in 2017 dollars

country comparison to the world: 34

GROSS NATIONAL SAVING:

20.8% of GDP (2017 est.)

20% of GDP (2016 est.)

20.5% of GDP (2015 est.)

country comparison to the world: 90

GDP - COMPOSITION, BY END USE:

household consumption: 57.8% (2017 est.)

government consumption: 20.8% (2017 est.)

investment in fixed capital: 23% (2017 est.)

investment in inventories: 0.7% (2017 est.)

exports of goods and services: 30.9% (2017 est.)

imports of goods and services: -33.2% (2017 est.)

GDP - COMPOSITION, BY SECTOR OF ORIGIN:

agriculture: 1.6% (2017 est.)

industry: 28.2% (2017 est.)

services: 70.2% (2017 est.)

AGRICULTURE - PRODUCTS:

wheat, barley, oilseed, tobacco, fruits, vegetables; dairy products; fish; forest products

INDUSTRIES:

transportation equipment, chemicals, processed and unprocessed minerals, food products, wood and paper products, fish products, petroleum, natural gas

INDUSTRIAL PRODUCTION GROWTH RATE:

4.9% (2017 est.)

country comparison to the world: 60

LABOR FORCE:

19.52 million (2017 est.)

country comparison to the world: 31

LABOR FORCE - BY OCCUPATION:

agriculture: 2%

industry: 13%

services: 6%

industry and services: 76%

manufacturing: 3% (2006 est.)

UNEMPLOYMENT RATE:

6.3% (2017 est.)

7% (2016 est.)

country comparison to the world: 94

POPULATION BELOW POVERTY LINE:

9.4% (2008 est.)

note: this figure is the Low Income Cut-Off, a calculation that results in higher figures than found in many comparable economies; Canada does not have an official poverty line

HOUSEHOLD INCOME OR CONSUMPTION BY PERCENTAGE SHARE:

lowest 10%: 24.8% (2000)

highest 10%: 24.8% (2000)

DISTRIBUTION OF FAMILY INCOME - GINI INDEX:

32.1 (2005)

31.5 (1994)

country comparison to the world: 119

BUDGET:

revenues: 649.6 billion (2017 est.)

expenditures: 665.7 billion (2017 est.)

TAXES AND OTHER REVENUES:

39.3% (of GDP) (2017 est.)

country comparison to the world: 48

BUDGET SURPLUS (+) OR DEFICIT (-):

-1% (of GDP) (2017 est.)

country comparison to the world: 77

PUBLIC DEBT:

89.7% of GDP (2017 est.)

91.1% of GDP (2016 est.)

note: figures are for gross general government debt, as opposed to net federal debt; gross general government debt includes both intragovernmental debt and the debt of public entities at the sub-national level

country comparison to the world: 25

FISCAL YEAR:

1 April - 31 March

INFLATION RATE (CONSUMER PRICES):

1.6% (2017 est.)

1.4% (2016 est.)

country comparison to the world: 87

CENTRAL BANK DISCOUNT RATE:

1% (31 December 2010)

0.25% (31 December 2009)

country comparison to the world: 133

COMMERCIAL BANK PRIME LENDING RATE:

3.2% (31 December 2017 est.)

2.7% (31 December 2016 est.)

country comparison to the world: 172

STOCK OF NARROW MONEY:

$748.9 billion (31 December 2017 est.)

$637.6 billion (31 December 2016 est.)

country comparison to the world: 9

STOCK OF BROAD MONEY:

$748.9 billion (31 December 2017 est.)

$637.6 billion (31 December 2016 est.)

country comparison to the world: 9

STOCK OF DOMESTIC CREDIT:

$3.219 trillion (31 December 2017 est.)

$2.802 trillion (31 December 2016 est.)

country comparison to the world: 8

MARKET VALUE OF PUBLICLY TRADED SHARES:

$1.593 trillion (31 December 2015 est.)

$2.095 trillion (31 December 2014 est.)

$2.114 trillion (31 December 2013 est.)

country comparison to the world: 7

CURRENT ACCOUNT BALANCE:

-$48.75 billion (2017 est.)

-$49.32 billion (2016 est.)

country comparison to the world: 204

EXPORTS:

$423.5 billion (2017 est.)

$393.5 billion (2016 est.)

country comparison to the world: 11

EXPORTS - PARTNERS:

US 76.4%, China 4.3% (2017)

EXPORTS - COMMODITIES:

motor vehicles and parts, industrial machinery, aircraft, telecommunications equipment; chemicals, plastics, fertilizers; wood pulp, timber, crude petroleum, natural gas, electricity, aluminum

IMPORTS:

$442.1 billion (2017 est.)

$413.4 billion (2016 est.)

country comparison to the world: 12

IMPORTS - COMMODITIES:

machinery and equipment, motor vehicles and parts, crude oil, chemicals, electricity, durable consumer goods

IMPORTS - PARTNERS:

US 51.5%, China 12.6%, Mexico 6.3% (2017)

RESERVES OF FOREIGN EXCHANGE AND GOLD:

$86.68 billion (31 December 2017 est.)

$82.72 billion (31 December 2016 est.)

country comparison to the world: 28

DEBT - EXTERNAL:

$1.608 trillion (31 March 2016 est.)

$1.55 trillion (31 March 2015 est.)

country comparison to the world: 13

STOCK OF DIRECT FOREIGN INVESTMENT - AT HOME:

$1.039 trillion (31 December 2017 est.)

$1.004 trillion (31 December 2016 est.)

country comparison to the world: 10

STOCK OF DIRECT FOREIGN INVESTMENT - ABROAD:

$1.371 trillion (31 December 2017 est.)

$1.277 trillion (31 December 2016 est.)

country comparison to the world: 11

EXCHANGE RATES:

Canadian dollars (CAD) per US dollar -

1.308 (2017 est.)

1.3256 (2016 est.)

1.3256 (2015 est.)

1.2788 (2014 est.)

1.0298 (2013 est.)

ENERGY :: CANADA

ELECTRICITY ACCESS:

electrification - total population: 100% (2016)

ELECTRICITY - PRODUCTION:

649.6 billion kWh (2016 est.)

country comparison to the world: 6

ELECTRICITY - CONSUMPTION:

522.2 billion kWh (2016 est.)

country comparison to the world: 7

ELECTRICITY - EXPORTS:

73.35 billion kWh (2016 est.)

country comparison to the world: 2

ELECTRICITY - IMPORTS:

2.682 billion kWh (2016 est.)

country comparison to the world: 52

ELECTRICITY - INSTALLED GENERATING CAPACITY:

143.5 million kW (2016 est.)

country comparison to the world: 8

ELECTRICITY - FROM FOSSIL FUELS:

23% of total installed capacity (2016 est.)

country comparison to the world: 191

ELECTRICITY - FROM NUCLEAR FUELS:

9% of total installed capacity (2017 est.)

country comparison to the world: 16

ELECTRICITY - FROM HYDROELECTRIC PLANTS:

56% of total installed capacity (2017 est.)

country comparison to the world: 30

ELECTRICITY - FROM OTHER RENEWABLE SOURCES:

12% of total installed capacity (2017 est.)

country comparison to the world: 73

CRUDE OIL - PRODUCTION:

3.977 million bbl/day (2017 est.)

country comparison to the world: 6

CRUDE OIL - EXPORTS:

2.818 million bbl/day (2017 est.)

country comparison to the world: 4

CRUDE OIL - IMPORTS:

806,700 bbl/day (2017 est.)

country comparison to the world: 14

CRUDE OIL - PROVED RESERVES:

170.5 billion bbl (1 January 2018 est.)

country comparison to the world: 3

REFINED PETROLEUM PRODUCTS - PRODUCTION:

2.009 million bbl/day (2017 est.)

country comparison to the world: 10

REFINED PETROLEUM PRODUCTS - CONSUMPTION:

2.445 million bbl/day (2017 est.)

country comparison to the world: 10

REFINED PETROLEUM PRODUCTS - EXPORTS:

1.115 million bbl/day (2017 est.)

country comparison to the world: 8

REFINED PETROLEUM PRODUCTS - IMPORTS:

405,700 bbl/day (2017 est.)

country comparison to the world: 21

NATURAL GAS - PRODUCTION:

159.1 billion cu m (2017 est.)

country comparison to the world: 5

NATURAL GAS - CONSUMPTION:

124.4 billion cu m (2017 est.)

country comparison to the world: 6

NATURAL GAS - EXPORTS:

83.96 billion cu m (2017 est.)

country comparison to the world: 5

NATURAL GAS - IMPORTS:

26.36 billion cu m (2017 est.)

country comparison to the world: 13

NATURAL GAS - PROVED RESERVES:

2.056 trillion cu m (1 January 2018 est.)

country comparison to the world: 16

CARBON DIOXIDE EMISSIONS FROM CONSUMPTION OF ENERGY:

640.6 million Mt (2017 est.)

country comparison to the world: 9

COMMUNICATIONS :: CANADA

TELEPHONES - FIXED LINES:

total subscriptions: 14,700,854 (2017 est.)

subscriptions per 100 inhabitants: 41 (2017 est.)

country comparison to the world: 15

TELEPHONES - MOBILE CELLULAR:

total subscriptions: 31,458,600 (2017 est.)

subscriptions per 100 inhabitants: 88 (2017 est.)

country comparison to the world: 43

TELEPHONE SYSTEM:

general assessment: excellent service provided by modern technology; consumer demand for mobile data services have promted telecos to invest and pomote LTE infrastructure, and further investment in 5G; government policy has aided the extension of broadband to rural and regional areas, with the result that services are almost universally accessible (2017)

domestic: comparatively low mobile penetration provides further room for growth; domestic satellite system with about 300 earth stations; 41 per 100 fixed-line; 88 per 100 mobile-cellular (2017)

international: country code - 1; submarine cables provide links to the US and Europe; satellite earth stations - 7 (5 Intelsat - 4 Atlantic Ocean and 1 Pacific Ocean, and 2 Intersputnik - Atlantic Ocean region) (2016)

BROADCAST MEDIA:

2 public TV broadcasting networks, 1 in English and 1 in French, each with a large number of network affiliates; several private-commercial networks also with multiple network affiliates; overall, about 150 TV stations; multi-channel satellite and cable systems provide access to a wide range of stations including US stations; mix of public and commercial radio broadcasters with the Canadian Broadcasting Corporation (CBC), the public radio broadcaster, operating 4 radio networks, Radio Canada International, and radio services to indigenous populations in the north; roughly 1,119 licensed radio stations (2016)

INTERNET COUNTRY CODE:

.ca

INTERNET USERS:

total: 31,770,034 (July 2016 est.)

percent of population: 89.8% (July 2016 est.)

country comparison to the world: 22

BROADBAND - FIXED SUBSCRIPTIONS:

total: 13,922,504 (2017 est.)

subscriptions per 100 inhabitants: 39 (2017 est.)

country comparison to the world: 14

TRANSPORTATION :: CANADA

NATIONAL AIR TRANSPORT SYSTEM:

number of registered air carriers: 51 (2015)

inventory of registered aircraft operated by air carriers: 879 (2015)

annual passenger traffic on registered air carriers: 80,228,301 (2015)

annual freight traffic on registered air carriers: 2,074,830,881 mt-km (2015)

CIVIL AIRCRAFT REGISTRATION COUNTRY CODE PREFIX:

C (2016)

AIRPORTS:

1,467 (2013)

country comparison to the world: 4

AIRPORTS - WITH PAVED RUNWAYS:

total: 523 (2017)

over 3,047 m: 21 (2017)

2,438 to 3,047 m: 19 (2017)

1,524 to 2,437 m: 147 (2017)

914 to 1,523 m: 257 (2017)

under 914 m: 79 (2017)

AIRPORTS - WITH UNPAVED RUNWAYS:

total: 944 (2013)

1,524 to 2,437 m: 75 (2013)

914 to 1,523 m: 385 (2013)

under 914 m: 484 (2013)

HELIPORTS:

26 (2013)

PIPELINES:

110000 km gas and liquid petroleum (2017)

RAILWAYS:

total: 77,932 km (2014)

standard gauge: 77,932 km 1.435-m gauge (2014)

country comparison to the world: 4

ROADWAYS:

total: 1,042,300 km (2011)

paved: 415,600 km (includes 17,000 km of expressways) (2011)

unpaved: 626,700 km (2011)

country comparison to the world: 7

WATERWAYS:

636 km (Saint Lawrence Seaway of 3,769 km, including the Saint Lawrence River of 3,058 km, shared with United States) (2011)

country comparison to the world: 77

MERCHANT MARINE:

total: 639 (2017)

by type: bulk carrier 16, container ship 1, general cargo 88, oil tanker 15, other 519 (2017)

country comparison to the world: 32

PORTS AND TERMINALS:

major seaport(s): Halifax, Saint John (New Brunswick), Vancouver

oil terminal(s): Lower Lakes terminal

container port(s) (TEUs): Montreal (1,447,566), Vancouver (2,929,585) (2016)

LNG terminal(s) (import): Saint John

river and lake port(s): Montreal, Quebec City, Sept-Isles (St. Lawrence)

dry bulk cargo port(s): Port-Cartier (iron ore and grain),

Fraser River Port (Fraser) Hamilton (Lake Ontario)

MILITARY AND SECURITY :: CANADA

MILITARY EXPENDITURES:

1.29% of GDP (2017)

1.16% of GDP (2016)

1.2% of GDP (2015)

1% of GDP (2014)

1% of GDP (2013)

country comparison to the world: 88

MILITARY BRANCHES:

Canadian Forces: Canadian Army, Royal Canadian Navy, Royal Canadian Air Force, Canadian Joint Operations Command (2015)

MILITARY SERVICE AGE AND OBLIGATION:

17 years of age for voluntary male and female military service (with parental consent); 16 years of age for Reserve and Military College applicants; Canadian citizenship or permanent residence status required; maximum 34 years of age; service obligation 3-9 years (2012)

TRANSNATIONAL ISSUES :: CANADA

DISPUTES - INTERNATIONAL:

managed maritime boundary disputes with the US at Dixon Entrance, Beaufort Sea, Strait of Juan de Fuca, and the Gulf of Maine, including the disputed Machias Seal Island and North RockCanada and the United States dispute how to divide the Beaufort Sea and the status of the Northwest Passage but continue to work cooperatively to survey the Arctic continental shelfUS works closely with Canada to intensify security measures for monitoring and controlling legal and illegal movement of people, transport, and commodities across the international bordersovereignty dispute with Denmark over Hans Island in the Kennedy Channel between Ellesmere Island and Greenlandcommencing the collection of technical evidence for submission to the Commission on the Limits of the Continental Shelf in support of claims for continental shelf beyond 200 nm from its declared baselines in the Arctic, as stipulated in Article 76, paragraph 8, of the UN Convention on the Law of the Sea

REFUGEES AND INTERNALLY DISPLACED PERSONS:

refugees (country of origin): 8,228 (Colombia), 7,356 (China), 6,774 (Haiti) (2016)

stateless persons: 3,790 (2017)

ILLICIT DRUGS:

illicit producer of cannabis for the domestic drug market and export to US; use of hydroponics technology permits growers to plant large quantities of high-quality marijuana indoors; increasing ecstasy production, some of which is destined for the US; vulnerable to narcotics money laundering because of its mature financial services sector

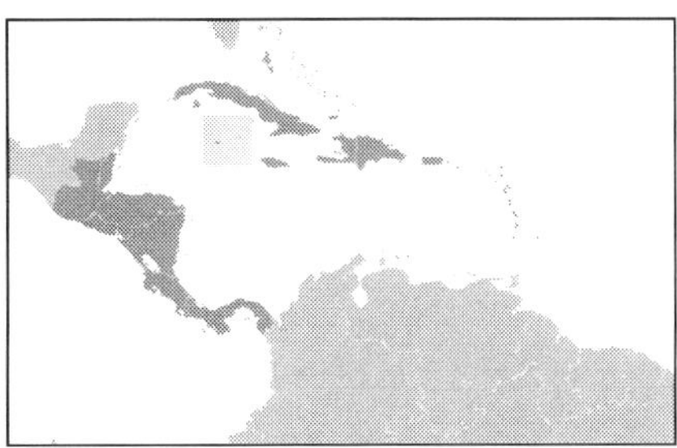

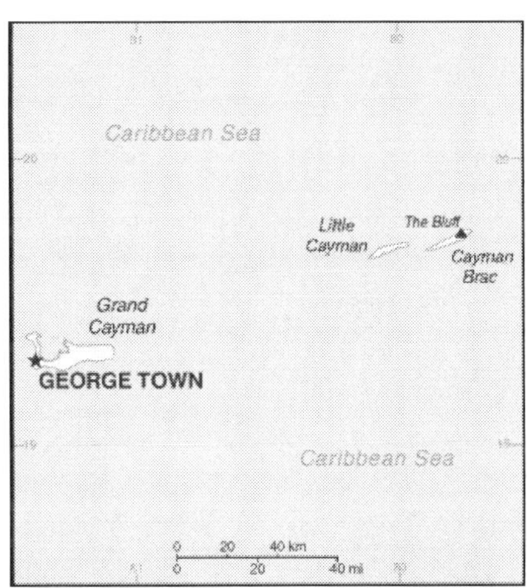

CENTRAL AMERICA :: CAYMAN ISLANDS

INTRODUCTION :: CAYMAN ISLANDS

BACKGROUND:

The Cayman Islands were colonized from Jamaica by the British during the 18th and 19th centuries and were administered by Jamaica after 1863. In 1959, the islands became a territory within the Federation of the West Indies. When the Federation dissolved in 1962, the Cayman Islands chose to remain a British dependency. The territory has transformed itself into a significant offshore financial center.

GEOGRAPHY :: CAYMAN ISLANDS

LOCATION:

Caribbean, three-island group (Grand Cayman, Cayman Brac, Little Cayman) in Caribbean Sea, 240 km south of Cuba and 268 km northwest of Jamaica

GEOGRAPHIC COORDINATES:

19 30 N, 80 30 W

MAP REFERENCES:

Central America and the Caribbean

AREA:

total: 264 sq km

land: 264 sq km

water: 0 sq km

country comparison to the world: 211

AREA - COMPARATIVE:

1.5 times the size of Washington, DC

LAND BOUNDARIES:

0 km

COASTLINE:

160 km

MARITIME CLAIMS:

territorial sea: 12 nm

exclusive fishing zone: 200 nm

CLIMATE:

tropical marine; warm, rainy summers (May to October) and cool, relatively dry winters (November to April)

TERRAIN:

low-lying limestone base surrounded by coral reefs

ELEVATION:

0 m lowest point: Caribbean Sea

50 highest point: 1 km SW of The Bluff on Cayman Brac

NATURAL RESOURCES:

fish, climate and beaches that foster tourism

LAND USE:

agricultural land: 11.2% (2011 est.)

arable land: 0.8% (2011 est.) / permanent crops: 2.1% (2011 est.) / permanent pasture: 8.3% (2011 est.)

forest: 52.9% (2011 est.)

other: 35.9% (2011 est.)

IRRIGATED LAND:

NA

POPULATION DISTRIBUTION:

majority of the population resides on Grand Cayman

NATURAL HAZARDS:

hurricanes (July to November)

ENVIRONMENT - CURRENT ISSUES:

no natural freshwater resources; drinking water supplies are met by reverse osmosis desalination plants and rainwater catchment; trash washing up on the beaches or being deposited there by residents; no recycling or waste treatment facilities; deforestation (trees being cut down to create space for commercial use)

GEOGRAPHY - NOTE:

important location between Cuba and Central America

PEOPLE AND SOCIETY :: CAYMAN ISLANDS

POPULATION:

59,613 (July 2018 est.)

note: most of the population lives on Grand Cayman

country comparison to the world: 205

NATIONALITY:

noun: Caymanian(s)

adjective: Caymanian

ETHNIC GROUPS:

mixed 40%, white 20%, black 20%, expatriates of various ethnic groups 20%

LANGUAGES:

English (official) 90.9%, Spanish 4%, Filipino 3.3%, other 1.7%, unspecified 0.1% (2010 est.)

RELIGIONS:

Protestant 67.8% (includes Church of God 22.6%, Seventh Day Adventist 9.4%, Presbyterian/United Church 8.6%, Baptist 8.3%, Pentecostal 7.1%, non-denominational 5.3%, Anglican 4.1%, Wesleyan Holiness 2.4%), Roman Catholic 14.1%, Jehovah's Witness 1.1%, other 7%, none 9.3%, unspecified 0.7% (2010 est.)

AGE STRUCTURE:

0-14 years: 17.91% (male 5,376 /female 5,298)

15-24 years: 12.2% (male 3,609 /female 3,662)

25-54 years: 42.12% (male 12,256 /female 12,855)

55-64 years: 14.64% (male 4,169 /female 4,558)

65 years and over: 13.13% (male 3,627 /female 4,203) (2018 est.)

MEDIAN AGE:

total: 40.2 years

male: 39.5 years

female: 40.9 years (2018 est.)

country comparison to the world: 50

POPULATION GROWTH RATE:

1.96% (2018 est.)

country comparison to the world: 49

BIRTH RATE:

12 births/1,000 population (2018 est.)

country comparison to the world: 166

DEATH RATE:

5.9 deaths/1,000 population (2018 est.)

country comparison to the world: 167

NET MIGRATION RATE:

13.8 migrant(s)/1,000 population (2017 est.)

note: major destination for Cubans trying to migrate to the US

country comparison to the world: 4

POPULATION DISTRIBUTION:

majority of the population resides on Grand Cayman

URBANIZATION:

urban population: 100% of total population (2018)

rate of urbanization: 1.27% annual rate of change (2015-20 est.)

MAJOR URBAN AREAS - POPULATION:

35,000 GEORGE TOWN (capital) (2018)

SEX RATIO:

at birth: 1.02 male(s)/female (2017 est.)

0-14 years: 1.01 male(s)/female (2017 est.)

15-24 years: 0.98 male(s)/female (2017 est.)

25-54 years: 0.95 male(s)/female (2017 est.)

55-64 years: 0.91 male(s)/female (2017 est.)

65 years and over: 0.89 male(s)/female (2017 est.)

total population: 0.95 male(s)/female (2017 est.)

INFANT MORTALITY RATE:

total: 5.7 deaths/1,000 live births (2018 est.)

male: 6.5 deaths/1,000 live births (2018 est.)

female: 4.9 deaths/1,000 live births (2018 est.)

country comparison to the world: 168

LIFE EXPECTANCY AT BIRTH:

total population: 81.4 years (2018 est.)

male: 78.7 years (2018 est.)

female: 84.2 years (2018 est.)

country comparison to the world: 28

TOTAL FERTILITY RATE:

1.84 children born/woman (2018 est.)

country comparison to the world: 145

DRINKING WATER SOURCE:

improved:

urban: 97.4% of population (2015 est.)

rural: NA (2015 est.)

total: 97.4% of population (2015 est.)

unimproved:

urban: 2.6% of population (2015 est.)

total: 2.6% of population (2015 est.)

SANITATION FACILITY ACCESS:

improved:

urban: 95.6% of population (2015 est.)

total: 95.6% of population (2015 est.)

unimproved:

urban: 4.4% of population (2015 est.)

total: 4.4% of population (2015 est.)

HIV/AIDS - ADULT PREVALENCE RATE:

NA

HIV/AIDS - PEOPLE LIVING WITH HIV/AIDS:

NA

HIV/AIDS - DEATHS:

NA

MAJOR INFECTIOUS DISEASES:

note: active local transmission of Zika virus by Aedes species mosquitoes has been identified in this country (as of August 2016); it poses an important risk (a large number of cases possible) among US citizens if bitten by an infective mosquito; other less common ways to get Zika are through sex, via blood transfusion, or during pregnancy, in which the pregnant woman passes Zika virus to her fetus

EDUCATION EXPENDITURES:

NA

LITERACY:

definition: age 15 and over has ever attended school (2007 est.)

total population: 98.9% (2007 est.)

male: 98.7% (2007 est.)

female: 99% (2007 est.)

UNEMPLOYMENT, YOUTH AGES 15-24:

total: 13.8% (2015 est.)

male: 16.4% (2015 est.)

female: 11.4% (2015 est.)

country comparison to the world: 95

GOVERNMENT :: CAYMAN ISLANDS

COUNTRY NAME:

conventional long form: none

conventional short form: Cayman Islands

etymology: the islands' name comes from the native Carib word "caiman," describing the marine crocodiles living there

DEPENDENCY STATUS:

overseas territory of the UK

GOVERNMENT TYPE:

parliamentary democracy (Legislative Assembly); self-governing overseas territory of the UK

CAPITAL:

name: George Town (on Grand Cayman)

geographic coordinates: 19 18 N, 81 23 W

time difference: UTC-5 (same time as Washington, DC, during Standard Time)

ADMINISTRATIVE DIVISIONS:

6 districts; Bodden Town, Cayman Brac and Little Cayman, East End, George Town, North Side, West Bay

INDEPENDENCE:

none (overseas territory of the UK)

NATIONAL HOLIDAY:

Constitution Day, first Monday in July (1959)

CONSTITUTION:

history: several previous; latest approved 10 June 2009, entered into force 6 November 2009 (The Cayman

Islands Constitution Order 2009) (2018)

amendments: amended several times, last in 2016 (2018)

LEGAL SYSTEM:

English common law and local statutes

CITIZENSHIP:

see United Kingdom

SUFFRAGE:

18 years of age; universal

EXECUTIVE BRANCH:

chief of state: Queen ELIZABETH II (since 6 February 1952); represented by Governor Martyn ROPER (since 29 October 2018)

head of government: Premier Alden MCLAUGHLIN (since 29 May 2013)

cabinet: Cabinet selected from the Legislative Assembly and appointed by the governor on the advice of the premier

elections/appointments: the monarchy is hereditary; governor appointed by the monarch; following legislative elections, the leader of the majority party or majority coalition appointed premier by the governor

LEGISLATIVE BRANCH:

description: unicameral Legislative Assembly (21 seats; 19 members directly elected by majority vote and 2 ex officio members - the deputy governor and attorney general - appointed by the governor; members serve 4-year terms)

elections: last held on 24 May 2017 (next to be held in 2021)

election results: percent of vote by party - independent 44.7%, PPM 31.2%, CDP 24.1%; seats by party - independent 9, PPM 7, CDP 3

JUDICIAL BRANCH:

highest courts: Court of Appeal (consists of the court president and at least 2 judges); Grand Court (consists of the court president and at least 2 judges); note - appeals beyond the Court of Appeal are heard by the Judicial Committee of the Privy Council (in London)

judge selection and term of office: Court of Appeal and Grand Court judges appointed by the governor on the advice of the Judicial and Legal Services Commission, an 8-member independent body consisting of governor appointees, Court of Appeal president, and attorneys; Court of Appeal judges' tenure based on their individual instruments of appointment; Grand Court judges normally appointed until retirement at age 65 but can be extended until age 70

subordinate courts: Summary Court

POLITICAL PARTIES AND LEADERS:

People's Progressive Movement or PPM [Alden MCLAUGHLIN]
Cayman Democratic Party or CDP [McKeeva BUSH]

INTERNATIONAL ORGANIZATION PARTICIPATION:

Caricom (associate), CDB, Interpol (subbureau), IOC, UNESCO (associate), UPU

DIPLOMATIC REPRESENTATION IN THE US:

none (overseas territory of the UK)

DIPLOMATIC REPRESENTATION FROM THE US:

none (overseas territory of the UK); consular services provided through the US Embassy in Jamaica

FLAG DESCRIPTION:

a blue field with the flag of the UK in the upper hoist-side quadrant and the Caymanian coat of arms centered on the outer half of the flag; the coat of arms includes a crest with a pineapple, representing the connection with Jamaica, and a turtle, representing Cayman's seafaring tradition, above a shield bearing a golden lion, symbolizing Great Britain, below which are three green stars (representing the three islands) surmounting white and blue wavy lines representing the sea; a scroll below the shield bears the motto HE HATH FOUNDED IT UPON THE SEAS

NATIONAL SYMBOL(S):

green sea turtle

NATIONAL ANTHEM:

name: Beloved Isle Cayman

lyrics/music: Leila E. ROSS

note: adopted 1993; served as an unofficial anthem since 1930; as a territory of the United Kingdom, in addition to the local anthem, "God Save the Queen" is official (see United Kingdom)

ECONOMY :: CAYMAN ISLANDS

ECONOMY - OVERVIEW:

With no direct taxation, the islands are a thriving offshore financial center. More than 65,000 companies were registered in the Cayman Islands as of 2017, including more than 280 banks, 700 insurers, and 10,500 mutual funds. A stock exchange was opened in 1997. Nearly 90% of the islands' food and consumer goods must be imported. The Caymanians enjoy a standard of living comparable to that of Switzerland.

Tourism is also a mainstay, accounting for about 70% of GDP and 75% of foreign currency earnings. The tourist industry is aimed at the luxury market and caters mainly to visitors from North America. Total tourist arrivals exceeded 2.1 million in 2016, with more than three-quarters from the US.

GDP (PURCHASING POWER PARITY):

$2.507 billion (2014 est.)

$2.465 billion (2013 est.)

$2.435 billion (2012 est.)

country comparison to the world: 192

GDP (OFFICIAL EXCHANGE RATE):

$2.25 billion (2008 est.) (2008 est.)

GDP - REAL GROWTH RATE:

1.7% (2014 est.)

1.2% (2013 est.)

1.6% (2012 est.)

country comparison to the world: 163

GDP - PER CAPITA (PPP):

$43,800 (2004 est.)

country comparison to the world: 41

GDP - COMPOSITION, BY END USE:

household consumption: 62.3% (2017 est.)

government consumption: 14.5% (2017 est.)

investment in fixed capital: 22.1% (2017 est.)

investment in inventories: 0.1% (2017 est.)

exports of goods and services: 65.4% (2017 est.)

imports of goods and services: -64.2% (2017 est.)

GDP - COMPOSITION, BY SECTOR OF ORIGIN:

agriculture: 0.3% (2017 est.)

industry: 7.4% (2017 est.)

services: 92.3% (2017 est.)

AGRICULTURE - PRODUCTS:

vegetables, fruit; livestock; turtle farming

INDUSTRIES:

tourism, banking, insurance and finance, construction, construction materials, furniture

INDUSTRIAL PRODUCTION GROWTH RATE:

2.2% (2017 est.)

country comparison to the world: 124

LABOR FORCE:

39,000 (2007 est.)

note: nearly 55% are non-nationals

country comparison to the world: 197

LABOR FORCE - BY OCCUPATION:

agriculture: 1.9%

industry: 19.1%

services: 79% (2008 est.)

UNEMPLOYMENT RATE:

4% (2008)

4.4% (2004)

country comparison to the world: 51

POPULATION BELOW POVERTY LINE:

NA

HOUSEHOLD INCOME OR CONSUMPTION BY PERCENTAGE SHARE:

lowest 10%: NA

highest 10%: NA

BUDGET:

revenues: 874.5 million (2017 est.)

expenditures: 766.6 million (2017 est.)

TAXES AND OTHER REVENUES:

38.9% (of GDP) (2017 est.)

country comparison to the world: 51

BUDGET SURPLUS (+) OR DEFICIT (-):

4.8% (of GDP) (2017 est.)

country comparison to the world: 7

FISCAL YEAR:

1 April - 31 March

INFLATION RATE (CONSUMER PRICES):

2% (2017 est.)

-0.6% (2016 est.)

country comparison to the world: 104

COMMERCIAL BANK PRIME LENDING RATE:

14.9% (31 December 2017 est.)

14.9% (31 December 2016 est.)

country comparison to the world: 42

STOCK OF NARROW MONEY:

$334.3 million (31 December 2008)

country comparison to the world: 179

STOCK OF BROAD MONEY:

$5.564 billion (31 December 2008 est.)

country comparison to the world: 100

MARKET VALUE OF PUBLICLY TRADED SHARES:

$315.6 million (31 December 2015 est.)

$183.5 million (31 December 2007)

$188.4 million (31 December 2006)

country comparison to the world: 115

CURRENT ACCOUNT BALANCE:

-$492.6 million (2017 est.)

-$493.5 million (2016 est.)

country comparison to the world: 118

EXPORTS:

$421.9 million (2017 est.)

$47.6 million (2016 est.)

country comparison to the world: 182

EXPORTS - COMMODITIES:

turtle products, manufactured consumer goods

IMPORTS:

$787.3 million (2017 est.)

$810.1 million (2016 est.)

country comparison to the world: 189

IMPORTS - COMMODITIES:

foodstuffs, manufactured goods, fuels

STOCK OF DIRECT FOREIGN INVESTMENT - AT HOME:

NA

STOCK OF DIRECT FOREIGN INVESTMENT - ABROAD:

NA

EXCHANGE RATES:

Caymanian dollars (KYD) per US dollar -

0.82 (2017 est.)

0.82 (2016 est.)

0.82 (2015 est.)

0.82 (2014 est.)

0.83 (2013 est.)

ENERGY :: CAYMAN ISLANDS

ELECTRICITY ACCESS:

population without electricity: 5,726 (2012)

electrification - total population: 91% (2012)

electrification - urban areas: 91% (2012)

electrification - rural areas: 80% (2012)

ELECTRICITY - PRODUCTION:

650 million kWh (2016 est.)

country comparison to the world: 160

ELECTRICITY - CONSUMPTION:

612 million kWh (2016 est.)

country comparison to the world: 165

ELECTRICITY - EXPORTS:

0 kWh (2016 est.)

country comparison to the world: 118

ELECTRICITY - IMPORTS:

0 kWh (2016 est.)

country comparison to the world: 132

ELECTRICITY - INSTALLED GENERATING CAPACITY:

132,000 kW (2016 est.)

country comparison to the world: 174

ELECTRICITY - FROM FOSSIL FUELS:

100% of total installed capacity (2016 est.)

country comparison to the world: 6

ELECTRICITY - FROM NUCLEAR FUELS:

0% of total installed capacity (2017 est.)

country comparison to the world: 63

ELECTRICITY - FROM HYDROELECTRIC PLANTS:

0% of total installed capacity (2017 est.)

country comparison to the world: 163

ELECTRICITY - FROM OTHER RENEWABLE SOURCES:

0% of total installed capacity (2017 est.)

country comparison to the world: 180

CRUDE OIL - PRODUCTION:

0 bbl/day (2017 est.)

country comparison to the world: 119

CRUDE OIL - EXPORTS:

0 bbl/day (2015 est.)

country comparison to the world: 104

CRUDE OIL - IMPORTS:

0 bbl/day (2015 est.)

country comparison to the world: 107

CRUDE OIL - PROVED RESERVES:

0 bbl (1 January 2018 est.)

country comparison to the world: 116

REFINED PETROLEUM PRODUCTS - PRODUCTION:

0 bbl/day (2017 est.)

country comparison to the world: 128

REFINED PETROLEUM PRODUCTS - CONSUMPTION:

4,400 bbl/day (2016 est.)

country comparison to the world: 181

REFINED PETROLEUM PRODUCTS - EXPORTS:

0 bbl/day (2015 est.)

country comparison to the world: 141

REFINED PETROLEUM PRODUCTS - IMPORTS:

4,285 bbl/day (2015 est.)

country comparison to the world: 175

NATURAL GAS - PRODUCTION:

0 cu m (2017 est.)

country comparison to the world: 114

NATURAL GAS - CONSUMPTION:

0 cu m (2017 est.)

country comparison to the world: 130

NATURAL GAS - EXPORTS:

0 cu m (2017 est.)

country comparison to the world: 80

NATURAL GAS - IMPORTS:

0 cu m (2017 est.)

country comparison to the world: 104

NATURAL GAS - PROVED RESERVES:

0 cu m (1 January 2014 est.)

country comparison to the world: 120

CARBON DIOXIDE EMISSIONS FROM CONSUMPTION OF ENERGY:

643,800 Mt (2017 est.)

country comparison to the world: 178

COMMUNICATIONS :: CAYMAN ISLANDS

TELEPHONES - FIXED LINES:

total subscriptions: 34,116 (July 2016 est.)

subscriptions per 100 inhabitants: 60 (July 2016 est.)

country comparison to the world: 168

TELEPHONES - MOBILE CELLULAR:

total subscriptions: 95,656 (July 2016 est.)

subscriptions per 100 inhabitants: 164 (July 2016 est.)

country comparison to the world: 192

TELEPHONE SYSTEM:

general assessment: reasonably good overall telephone system with a high fixed-line teledensity; given the high dependence of tourism and activities such as fisheries and offshore financial services, the telecom sector provides a relatively high contribution to overall GDP; good competion in all sectors promotes advancement in mobile telephony and data segments (2018)

domestic: introduction of competition in the mobile-cellular market in 2004 boosted subscriptions dramatically; 60 per 100 fixed-line, 164 per 100 mobile-cellular (2018)

international: country code - 1-345; landing points for the Maya-1, Eastern Caribbean Fiber System (ECFS), and the Cayman-Jamaica Fiber System submarine cables that provide links to the US and parts of Central and South America; satellite earth station - 1 Intelsat (Atlantic Ocean) (2015)

BROADCAST MEDIA:

4 TV stations; cable and satellite subscription services offer a variety of international programming; government-owned Radio Cayman operates 2 networks broadcasting on 5 stations; 10 privately owned radio stations operate alongside Radio Cayman (2007)

INTERNET COUNTRY CODE:

.ky

INTERNET USERS:

total: 45,242 (July 2016 est.)

percent of population: 79% (July 2016 est.)

country comparison to the world: 197

BROADBAND - FIXED SUBSCRIPTIONS:

total: 24,535 (2017 est.)

subscriptions per 100 inhabitants: 42 (2017 est.)

country comparison to the world: 145

TRANSPORTATION :: CAYMAN ISLANDS

NATIONAL AIR TRANSPORT SYSTEM:

number of registered air carriers: 1 (2015)

inventory of registered aircraft operated by air carriers: 6 (2015)

CIVIL AIRCRAFT REGISTRATION COUNTRY CODE PREFIX:

VP-C (2016)

AIRPORTS:

3 (2013)

country comparison to the world: 194

AIRPORTS - WITH PAVED RUNWAYS:

total: 3 (2017)

1,524 to 2,437 m: 2 (2017)

914 to 1,523 m: 1 (2017)

AIRPORTS - WITH UNPAVED RUNWAYS:

total: 1 (2012)

914 to 1,523 m: 1 (2012)

ROADWAYS:

total: 785 km (2007)

paved: 785 km (2007)

country comparison to the world: 190

MERCHANT MARINE:

total: 161 (2017)

by type: bulk carrier 29, general cargo 4, oil tanker 16, other 112 (2017)

country comparison to the world: 70

PORTS AND TERMINALS:

major seaport(s): Cayman Brac, George Town

MILITARY AND SECURITY :: CAYMAN ISLANDS

MILITARY BRANCHES:

no regular military forces; Royal Cayman Islands Police Force (2012)

MILITARY - NOTE:

defense is the responsibility of the UK

TRANSNATIONAL ISSUES :: CAYMAN ISLANDS

DISPUTES - INTERNATIONAL:

none

ILLICIT DRUGS:

major offshore financial center; vulnerable to drug transshipment to the US and Europe

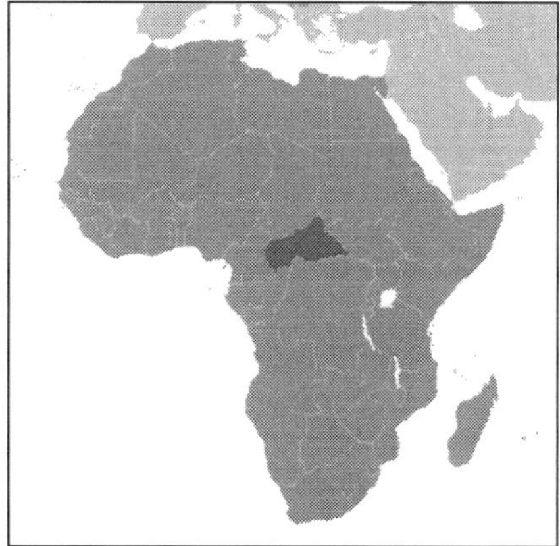

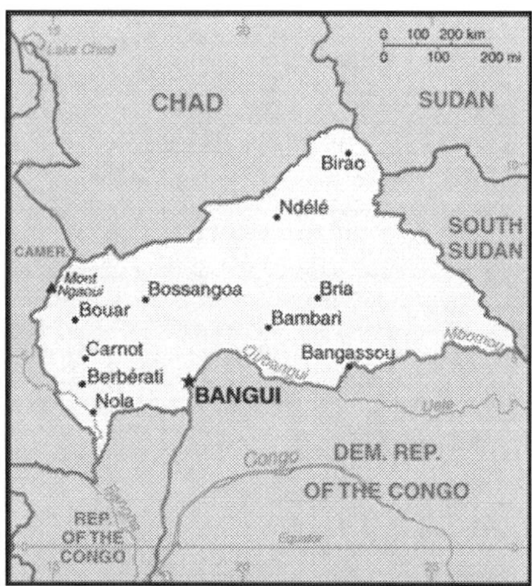

AFRICA :: CENTRAL AFRICAN REPUBLIC

INTRODUCTION :: CENTRAL AFRICAN REPUBLIC

BACKGROUND:

The former French colony of Ubangi-Shari became the Central African Republic upon independence in 1960. After three tumultuous decades of misrule - mostly by military governments - civilian rule was established in 1993 but lasted only a decade. In March 2003, President Ange-Felix PATASSE was deposed in a military coup led by General Francois BOZIZE, who established a transitional government. Elections held in 2005 affirmed General BOZIZE as president; he was reelected in 2011 in voting widely viewed as flawed. The government still lacks full control of the countryside, where lawlessness persists. Several rebel groups joined together in early December 2012 to launch a series of attacks that left them in control of numerous towns in the northern and central parts of the country. The rebels - unhappy with BOZIZE's government - participated in peace talks in early January 2013 which resulted in a coalition government including the rebellion's leadership. In March 2013, the coalition government dissolved, rebels seized the capital, and President BOZIZE fled the country. Rebel leader Michel DJOTODIA assumed the presidency and the following month established a National Transitional Council (CNT). In January 2014, the CNT elected Catherine SAMBA-PANZA as interim president. Elections completed in March 2016 installed independent candidate Faustin-Archange TOUADERA as president; he continues to work towards peace between the government and armed groups, and is developing a disarmament, demobilization, reintegration, and repatriation program to reintegrate the armed groups into society.

GEOGRAPHY :: CENTRAL AFRICAN REPUBLIC

LOCATION:

Central Africa, north of Democratic Republic of the Congo

GEOGRAPHIC COORDINATES:

7 00 N, 21 00 E

MAP REFERENCES:

Africa

AREA:

total: 622,984 sq km

land: 622,984 sq km

water: 0 sq km

country comparison to the world: 46

AREA - COMPARATIVE:

slightly smaller than Texas

LAND BOUNDARIES:

total: 5,920 km

border countries (6): Cameroon 901 km, Chad 1556 km, Democratic Republic of the Congo 1747 km, Republic of the Congo 487 km, South Sudan 1055 km, Sudan 174 km

COASTLINE:

0 km (landlocked)

MARITIME CLAIMS:

none (landlocked)

CLIMATE:

tropical; hot, dry winters; mild to hot, wet summers

TERRAIN:

vast, flat to rolling plateau; scattered hills in northeast and southwest

ELEVATION:

mean elevation: 635 m

elevation extremes: 335 m lowest point: Oubangui River

1410 highest point: Mont Ngaoui

NATURAL RESOURCES:

diamonds, uranium, timber, gold, oil, hydropower

LAND USE:

agricultural land: 8.1% (2011 est.)

arable land: 2.9% (2011 est.) / permanent crops: 0.1% (2011 est.) / permanent pasture: 5.1% (2011 est.)

forest: 36.2% (2011 est.)

other: 55.7% (2011 est.)

IRRIGATED LAND:

10 sq km (2012)

POPULATION DISTRIBUTION:

majority of residents live in the western and central areas of the country, especially in and around the capital of Bangui

NATURAL HAZARDS:

hot, dry, dusty harmattan winds affect northern areas; floods are common

ENVIRONMENT - CURRENT ISSUES:

water pollution; tap water is not potable; poaching and mismanagement have diminished the country's reputation as one of the last great wildlife refuges; desertification; deforestation; soil erosion

ENVIRONMENT - INTERNATIONAL AGREEMENTS:

party to: Biodiversity, Climate Change, Climate Change-Kyoto Protocol, Desertification, Endangered Species, Hazardous Wastes, Ozone Layer Protection, Tropical Timber 94, Wetlands

signed, but not ratified: Law of the Sea

GEOGRAPHY - NOTE:

landlocked; almost the precise center of Africa

PEOPLE AND SOCIETY :: CENTRAL AFRICAN REPUBLIC

POPULATION:

5,745,062 (July 2018 est.)

note: estimates for this country explicitly take into account the effects of excess mortality due to AIDS; this can result in lower life expectancy, higher infant mortality, higher death rates, lower population growth rates, and changes in the distribution of population by age and sex than would otherwise be expected

country comparison to the world: 116

NATIONALITY:

noun: Central African(s)

adjective: Central African

ETHNIC GROUPS:

Baya 33%, Banda 27%, Mandjia 13%, Sara 10%, Mboum 7%, M'Baka 4%, Yakoma 4%, other 2%

LANGUAGES:

French (official), Sangho (lingua franca and national language), tribal languages

RELIGIONS:

indigenous beliefs 35%, Protestant 25%, Roman Catholic 25%, Muslim 15%

note: animistic beliefs and practices strongly influence the Christian majority

DEMOGRAPHIC PROFILE:

The Central African Republic's (CAR) humanitarian crisis has worsened since a coup in March 2013. CAR's high mortality rate and low life expectancy are attributed to elevated rates of preventable and treatable diseases (including malaria and malnutrition), an inadequate health care system, precarious food security, and armed conflict. Some of the worst mortality rates are in western CAR's diamond mining region, which is impoverished because of government attempts to control the diamond trade and the fall in industrial diamond prices. To make matters worse, the government and international donors have reduced health funding in recent years. The CAR's weak educational system and low literacy rate have also suffered as a result of the country's ongoing conflict. Schools are closed, qualified teachers are scarce, infrastructure, funding, and supplies are lacking and subject to looting, and many students and teachers are displaced by violence.

Rampant poverty, human rights violations, unemployment, poor infrastructure, and a lack of security and stability have led to forced displacement internally and externally. Since the political crisis that resulted in CAR's March 2013 coup began in December 2012, approximately 370,000 people have fled to Chad, the Democratic Republic of the Congo (DRC), and other neighboring countries, while more than an estimated 600,000 are displaced internally as of October 2017. The UN has urged countries to refrain from repatriating CAR refugees amid the heightened lawlessness.

AGE STRUCTURE:

0-14 years: 39.89% (male 1,151,724 /female 1,140,083)

15-24 years: 19.91% (male 574,969 /female 568,942)

25-54 years: 32.64% (male 938,365 /female 936,948)

55-64 years: 4.17% (male 112,310 /female 127,045)

65 years and over: 3.39% (male 75,401 /female 119,275) (2018 est.)

DEPENDENCY RATIOS:

total dependency ratio: 90 (2015 est.)

youth dependency ratio: 83.1 (2015 est.)

elderly dependency ratio: 7 (2015 est.)

potential support ratio: 14.4 (2015 est.)

MEDIAN AGE:

total: 19.8 years

male: 19.5 years

female: 20.1 years (2018 est.)

country comparison to the world: 197

POPULATION GROWTH RATE:

2.11% (2018 est.)

country comparison to the world: 43

BIRTH RATE:

34 births/1,000 population (2018 est.)

country comparison to the world: 24

DEATH RATE:

12.9 deaths/1,000 population (2018 est.)

country comparison to the world: 11

NET MIGRATION RATE:

0 migrant(s)/1,000 population (2017 est.)

country comparison to the world: 78

POPULATION DISTRIBUTION:

majority of residents live in the western and central areas of the country, especially in and around the capital of Bangui

URBANIZATION:

urban population: 41.4% of total population (2018)

rate of urbanization: 2.52% annual rate of change (2015-20 est.)

MAJOR URBAN AREAS - POPULATION:

851,000 BANGUI (capital) (2018)

SEX RATIO:

at birth: 1.02 male(s)/female (2017 est.)

0-14 years: 1.01 male(s)/female (2017 est.)

15-24 years: 1.01 male(s)/female (2017 est.)

25-54 years: 1 male(s)/female (2017 est.)

55-64 years: 0.84 male(s)/female (2017 est.)

65 years and over: 0.64 male(s)/female (2017 est.)

total population: 0.98 male(s)/female (2017 est.)

MATERNAL MORTALITY RATE:

882 deaths/100,000 live births (2015 est.)

country comparison to the world: 2

INFANT MORTALITY RATE:

total: 84.3 deaths/1,000 live births (2018 est.)

male: 91.6 deaths/1,000 live births (2018 est.)

female: 76.7 deaths/1,000 live births (2018 est.)

country comparison to the world: 4

LIFE EXPECTANCY AT BIRTH:

total population: 53.3 years (2018 est.)

male: 51.9 years (2018 est.)

female: 54.7 years (2018 est.)

country comparison to the world: 219

TOTAL FERTILITY RATE:

4.25 children born/woman (2018 est.)

country comparison to the world: 29

CONTRACEPTIVE PREVALENCE RATE:

15.2% (2010/11)

HEALTH EXPENDITURES:

4.2% of GDP (2014)

country comparison to the world: 162

PHYSICIANS DENSITY:

0.05 physicians/1,000 population (2009)

HOSPITAL BED DENSITY:

1 beds/1,000 population (2011)

DRINKING WATER SOURCE:

improved:

urban: 89.6% of population

rural: 54.4% of population

total: 68.5% of population

unimproved:

urban: 10.4% of population

rural: 45.6% of population

total: 31.5% of population (2015 est.)

SANITATION FACILITY ACCESS:

improved:

urban: 43.6% of population (2015 est.)

rural: 7.2% of population (2015 est.)

total: 21.8% of population (2015 est.)

unimproved:

urban: 56.4% of population (2015 est.)

rural: 92.8% of population (2015 est.)

total: 78.2% of population (2015 est.)

HIV/AIDS - ADULT PREVALENCE RATE:

4% (2017 est.)

country comparison to the world: 15

HIV/AIDS - PEOPLE LIVING WITH HIV/AIDS:

110,000 (2017 est.)

country comparison to the world: 41

HIV/AIDS - DEATHS:

5,200 (2017 est.)

country comparison to the world: 26

MAJOR INFECTIOUS DISEASES:

degree of risk: very high (2016)

food or waterborne diseases: bacterial and protozoal diarrhea, hepatitis A and E, and typhoid fever (2016)

vectorborne diseases: malaria and dengue fever (2016)

water contact diseases: schistosomiasis (2016)

animal contact diseases: rabies (2016)

respiratory diseases: meningococcal meningitis (2016)

OBESITY - ADULT PREVALENCE RATE:

7.5% (2016)

country comparison to the world: 159

CHILDREN UNDER THE AGE OF 5 YEARS UNDERWEIGHT:

23.5% (2010)

country comparison to the world: 21

EDUCATION EXPENDITURES:

1.2% of GDP (2011)

country comparison to the world: 177

LITERACY:

definition: age 15 and over can read and write (2015 est.)

total population: 36.8% (2015 est.)

male: 50.7% (2015 est.)

female: 24.4% (2015 est.)

SCHOOL LIFE EXPECTANCY (PRIMARY TO TERTIARY EDUCATION):

total: 7 years (2012)

male: 8 years (2012)

female: 6 years (2012)

GOVERNMENT :: CENTRAL AFRICAN REPUBLIC

COUNTRY NAME:

conventional long form: Central African Republic

conventional short form: none

local long form: Republique Centrafricaine

local short form: none

former: Ubangi-Shari, Central African Empire

abbreviation: CAR

etymology: self-descriptive name specifying the country's location on the continent; "Africa" is derived from the Roman designation of the area corresponding to present-day Tunisia "Africa terra," which meant "Land of the Afri" (the tribe resident in that area), but which eventually came to mean the entire continent

GOVERNMENT TYPE:

presidential republic

CAPITAL:

name: Bangui

geographic coordinates: 4 22 N, 18 35 E

time difference: UTC+1 (6 hours ahead of Washington, DC, during Standard Time)

ADMINISTRATIVE DIVISIONS:

14 prefectures (prefectures, singular - prefecture), 2 economic prefectures* (prefectures economiques, singular - prefecture economique), and 1 commune**; Bamingui-Bangoran, Bangui**, Basse-Kotto, Haute-Kotto, Haut-Mbomou, Kemo, Lobaye, Mambere-Kadei, Mbomou, Nana-Grebizi*, Nana-Mambere, Ombella-Mpoko, Ouaka, Ouham, Ouham-Pende, Sangha-Mbaere*, Vakaga

INDEPENDENCE:

13 August 1960 (from France)

NATIONAL HOLIDAY:

Republic Day, 1 December (1958)

CONSTITUTION:

history: several previous; latest (interim constitution) approved by the Transitional Council 30 August 2015, adopted by referendum 13-14 December 2015, ratified 27 March 2016 (2017)

amendments: proposals require support of the government, two-thirds of the National Council of Transition, and assent by the "Mediator of the Central African" crisis; passage requires at least three-fourths majority vote by the National Council membership; non-amendable constitutional provisions include those on the secular and republican form of government, fundamental rights and freedoms, amendment procedures, or changes to the authorities of various high-level executive, parliamentary, and judicial officials (2017)

LEGAL SYSTEM:

civil law system based on the French model

INTERNATIONAL LAW ORGANIZATION PARTICIPATION:

has not submitted an ICJ jurisdiction declaration; accepts ICCt jurisdiction

CITIZENSHIP:

citizenship by birth: no

citizenship by descent only: least one parent must be a citizen of the Central African Republic

dual citizenship recognized: yes

residency requirement for naturalization: 35 years

SUFFRAGE:

18 years of age; universal

EXECUTIVE BRANCH:

chief of state: President Faustin-Archange TOUADERA (since 30 March 2016)

head of government: Prime Minister Simplice SARANDJI (since 2 April 2016)

cabinet: Council of Ministers appointed by the president

elections/appointments: under the 2015 constitution, the president is elected by universal direct suffrage for a period of 5 years (eligible for a second term); election last held 30 December 2015 with a runoff 20 February 2016 (next to be held in 2020)

election results: Faustin-Archange TOUADERA elected president in the second round; percent of vote in first round - Anicet-Georges DOLOGUELE (URCA) 23.7%, Faustin-Archange TOUADERA (independent) 19.1%, Desire KOLINGBA (RDC) 12.%, Martin ZIGUELE (MLPC) 11.4%, other 33.8%; percent of vote in second round - Faustin-Archange TOUADERA 62.7%, Anicet-Georges DOLOGUELE 37.3%

note: rebel forces seized the capital in March 2013, forcing former President BOZIZE to flee the country; Interim President Michel DJOTODIA assumed the presidency, reinstated the prime minister, and established a National Transitional Council (CNT) in April 2013; the NTC elected Catherine SAMBA-PANZA interim president in January 2014 to serve until February 2015, when new elections were to be held; her term was extended because instability delayed new elections and the transition did not take place until the end of March 2016

LEGISLATIVE BRANCH:

description: unicameral National Assembly or Assemblee Nationale (140 seats; members directly elected in single-seat constituencies by absolute majority vote with a second round if needed; members serve 5-year terms)

elections: last held 30 December 2015 (results annulled), 14 February 2016 - first round and 31 March 2016 - second round (next to be held in 2021)

election results: percent of vote by party - NA; seats by party - UNDP 16, URCA 11, RDC 8, MLPC 10, KNK 7, other 28, independent 60

JUDICIAL BRANCH:

highest courts: Supreme Court or Cour Supreme (consists of NA judges); Constitutional Court (consists of 9 judges, at least 3 of whom are women)

judge selection and term of office: Supreme Court judges appointed by the president; Constitutional Court judge appointments - 2 by the president, 1 by the speaker of the National Assembly, 2 elected by their peers, 2 are advocates elected by their peers, and 2 are law professors elected by their peers; judges serve 7-year non-renewable terms

subordinate courts: high courts; magistrates' courts

POLITICAL PARTIES AND LEADERS:

Action Party for Development or PAD [El Hadj Laurent NGON-BABA]
Alliance for Democracy and Progress or ADP [Clement BELIBANGA]
Central African Democratic Rally or RDC [Desire Nzanga KOLINGBA]
Movement for Democracy and Development or MDD [Louis PAPENIAH]
Movement for the Liberation of the Central African People or MLPC [Martin ZIGUELE]
National Convergence (also known as Kwa Na Kwa) or KNK [Francois BOZIZE]
National Union for Democracy and Progress or UNDP [Amine MICHEL]
New Alliance for Progress or NAP [Jean-Jacques DEMAFOUTH]
Social Democratic Party or PSD [Enoch LAKOUE]
Union for Central African Renewal or URCA [Anicet-Georges DOLOGUELE]

INTERNATIONAL ORGANIZATION PARTICIPATION:

ACP, AfDB, AU, BDEAC, CEMAC, EITI (compliant country) (suspended), FAO, FZ, G-77, IAEA, IBRD, ICAO, ICCt, ICRM, IDA, IFAD, IFC, IFRCS, ILO, IMF, Interpol, IOC, IOM, ITSO, ITU, ITUC (NGOs), MIGA, NAM, OIC (observer), OIF, OPCW, UN, UNCTAD, UNESCO, UNIDO, UNWTO, UPU, WCO, WHO, WIPO, WMO, WTO

DIPLOMATIC REPRESENTATION IN THE US:

chief of mission: Ambassador Martial NDOUBOU (since 17 September 2018)

chancery: 2704 Ontario Road NW, Washington, DC 20009

telephone: [1] (202) 483-7800

FAX: [1] (202) 332-9893

DIPLOMATIC REPRESENTATION FROM THE US:

chief of mission: Ambassador (vacant); Charge d'Affaires David P. BROWNSTEIN (since September 2017)

embassy: Avenue David Dacko, Bangui

mailing address: P.O. Box 924, Bangui

telephone: [236] 21 61 0200

FAX: [236] 21 61 4494

FLAG DESCRIPTION:

four equal horizontal bands of blue (top), white, green, and yellow with a vertical red band in center; a yellow five-pointed star to the hoist side of the blue band; banner combines the Pan-African and French flag colors; red symbolizes the blood spilled in the struggle for independence, blue represents the sky and freedom, white peace and dignity, green hope and faith, and yellow tolerance; the star represents aspiration towards a vibrant future

NATIONAL SYMBOL(S):

elephant; national colors: blue, white, green, yellow, red

NATIONAL ANTHEM:

name: "Le Renaissance" (The Renaissance)

lyrics/music: Barthelemy BOGANDA/Herbert PEPPER

note: adopted 1960; Barthelemy BOGANDA wrote the anthem's lyrics and was the first prime minister of the autonomous French territory

ECONOMY :: CENTRAL AFRICAN REPUBLIC

ECONOMY - OVERVIEW:

Subsistence agriculture, together with forestry and mining, remains the backbone of the economy of the Central African Republic (CAR), with about 60% of the population living in outlying areas. The agricultural sector generates more than half of estimated GDP, although statistics are unreliable in the conflict-prone country. Timber and diamonds account for most export earnings, followed by cotton. Important constraints to economic development include the CAR's landlocked geography, poor transportation system, largely unskilled work force, and legacy of misdirected macroeconomic policies. Factional fighting between the government and its opponents remains a drag on economic revitalization. Distribution of income is highly unequal and grants from the international community can only partially meet humanitarian needs. CAR shares a common currency with the Central African Monetary Union. The currency is pegged to the Euro.

Since 2009, the IMF has worked closely with the government to institute reforms that have resulted in some improvement in budget transparency, but other problems remain. The government's additional spending in the run-up to the 2011 election worsened CAR's fiscal situation. In 2012, the World Bank approved $125 million in funding for transport infrastructure and regional trade, focused on the route between CAR's capital and the port of Douala in Cameroon. In July 2016, the IMF approved a three-year extended credit facility valued at $116 million; in mid-2017, the IMF completed a review of CAR's fiscal performance and broadly approved of the government's management, although issues with revenue collection, weak government capacity, and transparency remain. The World Bank in late 2016 approved a $20 million grant to restore basic fiscal management, improve transparency, and assist with economic recovery.

Participation in the Kimberley Process, a commitment to remove conflict diamonds from the global supply chain, led to a partially lifted the ban on diamond exports from CAR in 2015, but persistent insecurity is likely to constrain real GDP growth.

GDP (PURCHASING POWER PARITY):

$3.39 billion (2017 est.)

$3.249 billion (2016 est.)

$3.108 billion (2015 est.)

note: data are in 2017 dollars

country comparison to the world: 185

GDP (OFFICIAL EXCHANGE RATE):

$1.937 billion (2017 est.) (2017 est.)

GDP - REAL GROWTH RATE:

4.3% (2017 est.)

4.5% (2016 est.)

4.8% (2015 est.)

country comparison to the world: 67

GDP - PER CAPITA (PPP):

$700 (2017 est.)

$700 (2016 est.)

$600 (2015 est.)

note: data are in 2017 dollars

country comparison to the world: 228

GROSS NATIONAL SAVING:

5.4% of GDP (2017 est.)

8.2% of GDP (2016 est.)

4.2% of GDP (2015 est.)

country comparison to the world: 175

GDP - COMPOSITION, BY END USE:

household consumption: 95.3% (2017 est.)

government consumption: 8.5% (2017 est.)

investment in fixed capital: 13.7% (2017 est.)

investment in inventories: 0% (2017 est.)

exports of goods and services: 12% (2017 est.)

imports of goods and services: -29.5% (2017 est.)

GDP - COMPOSITION, BY SECTOR OF ORIGIN:

agriculture: 43.2% (2017 est.)

industry: 16% (2017 est.)

services: 40.8% (2017 est.)

AGRICULTURE - PRODUCTS:

cotton, coffee, tobacco, cassava (manioc, tapioca), yams, millet, corn, bananas; timber

INDUSTRIES:

gold and diamond mining, logging, brewing, sugar refining

INDUSTRIAL PRODUCTION GROWTH RATE:

3.9% (2017 est.)

country comparison to the world: 77

LABOR FORCE:

2.242 million (2017 est.)

country comparison to the world: 120

UNEMPLOYMENT RATE:

6.9% (2017 est.)

country comparison to the world: 103

POPULATION BELOW POVERTY LINE:

62% NA (2008 est.)

HOUSEHOLD INCOME OR CONSUMPTION BY PERCENTAGE SHARE:

lowest 10%: 33% (2003)

highest 10%: 33% (2003)

DISTRIBUTION OF FAMILY INCOME - GINI INDEX:

43.6 (2003 est.)

61.3 (1993)

country comparison to the world: 46

BUDGET:

revenues: 282.9 million (2017 est.)

expenditures: 300.1 million (2017 est.)

TAXES AND OTHER REVENUES:

14.6% (of GDP) (2017 est.)

country comparison to the world: 198

BUDGET SURPLUS (+) OR DEFICIT (-):

-0.9% (of GDP) (2017 est.)

country comparison to the world: 71

PUBLIC DEBT:

52.9% of GDP (2017 est.)

56% of GDP (2016 est.)

country comparison to the world: 93

FISCAL YEAR:

calendar year

INFLATION RATE (CONSUMER PRICES):

4.1% (2017 est.)

4.6% (2016 est.)

country comparison to the world: 159

CENTRAL BANK DISCOUNT RATE:

4.25% (31 December 2009)

4.75% (31 December 2008)

country comparison to the world: 90

COMMERCIAL BANK PRIME LENDING RATE:

15.5% (31 December 2017 est.)

15.5% (31 December 2016 est.)

country comparison to the world: 35

STOCK OF NARROW MONEY:

$428.9 million (31 December 2017 est.)

$341.5 million (31 December 2016 est.)

country comparison to the world: 172

STOCK OF BROAD MONEY:

$428.9 million (31 December 2017 est.)

$341.5 million (31 December 2016 est.)

country comparison to the world: 176

STOCK OF DOMESTIC CREDIT:

$547 million (31 December 2017 est.)

$452.7 million (31 December 2016 est.)

country comparison to the world: 177

MARKET VALUE OF PUBLICLY TRADED SHARES:

NA

CURRENT ACCOUNT BALANCE:

-$163 million (2017 est.)

-$97 million (2016 est.)

country comparison to the world: 94

EXPORTS:

$113.7 million (2017 est.)

$101.5 million (2016 est.)

country comparison to the world: 196

EXPORTS - PARTNERS:

France 31.2%, Burundi 16.2%, China 12.5%, Cameroon 9.6%, Austria 7.8% (2017)

EXPORTS - COMMODITIES:

diamonds, timber, cotton, coffee

IMPORTS:

$393.1 million (2017 est.)

$342.2 million (2016 est.)

country comparison to the world: 199

IMPORTS - COMMODITIES:

food, textiles, petroleum products, machinery, electrical equipment, motor vehicles, chemicals, pharmaceuticals

IMPORTS - PARTNERS:

France 17.1%, US 12.3%, India 11.5%, China 8.2%, South Africa 7.4%, Japan 5.8%, Italy 5.1%, Cameroon 4.9%, Netherlands 4.6% (2017)

RESERVES OF FOREIGN EXCHANGE AND GOLD:

$304.3 million (31 December 2017 est.)

$252.5 million (31 December 2016 est.)

country comparison to the world: 168

DEBT - EXTERNAL:

$779.9 million (31 December 2017 est.)

$691.5 million (31 December 2016 est.)

country comparison to the world: 171

EXCHANGE RATES:

Cooperation Financiere en Afrique Centrale francs (XAF) per US dollar -

605.3 (2017 est.)

593.01 (2016 est.)

593.01 (2015 est.)

591.45 (2014 est.)

494.42 (2013 est.)

ENERGY :: CENTRAL AFRICAN REPUBLIC

ELECTRICITY ACCESS:

population without electricity: 4.5 million (2013)

electrification - total population: 3% (2013)

electrification - urban areas: 5% (2013)

electrification - rural areas: 1% (2013)

ELECTRICITY - PRODUCTION:

171.4 million kWh (2016 est.)

country comparison to the world: 194

ELECTRICITY - CONSUMPTION:

159.4 million kWh (2016 est.)

country comparison to the world: 196

ELECTRICITY - EXPORTS:

0 kWh (2016 est.)

country comparison to the world: 119

ELECTRICITY - IMPORTS:

0 kWh (2016 est.)

country comparison to the world: 133

ELECTRICITY - INSTALLED GENERATING CAPACITY:

38,300 kW (2016 est.)

country comparison to the world: 197

ELECTRICITY - FROM FOSSIL FUELS:

50% of total installed capacity (2016 est.)

country comparison to the world: 151

ELECTRICITY - FROM NUCLEAR FUELS:

0% of total installed capacity (2017 est.)

country comparison to the world: 64

ELECTRICITY - FROM HYDROELECTRIC PLANTS:

50% of total installed capacity (2017 est.)

country comparison to the world: 40

ELECTRICITY - FROM OTHER RENEWABLE SOURCES:

1% of total installed capacity (2017 est.)

country comparison to the world: 151

CRUDE OIL - PRODUCTION:

0 bbl/day (2017 est.)

country comparison to the world: 120

CRUDE OIL - EXPORTS:

0 bbl/day (2015 est.)

country comparison to the world: 105

CRUDE OIL - IMPORTS:

0 bbl/day (2015 est.)

country comparison to the world: 108

CRUDE OIL - PROVED RESERVES:

0 bbl (1 January 2018 est.)

country comparison to the world: 117

REFINED PETROLEUM PRODUCTS - PRODUCTION:

0 bbl/day (2017 est.)

country comparison to the world: 129

REFINED PETROLEUM PRODUCTS - CONSUMPTION:

2,800 bbl/day (2016 est.)

country comparison to the world: 189

REFINED PETROLEUM PRODUCTS - EXPORTS:

0 bbl/day (2015 est.)

country comparison to the world: 142

REFINED PETROLEUM PRODUCTS - IMPORTS:

2,799 bbl/day (2015 est.)

country comparison to the world: 185

NATURAL GAS - PRODUCTION:

0 cu m (2017 est.)

country comparison to the world: 115

NATURAL GAS - CONSUMPTION:

0 cu m (2017 est.)

country comparison to the world: 131

NATURAL GAS - EXPORTS:

0 cu m (2017 est.)

country comparison to the world: 81

NATURAL GAS - IMPORTS:

0 cu m (2017 est.)

country comparison to the world: 105

NATURAL GAS - PROVED RESERVES:

0 cu m (1 January 2014 est.)

country comparison to the world: 121

CARBON DIOXIDE EMISSIONS FROM CONSUMPTION OF ENERGY:

413,800 Mt (2017 est.)

country comparison to the world: 187

COMMUNICATIONS :: CENTRAL AFRICAN REPUBLIC

TELEPHONES - FIXED LINES:

total subscriptions: 1,964 (July 2016 est.)

subscriptions per 100 inhabitants: less than 1 (July 2016 est.)

country comparison to the world: 214

TELEPHONES - MOBILE CELLULAR:

total subscriptions: 1,248,346 (July 2016 est.)

subscriptions per 100 inhabitants: 22 (July 2016 est.)

country comparison to the world: 156

TELEPHONE SYSTEM:

general assessment: network consists principally of microwave radio relay and at low-capacity; ongoing conflict has obstructed telecommunication and media development, although there are ISP and mobile phone carriers, radio is the most-popular communications medium (2017)

domestic: very limited telephone service with less than 1 fixed-line connection per 100 persons; with the presence of multiple providers mobile-cellular service has reached 22 per 100 mobile-cellular subscribers; cellular usage is increasing from a low base; most fixed-line and mobile-cellular telephone services are concentrated in Bangui (2017)

international: country code - 236; satellite earth station - 1 Intelsat (Atlantic Ocean) (2015)

BROADCAST MEDIA:

government-owned network, Radiodiffusion Television Centrafricaine, provides limited domestic TV broadcasting; state-owned radio network is supplemented by a small number of privately owned broadcast stations as well as a few community radio stations; transmissions of at least 2 international broadcasters are available (2017)

INTERNET COUNTRY CODE:

.cf

INTERNET USERS:

total: 246,000 (July 2016 est.)

percent of population: 4.6% (July 2016 est.)

country comparison to the world: 166

TRANSPORTATION :: CENTRAL AFRICAN REPUBLIC

NATIONAL AIR TRANSPORT SYSTEM:

number of registered air carriers: 2 (2015)

inventory of registered aircraft operated by air carriers: 2 (2015)

annual passenger traffic on registered air carriers: 46,364 (2015)

annual freight traffic on registered air carriers: 0 mt-km (2015)

CIVIL AIRCRAFT REGISTRATION COUNTRY CODE PREFIX:

TL (2016)

AIRPORTS:

39 (2013)

country comparison to the world: 106

AIRPORTS - WITH PAVED RUNWAYS:

total: 2 (2017)

2,438 to 3,047 m: 1 (2017)

1,524 to 2,437 m: 1 (2017)

AIRPORTS - WITH UNPAVED RUNWAYS:

total: 37 (2013)

2,438 to 3,047 m: 1 (2013)

1,524 to 2,437 m: 11 (2013)

914 to 1,523 m: 19 (2013)

under 914 m: 6 (2013)

ROADWAYS:

total: 20,278 km (2010)

paved: 1,385 km (2010)

unpaved: 18,893 km (2010)

country comparison to the world: 109

WATERWAYS:

2,800 km (the primary navigable river is the Ubangi, which joins the River Congo; it was the traditional route for the export of products because it connected with the Congo-Ocean railway at Brazzaville; because of the warfare on both sides of the River Congo from 1997, importers and exporters preferred routes through Cameroon) (2011)

country comparison to the world: 34

PORTS AND TERMINALS:

river port(s): Bangui (Oubangui)

Nola (Sangha)

MILITARY AND SECURITY :: CENTRAL AFRICAN REPUBLIC

MILITARY BRANCHES:

Central African Armed Forces (Forces Armees Centrafricaines, FACA): Ground Forces (includes Military Air Service), General Directorate of Gendarmerie Inspection (DGIG), National Police (2017)

MILITARY SERVICE AGE AND OBLIGATION:

18 years of age for military service; no conscription (2017)

TRANSNATIONAL ISSUES :: CENTRAL AFRICAN REPUBLIC

DISPUTES - INTERNATIONAL:

periodic skirmishes persist over water and grazing rights among related pastoral populations along the border with southern Sudan

REFUGEES AND INTERNALLY DISPLACED PERSONS:

IDPs: 547,814 (clashes between army and rebel groups since 2005; tensions between ethnic groups) (2018)

TRAFFICKING IN PERSONS:

current situation: Central African Republic (CAR) is a source, transit, and destination country for children subjected to forced labor and sex trafficking, women subjected to forced prostitution, and adults subjected to forced labor; most victims appear to be CAR citizens exploited within the country, with a smaller number transported back and forth between the CAR and nearby countries; armed groups operating in the CAR, including those aligned with the former SELEKA Government and the Lord's Resistance Army, continue to recruit and re-recruit children for military activities and labor; children are also subject to domestic servitude, commercial sexual exploitation, and forced labor in agriculture, mines, shops, and street vending; women and girls are subject to domestic servitude, sexual slavery, commercial sexual exploitation, and forced marriage

tier rating: Tier 3 – the Central African Republic does not fully comply with the minimum standards for the elimination of trafficking and is not making significant efforts to do so;

the government conducted a limited number of investigations and prosecutions of cases of suspected human trafficking in 2014 but did not identify, provide protection to, or refer to care providers any trafficking victims; the government did not directly provide reintegration programs for demobilized child soldiers, leaving victims vulnerable to further exploitation or retrafficking by armed groups, including those affiliated with the government; in 2014, an NGO and the government began drafting a national action plan against trafficking but no efforts were reported to establish a policy against child soldiering or to raise awareness about existing laws prohibiting the use of children in the armed forces (2015)

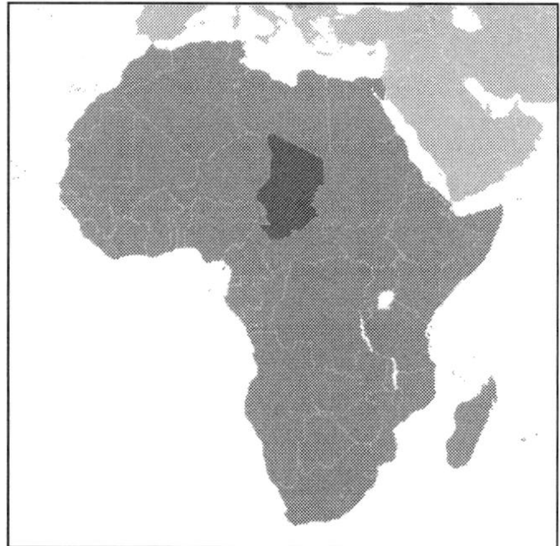

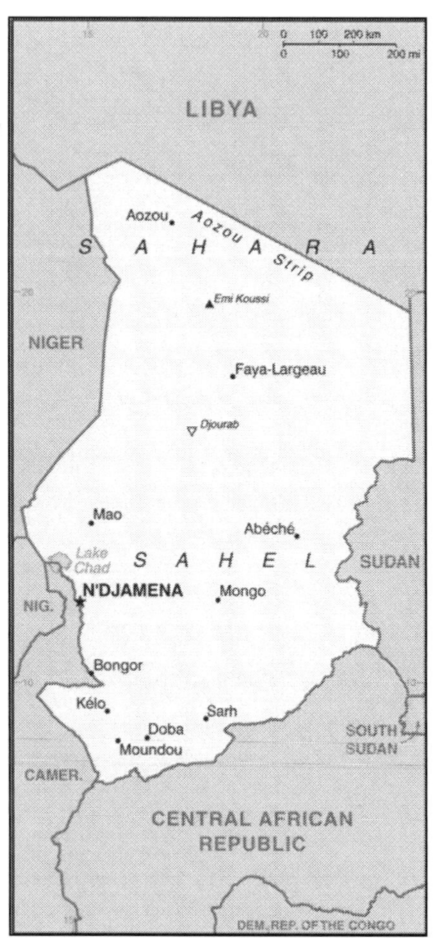

AFRICA :: CHAD

INTRODUCTION :: CHAD

BACKGROUND:

Chad, part of France's African holdings until 1960, endured three decades of civil warfare, as well as invasions by Libya, before peace was restored in 1990. The government eventually drafted a democratic constitution and held flawed presidential elections in 1996 and 2001. In 1998, a rebellion broke out in northern Chad, which has sporadically flared up despite several peace agreements between the government and insurgents. In June 2005, President Idriss DEBY held a referendum successfully removing constitutional term limits and won another controversial election in 2006. Sporadic rebel campaigns continued throughout 2006 and 2007. The capital experienced a significant insurrection in early 2008, but has had no significant rebel threats since then, in part due to Chad's 2010 rapprochement with Sudan, which previously used Chadian rebels as proxies. In late 2015, the government imposed a state of emergency in the Lake Chad region following multiple attacks by the terrorist group Boko Haram throughout the year; Boko Haram also launched several bombings in N'Djamena in mid-2015. DEBY in 2016 was reelected to his fifth term in an election that was peaceful but flawed. In December 2015, Chad completed a two-year rotation on the UN Security Council. In January 2017, DEBY completed a one-year term as Chairperson of the African Union Assembly.

GEOGRAPHY :: CHAD

LOCATION:

Central Africa, south of Libya

GEOGRAPHIC COORDINATES:

15 00 N, 19 00 E

MAP REFERENCES:

Africa

AREA:

total: 1.284 million sq km

land: 1,259,200 sq km

water: 24,800 sq km

country comparison to the world: 22

AREA - COMPARATIVE:

almost nine times the size of New York state; slightly more than three times the size of California

LAND BOUNDARIES:

total: 6,406 km

border countries (6): Cameroon 1116 km, Central African Republic 1556 km, Libya 1050 km, Niger 1196 km, Nigeria 85 km, Sudan 1403 km

COASTLINE:

0 km (landlocked)

MARITIME CLAIMS:

none (landlocked)

CLIMATE:

tropical in south, desert in north

TERRAIN:

broad, arid plains in center, desert in north, mountains in northwest, lowlands in south

ELEVATION:

mean elevation: 543 m

elevation extremes: 160 m lowest point: Djourab

3445 highest point: Emi Koussi

NATURAL RESOURCES:

petroleum, uranium, natron, kaolin, fish (Lake Chad), gold, limestone, sand and gravel, salt

LAND USE:

agricultural land: 39.6% (2011 est.)

arable land: 3.9% (2011 est.) / permanent crops: 0% (2011 est.) / permanent pasture: 35.7% (2011 est.)

forest: 9.1% (2011 est.)

other: 51.3% (2011 est.)

IRRIGATED LAND:

300 sq km (2012)

POPULATION DISTRIBUTION:

the population is unevenly distributed due to contrasts in climate and physical geography; the highest density is found in the southwest, particularly around Lake Chad and points south; the dry Saharan zone to the north is the least densely populated

NATURAL HAZARDS:

hot, dry, dusty harmattan winds occur in north; periodic droughts; locust plagues

ENVIRONMENT - CURRENT ISSUES:

inadequate supplies of potable water; improper waste disposal in rural areas and poor farming practices contribute to soil and water pollution; desertification

ENVIRONMENT - INTERNATIONAL AGREEMENTS:

party to: Biodiversity, Climate Change, Desertification, Endangered Species, Hazardous Wastes, Ozone Layer Protection, Wetlands

signed, but not ratified: Law of the Sea, Marine Dumping

GEOGRAPHY - NOTE:

note 1: Chad is the largest of Africa's 16 landlocked countries

note 2: not long ago - geologically speaking - what is today the Sahara was green savannah teeming with wildlife; during the African Humid Period, roughly 11,000 to 5,000 years ago, a vibrant animal community, including elephants, giraffes, hippos, and antelope lived there; the last remnant of the "Green Sahara" exists in the Lakes of Ounianga (oo-nee-ahn-ga) in northern Chad, a series of 18 interconnected freshwater, saline, and hypersaline lakes now protected as a World Heritage site

note 3: Lake Chad, the most significant water body in the Sahel, is a remnant of a former inland sea, paleolake Mega-Chad; at its greatest extent, sometime before 5000 B.C., Lake Mega-Chad was the largest of four Saharan paleolakes that existed during the African Humid Period; it covered an area of about 400,000 sq km (150,000 sq mi), roughly the size of today's Caspian Sea

PEOPLE AND SOCIETY :: CHAD

POPULATION:

15,833,116 (July 2018 est.)

country comparison to the world: 71

NATIONALITY:

noun: Chadian(s)

adjective: Chadian

ETHNIC GROUPS:

Sara (Ngambaye/Sara/Madjingaye/Mbaye) 30.5%, Kanembu/Bornu/Buduma 9.8%, Arab 9.7%, Wadai/Maba/Masalit/Mimi 7%, Gorane 5.8%, Masa/Musseye/Musgum 4.9%, Bulala/Medogo/Kuka 3.7%, Marba/Lele/Mesme 3.5%, Mundang 2.7%, Bidiyo/Migaama/Kenga/Dangleat 2.5%, Dadjo/Kibet/Muro 2.4%, Tupuri/Kera 2%, Gabri/Kabalaye/Nanchere/Somrai 2%, Fulani/Fulbe/Bodore 1.8%, Karo/Zime/Peve 1.3%, Baguirmi/Barma 1.2%, Zaghawa/Bideyat/Kobe 1.1%, Tama/Assongori/Mararit 1.1%, Mesmedje/Massalat/Kadjakse 0.8%, other Chadian ethnicities 3.4%, Chadians of foreign ethnicities 0.9%, foreign nationals 0.3%, unspecified 1.7% (2014-15 est.)

LANGUAGES:

French (official), Arabic (official), Sara (in south), Sara more than 120 different languages and dialects

RELIGIONS:

Muslim 52.1%, Protestant 23.9%, Roman Catholic 20%, animist 0.3%, other Christian 0.2%, none 2.8%, unspecified 0.7% (2014-15 est.)

DEMOGRAPHIC PROFILE:

Despite the start of oil production in 2003, 40% of Chad's population lives below the poverty line. The population will continue to grow rapidly because of the country's very high fertility rate and large youth cohort – more than 65% of the populace is under the age of 25 – although the mortality rate is high and life expectancy is low. Chad has the world's third highest maternal mortality rate. Among the primary risk factors are poverty, anemia, rural habitation, high fertility, poor education, and a lack of access to family planning and obstetric care. Impoverished, uneducated adolescents living in rural areas are most affected. To improve women's reproductive health and reduce fertility, Chad will need to increase women's educational attainment, job participation, and knowledge of and access to family planning. Only about a quarter of women are literate, less than 5% use contraceptives, and more than 40% undergo genital cutting.

As of October 2017, more than 320,000 refugees from Sudan and more than 75,000 from the Central African Republic strain Chad's limited resources and create tensions in host communities. Thousands of new refugees fled to Chad in 2013 to escape worsening violence in the Darfur region of Sudan. The large refugee populations are hesitant to return to their home countries because of continued instability. Chad was relatively stable in 2012 in comparison to other states in the region, but past fighting between government forces and opposition groups and inter-communal violence have left nearly 60,000 of its citizens displaced in the eastern part of the country.

AGE STRUCTURE:

0-14 years: 48.12% (male 3,856,001 /female 3,763,622)

15-24 years: 19.27% (male 1,532,687 /female 1,518,940)

25-54 years: 26.95% (male 2,044,795 /female 2,222,751)

55-64 years: 3.25% (male 228,930 /female 286,379)

65 years and over: 2.39% (male 164,257 /female 214,754) (2018 est.)

DEPENDENCY RATIOS:

total dependency ratio: 100.2 (2015 est.)

youth dependency ratio: 95.2 (2015 est.)

elderly dependency ratio: 4.9 (2015 est.)

potential support ratio: 20.3 (2015 est.)

MEDIAN AGE:

total: 15.8 years

male: 15.3 years

female: 16.3 years (2018 est.)

country comparison to the world: 226

POPULATION GROWTH RATE:

3.23% (2018 est.)

country comparison to the world: 5

BIRTH RATE:

43 births/1,000 population (2018 est.)

country comparison to the world: 4

DEATH RATE:

10.5 deaths/1,000 population (2018 est.)

country comparison to the world: 26

NET MIGRATION RATE:

-3.2 migrant(s)/1,000 population (2017 est.)

country comparison to the world: 176

POPULATION DISTRIBUTION:

the population is unevenly distributed due to contrasts in climate and physical geography; the highest density is found in the southwest, particularly around Lake Chad and points south; the dry Saharan zone to the north is the least densely populated

URBANIZATION:

urban population: 23.1% of total population (2018)

rate of urbanization: 3.88% annual rate of change (2015-20 est.)

MAJOR URBAN AREAS - POPULATION:

1.323 million N'DJAMENA (capital) (2018)

SEX RATIO:

at birth: 1.03 male(s)/female (2017 est.)

0-14 years: 1.03 male(s)/female (2017 est.)

15-24 years: 0.95 male(s)/female (2017 est.)

25-54 years: 0.83 male(s)/female (2017 est.)

55-64 years: 0.79 male(s)/female (2017 est.)

65 years and over: 0.71 male(s)/female (2017 est.)

total population: 0.93 male(s)/female (2017 est.)

MOTHER'S MEAN AGE AT FIRST BIRTH:

17.9 years (2014/15 est.)

note: median age at first birth among women 25-29

MATERNAL MORTALITY RATE:

856 deaths/100,000 live births (2015 est.)

country comparison to the world: 3

INFANT MORTALITY RATE:

total: 71.7 deaths/1,000 live births (2018 est.)

male: 77.8 deaths/1,000 live births (2018 est.)

female: 65.4 deaths/1,000 live births (2018 est.)

country comparison to the world: 6

LIFE EXPECTANCY AT BIRTH:

total population: 57.5 years (2018 est.)

male: 55.7 years (2018 est.)

female: 59.3 years (2018 est.)

country comparison to the world: 214

TOTAL FERTILITY RATE:

5.9 children born/woman (2018 est.)

country comparison to the world: 4

CONTRACEPTIVE PREVALENCE RATE:

5.7% (2014/15)

HEALTH EXPENDITURES:

3.6% of GDP (2014)

country comparison to the world: 169

PHYSICIANS DENSITY:

0.04 physicians/1,000 population (2013)

DRINKING WATER SOURCE:

improved:

urban: 71.8% of population

rural: 44.8% of population

total: 50.8% of population

unimproved:

urban: 28.2% of population

rural: 55.2% of population

total: 49.2% of population (2015 est.)

SANITATION FACILITY ACCESS:

improved:

urban: 31.4% of population (2015 est.)

rural: 6.5% of population (2015 est.)

total: 12.1% of population (2015 est.)

unimproved:

urban: 68.6% of population (2015 est.)

rural: 93.5% of population (2015 est.)

total: 87.9% of population (2015 est.)

HIV/AIDS - ADULT PREVALENCE RATE:

1.3% (2017 est.)

country comparison to the world: 36

HIV/AIDS - PEOPLE LIVING WITH HIV/AIDS:

110,000 (2017 est.)

country comparison to the world: 42

HIV/AIDS - DEATHS:

3,100 (2017 est.)

country comparison to the world: 38

MAJOR INFECTIOUS DISEASES:

degree of risk: very high (2016)

food or waterborne diseases: bacterial and protozoal diarrhea, hepatitis A and E, and typhoid fever (2016)

vectorborne diseases: malaria and dengue fever (2016)

water contact diseases: schistosomiasis (2016)

animal contact diseases: rabies (2016)

respiratory diseases: meningococcal meningitis (2016)

OBESITY - ADULT PREVALENCE RATE:

6.1% (2016)

country comparison to the world: 170

CHILDREN UNDER THE AGE OF 5 YEARS UNDERWEIGHT:

28.8% (2015)

country comparison to the world: 11

EDUCATION EXPENDITURES:

2.9% of GDP (2013)

country comparison to the world: 146

LITERACY:

definition: age 15 and over can read and write French or Arabic (2016 est.)

total population: 22.3% (2016 est.)

male: 31.3% (2016 est.)

female: 14% (2016 est.)

SCHOOL LIFE EXPECTANCY (PRIMARY TO TERTIARY EDUCATION):

total: 7 years (2011)

male: 9 years (2011)

female: 6 years (2011)

GOVERNMENT :: CHAD

COUNTRY NAME:

conventional long form: Republic of Chad

conventional short form: Chad

local long form: Republique du Tchad/Jumhuriyat Tshad

local short form: Tchad/Tshad

etymology: named for Lake Chad, which lies along the country's western border; the word "tsade" means "large body of water" or "lake" in several local native languages

note: the only country whose name is composed of a single syllable with a single vowel

GOVERNMENT TYPE:

presidential republic

CAPITAL:

name: N'Djamena

geographic coordinates: 12 06 N, 15 02 E

time difference: UTC+1 (6 hours ahead of Washington, DC, during Standard Time)

ADMINISTRATIVE DIVISIONS:

23 regions (regions, singular - region); Barh el Gazel, Batha, Borkou, Chari-Baguirmi, Ennedi-Est, Ennedi-Ouest, Guera, Hadjer-Lamis, Kanem, Lac, Logone Occidental, Logone Oriental, Mandoul, Mayo-Kebbi Est, Mayo-Kebbi Ouest, Moyen-Chari, Ouaddai, Salamat, Sila, Tandjile, Tibesti, Ville de N'Djamena, Wadi Fira

INDEPENDENCE:

11 August 1960 (from France)

NATIONAL HOLIDAY:

Independence Day, 11 August (1960)

CONSTITUTION:

history: several previous; latest approved 30 April 2018 by the National Assembly, entered into force 4 May 2018 (2018)

amendments: proposed as a revision by the president of the republic after a Council of Ministers (cabinet) decision or by the National Assembly; approval for consideration of a revision requires at least three-fifths majority vote by the Assembly; passage requires approval by referendum or at least two-thirds majority vote by the Assembly; amended 2005, 2013 (2018)

LEGAL SYSTEM:

mixed legal system of civil and customary law

INTERNATIONAL LAW ORGANIZATION PARTICIPATION:

has not submitted an ICJ jurisdiction declaration; accepts ICCt jurisdiction

CITIZENSHIP:

citizenship by birth: no

citizenship by descent only: both parents must be citizens of Chad

dual citizenship recognized: Chadian law does not address dual citizenship

residency requirement for naturalization: 15 years

SUFFRAGE:

18 years of age; universal

EXECUTIVE BRANCH:

chief of state: President Idriss DEBY Itno, Lt. Gen. (since 4 December 1990)

head of government: President Idriss DEBY Itno, Lt. Gen. (since 4 December 1990); prime minister position eliminated under the 2018 constitution

cabinet: Council of Ministers; members appointed by the president on the recommendation of the prime minister

elections/appointments: president directly elected by absolute majority popular vote in 2 rounds if needed for a 5-year term (no term limits); election last held on 10 April 2016 (next to be held in April 2021); prime minister appointed by the president

election results: Lt. Gen. Idriss DEBY Itno reelected president in first round; percent of vote - Lt. Gen. Idriss DEBY (MPS) 61.6%, Saleh KEBZABO (UNDR) 12.8%, Laokein Kourayo MEDAR (CTPD) 10.7%, Djimrangar DADNADJI (CAP-SUR) 5.1%, other 9.8%

LEGISLATIVE BRANCH:

description: unicameral National Assembly (188 seats; 163 directly elected in multi-seat constituencies by proportional representation vote and 25 directly elected in single-seat constituencies by absolute majority vote with a second round if needed; members serve 4-year terms)

elections: last held on 13 February and 6 May 2011 (next to be held in 2019)

election results: percent of vote by party - NA; seats by party - MPS 117, UNDR 10, RDP 9, RNDT/Le Reveil 8, URD 8, Viva-RNDP 5, FAR 4, CTPD 2, PDSA 2, PUR 2, UDR 2, other minor parties 19

note: the National Assembly mandate was extended to 2019, reportedly due to a lack of funding for the scheduled 2015 election

JUDICIAL BRANCH:

highest courts: Supreme Court (consists of the chief justice, 3 chamber presidents, and 12 judges or councilors and divided into 3 chambers); Constitutional Council (consists of 3 judges and 6 jurists)

judge selection and term of office: Supreme Court chief justice selected by the president; councilors - 8 designated by the president and 7 by the speaker of the National Assembly; chief justice and councilors appointed for life; Constitutional Council judges - 2 appointed by the president and 1 by the speaker of the National Assembly; jurists - 3 each by the president and by the speaker of the National Assembly; judges appointed for 9-year terms

subordinate courts: High Court of Justice; Courts of Appeal; tribunals; justices of the peace

POLITICAL PARTIES AND LEADERS:

Chadian Convention for Peace and Development or CTPD [Laoukein Kourayo MEDAR]
Federation Action for the Republic or FAR [Ngarledjy YORONGAR]
Framework of Popular Action for Solidarity and Unity of the Republic or CAP-SUR [Joseph Djimrangar DADNADJI]
National Rally for Development and Progress or Viva-RNDP [Dr. Nouradine Delwa Kassire COUMAKOYE]
National Union for Democracy and Renewal or UNDR [Saleh KEBZABO]
Party for Liberty and Development or PLD [Ahmat ALHABO]
Party for Unity and Reconciliation
Patriotic Salvation Movement or MPS [Idriss DEBY]Rally for Democracy and Progress or RDP [Mahamat Allahou TAHER]RNDT/Le Reveil [Albert Pahimi PADACKE]
Social Democratic Party for a Change-over of Power or PDSA
Union for Renewal and Democracy or URD [Sande NGARYIMBE]

INTERNATIONAL ORGANIZATION PARTICIPATION:

ACP, AfDB, AU, BDEAC, CEMAC, EITI (compliant country), FAO, FZ, G-77, IAEA, IBRD, ICAO, ICCt, ICRM, IDA, IDB, IFAD, IFC, IFRCS, ILO, IMF, Interpol, IOC, IOM, IPU, ITSO, ITU, ITUC (NGOs), MIGA, MINUSMA, NAM, OIC, OIF, OPCW, UN, UNCTAD, UNESCO, UNIDO, UNOCI, UNWTO, UPU, WCO, WHO, WIPO, WMO, WTO

DIPLOMATIC REPRESENTATION IN THE US:

chief of mission: Ambassador Ngote Gali KOUTOU (since 22 June 2018)

chancery: 2401 Massachusetts Avenue NW, Washington, DC 20008

telephone: [1] (202) 652-1312

FAX: [1] (202) 758-0431

DIPLOMATIC REPRESENTATION FROM THE US:

chief of mission: Ambassador Geeta PASI (since September 2016)

embassy: Chagoua Round Point, N'Djamena

mailing address: B. P. 413, N'Djamena

telephone: [235] 2251-5017

FAX: [235] 2253-9102

FLAG DESCRIPTION:

three equal vertical bands of blue (hoist side), gold, and red; the flag combines the blue and red French (former colonial) colors with the red and yellow (gold) of the Pan-African colors; blue symbolizes the sky, hope, and the south of the country, which is relatively well-watered; gold represents the sun, as well as the desert in the north of the country; red stands for progress, unity, and sacrifice

note: almost identical to the flag of Romania but with a darker shade of blue; also similar to the flags of Andorra and Moldova, both of which have a national coat of arms centered in the yellow band; design based on the flag of France

NATIONAL SYMBOL(S):

goat (north), lion (south); national colors: blue, yellow, red

NATIONAL ANTHEM:

name: "La Tchadienne" (The Chadian)

lyrics/music: Louis GIDROL and his students/Paul VILLARD

note: adopted 1960

ECONOMY :: CHAD

ECONOMY - OVERVIEW:

Chad's landlocked location results in high transportation costs for imported goods and dependence on neighboring countries. Oil and agriculture are mainstays of Chad's economy. Oil provides about 60% of export revenues, while cotton, cattle, livestock, and gum arabic provide the bulk of Chad's non-oil export earnings. The services sector contributes less than one-third of GDP and has attracted foreign investment mostly through telecommunications and banking.

Nearly all of Chad's fuel is provided by one domestic refinery, and unanticipated shutdowns occasionally result in shortages. The country regulates the price of domestic fuel, providing an incentive for black market sales.

Although high oil prices and strong local harvests supported the economy in the past, low oil prices now stress Chad's fiscal position and have resulted in significant government cutbacks. Chad relies on foreign assistance and foreign capital for most of its public and private sector investment. Investment in Chad is difficult due to its limited infrastructure, lack of trained workers, extensive government bureaucracy, and corruption. Chad obtained a three-year extended credit facility from the IMF in 2014 and was granted debt relief under the Heavily Indebted Poor Countries Initiative in April 2015.

In 2018, economic policy will be driven by efforts that started in 2016 to reverse the recession and to repair damage to public finances and exports. The government is implementing an emergency action plan to counterbalance the drop in oil revenue and to diversify the economy. Chad's national development plan (NDP) cost just over $9 billion with a financing gap of $6.7 billion. The NDP emphasized the importance of private sector participation in Chad's development, as well as the need to improve the business environment, particularly in priority sectors such as mining and agriculture.

The Government of Chad reached a deal with Glencore and four other banks on the restructuring of a $1.45 billion oil-backed loan in February 2018, after a long negotiation. The new terms include an extension of the maturity to 2030 from 2022, a two-year grace period on principal repayments, and a lower interest rate of the London Inter-bank Offer Rate (Libor) plus 2% - down from Libor plus 7.5%. The original Glencore loan was to be repaid with crude oil assets, however, Chad's oil sales were hit by the downturn in the price of oil. Chad had secured a $312 million credit from the IMF in June 2017, but release of those funds hinged on restructuring the Glencore debt. Chad had already cut public spending to try to meet the terms of the IMF program, but that prompted strikes and protests in a country where nearly 40% of the population lives below the poverty line. Multinational partners, such as the African Development Bank, the EU, and the World Bank are likely to continue budget support in 2018, but Chad will remain at high debt risk, given its dependence on oil revenue and pressure to spend on subsidies and security.

GDP (PURCHASING POWER PARITY):

$28.62 billion (2017 est.)

$29.55 billion (2016 est.)

$31.58 billion (2015 est.)

note: data are in 2017 dollars

country comparison to the world: 134

GDP (OFFICIAL EXCHANGE RATE):

$9.872 billion (2017 est.) (2017 est.)

GDP - REAL GROWTH RATE:

-3.1% (2017 est.)

-6.4% (2016 est.)

1.8% (2015 est.)

country comparison to the world: 211

GDP - PER CAPITA (PPP):

$2,300 (2017 est.)

$2,500 (2016 est.)

$2,700 (2015 est.)

note: data are in 2017 dollars

country comparison to the world: 202

GROSS NATIONAL SAVING:

15.5% of GDP (2017 est.)

7.5% of GDP (2016 est.)

13.3% of GDP (2015 est.)

country comparison to the world: 133

GDP - COMPOSITION, BY END USE:

household consumption: 75.1% (2017 est.)

government consumption: 4.4% (2017 est.)

investment in fixed capital: 24.1% (2017 est.)

investment in inventories: 0.7% (2017 est.)

exports of goods and services: 35.1% (2017 est.)

imports of goods and services: -39.4% (2017 est.)

GDP - COMPOSITION, BY SECTOR OF ORIGIN:

agriculture: 52.3% (2017 est.)

industry: 14.7% (2017 est.)

services: 33.1% (2017 est.)

AGRICULTURE - PRODUCTS:

cotton, sorghum, millet, peanuts, sesame, corn, rice, potatoes, onions, cassava (manioc, tapioca), cattle, sheep, goats, camels

INDUSTRIES:

oil, cotton textiles, brewing, natron (sodium carbonate), soap, cigarettes, construction materials

INDUSTRIAL PRODUCTION GROWTH RATE:

-4% (2017 est.)

country comparison to the world: 192

LABOR FORCE:

5.654 million (2017 est.)

country comparison to the world: 74

LABOR FORCE - BY OCCUPATION:

agriculture: 80%

industry: 20% (2006 est.)

UNEMPLOYMENT RATE:

NA

POPULATION BELOW POVERTY LINE:

46.7% (2011 est.)

HOUSEHOLD INCOME OR CONSUMPTION BY PERCENTAGE SHARE:

lowest 10%: 30.8% (2003)

highest 10%: 30.8% (2003)

DISTRIBUTION OF FAMILY INCOME - GINI INDEX:

43.3 (2011 est.)

country comparison to the world: 47

BUDGET:

revenues: 1.337 billion (2017 est.)

expenditures: 1.481 billion (2017 est.)

TAXES AND OTHER REVENUES:

13.5% (of GDP) (2017 est.)

country comparison to the world: 206

BUDGET SURPLUS (+) OR DEFICIT (-):

-1.5% (of GDP) (2017 est.)

country comparison to the world: 89

PUBLIC DEBT:

52.5% of GDP (2017 est.)

52.4% of GDP (2016 est.)

country comparison to the world: 94

FISCAL YEAR:

calendar year

INFLATION RATE (CONSUMER PRICES):

-0.9% (2017 est.)

-1.1% (2016 est.)

country comparison to the world: 2

CENTRAL BANK DISCOUNT RATE:

4.25% (31 December 2009)

4.75% (31 December 2008)

country comparison to the world: 91

COMMERCIAL BANK PRIME LENDING RATE:

15.5% (31 December 2017 est.)

15.5% (31 December 2016 est.)

country comparison to the world: 36

STOCK OF NARROW MONEY:

$1.397 billion (31 December 2017 est.)

$1.241 billion (31 December 2016 est.)

country comparison to the world: 144

STOCK OF BROAD MONEY:

$1.397 billion (31 December 2017 est.)

$1.241 billion (31 December 2016 est.)

country comparison to the world: 152

STOCK OF DOMESTIC CREDIT:

$2.681 billion (31 December 2017 est.)

$2.387 billion (31 December 2016 est.)

country comparison to the world: 143

MARKET VALUE OF PUBLICLY TRADED SHARES:

NA

CURRENT ACCOUNT BALANCE:

-$558 million (2017 est.)

-$926 million (2016 est.)

country comparison to the world: 121

EXPORTS:

$2.464 billion (2017 est.)

$2.187 billion (2016 est.)

country comparison to the world: 133

EXPORTS - PARTNERS:

US 38.7%, China 16.6%, Netherlands 15.7%, UAE 12.2%, India 6.3% (2017)

EXPORTS - COMMODITIES:

oil, livestock, cotton, sesame, gum arabic, shea butter

IMPORTS:

$2.16 billion (2017 est.)

$1.997 billion (2016 est.)

country comparison to the world: 163

IMPORTS - COMMODITIES:

machinery and transportation equipment, industrial goods, foodstuffs, textiles

IMPORTS - PARTNERS:

China 19.9%, Cameroon 17.2%, France 17%, US 5.4%, India 4.9%, Senegal 4.5% (2017)

RESERVES OF FOREIGN EXCHANGE AND GOLD:

$22.9 million (31 December 2017 est.)

$20.92 million (31 December 2016 est.)

country comparison to the world: 190

DEBT - EXTERNAL:

$1.724 billion (31 December 2017 est.)

$1.281 billion (31 December 2016 est.)

country comparison to the world: 154

STOCK OF DIRECT FOREIGN INVESTMENT - AT HOME:

$4.5 billion (2006 est.)

country comparison to the world: 107

STOCK OF DIRECT FOREIGN INVESTMENT - ABROAD:

NA

EXCHANGE RATES:

Cooperation Financiere en Afrique Centrale francs (XAF) per US dollar -

605.3 (2017 est.)

593.01 (2016 est.)

593.01 (2015 est.)

591.45 (2014 est.)

494.42 (2013 est.)

ENERGY :: CHAD

ELECTRICITY ACCESS:

population without electricity: 10,477,071 (2013)

electrification - total population: 4% (2013)

electrification - urban areas: 14% (2013)

electrification - rural areas: 1% (2013)

ELECTRICITY - PRODUCTION:

224.3 million kWh (2016 est.)

country comparison to the world: 190

ELECTRICITY - CONSUMPTION:

208.6 million kWh (2016 est.)

country comparison to the world: 192

ELECTRICITY - EXPORTS:

0 kWh (2016 est.)

country comparison to the world: 120

ELECTRICITY - IMPORTS:

0 kWh (2016 est.)

country comparison to the world: 134

ELECTRICITY - INSTALLED GENERATING CAPACITY:

48,200 kW (2016 est.)

country comparison to the world: 192

ELECTRICITY - FROM FOSSIL FUELS:

98% of total installed capacity (2016 est.)

country comparison to the world: 28

ELECTRICITY - FROM NUCLEAR FUELS:

0% of total installed capacity (2017 est.)

country comparison to the world: 65

ELECTRICITY - FROM HYDROELECTRIC PLANTS:

0% of total installed capacity (2017 est.)

country comparison to the world: 164

ELECTRICITY - FROM OTHER RENEWABLE SOURCES:

3% of total installed capacity (2017 est.)

country comparison to the world: 123

CRUDE OIL - PRODUCTION:

128,000 bbl/day (2017 est.)

country comparison to the world: 41

CRUDE OIL - EXPORTS:

70,440 bbl/day (2015 est.)

country comparison to the world: 37

CRUDE OIL - IMPORTS:

0 bbl/day (2015 est.)

country comparison to the world: 109

CRUDE OIL - PROVED RESERVES:

1.5 billion bbl (1 January 2018 est.)

country comparison to the world: 38

REFINED PETROLEUM PRODUCTS - PRODUCTION:

0 bbl/day (2015 est.)

country comparison to the world: 130

REFINED PETROLEUM PRODUCTS - CONSUMPTION:

2,300 bbl/day (2016 est.)

country comparison to the world: 193

REFINED PETROLEUM PRODUCTS - EXPORTS:

0 bbl/day (2015 est.)

country comparison to the world: 143

REFINED PETROLEUM PRODUCTS - IMPORTS:

2,285 bbl/day (2015 est.)

country comparison to the world: 189

NATURAL GAS - PRODUCTION:

0 cu m (2017 est.)

country comparison to the world: 116

NATURAL GAS - CONSUMPTION:

0 cu m (2017 est.)

country comparison to the world: 132

NATURAL GAS - EXPORTS:

0 cu m (2017 est.)

country comparison to the world: 82

NATURAL GAS - IMPORTS:

0 cu m (2017 est.)

country comparison to the world: 106

NATURAL GAS - PROVED RESERVES:

0 cu m (1 January 2014 est.)

country comparison to the world: 122

CARBON DIOXIDE EMISSIONS FROM CONSUMPTION OF ENERGY:

342,200 Mt (2017 est.)

country comparison to the world: 190

COMMUNICATIONS :: CHAD

TELEPHONES - FIXED LINES:

total subscriptions: 14,000 (July 2016 est.)

subscriptions per 100 inhabitants: less than 1 (July 2016 est.)

country comparison to the world: 189

TELEPHONES - MOBILE CELLULAR:

total subscriptions: 6,231,009 (July 2016 est.)

subscriptions per 100 inhabitants: 52 (July 2016 est.)

country comparison to the world: 112

TELEPHONE SYSTEM:

general assessment: inadequate system of radio telephone communication stations with high maintenance costs and low telephone density; Chad remains one of the least developed on the African continent, telecom infrastructure is particularly low, with penetration rates in all sectors - fixed, mobile and internet - well below African averages (2017)

domestic: fixed-line connections less than 1 per 100 persons, with mobile-cellular subscribership base of about 52 per 100 persons (2017)

international: country code - 235; satellite earth station - 1 Intelsat (Atlantic Ocean) (2016)

BROADCAST MEDIA:

1 state-owned TV station; 2 privately-owned TV stations; state-owned radio network, Radiodiffusion Nationale Tchadienne (RNT), operates national and regional stations; over 10 private radio stations; some stations rebroadcast programs from international broadcasters (2017)

INTERNET COUNTRY CODE:

.td

INTERNET USERS:

total: 592,623 (July 2016 est.)

percent of population: 5% (July 2016 est.)

country comparison to the world: 146

BROADBAND - FIXED SUBSCRIPTIONS:

total: 10,470 (2017 est.)

subscriptions per 100 inhabitants: less than 1 (2017 est.)

country comparison to the world: 168

TRANSPORTATION :: CHAD

NATIONAL AIR TRANSPORT SYSTEM:

number of registered air carriers: 1 (2015)

inventory of registered aircraft operated by air carriers: 1 (2015)

annual passenger traffic on registered air carriers: 28,332 (2015)

annual freight traffic on registered air carriers: mt-km (2015)

AIRPORTS:

59 (2013)

country comparison to the world: 82

AIRPORTS - WITH PAVED RUNWAYS:

total: 9 (2017)

over 3,047 m: 2 (2017)

2,438 to 3,047 m: 4 (2017)

1,524 to 2,437 m: 2 (2017)

under 914 m: 1 (2017)

AIRPORTS - WITH UNPAVED RUNWAYS:

total: 50 (2013)

over 3,047 m: 1 (2013)

2,438 to 3,047 m: 2 (2013)

1,524 to 2,437 m: 14 (2013)

914 to 1,523 m: 22 (2013)

under 914 m: 11 (2013)

PIPELINES:

582 km oil (2013)

ROADWAYS:

total: 40,000 km (2011)

note: consists of 25,000 km of national and regional roads and 15,000 km of local roads; 206 km of urban roads are paved

country comparison to the world: 88

WATERWAYS:

(Chari and Legone Rivers are navigable only in wet season) (2012)

MILITARY AND SECURITY :: CHAD

MILITARY EXPENDITURES:

2.79% of GDP (2016)

2.03% of GDP (2015)

2.82% of GDP (2014)

5.61% of GDP (2013)

country comparison to the world: 33

MILITARY BRANCHES:

Chadian National Army (Armee Nationale du Tchad, ANT): Ground Forces (l'Armee de Terre, AdT), Chadian Air Force (l'Armee de l'Air Tchadienne, AAT), National Gendarmerie, National and Nomadic Guard of Chad (GNNT) (2013)

MILITARY SERVICE AGE AND OBLIGATION:

20 is the legal minimum age for compulsory military service, with a 3-year service obligation; 18 is the legal minimum age for voluntary service; no minimum age restriction for volunteers with consent from a parent or guardian; women are subject to 1 year of compulsory military or civic service at age 21; while provisions for military service have not been

repealed, they have never been fully implemented (2015)

TERRORISM :: CHAD

TERRORIST GROUPS - FOREIGN BASED:

Boko Haram:
aim(s): establish an Islamic caliphate across Africa
area(s) of operation: conducts kidnappings, bombings, and assaults, including in the capital, N'Djamena
note: violently opposes any political or social activity associated with Western society, including voting, attending secular schools, and wearing Western dress (April 2018)

Islamic State of Iraq and ash-Sham (ISIS)-West Africa:
aim(s): implement ISIS's strict interpretation of Sharia; replace the Nigerian Government with an Islamic state
area(s) of operation: based primarily in Northeast Nigeria along the border with Niger, with its largest presence in northeast Nigeria and the Lake Chad region; targets primarily regional military installations (April 2018)

TRANSNATIONAL ISSUES :: CHAD

DISPUTES - INTERNATIONAL:

since 2003, ad hoc armed militia groups and the Sudanese military have driven hundreds of thousands of Darfur residents into ChadChad wishes to be a helpful mediator in resolving the Darfur conflict, and in 2010 established a joint border monitoring force with Sudan, which has helped to reduce cross-border banditry and violenceonly Nigeria and Cameroon have heeded the Lake Chad Commission's admonition to ratify the delimitation treaty, which also includes the Chad-Niger and Niger-Nigeria boundaries

REFUGEES AND INTERNALLY DISPLACED PERSONS:

refugees (country of origin): 336,295 (Sudan), 101,178 (Central African Republic), 11,319 (Nigeria) (2018)

IDPs: 162,755 (majority are in the east) (2018)

SOUTH AMERICA :: CHILE

INTRODUCTION :: CHILE

BACKGROUND:

Prior to the arrival of the Spanish in the 16th century, the Inca ruled northern Chile while an indigenous people, the Mapuche, inhabited central and southern Chile. Although Chile declared its independence in 1810, it did not achieve decisive victory over the Spanish until 1818. In the War of the Pacific (1879-83), Chile defeated Peru and Bolivia to win its present northern regions. In the 1880s, the Chilean central government gained control over the central and southern regions inhabited by the Mapuche. After a series of elected governments, the three-year-old Marxist government of Salvador ALLENDE was overthrown in 1973 by a military coup led by General Augusto PINOCHET, who ruled until a democratically-elected president was inaugurated in 1990. Sound economic policies, maintained consistently since the 1980s, contributed to steady growth, reduced poverty rates by over half, and helped secure the country's commitment to democratic and representative government. Chile has increasingly assumed regional and international leadership roles befitting its status as a stable, democratic nation.

GEOGRAPHY :: CHILE

LOCATION:

Southern South America, bordering the South Pacific Ocean, between Argentina and Peru

GEOGRAPHIC COORDINATES:

30 00 S, 71 00 W

MAP REFERENCES:

South America

AREA:

total: 756,102 sq km

land: 743,812 sq km

water: 12,290 sq km

note: includes Easter Island (Isla de Pascua) and Isla Sala y Gomez

country comparison to the world: 39

AREA - COMPARATIVE:

slightly smaller than twice the size of Montana

LAND BOUNDARIES:

total: 7,801 km

border countries (3): Argentina 6691 km, Bolivia 942 km, Peru 168 km

COASTLINE:

6,435 km

MARITIME CLAIMS:

territorial sea: 12 nm

exclusive economic zone: 200 nm

contiguous zone: 24 nm

continental shelf: 200/350 nm

CLIMATE:

temperate; desert in north; Mediterranean in central region; cool and damp in south

TERRAIN:

low coastal mountains, fertile central valley, rugged Andes in east

ELEVATION:

mean elevation: 1,871 m

elevation extremes: 0 m lowest point: Pacific Ocean

6880 highest point: Nevado Ojos del Salado

NATURAL RESOURCES:

copper, timber, iron ore, nitrates, precious metals, molybdenum, hydropower

LAND USE:

agricultural land: 21.1% (2011 est.)

arable land: 1.7% (2011 est.) / permanent crops: 0.6% (2011 est.) / permanent pasture: 18.8% (2011 est.)

forest: 21.9% (2011 est.)

other: 57% (2011 est.)

IRRIGATED LAND:

11,100 sq km (2012)

POPULATION DISTRIBUTION:

90% of the population is located in the middle third of the country around the capital of Santiago; the far north (anchored by the Atacama Desert) and the extreme south are relatively underpopulated

NATURAL HAZARDS:

severe earthquakes; active volcanism; tsunamis

volcanism: significant volcanic activity due to more than three-dozen active volcanoes along the Andes Mountains; Lascar (5,592 m), which last erupted in 2007, is the most active volcano in the northern Chilean Andes; Llaima (3,125 m) in central Chile, which last erupted in 2009, is another of the country's most active; Chaiten's 2008 eruption forced major evacuations; other notable historically active volcanoes include Cerro Hudson, Calbuco, Copahue, Guallatiri, Llullaillaco, Nevados de Chillan, Puyehue, San Pedro, and Villarrica; see note 2 under "Geography - note"

ENVIRONMENT - CURRENT ISSUES:

air pollution from industrial and vehicle emissions; water pollution from raw sewage; noise pollution; improper garbage disposal; soil degradation; widespread deforestation and mining threaten the environment; wildlife conservation

ENVIRONMENT - INTERNATIONAL AGREEMENTS:

party to: Antarctic-Environmental Protocol, Antarctic-Marine Living Resources, Antarctic Seals, Antarctic Treaty, Biodiversity, Climate Change, Climate Change-Kyoto Protocol, Desertification, Endangered Species, Environmental Modification, Hazardous Wastes, Law of the Sea, Marine Dumping, Ozone Layer Protection, Ship Pollution, Wetlands, Whaling

signed, but not ratified: none of the selected agreements

GEOGRAPHY - NOTE:

note 1: the longest north-south trending country in the world, extending across 39 degrees of latitude; strategic location relative to sea lanes between the Atlantic and Pacific Oceans (Strait of Magellan, Beagle Channel, Drake Passage)

note 2: Chile is one of the countries along the Ring of Fire, a belt of active volcanoes and earthquake epicenters bordering the Pacific Ocean; up to 90% of the world's earthquakes and some 75% of the world's volcanoes occur within the Ring of Fire

note 3: the Atacama Desert - the driest desert in the world - spreads across the northern part of the country; the small crater lake of Ojos del Salado is the world's highest lake (at 6,390 m)

PEOPLE AND SOCIETY :: CHILE

POPULATION:

17,925,262 (July 2018 est.)

country comparison to the world: 65

NATIONALITY:

noun: Chilean(s)

adjective: Chilean

ETHNIC GROUPS:

white and non-indigenous 88.9%, Mapuche 9.1%, Aymara 0.7%, other indigenous groups 1% (includes Rapa Nui, Likan Antai, Quechua, Colla, Diaguita, Kawesqar, Yagan or Yamana), unspecified 0.3% (2012 est.)

LANGUAGES:

Spanish 99.5% (official), English 10.2%, indigenous 1% (includes Mapudungun, Aymara, Quechua, Rapa Nui), other 2.3%, unspecified 0.2% (2012 est.)

note: shares sum to more than 100% because some respondents gave more than one answer on the census

RELIGIONS:

Roman Catholic 66.7%, Evangelical or Protestant 16.4%, Jehovah's Witness 1%, other 3.4%, none 11.5%, unspecified 1.1% (2012 est.)

DEMOGRAPHIC PROFILE:

Chile is in the advanced stages of demographic transition and is becoming an aging society - with fertility below replacement level, low mortality rates, and life expectancy on par with developed countries. Nevertheless, with its dependency ratio nearing its low point, Chile could benefit from its favorable age structure. It will need to keep its large working-age population productively employed, while preparing to provide for the needs of its growing proportion of elderly people, especially as women - the traditional caregivers - increasingly enter the workforce. Over the last two decades, Chile has made great strides in reducing its poverty rate, which is now lower than most Latin American countries. However, its severe income inequality ranks as the worst among members of the Organization for Economic Cooperation and Development. Unequal access to quality education perpetuates this uneven income distribution.

Chile has historically been a country of emigration but has slowly become more attractive to immigrants since transitioning to democracy in 1990 and improving its economic stability (other regional destinations have concurrently experienced deteriorating economic and political conditions). Most of Chile's small but growing foreign-born population consists of transplants from other Latin American countries, especially Peru.

AGE STRUCTURE:

0-14 years: 19.98% (male 1,827,657 /female 1,754,253)

15-24 years: 14.63% (male 1,337,663 /female 1,285,514)

25-54 years: 42.94% (male 3,851,775 /female 3,845,195)

55-64 years: 11.32% (male 957,872 /female 1,070,975)

65 years and over: 11.13% (male 836,489 /female 1,157,869) (2018 est.)

DEPENDENCY RATIOS:

total dependency ratio: 45.5 (2015 est.)

youth dependency ratio: 30.3 (2015 est.)

elderly dependency ratio: 15.2 (2015 est.)

potential support ratio: 6.6 (2015 est.)

MEDIAN AGE:

total: 34.8 years

male: 33.6 years

female: 36 years (2018 est.)

country comparison to the world: 85

POPULATION GROWTH RATE:

0.75% (2018 est.)

country comparison to the world: 135

BIRTH RATE:

13.4 births/1,000 population (2018 est.)

country comparison to the world: 141

DEATH RATE:

6.3 deaths/1,000 population (2018 est.)

country comparison to the world: 150

NET MIGRATION RATE:

0.3 migrant(s)/1,000 population (2017 est.)

country comparison to the world: 66

POPULATION DISTRIBUTION:

90% of the population is located in the middle third of the country around the capital of Santiago; the far north (anchored by the Atacama Desert) and the extreme south are relatively underpopulated

URBANIZATION:

urban population: 87.6% of total population (2018)

rate of urbanization: 0.87% annual rate of change (2015-20 est.)

MAJOR URBAN AREAS - POPULATION:

6.68 million SANTIAGO (capital), 967,000 Valparaiso, 857,000 Concepcion (2018)

SEX RATIO:

at birth: 1.04 male(s)/female (2017 est.)

0-14 years: 1.04 male(s)/female (2017 est.)

15-24 years: 1.04 male(s)/female (2017 est.)

25-54 years: 1 male(s)/female (2017 est.)

55-64 years: 0.89 male(s)/female (2017 est.)

65 years and over: 0.72 male(s)/female (2017 est.)

total population: 0.97 male(s)/female (2017 est.)

MATERNAL MORTALITY RATE:

22 deaths/100,000 live births (2015 est.)

country comparison to the world: 128

INFANT MORTALITY RATE:

total: 6.4 deaths/1,000 live births (2018 est.)

male: 6.9 deaths/1,000 live births (2018 est.)

female: 6 deaths/1,000 live births (2018 est.)

country comparison to the world: 163

LIFE EXPECTANCY AT BIRTH:

total population: 79.1 years (2018 est.)

male: 76 years (2018 est.)

female: 82.2 years (2018 est.)

country comparison to the world: 51

TOTAL FERTILITY RATE:

1.79 children born/woman (2018 est.)

country comparison to the world: 148

CONTRACEPTIVE PREVALENCE RATE:

76.3% (2015/16)

HEALTH EXPENDITURES:

7.8% of GDP (2014)

country comparison to the world: 58

PHYSICIANS DENSITY:

1.03 physicians/1,000 population (2009)

HOSPITAL BED DENSITY:

2.2 beds/1,000 population (2013)

DRINKING WATER SOURCE:

improved:

urban: 99.7% of population

rural: 93.3% of population

total: 99% of population

unimproved:

urban: 0.3% of population

rural: 6.7% of population

total: 1% of population (2015 est.)

SANITATION FACILITY ACCESS:

improved:

urban: 100% of population (2015 est.)

rural: 90.9% of population (2015 est.)

total: 99.1% of population (2015 est.)

unimproved:

urban: 0% of population (2015 est.)

rural: 9.1% of population (2015 est.)

total: 0.9% of population (2015 est.)

HIV/AIDS - ADULT PREVALENCE RATE:

0.6% (2017 est.)

country comparison to the world: 57

HIV/AIDS - PEOPLE LIVING WITH HIV/AIDS:

67,000 (2017 est.)

country comparison to the world: 53

HIV/AIDS - DEATHS:

NA

OBESITY - ADULT PREVALENCE RATE:

28% (2016)

country comparison to the world: 32

CHILDREN UNDER THE AGE OF 5 YEARS UNDERWEIGHT:

0.5% (2014)

country comparison to the world: 125

EDUCATION EXPENDITURES:

4.9% of GDP (2015)

country comparison to the world: 79

LITERACY:

definition: age 15 and over can read and write (2015 est.)

total population: 97.5% (2015 est.)

male: 97.6% (2015 est.)

female: 97.4% (2015 est.)

SCHOOL LIFE EXPECTANCY (PRIMARY TO TERTIARY EDUCATION):

total: 16 years (2015)

male: 16 years (2015)

female: 17 years (2015)

UNEMPLOYMENT, YOUTH AGES 15-24:

total: 17.2% (2017 est.)

male: 16.1% (2017 est.)

female: 18.8% (2017 est.)

country comparison to the world: 78

GOVERNMENT :: CHILE

COUNTRY NAME:

conventional long form: Republic of Chile

conventional short form: Chile

local long form: Republica de Chile

local short form: Chile

etymology: derivation of the name is unclear, but it may come from the Mapuche word "chilli" meaning "limit of the earth" or from the Quechua "chiri" meaning "cold"

GOVERNMENT TYPE:

presidential republic

CAPITAL:

name: Santiago; note - Valparaiso is the seat of the national legislature

geographic coordinates: 33 27 S, 70 40 W

time difference: UTC-3 (2 hours ahead of Washington, DC, during Standard Time)

daylight saving time: +1hr, begins second Sunday in August; ends second Sunday in May; note - Punta Arenas observes DST throughout the year

note: Chile has three time zones: the continental portion at UTC-3; the southern Magallanes region, which does not use daylight savings time and remains at UTC-3 for the summer months; and Easter Island at UTC-5

ADMINISTRATIVE DIVISIONS:

16 regions (regiones, singular - region); Aysen, Antofagasta, Araucania, Arica y Parinacota, Atacama, Biobio, Coquimbo, Libertador General Bernardo O'Higgins, Los Lagos, Los Rios, Magallanes y de la Antartica Chilena (Magallanes and Chilean Antarctica), Maule, Nuble, Region Metropolitana (Santiago), Tarapaca, Valparaiso

note: the US does not recognize any claims to Antarctica

INDEPENDENCE:

18 September 1810 (from Spain)

NATIONAL HOLIDAY:

Independence Day, 18 September (1810)

CONSTITUTION:

history: many previous; latest adopted 11 September 1980, effective 11 March 1981, note - in March 2018, days before her term ended, President BACHELET sent a proposal for a new constitution to the National Congress (2018)

amendments: proposed by members of either house of the National Congress or by the president of the republic; passage requires at least three-fifths majority vote of the membership in both houses and approval by the president; passage of amendments to constitutional articles such as the republican form of government, basic rights and freedoms, the Constitutional Tribunal, electoral justice, the Council of National Security, or the constitutional amendment process requires at least two-third majority vote by both houses of Congress and approval by the president; the president can opt to hold a referendum when Congress and the president disagree on an amendment; amended many times, last in 2017 (2018)

LEGAL SYSTEM:

civil law system influenced by several West European civil legal systems; judicial review of legislative acts by the Constitutional Tribunal

INTERNATIONAL LAW ORGANIZATION PARTICIPATION:

has not submitted an ICJ jurisdiction declaration; accepts ICCt jurisdiction

CITIZENSHIP:

citizenship by birth: yes

citizenship by descent only: yes

dual citizenship recognized: yes

residency requirement for naturalization: 5 years

SUFFRAGE:

18 years of age; universal

EXECUTIVE BRANCH:

chief of state: President Sebastian PINERA Echenique (since 11 March 2018); note - the president is both chief of state and head of government

head of government: President Sebastian PINERA Echenique (since 11 March 2018)

cabinet: Cabinet appointed by the president

elections/appointments: president directly elected by absolute majority popular vote in 2 rounds if needed for a single 4-year term; election last held on 19 November 2017 with a runoff held 17 December 2017 (next to be held in November 2021)

election results: Sebastian PINERA Echenique elected president in second round; percent of vote in first round - Sebastian PINERA Echenique (independent) 36.6%; Alejandro GUILLIER (independent) 22.7%; Beatriz SANCHEZ (independent) 20.3%; Jose Antonio KAST (independent) 7.9%; Carolina GOIC (PDC) 5.9%; Marco ENRIQUEZ-OMINAMI (PRO) 5.7%; other 0.9%; percent of vote in second round - Sebastian PINERA Echenique 54.6%, Alejandro GUILLIER 45.4%

LEGISLATIVE BRANCH:

description: bicameral National Congress or Congreso Nacional consists of:
Senate or Senado (43 seats following the 2017 election; to increase to 50 in 2022); members directly elected in multi-seat constituencies by open party-list proportional representation vote to serve 8-year terms with one-half of the membership renewed every 4 years)
Chamber of Deputies or Camara de Diputados (155 seats; members directly elected in multi-seat constituencies by oen party-list proportional representation vote to serve 4-year terms)

elections:
Senate - last held on 19 November 2017 (next to be held in 2021)
Chamber of Deputies - last held on 19 November 2017 (next to be held in 2021)

election results:
Senate - percent of vote by party - NA; seats by party - New Majority Coalition (formerly known as Concertacion) 19 (PDC 6, PS 6, PPD 6, MAS 1), Let's Go Chile Coalition (formerly known as the Coalition for Change and the Alianza coalition) 15 (RN 6, UDI 8, Amplitude Party 1), independent 4
Chamber of Deputies - percent of vote by party - NA; seats by party - New Majority 68 (PDC 21, PS 16, PPD 14, PC 6, PRSD 6, Citizen Left 1, independent 4), Coalition for Change 47 (UDI 29, RN 14, independent 3, EP 1), Liberal Party 1, independent 4

JUDICIAL BRANCH:

highest courts: Supreme Court or Corte Suprema (consists of a court president and 20 members or ministros); Constitutional Court (consists of 10 members); Elections Qualifying Court (consists of 5 members)

judge selection and term of office: Supreme Court president and judges (ministers) appointed by the president of the republic and ratified by the Senate from lists of candidates provided by the court itself; judges appointed for life with mandatory retirement at age 70; Constitutional Court members appointed - 3 by the Supreme Court, 3 by the president of the republic, 2 by the Chamber of Deputies, and 2 by the Senate; members serve 9-year terms with partial membership replacement every 3 years (the court reviews constitutionality of legislation); Elections Qualifying Court members appointed by lottery - 1 by the former president or vice-president of the Senate and 1 by the former president or vice-president of the Chamber of Deputies, 2 by the Supreme Court, and 1 by the Appellate Court of Valparaiso; members appointed for 4-year terms

subordinate courts: Courts of Appeal; oral criminal tribunals; military tribunals; local police courts; specialized tribunals and courts in matters such as family, labor, customs, taxes, and electoral affairs

POLITICAL PARTIES AND LEADERS:

Amplitude (Amplitud) [Lily PEREZ]
Broad Social Movement or MAS [Cristian TAPIA Ramos]
Christian Democratic Party or PDC [Carolina GOIC Boroevic]
Communist Party of Chile or PC [Guillermo TEILLIER del Valle]
Democratic Revolution or RD [Rodrigo ECHECOPAR]
Independent Democratic Union or UDI [Jacqueline VAN RYSSELBERGHE Herrera])
Independent Regionalist Party or PRI [Alejandra BRAVO Hidalgo]
Let's Go Chile Coalition (Chile Vamos) [Sebastian PINERA] (includes EVOPOLI, PRI, RN, UDI)
Liberal Party (Partido Liberal de Chile) [Vlado MIROSEVIC]
National Renewal or RN [Cristian MONCKEBERG Bruner]
New Majority Coalition (Nueva Mayoria) [Michelle BACHELET] (includes PDC, PC, PPD, PRSD, PS); note - dissolved in March 2018
Party for Democracy or PPD [Gonzalo NAVARRETE]
Political Evolution or EVOPOLI [Jorge SAINT JEAN]
Progressive Party or PRO [Patricia MORALES]
Radical Social Democratic Party or PRSD [Ernesto VELASCO Rodriguez],
Socialist Party or PS [Alvaro ELIZALDE Soto] (formerly known as Concertacion)

INTERNATIONAL ORGANIZATION PARTICIPATION:

APEC, BIS, CAN (associate), CD, CELAC, FAO, G-15, G-77, IADB, IAEA, IBRD, ICAO, ICC (national committees), ICCt, ICRM, IDA, IFAD, IFC, IFRCS, IHO, ILO, IMF, IMO, IMSO, Interpol, IOC, IOM, IPU, ISO, ITSO, ITU, ITUC (NGOs), LAES, LAIA, Mercosur (associate), MIGA, MINUSTAH, NAM, OAS, OECD (enhanced engagement), OPANAL, OPCW, Pacific Alliance, PCA, SICA (observer), UN, UNASUR, UNCTAD, UNESCO, UNFICYP, UNHCR, UNIDO, Union Latina, UNMOGIP, UNTSO, UNWTO, UPU, WCO, WFTU (NGOs), WHO, WIPO, WMO, WTO

DIPLOMATIC REPRESENTATION IN THE US:

chief of mission: Ambassador Oscar Alfonso Sebastian SILVA Navarro (since 17 September 2018)

chancery: 1732 Massachusetts Avenue NW, Washington, DC 20036

telephone: [1] (202) 785-1746

FAX: [1] (202) 887-5579

consulate(s) general: Chicago, Houston, Los Angeles, Miami, New York, San Francisco

DIPLOMATIC REPRESENTATION FROM THE US:

chief of mission: Ambassador Carol PEREZ (since 14 November 2016)

embassy: Avenida Andres Bello 2800, Las Condes, Santiago

mailing address: APO AA 34033

telephone: [56] (2) 2330-3000

FAX: [56] (2) 2330-3710, 2330-3160

FLAG DESCRIPTION:

two equal horizontal bands of white (top) and red; a blue square the same height as the white band at the hoist-side end of the white band; the square bears a white five-pointed star in the center representing a guide to progress and honor; blue symbolizes the sky, white is for the snow-covered Andes, and red represents the blood spilled to achieve independence

note: design influenced by the US flag

NATIONAL SYMBOL(S):

huemul (mountain deer), Andean condor; national colors: red, white, blue

NATIONAL ANTHEM:

name: "Himno Nacional de Chile" (National Anthem of Chile)

lyrics/music: Eusebio LILLO Robles and Bernardo DE VERA y Pintado/Ramon CARNICER y Battle

note: music adopted 1828, original lyrics adopted 1818, adapted lyrics adopted 1847; under Augusto PINOCHET's military rule, a verse glorifying the army was added; however, as a protest, some citizens refused to sing this verse; it was removed when democracy was restored in 1990

ECONOMY :: CHILE

ECONOMY - OVERVIEW:

Chile has a market-oriented economy characterized by a high level of foreign trade and a reputation for strong financial institutions and sound policy that have given it the strongest sovereign bond rating in South America. Exports of goods and services account for approximately one-third of GDP, with commodities making up some 60% of total exports. Copper is Chile's top export and provides 20% of government revenue.

From 2003 through 2013, real growth averaged almost 5% per year, despite a slight contraction in 2009 that resulted from the global financial crisis. Growth slowed to an estimated 1.4% in 2017. A continued drop in copper prices prompted Chile to experience its third consecutive year of slow growth.

Chile deepened its longstanding commitment to trade liberalization with the signing of a free trade agreement with the US, effective 1 January 2004. Chile has 26 trade agreements covering 60 countries including agreements with the EU, Mercosur, China, India, South Korea, and Mexico. In May 2010, Chile signed the OECD Convention, becoming the first South American country to join the OECD. In October 2015, Chile signed the Trans-Pacific Partnership trade agreement, which was finalized as the Comprehensive and Progressive Trans-Pacific Partnership (CPTPP) and signed at a ceremony in Chile in March 2018.

The Chilean Government has generally followed a countercyclical fiscal policy, under which it accumulates surpluses in sovereign wealth funds during periods of high copper prices and economic growth, and generally allows deficit spending only during periods of low copper prices and growth. As of 31 October 2016, those sovereign wealth funds - kept mostly outside the country and separate from Central Bank reserves - amounted to more than $23.5 billion. Chile used these funds to finance fiscal stimulus packages during the 2009 economic downturn.

In 2014, then-President Michelle BACHELET introduced tax reforms aimed at delivering her campaign promise to fight inequality and to provide access to education and health care. The reforms are expected to generate additional tax revenues equal to 3% of Chile's GDP, mostly by increasing corporate tax rates to OECD averages.

GDP (PURCHASING POWER PARITY):

$452.1 billion (2017 est.)

$445.5 billion (2016 est.)

$439.9 billion (2015 est.)

note: data are in 2017 dollars

country comparison to the world: 44

GDP (OFFICIAL EXCHANGE RATE):

$277 billion (2017 est.) (2017 est.)

GDP - REAL GROWTH RATE:

1.5% (2017 est.)

1.3% (2016 est.)

2.3% (2015 est.)

country comparison to the world: 170

GDP - PER CAPITA (PPP):

$24,600 (2017 est.)

$24,500 (2016 est.)

$24,400 (2015 est.)

note: data are in 2017 dollars

country comparison to the world: 82

GROSS NATIONAL SAVING:

20.5% of GDP (2017 est.)

20.9% of GDP (2016 est.)

21.4% of GDP (2015 est.)

country comparison to the world: 94

GDP - COMPOSITION, BY END USE:

household consumption: 62.3% (2017 est.)

government consumption: 14% (2017 est.)

investment in fixed capital: 21.5% (2017 est.)

investment in inventories: 0.5% (2017 est.)

exports of goods and services: 28.7% (2017 est.)

imports of goods and services: -27% (2017 est.)

GDP - COMPOSITION, BY SECTOR OF ORIGIN:

agriculture: 4.2% (2017 est.)

industry: 32.8% (2017 est.)

services: 63% (2017 est.)

AGRICULTURE - PRODUCTS:

grapes, apples, pears, onions, wheat, corn, oats, peaches, garlic, asparagus, beans; beef, poultry, wool; fish; timber

INDUSTRIES:

copper, lithium, other minerals, foodstuffs, fish processing, iron and steel, wood and wood products, transport equipment, cement, textiles

INDUSTRIAL PRODUCTION GROWTH RATE:

-0.4% (2017 est.)

country comparison to the world: 170

LABOR FORCE:

8.881 million (2017 est.)

country comparison to the world: 58

LABOR FORCE - BY OCCUPATION:

agriculture: 9.2%

industry: 23.7%

services: 67.1% (2013)

UNEMPLOYMENT RATE:

6.7% (2017 est.)

6.5% (2016 est.)

country comparison to the world: 99

POPULATION BELOW POVERTY LINE:

14.4% (2013)

HOUSEHOLD INCOME OR CONSUMPTION BY PERCENTAGE SHARE:

lowest 10%: 41.5% (2013 est.)

highest 10%: 41.5% (2013 est.)

DISTRIBUTION OF FAMILY INCOME - GINI INDEX:

50.5 (2013)

57.1 (2000)

country comparison to the world: 15

BUDGET:

revenues: 57.75 billion (2017 est.)

expenditures: 65.38 billion (2017 est.)

TAXES AND OTHER REVENUES:

20.8% (of GDP) (2017 est.)

country comparison to the world: 145

BUDGET SURPLUS (+) OR DEFICIT (-):

-2.8% (of GDP) (2017 est.)

country comparison to the world: 124

PUBLIC DEBT:

23.6% of GDP (2017 est.)

21% of GDP (2016 est.)

country comparison to the world: 182

FISCAL YEAR:

calendar year

INFLATION RATE (CONSUMER PRICES):

2.2% (2017 est.)

3.8% (2016 est.)

country comparison to the world: 113

CENTRAL BANK DISCOUNT RATE:

3.35% (31 December 2015)

3% (31 December 2014)

country comparison to the world: 104

COMMERCIAL BANK PRIME LENDING RATE:

4.6% (31 December 2017 est.)

5.59% (31 December 2016 est.)

country comparison to the world: 156

STOCK OF NARROW MONEY:

$52.54 billion (31 December 2017 est.)

$44.01 billion (31 December 2016 est.)

country comparison to the world: 53

STOCK OF BROAD MONEY:

$52.54 billion (31 December 2017 est.)

$44.01 billion (31 December 2016 est.)

country comparison to the world: 53

STOCK OF DOMESTIC CREDIT:

$244.3 billion (31 December 2017 est.)

$211.6 billion (31 December 2016 est.)

country comparison to the world: 43

MARKET VALUE OF PUBLICLY TRADED SHARES:

$190.4 billion (31 December 2015 est.)

$233.2 billion (31 December 2014 est.)

$265.2 billion (31 December 2013 est.)

country comparison to the world: 35

CURRENT ACCOUNT BALANCE:

-$4.102 billion (2017 est.)

-$3.484 billion (2016 est.)

country comparison to the world: 178

EXPORTS:

$69.23 billion (2017 est.)

$60.6 billion (2016 est.)

country comparison to the world: 42

EXPORTS - PARTNERS:

China 27.5%, US 14.5%, Japan 9.3%, South Korea 6.2%, Brazil 5% (2017)

EXPORTS - COMMODITIES:

copper, fruit, fish products, paper and pulp, chemicals, wine

IMPORTS:

$61.31 billion (2017 est.)

$55.29 billion (2016 est.)

country comparison to the world: 49

IMPORTS - COMMODITIES:

petroleum and petroleum products, chemicals, electrical and telecommunications equipment, industrial machinery, vehicles, natural gas

IMPORTS - PARTNERS:

China 23.9%, US 18.1%, Brazil 8.6%, Argentina 4.5%, Germany 4% (2017)

RESERVES OF FOREIGN EXCHANGE AND GOLD:

$38.98 billion (31 December 2017 est.)

$40.49 billion (31 December 2016 est.)

country comparison to the world: 44

DEBT - EXTERNAL:

$183.4 billion (31 December 2017 est.)

$158.1 billion (31 December 2016 est.)

country comparison to the world: 37

STOCK OF DIRECT FOREIGN INVESTMENT - AT HOME:

$206.2 billion (31 December 2017 est.)

$199.8 billion (31 December 2016 est.)

country comparison to the world: 31

STOCK OF DIRECT FOREIGN INVESTMENT - ABROAD:

$95.37 billion (31 December 2017 est.)

$90.54 billion (31 December 2016 est.)

country comparison to the world: 36

EXCHANGE RATES:

Chilean pesos (CLP) per US dollar -

653.9 (2017 est.)

676.94 (2016 est.)

676.94 (2015 est.)

658.93 (2014 est.)

570.37 (2013 est.)

ENERGY :: CHILE

ELECTRICITY ACCESS:

population without electricity: 70,600 (2012)

electrification - total population: 99.6% (2012)

electrification - urban areas: 100% (2012)

electrification - rural areas: 98% (2012)

ELECTRICITY - PRODUCTION:

76.09 billion kWh (2016 est.)

country comparison to the world: 39

ELECTRICITY - CONSUMPTION:

73.22 billion kWh (2016 est.)

country comparison to the world: 38

ELECTRICITY - EXPORTS:

0 kWh (2016 est.)

country comparison to the world: 121

ELECTRICITY - IMPORTS:

0 kWh (2016 est.)

country comparison to the world: 135

ELECTRICITY - INSTALLED GENERATING CAPACITY:

24.53 million kW (2016 est.)

country comparison to the world: 37

ELECTRICITY - FROM FOSSIL FUELS:

59% of total installed capacity (2016 est.)

country comparison to the world: 133

ELECTRICITY - FROM NUCLEAR FUELS:

0% of total installed capacity (2017 est.)

country comparison to the world: 66

ELECTRICITY - FROM HYDROELECTRIC PLANTS:

26% of total installed capacity (2017 est.)

country comparison to the world: 75

ELECTRICITY - FROM OTHER RENEWABLE SOURCES:

15% of total installed capacity (2017 est.)

country comparison to the world: 57

CRUDE OIL - PRODUCTION:

3,244 bbl/day (2017 est.)

country comparison to the world: 83

CRUDE OIL - EXPORTS:

0 bbl/day (2017 est.)

country comparison to the world: 106

CRUDE OIL - IMPORTS:

169,600 bbl/day (2017 est.)

country comparison to the world: 33

CRUDE OIL - PROVED RESERVES:

150 million bbl (1 January 2018 est.)

country comparison to the world: 60

REFINED PETROLEUM PRODUCTS - PRODUCTION:

216,200 bbl/day (2017 est.)

country comparison to the world: 49

REFINED PETROLEUM PRODUCTS - CONSUMPTION:

354,500 bbl/day (2017 est.)

country comparison to the world: 39

REFINED PETROLEUM PRODUCTS - EXPORTS:

7,359 bbl/day (2017 est.)

country comparison to the world: 87

REFINED PETROLEUM PRODUCTS - IMPORTS:

166,400 bbl/day (2017 est.)

country comparison to the world: 38

NATURAL GAS - PRODUCTION:

1.218 billion cu m (2017 est.)

country comparison to the world: 65

NATURAL GAS - CONSUMPTION:

5.125 billion cu m (2017 est.)

country comparison to the world: 58

NATURAL GAS - EXPORTS:

277.5 million cu m (2017 est.)

country comparison to the world: 43

NATURAL GAS - IMPORTS:

4.446 billion cu m (2017 est.)

country comparison to the world: 38

NATURAL GAS - PROVED RESERVES:

97.97 billion cu m (1 January 2018 est.)

country comparison to the world: 52

CARBON DIOXIDE EMISSIONS FROM CONSUMPTION OF ENERGY:

88.23 million Mt (2017 est.)

country comparison to the world: 47

COMMUNICATIONS :: CHILE

TELEPHONES - FIXED LINES:

total subscriptions: 3,193,131 (2017 est.)

subscriptions per 100 inhabitants: 18 (2017 est.)

country comparison to the world: 43

TELEPHONES - MOBILE CELLULAR:

total subscriptions: 23,013,147 (2017 est.)

subscriptions per 100 inhabitants: 129 (2017 est.)

country comparison to the world: 53

TELEPHONE SYSTEM:

general assessment: privatization began in 1988; most advanced telecommunications infrastructure in South America; modern system based on extensive microwave radio relay facilities; although Chile has one of the highest mobile penetration rates in the region, the number of subscribers has fallen due to subscribers ending multiple SIM card use; this downward trend is expected to be halted in 2018 as the availability of LTE networks and services broaden; in terms of available broadband speeds the country ranks second highest in South and Central America (2017)

domestic: number of fixed-line connections have stagnated to 18 per 100 in recent years as mobile-cellular usage continues to increase, reaching 130 telephones per 100 persons; domestic satellite system with 3 earth stations (2017)

international: country code - 56; landing points for the Pan American, South America-1, and South American Crossing/Latin America Nautilus submarine cables providing links to the US and to Central and South America; satellite earth stations - 2 Intelsat (Atlantic Ocean) (2016)

BROADCAST MEDIA:

national and local terrestrial TV channels, coupled with extensive cable TV networks; the state-owned Television Nacional de Chile (TVN) network is self-financed through commercial advertising revenues and is not under direct government control; large number of privately owned TV stations; about 250 radio stations (2007)

INTERNET COUNTRY CODE:

.cl

INTERNET USERS:

total: 11,650,840 (July 2016 est.)

percent of population: 66% (July 2016 est.)

country comparison to the world: 46

BROADBAND - FIXED SUBSCRIPTIONS:

total: 3,058,979 (2017 est.)

subscriptions per 100 inhabitants: 17 (2017 est.)

country comparison to the world: 40

TRANSPORTATION :: CHILE

NATIONAL AIR TRANSPORT SYSTEM:

number of registered air carriers: 9 (2015)

inventory of registered aircraft operated by air carriers: 173 (2015)

annual passenger traffic on registered air carriers: 15,006,762 (2015)

annual freight traffic on registered air carriers: 1,392,236,000 mt-km (2015)

CIVIL AIRCRAFT REGISTRATION COUNTRY CODE PREFIX:

CC (2016)

AIRPORTS:

481 (2013)

country comparison to the world: 15

AIRPORTS - WITH PAVED RUNWAYS:

total: 90 (2017)

over 3,047 m: 5 (2017)

2,438 to 3,047 m: 7 (2017)

1,524 to 2,437 m: 23 (2017)

914 to 1,523 m: 31 (2017)

under 914 m: 24 (2017)

AIRPORTS - WITH UNPAVED RUNWAYS:

total: 391 (2013)

2,438 to 3,047 m: 5 (2013)

1,524 to 2,437 m: 11 (2013)

914 to 1,523 m: 56 (2013)

under 914 m: 319 (2013)

HELIPORTS:

1 (2013)

PIPELINES:

3160 km gas, 781 km liquid petroleum gas, 985 km oil, 722 km refined products (2013)

RAILWAYS:

total: 7,282 km (2014)

narrow gauge: 3,853.5 km 1.000-m gauge (2014)

broad gauge: 3,428 km 1.676-m gauge (1,691 km electrified) (2014)

country comparison to the world: 30

ROADWAYS:

total: 77,764 km (2010)

paved: 18,119 km (includes 2,387 km of expressways) (2010)

unpaved: 59,645 km (2010)

country comparison to the world: 62

MERCHANT MARINE:

total: 211 (2017)

by type: bulk carrier 10, container ship 5, general cargo 54, oil tanker 12, other 130 (2017)

country comparison to the world: 64

PORTS AND TERMINALS:

major seaport(s): Coronel, Huasco, Lirquen, Puerto Ventanas, San Antonio, San Vicente, Valparaiso

LNG terminal(s) (import): Mejillones, Quintero

MILITARY AND SECURITY :: CHILE

MILITARY EXPENDITURES:

1.87% of GDP (2016)

1.91% of GDP (2015)

1.96% of GDP (2014)

country comparison to the world: 55

MILITARY BRANCHES:

Chilean Army, Chilean Navy (Armada de Chile, includes Naval Aviation, Marine Corps, and Maritime Territory and Merchant Marine Directorate (Directemar)), Chilean Air Force (Fuerza Aerea de Chile, FACh) (2015)

MILITARY SERVICE AGE AND OBLIGATION:

18-45 years of age for voluntary male and female military service, although the right to compulsory recruitment of males 18-45 is retained; service obligation is 12 months for Army and 22 months for Navy and Air Force (2015)

TRANSNATIONAL ISSUES :: CHILE

DISPUTES - INTERNATIONAL:

Chile and Peru rebuff Bolivia's reactivated claim to restore the Atacama corridor, ceded to Chile in 1884, but Chile has offered instead unrestricted but not sovereign maritime access through Chile to Bolivian natural gasChile rejects Peru's unilateral legislation to change its latitudinal maritime boundary with Chile to an equidistance line with a southwestern axis favoring Peru; in October 2007, Peru took its maritime complaint with Chile to the ICJterritorial claim in Antarctica (Chilean Antarctic Territory) partially overlaps Argentine and British claimsthe joint boundary commission, established by Chile and Argentina in 2001, has yet to map and demarcate the delimited boundary in the inhospitable Andean Southern Ice Field (Campo de Hielo Sur)

REFUGEES AND INTERNALLY DISPLACED PERSONS:

refugees (country of origin): 133,321 (Venezuela) (economic and political crisis; includes Venezuelans who have claimed asylum or have received alternative legal stay) (2018)

ILLICIT DRUGS:

transshipment country for cocaine destined for Europe and the region; some money laundering activity, especially through the Iquique Free Trade Zone; imported precursors passed on to Bolivia; domestic cocaine consumption is rising, making Chile a significant consumer of cocaine

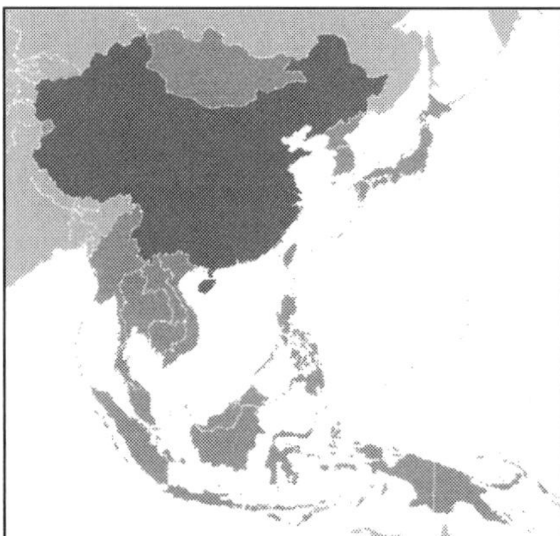

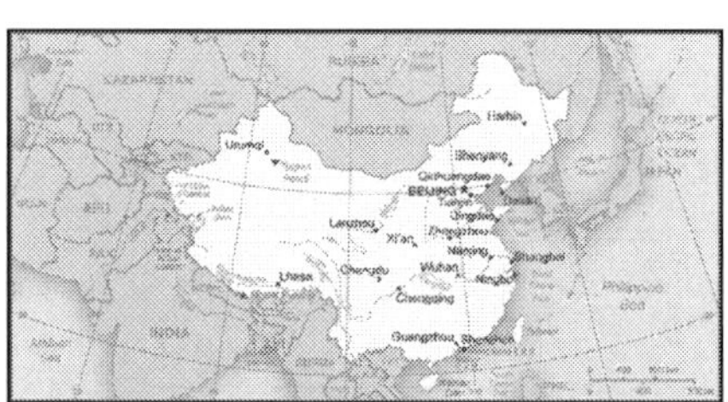

EAST ASIA / SOUTHEAST ASIA :: CHINA

INTRODUCTION :: CHINA

BACKGROUND:

China's historical civilization dates from at least 1200 B.C.; from the 3rd century B.C. and for the next two millennia, China alternated between periods of unity and disunity under a succession of imperial dynasties. In the 19th and early 20th centuries, the country was beset by civil unrest, major famines, military defeats, and foreign occupation. After World War II, the Chinese Communist Party under MAO Zedong established an autocratic socialist system that, while ensuring China's sovereignty, imposed strict controls over everyday life and cost the lives of tens of millions of people. After 1978, MAO's successor DENG Xiaoping and other leaders focused on market-oriented economic development and by 2000 output had quadrupled. For much of the population, living standards have improved dramatically but political controls remain tight. Since the early 1990s, China has increased its global outreach and participation in international organizations.

GEOGRAPHY :: CHINA

LOCATION:

Eastern Asia, bordering the East China Sea, Korea Bay, Yellow Sea, and South China Sea, between North Korea and Vietnam

GEOGRAPHIC COORDINATES:

35 00 N, 105 00 E

MAP REFERENCES:

Asia

AREA:

total: 9,596,960 sq km

land: 9,326,410 sq km

water: 270,550 sq km

country comparison to the world: 5

AREA - COMPARATIVE:

slightly smaller than the US

LAND BOUNDARIES:

total: 22,457 km

border countries (15): Afghanistan 91 km, Bhutan 477 km, Burma 2129 km, India 2659 km, Kazakhstan 1765 km, North Korea 1352 km, Kyrgyzstan 1063 km, Laos 475 km, Mongolia 4630 km, Nepal 1389 km, Pakistan 438 km, Russia (northeast) 4133 km, Russia (northwest) 46 km, Tajikistan 477 km, Vietnam 1297 km

COASTLINE:

14,500 km

MARITIME CLAIMS:

territorial sea: 12 nm

exclusive economic zone: 200 nm

contiguous zone: 24 nm

continental shelf: 200 nm or to the edge of the continental margin

CLIMATE:

extremely diverse; tropical in south to subarctic in north

TERRAIN:

mostly mountains, high plateaus, deserts in west; plains, deltas, and hills in east

ELEVATION:

mean elevation: 1,840 m

elevation extremes: -154 m lowest point: Turpan Pendi

8848 highest point: Mount Everest (highest peak in Asia and highest point on earth above sea level)

NATURAL RESOURCES:

coal, iron ore, petroleum, natural gas, mercury, tin, tungsten, antimony, manganese, molybdenum, vanadium, magnetite, aluminum, lead, zinc, rare earth elements, uranium, hydropower potential (world's largest), arable land

LAND USE:

agricultural land: 54.7% (2011 est.)

arable land: 11.3% (2011 est.) / permanent crops: 1.6% (2011 est.) / permanent pasture: 41.8% (2011 est.)

forest: 22.3% (2011 est.)

other: 23% (2011 est.)

IRRIGATED LAND:

690,070 sq km (2012)

POPULATION DISTRIBUTION:

overwhelming majority of the population is found in the eastern half of the country; the west, with its vast mountainous and desert areas, remains sparsely populated; though ranked first in the world in total population, overall density is less than that of many other countries in Asia and Europe; high population density is found along the Yangtze and Yellow River valleys, the Xi Jiang River delta, the Sichuan Basin (around Chengdu), in and around Beijing, and the industrial area around Shenyang

NATURAL HAZARDS:

frequent typhoons (about five per year along southern and eastern coasts); damaging floods; tsunamis; earthquakes; droughts; land subsidence

volcanism: China contains some historically active volcanoes including Changbaishan (also known as Baitoushan, Baegdu, or P'aektu-san), Hainan Dao, and Kunlun although most have been relatively inactive in recent centuries

ENVIRONMENT - CURRENT ISSUES:

air pollution (greenhouse gases, sulfur dioxide particulates) from reliance on coal produces acid rain; China is the world's largest single emitter of carbon dioxide from the burning of fossil fuels; water shortages, particularly in the north; water pollution from untreated wastes; coastal destruction due to land reclamation, industrial development, and aquaculture; deforestation and habitat destruction; poor land management leads to soil erosion, landslides, floods, droughts, dust storms, and desertification; trade in endangered species

ENVIRONMENT - INTERNATIONAL AGREEMENTS:

party to: Antarctic-Environmental Protocol, Antarctic Treaty, Biodiversity, Climate Change, Climate Change-Kyoto Protocol, Desertification, Endangered Species, Environmental Modification, Hazardous Wastes, Law of the Sea, Marine Dumping, Ozone Layer Protection, Ship Pollution, Tropical Timber 83, Tropical Timber 94, Wetlands, Whaling

signed, but not ratified: none of the selected agreements

GEOGRAPHY - NOTE:

world's fourth largest country (after Russia, Canada, and US) and largest country situated entirely in Asia; Mount Everest on the border with Nepal is the world's tallest peak above sea level

PEOPLE AND SOCIETY :: CHINA

POPULATION:

1,384,688,986 (July 2018 est.)

country comparison to the world: 1

NATIONALITY:

noun: Chinese (singular and plural)

adjective: Chinese

ETHNIC GROUPS:

Han Chinese 91.6%, Zhuang 1.3%, other (includes Hui, Manchu, Uighur, Miao, Yi, Tujia, Tibetan, Mongol, Dong, Buyei, Yao, Bai, Korean, Hani, Li, Kazakh, Dai, and other nationalities) 7.1% (2010 est.)

note: the Chinese Government officially recognizes 56 ethnic groups

LANGUAGES:

Standard Chinese or Mandarin (official; Putonghua, based on the Beijing dialect), Yue (Cantonese), Wu (Shanghainese), Minbei (Fuzhou), Minnan (Hokkien-Taiwanese), Xiang, Gan, Hakka dialects, minority languages (see Ethnic groups entry)

note: Zhuang is official in Guangxi Zhuang, Yue is official in Guangdong, Mongolian is official in Nei Mongol, Uighur is official in Xinjiang Uygur, Kyrgyz is official in Xinjiang Uygur, and Tibetan is official in Xizang (Tibet)

RELIGIONS:

Buddhist 18.2%, Christian 5.1%, Muslim 1.8%, folk religion 21.9%, Hindu < 0.1%, Jewish < 0.1%, other 0.7% (includes Daoist (Taoist)), unaffiliated 52.2% (2010 est.)

note: officially atheist

AGE STRUCTURE:

0-14 years: 17.22% (male 128,270,371 /female 110,120,535)

15-24 years: 12.32% (male 91,443,139 /female 79,181,726)

25-54 years: 47.84% (male 338,189,015 /female 324,180,103)

55-64 years: 11.35% (male 79,340,391 /female 77,857,806)

65 years and over: 11.27% (male 74,277,631 /female 81,828,269) (2018 est.)

DEPENDENCY RATIOS:

total dependency ratio: 37.7 (2015 est.)

youth dependency ratio: 24.3 (2015 est.)

elderly dependency ratio: 13.3 (2015 est.)

potential support ratio: 7.5 (2015 est.)

data do not include Hong Kong, Macau, and Taiwan

MEDIAN AGE:

total: 37.7 years

male: 36.8 years

female: 38.8 years (2018 est.)

country comparison to the world: 64

POPULATION GROWTH RATE:

0.37% (2018 est.)

country comparison to the world: 165

BIRTH RATE:

12.1 births/1,000 population (2018 est.)

country comparison to the world: 161

DEATH RATE:

8 deaths/1,000 population (2018 est.)

country comparison to the world: 89

NET MIGRATION RATE:

-0.4 migrant(s)/1,000 population (2017 est.)

country comparison to the world: 119

POPULATION DISTRIBUTION:

overwhelming majority of the population is found in the eastern half of the country; the west, with its vast mountainous and desert areas, remains sparsely populated; though ranked first in the world in total population, overall density is less than that of many other countries in Asia and Europe; high population density is found along the Yangtze and Yellow River valleys, the Xi Jiang River delta, the Sichuan Basin (around Chengdu), in and around Beijing, and the industrial area around Shenyang

URBANIZATION:

urban population: 59.2% of total population (2018)

rate of urbanization: 2.42% annual rate of change (2015-20 est.)

note: data do not include Hong Kong and Macau

MAJOR URBAN AREAS - POPULATION:

25.582 million Shanghai, 19.618 million BEIJING (capital), 14.838 million Chongqing, 12.683 million Guangdong, 13.215 million Tianjin, 11.908 million Shenzhen (2018)

SEX RATIO:

at birth: 1.14 male(s)/female (2017 est.)

0-14 years: 1.17 male(s)/female (2017 est.)

15-24 years: 1.14 male(s)/female (2017 est.)

25-54 years: 1.04 male(s)/female (2017 est.)

55-64 years: 1.02 male(s)/female (2017 est.)

65 years and over: 0.92 male(s)/female (2017 est.)

total population: 1.06 male(s)/female (2017 est.)

MATERNAL MORTALITY RATE:

27 deaths/100,000 live births (2015 est.)

country comparison to the world: 118

INFANT MORTALITY RATE:

total: 11.8 deaths/1,000 live births (2018 est.)

male: 12.2 deaths/1,000 live births (2018 est.)

female: 11.4 deaths/1,000 live births (2018 est.)

country comparison to the world: 118

LIFE EXPECTANCY AT BIRTH:

total population: 75.8 years (2018 est.)

male: 73.7 years (2018 est.)

female: 78.1 years (2018 est.)

country comparison to the world: 100

TOTAL FERTILITY RATE:

1.6 children born/woman (2018 est.)

country comparison to the world: 181

HEALTH EXPENDITURES:

5.5% of GDP (2014)

country comparison to the world: 125

PHYSICIANS DENSITY:

3.63 physicians/1,000 population (2015)

HOSPITAL BED DENSITY:

4.2 beds/1,000 population (2012)

DRINKING WATER SOURCE:

improved:

urban: 97.5% of population

rural: 93% of population

total: 95.5% of population

unimproved:

urban: 2.5% of population

rural: 7% of population

total: 4.5% of population (2015 est.)

SANITATION FACILITY ACCESS:

improved:

urban: 86.6% of population (2015 est.)

rural: 63.7% of population (2015 est.)

total: 76.5% of population (2015 est.)

unimproved:

urban: 13.4% of population (2015 est.)

rural: 36.3% of population (2015 est.)

total: 23.5% of population (2015 est.)

HIV/AIDS - ADULT PREVALENCE RATE:

NA

HIV/AIDS - PEOPLE LIVING WITH HIV/AIDS:

NA

HIV/AIDS - DEATHS:

NA

MAJOR INFECTIOUS DISEASES:

degree of risk: intermediate (2016)

food or waterborne diseases: bacterial diarrhea, hepatitis A, and typhoid fever (2016)

vectorborne diseases: Japanese encephalitis (2016)

soil contact diseases: hantaviral hemorrhagic fever with renal syndrome (HFRS) (2016)

OBESITY - ADULT PREVALENCE RATE:

6.2% (2016)

country comparison to the world: 169

CHILDREN UNDER THE AGE OF 5 YEARS UNDERWEIGHT:

2.4% (2013)

country comparison to the world: 107

EDUCATION EXPENDITURES:

NA

LITERACY:

definition: age 15 and over can read and write (2015 est.)

total population: 96.4% (2015 est.)

male: 98.2% (2015 est.)

female: 94.5% (2015 est.)

SCHOOL LIFE EXPECTANCY (PRIMARY TO TERTIARY EDUCATION):

total: 14 years (2015)

male: 14 years (2015)

female: 14 years (2015)

PEOPLE - NOTE:

in October 2015, the Chinese Government announced that it would change its rules to allow all couples to have two children, loosening a 1979 mandate that restricted many couples to one child; the new policy was implemented on 1 January 2016 to address China's rapidly aging population and economic needs

GOVERNMENT :: CHINA

COUNTRY NAME:

conventional long form: People's Republic of China

conventional short form: China

local long form: Zhonghua Renmin Gongheguo

local short form: Zhongguo

abbreviation: PRC

etymology: English name derives from the Qin (Chin) rulers of the 3rd century B.C., who comprised the first imperial dynasty of ancient China; the Chinese name Zhongguo translates as "Central Nation" or "Middle Kingdom"

GOVERNMENT TYPE:

communist party-led state

CAPITAL:

geographic coordinates: 39 55 N, 116 23 E

time difference: UTC+8 (13 hours ahead of Washington, DC, during Standard Time)

capital: Beijing

note: despite its size, all of China falls within one time zone

ADMINISTRATIVE DIVISIONS:

23 provinces (sheng, singular and plural), 5 autonomous regions (zizhiqu, singular and plural), and 4 municipalities (shi, singular and plural)

provinces: Anhui, Fujian, Gansu, Guangdong, Guizhou, Hainan, Hebei, Heilongjiang, Henan, Hubei, Hunan, Jiangsu, Jiangxi, Jilin, Liaoning, Qinghai, Shaanxi, Shandong, Shanxi, Sichuan, Yunnan, Zhejiang; (see note on Taiwan);

autonomous regions: Guangxi, Nei Mongol (Inner Mongolia), Ningxia, Xinjiang Uygur, Xizang (Tibet);

municipalities: Beijing, Chongqing, Shanghai, Tianjin

note: China considers Taiwan its 23rd province; see separate entries for the special administrative regions of Hong Kong and Macau

INDEPENDENCE:

1 October 1949 (People's Republic of China established); notable earlier dates:221 B.C. (unification under the Qin Dynasty);1 January 1912 (Qing Dynasty replaced by the Republic of China)

NATIONAL HOLIDAY:

National Day (anniversary of the founding of the People's Republic of China), 1 October (1949)

CONSTITUTION:

history: several previous; latest promulgated 4 December 1982 (2018)

amendments: proposed by the Standing Committee of the National People's Congress or supported by more than one-fifth of the National People's Congress membership; passage requires more than two-thirds majority vote of the Congress membership; amended several times, last in 2018 (2018)

LEGAL SYSTEM:

civil law influenced by Soviet and continental European civil law systems; legislature retains power to interpret statutes; note - in early 2017, the National People's Congress took the first step in adopting a new civil code by passing the General Provisions of the Civil Law

INTERNATIONAL LAW ORGANIZATION PARTICIPATION:

has not submitted an ICJ jurisdiction declaration; non-party state to the ICCt

CITIZENSHIP:

citizenship by birth: no

citizenship by descent only: least one parent must be a citizen of China

dual citizenship recognized: no

residency requirement for naturalization: while naturalization is theoretically possible, in practical terms it is extremely difficult; residency is required but not specified

SUFFRAGE:

18 years of age; universal

EXECUTIVE BRANCH:

head of government: Premier LI Keqiang (since 16 March 2013); Executive Vice Premiers HAN Zheng (since 19 March 2018), SUN Chunlan (since 19 March 2018), LIU He (since 19 March 2018), HU Chunhua (since 19 March 2018)

cabinet: State Council appointed by National People's Congress

elections/appointments: president and vice president indirectly elected by National People's Congress for a 5-year term (unlimited terms); election last held on 17 March 2018 (next to be held in March 2023); premier nominated by president, confirmed by National People's Congress

election results: XI Jinping reelected president; National People's Congress vote - 2,970 (unanimously); WANG Qishan elected vice president with 2,969 votes

President XI Jinping (since 14 March 2013); Vice President WANG Qishan (since 17 March 2018)

LEGISLATIVE BRANCH:

description: unicameral National People's Congress or Quanguo Renmin Daibiao Dahui (maximum of 3,000 seats; members indirectly elected by municipal, regional, and provincial people's congresses, and the People's Liberation Army; members serve 5-year terms); note - in practice, only members of the Chinese Communist Party (CCP), its 8 allied independent parties, and CCP-approved independent candidates are elected

elections: last held in December 2017-February 2018 (next to be held in late 2022 to early 2023)

election results: percent of vote - NA; seats by party - NA; composition - men 2,238, women 742, percent of women 24.9%

JUDICIAL BRANCH:

highest courts: Supreme People's Court (consists of over 340 judges including the chief justice, 13 grand justices organized into a civil committee and tribunals for civil, economic, administrative, complaint and appeal, and communication and transportation cases); note - in late December 2016, the third, fourth, fifth, and sixth circuit courts of the Supreme People's Court began operation

judge selection and term of office: chief justice appointed by the People's National Congress (NPC); limited to 2 consecutive 5-year-terms; other justices and judges nominated by the chief justice and appointed by the Standing Committee of the NPC; term of other justices and judges determined by the NPC

subordinate courts: Higher People's Courts; Intermediate People's Courts; District and County People's Courts; Autonomous Region People's Courts; International Commercial Courts; Special People's Courts for military, maritime, transportation, and forestry issues

note: in late 2014, China unveiled planned judicial reforms

POLITICAL PARTIES AND LEADERS:

Chinese Communist Party or CCP [XI Jinping]

note: China has 8 nominally independent small parties controlled by the CCP

INTERNATIONAL ORGANIZATION PARTICIPATION:

ADB, AfDB (nonregional member), APEC, Arctic Council (observer), ARF, ASEAN (dialogue partner), BIS, BRICS, CDB, CICA, EAS, FAO, FATF, G-20, G-24 (observer), G-5, G-77, IADB, IAEA, IBRD, ICAO, ICC (national committees), ICRM, IDA, IFAD, IFC, IFRCS, IHO, ILO, IMF, IMO, IMSO, Interpol, IOC, IOM (observer), IPU, ISO, ITSO, ITU, LAIA (observer), MIGA, MINURSO, MINUSMA, MONUSCO, NAM (observer), NSG, OAS (observer), OPCW, Pacific Alliance (observer), PCA, PIF (partner), SAARC (observer), SCO, SICA (observer), UN, UNAMID, UNCTAD, UNESCO, UNFICYP, UNHCR, UNIDO, UNIFIL, UNMIL, UNMISS, UNOCI, UN Security Council (permanent), UNTSO, UNWTO, UPU, WCO, WHO, WIPO, WMO, WTO, ZC

DIPLOMATIC REPRESENTATION IN THE US:

chief of mission: Ambassador CUI Tiankai (since 3 April 2013)

chancery: 3505 International Place NW, Washington, DC 20008

telephone: [1] (202) 495-2266

FAX: [1] (202) 495-2138

consulate(s) general: Chicago, Houston, Los Angeles, New York, San Francisco

DIPLOMATIC REPRESENTATION FROM THE US:

chief of mission: Ambassador Terry BRANSTAD (since 12 July 2017)

embassy: 55 An Jia Lou Lu, 100600 Beijing

mailing address: PSC 461, Box 50, FPO AP 96521-0002

telephone: [86] (10) 8531-3000

FAX: [86] (10) 8531-3300

consulate(s) general: Chengdu, Guangzhou, Shanghai, Shenyang, Wuhan

FLAG DESCRIPTION:

red with a large yellow five-pointed star and four smaller yellow five-pointed stars (arranged in a vertical arc toward the middle of the flag) in the upper hoist-side corner; the color red represents revolution, while the stars symbolize the four social classes - the working class, the peasantry, the urban petty bourgeoisie, and the national bourgeoisie (capitalists) - united under the Communist Party of China

NATIONAL SYMBOL(S):

dragon, giant panda; national colors: red, yellow

NATIONAL ANTHEM:

name: "Yiyongjun Jinxingqu" (The March of the Volunteers)

lyrics/music: TIAN Han/NIE Er

note: adopted 1949; the anthem, though banned during the Cultural Revolution, is more commonly known as "Zhongguo Guoge" (Chinese National Song); it was originally the theme song to the 1935 Chinese movie, "Sons and Daughters in a Time of Storm"

ECONOMY :: CHINA

ECONOMY - OVERVIEW:

Since the late 1970s, China has moved from a closed, centrally planned system to a more market-oriented one that plays a major global role. China has implemented reforms in a gradualist fashion, resulting in efficiency gains that have contributed to a more than tenfold increase in GDP since 1978. Reforms began with the phaseout of collectivized agriculture, and expanded to include the gradual liberalization of prices, fiscal decentralization, increased autonomy for state enterprises, growth of the private sector, development of stock markets and a modern banking system, and opening to foreign trade and investment. China continues to pursue an industrial policy, state support of key sectors, and a restrictive investment regime. From 2013 to 2017, China had one of the fastest growing economies in the world, averaging slightly more than 7% real growth per year. Measured on a purchasing power parity (PPP) basis that adjusts for price differences, China in 2017 stood as the largest economy in the world, surpassing the US in 2014 for the first time in modern history. China became the world's largest exporter in 2010, and the largest trading nation in 2013. Still, China's per capita income is below the world average.

In July 2005 moved to an exchange rate system that references a basket of currencies. From mid-2005 to late 2008, the renminbi (RMB) appreciated more than 20% against the US dollar, but the exchange rate remained virtually pegged to the dollar from the onset of the global financial crisis until June 2010, when Beijing announced it would resume a gradual appreciation. From 2013 until early 2015, the renminbi held steady against the dollar, but it depreciated 13% from mid-2015 until end-2016 amid strong capital outflows; in 2017 the RMB resumed appreciating against the dollar – roughly 7% from end-of-2016 to end-of-2017. In 2015, the People's Bank of China announced it would continue to carefully push for full convertibility of the renminbi, after the currency was accepted as part of the IMF's special drawing rights basket. However, since late 2015 the Chinese Government has strengthened capital controls and oversight of overseas investments to better manage the exchange rate and maintain financial stability.

The Chinese Government faces numerous economic challenges including: (a) reducing its high domestic savings rate and correspondingly low domestic household consumption; (b) managing its high corporate debt burden to maintain financial stability; (c) controlling off-balance sheet local government debt used to finance infrastructure stimulus; (d) facilitating higher-wage job opportunities for the aspiring middle class, including rural migrants and college graduates, while maintaining competitiveness; (e) dampening speculative investment in the real estate sector without sharply slowing the economy; (f) reducing industrial overcapacity; and (g) raising productivity growth rates through the more efficient allocation of capital and state-support for innovation. Economic development has progressed further in coastal provinces than in the interior, and by 2016 more than 169.3 million migrant workers and their dependents had relocated to urban areas to find work. One consequence of China's population control policy known as the "one-child policy" - which was relaxed in 2016 to permit all families to have two children - is that China is now one of the most rapidly aging countries in the world. Deterioration in the environment - notably air pollution, soil erosion, and the steady fall of the water table, especially in the North - is another long-term problem. China continues to lose arable land because of erosion and urbanization. The Chinese Government is seeking to add energy production capacity from sources other than coal and oil, focusing on natural gas, nuclear, and clean energy development. In 2016, China ratified the Paris Agreement, a multilateral agreement to combat climate change, and committed to peak its carbon dioxide emissions between 2025 and 2030.

The government's 13th Five-Year Plan, unveiled in March 2016, emphasizes the need to increase innovation and boost domestic consumption to make the economy less dependent on government investment, exports, and heavy industry. However, China has made more progress on subsidizing innovation than rebalancing the economy. Beijing has committed to giving the market a more decisive role in allocating resources, but the Chinese Government's policies continue to favor state-owned enterprises and emphasize stability. Chinese leaders in 2010 pledged to double China's GDP by 2020, and the 13th Five Year Plan includes annual economic growth targets of at least 6.5% through 2020 to achieve that goal. In recent years, China has renewed its support for state-owned enterprises in sectors considered important to "economic security," explicitly looking to foster globally competitive industries. Chinese leaders also have undermined some market-oriented reforms by reaffirming the "dominant" role of the state in the economy, a stance that threatens to discourage private initiative and make the economy less efficient over time. The slight acceleration in economic growth in 2017—the first such uptick since 2010—gives Beijing more latitude to pursue its economic reforms, focusing on financial sector deleveraging and its Supply-Side Structural Reform agenda, first announced in late 2015.

GDP (PURCHASING POWER PARITY):

$23.21 trillion (2017 est.)

$21.72 trillion (2016 est.)

$20.35 trillion (2015 est.)

note: data are in 2017 dollars

country comparison to the world: 1

GDP (OFFICIAL EXCHANGE RATE):

$12.01 trillion (2017 est.) (2017 est.)

note: because China's exchange rate is determined by fiat rather than by market forces, the official exchange rate measure of GDP is not an accurate measure of China's output; GDP at the official exchange rate substantially understates the actual level of China's output vis-a-vis the rest of the world; in China's situation, GDP at purchasing power parity provides the best measure for comparing output across countries

GDP - REAL GROWTH RATE:

6.9% (2017 est.)

6.7% (2016 est.)

6.9% (2015 est.)

country comparison to the world: 21

GDP - PER CAPITA (PPP):

$16,700 (2017 est.)

$15,700 (2016 est.)

$14,800 (2015 est.)

note: data are in 2017 dollars

country comparison to the world: 105

GROSS NATIONAL SAVING:

45.8% of GDP (2017 est.)

45.9% of GDP (2016 est.)

47.5% of GDP (2015 est.)

country comparison to the world: 6

GDP - COMPOSITION, BY END USE:

household consumption: 39.1% (2017 est.)

government consumption: 14.5% (2017 est.)

investment in fixed capital: 42.7% (2017 est.)

investment in inventories: 1.7% (2017 est.)

exports of goods and services: 20.4% (2017 est.)

imports of goods and services: -18.4% (2017 est.)

GDP - COMPOSITION, BY SECTOR OF ORIGIN:

agriculture: 7.9% (2017 est.)

industry: 40.5% (2017 est.)

services: 51.6% (2017 est.)

AGRICULTURE - PRODUCTS:

world leader in gross value of agricultural output; rice, wheat, potatoes, corn, tobacco, peanuts, tea, apples, cotton, pork, mutton, eggs; fish, shrimp

INDUSTRIES:

world leader in gross value of industrial output; mining and ore processing, iron, steel, aluminum, and other metals, coal; machine building; armaments; textiles and apparel; petroleum; cement; chemicals; fertilizer; consumer products (including footwear, toys, and electronics); food processing; transportation equipment, including automobiles, railcars and locomotives, ships, aircraft; telecommunications equipment, commercial space launch vehicles, satellites

INDUSTRIAL PRODUCTION GROWTH RATE:

6.1% (2017 est.)

country comparison to the world: 40

LABOR FORCE:

806.7 million (2017 est.)

note: by the end of 2012, China's working age population (15-64 years) was 1.004 billion

country comparison to the world: 1

LABOR FORCE - BY OCCUPATION:

agriculture: 27.7%

industry: 28.8%

services: 43.5% (2016 est.)

UNEMPLOYMENT RATE:

3.9% (2017 est.)

4% (2016 est.)

note: data are for registered urban unemployment, which excludes private enterprises and migrants

country comparison to the world: 48

POPULATION BELOW POVERTY LINE:

3.3% (2016 est.)

note: in 2011, China set a new poverty line at RMB 2300 (approximately US $400)

HOUSEHOLD INCOME OR CONSUMPTION BY PERCENTAGE SHARE:

lowest 10%: 31.4% (2012)

highest 10%: 31.4% (2012)

note: data are for urban households only

DISTRIBUTION OF FAMILY INCOME - GINI INDEX:

46.5 (2016 est.)

46.2 (2015 est.)

country comparison to the world: 31

BUDGET:

revenues: 2.553 trillion (2017 est.)

expenditures: 3.008 trillion (2017 est.)

TAXES AND OTHER REVENUES:

21.3% (of GDP) (2017 est.)

country comparison to the world: 141

BUDGET SURPLUS (+) OR DEFICIT (-):

-3.8% (of GDP) (2017 est.)

country comparison to the world: 152

PUBLIC DEBT:

47% of GDP (2017 est.)

44.2% of GDP (2016 est.)

note: official data; data cover both central and local government debt, including debt officially recognized by China's National Audit Office report in 2011; data exclude policy bank bonds, Ministry of Railway debt, and China Asset Management Company debt

country comparison to the world: 111

FISCAL YEAR:

calendar year

INFLATION RATE (CONSUMER PRICES):

1.6% (2017 est.)

2% (2016 est.)

country comparison to the world: 88

CENTRAL BANK DISCOUNT RATE:

2.25% (5 December 2017 est.)

2.25% (31 December 2016 est.)

country comparison to the world: 117

COMMERCIAL BANK PRIME LENDING RATE:

4.35% (31 December 2017 est.)

4.35% (31 December 2016 est.)

country comparison to the world: 160

STOCK OF NARROW MONEY:

$8.351 trillion (31 December 2017 est.)

$7.001 trillion (31 December 2016 est.)

country comparison to the world: 1

STOCK OF BROAD MONEY:

$8.351 trillion (31 December 2017 est.)

$7.001 trillion (31 December 2016 est.)

country comparison to the world: 1

STOCK OF DOMESTIC CREDIT:

$27.34 trillion (31 December 2017 est.)

$23.02 trillion (31 December 2016 est.)

country comparison to the world: 1

MARKET VALUE OF PUBLICLY TRADED SHARES:

$7.335 trillion (December 2016 est.)

$8.234 trillion (December 2015 est.)

$8.518 trillion (31 est.)

country comparison to the world: 2

CURRENT ACCOUNT BALANCE:

$164.9 billion (2017 est.)

$202.2 billion (2016 est.)

country comparison to the world: 3

EXPORTS:

$2.216 trillion (2017 est.)

$1.99 trillion (2016 est.)

country comparison to the world: 1

EXPORTS - PARTNERS:

US 19%, Hong Kong 12.4%, Japan 6%, South Korea 4.5% (2017)

EXPORTS - COMMODITIES:

electrical and other machinery, including computers and telecommunications equipment, apparel, furniture, textiles

IMPORTS:

$1.74 trillion (2017 est.)

$1.501 trillion (2016 est.)

country comparison to the world: 2

IMPORTS - COMMODITIES:

electrical and other machinery, including integrated circuits and other computer components, oil and mineral fuels; optical and medical equipment, metal ores, motor vehicles; soybeans

IMPORTS - PARTNERS:

South Korea 9.7%, Japan 9.1%, US 8.5%, Germany 5.3%, Australia 5.1% (2017)

RESERVES OF FOREIGN EXCHANGE AND GOLD:

$3.236 trillion (31 December 2017 est.)

$3.098 trillion (31 December 2016 est.)

country comparison to the world: 1

DEBT - EXTERNAL:

$1.598 trillion (31 December 2017 est.)

$1.429 trillion (31 December 2016 est.)

country comparison to the world: 14

STOCK OF DIRECT FOREIGN INVESTMENT - AT HOME:

$1.523 trillion (31 December 2017 est.)

$1.391 trillion (31 December 2016 est.)

country comparison to the world: 7

STOCK OF DIRECT FOREIGN INVESTMENT - ABROAD:

$1.383 trillion (31 December 2017 est.)

$1.227 trillion (31 December 2016 est.)

country comparison to the world: 10

EXCHANGE RATES:

Renminbi yuan (RMB) per US dollar -

7.76 (2017 est.)

6.6446 (2016 est.)

6.2275 (2015 est.)

6.1434 (2014 est.)

6.1958 (2013 est.)

ENERGY :: CHINA

ELECTRICITY ACCESS:

population without electricity: 1.2 million (2016)

electrification - total population: 99.9% (2016)

electrification - urban areas: 100% (2016)

electrification - rural areas: 99.8% (2016)

ELECTRICITY - PRODUCTION:

5.883 trillion kWh (2016 est.)

country comparison to the world: 1

ELECTRICITY - CONSUMPTION:

5.564 trillion kWh (2016 est.)

country comparison to the world: 1

ELECTRICITY - EXPORTS:

18.91 billion kWh (2016 est.)

country comparison to the world: 10

ELECTRICITY - IMPORTS:

6.185 billion kWh (2016 est.)

country comparison to the world: 33

ELECTRICITY - INSTALLED GENERATING CAPACITY:

1.653 billion kW (2016 est.)

country comparison to the world: 1

ELECTRICITY - FROM FOSSIL FUELS:

62% of total installed capacity (2016 est.)

country comparison to the world: 124

ELECTRICITY - FROM NUCLEAR FUELS:

2% of total installed capacity (2017 est.)

country comparison to the world: 25

ELECTRICITY - FROM HYDROELECTRIC PLANTS:

18% of total installed capacity (2017 est.)

country comparison to the world: 93

ELECTRICITY - FROM OTHER RENEWABLE SOURCES:

18% of total installed capacity (2017 est.)

country comparison to the world: 47

CRUDE OIL - PRODUCTION:

3.838 million bbl/day (2017 est.)

country comparison to the world: 7

CRUDE OIL - EXPORTS:

57,310 bbl/day (2015 est.)

country comparison to the world: 40

CRUDE OIL - IMPORTS:

6.71 million bbl/day (2015 est.)

country comparison to the world: 2

CRUDE OIL - PROVED RESERVES:

25.63 billion bbl (1 January 2018 est.)

country comparison to the world: 12

REFINED PETROLEUM PRODUCTS - PRODUCTION:

11.51 million bbl/day (2015 est.)

country comparison to the world: 2

REFINED PETROLEUM PRODUCTS - CONSUMPTION:

12.47 million bbl/day (2016 est.)

country comparison to the world: 2

REFINED PETROLEUM PRODUCTS - EXPORTS:

848,400 bbl/day (2015 est.)

country comparison to the world: 9

REFINED PETROLEUM PRODUCTS - IMPORTS:

1.16 million bbl/day (2015 est.)

country comparison to the world: 4

NATURAL GAS - PRODUCTION:

145.9 billion cu m (2017 est.)

country comparison to the world: 6

NATURAL GAS - CONSUMPTION:

238.6 billion cu m (2017 est.)

country comparison to the world: 3

NATURAL GAS - EXPORTS:

3.37 billion cu m (2017 est.)

country comparison to the world: 35

NATURAL GAS - IMPORTS:

97.63 billion cu m (2017 est.)

country comparison to the world: 3

NATURAL GAS - PROVED RESERVES:

5.44 trillion cu m (1 January 2018 est.)

country comparison to the world: 9

CARBON DIOXIDE EMISSIONS FROM CONSUMPTION OF ENERGY:

11.67 billion Mt (2017 est.)

country comparison to the world: 1

COMMUNICATIONS :: CHINA

TELEPHONES - FIXED LINES:

total subscriptions: 193.762 million (2017 est.)

subscriptions per 100 inhabitants: 14 (2017 est.)

country comparison to the world: 1

TELEPHONES - MOBILE CELLULAR:

total subscriptions: 1,474,097,000 (2017 est.)

subscriptions per 100 inhabitants: 107 (2017 est.)

country comparison to the world: 1

TELEPHONE SYSTEM:

general assessment: China has become the largest Internet market in the world, with the majority of users accessing the Internet through mobile devices; moderate growth is predicted over the next five years in the fixed broadband segment; one of the biggest drivers of commercial growth is its increasing urbanisation rate as rural residents move to cities; 80% of China's Internet users access the Internet through mobile devices; by 2015 China will be the world's largest 5G market (2017)

domestic: 14 per 100 fixed line and 107 per 100 moblie-cellular; a domestic satellite system with several earth stations is in place in 2018 (2017)

international: country code - 86; a number of submarine cables provide connectivity to Asia, the Middle East, Europe, and the US; satellite earth stations - 7 (5 Intelsat - 4 Pacific Ocean and 1 Indian Ocean; 1 Intersputnik - Indian Ocean region; and 1 Inmarsat - Pacific and Indian Ocean regions) (2017)

BROADCAST MEDIA:

all broadcast media are owned by, or affiliated with, the Communist Party of China or a government agency; no privately owned TV or radio stations; state-run Chinese Central TV, provincial, and municipal stations offer more than 2,000 channels; the Central Propaganda Department sends directives to all domestic media outlets to guide its reporting with the government maintaining authority to approve all programming; foreign-made TV programs must be approved prior to broadcast; increasingly, Chinese turn to online and satellite television to access Chinese and international films and television shows (2017)

INTERNET COUNTRY CODE:

.cn

INTERNET USERS:

total: 730,723,960 (July 2016 est.)

percent of population: 53.2% (July 2016 est.)

country comparison to the world: 1

BROADBAND - FIXED SUBSCRIPTIONS:

total: 378.54 million (2017 est.)

subscriptions per 100 inhabitants: 27 (2017 est.)

country comparison to the world: 1

TRANSPORTATION :: CHINA

NATIONAL AIR TRANSPORT SYSTEM:

number of registered air carriers: 56 (2015)

inventory of registered aircraft operated by air carriers: 2,890 (2015)

annual passenger traffic on registered air carriers: 436,183,969 (2015)

annual freight traffic on registered air carriers: 19.806 billion mt-km (2015)

CIVIL AIRCRAFT REGISTRATION COUNTRY CODE PREFIX:

B (2016)

AIRPORTS:

507 (2013)

country comparison to the world: 14

AIRPORTS - WITH PAVED RUNWAYS:

total: 463 (2017)

over 3,047 m: 71 (2017)

2,438 to 3,047 m: 158 (2017)

1,524 to 2,437 m: 123 (2017)

914 to 1,523 m: 25 (2017)

under 914 m: 86 (2017)

AIRPORTS - WITH UNPAVED RUNWAYS:

total: 44 (2013)

over 3,047 m: 4 (2013)

2,438 to 3,047 m: 7 (2013)

1,524 to 2,437 m: 6 (2013)

914 to 1,523 m: 9 (2013)

under 914 m: 18 (2013)

HELIPORTS:

47 (2013)

PIPELINES:

70000 km gas, 22900 km crude oil, 25500 km refined petroleum products, 710206 km water (2015)

RAILWAYS:

total: 124,000 km (2017)

standard gauge: 124,000 km 1.435-m gauge (80,000 km electrified); 102,000 traditional, 22,000 high-speed (2017)

country comparison to the world: 2

ROADWAYS:

total: 4,577,300 km (2015)

paved: 4,046,300 km (includes 123,500 km of expressways) (2015)

unpaved: 531,000 km (2015)

country comparison to the world: 3

WATERWAYS:

110,000 km (navigable waterways) (2011)

country comparison to the world: 1

MERCHANT MARINE:

total: 4,287 (2017)

by type: bulk carrier 1069, container ship 198, general cargo 697, oil tanker 480, other 1843 (2017)

country comparison to the world: 4

PORTS AND TERMINALS:

major seaport(s): Dalian, Ningbo, Qingdao, Qinhuangdao, Shanghai, Shenzhen, Tianjin

container port(s) (TEUs): Dalian (9,614,000), Guangzhou (18,857,700), Ningbo (21,560,000), Qingdao (18,010,000), Shanghai (37,133,000), Shenzhen (23,979,300), Tianjin (14,490,000) (2016)

LNG terminal(s) (import): Fujian, Guangdong, Jiangsu, Shandong, Shanghai, Tangshan, Zhejiang

river port(s): Guangzhou (Pearl)

TRANSPORTATION - NOTE:

seven of the world's ten largest container ports are in China

MILITARY AND SECURITY :: CHINA

MILITARY EXPENDITURES:

2% of GDP (2017)

1.9% of GDP (2016)

1.95% of GDP (2015)

1.9% of GDP (2014)

1.85% of GDP (2013)

country comparison to the world: 51

MILITARY BRANCHES:

People's Liberation Army (PLA): Army, Navy (PLAN, includes marines and naval aviation), Air Force (PLAAF, includes airborne forces), Rocket Force (strategic missile force), and Strategic Support Force (space and cyber forces); People's Armed Police (PAP); PLA Reserve Force (2018)

MILITARY SERVICE AGE AND OBLIGATION:

18-22 years of age for selective compulsory military service, with a 2-year service obligation; no minimum age for voluntary service (all officers are volunteers); 18-19 years of age for women high school graduates who meet requirements for specific military jobs (2018)

TRANSNATIONAL ISSUES :: CHINA

DISPUTES - INTERNATIONAL:

continuing talks and confidence-building measures work toward reducing tensions over Kashmir that nonetheless remains militarized with portions under the de facto administration of China (Aksai Chin), India (Jammu and Kashmir), and Pakistan (Azad Kashmir and Northern Areas)India does not recognize Pakistan's ceding historic Kashmir lands to China in 1964China and India continue their security and foreign policy dialogue started in 2005 related to the dispute over most of their rugged, militarized boundary, regional nuclear proliferation, and other mattersChina claims most of India's Arunachal Pradesh to the base of the Himalayaslacking any treaty describing the boundary, Bhutan and China continue negotiations to establish a common boundary alignment to resolve territorial disputes arising from substantial cartographic discrepancies, the most contentious of which lie in Bhutan's west along China's Chumbi salientBurmese forces attempting to dig in to the largely autonomous Shan State to rout local militias tied to the drug trade, prompts local residents to periodically flee into neighboring Yunnan Province in ChinaChinese maps show an international boundary symbol off the coasts of the littoral states of the South China Seas, where China has interrupted Vietnamese hydrocarbon explorationChina asserts sovereignty over Scarborough Reef along with the Philippines and Taiwan, and over the Spratly Islands together with Malaysia, the Philippines, Taiwan, Vietnam, and Bruneithe 2002 Declaration on the Conduct of Parties in the South China Sea eased tensions in the Spratlys but is not the legally binding code of conduct sought by some partiesVietnam and China continue to expand construction of facilities in the Spratlys and in March 2005, the national oil companies of China, the Philippines, and Vietnam signed a joint accord on marine seismic activities in the Spratly Islands;China and ASEAN began formal South China Sea Code of Conduct negotiations in March 2018, but it remains unclear the timeline for a final agreement and how it would be enforced;

China occupies some of the Paracel Islands also claimed by Vietnam and Taiwanthe Japanese-administered Senkaku Islands are also claimed by China and Taiwancertain islands in the Yalu and Tumen Rivers are in dispute with North KoreaNorth Korea and China seek to stem illegal migration to China by North Koreans, fleeing privations and oppression, by building a fence along portions of the border and imprisoning North Koreans deported by ChinaChina and Russia have demarcated the once disputed islands at the Amur and Ussuri confluence and in the Argun River in accordance with their 2004 AgreementChina and Tajikistan have begun demarcating the revised boundary agreed to in the delimitation of 2002the decade-long demarcation of the China-Vietnam land boundary was completed in 2009citing environmental, cultural, and social concerns, China has reconsidered construction of 13 dams on the Salween River, but, as of 2016, energy-starved Burma, with backing from Thailand, remained intent on building seven hydro-electric dams downstream despite regional and international protests

Chinese and Hong Kong authorities met in March 2008 to resolve ownership and use of lands recovered in Shenzhen River channelization, including 96-hectare Lok Ma Chau Loop

REFUGEES AND INTERNALLY DISPLACED PERSONS:

refugees (country of origin): 317,098 (Vietnam), undetermined (North Korea) (2016)

IDPs: undetermined (2014)

TRAFFICKING IN PERSONS:

current situation: China is a source, transit, and destination country for men, women, and children subjected to sex trafficking and forced labor; Chinese adults and children are forced into prostitution and various forms of forced labor, including begging and working in brick kilns, coal mines, and factories; women and children are recruited from rural areas and taken to urban centers for sexual exploitation, often lured by criminal syndicates or gangs with fraudulent job offers; state-sponsored forced labor, where detainees work for up to four years often with no remuneration, continues to be a serious concern; Chinese men, women, and children also may be subjected to conditions of sex trafficking and forced labor worldwide, particularly in overseas Chinese communities; women and children are trafficked to China from neighboring countries, as well as Africa and the Americas, for forced labor and prostitution

tier rating: Tier 2 Watch List - China does not fully comply with the minimum standards for the elimination of trafficking; however, it is making significant efforts to do so; official data for 2014 states that 194 alleged traffickers were arrested and at least 35 were convicted, but the government's conflation of human trafficking with other crimes makes it difficult to assess law enforcement efforts to investigate and to prosecute trafficking offenses according to international law; despite reports of complicity, no government officials were investigated, prosecuted, or convicted for their roles in trafficking offenses; authorities did not adequately protect victims and did not provide the data needed to ascertain the number of victims identified or assisted or the services provided; the National People's Congress ratified a decision to abolish "reform through labor" in 2013, but some continued to operate as state-sponsored drug detention or "custody and education" centers that force inmates to perform manual labor; some North Korean refugees continued to be forcibly repatriated as illegal economic migrants, despite reports that some were trafficking victims (2015)

ILLICIT DRUGS:

major transshipment point for heroin produced in the Golden Triangle region of Southeast Asia; growing domestic consumption of synthetic drugs, and heroin from Southeast and Southwest Asia; source country for methamphetamine and heroin chemical precursors, despite new regulations on its large chemical industry; more people believed to be convicted and executed for drug offences than anywhere else in the world, according to NGOs

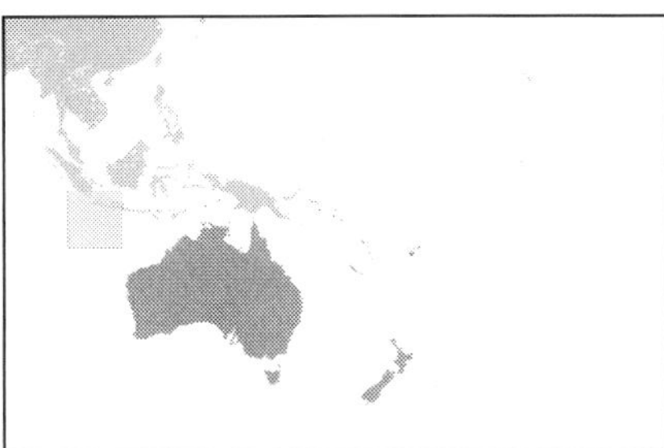

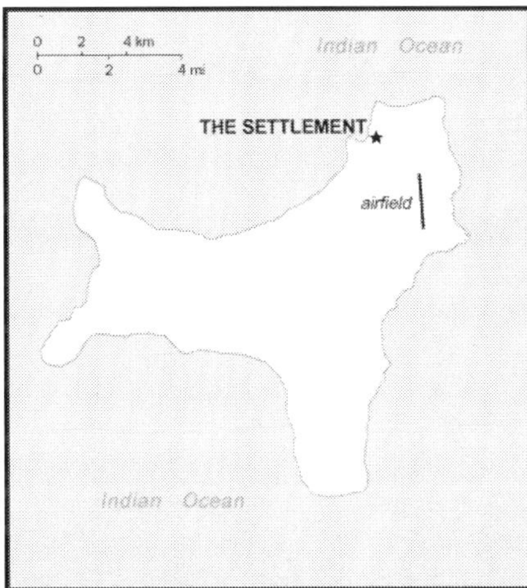

AUSTRALIA - OCEANIA :: CHRISTMAS ISLAND

INTRODUCTION :: CHRISTMAS ISLAND

BACKGROUND:

Named in 1643 for the day of its discovery, the island was annexed and settlement began by the UK in 1888 with the discovery of the island's phosphate deposits. Following the Second World War, Christmas Island came under the jurisdiction of the new British Colony of Singapore. The island existed as a separate Crown colony from 1 January 1958 to 1 October 1958 when its transfer to Australian jurisdiction was finalized. That date is still celebrated on the first Monday in October as Territory Day. Almost two-thirds of the island has been declared a national park.

GEOGRAPHY :: CHRISTMAS ISLAND

LOCATION:

Southeastern Asia, island in the Indian Ocean, south of Indonesia

GEOGRAPHIC COORDINATES:

10 30 S, 105 40 E

MAP REFERENCES:

Southeast Asia

AREA:

total: 135 sq km

land: 135 sq km

water: 0 sq km

country comparison to the world: 222

AREA - COMPARATIVE:

about three-quarters the size of Washington, DC

LAND BOUNDARIES:

0 km

COASTLINE:

138.9 km

MARITIME CLAIMS:

territorial sea: 12 nm

contiguous zone: 12 nm

exclusive fishing zone: 200 nm

CLIMATE:

tropical with a wet season (December to April) and dry season; heat and humidity moderated by trade winds

TERRAIN:

steep cliffs along coast rise abruptly to central plateau

ELEVATION:

0 m lowest point: Indian Ocean

361 highest point: Murray Hill

NATURAL RESOURCES:

phosphate, beaches

LAND USE:

agricultural land: 0% (2011 est.)

arable land: 0% (2011 est.) / permanent crops: 0% (2011 est.) / permanent pasture: 0% (2011 est.)

other: 100% (2011 est.)

IRRIGATED LAND:

NA

POPULATION DISTRIBUTION:

majority of the population lives on the northern tip of the island

NATURAL HAZARDS:

the narrow fringing reef surrounding the island can be a maritime hazard

ENVIRONMENT - CURRENT ISSUES:

loss of rainforest; impact of phosphate mining

GEOGRAPHY - NOTE:

located along major sea lanes of the Indian Ocean

PEOPLE AND SOCIETY :: CHRISTMAS ISLAND

POPULATION:

2,205 (July 2016 est.)

country comparison to the world: 231

NATIONALITY:

noun: Christmas Islander(s)

adjective: Christmas Island

ETHNIC GROUPS:

Chinese 70%, European 20%, Malay 10% (2001)

note: no indigenous population

LANGUAGES:

English (official) 27.6%, Mandarin 17.2%, Malay 17.1%, Cantonese 3.9%, Min Nan 1.6%, Tagalog 1%, other 4.5%, unspecified 27.1% (2016 est.)

note: data represent language spoken at home

RELIGIONS:

Muslim 19.4%, Buddhist 18.3%, Roman Catholic 8.8%, Protestant 6.5% (includes Anglican 3.6%, Uniting Church 1.2%, other 1.7%), other Christian 3.3%, other 0.6%, none 15.3%, unspecified 27.7% (2016 est.)

AGE STRUCTURE:

0-14 years: 12.79% (male 147/female 135) (2017 est.)

15-24 years: 12.2% (male 202/female 67) (2017 est.)

25-54 years: 57.91% (male 955/female 322) (2017 est.)

55-64 years: 11.66% (male 172/female 85) (2017 est.)

65 years and over: 5.44% (male 84/female 36) (2017 est.)

POPULATION GROWTH RATE:

1.11% (2014 est.)

country comparison to the world: 97

POPULATION DISTRIBUTION:

majority of the population lives on the northern tip of the island

SEX RATIO:

NA

INFANT MORTALITY RATE:

total: NA

male: NA

female: NA

LIFE EXPECTANCY AT BIRTH:

total population: NA (2017 est.)

male: NA (2017 est.)

female: NA (2017 est.)

TOTAL FERTILITY RATE:

NA

HIV/AIDS - ADULT PREVALENCE RATE:

NA

HIV/AIDS - PEOPLE LIVING WITH HIV/AIDS:

NA

HIV/AIDS - DEATHS:

NA

GOVERNMENT :: CHRISTMAS ISLAND

COUNTRY NAME:

conventional long form: Territory of Christmas Island

conventional short form: Christmas Island

etymology: named by English Captain William MYNORS for the day of its discovery, Christmas Day (25 December 1643)

DEPENDENCY STATUS:

non-self governing territory of Australia; administered from Canberra by the Department of Regional Australia, Local Government, Arts and Sport

GOVERNMENT TYPE:

non-self-governing overseas territory of Australia

CAPITAL:

name: The Settlement

geographic coordinates: 10 25 S, 105 43 E

time difference: UTC+7 (12 hours ahead of Washington, DC, during Standard Time)

ADMINISTRATIVE DIVISIONS:

none (territory of Australia)

INDEPENDENCE:

none (territory of Australia)

NATIONAL HOLIDAY:

Australia Day (commemorates the arrival of the First Fleet of Australian settlers), 26 January (1788)

CONSTITUTION:

history: 1 October 1958 (Christmas Island Act 1958) (2017)

amendments: amended many times, last in 2016 (2017)

LEGAL SYSTEM:

legal system is under the authority of the governor general of Australia and Australian law

CITIZENSHIP:

see Australia

SUFFRAGE:

18 years of age

EXECUTIVE BRANCH:

chief of state: Queen ELIZABETH II (since 6 February 1952); represented by Governor General of the Commonwealth of Australia General Sir Peter COSGROVE (since 28 March 2014)

head of government: Administrator Natasha GRIGGS (since 5 October 2018)

elections/appointments: the monarchy is hereditary; governor general appointed by the monarch on the recommendation of the Australian prime minister; administrator appointed by the governor general of Australia for a 2-year term and represents the monarch and Australia

LEGISLATIVE BRANCH:

description: unicameral Christmas Island Shire Council (9 seats; members directly elected by simple majority vote to serve 4-year terms with a portion of the membership renewed every 2 years)

elections: held every 2 years with half the members standing for election; last held on 17 October 2015 (next to be held on 21 October 2017)

election results: percent of vote - NA; seats by party - independent 9; composition as of 17 October 2015 - men 6, women 3, percent of women 33.3%

JUDICIAL BRANCH:

under the terms of the Territorial Law Reform Act 1992, Western Australia provides court services as needed for the island, including the Supreme Court and subordinate courts (District Court, Magistrate Court, Family Court, Children's Court, and Coroners' Court)

POLITICAL PARTIES AND LEADERS:

none

INTERNATIONAL ORGANIZATION PARTICIPATION:

none

DIPLOMATIC REPRESENTATION IN THE US:

none (territory of Australia)

DIPLOMATIC REPRESENTATION FROM THE US:

none (territory of Australia)

FLAG DESCRIPTION:

territorial flag; divided diagonally from upper hoist to lower fly; the upper triangle is green with a yellow image of the Golden Bosun Bird superimposed; the lower triangle is blue with the Southern Cross constellation, representing Australia, superimposed; a centered yellow disk displays a green map of the island

note: the flag of Australia is used for official purposes

NATIONAL SYMBOL(S):

golden bosun bird

NATIONAL ANTHEM:

note: as a territory of Australia, "Advance Australia Fair" remains official as the national anthem, while "God Save the Queen" serves as the royal anthem (see Australia)

ECONOMY :: CHRISTMAS ISLAND

ECONOMY - OVERVIEW:

The main economic activities on Christmas Island are the mining of low grade phosphate, limited tourism, the provision of government services and, since 2005, the construction and operation of the Immigration Detention Center. The government sector includes administration, health, education, policing, customs, quarantine, and defense.

GDP (PURCHASING POWER PARITY):

NA

AGRICULTURE - PRODUCTS:

NA

INDUSTRIES:

tourism, phosphate extraction (near depletion)

LABOR FORCE:

NA

BUDGET:

revenues: NA

expenditures: NA

FISCAL YEAR:

1 July - 30 June

EXPORTS:

NA

EXPORTS - COMMODITIES:

phosphate

IMPORTS:

NA

IMPORTS - COMMODITIES:

consumer goods

STOCK OF DIRECT FOREIGN INVESTMENT - AT HOME:

(31 December 2009 est.)

EXCHANGE RATES:

Australian dollars (AUD) per US dollar -

1.311 (2017 est.)

1.3442 (2016 est.)

1.3442 (2015)

1.3291 (2014 est.)

1.1094 (2013 est.)

COMMUNICATIONS :: CHRISTMAS ISLAND

TELEPHONE SYSTEM:

general assessment: service provided by the Australian network (2017)

domestic: local area code - 08; GSM mobile-cellular telephone service is provided by Telstra as part of the Australian network (2017)

international: international code - 61 8; satellite earth station - 1 (Intelsat provides telephone and telex service) (2017)

BROADCAST MEDIA:

1 community radio station; satellite broadcasts of several Australian radio and TV stations (2017)

INTERNET COUNTRY CODE:

.cx

INTERNET USERS:

total: 790 (July 2016 est.)

percent of population: 35.8% (July 2016 est.)

country comparison to the world: 225

TRANSPORTATION :: CHRISTMAS ISLAND

AIRPORTS:

1 (2013)

country comparison to the world: 217

AIRPORTS - WITH PAVED RUNWAYS:

total: 1 (2017)

1,524 to 2,437 m: 1 (2017)

RAILWAYS:

total: 18 km (2017)

standard gauge: 18 km 1.435-m (not in operation) (2017)

note: the 18-km Christmas Island Phosphate Company Railway between Flying Fish Cove and South Point was decommissioned in 1987; some tracks and scrap remain in place

country comparison to the world: 134

ROADWAYS:

total: 140 km (2011)

paved: 30 km (2011)

unpaved: 110 km (2011)

country comparison to the world: 213

PORTS AND TERMINALS:

major seaport(s): Flying Fish Cove

MILITARY AND SECURITY :: CHRISTMAS ISLAND

MILITARY - NOTE:

defense is the responsibility of Australia

TRANSNATIONAL ISSUES :: CHRISTMAS ISLAND

DISPUTES - INTERNATIONAL:

none

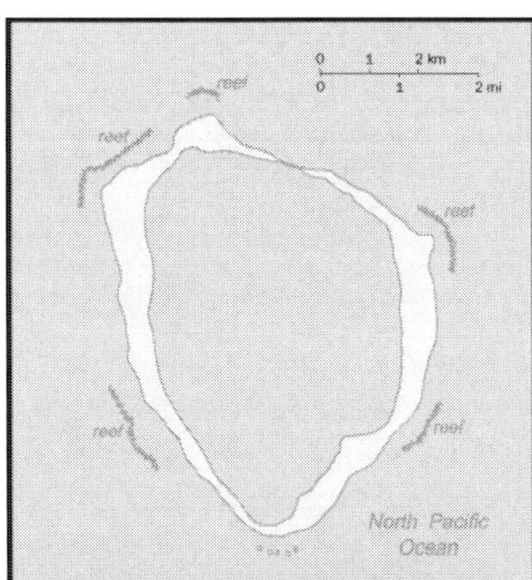

NORTH AMERICA :: CLIPPERTON ISLAND

INTRODUCTION :: CLIPPERTON ISLAND

BACKGROUND:

This isolated atoll was named for John CLIPPERTON, an English pirate who was rumored to have made it his hideout early in the 18th century. Annexed by France in 1855 and claimed by the US, it was seized by Mexico in 1897. Arbitration eventually awarded the island to France in 1931, which took possession in 1935.

GEOGRAPHY :: CLIPPERTON ISLAND

LOCATION:

Middle America, atoll in the North Pacific Ocean, 1,120 km southwest of Mexico

GEOGRAPHIC COORDINATES:

10 17 N, 109 13 W

MAP REFERENCES:

Political Map of the World

AREA:

total: 6 sq km

land: 6 sq km

water: 0 sq km

country comparison to the world: 248

AREA - COMPARATIVE:

about 12 times the size of The Mall in Washington, DC

LAND BOUNDARIES:

0 km

COASTLINE:

11.1 km

MARITIME CLAIMS:

territorial sea: 12 nm

exclusive economic zone: 200 nm

CLIMATE:

tropical; humid, average temperature 20-32 degrees Celsius, wet season (May to October)

TERRAIN:

coral atoll

ELEVATION:

0 m lowest point: Pacific Ocean

29 highest point: Rocher Clipperton

NATURAL RESOURCES:

fish

LAND USE:

agricultural land: 0% (2011 est.)

arable land: 0% (2011 est.) / permanent crops: 0% (2011 est.) / permanent pasture: 0% (2011 est.)

forest: 0% (2011 est.)

other: 100% (2011 est.)

NATURAL HAZARDS:

subject to tropical storms and hurricanes from May to October

ENVIRONMENT - CURRENT ISSUES:

no natural resources, guano deposits depleted; the ring-shaped atoll encloses a stagnant fresh-water lagoon

GEOGRAPHY - NOTE:

the atoll reef is approximately 12 km (7.5 mi) in circumference; an attempt to colonize the atoll in the early 20th century ended in disaster and was abandoned in 1917

PEOPLE AND SOCIETY :: CLIPPERTON ISLAND

POPULATION:

uninhabited

GOVERNMENT :: CLIPPERTON ISLAND

COUNTRY NAME:

conventional long form: none

conventional short form: Clipperton Island

local long form: none

local short form: Ile Clipperton

former: sometimes referred to as Ile de la Passion or Atoll Clipperton

etymology: named after an 18th-century English pirate who supposedly used the island as a base

DEPENDENCY STATUS:

possession of France; administered directly by the Minister of Overseas France

LEGAL SYSTEM:

the laws of France apply

FLAG DESCRIPTION:

the flag of France is used

ECONOMY :: CLIPPERTON ISLAND

ECONOMY - OVERVIEW:

Although 115 species of fish have been identified in the territorial waters of Clipperton Island, tuna fishing is the only economically viable species.

TRANSPORTATION :: CLIPPERTON ISLAND

PORTS AND TERMINALS:

none; offshore anchorage only

MILITARY AND SECURITY :: CLIPPERTON ISLAND

MILITARY - NOTE:

defense is the responsibility of France

TRANSNATIONAL ISSUES :: CLIPPERTON ISLAND

DISPUTES - INTERNATIONAL:

none

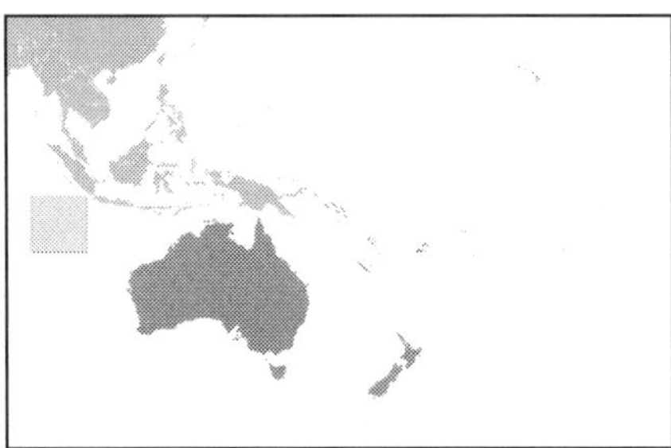

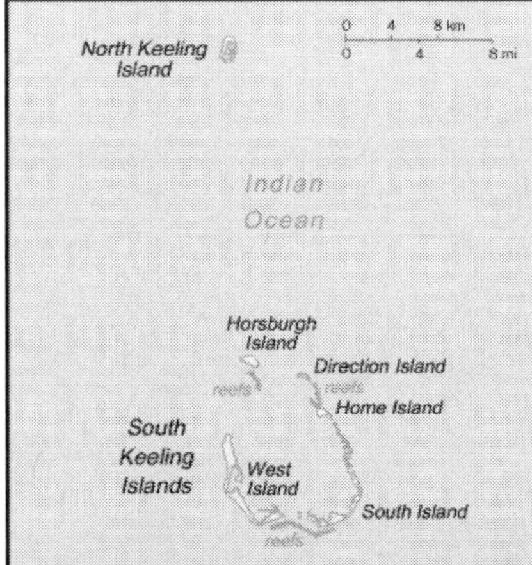

AUSTRALIA - OCEANIA :: COCOS (KEELING) ISLANDS

INTRODUCTION :: COCOS (KEELING) ISLANDS

BACKGROUND:

There are 27 coral islands in the group. Captain William KEELING discovered the islands in 1609, but they remained uninhabited until the 19th century. From the 1820s to 1978, members of the CLUNIES-ROSS family controlled the islands and the copra produced from local coconuts. Annexed by the UK in 1857, the Cocos Islands were transferred to the Australian Government in 1955. Apart from North Keeling Island, which lies 30 kilometers north of the main group, the islands form a horseshoe-shaped atoll surrounding a lagoon. North Keeling Island was declared a national park in 1995 and is administered by Parks Australia. The population on the two inhabited islands generally is split between the ethnic Europeans on West Island and the ethnic Malays on Home Island.

GEOGRAPHY :: COCOS (KEELING) ISLANDS

LOCATION:

Southeastern Asia, group of islands in the Indian Ocean, southwest of Indonesia, about halfway between Australia and Sri Lanka

GEOGRAPHIC COORDINATES:

12 30 S, 96 50 E

MAP REFERENCES:

Southeast Asia

AREA:

total: 14 sq km

land: 14 sq km

water: 0 sq km

note: includes the two main islands of West Island and Home Island

country comparison to the world: 241

AREA - COMPARATIVE:

about 24 times the size of The Mall in Washington, DC

LAND BOUNDARIES:

0 km

COASTLINE:

26 km

MARITIME CLAIMS:

territorial sea: 12 nm

exclusive fishing zone: 200 nm

CLIMATE:

tropical with high humidity, moderated by the southeast trade winds for about nine months of the year

TERRAIN:

flat, low-lying coral atolls

ELEVATION:

0 m lowest point: Indian Ocean

9 highest point: South Point on South Island

NATURAL RESOURCES:

fish

LAND USE:

agricultural land: 0% (2011 est.)

arable land: 0% (2011 est.) / permanent crops: 0% (2011 est.) / permanent pasture: 0% (2011 est.)

forest: 0% (2011 est.)

other: 100% (2011 est.)

IRRIGATED LAND:

NA

POPULATION DISTRIBUTION:

only Home Island and West Island are populated

NATURAL HAZARDS:

cyclone season is October to April

ENVIRONMENT - CURRENT ISSUES:

freshwater resources are limited to rainwater accumulations in natural underground reservoirs; illegal fishing a concern

GEOGRAPHY - NOTE:

islands are thickly covered with coconut palms and other vegetation; site of a World War I naval battle in November 1914 between the Australian light cruiser HMAS Sydney and the German raider SMS Emden; after being heavily damaged in the engagement, the Emden was beached by her captain on North Keeling Island

PEOPLE AND SOCIETY :: COCOS (KEELING) ISLANDS

POPULATION:

596 (July 2014 est.)

country comparison to the world: 237

NATIONALITY:

noun: Cocos Islander(s)

adjective: Cocos Islander

ETHNIC GROUPS:

Europeans, Cocos Malays

LANGUAGES:

English 22.3%, Malay (Cocos dialect) 68.8%, unspecified 8.9% (2016 est.)

note: data represent language spoken at home

RELIGIONS:

Muslim (predominantly Sunni) 75%, Anglican 3.5%, Roman Catholic 2.2%, none 12.9%, unspecified 6.3% (2016 est.)

POPULATION GROWTH RATE:

0% (2014 est.)

country comparison to the world: 193

POPULATION DISTRIBUTION:

only Home Island and West Island are populated

INFANT MORTALITY RATE:

total: NA

male: NA

female: NA

LIFE EXPECTANCY AT BIRTH:

total population: NA (2017 est.)

male: NA (2017 est.)

female: NA (2017 est.)

TOTAL FERTILITY RATE:

NA

HIV/AIDS - ADULT PREVALENCE RATE:

NA

HIV/AIDS - PEOPLE LIVING WITH HIV/AIDS:

NA

HIV/AIDS - DEATHS:

NA

GOVERNMENT :: COCOS (KEELING) ISLANDS

COUNTRY NAME:

conventional long form: Territory of Cocos (Keeling) Islands

conventional short form: Cocos (Keeling) Islands

etymology: the name refers to the abundant coconut trees on the islands and to English Captain William KEELING, the first European to sight the islands in 1609

DEPENDENCY STATUS:

non-self governing territory of Australia; administered from Canberra by the Department of Regional Australia, Local Government, Arts and Sport

GOVERNMENT TYPE:

non-self-governing overseas territory of Australia

CAPITAL:

name: West Island

geographic coordinates: 12 10 S, 96 50 E

time difference: UTC+6.5 (11.5 hours ahead of Washington, DC, during Standard Time)

ADMINISTRATIVE DIVISIONS:

none (territory of Australia)

INDEPENDENCE:

none (territory of Australia)

NATIONAL HOLIDAY:

Australia Day (commemorates the arrival of the First Fleet of Australian settlers), 26 January (1788)

CONSTITUTION:

history: 23 November 1955 (Cocos (Keeling) Islands Act 1955) (2017)

amendments: amended many times, last in 2016 (2017)

LEGAL SYSTEM:

common law based on the Australian model

CITIZENSHIP:

see Australia

SUFFRAGE:

18 years of age

EXECUTIVE BRANCH:

chief of state: Queen ELIZABETH II (since 6 February 1952); represented by Governor General of the Commonwealth of Australia General Sir Peter COSGROVE (since 28 March 2014)

head of government: Administrator Natasha GRIGGS (since 5 October 2018)

cabinet: NA

elections/appointments: the monarchy is hereditary; governor general appointed by the monarch on the recommendation of the Australian prime minister; administrator appointed by the governor general for a 2-year term and represents the monarch and Australia

LEGISLATIVE BRANCH:

description: unicameral Cocos (Keeling) Islands Shire Council (7 seats; members directly elected by simple majority vote to serve 4-year terms with half the membership renewed every 2 years)

elections: last held in October 2017 (next to be held in October 2019)

election results: percent of vote by party - NA; seats by party - NA; composition - men 5, women 2, percent of women 28.6%

JUDICIAL BRANCH:

under the terms of the Territorial Law Reform Act 1992, Western Australia provides court services as needed for the island including the Supreme Court and subordinate courts (District Court, Magistrate Court, Family Court, Children's Court, and Coroners' Court)

POLITICAL PARTIES AND LEADERS:

none

INTERNATIONAL ORGANIZATION PARTICIPATION:

none

DIPLOMATIC REPRESENTATION IN THE US:

none (territory of Australia)

DIPLOMATIC REPRESENTATION FROM THE US:

none (territory of Australia)

FLAG DESCRIPTION:

the flag of Australia is used

NATIONAL ANTHEM:

note: as a territory of Australia, "Advance Australia Fair" remains official as the national anthem, while "God Save the Queen" serves as the royal anthem (see Australia)

ECONOMY :: COCOS (KEELING) ISLANDS

ECONOMY - OVERVIEW:

Coconuts, grown throughout the islands, are the sole cash crop. Small local gardens and fishing contribute to the food supply, but additional food and most other necessities must be imported from Australia. There is a small tourist industry.

GDP (PURCHASING POWER PARITY):

NA

GDP - REAL GROWTH RATE:

1% (2003)

country comparison to the world: 183

AGRICULTURE - PRODUCTS:

vegetables, bananas, pawpaws, coconuts

INDUSTRIES:

copra products, tourism

LABOR FORCE:

NA

LABOR FORCE - BY OCCUPATION:

note: the Cocos Islands Cooperative Society Ltd. employs construction workers, stevedores, and lighterage workers; tourism is the other main source of employment

UNEMPLOYMENT RATE:

0.1% (2011)

60% (2000 est.)

country comparison to the world: 1

BUDGET:

revenues: NA

expenditures: NA

FISCAL YEAR:

1 July - 30 June

EXPORTS:

NA

EXPORTS - COMMODITIES:

copra

IMPORTS:

NA

IMPORTS - COMMODITIES:

foodstuffs

EXCHANGE RATES:

Australian dollars (AUD) per US dollar -

1.311 (2017 est.)

1.3442 (2016 est.)

1.3442 (2015)

1.3291 (2014)

1.1094 (2013)

COMMUNICATIONS :: COCOS (KEELING) ISLANDS

TELEPHONE SYSTEM:

general assessment: telephone service is part of the Australian network; an operational local mobile-cellular network available; wireless Internet connectivity available (2017)

domestic: local area code - 08 (2017)

international: international code - 61 8; telephone, telex, and facsimile communications with Australia and elsewhere via satellite; satellite earth station - 1 (Intelsat) (2017)

BROADCAST MEDIA:

1 local radio station staffed by community volunteers; satellite broadcasts of several Australian radio and TV stations available (2017)

INTERNET COUNTRY CODE:

.cc

TRANSPORTATION :: COCOS (KEELING) ISLANDS

AIRPORTS:

1 (2013)

country comparison to the world: 218

AIRPORTS - WITH PAVED RUNWAYS:

total: 1 (2017)

2,438 to 3,047 m: 1 (2017)

ROADWAYS:

total: 22 km (2007)

paved: 10 km (2007)

unpaved: 12 km (2007)

country comparison to the world: 222

PORTS AND TERMINALS:

major seaport(s): Port Refuge

MILITARY AND SECURITY :: COCOS (KEELING) ISLANDS

MILITARY - NOTE:

defense is the responsibility of Australia; the territory has a five-person police force

TRANSNATIONAL ISSUES :: COCOS (KEELING) ISLANDS

DISPUTES - INTERNATIONAL:

none

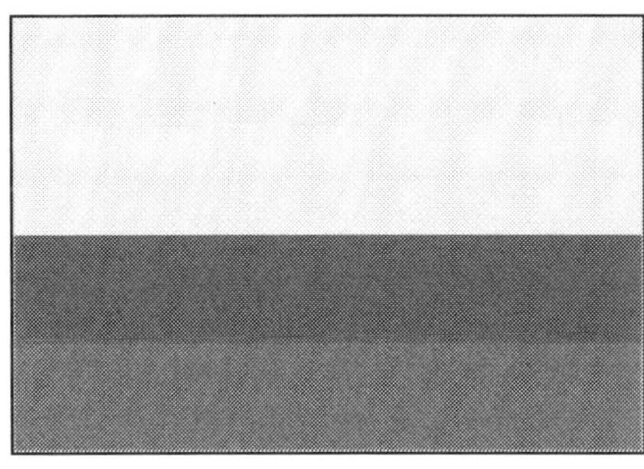

SOUTH AMERICA :: COLOMBIA

INTRODUCTION :: COLOMBIA

BACKGROUND:

Colombia was one of the three countries that emerged after the dissolution of Gran Colombia in 1830 (the others are Ecuador and Venezuela). A decades-long conflict between government forces, paramilitaries, and antigovernment insurgent groups heavily funded by the drug trade, principally the Revolutionary Armed Forces of Colombia (FARC), escalated during the 1990s. More than 31,000 former United Self Defense Forces of Colombia (AUC) paramilitaries demobilized by the end of 2006, and the AUC as a formal organization ceased to operate. In the wake of the paramilitary demobilization, illegal armed groups arose, whose members include some former paramilitaries. After four years of formal peace negotiations, the Colombian Government signed a final peace accord with the FARC in November 2016, which was subsequently ratified by the Colombian Congress. The accord calls for members of the FARC to demobilize, disarm, and reincorporate into society and politics. The accord also committed the Colombian Government to create three new institutions to form a 'comprehensive system for truth, justice, reparation, and non-repetition,' to include a truth commission, a special unit to coordinate the search for those who disappeared during the conflict, and a 'Special Jurisdiction for Peace' to administer justice for conflict-related crimes. The Colombian Government has stepped up efforts to expand its presence into every one of its administrative departments. Despite decades of internal conflict and drug-related security challenges, Colombia maintains relatively strong democratic institutions characterized by peaceful, transparent elections and the protection of civil liberties.

GEOGRAPHY :: COLOMBIA

LOCATION:

Northern South America, bordering the Caribbean Sea, between Panama and Venezuela, and bordering the North Pacific Ocean, between Ecuador and Panama

GEOGRAPHIC COORDINATES:

4 00 N, 72 00 W

MAP REFERENCES:

South America

AREA:

total: 1,138,910 sq km

land: 1,038,700 sq km

water: 100,210 sq km

note: includes Isla de Malpelo, Roncador Cay, and Serrana Bank

country comparison to the world: 27

AREA - COMPARATIVE:

slightly less than twice the size of Texas

LAND BOUNDARIES:

total: 6,672 km

border countries (5): Brazil 1790 km, Ecuador 708 km, Panama 339 km, Peru 1494 km, Venezuela 2341 km

COASTLINE:

3,208 km (Caribbean Sea 1,760 km, North Pacific Ocean 1,448 km)

MARITIME CLAIMS:

territorial sea: 12 nm

exclusive economic zone: 200 nm

continental shelf: 200-m depth or to the depth of exploitation

CLIMATE:

tropical along coast and eastern plains; cooler in highlands

TERRAIN:

flat coastal lowlands, central highlands, high Andes Mountains, eastern lowland plains (Llanos)

ELEVATION:

mean elevation: 593 m

elevation extremes: 0 m lowest point: Pacific Ocean

5730 highest point: Pico Cristobal Colon

note: nearby Pico Simon Bolivar also has the same elevation

NATURAL RESOURCES:

petroleum, natural gas, coal, iron ore, nickel, gold, copper, emeralds, hydropower

LAND USE:

agricultural land: 37.5% (2011 est.)

arable land: 1.4% (2011 est.) / permanent crops: 1.6% (2011 est.) / permanent pasture: 34.5% (2011 est.)

forest: 54.4% (2011 est.)

other: 8.1% (2011 est.)

IRRIGATED LAND:

10,900 sq km (2012)

POPULATION DISTRIBUTION:

the majority of people live in the north and west where agricultural opportunities and natural resources are found; the vast grasslands of the llanos to the south and east, which make up approximately 60% of the country, are sparsely populated

NATURAL HAZARDS:

highlands subject to volcanic eruptions; occasional earthquakes; periodic droughts

volcanism: Galeras (4,276 m) is one of Colombia's most active volcanoes, having erupted in 2009 and 2010 causing major evacuations; it has been deemed a Decade Volcano by the International Association of Volcanology and Chemistry of the Earth's Interior, worthy of study due to its explosive history and close proximity to human populations; Nevado del Ruiz (5,321 m), 129 km (80 mi) west of Bogota, erupted in 1985 producing lahars (mudflows) that killed 23,000 people; the volcano last erupted in 1991; additionally, after 500 years of dormancy, Nevado del Huila reawakened in 2007 and has experienced frequent eruptions since then; other historically active volcanoes include Cumbal, Dona Juana, Nevado del Tolima, and Purace

ENVIRONMENT - CURRENT ISSUES:

deforestation resulting from timber exploitation in the jungles of the Amazon and the region of Chocó; illicit drug crops grown by peasants in the national parks; soil erosion; soil and water quality damage from overuse of pesticides; air pollution, especially in Bogota, from vehicle emissions

ENVIRONMENT - INTERNATIONAL AGREEMENTS:

party to: Antarctic Treaty, Biodiversity, Climate Change, Climate Change-Kyoto Protocol, Desertification, Endangered Species, Hazardous Wastes, Marine Life Conservation, Ozone Layer Protection, Ship Pollution, Tropical Timber 83, Tropical Timber 94, Wetlands

signed, but not ratified: Law of the Sea

GEOGRAPHY - NOTE:

only South American country with coastlines on both the North Pacific Ocean and Caribbean Sea

PEOPLE AND SOCIETY :: COLOMBIA

POPULATION:

48,168,996 (July 2018 est.)

country comparison to the world: 30

NATIONALITY:

noun: Colombian(s)

adjective: Colombian

ETHNIC GROUPS:

mestizo and white 84.2%, Afro-Colombian (includes mulatto, Raizal, and Palenquero) 10.4%, Amerindian 3.4%, Romani (2005 est.)

LANGUAGES:

Spanish (official)

RELIGIONS:

Roman Catholic 79%, Protestant 14% (includes Pentecostal 6%, mainline Protestant 2%, other 6%), other 2%, unspecified 5% (2014 est.)

DEMOGRAPHIC PROFILE:

Colombia is in the midst of a demographic transition resulting from steady declines in its fertility, mortality, and population growth rates. The birth rate has fallen from more than 6 children per woman in the 1960s to just above replacement level today as a result of increased literacy, family planning services, and urbanization. However, income inequality is among the worst in the world, and more than a third of the population lives below the poverty line.

Colombia experiences significant legal and illegal economic emigration and refugee outflows. Large-scale labor emigration dates to the 1960s; the United States and, until recently, Venezuela have been the main host countries. Emigration to Spain picked up in the 1990s because of its economic growth, but this flow has since diminished because of Spain's ailing economy and high unemployment. Colombia has been the largest source of Latin American refugees in Latin America, nearly 400,000 of whom live primarily in Venezuela and Ecuador. Venezuela's political and economic crisis since 2015, however, has created a reverse flow, consisting largely of Colombians returning home.

Forced displacement continues to be prevalent because of violence among guerrillas, paramilitary groups, and Colombian security forces. Afro-Colombian and indigenous populations are disproportionately affected. Even with the Colombian Government's December 2016 peace agreement with the Revolutionary Armed Forces of Colombia (FARC), the risk of displacement remains as other rebel groups fill the void left by the FARC. Between 1985 and September 2017, nearly 7.6 million persons have been internally displaced, the highest total in the world. These estimates may undercount actual numbers because many internally displaced persons are not registered. Historically, Colombia also has one of the world's highest levels of forced disappearances. About 30,000 cases have been recorded over the last four decades—although the number is likely to be much higher—including human rights activists, trade unionists, Afro-Colombians, indigenous people, and farmers in rural conflict zones.

Because of political violence and economic problems, Colombia received limited numbers of immigrants during the 19th and 20th centuries, mostly from the Middle East, Europe, and Japan. More recently, growth in the oil, mining, and manufacturing sectors has attracted increased labor migration; the primary source countries are Venezuela, the US, Mexico, and Argentina. Colombia has also become a transit area for illegal migrants from Africa, Asia, and the Caribbean -- especially Haiti and Cuba -- who are en route to the US or Canada.

AGE STRUCTURE:

0-14 years: 23.89% (male 5,895,637 /female 5,611,298)

15-24 years: 16.96% (male 4,161,661 /female 4,006,875)

25-54 years: 41.98% (male 10,043,080 /female 10,177,042)

55-64 years: 9.44% (male 2,145,031 /female 2,404,090)

65 years and over: 7.73% (male 1,555,848 /female 2,168,434) (2018 est.)

DEPENDENCY RATIOS:

total dependency ratio: 45.6 (2015 est.)

youth dependency ratio: 35.4 (2015 est.)

elderly dependency ratio: 10.2 (2015 est.)

potential support ratio: 9.8 (2015 est.)

MEDIAN AGE:

total: 30.4 years

male: 29.4 years

female: 31.4 years (2018 est.)

country comparison to the world: 117

POPULATION GROWTH RATE:

0.97% (2018 est.)

country comparison to the world: 112

BIRTH RATE:

15.8 births/1,000 population (2018 est.)

country comparison to the world: 114

DEATH RATE:

5.5 deaths/1,000 population (2018 est.)

country comparison to the world: 177

NET MIGRATION RATE:

-0.6 migrant(s)/1,000 population (2017 est.)

country comparison to the world: 129

POPULATION DISTRIBUTION:

the majority of people live in the north and west where agricultural opportunities and natural resources are found; the vast grasslands of the llanos to the south and east, which make up approximately 60% of the country, are sparsely populated

URBANIZATION:

urban population: 80.8% of total population (2018)

rate of urbanization: 1.22% annual rate of change (2015-20 est.)

MAJOR URBAN AREAS - POPULATION:

10.574 million BOGOTA (capital), 3.934 million Medellin, 2.726 million Cali, 2.218 million Barranquilla, 1.295 million Bucaramanga, 1.047 million Cartagena (2018)

SEX RATIO:

at birth: 1.05 male(s)/female (2017 est.)

0-14 years: 1.05 male(s)/female (2017 est.)

15-24 years: 1.04 male(s)/female (2017 est.)

25-54 years: 0.98 male(s)/female (2017 est.)

55-64 years: 0.88 male(s)/female (2017 est.)

65 years and over: 0.72 male(s)/female (2017 est.)

total population: 0.98 male(s)/female (2017 est.)

MOTHER'S MEAN AGE AT FIRST BIRTH:

21.7 years (2015 est.)

note: median age at first birth among women 25-29

MATERNAL MORTALITY RATE:

64 deaths/100,000 live births (2015 est.)

country comparison to the world: 86

INFANT MORTALITY RATE:

total: 13.2 deaths/1,000 live births (2018 est.)

male: 16 deaths/1,000 live births (2018 est.)

female: 10.2 deaths/1,000 live births (2018 est.)

country comparison to the world: 105

LIFE EXPECTANCY AT BIRTH:

total population: 76.2 years (2018 est.)

male: 73 years (2018 est.)

female: 79.5 years (2018 est.)

country comparison to the world: 90

TOTAL FERTILITY RATE:

1.98 children born/woman (2018 est.)

country comparison to the world: 121

CONTRACEPTIVE PREVALENCE RATE:

81% (2015/16)

HEALTH EXPENDITURES:

7.2% of GDP (2014)

country comparison to the world: 76

PHYSICIANS DENSITY:

1.82 physicians/1,000 population (2014)

HOSPITAL BED DENSITY:

1.5 beds/1,000 population (2014)

DRINKING WATER SOURCE:

improved:

urban: 96.8% of population (2015 est.)

rural: 73.8% of population (2015 est.)

total: 91.4% of population (2015 est.)

unimproved:

urban: 3.2% of population (2015 est.)

rural: 26.2% of population (2015 est.)

total: 8.6% of population (2015 est.)

SANITATION FACILITY ACCESS:

improved:

urban: 85.2% of population (2015 est.)

rural: 67.9% of population (2015 est.)

total: 81.1% of population (2015 est.)

unimproved:

urban: 14.8% of population (2015 est.)

rural: 32.1% of population (2015 est.)

total: 18.9% of population (2015 est.)

HIV/AIDS - ADULT PREVALENCE RATE:

0.5% (2017 est.)

country comparison to the world: 65

HIV/AIDS - PEOPLE LIVING WITH HIV/AIDS:

150,000 (2017 est.)

country comparison to the world: 31

HIV/AIDS - DEATHS:

4,400 (2017 est.)

country comparison to the world: 32

MAJOR INFECTIOUS DISEASES:

degree of risk: high (2016)

food or waterborne diseases: bacterial diarrhea (2016)

vectorborne diseases: dengue fever, malaria, and yellow fever (2016)

note: active local transmission of Zika virus by Aedes species mosquitoes has been identified in this country (as of August 2016); it poses an important risk (a large number of cases possible) among US citizens if bitten by an infective mosquito; other less common ways to get Zika are through sex, via blood transfusion, or during pregnancy, in which the pregnant woman passes Zika virus to her fetus

OBESITY - ADULT PREVALENCE RATE:

22.3% (2016)

country comparison to the world: 78

CHILDREN UNDER THE AGE OF 5 YEARS UNDERWEIGHT:

3.4% (2010)

country comparison to the world: 94

EDUCATION EXPENDITURES:

4.5% of GDP (2016)

country comparison to the world: 92

LITERACY:

definition: age 15 and over can read and write (2015 est.)

total population: 94.2% (2015 est.)

male: 94.1% (2015 est.)

female: 94.4% (2015 est.)

SCHOOL LIFE EXPECTANCY (PRIMARY TO TERTIARY EDUCATION):

total: 14 years (2015)

male: 14 years (2015)

female: 15 years (2015)

UNEMPLOYMENT, YOUTH AGES 15-24:

total: 17.5% (2016 est.)

male: 13.7% (2016 est.)

female: 22.7% (2016 est.)

country comparison to the world: 75

GOVERNMENT :: COLOMBIA

COUNTRY NAME:

conventional long form: Republic of Colombia

conventional short form: Colombia

local long form: Republica de Colombia

local short form: Colombia

etymology: the country is named after explorer Christopher COLUMBUS

GOVERNMENT TYPE:

presidential republic

CAPITAL:

name: Bogota

geographic coordinates: 4 36 N, 74 05 W

time difference: UTC-5 (same time as Washington, DC, during Standard Time)

ADMINISTRATIVE DIVISIONS:

32 departments (departamentos, singular - departamento) and 1 capital district* (distrito capital); Amazonas, Antioquia, Arauca, Atlantico, Bogota*, Bolivar, Boyaca, Caldas, Caqueta, Casanare, Cauca, Cesar, Choco, Cordoba, Cundinamarca, Guainia, Guaviare, Huila, La Guajira, Magdalena, Meta, Narino, Norte de Santander, Putumayo, Quindio, Risaralda, Archipielago de San Andres, Providencia y Santa Catalina (colloquially San Andres y Providencia), Santander, Sucre, Tolima, Valle del Cauca, Vaupes, Vichada

INDEPENDENCE:

20 July 1810 (from Spain)

NATIONAL HOLIDAY:

Independence Day, 20 July (1810)

CONSTITUTION:

history: several previous; latest promulgated 5 July 1991 (2018)

amendments: proposed by the government, by Congress, by a constituent assembly, or by public petition; passage requires a majority vote by Congress in each of two consecutive sessions; passage of amendments to constitutional articles on citizen rights, guarantees, and duties also require approval in a referendum by over one-half of voters and participation of over one-fourth of citizens registered to vote; amended many times, last in 2018 (2018)

LEGAL SYSTEM:

civil law system influenced by the Spanish and French civil codes

INTERNATIONAL LAW ORGANIZATION PARTICIPATION:

has not submitted an ICJ jurisdiction declaration; accepts ICCt jurisdiction

CITIZENSHIP:

citizenship by birth: no

citizenship by descent only: least one parent must be a citizen or permanent resident of Colombia

dual citizenship recognized: yes

residency requirement for naturalization: 5 years

SUFFRAGE:

18 years of age; universal

EXECUTIVE BRANCH:

chief of state: President Ivan DUQUE Marquez (since 7 August 2018); Vice President Marta Lucia RAMIREZ Blanco (since 7 August 2018); the president is both chief of state and head of government

head of government: President Ivan DUQUE Marquez (since 7 August 2018); Vice President Marta Lucia RAMIREZ Blanco (since 7 August 2018)

cabinet: Cabinet appointed by the president

elections/appointments: president directly elected by absolute majority vote in 2 rounds if needed for a single 4-year term (beginning in 2018); election last held on 27 May 2018 with a runoff held on 17 June 2018 (next to be held in 2022); note - political reform in 2015 eliminated presidential reelection

election results: Ivan DUQUE Marquez elected president in second round; percent of vote - Ivan DUQUE Marquez (CD) 54%, Gustavo PETRO (Humane Colombia) 41.8%, other/blank/invalid 4.2%

LEGISLATIVE BRANCH:

description: bicameral Congress or Congreso consists of:
Senate or Senado (108 seats; 102 members elected in a single nationwide constituency by party-list proportional representation vote, 2 members elected in a special nationwide constituency for indigenous communities, 5 members of the People's Alternative Revolutionary Force (FARC) political party for the 2018 and 2022 elections only as per the 2016 peace accord, and 1 seat reserved for the runner-up presidential candidate in the recent election; all members serve 4-year terms)
Chamber of Representatives or Camara de Representantes (172 seats; 166 members elected in multi-seat constituencies by party-list proportional representation vote, 5 members of the FARC for the 2018 and 2022 elections only as per the 2016 peace, and 1 seat reserved for the runner-up vice presidential candidate in the recent election; all members serve 4-year terms)

elections:
Senate - last held on 11 March 2018 (next to be held in March 2022)
Chamber of Representatives - last held on 11 March 2018 (next to be held in March 2022)

election results:
Senate - percent of vote by party - NA; seats by party - CD 19, CR 16, PC 15, PL 14, U Party 14, Green Alliance 10, PDA 5, other 9
Chamber of Representatives - percent of vote by party - NA; seats by party - PL 35, CD 32, CR 30, U Party 25, PC 21, Green Alliance 9, other 13

JUDICIAL BRANCH:

highest courts: Supreme Court of Justice or Corte Suprema de Justicia (consists of the Civil-Agrarian and Labor Chambers each with 7 judges, and the Penal Chamber with 9 judges); Constitutional Court (consists of 9 magistrates); Council of State (consists of 31 members); Superior Judiciary Council (consists of 13 magistrates)

judge selection and term of office:
Supreme Court judges appointed by the Supreme Court members from candidates submitted by the Superior Judiciary Council; judges elected for individual 8-year terms;
Constitutional Court magistrates - nominated by the president, by the Supreme Court, and elected by the Senate; judges elected for individual 8-year terms; Council of State members appointed by the State Council

plenary from lists nominated by the Superior Judiciary Council

subordinate courts: Superior Tribunals (appellate courts for each of the judicial districts); regional courts; civil municipal courts; Superior Military Tribunal; first instance administrative courts

POLITICAL PARTIES AND LEADERS:

Alternative Democratic Pole or PDA [Clara LOPEZ]
Citizens Option (Opcion Ciudadana) or OC [Angel ALIRIO Moreno] (formerly known as the National Integration Party or PIN)
Conservative Party or PC [David BARGUIL]
Democratic Center Party or CD [Alvaro URIBE Velez, Oscar Ivan ZULUAGA, Carlos HOLMES TRUJILLO, Ivan DUQUE]
Green Alliance [Jorge LONDONO, Antonio SANGUINO, Luis AVELLANEDA, Camilo ROMERO]
Humane Colombia [Gustavo PETRO]
Liberal Party or PL [Horacio SERPA]
People's Alternative Revolutionary Force or FARC [Timoleon JIMENEZ]
Radical Change or CR [Carlos Fernando GALAN]
Social National Unity Party or U Party [Roy BARRERAS, Jose David NAME]

note: Colombia has numerous smaller political movements

INTERNATIONAL ORGANIZATION PARTICIPATION:

BCIE, BIS, CAN, Caricom (observer), CD, CDB, CELAC, EITI (candidate country), FAO, G-3, G-24, G-77, IADB, IAEA, IBRD, ICAO, ICC (national committees), ICCt, ICRM, IDA, IFAD, IFC, IFRCS, IHO, ILO, IMF, IMO, IMSO, Interpol, IOC, IOM, IPU, ISO, ITSO, ITU, ITUC (NGOs), LAES, LAIA, Mercosur (associate), MIGA, NAM, OAS, OPANAL, OPCW, Pacific Alliance, PCA, UN, UNASUR, UNCTAD, UNESCO, UNHCR, UNIDO, Union Latina, UNWTO, UPU, WCO, WFTU (NGOs), WHO, WIPO, WMO, WTO

DIPLOMATIC REPRESENTATION IN THE US:

chief of mission: Ambassador Francisco SANTOS Calderon (since 17 September 2018)

chancery: 1724 Massachusetts Ave, NW, Washington, DC 20036

telephone: [1] (202) 387-8338

FAX: [1] (202) 232-8643

consulate(s) general: Atlanta, Houston, Los Angeles, Miami, New York, Newark (NJ), Orlando, San Juan (Puerto Rico)

consulate(s): Boston, Chicago, San Francisco

DIPLOMATIC REPRESENTATION FROM THE US:

chief of mission: Ambassador Kevin WHITAKER (since 11 June 2014)

embassy: Calle 24 Bis No. 48-50, Bogota, D.C.

mailing address: Carrera 45 No. 24B-27, Bogota, D.C.

telephone: [57] (1) 275-2000

FAX: [57] (1) 275-4600

FLAG DESCRIPTION:

three horizontal bands of yellow (top, double-width), blue, and red; the flag retains the three main colors of the banner of Gran Colombia, the short-lived South American republic that broke up in 1830; various interpretations of the colors exist and include: yellow for the gold in Colombia's land, blue for the seas on its shores, and red for the blood spilled in attaining freedom; alternatively, the colors have been described as representing more elemental concepts such as sovereignty and justice (yellow), loyalty and vigilance (blue), and valor and generosity (red); or simply the principles of liberty, equality, and fraternity

note: similar to the flag of Ecuador, which is longer and bears the Ecuadorian coat of arms superimposed in the center

NATIONAL SYMBOL(S):

Andean condor; national colors: yellow, blue, red

NATIONAL ANTHEM:

name: "Himno Nacional de la Republica de Colombia" (National Anthem of the Republic of Colombia)

lyrics/music: Rafael NUNEZ/Oreste SINDICI

note: adopted 1920; the anthem was created from an inspirational poem written by President Rafael NUNEZ

ECONOMY :: COLOMBIA

ECONOMY - OVERVIEW:

Colombia heavily depends on energy and mining exports, making it vulnerable to fluctuations in commodity prices. Colombia is Latin America's fourth largest oil producer and the world's fourth largest coal producer, third largest coffee exporter, and second largest cut flowers exporter. Colombia's economic development is hampered by inadequate infrastructure, poverty, narcotrafficking, and an uncertain security situation, in addition to dependence on primary commodities (goods that have little value-added from processing or labor inputs).

Colombia's economy slowed in 2017 because of falling world market prices for oil and lower domestic oil production due to insurgent attacks on pipeline infrastructure. Although real GDP growth averaged 4.7% during the past decade, it fell to an estimated 1.8% in 2017. Declining oil prices also have contributed to reduced government revenues. In 2016, oil revenue dropped below 4% of the federal budget and likely remained below 4% in 2017. A Western credit rating agency in December 2017 downgraded Colombia's sovereign credit rating to BBB-, because of weaker-than-expected growth and increasing external debt. Colombia has struggled to address local referendums against foreign investment, which have slowed its expansion, especially in the oil and mining sectors. Colombia's FDI declined by 3% to $10.2 billion between January and September 2017.

Colombia has signed or is negotiating Free Trade Agreements (FTA) with more than a dozen countries; the US-Colombia FTA went into effect in May 2012. Colombia is a founding member of the Pacific Alliance—a regional trade block formed in 2012 by Chile, Colombia, Mexico, and Peru to promote regional trade and economic integration. The Colombian government took steps in 2017 to address several bilateral trade irritants with the US, including those on truck scrappage, distilled spirits, pharmaceuticals, ethanol imports, and labor rights. Colombia hopes to accede to the Organization for Economic Cooperation and Development.

GDP (PURCHASING POWER PARITY):

$711.6 billion (2017 est.)

$699.1 billion (2016 est.)

$685.6 billion (2015 est.)

note: data are in 2017 dollars

country comparison to the world: 31

GDP (OFFICIAL EXCHANGE RATE):

$314.5 billion (2017 est.) (2017 est.)

GDP - REAL GROWTH RATE:

1.8% (2017 est.)

2% (2016 est.)

3% (2015 est.)

country comparison to the world: 160

GDP - PER CAPITA (PPP):

$14,400 (2017 est.)

$14,300 (2016 est.)

$14,200 (2015 est.)

note: data are in 2017 dollars

country comparison to the world: 116

GROSS NATIONAL SAVING:

18.9% of GDP (2017 est.)

19% of GDP (2016 est.)

17.4% of GDP (2015 est.)

country comparison to the world: 104

GDP - COMPOSITION, BY END USE:

household consumption: 68.2% (2017 est.)

government consumption: 14.8% (2017 est.)

investment in fixed capital: 22.2% (2017 est.)

investment in inventories: 0.2% (2017 est.)

exports of goods and services: 14.6% (2017 est.)

imports of goods and services: -19.7% (2017 est.)

GDP - COMPOSITION, BY SECTOR OF ORIGIN:

agriculture: 7.2% (2017 est.)

industry: 30.8% (2017 est.)

services: 62.1% (2017 est.)

AGRICULTURE - PRODUCTS:

coffee, cut flowers, bananas, rice, tobacco, corn, sugarcane, cocoa beans, oilseed, vegetables; shrimp; forest products

INDUSTRIES:

textiles, food processing, oil, clothing and footwear, beverages, chemicals, cement; gold, coal, emeralds

INDUSTRIAL PRODUCTION GROWTH RATE:

-2.2% (2017 est.)

country comparison to the world: 185

LABOR FORCE:

25.76 million (2017 est.)

country comparison to the world: 25

LABOR FORCE - BY OCCUPATION:

agriculture: 17%

industry: 21%

services: 62% (2011 est.)

UNEMPLOYMENT RATE:

9.3% (2017 est.)

9.2% (2016 est.)

country comparison to the world: 134

POPULATION BELOW POVERTY LINE:

28% (2017 est.)

HOUSEHOLD INCOME OR CONSUMPTION BY PERCENTAGE SHARE:

lowest 10%: 39.6% (2015 est.)

highest 10%: 39.6% (2015 est.)

DISTRIBUTION OF FAMILY INCOME - GINI INDEX:

51.1 (2015)

53.5 (2014)

country comparison to the world: 12

BUDGET:

revenues: 83.35 billion (2017 est.)

expenditures: 91.73 billion (2017 est.)

TAXES AND OTHER REVENUES:

26.5% (of GDP) (2017 est.)

country comparison to the world: 109

BUDGET SURPLUS (+) OR DEFICIT (-):

-2.7% (of GDP) (2017 est.)

country comparison to the world: 119

PUBLIC DEBT:

49.4% of GDP (2017 est.)

49.8% of GDP (2016 est.)

note: data cover general government debt, and includes debt instruments issued (or owned) by government entities other than the treasury; the data include treasury debt held by foreign entities; the data include debt issued by subnational entities

country comparison to the world: 102

FISCAL YEAR:

calendar year

INFLATION RATE (CONSUMER PRICES):

4.3% (2017 est.)

7.5% (2016 est.)

country comparison to the world: 163

CENTRAL BANK DISCOUNT RATE:

4.75% (12 December 2017)

7.5% (31 December 2016)

country comparison to the world: 84

COMMERCIAL BANK PRIME LENDING RATE:

13.69% (31 December 2017 est.)

14.65% (31 December 2016 est.)

country comparison to the world: 52

STOCK OF NARROW MONEY:

$36.37 billion (31 December 2017 est.)

$34.01 billion (31 December 2016 est.)

country comparison to the world: 57

STOCK OF BROAD MONEY:

$36.37 billion (31 December 2017 est.)

$34.01 billion (31 December 2016 est.)

country comparison to the world: 57

STOCK OF DOMESTIC CREDIT:

$173.7 billion (31 December 2017 est.)

$153.1 billion (31 December 2016 est.)

country comparison to the world: 47

MARKET VALUE OF PUBLICLY TRADED SHARES:

$85.96 billion (31 December 2015 est.)

$146.7 billion (31 December 2014 est.)

$202.7 billion (31 December 2013 est.)

country comparison to the world: 43

CURRENT ACCOUNT BALANCE:

-$10.36 billion (2017 est.)

-$12.13 billion (2016 est.)

country comparison to the world: 191

EXPORTS:

$39.48 billion (2017 est.)

$31.39 billion (2016 est.)

country comparison to the world: 56

EXPORTS - PARTNERS:

US 28.5%, Panama 8.6%, China 5.1% (2017)

EXPORTS - COMMODITIES:

petroleum, coal, emeralds, coffee, nickel, cut flowers, bananas, apparel

IMPORTS:

$44.24 billion (2017 est.)

$43.24 billion (2016 est.)

country comparison to the world: 57

IMPORTS - COMMODITIES:

industrial equipment, transportation equipment, consumer goods, chemicals, paper products, fuels, electricity

IMPORTS - PARTNERS:

US 26.3%, China 19.3%, Mexico 7.5%, Brazil 5%, Germany 4.1% (2017)

RESERVES OF FOREIGN EXCHANGE AND GOLD:

$47.13 billion (31 December 2017 est.)

$46.18 billion (31 December 2016 est.)

country comparison to the world: 42

DEBT - EXTERNAL:

$124.6 billion (31 December 2017 est.)

$115 billion (31 December 2016 est.)

country comparison to the world: 46

STOCK OF DIRECT FOREIGN INVESTMENT - AT HOME:

$179.6 billion (31 December 2017 est.)

$164.3 billion (31 December 2016 est.)

country comparison to the world: 36

STOCK OF DIRECT FOREIGN INVESTMENT - ABROAD:

$55.51 billion (31 December 2017 est.)

$51.82 billion (31 December 2016 est.)

country comparison to the world: 42

EXCHANGE RATES:

Colombian pesos (COP) per US dollar -

2,957 (2017 est.)

3,055.3 (2016 est.)

3,055.3 (2015 est.)

2,001 (2014 est.)

2,001.1 (2013 est.)

ENERGY :: COLOMBIA

ELECTRICITY ACCESS:

population without electricity: 1.2 million (2013)

electrification - total population: 97% (2013)

electrification - urban areas: 100% (2013)

electrification - rural areas: 88% (2013)

ELECTRICITY - PRODUCTION:

74.92 billion kWh (2016 est.)

country comparison to the world: 41

ELECTRICITY - CONSUMPTION:

68.25 billion kWh (2016 est.)

country comparison to the world: 40

ELECTRICITY - EXPORTS:

460 million kWh (2015 est.)

country comparison to the world: 69

ELECTRICITY - IMPORTS:

378 million kWh (2016 est.)

country comparison to the world: 82

ELECTRICITY - INSTALLED GENERATING CAPACITY:

16.89 million kW (2016 est.)

country comparison to the world: 49

ELECTRICITY - FROM FOSSIL FUELS:

29% of total installed capacity (2016 est.)

country comparison to the world: 184

ELECTRICITY - FROM NUCLEAR FUELS:

0% of total installed capacity (2017 est.)

country comparison to the world: 67

ELECTRICITY - FROM HYDROELECTRIC PLANTS:

69% of total installed capacity (2017 est.)

country comparison to the world: 17

ELECTRICITY - FROM OTHER RENEWABLE SOURCES:

2% of total installed capacity (2017 est.)

country comparison to the world: 137

CRUDE OIL - PRODUCTION:

853,600 bbl/day (2017 est.)

country comparison to the world: 22

CRUDE OIL - EXPORTS:

726,700 bbl/day (2015 est.)

country comparison to the world: 18

CRUDE OIL - IMPORTS:

0 bbl/day (2015 est.)

country comparison to the world: 110

CRUDE OIL - PROVED RESERVES:

1.665 billion bbl (1 January 2018 est.)

country comparison to the world: 36

REFINED PETROLEUM PRODUCTS - PRODUCTION:

303,600 bbl/day (2015 est.)

country comparison to the world: 41

REFINED PETROLEUM PRODUCTS - CONSUMPTION:

333,000 bbl/day (2016 est.)

country comparison to the world: 40

REFINED PETROLEUM PRODUCTS - EXPORTS:

56,900 bbl/day (2015 est.)

country comparison to the world: 52

REFINED PETROLEUM PRODUCTS - IMPORTS:

57,170 bbl/day (2015 est.)

country comparison to the world: 74

NATURAL GAS - PRODUCTION:

10.02 billion cu m (2017 est.)

country comparison to the world: 41

NATURAL GAS - CONSUMPTION:

10.08 billion cu m (2017 est.)

country comparison to the world: 48

NATURAL GAS - EXPORTS:

0 cu m (2017 est.)

country comparison to the world: 83

NATURAL GAS - IMPORTS:

48.14 million cu m (2017 est.)

country comparison to the world: 76

NATURAL GAS - PROVED RESERVES:

113.9 billion cu m (1 January 2018 est.)

country comparison to the world: 49

CARBON DIOXIDE EMISSIONS FROM CONSUMPTION OF ENERGY:

95.59 million Mt (2017 est.)

country comparison to the world: 45

COMMUNICATIONS :: COLOMBIA

TELEPHONES - FIXED LINES:

total subscriptions: 6,987,654 (2017 est.)

subscriptions per 100 inhabitants: 15 (2017 est.)

country comparison to the world: 23

TELEPHONES - MOBILE CELLULAR:

total subscriptions: 62,222,011 (2017 est.)

subscriptions per 100 inhabitants: 130 (2017 est.)

country comparison to the world: 25

TELEPHONE SYSTEM:

general assessment: modern system in many respects with a nationwide microwave radio relay system, a domestic satellite system with 41 earth stations, and a fiber-optic network linking 50 cities; the cable sector commands about half of the market by subscribers, with DSL having a declining share and with fibre-based broadband developing strongly; competion among the MVNO (mobile virtual network operator) sector has promoted 2.9 million subscribers as of mid-2018; though most infrastructure as yet is primarily in high-density urban areas (2017)

domestic: fixed-line connections stand at about 15 per 100 persons; mobile cellular telephone subscribership is about 130 per 100 persons; competition among cellular service providers is resulting in falling local and international calling rates and contributing to the steep decline in the market share of fixed-line services (2017)

international: country code - 57; multiple submarine cable systems provide links to the US, parts of the Caribbean, and Central and South America; satellite earth stations - 10 (6 Intelsat, 1 Inmarsat, 3 fully digitalized international switching centers) (2016)

BROADCAST MEDIA:

combination of state-owned and privately owned broadcast media provide service; more than 500 radio stations and many national, regional, and local TV stations (2007)

INTERNET COUNTRY CODE:

.co

INTERNET USERS:

total: 27,452,550 (July 2016 est.)

percent of population: 58.1% (July 2016 est.)

country comparison to the world: 28

BROADBAND - FIXED SUBSCRIPTIONS:

total: 6,318,936 (2017 est.)

subscriptions per 100 inhabitants: 13 (2017 est.)

country comparison to the world: 24

TRANSPORTATION :: COLOMBIA

NATIONAL AIR TRANSPORT SYSTEM:

number of registered air carriers: 12 (2015)

inventory of registered aircraft operated by air carriers: 157 (2015)

annual passenger traffic on registered air carriers: 30,742,928 (2015)

annual freight traffic on registered air carriers: 1,317,562,271 mt-km (2015)

CIVIL AIRCRAFT REGISTRATION COUNTRY CODE PREFIX:

HJ, HK (2016)

AIRPORTS:

836 (2013)

country comparison to the world: 8

AIRPORTS - WITH PAVED RUNWAYS:

total: 121 (2017)

over 3,047 m: 2 (2017)

2,438 to 3,047 m: 9 (2017)

1,524 to 2,437 m: 39 (2017)

914 to 1,523 m: 53 (2017)

under 914 m: 18 (2017)

AIRPORTS - WITH UNPAVED RUNWAYS:

total: 715 (2013)

over 3,047 m: 1 (2013)

1,524 to 2,437 m: 25 (2013)

914 to 1,523 m: 201 (2013)

under 914 m: 488 (2013)

HELIPORTS:

3 (2013)

PIPELINES:

4991 km gas, 6796 km oil, 3429 km refined products (2013)

RAILWAYS:

total: 2,141 km (2015)

standard gauge: 150 km 1.435-m gauge (2015)

narrow gauge: 1,991 km 0.914-m gauge (2015)

country comparison to the world: 73

ROADWAYS:

total: 206,500 km (2016)

country comparison to the world: 25

WATERWAYS:

24,725 km (18,300 km navigable; the most important waterway, the River Magdalena, of which 1,488 km is navigable, is dredged regularly to ensure safe passage of cargo vessels and container barges) (2012)

country comparison to the world: 6

MERCHANT MARINE:

total: 103 (2017)

by type: general cargo 17, oil tanker 9, other 77 (2017)

country comparison to the world: 84

PORTS AND TERMINALS:

major seaport(s): Atlantic Ocean (Caribbean) - Cartagena, Santa Marta, Turbo

oil terminal(s): Covenas offshore terminal

container port(s) (TEUs): Cartagena (2,510,093) (2016)

river port(s): Barranquilla (Rio Magdalena)

dry bulk cargo port(s): Puerto Bolivar (coal)

Pacific Ocean - Buenaventura

MILITARY AND SECURITY :: COLOMBIA

MILITARY EXPENDITURES:

3.5% of GDP (2018 est.)

3.39% of GDP (2016)

3.13% of GDP (2015)

country comparison to the world: 21

MILITARY BRANCHES:

National Army (Ejercito Nacional), Republic of Colombia Navy (Armada Republica de Colombia, ARC, includes Naval Aviation, Naval Infantry (Infanteria de Marina, IM), and Coast Guard), Colombian Air Force (Fuerza Aerea de Colombia, FAC) (2012)

MILITARY SERVICE AGE AND OBLIGATION:

18-24 years of age for compulsory and voluntary military service; service obligation is 18 months (2012)

TERRORISM :: COLOMBIA

TERRORIST GROUPS - HOME BASED:

National Liberation Army (Ejercito de Liberacion Nacional, ELN):
aim(s): represent the rural poor against the nation's wealthy and block the privatization of national resources
area(s) of operation: the nation's largest remaining insurgent group operates mainly in the rural and mountainous areas in the northeast, especially Arauca Department, and is active in the northern and southwestern regions and along the borders with Venezuela and Ecuador
note: the group has a long history of engaging in narcotics production and trafficking, extortion, and kidnappings for ransom to fund operations (April 2018)

Revolutionary Armed Forces of Colombia (Fuerzas Armadas Revolucionarias de Colombia, FARC):
aim(s): signed a peace accord with the Colombian Government in 2016 and entered the political arena in September 2017 as the People's Alternative Revolutionary Force (also known as FARC) in order to change Colombia's economic model, push an agenda focused on social justice and development of rural areas; historically, FARC's aim has been to install a Marxist-Leninist regime in Colombia through a violent revolution
area(s) of operation: NA
note: on 30 November 2016, the Colombian Congress approved a peace accord between the FARC and Colombian Government; the government allowed FARC to form an official political party and integrate former fighters into society through measures such as funding education programs (April 2018)

TRANSNATIONAL ISSUES :: COLOMBIA

DISPUTES - INTERNATIONAL:

in December 2007, ICJ allocated San Andres, Providencia, and Santa Catalina islands to Colombia under 1928 Treaty but did not rule on 82 degrees W meridian as maritime boundary with Nicaraguamanaged dispute with Venezuela over maritime boundary and Venezuelan-administered Los Monjes Islands near the Gulf of VenezuelaColombian-organized illegal narcotics, guerrilla, and paramilitary activities penetrate all neighboring borders and have caused Colombian citizens to flee mostly into neighboring countriesColombia, Honduras, Nicaragua, Jamaica, and the US assert various claims to Bajo Nuevo and Serranilla Bank

REFUGEES AND INTERNALLY DISPLACED PERSONS:

refugees (country of origin): 417,355 (Venezuela) (economic and political crisis; includes Venezuelans who have claimed asylum or have received alternative legal stay) (2018)

IDPs: 7,708,465 (conflict between government and illegal armed groups and drug traffickers since 1985; about 300,000 new IDPs each year since 2000) (2018)

stateless persons: 11 (2016)

ILLICIT DRUGS:

illicit producer of coca, opium poppy, and cannabis; world's leading coca cultivator with 188,000 hectares in coca cultivation in 2016, a 18% increase over 2015, producing a potential of 710 mt of pure cocaine; the world's largest producer of coca derivatives; supplies cocaine to nearly all of the US market and the great majority of other international drug markets; in 2016, the Colombian government reported manual eradication of 17,642 hectares; Colombia suspended aerial eradication in October 2015 making 2016 the first full year without aerial eradication; a significant portion of narcotics proceeds are either laundered or invested in Colombia through the black market peso exchange; Colombia probably remains the second largest supplier of heroin to the US market; opium poppy cultivation was estimated to be 1,100 hectares in 2015, sufficient to potentially produce three metric tons of pure heroin

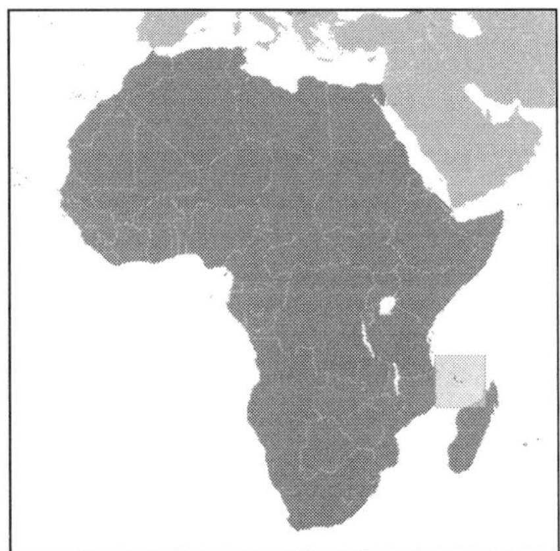

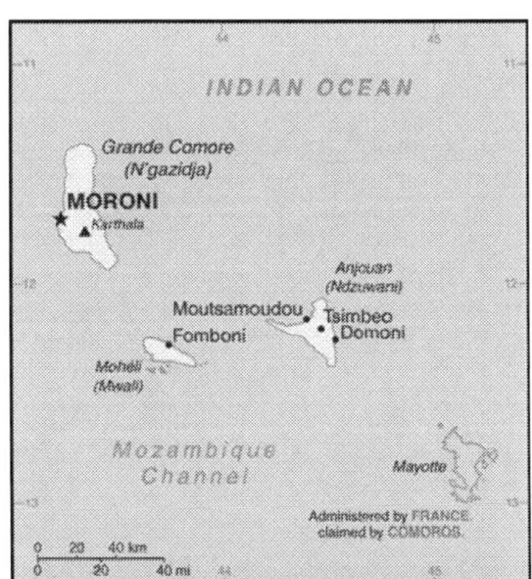

AFRICA :: COMOROS

INTRODUCTION :: COMOROS

BACKGROUND:

The archipelago of the Comoros in the Indian Ocean, composed of the islands of Mayotte, Anjouan, Moheli, and Grand Comore declared independence from France on 6 July 1975. France did not recognize the independence of Mayotte, which remains under French administration. Since independence, Comoros has endured political instability through realized and attempted coups. In 1997, the islands of Anjouan and Moheli declared independence from Comoros. In 1999, military chief Col. AZALI Assoumani seized power of the entire government in a bloodless coup; he initiated the 2000 Fomboni Accords, a power-sharing agreement in which the federal presidency rotates among the three islands, and each island maintains its local government. AZALI won the 2002 federal presidential election as president of the Union of the Comoros from Grand Comore Island, which held the first four-year term. AZALI stepped down in 2006 and President Ahmed Abdallah Mohamed SAMBI was elected to office as president from Anjouan. In 2007, Mohamed BACAR effected Anjouan's de-facto secession from the Union of the Comoros, refusing to step down when Comoros' other islands held legitimate elections in July. The African Union (AU) initially attempted to resolve the political crisis by applying sanctions and a naval blockade to Anjouan, but in March 2008 the AU and Comoran soldiers seized the island. The island's inhabitants generally welcomed the move. In 2009, the Comorian population approved a constitutional referendum extending the term of the president from four years to five years. In May 2011, Ikililou DHOININE won the presidency in peaceful elections widely deemed to be free and fair. In closely contested elections in 2016, former President AZALI Assoumani won a second term, when the rotating presidency returned to Grande Comore.

GEOGRAPHY :: COMOROS

LOCATION:

Southern Africa, group of islands at the northern mouth of the Mozambique Channel, about two-thirds of the way between northern Madagascar and northern Mozambique

GEOGRAPHIC COORDINATES:

12 10 S, 44 15 E

MAP REFERENCES:

Africa

AREA:

total: 2,235 sq km

land: 2,235 sq km

water: 0 sq km

country comparison to the world: 180

AREA - COMPARATIVE:

slightly more than 12 times the size of Washington, DC

LAND BOUNDARIES:

0 km

COASTLINE:

340 km

MARITIME CLAIMS:

territorial sea: 12 nm

exclusive economic zone: 200 nm

CLIMATE:

tropical marine; rainy season (November to May)

TERRAIN:

volcanic islands, interiors vary from steep mountains to low hills

ELEVATION:

0 m lowest point: Indian Ocean

2360 highest point: Karthala

NATURAL RESOURCES:

fish

LAND USE:

agricultural land: 84.4% (2011 est.)

arable land: 46.7% (2011 est.) / permanent crops: 29.6% (2011 est.) / permanent pasture: 8.1% (2011 est.)

forest: 1.4% (2011 est.)

other: 14.2% (2011 est.)

IRRIGATED LAND:

1.3 sq km (2012)

POPULATION DISTRIBUTION:

the capital city of Maroni, located on the western side of the island of Grande Comore, is the country's largest city; however, of the three islands that comprise Comoros, it is Anjouan that is the most densely populated

NATURAL HAZARDS:

cyclones possible during rainy season (December to April); volcanic activity on Grand Comore

volcanism: Karthala (2,361 m) on Grand Comore Island last erupted in 2007; a 2005 eruption forced thousands of people to be evacuated and produced a large ash cloud

ENVIRONMENT - CURRENT ISSUES:

deforestation; soil degradation and erosion results from forest loss and from crop cultivation on slopes without proper terracing; marine biodiversity affected as soil erosion leads to the silting of coral reefs

ENVIRONMENT - INTERNATIONAL AGREEMENTS:

party to: Biodiversity, Climate Change, Climate Change-Kyoto Protocol, Desertification, Endangered Species, Hazardous Wastes, Law of the Sea, Ozone Layer Protection, Ship Pollution, Wetlands

signed, but not ratified: none of the selected agreements

GEOGRAPHY - NOTE:

important location at northern end of Mozambique Channel

PEOPLE AND SOCIETY :: COMOROS

POPULATION:

821,164 (July 2018 est.)

country comparison to the world: 163

NATIONALITY:

noun: Comoran(s)

adjective: Comoran

ETHNIC GROUPS:

Antalote, Cafre, Makoa, Oimatsaha, Sakalava

LANGUAGES:

Arabic (official), French (official), Shikomoro (official; a blend of Swahili and Arabic) (Comorian)

RELIGIONS:

Sunni Muslim 98%, other (including Shia Muslim, Roman Catholic, Jehovah's Witness, Protestant) 2%

note: Islam is the state religion

DEMOGRAPHIC PROFILE:

Comoros' population is a melange of Arabs, Persians, Indonesians, Africans, and Indians, and the much smaller number of Europeans that settled on the islands between the 8th and 19th centuries, when they served as a regional trade hub. The Arab and Persian influence is most evident in the islands' overwhelmingly Muslim majority – about 98% of Comorans are Sunni Muslims. The country is densely populated, averaging nearly 350 people per square mile, although this varies widely among the islands, with Anjouan being the most densely populated. Given the large share of land dedicated to agriculture and Comoros' growing population, habitable land is becoming increasingly crowded. The combination of increasing population pressure on limited land and resources, widespread poverty, and poor job prospects motivates thousands of Comorans each year to attempt to illegally migrate using small fishing boats to the neighboring island of Mayotte, which is a French territory. The majority of legal Comoran migration to France came after Comoros' independence from France in 1975, with the flow peaking in the mid-1980s.

At least 150,000 to 200,000 people of Comoran citizenship or descent live abroad, mainly in France, where they have gone seeking a better quality of life, job opportunities, higher education (Comoros has no universities), advanced health care, and to finance elaborate traditional wedding ceremonies (aada). Remittances from the diaspora are an economic mainstay, in 2013 representing approximately 25% of Comoros' GDP and significantly more than the value of its exports of goods and services (only 15% of GDP). Grand Comore, Comoros' most populous island, is both the primary source of emigrants and the main recipient of remittances. Most remittances are spent on private consumption, but this often goes toward luxury goods and the aada and does not contribute to economic development or poverty reduction. Although the majority of the diaspora is now French-born with more distant ties to Comoros, it is unclear whether they will sustain the current level of remittances.

AGE STRUCTURE:

0-14 years: 38.54% (male 157,764 /female 158,676)

15-24 years: 19.89% (male 79,133 /female 84,181)

25-54 years: 33.25% (male 129,645 /female 143,408)

55-64 years: 4.34% (male 15,957 /female 19,690)

65 years and over: 3.98% (male 14,881 /female 17,829) (2018 est.)

DEPENDENCY RATIOS:

total dependency ratio: 75.5 (2015 est.)

youth dependency ratio: 70.5 (2015 est.)

elderly dependency ratio: 5.1 (2015 est.)

potential support ratio: 19.7 (2015 est.)

MEDIAN AGE:

total: 20.2 years

male: 19.5 years

female: 20.8 years (2018 est.)

country comparison to the world: 188

POPULATION GROWTH RATE:

1.57% (2018 est.)

country comparison to the world: 66

BIRTH RATE:

25.3 births/1,000 population (2018 est.)

country comparison to the world: 49

DEATH RATE:

7.1 deaths/1,000 population (2018 est.)

country comparison to the world: 125

NET MIGRATION RATE:

-2.4 migrant(s)/1,000 population (2017 est.)

country comparison to the world: 168

POPULATION DISTRIBUTION:

the capital city of Maroni, located on the western side of the island of Grande Comore, is the country's largest city; however, of the three islands that comprise Comoros, it is Anjouan that is the most densely populated

URBANIZATION:

urban population: 29% of total population (2018)

rate of urbanization: 2.87% annual rate of change (2015-20 est.)

MAJOR URBAN AREAS - POPULATION:

62,000 MORONI (capital) (2018)

SEX RATIO:

at birth: 1.02 male(s)/female (2017 est.)

0-14 years: 0.99 male(s)/female (2017 est.)

15-24 years: 0.94 male(s)/female (2017 est.)

25-54 years: 0.9 male(s)/female (2017 est.)

55-64 years: 0.8 male(s)/female (2017 est.)

65 years and over: 0.88 male(s)/female (2017 est.)

total population: 0.94 male(s)/female (2017 est.)

MOTHER'S MEAN AGE AT FIRST BIRTH:

24.6 years (2012 est.)

note: median age at first birth among women 25-29

MATERNAL MORTALITY RATE:

335 deaths/100,000 live births (2015 est.)

country comparison to the world: 38

INFANT MORTALITY RATE:

total: 58.3 deaths/1,000 live births (2018 est.)

male: 68.4 deaths/1,000 live births (2018 est.)

female: 47.9 deaths/1,000 live births (2018 est.)

country comparison to the world: 17

LIFE EXPECTANCY AT BIRTH:

total population: 64.9 years (2018 est.)

male: 62.6 years (2018 est.)

female: 67.4 years (2018 est.)

country comparison to the world: 185

TOTAL FERTILITY RATE:

3.21 children born/woman (2018 est.)

country comparison to the world: 46

CONTRACEPTIVE PREVALENCE RATE:

19.4% (2012)

HEALTH EXPENDITURES:

6.7% of GDP (2014)

country comparison to the world: 88

HOSPITAL BED DENSITY:

2.2 beds/1,000 population (2010)

DRINKING WATER SOURCE:

improved:

urban: 92.6% of population (2015 est.)

rural: 89.1% of population (2015 est.)

total: 90.1% of population (2015 est.)

unimproved:

urban: 7.4% of population (2015 est.)

rural: 10.9% of population (2015 est.)

total: 9.9% of population (2015 est.)

SANITATION FACILITY ACCESS:

improved:

urban: 48.3% of population (2015 est.)

rural: 30.9% of population (2015 est.)

total: 35.8% of population (2015 est.)

unimproved:

urban: 51.7% of population (2015 est.)

rural: 69.1% of population (2015 est.)

total: 64.2% of population (2015 est.)

HIV/AIDS - ADULT PREVALENCE RATE:

<.1% (2017 est.)

HIV/AIDS - PEOPLE LIVING WITH HIV/AIDS:

<200 (2017 est.)

HIV/AIDS - DEATHS:

<100 (2017 est.)

OBESITY - ADULT PREVALENCE RATE:

7.8% (2016)

country comparison to the world: 157

CHILDREN UNDER THE AGE OF 5 YEARS UNDERWEIGHT:

16.9% (2012)

country comparison to the world: 35

EDUCATION EXPENDITURES:

4.3% of GDP (2015)

country comparison to the world: 102

LITERACY:

definition: age 15 and over can read and write (2015 est.)

total population: 77.8% (2015 est.)

male: 81.8% (2015 est.)

female: 73.7% (2015 est.)

SCHOOL LIFE EXPECTANCY (PRIMARY TO TERTIARY EDUCATION):

total: 11 years (2014)

male: 11 years (2014)

female: 11 years (2014)

GOVERNMENT :: COMOROS

COUNTRY NAME:

conventional long form: Union of the Comoros

conventional short form: Comoros

local long form: Udzima wa Komori (Comorian)

local short form: Komori (Comorian)

etymology: name derives from the Arabic designation "Juzur al Qamar" meaning "Islands of the Moon"

Union des Comores (French) Jumhuriyat al Qamar al Muttahidah (Arabic) Comores (French) Juzur al Qamar (Arabic)

GOVERNMENT TYPE:

federal presidential republic

CAPITAL:

name: Moroni

geographic coordinates: 11 42 S, 43 14 E

time difference: UTC+3 (8 hours ahead of Washington, DC, during Standard Time)

ADMINISTRATIVE DIVISIONS:

3 islands and 4 municipalities*; Anjouan (Ndzuwani), Domoni*, Fomboni*, Grande Comore (N'gazidja), Moheli (Mwali), Moroni*, Moutsamoudou*

INDEPENDENCE:

6 July 1975 (from France)

NATIONAL HOLIDAY:

Independence Day, 6 July (1975)

CONSTITUTION:

history: previous 1996; latest ratified 23 December 2001 (2018)

amendments: proposed by the president of the union or supported by at least one-third of the Assembly of the Union membership; passage requires approval by at least two-thirds majority of the total Assembly membership and approval by at least two-thirds of the membership of the Island Councils, or approval in a referendum; amended 2009, 2014, 2018 (2018)

LEGAL SYSTEM:

mixed legal system of Islamic religious law, the French civil code of 1975, and customary law

INTERNATIONAL LAW ORGANIZATION PARTICIPATION:

has not submitted an ICJ jurisdiction declaration; accepts ICCt jurisdiction

CITIZENSHIP:

citizenship by birth: no

citizenship by descent only: at least one parent must be a citizen of the Comoros

dual citizenship recognized: no

residency requirement for naturalization: 10 years

SUFFRAGE:

18 years of age; universal

EXECUTIVE BRANCH:

chief of state: President AZALI Assoumani(since 26 May 2016); note - the president is both chief of state and head of government; Abdallah Said SAROUMA (since 26 May 2016), is vice president of Transportation,

Posts, Telecommunication, etc.; Djaffer Ahmed SAID (since 26 May 2016), is vice president of Economy, Planning, Industry Crafts,etc.; Moustadroine ABDOU (since 26 May 2016), is vice president of Agriculture, Fishing, and the Environment

head of government: President AZALI Assoumani (since 26 May 2016); Vice Presidents: Abdallah Said SAROUMA, (since 26 May 2016), Djaffer Ahmed SAID (since 26 May 2016), and Moustadroine ABDOU (since 26 May 2016)

cabinet: Council of Ministers appointed by the president

elections/appointments: president directly elected by simple majority popular vote in 2 rounds for a 5-year term (eligible for a second term); election last held on 21 February 2016 and second round held 10 April 2016 (next originally scheduled for 2021 but rescheduled for 2019)

election results: AZALI Assoumani (CRC) elected president in the second round; percent of vote in first round - Mohamed Ali SOILIHI (UPDC)17.6%, Mouigni BARAKA (RDC) 15.1%, AZALI Assoumani (CRC) 15.%, Fahmi Said IBRAHIM (PEC) 14.5%; percent of vote in second round - AZALI Assoumani (CRC) 41.%, Mohamed Ali SOILIHI (UPDC) 39.9%; Mouigni BARAKA (RDC)19.1%

note: a referendum held on 30 July 2018 overwhelmingly approved a constitutional amendment that extends the term limits of the president and ends the rotation of the Union presidents among the three main islands

LEGISLATIVE BRANCH:

description: unicameral Assembly of the Union (33 seats; 24 members directly elected by absolute majority vote in 2 rounds if needed and 9 members indirectly elected by the 3 island assemblies; members serve 5-year terms) (2017)

elections: last held on 25 January 2015 with a runoff on 22 February 2015 (next to be held in 2020) (2017)

election results: percent of vote by party - UPDC 29.1%, PJ 20.5%, RDC 21.3%, other 29.1%; seats by party - UPDC 8, PJ 7, RDC 2, CRC 2, RADHI 1, PEC 1, independent 3; note - in addition 9 seats will be filled by nominations from the 3 island assemblies

JUDICIAL BRANCH:

highest courts: Supreme Court or Cour Supreme (consists of 7 judges); Constitutional Court (consists of 8 members)

judge selection and term of office: Supreme Court judges - 2 selected by the president of the Union, 2 by the Assembly of the Union, and 1 each by the 3 island councils; judges appointed for life; Constitutional Court members appointed - 1 by the president, 1 each by the 3 vice presidents, 1 by the Assembly, and 1 each by the island executives; all members serve 6-year renewable terms

subordinate courts: Court of Appeals (in Moroni); Tribunal de premiere instance; island village (community) courts; religious courts

POLITICAL PARTIES AND LEADERS:

Convention for the Renewal of the Comoros or CRC [AZALI Assoumani]
Democratic Rally of the Comoros or RDC [Mouigni BARAKA]
Juwa Party or PJ [Ahmed Abdallah SAMBI]
Party for the Comorian Agreement (Partie Pour l'Entente Commorienne) or PEC [Fahmi Said IBRAHIM]
Rally for an Alternative of Harmonious and Integrated Development or RADHI [Abdou SOEFO]
Rally with a Development Initiative for Enlightened Youth or RIDJA [Said LARIFOU]
Union for the Development of the Comoros or UPDC [Mohamed HALIFA]

INTERNATIONAL ORGANIZATION PARTICIPATION:

ACP, AfDB, AMF, AOSIS, AU, CAEU (candidates), COMESA, FAO, FZ, G-77, IBRD, ICAO, ICCt, ICRM, IDA, IDB, IFAD, IFC, IFRCS, ILO, IMF, IMO, IMSO, InOC, Interpol, IOC, IOM, ITSO, ITU, ITUC (NGOs), LAS, MIGA, NAM, OIC, OIF, OPCW, UN, UNCTAD, UNESCO, UNIDO, UPU, WCO, WHO, WIPO, WMO, WTO (observer)

DIPLOMATIC REPRESENTATION IN THE US:

chief of mission: Ambassador Soilihi Mohamed SOILIHI (since 18 November 2014)

chancery: Mission to the US, 866 United Nations Plaza, Suite 418, New York, NY 10017

telephone: [1] (212) 750-1637

FAX: [1] (212) 750-1657

DIPLOMATIC REPRESENTATION FROM THE US:

the US does not have an embassy in Comoros; the US Ambassador to Madagascar is accredited to Comoros

FLAG DESCRIPTION:

four equal horizontal bands of yellow (top), white, red, and blue, with a green isosceles triangle based on the hoist; centered within the triangle is a white crescent with the convex side facing the hoist and four white, five-pointed stars placed vertically in a line between the points of the crescent; the horizontal bands and the four stars represent the four main islands of the archipelago - Mwali, N'gazidja, Ndzuwani, and Mahore (Mayotte - department of France, but claimed by Comoros)

note: the crescent, stars, and color green are traditional symbols of Islam

NATIONAL SYMBOL(S):

four stars and crescent; national colors: green, white

NATIONAL ANTHEM:

name: "Udzima wa ya Masiwa" (The Union of the Great Islands)

lyrics/music: Said Hachim SIDI ABDEREMANE/Said Hachim SIDI ABDEREMANE and Kamildine ABDALLAH

note: adopted 1978

ECONOMY :: COMOROS

ECONOMY - OVERVIEW:

One of the world's poorest and smallest economies, the Comoros is made up of three islands that are hampered by inadequate transportation links, a young and rapidly increasing population, and few natural resources. The low educational level of the labor force contributes to a subsistence level of economic activity and a heavy dependence on foreign grants and technical assistance. Agriculture, including fishing, hunting, and forestry, accounts for about 50% of GDP, employs a majority of the labor force, and provides most of the exports. Export income is heavily reliant on the three main crops of vanilla, cloves, and ylang ylang (perfume essence); and the Comoros' export earnings are easily disrupted by disasters such as fires and extreme weather. Despite agriculture's importance to the economy, the country imports roughly 70% of its food; rice, the main staple, and other dried vegetables account for more than 25% of imports. Remittances from about 300,000 Comorans contribute about 25% of the country's GDP. France, Comoros's colonial power, remains a key trading partner and bilateral donor.

Comoros faces an education system in need of upgrades, limited opportunities for private commercial and industrial enterprises, poor health services, limited exports, and a high population growth rate. Recurring political instability, sometimes initiated from outside the country, and an ongoing electricity crisis have inhibited growth. The government, elected in mid-2016, has moved to improve revenue mobilization, reduce expenditures, and improve electricity access, although the public sector wage bill remains one of the highest in sub-Saharan Africa. In mid-2017, Comoros joined the Southern African Development Community with 15 other regional member states.

GDP (PURCHASING POWER PARITY):

$1.319 billion (2017 est.)

$1.284 billion (2016 est.)

$1.257 billion (2015 est.)

note: data are in 2017 dollars

country comparison to the world: 201

GDP (OFFICIAL EXCHANGE RATE):

$652 million (2017 est.) (2017 est.)

GDP - REAL GROWTH RATE:

2.7% (2017 est.)

2.2% (2016 est.)

1% (2015 est.)

country comparison to the world: 125

GDP - PER CAPITA (PPP):

$1,600 (2017 est.)

$1,600 (2016 est.)

$1,600 (2015 est.)

note: data are in 2017 dollars

country comparison to the world: 216

GROSS NATIONAL SAVING:

17.3% of GDP (2017 est.)

13.6% of GDP (2016 est.)

18% of GDP (2015 est.)

country comparison to the world: 117

GDP - COMPOSITION, BY END USE:

household consumption: 92.6% (2017 est.)

government consumption: 20.4% (2017 est.)

investment in fixed capital: 20% (2017 est.)

investment in inventories: -3.1% (2017 est.)

exports of goods and services: 17.2% (2017 est.)

imports of goods and services: -47.1% (2017 est.)

GDP - COMPOSITION, BY SECTOR OF ORIGIN:

agriculture: 47.7% (2017 est.)

industry: 11.8% (2017 est.)

services: 40.5% (2017 est.)

AGRICULTURE - PRODUCTS:

vanilla, cloves, ylang-ylang (perfume essence), coconuts, bananas, cassava (manioc)

INDUSTRIES:

fishing, tourism, perfume distillation

INDUSTRIAL PRODUCTION GROWTH RATE:

1% (2017 est.)

country comparison to the world: 154

LABOR FORCE:

278,500 (2016 est.)

country comparison to the world: 166

LABOR FORCE - BY OCCUPATION:

agriculture: 80%

industry: 20% (1996 est.)

industry and services: 20% (1996 est.)

UNEMPLOYMENT RATE:

6.5% (2014 est.)

country comparison to the world: 96

POPULATION BELOW POVERTY LINE:

44.8% (2004 est.)

HOUSEHOLD INCOME OR CONSUMPTION BY PERCENTAGE SHARE:

lowest 10%: 55.2% (2004)

highest 10%: 55.2% (2004)

DISTRIBUTION OF FAMILY INCOME - GINI INDEX:

55.9 (2004 est.)

country comparison to the world: 8

BUDGET:

revenues: 165.2 million (2017 est.)

expenditures: 207.3 million (2017 est.)

TAXES AND OTHER REVENUES:

25.3% (of GDP) (2017 est.)

country comparison to the world: 117

BUDGET SURPLUS (+) OR DEFICIT (-):

-6.5% (of GDP) (2017 est.)

country comparison to the world: 188

PUBLIC DEBT:

32.4% of GDP (2017 est.)

27.7% of GDP (2016 est.)

country comparison to the world: 160

FISCAL YEAR:

calendar year

INFLATION RATE (CONSUMER PRICES):

1% (2017 est.)

1.8% (2016 est.)

country comparison to the world: 50

CENTRAL BANK DISCOUNT RATE:

1.93% (31 December 2010)

2.21% (31 December 2009)

country comparison to the world: 120

COMMERCIAL BANK PRIME LENDING RATE:

10.5% (31 December 2017 est.)

10.5% (31 December 2016 est.)

country comparison to the world: 81

STOCK OF NARROW MONEY:

$200.8 million (31 December 2017 est.)

$180.5 million (31 December 2016 est.)

country comparison to the world: 183

STOCK OF BROAD MONEY:

$200.8 million (31 December 2017 est.)

$180.5 million (31 December 2016 est.)

country comparison to the world: 186

STOCK OF DOMESTIC CREDIT:

$208.5 million (31 December 2017 est.)

$183.9 million (31 December 2016 est.)

country comparison to the world: 184

CURRENT ACCOUNT BALANCE:

-$27 million (2017 est.)

-$45 million (2016 est.)

country comparison to the world: 74

EXPORTS:

$18.9 million (2017 est.)

$17.9 million (2016 est.)

country comparison to the world: 212

EXPORTS - PARTNERS:

France 36.5%, India 12.2%, Germany 8.2%, Pakistan 6.3%, Switzerland 5.8%, South Korea 4.7%, Russia 4.3% (2017)

EXPORTS - COMMODITIES:

vanilla, ylang-ylang (perfume essence), cloves

IMPORTS:

$207.8 million (2017 est.)

$189.9 million (2016 est.)

country comparison to the world: 208

IMPORTS - COMMODITIES:

rice and other foodstuffs, consumer goods, petroleum products, cement and construction materials, transport equipment

IMPORTS - PARTNERS:

UAE 32.8%, France 17.3%, China 13.2%, Madagascar 6.1%, Pakistan 4.5%, India 4.3% (2017)

RESERVES OF FOREIGN EXCHANGE AND GOLD:

$208 million (31 December 2017 est.)

$159.5 million (31 December 2016 est.)

country comparison to the world: 173

DEBT - EXTERNAL:

$199.8 million (31 December 2017 est.)

$132 million (31 December 2016 est.)

country comparison to the world: 189

EXCHANGE RATES:

Comoran francs (KMF) per US dollar -

458.2 (2017 est.)

444.76 (2016 est.)

444.76 (2015 est.)

443.6 (2014 est.)

370.81 (2013 est.)

ENERGY :: COMOROS

ELECTRICITY ACCESS:

population without electricity: 200,000 (2013)

electrification - total population: 69% (2013)

electrification - urban areas: 89% (2013)

electrification - rural areas: 62% (2013)

ELECTRICITY - PRODUCTION:

42 million kWh (2016 est.)

country comparison to the world: 207

ELECTRICITY - CONSUMPTION:

39.06 million kWh (2016 est.)

country comparison to the world: 207

ELECTRICITY - EXPORTS:

0 kWh (2016 est.)

country comparison to the world: 122

ELECTRICITY - IMPORTS:

0 kWh (2016 est.)

country comparison to the world: 136

ELECTRICITY - INSTALLED GENERATING CAPACITY:

27,000 kW (2016 est.)

country comparison to the world: 203

ELECTRICITY - FROM FOSSIL FUELS:

96% of total installed capacity (2016 est.)

country comparison to the world: 38

ELECTRICITY - FROM NUCLEAR FUELS:

0% of total installed capacity (2017 est.)

country comparison to the world: 68

ELECTRICITY - FROM HYDROELECTRIC PLANTS:

4% of total installed capacity (2017 est.)

country comparison to the world: 131

ELECTRICITY - FROM OTHER RENEWABLE SOURCES:

0% of total installed capacity (2017 est.)

country comparison to the world: 181

CRUDE OIL - PRODUCTION:

0 bbl/day (2017 est.)

country comparison to the world: 121

CRUDE OIL - EXPORTS:

0 bbl/day (2015 est.)

country comparison to the world: 107

CRUDE OIL - IMPORTS:

0 bbl/day (2015 est.)

country comparison to the world: 111

CRUDE OIL - PROVED RESERVES:

0 bbl (1 January 2018 est.)

country comparison to the world: 118

REFINED PETROLEUM PRODUCTS - PRODUCTION:

0 bbl/day (2015 est.)

country comparison to the world: 131

REFINED PETROLEUM PRODUCTS - CONSUMPTION:

1,300 bbl/day (2016 est.)

country comparison to the world: 202

REFINED PETROLEUM PRODUCTS - EXPORTS:

0 bbl/day (2015 est.)

country comparison to the world: 144

REFINED PETROLEUM PRODUCTS - IMPORTS:

1,241 bbl/day (2015 est.)

country comparison to the world: 198

NATURAL GAS - PRODUCTION:

0 cu m (2017 est.)

country comparison to the world: 117

NATURAL GAS - CONSUMPTION:

0 cu m (2017 est.)

country comparison to the world: 133

NATURAL GAS - EXPORTS:

0 cu m (2017 est.)

country comparison to the world: 84

NATURAL GAS - IMPORTS:

0 cu m (2017 est.)

country comparison to the world: 107

NATURAL GAS - PROVED RESERVES:

0 cu m (1 January 2014 est.)

country comparison to the world: 123

CARBON DIOXIDE EMISSIONS FROM CONSUMPTION OF ENERGY:

193,600 Mt (2017 est.)

country comparison to the world: 201

COMMUNICATIONS :: COMOROS

TELEPHONES - FIXED LINES:

total subscriptions: 17,212 (2017 est.)

subscriptions per 100 inhabitants: 2 (2017 est.)

country comparison to the world: 183

TELEPHONES - MOBILE CELLULAR:

total subscriptions: 446,868 (2017 est.)

subscriptions per 100 inhabitants: 55 (2017 est.)

country comparison to the world: 173

TELEPHONE SYSTEM:

general assessment: sparse system of microwave radio relay and HF radiotelephone communication stations; telephone service limited to the islands' few towns (2017)

domestic: fixed-line connections only about 2 per 100 persons; mobile-cellular usage over 55 per 100 persons; two companies, Comoros Telecom and Telma, provide domestic and international mobile service and wireless data (2017)

international: country code - 269; landing point for the EASSy fiber-optic submarine cable system connecting East Africa with Europe and North America; HF radiotelephone communications to Madagascar and Reunion (2018)

BROADCAST MEDIA:

national state-owned TV station and a TV station run by Anjouan regional government; national state-owned radio; regional governments on the islands of Grande Comore and Anjouan each operate a radio station; a few independent and small community radio stations operate on the islands of Grande Comore and Moheli, and these two islands have access to Mayotte Radio and French TV (2007)

INTERNET COUNTRY CODE:

.km

INTERNET USERS:

total: 63,084 (July 2016 est.)

percent of population: 7.9% (July 2016 est.)

country comparison to the world: 185

BROADBAND - FIXED SUBSCRIPTIONS:

total: 1,644 (2017 est.)

subscriptions per 100 inhabitants: less than 1 (2017 est.)

country comparison to the world: 185

TRANSPORTATION :: COMOROS

NATIONAL AIR TRANSPORT SYSTEM:

number of registered air carriers: 2 (2015)

inventory of registered aircraft operated by air carriers: 9 (2015)

CIVIL AIRCRAFT REGISTRATION COUNTRY CODE PREFIX:

D6 (2016)

AIRPORTS:

4 (2013)

country comparison to the world: 186

AIRPORTS - WITH PAVED RUNWAYS:

total: 4 (2017)

2,438 to 3,047 m: 1 (2017)

914 to 1,523 m: 3 (2017)

ROADWAYS:

total: 880 km (2002)

paved: 673 km (2002)

unpaved: 207 km (2002)

country comparison to the world: 188

MERCHANT MARINE:

total: 203 (2017)

by type: bulk carrier 4, container ship 1, general cargo 86, oil tanker 26, other 86 (2017)

country comparison to the world: 65

PORTS AND TERMINALS:

major seaport(s): Moroni, Moutsamoudou

MILITARY AND SECURITY :: COMOROS

MILITARY BRANCHES:

National Army for Development (l'Armee Nationale de Developpement, AND): Comoran Security Force (also called Comoran Defense Force (Force Comorienne de Defense, FCD), includes Gendarmerie), Comoran Coast Guard, Comoran Federal Police (2015)

MILITARY SERVICE AGE AND OBLIGATION:

18 years of age for 2-year voluntary male and female military service; no conscription (2015)

TRANSNATIONAL ISSUES :: COMOROS

DISPUTES - INTERNATIONAL:

claims French-administered Mayotte and challenges France's and Madagascar's claims to Banc du Geyser, a drying reef in the Mozambique Channel

TRAFFICKING IN PERSONS:

current situation: Comoros is a source country for children subjected to forced labor and, reportedly, sex trafficking domestically, and women and children are subjected to forced labor in Mayotte; it is possibly a transit and destination country for Malagasy women and girls and a transit country for East African women and girls exploited in domestic service in the Middle East; Comoran children are forced to labor in domestic service, roadside and street vending, baking, fishing, and agriculture; some Comoran students at Koranic schools are exploited for forced agricultural or domestic labor, sometimes being subjected to physical and sexual abuse; Comoros may be particularly vulnerable to transnational trafficking because of inadequate border controls, government corruption, and the presence of international criminal networks

tier rating: Tier 3 – Comoros does not fully comply with the minimum standards for the elimination of trafficking and was placed on Tier 3 after being on the Tier 2 Watch List for two consecutive years without making progress; Parliament passed revisions to the penal code in 2014, including anti-trafficking provisions and enforcement guidelines, but these amendments have not yet been passed approved by the President and put into effect; a new child labor law was passed in 2015 prohibiting child trafficking, but existing laws do not criminalize the forced prostitution of adults; authorities did not investigate, prosecute, or convict alleged trafficking offenders, including complicit officials; the government lacked victim identification and care referral procedures, did not assist any victims during 2014, and provided minimal support to NGOs offering victims psychosocial services (2015)

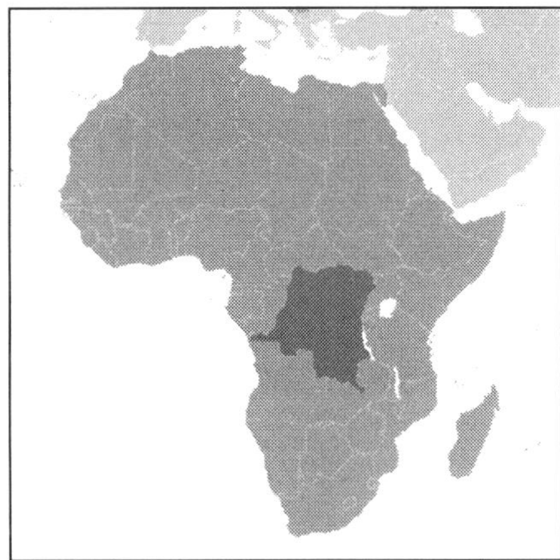

AFRICA :: CONGO, DEMOCRATIC REPUBLIC OF THE

INTRODUCTION :: CONGO, DEMOCRATIC REPUBLIC OF THE

BACKGROUND:

Established as an official Belgian colony in 1908, the then-Republic of the Congo gained its independence in 1960, but its early years were marred by political and social instability. Col. Joseph MOBUTU seized power and declared himself president in a November 1965 coup. He subsequently changed his name - to MOBUTU Sese Seko - as well as that of the country - to Zaire. MOBUTU retained his position for 32 years through several sham elections, as well as through brutal force. Ethnic strife and civil war, touched off by a massive inflow of refugees in 1994 from fighting in Rwanda and Burundi, led in May 1997 to the toppling of the MOBUTU regime by a rebellion backed by Rwanda and Uganda and fronted by Laurent KABILA. KABILA renamed the country the Democratic Republic of the Congo (DRC), but in August 1998 his regime was itself challenged by a second insurrection again backed by Rwanda and Uganda. Troops from Angola, Chad, Namibia, Sudan, and Zimbabwe intervened to support KABILA's regime. In January 2001, KABILA was assassinated and his son, Joseph KABILA, was named head of state. In October 2002, the new president was successful in negotiating the withdrawal of Rwandan forces occupying the eastern DRC; two months later, the Pretoria Accord was signed by all remaining warring parties to end the fighting and establish a government of national unity. A transitional government was set up in July 2003; it held a successful constitutional referendum in December 2005 and elections for the presidency, National Assembly, and provincial legislatures took place in 2006.

In 2009, following a resurgence of conflict in the eastern DRC, the government signed a peace agreement with the National Congress for the Defense of the People (CNDP), a primarily Tutsi rebel group. An attempt to integrate CNDP members into the Congolese military failed, prompting their defection in 2012 and the formation of the M23 armed group - named after the 23 March 2009 peace agreements. Renewed conflict led to large population displacements and significant human rights abuses before the M23 was pushed out of DRC to Uganda and Rwanda in late 2013 by a joint DRC and UN offensive. In addition, the DRC continues to experience violence committed by other armed groups including the Democratic Forces for the Liberation of Rwanda, the Allied Democratic Forces, and assorted Mai Mai militias. In the most recent national elections, held in November 2011, disputed results allowed Joseph KABILA to be reelected to the presidency. The DRC Constitution bars President KABILA from running for a third term, but the DRC Government has delayed national elections, originally slated for November 2016, to December 2018. The failure to hold elections as scheduled has fueled sporadic street protests by KABILA's opponents and has exacerbated tensions in the tumultuous eastern DRC regions.

GEOGRAPHY :: CONGO, DEMOCRATIC REPUBLIC OF THE

LOCATION:

Central Africa, northeast of Angola

GEOGRAPHIC COORDINATES:

0 00 N, 25 00 E

MAP REFERENCES:

Africa

AREA:

total: 2,344,858 sq km

land: 2,267,048 sq km

water: 77,810 sq km

country comparison to the world: 12

AREA - COMPARATIVE:

slightly less than one-fourth the size of the US

LAND BOUNDARIES:

total: 10,481 km

border countries (9): Angola 2646 km (of which 225 km is the boundary of Angola's discontiguous Cabinda Province), Burundi 236 km, Central African Republic 1747 km, Republic of the Congo 1229 km, Rwanda 221 km, South Sudan 714 km, Tanzania 479 km, Uganda 877 km, Zambia 2332 km

COASTLINE:

37 km

MARITIME CLAIMS:

territorial sea: 12 nm

exclusive economic zone: since 2011 the DRC has a Common Interest Zone agreement with Angola for the mutual development of off-shore resources

CLIMATE:

tropical; hot and humid in equatorial river basin; cooler and drier in southern highlands; cooler and wetter in eastern highlands; north of Equator - wet season (April to October), dry season (December to February); south of Equator - wet season (November to March), dry season (April to October)

TERRAIN:

vast central basin is a low-lying plateau; mountains in east

ELEVATION:

mean elevation: 726 m

elevation extremes: 0 m lowest point: Atlantic Ocean

5110 highest point: Pic Marguerite on Mont Ngaliema (Mount Stanley)

NATURAL RESOURCES:

cobalt, copper, niobium, tantalum, petroleum, industrial and gem diamonds, gold, silver, zinc, manganese, tin, uranium, coal, hydropower, timber

LAND USE:

agricultural land: 11.4% (2011 est.)

arable land: 3.1% (2011 est.) / permanent crops: 0.3% (2011 est.) / permanent pasture: 8% (2011 est.)

forest: 67.9% (2011 est.)

other: 20.7% (2011 est.)

IRRIGATED LAND:

110 sq km (2012)

POPULATION DISTRIBUTION:

urban clusters are spread throughout the country, particularly in the northeast along the boarder with Uganda, Rwanda, and Burundi; the largest city is the capital, Kinshasha, located in the west along the Congo River; the south is least densely populated

NATURAL HAZARDS:

periodic droughts in south; Congo River floods (seasonal); active volcanoes in the east along the Great Rift Valley

volcanism: Nyiragongo (3,470 m), which erupted in 2002 and is experiencing ongoing activity, poses a major threat to the city of Goma, home to a quarter million people; the volcano produces unusually fast-moving lava, known to travel up to 100 km /hr; Nyiragongo has been deemed a Decade Volcano by the International Association of Volcanology and Chemistry of the Earth's Interior, worthy of study due to its explosive history and close proximity to human populations; its neighbor, Nyamuragira, which erupted in 2010, is Africa's most active volcano; Visoke is the only other historically active volcano

ENVIRONMENT - CURRENT ISSUES:

poaching threatens wildlife populations; water pollution; deforestation (forests endangered by fires set to clean the land for agricultural purposes; forests also used as a source of fuel); soil erosion; mining (diamonds, gold, coltan - a mineral used in creating capacitors for electronic devices) causing environmental damage

ENVIRONMENT - INTERNATIONAL AGREEMENTS:

party to: Biodiversity, Climate Change, Climate Change-Kyoto Protocol, Desertification, Endangered Species, Hazardous Wastes, Law of the Sea, Marine Dumping, Ozone Layer Protection, Tropical Timber 83, Tropical Timber 94, Wetlands

signed, but not ratified: Environmental Modification

GEOGRAPHY - NOTE:

note 1: second largest country in Africa (after Algeria) and largest country in Sub-Saharan Africa; straddles the equator; dense tropical rain forest in central river basin and eastern highlands; the narrow strip of land that controls the lower Congo River is the DRC's only outlet to the South Atlantic Ocean

note 2: because of its speed, cataracts, rapids, and turbulence the Congo River, most of which flows through the DRC, has never been accurately measured along much of its length; nonetheless, it is conceded to be the deepest river in the world; estimates of its greatest depth vary between 220 and 250 meters

PEOPLE AND SOCIETY :: CONGO, DEMOCRATIC REPUBLIC OF THE

POPULATION:

85,281,024 (July 2018 est.)

note: estimates for this country explicitly take into account the effects of excess mortality due to AIDS; this can result in lower life expectancy, higher infant mortality, higher death rates, lower population growth rates, and changes in the distribution of population by age and sex than would otherwise be expected

country comparison to the world: 16

NATIONALITY:

noun: Congolese (singular and plural)

adjective: Congolese or Congo

ETHNIC GROUPS:

other and unspecified over 200 African ethnic groups of which the majority are Bantu; the four largest tribes - Mongo, Luba, Kongo (all Bantu), and the Mangbetu-Azande (Hamitic) - make up about 45% of the population

LANGUAGES:

French (official), Lingala (a lingua franca trade language), Kingwana (a dialect of Kiswahili or Swahili), Kikongo, Tshiluba

RELIGIONS:

Roman Catholic 50%, Protestant 20%, Kimbanguist 10%, Muslim 10%, other (includes syncretic sects and indigenous beliefs) 10%

DEMOGRAPHIC PROFILE:

Despite a wealth of fertile soil, hydroelectric power potential, and mineral resources, the Democratic Republic of the Congo (DRC) struggles with many socioeconomic problems, including high infant and maternal mortality rates, malnutrition, poor vaccination coverage, lack of access to improved water sources and sanitation, and frequent and early fertility. Ongoing conflict, mismanagement of resources, and a lack of investment have resulted in food insecurity; almost 30 percent of children under the age of 5 are malnourished. The overall coverage of basic public services – education, health, sanitation, and potable water – is very limited and piecemeal, with substantial regional and rural/urban disparities. Fertility remains high at almost 5 children per woman and is likely to remain high because of the low use of contraception and the cultural preference for larger families.

The DRC is a source and host country for refugees. Between 2012 and 2014, more than 119,000 Congolese refugees returned from the Republic of Congo to the relative stability of northwest DRC, but more than 540,000

Congolese refugees remained abroad as of year-end 2015. In addition, an estimated 3.9 million Congolese were internally displaced as of October 2017, the vast majority fleeing violence between rebel group and Congolese armed forces. Thousands of refugees have come to the DRC from neighboring countries, including Rwanda, the Central African Republic, and Burundi.

AGE STRUCTURE:

0-14 years: 41.25% (male 17,735,697 /female 17,446,866)

15-24 years: 21.46% (male 9,184,871 /female 9,117,462)

25-54 years: 30.96% (male 13,176,714 /female 13,225,429)

55-64 years: 3.63% (male 1,472,758 /female 1,625,637)

65 years and over: 2.69% (male 974,293 /female 1,321,297) (2018 est.)

DEPENDENCY RATIOS:

total dependency ratio: 97.5 (2015 est.)

youth dependency ratio: 91.5 (2015 est.)

elderly dependency ratio: 6 (2015 est.)

potential support ratio: 16.8 (2015 est.)

MEDIAN AGE:

total: 18.8 years

male: 18.6 years

female: 19 years (2018 est.)

country comparison to the world: 206

POPULATION GROWTH RATE:

2.33% (2018 est.)

country comparison to the world: 31

BIRTH RATE:

32.8 births/1,000 population (2018 est.)

country comparison to the world: 29

DEATH RATE:

9.4 deaths/1,000 population (2018 est.)

country comparison to the world: 50

NET MIGRATION RATE:

-0.1 migrant(s)/1,000 population (2018 est.)

country comparison to the world: 105

POPULATION DISTRIBUTION:

urban clusters are spread throughout the country, particularly in the northeast along the boarder with Uganda, Rwanda, and Burundi; the largest city is the capital, Kinshasha, located in the west along the Congo River; the south is least densely populated

URBANIZATION:

urban population: 44.5% of total population (2018)

rate of urbanization: 4.53% annual rate of change (2015-20 est.)

MAJOR URBAN AREAS - POPULATION:

13.171 million KINSHASA (capital), 2.305 million Mbuji-Mayi, 2.281 million Lubumbashi, 1.335 million Kananga, 1.167 million Kisangani, 973,000 Bukavu (2018)

SEX RATIO:

at birth: 1.03 male(s)/female (2017 est.)

0-14 years: 1.02 male(s)/female (2017 est.)

15-24 years: 1.01 male(s)/female (2017 est.)

25-54 years: 1 male(s)/female (2017 est.)

55-64 years: 0.89 male(s)/female (2017 est.)

65 years and over: 0.73 male(s)/female (2017 est.)

total population: 1 male(s)/female (2017 est.)

MOTHER'S MEAN AGE AT FIRST BIRTH:

19.9 years (2013/14 est.)

note: median age at first birth among women 25-29

MATERNAL MORTALITY RATE:

693 deaths/100,000 live births (2015 est.)

country comparison to the world: 10

INFANT MORTALITY RATE:

total: 66.7 deaths/1,000 live births (2018 est.)

male: 70.1 deaths/1,000 live births (2018 est.)

female: 63.1 deaths/1,000 live births (2018 est.)

country comparison to the world: 8

LIFE EXPECTANCY AT BIRTH:

total population: 58.1 years (2018 est.)

male: 56.5 years (2018 est.)

female: 59.7 years (2018 est.)

country comparison to the world: 213

TOTAL FERTILITY RATE:

4.54 children born/woman (2018 est.)

country comparison to the world: 25

CONTRACEPTIVE PREVALENCE RATE:

20.4% (2013/14)

HEALTH EXPENDITURES:

4.3% of GDP (2014)

country comparison to the world: 159

PHYSICIANS DENSITY:

0.09 physicians/1,000 population (2009)

DRINKING WATER SOURCE:

improved:

urban: 81.1% of population

rural: 31.2% of population

total: 52.4% of population

unimproved:

urban: 18.9% of population

rural: 68.8% of population

total: 47.6% of population (2015 est.)

SANITATION FACILITY ACCESS:

improved:

urban: 28.5% of population (2015 est.)

rural: 28.7% of population (2015 est.)

total: 28.7% of population (2015 est.)

unimproved:

urban: 71.5% of population (2015 est.)

rural: 71.3% of population (2015 est.)

total: 71.3% of population (2015 est.)

HIV/AIDS - ADULT PREVALENCE RATE:

0.7% (2017 est.)

country comparison to the world: 52

HIV/AIDS - PEOPLE LIVING WITH HIV/AIDS:

390,000 (2017 est.)

country comparison to the world: 18

HIV/AIDS - DEATHS:

17,000 (2017 est.)

country comparison to the world: 12

MAJOR INFECTIOUS DISEASES:

degree of risk: very high (2016)

food or waterborne diseases: bacterial and protozoal diarrhea, hepatitis A, and typhoid fever (2016)

vectorborne diseases: malaria, dengue fever, and trypanosomiasis-gambiense (African sleeping sickness) (2016)

water contact diseases: schistosomiasis (2016)

animal contact diseases: rabies (2016)

OBESITY - ADULT PREVALENCE RATE:

6.7% (2016)

country comparison to the world: 164

CHILDREN UNDER THE AGE OF 5 YEARS UNDERWEIGHT:

23.4% (2013)

country comparison to the world: 22

EDUCATION EXPENDITURES:

2.3% of GDP (2015)

country comparison to the world: 168

LITERACY:

definition: age 15 and over can read and write French, Lingala, Kingwana, or Tshiluba (2016 est.)

total population: 77% (2016 est.)

male: 88.5% (2016 est.)

female: 66.5% (2016 est.)

SCHOOL LIFE EXPECTANCY (PRIMARY TO TERTIARY EDUCATION):

total: 9 years (2013)

male: 10 years (2013)

female: 8 years (2013)

UNEMPLOYMENT, YOUTH AGES 15-24:

total: 8.7% (2012 est.)

male: 11.3% (2012 est.)

female: 6.8% (2012 est.)

country comparison to the world: 134

GOVERNMENT :: CONGO, DEMOCRATIC REPUBLIC OF THE

COUNTRY NAME:

conventional long form: Democratic Republic of the Congo

conventional short form: DRC

local long form: Republique Democratique du Congo

local short form: RDC

former: Congo Free State, Belgian Congo, Congo/Leopoldville, Congo/Kinshasa, Zaire

abbreviation: DRC (or DROC)

etymology: named for the Congo River, most of which lies within the DRC; the river name derives from Kongo, a Bantu kingdom that occupied its mouth at the time of Portuguese discovery in the late 15th century and whose name stems from its people the Bakongo, meaning "hunters"

GOVERNMENT TYPE:

semi-presidential republic

CAPITAL:

name: Kinshasa

geographic coordinates: 4 19 S, 15 18 E

time difference: UTC+1 (6 hours ahead of Washington, DC, during Standard Time)

note: the DRC has two time zones

ADMINISTRATIVE DIVISIONS:

26 provinces (provinces, singular - province); Bas-Uele (Lower Uele), Equateur, Haut-Katanga (Upper Katanga), Haut-Lomami (Upper Lomami), Haut-Uele (Upper Uele), Ituri, Kasai, Kasai-Central, Kasai-Oriental (East Kasai), Kinshasa, Kongo Central, Kwango, Kwilu, Lomami, Lualaba, Mai-Ndombe, Maniema, Mongala, Nord-Kivu (North Kivu), Nord-Ubangi (North Ubangi), Sankuru, Sud-Kivu (South Kivu), Sud-Ubangi (South Ubangi), Tanganyika, Tshopo, Tshuapa

INDEPENDENCE:

30 June 1960 (from Belgium)

NATIONAL HOLIDAY:

Independence Day, 30 June (1960)

CONSTITUTION:

history: several previous; latest adopted 13 May 2005, approved by referendum 18-19 December 2005, promulgated 18 February 2006 (2017)

amendments: proposed by the president of the republic, by the government, by either house of Parliament, or by public petition; agreement on the substance of a proposed bill requires absolute majority vote in both houses; passage requires a referendum only if both houses in joint meeting fail to achieve three-fifths majority vote; constitutional articles including the form of government, universal suffrage, judicial independence, political pluralism, and personal freedoms cannot be amended; amended 2011 (2017)

LEGAL SYSTEM:

civil law system primarily based on Belgian law, but also customary and tribal law

INTERNATIONAL LAW ORGANIZATION PARTICIPATION:

accepts compulsory ICJ jurisdiction with reservations; accepts ICCt jurisdiction

CITIZENSHIP:

citizenship by birth: no

citizenship by descent only: at least one parent must be a citizen of the Democratic Republic of the Congo

dual citizenship recognized: no

residency requirement for naturalization: 5 years

SUFFRAGE:

18 years of age; universal and compulsory

EXECUTIVE BRANCH:

chief of state: President Joseph KABILA (since 17 January 2001)

head of government: Prime Minister Bruno TSHIBALA (since 7 April 2017); Deputy Prime Ministers Jose MAKILA, Leonard She OKITUNDU, Henri MOVA Sankanyi (since February 2018)

cabinet: Ministers of State appointed by the president

elections/appointments: president directly elected by simple majority vote for a 5-year term (eligible for a second term); election last held on 28 November 2011 (next originally scheduled for 27 November 2016 but now scheduled for 23 December 2018); prime minister appointed by the president

election results: Joseph KABILA reelected president; percent of vote - Joseph KABILA (PPRD) 49%, Etienne TSHISEKEDI (UDPS) 32.3%, other 18.7%; note - election marred by serious voting irregularities

LEGISLATIVE BRANCH:

description: bicameral Parliament or Parlement consists of:
Senate (108 seats; members indirectly elected by provincial assemblies by proportional representation vote; members serve 5-year terms)
National Assembly (500 seats; 439 members directly elected in multi-seat constituencies by proportional representation vote and 61 directly elected in single-seat constituencies by simple majority vote; members serve 5-year terms)

elections:
Senate - last held on 19 January 2007 (follow-on election has been delayed)
National Assembly - last held on 28 November 2011 (next originally scheduled for 27 November 2016 but postponed

election results:
Senate - percent of vote by party - NA; seats by party - PPRD 22, MLC 14, FR 7, RCD 7, PDC 6, CDC 3, MSR 3,

PALU 2, other 18, independent 26
National Assembly - percent of vote by party - NA; seats by party - PPRD 62, UDPS 41, PPPD 29, MSR 27, MLC 22, PALU 19, UNC 17, ARC 16, AFDC 15, ECT 11, RRC 11, other 214 (includes numerous political parties that won 10 or fewer seats and 2 constituencies where voting was halted), independent 16; note - the November 2011 election was marred by violence including the destruction of ballots in 2 constituencies resulting in the closure of polling sites; election results were delayed 3 months, strongly contested, and continue to be unresolved

JUDICIAL BRANCH:

highest courts: Court of Cassation or Cour de Cassation (consists of 26 justices and organized into legislative and judiciary sections); Constitutional Court (consists of 9 judges)

judge selection and term of office: Court of Cassation judges nominated by the Judicial Service Council, an independent body of public prosecutors and selected judges of the lower courts; judge tenure NA; Constitutional Court judges - 3 nominated by the president, 3 by the Judicial Service Council, and 3 by the legislature; judges appointed by the president to serve 9-year non-renewable terms with one-third of the membership renewed every 3 years

subordinate courts: State Security Court; Court of Appeals (organized into administrative and judiciary sections); Tribunal de Grande; magistrates' courts; customary courts

POLITICAL PARTIES AND LEADERS:

Christian Democrat Party or PDC [Jose ENDUNDO]
Congolese Rally for Democracy or RCD [Azarias RUBERWA]
Convention of Christian Democrats or CDC
Forces of Renewal or FR [Mbusa NYAMWISI]
Movement for the Liberation of the Congo or MLC [Jean-Pierre BEMBA]
People's Party for Reconstruction and Democracy or PPRD [Henri MOVA Sakanyi]
Social Movement for Renewal or MSR [Pierre LUMBI]
Unified Lumumbist Party or PALU [Antoine GIZENGA]
Union for the Congolese Nation or UNC [Vital KAMERHE]
Union for Democracy and Social Progress or UDPS [Felix TSHISEKEDI]

INTERNATIONAL ORGANIZATION PARTICIPATION:

ACP, AfDB, AU, CEMAC, CEPGL, COMESA, EITI (compliant country), FAO, G-24, G-77, IAEA, IBRD, ICAO, ICC (NGOs), ICCt, ICRM, IDA, IFAD, IFC, IFRCS, IHO, ILO, IMF, IMO, Interpol, IOC, IOM, IPU, ISO, ITSO, ITU, ITUC (NGOs), MIGA, NAM, OIF, OPCW, PCA, SADC, UN, UNCTAD, UNESCO, UNHCR, UNIDO, UNWTO, UPU, WCO, WFTU (NGOs), WHO, WIPO, WMO, WTO

DIPLOMATIC REPRESENTATION IN THE US:

chief of mission: Ambassador Francois Nkuna BALUMUENE (since 23 September 2015)

chancery: 1726 M Street, NW, Suite 601, Washington, DC, 20036

telephone: [1] (202) 234-7690 through 7691

FAX: [1] (202) 234-2609

representative office: New York New York

DIPLOMATIC REPRESENTATION FROM THE US:

chief of mission: Ambassador (vacant); Charge d'Affaires Jennifer HASKELL (since 31 December 2016)

embassy: 310 Avenue des Aviateurs, Kinshasa, Gombe

mailing address: Unit 2220, DPO AE 09828

telephone: [243] 081 556-0151

FAX: [243] 81 556-0175

FLAG DESCRIPTION:

sky blue field divided diagonally from the lower hoist corner to upper fly corner by a red stripe bordered by two narrow yellow stripes; a yellow, five-pointed star appears in the upper hoist corner; blue represents peace and hope, red the blood of the country's martyrs, and yellow the country's wealth and prosperity; the star symbolizes unity and the brilliant future for the country

NATIONAL SYMBOL(S):

leopard; national colors: sky blue, red, yellow

NATIONAL ANTHEM:

name: "Debout Congolaise" (Arise Congolese)

lyrics/music: Joseph LUTUMBA/Simon-Pierre BOKA di Mpasi Londi

note: adopted 1960; replaced when the country was known as Zaire; but readopted in 1997

ECONOMY :: CONGO, DEMOCRATIC REPUBLIC OF THE

ECONOMY - OVERVIEW:

The economy of the Democratic Republic of the Congo - a nation endowed with vast natural resource wealth - continues to perform poorly. Systemic corruption since independence in 1960, combined with countrywide instability and intermittent conflict that began in the early-90s, has reduced national output and government revenue, and increased external debt. With the installation of a transitional government in 2003 after peace accords, economic conditions slowly began to improve as the government reopened relations with international financial institutions and international donors, and President KABILA began implementing reforms. Progress on implementing substantive economic reforms remains slow because of political instability, bureaucratic inefficiency, corruption, and patronage, which also dampen international investment prospects.

Renewed activity in the mining sector, the source of most export income, boosted Kinshasa's fiscal position and GDP growth until 2015, but low commodity prices have led to slower growth, volatile inflation, currency depreciation, and a growing fiscal deficit. An uncertain legal framework, corruption, and a lack of transparency in government policy are long-term problems for the large mining sector and for the economy as a whole. Much economic activity still occurs in the informal sector and is not reflected in GDP data.

Poverty remains widespread in DRC, and the country failed to meet any Millennium Development Goals by 2015. DRC also concluded its program with the IMF in 2015. The price of copper – the DRC's primary export - plummeted in 2015 and remained at record lows during 2016-17, reducing government revenues, expenditures, and foreign exchange reserves, while inflation reached nearly 50% in mid-2017 – its highest level since the early 2000s.

GDP (PURCHASING POWER PARITY):

$68.6 billion (2017 est.)

$66.33 billion (2016 est.)

$64.78 billion (2015 est.)

note: data are in 2017 dollars

country comparison to the world: 103

GDP (OFFICIAL EXCHANGE RATE):

$41.44 billion (2017 est.) (2017 est.)

GDP - REAL GROWTH RATE:

3.4% (2017 est.)

2.4% (2016 est.)

6.9% (2015 est.)

country comparison to the world: 101

GDP - PER CAPITA (PPP):

$800 (2017 est.)

$800 (2016 est.)

$800 (2015 est.)

note: data are in 2017 dollars

country comparison to the world: 226

GROSS NATIONAL SAVING:

11.5% of GDP (2017 est.)

8.7% of GDP (2016 est.)

16.5% of GDP (2015 est.)

country comparison to the world: 154

GDP - COMPOSITION, BY END USE:

household consumption: 78.5% (2017 est.)

government consumption: 12.7% (2017 est.)

investment in fixed capital: 15.9% (2017 est.)

investment in inventories: 0% (2017 est.)

exports of goods and services: 25.7% (2017 est.)

imports of goods and services: -32.8% (2017 est.)

GDP - COMPOSITION, BY SECTOR OF ORIGIN:

agriculture: 19.7% (2017 est.)

industry: 43.6% (2017 est.)

services: 36.7% (2017 est.)

AGRICULTURE - PRODUCTS:

coffee, sugar, palm oil, rubber, tea, cotton, cocoa, quinine, cassava (manioc, tapioca), bananas, plantains, peanuts, root crops, corn, fruits; wood products

INDUSTRIES:

mining (copper, cobalt, gold, diamonds, coltan, zinc, tin, tungsten), mineral processing, consumer products (textiles, plastics, footwear, cigarettes), metal products, processed foods and beverages, timber, cement, commercial ship repair

INDUSTRIAL PRODUCTION GROWTH RATE:

1.6% (2017 est.)

country comparison to the world: 140

LABOR FORCE:

31.36 million (2017 est.)

country comparison to the world: 18

LABOR FORCE - BY OCCUPATION:

agriculture: NA

industry: NA

services: NA

UNEMPLOYMENT RATE:

NA

POPULATION BELOW POVERTY LINE:

63% (2014 est.)

HOUSEHOLD INCOME OR CONSUMPTION BY PERCENTAGE SHARE:

lowest 10%: 34.7% (2006)

highest 10%: 34.7% (2006)

DISTRIBUTION OF FAMILY INCOME - GINI INDEX:

42.1 (2012 est.)

country comparison to the world: 53

BUDGET:

revenues: 4.634 billion (2017 est.)

expenditures: 5.009 billion (2017 est.)

TAXES AND OTHER REVENUES:

11.2% (of GDP) (2017 est.)

country comparison to the world: 211

BUDGET SURPLUS (+) OR DEFICIT (-):

-0.9% (of GDP) (2017 est.)

country comparison to the world: 72

PUBLIC DEBT:

18.1% of GDP (2017 est.)

19.3% of GDP (2016 est.)

country comparison to the world: 192

FISCAL YEAR:

calendar year

INFLATION RATE (CONSUMER PRICES):

41.5% (2017 est.)

18.2% (2016 est.)

country comparison to the world: 224

CENTRAL BANK DISCOUNT RATE:

20% (31 December 2017)

20% (31 December 2011)

country comparison to the world: 4

COMMERCIAL BANK PRIME LENDING RATE:

20.62% (31 December 2017 est.)

19.05% (31 December 2016 est.)

country comparison to the world: 13

STOCK OF NARROW MONEY:

$1.044 billion (31 December 2017 est.)

$1.192 billion (31 December 2016 est.)

country comparison to the world: 157

STOCK OF BROAD MONEY:

$1.044 billion (31 December 2017 est.)

$1.192 billion (31 December 2016 est.)

country comparison to the world: 162

STOCK OF DOMESTIC CREDIT:

$3.252 billion (31 December 2017 est.)

$3.582 billion (31 December 2016 est.)

country comparison to the world: 136

MARKET VALUE OF PUBLICLY TRADED SHARES:

NA

CURRENT ACCOUNT BALANCE:

-$200 million (2017 est.)

-$1.215 billion (2016 est.)

country comparison to the world: 98

EXPORTS:

$10.98 billion (2017 est.)

$8.228 billion (2016 est.)

country comparison to the world: 91

EXPORTS - PARTNERS:

China 41.4%, Zambia 22.7%, South Korea 7.2%, Finland 6.2% (2017)

EXPORTS - COMMODITIES:

diamonds, copper, gold, cobalt, wood products, crude oil, coffee

IMPORTS:

$10.82 billion (2017 est.)

$10.21 billion (2016 est.)

country comparison to the world: 101

IMPORTS - COMMODITIES:

foodstuffs, mining and other machinery, transport equipment, fuels

IMPORTS - PARTNERS:

China 19.9%, South Africa 18%, Zambia 10.4%, Belgium 9.1%, India 4.3%, Tanzania 4.2% (2017)

RESERVES OF FOREIGN EXCHANGE AND GOLD:

$457.5 million (31 December 2017 est.)

$708.2 million (31 December 2016 est.)

country comparison to the world: 155

DEBT - EXTERNAL:

$4.963 billion (31 December 2017 est.)

$5.35 billion (31 December 2016 est.)

country comparison to the world: 134

EXCHANGE RATES:

Congolese francs (CDF) per US dollar -

1,546.8 (2017 est.)

1,010.3 (2016 est.)

1,010.3 (2015 est.)

925.99 (2014 est.)

925.23 (2013 est.)

ENERGY :: CONGO, DEMOCRATIC REPUBLIC OF THE

ELECTRICITY ACCESS:

population without electricity: 61.4 million (2013)

electrification - total population: 9% (2013)

electrification - urban areas: 19% (2013)

electrification - rural areas: 2% (2013)

ELECTRICITY - PRODUCTION:

9.046 billion kWh (2016 est.)

country comparison to the world: 106

ELECTRICITY - CONSUMPTION:

7.43 billion kWh (2016 est.)

country comparison to the world: 106

ELECTRICITY - EXPORTS:

422 million kWh (2015 est.)

country comparison to the world: 70

ELECTRICITY - IMPORTS:

20 million kWh (2016 est.)

country comparison to the world: 113

ELECTRICITY - INSTALLED GENERATING CAPACITY:

2.587 million kW (2016 est.)

country comparison to the world: 105

ELECTRICITY - FROM FOSSIL FUELS:

2% of total installed capacity (2016 est.)

country comparison to the world: 210

ELECTRICITY - FROM NUCLEAR FUELS:

0% of total installed capacity (2017 est.)

country comparison to the world: 69

ELECTRICITY - FROM HYDROELECTRIC PLANTS:

98% of total installed capacity (2017 est.)

country comparison to the world: 4

ELECTRICITY - FROM OTHER RENEWABLE SOURCES:

0% of total installed capacity (2017 est.)

country comparison to the world: 182

CRUDE OIL - PRODUCTION:

19,160 bbl/day (2017 est.)

country comparison to the world: 65

CRUDE OIL - EXPORTS:

20,000 bbl/day (2015 est.)

country comparison to the world: 49

CRUDE OIL - IMPORTS:

0 bbl/day (2015 est.)

country comparison to the world: 112

CRUDE OIL - PROVED RESERVES:

180 million bbl (1 January 2018 est.)

country comparison to the world: 58

REFINED PETROLEUM PRODUCTS - PRODUCTION:

0 bbl/day (2017 est.)

country comparison to the world: 132

REFINED PETROLEUM PRODUCTS - CONSUMPTION:

21,000 bbl/day (2016 est.)

country comparison to the world: 136

REFINED PETROLEUM PRODUCTS - EXPORTS:

0 bbl/day (2015 est.)

country comparison to the world: 145

REFINED PETROLEUM PRODUCTS - IMPORTS:

21,140 bbl/day (2015 est.)

country comparison to the world: 115

NATURAL GAS - PRODUCTION:

0 cu m (2017 est.)

country comparison to the world: 118

NATURAL GAS - CONSUMPTION:

0 cu m (2017 est.)

country comparison to the world: 134

NATURAL GAS - EXPORTS:

0 cu m (2017 est.)

country comparison to the world: 85

NATURAL GAS - IMPORTS:

0 cu m (2017 est.)

country comparison to the world: 108

NATURAL GAS - PROVED RESERVES:

991.1 million cu m (1 January 2018 est.)

country comparison to the world: 99

CARBON DIOXIDE EMISSIONS FROM CONSUMPTION OF ENERGY:

3.146 million Mt (2017 est.)

country comparison to the world: 145

COMMUNICATIONS :: CONGO, DEMOCRATIC REPUBLIC OF THE

TELEPHONES - FIXED LINES:

total subscriptions: NA (2017 est.)

subscriptions per 100 inhabitants: NA (2017 est.)

TELEPHONES - MOBILE CELLULAR:

total subscriptions: 35,270,156 (2017 est.)

subscriptions per 100 inhabitants: 42 (2017 est.)

country comparison to the world: 39

TELEPHONE SYSTEM:

general assessment: barely adequate wire and microwave radio relay service in and between urban areas; domestic satellite system with 14 earth stations; inadequate fixed-line infrastructure; efforts have been made to improve regulating the telecom sector; wars and social upheavel have not promoted advancement; a revised Telecommunications Act adopted in May 2018, though the practical implementation of the Act's measures remains dubious (2017)

domestic: fixed-line connections only about 8 per 100 persons; given the backdrop of a wholly inadequate fixed-line infrastructure, the use of mobile-cellular services has surged and mobile teledensity is over 42 per 100 persons (2017)

international: country code - 243; satellite earth station - 1 Intelsat (Atlantic Ocean); the country was finally connected to low-cost, high-quality international bandwidth through the WACS submarine fibre optic cable in 2013, and SCPT is rolling out a fibre optic national backbone network with support from China (2017)

BROADCAST MEDIA:

state-owned TV broadcast station with near national coverage; more than a dozen privately owned TV stations - 2 with near national coverage; 2 state-owned radio stations are supplemented by more than 100 private radio stations; transmissions of at least 2 international broadcasters are available (2007)

INTERNET COUNTRY CODE:

.cd

INTERNET USERS:

total: 3.016 million (July 2016 est.)

percent of population: 3.8% (July 2016 est.)

country comparison to the world: 97

BROADBAND - FIXED SUBSCRIPTIONS:

total: 1,000 (2017 est.)

subscriptions per 100 inhabitants: less than 1 (2017 est.)

country comparison to the world: 191

TRANSPORTATION :: CONGO, DEMOCRATIC REPUBLIC OF THE

NATIONAL AIR TRANSPORT SYSTEM:

number of registered air carriers: 8 (2015)

inventory of registered aircraft operated by air carriers: 13 (2015)

annual passenger traffic on registered air carriers: 476,352 (2015)

annual freight traffic on registered air carriers: 85,839 mt-km (2015)

CIVIL AIRCRAFT REGISTRATION COUNTRY CODE PREFIX:

9Q (2016)

AIRPORTS:

198 (2013)

country comparison to the world: 27

AIRPORTS - WITH PAVED RUNWAYS:

total: 26 (2017)

over 3,047 m: 3 (2017)

2,438 to 3,047 m: 3 (2017)

1,524 to 2,437 m: 17 (2017)

914 to 1,523 m: 2 (2017)

under 914 m: 1 (2017)

AIRPORTS - WITH UNPAVED RUNWAYS:

total: 172 (2013)

1,524 to 2,437 m: 20 (2013)

914 to 1,523 m: 87 (2013)

under 914 m: 65 (2013)

HELIPORTS:

1 (2013)

PIPELINES:

62 km gas, 77 km oil, 756 km refined products (2013)

RAILWAYS:

total: 4,007 km (2014)

narrow gauge: 3,882 km 1.067-m gauge (858 km electrified) (2014)

125 1.000-m gauge

country comparison to the world: 47

ROADWAYS:

total: 153,497 km (2004)

paved: 2,794 km (2004)

unpaved: 150,703 km (2004)

country comparison to the world: 34

WATERWAYS:

15,000 km (including the Congo River, its tributaries, and unconnected lakes) (2011)

country comparison to the world: 8

MERCHANT MARINE:

total: 33 (2017)

by type: general cargo 18, oil tanker 1, other 14 (2017)

country comparison to the world: 125

PORTS AND TERMINALS:

major seaport(s): Banana

river or lake port(s): Boma, Bumba, Kinshasa, Kisangani, Matadi, Mbandaka (Congo)

Kindu (Lualaba) Bukavu, Goma (Lake Kivu) Kalemie (Lake Tanganyika)

MILITARY AND SECURITY :: CONGO, DEMOCRATIC REPUBLIC OF THE

MILITARY EXPENDITURES:

1.34% of GDP (2016)

1.36% of GDP (2015)

1% of GDP (2014)

1.25% of GDP (2013)

1.21% of GDP (2012)

country comparison to the world: 85

MILITARY BRANCHES:

Armed Forces of the Democratic Republic of the Congo (Forces d'Armees de la Republique Democratique du Congo, FARDC): Army, National Navy (La Marine Nationale), Congolese Air Force (Force Aerienne Congolaise, FAC) (2011)

MILITARY SERVICE AGE AND OBLIGATION:

18-45 years of age for voluntary and compulsory military service (2012)

TRANSNATIONAL ISSUES :: CONGO, DEMOCRATIC REPUBLIC OF THE

DISPUTES - INTERNATIONAL:

heads of the Great Lakes states and UN pledged in 2004 to abate tribal, rebel, and militia fighting in the region, including northeast Congo, where the UN Organization Mission in the Democratic Republic of the Congo (MONUC), organized in 1999, maintains over 16,500 uniformed peacekeepersmembers of Uganda's Lord's Resistance Army forces continue to seek refuge in Congo's Garamba National Park as peace talks with the Uganda Government evolvethe location of the boundary in the broad Congo River with the Republic of the Congo is indefinite except in the Pool Malebo/Stanley Pool areaUganda and DRC dispute Rukwanzi Island in Lake Albert and other areas on the Semliki River with hydrocarbon potentialboundary commission continues discussions over Congolese-administered triangle of land on the right bank of the Lunkinda River claimed by Zambia near the DRC village of Pweto

REFUGEES AND INTERNALLY DISPLACED PERSONS:

refugees (country of origin): 219,489 (Rwanda), 171,966 (Central African Republic), 95,438 (South Sudan) (refugees and asylum seekers), 42,309 (Burundi) (2018)

IDPs: 4.5 million (fighting between government forces and rebels since mid-1990s; conflict in Kasai region since 2016) (2017)

TRAFFICKING IN PERSONS:

current situation: The Democratic Republic of the Congo is a source, destination, and possibly a transit country for men, women, and children subjected to forced labor and sex trafficking; the majority of this trafficking is internal, and much of it is perpetrated by armed groups and rogue government forces outside official control in the country's unstable eastern provinces; Congolese adults are subjected to forced labor, including debt bondage, in unlicensed mines, and women may be forced into prostitution; Congolese women and girls are subjected to forced marriages where they are vulnerable to domestic servitude or sex trafficking, while children are forced to work in agriculture, mining, mineral smuggling, vending, portering, and begging; Congolese women and children migrate to countries in Africa, the Middle East, and Europe where some are subjected to forced prostitution, domestic servitude, and forced labor in agriculture and diamond mining; indigenous and foreign armed groups, including the Lord's Resistance Army, abduct and forcibly recruit Congolese adults and children to serve as laborers, porters, domestics, combatants, and sex slaves; some elements of the Congolese national army (FARDC) also forced adults to carry supplies, equipment, and looted goods, but no cases of the FARDC recruiting child soldiers were reported in 2014 – a significant change

tier rating: Tier 2 Watch List - The Democratic Republic of the Congo does not fully comply with the minimum standards for the elimination of trafficking; however, it is making significant efforts to do so; the government took significant steps to hold military and police officials complicit in human trafficking accountable with convictions for sex slavery and arrests of armed group commanders for the recruitment and use of child soldiers; the government appears to have ceased the recruitment of child soldiers through the implementation of a UN-backed action plan; little effort was made to address labor and sex trafficking crimes committed by persons other than officials, or to identify the victims, or to provide or refer the victims to care services; awareness of various forms of trafficking is limited among law enforcement personnel and training and resources are inadequate to conduct investigations (2015)

ILLICIT DRUGS:

traffickers exploit lax shipping controls to transit pseudoephedrine through the capital; while rampant corruption and inadequate supervision leave the banking system vulnerable to money laundering, the lack of a well-developed financial system limits the country's utility as a money-laundering center

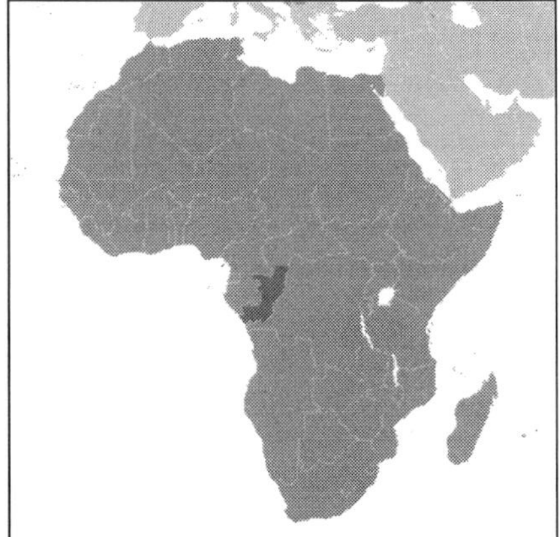

AFRICA :: CONGO, REPUBLIC OF THE

INTRODUCTION :: CONGO, REPUBLIC OF THE

BACKGROUND:

Upon independence in 1960, the former French region of Middle Congo became the Republic of the Congo. A quarter century of experimentation with Marxism was abandoned in 1990 and a democratically elected government took office in 1992. A brief civil war in 1997 restored former Marxist President Denis SASSOU-Nguesso, and ushered in a period of ethnic and political unrest. Southern-based rebel groups agreed to a final peace accord in March 2003. The Republic of Congo is one of Africa's largest petroleum producers, but with declining production it will need new offshore oil finds to sustain its oil earnings over the long term.

GEOGRAPHY :: CONGO, REPUBLIC OF THE

LOCATION:

Central Africa, bordering the South Atlantic Ocean, between Angola and Gabon

GEOGRAPHIC COORDINATES:

1 00 S, 15 00 E

MAP REFERENCES:

Africa

AREA:

total: 342,000 sq km

land: 341,500 sq km

water: 500 sq km

country comparison to the world: 65

AREA - COMPARATIVE:

slightly smaller than Montana

LAND BOUNDARIES:

total: 5,008 km

border countries (5): Angola 231 km, Cameroon 494 km, Central African Republic 487 km, Democratic Republic of the Congo 1229 km, Gabon 2567 km

COASTLINE:

169 km

MARITIME CLAIMS:

territorial sea: 12 nm

exclusive economic zone: 200 nm

contiguous zone: 24 nm

CLIMATE:

tropical; rainy season (March to June); dry season (June to October); persistent high temperatures and humidity; particularly enervating climate astride the Equator

TERRAIN:

coastal plain, southern basin, central plateau, northern basin

ELEVATION:

mean elevation: 430 m

elevation extremes: 0 m lowest point: Atlantic Ocean

903 highest point: Mount Berongou

NATURAL RESOURCES:

petroleum, timber, potash, lead, zinc, uranium, copper, phosphates, gold, magnesium, natural gas, hydropower

LAND USE:

agricultural land: 31.1% (2011 est.)

arable land: 1.6% (2011 est.) / permanent crops: 0.2% (2011 est.) / permanent pasture: 29.3% (2011 est.)

forest: 65.6% (2011 est.)

other: 3.3% (2011 est.)

IRRIGATED LAND:

20 sq km (2012)

POPULATION DISTRIBUTION:

the population is primarily located in the south, in and around the capital of Brazzaville

NATURAL HAZARDS:

seasonal flooding

ENVIRONMENT - CURRENT ISSUES:

air pollution from vehicle emissions; water pollution from raw sewage; tap water is not potable; deforestation; wildlife protection

ENVIRONMENT - INTERNATIONAL AGREEMENTS:

party to: Biodiversity, Climate Change, Climate Change-Kyoto Protocol, Desertification, Endangered Species, Hazardous Wastes, Law of the Sea, Ozone Layer Protection, Ship Pollution, Tropical Timber 83, Tropical Timber 94, Wetlands

signed, but not ratified: none of the selected agreements

GEOGRAPHY - NOTE:

about 70% of the population lives in Brazzaville, Pointe-Noire, or along the railroad between them

PEOPLE AND SOCIETY :: CONGO, REPUBLIC OF THE

POPULATION:

5,062,021 (July 2018 est.)

note: estimates for this country explicitly take into account the effects of excess mortality due to AIDS; this can result in lower life expectancy, higher infant mortality, higher death rates, lower population growth rates, and changes in the distribution of population by age and sex than would otherwise be expected

country comparison to the world: 122

NATIONALITY:

noun: Congolese (singular and plural)

adjective: Congolese or Congo

ETHNIC GROUPS:

Kongo 40.5%, Teke 16.9%, Mbochi 13.1%, foreigner 8.2%, Sangha 5.6%, Mbere/Mbeti/Kele 4.4%, Punu 4.3%, Pygmy 1.6%, Oubanguiens 1.6%, Duma 1.5%, Makaa 1.3%, other and unspecified 1% (2014-15 est.)

LANGUAGES:

French (official), French Lingala and Monokutuba (lingua franca trade languages), many local languages and dialects (of which Kikongo is the most widespread)

RELIGIONS:

Roman Catholic 33.1%, Awakening Churches/Christian Revival 22.3%, Protestant 19.9%, Salutiste 2.2%, Muslim 1.6%, Kimbanguiste 1.5%, other 8.1%, none 11.3% (2010 est.)

AGE STRUCTURE:

0-14 years: 41.75% (male 1,066,474 /female 1,046,924)

15-24 years: 16.99% (male 431,279 /female 428,999)

25-54 years: 33.77% (male 857,596 /female 851,712)

55-64 years: 4.39% (male 112,669 /female 109,429)

65 years and over: 3.1% (male 69,621 /female 87,318) (2018 est.)

DEPENDENCY RATIOS:

total dependency ratio: 84.5 (2015 est.)

youth dependency ratio: 78.3 (2015 est.)

elderly dependency ratio: 6.2 (2015 est.)

potential support ratio: 16.1 (2015 est.)

MEDIAN AGE:

total: 19.6 years

male: 19.4 years

female: 19.8 years (2018 est.)

country comparison to the world: 199

POPULATION GROWTH RATE:

2.17% (2018 est.)

country comparison to the world: 38

BIRTH RATE:

33.7 births/1,000 population (2018 est.)

country comparison to the world: 26

DEATH RATE:

9.2 deaths/1,000 population (2018 est.)

country comparison to the world: 58

NET MIGRATION RATE:

-2.8 migrant(s)/1,000 population (2018 est.)

country comparison to the world: 172

POPULATION DISTRIBUTION:

the population is primarily located in the south, in and around the capital of Brazzaville

URBANIZATION:

urban population: 66.9% of total population (2018)

rate of urbanization: 3.28% annual rate of change (2015-20 est.)

MAJOR URBAN AREAS - POPULATION:

2.23 million BRAZZAVILLE (capital), 1.138 million Pointe-Noire (2018)

SEX RATIO:

at birth: 1.02 male(s)/female (2017 est.)

0-14 years: 1.02 male(s)/female (2017 est.)

15-24 years: 1 male(s)/female (2017 est.)

25-54 years: 1.01 male(s)/female (2017 est.)

55-64 years: 0.99 male(s)/female (2017 est.)

65 years and over: 0.78 male(s)/female (2017 est.)

total population: 1.01 male(s)/female (2017 est.)

MOTHER'S MEAN AGE AT FIRST BIRTH:

19.8 years (2011/12 est.)

note: median age at first birth among women 25-29

MATERNAL MORTALITY RATE:

442 deaths/100,000 live births (2015 est.)

country comparison to the world: 25

INFANT MORTALITY RATE:

total: 53.5 deaths/1,000 live births (2018 est.)

male: 58.3 deaths/1,000 live births (2018 est.)

female: 48.5 deaths/1,000 live births (2018 est.)

country comparison to the world: 23

LIFE EXPECTANCY AT BIRTH:

total population: 60.3 years (2018 est.)

male: 59 years (2018 est.)

female: 61.6 years (2018 est.)

country comparison to the world: 208

TOTAL FERTILITY RATE:

4.26 children born/woman (2018 est.)

country comparison to the world: 28

CONTRACEPTIVE PREVALENCE RATE:

30.1% (2014/15)

HEALTH EXPENDITURES:

5.2% of GDP (2014)

country comparison to the world: 133

DRINKING WATER SOURCE:

improved:

urban: 95.8% of population (2015 est.)

rural: 40% of population (2015 est.)

total: 76.5% of population (2015 est.)

unimproved:

urban: 4.2% of population (2015 est.)

rural: 60% of population (2015 est.)

total: 23.5% of population (2015 est.)

SANITATION FACILITY ACCESS:

improved:

urban: 20% of population (2015 est.)

rural: 5.6% of population (2015 est.)

total: 15% of population (2015 est.)

unimproved:

urban: 80% of population (2015 est.)

rural: 94.4% of population (2015 est.)

total: 85% of population (2015 est.)

HIV/AIDS - ADULT PREVALENCE RATE:

3.1% (2017 est.)

country comparison to the world: 18

HIV/AIDS - PEOPLE LIVING WITH HIV/AIDS:

100,000 (2017 est.)

country comparison to the world: 44

HIV/AIDS - DEATHS:

4,900 (2017 est.)

country comparison to the world: 28

MAJOR INFECTIOUS DISEASES:

degree of risk: very high (2016)

food or waterborne diseases: bacterial and protozoal diarrhea, hepatitis A, and typhoid fever (2016)

vectorborne diseases: malaria and dengue fever (2016)

water contact diseases: schistosomiasis (2016)

animal contact diseases: rabies (2016)

OBESITY - ADULT PREVALENCE RATE:

9.6% (2016)

country comparison to the world: 143

CHILDREN UNDER THE AGE OF 5 YEARS UNDERWEIGHT:

12.3% (2015)

country comparison to the world: 55

EDUCATION EXPENDITURES:

6.2% of GDP (2010)

country comparison to the world: 30

LITERACY:

definition: age 15 and over can read and write (2015 est.)

total population: 79.3% (2015 est.)

male: 86.4% (2015 est.)

female: 72.9% (2015 est.)

SCHOOL LIFE EXPECTANCY (PRIMARY TO TERTIARY EDUCATION):

total: 11 years (2012)

male: 11 years (2012)

female: 11 years (2012)

GOVERNMENT :: CONGO, REPUBLIC OF THE

COUNTRY NAME:

conventional long form: Republic of the Congo

conventional short form: Congo (Brazzaville)

local long form: Republique du Congo

local short form: Congo

former: French Congo, Middle Congo, People's Republic of the Congo, Congo/Brazzaville

etymology: named for the Congo River, which makes up much of the country's eastern border; the river name derives from Kongo, a Bantu kingdom that occupied its mouth at the time of Portuguese discovery in the late 15th century and whose name stems from its people the Bakongo, meaning "hunters"

GOVERNMENT TYPE:

presidential republic

CAPITAL:

name: Brazzaville

geographic coordinates: 4 15 S, 15 17 E

time difference: UTC+1 (6 hours ahead of Washington, DC, during Standard Time)

ADMINISTRATIVE DIVISIONS:

12 departments (departments, singular - department); Bouenza, Brazzaville, Cuvette, Cuvette-Ouest, Kouilou, Lekoumou, Likouala, Niari, Plateaux, Pointe-Noire, Pool, Sangha

INDEPENDENCE:

15 August 1960 (from France)

NATIONAL HOLIDAY:

Independence Day, 15 August (1960)

CONSTITUTION:

history: several previous; latest approved by referendum 25 October 2015 (2017)

amendments: proposed by the president of the republic or by Parliament; passage of presidential proposals requires Supreme Court review followed by approval in a referendum; such proposals may also be submitted directly to Parliament, in which case passage requires at least three-quarters majority vote of both houses in joint session; proposals by Parliament require three-fourths majority vote of both houses in joint session; constitutional articles including those affecting the country's territory, republican form of government, and secularity of the state are not amendable (2017)

LEGAL SYSTEM:

mixed legal system of French civil law and customary law

INTERNATIONAL LAW ORGANIZATION PARTICIPATION:

has not submitted an ICJ jurisdiction declaration; accepts ICCt jurisdiction

CITIZENSHIP:

citizenship by birth: no

citizenship by descent only: at least one parent must be a citizen of the Republic of the Congo

dual citizenship recognized: no

residency requirement for naturalization: 10 years

SUFFRAGE:

18 years of age; universal

EXECUTIVE BRANCH:

chief of state: President Denis SASSOU-Nguesso (since 25 October 1997)

head of government: Prime Minister (vacant); Prime Minister Clement MOUAMBA (since 23 April 2016) resigned on 18 August 2017; note - a constitutional referendum held in 2015 approved the change of the head of government from the president to the prime minister

cabinet: Council of Ministers appointed by the president

elections/appointments: president directly elected by absolute majority popular vote in 2 rounds if needed for a 5-year term (eligible for 2 additional terms); election last held on 20 March 2016 (next to be held in 2021)

election results: Denis SASSOU-Nguesso reelected president in the first round; percent of vote - Denis SASSOU-Nguesso (PCT) 60.4%, Guy Price Parfait KOLELAS (MCDDI) 15.1%, Jean-Marie MOKOKO (independent) 13.9%, Pascal Tsaty MABIALA (UPADS) 4.4%, other 6.2%

LEGISLATIVE BRANCH:

description: bicameral Parliament or Parlement consists of:
Senate (72 seats; members indirectly elected by regional councils by simple majority vote to serve 6-year terms with one-half of membership renewed every 3 years)
National Assembly (151 seats; members directly elected in single-seat constituencies by absolute majority popular vote in 2 rounds if needed; members serve 5-year terms)

elections:
Senate - last held on 31 August 2017 for expiry of half the seats (next to be held in 2020)
National Assembly - last held on 16 and 30 July 2017 (next to be held in July 2022)

election results:
Senate - percent of vote by party - NA; seats by party - PCT 46, independent

12, MAR 2, RDPS 2, UPADS 2, DRD 1, FP 1, MCDDI 1, PRL 1, Pulp 1, PUR 1, RC 1
National Assembly - percent of vote by party - NA; seats by party - PCT 96, UPADS 8, MCDDI 4, other 23 (less than 4 seats) independent 20

JUDICIAL BRANCH:

highest courts: Supreme Court or Cour Supreme (consists of NA judges); Constitutional Court (consists of 9 members); note - a High Court of Justice, outside the judicial authority, tries cases involving treason by the president of the republic

judge selection and term of office: Supreme Court judges elected by Parliament and serve until age 65; Constitutional Court members appointed by the president of the republic - 3 directly by the president and 6 nominated by Parliament; members appointed for renewable 9-year terms with one-third of the membership renewed every 3 years

subordinate courts: Court of Audit and Budgetary Discipline; courts of appeal; regional and district courts; employment tribunals; juvenile courts

POLITICAL PARTIES AND LEADERS:

Action Movement for Renewal or MAR [Roland BOUITI-VIAUDO]
Citizen's Rally or RC [Claude Alphonse NSILOU]
Congolese Labour Party or PCT [Denis SASSOU-NGUESSO]
Congolese Movement for Democracy and Integral Development or MCDDI [Guy Price Parfait KOLELAS]
Movement for Unity, Solidarity, and Work or MUST [Claudine MUNARI]
Pan-African Union for Social Development or UPADS [Pascal Tsaty MABIALA]
Party for the Unity of the Republic or PUR
Patriotic Union for Democracy and Progress or UPDP [Auguste-Celestin GONGARD NKOUA]
Prospects and Realities Club or CPR
Rally for Democracy and Social Progress or RDPS [Bernard BATCHI]
Rally of the Presidential Majority or RMP
Republican and Liberal Party or PRL [Bonaventure MIZIDY]
Union for the Republic or UR
Union of Democratic Forces or UDF
Union for Democracy and Republic or UDR
many smaller parties

INTERNATIONAL ORGANIZATION PARTICIPATION:

ACP, AfDB, AU, BDEAC, CEMAC, EITI (compliant country), FAO, FZ, G-77, IAEA, IBRD, ICAO, ICCt, ICRM, IDA, IFAD, IFC, IFRCS, ILO, IMF, IMO, Interpol, IOC, IOM, IPU, ISO (correspondent), ITSO, ITU, ITUC (NGOs), MIGA, NAM, OIF, OPCW, UN, UNCTAD, UNESCO, UNHCR, UNIDO, UNITAR, UNWTO, UPU, WCO, WFTU (NGOs), WHO, WIPO, WMO, WTO

DIPLOMATIC REPRESENTATION IN THE US:

chief of mission: Ambassador Serge MOMBOULI (since 31 July 2001)

chancery: 1720 16th Street NW, Washington, DC 20009

telephone: [1] (202) 726-5500

FAX: [1] (202) 726-1860

DIPLOMATIC REPRESENTATION FROM THE US:

chief of mission: Ambassador Todd P. HASKELL (since July 2017)

embassy: 70-83 Section D, Maya-Maya Boulevard, Brazzaville

mailing address: B.P. 1015, Brazzaville

telephone: [242] 06 612-2000

FLAG DESCRIPTION:

divided diagonally from the lower hoist side by a yellow band; the upper triangle (hoist side) is green and the lower triangle is red; green symbolizes agriculture and forests, yellow the friendship and nobility of the people, red is unexplained but has been associated with the struggle for independence

note: uses the popular Pan-African colors of Ethiopia

NATIONAL SYMBOL(S):

lion, elephant; national colors: green, yellow, red

NATIONAL ANTHEM:

name: "La Congolaise" (The Congolese)

lyrics/music: Jacques TONDRA and Georges KIBANGHI/Jean ROYER and Joseph SPADILIERE

note: originally adopted 1959, restored 1991

ECONOMY :: CONGO, REPUBLIC OF THE

ECONOMY - OVERVIEW:

The Republic of the Congo's economy is a mixture of subsistence farming, an industrial sector based largely on oil and support services, and government spending. Oil has supplanted forestry as the mainstay of the economy, providing a major share of government revenues and exports. Natural gas is increasingly being converted to electricity rather than being flared, greatly improving energy prospects. New mining projects, particularly iron ore, which entered production in late 2013, may add as much as $1 billion to annual government revenue. The Republic of the Congo is a member of the Central African Economic and Monetary Community (CEMAC) and shares a common currency – the Central African Franc – with five other member states in the region.

The current administration faces difficult economic challenges of stimulating recovery and reducing poverty. The drop in oil prices that began in 2014 has constrained government spending; lower oil prices forced the government to cut more than $1 billion in planned spending. The fiscal deficit amounted to 11% of GDP in 2017. The government's inability to pay civil servant salaries has resulted in multiple rounds of strikes by many groups, including doctors, nurses, and teachers. In the wake of a multi-year recession, the country reached out to the IMF in 2017 for a new program; the IMF noted that the country's continued dependence on oil, unsustainable debt, and significant governance weakness are key impediments to the country's economy. In 2018, the country's external debt level will approach 120% of GDP. The IMF urged the government to renegotiate debts levels to sustainable levels before it agreed to a new macroeconomic adjustment package.

GDP (PURCHASING POWER PARITY):

$29.39 billion (2017 est.)

$30.33 billion (2016 est.)

$31.22 billion (2015 est.)

note: data are in 2017 dollars

country comparison to the world: 133

GDP (OFFICIAL EXCHANGE RATE):

$8.718 billion (2017 est.) (2017 est.)

GDP - REAL GROWTH RATE:

-3.1% (2017 est.)

-2.8% (2016 est.)

2.6% (2015 est.)

country comparison to the world: 212

GDP - PER CAPITA (PPP):

$6,800 (2017 est.)

$7,200 (2016 est.)

$7,500 (2015 est.)

note: data are in 2017 dollars

country comparison to the world: 161

GROSS NATIONAL SAVING:

19.5% of GDP (2017 est.)

-12.8% of GDP (2016 est.)

6.6% of GDP (2015 est.)

country comparison to the world: 101

GDP - COMPOSITION, BY END USE:

household consumption: 47.6% (2017 est.)

government consumption: 9.6% (2017 est.)

investment in fixed capital: 42.5% (2017 est.)

investment in inventories: 0.1% (2017 est.)

exports of goods and services: 62.9% (2017 est.)

imports of goods and services: -62.7% (2017 est.)

GDP - COMPOSITION, BY SECTOR OF ORIGIN:

agriculture: 9.3% (2017 est.)

industry: 51% (2017 est.)

services: 39.7% (2017 est.)

AGRICULTURE - PRODUCTS:

cassava (manioc, tapioca), sugar, rice, corn, peanuts, vegetables, coffee, cocoa; forest products

INDUSTRIES:

petroleum extraction, cement, lumber, brewing, sugar, palm oil, soap, flour, cigarettes

INDUSTRIAL PRODUCTION GROWTH RATE:

-3% (2017 est.)

country comparison to the world: 187

LABOR FORCE:

2.055 million (2016 est.)

country comparison to the world: 124

LABOR FORCE - BY OCCUPATION:

agriculture: 35.4%

industry: 20.6%

services: 44% (2005 est.)

UNEMPLOYMENT RATE:

36% (2014 est.)

country comparison to the world: 211

POPULATION BELOW POVERTY LINE:

46.5% (2011 est.)

HOUSEHOLD INCOME OR CONSUMPTION BY PERCENTAGE SHARE:

lowest 10%: 37.1% (2005)

highest 10%: 37.1% (2005)

DISTRIBUTION OF FAMILY INCOME - GINI INDEX:

48.9 (2011 est.)

country comparison to the world: 20

BUDGET:

revenues: 1.965 billion (2017 est.)

expenditures: 2.578 billion (2017 est.)

TAXES AND OTHER REVENUES:

22.5% (of GDP) (2017 est.)

country comparison to the world: 132

BUDGET SURPLUS (+) OR DEFICIT (-):

-7% (of GDP) (2017 est.)

country comparison to the world: 194

PUBLIC DEBT:

130.8% of GDP (2017 est.)

128.7% of GDP (2016 est.)

country comparison to the world: 7

FISCAL YEAR:

calendar year

INFLATION RATE (CONSUMER PRICES):

0.5% (2017 est.)

3.2% (2016 est.)

country comparison to the world: 26

CENTRAL BANK DISCOUNT RATE:

4.25% (31 December 2009)

4.75% (31 December 2008)

country comparison to the world: 92

COMMERCIAL BANK PRIME LENDING RATE:

14.6% (31 December 2017 est.)

14% (31 December 2016 est.)

country comparison to the world: 44

STOCK OF NARROW MONEY:

$2.585 billion (31 December 2017 est.)

$2.456 billion (31 December 2016 est.)

country comparison to the world: 126

STOCK OF BROAD MONEY:

$2.585 billion (31 December 2017 est.)

$2.456 billion (31 December 2016 est.)

country comparison to the world: 133

STOCK OF DOMESTIC CREDIT:

$3.036 billion (31 December 2017 est.)

$2.901 billion (31 December 2016 est.)

country comparison to the world: 139

MARKET VALUE OF PUBLICLY TRADED SHARES:

NA

CURRENT ACCOUNT BALANCE:

-$1.128 billion (2017 est.)

-$5.735 billion (2016 est.)

country comparison to the world: 145

EXPORTS:

$4.193 billion (2017 est.)

$4.116 billion (2016 est.)

country comparison to the world: 116

EXPORTS - PARTNERS:

China 53.8%, Angola 6.2%, Gabon 5.7%, Italy 5.4%, Spain 5.4%, Australia 4.8% (2017)

EXPORTS - COMMODITIES:

petroleum, lumber, plywood, sugar, cocoa, coffee, diamonds

IMPORTS:

$2.501 billion (2017 est.)

$5.639 billion (2016 est.)

country comparison to the world: 158

IMPORTS - COMMODITIES:

capital equipment, construction materials, foodstuffs

IMPORTS - PARTNERS:

France 15%, China 14%, Belgium 12.2%, Norway 8.1% (2017)

RESERVES OF FOREIGN EXCHANGE AND GOLD:

$505.7 million (31 December 2017 est.)

$727.1 million (31 December 2016 est.)

country comparison to the world: 151

DEBT - EXTERNAL:

$4.605 billion (31 December 2017 est.)

$4.721 billion (31 December 2016 est.)

country comparison to the world: 135

STOCK OF DIRECT FOREIGN INVESTMENT - AT HOME:

NA

EXCHANGE RATES:

Cooperation Financiere en Afrique Centrale francs (XAF) per US dollar -

579.8 (2017 est.)

593.01 (2016 est.)

593.01 (2015 est.)

591.45 (2014 est.)

494.42 (2013 est.)

ENERGY :: CONGO, REPUBLIC OF THE

ELECTRICITY ACCESS:

population without electricity: 2.6 million (2013)

electrification - total population: 42% (2013)

electrification - urban areas: 62% (2013)

electrification - rural areas: 5% (2013)

ELECTRICITY - PRODUCTION:

1.696 billion kWh (2016 est.)

country comparison to the world: 143

ELECTRICITY - CONSUMPTION:

912 million kWh (2016 est.)

country comparison to the world: 157

ELECTRICITY - EXPORTS:

22 million kWh (2015 est.)

country comparison to the world: 90

ELECTRICITY - IMPORTS:

18 million kWh (2016 est.)

country comparison to the world: 115

ELECTRICITY - INSTALLED GENERATING CAPACITY:

591,500 kW (2016 est.)

country comparison to the world: 139

ELECTRICITY - FROM FOSSIL FUELS:

64% of total installed capacity (2016 est.)

country comparison to the world: 121

ELECTRICITY - FROM NUCLEAR FUELS:

0% of total installed capacity (2017 est.)

country comparison to the world: 70

ELECTRICITY - FROM HYDROELECTRIC PLANTS:

36% of total installed capacity (2017 est.)

country comparison to the world: 59

ELECTRICITY - FROM OTHER RENEWABLE SOURCES:

0% of total installed capacity (2017 est.)

country comparison to the world: 183

CRUDE OIL - PRODUCTION:

244,200 bbl/day (2017 est.)

country comparison to the world: 33

CRUDE OIL - EXPORTS:

254,100 bbl/day (2015 est.)

country comparison to the world: 28

CRUDE OIL - IMPORTS:

0 bbl/day (2015 est.)

country comparison to the world: 113

CRUDE OIL - PROVED RESERVES:

1.6 billion bbl (1 January 2018 est.)

country comparison to the world: 37

REFINED PETROLEUM PRODUCTS - PRODUCTION:

15,760 bbl/day (2015 est.)

country comparison to the world: 93

REFINED PETROLEUM PRODUCTS - CONSUMPTION:

17,000 bbl/day (2016 est.)

country comparison to the world: 149

REFINED PETROLEUM PRODUCTS - EXPORTS:

5,766 bbl/day (2015 est.)

country comparison to the world: 89

REFINED PETROLEUM PRODUCTS - IMPORTS:

7,162 bbl/day (2015 est.)

country comparison to the world: 156

NATURAL GAS - PRODUCTION:

1.387 billion cu m (2017 est.)

country comparison to the world: 61

NATURAL GAS - CONSUMPTION:

1.387 billion cu m (2017 est.)

country comparison to the world: 85

NATURAL GAS - EXPORTS:

0 cu m (2017 est.)

country comparison to the world: 86

NATURAL GAS - IMPORTS:

0 cu m (2017 est.)

country comparison to the world: 109

NATURAL GAS - PROVED RESERVES:

90.61 billion cu m (1 January 2018 est.)

country comparison to the world: 54

CARBON DIOXIDE EMISSIONS FROM CONSUMPTION OF ENERGY:

5.239 million Mt (2017 est.)

country comparison to the world: 134

COMMUNICATIONS :: CONGO, REPUBLIC OF THE

TELEPHONES - FIXED LINES:

total subscriptions: 17,000 (July 2016 est.)

subscriptions per 100 inhabitants: less than 1 (July 2016 est.)

country comparison to the world: 184

TELEPHONES - MOBILE CELLULAR:

total subscriptions: 5.056 million (2017 est.)

subscriptions per 100 inhabitants: 102 (2017 est.)

country comparison to the world: 120

TELEPHONE SYSTEM:

general assessment: primary network consists of microwave radio relay and coaxial cable with services barely adequate for government use; key exchanges are in Brazzaville, Pointe-Noire, and Loubomo; intercity lines frequently out of order (2017)

domestic: fixed-line infrastructure inadequate, providing less than 1 connection per 100 persons; in the absence of an adequate fixed-line infrastructure, mobile-cellular subscribership has surged to 102 per 100 persons (2017)

international: country code - 242; satellite earth station - 1 Intelsat (Atlantic Ocean) (2015)

BROADCAST MEDIA:

1 state-owned TV and 3 state-owned radio stations; several privately owned TV and radio stations; satellite TV service is available; rebroadcasts of several international broadcasters are available (2007)

INTERNET COUNTRY CODE:

.cg

INTERNET USERS:

total: 362,000 (July 2016 est.)

percent of population: 7.6% (July 2016 est.)

country comparison to the world: 155

TRANSPORTATION :: CONGO, REPUBLIC OF THE

NATIONAL AIR TRANSPORT SYSTEM:

number of registered air carriers: 3 (2015)

inventory of registered aircraft operated by air carriers: 12 (2015)

annual passenger traffic on registered air carriers: 657,926 (2015)

annual freight traffic on registered air carriers: 2,987,493 mt-km (2015)

CIVIL AIRCRAFT REGISTRATION COUNTRY CODE PREFIX:

TN (2016)

AIRPORTS:

27 (2013)

country comparison to the world: 124

AIRPORTS - WITH PAVED RUNWAYS:

total: 8 (2017)

over 3,047 m: 2 (2017)

2,438 to 3,047 m: 1 (2017)

1,524 to 2,437 m: 5 (2017)

AIRPORTS - WITH UNPAVED RUNWAYS:

total: 19 (2013)

1,524 to 2,437 m: 8 (2013)

914 to 1,523 m: 9 (2013)

under 914 m: 2 (2013)

PIPELINES:

232 km gas, 4 km liquid petroleum gas, 982 km oil (2013)

RAILWAYS:

total: 510 km (2014)

narrow gauge: 510 km 1.067-m gauge (2014)

country comparison to the world: 112

ROADWAYS:

total: 17,000 km (2006)

paved: 1,212 km (2006)

unpaved: 15,788 km (2006)

country comparison to the world: 120

WATERWAYS:

1,120 km (commercially navigable on Congo and Oubanqui Rivers above Brazzaville; there are many ferries across the river to Kinshasa; the Congo south of Brazzaville-Kinshasa to the coast is not navigable because of rapids, necessitating a rail connection to Pointe Noire; other rivers are used for local traffic only) (2011)

country comparison to the world: 61

MERCHANT MARINE:

total: 40 (2017)

by type: general cargo 27, oil tanker 2, other 11 (2017)

country comparison to the world: 122

PORTS AND TERMINALS:

major seaport(s): Pointe-Noire

oil terminal(s): Djeno

river port(s): Brazzaville (Congo)

Impfondo (Oubangi) Ouesso (Sangha) Oyo (Alima)

MILITARY AND SECURITY :: CONGO, REPUBLIC OF THE

MILITARY EXPENDITURES:

7.17% of GDP (2016)

4.97% of GDP (2014)

2.61% of GDP (2013)

country comparison to the world: 4

MILITARY BRANCHES:

Congolese Armed Forces (Forces Armees Congolaises, FAC): Army (Armee de Terre), Navy, Congolese Air Force (Armee de l'Air Congolaise); Gendarmerie; Special Presidential Security Guard (GSSP) (2013)

MILITARY SERVICE AGE AND OBLIGATION:

18 years of age for voluntary military service; women may serve in the Armed Forces (2012)

TRANSNATIONAL ISSUES :: CONGO, REPUBLIC OF THE

DISPUTES - INTERNATIONAL:

the location of the boundary in the broad Congo River with the Democratic Republic of the Congo is undefined except in the Pool Malebo/Stanley Pool area

REFUGEES AND INTERNALLY DISPLACED PERSONS:

refugees (country of origin): 9,202 (Rwanda) (2016), 31,688 (Central African Republic) (2017), 15,715 (Democratic Republic of the Congo) (refugees and asylum seekers) (2018)

IDPs: 108,000 (multiple civil wars since 1992) (2017)

TRAFFICKING IN PERSONS:

current situation: the Republic of the Congo is a source and destination country for children, men, and women, subjected to forced labor and sex trafficking; most trafficking victims are from Benin, the Democratic Republic of the Congo (DRC), and, to a lesser extent, other neighboring countries and are subjected to domestic servitude and market vending by West African and Congolese nationals; adults and children, the majority from the DRC, are also sex trafficked in Congo, mainly Brazzaville; internal trafficking victims, often from rural areas, are exploited as domestic servants or forced to work in quarries, bakeries, fishing, and agriculture

tier rating: Tier 2 Watch List - the Republic of the Congo does not fully comply with the minimum standards for the elimination of trafficking; however, it is making significant efforts to do so; the country drafted an action plan based on anti-trafficking legislation, which remains pending in the Supreme Court; the government made minimal anti-trafficking law enforcement efforts in 2014, failing to prosecute or convict suspected traffickers from cases dating back to 2010; serious allegations of official complicity continue to be reported; the government lacks a systematic means of identifying victims and relies on NGOs and international organizations to identify victims and NGOs and foster families to provide care to victims; the quality of care varied widely because the foster care system was allegedly undermined by inadequate security and official complicity (2015)

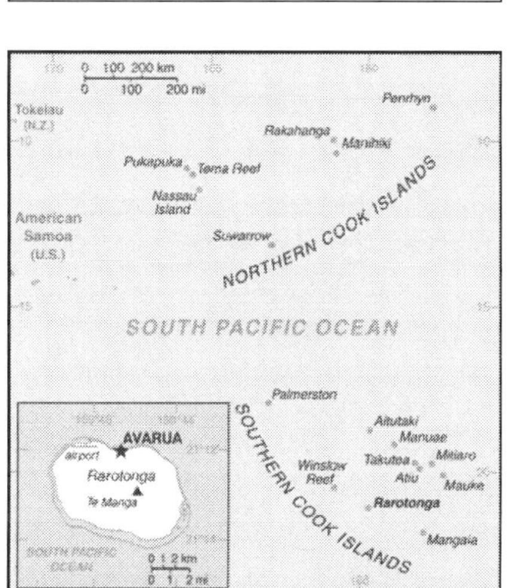

AUSTRALIA - OCEANIA :: COOK ISLANDS

INTRODUCTION :: COOK ISLANDS

BACKGROUND:

Named after Captain COOK, who sighted them in the 1770s, the islands became a British protectorate in 1888. By 1900, administrative control was transferred to New Zealand; in 1965, residents chose self-government in free association with New Zealand. The emigration of skilled workers to New Zealand, government deficits, and limited natural resources are of continuing concern.

GEOGRAPHY :: COOK ISLANDS

LOCATION:

Oceania, group of islands in the South Pacific Ocean, about halfway between Hawaii and New Zealand

GEOGRAPHIC COORDINATES:

21 14 S, 159 46 W

MAP REFERENCES:

Oceania

AREA:

total: 236 sq km

land: 236 sq km

water: 0 sq km

country comparison to the world: 215

AREA - COMPARATIVE:

1.3 times the size of Washington, DC

LAND BOUNDARIES:

0 km

COASTLINE:

120 km

MARITIME CLAIMS:

territorial sea: 12 nm

exclusive economic zone: 200 nm

continental shelf: 200 nm or to the edge of the continental margin

CLIMATE:

tropical oceanic; moderated by trade winds; a dry season from April to November and a more humid season from December to March

TERRAIN:

low coral atolls in north; volcanic, hilly islands in south

ELEVATION:

0 m lowest point: Pacific Ocean

652 highest point: Te Manga

NATURAL RESOURCES:

coconuts (copra)

LAND USE:

agricultural land: 8.4% (2011 est.)

arable land: 4.2% (2011 est.) / permanent crops: 4.2% (2011 est.) / permanent pasture: 0% (2011 est.)

forest: 64.6% (2011 est.)

other: 27% (2011 est.)

IRRIGATED LAND:

NA

POPULATION DISTRIBUTION:

most of the population is found on the island of Rarotonga

NATURAL HAZARDS:

tropical cyclones (November to March)

ENVIRONMENT - CURRENT ISSUES:

limited land presents solid and liquid waste disposal problems; soil destruction and deforestation; environmental degradation due to indiscriminant use of pesticides; improper disposal of pollutants; overfishing and destructive fishing practices; over dredging of lagoons and coral rubble beds; unregulated building

ENVIRONMENT - INTERNATIONAL AGREEMENTS:

party to: Biodiversity, Climate Change, Climate Change-Kyoto Protocol, Desertification, Hazardous Wastes, Law of the Sea, Ozone Layer Protection

GEOGRAPHY - NOTE:

the northern Cook Islands are seven low-lying, sparsely populated, coral atolls; the southern Cook Islands, where most of the population lives, consist of eight elevated, fertile, volcanic isles, including the largest, Rarotonga, at 67 sq km

PEOPLE AND SOCIETY :: COOK ISLANDS

POPULATION:

9,038 (July 2017 est.) (July 2018 est.)

note: the Cook Islands' Ministry of Finance & Economic Management estimated the resident population to have been 11,700 in September 2016

country comparison to the world: 224

NATIONALITY:

noun: Cook Islander(s)

adjective: Cook Islander

ETHNIC GROUPS:

Cook Island Maori (Polynesian) 81.3%, part Cook Island Maori 6.7%, other 11.9% (2011 est.)

LANGUAGES:

English (official) 86.4%, Cook Islands Maori (Rarotongan) (official) 76.2%, other 8.3% (2011 est.)

note: shares sum to more than 100% because some respondents gave more than one answer on the census

RELIGIONS:

Protestant 62.8% (Cook Islands Christian Church 49.1%, Seventh Day Adventist 7.9%, Assemblies of God 3.7%, Apostolic Church 2.1%), Roman Catholic 17%, Mormon 4.4%, other 8%, none 5.6%, no response 2.2% (2011 est.)

AGE STRUCTURE:

0-14 years: 20.68% (male 987 /female 882)

15-24 years: 15.99% (male 774 /female 671)

25-54 years: 38.06% (male 1,710 /female 1,730)

55-64 years: 12.72% (male 627 /female 523)

65 years and over: 12.55% (male 558 /female 576) (2018 est.)

MEDIAN AGE:

total: 37.2 years

male: 36.7 years

female: 37.6 years (2018 est.)

country comparison to the world: 67

POPULATION GROWTH RATE:

-2.72% (2018 est.)

country comparison to the world: 233

BIRTH RATE:

13.7 births/1,000 population (2018 est.)

country comparison to the world: 138

DEATH RATE:

8.6 deaths/1,000 population (2018 est.)

country comparison to the world: 75

POPULATION DISTRIBUTION:

most of the population is found on the island of Rarotonga

URBANIZATION:

urban population: 75.1% of total population (2018)

rate of urbanization: 0.37% annual rate of change (2015-20 est.)

SEX RATIO:

at birth: 1.07 male(s)/female (2017 est.)

0-14 years: 1.12 male(s)/female (2017 est.)

15-24 years: 1.14 male(s)/female (2017 est.)

25-54 years: 1 male(s)/female (2017 est.)

55-64 years: 1.17 male(s)/female (2017 est.)

65 years and over: 0.97 male(s)/female (2017 est.)

total population: 1.07 male(s)/female (2017 est.)

INFANT MORTALITY RATE:

total: 12.6 deaths/1,000 live births (2018 est.)

male: 15.3 deaths/1,000 live births (2018 est.)

female: 9.8 deaths/1,000 live births (2018 est.)

country comparison to the world: 107

LIFE EXPECTANCY AT BIRTH:

total population: 76.2 years (2018 est.)

male: 73.4 years (2018 est.)

female: 79.2 years (2018 est.)

country comparison to the world: 91

TOTAL FERTILITY RATE:

2.16 children born/woman (2018 est.)

country comparison to the world: 97

HEALTH EXPENDITURES:

3.4% of GDP (2014)

country comparison to the world: 174

PHYSICIANS DENSITY:

1.19 physicians/1,000 population (2009)

DRINKING WATER SOURCE:

improved:

urban: 99.9% of population

rural: 99.9% of population

total: 99.9% of population

unimproved:

urban: 0.1% of population

rural: 0.1% of population

total: 0.1% of population (2015 est.)

SANITATION FACILITY ACCESS:

improved:

urban: 97.6% of population (2015 est.)

rural: 97.6% of population (2015 est.)

total: 97.6% of population (2015 est.)

unimproved:

urban: 2.4% of population (2015 est.)

rural: 2.4% of population (2015 est.)

total: 2.4% of population (2015 est.)

HIV/AIDS - ADULT PREVALENCE RATE:

NA

HIV/AIDS - PEOPLE LIVING WITH HIV/AIDS:

NA

HIV/AIDS - DEATHS:

NA

OBESITY - ADULT PREVALENCE RATE:

55.9% (2016)

country comparison to the world: 2

EDUCATION EXPENDITURES:

4.7% of GDP (2016)

country comparison to the world: 86

SCHOOL LIFE EXPECTANCY (PRIMARY TO TERTIARY EDUCATION):

total: 15 years (2015)

male: 15 years (2015)

female: 16 years (2015)

GOVERNMENT :: COOK ISLANDS

COUNTRY NAME:

conventional long form: none

conventional short form: Cook Islands

former: Hervey Islands

etymology: named after Captain James COOK, the British explorer who visited the islands in 1773 and 1777

DEPENDENCY STATUS:

self-governing in free association with New Zealand; Cook Islands is fully responsible for internal affairs; New Zealand retains responsibility for external affairs and defense in consultation with the Cook Islands

GOVERNMENT TYPE:

self-governing parliamentary democracy (Parliament of the Cook Islands) in free association with New Zealand

CAPITAL:

name: Avarua

geographic coordinates: 21 12 S, 159 46 W

time difference: UTC-10 (5 hours behind Washington, DC, during Standard Time)

ADMINISTRATIVE DIVISIONS:

none

INDEPENDENCE:

none (became self-governing in free association with New Zealand on 4 August 1965 and has the right at any time to move to full independence by unilateral action)

NATIONAL HOLIDAY:

Constitution Day, first Monday in August (1965)

CONSTITUTION:

history: 4 August 1965 (Cook Islands Constitution Act 1964) (2017)

amendments: proposed by Parliament; passage requires at least two-thirds majority vote by the Parliament membership in each of several readings and assent to by the chief of state's representative; passage of amendments relating to the chief of state also requires two-thirds majority approval in a referendum; amended many times, last in 2004 (2017)

LEGAL SYSTEM:

common law similar to New Zealand common law

INTERNATIONAL LAW ORGANIZATION PARTICIPATION:

has not submitted an ICJ jurisdiction declaration (New Zealand normally retains responsibility for external affairs); accepts ICCt jurisdiction

SUFFRAGE:

18 years of age; universal

EXECUTIVE BRANCH:

chief of state: Queen ELIZABETH II (since 6 February 1952); represented by Tom J. MARSTERS (since 9 August 2013); New Zealand High Commissioner Peter MARSHALL (since 10 January 2017)

head of government: Prime Minister Henry PUNA (since 30 November 2010)

cabinet: Cabinet chosen by the prime minister

elections/appointments: the monarchy is hereditary; UK representative appointed by the monarch; New Zealand high commissioner appointed by the New Zealand Government; following legislative elections, the leader of the majority party or majority coalition usually becomes prime minister

LEGISLATIVE BRANCH:

description: unicameral Parliament, formerly the Legislative Assembly (24 seats; members directly elected in single-seat constituencies by simple majority vote to serve 4-year terms); note - the House of Ariki, a 24-member parliamentary body of traditional leaders appointed by the Queen's representative serves as a consultative body to the Parliament

elections: last held on 14 June 2018 (next to be held by 2022)

election results: percent of vote by party - NA; seats by party - Demo 11, CIP 10, One Cook Islands Movement 1, independent 2; composition - men 15, women 9, percent of women 37.5%

JUDICIAL BRANCH:

highest courts: Court of Appeal (consists of the chief justice and 3 judges of the High Court); High Court (consists of the chief justice and at least 4 judges and organized into civil, criminal, and land divisions); note - appeals beyond the Cook Islands Court of Appeal are heard by the Judicial Committee of the Privy Council (in London)

judge selection and term of office: High Court chief justice appointed by the Queen's Representative on the advice of the Executive Council tendered by the prime minister; other judges appointed by the Queen's Representative, on the advice of the Executive Council tendered by the chief justice, High Court chief justice, and the minister of justice; chief justice and judges appointed for 3-year renewable terms

subordinate courts: justices of the peace

POLITICAL PARTIES AND LEADERS:

Cook Islands Party or CIP [Henry PUNA]
Democratic Party or Demo [Tina BROWNE]
One Cook Islands Movement [Teina BISHOP]

INTERNATIONAL ORGANIZATION PARTICIPATION:

ACP, ADB, AOSIS, FAO, ICAO, ICCt, ICRM, IFAD, IFRCS, IMO, IMSO, IOC, ITUC (NGOs), OPCW, PIF, Sparteca, SPC, UNESCO, UPU, WHO, WMO

DIPLOMATIC REPRESENTATION IN THE US:

none (self-governing in free association with New Zealand)

DIPLOMATIC REPRESENTATION FROM THE US:

none (self-governing in free association with New Zealand)

FLAG DESCRIPTION:

blue with the flag of the UK in the upper hoist-side quadrant and a large circle of 15 white five-pointed stars (one for every island) centered in the outer half of the flag

NATIONAL SYMBOL(S):

a circle of 15, five-pointed, white stars on a blue field, Tiare maori (Gardenia taitensis) flower; national colors: green, white

NATIONAL ANTHEM:

name: "Te Atua Mou E" (To God Almighty)

lyrics/music: Tepaeru Te RITO/Thomas DAVIS

note: adopted 1982; as prime minister, Sir Thomas DAVIS composed the anthem; his wife, a tribal chief, wrote the lyrics

ECONOMY :: COOK ISLANDS

ECONOMY - OVERVIEW:

Like many other South Pacific island nations, the Cook Islands' economic development is hindered by the isolation of the country from foreign markets, the limited size of domestic markets, lack of natural resources, periodic devastation from natural disasters, and inadequate infrastructure. Agriculture, employing more than one-quarter of the working population, provides the economic base with major exports of copra and citrus fruit. Black pearls are the Cook Islands' leading export. Manufacturing activities are limited to fruit processing, clothing, and handicrafts. Trade deficits are offset by remittances from emigrants and by foreign aid overwhelmingly from New Zealand. In the 1980s and 1990s, the country became overextended, maintaining a bloated public service and accumulating a large foreign debt. Subsequent reforms, including the sale of state assets, the strengthening of economic management, the encouragement of tourism, and a debt restructuring agreement, have rekindled investment and growth. The government is targeting fisheries and seabed mining as sectors for future economic growth.

GDP (PURCHASING POWER PARITY):

$299.9 million (2016 est.)

$183.2 million (2005 est.)

country comparison to the world: 216

GDP (OFFICIAL EXCHANGE RATE):

$299.9 million (2016 est.) (2016 est.)

GDP - REAL GROWTH RATE:

0.1% (2005 est.)

country comparison to the world: 195

GDP - PER CAPITA (PPP):

$16,700 (2016 est.)

$9,100 (2005 est.)

country comparison to the world: 106

GDP - COMPOSITION, BY SECTOR OF ORIGIN:

agriculture: 5.1% (2010 est.)

industry: 12.7% (2010 est.)

services: 82.1% (2010 est.)

AGRICULTURE - PRODUCTS:

copra, citrus, pineapples, tomatoes, beans, pawpaws, bananas, yams, taro, coffee; pigs, poultry

INDUSTRIES:

fishing, fruit processing, tourism, clothing, handicrafts

INDUSTRIAL PRODUCTION GROWTH RATE:

1% (2002)

country comparison to the world: 155

LABOR FORCE:

6,820 (2001)

country comparison to the world: 218

LABOR FORCE - BY OCCUPATION:

agriculture: 29%

industry: 15%

services: 56% (1995)

UNEMPLOYMENT RATE:

13.1% (2005)

country comparison to the world: 167

POPULATION BELOW POVERTY LINE:

NA

HOUSEHOLD INCOME OR CONSUMPTION BY PERCENTAGE SHARE:

lowest 10%: NA

highest 10%: NA

BUDGET:

revenues: 86.9 million (2010)

expenditures: 77.9 million (2010)

TAXES AND OTHER REVENUES:

29% (of GDP) (2010 est.)

country comparison to the world: 86

BUDGET SURPLUS (+) OR DEFICIT (-):

3% (of GDP) (2010 est.)

country comparison to the world: 13

FISCAL YEAR:

1 April - 31 March

INFLATION RATE (CONSUMER PRICES):

2.2% (2011 est.)

country comparison to the world: 114

STOCK OF NARROW MONEY:

$38.99 million (31 December 2011 est.)

country comparison to the world: 191

STOCK OF BROAD MONEY:

$148.2 million (31 December 2011 est.)

$170.9 million (31 December 2010 est.)

country comparison to the world: 190

CURRENT ACCOUNT BALANCE:

$26.67 million (2005)

country comparison to the world: 59

EXPORTS:

$3.125 million (2011 est.)

$5.163 million (2010 est.)

country comparison to the world: 219

EXPORTS - COMMODITIES:

fish; copra, papayas, fresh and canned citrus fruit, coffee; pearls and pearl shells; clothing

IMPORTS:

$109.3 million (2011 est.)

$90.62 million (2010 est.)

country comparison to the world: 213

IMPORTS - COMMODITIES:

foodstuffs, textiles, fuels, timber, capital goods

DEBT - EXTERNAL:

$141 million (1996 est.)

country comparison to the world: 191

EXCHANGE RATES:

NZ dollars (NZD) per US dollar -

1.416 (2017 est.)

1.4341 (2016 est.)

1.4341 (2015 est.)

1.441 (2014 est.)

1.4279 (2013 est.)

ENERGY :: COOK ISLANDS

ELECTRICITY - PRODUCTION:

34 million kWh (2016 est.)

country comparison to the world: 209

ELECTRICITY - CONSUMPTION:

31.62 million kWh (2016 est.)

country comparison to the world: 209

ELECTRICITY - EXPORTS:

0 kWh (2016 est.)

country comparison to the world: 123

ELECTRICITY - IMPORTS:

0 kWh (2016 est.)

country comparison to the world: 137

ELECTRICITY - INSTALLED GENERATING CAPACITY:

14,000 kW (2016 est.)

country comparison to the world: 207

ELECTRICITY - FROM FOSSIL FUELS:

79% of total installed capacity (2016 est.)

country comparison to the world: 85

ELECTRICITY - FROM NUCLEAR FUELS:

0% of total installed capacity (2017 est.)

country comparison to the world: 71

ELECTRICITY - FROM HYDROELECTRIC PLANTS:

0% of total installed capacity (2017 est.)

country comparison to the world: 165

ELECTRICITY - FROM OTHER RENEWABLE SOURCES:

21% of total installed capacity (2017 est.)

country comparison to the world: 36

CRUDE OIL - PRODUCTION:

0 bbl/day (2017 est.)

country comparison to the world: 122

CRUDE OIL - EXPORTS:

0 bbl/day (2015 est.)

country comparison to the world: 108

CRUDE OIL - IMPORTS:

0 bbl/day (2015 est.)

country comparison to the world: 114

CRUDE OIL - PROVED RESERVES:

0 bbl (1 January 2018 est.)

country comparison to the world: 119

REFINED PETROLEUM PRODUCTS - PRODUCTION:

0 bbl/day (2015 est.)

country comparison to the world: 133

REFINED PETROLEUM PRODUCTS - CONSUMPTION:

600 bbl/day (2016 est.)

country comparison to the world: 209

REFINED PETROLEUM PRODUCTS - EXPORTS:

0 bbl/day (2015 est.)

country comparison to the world: 146

REFINED PETROLEUM PRODUCTS - IMPORTS:

611 bbl/day (2015 est.)

country comparison to the world: 205

NATURAL GAS - PRODUCTION:

0 cu m (2017 est.)

country comparison to the world: 119

NATURAL GAS - CONSUMPTION:

0 cu m (2017 est.)

country comparison to the world: 135

NATURAL GAS - EXPORTS:

0 cu m (2017 est.)

country comparison to the world: 87

NATURAL GAS - IMPORTS:

0 cu m (2017 est.)

country comparison to the world: 110

NATURAL GAS - PROVED RESERVES:

0 cu m (1 January 2014 est.)

country comparison to the world: 124

CARBON DIOXIDE EMISSIONS FROM CONSUMPTION OF ENERGY:

88,810 Mt (2017 est.)

country comparison to the world: 207

COMMUNICATIONS :: COOK ISLANDS

TELEPHONES - FIXED LINES:

total subscriptions: 7,800 (July 2016 est.)

subscriptions per 100 inhabitants: 75 (July 2016 est.)

country comparison to the world: 199

TELEPHONES - MOBILE CELLULAR:

total subscriptions: 11,000 (July 2016 est.)

subscriptions per 100 inhabitants: 105 (July 2016 est.)

country comparison to the world: 211

TELEPHONE SYSTEM:

general assessment: Telecom Cook Islands offers international direct dialing, Internet, email, and fax; individual islands are connected by a combination of satellite earth stations, microwave systems, and VHF and HF radiotelephone (2017)

domestic: service is provided by small exchanges connected to subscribers by open-wire, cable, and fiber-optic cable; 75 per 100 fixed-line, 105 per 100 mobile-cellular (2017)

international: country code - 682; satellite earth station - 1 Intelsat (Pacific Ocean); the topography of the South Pacific region has made internet connectivity a serious issue for many of the remote islands; submarine fibre-optic networks are expensive to build and maintain, with capital costs prohibitive for the smaller island communities; some countries have to rely solely on geostationary satellites; as a result, bandwidth is limited and broadband prices are expensive (2017)

BROADCAST MEDIA:

1 privately owned TV station broadcasts from Rarotonga providing a mix of local news and overseas-sourced programs (2016)

INTERNET COUNTRY CODE:

.ck

INTERNET USERS:

total: 5,160 (July 2016 est.)

percent of population: 54% (July 2016 est.)

country comparison to the world: 213

TRANSPORTATION :: COOK ISLANDS

NATIONAL AIR TRANSPORT SYSTEM:

number of registered air carriers: 1 (2015)

inventory of registered aircraft operated by air carriers: 1 (2015)

CIVIL AIRCRAFT REGISTRATION COUNTRY CODE PREFIX:

E5 (2016)

AIRPORTS:

11 (2013)

country comparison to the world: 154

AIRPORTS - WITH PAVED RUNWAYS:

total: 1 (2017)

1,524 to 2,437 m: 1 (2017)

AIRPORTS - WITH UNPAVED RUNWAYS:

total: 10 (2013)

1,524 to 2,437 m: 2 (2013)

914 to 1,523 m: 7 (2013)

under 914 m: 1 (2013)

ROADWAYS:

total: 320 km (2003)

paved: 33 km (2003)

unpaved: 287 km (2003)

country comparison to the world: 205

MERCHANT MARINE:

total: 218 (2017)

by type: bulk carrier 27, container ship 5, general cargo 102, oil tanker 17, other 67 (2017)

country comparison to the world: 63

PORTS AND TERMINALS:

major seaport(s): Avatiu

MILITARY AND SECURITY :: COOK ISLANDS

MILITARY BRANCHES:

no regular military forces; National Police Department

MILITARY - NOTE:

defense is the responsibility of New Zealand in consultation with the Cook Islands and at its request

TRANSNATIONAL ISSUES :: COOK ISLANDS

DISPUTES - INTERNATIONAL:

none

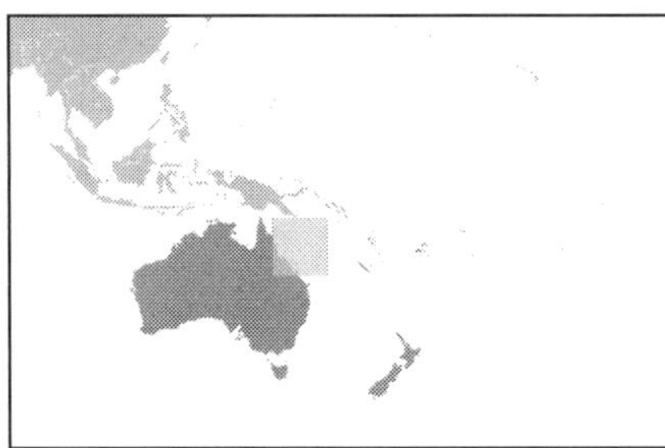

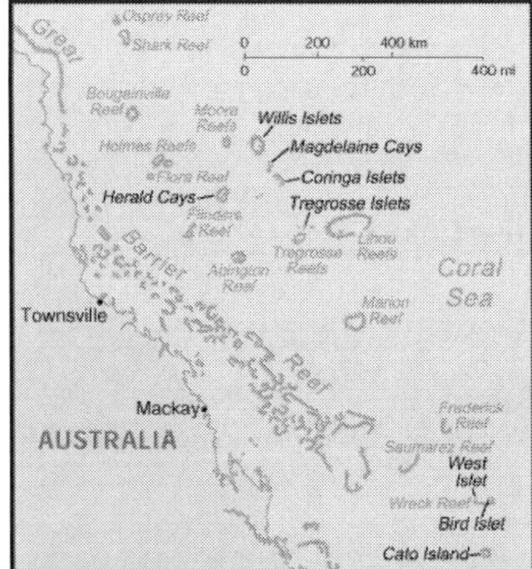

AUSTRALIA - OCEANIA :: CORAL SEA ISLANDS

INTRODUCTION :: CORAL SEA ISLANDS

BACKGROUND:

Scattered over more than three-quarters of a million square kilometers of ocean, the Coral Sea Islands were declared a territory of Australia in 1969. They are uninhabited except for a small meteorological staff on the Willis Islets. Automated weather stations, beacons, and a lighthouse occupy many other islands and reefs. The Coral Sea Islands Act 1969 was amended in 1997 to extend the boundaries of the Coral Sea Islands Territory around Elizabeth and Middleton Reefs.

GEOGRAPHY :: CORAL SEA ISLANDS

LOCATION:

Oceania, islands in the Coral Sea, northeast of Australia

GEOGRAPHIC COORDINATES:

18 00 S, 152 00 E

MAP REFERENCES:

Oceania

AREA:

total: 3 sq km less than

land: 3 sq km less than

water: 0 sq km

note: includes numerous small islands and reefs scattered over a sea area of about 780,000 sq km (300,000 sq mi) with the Willis Islets the most important

country comparison to the world: 253

AREA - COMPARATIVE:

about four times the size of the National Mall in Washington, DC

LAND BOUNDARIES:

0 km

COASTLINE:

3,095 km

MARITIME CLAIMS:

territorial sea: 3 nm

exclusive fishing zone: 200 nm

CLIMATE:

tropical

TERRAIN:

sand and coral reefs and islands (cays)

ELEVATION:

0 m lowest point: Pacific Ocean

9 highest point: unnamed location on Cato Island

NATURAL RESOURCES:

fish

LAND USE:

agricultural land: 0% (2011 est.)

arable land: 0% (2011 est.) / permanent crops: 0% (2011 est.) / permanent pasture: 0% (2011 est.)

forest: 0% (2011 est.)

other: 100% (2011 est.)

NATURAL HAZARDS:

occasional tropical cyclones

ENVIRONMENT - CURRENT ISSUES:

no permanent freshwater resources; damaging activities include coral mining, destructive fishing practices (overfishing, blast fishing)

GEOGRAPHY - NOTE:

important nesting area for birds and turtles

PEOPLE AND SOCIETY :: CORAL SEA ISLANDS

POPULATION:

no indigenous inhabitants (2017 est.)

note: there is a staff of four at the meteorological station on Willis Island

GOVERNMENT :: CORAL SEA ISLANDS

COUNTRY NAME:

conventional long form: Coral Sea Islands Territory

conventional short form: Coral Sea Islands

etymology: self-descriptive name to reflect the islands' position in the Coral Sea off the northeastern coast of Australia

DEPENDENCY STATUS:

territory of Australia; administered from Canberra by the Department of Regional Australia, Local Government, Arts and Sport

LEGAL SYSTEM:

the common law legal system of Australia, where applicable, applies

CITIZENSHIP:

see Australia

DIPLOMATIC REPRESENTATION IN THE US:

none (territory of Australia)

DIPLOMATIC REPRESENTATION FROM THE US:

none (territory of Australia)

FLAG DESCRIPTION:

the flag of Australia is used

ECONOMY :: CORAL SEA ISLANDS

ECONOMY - OVERVIEW:

no economic activity

COMMUNICATIONS :: CORAL SEA ISLANDS

COMMUNICATIONS - NOTE:

automatic weather stations on many of the isles and reefs relay data to the mainland

TRANSPORTATION :: CORAL SEA ISLANDS

PORTS AND TERMINALS:

none; offshore anchorage only

MILITARY AND SECURITY :: CORAL SEA ISLANDS

MILITARY - NOTE:

defense is the responsibility of Australia

TRANSNATIONAL ISSUES :: CORAL SEA ISLANDS

DISPUTES - INTERNATIONAL:

none

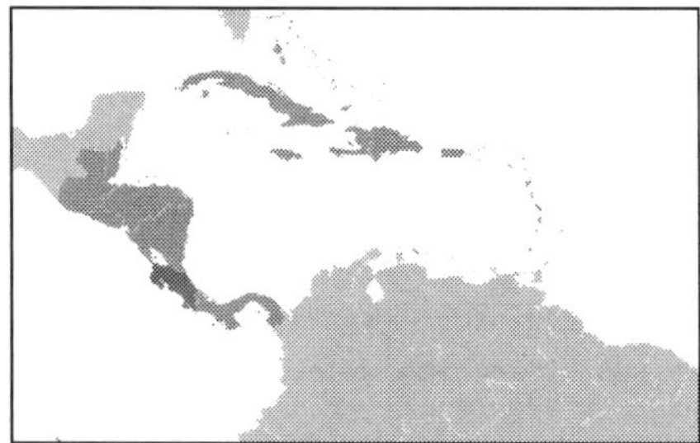

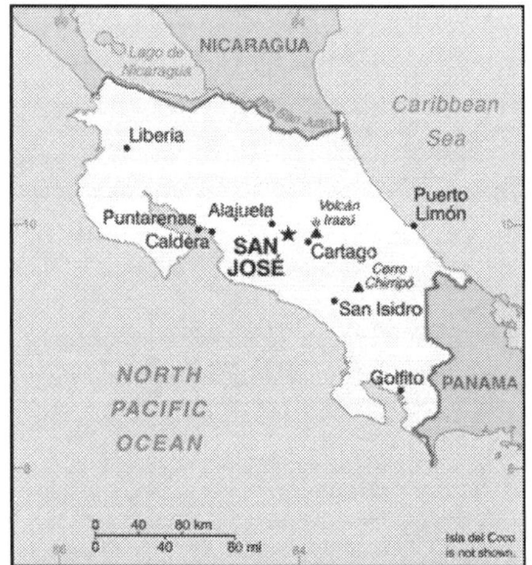

CENTRAL AMERICA :: COSTA RICA

INTRODUCTION :: COSTA RICA

BACKGROUND:

Although explored by the Spanish early in the 16th century, initial attempts at colonizing Costa Rica proved unsuccessful due to a combination of factors, including disease from mosquito-infested swamps, brutal heat, resistance by natives, and pirate raids. It was not until 1563 that a permanent settlement of Cartago was established in the cooler, fertile central highlands. The area remained a colony for some two and a half centuries. In 1821, Costa Rica became one of several Central American provinces that jointly declared their independence from Spain. Two years later it joined the United Provinces of Central America, but this federation disintegrated in 1838, at which time Costa Rica proclaimed its sovereignty and independence. Since the late 19th century, only two brief periods of violence have marred the country's democratic development. On 1 December 1948, Costa Rica dissolved its armed forces. Although it still maintains a large agricultural sector, Costa Rica has expanded its economy to include strong technology and tourism industries. The standard of living is relatively high. Land ownership is widespread.

GEOGRAPHY :: COSTA RICA

LOCATION:

Central America, bordering both the Caribbean Sea and the North Pacific Ocean, between Nicaragua and Panama

GEOGRAPHIC COORDINATES:

10 00 N, 84 00 W

MAP REFERENCES:

Central America and the Caribbean

AREA:

total: 51,100 sq km

land: 51,060 sq km

water: 40 sq km

note: includes Isla del Coco

country comparison to the world: 130

AREA - COMPARATIVE:

slightly smaller than West Virginia

LAND BOUNDARIES:

total: 661 km

border countries (2): Nicaragua 313 km, Panama 348 km

COASTLINE:

1,290 km

MARITIME CLAIMS:

territorial sea: 12 nm

exclusive economic zone: 200 nm

continental shelf: 200 nm

CLIMATE:

tropical and subtropical; dry season (December to April); rainy season (May to November); cooler in highlands

TERRAIN:

coastal plains separated by rugged mountains including over 100 volcanic cones, of which several are major active volcanoes

ELEVATION:

mean elevation: 746 m

elevation extremes: 0 m lowest point: Pacific Ocean

3819 highest point: Cerro Chirripo

NATURAL RESOURCES:

hydropower

LAND USE:

agricultural land: 37.1% (2011 est.)

arable land: 4.9% (2011 est.) / permanent crops: 6.7% (2011 est.) / permanent pasture: 25.5% (2011 est.)

forest: 51.5% (2011 est.)

other: 11.4% (2011 est.)

IRRIGATED LAND:

1,015 sq km (2012)

POPULATION DISTRIBUTION:

roughly half of the nation's population resides in urban areas; the capital of San Jose is the largest city and home to approximately one-fifth of the population

NATURAL HAZARDS:

occasional earthquakes, hurricanes along Atlantic coast; frequent flooding of lowlands at onset of rainy season and landslides; active volcanoes

volcanism: Arenal (1,670 m), which erupted in 2010, is the most active volcano in Costa Rica; a 1968 eruption destroyed the town of Tabacon; Irazu (3,432 m), situated just east of San Jose, has the potential to spew ash over the capital city as it did between 1963 and 1965; other historically active volcanoes include Miravalles, Poas, Rincon de la Vieja, and Turrialba

ENVIRONMENT - CURRENT ISSUES:

deforestation and land use change, largely a result of the clearing of land for cattle ranching and agriculture; soil erosion; coastal marine pollution; fisheries protection; solid waste management; air pollution

ENVIRONMENT - INTERNATIONAL AGREEMENTS:

party to: Biodiversity, Climate Change, Climate Change-Kyoto Protocol, Desertification, Endangered Species, Environmental Modification, Hazardous Wastes, Law of the Sea, Marine Dumping, Ozone Layer Protection, Wetlands, Whaling

signed, but not ratified: Marine Life Conservation

GEOGRAPHY - NOTE:

four volcanoes, two of them active, rise near the capital of San Jose in the center of the country; one of the volcanoes, Irazu, erupted destructively in 1963-65

PEOPLE AND SOCIETY :: COSTA RICA

POPULATION:

4,987,142 (July 2018 est.)

country comparison to the world: 123

NATIONALITY:

noun: Costa Rican(s)

adjective: Costa Rican

ETHNIC GROUPS:

white or mestizo 83.6%, mulatto 6.7%, indigenous 2.4%, black of African descent 1.1%, other 1.1%, none 2.9%, unspecified 2.2% (2011 est.)

LANGUAGES:

Spanish (official), English

RELIGIONS:

Roman Catholic 71.8%, Evangelical and Pentecostal 12.3%, other Protestant 2.6%, Jehovah's Witness 0.5%, other 2.4%, none 10.4% (2016 est.)

DEMOGRAPHIC PROFILE:

Costa Rica's political stability, high standard of living, and well-developed social benefits system set it apart from its Central American neighbors. Through the government's sustained social spending - almost 20% of GDP annually - Costa Rica has made tremendous progress toward achieving its goal of providing universal access to education, healthcare, clean water, sanitation, and electricity. Since the 1970s, expansion of these services has led to a rapid decline in infant mortality, an increase in life expectancy at birth, and a sharp decrease in the birth rate. The average number of children born per women has fallen from about 7 in the 1960s to 3.5 in the early 1980s to below replacement level today. Costa Rica's poverty rate is lower than in most Latin American countries, but it has stalled at around 20% for almost two decades.

Costa Rica is a popular regional immigration destination because of its job opportunities and social programs. Almost 9% of the population is foreign-born, with Nicaraguans comprising nearly three-quarters of the foreign population. Many Nicaraguans who perform unskilled seasonal labor enter Costa Rica illegally or overstay their visas, which continues to be a source of tension. Less than 3% of Costa Rica's population lives abroad. The overwhelming majority of expatriates have settled in the United States after completing a university degree or in order to work in a highly skilled field.

AGE STRUCTURE:

0-14 years: 22.43% (male 572,172 /female 546,464)

15-24 years: 15.94% (male 405,515 /female 389,433)

25-54 years: 44.04% (male 1,105,944 /female 1,090,434)

55-64 years: 9.48% (male 229,928 /female 242,696)

65 years and over: 8.11% (male 186,531 /female 218,025) (2018 est.)

DEPENDENCY RATIOS:

total dependency ratio: 45.4 (2015 est.)

youth dependency ratio: 32.4 (2015 est.)

elderly dependency ratio: 12.9 (2015 est.)

potential support ratio: 7.7 (2015 est.)

MEDIAN AGE:

total: 31.7 years

male: 31.2 years

female: 32.2 years (2018 est.)

country comparison to the world: 109

POPULATION GROWTH RATE:

1.13% (2018 est.)

country comparison to the world: 95

BIRTH RATE:

15.3 births/1,000 population (2018 est.)

country comparison to the world: 121

DEATH RATE:

4.8 deaths/1,000 population (2018 est.)

country comparison to the world: 200

NET MIGRATION RATE:

0.8 migrant(s)/1,000 population (2017 est.)

country comparison to the world: 59

POPULATION DISTRIBUTION:

roughly half of the nation's population resides in urban areas; the capital of San Jose is the largest city and home to approximately one-fifth of the population

URBANIZATION:

urban population: 79.3% of total population (2018)

rate of urbanization: 1.5% annual rate of change (2015-20 est.)

MAJOR URBAN AREAS - POPULATION:

1.358 million SAN JOSE (capital) (2018)

SEX RATIO:

at birth: 1.05 male(s)/female (2017 est.)

0-14 years: 1.05 male(s)/female (2017 est.)

15-24 years: 1.04 male(s)/female (2017 est.)

25-54 years: 1.01 male(s)/female (2017 est.)

55-64 years: 0.95 male(s)/female (2017 est.)

65 years and over: 0.86 male(s)/female (2017 est.)

total population: 1.01 male(s)/female (2017 est.)

MATERNAL MORTALITY RATE:

25 deaths/100,000 live births (2015 est.)

country comparison to the world: 122

INFANT MORTALITY RATE:

total: 7.8 deaths/1,000 live births (2018 est.)

male: 8.6 deaths/1,000 live births (2018 est.)

female: 7.1 deaths/1,000 live births (2018 est.)

country comparison to the world: 153

LIFE EXPECTANCY AT BIRTH:

total population: 78.9 years (2018 est.)

male: 76.2 years (2018 est.)

female: 81.7 years (2018 est.)

country comparison to the world: 55

TOTAL FERTILITY RATE:

1.89 children born/woman (2018 est.)

country comparison to the world: 135

CONTRACEPTIVE PREVALENCE RATE:

76.2% (2011)

HEALTH EXPENDITURES:

9.3% of GDP (2014)

country comparison to the world: 33

PHYSICIANS DENSITY:

1.15 physicians/1,000 population (2013)

HOSPITAL BED DENSITY:

1.1 beds/1,000 population (2014)

DRINKING WATER SOURCE:

improved:

urban: 99.6% of population (2015 est.)

rural: 91.9% of population (2015 est.)

total: 97.8% of population (2015 est.)

unimproved:

urban: 0.4% of population (2015 est.)

rural: 8.1% of population (2015 est.)

total: 2.2% of population (2015 est.)

SANITATION FACILITY ACCESS:

improved:

urban: 95.2% of population (2015 est.)

rural: 92.3% of population (2015 est.)

total: 94.5% of population (2015 est.)

unimproved:

urban: 4.8% of population (2015 est.)

rural: 7.7% of population (2015 est.)

total: 5.5% of population (2015 est.)

HIV/AIDS - ADULT PREVALENCE RATE:

0.4% (2017 est.)

country comparison to the world: 70

HIV/AIDS - PEOPLE LIVING WITH HIV/AIDS:

13,000 (2017 est.)

country comparison to the world: 93

HIV/AIDS - DEATHS:

<200 (2017 est.)

MAJOR INFECTIOUS DISEASES:

degree of risk: intermediate (2016)

food or waterborne diseases: bacterial diarrhea (2016)

vectorborne diseases: dengue fever (2016)

note: active local transmission of Zika virus by Aedes species mosquitoes has been identified in this country (as of August 2016); it poses an important risk (a large number of cases possible) among US citizens if bitten by an infective mosquito; other less common ways to get Zika are through sex, via blood transfusion, or during pregnancy, in which the pregnant woman passes Zika virus to her fetus

OBESITY - ADULT PREVALENCE RATE:

25.7% (2016)

country comparison to the world: 48

CHILDREN UNDER THE AGE OF 5 YEARS UNDERWEIGHT:

1.1% (2008)

country comparison to the world: 121

EDUCATION EXPENDITURES:

7.1% of GDP (2016)

country comparison to the world: 19

LITERACY:

definition: age 15 and over can read and write (2015 est.)

total population: 97.8% (2015 est.)

male: 97.7% (2015 est.)

female: 97.8% (2015 est.)

SCHOOL LIFE EXPECTANCY (PRIMARY TO TERTIARY EDUCATION):

total: 15 years (2015)

male: 15 years (2015)

female: 16 years (2015)

UNEMPLOYMENT, YOUTH AGES 15-24:

total: 20.6% (2017 est.)

male: 17.6% (2017 est.)

female: 25.9% (2017 est.)

country comparison to the world: 61

GOVERNMENT :: COSTA RICA

COUNTRY NAME:

conventional long form: Republic of Costa Rica

conventional short form: Costa Rica

local long form: Republica de Costa Rica

local short form: Costa Rica

etymology: the name means "rich coast" in Spanish and was first applied in the early colonial period of the 16th century

GOVERNMENT TYPE:

presidential republic

CAPITAL:

name: San Jose

geographic coordinates: 9 56 N, 84 05 W

time difference: UTC-6 (1 hour behind Washington, DC, during Standard Time)

ADMINISTRATIVE DIVISIONS:

7 provinces (provincias, singular - provincia); Alajuela, Cartago, Guanacaste, Heredia, Limon, Puntarenas, San Jose

INDEPENDENCE:

15 September 1821 (from Spain)

NATIONAL HOLIDAY:

Independence Day, 15 September (1821)

CONSTITUTION:

history: many previous; latest effective 8 November 1949 (2018)

amendments: proposals require the signatures of at least 10 Legislative Assembly members or by petition of at least 5% of qualified voters; consideration of proposals requires two-thirds majority approval in each of 3 readings by the Assembly, followed by preparation of the proposal as a legislative bill and its approval by simple majority of the Assembly; passage requires at least two-thirds majority vote of the Assembly membership; a referendum is required only if approved by at least two-thirds of the Assembly; amended many times, last in 2015 (2018)

LEGAL SYSTEM:

civil law system based on Spanish civil code; judicial review of legislative acts in the Supreme Court

INTERNATIONAL LAW ORGANIZATION PARTICIPATION:

accepts compulsory ICJ jurisdiction; accepts ICCt jurisdiction

CITIZENSHIP:

citizenship by birth: yes

citizenship by descent only: yes

dual citizenship recognized: yes

residency requirement for naturalization: 7 years

SUFFRAGE:

18 years of age; universal and compulsory

EXECUTIVE BRANCH:

chief of state: President Carlos ALVARADO Quesada (since 8 May 2018); First Vice President Epsy CAMPBELL Barr (since 8 May 2018); Second Vice President Marvin RODRIGUEZ Cordero (since 8 May

2018); note - the president is both chief of state and head of government

head of government: President Carlos ALVARADO Quesada (since 8 May 2018); First Vice President Epsy CAMPBELL Barr (since 8 May 2018); Second Vice President Marvin RODRIGUEZ Cordero (since 8 May 2018)

cabinet: Cabinet selected by the president

elections/appointments: president and vice presidents directly elected on the same ballot by modified majority popular vote (40% threshold) for a 4-year term (eligible for non-consecutive terms); election last held on 4 February 2018 with a runoff on 1 April 2018 (next to be held in February 2022)

election results: Carlos ALVARADO Quesada elected president in second round; percent of vote in first round - Fabricio ALVARADO Munoz (PRN) 25%; Carlos ALVARADO Quesada (PAC) 21.6%; Antonio ALVAREZ (PLN) 18.6%; Rodolfo PIZA (PUSC) 16%; Juan Diego CASTRO (PIN) 9.5%; Rodolfo HERNANDEZ (PRS) 4.9%, other 4.4%; percent of vote in second round - Carlos ALVARADO Quesada (PAC) 60.7%; Fabricio ALVARADO Munoz (PRN) 39.3%

LEGISLATIVE BRANCH:

description: unicameral Legislative Assembly or Asamblea Legislativa (57 seats; members directly elected in multi-seat constituencies - corresponding to the country's 7 provinces - by closed list proportional representation vote; members serve 4-year terms)

elections: last held on 4 February 2018 (next to be held in February 2022)

election results: percent of vote by party - PLN 19.5%, PRN 18.2%, PAC 16.3%, PUSC 14.6%, PLN 7.7%, PRS 4.2%, PFA 4%, ADC 2.5%, ML 2.3%, PASE 2.3%, PNG 2.2%, other 6.2%; seats by party - PLN 17, PRN 14, PAC 10, PUSC 9, PLN 4, PRS 2, PFA 1

JUDICIAL BRANCH:

highest courts: Supreme Court of Justice (consists of 22 judges organized into 3 cassation chambers each with 5 judges and the Constitutional Chamber with 7 judges)

judge selection and term of office: Supreme Court of Justice judges elected by the National Assembly for 8-year terms with renewal decided by the National Assembly

subordinate courts: appellate courts; trial courts; first instance and justice of the peace courts; Superior Electoral Tribunal

POLITICAL PARTIES AND LEADERS:

Accessibility Without Exclusion or PASE [Oscar Andres LOPEZ Arias]
Broad Front (Frente Amplio) or PFA [Ana Patricia MORA Castellanos]
Christian Democratic Alliance or ADC [Mario REDONDO Poveda]
Citizen Action Party or PAC [Marcia GONZALEZ Aguiluz]
Costa Rican Renovation Party or PRC [Gonzalo Alberto RAMIREZ Zamora]
Libertarian Movement Party or ML [Victor Danilo CUBERO Corrales]
National Integration Party or PIN [Walter MUNOZ Cespedes]
National Liberation Party or PLN [Jorge Julio PATTONI Saenz]
National Restoration Party or PRN [Carlos Luis AVENDANO Calvo]
New Generation or PNG [Sergio MENA]
Patriotic Alliance [Jorge ARAYA Westover]
Social Christian Republican Party or PRS [Dragos DOLANESCU Valenciano]
Social Christian Unity Party or PUSC [Pedro MUNOZ Fonseca]

INTERNATIONAL ORGANIZATION PARTICIPATION:

BCIE, CACM, CD, CELAC, FAO, G-77, IADB, IAEA, IBRD, ICAO, ICC (national committees), ICCt, ICRM, IDA, IFAD, IFC, IFRCS, ILO, IMF, IMO, IMSO, Interpol, IOC, IOM, IPU, ISO, ITSO, ITU, ITUC (NGOs), LAES, LAIA (observer), MIGA, NAM (observer), OAS, OIF (observer), OPANAL, OPCW, Pacific Alliance (observer), PCA, SICA, UN, UNCTAD, UNESCO, UNHCR, UNIDO, Union Latina, UNWTO, UPU, WCO, WFTU (NGOs), WHO, WIPO, WMO, WTO

DIPLOMATIC REPRESENTATION IN THE US:

chief of mission: Ambassador Fernando LLORCA Castro (since 17 September 2018)

chancery: 2114 S Street NW, Washington, DC 20008

telephone: [1] (202) 480-2200

FAX: [1] (202) 265-4795

consulate(s) general: Atlanta, Chicago, Houston, Los Angeles, Miami, New York, Washington DC

consulate(s): Saint Paul (MN), San Juan (Puerto Rico), Tucson (AZ)

DIPLOMATIC REPRESENTATION FROM THE US:

chief of mission: Ambassador Sharon DAY (since 5 October 2017)

embassy: Calle 98 Via 104, Pavas, San Jose

mailing address: APO AA 34020

telephone: [506] 2519-2000

FAX: [506] 2519-2305

FLAG DESCRIPTION:

five horizontal bands of blue (top), white, red (double width), white, and blue, with the coat of arms in a white elliptical disk placed toward the hoist side of the red band; Costa Rica retained the earlier blue-white-blue flag of Central America until 1848 when, in response to revolutionary activity in Europe, it was decided to incorporate the French colors into the national flag and a central red stripe was added; today the blue color is said to stand for the sky, opportunity, and perseverance, white denotes peace, happiness, and wisdom, while red represents the blood shed for freedom, as well as the generosity and vibrancy of the people

note: somewhat resembles the flag of North Korea; similar to the flag of Thailand but with the blue and red colors reversed

NATIONAL SYMBOL(S):

yiguirro (clay-colored robin); national colors: blue, white, red

NATIONAL ANTHEM:

name: "Himno Nacional de Costa Rica" (National Anthem of Costa Rica)

lyrics/music: Jose Maria ZELEDON Brenes/Manuel Maria GUTIERREZ

note: adopted 1949; the anthem's music was originally written for an 1853 welcome ceremony for diplomatic missions from the US and UK; the lyrics were added in 1903

ECONOMY :: COSTA RICA

ECONOMY - OVERVIEW:

Since 2010, Costa Rica has enjoyed strong and stable economic growth - 3.8% in 2017. Exports of bananas, coffee, sugar, and beef are the backbone of its commodity exports. Various industrial and processed agricultural products have broadened exports in recent years, as have high value-added goods, including medical devices. Costa Rica's impressive biodiversity also makes it a key destination for ecotourism.

Foreign investors remain attracted by the country's political stability and relatively high education levels, as well as the incentives offered in the free-trade zones; Costa Rica has attracted one of the highest levels of foreign direct investment per capita in Latin America. The US-Central American-Dominican Republic Free Trade Agreement (CAFTA-DR), which became effective for Costa Rica in 2009, helped increase foreign direct investment in key sectors of the economy, including insurance and telecommunication. However, poor infrastructure, high energy costs, a complex bureaucracy, weak investor protection, and uncertainty of contract enforcement impede greater investment.

Costa Rica's economy also faces challenges due to a rising fiscal deficit, rising public debt, and relatively low levels of domestic revenue. Poverty has remained around 20-25% for nearly 20 years, and the government's strong social safety net has eroded due to increased constraints on its expenditures. Costa Rica's credit rating was downgraded from stable to negative in 2015 and again in 2017, upping pressure on lending rates - which could hurt small business, on the budget deficit - which could hurt infrastructure development, and on the rate of return on investment - which could soften foreign direct investment (FDI). Unlike the rest of Central America, Costa Rica is not highly dependent on remittances - which represented just 1 % of GDP in 2016, but instead relies on FDI - which accounted for 5.1% of GDP.

GDP (PURCHASING POWER PARITY):

$83.94 billion (2017 est.)

$81.27 billion (2016 est.)

$77.96 billion (2015 est.)

note: data are in 2017 dollars

country comparison to the world: 93

GDP (OFFICIAL EXCHANGE RATE):

$58.27 billion (2017 est.) (2017 est.)

GDP - REAL GROWTH RATE:

3.3% (2017 est.)

4.2% (2016 est.)

3.6% (2015 est.)

country comparison to the world: 104

GDP - PER CAPITA (PPP):

$16,900 (2017 est.)

$16,600 (2016 est.)

$16,100 (2015 est.)

note: data are in 2017 dollars

country comparison to the world: 104

GROSS NATIONAL SAVING:

15.1% of GDP (2017 est.)

16.1% of GDP (2016 est.)

15% of GDP (2015 est.)

country comparison to the world: 135

GDP - COMPOSITION, BY END USE:

household consumption: 64.2% (2017 est.)

government consumption: 17.3% (2017 est.)

investment in fixed capital: 17.1% (2017 est.)

investment in inventories: 1% (2017 est.)

exports of goods and services: 33.3% (2017 est.)

imports of goods and services: -32.9% (2017 est.)

GDP - COMPOSITION, BY SECTOR OF ORIGIN:

agriculture: 5.5% (2017 est.)

industry: 20.6% (2017 est.)

services: 73.9% (2017 est.)

AGRICULTURE - PRODUCTS:

bananas, pineapples, coffee, melons, ornamental plants, sugar, corn, rice, beans, potatoes; beef, poultry, dairy; timber

INDUSTRIES:

medical equipment, food processing, textiles and clothing, construction materials, fertilizer, plastic products

INDUSTRIAL PRODUCTION GROWTH RATE:

1.3% (2017 est.)

country comparison to the world: 147

LABOR FORCE:

2.229 million (2017 est.)

note: official estimate; excludes Nicaraguans living in Costa Rica

country comparison to the world: 121

LABOR FORCE - BY OCCUPATION:

agriculture: 14%

industry: 22%

services: 64% (2006 est.)

UNEMPLOYMENT RATE:

8.1% (2017 est.)

9.5% (2016 est.)

country comparison to the world: 117

POPULATION BELOW POVERTY LINE:

21.7% (2014 est.)

HOUSEHOLD INCOME OR CONSUMPTION BY PERCENTAGE SHARE:

lowest 10%: 36.9% (2014 est.)

highest 10%: 36.9% (2014 est.)

DISTRIBUTION OF FAMILY INCOME - GINI INDEX:

48.5 (2014)

49.2 (2013)

country comparison to the world: 22

BUDGET:

revenues: 8.357 billion (2017 est.)

expenditures: 11.92 billion (2017 est.)

TAXES AND OTHER REVENUES:

14.3% (of GDP) (2017 est.)

country comparison to the world: 200

BUDGET SURPLUS (+) OR DEFICIT (-):

-6.1% (of GDP) (2017 est.)

country comparison to the world: 185

PUBLIC DEBT:

48.9% of GDP (2017 est.)

44.9% of GDP (2016 est.)

country comparison to the world: 105

FISCAL YEAR:

calendar year

INFLATION RATE (CONSUMER PRICES):

1.6% (2017 est.)

0% (2016 est.)

country comparison to the world: 89

CENTRAL BANK DISCOUNT RATE:

3.5% (31 December 2016 est.)

21.5% (31 December 2010)

country comparison to the world: 102

COMMERCIAL BANK PRIME LENDING RATE:

11.37% (31 December 2017 est.)

11.64% (31 December 2016 est.)

country comparison to the world: 71

STOCK OF NARROW MONEY:

$5.356 billion (31 December 2017 est.)

$5.63 billion (31 December 2016 est.)

country comparison to the world: 100

STOCK OF BROAD MONEY:

$5.356 billion (31 December 2017 est.)

$5.63 billion (31 December 2016 est.)

country comparison to the world: 103

STOCK OF DOMESTIC CREDIT:

$41.04 billion (31 December 2017 est.)

$38.21 billion (31 December 2016 est.)

country comparison to the world: 69

MARKET VALUE OF PUBLICLY TRADED SHARES:

$2.015 billion (31 December 2012 est.)

$1.443 billion (31 December 2011 est.)

$1.445 billion (31 December 2010 est.)

country comparison to the world: 99

CURRENT ACCOUNT BALANCE:

-$1.692 billion (2017 est.)

-$1.326 billion (2016 est.)

country comparison to the world: 160

EXPORTS:

$10.81 billion (2017 est.)

$10.15 billion (2016 est.)

country comparison to the world: 92

EXPORTS - PARTNERS:

US 40.9%, Belgium 6.3%, Panama 5.6%, Netherlands 5.6%, Nicaragua 5.1%, Guatemala 5% (2017)

EXPORTS - COMMODITIES:

bananas, pineapples, coffee, melons, ornamental plants, sugar; beef; seafood; electronic components, medical equipment

IMPORTS:

$15.15 billion (2017 est.)

$14.53 billion (2016 est.)

country comparison to the world: 90

IMPORTS - COMMODITIES:

raw materials, consumer goods, capital equipment, petroleum, construction materials

IMPORTS - PARTNERS:

US 38.1%, China 13.1%, Mexico 7.3% (2017)

RESERVES OF FOREIGN EXCHANGE AND GOLD:

$7.15 billion (31 December 2017 est.)

$7.574 billion (31 December 2016 est.)

country comparison to the world: 86

DEBT - EXTERNAL:

$26.83 billion (31 December 2017 est.)

$24.3 billion (31 December 2016 est.)

country comparison to the world: 86

STOCK OF DIRECT FOREIGN INVESTMENT - AT HOME:

$33.92 billion (31 December 2017 est.)

$31.84 billion (31 December 2016 est.)

country comparison to the world: 68

STOCK OF DIRECT FOREIGN INVESTMENT - ABROAD:

$4.007 billion (31 December 2017 est.)

$3.781 billion (31 December 2016 est.)

country comparison to the world: 78

EXCHANGE RATES:

Costa Rican colones (CRC) per US dollar -

573.5 (2017 est.)

544.74 (2016 est.)

544.74 (2015 est.)

534.57 (2014 est.)

538.32 (2013 est.)

ENERGY :: COSTA RICA

ELECTRICITY ACCESS:

population without electricity: 24,362 (2013)

electrification - total population: 99.5% (2013)

electrification - urban areas: 99.9% (2013)

electrification - rural areas: 98.3% (2013)

ELECTRICITY - PRODUCTION:

10.79 billion kWh (2016 est.)

country comparison to the world: 100

ELECTRICITY - CONSUMPTION:

9.812 billion kWh (2016 est.)

country comparison to the world: 98

ELECTRICITY - EXPORTS:

643 million kWh (2015 est.)

country comparison to the world: 64

ELECTRICITY - IMPORTS:

807 million kWh (2016 est.)

country comparison to the world: 72

ELECTRICITY - INSTALLED GENERATING CAPACITY:

3.584 million kW (2016 est.)

country comparison to the world: 94

ELECTRICITY - FROM FOSSIL FUELS:

18% of total installed capacity (2016 est.)

country comparison to the world: 196

ELECTRICITY - FROM NUCLEAR FUELS:

0% of total installed capacity (2017 est.)

country comparison to the world: 72

ELECTRICITY - FROM HYDROELECTRIC PLANTS:

64% of total installed capacity (2017 est.)

country comparison to the world: 25

ELECTRICITY - FROM OTHER RENEWABLE SOURCES:

18% of total installed capacity (2017 est.)

country comparison to the world: 48

CRUDE OIL - PRODUCTION:

0 bbl/day (2017 est.)

country comparison to the world: 123

CRUDE OIL - EXPORTS:

0 bbl/day (2015 est.)

country comparison to the world: 109

CRUDE OIL - IMPORTS:

0 bbl/day (2015 est.)

country comparison to the world: 115

CRUDE OIL - PROVED RESERVES:

0 bbl (1 January 2018 est.)

country comparison to the world: 120

REFINED PETROLEUM PRODUCTS - PRODUCTION:

0 bbl/day (2015 est.)

country comparison to the world: 134

REFINED PETROLEUM PRODUCTS - CONSUMPTION:

53,000 bbl/day (2016 est.)

country comparison to the world: 100

REFINED PETROLEUM PRODUCTS - EXPORTS:

0 bbl/day (2015 est.)

country comparison to the world: 147

REFINED PETROLEUM PRODUCTS - IMPORTS:

51,320 bbl/day (2015 est.)

country comparison to the world: 80

NATURAL GAS - PRODUCTION:

0 cu m (2017 est.)

country comparison to the world: 120

NATURAL GAS - CONSUMPTION:

0 cu m (2017 est.)

country comparison to the world: 136

NATURAL GAS - EXPORTS:

0 cu m (2017 est.)

country comparison to the world: 88

NATURAL GAS - IMPORTS:

0 cu m (2017 est.)

country comparison to the world: 111

NATURAL GAS - PROVED RESERVES:

0 cu m (1 January 2014 est.)

country comparison to the world: 125

CARBON DIOXIDE EMISSIONS FROM CONSUMPTION OF ENERGY:

7.653 million Mt (2017 est.)

country comparison to the world: 120

COMMUNICATIONS :: COSTA RICA

TELEPHONES - FIXED LINES:

total subscriptions: 843,148 (2017 est.)

subscriptions per 100 inhabitants: 17 (2017 est.)

country comparison to the world: 79

TELEPHONES - MOBILE CELLULAR:

total subscriptions: 8,840,342 (2017 est.)

subscriptions per 100 inhabitants: 179 (2017 est.)

country comparison to the world: 88

TELEPHONE SYSTEM:

general assessment: good domestic telephone service in terms of breadth of coverage; in recent years growth has been achieve from liberalistion of the telecom sector and has seen substantial expansion in all sectors; Costa Rica's broadband market is the most advanced in Central America, with the highest broadband penetration for this sub-region; broadband penetration does lag behind many South American countries; with the implementation of number portability there is greater opportunity for increased competition in the future (2017)

domestic: point-to-point and point-to-multi-point microwave, fiber-optic, and coaxial cable link rural areas; Internet service is available; 17 per 100 fixed-line, 179 per 100 mobile-cellular (2017)

international: country code - 506; landing points for the Americas Region Caribbean Ring System (ARCOS-1), MAYA-1, and the Pan American Crossing submarine cables that provide links to South and Central America, parts of the Caribbean, and the US; connected to Central American Microwave System; satellite earth stations - 2 Intelsat (Atlantic Ocean) (2015)

BROADCAST MEDIA:

multiple privately owned TV stations and 1 publicly owned TV station; cable network services are widely available; more than 100 privately owned radio stations and a public radio network (2017)

INTERNET COUNTRY CODE:

.cr

INTERNET USERS:

total: 3,217,277 (July 2016 est.)

percent of population: 66% (July 2016 est.)

country comparison to the world: 95

BROADBAND - FIXED SUBSCRIPTIONS:

total: 744,059 (2017 est.)

subscriptions per 100 inhabitants: 15 (2017 est.)

country comparison to the world: 74

TRANSPORTATION :: COSTA RICA

NATIONAL AIR TRANSPORT SYSTEM:

number of registered air carriers: 1 (2015)

inventory of registered aircraft operated by air carriers: 39 (2015)

annual passenger traffic on registered air carriers: 1,617,075 (2015)

annual freight traffic on registered air carriers: 9,284,160 mt-km (2015)

CIVIL AIRCRAFT REGISTRATION COUNTRY CODE PREFIX:

TI (2016)

AIRPORTS:

161 (2013)

country comparison to the world: 35

AIRPORTS - WITH PAVED RUNWAYS:

total: 47 (2017)

2,438 to 3,047 m: 2 (2017)

1,524 to 2,437 m: 2 (2017)

914 to 1,523 m: 27 (2017)

under 914 m: 16 (2017)

AIRPORTS - WITH UNPAVED RUNWAYS:

total: 114 (2013)

914 to 1,523 m: 18 (2013)

under 914 m: 96 (2013)

PIPELINES:

662 km refined products (2013)

RAILWAYS:

total: 278 km (2014)

narrow gauge: 278 km 1.067-m gauge (2014)

note: the entire rail network fell into disrepair and out of use at the end of the 20th century; since 2005, certain sections of rail have been rehabilitated

country comparison to the world: 123

ROADWAYS:

total: 39,018 km (2010)

paved: 10,133 km (2010)

unpaved: 28,885 km (2010)

country comparison to the world: 90

WATERWAYS:

730 km (seasonally navigable by small craft) (2011)

country comparison to the world: 74

MERCHANT MARINE:

total: 10 (2017)

by type: general cargo 2, other 8 (2017)

country comparison to the world: 147

PORTS AND TERMINALS:

major seaport(s): Atlantic Ocean (Caribbean) - Puerto Limon

Pacific Ocean - Caldera

MILITARY AND SECURITY :: COSTA RICA

MILITARY BRANCHES:

no regular military forces; Ministry of Public Security, Government, and Police (2011)

TRANSNATIONAL ISSUES :: COSTA RICA

DISPUTES - INTERNATIONAL:

Costa Rica and Nicaragua regularly file border dispute cases over the delimitations of the San Juan River and the northern tip of Calero Island to the International Court of Justice (ICJ); in 2009, the ICJ ruled that Costa Rican vessels carrying out police activities could not use the river, but official Costa Rican vessels providing essential services to riverside inhabitants and Costa Rican tourists could travel freely on the river; in 2011, the ICJ provisionally ruled that both countries must remove personnel from the disputed area; in 2013, the ICJ rejected Nicaragua's 2012 suit to halt Costa Rica's construction of a highway paralleling the river on the grounds of irreparable environmental damage; in 2013, the ICJ, regarding the disputed territory, ordered that Nicaragua should refrain from dredging or canal construction and refill and repair damage caused by trenches connecting the river to the Caribbean and upheld its 2010 ruling that Nicaragua must remove all personnel; in early 2014, Costa Rica brought Nicaragua to the ICJ over offshore oil concessions in the disputed region

REFUGEES AND INTERNALLY DISPLACED PERSONS:

refugees (country of origin): 9,655 (Venezuela) (economic and political crisis; includes Venezuelans who have claimed asylum or have received alternative legal stay) (2018)

stateless persons: 71 (2017)

TRAFFICKING IN PERSONS:

current situation: Costa Rica is a source, transit, and destination country for men, women, and children subjected to sex trafficking and forced labor; Costa Rican women and children, as well as those from Nicaragua, the Dominican Republic, and other Latin American countries, are sex trafficked in Costa Rica; child sex tourism is a particular problem with offenders coming from the US and Europe; men and children from Central America, including indigenous Panamanians, and Asia are exploited in agriculture, construction, fishing, and commerce; Nicaraguans transit Costa Rica to reach Panama, where some are subjected to forced labor or sex trafficking

tier rating: Tier 2 Watch List – Costa Rica does not fully comply with the minimum standards for the elimination of trafficking; however, it is making significant efforts to do so; anti-trafficking law enforcement efforts declined in 2014, with fewer prosecutions and no convictions and no actions taken against complicit government personnel; some officials conflated trafficking with smuggling, and authorities reported the diversion of funds to combat smuggling hindered anti-trafficking efforts; the government identified more victims than the previous year but did not make progress in ensuring that victims received adequate protective services; specialized services were limited and mostly provided by NGOs without government support, even from a dedicated fund for anti-trafficking efforts; victims services were virtually non-existent outside of the capital (2015)

ILLICIT DRUGS:

transshipment country for cocaine and heroin from South America; illicit production of cannabis in remote areas; domestic cocaine consumption, particularly crack cocaine, is rising; significant consumption of amphetamines; seizures of smuggled cash in Costa Rica and at the main border crossing to enter Costa Rica from Nicaragua have risen in recent years

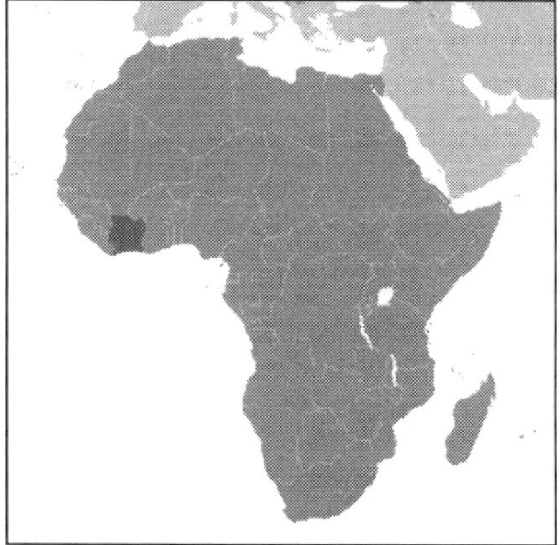

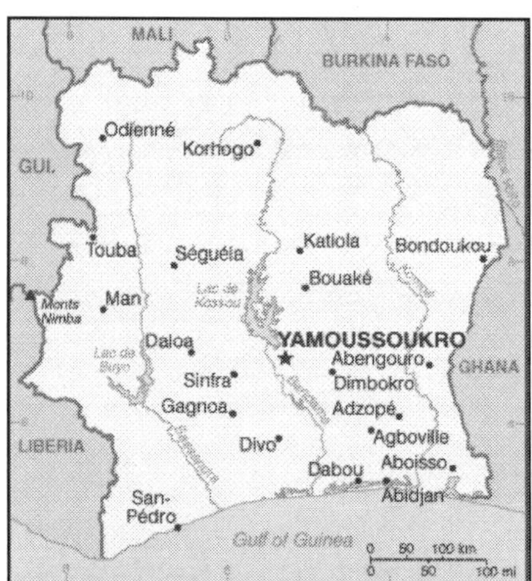

AFRICA :: COTE D'IVOIRE

INTRODUCTION :: COTE D'IVOIRE

BACKGROUND:

Close ties to France following independence in 1960, the development of cocoa production for export, and foreign investment all made Cote d'Ivoire one of the most prosperous of the West African states but did not protect it from political turmoil. In December 1999, a military coup - the first ever in Cote d'Ivoire's history - overthrew the government. Junta leader Robert GUEI blatantly rigged elections held in late 2000 and declared himself the winner. Popular protest forced him to step aside and an election brought Laurent GBAGBO into power. Ivoirian dissidents and disaffected members of the military launched a failed coup attempt in September 2002 that developed into a rebellion and then a civil war. In 2003, a cease-fire resulted in the country being divided with the rebels holding the north, the government the south, and peacekeeping forces a buffer zone between the two. In March 2007, President GBAGBO and former New Forces rebel leader Guillaume SORO signed an agreement in which SORO joined GBAGBO's government as prime minister and the two agreed to reunite the country by dismantling the buffer zone, integrating rebel forces into the national armed forces, and holding elections. Difficulties in preparing electoral registers delayed balloting until 2010. In November 2010, Alassane Dramane OUATTARA won the presidential election over GBAGBO, but GBAGBO refused to hand over power, resulting in a five-month resumption of violent conflict. In April 2011, after widespread fighting, GBAGBO was formally forced from office by armed OUATTARA supporters with the help of UN and French forces. The UN peacekeeping mission departed in June 2017. OUATTARA is focused on rebuilding the country's economy and infrastructure while rebuilding the security forces. GBAGBO is in The Hague on trial for crimes against humanity.

GEOGRAPHY :: COTE D'IVOIRE

LOCATION:

Western Africa, bordering the North Atlantic Ocean, between Ghana and Liberia

GEOGRAPHIC COORDINATES:

8 00 N, 5 00 W

MAP REFERENCES:

Africa

AREA:

total: 322,463 sq km

land: 318,003 sq km

water: 4,460 sq km

country comparison to the world: 70

AREA - COMPARATIVE:

slightly larger than New Mexico

LAND BOUNDARIES:

total: 3,458 km

border countries (5): Burkina Faso 545 km, Ghana 720 km, Guinea 816 km, Liberia 778 km, Mali 599 km

COASTLINE:

515 km

MARITIME CLAIMS:

territorial sea: 12 nm

exclusive economic zone: 200 nm

continental shelf: 200 nm

CLIMATE:

tropical along coast, semiarid in far north; three seasons - warm and dry (November to March), hot and dry (March to May), hot and wet (June to October)

TERRAIN:

mostly flat to undulating plains; mountains in northwest

ELEVATION:

mean elevation: 250 m

elevation extremes: 0 m lowest point: Gulf of Guinea

1752 highest point: Monts Nimba

NATURAL RESOURCES:

petroleum, natural gas, diamonds, manganese, iron ore, cobalt, bauxite, copper, gold, nickel, tantalum, silica sand, clay, cocoa beans, coffee, palm oil, hydropower

LAND USE:

agricultural land: 64.8% (2011 est.)

arable land: 9.1% (2011 est.) / permanent crops: 14.2% (2011 est.) / permanent pasture: 41.5% (2011 est.)

forest: 32.7% (2011 est.)

other: 2.5% (2011 est.)

IRRIGATED LAND:

730 sq km (2012)

POPULATION DISTRIBUTION:

the population is primarily located in the forested south, with the highest concentration of people residing in and around the cities on the Atlantic coast; most of the northern savanna remains sparsely populated with higher concentrations located along transportation corridors

NATURAL HAZARDS:

coast has heavy surf and no natural harbors; during the rainy season torrential flooding is possible

ENVIRONMENT - CURRENT ISSUES:

deforestation (most of the country's forests - once the largest in West Africa - have been heavily logged); water pollution from sewage, and from industrial, mining, and agricultural effluents

ENVIRONMENT - INTERNATIONAL AGREEMENTS:

party to: Biodiversity, Climate Change, Climate Change-Kyoto Protocol, Desertification, Endangered Species, Hazardous Wastes, Law of the Sea, Marine Dumping, Ozone Layer Protection, Ship Pollution, Tropical Timber 83, Tropical Timber 94, Wetlands, Whaling

signed, but not ratified: none of the selected agreements

GEOGRAPHY - NOTE:

most of the inhabitants live along the sandy coastal region; apart from the capital area, the forested interior is sparsely populated

PEOPLE AND SOCIETY :: COTE D'IVOIRE

POPULATION:

26,260,582 (July 2018 est.)

note: estimates for this country explicitly take into account the effects of excess mortality due to AIDS; this can result in lower life expectancy, higher infant mortality, higher death rates, lower population growth rates, and changes in the distribution of population by age and sex than would otherwise be expected

country comparison to the world: 51

NATIONALITY:

noun: Ivoirian(s)

adjective: Ivoirian

ETHNIC GROUPS:

Akan 28.8%, Voltaique or Gur 16.1%, Northern Mande 14.5%, Kru 8.5%, Southern Mande 6.9%, unspecified 0.9%, non-Ivoirian 42.3% (2014 est.)

LANGUAGES:

French (official), 60 native dialects of which Dioula is the most widely spoken

RELIGIONS:

Muslim 42.9%, Catholic 17.2%, Evangelical 11.8%, Methodist 1.7%, other Christian 3.2%, animist 3.6%, other religion 0.5%, none 19.1% (2014 est.)

note: the majority of foreign migrant workers are Muslim (72.7%) and Christian (17.7%)

DEMOGRAPHIC PROFILE:

Cote d'Ivoire's population is likely to continue growing for the foreseeable future because almost 60% of the populace is younger than 25, the total fertility rate is holding steady at about 3.5 children per woman, and contraceptive use is under 20%. The country will need to improve education, health care, and gender equality in order to turn its large and growing youth cohort into human capital. Even prior to 2010 unrest that shuttered schools for months, access to education was poor, especially for women. As of 2015, only 53% of men and 33% of women were literate. The lack of educational attainment contributes to Cote d'Ivoire's high rates of unskilled labor, adolescent pregnancy, and HIV/AIDS prevalence.

Following its independence in 1960, Cote d'Ivoire's stability and the blossoming of its labor-intensive cocoa and coffee industries in the southwest made it an attractive destination for migrants from other parts of the country and its neighbors, particularly Burkina Faso. The HOUPHOUET-BOIGNY administration continued the French colonial policy of encouraging labor immigration by offering liberal land ownership laws. Foreigners from West Africa, Europe (mainly France), and Lebanon composed about 25% of the population by 1998.

Ongoing economic decline since the 1980s and the power struggle after HOUPHOUET-BOIGNY's death in 1993 ushered in the politics of "Ivoirite," institutionalizing an Ivoirian identity that further marginalized northern Ivoirians and scapegoated immigrants. The hostile Muslim north-Christian south divide snowballed into a 2002 civil war, pushing tens of thousands of foreign migrants, Liberian refugees, and Ivoirians to flee to war-torn Liberia or other regional countries and more than a million people to be internally displaced. Subsequently, violence following the contested 2010 presidential election prompted some 250,000 people to seek refuge in Liberia and other neighboring countries and again internally displaced as many as a million people. By July 2012, the majority had returned home, but ongoing inter-communal tension and armed conflict continue to force people from their homes.

AGE STRUCTURE:

0-14 years: 39.59% (male 5,213,630 /female 5,182,872)

15-24 years: 19.91% (male 2,613,772 /female 2,615,680)

25-54 years: 34.25% (male 4,577,394 /female 4,416,408)

55-64 years: 3.47% (male 460,048 /female 451,604)

65 years and over: 2.78% (male 325,510 /female 403,664) (2018 est.)

DEPENDENCY RATIOS:

total dependency ratio: 83.8 (2015 est.)

youth dependency ratio: 78.5 (2015 est.)

elderly dependency ratio: 5.3 (2015 est.)

potential support ratio: 18.9 (2015 est.)

MEDIAN AGE:

total: 19.9 years

male: 20 years

female: 19.8 years (2018 est.)

country comparison to the world: 192

POPULATION GROWTH RATE:

2.3% (2018 est.)

country comparison to the world: 33

BIRTH RATE:

30.1 births/1,000 population (2018 est.)

country comparison to the world: 36

DEATH RATE:

8.4 deaths/1,000 population (2018 est.)

country comparison to the world: 80

NET MIGRATION RATE:

0 migrant(s)/1,000 population (2017 est.)

country comparison to the world: 79

POPULATION DISTRIBUTION:

the population is primarily located in the forested south, with the highest concentration of people residing in and around the cities on the Atlantic coast; most of the northern savanna remains sparsely populated with higher concentrations located along transportation corridors

URBANIZATION:

urban population: 50.8% of total population (2018)

rate of urbanization: 3.38% annual rate of change (2015-20 est.)

MAJOR URBAN AREAS - POPULATION:

4.921 million ABIDJAN (seat of government), 231,000 YAMOUSSOUKRO (capital) (2018)

SEX RATIO:

at birth: 1.02 male(s)/female (2017 est.)

0-14 years: 1.02 male(s)/female (2017 est.)

15-24 years: 1.02 male(s)/female (2017 est.)

25-54 years: 1.05 male(s)/female (2017 est.)

55-64 years: 1.01 male(s)/female (2017 est.)

65 years and over: 0.93 male(s)/female (2017 est.)

total population: 1.02 male(s)/female (2017 est.)

MOTHER'S MEAN AGE AT FIRST BIRTH:

19.8 years (2011/12 est.)

note: median age at first birth among women 25-29

MATERNAL MORTALITY RATE:

645 deaths/100,000 live births (2015 est.)

country comparison to the world: 12

INFANT MORTALITY RATE:

total: 62.6 deaths/1,000 live births (2018 est.)

male: 70.6 deaths/1,000 live births (2018 est.)

female: 54.4 deaths/1,000 live births (2018 est.)

country comparison to the world: 14

LIFE EXPECTANCY AT BIRTH:

total population: 60.1 years (2018 est.)

male: 58 years (2018 est.)

female: 62.4 years (2018 est.)

country comparison to the world: 209

TOTAL FERTILITY RATE:

3.83 children born/woman (2018 est.)

country comparison to the world: 38

CONTRACEPTIVE PREVALENCE RATE:

15.5% (2016)

HEALTH EXPENDITURES:

5.7% of GDP (2014)

country comparison to the world: 115

PHYSICIANS DENSITY:

0.14 physicians/1,000 population (2008)

DRINKING WATER SOURCE:

improved:

urban: 93.1% of population (2015 est.)

rural: 68.8% of population (2015 est.)

total: 81.9% of population (2015 est.)

unimproved:

urban: 6.9% of population (2015 est.)

rural: 31.2% of population (2015 est.)

total: 18.1% of population (2015 est.)

SANITATION FACILITY ACCESS:

improved:

urban: 32.8% of population (2015 est.)

rural: 10.3% of population (2015 est.)

total: 22.5% of population (2015 est.)

unimproved:

urban: 67.2% of population (2015 est.)

rural: 89.7% of population (2015 est.)

total: 77.5% of population (2015 est.)

HIV/AIDS - ADULT PREVALENCE RATE:

2.8% (2017 est.)

country comparison to the world: 19

HIV/AIDS - PEOPLE LIVING WITH HIV/AIDS:

500,000 (2017 est.)

country comparison to the world: 16

HIV/AIDS - DEATHS:

24,000 (2017 est.)

country comparison to the world: 10

MAJOR INFECTIOUS DISEASES:

degree of risk: very high (2016)

food or waterborne diseases: bacterial diarrhea, hepatitis A, and typhoid fever (2016)

vectorborne diseases: malaria, dengue fever, and yellow fever (2016)

water contact diseases: schistosomiasis (2016)

animal contact diseases: rabies (2016)

respiratory diseases: meningococcal meningitis (2016)

OBESITY - ADULT PREVALENCE RATE:

10.3% (2016)

country comparison to the world: 138

CHILDREN UNDER THE AGE OF 5 YEARS UNDERWEIGHT:

12.8% (2016)

country comparison to the world: 53

EDUCATION EXPENDITURES:

4.8% of GDP (2015)

country comparison to the world: 84

LITERACY:

definition: age 15 and over can read and write (2015 est.)

total population: 43.1% (2015 est.)

male: 53.1% (2015 est.)

female: 32.5% (2015 est.)

SCHOOL LIFE EXPECTANCY (PRIMARY TO TERTIARY EDUCATION):

total: 9 years (2015)

male: 10 years (2015)

female: 8 years (2015)

UNEMPLOYMENT, YOUTH AGES 15-24:

total: 3.9% (2016 est.)

male: 2.8% (2016 est.)

female: 5.1% (2016 est.)

country comparison to the world: 157

GOVERNMENT :: COTE D'IVOIRE

COUNTRY NAME:

conventional long form: Republic of Cote d'Ivoire

conventional short form: Cote d'Ivoire

local long form: Republique de Cote d'Ivoire

local short form: Cote d'Ivoire

former: Ivory Coast

etymology: name reflects the intense ivory trade that took place in the region from the 15th to 17th centuries

note: pronounced coat-div-whar

GOVERNMENT TYPE:

presidential republic

CAPITAL:

name: Yamoussoukro (legislative capital), Abidjan (administrative capital); note - although Yamoussoukro has been the official capital since 1983, Abidjan remains the administrative capital as well as the officially designated commercial capital; the US, like other countries, maintains its Embassy in Abidjan

geographic coordinates: 6 49 N, 5 16 W

time difference: UTC 0 (5 hours ahead of Washington, DC, during Standard Time)

ADMINISTRATIVE DIVISIONS:

12 districts and 2 autonomous districts*; Abidjan*, Bas-Sassandra, Comoe, Denguele, Goh-Djiboua, Lacs, Lagunes, Montagnes, Sassandra-Marahoue, Savanes, Vallee du Bandama, Woroba, Yamoussoukro*, Zanzan

INDEPENDENCE:

7 August 1960 (from France)

NATIONAL HOLIDAY:

Independence Day, 7 August (1960)

CONSTITUTION:

history: previous 1960, 2000; latest draft completed 24 September 2016, approved by the National Assembly 11 October 2016, approved by referendum 30 October 2016, promulgated 8 November 2016 (2017)

amendments: proposed by the president of the republic or by Parliament; consideration of drafts or proposals requires an absolute majority vote by the parliamentary membership; passage of amendments affecting presidential elections, presidential term of office and vacancies, and amendment procedures requires approval by absolute majority in a referendum; passage of other proposals by the president requires at least four-fifths majority vote by Parliament; constitutional articles on the sovereignty of the state and its republican and secular form of government cannot be amended (2017)

LEGAL SYSTEM:

civil law system based on the French civil code; judicial review of legislation held in the Constitutional Chamber of the Supreme Court

INTERNATIONAL LAW ORGANIZATION PARTICIPATION:

accepts compulsory ICJ jurisdiction with reservations; accepts ICCt jurisdiction

CITIZENSHIP:

citizenship by birth: no

citizenship by descent only: at least one parent must be a citizen of Cote d'Ivoire

dual citizenship recognized: no

residency requirement for naturalization: 5 years

SUFFRAGE:

18 years of age; universal

EXECUTIVE BRANCH:

chief of state: President Alassane Dramane OUATTARA (since 4 December 2010); Vice President Daniel Kablan DUNCAN (since 16 January 2017); note - the 2016 constitution calls for the establishment of the position of vice-president

head of government: Prime Minister Amadou Gon COULIBALY (since 11 January 2017)

cabinet: Council of Ministers appointed by the president

elections/appointments: president directly elected by absolute majority popular vote in 2 rounds if needed for a 5-year term (no term limits); election last held on 25 October 2015 (next to be held in 2020); prime minister appointed by the president; note - the 2016 constitution limits the presidential tenure to 2 terms beginning with the 2020 election; the vice president is named by the president

election results: Alassane OUATTARA reelected president; percent of vote - Alassane OUATTARA (RDR) 83.7%, Pascal Affi N'GUESSAN (FPI) 9.3%, Konan Bertin KOUADIO (independent) 3.9%, other 3.1%

LEGISLATIVE BRANCH:

description: bicameral Parliament consists of:
Senate or Senat (99 seats; 66 members indirectly elected by the National Assembly and members of municipal, autonomous districts, and regional councils, and 33 members appointed by the president; members serve 5-year terms)
National Assembly (255 seats; members directly elected in single- and multi-seat constituencies by simple majority vote to serve 5-year terms)

elections:
Senate - first ever held on 25 March 2018 (next to be held in 2023)
National Assembly - last held on 18 December 2016 (next to be held in 2021)

election results:
Senate - percent by party NA; seats by party - RHDP 50, independent 16
National Assembly - percent of vote by party - RHDP 50.3%, FPI 5.8%, UDPCI 1%, other 1.4%, independent 38.5%; seats by party - RHDP, 167, UDPCI 6, FPI 3, UPCI 3, independent 76

note: the new constitution of November 2016 called for a bicameral Parliament with the creation of the Senate

JUDICIAL BRANCH:

highest courts: Supreme Court or Cour Supreme (organized into Judicial, Audit, Constitutional, and Administrative Chambers; consists of the court president, 3 vice-presidents for the Judicial, Audit, and Administrative chambers, and 9 associate justices or magistrates)

judge selection and term of office: judges nominated by the Superior Council of the Magistrature, a 7-member body consisting of the national president (chairman), 3 "bench" judges, and 3 public prosecutors; judges appointed for life

subordinate courts: Courts of Appeal (organized into civil, criminal, and social chambers); first instance courts; peace courts

POLITICAL PARTIES AND LEADERS:

Democratic Party of Cote d'Ivoire or PDCI [Henri Konan BEDIE]
Ivorian Popular Front or FPI [former pres. Laurent GBAGBO]
Liberty and Democracy for the Republic or LIDER [Mamadou KOULIBALY]
Movement of the Future Forces or MFA [Innocent Augustin ANAKY KOBENA]
Rally of Houphouetists for Democracy and Peace or RHDP [Alassane OUATTARA] (alliance includes MFA, PDCI, RDR, UDPCI, UPCI)
Rally of the Republicans or RDR [Henriette DIABATE]
Union for Cote d'Ivoire or UPCI [Gnamien KONAN]
Union for Democracy and Peace in Cote d'Ivoire or UDPCI [Albert Toikeusse MABRI]
other: more than 144 smaller registered parties

INTERNATIONAL ORGANIZATION PARTICIPATION:

ACP, AfDB, AU, ECOWAS, EITI (compliant country), Entente, FAO, FZ, G-24, G-77, IAEA, IBRD, ICAO, ICC, ICCt, ICRM, IDA, IDB, IFAD, IFC, IFRCS, ILO, IMF, IMO, Interpol, IOC, IOM, IPU, ISO, ITSO, ITU, ITUC (NGOs), MIGA, MINUSMA, MONUSCO, NAM, OIC, OIF, OPCW, UN, UNCTAD,

UNESCO, UNHCR, UNIDO, Union Latina, UN Security Council (temporary), UNWTO, UPU, WADB (regional), WAEMU, WCO, WFTU (NGOs), WHO, WIPO, WMO, WTO

DIPLOMATIC REPRESENTATION IN THE US:

chief of mission: Ambassador Mamadou HAIDARA (since 28 March 2018)

chancery: 2424 Massachusetts Avenue NW, Washington, DC 20008

telephone: [1] (202) 797-0300

FAX: [1] (202) 462-9444

DIPLOMATIC REPRESENTATION FROM THE US:

chief of mission: Ambassador (vacant); Charge d'Affaires Katherine BRUCKER (since 28 August 2017)

embassy: Cocody Riviera Golf 01, Abidjan

mailing address: B. P. 1712, Abidjan 01

telephone: [225] 22 49 40 00

FAX: [225] 22 49 43 23

FLAG DESCRIPTION:

three equal vertical bands of orange (hoist side), white, and green; orange symbolizes the land (savannah) of the north and fertility, white stands for peace and unity, green represents the forests of the south and the hope for a bright future

note: similar to the flag of Ireland, which is longer and has the colors reversed - green (hoist side), white, and orange; also similar to the flag of Italy, which is green (hoist side), white, and red; design was based on the flag of France

NATIONAL SYMBOL(S):

elephant; national colors: orange, white, green

NATIONAL ANTHEM:

name: "L'Abidjanaise" (Song of Abidjan)

lyrics/music: Mathieu EKRA, Joachim BONY, and Pierre Marie COTY/Pierre Marie COTY and Pierre Michel PANGO

note: adopted 1960; although the nation's capital city moved from Abidjan to Yamoussoukro in 1983, the anthem still owes its name to the former capital

ECONOMY :: COTE D'IVOIRE

ECONOMY - OVERVIEW:

For the last 5 years Cote d'Ivoire's growth rate has been among the highest in the world. Cote d'Ivoire is heavily dependent on agriculture and related activities, which engage roughly two-thirds of the population. Cote d'Ivoire is the world's largest producer and exporter of cocoa beans and a significant producer and exporter of coffee and palm oil. Consequently, the economy is highly sensitive to fluctuations in international prices for these products and to climatic conditions. Cocoa, oil, and coffee are the country's top export revenue earners, but the country has targeted agricultural processing of cocoa, cashews, mangoes, and other commodities as a high priority. Mining gold and exporting electricity are growing industries outside agriculture.

Following the end of more than a decade of civil conflict in 2011, Cote d'Ivoire has experienced a boom in foreign investment and economic growth. In June 2012, the IMF and the World Bank announced $4.4 billion in debt relief for Cote d'Ivoire under the Highly Indebted Poor Countries Initiative.

GDP (PURCHASING POWER PARITY):

$97.16 billion (2017 est.)

$90.12 billion (2016 est.)

$83.19 billion (2015 est.)

note: data are in 2017 dollars

country comparison to the world: 86

GDP (OFFICIAL EXCHANGE RATE):

$40.47 billion (2017 est.) (2017 est.)

GDP - REAL GROWTH RATE:

7.8% (2017 est.)

8.3% (2016 est.)

8.8% (2015 est.)

country comparison to the world: 10

GDP - PER CAPITA (PPP):

$3,900 (2017 est.)

$3,700 (2016 est.)

$3,500 (2015 est.)

note: data are in 2017 dollars

country comparison to the world: 179

GROSS NATIONAL SAVING:

15.9% of GDP (2017 est.)

19.2% of GDP (2016 est.)

19.5% of GDP (2015 est.)

country comparison to the world: 131

GDP - COMPOSITION, BY END USE:

household consumption: 61.7% (2017 est.)

government consumption: 14.9% (2017 est.)

investment in fixed capital: 22.4% (2017 est.)

investment in inventories: 0.3% (2017 est.)

exports of goods and services: 30.8% (2017 est.)

imports of goods and services: -30.1% (2017 est.)

GDP - COMPOSITION, BY SECTOR OF ORIGIN:

agriculture: 20.1% (2017 est.)

industry: 26.6% (2017 est.)

services: 53.3% (2017 est.)

AGRICULTURE - PRODUCTS:

coffee, cocoa beans, bananas, palm kernels, corn, rice, cassava (manioc, tapioca), sweet potatoes, sugar, cotton, rubber; timber

INDUSTRIES:

foodstuffs, beverages; wood products, oil refining, gold mining, truck and bus assembly, textiles, fertilizer, building materials, electricity

INDUSTRIAL PRODUCTION GROWTH RATE:

4.2% (2017 est.)

country comparison to the world: 71

LABOR FORCE:

8.747 million (2017 est.)

country comparison to the world: 59

LABOR FORCE - BY OCCUPATION:

agriculture: 68% (2007 est.)

UNEMPLOYMENT RATE:

9.4% (2013 est.)

country comparison to the world: 135

POPULATION BELOW POVERTY LINE:

46.3% (2015 est.)

HOUSEHOLD INCOME OR CONSUMPTION BY PERCENTAGE SHARE:

lowest 10%: 31.8% (2008)

highest 10%: 31.8% (2008)

DISTRIBUTION OF FAMILY INCOME - GINI INDEX:

41.5 (2008)

36.7 (1995)

country comparison to the world: 56

BUDGET:

revenues: 7.749 billion (2017 est.)

expenditures: 9.464 billion (2017 est.)

TAXES AND OTHER REVENUES:

19.1% (of GDP) (2017 est.)

country comparison to the world: 156

BUDGET SURPLUS (+) OR DEFICIT (-):

-4.2% (of GDP) (2017 est.)

country comparison to the world: 159

PUBLIC DEBT:

47% of GDP (2017 est.)

47% of GDP (2016 est.)

country comparison to the world: 112

FISCAL YEAR:

calendar year

INFLATION RATE (CONSUMER PRICES):

0.8% (2017 est.)

0.7% (2016 est.)

country comparison to the world: 40

CENTRAL BANK DISCOUNT RATE:

4.25% (31 December 2010)

4.25% (31 December 2009)

country comparison to the world: 93

COMMERCIAL BANK PRIME LENDING RATE:

5.4% (31 December 2017 est.)

5.3% (31 December 2016 est.)

country comparison to the world: 136

STOCK OF NARROW MONEY:

$11.63 billion (31 December 2017 est.)

$8.861 billion (31 December 2016 est.)

country comparison to the world: 81

STOCK OF BROAD MONEY:

$11.63 billion (31 December 2017 est.)

$8.861 billion (31 December 2016 est.)

country comparison to the world: 83

STOCK OF DOMESTIC CREDIT:

$14.56 billion (31 December 2017 est.)

$10.9 billion (31 December 2016 est.)

country comparison to the world: 98

MARKET VALUE OF PUBLICLY TRADED SHARES:

$12.49 billion (31 December 2015 est.)

$11.71 billion (31 December 2014 est.)

$11.82 billion (31 December 2013 est.)

country comparison to the world: 72

CURRENT ACCOUNT BALANCE:

-$1.86 billion (2017 est.)

-$414 million (2016 est.)

country comparison to the world: 161

EXPORTS:

$11.74 billion (2017 est.)

$11.77 billion (2016 est.)

country comparison to the world: 84

EXPORTS - PARTNERS:

Netherlands 11.8%, US 7.9%, France 6.4%, Belgium 6.4%, Germany 5.8%, Burkina Faso 4.5%, India 4.4%, Mali 4.2% (2017)

EXPORTS - COMMODITIES:

cocoa, coffee, timber, petroleum, cotton, bananas, pineapples, palm oil, fish

IMPORTS:

$9.447 billion (2017 est.)

$7.81 billion (2016 est.)

country comparison to the world: 105

IMPORTS - COMMODITIES:

fuel, capital equipment, foodstuffs

IMPORTS - PARTNERS:

Nigeria 15%, France 13.4%, China 11.3%, US 4.3% (2017)

RESERVES OF FOREIGN EXCHANGE AND GOLD:

$6.257 billion (31 December 2017 est.)

$4.935 billion (31 December 2016 est.)

country comparison to the world: 91

DEBT - EXTERNAL:

$13.07 billion (31 December 2017 est.)

$11.02 billion (31 December 2016 est.)

country comparison to the world: 105

STOCK OF DIRECT FOREIGN INVESTMENT - AT HOME:

NA

STOCK OF DIRECT FOREIGN INVESTMENT - ABROAD:

NA

EXCHANGE RATES:

Communaute Financiere Africaine francs (XOF) per US dollar -

594.3 (2017 est.)

593.01 (2016 est.)

593.01 (2015 est.)

591.45 (2014 est.)

494.42 (2013 est.)

ENERGY :: COTE D'IVOIRE

ELECTRICITY ACCESS:

population without electricity: 15 million (2013)

electrification - total population: 26% (2013)

electrification - urban areas: 42% (2013)

electrification - rural areas: 8% (2013)

ELECTRICITY - PRODUCTION:

9.73 billion kWh (2016 est.)

country comparison to the world: 104

ELECTRICITY - CONSUMPTION:

6.245 billion kWh (2016 est.)

country comparison to the world: 114

ELECTRICITY - EXPORTS:

872 million kWh (2015 est.)

country comparison to the world: 61

ELECTRICITY - IMPORTS:

19 million kWh (2016 est.)

country comparison to the world: 114

ELECTRICITY - INSTALLED GENERATING CAPACITY:

1.914 million kW (2016 est.)

country comparison to the world: 114

ELECTRICITY - FROM FOSSIL FUELS:

60% of total installed capacity (2016 est.)

country comparison to the world: 130

ELECTRICITY - FROM NUCLEAR FUELS:

0% of total installed capacity (2017 est.)

country comparison to the world: 73

ELECTRICITY - FROM HYDROELECTRIC PLANTS:

40% of total installed capacity (2017 est.)

country comparison to the world: 51

ELECTRICITY - FROM OTHER RENEWABLE SOURCES:

0% of total installed capacity (2017 est.)

country comparison to the world: 184

CRUDE OIL - PRODUCTION:

54,000 bbl/day (2017 est.)

country comparison to the world: 50

CRUDE OIL - EXPORTS:

26,700 bbl/day (2015 est.)

country comparison to the world: 47

CRUDE OIL - IMPORTS:

62,350 bbl/day (2015 est.)

country comparison to the world: 52

CRUDE OIL - PROVED RESERVES:

100 million bbl (1 January 2018 est.)

country comparison to the world: 69

REFINED PETROLEUM PRODUCTS - PRODUCTION:

69,360 bbl/day (2017 est.)

country comparison to the world: 72

REFINED PETROLEUM PRODUCTS - CONSUMPTION:

51,000 bbl/day (2016 est.)

country comparison to the world: 104

REFINED PETROLEUM PRODUCTS - EXPORTS:

31,450 bbl/day (2015 est.)

country comparison to the world: 61

REFINED PETROLEUM PRODUCTS - IMPORTS:

7,405 bbl/day (2015 est.)

country comparison to the world: 154

NATURAL GAS - PRODUCTION:

2.322 billion cu m (2017 est.)

country comparison to the world: 59

NATURAL GAS - CONSUMPTION:

2.322 billion cu m (2017 est.)

country comparison to the world: 82

NATURAL GAS - EXPORTS:

0 cu m (2017 est.)

country comparison to the world: 89

NATURAL GAS - IMPORTS:

0 cu m (2017 est.)

country comparison to the world: 112

NATURAL GAS - PROVED RESERVES:

28.32 billion cu m (1 January 2018 est.)

country comparison to the world: 68

CARBON DIOXIDE EMISSIONS FROM CONSUMPTION OF ENERGY:

11.54 million Mt (2017 est.)

country comparison to the world: 101

COMMUNICATIONS :: COTE D'IVOIRE

TELEPHONES - FIXED LINES:

total subscriptions: 305,562 (2017 est.)

subscriptions per 100 inhabitants: 1 (2017 est.)

country comparison to the world: 111

TELEPHONES - MOBILE CELLULAR:

total subscriptions: 31,747,233 (2017 est.)

subscriptions per 100 inhabitants: 131 (2017 est.)

country comparison to the world: 42

TELEPHONE SYSTEM:

general assessment: well-developed by African standards; telecommunications sector privatized in late 1990s and operational fixed lines have increased since that time with 2 fixed-line providers operating over open-wire lines, microwave radio relay, and fiber-optics; 90% digitalized; Côte d'Ivoire continues to benefit from strong economic growth; the fixed internet and broadband sectors have remained lagging (2017)

domestic: less than 1 per 100 fixed-line, with multiple mobile-cellular service providers competing in the market, usage has increased sharply to about 131 per 100 persons (2017)

international: country code - 225; landing point for the SAT-3/WASC fiber-optic submarine cable that provides connectivity to Europe and Asia; satellite earth stations - 2 Intelsat (1 Atlantic Ocean and 1 Indian Ocean) (2016)

BROADCAST MEDIA:

2 state-owned TV stations; no private terrestrial TV stations, but satellite TV subscription service is available; 2 state-owned radio stations; some private radio stations; transmissions of several international broadcasters are available (2007)

INTERNET COUNTRY CODE:

.ci

INTERNET USERS:

total: 6,297,676 (July 2016 est.)

percent of population: 26.5% (July 2016 est.)

country comparison to the world: 66

BROADBAND - FIXED SUBSCRIPTIONS:

total: 142,825 (2017 est.)

subscriptions per 100 inhabitants: 1 (2017 est.)

country comparison to the world: 114

TRANSPORTATION :: COTE D'IVOIRE

NATIONAL AIR TRANSPORT SYSTEM:

number of registered air carriers: 1 (2015)

inventory of registered aircraft operated by air carriers: 10 (2015)

annual passenger traffic on registered air carriers: 359,260 (2015)

annual freight traffic on registered air carriers: 4,719,120 mt-km (2015)

CIVIL AIRCRAFT REGISTRATION COUNTRY CODE PREFIX:

TU (2016)

AIRPORTS:

27 (2013)

country comparison to the world: 125

AIRPORTS - WITH PAVED RUNWAYS:

total: 7 (2017)

over 3,047 m: 1 (2017)

2,438 to 3,047 m: 2 (2017)

1,524 to 2,437 m: 4 (2017)

AIRPORTS - WITH UNPAVED RUNWAYS:

total: 20 (2013)

1,524 to 2,437 m: 6 (2013)

914 to 1,523 m: 11 (2013)

under 914 m: 3 (2013)

HELIPORTS:

1 (2013)

PIPELINES:

101 km condensate, 256 km gas, 118 km oil, 5 km oil/gas/water, 7 km water (2013)

RAILWAYS:

total: 660 km (2008)

narrow gauge: 660 km 1.000-m gauge (2008)

note: an additional 622 km of this railroad extends into Burkina Faso

country comparison to the world: 104

ROADWAYS:

total: 81,996 km (2007)

paved: 6,502 km (2007)

unpaved: 75,494 km (2007)

note: includes intercity and urban roads; another 20,000 km of dirt roads are in poor condition and 150,000 km of dirt roads are impassable

country comparison to the world: 61

WATERWAYS:

980 km (navigable rivers, canals, and numerous coastal lagoons) (2011)

country comparison to the world: 66

MERCHANT MARINE:

total: 9 (2017)

by type: oil tanker 2, other 7 (2017)

country comparison to the world: 150

PORTS AND TERMINALS:

major seaport(s): Abidjan, San-Pedro

oil terminal(s): Espoir Offshore Terminal

MILITARY AND SECURITY :: COTE D'IVOIRE

MILITARY EXPENDITURES:

1.18% of GDP (2016)

1.74% of GDP (2015)

1.48% of GDP (2014)

country comparison to the world: 98

MILITARY BRANCHES:

Armed Forces of Cote d'Ivoire (Force Armee de Cote d'Ivoire, FACI): Army, Navy, Cote d'Ivoire Air Force (Force Aerienne de la Cote d'Ivoire) (2017)

MILITARY SERVICE AGE AND OBLIGATION:

18-25 years of age for compulsory and voluntary male and female military service; conscription is not enforced; voluntary recruitment of former rebels into the new national army is restricted to ages 22-29 (2012)

TRANSNATIONAL ISSUES :: COTE D'IVOIRE

DISPUTES - INTERNATIONAL:

disputed maritime border between Cote d'Ivoire and Ghana

REFUGEES AND INTERNALLY DISPLACED PERSONS:

IDPs: 16,000 (post-election conflict in 2010-11, as well as civil war from 2002-04; most pronounced in western and southwestern regions) (2017)

stateless persons: 692,000 (2017); note - many Ivoirians lack documentation proving their nationality, which prevent them from accessing education and healthcare; birth on Ivorian soil does not automatically result in citizenship; disputes over citizenship and the associated rights of the large population descended from migrants from neighboring countries is an ongoing source of tension and contributed to the country's 2002 civil war; some observers believe the government's mass naturalizations of thousands of people over the last couple of years is intended to boost its electoral support base; the government in October 2013 acceded to international conventions on statelessness and in August 2013 reformed its nationality law, key steps to clarify the nationality of thousands of residents; since the adoption of the Abidjan Declaration to eradicate statelessness in West Africa in February 2015, 6,400 people have received nationality papers

ILLICIT DRUGS:

illicit producer of cannabis, mostly for local consumption; utility as a narcotic transshipment point to Europe reduced by ongoing political instability; while rampant corruption and inadequate supervision leave the banking system vulnerable to money laundering, the lack of a developed financial system limits the country's utility as a major money-laundering center

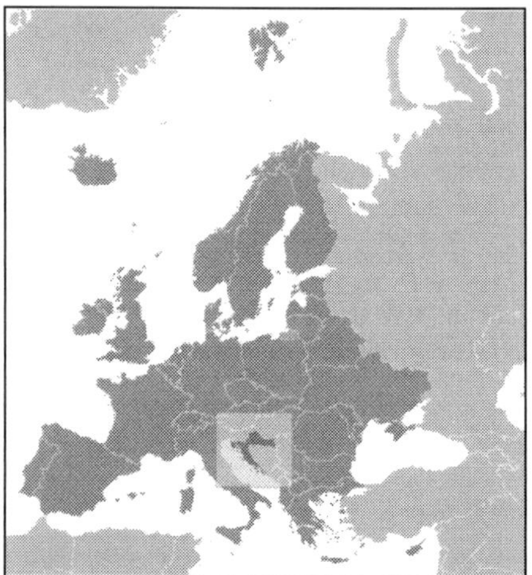

EUROPE :: CROATIA

INTRODUCTION :: CROATIA

BACKGROUND:

The lands that today comprise Croatia were part of the Austro-Hungarian Empire until the close of World War I. In 1918, the Croats, Serbs, and Slovenes formed a kingdom known after 1929 as Yugoslavia. Following World War II, Yugoslavia became a federal independent communist state consisting of six socialist republics under the strong hand of Marshal Josip Broz, aka TITO. Although Croatia declared its independence from Yugoslavia in 1991, it took four years of sporadic, but often bitter, fighting before occupying Serb armies were mostly cleared from Croatian lands, along with a majority of Croatia's ethnic Serb population. Under UN supervision, the last Serb-held enclave in eastern Slavonia was returned to Croatia in 1998. The country joined NATO in April 2009 and the EU in July 2013.

GEOGRAPHY :: CROATIA

LOCATION:

Southeastern Europe, bordering the Adriatic Sea, between Bosnia and Herzegovina and Slovenia

GEOGRAPHIC COORDINATES:

45 10 N, 15 30 E

MAP REFERENCES:

Europe

AREA:

total: 56,594 sq km

land: 55,974 sq km

water: 620 sq km

country comparison to the world: 128

AREA - COMPARATIVE:

slightly smaller than West Virginia

LAND BOUNDARIES:

total: 2,237 km

border countries (5): Bosnia and Herzegovina 956 km, Hungary 348 km, Montenegro 19 km, Serbia 314 km, Slovenia 600 km

COASTLINE:

5,835 km (mainland 1,777 km, islands 4,058 km)

MARITIME CLAIMS:

territorial sea: 12 nm

continental shelf: 200-m depth or to the depth of exploitation

CLIMATE:

Mediterranean and continental; continental climate predominant with hot summers and cold winters; mild winters, dry summers along coast

TERRAIN:

geographically diverse; flat plains along Hungarian border, low mountains and highlands near Adriatic coastline and islands

ELEVATION:

mean elevation: 331 m

elevation extremes: 0 m lowest point: Adriatic Sea

1831 highest point: Dinara

NATURAL RESOURCES:

oil, some coal, bauxite, low-grade iron ore, calcium, gypsum, natural asphalt, silica, mica, clays, salt, hydropower

LAND USE:

agricultural land: 23.7% (2011 est.)

arable land: 16% (2011 est.) / permanent crops: 1.5% (2011 est.) / permanent pasture: 6.2% (2011 est.)

forest: 34.4% (2011 est.)

other: 41.9% (2011 est.)

IRRIGATED LAND:

240 sq km (2012)

POPULATION DISTRIBUTION:

more of the population lives in the northern half of the country, with approximately a quarter of the populace residing in and around the capital of Zagreb; many of the islands are sparsely populated

NATURAL HAZARDS:

destructive earthquakes

ENVIRONMENT - CURRENT ISSUES:

air pollution improving but still a concern in urban settings and in emissions arriving from neighboring countries; surface water pollution in the Danube River Basin

ENVIRONMENT - INTERNATIONAL AGREEMENTS:

party to: Air Pollution, Air Pollution-Nitrogen Oxides, Air Pollution-Persistent Organic Pollutants, Air Pollution-Sulfur 94, Air Pollution-Volatile Organic Compounds, Biodiversity, Climate Change, Climate Change-Kyoto Protocol, Desertification, Endangered Species, Hazardous Wastes, Law of the Sea, Marine Dumping, Ozone Layer Protection, Ship Pollution, Wetlands, Whaling

signed, but not ratified: none of the selected agreements

GEOGRAPHY - NOTE:

controls most land routes from Western Europe to Aegean Sea and Turkish Straits; most Adriatic Sea islands lie off the coast of Croatia -

some 1,200 islands, islets, ridges, and rocks

PEOPLE AND SOCIETY :: CROATIA

POPULATION:

4,270,480 (July 2018 est.)

country comparison to the world: 127

NATIONALITY:

noun: Croat(s), Croatian(s)

adjective: Croatian

note: the French designation of "Croate" to Croatian mercenaries in the 17th century eventually became "Cravate" and later came to be applied to the soldiers' scarves - the cravat; Croatia celebrates Cravat Day every 18 October

ETHNIC GROUPS:

Croat 90.4%, Serb 4.4%, other 4.4% (including Bosniak, Hungarian, Slovene, Czech, and Romani), unspecified 0.8% (2011 est.)

LANGUAGES:

Croatian (official) 95.6%, Serbian 1.2%, other 3% (including Hungarian, Czech, Slovak, and Albanian), unspecified 0.2% (2011 est.)

RELIGIONS:

Roman Catholic 86.3%, Orthodox 4.4%, Muslim 1.5%, other 1.5%, unspecified 2.5%, not religious or atheist 3.8% (2011 est.)

AGE STRUCTURE:

0-14 years: 14.21% (male 312,805 /female 293,931)

15-24 years: 11.09% (male 242,605 /female 230,853)

25-54 years: 40.15% (male 858,025 /female 856,455)

55-64 years: 14.65% (male 304,054 /female 321,543)

65 years and over: 19.91% (male 342,025 /female 508,184) (2018 est.)

DEPENDENCY RATIOS:

total dependency ratio: 50.9 (2015 est.)

youth dependency ratio: 22.4 (2015 est.)

elderly dependency ratio: 28.5 (2015 est.)

potential support ratio: 3.5 (2015 est.)

MEDIAN AGE:

total: 43.3 years

male: 41.4 years

female: 45.3 years (2018 est.)

country comparison to the world: 20

POPULATION GROWTH RATE:

-0.51% (2018 est.)

country comparison to the world: 221

BIRTH RATE:

8.8 births/1,000 population (2018 est.)

country comparison to the world: 208

DEATH RATE:

12.4 deaths/1,000 population (2018 est.)

country comparison to the world: 16

NET MIGRATION RATE:

-1.7 migrant(s)/1,000 population (2017 est.)

country comparison to the world: 151

POPULATION DISTRIBUTION:

more of the population lives in the northern half of the country, with approximately a quarter of the populace residing in and around the capital of Zagreb; many of the islands are sparsely populated

URBANIZATION:

urban population: 56.9% of total population (2018)

rate of urbanization: -0.08% annual rate of change (2015-20 est.)

MAJOR URBAN AREAS - POPULATION:

686,000 ZAGREB (capital) (2018)

SEX RATIO:

at birth: 1.06 male(s)/female (2017 est.)

0-14 years: 1.06 male(s)/female (2017 est.)

15-24 years: 1.05 male(s)/female (2017 est.)

25-54 years: 1 male(s)/female (2017 est.)

55-64 years: 0.96 male(s)/female (2017 est.)

65 years and over: 0.69 male(s)/female (2017 est.)

total population: 0.93 male(s)/female (2017 est.)

MOTHER'S MEAN AGE AT FIRST BIRTH:

28 years (2014 est.)

MATERNAL MORTALITY RATE:

8 deaths/100,000 live births (2015 est.)

country comparison to the world: 156

INFANT MORTALITY RATE:

total: 9.1 deaths/1,000 live births (2018 est.)

male: 8.8 deaths/1,000 live births (2018 est.)

female: 9.3 deaths/1,000 live births (2018 est.)

country comparison to the world: 144

LIFE EXPECTANCY AT BIRTH:

total population: 76.3 years (2018 est.)

male: 73.2 years (2018 est.)

female: 79.6 years (2018 est.)

country comparison to the world: 87

TOTAL FERTILITY RATE:

1.41 children born/woman (2018 est.)

country comparison to the world: 212

HEALTH EXPENDITURES:

7.8% of GDP (2014)

country comparison to the world: 59

PHYSICIANS DENSITY:

3.13 physicians/1,000 population (2014)

HOSPITAL BED DENSITY:

5.6 beds/1,000 population (2015)

DRINKING WATER SOURCE:

improved:

urban: 99.6% of population (2015 est.)

rural: 99.7% of population (2015 est.)

total: 99.6% of population (2015 est.)

unimproved:

urban: 0.4% of population (2015 est.)

rural: 0.3% of population (2015 est.)

total: 0.4% of population (2015 est.)

SANITATION FACILITY ACCESS:

improved:

urban: 97.8% of population (2015 est.)

rural: 95.8% of population (2015 est.)

total: 97% of population (2015 est.)

unimproved:

urban: 2.2% of population (2015 est.)

rural: 4.2% of population (2015 est.)

total: 3% of population (2015 est.)

HIV/AIDS - ADULT PREVALENCE RATE:

<.1% (2016 est.)

HIV/AIDS - PEOPLE LIVING WITH HIV/AIDS:

1,500 (2016 est.)

country comparison to the world: 131

HIV/AIDS - DEATHS:

<100 (2016 est.)

MAJOR INFECTIOUS DISEASES:

degree of risk: intermediate (2016)

vectorborne diseases: tickborne encephalitis (2016)

OBESITY - ADULT PREVALENCE RATE:

24.4% (2016)

country comparison to the world: 59

EDUCATION EXPENDITURES:

4.6% of GDP (2013)

country comparison to the world: 88

LITERACY:

definition: age 15 and over can read and write (2015 est.)

total population: 99.3% (2015 est.)

male: 99.7% (2015 est.)

female: 98.9% (2015 est.)

SCHOOL LIFE EXPECTANCY (PRIMARY TO TERTIARY EDUCATION):

total: 15 years (2014)

male: 15 years (2014)

female: 16 years (2014)

UNEMPLOYMENT, YOUTH AGES 15-24:

total: 31.3% (2016 est.)

male: 31.2% (2016 est.)

female: 31.3% (2016 est.)

country comparison to the world: 26

GOVERNMENT :: CROATIA

COUNTRY NAME:

conventional long form: Republic of Croatia

conventional short form: Croatia

local long form: Republika Hrvatska

local short form: Hrvatska

former: People's Republic of Croatia, Socialist Republic of Croatia

etymology: name derives from the Croats, a Slavic tribe who migrated to the Balkans in the 7th century A.D.

GOVERNMENT TYPE:

parliamentary republic

CAPITAL:

name: Zagreb

geographic coordinates: 45 48 N, 16 00 E

time difference: UTC+1 (6 hours ahead of Washington, DC, during Standard Time)

daylight saving time: +1hr, begins last Sunday in March; ends last Sunday in October

ADMINISTRATIVE DIVISIONS:

20 counties (zupanije, zupanija - singular) and 1 city* (grad - singular) with special county status; Bjelovarsko-Bilogorska(Bjelovar-Bilogora), Brodsko-Posavska (Brod-Posavina), Dubrovacko-Neretvanska (Dubrovnik-Neretva), Istarska (Istria), Karlovacka (Karlovac), Koprivnicko-Krizevacka (Koprivnica-Krizevci), Krapinsko-Zagorska (Krapina-Zagorje), Licko-Senjska (Lika-Senj), Medimurska (Medimurje), Osijecko-Baranjska (Osijek-Baranja), Pozesko-Slavonska (Pozega-Slavonia), Primorsko-Goranska (Primorje-Gorski Kotar), Sibensko-Kninska (Sibenik-Knin), Sisacko-Moslavacka (Sisak-Moslavina), Splitsko-Dalmatinska (Split-Dalmatia), Varazdinska (Varazdin), Viroviticko-Podravska (Virovitica-Podravina), Vukovarsko-Srijemska (Vukovar-Syrmia), Zadarska (Zadar), Zagreb*, Zagrebacka (Zagreb county)

INDEPENDENCE:

25 June 1991 (from Yugoslavia); notable earlier dates: ca. 925 (Kingdom of Croatia established); 1 December 1918 (Kingdom of Serbs, Croats, and Slovenes (Yugoslavia) established)

NATIONAL HOLIDAY:

Independence Day, 8 October (1991) and Statehood Day, 25 June (1991); note - 25 June 1991 was the day the Croatian parliament voted for independence; following a three-month moratorium to allow the European Community to solve the Yugoslav crisis peacefully, parliament adopted a decision on 8 October 1991 to sever constitutional relations with Yugoslavia

CONSTITUTION:

history: several previous; latest adopted 22 December 1990 (2016)

amendments: proposed by at least one-fifth of the Assembly membership, by the president of the republic, by the Government of Croatia, or through petition by at least 10% of the total electorate; proceedings to amend require majority vote by the Assembly; passage requires two-thirds majority vote by the Assembly; passage by petition requires a majority vote in a referendum and promulgation by the Assembly; amended several times, last in 2014 (2016)

LEGAL SYSTEM:

civil law system influenced by legal heritage of Austria-Hungary; note - Croatian law was fully harmonized with the European Community acquis as of the June 2010 completion of EU accession negotiations

INTERNATIONAL LAW ORGANIZATION PARTICIPATION:

has not submitted an ICJ jurisdiction declaration; accepts ICCt jurisdiction

CITIZENSHIP:

citizenship by birth: no

citizenship by descent only: at least one parent must be a citizen of Croatia

dual citizenship recognized: yes

residency requirement for naturalization: 5 years

SUFFRAGE:

18 years of age; universal

EXECUTIVE BRANCH:

chief of state: President Kolinda GRABAR-KITAROVIC (since 19 February 2015)

head of government: Prime Minister Andrej PLENKOVIC (since 19 October 2016); Deputy Prime Ministers Damir KRSTICEVIC (since 19 October 2016), Predrag STROMAR (since 9 June 2017), Marija Pejcinovic BURIC (since 19 June 2017), and Tomislav TOLUSIC (since 25 May 2018)

cabinet: Council of Ministers named by the prime minister and approved by the Assembly

elections/appointments: president directly elected by absolute majority popular vote in 2 rounds if needed for a 5-year term (eligible for a second term); election last held on 28 December 2014 and 11 January 2015 (next to be held in 2019); the leader of the majority party or majority coalition usually appointed prime minister by the president and approved by the Assembly

election results: Kolinda GRABAR-KITAROVIC elected president in second round; percent of vote - Kolinda GRABAR-KITAROVIC (HDZ) 50.7%, Ivo JOSIPOVIC (Forward Croatia Progressive Alliance) 49.3%

LEGISLATIVE BRANCH:

description: unicameral Assembly or Hrvatski Sabor (151 seats; 140

members in 10 multi-seat constituencies and 3 members in a single constituency for Croatian diaspora directly elected by proportional representation vote using the D'Hondt method with a 5% threshold; an additional 8 members elected from a nationwide constituency by simple majority by voters belonging to minorities recognized by Croatia; the Serb minority elects 3 Assembly members, the Hungarian and Italian minorities elect 1 each, the Czech and Slovak minorities elect 1 jointly, and all other minorities elect 2; all members serve 4-year terms

elections: last held on 11 September 2016 as a snap election following dissolution of the Assembly on 15 July 2016 (next to be held by 23 December 2020)

election results: seats by party as of August 2017 - HDZ 55, SDP 37, MOST-NL 12, HNS 5, GLAS 4, Human Blockade 3, IDS 3, SDSS 3, HDS 2, PH 2, other 7, independent 13; composition as of September 2016 - men 123, women 28, percent of women 18.5%

note: as of August 2017, seats by party - HDZ 55, SDP 37, MOST-NL 12, HNS 5, HSS 5, GLAS 4, Human Blockade 3, IDS 3, SDSS 3, HDS 2, PH 2, other 7, independent 13

JUDICIAL BRANCH:

highest courts: Supreme Court (consists of the court president and vice president, 25 civil department justices, and 16 criminal department justices)

judge selection and term of office: president of Supreme Court nominated by president of Croatia and elected by Croatian Sabor for a 4-year term; other Supreme Court justices appointed by National Judicial Council; all judges serve until age 70

subordinate courts: Administrative Court; county, municipal, and specialized courts; note - there is an 11-member Constitutional Court with jurisdiction limited to constitutional issues but is outside Croatia's judicial system

POLITICAL PARTIES AND LEADERS:

Bloc of Pensioners Together or BUZ [Milivoj SPIKA]
Bridge of Independent Lists or Most-NL [Bozo PETROV]
Civic Liberal Alliance or GLAS [Ankar Mrak TARITAS]
Croatian Christian Democratic Party or HDS [Goran DODIG]
Croatian Democratic Congress of Slavonia and Baranja or HDSSB [Branimir GLAVAS]
Croatian Democratic Union or HDZ [Andrej PLENKOVIC]
Croatian Laborists - Labor Party or HL [David BREGOVAC]
Croatian Party of Rights - Dr. Ante Starcevic or HSP AS [Hrvoje NICE]
Croatian Peasant Party or HSS [Kreso BELJAK]
Croatian Pensioner Party or HSU [Silvano HRELJA]
Croatian People's Party - Liberal Democrats or HNS [Ivan VRDOLJAK]
Croatian Social Liberal Party or HSLS [Darinko KOSOR]
Forward Croatia Progressive Alliance [Ivo JOSIPOVIC]
Human Blockade ("Living Wall") [Ivan SINCIC]
Independent Democratic Serb Party or SDSS [Milorad PUPOVAC]
Istrian Democratic Assembly or IDS [Boris MILETIC]
Let's Change Croatia or PH [Ivan LOVRINOVIC]
Milan Bandic 365 - Party of Labor and Solidarity or BM365-SRS [Milan BANDIC]
Movement for Successful Croatia or HRAST [Ladislav ILCIC]
People's Party - Reformists Party [Radimir CACIC]
Smart Party or PAMETNO [Marijana PULJAK]
Social Democratic Party of Croatia or SDP [Davor BERNARDIC]

INTERNATIONAL ORGANIZATION PARTICIPATION:

Australia Group, BIS, BSEC (observer), CD, CE, CEI, EAPC, EBRD, ECB, EMU, EU, FAO, G-11, IADB, IAEA, IBRD, ICAO, ICC (national committees), ICCt, ICRM, IDA, IFAD, IFC, IFRCS, IHO, ILO, IMF, IMO, IMSO, Interpol, IOC, IOM, IPU, ISO, ITSO, ITU, ITUC (NGOs), MIGA, MINURSO, NAM (observer), NATO, NSG, OAS (observer), OIF (observer), OPCW, OSCE, PCA, SELEC, UN, UNCTAD, UNESCO, UNFICYP, UNHCR, UNIDO, UNIFIL, UNMIL, UNMOGIP, UNWTO, UPU, WCO, WHO, WIPO, WMO, WTO, ZC

DIPLOMATIC REPRESENTATION IN THE US:

chief of mission: Ambassador Pjer SIMUNOVIC (since 8 September 2017)

chancery: 2343 Massachusetts Avenue NW, Washington, DC 20008

telephone: [1] (202) 588-5899

FAX: [1] (202) 588-8936

consulate(s) general: Chicago, Los Angeles, New York

DIPLOMATIC REPRESENTATION FROM THE US:

chief of mission: Ambassador W. Robert KOHORST (since 12 January 2018)

embassy: 2 Thomas Jefferson Street, 10010 Zagreb

mailing address: use embassy street address

telephone: [385] (1) 661-2200

FAX: [385] (1) 661-2373

FLAG DESCRIPTION:

three equal horizontal bands of red (top), white, and blue - the Pan-Slav colors - superimposed by the Croatian coat of arms; the coat of arms consists of one main shield (a checkerboard of 13 red and 12 silver (white) fields) surmounted by five smaller shields that form a crown over the main shield; the five small shields represent five historic regions (from left to right): Croatia, Dubrovnik, Dalmatia, Istria, and Slavonia

note: the Pan-Slav colors were inspired by the 19th-century flag of Russia

NATIONAL SYMBOL(S):

red-white checkerboard; national colors: red, white, blue

NATIONAL ANTHEM:

name: "Lijepa nasa domovino" (Our Beautiful Homeland)

lyrics/music: Antun MIHANOVIC/Josip RUNJANIN

note: adopted in 1972 while still part of Yugoslavia; "Lijepa nasa domovino," whose lyrics were written in 1835, served as an unofficial anthem beginning in 1891

ECONOMY :: CROATIA

ECONOMY - OVERVIEW:

Though still one of the wealthiest of the former Yugoslav republics, Croatia's economy suffered badly during the 1991-95 war. The country's output during that time collapsed, and Croatia missed the early waves of investment in Central and Eastern Europe that followed the fall of the Berlin Wall. Between 2000 and 2007, however, Croatia's economic fortunes began to improve with moderate but steady GDP growth between 4% and 6%, led by a rebound in tourism and credit-driven consumer spending. Inflation over the same period remained tame and the currency, the kuna, stable.

Croatia experienced an abrupt slowdown in the economy in 2008; economic growth was stagnant or negative in each year between 2009 and 2014, but has picked up since the third quarter of 2014, ending 2017 with an average of 2.8% growth. Challenges remain including uneven regional development, a difficult investment climate, an inefficient judiciary, and loss of educated young professionals seeking higher salaries elsewhere in the EU. In 2016, Croatia revised its tax code to stimulate growth from domestic consumption and foreign investment. Income tax reduction began in 2017, and in 2018 various business costs were removed from income tax calculations. At the start of 2018, the government announced its economic reform plan, slated for implementation in 2019.

Tourism is one of the main pillars of the Croatian economy, comprising 19.6% of Croatia's GDP. Croatia is working to become a regional energy hub, and is undertaking plans to open a floating liquefied natural gas (LNG) regasification terminal by the end of 2019 or early in 2020 to import LNG for re-distribution in southeast Europe.

Croatia joined the EU on July 1, 2013, following a decade-long accession process. Croatia has developed a plan for Eurozone accession, and the government projects Croatia will adopt the Euro by 2024. In 2017, the Croatian government decreased public debt to 78% of GDP, from an all-time high of 84% in 2014, and realized a 0.8% budget surplus - the first surplus since independence in 1991. The government has also sought to accelerate privatization of non-strategic assets with mixed success. Croatia's economic recovery is still somewhat fragile; Croatia's largest private company narrowly avoided collapse in 2017, thanks to a capital infusion from an American investor. Restructuring is ongoing, and projected to finish by mid-July 2018.

GDP (PURCHASING POWER PARITY):

$102.1 billion (2017 est.)

$99.37 billion (2016 est.)

$95.97 billion (2015 est.)

note: data are in 2017 dollars

country comparison to the world: 85

GDP (OFFICIAL EXCHANGE RATE):

$54.76 billion (2017 est.) (2017 est.)

GDP - REAL GROWTH RATE:

2.8% (2017 est.)

3.5% (2016 est.)

2.4% (2015 est.)

country comparison to the world: 121

GDP - PER CAPITA (PPP):

$24,700 (2017 est.)

$23,800 (2016 est.)

$22,800 (2015 est.)

note: data are in 2017 dollars

country comparison to the world: 81

GROSS NATIONAL SAVING:

24.7% of GDP (2017 est.)

23.4% of GDP (2016 est.)

24.5% of GDP (2015 est.)

country comparison to the world: 62

GDP - COMPOSITION, BY END USE:

household consumption: 57.3% (2017 est.)

government consumption: 19.5% (2017 est.)

investment in fixed capital: 20% (2017 est.)

investment in inventories: 0% (2017 est.)

exports of goods and services: 51.1% (2017 est.)

imports of goods and services: -48.8% (2017 est.)

GDP - COMPOSITION, BY SECTOR OF ORIGIN:

agriculture: 3.7% (2017 est.)

industry: 26.2% (2017 est.)

services: 70.1% (2017 est.)

AGRICULTURE - PRODUCTS:

arable crops (wheat, corn, barley, sugar beet, sunflower, rapeseed, alfalfa, clover); vegetables (potatoes, cabbage, onion, tomato, pepper); fruits (apples, plum, mandarins, olives), grapes for wine; livestock (cattle, cows, pigs); dairy products

INDUSTRIES:

chemicals and plastics, machine tools, fabricated metal, electronics, pig iron and rolled steel products, aluminum, paper, wood products, construction materials, textiles, shipbuilding, petroleum and petroleum refining, food and beverages, tourism

INDUSTRIAL PRODUCTION GROWTH RATE:

1.2% (2017 est.)

country comparison to the world: 148

LABOR FORCE:

1.559 million (2017 est.)

country comparison to the world: 130

LABOR FORCE - BY OCCUPATION:

agriculture: 1.9%

industry: 27.3%

services: 70.8% (2017 est.)

UNEMPLOYMENT RATE:

12.4% (2017 est.)

15% (2016 est.)

country comparison to the world: 164

POPULATION BELOW POVERTY LINE:

19.5% (2015 est.)

HOUSEHOLD INCOME OR CONSUMPTION BY PERCENTAGE SHARE:

lowest 10%: 23% (2015 est.)

highest 10%: 23% (2015 est.)

DISTRIBUTION OF FAMILY INCOME - GINI INDEX:

30.8 (2015 est.)

32.1 (2014 est.)

country comparison to the world: 127

BUDGET:

revenues: 25.24 billion (2017 est.)

expenditures: 24.83 billion (2017 est.)

TAXES AND OTHER REVENUES:

46.1% (of GDP) (2017 est.)

country comparison to the world: 21

BUDGET SURPLUS (+) OR DEFICIT (-):

0.8% (of GDP) (2017 est.)

country comparison to the world: 35

PUBLIC DEBT:

77.8% of GDP (2017 est.)

82.3% of GDP (2016 est.)

country comparison to the world: 38

FISCAL YEAR:

calendar year

INFLATION RATE (CONSUMER PRICES):

1.1% (2017 est.)

-1.1% (2016 est.)

country comparison to the world: 57

CENTRAL BANK DISCOUNT RATE:

3% (31 December 2017)

3.5% (31 December 2016)

country comparison to the world: 109

COMMERCIAL BANK PRIME LENDING RATE:

4.23% (31 December 2017 est.)

4.97% (31 December 2016 est.)

country comparison to the world: 162

STOCK OF NARROW MONEY:

$14.2 billion (31 December 2017 est.)

$11.64 billion (31 December 2016 est.)

country comparison to the world: 75

STOCK OF BROAD MONEY:

$14.2 billion (31 December 2017 est.)

$11.64 billion (31 December 2016 est.)

country comparison to the world: 76

STOCK OF DOMESTIC CREDIT:

$39.97 billion (31 December 2017 est.)

$41.38 billion (31 December 2016 est.)

country comparison to the world: 70

MARKET VALUE OF PUBLICLY TRADED SHARES:

$18.33 billion (31 December 2017 est.)

$19.98 billion (31 December 2016 est.)

$22.6 billion (31 December 2015 est.)

country comparison to the world: 66

CURRENT ACCOUNT BALANCE:

$2.15 billion (2017 est.)

$1.338 billion (2016 est.)

country comparison to the world: 39

EXPORTS:

$13.15 billion (2017 est.)

$13.88 billion (2016 est.)

country comparison to the world: 82

EXPORTS - PARTNERS:

Italy 13.4%, Germany 12.2%, Slovenia 10.6%, Bosnia and Herzegovina 9.8%, Austria 6.2%, Serbia 4.8% (2017)

EXPORTS - COMMODITIES:

transport equipment, machinery, textiles, chemicals, foodstuffs, fuels

IMPORTS:

$22.34 billion (2017 est.)

$19.76 billion (2016 est.)

country comparison to the world: 72

IMPORTS - COMMODITIES:

machinery, transport and electrical equipment; chemicals, fuels and lubricants; foodstuffs

IMPORTS - PARTNERS:

Germany 15.7%, Italy 12.9%, Slovenia 10.7%, Hungary 7.5%, Austria 7.5% (2017)

RESERVES OF FOREIGN EXCHANGE AND GOLD:

$18.82 billion (31 December 2017 est.)

$14.24 billion (31 December 2016 est.)

country comparison to the world: 60

DEBT - EXTERNAL:

$48.1 billion (31 December 2017 est.)

$46.96 billion (31 December 2016 est.)

country comparison to the world: 67

STOCK OF DIRECT FOREIGN INVESTMENT - AT HOME:

$43.71 billion (31 December 2017 est.)

$35.65 billion (31 December 2016 est.)

country comparison to the world: 61

STOCK OF DIRECT FOREIGN INVESTMENT - ABROAD:

$8.473 billion (31 December 2017 est.)

$6.358 billion (31 December 2016 est.)

country comparison to the world: 67

EXCHANGE RATES:

kuna (HRK) per US dollar -

6.62 (2017 est.)

6.8 (2016 est.)

6.806 (2015 est.)

6.8583 (2014 est.)

5.7482 (2013 est.)

ENERGY :: CROATIA

ELECTRICITY ACCESS:

electrification - total population: 100% (2016)

ELECTRICITY - PRODUCTION:

12.2 billion kWh (2016 est.)

country comparison to the world: 95

ELECTRICITY - CONSUMPTION:

15.93 billion kWh (2016 est.)

country comparison to the world: 76

ELECTRICITY - EXPORTS:

3.2 billion kWh (2016 est.)

country comparison to the world: 42

ELECTRICITY - IMPORTS:

8.702 billion kWh (2016 est.)

country comparison to the world: 28

ELECTRICITY - INSTALLED GENERATING CAPACITY:

4.921 million kW (2016 est.)

country comparison to the world: 80

ELECTRICITY - FROM FOSSIL FUELS:

45% of total installed capacity (2016 est.)

country comparison to the world: 160

ELECTRICITY - FROM NUCLEAR FUELS:

0% of total installed capacity (2017 est.)

country comparison to the world: 74

ELECTRICITY - FROM HYDROELECTRIC PLANTS:

40% of total installed capacity (2017 est.)

country comparison to the world: 52

ELECTRICITY - FROM OTHER RENEWABLE SOURCES:

16% of total installed capacity (2017 est.)

country comparison to the world: 50

CRUDE OIL - PRODUCTION:

14,000 bbl/day (2017 est.)

country comparison to the world: 73

CRUDE OIL - EXPORTS:

0 bbl/day (2015 est.)

country comparison to the world: 110

CRUDE OIL - IMPORTS:

55,400 bbl/day (2015 est.)

country comparison to the world: 55

CRUDE OIL - PROVED RESERVES:

71 million bbl (1 January 2018 est.)

country comparison to the world: 74

REFINED PETROLEUM PRODUCTS - PRODUCTION:

74,620 bbl/day (2015 est.)

country comparison to the world: 70

REFINED PETROLEUM PRODUCTS - CONSUMPTION:

73,000 bbl/day (2016 est.)

country comparison to the world: 91

REFINED PETROLEUM PRODUCTS - EXPORTS:

40,530 bbl/day (2015 est.)

country comparison to the world: 58

REFINED PETROLEUM PRODUCTS - IMPORTS:

35,530 bbl/day (2015 est.)

country comparison to the world: 94

NATURAL GAS - PRODUCTION:

1.048 billion cu m (2017 est.)

country comparison to the world: 67

NATURAL GAS - CONSUMPTION:

2.577 billion cu m (2017 est.)

country comparison to the world: 77

NATURAL GAS - EXPORTS:

172.7 million cu m (2017 est.)

country comparison to the world: 46

NATURAL GAS - IMPORTS:

1.841 billion cu m (2017 est.)

country comparison to the world: 54

NATURAL GAS - PROVED RESERVES:

24.92 billion cu m (1 January 2018 est.)

country comparison to the world: 71

CARBON DIOXIDE EMISSIONS FROM CONSUMPTION OF ENERGY:

17.96 million Mt (2017 est.)

country comparison to the world: 89

COMMUNICATIONS :: CROATIA

TELEPHONES - FIXED LINES:

total subscriptions: 1,401,354 (2017 est.)

subscriptions per 100 inhabitants: 33 (2017 est.)

country comparison to the world: 64

TELEPHONES - MOBILE CELLULAR:

total subscriptions: 4,315,580 (2017 est.)

subscriptions per 100 inhabitants: 101 (2017 est.)

country comparison to the world: 125

TELEPHONE SYSTEM:

general assessment: the telecommunications network has improved steadily since the mid-1990s, covering much of what were once inaccessible areas; local lines are digital; telecoms market in Croatia has been shaped by Croatia becoming part of the European Union in 2013, a process which opened up the market and the creation of a regulatory environment leading to competition; mobile market has one of the highest penetration rates in the Balkans region; Government abolishes 6% tax on mobile services revenue; trials 5G technologies (2017)

domestic: fixed-line teledensity has dropped somewhat to about 33 per 100 persons; mobile-cellular telephone subscriptions 101 per 100 (2017)

international: country code - 385; digital international service is provided through the main switch in Zagreb; Croatia participates in the Trans-Asia-Europe fiber-optic project, which consists of 2 fiber-optic trunk connections with Slovenia and a fiber-optic trunk line from Rijeka to Split and Dubrovnik; the ADRIA-1 submarine cable provides connectivity to Albania and Greece (2016)

BROADCAST MEDIA:

the national state-owned public broadcaster, Croatian Radiotelevision, operates 4 terrestrial TV networks, a satellite channel that rebroadcasts programs for Croatians living abroad, and 6 regional TV centers; 2 private broadcasters operate national terrestrial networks; roughly 25 privately owned regional TV stations; multi-channel cable and satellite TV subscription services are available; state-owned public broadcaster operates 3 national radio networks and 9 regional radio stations; 2 privately owned national radio networks and more than 170 regional, county, city, and community radio stations (2012)

INTERNET COUNTRY CODE:

.hr

INTERNET USERS:

total: 3,135,949 (July 2016 est.)

percent of population: 72.7% (July 2016 est.)

country comparison to the world: 96

BROADBAND - FIXED SUBSCRIPTIONS:

total: 1,095,881 (2017 est.)

subscriptions per 100 inhabitants: 26 (2017 est.)

country comparison to the world: 69

TRANSPORTATION :: CROATIA

NATIONAL AIR TRANSPORT SYSTEM:

number of registered air carriers: 3 (2015)

inventory of registered aircraft operated by air carriers: 46 (2015)

annual passenger traffic on registered air carriers: 1,782,666 (2015)

annual freight traffic on registered air carriers: 775,320 mt-km (2015)

CIVIL AIRCRAFT REGISTRATION COUNTRY CODE PREFIX:

9A (2016)

AIRPORTS:

69 (2013)

country comparison to the world: 72

AIRPORTS - WITH PAVED RUNWAYS:

total: 24 (2017)

over 3,047 m: 2 (2017)

2,438 to 3,047 m: 6 (2017)

1,524 to 2,437 m: 3 (2017)

914 to 1,523 m: 3 (2017)

under 914 m: 10 (2017)

AIRPORTS - WITH UNPAVED RUNWAYS:

total: 45 (2013)

1,524 to 2,437 m: 1 (2013)

914 to 1,523 m: 6 (2013)

under 914 m: 38 (2013)

HELIPORTS:

1 (2013)

PIPELINES:

2410 km gas, 610 km oil (2011)

RAILWAYS:

total: 2,722 km (2014)

standard gauge: 2,722 km 1.435-m gauge (985 km electrified) (2014)

country comparison to the world: 64

ROADWAYS:

total: 26,958 km (includes 1,416 km of expressways) (2015)

country comparison to the world: 99

WATERWAYS:

785 km (2009)

country comparison to the world: 73

MERCHANT MARINE:

total: 288 (2017)

by type: bulk carrier 17, general cargo 39, oil tanker 18, other 214 (2017)

country comparison to the world: 54

PORTS AND TERMINALS:

major seaport(s): Ploce, Rijeka, Sibenik, Split

oil terminal(s): Omisalj

river port(s): Vukovar (Danube)

MILITARY AND SECURITY :: CROATIA

MILITARY EXPENDITURES:

1.27% of GDP (2017)

1.38% of GDP (2016)

1.55% of GDP (2015)

country comparison to the world: 90

MILITARY BRANCHES:

Armed Forces of the Republic of Croatia (Oruzane Snage Republike Hrvatske, OSRH) consists of five major commands directly subordinate to a General Staff: Ground Forces (Hrvatska Kopnena Vojska, HKoV), Naval Forces (Hrvatska Ratna Mornarica, HRM, includes coast guard), Air Force and Air Defense Command (Hrvatsko Ratno Zrakoplovstvo I Protuzracna Obrana),

Joint Education and Training Command, Logistics Command; Military Police Force supports each of the three Croatian military forces (2017)

MILITARY SERVICE AGE AND OBLIGATION:

18-27 years of age for voluntary military service; conscription abolished in 2008 (2017)

TRANSNATIONAL ISSUES :: CROATIA

DISPUTES - INTERNATIONAL:

dispute remains with Bosnia and Herzegovina over several small sections of the boundary related to maritime access that hinders ratification of the 1999 border agreementsince the breakup of Yugoslavia in the early 1990s, Croatia and Slovenia have each claimed sovereignty over Piranski Bay and four villages, and Slovenia has objected to Croatia's claim of an exclusive economic zone in the Adriatic Sea; in 2009, however Croatia and Slovenia signed a binding international arbitration agreement to define their disputed land and maritime borders, which led to Slovenia lifting its objections to Croatia joining the EU; Slovenia continues to impose a hard border Schengen regime with Croatia, which joined the EU in 2013 but has not yet fulfilled Schengen requirementsSerbia and Croatia have an unresolved border dispute along the Danube river and numerous other unresolved bilateral issues dating back to the conflicts in the 1990s

REFUGEES AND INTERNALLY DISPLACED PERSONS:

stateless persons: 2,873 (2017)

note: 659,105 estimated refugee and migrant arrivals (January 2015-December 2016); flows have slowed considerably in 2017; Croatia is predominantly a transit country and hosts about 340 asylum seekers as of the end of June 2018

ILLICIT DRUGS:

primarily a transit country along the Balkan route for maritime shipments of South American cocaine bound for Western Europe and other illicit drugs and chemical precursors to and from Western Europe; no significant domestic production of illicit drugs

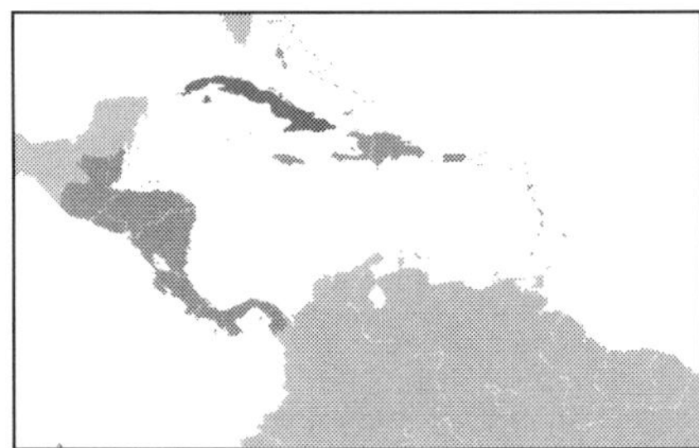

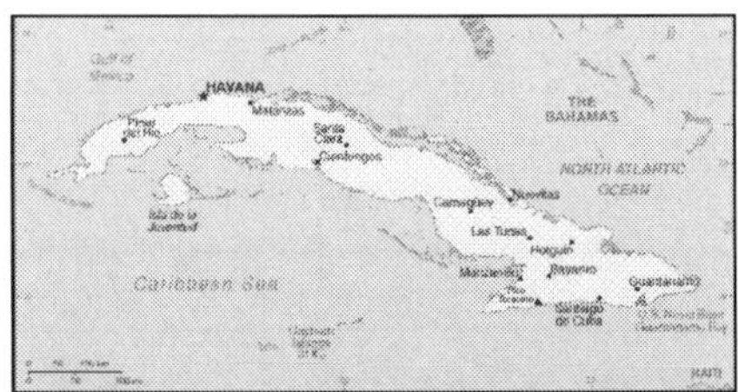

CENTRAL AMERICA :: CUBA

INTRODUCTION :: CUBA

BACKGROUND:

The native Amerindian population of Cuba began to decline after the European discovery of the island by Christopher COLUMBUS in 1492 and following its development as a Spanish colony during the next several centuries. Large numbers of African slaves were imported to work the coffee and sugar plantations, and Havana became the launching point for the annual treasure fleets bound for Spain from Mexico and Peru. Spanish rule eventually provoked an independence movement and occasional rebellions that were harshly suppressed. US intervention during the Spanish-American War in 1898 assisted the Cubans in overthrowing Spanish rule. The Treaty of Paris established Cuban independence from Spain in 1898 and, following three-and-a-half years of subsequent US military rule, Cuba became an independent republic in 1902 after which the island experienced a string of governments mostly dominated by the military and corrupt politicians. Fidel CASTRO led a rebel army to victory in 1959; his authoritarian rule held the subsequent regime together for nearly five decades. He stepped down as president in February 2008 in favor of his younger brother Raul CASTRO. Cuba's communist revolution, with Soviet support, was exported throughout Latin America and Africa during the 1960s, 1970s, and 1980s. On 8-9 September 2017, Hurricane Irma passed along the north coast of Cuba causing extensive damage to structures, roads, and power supplies. Miguel DIAZ-CANEL Bermudez, hand-picked by Raul CASTRO to succeed him, was approved as president by the National Assembly and took office on 19 April 2018.

The country faced a severe economic downturn in 1990 following the withdrawal of former Soviet subsidies worth $4-6 billion annually. Cuba at times portrays the US embargo, in place since 1961, as the source of its difficulties. Over the past decade, there has been growing communication with the Cuban Government to address national interests. As a result of efforts begun in December 2014 to re-establish diplomatic relations with the Cuban Government, which were severed in January 1961, the US and Cuba reopened embassies in their respective countries on 20 July 2015. However, the embargo remains in place.

Illicit migration of Cuban nationals to the US via maritime and overland routes has been a longstanding challenge. On 12 January 2017, the US and Cuba signed a Joint Statement ending the so-called "wet-foot, dry-foot" policy – by which Cuban nationals who reached US soil were permitted to stay – facilitating the repatriation of Cuban migrants. Illicit Cuban migration has since dropped significantly. In FY 2017, the US Coast Guard interdicted 1,606 Cuban nationals at sea. Also in FY 2017, 20,995 Cuban migrants presented themselves at various land border ports of entry throughout the US.

GEOGRAPHY :: CUBA

LOCATION:

Caribbean, island between the Caribbean Sea and the North Atlantic Ocean, 150 km south of Key West, Florida

GEOGRAPHIC COORDINATES:

21 30 N, 80 00 W

MAP REFERENCES:

Central America and the Caribbean

AREA:

total: 110,860 sq km

land: 109,820 sq km

water: 1,040 sq km

country comparison to the world: 107

AREA - COMPARATIVE:

slightly smaller than Pennsylvania

LAND BOUNDARIES:

total: 28.5 km

border countries (1): US Naval Base at Guantanamo Bay 28.5 km

note: Guantanamo Naval Base is leased by the US and remains part of Cuba

COASTLINE:

3,735 km

MARITIME CLAIMS:

territorial sea: 12 nm

exclusive economic zone: 200 nm

contiguous zone: 24 nm

CLIMATE:

tropical; moderated by trade winds; dry season (November to April); rainy season (May to October)

TERRAIN:

mostly flat to rolling plains, with rugged hills and mountains in the southeast

ELEVATION:

mean elevation: 108 m

elevation extremes: 0 m lowest point: Caribbean Sea

1974 highest point: Pico Turquino

NATURAL RESOURCES:

cobalt, nickel, iron ore, chromium, copper, salt, timber, silica, petroleum, arable land

LAND USE:

agricultural land: 60.3% (2011 est.)

arable land: 33.8% (2011 est.) / permanent crops: 3.6% (2011 est.) / permanent pasture: 22.9% (2011 est.)

forest: 27.3% (2011 est.)

other: 12.4% (2011 est.)

IRRIGATED LAND:

8,700 sq km (2012)

POPULATION DISTRIBUTION:

large population clusters found throughout the country, the more significant ones being in the larger towns and cities, particularly the capital of Havana

NATURAL HAZARDS:

the east coast is subject to hurricanes from August to November (in general, the country averages about one hurricane every other year); droughts are common

ENVIRONMENT - CURRENT ISSUES:

soil degradation and desertification (brought on by poor farming techniques and natural disasters) are the main environmental problems; biodiversity loss; deforestation; air and water pollution

ENVIRONMENT - INTERNATIONAL AGREEMENTS:

party to: Antarctic Treaty, Biodiversity, Climate Change, Climate Change-Kyoto Protocol, Desertification, Endangered Species, Environmental Modification, Hazardous Wastes, Law of the Sea, Marine Dumping, Ozone Layer Protection, Ship Pollution, Wetlands

signed, but not ratified: Marine Life Conservation

GEOGRAPHY - NOTE:

largest country in Caribbean and westernmost island of the Greater Antilles

PEOPLE AND SOCIETY :: CUBA

POPULATION:

11,116,396 (July 2018 est.)

country comparison to the world: 82

NATIONALITY:

noun: Cuban(s)

adjective: Cuban

ETHNIC GROUPS:

white 64.1%, mulatto or mixed 26.6%, black 9.3% (2012 est.)

note: data represent racial self-identification from Cuba's 2012 national census

LANGUAGES:

Spanish (official)

RELIGIONS:

nominally Roman Catholic 85%, Protestant, Jehovah's Witnesses, Jewish, Santeria

note: prior to CASTRO assuming power

AGE STRUCTURE:

0-14 years: 16.44% (male 940,787 /female 886,996)

15-24 years: 12.1% (male 698,220 /female 646,684)

25-54 years: 43.69% (male 2,443,190 /female 2,414,119)

55-64 years: 12.54% (male 677,304 /female 716,704)

65 years and over: 15.22% (male 773,636 /female 918,756) (2018 est.)

DEPENDENCY RATIOS:

total dependency ratio: 43.3 (2015 est.)

youth dependency ratio: 23.3 (2015 est.)

elderly dependency ratio: 19.9 (2015 est.)

potential support ratio: 5 (2015 est.)

MEDIAN AGE:

total: 41.8 years

male: 40.2 years

female: 43.1 years (2018 est.)

country comparison to the world: 36

POPULATION GROWTH RATE:

-0.27% (2018 est.)

country comparison to the world: 215

BIRTH RATE:

10.6 births/1,000 population (2018 est.)

country comparison to the world: 185

DEATH RATE:

8.9 deaths/1,000 population (2018 est.)

country comparison to the world: 63

NET MIGRATION RATE:

-4.9 migrant(s)/1,000 population (2017 est.)

country comparison to the world: 190

POPULATION DISTRIBUTION:

large population clusters found throughout the country, the more significant ones being in the larger towns and cities, particularly the capital of Havana

URBANIZATION:

urban population: 77% of total population (2018)

rate of urbanization: 0.14% annual rate of change (2015-20 est.)

MAJOR URBAN AREAS - POPULATION:

2.136 million HAVANA (capital) (2018)

SEX RATIO:

at birth: 1.06 male(s)/female (2017 est.)

0-14 years: 1.06 male(s)/female (2017 est.)

15-24 years: 1.08 male(s)/female (2017 est.)

25-54 years: 1.01 male(s)/female (2017 est.)

55-64 years: 0.94 male(s)/female (2017 est.)

65 years and over: 0.81 male(s)/female (2017 est.)

total population: 0.99 male(s)/female (2017 est.)

MATERNAL MORTALITY RATE:

39 deaths/100,000 live births (2015 est.)

country comparison to the world: 106

INFANT MORTALITY RATE:

total: 4.4 deaths/1,000 live births (2018 est.)

male: 4.9 deaths/1,000 live births (2018 est.)

female: 3.9 deaths/1,000 live births (2018 est.)

country comparison to the world: 182

LIFE EXPECTANCY AT BIRTH:

total population: 78.9 years (2018 est.)

male: 76.6 years (2018 est.)

female: 81.4 years (2018 est.)

country comparison to the world: 56

TOTAL FERTILITY RATE:

1.71 children born/woman (2018 est.)

country comparison to the world: 170

CONTRACEPTIVE PREVALENCE RATE:

73.7% (2014)

HEALTH EXPENDITURES:

11.1% of GDP (2014)

country comparison to the world: 12

PHYSICIANS DENSITY:

7.52 physicians/1,000 population (2014)

HOSPITAL BED DENSITY:

5.2 beds/1,000 population (2014)

DRINKING WATER SOURCE:

improved:

urban: 96.4% of population (2015 est.)

rural: 89.8% of population (2015 est.)

total: 94.9% of population (2015 est.)

unimproved:

urban: 3.6% of population (2015 est.)

rural: 10.2% of population (2015 est.)

total: 5.1% of population (2015 est.)

SANITATION FACILITY ACCESS:

improved:

urban: 94.4% of population (2015 est.)

rural: 89.1% of population (2015 est.)

total: 93.2% of population (2015 est.)

unimproved:

urban: 5.6% of population (2015 est.)

rural: 10.9% of population (2015 est.)

total: 6.8% of population (2015 est.)

HIV/AIDS - ADULT PREVALENCE RATE:

0.4% (2017 est.)

country comparison to the world: 71

HIV/AIDS - PEOPLE LIVING WITH HIV/AIDS:

30,000 (2017 est.)

country comparison to the world: 72

HIV/AIDS - DEATHS:

<500 (2017 est.)

MAJOR INFECTIOUS DISEASES:

degree of risk: intermediate (2016)

food or waterborne diseases: bacterial diarrhea and hepatitis A (2016)

vectorborne diseases: dengue fever (2016)

note: active local transmission of Zika virus by Aedes species mosquitoes has been identified in this country (as of August 2016); it poses an important risk (a large number of cases possible) among US citizens if bitten by an infective mosquito; other less common ways to get Zika are through sex, via blood transfusion, or during pregnancy, in which the pregnant woman passes Zika virus to her fetus

OBESITY - ADULT PREVALENCE RATE:

24.6% (2016)

country comparison to the world: 56

EDUCATION EXPENDITURES:

12.8% of GDP (2010)

country comparison to the world: 1

LITERACY:

definition: age 15 and over can read and write (2015 est.)

total population: 99.8% (2015 est.)

male: 99.9% (2015 est.)

female: 99.8% (2015 est.)

SCHOOL LIFE EXPECTANCY (PRIMARY TO TERTIARY EDUCATION):

total: 14 years (2015)

male: 13 years (2015)

female: 14 years (2015)

UNEMPLOYMENT, YOUTH AGES 15-24:

total: 6.1% (2010 est.)

male: 6.4% (2010 est.)

female: 5.6% (2010 est.)

country comparison to the world: 150

PEOPLE - NOTE:

illicit emigration is a continuing problem; Cubans attempt to depart the island and enter the US using homemade rafts, alien smugglers, direct flights, or falsified visas; Cubans also use non-maritime routes to enter the US including direct flights to Miami and overland via the southwest border; the number of Cubans migrating to the US surged after the announcement of normalization of US-Cuban relations in late December 2014 but has decreased since the end of the so-called "wet-foot, dry-foot" policy on 12 January 2017

GOVERNMENT :: CUBA

COUNTRY NAME:

conventional long form: Republic of Cuba

conventional short form: Cuba

local long form: Republica de Cuba

local short form: Cuba

etymology: name derives from the Taino Indian designation for the island "coabana" meaning "great place"

GOVERNMENT TYPE:

communist state

CAPITAL:

name: Havana

geographic coordinates: 23 07 N, 82 21 W

time difference: UTC-5 (same time as Washington, DC, during Standard Time)

daylight saving time: +1hr, begins second Sunday in March; ends first Sunday in November; note - Cuba has been known to alter the schedule of DST on short notice in an attempt to conserve electricity for lighting

ADMINISTRATIVE DIVISIONS:

15 provinces (provincias, singular - provincia) and 1 special municipality* (municipio especial); Artemisa, Camaguey, Ciego de Avila, Cienfuegos, Granma, Guantanamo, Holguin, Isla de la Juventud*, La Habana, Las Tunas, Matanzas, Mayabeque, Pinar del Rio, Sancti Spiritus, Santiago de Cuba, Villa Clara

INDEPENDENCE:

20 May 1902 (from Spain 10 December 1898; administered by the US from 1898 to 1902); not acknowledged by the Cuban Government as a day of independence

NATIONAL HOLIDAY:

Triumph of the Revolution (Liberation Day), 1 January (1959)

CONSTITUTION:

history: several previous; latest adopted by referendum 15 February 1976, effective 24 February 1976; note - in early June 2018, the Cuban Government announced that Raul CASTRO would head a commission to rewrite the country's constitution (2018)

amendments: proposed by the National Assembly of People's Power; passage requires approval of at least two-thirds majority of the National Assembly membership; amendments to constitutional articles on the authorities of the National Assembly, Council of State, or any rights and duties in the constitution also require approval in a referendum; constitutional articles on the Cuban political, social, and economic system cannot be amended; amended 1978, 1992, 2002 (2018)

LEGAL SYSTEM:

civil law system based on Spanish civil code

INTERNATIONAL LAW ORGANIZATION PARTICIPATION:

has not submitted an ICJ jurisdiction declaration; non-party state to the ICCt

CITIZENSHIP:

citizenship by birth: yes

citizenship by descent only: yes

dual citizenship recognized: no

residency requirement for naturalization: unknown

SUFFRAGE:

16 years of age; universal

EXECUTIVE BRANCH:

chief of state: President of the Council of State and President of the Council of Ministers Miguel DIAZ-CANEL Bermudez (since 19 April 2018); First Vice President of the Council of State and First Vice President of the Council of Ministers Salvador Antonio VALDES Mesa (since 19 April 2018); note - the president is both chief of state and head of government

head of government: President of the Council of State and President of the Council of Ministers Miguel DIAZ-CANEL Bermudez (since 19 April 2018); First Vice President of the Council of State and First Vice President of the Council of Ministers Salvador Antonio VALDES Mesa (since 19 April 2018)

cabinet: Council of Ministers proposed by the president of the Council of State and appointed by the National Assembly; it is subordinate to the 31-member Council of State, which is elected by the Assembly to act on its behalf when it is not in session

elections/appointments: president and vice presidents indirectly elected by the National Assembly for a 5-year term (may be reelected for another 5-year term); election last held on 19 April 2018 (next to be held in 2023)

election results: Miguel DIAZ-CANEL Bermudez (PCC) elected president; percent of National Assembly vote - 98.8%; Salvador Antonio VALDES Mesa (PCC) elected vice president; percent of National Assembly vote - 100%

LEGISLATIVE BRANCH:

description: unicameral National Assembly of People's Power or Asamblea Nacional del Poder Popular (605 seats; members directly elected by absolute majority vote; members serve 5-year terms); note - the National Candidature Commission submits a slate of approved candidates; to be elected, candidates must receive more than 50% of valid votes otherwise the seat remains vacant or the Council of State can declare another election

elections: last held on 11 March 2018 (next to be held in early 2023)

election results: Cuba's Communist Party is the only legal party, and officially sanctioned candidates run unopposed

JUDICIAL BRANCH:

highest courts: People's Supreme Court (consists of court president, vice president, 41 professional justices, and NA lay judges); organization includes the State Council, criminal, civil, administrative, labor, crimes against the state, and military courts)

judge selection and term of office: professional judges elected by the National Assembly are not subject to a specific term; lay judges nominated by workplace collectives and neighborhood associations and elected by municipal or provincial assemblies; lay judges appointed for 5-year terms and serve up to 30 days per year

subordinate courts: People's Provincial Courts; People's Regional Courts; People's Courts

POLITICAL PARTIES AND LEADERS:

Cuban Communist Party or PCC [Raul CASTRO Ruz]

INTERNATIONAL ORGANIZATION PARTICIPATION:

ACP, ALBA, AOSIS, CELAC, FAO, G-77, IAEA, ICAO, ICC (national committees), ICRM, IFAD, IFRCS, IHO, ILO, IMO, IMSO, Interpol, IOC, IOM (observer), IPU, ISO, ITSO, ITU, LAES, LAIA, NAM, OAS (excluded from formal participation since 1962), OPANAL, OPCW, PCA, Petrocaribe, PIF (partner), UN, UNCTAD, UNESCO, UNIDO, Union Latina, UNWTO, UPU, WCO, WFTU (NGOs), WHO, WIPO, WMO, WTO

DIPLOMATIC REPRESENTATION IN THE US:

chief of mission: Ambassador Jose Ramon CABANAS Rodriguez (since 17 September 2015)

chancery: 2630 16th Street NW, Washington, DC 20009

telephone: [1] (202) 797-8518

FAX: NA

consulate(s) general: NA

DIPLOMATIC REPRESENTATION FROM THE US:

chief of mission: Ambassador (vacant); Charge d'Affaires Phillip GOLDBERG (Since February 2018)

embassy: Calzada between L & M Streets, Vedado, Havana

mailing address: use embassy street address

telephone: [53] (7) 839-4100

FAX: NA

FLAG DESCRIPTION:

five equal horizontal bands of blue (top, center, and bottom) alternating with white; a red equilateral triangle based on the hoist side bears a white, five-pointed star in the center; the blue bands refer to the three old divisions of the island: central, occidental, and oriental; the white bands describe the purity of the independence ideal; the triangle symbolizes liberty, equality, and fraternity, while the red color stands for the blood shed in the independence struggle; the white star, called La Estrella Solitaria (the Lone Star) lights the way to freedom and was taken from the flag of Texas

note: design similar to the Puerto Rican flag, with the colors of the bands and triangle reversed

NATIONAL SYMBOL(S):

royal palm; national colors: red, white, blue

NATIONAL ANTHEM:

name: "La Bayamesa" (The Bayamo Song)

lyrics/music: Pedro FIGUEREDO

note: adopted 1940; Pedro FIGUEREDO first performed "La Bayamesa" in 1868 during the Ten Years War against the Spanish; a leading figure in the uprising, FIGUEREDO was captured in 1870 and executed by a firing squad; just prior to the fusillade he is reputed to have shouted, "Morir por la Patria es vivir" (To die for the country is to live), a line from the anthem

ECONOMY :: CUBA

ECONOMY - OVERVIEW:

The government continues to balance the need for loosening its socialist economic system against a desire for firm political control. In April 2011, the government held the first Cuban Communist Party Congress in almost 13 years, during which leaders approved a plan for wide-ranging economic changes. Since then, the government has slowly and incrementally implemented limited economic reforms, including allowing Cubans to buy electronic appliances and cell phones, stay in hotels, and buy and sell used cars. The government has cut state sector jobs as part of the reform process, and it has opened up some retail services to "self-employment," leading to the rise of so-called "cuentapropistas" or entrepreneurs. More than 500,000

Cuban workers are currently registered as self-employed.

The Cuban regime has updated its economic model to include permitting the private ownership and sale of real estate and new vehicles, allowing private farmers to sell agricultural goods directly to hotels, allowing the creation of non-agricultural cooperatives, adopting a new foreign investment law, and launching a "Special Development Zone" around the Mariel port.

Since 2016, Cuba has attributed slowed economic growth in part to problems with petroleum product deliveries from Venezuela. Since late 2000, Venezuela provided petroleum products to Cuba on preferential terms, supplying at times nearly 100,000 barrels per day. Cuba paid for the oil, in part, with the services of Cuban personnel in Venezuela, including some 30,000 medical professionals.

GDP (PURCHASING POWER PARITY):

$137 billion (2017 est.)

$134.8 billion (2016 est.)

$134.2 billion (2015 est.)

note: data are in 2016 US dollars

country comparison to the world: 79

GDP (OFFICIAL EXCHANGE RATE):

$93.79 billion (2017 est.) (2017 est.)

note: data are in Cuban Pesos at 1 CUP = 1 US$; official exchange rate

GDP - REAL GROWTH RATE:

1.6% (2017 est.)

0.5% (2016 est.)

4.4% (2015 est.)

country comparison to the world: 167

GDP - PER CAPITA (PPP):

$12,300 (2016 est.)

$12,200 (2015 est.)

$12,100 (2014 est.)

note: data are in 2016 US dollars

country comparison to the world: 128

GROSS NATIONAL SAVING:

11.4% of GDP (2017 est.)

12.3% of GDP (2016 est.)

12.1% of GDP (2015 est.)

country comparison to the world: 156

GDP - COMPOSITION, BY END USE:

household consumption: 57% (2017 est.)

government consumption: 31.6% (2017 est.)

investment in fixed capital: 9.6% (2017 est.)

investment in inventories: 0% (2017 est.)

exports of goods and services: 14.6% (2017 est.)

imports of goods and services: -12.7% (2017 est.)

GDP - COMPOSITION, BY SECTOR OF ORIGIN:

agriculture: 4% (2017 est.)

industry: 22.7% (2017 est.)

services: 73.4% (2017 est.)

AGRICULTURE - PRODUCTS:

sugar, tobacco, citrus, coffee, rice, potatoes, beans; livestock

INDUSTRIES:

petroleum, nickel, cobalt, pharmaceuticals, tobacco, construction, steel, cement, agricultural machinery, sugar

INDUSTRIAL PRODUCTION GROWTH RATE:

-1.2% (2017 est.)

country comparison to the world: 179

LABOR FORCE:

4.691 million (2017 est.)

note: state sector 72.3%, non-state sector 27.7%

country comparison to the world: 86

LABOR FORCE - BY OCCUPATION:

agriculture: 18%

industry: 10%

services: 72% (2016 est.)

UNEMPLOYMENT RATE:

2.6% (2017 est.)

2.4% (2016 est.)

note: data are official rates; unofficial estimates are about double

country comparison to the world: 27

POPULATION BELOW POVERTY LINE:

NA

HOUSEHOLD INCOME OR CONSUMPTION BY PERCENTAGE SHARE:

lowest 10%: NA

highest 10%: NA

BUDGET:

revenues: 54.52 billion (2017 est.)

expenditures: 64.64 billion (2017 est.)

TAXES AND OTHER REVENUES:

58.1% (of GDP) (2017 est.)

country comparison to the world: 8

BUDGET SURPLUS (+) OR DEFICIT (-):

-10.8% (of GDP) (2017 est.)

country comparison to the world: 214

PUBLIC DEBT:

47.7% of GDP (2017 est.)

42.7% of GDP (2016 est.)

country comparison to the world: 110

FISCAL YEAR:

calendar year

INFLATION RATE (CONSUMER PRICES):

5.5% (2017 est.)

4.5% (2016 est.)

country comparison to the world: 178

CENTRAL BANK DISCOUNT RATE:

NA

COMMERCIAL BANK PRIME LENDING RATE:

NA

STOCK OF NARROW MONEY:

$23.26 billion (31 December 2017 est.)

$21.92 billion (31 December 2016 est.)

country comparison to the world: 66

STOCK OF BROAD MONEY:

$23.26 billion (31 December 2017 est.)

$21.92 billion (31 December 2016 est.)

country comparison to the world: 66

STOCK OF DOMESTIC CREDIT:

NA

CURRENT ACCOUNT BALANCE:

$985.4 million (2017 est.)

$2.008 billion (2016 est.)

country comparison to the world: 50

EXPORTS:

$2.63 billion (2017 est.)

$2.546 billion (2016 est.)

country comparison to the world: 132

EXPORTS - PARTNERS:

Venezuela 17.8%, Spain 12.2%, Russia 7.9%, Lebanon 6.1%, Indonesia 4.5%, Germany 4.3% (2017)

EXPORTS - COMMODITIES:

petroleum, nickel, medical products, sugar, tobacco, fish, citrus, coffee

IMPORTS:

$11.06 billion (2017 est.)

$10.28 billion (2016 est.)

country comparison to the world: 99

IMPORTS - COMMODITIES:

petroleum, food, machinery and equipment, chemicals

IMPORTS - PARTNERS:

China 22%, Spain 14%, Russia 5%, Brazil 5%, Mexico 4.9%, Italy 4.8%, US 4.5% (2017)

RESERVES OF FOREIGN EXCHANGE AND GOLD:

$11.35 billion (31 December 2017 est.)

$12.3 billion (31 December 2016 est.)

country comparison to the world: 72

DEBT - EXTERNAL:

$30.06 billion (31 December 2017 est.)

$29.89 billion (31 December 2016 est.)

country comparison to the world: 80

STOCK OF DIRECT FOREIGN INVESTMENT - AT HOME:

NA

STOCK OF DIRECT FOREIGN INVESTMENT - ABROAD:

$4.138 billion (2006 est.)

country comparison to the world: 77

EXCHANGE RATES:

Cuban pesos (CUP) per US dollar -

1 (2017 est.)

1 (2016 est.)

1 (2015 est.)

1 (2014 est.)

22.7 (2013 est.)

ENERGY :: CUBA

ELECTRICITY ACCESS:

population without electricity: 200,000 (2013)

electrification - total population: 99.9% (2013)

electrification - urban areas: 100% (2013)

electrification - rural areas: 95% (2013)

ELECTRICITY - PRODUCTION:

19.28 billion kWh (2016 est.)

country comparison to the world: 76

ELECTRICITY - CONSUMPTION:

16.16 billion kWh (2016 est.)

country comparison to the world: 75

ELECTRICITY - EXPORTS:

0 kWh (2016 est.)

country comparison to the world: 124

ELECTRICITY - IMPORTS:

0 kWh (2016 est.)

country comparison to the world: 138

ELECTRICITY - INSTALLED GENERATING CAPACITY:

6.998 million kW (2016 est.)

country comparison to the world: 74

ELECTRICITY - FROM FOSSIL FUELS:

91% of total installed capacity (2016 est.)

country comparison to the world: 53

ELECTRICITY - FROM NUCLEAR FUELS:

0% of total installed capacity (2017 est.)

country comparison to the world: 75

ELECTRICITY - FROM HYDROELECTRIC PLANTS:

1% of total installed capacity (2017 est.)

country comparison to the world: 147

ELECTRICITY - FROM OTHER RENEWABLE SOURCES:

8% of total installed capacity (2017 est.)

country comparison to the world: 85

CRUDE OIL - PRODUCTION:

50,000 bbl/day (2017 est.)

country comparison to the world: 51

CRUDE OIL - EXPORTS:

0 bbl/day (2015 est.)

country comparison to the world: 111

CRUDE OIL - IMPORTS:

112,400 bbl/day (2015 est.)

country comparison to the world: 41

CRUDE OIL - PROVED RESERVES:

124 million bbl (1 January 2018 est.)

country comparison to the world: 68

REFINED PETROLEUM PRODUCTS - PRODUCTION:

104,100 bbl/day (2015 est.)

country comparison to the world: 67

REFINED PETROLEUM PRODUCTS - CONSUMPTION:

175,000 bbl/day (2016 est.)

country comparison to the world: 60

REFINED PETROLEUM PRODUCTS - EXPORTS:

24,190 bbl/day (2015 est.)

country comparison to the world: 69

REFINED PETROLEUM PRODUCTS - IMPORTS:

52,750 bbl/day (2015 est.)

country comparison to the world: 78

NATURAL GAS - PRODUCTION:

1.189 billion cu m (2017 est.)

country comparison to the world: 66

NATURAL GAS - CONSUMPTION:

1.189 billion cu m (2017 est.)

country comparison to the world: 90

NATURAL GAS - EXPORTS:

0 cu m (2017 est.)

country comparison to the world: 90

NATURAL GAS - IMPORTS:

0 cu m (2017 est.)

country comparison to the world: 113

NATURAL GAS - PROVED RESERVES:

70.79 billion cu m (1 January 2018 est.)

country comparison to the world: 57

CARBON DIOXIDE EMISSIONS FROM CONSUMPTION OF ENERGY:

26.94 million Mt (2017 est.)

country comparison to the world: 78

COMMUNICATIONS :: CUBA

TELEPHONES - FIXED LINES:

total subscriptions: 1,349,188 (2017 est.)

subscriptions per 100 inhabitants: 12 (2017 est.)

country comparison to the world: 67

TELEPHONES - MOBILE CELLULAR:

total subscriptions: 4,613,782 (2017 est.)

subscriptions per 100 inhabitants: 41 (2017 est.)

country comparison to the world: 123

TELEPHONE SYSTEM:

general assessment: fixed-line and mobile services run by the state-run ETESCA; mobile-cellular telephone service is expensive and must be paid in convertible pesos; Cuban Government has opened several hundred Wi-Fi hotspots around the island, which are expensive, and launched a new residential Internet pilot in Havana and other provinces; ongoing normalisation of relations with the US warrants considerable economic prosperity for Cuba (2017)

domestic: fixed-line density remains low at about 12 per 100 inhabitants; mobile-cellular service is expanding to about 41 per 100 persons (2017)

international: country code - 53; the ALBA-1 fiber-optic submarine cable links Cuba, Jamaica, and Venezuela; January 2016 the FCC allowed US firms to do business directly with the Cuban telecom sector, the government has looked favourably on proposals for a new subsea cable to link Cuba directly with Florida, which would supplement the only direct international cable access, via the ALBA-1 cable from Venezuela; satellite earth station - 1 Intersputnik (Atlantic Ocean region); several US telecommunication companies have signed voice and data deals to serve their customers while in Cuba (2017)

BROADCAST MEDIA:

government owns and controls all broadcast media with private ownership of electronic media prohibited; however, several online independent news sites exist and those that are not openly critical of the government are often tolerated; government operates 5 national TV networks and many local TV stations; government operates 6 national radio networks, an international station, and many local radio stations; Radio-TV Marti is beamed from the US (2017)

INTERNET COUNTRY CODE:

.cu

INTERNET USERS:

total: 4,334,022 (July 2016 est.)

percent of population: 38.8% (July 2016 est.)

note: private citizens are prohibited from buying computers or accessing the Internet without special authorization; foreigners may access the Internet in large hotels but are subject to firewalls; some Cubans buy illegal passwords on the black market or take advantage of public outlets to access limited email and the government-controlled "intranet"

country comparison to the world: 84

BROADBAND - FIXED SUBSCRIPTIONS:

total: 33,536 (2017 est.)

subscriptions per 100 inhabitants: less than 1 (2017 est.)

country comparison to the world: 138

TRANSPORTATION :: CUBA

NATIONAL AIR TRANSPORT SYSTEM:

number of registered air carriers: 4 (2015)

inventory of registered aircraft operated by air carriers: 18 (2015)

annual passenger traffic on registered air carriers: 1,294,458 (2015)

annual freight traffic on registered air carriers: 20,919,645 mt-km (2015)

CIVIL AIRCRAFT REGISTRATION COUNTRY CODE PREFIX:

CU (2016)

AIRPORTS:

133 (2017)

country comparison to the world: 42

AIRPORTS - WITH PAVED RUNWAYS:

total: 64 (2017)

over 3,047 m: 7 (2017)

2,438 to 3,047 m: 10 (2017)

1,524 to 2,437 m: 16 (2017)

914 to 1,523 m: 4 (2017)

under 914 m: 27 (2017)

AIRPORTS - WITH UNPAVED RUNWAYS:

total: 69 (2013)

914 to 1,523 m: 11 (2013)

under 914 m: 58 (2013)

PIPELINES:

41 km gas, 230 km oil (2013)

RAILWAYS:

total: 8,367 km (2015)

standard gauge: 8,195 km 1.435-m gauge (124 km electrified) (2015)

narrow gauge: 172 km 1.000-m gauge (2015)

note: 70 km of standard gauge track is not for public use

country comparison to the world: 26

ROADWAYS:

total: 60,858 km (2001)

paved: 29,820 km (includes 639 km of expressways) (2001)

unpaved: 31,038 km (2001)

country comparison to the world: 69

WATERWAYS:

240 km (almost all navigable inland waterways are near the mouths of rivers) (2011)

country comparison to the world: 94

MERCHANT MARINE:

total: 43 (2017)

by type: general cargo 11, oil tanker 3, other 29 (2017)

country comparison to the world: 118

PORTS AND TERMINALS:

major seaport(s): Antilla, Cienfuegos, Guantanamo, Havana, Matanzas, Mariel, Nuevitas Bay, Santiago de Cuba

MILITARY AND SECURITY :: CUBA

MILITARY EXPENDITURES:

3.08% of GDP (2015)

3.54% of GDP (2014)

3.51% of GDP (2013)

country comparison to the world: 28

MILITARY BRANCHES:

Revolutionary Armed Forces (Fuerzas Armadas Revolucionarias, FAR): Revolutionary Army (Ejercito Revolucionario, ER, includes Territorial Militia Troops (Milicia de Tropas de Territoriales, MTT)), Revolutionary Navy (Marina de Guerra Revolucionaria, MGR, includes Marine Corps), Revolutionary Air and Air Defense Forces (Defensas Anti-Aereas y Fuerza Aerea Revolucionaria, DAAFAR); Youth Labor Army (Ejercito Juvenil del Trabajo, EJT) (2013)

MILITARY SERVICE AGE AND OBLIGATION:

17-28 years of age for compulsory military service; 2-year service obligation for males, optional for females (2017)

MILITARY - NOTE:

the collapse of the Soviet Union deprived the Cuban military of its major economic and logistic support and had a significant impact on the state of Cuban equipment; the army remains well trained and professional in nature; the lack of replacement parts for its existing equipment has increasingly affected operational capabilities (2013)

TRANSNATIONAL ISSUES :: CUBA

DISPUTES - INTERNATIONAL:

US Naval Base at Guantanamo Bay is leased to the United States and only mutual agreement or US abandonment of the facility can terminate the lease

TRAFFICKING IN PERSONS:

current situation: Cuba is a source country for adults and children subjected to sex trafficking and forced labor; child sex trafficking and child sex tourism occur in Cuba, while some Cubans are forced into prostitution in South America and the Caribbean;

allegations have been made that some Cubans have been forced or coerced to work at Cuban medical missions abroad; assessing the scope of trafficking within Cuba is difficult because of the lack of information

tier rating: Tier 2 Watch List - Cuba does not fully comply with the minimum standards for the elimination of trafficking; however, it is making significant efforts to do so; Cuba's penal code does not criminalize all forms of human trafficking, but the government reported that it is in the process of amending its criminal code to comply with the 2000 UN TIP Protocol, to which it acceded in 2013; the government in 2014 prosecuted and convicted 13 sex traffickers and provided services to the victims in those cases but does not have shelters specifically for trafficking victims; the government did not recognize forced labor as a problem and took no action to address it; state media produced newspaper articles and TV and radio programs to raise public awareness about sex trafficking (2015)

ILLICIT DRUGS:

territorial waters and air space serve as transshipment zone for US- and European-bound drugs; established the death penalty for certain drug-related crimes in 1999

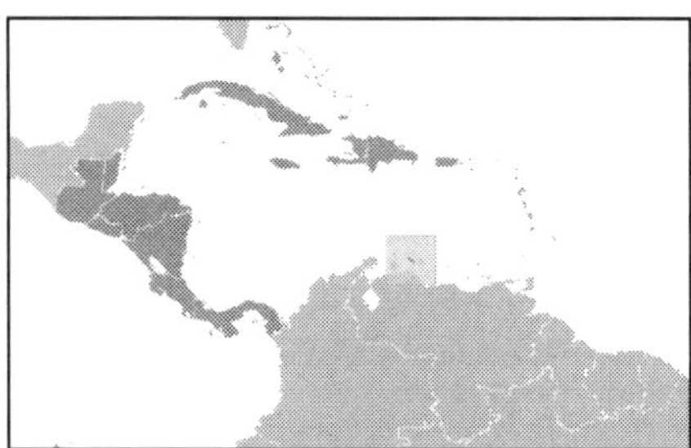

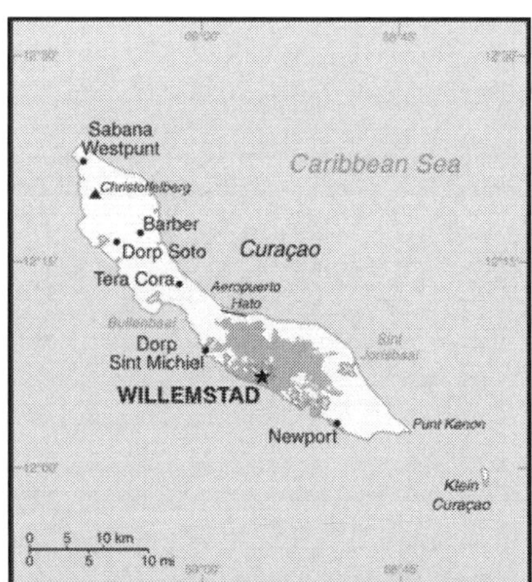

CENTRAL AMERICA :: CURACAO

INTRODUCTION :: CURACAO

BACKGROUND:

Originally settled by Arawak Indians, Curacao was seized by the Dutch in 1634 along with the neighboring island of Bonaire. Once the center of the Caribbean slave trade, Curacao was hard hit economically by the abolition of slavery in 1863. Its prosperity (and that of neighboring Aruba) was restored in the early 20th century with the construction of the Isla Refineria to service the newly discovered Venezuelan oil fields. In 1954, Curacao and several other Dutch Caribbean possessions were reorganized as the Netherlands Antilles, part of the Kingdom of the Netherlands. In referenda in 2005 and 2009, the citizens of Curacao voted to become a self-governing country within the Kingdom of the Netherlands. The change in status became effective in October 2010 with the dissolution of the Netherlands Antilles.

GEOGRAPHY :: CURACAO

LOCATION:

Caribbean, an island in the Caribbean Sea, 55 km off the coast of Venezuela

GEOGRAPHIC COORDINATES:

12 10 N, 69 00 W

MAP REFERENCES:

Central America and the Caribbean

AREA:

total: 444 sq km

land: 444 sq km

water: 0 sq km

country comparison to the world: 200

AREA - COMPARATIVE:

more than twice the size of Washington, DC

LAND BOUNDARIES:

0

COASTLINE:

364 km

MARITIME CLAIMS:

territorial sea: 12 nm

exclusive economic zone: 200 nm

CLIMATE:

tropical marine climate, ameliorated by northeast trade winds, results in mild temperatures; semiarid with average rainfall of 60 cm/year

TERRAIN:

generally low, hilly terrain

ELEVATION:

mean elevation: NA

elevation extremes: 0 m lowest point: Caribbean Sea

372 m highest point: Mt. Christoffel

NATURAL RESOURCES:

calcium phosphates, aloes, sorghum, peanuts, vegetables, tropical fruit

LAND USE:

agricultural land: 10% (2011 est.)

arable land: 10% / permanent crops: 0% / permanent pasture: 0% (2011 est.)

forest: 0% (2011 est.)

other: 90% (2011 est.)

IRRIGATED LAND:

NA

POPULATION DISTRIBUTION:

largest concentration on the island is Willemstad; smaller settlements near the coast can be found throughout the island, particularly in the northwest

NATURAL HAZARDS:

Curacao is south of the Caribbean hurricane belt and is rarely threatened

ENVIRONMENT - CURRENT ISSUES:

problems in waste management that threaten environmental sustainability on the island include pollution of marine areas from domestic sewage, inadequate sewage treatment facilities, industrial effluents and agricultural runoff, the mismanagement of toxic substances, and ineffective regulations; the refinery in Sint Anna Bay, at the eastern edge of Willemstad's large natural harbor, processes heavy crude oil from Venezuela; it has caused significant environmental damage to the surrounding area because of neglect and a lack of strict environmental controls; the release of noxious fumes and potentially hazardous particles causes schools downwind to regularly close

GEOGRAPHY - NOTE:

Curacao is a part of the Windward Islands (southern) group in the Lesser Antilles

PEOPLE AND SOCIETY :: CURACAO

POPULATION:

150,241 (July 2018 est.)

country comparison to the world: 188

NATIONALITY:

noun: Curacaoan

adjective: Curacaoan; Dutch

ETHNIC GROUPS:

Curacaoan 75.4%, Dutch 6%, Dominican 3.6%, Colombian 3%, Bonairean, Sint Eustatian, Saban 1.5%, Haitian 1.2%, Surinamese 1.2%,

Venezuelan 1.1%, Aruban 1.1%, other 5%, unspecified 0.9% (2011 est.)

LANGUAGES:

Papiamento (official) (a creole language that is a mixture of Portuguese, Spanish, Dutch, English, and, to a lesser extent, French, as well as elements of African languages and the language of the Arawak) 81.2%, Dutch (official) 8%, Spanish 4%, English (official) 2.9%, other 3.9% (2001 census)

RELIGIONS:

Roman Catholic 72.8%, Pentecostal6.6%, Protestant 3.2%, Adventist 3%, Jehovah's Witness2%, Evangelical 1.9%, other 3.8%, none 6%, unspecified 0.6% (2011 est.)

AGE STRUCTURE:

0-14 years: 19.88% (male 15,250 /female 14,613)

15-24 years: 14.05% (male 10,957 /female 10,158)

25-54 years: 36.66% (male 27,278 /female 27,802)

55-64 years: 13.84% (male 9,018 /female 11,769)

65 years and over: 15.57% (male 9,547 /female 13,849) (2018 est.)

DEPENDENCY RATIOS:

total dependency ratio: 52.4 (2015 est.)

youth dependency ratio: 28.7 (2015 est.)

elderly dependency ratio: 23.6 (2015 est.)

potential support ratio: 4.2 (2015 est.)

MEDIAN AGE:

total: 36.3 years

male: 33.8 years

female: 39.6 years (2018 est.)

country comparison to the world: 75

POPULATION GROWTH RATE:

0.39% (2018 est.)

country comparison to the world: 163

BIRTH RATE:

13.7 births/1,000 population (2018 est.)

country comparison to the world: 139

DEATH RATE:

8.5 deaths/1,000 population (2018 est.)

country comparison to the world: 77

NET MIGRATION RATE:

-1.3 migrant(s)/1,000 population (2017 est.)

country comparison to the world: 144

POPULATION DISTRIBUTION:

largest concentration on the island is Willemstad; smaller settlements near the coast can be found throughout the island, particularly in the northwest

URBANIZATION:

urban population: 89.1% of total population (2018)

rate of urbanization: 0.62% annual rate of change (2015-20 est.)

MAJOR URBAN AREAS - POPULATION:

144000 WILLEMSTAD (capital) (2018)

SEX RATIO:

at birth: 1.05 male(s)/female (2017 est.)

0-14 years: 1.04 male(s)/female (2017 est.)

15-24 years: 1.09 male(s)/female (2017 est.)

25-54 years: 0.96 male(s)/female (2017 est.)

55-64 years: 0.76 male(s)/female (2017 est.)

65 years and over: 0.7 male(s)/female (2017 est.)

total population: 0.92 male(s)/female (2017 est.)

INFANT MORTALITY RATE:

total: 7.3 deaths/1,000 live births (2018 est.)

male: 7.9 deaths/1,000 live births (2018 est.)

female: 6.8 deaths/1,000 live births (2018 est.)

country comparison to the world: 159

LIFE EXPECTANCY AT BIRTH:

total population: 78.6 years (2018 est.)

male: 76.3 years (2018 est.)

female: 81.1 years (2018 est.)

country comparison to the world: 61

TOTAL FERTILITY RATE:

2.03 children born/woman (2018 est.)

country comparison to the world: 113

HIV/AIDS - ADULT PREVALENCE RATE:

NA

HIV/AIDS - PEOPLE LIVING WITH HIV/AIDS:

NA

HIV/AIDS - DEATHS:

NA

MAJOR INFECTIOUS DISEASES:

note: active local transmission of Zika virus by Aedes species mosquitoes has been identified in this country (as of August 2016); it poses an important risk (a large number of cases possible) among US citizens if bitten by an infective mosquito; other less common ways to get Zika are through sex, via blood transfusion, or during pregnancy, in which the pregnant woman passes Zika virus to her fetus

EDUCATION EXPENDITURES:

4.9% of GDP (2013)

country comparison to the world: 80

SCHOOL LIFE EXPECTANCY (PRIMARY TO TERTIARY EDUCATION):

total: 18 years (2013)

male: 18 years (2013)

female: 19 years (2013)

UNEMPLOYMENT, YOUTH AGES 15-24:

total: 29.7% (2015 est.)

male: NA (2015 est.)

female: NA (2015 est.)

country comparison to the world: 32

GOVERNMENT :: CURACAO

COUNTRY NAME:

conventional long form: none

conventional short form: Curacao

local long form: Land Curacao (Dutch); Pais Korsou (Papiamento)

local short form: Curacao (Dutch); Korsou (Papiamento)

former: Netherlands Antilles; Curacao and Dependencies

etymology: the most plausible name derivation is that the island was designated Isla de la Curacion (Spanish meaning "Island of the Cure" or "Island of Healing") or Ilha da Curacao (Portuguese meaning the same) to reflect the locale's function as a recovery stop for sick crewmen

DEPENDENCY STATUS:

constituent country within the Kingdom of the Netherlands; full autonomy in internal affairs granted in 2010; Dutch Government responsible for defense and foreign affairs

GOVERNMENT TYPE:

parliamentary democracy

CAPITAL:

name: Willemstad

geographic coordinates: 12 06 N, 68 55 W

time difference: UTC-4 (1 hour ahead of Washington, DC, during Standard Time)

ADMINISTRATIVE DIVISIONS:

none (part of the Kingdom of the Netherlands)

note: Curacao is one of four constituent countries of the Kingdom of the Netherlands; the other three are the Netherlands, Aruba, and Sint Maarten

INDEPENDENCE:

none (part of the Kingdom of the Netherlands)

NATIONAL HOLIDAY:

King's Day (birthday of King WILLEM-ALEXANDER), 27 April (1967); note - King's or Queen's Day are observed on the ruling monarch's birthday; celebrated on 26 April if 27 April is a Sunday

CONSTITUTION:

previous 1947, 1955; latest adopted 5 September 2010, entered into force 10 October 2010 (regulates governance of Curacao but is subordinate to the Charter for the Kingdom of the Netherlands); note - in October 2010, with the dissolution of the Netherlands Antilles, Curacao became a constituent country within the Kingdom of the Netherlands (2018)

LEGAL SYSTEM:

based on Dutch civil law system with some English common law influence

CITIZENSHIP:

see the Netherlands

SUFFRAGE:

18 years of age; universal

EXECUTIVE BRANCH:

chief of state: King WILLEM-ALEXANDER of the Netherlands (since 30 April 2013); represented by Governor Lucille A. GEORGE-WOUT (since 4 November 2013)

head of government: Prime Minister Ivar ASJES (since 7 June 2013)

cabinet: Cabinet appointed by the governor

elections/appointments: the monarch is hereditary; governor appointed by the monarch; following legislative elections, the leader of the majority party usually elected prime minister by the legislature (Estates of Curacao); next election scheduled for 2016

LEGISLATIVE BRANCH:

description: unicameral Estates of Curacao (21 seats; members directly elected by proportional representation vote to serve 4-year terms)

elections: last held on 28 April 2017 (next to be held in 2021); early elections were held after Prime Minister Hensley KOEIMAN resigned on 12 February 2017, when the coalition government lost its majority

election results: percent of vote by party - PAR 23.3%, MAN 20.4%, MFK 19.9%, KdnT 9.4%, PIN 5.3%, PS 5.1%, MP 4.9%, other 11.7%; seats by party - PAR 6, MAN 5, MFK 5, KdnT 2, PIN 1, PS 1, MP 1

JUDICIAL BRANCH:

highest courts: Joint Court of Justice of Aruba, Curacao, Sint Maarten, and of Bonaire, Sint Eustatitus and Saba or "Joint Court of Justice" (sits as a 3-judge panel); final appeals heard by the Supreme Court, in The Hague, Netherlands

judge selection and term of office: Joint Court judges appointed by the monarch for life

subordinate courts: first instance courts, appeals court; specialized courts

POLITICAL PARTIES AND LEADERS:

Korsou di Nos Tur or KdnT [Amparo dos SANTOS]
Mayors for Liberec Region (Starostove pro Liberecky Kraj) or SLK [Martin PUTA]
Movementu Futuro Korsou or MFK [Gerrit SCHOTTE]
Movementu Progresivo or MP [Marylin MOSES]
Movishon Antia Nobo or MAN [Hensley KOEIMAN]
Partido Antia Restruktura or PAR [Eugene RHUGGENAATH]
Partido Inovashon Nashonal or PIN [Suzanne CAMELIA-ROMER]
Partido pa Adelanto I Inovashon Soshal or PAIS [Alex ROSARIA]
Partido Nashonal di Pueblo or PNP [Humphrey DAVELAAR]
Pueblo Soberano or PS
Un Korsou Hustu [Omayra LEEFLANG]

INTERNATIONAL ORGANIZATION PARTICIPATION:

Caricom (observer), FATF, ILO, ITU, UNESCO (associate), UPU

DIPLOMATIC REPRESENTATION IN THE US:

none (represented by the Kingdom of the Netherlands)

DIPLOMATIC REPRESENTATION FROM THE US:

chief of mission: Consul General Margaret HAWTHORNE (since April 2016); note - also accredited to Aruba and Sint Maarten

mailing address: P. O. Box 158, Willemstad, Curacao

telephone: [599] (9) 4613066

FAX: [599] (9) 4616489

consulate(s) general: J. B. Gorsiraweg #1, Willemstad, Curacao

FLAG DESCRIPTION:

on a blue field a horizontal yellow band somewhat below the center divides the flag into proportions of 5:1:2; two five-pointed white stars - the smaller above and to the left of the larger - appear in the canton; the blue of the upper and lower sections symbolizes the sky and sea respectively; yellow represents the sun; the stars symbolize Curacao and its uninhabited smaller sister island of Klein Curacao; the five star points signify the five continents from which Curacao's people derive

NATIONAL SYMBOL(S):

laraha (citrus tree); national colors: blue, yellow, white

NATIONAL ANTHEM:

name: Himmo di Korsou (Anthem of Curacao)

lyrics/music: Guillermo ROSARIO, Mae HENRIQUEZ, Enrique MULLER, Betty DORAN/Frater Candidus NOWENS, Errol "El Toro" COLINA

note: adapted 1978; the lyrics, originally written in 1899, were rewritten in 1978 to make them less colonial in nature

ECONOMY :: CURACAO

ECONOMY - OVERVIEW:

Most of Curacao's GDP results from services. Tourism, petroleum refining and bunkering, offshore finance, and transportation and communications are the mainstays of this small island economy, which is closely tied to the outside world. Curacao has limited natural resources, poor soil, and inadequate water supplies, and budgetary problems complicate reform of the health and education systems. Although GDP grew only slightly during the past decade, Curacao enjoys a high per capita income and a well-developed infrastructure compared to other countries in the region.

Curacao has an excellent natural harbor that can accommodate large oil tankers, and the port of Willemstad hosts a free trade zone and a dry dock. Venezuelan state-owned oil company PdVSA, under a contract in effect until 2019, leases the single refinery on the island from the government, directly employing some 1,000 people. Most of the oil for the refinery is imported from Venezuela and most of the refined products are exported to the US and Asia. Almost all consumer and capital goods are imported, with the US, the Netherlands, and Venezuela being the major suppliers.

The government is attempting to diversify its industry and trade. Curacao is an Overseas Countries and Territories (OCT) of the European Union. Nationals of Curacao are citizens of the European Union, even though it is not a member. Based on its OCT status, products that originate in Curacao have preferential access to the EU and are exempt from import duties. Curacao is a beneficiary of the Caribbean Basin Initiative and, as a result, products originating in Curacao can be imported tax free into the US if at least 35% has been added to the value of these products in Curacao. The island has state-of-the-art information and communication technology connectivity with the rest of the world, including a Tier IV datacenter. With several direct satellite and submarine optic fiber cables, Curacao has one of the best Internet speeds and reliability in the Western Hemisphere.

GDP (PURCHASING POWER PARITY):

$3.128 billion (2012 est.)

$3.02 billion (2011 est.)

$2.96 billion (2010 est.)

note: data are in 2012 US dollars

country comparison to the world: 189

GDP (OFFICIAL EXCHANGE RATE):

$5.6 billion (2012 est.)

GDP - REAL GROWTH RATE:

3.6% (2012 est.)

2% (2011 est.)

0.1% (2010 est.)

country comparison to the world: 95

GDP - PER CAPITA (PPP):

$15,000 (2004 est.)

country comparison to the world: 112

GDP - COMPOSITION, BY END USE:

household consumption: 66.9% (2016 est.)

government consumption: 33.6% (2016 est.)

investment in fixed capital: 19.4% (2016 est.)

investment in inventories: 0% (2016 est.)

exports of goods and services: 17.5% (2016 est.)

imports of goods and services: -37.5% (2016 est.)

GDP - COMPOSITION, BY SECTOR OF ORIGIN:

agriculture: 0.7% (2012 est.)

industry: 15.5% (2012 est.)

services: 83.8% (2012 est.)

AGRICULTURE - PRODUCTS:

aloe, sorghum, peanuts, vegetables, tropical fruit

INDUSTRIES:

tourism, petroleum refining, petroleum transshipment, light manufacturing, financial and business services

INDUSTRIAL PRODUCTION GROWTH RATE:

NA

LABOR FORCE:

73,010 (2013)

country comparison to the world: 185

LABOR FORCE - BY OCCUPATION:

agriculture: 1.2%

industry: 16.9%

services: 81.8% (2008 est.)

UNEMPLOYMENT RATE:

13% (2013 est.)

9.8% (2011 est.)

country comparison to the world: 166

BUDGET:

TAXES AND OTHER REVENUES:

16.6% (of GDP) (2012 est.)

country comparison to the world: 177

BUDGET SURPLUS (+) OR DEFICIT (-):

-0.4% (of GDP) (2012 est.)

country comparison to the world: 56

PUBLIC DEBT:

33.2% of GDP (2012 est.)

40.6% of GDP (2011 est.)

country comparison to the world: 158

INFLATION RATE (CONSUMER PRICES):

2.6% (2013 est.)

2.8% (2012 est.)

country comparison to the world: 124

CENTRAL BANK DISCOUNT RATE:

NA% (31 December 2010)

COMMERCIAL BANK PRIME LENDING RATE:

14.5% (31 December 2011 est.)

14.5% (31 December 2010 est.)

country comparison to the world: 45

STOCK OF NARROW MONEY:

$1.728 billion (31 December 2011 est.)

$1.618 billion (31 December 2010 est.)

country comparison to the world: 138

STOCK OF BROAD MONEY:

$4.953 billion (31 December 2011 est.)

$4.31 billion (31 December 2009 est.)

country comparison to the world: 109

STOCK OF DOMESTIC CREDIT:

$3.882 billion (31 December 2011 est.)

$3.799 billion (31 December 2010 est.)

country comparison to the world: 133

CURRENT ACCOUNT BALANCE:

-$400 million (2011 est.)

-$600 million (2010 est.)

country comparison to the world: 112

EXPORTS:

$555.6 billion (2017 est.)

$1.44 billion (2010 est.)

country comparison to the world: 6

EXPORTS - COMMODITIES:

petroleum products

IMPORTS:

$540.3 billion (2018 est.)

$453.8 billion (2017 est.)

country comparison to the world: 8

IMPORTS - COMMODITIES:

crude petroleum, food, manufactures

RESERVES OF FOREIGN EXCHANGE AND GOLD:

$0 (31 December 2017 est.)

country comparison to the world: 191

EXCHANGE RATES:

Netherlands Antillean guilders (ANG) per US dollar -

1.79 (2017 est.)

1.79 (2016 est.)

1.79 (2015 est.)

1.79 (2014 est.)

1.79 (2013 est.)

ENERGY :: CURACAO

ELECTRICITY ACCESS:

population without electricity: 14,903 (2012)

electrification - total population: 91% (2012)

electrification - urban areas: 91% (2012)

electrification - rural areas: 80% (2012)

ELECTRICITY - PRODUCTION:

1.785 billion kWh (2012 est.)

country comparison to the world: 139

ELECTRICITY - CONSUMPTION:

968 million kWh (2008 est.)

country comparison to the world: 156

ELECTRICITY - EXPORTS:

0 kWh (2009 est.)

country comparison to the world: 125

ELECTRICITY - IMPORTS:

0 kWh (2009 est.)

country comparison to the world: 139

CRUDE OIL - PRODUCTION:

0 bbl/day (2017 est.)

country comparison to the world: 124

CRUDE OIL - EXPORTS:

0 bbl/day (2015 est.)

country comparison to the world: 112

CRUDE OIL - IMPORTS:

191,300 bbl/day (2015 est.)

country comparison to the world: 31

CRUDE OIL - PROVED RESERVES:

0 bbl (1 January 2011 est.)

country comparison to the world: 121

REFINED PETROLEUM PRODUCTS - PRODUCTION:

189,800 bbl/day (2015 est.)

country comparison to the world: 53

REFINED PETROLEUM PRODUCTS - CONSUMPTION:

70,000 bbl/day (2016 est.)

country comparison to the world: 93

REFINED PETROLEUM PRODUCTS - EXPORTS:

167,500 bbl/day (2015 est.)

country comparison to the world: 33

REFINED PETROLEUM PRODUCTS - IMPORTS:

45,800 bbl/day (2015 est.)

country comparison to the world: 85

NATURAL GAS - PRODUCTION:

0 cu m (2009 est.)

country comparison to the world: 121

NATURAL GAS - CONSUMPTION:

0 cu m (2009 est.)

country comparison to the world: 137

NATURAL GAS - EXPORTS:

0 cu m (2009 est.)

country comparison to the world: 91

NATURAL GAS - IMPORTS:

0 cu m (2009 est.)

country comparison to the world: 114

NATURAL GAS - PROVED RESERVES:

0 cu m (1 January 2011 est.)

country comparison to the world: 126

COMMUNICATIONS :: CURACAO

TELEPHONE SYSTEM:

international: country code - 599

BROADCAST MEDIA:

government-run TeleCuracao operates a TV station and a radio station; 3 other privately owned TV stations and several privately owned radio stations (2017)

INTERNET COUNTRY CODE:

.cw

INTERNET USERS:

total: 138,750 (July 2016 est.)

percent of population: 93.9% (July 2016 est.)

country comparison to the world: 174

TRANSPORTATION :: CURACAO

NATIONAL AIR TRANSPORT SYSTEM:

number of registered air carriers: 2 (2015)

inventory of registered aircraft operated by air carriers: 11 (2015)

CIVIL AIRCRAFT REGISTRATION COUNTRY CODE PREFIX:

PJ (2016)

AIRPORTS:

1 (2017)

country comparison to the world: 219

AIRPORTS - WITH PAVED RUNWAYS:

over 3,047 m: 1 (2017)

ROADWAYS:

total: 550 km

country comparison to the world: 194

MERCHANT MARINE:

total: 92 (2017)

by type: general cargo 18, oil tanker 1, other 73 (2017)

country comparison to the world: 89

PORTS AND TERMINALS:

major seaport(s): Willemstad

oil terminal(s): Bullen Baai (Curacao Terminal)

bulk cargo port(s): Fuik Bay (phosphate rock)

MILITARY AND SECURITY :: CURACAO

MILITARY BRANCHES:

no regular military forces; the Dutch Government controls foreign and defense policy (2012)

MILITARY SERVICE AGE AND OBLIGATION:

no conscription (2010)

MILITARY - NOTE:

defense is the responsibility of the Kingdom of the Netherlands

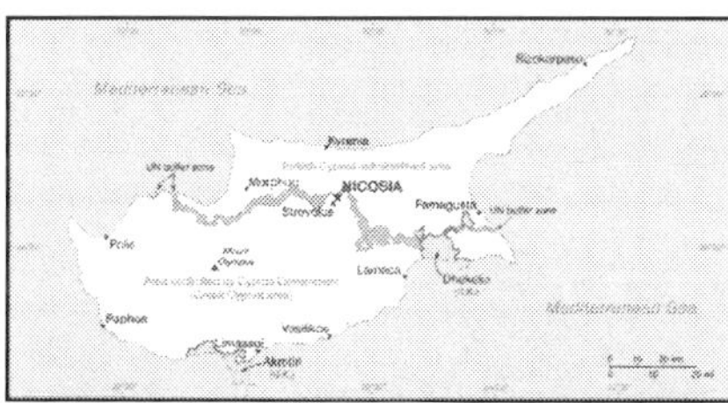

EUROPE :: CYPRUS

INTRODUCTION :: CYPRUS

BACKGROUND:

A former British colony, Cyprus became independent in 1960 following years of resistance to British rule. Tensions between the Greek Cypriot majority and Turkish Cypriot minority came to a head in December 1963, when violence broke out in the capital of Nicosia. Despite the deployment of UN peacekeepers in 1964, sporadic intercommunal violence continued, forcing most Turkish Cypriots into enclaves throughout the island. In 1974, a Greek Government-sponsored attempt to overthrow the elected president of Cyprus was met by military intervention from Turkey, which soon controlled more than a third of the island. In 1983, the Turkish Cypriot administered area declared itself the "Turkish Republic of Northern Cyprus" ("TRNC"), but it is recognized only by Turkey. A UN-mediated agreement, the Annan Plan, failed to win approval by both communities in 2004. In February 2014, after a hiatus of nearly two years, the leaders of the two communities resumed formal discussions under UN auspices aimed at reuniting the divided island. The most recent round of negotiations to reunify the island were suspended in July 2017 after failure to achieve a breakthrough. The entire island entered the EU on 1 May 2004, although the EU acquis - the body of common rights and obligations - applies only to the areas under the internationally recognized government, and is suspended in the area administered by Turkish Cypriots. However, individual Turkish Cypriots able to document their eligibility for Republic of Cyprus citizenship legally enjoy the same rights accorded to other citizens of EU states.

GEOGRAPHY :: CYPRUS

LOCATION:

Middle East, island in the Mediterranean Sea, south of Turkey; note - Cyprus views itself as part of Europe; geopolitically, it can be classified as falling within Europe, the Middle East, or both

GEOGRAPHIC COORDINATES:

35 00 N, 33 00 E

MAP REFERENCES:

Middle East

AREA:

total: 9,251 sq km (of which 3,355 sq km are in north Cyprus)

land: 9,241 sq km

water: 10 sq km

country comparison to the world: 170

AREA - COMPARATIVE:

about 0.6 times the size of Connecticut

LAND BOUNDARIES:

total: 156 km

border sovereign base areas: Akrotiri 48 km, Dhekelia 108 km

COASTLINE:

648 km

MARITIME CLAIMS:

territorial sea: 12 nm

contiguous zone: 24 nm

continental shelf: 200-m depth or to the depth of exploitation

CLIMATE:

temperate; Mediterranean with hot, dry summers and cool winters

TERRAIN:

central plain with mountains to north and south; scattered but significant plains along southern coast

ELEVATION:

mean elevation: 91 m

elevation extremes: 0 m lowest point: Mediterranean Sea

1951 highest point: Mount Olympus

NATURAL RESOURCES:

copper, pyrites, asbestos, gypsum, timber, salt, marble, clay earth pigment

LAND USE:

agricultural land: 13.4% (2011 est.)

arable land: 9.8% (2011 est.) / permanent crops: 3.2% (2011 est.) / permanent pasture: 0.4% (2011 est.)

forest: 18.8% (2011 est.)

other: 67.8% (2011 est.)

IRRIGATED LAND:

460 sq km (2012)

POPULATION DISTRIBUTION:

population concentrated in central Nicosia and in the major cities of the south: Paphos, Limassol, and Larnaca

NATURAL HAZARDS:

moderate earthquake activity; droughts

ENVIRONMENT - CURRENT ISSUES:

water resource problems (no natural reservoir catchments, seasonal disparity in rainfall, sea water intrusion to island's largest aquifer, increased salination in the north); water pollution from sewage, industrial wastes, and pesticides; coastal degradation; erosion; loss of wildlife habitats from urbanization

ENVIRONMENT - INTERNATIONAL AGREEMENTS:

party to: Air Pollution, Air Pollution-Nitrogen Oxides, Air Pollution-Persistent Organic Pollutants, Air Pollution-Sulfur 94, Biodiversity, Climate Change, Climate Change-Kyoto Protocol, Desertification, Endangered Species, Environmental Modification, Hazardous Wastes, Law of the Sea, Marine Dumping, Ozone Layer Protection, Ship Pollution, Wetlands

signed, but not ratified: none of the selected agreements

GEOGRAPHY - NOTE:

the third largest island in the Mediterranean Sea (after Sicily and Sardinia); several small Cypriot enclaves exist within the Dhekelia Sovereign Base Area

PEOPLE AND SOCIETY :: CYPRUS

POPULATION:

1,237,088 (July 2018 est.)

country comparison to the world: 158

NATIONALITY:

noun: Cypriot(s)

adjective: Cypriot

ETHNIC GROUPS:

Greek 98.8%, other 1% (includes Maronite, Armenian, Turkish-Cypriot), unspecified 0.2% (2011 est.)

note: data represent only the government-controlled area of Cyprus

LANGUAGES:

Greek (official) 80.9%, Turkish (official) 0.2%, English 4.1%, Romanian 2.9%, Russian 2.5%, Bulgarian 2.2%, Arabic 1.2%, Filipino 1.1%, other 4.3%, unspecified 0.6% (2011 est.)

note: data represent only the government-controlled area of Cyprus

RELIGIONS:

Orthodox Christian 89.1%, Roman Catholic 2.9%, Protestant/Anglican 2%, Muslim 1.8%, Buddhist 1%, other (includes Maronite, Armenian Church, Hindu) 1.4%, unknown 1.1%, none/atheist 0.6% (2011 est.)

note: data represent only the government-controlled area of Cyprus

AGE STRUCTURE:

0-14 years: 15.64% (male 99,390 /female 94,053)

15-24 years: 13.25% (male 89,265 /female 74,607)

25-54 years: 47.11% (male 308,190 /female 274,632)

55-64 years: 11.62% (male 68,952 /female 74,842)

65 years and over: 12.38% (male 66,209 /female 86,948) (2018 est.)

DEPENDENCY RATIOS:

total dependency ratio: 42.3 (2015 est.)

youth dependency ratio: 24 (2015 est.)

elderly dependency ratio: 18.3 (2015 est.)

potential support ratio: 5.5 (2015 est.)

note: data represent the whole country

MEDIAN AGE:

total: 37.2 years

male: 35.9 years

female: 38.7 years (2018 est.)

country comparison to the world: 68

POPULATION GROWTH RATE:

1.27% (2018 est.)

country comparison to the world: 86

BIRTH RATE:

11.2 births/1,000 population (2018 est.)

country comparison to the world: 174

DEATH RATE:

6.8 deaths/1,000 population (2018 est.)

country comparison to the world: 133

NET MIGRATION RATE:

8.7 migrant(s)/1,000 population (2017 est.)

country comparison to the world: 12

POPULATION DISTRIBUTION:

population concentrated in central Nicosia and in the major cities of the south: Paphos, Limassol, and Larnaca

URBANIZATION:

urban population: 66.8% of total population (2018)

rate of urbanization: 0.75% annual rate of change (2015-20 est.)

MAJOR URBAN AREAS - POPULATION:

269,000 NICOSIA (capital) (2018)

SEX RATIO:

at birth: 1.05 male(s)/female (2017 est.)

0-14 years: 1.06 male(s)/female (2017 est.)

15-24 years: 1.19 male(s)/female (2017 est.)

25-54 years: 1.11 male(s)/female (2017 est.)

55-64 years: 0.92 male(s)/female (2017 est.)

65 years and over: 0.77 male(s)/female (2017 est.)

total population: 1.04 male(s)/female (2017 est.)

MOTHER'S MEAN AGE AT FIRST BIRTH:

28.8 years (2014 est.)

note: data represent only government-controlled areas

MATERNAL MORTALITY RATE:

7 deaths/100,000 live births (2015 est.)

country comparison to the world: 162

INFANT MORTALITY RATE:

total: 7.7 deaths/1,000 live births (2018 est.)

male: 9 deaths/1,000 live births (2018 est.)

female: 6.2 deaths/1,000 live births (2018 est.)

country comparison to the world: 155

LIFE EXPECTANCY AT BIRTH:

total population: 79 years (2018 est.)

male: 76.2 years (2018 est.)

female: 81.9 years (2018 est.)

country comparison to the world: 52

TOTAL FERTILITY RATE:

1.47 children born/woman (2018 est.)

country comparison to the world: 202

HEALTH EXPENDITURES:

7.4% of GDP (2014)

country comparison to the world: 68

PHYSICIANS DENSITY:

2.5 physicians/1,000 population (2014)

HOSPITAL BED DENSITY:

3.4 beds/1,000 population (2013)

DRINKING WATER SOURCE:

improved:

urban: 100% of population

rural: 100% of population

total: 100% of population

unimproved:

urban: 0% of population

rural: 0% of population

total: 0% of population (2015 est.)

SANITATION FACILITY ACCESS:

improved:

urban: 100% of population (2015 est.)

rural: 100% of population (2015 est.)

total: 100% of population (2015 est.)

unimproved:

urban: 0% of population (2015 est.)

rural: 0% of population (2015 est.)

total: 0% of population (2015 est.)

HIV/AIDS - ADULT PREVALENCE RATE:

0.1% (2017 est.)

country comparison to the world: 109

HIV/AIDS - PEOPLE LIVING WITH HIV/AIDS:

<1000 (2017 est.)

HIV/AIDS - DEATHS:

<100 (2017 est.)

OBESITY - ADULT PREVALENCE RATE:

21.8% (2016)

country comparison to the world: 84

EDUCATION EXPENDITURES:

6.1% of GDP (2014)

country comparison to the world: 33

LITERACY:

definition: age 15 and over can read and write (2015 est.)

total population: 99.1% (2015 est.)

male: 99.5% (2015 est.)

female: 98.7% (2015 est.)

SCHOOL LIFE EXPECTANCY (PRIMARY TO TERTIARY EDUCATION):

total: 15 years (2015)

male: 14 years (2015)

female: 15 years (2015)

UNEMPLOYMENT, YOUTH AGES 15-24:

total: 29.1% (2016 est.)

male: 25.8% (2016 est.)

female: 31.8% (2016 est.)

country comparison to the world: 38

PEOPLE - NOTE:

demographic data for Cyprus represent the population of the government-controlled area and the area administered by Turkish Cypriots, unless otherwise indicated

GOVERNMENT :: CYPRUS

COUNTRY NAME:

conventional long form: Republic of Cyprus

conventional short form: Cyprus

local long form: Kypriaki Dimokratia/Kibris Cumhuriyeti

local short form: Kypros/Kibris

etymology: the derivation of the name "Cyprus" is unknown, but the extensive mining of copper metal on the island in antiquity gave rise to the Latin word "cuprum" for copper

note: the Turkish Cypriot community, which administers the northern part of the island, refers to itself as the "Turkish Republic of Northern Cyprus" or "TRNC" ("Kuzey Kibris Turk Cumhuriyeti" or "KKTC")

GOVERNMENT TYPE:

Republic of Cyprus - presidential democracy; Turkish Republic of Northern Cyprus (self-declared) - semi-presidential democracy

note: a separation of the two main ethnic communities inhabiting the island began following the outbreak of communal strife in 1963; this separation was further solidified when a Greek military-junta-supported coup attempt prompted the Turkish intervention in July 1974 that gave the Turkish Cypriots de facto control in the north; Greek Cypriots control the only internationally recognized government on the island; on 15 November 1983, then Turkish Cypriot "President" Rauf DENKTAS declared independence and the formation of a "Turkish Republic of Northern Cyprus" ("TRNC"), which is recognized only by Turkey

CAPITAL:

name: Nicosia (Lefkosia/Lefkosa)

geographic coordinates: 35 10 N, 33 22 E

time difference: UTC+2 (7 hours ahead of Washington, DC, during Standard Time)

daylight saving time: +1hr, begins last Sunday in March; ends last Sunday in October

ADMINISTRATIVE DIVISIONS:

6 districts; Ammochostos (Famagusta); (all but a small part located in the Turkish Cypriot community), Keryneia (Kyrenia; the only district located entirely in the Turkish Cypriot community), Larnaka (Larnaca; with a small part located in the Turkish Cypriot community), Lefkosia (Nicosia; a small part administered by Turkish Cypriots), Lemesos (Limassol), Pafos (Paphos); note - the 5 "districts" of the "TRNC" are Gazimagusa (Famagusta), Girne (Kyrenia), Guzelyurt (Morphou), Iskele (Trikomo), Lefkosa (Nicosia)

INDEPENDENCE:

16 August 1960 (from the UK); note - Turkish Cypriots proclaimed self-rule on 13 February 1975 and independence in 1983, but these proclamations are recognized only by Turkey

NATIONAL HOLIDAY:

Independence Day, 1 October (1960); note - Turkish Cypriots celebrate 15 November (1983) as "Republic Day"

CONSTITUTION:

history: ratified 16 August 1960; note - in 1963, the constitution was partly suspended as Turkish Cypriots withdrew from the government; Turkish-held territory in 1983 was declared the "Turkish Republic of Northern Cyprus" ("TRNC"); in 1985, the "TRNC" approved its own constitution (2016)

amendments: constitution of the Republic of Cyprus - proposed by the House of Representatives; passage requires at least two-thirds majority vote of the total membership of the "Greek Community" and the "Turkish Community"; however, all seats of Turkish Cypriot members have remained vacant since 1964; amended several times, last in 2016 (2016)

constitution of the “Turkish Republic of Northern Cyprus” - proposed by at least 10 members of the Assembly of the Republic; passage requires at least two-thirds majority vote of the total Assembly membership and approval by referendum; amended 2014

LEGAL SYSTEM:

mixed legal system of English common law and civil law with European law supremacy

INTERNATIONAL LAW ORGANIZATION PARTICIPATION:

accepts compulsory ICJ jurisdiction with reservations; accepts ICCt jurisdiction

CITIZENSHIP:

citizenship by birth: no

citizenship by descent only: at least one parent must be a citizen of Cyprus

dual citizenship recognized: yes

residency requirement for naturalization: 7 years

SUFFRAGE:

18 years of age; universal

EXECUTIVE BRANCH:

chief of state: President Nikos ANASTASIADES (since 28 February 2013); the president is both chief of state and head of government; note - vice presidency reserved for a Turkish Cypriot, but vacant since 1974 because Turkish Cypriots do not participate in the Cyprus Government

head of government: President Nikos ANASTASIADES (since 28 February 2013)

cabinet: Council of Ministers appointed by the president; note - under the 1960 constitution, 3 of the ministerial posts reserved for Turkish Cypriots, appointed by the vice president; positions currently filled by Greek Cypriots

elections/appointments: president directly elected by absolute majority popular vote in 2 rounds if needed for a 5-year term; election last held on 28 January 2018 with a runoff on 4 February 2018 (next to be held in February 2023)

election results: Nikos ANASTASIADES reelected president in second round; percent of vote in first round - Nikos ANASTASIADES (DISY) 35.5%, Stavros MALAS (AKEL) 30.2%, Niolas PAPADOPOULOS (DIKO) 25.7%, other 8.6%; percent of vote in second round - Nikos ANASTASIADES 56%, Savros MALAS 44%

note: Mustafa AKINCI assumed office as "president" of the "TRNC" on 30 April 2015; percent of vote in first round (19 April 2015) - Dervis EROGLU 28.2%, Mustafa AKINCI 26.9%, other 44.9%; percent of vote in runoff (26 April 2015) - AKINCI 60.5%, EROGLU 39.5%; Tufan ERHURMAN is "TRNC prime minister" (since 2 February 2018)

LEGISLATIVE BRANCH:

description: area under government control: unicameral House of Representatives or Vouli Antiprosopon (80 seats; 56 assigned to Greek Cypriots, 24 to Turkish Cypriots, but only those assigned to Greek Cypriots are filled; members directly elected by both proportional representation and preferential vote; members serve 5-year terms); area administered by Turkish Cypriots: unicameral Assembly of the Republic or Cumhuriyet Meclisi (50 seats; members directly elected by proportional representation vote to serve 5-year terms)

elections: area under government control: last held on 22 May 2016 (next to be held in May 2021); area administered by Turkish Cypriots: last held on 7 January 2018 (next to be held in 2023)

election results: area under government control: House of Representatives - percent of vote by party - DISY 30.7%, AKEL 25.7%, DIKO 14.5%, KS-EDEK 6.2%, SP 6% Solidarity Movement 5.2%, other 11.7%; seats by party - DISY 18, AKEL 16, DIKO 9, KS-EDEK 3, Citizen's Alliance 3 (2 left the party in 2017 and 2018 due to disagreements over the party's policy regarding the presidential election campaign; the two became independent MPs), Solidarity Movement 3, other 4; area administered by Turkish Cypriots: "Assembly of the Republic" - percent of vote by party - UBP 35.6%, CTP 20.9%, HP 17.1%, TDP 8.6%, DP 7.8%, YDP 7%, 3%; seats by party - UBP 21, CTP 12, HP 9, DP 3, TDP 3, YDP 2

JUDICIAL BRANCH:

highest courts: Supreme Court of Cyprus (consists of 13 judges including the court president); note - the highest court in the "Turkish Republic of Northern Cyprus (TRNC)" is the "Supreme Court" (consists of 8 "judges" including the "court president")

judge selection and term of office: Republic of Cyprus Supreme Court judges appointed by the president of the republic upon the recommendation of the Supreme Court judges; judges can serve until age 68; "TRNC Supreme Court" judges appointed by the "Supreme Council of Judicature," a 12-member body of judges, the attorney general, appointees - 1 each by the president of the "TRNC" and by the "Legislative Assembly" - and 1 member elected by the bar association; judge tenure NA

subordinate courts: Republic of Cyprus district courts; Assize Courts; Administrative Court; specialized courts for issues relating to family, industrial disputes, military, and rent control; "TRNC Assize Courts"; "district and family courts"

POLITICAL PARTIES AND LEADERS:

area under government control:
Citizens' Alliance or SP [Giorgos LILLIKAS];
Democratic Party or DIKO [Nicolas PAPADOPOULOS];
Democratic Rally or DISY [Averof NEOPHYTOU];
Ecological and Environmental Movement or KOP (Green party) [Giorgos PERDIKIS];
Movement of Social Democrats-United Democratic Center Union or KS-EDEK [Marinos SIZOPOULOS];
National Popular Front or ELAM [Christos CHRISTOU];
Progressive Party of the Working People or AKEL (Communist party) [Andros KYPRIANOU];
Solidarity Movement [Eleni THEOCHAROUS];
United Democrats or EDI [Praxoula ANTONIADOU];

area administered by Turkish Cypriots:
Communal Democracy Party or TDP [Cemal OZYIGIT];
Communist Liberation Party-New Forces or TKP-YG [Mehmet CAKICI];
Democratic Party or DP [Serdar DENKTAS];
National Democratic Party or NDP [Buray BUSKUVUTCU];
National Unity Party or UBP [Huseyin OZGURGUN];
People's Party or HP [Kudret OZERSAY];
Rebirth Party or YDP [Erhan ARIKLI];
Republican Turkish Party or CTP [Tufan ERHURMAN];
United Cyprus Party or BKP [Izzet IZCAN]

INTERNATIONAL ORGANIZATION PARTICIPATION:

Australia Group, C, CD, CE, EBRD, ECB, EIB, EMU, EU, FAO, IAEA, IBRD, ICAO, ICC (national committees), ICCt, ICRM, IDA, IFAD, IFC, IFRCS, IHO, ILO, IMF, IMO, IMSO, Interpol, IOC, IOM, IPU, ISO, ITSO, ITU, ITUC (NGOs), MIGA, NAM, NSG, OAS (observer), OIF, OPCW, OSCE, PCA, UN, UNCTAD, UNESCO, UNHCR, UNIDO, UNIFIL, UNWTO, UPU, WCO, WFTU (NGOs), WHO, WIPO, WMO, WTO

DIPLOMATIC REPRESENTATION IN THE US:

chief of mission: Ambassador Mario LYSIOTIS (since 17 September 2018)

chancery: 2211 R Street NW, Washington, DC 20008

telephone: [1] (202) 462-5772, 462-0873

FAX: [1] (202) 483-6710

consulate(s) general: New York

note: representative of the Turkish Cypriot community in the US is Ismet

KORUKOGLU; office at 1667 K Street NW, Washington, DC; telephone [1] (202) 887-6198

DIPLOMATIC REPRESENTATION FROM THE US:

chief of mission: Ambassador Kathleen Ann DOHERTY (since 7 October 2015)

embassy: corner of Metochiou and Ploutarchou Streets, 2407 Engomi, Nicosia

mailing address: P. O. Box 24536, 1385 Nicosia

telephone: [357] (22) 393939

FAX: [357] (22) 393344

FLAG DESCRIPTION:

centered on a white field is a copper-colored silhouette of the island (the island has long been famous for its copper deposits) above two olive-green-colored, crossed olive branches; the branches symbolize the hope for peace and reconciliation between the Greek and Turkish communities

note: one of only two national flags that uses a map as a design element; the flag of Kosovo is the other

note: the "Turkish Republic of Northern Cyprus" flag retains the white field of the Cyprus national flag but displays narrow horizontal red stripes positioned a small distance from the top and bottom edges between which are centered a red crescent and a red five-pointed star; the banner is modeled after the Turkish national flag but with the colors reversed

NATIONAL SYMBOL(S):

Cypriot mouflon (wild sheep), white dove; national colors: blue, white

NATIONAL ANTHEM:

name: "Ymnos eis tin Eleftherian" (Hymn to Liberty)

lyrics/music: Dionysios SOLOMOS/Nikolaos MANTZAROS

note: adopted 1960; Cyprus adopted the Greek national anthem as its own; the Turkish Cypriot community in Cyprus uses the anthem of Turkey

ECONOMY :: CYPRUS

ECONOMY - OVERVIEW:

The area of the Republic of Cyprus under government control has a market economy dominated by a services sector that accounts for more than four-fifths of GDP. Tourism, finance, shipping, and real estate have traditionally been the most important services. Cyprus has been a member of the EU since May 2004 and adopted the euro as its national currency in January 2008.

During the first five years of EU membership, the Cyprus economy grew at an average rate of about 4%, with unemployment between 2004 and 2008 averaging about 4%. However, the economy tipped into recession in 2009 as the ongoing global financial crisis and resulting low demand hit the tourism and construction sectors. An overextended banking sector with excessive exposure to Greek debt added to the contraction. Cyprus' biggest two banks were among the largest holders of Greek bonds in Europe and had a substantial presence in Greece through bank branches and subsidiaries. Following numerous downgrades of its credit rating, Cyprus lost access to international capital markets in May 2011. In July 2012, Cyprus became the fifth euro-zone government to request an economic bailout program from the European Commission, European Central Bank and the International Monetary Fund - known collectively as the "Troika."

Shortly after the election of President Nikos ANASTASIADES in February 2013, Cyprus reached an agreement with the Troika on a $13 billion bailout that triggered a two-week bank closure and the imposition of capital controls that remained partially in place until April 2015. Cyprus' two largest banks merged and the combined entity was recapitalized through conversion of some large bank deposits to shares and imposition of losses on bank bondholders. As with other EU countries, the Troika conditioned the bailout on passing financial and structural reforms and privatizing state-owned enterprises. Despite downsizing and restructuring, the Cypriot financial sector remains burdened by the largest stock of non-performing loans in the euro zone, equal to nearly half of all loans. Since the bailout, Cyprus has received positive appraisals by the Troika and outperformed fiscal targets but has struggled to overcome political opposition to bailout-mandated legislation, particularly regarding privatizations. The rate of non-performing loans (NPLs) is still very high at around 49%, and growth would accelerate if Cypriot banks could increase the pace of resolution of the NPLs.

In October 2013, a US-Israeli consortium completed preliminary appraisals of hydrocarbon deposits in Cyprus' exclusive economic zone (EEZ), which estimated gross mean reserves of about 130 billion cubic meters. Though exploration continues in Cyprus' EEZ, no additional commercially exploitable reserves have been identified. Developing offshore hydrocarbon resources remains a critical component of the government's economic recovery efforts, but development has been delayed as a result of regional developments and disagreements about exploitation methods.

GDP (PURCHASING POWER PARITY):

$31.78 billion (2017 est.)

$30.59 billion (2016 est.)

$29.58 billion (2015 est.)

note: data are in 2017 dollars

country comparison to the world: 129

GDP (OFFICIAL EXCHANGE RATE):

$21.7 billion (2017 est.) (2017 est.)

GDP - REAL GROWTH RATE:

3.9% (2017 est.)

3.4% (2016 est.)

2% (2015 est.)

country comparison to the world: 81

GDP - PER CAPITA (PPP):

$37,200 (2017 est.)

$36,100 (2016 est.)

$34,900 (2015 est.)

note: data are in 2017 dollars

country comparison to the world: 53

GROSS NATIONAL SAVING:

13.7% of GDP (2017 est.)

11.9% of GDP (2016 est.)

12.8% of GDP (2015 est.)

country comparison to the world: 140

GDP - COMPOSITION, BY END USE:

household consumption: 68.7% (2017 est.)

government consumption: 14.9% (2017 est.)

investment in fixed capital: 21.1% (2017 est.)

investment in inventories: -0.7% (2017 est.)

exports of goods and services: 63.8% (2017 est.)

imports of goods and services: -67.8% (2017 est.)

GDP - COMPOSITION, BY SECTOR OF ORIGIN:

agriculture: 2% (2017 est.)

industry: 12.5% (2017 est.)

services: 85.5% (2017 est.)

AGRICULTURE - PRODUCTS:

citrus, vegetables, barley, grapes, olives, vegetables; poultry, pork, lamb; dairy, cheese

INDUSTRIES:

tourism, food and beverage processing, cement and gypsum, ship repair and refurbishment, textiles, light chemicals, metal products, wood, paper, stone and clay products

INDUSTRIAL PRODUCTION GROWTH RATE:

13.4% (2017 est.)

country comparison to the world: 5

LABOR FORCE:

426,600 (2017 est.)

country comparison to the world: 158

LABOR FORCE - BY OCCUPATION:

agriculture: 3.8%

industry: 15.2%

services: 81% (2014 est.)

UNEMPLOYMENT RATE:

11.1% (2017 est.)

13% (2016 est.)

country comparison to the world: 150

POPULATION BELOW POVERTY LINE:

NA

HOUSEHOLD INCOME OR CONSUMPTION BY PERCENTAGE SHARE:

lowest 10%: 28.8% (2014)

highest 10%: 28.8% (2014)

DISTRIBUTION OF FAMILY INCOME - GINI INDEX:

34.8 (2014 est.)

32.4 (2013 est.)

country comparison to the world: 99

BUDGET:

revenues: 8.663 billion (2017 est.)

expenditures: 8.275 billion (2017 est.)

TAXES AND OTHER REVENUES:

39.9% (of GDP) (2017 est.)

country comparison to the world: 40

BUDGET SURPLUS (+) OR DEFICIT (-):

1.8% (of GDP) (2017 est.)

country comparison to the world: 17

PUBLIC DEBT:

97.5% of GDP (2017 est.)

106.6% of GDP (2016 est.)

note: data cover general government debt and include debt instruments issued (or owned) by government entities other than the treasury; the data include treasury debt held by foreign entities; the data exclude debt issued by subnational entities, as well as intragovernmental debt; intragovernmental debt consists of treasury borrowings from surpluses in the social funds, such as for retirement, medical care, and unemployment

country comparison to the world: 19

FISCAL YEAR:

calendar year

INFLATION RATE (CONSUMER PRICES):

0.7% (2017 est.)

-1.2% (2016 est.)

country comparison to the world: 35

CENTRAL BANK DISCOUNT RATE:

0% (31 December 2017)

0% (31 December 2010)

note: this is the European Central Bank's rate on the marginal lending facility, which offers overnight credit to banks in the euro area

country comparison to the world: 150

COMMERCIAL BANK PRIME LENDING RATE:

4.13% (31 December 2017 est.)

4.33% (31 December 2016 est.)

country comparison to the world: 164

STOCK OF NARROW MONEY:

$5.152 billion (31 December 2017 est.)

$4.174 billion (31 December 2016 est.)

note: see entry for the European Union for money supply for the entire euro area; the European Central Bank (ECB) controls monetary policy for the 18 members of the Economic and Monetary Union (EMU); individual members of the EMU do not control the quantity of money circulating within their own borders

country comparison to the world: 102

STOCK OF BROAD MONEY:

$5.152 billion (31 December 2017 est.)

$4.174 billion (31 December 2016 est.)

country comparison to the world: 105

STOCK OF DOMESTIC CREDIT:

$55.61 billion (31 December 2017 est.)

$50.84 billion (31 December 2016 est.)

country comparison to the world: 63

MARKET VALUE OF PUBLICLY TRADED SHARES:

$2.692 billion (31 December 2015 est.)

$4.031 billion (31 December 2014 est.)

$2.105 billion (31 December 2013 est.)

country comparison to the world: 96

CURRENT ACCOUNT BALANCE:

-$1.458 billion (2017 est.)

-$984 million (2016 est.)

country comparison to the world: 154

EXPORTS:

$2.805 billion (2017 est.)

$2.7 billion (2016 est.)

country comparison to the world: 131

EXPORTS - PARTNERS:

Libya 9.4%, Greece 7.7%, Norway 6.7%, UK 5.3%, Germany 4.1% (2017)

EXPORTS - COMMODITIES:

citrus, potatoes, pharmaceuticals, cement, clothing

IMPORTS:

$7.935 billion (2017 est.)

$7.153 billion (2016 est.)

country comparison to the world: 111

IMPORTS - COMMODITIES:

consumer goods, petroleum and lubricants, machinery, transport equipment

IMPORTS - PARTNERS:

Greece 19%, Italy 7.5%, China 7.4%, South Korea 7.3%, Germany 7%, Netherlands 5.1%, UK 5%, Israel 4.1% (2017)

RESERVES OF FOREIGN EXCHANGE AND GOLD:

$888.2 million (31 December 2017 est.)

$817.7 million (31 December 2016 est.)

country comparison to the world: 136

DEBT - EXTERNAL:

$95.28 billion (31 December 2013 est.)

$103.5 billion (31 December 2012 est.)

country comparison to the world: 50

STOCK OF DIRECT FOREIGN INVESTMENT - AT HOME:

$232.5 billion (31 December 2017 est.)

$174.5 billion (31 December 2016 est.)

country comparison to the world: 28

STOCK OF DIRECT FOREIGN INVESTMENT - ABROAD:

$222.9 billion (31 December 2017 est.)

$175.3 billion (31 December 2016 est.)

country comparison to the world: 26

EXCHANGE RATES:

euros (EUR) per US dollar -

0.885 (2017 est.)

0.903 (2016 est.)

0.9214 (2015 est.)

0.885 (2014 est.)

0.7634 (2013 est.)

ECONOMY OF THE AREA ADMINISTERED BY TURKISH CYPRIOTS:

Economy - overview: Even though the whole of the island is part of the EU, implementation of the EU "acquis communautaire" has been suspended in the area administered by Turkish Cypriots, known locally as the "Turkish Republic of Northern Cyprus" ("TRNC"), until political conditions permit the reunification of the island. The market-based economy of the "TRNC" is roughly one-fifth the size of its southern neighbor and is likewise dominated by the service sector with a large portion of the population employed by the government. In 2012 - the latest year for which data are available - the services sector, which includes the public sector, trade, tourism, and education, contributed 58.7% to economic output. In the same year, light manufacturing and agriculture contributed 2.7% and 6.2%, respectively. Manufacturing is limited mainly to food and beverages, furniture and fixtures, construction materials, metal and non-metal products, textiles and clothing. The "TRNC" maintains few economic ties with the Republic of Cyprus outside of trade in construction materials. Since its creation, the "TRNC" has heavily relied on financial assistance from Turkey, which supports the "TRNC" defense, telecommunications, water and postal services. The Turkish Lira is the preferred currency, though foreign currencies are widely accepted in business transactions. The "TRNC" remains vulnerable to the Turkish market and monetary policy because of its use of the Turkish Lira. The "TRNC" weathered the European financial crisis relatively unscathed - compared to the Republic of Cyprus - because of the lack of financial sector development, the health of the Turkish economy, and its separation from the rest of the island. The "TRNC" economy experienced growth estimated at 2.8% in 2013 and 2.3% in 2014 and is projected to grow 3.8% in 2015.;

GDP (purchasing power parity): $1.829 billion (2007 est.);

GDP - real growth rate: 2.3% (2014 est.);

2.8% (2013 est.);

GDP - per capita: $11,700 (2007 est.);

GDP - composition by sector: agriculture: 6.2%,; industry: 35.1%,; services: 58.7% (2012 est.);

Labor force: 95,030 (2007 est.);

Labor force - by occupation: agriculture: 14.5%,; industry: 29%,; services: 56.5% (2004);

Unemployment rate: 9.4% (2005 est.);

Population below poverty line: %NA;

Inflation rate: 11.4% (2006);

Budget: revenues: $2.5 billion,; expenditures: $2.5 billion (2006);

Agriculture - products: citrus fruit, dairy, potatoes, grapes, olives, poultry, lamb;

Industries: foodstuffs, textiles, clothing, ship repair, clay, gypsum, copper, furniture;

Industrial production growth rate: -0.3% (2007 est.);

Electricity production: 998.9 million kWh (2005);

Electricity consumption: 797.9 million kWh (2005);

Exports: $68.1 million, f.o.b. (2007 est.);

Export - commodities: citrus, dairy, potatoes, textiles;

Export - partners: Turkey 40%; direct trade between the area administered by Turkish Cypriots and the area under government control remains limited;

Imports: $1.2 billion, f.o.b. (2007 est.);

Import - commodities: vehicles, fuel, cigarettes, food, minerals, chemicals, machinery;

Import - partners: Turkey 60%; direct trade between the area administered by Turkish Cypriots and the area under government control remains limited;

Reserves of foreign exchange and gold: NA;

Debt - external: NA;

Currency (code): Turkish new lira (YTL);

Exchange rates: Turkish new lira per US dollar:; 1.9 (2013); 1.8 (2012); 1.668 (2011); 1.5026 (2010); 1.55 (2009);

ENERGY :: CYPRUS

ELECTRICITY ACCESS:

electrification - total population: 100% (2016)

ELECTRICITY - PRODUCTION:

4.618 billion kWh (2016 est.)

country comparison to the world: 123

ELECTRICITY - CONSUMPTION:

4.355 billion kWh (2016 est.)

country comparison to the world: 126

ELECTRICITY - EXPORTS:

0 kWh (2016 est.)

country comparison to the world: 126

ELECTRICITY - IMPORTS:

0 kWh (2016 est.)

country comparison to the world: 140

ELECTRICITY - INSTALLED GENERATING CAPACITY:

1.77 million kW (2016 est.)

country comparison to the world: 117

ELECTRICITY - FROM FOSSIL FUELS:

85% of total installed capacity (2016 est.)

country comparison to the world: 70

ELECTRICITY - FROM NUCLEAR FUELS:

0% of total installed capacity (2017 est.)

country comparison to the world: 76

ELECTRICITY - FROM HYDROELECTRIC PLANTS:

0% of total installed capacity (2017 est.)

country comparison to the world: 166

ELECTRICITY - FROM OTHER RENEWABLE SOURCES:

15% of total installed capacity (2017 est.)

country comparison to the world: 58

CRUDE OIL - PRODUCTION:

0 bbl/day (2017 est.)

country comparison to the world: 125

CRUDE OIL - EXPORTS:

0 bbl/day (2015 est.)

country comparison to the world: 113

CRUDE OIL - IMPORTS:

0 bbl/day (2015 est.)

country comparison to the world: 116

CRUDE OIL - PROVED RESERVES:

0 bbl (1 January 2018 est.)

country comparison to the world: 122

REFINED PETROLEUM PRODUCTS - PRODUCTION:

0 bbl/day (2015 est.)

country comparison to the world: 135

REFINED PETROLEUM PRODUCTS - CONSUMPTION:

49,000 bbl/day (2016 est.)

country comparison to the world: 106

REFINED PETROLEUM PRODUCTS - EXPORTS:

500 bbl/day (2015 est.)

country comparison to the world: 110

REFINED PETROLEUM PRODUCTS - IMPORTS:

49,240 bbl/day (2015 est.)

country comparison to the world: 84

NATURAL GAS - PRODUCTION:

0 cu m (2017 est.)

country comparison to the world: 122

NATURAL GAS - CONSUMPTION:

0 cu m (2017 est.)

country comparison to the world: 138

NATURAL GAS - EXPORTS:

0 cu m (2017 est.)

country comparison to the world: 92

NATURAL GAS - IMPORTS:

0 cu m (2017 est.)

country comparison to the world: 115

NATURAL GAS - PROVED RESERVES:

141.6 billion cu m (1 January 2014 est.)

country comparison to the world: 47

CARBON DIOXIDE EMISSIONS FROM CONSUMPTION OF ENERGY:

7.72 million Mt (2017 est.)

country comparison to the world: 118

COMMUNICATIONS :: CYPRUS

TELEPHONES - FIXED LINES:

total subscriptions: 317,241 (2017 est.)

subscriptions per 100 inhabitants: 26 (2017 est.)

country comparison to the world: 110

TELEPHONES - MOBILE CELLULAR:

total subscriptions: 1,176,801 (2017 est.)

subscriptions per 100 inhabitants: 96 (2017 est.)

country comparison to the world: 157

TELEPHONE SYSTEM:

general assessment: despite the growth of Cyprus's telecom sector, the market overall continues to be dominated by the incumbent, Cyta, which is still fully-owned by the state; improved regulatory circumstances, especially in relation to network interconnection and access, has given competing operators the certainty to invest in network infrastructure, to launch competing services (2017)

domestic: open-wire, fiber-optic cable, and microwave radio relay; fixed-line teledisity is 26 per 100, 96 per 100 for mobile-cellular (2017)

international: country code - 357 (area administered by Turkish Cypriots uses the country code of Turkey - 90); a number of submarine cables, including the SEA-ME-WE-3, combine to provide connectivity to Western Europe, the Middle East, and Asia; tropospheric scatter; satellite earth stations - 8 (3 Intelsat - 1 Atlantic Ocean and 2 Indian Ocean, 2 Eutelsat, 2 Intersputnik, and 1 Arabsat); Quantum Cable contracts for new submarine cable linking to Greece and Israel; Telecom Italy Sparkle and Cyta complete the Kimonas cable subsystem linking Cyprus with Crete; Cyta upgrades transmission capacity on the TE-North Cable System to 500Gb/s (2017)

BROADCAST MEDIA:

mixture of state and privately run TV and radio services; the public broadcaster operates 2 TV channels and 4 radio stations; 6 private TV broadcasters, satellite and cable TV services including telecasts from Greece and Turkey, and a number of private radio stations are available; in areas administered by Turkish Cypriots, there are 2 public TV stations, 4 public radio stations, and 7 privately owned TV and 21 radio broadcast stations plus 6 radio and 4 TV channels of local universities, plus 1 radio station of military, security forces and 1 radio station of civil defense cooperation, as well as relay stations from Turkey (2017)

INTERNET COUNTRY CODE:

.cy

INTERNET USERS:

total: 915,036 (July 2016 est.)

percent of population: 75.9% (July 2016 est.)

country comparison to the world: 134

BROADBAND - FIXED SUBSCRIPTIONS:

total: 295,686 (2017 est.)

subscriptions per 100 inhabitants: 24 (2017 est.)

country comparison to the world: 95

TRANSPORTATION :: CYPRUS

NATIONAL AIR TRANSPORT SYSTEM:

number of registered air carriers: 2 (2015)

inventory of registered aircraft operated by air carriers: 6 (2015)

annual passenger traffic on registered air carriers: 23,404 (2015)

annual freight traffic on registered air carriers: 230,600 mt-km (2015)

CIVIL AIRCRAFT REGISTRATION COUNTRY CODE PREFIX:

5B (2016)

AIRPORTS:

15 (2013)

country comparison to the world: 145

AIRPORTS - WITH PAVED RUNWAYS:

total: 13 (2017)

2,438 to 3,047 m: 7 (2017)

1,524 to 2,437 m: 2 (2017)

914 to 1,523 m: 3 (2017)

under 914 m: 1 (2017)

AIRPORTS - WITH UNPAVED RUNWAYS:

total: 2 (2013)

under 914 m: 2 (2013)

HELIPORTS:

9 (2013)

PIPELINES:

0 km oil

ROADWAYS:

total: 20,006 km (2011)

government control: 13,006 km (includes 2,277 km of expressways) (2011)

paved: 8,564 km (2011)

unpaved: 4,442 km (2011)

Turkish Cypriot control: 7,000 km (2011)

country comparison to the world: 110

MERCHANT MARINE:

total: 1,022 (2017)

by type: bulk carrier 307, container ship 183, general cargo 164, oil tanker 57, other 311 (2017)

country comparison to the world: 24

PORTS AND TERMINALS:

major seaport(s): area under government control: Larnaca, Limassol, Vasilikos

area administered by Turkish Cypriots: Famagusta, Kyrenia

MILITARY AND SECURITY :: CYPRUS

MILITARY EXPENDITURES:

1.78% of GDP (2016)

1.68% of GDP (2015)

1.54% of GDP (2014)

1.6% of GDP (2013)

1.66% of GDP (2012)

country comparison to the world: 62

MILITARY BRANCHES:

Republic of Cyprus: Cypriot National Guard (Ethniki Froura, EF, includes naval and air elements); Northern Cyprus: Turkish Cypriot Security Force (GKK) (2014)

MILITARY SERVICE AGE AND OBLIGATION:

Cypriot National Guard (CNG): 18-50 years of age for compulsory military service for all Greek Cypriot males; 17 years of age for voluntary service; 14-month service obligation (2016)

TRANSNATIONAL ISSUES :: CYPRUS

DISPUTES - INTERNATIONAL:

hostilities in 1974 divided the island into two de facto autonomous entities, the internationally recognized Cypriot Government and a Turkish-Cypriot community (north Cyprus)the 1,000-strong UN Peacekeeping Force in Cyprus (UNFICYP) has served in Cyprus since 1964 and maintains the buffer zone between north and southon 1 May 2004, Cyprus entered the EU still divided, with the EU's body of legislation and standards (acquis communitaire) suspended in the northTurkey protests Cypriot Government creating hydrocarbon blocks and maritime boundary with Lebanon in March 2007

REFUGEES AND INTERNALLY DISPLACED PERSONS:

IDPs: 217,000 (both Turkish and Greek Cypriots; many displaced since 1974) (2017)

ILLICIT DRUGS:

minor transit point for heroin and hashish via air routes and container traffic to Europe, especially from Lebanon and Turkey; some cocaine transits as well; despite a strengthening of anti-money-laundering legislation, remains vulnerable to money laundering; reporting of suspicious transactions in offshore sector remains weak

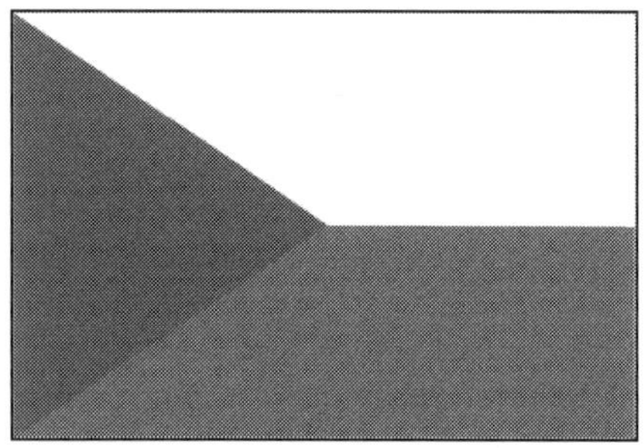

EUROPE :: CZECHIA

INTRODUCTION :: CZECHIA

BACKGROUND:

At the close of World War I, the Czechs and Slovaks of the former Austro-Hungarian Empire merged to form Czechoslovakia. During the interwar years, having rejected a federal system, the new country's predominantly Czech leaders were frequently preoccupied with meeting the increasingly strident demands of other ethnic minorities within the republic, most notably the Slovaks, the Sudeten Germans, and the Ruthenians (Ukrainians). On the eve of World War II, Nazi Germany occupied the territory that today comprises Czechia, and Slovakia became an independent state allied with Germany. After the war, a reunited but truncated Czechoslovakia (less Ruthenia) fell within the Soviet sphere of influence. In 1968, an invasion by Warsaw Pact troops ended the efforts of the country's leaders to liberalize communist rule and create "socialism with a human face," ushering in a period of repression known as "normalization." The peaceful "Velvet Revolution" swept the Communist Party from power at the end of 1989 and inaugurated a return to democratic rule and a market economy. On 1 January 1993, the country underwent a nonviolent "velvet divorce" into its two national components, the Czech Republic and Slovakia. The Czech Republic joined NATO in 1999 and the European Union in 2004. The country added the short-form name Czechia in 2016, while continuing to use the full form name, Czech Republic.

GEOGRAPHY :: CZECHIA

LOCATION:

Central Europe, between Germany, Poland, Slovakia, and Austria

GEOGRAPHIC COORDINATES:

49 45 N, 15 30 E

MAP REFERENCES:

Europe

AREA:

total: 78,867 sq km

land: 77,247 sq km

water: 1,620 sq km

country comparison to the world: 117

AREA - COMPARATIVE:

about two-thirds the size of Pennsylvania; slightly smaller than South Carolina

LAND BOUNDARIES:

total: 2,143 km

border countries (4): Austria 402 km, Germany 704 km, Poland 796 km, Slovakia 241 km

COASTLINE:

0 km (landlocked)

MARITIME CLAIMS:

none (landlocked)

CLIMATE:

temperate; cool summers; cold, cloudy, humid winters

TERRAIN:

Bohemia in the west consists of rolling plains, hills, and plateaus surrounded by low mountains; Moravia in the east consists of very hilly country

ELEVATION:

mean elevation: 433 m

elevation extremes: 115 m lowest point: Labe (Elbe) River

1602 highest point: Snezka

NATURAL RESOURCES:

hard coal, soft coal, kaolin, clay, graphite, timber, arable land

LAND USE:

agricultural land: 54.8% (2011 est.)

arable land: 41% (2011 est.) / permanent crops: 1% (2011 est.) / permanent pasture: 12.8% (2011 est.)

forest: 34.4% (2011 est.)

other: 10.8% (2011 est.)

IRRIGATED LAND:

320 sq km (2012)

POPULATION DISTRIBUTION:

a fairly even distribution throughout most of the country, but the northern and eastern regions tend to have larger urban concentrations

NATURAL HAZARDS:

flooding

ENVIRONMENT - CURRENT ISSUES:

air and water pollution in areas of northwest Bohemia and in northern Moravia around Ostrava present health risks; acid rain damaging forests; land pollution caused by industry, mining, and agriculture

ENVIRONMENT - INTERNATIONAL AGREEMENTS:

party to: Air Pollution, Air Pollution-Nitrogen Oxides, Air Pollution-Persistent Organic Pollutants, Air Pollution-Sulfur 85, Air Pollution-Sulfur 94, Air Pollution-Volatile Organic Compounds, Antarctic-

Environmental Protocol, Antarctic Treaty, Biodiversity, Climate Change, Climate Change-Kyoto Protocol, Desertification, Endangered Species, Environmental Modification, Hazardous Wastes, Law of the Sea, Ozone Layer Protection, Ship Pollution, Wetlands, Whaling

signed, but not ratified: none of the selected agreements

GEOGRAPHY - NOTE:

landlocked; strategically located astride some of oldest and most significant land routes in Europe; Moravian Gate is a traditional military corridor between the North European Plain and the Danube in central Europe

PEOPLE AND SOCIETY :: CZECHIA

POPULATION:

10,686,269 (July 2018 est.)

country comparison to the world: 85

NATIONALITY:

noun: Czech(s)

adjective: Czech

ETHNIC GROUPS:

Czech 64.3%, Moravian 5%, Slovak 1.4%, other 1.8%, unspecified 27.5% (2011 est.)

LANGUAGES:

Czech (official) 95.4%, Slovak 1.6%, other 3% (2011 census)

RELIGIONS:

Roman Catholic 10.4%, Protestant (includes Czech Brethren and Hussite) 1.1%, other and unspecified 54%, none 34.5% (2011 est.)

AGE STRUCTURE:

0-14 years: 15.21% (male 834,800 /female 790,128)

15-24 years: 9.34% (male 514,728 /female 483,546)

25-54 years: 43.79% (male 2,404,724 /female 2,275,309)

55-64 years: 12.24% (male 638,130 /female 669,959)

65 years and over: 19.42% (male 865,455 /female 1,209,490) (2018 est.)

DEPENDENCY RATIOS:

total dependency ratio: 49.5 (2015 est.)

youth dependency ratio: 22.6 (2015 est.)

elderly dependency ratio: 26.9 (2015 est.)

potential support ratio: 3.7 (2015 est.)

MEDIAN AGE:

total: 42.5 years

male: 41.2 years

female: 43.8 years (2018 est.)

country comparison to the world: 29

POPULATION GROWTH RATE:

0.1% (2018 est.)

country comparison to the world: 186

BIRTH RATE:

9.2 births/1,000 population (2018 est.)

country comparison to the world: 203

DEATH RATE:

10.5 deaths/1,000 population (2018 est.)

country comparison to the world: 27

NET MIGRATION RATE:

2.3 migrant(s)/1,000 population (2017 est.)

country comparison to the world: 40

POPULATION DISTRIBUTION:

a fairly even distribution throughout most of the country, but the northern and eastern regions tend to have larger urban concentrations

URBANIZATION:

urban population: 73.8% of total population (2018)

rate of urbanization: 0.21% annual rate of change (2015-20 est.)

MAJOR URBAN AREAS - POPULATION:

1.292 million PRAGUE (capital) (2018)

SEX RATIO:

at birth: 1.06 male(s)/female (2017 est.)

0-14 years: 1.06 male(s)/female (2017 est.)

15-24 years: 1.06 male(s)/female (2017 est.)

25-54 years: 1.05 male(s)/female (2017 est.)

55-64 years: 0.94 male(s)/female (2017 est.)

65 years and over: 0.7 male(s)/female (2017 est.)

total population: 0.97 male(s)/female (2017 est.)

MOTHER'S MEAN AGE AT FIRST BIRTH:

28.1 years (2014 est.)

MATERNAL MORTALITY RATE:

4 deaths/100,000 live births (2015 est.)

country comparison to the world: 177

INFANT MORTALITY RATE:

total: 2.6 deaths/1,000 live births (2018 est.)

male: 2.8 deaths/1,000 live births (2018 est.)

female: 2.5 deaths/1,000 live births (2018 est.)

country comparison to the world: 214

LIFE EXPECTANCY AT BIRTH:

total population: 78.9 years (2018 est.)

male: 76 years (2018 est.)

female: 82.1 years (2018 est.)

country comparison to the world: 57

TOTAL FERTILITY RATE:

1.46 children born/woman (2018 est.)

country comparison to the world: 203

CONTRACEPTIVE PREVALENCE RATE:

86.3% (2008)

note: percent of women aged 18-44

HEALTH EXPENDITURES:

7.4% of GDP (2014)

country comparison to the world: 69

PHYSICIANS DENSITY:

3.68 physicians/1,000 population (2013)

HOSPITAL BED DENSITY:

6.5 beds/1,000 population (2015)

DRINKING WATER SOURCE:

improved:

urban: 100% of population (2015 est.)

rural: 100% of population (2015 est.)

total: 100% of population (2015 est.)

unimproved:

urban: 0% of population (2015 est.)

rural: 0% of population (2015 est.)

total: 0% of population (2015 est.)

SANITATION FACILITY ACCESS:

improved:

urban: 99.1% of population (2015 est.)

rural: 99.2% of population (2015 est.)

total: 99.1% of population (2015 est.)

unimproved:

urban: 0.9% of population (2015 est.)

rural: 0.8% of population (2015 est.)

total: 0.9% of population (2015 est.)

HIV/AIDS - ADULT PREVALENCE RATE:

<.1% (2017 est.)

HIV/AIDS - PEOPLE LIVING WITH HIV/AIDS:

2,900 (2017 est.)

country comparison to the world: 123

HIV/AIDS - DEATHS:

<100 (2017 est.)

OBESITY - ADULT PREVALENCE RATE:

26% (2016)

country comparison to the world: 46

EDUCATION EXPENDITURES:

4% of GDP (2014)

country comparison to the world: 110

LITERACY:

definition: NA (2011 est.)

total population: 99% (2011 est.)

male: 99% (2011 est.)

female: 99% (2011 est.)

SCHOOL LIFE EXPECTANCY (PRIMARY TO TERTIARY EDUCATION):

total: 17 years (2014)

male: 16 years (2014)

female: 18 years (2014)

UNEMPLOYMENT, YOUTH AGES 15-24:

total: 10.5% (2016 est.)

male: 9.9% (2016 est.)

female: 11.4% (2016 est.)

country comparison to the world: 122

GOVERNMENT :: CZECHIA

COUNTRY NAME:

conventional long form: Czech Republic

conventional short form: Czechia

local long form: Ceska republika

local short form: Cesko

etymology: name derives from the Czechs, a West Slavic tribe who rose to prominence in the late 9th century A.D.

GOVERNMENT TYPE:

parliamentary republic

CAPITAL:

name: Prague

geographic coordinates: 50 05 N, 14 28 E

time difference: UTC+1 (6 hours ahead of Washington, DC, during Standard Time)

daylight saving time: +1hr, begins last Sunday in March; ends last Sunday in October

ADMINISTRATIVE DIVISIONS:

13 regions (kraje, singular - kraj) and 1 capital city* (hlavni mesto); Jihocesky (South Bohemia), Jihomoravsky (South Moravia), Karlovarsky (Karlovy Vary), Kralovehradecky (Hradec Kralove), Liberecky (Liberec), Moravskoslezsky (Moravia-Silesia), Olomoucky (Olomouc), Pardubicky (Pardubice), Plzensky (Pilsen), Praha (Prague)*, Stredocesky (Central Bohemia), Ustecky (Usti), Vysocina (Highlands), Zlinsky (Zlin)

INDEPENDENCE:

1 January 1993 (Czechoslovakia split into the Czech Republic and Slovakia); note - although 1 January is the day the Czech Republic came into being, the Czechs commemorate 28 October 1918, the day the former Czechoslovakia declared its independence from the Austro-Hungarian Empire, as their independence day

NATIONAL HOLIDAY:

Czechoslovak Founding Day, 28 October (1918)

CONSTITUTION:

history: previous 1960; latest ratified 16 December 1992, effective 1 January 1993 (2017)

amendments: passage requires at least three-fifths concurrence by members present in both houses of Parliament; amended several times, last in 2013 (2017)

LEGAL SYSTEM:

new civil code enacted in 2014, replacing civil code of 1964 - based on former Austro-Hungarian civil codes and socialist theory - and reintroducing former Czech legal terminology

INTERNATIONAL LAW ORGANIZATION PARTICIPATION:

has not submitted an ICJ jurisdiction declaration; accepts ICCt jurisdiction

CITIZENSHIP:

citizenship by birth: no

citizenship by descent only: at least one parent must be a citizen of Czechia

dual citizenship recognized: no

residency requirement for naturalization: 5 years

SUFFRAGE:

18 years of age; universal

EXECUTIVE BRANCH:

chief of state: President Milos ZEMAN (since 8 March 2013)

head of government: Prime Minister Andrej BABIS (since 13 December 2017); First Deputy Prime Minister Jan HAMACEK (since 27 June 2018), Deputy Prime Minister Richard BRABEC (since 13 December 2017); note - the current government of Prime Minister Andrej BABIS was sworn in on 13 December 2017 but lost a confidence vote on 16 January 2018 and resigned the next day; President Milos ZEMAN accepted the resignation on 24 January 2018; the government is currently ruling in resignation

cabinet: Cabinet appointed by the president on the recommendation of the prime minister

elections/appointments: president directly elected by absolute majority popular vote in 2 rounds if needed for a 5-year term (limited to 2 consecutive terms); elections last held on 12-13 January 2018 with a runoff on 26-27 January 2018 (next to be held in January 2023); prime minister appointed by the president for a 4-year term

election results: Milos ZEMAN reelected president in the second round; percent of vote - Milos ZEMAN (SPO) 51.4%, Jiri DRAHOS (independent) 48.6%

LEGISLATIVE BRANCH:

description: bicameral Parliament or Parlament consists of:
Senate or Senat (81 seats; members directly elected in single-seat constituencies by absolute majority vote in 2 rounds if needed; members serve 6-year terms with one-third of the membership renewed every 2 years)
Chamber of Deputies or Poslanecka Snemovna (200 seats; members directly elected in 14 multi-seat constituencies by proportional representation vote with a 5% threshold required to fill a seat; members serve 4-year terms)

elections:
Senate - last held in 2 rounds on 5-6 and 12-13 October 2018 (next to be held in October 2020)
Chamber of Deputies - last held on 20-

21 October 2017 (next to be held by October 2021)

election results:
Senate - percent of vote by party - NA; ODS 16, KDU-CSL 16, CSSD 13, STAN 10, ANO 7, SEN 21 6, TOP 09 3, SZ 1, Movement for Prague 1, Pirates 1, SsCR 1, independent 6; composition NA

Chamber of Deputies - percent of vote by party - ANO 29.6%, ODS 11.3%, Pirates 10.8%, SPD 10.6%, KSCM 7.8%, CSSD 7.3%, KDU-CSL 5.8%, TOP 09 5.3%, STAN 5.2%, other 6.3%; seats by party - ANO 78, ODS 25, Pirates 22, SPD 22, CSSD 15, KSCM 15, KDU-CSL 10, TOP 09 7, STAN 6; composition - men 156, women 44, percent of women 22%; note - total Parliament percent of women NA

JUDICIAL BRANCH:

highest courts: Supreme Court (organized into Civil Law and Commercial Division, and Criminal Division each with a court chief justice, vice justice, and several judges); Constitutional Court (consists of 15 justices); Supreme Administrative Court (consists of 28 judges)

judge selection and term of office: Supreme Court judges proposed by the Chamber of Deputies and appointed by the president; judges appointed for life; Constitutional Court judges appointed by the president and confirmed by the Senate; judges appointed for 10-year, renewable terms; Supreme Administrative Court judges selected by the president of the Court; unlimited terms

subordinate courts: High Court; regional and district courts

POLITICAL PARTIES AND LEADERS:

Christian Democratic Union-Czechoslovak People's Party or KDU-CSL [Pavel BELOBRADEK]
Civic Democratic Party or ODS [Petr FIALA]
Communist Party of Bohemia and Moravia or KSCM [Vojtech FILIP]
Czech Social Democratic Party or CSSD [Jan HAMACEK]
Dawn - National Coalition or Usvit-NK [Miroslav LIDINSKY]
Free Citizens Party or Svobodni [Petr MACH]
Freedom and Direct Democracy or SPD [Tomio OKAMURA]
Green Party or SZ [Petr STEPANEK]
Mayors and Independents or STAN [Petr GAZDIK]
Mayors for the Liberec Region or SLK [Martin PUTA]
Movement for Prague
Movement of Dissatisfied Citizens or ANO [Andrej BABIS]
Nestranici (Non-Partisans) or NK [Vera RYBOVA]
North Bohemians or S.cz [Bronislav SCHWARZ]
Party of Civic Rights or SPO [Lubomir NECAS]
Pirate Party or Pirates [Ivan BARTOS]
Tradition Responsibility Prosperity 09 or TOP 09 [Jiri POSPISIL]

INTERNATIONAL ORGANIZATION PARTICIPATION:

Australia Group, BIS, BSEC (observer), CD, CE, CEI, CERN, EAPC, EBRD, ECB, EIB, ESA, EU, FAO, IAEA, IBRD, ICAO, ICC (national committees), ICCt, ICRM, IDA, IEA, IFC, IFRCS, ILO, IMF, IMO, IMSO, Interpol, IOC, IOM, IPU, ISO, ITSO, ITU, ITUC (NGOs), MIGA, MONUSCO, NATO, NEA, NSG, OAS (observer), OECD, OIF (observer), OPCW, OSCE, PCA, Schengen Convention, SELEC, UN, UNCTAD, UNESCO, UNHCR, UNIDO, UNWTO, UPU, WCO, WFTU (NGOs), WHO, WIPO, WMO, WTO, ZC

DIPLOMATIC REPRESENTATION IN THE US:

chief of mission: Ambassador Hynek KMONICEK (since 24 April 2017)

chancery: 3900 Spring of Freedom Street NW, Washington, DC 20008

telephone: [1] (202) 274-9100

FAX: [1] (202) 966-8540

consulate(s) general: Chicago, Los Angeles, New York

DIPLOMATIC REPRESENTATION FROM THE US:

chief of mission: Ambassador Stephen B. KING (since 6 December 2017)

embassy: Trziste 15, 118 01 Prague 1 - Mala Strana

mailing address: use embassy street address

telephone: [420] 257 022 000

FAX: [420] 257 022 809

FLAG DESCRIPTION:

two equal horizontal bands of white (top) and red with a blue isosceles triangle based on the hoist side

note: combines the white and red colors of Bohemia with blue from the arms of Moravia; is identical to the flag of the former Czechoslovakia

NATIONAL SYMBOL(S):

silver (or white), double-tailed, rampant lion; national colors: white, red, blue

NATIONAL ANTHEM:

name: "Kde domov muj?" (Where is My Home?)

lyrics/music: Josef Kajetan TYL/Frantisek Jan SKROUP

note: adopted 1993; the anthem was originally written as incidental music to the play "Fidlovacka" (1834), it soon became very popular as an unofficial anthem of the Czech nation; its first verse served as the official Czechoslovak anthem beginning in 1918, while the second verse (Slovak) was dropped after the split of Czechoslovakia in 1993

ECONOMY :: CZECHIA

ECONOMY - OVERVIEW:

Czechia is a prosperous market economy that boasts one of the highest GDP growth rates and lowest unemployment levels in the EU, but its dependence on exports makes economic growth vulnerable to contractions in external demand. Czechia's exports comprise some 80% of GDP and largely consist of automobiles, the country's single largest industry. Czechia acceded to the EU in 2004 but has yet to join the euro-zone. While the flexible koruna helps Czechia weather external shocks, it was one of the world's strongest performing currencies in 2017, appreciating approximately 16% relative to the US dollar after the central bank (Czech National Bank - CNB) ended its cap on the currency's value in early April 2017, which it had maintained since November 2013. The CNB hiked rates in August and November 2017 - the first rate changes in nine years - to address rising inflationary pressures brought by strong economic growth and a tight labor market.

Since coming to power in 2014, the new government has undertaken some reforms to try to reduce corruption, attract investment, and improve social welfare programs, which could help increase the government's revenues and improve living conditions for Czechs. The government introduced in December 2016 an online tax reporting system intended to reduce tax evasion and increase revenues. The government also plans to remove labor market rigidities to improve the business climate, bring procurement procedures in line with EU best practices, and boost wages. The country's low unemployment rate has led to steady increases in salaries, and the government is facing pressure from businesses to allow greater migration of qualified workers, at least from Ukraine and neighboring Central European countries.

Long-term challenges include dealing with a rapidly aging population, a shortage of skilled workers, a lagging education system, funding an unsustainable pension and health care system, and diversifying away from manufacturing and toward a more high-tech, services-based, knowledge economy.

GDP (PURCHASING POWER PARITY):

$375.9 billion (2017 est.)

$360.5 billion (2016 est.)

$351.9 billion (2015 est.)

note: data are in 2017 dollars

country comparison to the world: 49

GDP (OFFICIAL EXCHANGE RATE):

$215.8 billion (2017 est.) (2017 est.)

GDP - REAL GROWTH RATE:

4.3% (2017 est.)

2.5% (2016 est.)

5.3% (2015 est.)

country comparison to the world: 68

GDP - PER CAPITA (PPP):

$35,500 (2017 est.)

$34,200 (2016 est.)

$33,400 (2015 est.)

note: data are in 2017 dollars

country comparison to the world: 57

GROSS NATIONAL SAVING:

26.9% of GDP (2017 est.)

27.5% of GDP (2016 est.)

28.2% of GDP (2015 est.)

country comparison to the world: 45

GDP - COMPOSITION, BY END USE:

household consumption: 47.4% (2017 est.)

government consumption: 19.2% (2017 est.)

investment in fixed capital: 24.7% (2017 est.)

investment in inventories: 1.1% (2017 est.)

exports of goods and services: 79.9% (2017 est.)

imports of goods and services: -72.3% (2017 est.)

GDP - COMPOSITION, BY SECTOR OF ORIGIN:

agriculture: 2.3% (2017 est.)

industry: 36.9% (2017 est.)

services: 60.8% (2017 est.)

AGRICULTURE - PRODUCTS:

wheat, potatoes, sugar beets, hops, fruit; pigs, poultry

INDUSTRIES:

motor vehicles, metallurgy, machinery and equipment, glass, armaments

INDUSTRIAL PRODUCTION GROWTH RATE:

7.5% (2017 est.)

country comparison to the world: 27

LABOR FORCE:

5.427 million (2017 est.)

country comparison to the world: 76

LABOR FORCE - BY OCCUPATION:

agriculture: 2.8%

industry: 38%

services: 59.2% (2015)

UNEMPLOYMENT RATE:

2.9% (2017 est.)

3.9% (2016 est.)

country comparison to the world: 33

POPULATION BELOW POVERTY LINE:

9.7% (2015 est.)

HOUSEHOLD INCOME OR CONSUMPTION BY PERCENTAGE SHARE:

lowest 10%: 21.7% (2015 est.)

highest 10%: 21.7% (2015 est.)

DISTRIBUTION OF FAMILY INCOME - GINI INDEX:

25 (2015)

25.1 (2014)

country comparison to the world: 152

BUDGET:

revenues: 87.37 billion (2017 est.)

expenditures: 83.92 billion (2017 est.)

TAXES AND OTHER REVENUES:

40.5% (of GDP) (2017 est.)

country comparison to the world: 37

BUDGET SURPLUS (+) OR DEFICIT (-):

1.6% (of GDP) (2017 est.)

country comparison to the world: 19

PUBLIC DEBT:

34.7% of GDP (2017 est.)

36.8% of GDP (2016 est.)

country comparison to the world: 153

FISCAL YEAR:

calendar year

INFLATION RATE (CONSUMER PRICES):

2.4% (2017 est.)

0.7% (2016 est.)

country comparison to the world: 118

CENTRAL BANK DISCOUNT RATE:

0.05% (31 December 2017)

0.05% (31 December 2016)

note: this is the two-week repo, the main rate CNB uses

country comparison to the world: 143

COMMERCIAL BANK PRIME LENDING RATE:

3.59% (31 December 2017 est.)

3.91% (31 December 2016 est.)

country comparison to the world: 168

STOCK OF NARROW MONEY:

$177.2 billion (31 December 2017 est.)

$133.5 billion (31 December 2016 est.)

country comparison to the world: 27

STOCK OF BROAD MONEY:

$177.2 billion (31 December 2017 est.)

$133.5 billion (31 December 2016 est.)

country comparison to the world: 27

STOCK OF DOMESTIC CREDIT:

$147.1 billion (31 December 2017 est.)

$124.3 billion (31 December 2016 est.)

country comparison to the world: 50

MARKET VALUE OF PUBLICLY TRADED SHARES:

$58.83 billion (31 December 2017 est.)

$40.74 billion (31 December 2016 est.)

$44.5 billion (31 December 2015 est.)

country comparison to the world: 48

CURRENT ACCOUNT BALANCE:

$2.317 billion (2017 est.)

$3.037 billion (2016 est.)

country comparison to the world: 38

EXPORTS:

$144.8 billion (2017 est.)

$131.1 billion (2016 est.)

country comparison to the world: 33

EXPORTS - PARTNERS:

Germany 32.8%, Slovakia 7.8%, Poland 6.1%, France 5.1%, UK 4.9%, Austria 4.4%, Italy 4.1% (2017)

EXPORTS - COMMODITIES:

machinery and transport equipment, raw materials, fuel, chemicals

IMPORTS:

$134.7 billion (2017 est.)

$120.5 billion (2016 est.)

country comparison to the world: 32

IMPORTS - COMMODITIES:

machinery and transport equipment, raw materials and fuels, chemicals

IMPORTS - PARTNERS:

Germany 29.8%, Poland 9.1%, China 7.4%, Slovakia 5.8%, Netherlands 5.3%, Italy 4% (2017)

RESERVES OF FOREIGN EXCHANGE AND GOLD:

$148 billion (31 December 2017 est.)

$85.73 billion (31 December 2016 est.)

country comparison to the world: 18

DEBT - EXTERNAL:

$205.2 billion (31 December 2017 est.)

$138 billion (31 December 2016 est.)

country comparison to the world: 35

STOCK OF DIRECT FOREIGN INVESTMENT - AT HOME:

$185.6 billion (31 December 2017 est.)

$139.6 billion (31 December 2016 est.)

country comparison to the world: 34

STOCK OF DIRECT FOREIGN INVESTMENT - ABROAD:

$54.39 billion (31 December 2017 est.)

$43.09 billion (31 December 2016 est.)

country comparison to the world: 43

EXCHANGE RATES:

koruny (CZK) per US dollar -

23.34 (2017 est.)

24.44 (2016 est.)

24.44 (2015 est.)

24.599 (2014 est.)

20.758 (2013 est.)

ENERGY :: CZECHIA

ELECTRICITY ACCESS:

electrification - total population: 100% (2016)

ELECTRICITY - PRODUCTION:

77.39 billion kWh (2016 est.)

country comparison to the world: 38

ELECTRICITY - CONSUMPTION:

62.34 billion kWh (2016 est.)

country comparison to the world: 42

ELECTRICITY - EXPORTS:

24.79 billion kWh (2016 est.)

country comparison to the world: 7

ELECTRICITY - IMPORTS:

13.82 billion kWh (2016 est.)

country comparison to the world: 18

ELECTRICITY - INSTALLED GENERATING CAPACITY:

21.63 million kW (2016 est.)

country comparison to the world: 40

ELECTRICITY - FROM FOSSIL FUELS:

60% of total installed capacity (2016 est.)

country comparison to the world: 131

ELECTRICITY - FROM NUCLEAR FUELS:

19% of total installed capacity (2017 est.)

country comparison to the world: 10

ELECTRICITY - FROM HYDROELECTRIC PLANTS:

5% of total installed capacity (2017 est.)

country comparison to the world: 130

ELECTRICITY - FROM OTHER RENEWABLE SOURCES:

16% of total installed capacity (2017 est.)

country comparison to the world: 51

CRUDE OIL - PRODUCTION:

2,000 bbl/day (2017 est.)

country comparison to the world: 87

CRUDE OIL - EXPORTS:

446 bbl/day (2017 est.)

country comparison to the world: 78

CRUDE OIL - IMPORTS:

155,900 bbl/day (2017 est.)

country comparison to the world: 36

CRUDE OIL - PROVED RESERVES:

15 million bbl (1 January 2018 est.)

country comparison to the world: 85

REFINED PETROLEUM PRODUCTS - PRODUCTION:

177,500 bbl/day (2017 est.)

country comparison to the world: 56

REFINED PETROLEUM PRODUCTS - CONSUMPTION:

213,700 bbl/day (2017 est.)

country comparison to the world: 56

REFINED PETROLEUM PRODUCTS - EXPORTS:

52,200 bbl/day (2017 est.)

country comparison to the world: 54

REFINED PETROLEUM PRODUCTS - IMPORTS:

83,860 bbl/day (2017 est.)

country comparison to the world: 60

NATURAL GAS - PRODUCTION:

229.4 million cu m (2017 est.)

country comparison to the world: 78

NATURAL GAS - CONSUMPTION:

8.721 billion cu m (2017 est.)

country comparison to the world: 51

NATURAL GAS - EXPORTS:

0 cu m (2017 est.)

country comparison to the world: 93

NATURAL GAS - IMPORTS:

8.891 billion cu m (2017 est.)

country comparison to the world: 28

NATURAL GAS - PROVED RESERVES:

3.964 billion cu m (1 January 2018 est.)

country comparison to the world: 93

CARBON DIOXIDE EMISSIONS FROM CONSUMPTION OF ENERGY:

115.8 million Mt (2017 est.)

country comparison to the world: 39

COMMUNICATIONS :: CZECHIA

TELEPHONES - FIXED LINES:

total subscriptions: 1,616,631 (2017 est.)

subscriptions per 100 inhabitants: 15 (2017 est.)

country comparison to the world: 62

TELEPHONES - MOBILE CELLULAR:

total subscriptions: 12,634,937 (2017 est.)

subscriptions per 100 inhabitants: 118 (2017 est.)

country comparison to the world: 73

TELEPHONE SYSTEM:

general assessment: good telephone and Internet service; the Czech Republic has a sophisticated telecom market, with good competition in all sectors provided by a number of alternate operators; the incumbent telco O2 Czech Republic remains the dominant player though other operators are gaining market share, through merger and acquisition activity; regulator makes progress for 5G services; fixed wireless broadband remains strong, with penetration among the highest in the EU (2017)

domestic: access to the fixed-line telephone network expanded throughout the 1990s, 15 per 100 fixed-line, but the number of fixed-line connections has been dropping since then; mobile telephone usage increased sharply 118 per 100 mobile-cellular, and the number of cellular telephone subscriptions now greatly exceeds the population (2017)

international: country code - 420; satellite earth stations - 6 (2 Intersputnik - Atlantic and Indian Ocean regions, 1 Intelsat, 1 Eutelsat, 1 Inmarsat, 1 Globalstar) (2017)

BROADCAST MEDIA:

22 TV stations operate nationally, with 17 of them in private hands; publicly operated Czech Television has 5 national channels; throughout the country, there are some 350 TV channels in operation, many through cable, satellite, and IPTV subscription services; 63 radio broadcasters are registered, operating over 80 radio stations, including 7 multiregional radio stations or networks; publicly operated broadcaster Czech Radio operates 4 national, 14 regional, and 4 Internet stations; both Czech Radio and Czech Television are partially financed through a license fee (2018)

INTERNET COUNTRY CODE:

.cz

INTERNET USERS:

total: 8,141,303 (July 2016 est.)

percent of population: 76.5% (July 2016 est.)

country comparison to the world: 52

BROADBAND - FIXED SUBSCRIPTIONS:

total: 3,060,597 (2017 est.)

subscriptions per 100 inhabitants: 29 (2017 est.)

country comparison to the world: 39

TRANSPORTATION :: CZECHIA

NATIONAL AIR TRANSPORT SYSTEM:

number of registered air carriers: 4 (2015)

inventory of registered aircraft operated by air carriers: 48 (2015)

annual passenger traffic on registered air carriers: 4,971,616 (2015)

annual freight traffic on registered air carriers: 26,619,650 mt-km (2015)

CIVIL AIRCRAFT REGISTRATION COUNTRY CODE PREFIX:

OK (2016)

AIRPORTS:

128 (2013)

country comparison to the world: 46

AIRPORTS - WITH PAVED RUNWAYS:

total: 41 (2017)

over 3,047 m: 2 (2017)

2,438 to 3,047 m: 9 (2017)

1,524 to 2,437 m: 12 (2017)

914 to 1,523 m: 2 (2017)

under 914 m: 16 (2017)

AIRPORTS - WITH UNPAVED RUNWAYS:

total: 87 (2013)

1,524 to 2,437 m: 1 (2013)

914 to 1,523 m: 25 (2013)

under 914 m: 61 (2013)

HELIPORTS:

1 (2013)

PIPELINES:

7160 km gas, 536 km oil, 94 km refined products (2013)

RAILWAYS:

total: 9,622 km (2014)

standard gauge: 9,519.5 km 1.435-m gauge (3,240.5 km electrified) (2014)

narrow gauge: 102 km 0.760-m gauge (2014)

country comparison to the world: 24

ROADWAYS:

total: 130,661 km (includes urban roads) (2011)

paved: 130,661 km (includes 730 km of expressways) (2011)

country comparison to the world: 40

WATERWAYS:

664 km (principally on Elbe, Vltava, Oder, and other navigable rivers, lakes, and canals) (2010)

country comparison to the world: 76

PORTS AND TERMINALS:

river port(s): Prague (Vltava)

Decin, Usti nad Labem (Elbe)

MILITARY AND SECURITY :: CZECHIA

MILITARY EXPENDITURES:

0.98% of GDP (2016)

0.96% of GDP (2015)

0.97% of GDP (2014)

country comparison to the world: 115

MILITARY BRANCHES:

Army of the Czech Republic (Armada Ceske Republiky): General Staff (Generalni Stab, includes Land Forces (Pozemni sily) and Air Forces (Vzdusne sily)) (2018)

MILITARY SERVICE AGE AND OBLIGATION:

18-28 years of age for male and female voluntary military service; no conscription (2012)

TRANSNATIONAL ISSUES :: CZECHIA

DISPUTES - INTERNATIONAL:

none

REFUGEES AND INTERNALLY DISPLACED PERSONS:

stateless persons: 1,502 (2017)

ILLICIT DRUGS:

transshipment point for Southwest Asian heroin and minor transit point for Latin American cocaine to Western Europe; producer of synthetic drugs for local and regional markets; susceptible to money laundering related to drug trafficking, organized crime; significant consumer of ecstasy

EUROPE :: DENMARK

INTRODUCTION :: DENMARK

BACKGROUND:

Once the seat of Viking raiders and later a major north European power, Denmark has evolved into a modern, prosperous nation that is participating in the general political and economic integration of Europe. It joined NATO in 1949 and the EEC (now the EU) in 1973. However, the country has opted out of certain elements of the EU's Maastricht Treaty, including the European Economic and Monetary Union, European defense cooperation, and issues concerning certain justice and home affairs.

GEOGRAPHY :: DENMARK

LOCATION:

Northern Europe, bordering the Baltic Sea and the North Sea, on a peninsula north of Germany (Jutland); also includes several major islands (Sjaelland, Fyn, and Bornholm)

GEOGRAPHIC COORDINATES:

56 00 N, 10 00 E

MAP REFERENCES:

Europe

AREA:

total: 43,094 sq km

land: 42,434 sq km

water: 660 sq km

note: includes the island of Bornholm in the Baltic Sea and the rest of metropolitan Denmark (the Jutland Peninsula, and the major islands of Sjaelland and Fyn), but excludes the Faroe Islands and Greenland

country comparison to the world: 134

AREA - COMPARATIVE:

slightly less than twice the size of Massachusetts

LAND BOUNDARIES:

total: 140 km

border countries (1): Germany 140 km

COASTLINE:

7,314 km

MARITIME CLAIMS:

territorial sea: 12 nm

exclusive economic zone: 200 nm

contiguous zone: 24 nm

continental shelf: 200-m depth or to the depth of exploitation

CLIMATE:

temperate; humid and overcast; mild, windy winters and cool summers

TERRAIN:

low and flat to gently rolling plains

ELEVATION:

mean elevation: 34 m

elevation extremes: -7 m lowest point: Lammefjord

171 highest point: Mollehoj/Ejer Bavnehoj

NATURAL RESOURCES:

petroleum, natural gas, fish, arable land, salt, limestone, chalk, stone, gravel and sand

LAND USE:

agricultural land: 63.4% (2011 est.)

arable land: 58.9% (2011 est.) / permanent crops: 0.1% (2011 est.) / permanent pasture: 4.4% (2011 est.)

forest: 12.9% (2011 est.)

other: 23.7% (2011 est.)

note: highest percentage of arable land for any country in the world

IRRIGATED LAND:

4,350 sq km (2012)

POPULATION DISTRIBUTION:

with excellent access to the North Sea, Skagerrak, Kattegat, and the Baltic Sea, population centers tend to be along coastal areas, particularly in Copenhagen and the eastern side of the country's mainland

NATURAL HAZARDS:

flooding is a threat in some areas of the country (e.g., parts of Jutland, along the southern coast of the island of Lolland) that are protected from the sea by a system of dikes

ENVIRONMENT - CURRENT ISSUES:

air pollution, principally from vehicle and power plant emissions; nitrogen and phosphorus pollution of the North Sea; drinking and surface water becoming polluted from animal wastes and pesticides; much of country's household and industrial waste is recycled

ENVIRONMENT - INTERNATIONAL AGREEMENTS:

party to: Air Pollution, Air Pollution-Nitrogen Oxides, Air Pollution-Persistent Organic Pollutants, Air Pollution-Sulfur 85, Air Pollution-Sulfur 94, Air Pollution-Volatile Organic Compounds, Antarctic Treaty, Biodiversity, Climate Change, Climate Change-Kyoto Protocol,

Desertification, Endangered Species, Environmental Modification, Hazardous Wastes, Law of the Sea, Marine Dumping, Marine Life Conservation, Ozone Layer Protection, Ship Pollution, Tropical Timber 83, Tropical Timber 94, Wetlands, Whaling

signed, but not ratified: none of the selected agreements

GEOGRAPHY - NOTE:

composed of the Jutland Peninsula and a group of more than 400 islands (Danish Archipelago); controls Danish Straits (Skagerrak and Kattegat) linking Baltic and North Seas; about one-quarter of the population lives in greater Copenhagen

PEOPLE AND SOCIETY :: DENMARK

POPULATION:

5,809,502 (July 2018 est.)

country comparison to the world: 115

NATIONALITY:

noun: Dane(s)

adjective: Danish

ETHNIC GROUPS:

Danish (includes Greenlandic (who are predominantly Inuit) and Faroese) 86.3%, Turkish 1.1%, other 12.6% (largest groups are Polish, Syrian, German, Iraqi, and Romanian) (2018 est.)

note: data represent population by ancestry

LANGUAGES:

Danish, Faroese, Greenlandic (an Inuit dialect), German (small minority)

note: English is the predominant second language

RELIGIONS:

Evangelical Lutheran (official) 74.8%, Muslim 5.3%, other (denominations of less than 1% each, include Roman Catholic, Jehovah's Witness, Serbian Orthodox Christian, Jewish, Baptist, and Buddhist) 19.9% (2017 est.)

AGE STRUCTURE:

0-14 years: 16.57% (male 493,829 /female 468,548)

15-24 years: 12.67% (male 377,094 /female 358,807)

25-54 years: 39.03% (male 1,147,196 /female 1,119,967)

55-64 years: 12.33% (male 356,860 /female 359,264)

65 years and over: 19.42% (male 518,200 /female 609,737) (2018 est.)

DEPENDENCY RATIOS:

total dependency ratio: 56 (2015 est.)

youth dependency ratio: 26.3 (2015 est.)

elderly dependency ratio: 29.7 (2015 est.)

potential support ratio: 3.4 (2015 est.)

MEDIAN AGE:

total: 41.9 years

male: 40.8 years

female: 42.9 years (2018 est.)

country comparison to the world: 35

POPULATION GROWTH RATE:

0.59% (2018 est.)

country comparison to the world: 148

BIRTH RATE:

10.9 births/1,000 population (2018 est.)

country comparison to the world: 178

DEATH RATE:

9.3 deaths/1,000 population (2018 est.)

country comparison to the world: 55

NET MIGRATION RATE:

2.1 migrant(s)/1,000 population (2017 est.)

country comparison to the world: 46

POPULATION DISTRIBUTION:

with excellent access to the North Sea, Skagerrak, Kattegat, and the Baltic Sea, population centers tend to be along coastal areas, particularly in Copenhagen and the eastern side of the country's mainland

URBANIZATION:

urban population: 87.9% of total population (2018)

rate of urbanization: 0.51% annual rate of change (2015-20 est.)

MAJOR URBAN AREAS - POPULATION:

1.321 million COPENHAGEN (capital) (2018)

SEX RATIO:

at birth: 1.05 male(s)/female (2017 est.)

0-14 years: 1.05 male(s)/female (2017 est.)

15-24 years: 1.04 male(s)/female (2017 est.)

25-54 years: 0.99 male(s)/female (2017 est.)

55-64 years: 0.99 male(s)/female (2017 est.)

65 years and over: 0.81 male(s)/female (2017 est.)

total population: 0.97 male(s)/female (2017 est.)

MOTHER'S MEAN AGE AT FIRST BIRTH:

29.1 years (2015 est.)

MATERNAL MORTALITY RATE:

6 deaths/100,000 live births (2015 est.)

country comparison to the world: 166

INFANT MORTALITY RATE:

total: 3.2 deaths/1,000 live births (2018 est.)

male: 3.6 deaths/1,000 live births (2018 est.)

female: 2.7 deaths/1,000 live births (2018 est.)

country comparison to the world: 208

LIFE EXPECTANCY AT BIRTH:

total population: 81 years (2018 est.)

male: 79.1 years (2018 est.)

female: 83.1 years (2018 est.)

country comparison to the world: 34

TOTAL FERTILITY RATE:

1.78 children born/woman (2018 est.)

country comparison to the world: 152

HEALTH EXPENDITURES:

10.8% of GDP (2014)

country comparison to the world: 16

PHYSICIANS DENSITY:

3.66 physicians/1,000 population (2014)

HOSPITAL BED DENSITY:

2.5 beds/1,000 population (2015)

DRINKING WATER SOURCE:

improved:

urban: 100% of population

rural: 100% of population

total: 100% of population

unimproved:

urban: 0% of population

rural: 0% of population

total: 0% of population (2015 est.)

SANITATION FACILITY ACCESS:

improved:

urban: 99.6% of population (2015 est.)

rural: 99.6% of population (2015 est.)

total: 99.6% of population (2015 est.)

unimproved:

urban: 0.4% of population (2015 est.)

rural: 0.4% of population (2015 est.)

total: 0.4% of population (2015 est.)

HIV/AIDS - ADULT PREVALENCE RATE:

0.1% (2017 est.)

country comparison to the world: 110

HIV/AIDS - PEOPLE LIVING WITH HIV/AIDS:

6,400 (2017 est.)

country comparison to the world: 113

HIV/AIDS - DEATHS:

<100 (2017 est.)

OBESITY - ADULT PREVALENCE RATE:

19.7% (2016)

country comparison to the world: 109

EDUCATION EXPENDITURES:

7.6% of GDP (2014)

country comparison to the world: 12

SCHOOL LIFE EXPECTANCY (PRIMARY TO TERTIARY EDUCATION):

total: 19 years (2014)

male: 18 years (2014)

female: 20 years (2014)

UNEMPLOYMENT, YOUTH AGES 15-24:

total: 12% (2016 est.)

male: 13.1% (2016 est.)

female: 10.9% (2016 est.)

country comparison to the world: 109

GOVERNMENT :: DENMARK

COUNTRY NAME:

conventional long form: Kingdom of Denmark

conventional short form: Denmark

local long form: Kongeriget Danmark

local short form: Danmark

etymology: the name derives from the words "Dane(s)" and "mark"; the latter referring to a march (borderland) or forest

GOVERNMENT TYPE:

parliamentary constitutional monarchy

CAPITAL:

name: Copenhagen

geographic coordinates: 55 40 N, 12 35 E

time difference: UTC+1 (6 hours ahead of Washington, DC, during Standard Time)

daylight saving time: +1hr, begins last Sunday in March; ends last Sunday in October

note: applies to continental Denmark only, not to its North Atlantic components

ADMINISTRATIVE DIVISIONS:

metropolitan Denmark - 5 regions (regioner, singular - region); Hovedstaden (Capital), Midtjylland (Central Jutland), Nordjylland (North Jutland), Sjaelland (Zealand), Syddanmark (Southern Denmark)

note: an extensive local government reform merged 271 municipalities into 98 and 13 counties into five regions, effective 1 January 2007

INDEPENDENCE:

ca. 965 (unified and Christianized under HARALD I Gormson); 5 June 1849 (became a parliamentary constitutional monarchy)

NATIONAL HOLIDAY:

Constitution Day, 5 June (1849); note - closest equivalent to a national holiday

CONSTITUTION:

history: several previous; latest adopted 5 June 1953 (2016)

amendments: proposed by the Folketing with consent of the government; passage requires approval by the next Folketing following a general election, approval by simple majority vote of at least 40% of voters in a referendum, and assent by the chief of state; changed several times, last in 2009 (Danish Act of Succession) (2016)

LEGAL SYSTEM:

civil law; judicial review of legislative acts

INTERNATIONAL LAW ORGANIZATION PARTICIPATION:

accepts compulsory ICJ jurisdiction with reservations; accepts ICCt jurisdiction

CITIZENSHIP:

citizenship by birth: no

citizenship by descent only: at least one parent must be a citizen of Denmark

dual citizenship recognized: yes

residency requirement for naturalization: 7 years

SUFFRAGE:

18 years of age; universal

EXECUTIVE BRANCH:

chief of state: Queen MARGRETHE II (since 14 January 1972); Heir Apparent Crown Prince FREDERIK (elder son of the monarch, born on 26 May 1968)

head of government: Prime Minister Lars LOKKE RASMUSSEN (since 28 June 2015)

cabinet: Council of State appointed by the monarch

elections/appointments: the monarchy is hereditary; following legislative elections, the leader of the majority party or majority coalition usually appointed prime minister by the monarch

LEGISLATIVE BRANCH:

description: unicameral People's Assembly or Folketing (179 seats, including 2 each representing Greenland and the Faroe Islands; members directly elected in multi-seat constituencies by proportional representation vote; members serve 4-year terms unless the Folketing is dissolved earlier)

elections: last held on 18 June 2015 (next to be held by June 2019)

election results: percent of vote by party - SDP 26.3%, DF 21.1%, V 19.5%, EL 7.8%, LA 7.5%, AP 4.8%, SLP 4.6%, SF 4.2%, C 3.4%, other 0.9%; seats by party - SDP 47, DF 37, V 34, EL 14, LA 13, AP 9, SLP 8, SF 7, C 6; composition - men 112, women 67, percent of women 37.4%; note - does not include each of the 2 seats from Greenland and the Faroe Islands

JUDICIAL BRANCH:

highest courts: Supreme Court (consists of the court president and 18 judges)

judge selection and term of office: judges appointed by the monarch upon the recommendation of the Minister of Justice with the advice of the Judicial Appointments Council, a 6-member independent body of judges and lawyers; judges appointed for life with retirement at age 70

subordinate courts: Special Court of Indictment and Revision; 2 High Courts; Maritime and Commercial Court; county courts

POLITICAL PARTIES AND LEADERS:

The Alternative A or AP [Uffe ELBAEK]
Conservative People's Party or DKF or C [Soren PAPE POULSEN]
Danish People's Party or DF or O [Kristian THULESEN DAHL]
Liberal Alliance or LA [Anders SAMUELSEN]
Liberal Party (Venstre) or V [Lars LOKKE RASMUSSEN]
Red-Green Alliance (Unity List) or EL [collective leadership, Pernille SKIPPER, spokesperson]
Social Democratic Party or SDP
Social Democrats or A [Mette FREDERIKSEN]
Social Liberal Party or B or SLP [Morten OSTERGAARD]
Socialist People's Party or SF [Pia OLSEN DYHR]

INTERNATIONAL ORGANIZATION PARTICIPATION:

ADB (nonregional member), AfDB (nonregional member), Arctic Council, Australia Group, BIS, CBSS, CD, CE, CERN, EAPC, EBRD, ECB, EIB, EITI (implementing country), ESA, EU, FAO, FATF, G-9, IADB, IAEA, IBRD, ICAO, ICC (national committees), ICCt, ICRM, IDA, IEA, IFAD, IFC, IFRCS, IGAD (partners), IHO, ILO, IMF, IMO, IMSO, Interpol, IOC, IOM, IPU, ISO, ITSO, ITU, ITUC (NGOs), MIGA, MINUSMA, NATO, NC, NEA, NIB, NSG, OAS (observer), OECD, OPCW, OSCE, Paris Club, PCA, Schengen Convention, UN, UNCTAD, UNESCO, UNHCR, UNIDO, UNMIL, UNMISS, UNRWA, UNTSO, UPU, WCO, WHO, WIPO, WMO, WTO, ZC

DIPLOMATIC REPRESENTATION IN THE US:

chief of mission: Ambassador Lars Gert LOSE (since 17 September 2015)

chancery: 3200 Whitehaven Street NW, Washington, DC 20008

telephone: [1] (202) 234-4300

FAX: [1] (202) 328-1470

consulate(s) general: Chicago, Houston, New York

DIPLOMATIC REPRESENTATION FROM THE US:

chief of mission: Ambassador Carla SANDS (since 15 December 2017)

embassy: Dag Hammarskjolds Alle 24, 2100 Copenhagen 0

mailing address: Unit 5280, DPO, AE 09716

telephone: [45] 33 41 71 00

FAX: [45] 35 43 02 23

FLAG DESCRIPTION:

red with a white cross that extends to the edges of the flag; the vertical part of the cross is shifted to the hoist side; the banner is referred to as the Dannebrog (Danish flag) and is one of the oldest national flags in the world; traditions as to the origin of the flag design vary, but the best known is a legend that the banner fell from the sky during an early-13th century battle; caught up by the Danish king before it ever touched the earth, this heavenly talisman inspired the royal army to victory; in actuality, the flag may derive from a crusade banner or ensign

note: the shifted cross design element was subsequently adopted by the other Nordic countries of Finland, Iceland, Norway, and Sweden

NATIONAL SYMBOL(S):

lion, mute swan; national colors: red, white

NATIONAL ANTHEM:

name: "Der er et yndigt land" (There is a Lovely Country); "Kong Christian" (King Christian)

lyrics/music: Adam Gottlob OEHLENSCHLAGER/Hans Ernst KROYER; Johannes EWALD/unknown

note: Denmark has two national anthems with equal status; "Der er et yndigt land," adopted 1844, is a national anthem, while "Kong Christian," adopted 1780, serves as both a national and royal anthem; "Kong Christian" is also known as "Kong Christian stod ved hojen mast" (King Christian Stood by the Lofty Mast) and "Kongesangen" (The King's Anthem); within Denmark, the royal anthem is played only when royalty is present and is usually followed by the national anthem; when royalty is not present, only the national anthem is performed; outside Denmark, the royal anthem is played, unless the national anthem is requested

ECONOMY :: DENMARK

ECONOMY - OVERVIEW:

This thoroughly modern market economy features advanced industry with world-leading firms in pharmaceuticals, maritime shipping, and renewable energy, and a high-tech agricultural sector. Danes enjoy a high standard of living, and the Danish economy is characterized by extensive government welfare measures and an equitable distribution of income. An aging population will be a long-term issue.

Denmark's small open economy is highly dependent on foreign trade, and the government strongly supports trade liberalization. Denmark is a net exporter of food, oil, and gas and enjoys a comfortable balance of payments surplus, but depends on imports of raw materials for the manufacturing sector.

Denmark is a member of the EU but not the eurozone. Despite previously meeting the criteria to join the European Economic and Monetary Union, Denmark has negotiated an opt-out with the EU and is not required to adopt the euro.

Denmark is experiencing a modest economic expansion. The economy grew by 2.0% in 2016 and 2.1% in 2017. The expansion is expected to decline slightly in 2018. Unemployment stood at 5.5% in 2017, based on the national labor survey. The labor market was tight in 2017, with corporations experiencing some difficulty finding appropriately-skilled workers to fill billets. The Danish Government offers extensive programs to train unemployed persons to work in sectors that need qualified workers.

Denmark maintained a healthy budget surplus for many years up to 2008, but the global financial crisis swung the budget balance into deficit. Since 2014 the balance has shifted between surplus and deficit. In 2017 there was a surplus of 1.0%. The government projects a lower deficit in 2018 and 2019 of 0.7%, and public debt (EMU debt) as a share of GDP is expected to decline to 35.6% in 2018 and 34.8% in 2019. The Danish Government plans to address increasing municipal, public housing and integration spending in 2018.

GDP (PURCHASING POWER PARITY):

$287.8 billion (2017 est.)

$281.4 billion (2016 est.)

$276 billion (2015 est.)

note: data are in 2017 dollars

country comparison to the world: 60

GDP (OFFICIAL EXCHANGE RATE):

$325.6 billion (2017 est.) (2017 est.)

GDP - REAL GROWTH RATE:

2.3% (2017 est.)

2% (2016 est.)

1.6% (2015 est.)

country comparison to the world: 139

GDP - PER CAPITA (PPP):

$50,100 (2017 est.)

$49,300 (2016 est.)

$48,800 (2015 est.)

note: data are in 2017 dollars

country comparison to the world: 30

GROSS NATIONAL SAVING:

28.8% of GDP (2017 est.)

28.3% of GDP (2016 est.)

28.7% of GDP (2015 est.)

country comparison to the world: 35

GDP - COMPOSITION, BY END USE:

household consumption: 48% (2017 est.)

government consumption: 25.2% (2017 est.)

investment in fixed capital: 20% (2017 est.)

investment in inventories: -0.2% (2017 est.)

exports of goods and services: 54.5% (2017 est.)

imports of goods and services: -47.5% (2017 est.)

GDP - COMPOSITION, BY SECTOR OF ORIGIN:

agriculture: 1.3% (2017 est.)

industry: 22.9% (2017 est.)

services: 75.8% (2017 est.)

AGRICULTURE - PRODUCTS:

barley, wheat, potatoes, sugar beets; pork, dairy products; fish

INDUSTRIES:

wind turbines, pharmaceuticals, medical equipment, shipbuilding and refurbishment, iron, steel, nonferrous metals, chemicals, food processing, machinery and transportation equipment, textiles and clothing, electronics, construction, furniture and other wood products

INDUSTRIAL PRODUCTION GROWTH RATE:

2.5% (2017 est.)

country comparison to the world: 116

LABOR FORCE:

2.998 million (2017 est.)

country comparison to the world: 104

LABOR FORCE - BY OCCUPATION:

agriculture: 2.4%

industry: 18.3%

services: 79.3% (2016 est.)

UNEMPLOYMENT RATE:

5.7% (2017 est.)

6.2% (2016 est.)

country comparison to the world: 84

POPULATION BELOW POVERTY LINE:

13.4% (2011 est.)

note: excludes students

HOUSEHOLD INCOME OR CONSUMPTION BY PERCENTAGE SHARE:

lowest 10%: 23.4% (2016 est.)

highest 10%: 23.4% (2016 est.)

DISTRIBUTION OF FAMILY INCOME - GINI INDEX:

29 (2016 est.)

27.5 (2010 est.)

country comparison to the world: 139

BUDGET:

revenues: 172.5 billion (2017 est.)

expenditures: 168.9 billion (2017 est.)

TAXES AND OTHER REVENUES:

53% (of GDP) (2017 est.)

country comparison to the world: 12

BUDGET SURPLUS (+) OR DEFICIT (-):

1.1% (of GDP) (2017 est.)

country comparison to the world: 30

PUBLIC DEBT:

35.3% of GDP (2017 est.)

37.9% of GDP (2016 est.)

note: data cover general government debt and include debt instruments issued (or owned) by government entities other than the treasury; the data include treasury debt held by foreign entities; the data include debt issued by subnational entities, as well as intra-governmental debt; intragovernmental debt consists of treasury borrowings from surpluses in the social funds, such as for retirement, medical care, and unemployment; debt instruments for the social funds are not sold at public auctions

country comparison to the world: 151

FISCAL YEAR:

calendar year

INFLATION RATE (CONSUMER PRICES):

1.1% (2017 est.)

0.3% (2016 est.)

country comparison to the world: 58

CENTRAL BANK DISCOUNT RATE:

0% (31 December 2017)

0% (31 December 2016)

country comparison to the world: 151

COMMERCIAL BANK PRIME LENDING RATE:

2.84% (31 December 2017 est.)

3.25% (31 December 2016 est.)

country comparison to the world: 176

STOCK OF NARROW MONEY:

$193.2 billion (31 December 2017 est.)

$159.3 billion (31 December 2016 est.)

country comparison to the world: 25

STOCK OF BROAD MONEY:

$193.2 billion (31 December 2017 est.)

$159.3 billion (31 December 2016 est.)

country comparison to the world: 25

STOCK OF DOMESTIC CREDIT:

$693.8 billion (31 December 2017 est.)

$630.5 billion (31 December 2016 est.)

country comparison to the world: 21

MARKET VALUE OF PUBLICLY TRADED SHARES:

$361.2 billion (31 December 2016 est.)

$352 billion (31 December 2015 est.)

$271.4 billion (31 December 2014 est.)

country comparison to the world: 28

CURRENT ACCOUNT BALANCE:

$24.82 billion (2017 est.)

$22.47 billion (2016 est.)

country comparison to the world: 14

EXPORTS:

$113.6 billion (2017 est.)

$103.6 billion (2016 est.)

country comparison to the world: 34

EXPORTS - PARTNERS:

Germany 15.5%, Sweden 11.6%, UK 8.2%, US 7.5%, Norway 6%, China 4.4%, Netherlands 4.4% (2017)

EXPORTS - COMMODITIES:

wind turbines, pharmaceuticals, machinery and instruments, meat and meat products, dairy products, fish, furniture and design

IMPORTS:

$94.93 billion (2017 est.)

$86.81 billion (2016 est.)

country comparison to the world: 37

IMPORTS - COMMODITIES:

machinery and equipment, raw materials and semimanufactures for industry, chemicals, grain and foodstuffs, consumer goods

IMPORTS - PARTNERS:

Germany 21.3%, Sweden 11.9%, Netherlands 7.8%, China 7.1%, Norway 6.3%, Poland 4% (2017)

RESERVES OF FOREIGN EXCHANGE AND GOLD:

$75.25 billion (31 December 2017 est.)

$64.25 billion (31 December 2016 est.)

country comparison to the world: 30

DEBT - EXTERNAL:

$484.8 billion (31 March 2016 est.)

$519.8 billion (31 March 2015 est.)

country comparison to the world: 25

STOCK OF DIRECT FOREIGN INVESTMENT - AT HOME:

$188.7 billion (31 December 2017 est.)

$147.9 billion (31 December 2016 est.)

country comparison to the world: 32

STOCK OF DIRECT FOREIGN INVESTMENT - ABROAD:

$287.9 billion (31 December 2017 est.)

$235.4 billion (31 December 2016 est.)

country comparison to the world: 23

EXCHANGE RATES:

Danish kroner (DKK) per US dollar -

6.586 (2017 est.)

6.7309 (2016 est.)

6.7309 (2015 est.)

6.7236 (2014 est.)

5.6125 (2013 est.)

ENERGY :: DENMARK

ELECTRICITY ACCESS:

electrification - total population: 100% (2016)

ELECTRICITY - PRODUCTION:

29.84 billion kWh (2016 est.)

country comparison to the world: 65

ELECTRICITY - CONSUMPTION:

33.02 billion kWh (2016 est.)

country comparison to the world: 59

ELECTRICITY - EXPORTS:

9.919 billion kWh (2016 est.)

country comparison to the world: 20

ELECTRICITY - IMPORTS:

14.98 billion kWh (2016 est.)

country comparison to the world: 14

ELECTRICITY - INSTALLED GENERATING CAPACITY:

14.34 million kW (2016 est.)

country comparison to the world: 52

ELECTRICITY - FROM FOSSIL FUELS:

46% of total installed capacity (2016 est.)

country comparison to the world: 158

ELECTRICITY - FROM NUCLEAR FUELS:

0% of total installed capacity (2017 est.)

country comparison to the world: 77

ELECTRICITY - FROM HYDROELECTRIC PLANTS:

0% of total installed capacity (2017 est.)

country comparison to the world: 167

ELECTRICITY - FROM OTHER RENEWABLE SOURCES:

54% of total installed capacity (2017 est.)

country comparison to the world: 3

CRUDE OIL - PRODUCTION:

137,100 bbl/day (2017 est.)

country comparison to the world: 40

CRUDE OIL - EXPORTS:

82,980 bbl/day (2017 est.)

country comparison to the world: 36

CRUDE OIL - IMPORTS:

98,240 bbl/day (2017 est.)

country comparison to the world: 44

CRUDE OIL - PROVED RESERVES:

439 million bbl (1 January 2018 est.)

country comparison to the world: 46

REFINED PETROLEUM PRODUCTS - PRODUCTION:

183,900 bbl/day (2017 est.)

country comparison to the world: 55

REFINED PETROLEUM PRODUCTS - CONSUMPTION:

158,500 bbl/day (2017 est.)

country comparison to the world: 64

REFINED PETROLEUM PRODUCTS - EXPORTS:

133,700 bbl/day (2017 est.)

country comparison to the world: 38

REFINED PETROLEUM PRODUCTS - IMPORTS:

109,700 bbl/day (2017 est.)

country comparison to the world: 51

NATURAL GAS - PRODUCTION:

4.842 billion cu m (2017 est.)

country comparison to the world: 52

NATURAL GAS - CONSUMPTION:

3.115 billion cu m (2017 est.)

country comparison to the world: 73

NATURAL GAS - EXPORTS:

2.237 billion cu m (2017 est.)

country comparison to the world: 37

NATURAL GAS - IMPORTS:

509.7 million cu m (2017 est.)

country comparison to the world: 65

NATURAL GAS - PROVED RESERVES:

12.86 billion cu m (1 January 2018 est.)

country comparison to the world: 77

CARBON DIOXIDE EMISSIONS FROM CONSUMPTION OF ENERGY:

37.45 million Mt (2017 est.)

country comparison to the world: 70

COMMUNICATIONS :: DENMARK

TELEPHONES - FIXED LINES:

total subscriptions: 1,439,695 (2017 est.)

subscriptions per 100 inhabitants: 26 (2017 est.)

country comparison to the world: 63

TELEPHONES - MOBILE CELLULAR:

total subscriptions: 6,978,348 (2017 est.)

subscriptions per 100 inhabitants: 124 (2017 est.)

country comparison to the world: 106

TELEPHONE SYSTEM:

general assessment: excellent telephone and Internet services; Denmark's competitive telecom market has led to the country having the second highest broadband penetration rate in Europe; the fixed-line sector continues to see a decline in revenue while customers move to VoIP (Voice over Internet Protocol) and mobile alternatives; growth has been stimulated by the availability of LTE services; the government is able to offer broadband coverage in rural areas (2017)

domestic: buried and submarine cables and microwave radio relay form trunk network; multiple mobile-cellular communications systems; fixed-line 26 per 100, 124 per 100 for mobile-cellular (2017)

international: country code - 45; a series of fiber-optic submarine cables link Denmark with Canada, Faroe Islands, Germany, Iceland, Netherlands, Norway, Poland, Russia, Sweden, and UK; satellite earth stations - 18 (6 Intelsat, 10 Eutelsat, 1 Orion, 1 Inmarsat (Blaavand-Atlantic-East)); note - the Nordic countries (Denmark, Finland, Iceland, Norway, and Sweden) share the Danish earth station and the Eik, Norway, station for worldwide Inmarsat access (2015)

BROADCAST MEDIA:

strong public-sector TV presence with state-owned Danmarks Radio (DR) operating 6 channels and publicly owned TV2 operating roughly a half-dozen channels; broadcasts of privately owned stations are available via satellite and cable feed; DR operates 4 nationwide FM radio stations, 10 digital audio broadcasting stations, and 14 web-based radio stations; in 2010, there were 140 commercial and 187 community (non-commercial) radio stations (2012)

INTERNET COUNTRY CODE:

.dk

INTERNET USERS:

total: 5,424,169 (July 2016 est.)

percent of population: 97% (July 2016 est.)

country comparison to the world: 72

BROADBAND - FIXED SUBSCRIPTIONS:

total: 2,475,382 (2017 est.)

subscriptions per 100 inhabitants: 44 (2017 est.)

country comparison to the world: 48

TRANSPORTATION :: DENMARK

NATIONAL AIR TRANSPORT SYSTEM:

number of registered air carriers: 10 (2015)

inventory of registered aircraft operated by air carriers: 76 (2015)

annual passenger traffic on registered air carriers: 582,011 (2015)

annual freight traffic on registered air carriers: 0 mt-km (2015)

CIVIL AIRCRAFT REGISTRATION COUNTRY CODE PREFIX:

OY (2016)

AIRPORTS:

80 (2013)

country comparison to the world: 68

AIRPORTS - WITH PAVED RUNWAYS:

total: 28 (2017)

over 3,047 m: 2 (2017)

2,438 to 3,047 m: 7 (2017)

1,524 to 2,437 m: 5 (2017)

914 to 1,523 m: 12 (2017)

under 914 m: 2 (2017)

AIRPORTS - WITH UNPAVED RUNWAYS:

total: 52 (2013)

914 to 1,523 m: 5 (2013)

under 914 m: 47 (2013)

PIPELINES:

1536 km gas, 330 km oil (2015)

RAILWAYS:

total: 3,476 km (2017)

standard gauge: 3,476 km 1.435-m gauge (1,756 km electrified) (2017)

country comparison to the world: 56

ROADWAYS:

total: 74,558 km (2017)

paved: 74,558 km (includes 1,205 km of expressways) (2017)

country comparison to the world: 64

WATERWAYS:

400 km (2010)

country comparison to the world: 87

MERCHANT MARINE:

total: 654 (2017)

by type: bulk carrier 7, container ship 114, general cargo 77, oil tanker 75, other 381 (2017)

country comparison to the world: 31

PORTS AND TERMINALS:

major seaport(s): Baltic Sea - Aarhus, Copenhagen, Fredericia, Kalundborg

cruise port(s): Copenhagen

river port(s): Aalborg (Langerak)

dry bulk cargo port(s): Ensted (coal)

North Sea - Esbjerg,

MILITARY AND SECURITY :: DENMARK

MILITARY EXPENDITURES:

1.21% of GDP (2018)

1.15% of GDP (2016)

1.12% of GDP (2015)

1.15% of GDP (2014)

1.23% of GDP (2013)

country comparison to the world: 97

MILITARY BRANCHES:

Danish Army, Royal Danish Navy, Royal Danish Air Force (2017)

MILITARY SERVICE AGE AND OBLIGATION:

18 years of age for compulsory and voluntary military service; conscripts serve an initial training period that varies from 4 to 12 months according to specialization; former conscripts are assigned to mobilization units; women eligible to volunteer for military service; in addition to full time employment, the Danish Military offers reserve contracts in all three branches (2016)

TRANSNATIONAL ISSUES :: DENMARK

DISPUTES - INTERNATIONAL:

Iceland, the UK, and Ireland dispute Denmark's claim that the Faroe Islands' continental shelf extends beyond 200 nmsovereignty dispute with Canada over Hans Island in the Kennedy Channel between Ellesmere Island and GreenlandDenmark (Greenland) and Norway have made submissions to the Commission on the Limits of the Continental Shelf (CLCS) and Russia is collecting additional data to augment its 2001 CLCS submission

REFUGEES AND INTERNALLY DISPLACED PERSONS:

refugees (country of origin): 18,215 (Syria) (2016)

stateless persons: 7,990 (2017)

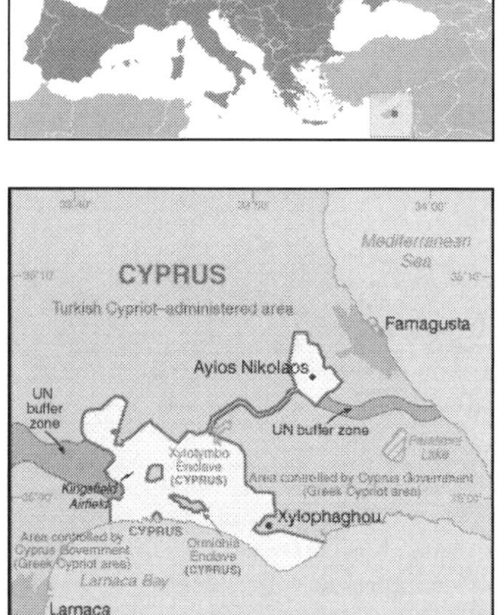

EUROPE :: DHEKELIA

INTRODUCTION :: DHEKELIA

BACKGROUND:

By terms of the 1960 Treaty of Establishment that created the independent Republic of Cyprus, the UK retained full sovereignty and jurisdiction over two areas of almost 254 square kilometers - Akrotiri and Dhekelia. The larger of these is the Dhekelia Sovereign Base Area, which is also referred to as the Eastern Sovereign Base Area.

GEOGRAPHY :: DHEKELIA

LOCATION:

Eastern Mediterranean, on the southeast coast of Cyprus near Famagusta

GEOGRAPHIC COORDINATES:

34 59 N, 33 45 E

MAP REFERENCES:

Middle East

AREA:

total: 130.8 sq km

note: area surrounds three Cypriot enclaves

country comparison to the world: 223

AREA - COMPARATIVE:

about three-quarters the size of Washington, DC

LAND BOUNDARIES:

total: 108 km

border countries (1): Cyprus 108 km

COASTLINE:

27.5 km

CLIMATE:

temperate; Mediterranean with hot, dry summers and cool winters

ENVIRONMENT - CURRENT ISSUES:

netting and trapping of small migrant songbirds in the spring and autumn

GEOGRAPHY - NOTE:

British extraterritorial rights also extended to several small off-post sites scattered across Cyprus; several small Cypriot enclaves exist within the Sovereign Base Area (SBA); of the SBA land, 60% is privately owned and farmed, 20% is owned by the Ministry of Defense, and 20% is SBA Crown land

PEOPLE AND SOCIETY :: DHEKELIA

POPULATION:

approximately 15,500 on the Sovereign Base Areas of Akrotiri and Dhekelia including 9,700 Cypriots and 5,800 Service and UK-based contract personnel and dependents

LANGUAGES:

English, Greek

HIV/AIDS - ADULT PREVALENCE RATE:

NA

GOVERNMENT :: DHEKELIA

COUNTRY NAME:

conventional long form: none

conventional short form: Dhekelia

DEPENDENCY STATUS:

a special form of UK overseas territory; administered by an administrator who is also the Commander, British Forces Cyprus

CAPITAL:

name: Episkopi Cantonment (base administrative center for Akrotiri and Dhekelia); located in Akrotiri

geographic coordinates: 34 40 N, 32 51 E

time difference: UTC+2 (7 hours ahead of Washington, DC, during Standard Time)

daylight saving time: +1hr, begins last Sunday in March; ends last Sunday in October

etymology: "Episkopi" means "episcopal" in Greek and stems from the fact that the site previously served as the bishop's seat of an Orthodox diocese

CONSTITUTION:

presented 3 August 1960, effective 16 August 1960 (The Sovereign Base Areas of Akrotiri and Dhekelia Order in Council 1960, serves as a basic legal document); amended 1966 (2016)

LEGAL SYSTEM:

laws applicable to the Cypriot population are, as far as possible, the same as the laws of the Republic of Cyprus; note - the Sovereign Base Area Administration has its own court system to deal with civil and criminal matters

EXECUTIVE BRANCH:

chief of state: Queen ELIZABETH II (since 6 February 1952)

head of government: Administrator Major General James ILLINGWORTH (since 14 March 2017); note - reports to the British Ministry of Defense

elections/appointments: the monarchy is hereditary; administrator appointed by the monarch on the advice of the Ministry of Defense

JUDICIAL BRANCH:

highest courts: Senior Judges' Court (consists of several visiting judges from England and Wales)

judge selection and term of office: see entry for United Kingdom

subordinate courts: Resident Judges' Court; military courts

DIPLOMATIC REPRESENTATION IN THE US:

none (overseas territory of the UK)

DIPLOMATIC REPRESENTATION FROM THE US:

none (overseas territory of the UK)

FLAG DESCRIPTION:

the flag of the UK is used

NATIONAL ANTHEM:

note: as a United Kingdom area of special sovereignty, "God Save the Queen" is official (see United Kingdom)

ECONOMY :: DHEKELIA

ECONOMY - OVERVIEW:

Economic activity is limited to providing services to the military and their families located in Dhekelia. All food and manufactured goods must be imported.

INDUSTRIES:

none

EXCHANGE RATES:

note: uses the euro

COMMUNICATIONS :: DHEKELIA

BROADCAST MEDIA:

British Forces Broadcast Service (BFBS) provides multi-channel satellite TV service as well as BFBS radio broadcasts to the Dhekelia Sovereign Base (2009)

MILITARY AND SECURITY :: DHEKELIA

MILITARY - NOTE:

defense is the responsibility of the UK; includes Dhekelia Garrison and Ayios Nikolaos Station connected by a roadway

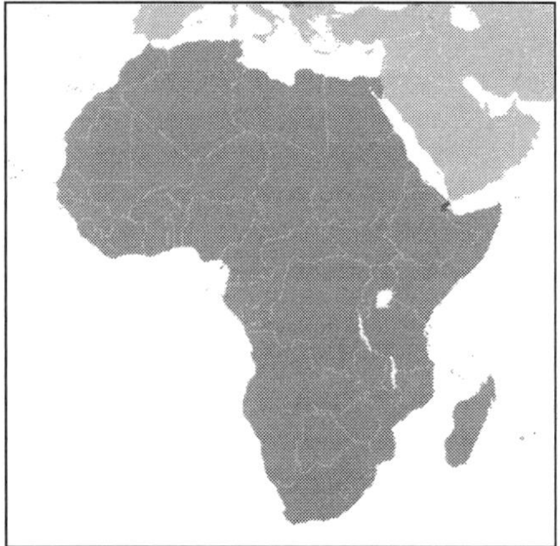

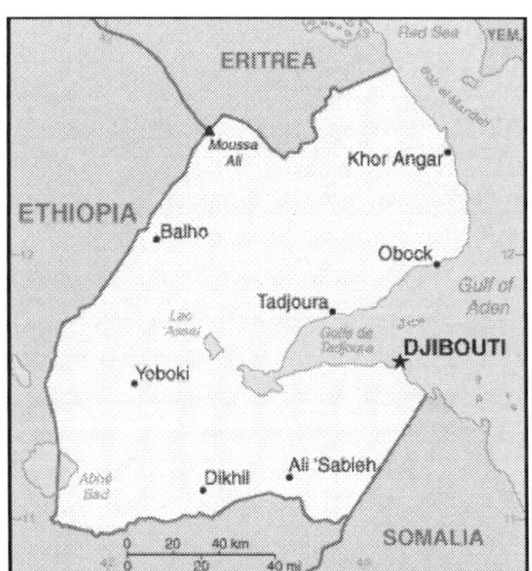

AFRICA :: DJIBOUTI

INTRODUCTION :: DJIBOUTI

BACKGROUND:

The French Territory of the Afars and the Issas became Djibouti in 1977. Hassan Gouled APTIDON installed an authoritarian one-party state and proceeded to serve as president until 1999. Unrest among the Afar minority during the 1990s led to a civil war that ended in 2001 with a peace accord between Afar rebels and the Somali Issa-dominated government. In 1999, Djibouti's first multiparty presidential election resulted in the election of Ismail Omar GUELLEH as president; he was reelected to a second term in 2005 and extended his tenure in office via a constitutional amendment, which allowed him to serve a third term in 2011 and begin a fourth term in 2016. Djibouti occupies a strategic geographic location at the intersection of the Red Sea and the Gulf of Aden and serves as an important shipping portal for goods entering and leaving the east African highlands and transshipments between Europe, the Middle East, and Asia. The government holds longstanding ties to France, which maintains a significant military presence in the country, and has strong ties with the US. Djibouti hosts several thousand members of US armed services at US-run Camp Lemonnier.

GEOGRAPHY :: DJIBOUTI

LOCATION:

Eastern Africa, bordering the Gulf of Aden and the Red Sea, between Eritrea and Somalia

GEOGRAPHIC COORDINATES:

11 30 N, 43 00 E

MAP REFERENCES:

Africa

AREA:

total: 23,200 sq km

land: 23,180 sq km

water: 20 sq km

country comparison to the world: 151

AREA - COMPARATIVE:

slightly smaller than New Jersey

LAND BOUNDARIES:

total: 528 km

border countries (3): Eritrea 125 km, Ethiopia 342 km, Somalia 61 km

COASTLINE:

314 km

MARITIME CLAIMS:

territorial sea: 12 nm

exclusive economic zone: 200 nm

contiguous zone: 24 nm

CLIMATE:

desert; torrid, dry

TERRAIN:

coastal plain and plateau separated by central mountains

ELEVATION:

mean elevation: 430 m

elevation extremes: -155 m lowest point: Lac Assal

2021 highest point: Moussa Ali

NATURAL RESOURCES:

potential geothermal power, gold, clay, granite, limestone, marble, salt, diatomite, gypsum, pumice, petroleum

LAND USE:

agricultural land: 73.4% (2011 est.)

arable land: 0.1% (2011 est.) / permanent crops: 0% (2011 est.) / permanent pasture: 73.3% (2011 est.)

forest: 0.2% (2011 est.)

other: 26.4% (2011 est.)

IRRIGATED LAND:

10 sq km (2012)

POPULATION DISTRIBUTION:

most densely populated areas are in the east; the largest city is Djibouti, with a population over 600,000; no other city in the country has a total population over 50,000

NATURAL HAZARDS:

earthquakes; droughts; occasional cyclonic disturbances from the Indian Ocean bring heavy rains and flash floods

volcanism: experiences limited volcanic activity; Ardoukoba (298 m) last erupted in 1978; Manda-Inakir, located along the Ethiopian border, is also historically active

ENVIRONMENT - CURRENT ISSUES:

inadequate supplies of potable water; water pollution; limited arable land; deforestation (forests threatened by agriculture and the use of wood for fuel); desertification; endangered species

ENVIRONMENT - INTERNATIONAL AGREEMENTS:

party to: Biodiversity, Climate Change, Climate Change-Kyoto Protocol, Desertification, Endangered Species, Hazardous Wastes, Law of the Sea, Ozone Layer Protection, Ship Pollution, Wetlands

signed, but not ratified: none of the selected agreements

GEOGRAPHY - NOTE:

strategic location near world's busiest shipping lanes and close to Arabian oilfields; terminus of rail traffic into Ethiopia; mostly wasteland; Lac Assal (Lake Assal) is the lowest point in Africa and the saltiest lake in the world

PEOPLE AND SOCIETY :: DJIBOUTI

POPULATION:

884,017 (July 2018 est.)

country comparison to the world: 162

NATIONALITY:

noun: Djiboutian(s)

adjective: Djiboutian

ETHNIC GROUPS:

Somali 60%, Afar 35%, other 5% (includes French, Arab, Ethiopian, and Italian)

LANGUAGES:

French (official), Arabic (official), Somali, Afar

RELIGIONS:

Muslim 94%, Christian 6%

DEMOGRAPHIC PROFILE:

Djibouti is a poor, predominantly urban country, characterized by high rates of illiteracy, unemployment, and childhood malnutrition. More than 75% of the population lives in cities and towns (predominantly in the capital, Djibouti). The rural population subsists primarily on nomadic herding. Prone to droughts and floods, the country has few natural resources and must import more than 80% of its food from neighboring countries or Europe. Health care, particularly outside the capital, is limited by poor infrastructure, shortages of equipment and supplies, and a lack of qualified personnel. More than a third of health care recipients are migrants because the services are still better than those available in their neighboring home countries. The nearly universal practice of female genital cutting reflects Djibouti's lack of gender equality and is a major contributor to obstetrical complications and its high rates of maternal and infant mortality. A 1995 law prohibiting the practice has never been enforced.

Because of its political stability and its strategic location at the confluence of East Africa and the Gulf States along the Gulf of Aden and the Red Sea, Djibouti is a key transit point for migrants and asylum seekers heading for the Gulf States and beyond. Each year some hundred thousand people, mainly Ethiopians and some Somalis, journey through Djibouti, usually to the port of Obock, to attempt a dangerous sea crossing to Yemen. However, with the escalation of the ongoing Yemen conflict, Yemenis began fleeing to Djibouti in March 2015, with almost 20,000 arriving by August 2017. Most Yemenis remain unregistered and head for Djibouti City rather than seeking asylum at one of Djibouti's three spartan refugee camps. Djibouti has been hosting refugees and asylum seekers, predominantly Somalis and lesser numbers of Ethiopians and Eritreans, at camps for 20 years, despite lacking potable water, food shortages, and unemployment.

AGE STRUCTURE:

0-14 years: 30.71% (male 136,191 /female 135,263)

15-24 years: 21.01% (male 87,520 /female 98,239)

25-54 years: 39.63% (male 145,427 /female 204,927)

55-64 years: 4.82% (male 18,967 /female 23,639)

65 years and over: 3.83% (male 15,136 /female 18,708) (2018 est.)

DEPENDENCY RATIOS:

total dependency ratio: 56.5 (2015 est.)

youth dependency ratio: 50.1 (2015 est.)

elderly dependency ratio: 6.4 (2015 est.)

potential support ratio: 15.6 (2015 est.)

MEDIAN AGE:

total: 24.2 years

male: 22.4 years

female: 25.7 years (2018 est.)

country comparison to the world: 165

POPULATION GROWTH RATE:

2.13% (2018 est.)

country comparison to the world: 42

BIRTH RATE:

23.3 births/1,000 population (2018 est.)

country comparison to the world: 59

DEATH RATE:

7.5 deaths/1,000 population (2018 est.)

country comparison to the world: 109

NET MIGRATION RATE:

5.7 migrant(s)/1,000 population (2017 est.)

country comparison to the world: 19

POPULATION DISTRIBUTION:

most densely populated areas are in the east; the largest city is Djibouti, with a population over 600,000; no other city in the country has a total population over 50,000

URBANIZATION:

urban population: 77.8% of total population (2018)

rate of urbanization: 1.67% annual rate of change (2015-20 est.)

MAJOR URBAN AREAS - POPULATION:

562,000 DJIBOUTI (capital) (2018)

SEX RATIO:

at birth: 1.02 male(s)/female (2017 est.)

0-14 years: 1.01 male(s)/female (2017 est.)

15-24 years: 0.89 male(s)/female (2017 est.)

25-54 years: 0.71 male(s)/female (2017 est.)

55-64 years: 0.85 male(s)/female (2017 est.)

65 years and over: 0.82 male(s)/female (2017 est.)

total population: 0.84 male(s)/female (2017 est.)

MATERNAL MORTALITY RATE:

229 deaths/100,000 live births (2015 est.)

country comparison to the world: 46

INFANT MORTALITY RATE:

total: 44.3 deaths/1,000 live births (2018 est.)

male: 50.9 deaths/1,000 live births (2018 est.)

female: 37.5 deaths/1,000 live births (2018 est.)

country comparison to the world: 39

LIFE EXPECTANCY AT BIRTH:

total population: 64 years (2018 est.)

male: 61.4 years (2018 est.)

female: 66.6 years (2018 est.)

country comparison to the world: 191

TOTAL FERTILITY RATE:

2.27 children born/woman (2018 est.)

country comparison to the world: 90

CONTRACEPTIVE PREVALENCE RATE:

19% (2012)

HEALTH EXPENDITURES:

10.6% of GDP (2014)

country comparison to the world: 18

PHYSICIANS DENSITY:

0.23 physicians/1,000 population (2014)

HOSPITAL BED DENSITY:

1.4 beds/1,000 population (2014)

DRINKING WATER SOURCE:

improved:

urban: 97.4% of population (2015 est.)

rural: 64.7% of population (2015 est.)

total: 90% of population (2015 est.)

unimproved:

urban: 2.6% of population (2015 est.)

rural: 35.3% of population (2015 est.)

total: 10% of population (2015 est.)

SANITATION FACILITY ACCESS:

improved:

urban: 59.8% of population (2015 est.)

rural: 5.1% of population (2015 est.)

total: 47.4% of population (2015 est.)

unimproved:

urban: 40.2% of population (2015 est.)

rural: 94.9% of population (2015 est.)

total: 52.6% of population (2015 est.)

HIV/AIDS - ADULT PREVALENCE RATE:

1.3% (2017 est.)

country comparison to the world: 37

HIV/AIDS - PEOPLE LIVING WITH HIV/AIDS:

9,100 (2017 est.)

country comparison to the world: 101

HIV/AIDS - DEATHS:

<1000 (2017 est.)

MAJOR INFECTIOUS DISEASES:

degree of risk: high (2016)

food or waterborne diseases: bacterial and protozoal diarrhea, hepatitis A, and typhoid fever (2016)

vectorborne diseases: dengue fever (2016)

OBESITY - ADULT PREVALENCE RATE:

13.5% (2016)

country comparison to the world: 131

CHILDREN UNDER THE AGE OF 5 YEARS UNDERWEIGHT:

29.8% (2012)

country comparison to the world: 9

EDUCATION EXPENDITURES:

4.5% of GDP (2010)

country comparison to the world: 93

SCHOOL LIFE EXPECTANCY (PRIMARY TO TERTIARY EDUCATION):

total: 6 years (2011)

male: 7 years (2011)

female: 6 years (2011)

GOVERNMENT :: DJIBOUTI

COUNTRY NAME:

conventional long form: Republic of Djibouti

conventional short form: Djibouti

local long form: Republique de Djibouti/Jumhuriyat Jibuti

local short form: Djibouti/Jibuti

former: French Somaliland, French Territory of the Afars and Issas

etymology: the country name derives from the capital city of Djibouti

GOVERNMENT TYPE:

semi-presidential republic

CAPITAL:

name: Djibouti

geographic coordinates: 11 35 N, 43 09 E

time difference: UTC+3 (8 hours ahead of Washington, DC, during Standard Time)

ADMINISTRATIVE DIVISIONS:

6 districts (cercles, singular - cercle); Ali Sabieh, Arta, Dikhil, Djibouti, Obock, Tadjourah

INDEPENDENCE:

27 June 1977 (from France)

NATIONAL HOLIDAY:

Independence Day, 27 June (1977)

CONSTITUTION:

history: approved by referendum 4 September 1992 (2017)

amendments: proposed by the president of the republic or by the National Assembly; Assembly consideration of proposals requires assent by at least one-third of the membership; passage requires a simple majority vote by the Assembly and approval by simple majority vote in a referendum; the president can opt to bypass a referendum if adopted by at least two-thirds majority vote of the Assembly; constitutional articles on the sovereignty of Djibouti, its republican form of government, and its pluralist form of democracy cannot by amended; amended 2006, 2008, 2010 (2017)

LEGAL SYSTEM:

mixed legal system based primarily on the French civil code (as it existed in 1997), Islamic religious law (in matters of family law and successions), and customary law

INTERNATIONAL LAW ORGANIZATION PARTICIPATION:

accepts compulsory ICJ jurisdiction with reservations; accepts ICCt jurisdiction

CITIZENSHIP:

citizenship by birth: no

citizenship by descent only: the mother must be a citizen of Djibouti

dual citizenship recognized: no

residency requirement for naturalization: 10 years

SUFFRAGE:

18 years of age; universal

EXECUTIVE BRANCH:

chief of state: President Ismail Omar GUELLEH (since 8 May 1999)

head of government: Prime Minister Abdoulkader Kamil MOHAMED (since 1 April 2013)

cabinet: Council of Ministers appointed by the prime minister

elections/appointments: president directly elected by absolute majority popular vote in 2 rounds if needed for a 5-year term; election last held on 8 April 2016 (next to be held by 2021); prime minister appointed by the president

election results: Ismail Omar GUELLEH reelected president for a fourth term; percent of vote - Ismail Omar GUELLEH (RPP) 87%, Omar Elmi KHAIREH (CDU) 7.3%, other 5.6%

LEGISLATIVE BRANCH:

description: unicameral National Assembly or Assemblee Nationale, formerly the Chamber of Deputies (65 seats; members directly elected in multi-seat constituencies by party-list proportional representation vote; members serve 5-year terms)

elections: last held on 23 February 2018 (next to be held in February 2023)

election results: percent of vote by party - NA; seats by party - UMP 57, UDJ-PDD 7, CDU 1

JUDICIAL BRANCH:

highest courts: Supreme Court or Cour Supreme (consists of NA magistrates); Constitutional Council (consists of 6 magistrates)

judge selection and term of office: Supreme Court magistrates appointed by the president with the advice of the Superior Council of the Magistracy or CSM, a 10-member body consisting of 4 judges, 3 members (non parliamentarians and judges) appointed by the president, and 3 appointed by the National Assembly president or speaker; magistrates appointed for life with retirement at age 65; Constitutional Council magistrate appointments - 2 by the president of the republic, 2 by the president of the National Assembly, and 2 by the CSM; magistrates appointed for 8-year, non-renewable terms

subordinate courts: High Court of Appeal; 5 Courts of First Instance; customary courts; State Court (replaced sharia courts in 2003)

POLITICAL PARTIES AND LEADERS:

Center for United Democrats or CDU [Omar Elmi KHAIREH, chairman]
Democratic Renewal Party or PRD [Abdillahi HAMARITEH]
Djibouti Development Party or PDD [Mohamed Daoud CHEHEM]
Front for Restoration of Unity and Democracy (Front pour la Restauration de l'Unite Democratique) or FRUD [Ali Mohamed DAOUD]
Movement for Democratic Renewal and Development [Daher Ahmed FARAH]
Movement for Development and Liberty or MoDel [Ismail Ahmed WABERI]
National Democratic Party or PND [Aden Robleh AWALEH]
People's Rally for Progress or RPP [Ismail Omar GUELLEH] (governing party)
Peoples Social Democratic Party or PPSD [Hasna Moumin BAHDON]
Republican Alliance for Democracy or ARD
Union for a Presidential Majority or UMP (coalition includes RPP, FRUD, PND, PPSD)
Union for Democracy and Justice or UDJ [Ilya Ismail GUEDI Hared]
Union for National Salvation or USN [Ahmed Youssouf HOUMED] (coalition includes ARD, MoDel, MRD, PDD, PND, UDJ)

INTERNATIONAL ORGANIZATION PARTICIPATION:

ACP, AfDB, AFESD, AMF, AU, CAEU (candidates), COMESA, FAO, G-77, IBRD, ICAO, ICCt, ICRM, IDA, IDB, IFAD, IFC, IFRCS, IGAD, ILO, IMF, IMO, Interpol, IOC, IOM, IPU, ITU, ITUC (NGOs), LAS, MIGA, MINURSO, NAM, OIC, OIF, OPCW, UN, UNCTAD, UNESCO, UNHCR, UNIDO, UNWTO, UPU, WCO, WFTU (NGOs), WHO, WIPO, WMO, WTO

DIPLOMATIC REPRESENTATION IN THE US:

chief of mission: Ambassador Mohamed Said DOUALEH (28 December 2016)

chancery: 1156 15th Street NW, Suite 515, Washington, DC 20005

telephone: [1] (202) 331-0270

FAX: [1] (202) 331-0302

DIPLOMATIC REPRESENTATION FROM THE US:

chief of mission: Ambassador Larry Edward ANDRE, Jr. (since 20 November 2017)

embassy: Lot 350-B, Haramouss

mailing address: B.P. 185, Djibouti

telephone: [253] 21 45 30 00

FAX: [253] 21 45 31 29

FLAG DESCRIPTION:

two equal horizontal bands of light blue (top) and light green with a white isosceles triangle based on the hoist side bearing a red five-pointed star in the center; blue stands for sea and sky and the Issa Somali people; green symbolizes earth and the Afar people; white represents peace; the red star recalls the struggle for independence and stands for unity

NATIONAL SYMBOL(S):

red star; national colors: light blue, green, white, red

NATIONAL ANTHEM:

name: "Jabuuti" (Djibouti)

lyrics/music: Aden ELMI/Abdi ROBLEH

note: adopted 1977

ECONOMY :: DJIBOUTI

ECONOMY - OVERVIEW:

Djibouti's economy is based on service activities connected with the country's strategic location as a deepwater port on the Red Sea. Three-fourths of Djibouti's inhabitants live in the capital city; the remainder are mostly nomadic herders. Scant rainfall and less than 4% arable land limits crop production to small quantities of fruits and vegetables, and most food must be imported.

Djibouti provides services as both a transit port for the region and an international transshipment and refueling center. Imports, exports, and reexports represent 70% of port activity at Djibouti's container terminal. Reexports consist primarily of coffee from landlocked neighbor Ethiopia. Djibouti has few natural resources and little industry. The nation is, therefore, heavily dependent on foreign assistance to support its balance of payments and to finance development projects. An official unemployment rate of nearly 40% - with youth unemployment near 80% - continues to be a major problem. Inflation was a modest 3% in 2014-2017, due to low international food prices and a decline in electricity tariffs.

Djibouti's reliance on diesel-generated electricity and imported food and water leave average consumers vulnerable to global price shocks, though in mid-2015 Djibouti passed new legislation to liberalize the energy sector. The government has emphasized infrastructure development for transportation and energy and Djibouti – with the help of foreign partners, particularly China – has begun to increase and modernize its port capacity. In 2017, Djibouti opened two of the largest projects in its history, the Doraleh Port and Djibouti-Addis Ababa Railway, funded by China as part of the "Belt and Road Initiative," which will increase the country's ability to capitalize on its strategic location.

GDP (PURCHASING POWER PARITY):

$3.64 billion (2017 est.)

$3.411 billion (2016 est.)

$3.203 billion (2015 est.)

note: data are in 2017 dollars

country comparison to the world: 183

GDP (OFFICIAL EXCHANGE RATE):

$2.029 billion (2017 est.) (2017 est.)

GDP - REAL GROWTH RATE:

6.7% (2017 est.)

6.5% (2016 est.)

6.5% (2015 est.)

country comparison to the world: 26

GDP - PER CAPITA (PPP):

$3,600 (2017 est.)

$3,400 (2016 est.)

$3,300 (2015 est.)

note: data are in 2017 dollars

country comparison to the world: 185

GROSS NATIONAL SAVING:

22.3% of GDP (2017 est.)

38.1% of GDP (2016 est.)

19% of GDP (2015 est.)

country comparison to the world: 81

GDP - COMPOSITION, BY END USE:

household consumption: 56.5% (2017 est.)

government consumption: 29.2% (2017 est.)

investment in fixed capital: 41.8% (2017 est.)

investment in inventories: 0.3% (2017 est.)

exports of goods and services: 38.6% (2017 est.)

imports of goods and services: -66.4% (2017 est.)

GDP - COMPOSITION, BY SECTOR OF ORIGIN:

agriculture: 2.4% (2017 est.)

industry: 17.3% (2017 est.)

services: 80.2% (2017 est.)

AGRICULTURE - PRODUCTS:

fruits, vegetables; goats, sheep, camels, animal hides

INDUSTRIES:

construction, agricultural processing, shipping

INDUSTRIAL PRODUCTION GROWTH RATE:

2.7% (2017 est.)

country comparison to the world: 112

LABOR FORCE:

294,600 (2012)

country comparison to the world: 163

LABOR FORCE - BY OCCUPATION:

agriculture: NA

industry: NA

services: NA

UNEMPLOYMENT RATE:

40% (2017 est.)

60% (2014 est.)

country comparison to the world: 213

POPULATION BELOW POVERTY LINE:

23% (2015 est.)

note: percent of population below $1.25 per day at purchasing power parity

HOUSEHOLD INCOME OR CONSUMPTION BY PERCENTAGE SHARE:

lowest 10%: 30.9% (2002)

highest 10%: 30.9% (2002)

DISTRIBUTION OF FAMILY INCOME - GINI INDEX:

40.9 (2002)

country comparison to the world: 60

BUDGET:

revenues: 717 million (2017 est.)

expenditures: 899.2 million (2017 est.)

TAXES AND OTHER REVENUES:

35.3% (of GDP) (2017 est.)

country comparison to the world: 62

BUDGET SURPLUS (+) OR DEFICIT (-):

-9% (of GDP) (2017 est.)

country comparison to the world: 205

PUBLIC DEBT:

31.8% of GDP (2017 est.)

33.7% of GDP (2016 est.)

country comparison to the world: 161

FISCAL YEAR:

calendar year

INFLATION RATE (CONSUMER PRICES):

0.7% (2017 est.)

2.7% (2016 est.)

country comparison to the world: 36

COMMERCIAL BANK PRIME LENDING RATE:

11.3% (31 December 2017 est.)

11.45% (31 December 2016 est.)

country comparison to the world: 72

STOCK OF NARROW MONEY:

$1.475 billion (31 December 2017 est.)

$1.361 billion (31 December 2016 est.)

country comparison to the world: 143

STOCK OF BROAD MONEY:

$1.475 billion (31 December 2017 est.)

$1.361 billion (31 December 2016 est.)

country comparison to the world: 151

STOCK OF DOMESTIC CREDIT:

$673.1 million (31 December 2017 est.)

$659.4 million (31 December 2016 est.)

country comparison to the world: 172

CURRENT ACCOUNT BALANCE:

-$280 million (2017 est.)

-$178 million (2016 est.)

country comparison to the world: 102

EXPORTS:

$161.4 million (2017 est.)

$139.9 million (2016 est.)

country comparison to the world: 192

EXPORTS - PARTNERS:

Ethiopia 38.8%, Somalia 17.1%, Qatar 9.1%, Brazil 8.9%, Yemen 4.9%, US 4.6% (2017)

EXPORTS - COMMODITIES:

reexports, hides and skins, scrap metal

IMPORTS:

$726.4 million (2017 est.)

$705.2 million (2016 est.)

country comparison to the world: 191

IMPORTS - COMMODITIES:

foods, beverages, transport equipment, chemicals, petroleum products, clothing

IMPORTS - PARTNERS:

UAE 25%, France 15.2%, Saudi Arabia 11%, China 9.6%, Ethiopia 6.8%, Yemen 4.6% (2017)

RESERVES OF FOREIGN EXCHANGE AND GOLD:

$547.7 million (31 December 2017 est.)

$398.5 million (31 December 2016 est.)

country comparison to the world: 148

DEBT - EXTERNAL:

$1.954 billion (31 December 2017 est.)

$1.519 billion (31 December 2016 est.)

country comparison to the world: 153

STOCK OF DIRECT FOREIGN INVESTMENT - AT HOME:

$1.47 billion (31 December 2017 est.)

$1.483 billion (31 December 2016 est.)

country comparison to the world: 121

EXCHANGE RATES:

Djiboutian francs (DJF) per US dollar -

177.7 (2017 est.)

177.72 (2016 est.)

177.72 (2015 est.)

177.72 (2014 est.)

177.72 (2013 est.)

ENERGY :: DJIBOUTI

ELECTRICITY ACCESS:

population without electricity: 400,000 (2013)

electrification - total population: 50% (2013)

electrification - urban areas: 61% (2013)

electrification - rural areas: 14% (2013)

ELECTRICITY - PRODUCTION:

405.5 million kWh (2016 est.)

country comparison to the world: 170

ELECTRICITY - CONSUMPTION:

377.1 million kWh (2016 est.)

country comparison to the world: 177

ELECTRICITY - EXPORTS:

0 kWh (2016 est.)

country comparison to the world: 127

ELECTRICITY - IMPORTS:

0 kWh (2016 est.)

country comparison to the world: 141

ELECTRICITY - INSTALLED GENERATING CAPACITY:

130,300 kW (2016 est.)

country comparison to the world: 175

ELECTRICITY - FROM FOSSIL FUELS:

100% of total installed capacity (2016 est.)

country comparison to the world: 7

ELECTRICITY - FROM NUCLEAR FUELS:

0% of total installed capacity (2017 est.)

country comparison to the world: 78

ELECTRICITY - FROM HYDROELECTRIC PLANTS:

0% of total installed capacity (2017 est.)

country comparison to the world: 168

ELECTRICITY - FROM OTHER RENEWABLE SOURCES:

0% of total installed capacity (2017 est.)

country comparison to the world: 185

CRUDE OIL - PRODUCTION:

0 bbl/day (2017 est.)

country comparison to the world: 126

CRUDE OIL - EXPORTS:

0 bbl/day (2015 est.)

country comparison to the world: 114

CRUDE OIL - IMPORTS:

0 bbl/day (2015 est.)

country comparison to the world: 117

CRUDE OIL - PROVED RESERVES:

0 bbl (1 January 2018 est.)

country comparison to the world: 123

REFINED PETROLEUM PRODUCTS - PRODUCTION:

0 bbl/day (2015 est.)

country comparison to the world: 136

REFINED PETROLEUM PRODUCTS - CONSUMPTION:

6,360 bbl/day (2016 est.)

country comparison to the world: 170

REFINED PETROLEUM PRODUCTS - EXPORTS:

403 bbl/day (2015 est.)

country comparison to the world: 112

REFINED PETROLEUM PRODUCTS - IMPORTS:

6,692 bbl/day (2015 est.)

country comparison to the world: 161

NATURAL GAS - PRODUCTION:

0 cu m (2017 est.)

country comparison to the world: 123

NATURAL GAS - CONSUMPTION:

0 cu m (2017 est.)

country comparison to the world: 139

NATURAL GAS - EXPORTS:

0 cu m (2017 est.)

country comparison to the world: 94

NATURAL GAS - IMPORTS:

0 cu m (2017 est.)

country comparison to the world: 116

NATURAL GAS - PROVED RESERVES:

0 cu m (1 January 2014 est.)

country comparison to the world: 127

CARBON DIOXIDE EMISSIONS FROM CONSUMPTION OF ENERGY:

950,200 Mt (2017 est.)

country comparison to the world: 171

COMMUNICATIONS :: DJIBOUTI

TELEPHONES - FIXED LINES:

total subscriptions: 36,582 (2017 est.)

subscriptions per 100 inhabitants: 4 (2017 est.)

country comparison to the world: 163

TELEPHONES - MOBILE CELLULAR:

total subscriptions: 373,052 (2017 est.)

subscriptions per 100 inhabitants: 43 (2017 est.)

country comparison to the world: 175

TELEPHONE SYSTEM:

general assessment: telephone facilities in the city of Djibouti are adequate, as are the microwave radio relay connections to outlying areas of the country; Djibouti is one of the few remaining countries in which the national telco, Djibouti Telecom (DT), has a monopoly on all telecom services, including fixed lines, mobile, internet and broadband; the lack of competition has meant that the market has not lived up to its potential (2017)

domestic: Djibouti Telecom (DT) is the sole provider of telecommunications services and utilizes mostly a microwave radio relay network; fiber-optic cable is installed in the capital; rural areas connected via wireless local loop radio systems; mobile cellular coverage is primarily limited to the area in and around Djibouti city; 4 per 100 fixed-line, 43 per 100 moblie-cellular (2017)

international: country code - 253; landing point for the SEA-ME-WE-3 and EASSy fiber-optic submarine cable systems providing links to Asia, the Middle East, Europe and North America; satellite earth stations - 2 (1 Intelsat - Indian Ocean and 1 Arabsat); work starts on the PEACE submarine cable linking Djibouti with Pakistan; Djibouti Telecom joins six other regional telcos to build the DARE submarine cable system, is contracted to manage the Australia West Cable landing; Djibouti Internet Exchange (DjIX) joins the African IXP Association; Djibouti Telecom signs an agreement to peer IP traffic through France-IX's IXPs in Paris and Marseille; growth in the mobile and internet sectors accelerates with 3G launch (2017)

BROADCAST MEDIA:

state-owned Radiodiffusion-Television de Djibouti operates the sole terrestrial TV station, as well as the only 2 domestic radio networks; no private TV or radio stations; transmissions of several international broadcasters are available (2007)

INTERNET COUNTRY CODE:

.dj

INTERNET USERS:

total: 111,212 (July 2016 est.)

percent of population: 13.1% (July 2016 est.)

country comparison to the world: 176

BROADBAND - FIXED SUBSCRIPTIONS:

total: 24,389 (2017 est.)

subscriptions per 100 inhabitants: 3 (2017 est.)

country comparison to the world: 147

TRANSPORTATION :: DJIBOUTI

NATIONAL AIR TRANSPORT SYSTEM:

number of registered air carriers: 2 (2015)

inventory of registered aircraft operated by air carriers: 4 (2015)

CIVIL AIRCRAFT REGISTRATION COUNTRY CODE PREFIX:

J2 (2016)

AIRPORTS:

13 (2013)

country comparison to the world: 151

AIRPORTS - WITH PAVED RUNWAYS:

total: 3 (2017)

over 3,047 m: 1 (2017)

2,438 to 3,047 m: 1 (2017)

1,524 to 2,437 m: 1 (2017)

AIRPORTS - WITH UNPAVED RUNWAYS:

total: 10 (2013)

1,524 to 2,437 m: 1 (2013)

914 to 1,523 m: 7 (2013)

under 914 m: 2 (2013)

RAILWAYS:

total: 97 km (Djibouti segment of the 756 km Addis Ababa-Djibouti railway) (2017)

standard gauge: 97 km 1.435-m gauge (2017)

country comparison to the world: 127

ROADWAYS:

total: 3,065 km (2000)

paved: 1,379 km (2000)

unpaved: 1,686 km (2000)

country comparison to the world: 165

MERCHANT MARINE:

total: 18 (2017)

by type: oil tanker 2, other 16 (2017)

country comparison to the world: 141

PORTS AND TERMINALS:

major seaport(s): Djibouti

MILITARY AND SECURITY :: DJIBOUTI

MILITARY BRANCHES:

Djibouti Armed Forces (Forces Armees Djiboutiennes, FAD): Djibouti National Army (includes Navy, Djiboutian Air Force (Force Aerienne Djiboutienne, FAD), National Gendarmerie (GN)) (2013)

MILITARY SERVICE AGE AND OBLIGATION:

18 years of age for voluntary military service; 16-25 years of age for voluntary military training; no conscription (2012)

MARITIME THREATS:

the International Maritime Bureau reports offshore waters in the Red Sea and Gulf of Aden remain a high risk for piracy; the presence of several naval task forces in the Gulf of Aden and additional anti-piracy measures on the part of ship operators, including the use of on-board armed security teams, contributed to the drop in incidents; there were three incidents in the Gulf of Aden and one in the Red Sea in 2017; Operation Ocean Shield, the NATO/EUNAVFOR naval task force established in 2009 to combat Somali piracy, concluded its operations in December 2016 as a result of the drop in reported incidents over the last few years; the EU naval mission, Operation ATALANTA, continues its operations in the Gulf of Aden and Indian Ocean through 2020; naval units from Japan, India, and China also operate in conjuction with EU forces; China has established a logistical base in Djibouti to support its deployed naval units in the Horn of Africa

TERRORISM :: DJIBOUTI

TERRORIST GROUPS - FOREIGN BASED:

al-Shabaab:

aim(s): punish Djibouti for participating in the African Union Mission in Somalia; compel Djibouti to withdraw troops from Somalia
area(s) of operation: maintains minimal operational presence (April 2018)

TRANSNATIONAL ISSUES :: DJIBOUTI

DISPUTES - INTERNATIONAL:

Djibouti maintains economic ties and border accords with "Somaliland" leadership while maintaining some political ties to various factions in SomaliaKuwait is chief investor in the 2008 restoration and upgrade of the Ethiopian-Djibouti rail linkin 2008, Eritrean troops moved across the border on Ras Doumera peninsula and occupied Doumera Island with undefined sovereignty in the Red Sea

REFUGEES AND INTERNALLY DISPLACED PERSONS:

refugees (country of origin): 19,636 (Yemen) (2017), 12,139 (Somalia) (2018)

TRAFFICKING IN PERSONS:

current situation: Djibouti is a transit, source, and destination country for men, women, and children subjected to forced labor and sex trafficking; economic migrants from East Africa en route to Yemen and other Middle East locations are vulnerable to exploitation in Djibouti; some women and girls may be forced into domestic servitude or prostitution after reaching Djibouti City, the Ethiopia-Djibouti trucking corridor, or Obock – the main crossing point into Yemen; Djiboutian and foreign children may be forced to beg, to work as domestic servants, or to commit theft and other petty crimes

tier rating: Tier 2 Watch List – Djibouti does not fully comply with the minimum standards for the elimination of trafficking; however, it is making significant efforts to do so; in 2014, Djibouti was granted a waiver from an otherwise required downgrade to Tier 3 because its government has a written plan that, if implemented would constitute making significant efforts to bring itself into compliance with the minimum standards for the elimination of trafficking; one forced labor trafficker was convicted in 2014 but received a suspended sentence inadequate to deter trafficking; authorities did not investigate or prosecute any other forced labor crimes, any sex trafficking offenses, or any officials complicit in human trafficking, and remained limited in their ability to recognize or protect trafficking victims; official round-ups, detentions, and deportations of non-Djiboutian residents, including children without screening for trafficking victims remained routine; the government did not provide care to victims but supported local NGOs operating centers that assisted victims (2015)

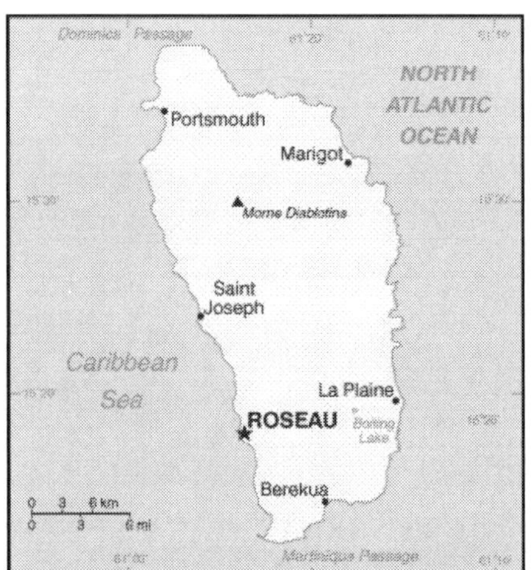

CENTRAL AMERICA :: DOMINICA

INTRODUCTION :: DOMINICA

BACKGROUND:

Dominica was the last of the Caribbean islands to be colonized by Europeans due chiefly to the fierce resistance of the native Caribs. France ceded possession to Great Britain in 1763, which colonized the island in 1805. In 1980, two years after independence, Dominica's fortunes improved when a corrupt and tyrannical administration was replaced by that of Mary Eugenia CHARLES, the first female prime minister in the Caribbean, who remained in office for 15 years. On 18 September 2017, Hurricane Maria passed over the island causing extensive damage to structures, roads, communications, and the power supply, and largely destroying critical agricultural areas.

GEOGRAPHY :: DOMINICA

LOCATION:

Caribbean, island between the Caribbean Sea and the North Atlantic Ocean, about halfway between Puerto Rico and Trinidad and Tobago

GEOGRAPHIC COORDINATES:

15 25 N, 61 20 W

MAP REFERENCES:

Central America and the Caribbean

AREA:

total: 751 sq km

land: 751 sq km

water: NEGL

country comparison to the world: 189

AREA - COMPARATIVE:

slightly more than four times the size of Washington, DC

LAND BOUNDARIES:

0 km

COASTLINE:

148 km

MARITIME CLAIMS:

territorial sea: 12 nm

exclusive economic zone: 200 nm

contiguous zone: 24 nm

CLIMATE:

tropical; moderated by northeast trade winds; heavy rainfall

TERRAIN:

rugged mountains of volcanic origin

ELEVATION:

0 m lowest point: Caribbean Sea

1447 highest point: Morne Diablotins

NATURAL RESOURCES:

timber, hydropower, arable land

LAND USE:

agricultural land: 34.7% (2011 est.)

arable land: 8% (2011 est.) / permanent crops: 24% (2011 est.) / permanent pasture: 2.7% (2011 est.)

forest: 59.2% (2011 est.)

other: 6.1% (2011 est.)

IRRIGATED LAND:

NA

POPULATION DISTRIBUTION:

population is mosly clustered along the coast, with roughly a third living in the parish of St. George, in or around the capital of Roseau; the volcanic interior is sparsely populated

NATURAL HAZARDS:

flash floods are a constant threat; destructive hurricanes can be expected during the late summer months

volcanism: Dominica was the last island to be formed in the Caribbean some 26 million years ago, it lies in the middle of the volcanic island arc of the Lesser Antilles that extends from the island of Saba in the north to Grenada in the south; of the 16 volcanoes that make up this arc, five are located on Dominica, more than any other island in the Caribbean: Morne aux Diables (861 m), Morne Diablotins (1,430 m), Morne Trois Pitons (1,387 m), Watt Mountain (1,224 m), which last erupted in 1997, and Morne Plat Pays (940 m); the two best known volcanic features on Dominica, the Valley of Desolation and the Boiling Lake thermal areas, lie on the flanks of Watt Mountain and both are popular tourist destinations

ENVIRONMENT - CURRENT ISSUES:

water shortages a continuing concern; pollution from agrochemicals and from untreated sewage; forests endangered by the expansion of farming; soil erosion; pollution of the coastal zone by agricultural and industrial chemicals, and untreated sewage

ENVIRONMENT - INTERNATIONAL AGREEMENTS:

party to: Biodiversity, Climate Change, Climate Change-Kyoto Protocol, Desertification, Endangered Species, Environmental Modification, Hazardous Wastes, Law of the Sea, Ozone Layer Protection, Ship Pollution, Whaling

signed, but not ratified: none of the selected agreements

GEOGRAPHY - NOTE:

known as "The Nature Island of the Caribbean" due to its spectacular, lush, and varied flora and fauna, which are protected by an extensive natural park system; the most mountainous of the Lesser Antilles, its volcanic peaks are cones of lava craters and include Boiling Lake, the second-largest, thermally active lake in the world

PEOPLE AND SOCIETY :: DOMINICA

POPULATION:

74,027 (July 2018 est.)

country comparison to the world: 202

NATIONALITY:

noun: Dominican(s)

adjective: Dominican

ETHNIC GROUPS:

black 86.6%, mixed 9.1%, indigenous 2.9%, other 1.3%, unspecified 0.2% (2001 est.)

LANGUAGES:

English (official), French patois

RELIGIONS:

Roman Catholic 61.4%, Protestant 28.6% (includes Evangelical 6.7%, Seventh Day Adventist 6.1%, Pentecostal 5.6%, Baptist 4.1%, Methodist 3.7%, Church of God 1.2%, other 1.2%), Rastafarian 1.3%, Jehovah's Witness 1.2%, other 0.3%, none 6.1%, unspecified 1.1% (2001 est.)

AGE STRUCTURE:

0-14 years: 21.62% (male 8,187 /female 7,815)

15-24 years: 14.37% (male 5,473 /female 5,167)

25-54 years: 42.59% (male 15,985 /female 15,541)

55-64 years: 9.99% (male 3,927 /female 3,470)

65 years and over: 11.43% (male 3,814 /female 4,648) (2018 est.)

MEDIAN AGE:

total: 34 years

male: 33.5 years

female: 34.5 years (2018 est.)

country comparison to the world: 88

POPULATION GROWTH RATE:

0.17% (2018 est.)

country comparison to the world: 182

BIRTH RATE:

15 births/1,000 population (2018 est.)

country comparison to the world: 125

DEATH RATE:

7.9 deaths/1,000 population (2018 est.)

country comparison to the world: 92

NET MIGRATION RATE:

-5.4 migrant(s)/1,000 population (2017 est.)

country comparison to the world: 193

POPULATION DISTRIBUTION:

population is mosly clustered along the coast, with roughly a third living in the parish of St. George, in or around the capital of Roseau; the volcanic interior is sparsely populated

URBANIZATION:

urban population: 70.5% of total population (2018)

rate of urbanization: 0.94% annual rate of change (2015-20 est.)

MAJOR URBAN AREAS - POPULATION:

15,000 ROSEAU (capital) (2018)

SEX RATIO:

at birth: 1.04 male(s)/female (2017 est.)

0-14 years: 1.05 male(s)/female (2017 est.)

15-24 years: 1.06 male(s)/female (2017 est.)

25-54 years: 1.03 male(s)/female (2017 est.)

55-64 years: 1.15 male(s)/female (2017 est.)

65 years and over: 0.79 male(s)/female (2017 est.)

total population: 1.02 male(s)/female (2017 est.)

INFANT MORTALITY RATE:

total: 10.3 deaths/1,000 live births (2018 est.)

male: 13.6 deaths/1,000 live births (2018 est.)

female: 6.8 deaths/1,000 live births (2018 est.)

country comparison to the world: 132

LIFE EXPECTANCY AT BIRTH:

total population: 77.4 years (2018 est.)

male: 74.4 years (2018 est.)

female: 80.5 years (2018 est.)

country comparison to the world: 73

TOTAL FERTILITY RATE:

2.03 children born/woman (2018 est.)

country comparison to the world: 114

HEALTH EXPENDITURES:

5.5% of GDP (2014)

country comparison to the world: 126

HOSPITAL BED DENSITY:

3.8 beds/1,000 population (2010)

DRINKING WATER SOURCE:

improved:

urban: 95.7% of population (2015 est.)

unimproved:

urban: 4.3% of population (2015 est.)

SANITATION FACILITY ACCESS:

improved:

urban: 79.6% of population (2007 est.)

rural: 84.3% of population (2007 est.)

total: 81.1% of population (2007 est.)

unimproved:

urban: 20.4% of population (2007 est.)

rural: 15.7% of population (2007 est.)

total: 18.9% of population (2007 est.)

HIV/AIDS - ADULT PREVALENCE RATE:

NA

HIV/AIDS - PEOPLE LIVING WITH HIV/AIDS:

NA

HIV/AIDS - DEATHS:

NA

MAJOR INFECTIOUS DISEASES:

note: active local transmission of Zika virus by Aedes species mosquitoes has been identified in this country (as of August 2016); it poses an important risk (a large number of cases possible) among US citizens if bitten by an infective mosquito; other less common ways to get Zika are through sex, via blood transfusion, or during pregnancy, in which the pregnant woman passes Zika virus to her fetus

OBESITY - ADULT PREVALENCE RATE:

27.9% (2016)

country comparison to the world: 33

EDUCATION EXPENDITURES:

3.4% of GDP (2015)

country comparison to the world: 133

PEOPLE - NOTE:

3,000-3,500 Kalinago (Carib) still living on Dominica are the only pre-Columbian population remaining in the Caribbean; only 70-100 may be "pure" Kalinago because of years of integration into the broader population

GOVERNMENT :: DOMINICA

COUNTRY NAME:

conventional long form: Commonwealth of Dominica

conventional short form: Dominica

etymology: the island was named by explorer Christopher COLUMBUS for the day of the week on which he spotted it, Sunday ("Domingo" in Latin), 3 November 1493

GOVERNMENT TYPE:

parliamentary republic

CAPITAL:

name: Roseau

geographic coordinates: 15 18 N, 61 24 W

time difference: UTC-4 (1 hour ahead of Washington, DC, during Standard Time)

ADMINISTRATIVE DIVISIONS:

10 parishes; Saint Andrew, Saint David, Saint George, Saint John, Saint Joseph, Saint Luke, Saint Mark, Saint Patrick, Saint Paul, Saint Peter

INDEPENDENCE:

3 November 1978 (from the UK)

NATIONAL HOLIDAY:

Independence Day, 3 November (1978)

CONSTITUTION:

history: previous 1967 (preindependence); latest presented 25 July 1978, entered into force 3 November 1978 (2018)

amendments: proposed by the House of Assembly; passage of amendments to constitutional sections such as fundamental rights and freedoms, the government structure, and constitutional amendment procedures requires approval by three-fourths of the Assembly membership in the final reading of the amendment bill, approval by simple majority in a referendum, and assent to by the president; amended several times, last in 2015 (2018)

LEGAL SYSTEM:

common law based on the English model

INTERNATIONAL LAW ORGANIZATION PARTICIPATION:

accepts compulsory ICJ jurisdiction; accepts ICCt jurisdiction

CITIZENSHIP:

citizenship by birth: yes

citizenship by descent only: yes

dual citizenship recognized: yes

residency requirement for naturalization: 5 years

SUFFRAGE:

18 years of age; universal

EXECUTIVE BRANCH:

chief of state: President Charles A. SAVARIN (since 2 October 2013)

head of government: Prime Minister Roosevelt SKERRIT (since 8 January 2004)

cabinet: Cabinet appointed by the president on the advice of the prime minister

elections/appointments: president nominated by the prime minister and leader of the opposition party and elected by the House of Assembly for a 5-year term (eligible for a second term); election last held on 1 October 2018 (next to be held in October 2023); prime minister appointed by the president

election results: Charles A. SAVARIN (DLP) reelected president unopposed

LEGISLATIVE BRANCH:

description: unicameral House of Assembly (32 seats; 21 representatives directly elected in single-seat constituencies by simple majority vote, 9 senators appointed by the Assembly, and 2 ex-officio members - the House Speaker and the Clerk of the House; members serve 5-year terms)

elections: last held on 8 December 2014 (next to be held in 2019); note - tradition dictates that the election is held within 5 years of the last election, but technically it is 5 years from the first seating of parliament plus a 90-day grace period

election results: percent of vote by party - DLP 57.0%, UWP 42.9%, other 0.1%; seats by party - DLP 15, UWP 6

JUDICIAL BRANCH:

highest courts: the Eastern Caribbean Supreme Court (ECSC) is the superior court of the Organization of Eastern Caribbean States; the ECSC - headquartered on St. Lucia - consists of the Court of Appeal - headed by the chief justice and 4 judges - and the High Court with 18 judges; the Court of Appeal is itinerant, travelling to member states on a schedule to hear appeals from the High Court and subordinate courts; High Court judges reside at the member states with 2 in Dominica; note - in 2015, Dominica acceded to the Caribbean Court of Justice as final court of appeal, replacing that of the Judicial Commmitte of the Privy Council in London

judge selection and term of office: chief justice of Eastern Caribbean Supreme Court appointed by the Her Majesty, Queen ELIZABETH II; other justices and judges appointed by the Judicial and Legal Services Commission, an independent body of judicial officials; Court of Appeal justices appointed for life with mandatory retirement at age 65; High Court judges appointed for life with mandatory retirement at age 62

subordinate courts: Court of Summary Jurisdiction; magistrates' courts

POLITICAL PARTIES AND LEADERS:

Dominica Freedom Party or DFP [Judith PESTAINA]
Dominica Labor Party or DLP [Roosevelt SKERRIT]
Dominica United Workers Party or UWP [Lennox LINTON]

INTERNATIONAL ORGANIZATION PARTICIPATION:

ACP, AOSIS, C, Caricom, CD, CDB, CELAC, Commonwealth of Nations, ECCU, FAO, G-77, IAEA, IBRD, ICCt, ICRM, IDA, IFAD, IFC, IFRCS, ILO, IMF, IMO, Interpol, IOC, ISO (correspondent), ITU, ITUC (NGOs), MIGA, NAM, OAS, OECS, OIF, OPANAL, OPCW, Petrocaribe, UN, UNCTAD, UNESCO, UNIDO, UPU, WFTU, WHO, WIPO, WMO, WTO

DIPLOMATIC REPRESENTATION IN THE US:

chief of mission: Ambassador Vince HENDERSON (since 18 January 2017)

chancery: 3216 New Mexico Avenue NW, Washington, DC 20016

telephone: [1] (202) 364-6781

FAX: [1] (202) 364-6791

consulate(s) general: New York

DIPLOMATIC REPRESENTATION FROM THE US:

the US does not have an embassy in Dominica; the US Ambassador to Barbados is accredited to Dominica

FLAG DESCRIPTION:

green with a centered cross of three equal bands - the vertical part is yellow (hoist side), black, and white and the horizontal part is yellow (top), black, and white; superimposed in the center of the cross is a red disk bearing a Sisserou parrot, unique to Dominica, encircled by 10 green, five-pointed stars edged in yellow; the 10 stars represent the 10 administrative divisions (parishes); green symbolizes the island's lush vegetation; the triple-colored cross represents the Christian Trinity; the yellow color denotes sunshine, the main agricultural products (citrus and bananas), and the native Carib Indians; black is for the rich soil and the African heritage of most citizens; white signifies rivers, waterfalls, and the purity of aspirations; the red disc stands for social justice

NATIONAL SYMBOL(S):

Sisserou parrot, Carib Wood flower; national colors: green, yellow, black, white, red

NATIONAL ANTHEM:

name: Isle of Beauty

lyrics/music: Wilfred Oscar Morgan POND/Lemuel McPherson CHRISTIAN

note: adopted 1967

ECONOMY :: DOMINICA

ECONOMY - OVERVIEW:

The Dominican economy was dependent on agriculture - primarily bananas - in years past, but increasingly has been driven by tourism, as the government seeks to promote Dominica as an "ecotourism" destination. However, Hurricane Maria, which passed through the island in September 2017, destroyed much of the country's agricultural sector and caused damage to all of the country's transportation and physical infrastructure. Before Hurricane Maria, the government had attempted to foster an offshore financial industry and planned to sign agreements with the private sector to develop geothermal energy resources. At a time when government finances are fragile, the government's focus has been to get the country back in shape to service cruise ships. The economy contracted in 2015 and recovered to positive growth in 2016 due to a recovery of agriculture and tourism. Dominica suffers from high debt levels, which increased from 67% of GDP in 2010 to 77% in 2016. Dominica is one of five countries in the East Caribbean that have citizenship by investment programs whereby foreigners can obtain passports for a fee and revenue from this contribute to government budgets.

GDP (PURCHASING POWER PARITY):

$783 million (2017 est.)

$821.5 million (2016 est.)

$800.4 million (2015 est.)

note: data are in 2017 dollars

country comparison to the world: 206

GDP (OFFICIAL EXCHANGE RATE):

$557 million (2017 est.) (2017 est.)

GDP - REAL GROWTH RATE:

-4.7% (2017 est.)

2.6% (2016 est.)

-3.7% (2015 est.)

country comparison to the world: 217

GDP - PER CAPITA (PPP):

$11,000 (2017 est.)

$11,600 (2016 est.)

$11,300 (2015 est.)

note: data are in 2017 dollars

country comparison to the world: 136

GROSS NATIONAL SAVING:

10.8% of GDP (2017 est.)

20% of GDP (2016 est.)

14.3% of GDP (2015 est.)

country comparison to the world: 160

GDP - COMPOSITION, BY END USE:

household consumption: 60.6% (2017 est.)

government consumption: 26.2% (2017 est.)

investment in fixed capital: 21.5% (2017 est.)

investment in inventories: 0% (2017 est.)

exports of goods and services: 54.4% (2017 est.)

imports of goods and services: -62.7% (2017 est.)

GDP - COMPOSITION, BY SECTOR OF ORIGIN:

agriculture: 22.3% (2017 est.)

industry: 12.6% (2017 est.)

services: 65.1% (2017 est.)

AGRICULTURE - PRODUCTS:

bananas, citrus, mangos, root crops, coconuts, cocoa

note: forest and fishery potential not exploited

INDUSTRIES:

soap, coconut oil, tourism, copra, furniture, cement blocks, shoes

INDUSTRIAL PRODUCTION GROWTH RATE:

-13% (2017 est.)

country comparison to the world: 199

LABOR FORCE:

25,000 (2000 est.)

country comparison to the world: 208

LABOR FORCE - BY OCCUPATION:

agriculture: 40%

industry: 32%

services: 28% (2002 est.)

UNEMPLOYMENT RATE:

23% (2000 est.)

country comparison to the world: 192

POPULATION BELOW POVERTY LINE:

29% (2009 est.)

HOUSEHOLD INCOME OR CONSUMPTION BY PERCENTAGE SHARE:

lowest 10%: NA

highest 10%: NA

BUDGET:

revenues: 227.8 million (2017 est.)

expenditures: 260.4 million (2017 est.)

TAXES AND OTHER REVENUES:

40.9% (of GDP) (2017 est.)

country comparison to the world: 34

BUDGET SURPLUS (+) OR DEFICIT (-):

-5.9% (of GDP) (2017 est.)

country comparison to the world: 181

PUBLIC DEBT:

82.7% of GDP (2017 est.)

71.7% of GDP (2016 est.)

country comparison to the world: 33

FISCAL YEAR:

1 July - 30 June

INFLATION RATE (CONSUMER PRICES):

0.6% (2017 est.)

0% (2016 est.)

country comparison to the world: 32

CENTRAL BANK DISCOUNT RATE:

6.5% (31 December 2010)

6.5% (31 December 2009)

country comparison to the world: 58

COMMERCIAL BANK PRIME LENDING RATE:

8.08% (31 December 2017 est.)

8.28% (31 December 2016 est.)

country comparison to the world: 108

STOCK OF NARROW MONEY:

$113.2 million (31 December 2017 est.)

$112 million (31 December 2016 est.)

country comparison to the world: 188

STOCK OF BROAD MONEY:

$113.2 million (31 December 2017 est.)

$112 million (31 December 2016 est.)

country comparison to the world: 193

STOCK OF DOMESTIC CREDIT:

$182.2 million (31 December 2017 est.)

$195.9 million (31 December 2016 est.)

country comparison to the world: 185

CURRENT ACCOUNT BALANCE:

-$70 million (2017 est.)

$5 million (2016 est.)

country comparison to the world: 82

EXPORTS:

$28 million (2017 est.)

$43.7 million (2016 est.)

country comparison to the world: 206

EXPORTS - PARTNERS:

Saudi Arabia 42.6%, Trinidad and Tobago 9.3%, Jamaica 8.1%, St. Kitts and Nevis 7.1%, Guyana 6.7% (2017)

EXPORTS - COMMODITIES:

bananas, soap, bay oil, vegetables, grapefruit, oranges

IMPORTS:

$206.6 million (2017 est.)

$188.4 million (2016 est.)

country comparison to the world: 209

IMPORTS - COMMODITIES:

manufactured goods, machinery and equipment, food, chemicals

IMPORTS - PARTNERS:

US 61.3%, Trinidad and Tobago 9.8% (2017)

RESERVES OF FOREIGN EXCHANGE AND GOLD:

$212.3 million (31 December 2017 est.)

$221.9 million (31 December 2016 est.)

country comparison to the world: 172

DEBT - EXTERNAL:

$280.4 million (31 December 2017 est.)

$314.2 million (31 December 2015 est.)

country comparison to the world: 186

STOCK OF DIRECT FOREIGN INVESTMENT - AT HOME:

$372.7 million (31 December 2017 est.)

country comparison to the world: 132

STOCK OF DIRECT FOREIGN INVESTMENT - ABROAD:

$220,000 (31 December 2017 est.)

country comparison to the world: 119

EXCHANGE RATES:

East Caribbean dollars (XCD) per US dollar -

2.7 (2017 est.)

2.7 (2016 est.)

2.7 (2015 est.)

2.7 (2014 est.)

2.7 (2013 est.)

ENERGY :: DOMINICA

ELECTRICITY ACCESS:

population without electricity: 5,900 (2012)

electrification - total population: 93% (2012)

electrification - urban areas: 99% (2012)

electrification - rural areas: 80% (2012)

ELECTRICITY - PRODUCTION:

111.4 million kWh (2016 est.)

country comparison to the world: 199

ELECTRICITY - CONSUMPTION:

103.6 million kWh (2016 est.)

country comparison to the world: 201

ELECTRICITY - EXPORTS:

0 kWh (2016 est.)

country comparison to the world: 128

ELECTRICITY - IMPORTS:

0 kWh (2016 est.)

country comparison to the world: 142

ELECTRICITY - INSTALLED GENERATING CAPACITY:

27,800 kW (2016 est.)

country comparison to the world: 201

ELECTRICITY - FROM FOSSIL FUELS:

72% of total installed capacity (2016 est.)

country comparison to the world: 102

ELECTRICITY - FROM NUCLEAR FUELS:

0% of total installed capacity (2017 est.)

country comparison to the world: 79

ELECTRICITY - FROM HYDROELECTRIC PLANTS:

25% of total installed capacity (2017 est.)

country comparison to the world: 76

ELECTRICITY - FROM OTHER RENEWABLE SOURCES:

3% of total installed capacity (2017 est.)

country comparison to the world: 124

CRUDE OIL - PRODUCTION:

0 bbl/day (2017 est.)

country comparison to the world: 127

CRUDE OIL - EXPORTS:

0 bbl/day (2015 est.)

country comparison to the world: 115

CRUDE OIL - IMPORTS:

0 bbl/day (2015 est.)

country comparison to the world: 118

CRUDE OIL - PROVED RESERVES:

0 bbl (1 January 2018 est.)

country comparison to the world: 124

REFINED PETROLEUM PRODUCTS - PRODUCTION:

0 bbl/day (2015 est.)

country comparison to the world: 137

REFINED PETROLEUM PRODUCTS - CONSUMPTION:

1,300 bbl/day (2016 est.)

country comparison to the world: 203

REFINED PETROLEUM PRODUCTS - EXPORTS:

0 bbl/day (2015 est.)

country comparison to the world: 148

REFINED PETROLEUM PRODUCTS - IMPORTS:

1,237 bbl/day (2015 est.)

country comparison to the world: 199

NATURAL GAS - PRODUCTION:

0 cu m (2017 est.)

country comparison to the world: 124

NATURAL GAS - CONSUMPTION:

0 cu m (2017 est.)

country comparison to the world: 140

NATURAL GAS - EXPORTS:

0 cu m (2017 est.)

country comparison to the world: 95

NATURAL GAS - IMPORTS:

0 cu m (2017 est.)

country comparison to the world: 117

NATURAL GAS - PROVED RESERVES:

0 cu m (1 January 2014 est.)

country comparison to the world: 128

CARBON DIOXIDE EMISSIONS FROM CONSUMPTION OF ENERGY:

199,600 Mt (2017 est.)

country comparison to the world: 200

COMMUNICATIONS :: DOMINICA

TELEPHONES - FIXED LINES:

total subscriptions: 13,328 (July 2016 est.)

subscriptions per 100 inhabitants: 18 (July 2016 est.)

country comparison to the world: 190

TELEPHONES - MOBILE CELLULAR:

total subscriptions: 78,444 (July 2016 est.)

subscriptions per 100 inhabitants: 106 (July 2016 est.)

country comparison to the world: 195

TELEPHONE SYSTEM:

general assessment: fully automatic network; there are multiple operators licensed to provide services, most of them are small and localised; the telecom sector across the Caribbean region remains one of the key growth areas (2017)

domestic: fixed-line connections continued to decline slowly with the two active operators providing about 18 fixed-line connections per 100 persons; subscribership among the three mobile-cellular providers is about 106 per 100 persons (2017)

international: country code - 1-767; landing points for the East Caribbean Fiber Optic System (ECFS) and the Global Caribbean Network (GCN) submarine cables providing connectivity to other islands in the eastern Caribbean extending from the British Virgin Islands to Trinidad; microwave radio relay and SHF radiotelephone links to Martinique and Guadeloupe; VHF and UHF radiotelephone links to Saint Lucia (2016)

BROADCAST MEDIA:

no terrestrial TV service available; subscription cable TV provider offers some locally produced programming plus channels from the US, Latin America, and the Caribbean; state-operated radio broadcasts on 6 stations; privately owned radio broadcasts on about 15 stations (2007)

INTERNET COUNTRY CODE:

.dm

INTERNET USERS:

total: 49,439 (July 2016 est.)

percent of population: 67% (July 2016 est.)

country comparison to the world: 195

BROADBAND - FIXED SUBSCRIPTIONS:

total: 15,487 (2017 est.)

subscriptions per 100 inhabitants: 21 (2017 est.)

country comparison to the world: 160

TRANSPORTATION :: DOMINICA

NATIONAL AIR TRANSPORT SYSTEM:

number of registered air carriers: 0 (2015)

inventory of registered aircraft operated by air carriers: 0 (2015)

annual passenger traffic on registered air carriers: 0 (2015)

annual freight traffic on registered air carriers: 0 mt-km (2015)

CIVIL AIRCRAFT REGISTRATION COUNTRY CODE PREFIX:

J7 (2016)

AIRPORTS:

2 (2013)

country comparison to the world: 199

AIRPORTS - WITH PAVED RUNWAYS:

total: 2 (2017)

1,524 to 2,437 m: 1 (2017)

914 to 1,523 m: 1 (2017)

ROADWAYS:

total: 1,512 km (2010)

paved: 762 km (2010)

unpaved: 750 km (2010)

country comparison to the world: 177

MERCHANT MARINE:

total: 76 (2017)

by type: general cargo 24, oil tanker 15, other 37 (2017)

country comparison to the world: 101

PORTS AND TERMINALS:

major seaport(s): Portsmouth, Roseau

MILITARY AND SECURITY :: DOMINICA

MILITARY BRANCHES:

no regular military forces; Commonwealth of Dominica Police Force (includes Coast Guard) (2012)

TRANSNATIONAL ISSUES :: DOMINICA

DISPUTES - INTERNATIONAL:

Dominica is the only Caribbean state to challenge Venezuela's sovereignty claim over Aves Island and joins the other island nations in challenging whether the feature sustains human habitation, a criterion under the UN Convention on the Law of the Sea, which permits Venezuela to extend its EEZ and continental shelf claims over a large portion of the eastern Caribbean Sea

ILLICIT DRUGS:

transshipment point for narcotics bound for the US and Europe; minor cannabis producer

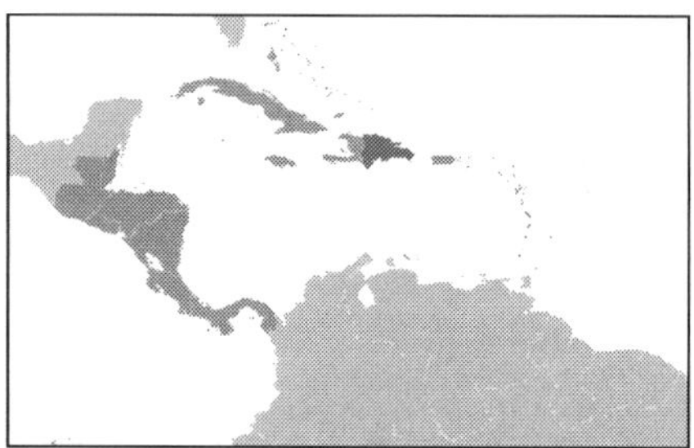

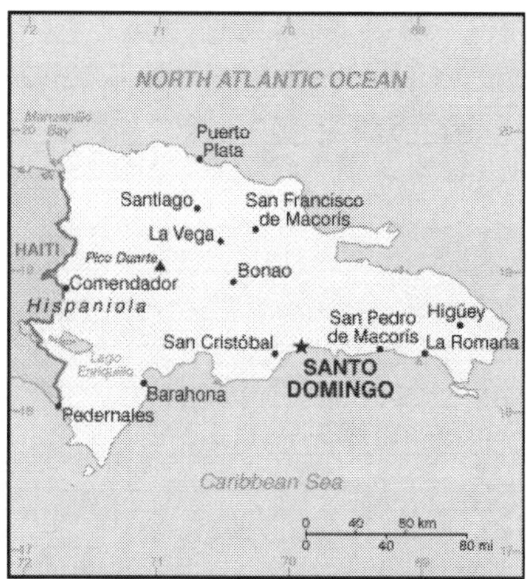

CENTRAL AMERICA :: DOMINICAN REPUBLIC

INTRODUCTION :: DOMINICAN REPUBLIC

BACKGROUND:

The Taino - indigenous inhabitants of Hispaniola prior to the arrival of the Europeans - divided the island into five chiefdoms and territories. Christopher COLUMBUS explored and claimed the island on his first voyage in 1492; it became a springboard for Spanish conquest of the Caribbean and the American mainland. In 1697, Spain recognized French dominion over the western third of the island, which in 1804 became Haiti. The remainder of the island, by then known as Santo Domingo, sought to gain its own independence in 1821 but was conquered and ruled by the Haitians for 22 years; it finally attained independence as the Dominican Republic in 1844. In 1861, the Dominicans voluntarily returned to the Spanish Empire, but two years later they launched a war that restored independence in 1865. A legacy of unsettled, mostly non-representative rule followed, capped by the dictatorship of Rafael Leonidas TRUJILLO from 1930 to 1961. Juan BOSCH was elected president in 1962 but was deposed in a military coup in 1963. In 1965, the US led an intervention in the midst of a civil war sparked by an uprising to restore BOSCH. In 1966, Joaquin BALAGUER defeated BOSCH in the presidential election. BALAGUER maintained a tight grip on power for most of the next 30 years when international reaction to flawed elections forced him to curtail his term in 1996. Since then, regular competitive elections have been held in which opposition candidates have won the presidency. Former President Leonel FERNANDEZ Reyna (first term 1996-2000) won elected to a new term in 2004 following a constitutional amendment allowing presidents to serve more than one term, and was later reelected to a second consecutive term. In 2012, Danilo MEDINA Sanchez became president; he was reelected in 2016.

GEOGRAPHY :: DOMINICAN REPUBLIC

LOCATION:

Caribbean, eastern two-thirds of the island of Hispaniola, between the Caribbean Sea and the North Atlantic Ocean, east of Haiti

GEOGRAPHIC COORDINATES:

19 00 N, 70 40 W

MAP REFERENCES:

Central America and the Caribbean

AREA:

total: 48,670 sq km

land: 48,320 sq km

water: 350 sq km

country comparison to the world: 132

AREA - COMPARATIVE:

slightly more than twice the size of New Jersey

LAND BOUNDARIES:

total: 376 km

border countries (1): Haiti 376 km

COASTLINE:

1,288 km

MARITIME CLAIMS:

territorial sea: 12 nm

exclusive economic zone: 200 nm

contiguous zone: 24 nm

continental shelf: 200 nm or to the edge of the continental margin

measured from claimed archipelagic straight baselines

CLIMATE:

tropical maritime; little seasonal temperature variation; seasonal variation in rainfall

TERRAIN:

rugged highlands and mountains interspersed with fertile valleys

ELEVATION:

mean elevation: 424 m

elevation extremes: -46 m lowest point: Lago Enriquillo

3098 highest point: Pico Duarte

NATURAL RESOURCES:

nickel, bauxite, gold, silver, arable land

LAND USE:

agricultural land: 51.5% (2011 est.)

arable land: 16.6% (2011 est.) / permanent crops: 10.1% (2011 est.) / permanent pasture: 24.8% (2011 est.)

forest: 40.8% (2011 est.)

other: 7.7% (2011 est.)

IRRIGATED LAND:

3,070 sq km (2012)

POPULATION DISTRIBUTION:

coastal development is significant, especially in the southern coastal plains and the Cibao Valley, where population density is highest; smaller population clusters exist in the interior mountains (Cordillera Central)

NATURAL HAZARDS:

lies in the middle of the hurricane belt and subject to severe storms from June to October; occasional flooding; periodic droughts

ENVIRONMENT - CURRENT ISSUES:

water shortages; soil eroding into the sea damages coral reefs; deforestation

ENVIRONMENT - INTERNATIONAL AGREEMENTS:

party to: Biodiversity, Climate Change, Climate Change-Kyoto Protocol, Desertification, Endangered Species, Hazardous Wastes, Marine Dumping, Marine Life Conservation, Ozone Layer Protection, Ship Pollution, Wetlands

signed, but not ratified: Law of the Sea

GEOGRAPHY - NOTE:

shares island of Hispaniola with Haiti (eastern two-thirds makes up the Dominican Republic, western one-third is Haiti); the second largest country in the Antilles (after Cuba); geographically diverse with the Caribbean's tallest mountain, Pico Duarte, and lowest elevation and largest lake, Lago Enriquillo

PEOPLE AND SOCIETY :: DOMINICAN REPUBLIC

POPULATION:

10,298,756 (July 2018 est.)

country comparison to the world: 88

NATIONALITY:

noun: Dominican(s)

adjective: Dominican

ETHNIC GROUPS:

mixed 70.4% (mestizo/indio 58%, mulatto 12.4%), black 15.8%, white 13.5%, other 0.3% (2014 est.)

note: respondents self-identified their race; the term "indio" in the Dominican Republic is not associated with people of indigenous ancestry but people of mixed ancestry or skin color between light and dark

LANGUAGES:

Spanish (official)

RELIGIONS:

Roman Catholic 95%, other 5%

AGE STRUCTURE:

0-14 years: 27.56% (male 1,442,926 /female 1,395,809)

15-24 years: 18.52% (male 969,467 /female 937,765)

25-54 years: 40.28% (male 2,112,813 /female 2,035,902)

55-64 years: 7.71% (male 397,821 /female 396,172)

65 years and over: 5.92% (male 286,300 /female 323,781) (2018 est.)

DEPENDENCY RATIOS:

total dependency ratio: 57.8 (2015 est.)

youth dependency ratio: 47.3 (2015 est.)

elderly dependency ratio: 10.5 (2015 est.)

potential support ratio: 9.5 (2015 est.)

MEDIAN AGE:

total: 27.3 years

male: 27.1 years

female: 27.4 years (2018 est.)

country comparison to the world: 145

POPULATION GROWTH RATE:

0.99% (2018 est.)

country comparison to the world: 109

BIRTH RATE:

18.9 births/1,000 population (2018 est.)

country comparison to the world: 84

DEATH RATE:

6.4 deaths/1,000 population (2018 est.)

country comparison to the world: 145

NET MIGRATION RATE:

-1.9 migrant(s)/1,000 population (2017 est.)

country comparison to the world: 157

POPULATION DISTRIBUTION:

coastal development is significant, especially in the southern coastal plains and the Cibao Valley, where population density is highest; smaller population clusters exist in the interior mountains (Cordillera Central)

URBANIZATION:

urban population: 81.1% of total population (2018)

rate of urbanization: 2.06% annual rate of change (2015-20 est.)

MAJOR URBAN AREAS - POPULATION:

3.172 million SANTO DOMINGO (capital) (2018)

SEX RATIO:

at birth: 1.04 male(s)/female (2017 est.)

0-14 years: 1.04 male(s)/female (2017 est.)

15-24 years: 1.04 male(s)/female (2017 est.)

25-54 years: 1.05 male(s)/female (2017 est.)

55-64 years: 1.01 male(s)/female (2017 est.)

65 years and over: 0.86 male(s)/female (2017 est.)

total population: 1.03 male(s)/female (2017 est.)

MOTHER'S MEAN AGE AT FIRST BIRTH:

21.3 years (2013 est.)

note: median age at first birth among women 25-29

MATERNAL MORTALITY RATE:

92 deaths/100,000 live births (2015 est.)

country comparison to the world: 75

INFANT MORTALITY RATE:

total: 22.7 deaths/1,000 live births (2018 est.)

male: 25 deaths/1,000 live births (2018 est.)

female: 20.3 deaths/1,000 live births (2018 est.)

country comparison to the world: 72

LIFE EXPECTANCY AT BIRTH:

total population: 71.3 years (2018 est.)

male: 69.7 years (2018 est.)

female: 73.1 years (2018 est.)

country comparison to the world: 151

TOTAL FERTILITY RATE:

2.28 children born/woman (2018 est.)

country comparison to the world: 88

CONTRACEPTIVE PREVALENCE RATE:

69.5% (2014)

HEALTH EXPENDITURES:

4.4% of GDP (2014)

country comparison to the world: 157

PHYSICIANS DENSITY:

1.49 physicians/1,000 population (2011)

HOSPITAL BED DENSITY:

1.6 beds/1,000 population (2014)

DRINKING WATER SOURCE:

improved:

urban: 85.4% of population (2015 est.)

rural: 81.9% of population (2015 est.)

total: 84.7% of population (2015 est.)

unimproved:

urban: 14.6% of population (2015 est.)

rural: 18.1% of population (2015 est.)

total: 15.3% of population (2015 est.)

SANITATION FACILITY ACCESS:

improved:

urban: 86.2% of population (2015 est.)

rural: 75.7% of population (2015 est.)

total: 84% of population (2015 est.)

unimproved:

urban: 13.8% of population (2015 est.)

rural: 24.3% of population (2015 est.)

total: 16% of population (2015 est.)

HIV/AIDS - ADULT PREVALENCE RATE:

0.9% (2017 est.)

country comparison to the world: 46

HIV/AIDS - PEOPLE LIVING WITH HIV/AIDS:

67,000 (2017 est.)

country comparison to the world: 54

HIV/AIDS - DEATHS:

2,600 (2017 est.)

country comparison to the world: 42

MAJOR INFECTIOUS DISEASES:

degree of risk: high (2016)

food or waterborne diseases: bacterial diarrhea, hepatitis A, and typhoid fever (2016)

vectorborne diseases: dengue fever (2016)

note: active local transmission of Zika virus by Aedes species mosquitoes has been identified in this country (as of August 2016); it poses an important risk (a large number of cases possible) among US citizens if bitten by an infective mosquito; other less common ways to get Zika are through sex, via blood transfusion, or during pregnancy, in which the pregnant woman passes Zika virus to her fetus

OBESITY - ADULT PREVALENCE RATE:

27.6% (2016)

country comparison to the world: 37

CHILDREN UNDER THE AGE OF 5 YEARS UNDERWEIGHT:

4% (2013)

country comparison to the world: 87

LITERACY:

definition: age 15 and over can read and write (2015 est.)

total population: 91.8% (2015 est.)

male: 91.2% (2015 est.)

female: 92.3% (2015 est.)

SCHOOL LIFE EXPECTANCY (PRIMARY TO TERTIARY EDUCATION):

total: 13 years (2014)

male: 13 years (2014)

female: 14 years (2014)

UNEMPLOYMENT, YOUTH AGES 15-24:

total: 13.4% (2016 est.)

male: 8.5% (2016 est.)

female: 21.7% (2016 est.)

country comparison to the world: 97

GOVERNMENT :: DOMINICAN REPUBLIC

COUNTRY NAME:

conventional long form: Dominican Republic

conventional short form: The Dominican

local long form: Republica Dominicana

local short form: La Dominicana

etymology: the country name derives from the capital city of Santo Domingo (Saint Dominic)

GOVERNMENT TYPE:

presidential republic

CAPITAL:

name: Santo Domingo

geographic coordinates: 18 28 N, 69 54 W

time difference: UTC-4 (1 hour ahead of Washington, DC, during Standard Time)

ADMINISTRATIVE DIVISIONS:

10 regions (regiones, singular - region); Cibao Nordeste, Cibao Noroeste, Cibao Norte, Cibao Sur, El Valle, Enriquillo, Higuamo, Ozama, Valdesia, Yuma

INDEPENDENCE:

27 February 1844 (from Haiti)

NATIONAL HOLIDAY:

Independence Day, 27 February (1844)

CONSTITUTION:

history: many previous (38 total); latest proclaimed 13 June 2015 (2018)

amendments: proposed by a special session of the National Congress called the National Revisory Assembly; passage requires at least two-thirds majority approval by at least one-half of those present in both houses of the Assembly; passage of amendments to constitutional articles such as fundamental rights and guarantees, territorial composition, nationality, or the procedures for constitutional reform also requires approval in a referendum; amended many times, last in 2017 (2018)

LEGAL SYSTEM:

civil law system based on the French civil code; Criminal Procedures Code modified in 2004 to include important elements of an accusatory system

INTERNATIONAL LAW ORGANIZATION PARTICIPATION:

accepts compulsory ICJ jurisdiction; accepts ICCt jurisdiction

CITIZENSHIP:

citizenship by birth: no

citizenship by descent only: at least one parent must be a citizen of the Dominican Republic

dual citizenship recognized: yes

residency requirement for naturalization: 2 years

SUFFRAGE:

18 years of age; universal and compulsory; married persons regardless of age can vote; note - members of the armed forces and national police by law cannot vote

EXECUTIVE BRANCH:

chief of state: President Danilo MEDINA Sanchez (since 16 August 2012); Vice President Margarita CEDENO DE FERNANDEZ (since 16 August 2012); note - the president is both chief of state and head of government

head of government: President Danilo MEDINA Sanchez (since 16 August 2012); Vice President Margarita CEDENO DE FERNANDEZ (since 16 August 2012)

cabinet: Cabinet nominated by the president

elections/appointments: president and vice president directly elected on the same ballot by absolute vote in 2 rounds if needed for a 4-year term (eligible for consecutive terms);

election last held on 15 May 2016 (next to be held in 2020)

election results: Danilo MEDINA Sanchez reelected president in first round; percent of vote - Danilo MEDINA Sanchez (PLD) 61.7%, Luis Rodolfo ABINADER Corona (PRM) 35%, other 3.3%; Margarita CEDENO DE FERNANDEZ (PLD) reelected vice president

LEGISLATIVE BRANCH:

description: bicameral National Congress or Congreso Nacional consists of:
Senate or Senado (32 seats; members directly elected in single-seat constituencies by simple majority vote to serve 4-year terms)
House of Representatives or Camara de Diputados (190 seats; members directly elected in multi-seat constituencies by proportional representation vote; members serve 4-year terms)

elections:
Senate - last held on 15 May 2016 (next to be held in May 2020)
House of Representatives - last held on 15 May 2016 (next to be held in May 2020)

election results:
Senate - percent of vote by party - NA; seats by party - PLD 26, PRM 2, BIS 1, PLRD 1, PRD 1, PRSC 1
House of Representatives - percent of vote by party - NA; seats by party - PLD 106, PRM 42, PRSC 18, PRD 16, PLRD 3, other 5

JUDICIAL BRANCH:

highest courts: Supreme Court of Justice or Suprema Corte de Justicia (consists of a minimum of 16 magistrates); Constitutional Court or Tribunal Constitucional (consists of 13 judges); note - the Constitutional Court was established in 2010 by constitutional amendment

judge selection and term of office: Supreme Court and Constitutional Court judges appointed by the National Council of the Judiciary comprised of the president, the leaders of both chambers of congress, the president of the Supreme Court, and a non-governing party congressional representative; Supreme Court judges appointed for 7-year terms; Constitutional Court judges appointed for 9-year terms

subordinate courts: courts of appeal; courts of first instance; justices of the peace; special courts for juvenile, labor, and land cases; Contentious Administrative Court for cases filed against the government

POLITICAL PARTIES AND LEADERS:

Dominican Liberation Party or PLD [Leonel FERNANDEZ Reyna]
Dominican Revolutionary Party or PRD [Miguel VARGAS Maldonado]
Institutional Social Democratic Bloc or BIS
Liberal Reformist Party or PRL (formerly the Liberal Party of the Dominican Republic or PLRD)
Modern Revolutionary Party or PRM [Andres BAUTISTA Garcia]
National Progressive Front or FNP [Vinicio CASTILLO, Pelegrin CASTILLO]
Social Christian Reformist Party or PRSC [Federico ANTUN]

INTERNATIONAL ORGANIZATION PARTICIPATION:

ACP, AOSIS, BCIE, Caricom (observer), CD, CELAC, FAO, G-77, IADB, IAEA, IBRD, ICAO, ICC (national committees), ICCt, ICRM, IDA, IFAD, IFC, IFRCS, IHO, ILO, IMF, IMO, Interpol, IOC, IOM, IPU, ISO (correspondent), ITSO, ITU, ITUC (NGOs), LAES, LAIA, MIGA, MINUSMA, NAM, OAS, OIF (observer), OPANAL, OPCW, Pacific Alliance (observer), PCA, Petrocaribe, SICA (associated member), UN, UNCTAD, UNESCO, UNIDO, Union Latina, UNWTO, UPU, WCO, WFTU (NGOs), WHO, WIPO, WMO, WTO

DIPLOMATIC REPRESENTATION IN THE US:

chief of mission: Ambassador Jose Tomas PEREZ Vazquez(since 23 February 2015)

chancery: 1715 22nd Street NW, Washington, DC 20008

telephone: [1] (202) 332-6280

FAX: [1] (202) 265-8057

consulate(s) general: Boston, Chicago, Los Angeles, Mayaguez (Puerto Rico), Miami, New Orleans, New York, San Juan (Puerto Rico)

consulate(s): San Francisco

DIPLOMATIC REPRESENTATION FROM THE US:

chief of mission: Ambassador (vacant); Charge d'Affaires Robert COPLEY (since 21 July 2017)

embassy: Av. Republica de Colombia # 57, Santo Domingo

mailing address: Unit 5500, APO AA 34041-5500

telephone: [1] (809) 567-7775

FAX: [1] (809) 686-7437

FLAG DESCRIPTION:

a centered white cross that extends to the edges divides the flag into four rectangles - the top ones are ultramarine blue (hoist side) and vermilion red, and the bottom ones are vermilion red (hoist side) and ultramarine blue; a small coat of arms featuring a shield supported by a laurel branch (left) and a palm branch (right) is at the center of the cross; above the shield a blue ribbon displays the motto, DIOS, PATRIA, LIBERTAD (God, Fatherland, Liberty), and below the shield, REPUBLICA DOMINICANA appears on a red ribbon; in the shield a bible is opened to a verse that reads "Y la verdad nos hara libre" (And the truth shall set you free); blue stands for liberty, white for salvation, and red for the blood of heroes

NATIONAL SYMBOL(S):

palmchat (bird); national colors: red, white, blue

NATIONAL ANTHEM:

name: "Himno Nacional" (National Anthem)

lyrics/music: Emilio PRUD'HOMME/Jose REYES

note: adopted 1934; also known as "Quisqueyanos valientes" (Valient Sons of Quisqueye); the anthem never refers to the people as Dominican but rather calls them "Quisqueyanos," a reference to the indigenous name of the island

ECONOMY :: DOMINICAN REPUBLIC

ECONOMY - OVERVIEW:

The Dominican Republic was for most of its history primarily an exporter of sugar, coffee, and tobacco, but over the last three decades the economy has become more diversified as the service sector has overtaken agriculture as the economy's largest employer, due to growth in construction, tourism, and free trade zones. The mining sector has also played a greater role in the export market since late 2012 with the commencement of the extraction phase of the Pueblo Viejo Gold and Silver mine, one of the largest gold mines in the world.

For the last 20 years, the Dominican Republic has been one of the fastest growing economies in Latin America. The economy rebounded from the global recession in 2010-16, and the fiscal situation is improving. A tax reform package passed in November 2012, a reduction in government spending, and lower energy costs helped to narrow the central government budget deficit from 6.6% of GDP in 2012 to 2.6% in 2016, and public debt is declining. Marked income inequality, high unemployment, and underemployment remain important long-term challenges; the poorest half of the population receives less than one-fifth of GDP, while the richest 10% enjoys nearly 40% of GDP.

The economy is highly dependent upon the US, the destination for approximately half of exports and the source of 40% of imports. Remittances from the US amount to about 7% of GDP, equivalent to about a third of exports and two-thirds of tourism receipts. The Central America-Dominican Republic Free Trade Agreement came into force in March 2007, boosting investment and manufacturing exports.

GDP (PURCHASING POWER PARITY):

$173 billion (2017 est.)

$165.4 billion (2016 est.)

$155.2 billion (2015 est.)

note: data are in 2017 dollars

country comparison to the world: 72

GDP (OFFICIAL EXCHANGE RATE):

$76.09 billion (2017 est.) (2017 est.)

GDP - REAL GROWTH RATE:

4.6% (2017 est.)

6.6% (2016 est.)

7% (2015 est.)

country comparison to the world: 61

GDP - PER CAPITA (PPP):

$17,000 (2017 est.)

$16,400 (2016 est.)

$15,500 (2015 est.)

note: data are in 2017 dollars

country comparison to the world: 102

GROSS NATIONAL SAVING:

21.6% of GDP (2017 est.)

20.8% of GDP (2016 est.)

20.7% of GDP (2015 est.)

country comparison to the world: 84

GDP - COMPOSITION, BY END USE:

household consumption: 69.3% (2017 est.)

government consumption: 12.2% (2017 est.)

investment in fixed capital: 21.9% (2017 est.)

investment in inventories: -0.1% (2017 est.)

exports of goods and services: 24.8% (2017 est.)

imports of goods and services: -28.1% (2017 est.)

GDP - COMPOSITION, BY SECTOR OF ORIGIN:

agriculture: 5.6% (2017 est.)

industry: 33% (2017 est.)

services: 61.4% (2017 est.)

AGRICULTURE - PRODUCTS:

cocoa, tobacco, sugarcane, coffee, cotton, rice, beans, potatoes, corn, bananas; cattle, pigs, dairy products, beef, eggs

INDUSTRIES:

tourism, sugar processing, gold mining, textiles, cement, tobacco, electrical components, medical devices

INDUSTRIAL PRODUCTION GROWTH RATE:

3.1% (2017 est.)

country comparison to the world: 99

LABOR FORCE:

4.732 million (2017 est.)

country comparison to the world: 85

LABOR FORCE - BY OCCUPATION:

agriculture: 14.4%

industry: 20.8% (2014)

services: 64.7% (2014 est.)

UNEMPLOYMENT RATE:

5.1% (2017 est.)

5.5% (2016 est.)

country comparison to the world: 76

POPULATION BELOW POVERTY LINE:

30.5% (2016 est.)

HOUSEHOLD INCOME OR CONSUMPTION BY PERCENTAGE SHARE:

lowest 10%: 37.4% (2013 est.)

highest 10%: 37.4% (2013 est.)

DISTRIBUTION OF FAMILY INCOME - GINI INDEX:

47.1 (2013 est.)

45.7 (2012 est.)

country comparison to the world: 25

BUDGET:

revenues: 11.33 billion (2017 est.)

expenditures: 13.62 billion (2017 est.)

TAXES AND OTHER REVENUES:

14.9% (of GDP) (2017 est.)

country comparison to the world: 194

BUDGET SURPLUS (+) OR DEFICIT (-):

-3% (of GDP) (2017 est.)

country comparison to the world: 132

PUBLIC DEBT:

37.2% of GDP (2017 est.)

34.6% of GDP (2016 est.)

country comparison to the world: 140

FISCAL YEAR:

calendar year

INFLATION RATE (CONSUMER PRICES):

3.3% (2017 est.)

1.6% (2016 est.)

country comparison to the world: 137

COMMERCIAL BANK PRIME LENDING RATE:

13.91% (31 December 2017 est.)

15.08% (31 December 2016 est.)

country comparison to the world: 50

STOCK OF NARROW MONEY:

$7.011 billion (31 December 2017 est.)

$6.491 billion (31 December 2016 est.)

country comparison to the world: 92

STOCK OF BROAD MONEY:

$7.011 billion (31 December 2017 est.)

$6.491 billion (31 December 2016 est.)

country comparison to the world: 94

STOCK OF DOMESTIC CREDIT:

$35.42 billion (31 December 2017 est.)

$33.6 billion (31 December 2016 est.)

country comparison to the world: 74

MARKET VALUE OF PUBLICLY TRADED SHARES:

NA

CURRENT ACCOUNT BALANCE:

-$165 million (2017 est.)

-$815 million (2016 est.)

country comparison to the world: 95

EXPORTS:

$10.12 billion (2017 est.)

$9.86 billion (2016 est.)

country comparison to the world: 93

EXPORTS - PARTNERS:

US 50.3%, Haiti 9.1%, Canada 8.2%, India 5.6% (2017)

EXPORTS - COMMODITIES:

gold, silver, cocoa, sugar, coffee, tobacco, meats, consumer goods

IMPORTS:

$17.7 billion (2017 est.)

$17.4 billion (2016 est.)

country comparison to the world: 83

IMPORTS - COMMODITIES:

petroleum, foodstuffs, cotton and fabrics, chemicals and pharmaceuticals

IMPORTS - PARTNERS:

US 41.4%, China 13.9%, Mexico 4.5%, Brazil 4.3% (2017)

RESERVES OF FOREIGN EXCHANGE AND GOLD:

$6.873 billion (31 December 2017 est.)

$6.134 billion (31 December 2016 est.)

country comparison to the world: 87

DEBT - EXTERNAL:

$29.16 billion (31 December 2017 est.)

$27.7 billion (31 December 2016 est.)

country comparison to the world: 83

STOCK OF DIRECT FOREIGN INVESTMENT - AT HOME:

$37.15 billion (31 December 2017 est.)

$33.56 billion (31 December 2016 est.)

country comparison to the world: 65

STOCK OF DIRECT FOREIGN INVESTMENT - ABROAD:

$408.6 million (31 December 2017 est.)

$387.8 million (31 December 2016 est.)

country comparison to the world: 99

EXCHANGE RATES:

Dominican pesos (DOP) per US dollar -

47.42 (2017 est.)

46.078 (2016 est.)

46.078 (2015 est.)

45.052 (2014 est.)

43.556 (2013 est.)

ENERGY :: DOMINICAN REPUBLIC

ELECTRICITY ACCESS:

population without electricity: 300,000 (2013)

electrification - total population: 98% (2013)

electrification - urban areas: 99% (2013)

electrification - rural areas: 97% (2013)

ELECTRICITY - PRODUCTION:

18.03 billion kWh (2016 est.)

country comparison to the world: 81

ELECTRICITY - CONSUMPTION:

15.64 billion kWh (2016 est.)

country comparison to the world: 78

ELECTRICITY - EXPORTS:

0 kWh (2016 est.)

country comparison to the world: 129

ELECTRICITY - IMPORTS:

0 kWh (2016 est.)

country comparison to the world: 143

ELECTRICITY - INSTALLED GENERATING CAPACITY:

3.839 million kW (2016 est.)

country comparison to the world: 91

ELECTRICITY - FROM FOSSIL FUELS:

77% of total installed capacity (2016 est.)

country comparison to the world: 92

ELECTRICITY - FROM NUCLEAR FUELS:

0% of total installed capacity (2017 est.)

country comparison to the world: 80

ELECTRICITY - FROM HYDROELECTRIC PLANTS:

16% of total installed capacity (2017 est.)

country comparison to the world: 99

ELECTRICITY - FROM OTHER RENEWABLE SOURCES:

7% of total installed capacity (2017 est.)

country comparison to the world: 93

CRUDE OIL - PRODUCTION:

0 bbl/day (2017 est.)

country comparison to the world: 128

CRUDE OIL - EXPORTS:

0 bbl/day (2015 est.)

country comparison to the world: 116

CRUDE OIL - IMPORTS:

16,980 bbl/day (2015 est.)

country comparison to the world: 67

CRUDE OIL - PROVED RESERVES:

0 bbl (1 January 2018 est.)

country comparison to the world: 125

REFINED PETROLEUM PRODUCTS - PRODUCTION:

16,060 bbl/day (2015 est.)

country comparison to the world: 92

REFINED PETROLEUM PRODUCTS - CONSUMPTION:

134,000 bbl/day (2016 est.)

country comparison to the world: 70

REFINED PETROLEUM PRODUCTS - EXPORTS:

0 bbl/day (2015 est.)

country comparison to the world: 149

REFINED PETROLEUM PRODUCTS - IMPORTS:

108,500 bbl/day (2015 est.)

country comparison to the world: 52

NATURAL GAS - PRODUCTION:

0 cu m (2017 est.)

country comparison to the world: 125

NATURAL GAS - CONSUMPTION:

1.161 billion cu m (2017 est.)

country comparison to the world: 92

NATURAL GAS - EXPORTS:

0 cu m (2017 est.)

country comparison to the world: 96

NATURAL GAS - IMPORTS:

1.161 billion cu m (2017 est.)

country comparison to the world: 60

NATURAL GAS - PROVED RESERVES:

0 cu m (1 January 2014 est.)

country comparison to the world: 129

CARBON DIOXIDE EMISSIONS FROM CONSUMPTION OF ENERGY:

23.79 million Mt (2017 est.)

country comparison to the world: 81

COMMUNICATIONS :: DOMINICAN REPUBLIC

TELEPHONES - FIXED LINES:

total subscriptions: 1,329,852 (2017 est.)

subscriptions per 100 inhabitants: 12 (2017 est.)

country comparison to the world: 68

TELEPHONES - MOBILE CELLULAR:

total subscriptions: 8,769,127 (2017 est.)

subscriptions per 100 inhabitants: 82 (2017 est.)

country comparison to the world: 92

TELEPHONE SYSTEM:

general assessment: relatively efficient system based on island-wide microwave radio relay network; there are multiple operators licensed to provide services, most of them are small and localised; the telecom sector across the Caribbean region remains one of the key growth areas (2017)

domestic: fixed-line teledensity is about 12 per 100 persons; multiple providers of mobile-cellular service with a subscribership of over 80 per 100 persons (2017)

international: country code - 1-809; 1-829; 1-849; landing point for the Americas Region Caribbean Ring System (ARCOS-1), Antillas 1, AMX-1, and the Fibralink submarine cables that provide links to South and Central America, parts of the Caribbean, and US; satellite earth station - 1 Intelsat (Atlantic Ocean) (2016)

BROADCAST MEDIA:

combination of state-owned and privately owned broadcast media; 1 state-owned TV network and a number of private TV networks; networks operate repeaters to extend signals throughout country; combination of state-owned and privately owned radio stations with more than 300 radio stations operating (2015)

INTERNET COUNTRY CODE:

.do

INTERNET USERS:

total: 6,504,998 (July 2016 est.)

percent of population: 61.3% (July 2016 est.)

country comparison to the world: 65

TRANSPORTATION :: DOMINICAN REPUBLIC

NATIONAL AIR TRANSPORT SYSTEM:

number of registered air carriers: 1 (2015)

inventory of registered aircraft operated by air carriers: 6 (2015)

annual passenger traffic on registered air carriers: 14,463 (2015)

annual freight traffic on registered air carriers: 0 mt-km (2015)

CIVIL AIRCRAFT REGISTRATION COUNTRY CODE PREFIX:

HI (2016)

AIRPORTS:

36 (2013)

country comparison to the world: 109

AIRPORTS - WITH PAVED RUNWAYS:

total: 16 (2017)

over 3,047 m: 3 (2017)

2,438 to 3,047 m: 4 (2017)

1,524 to 2,437 m: 4 (2017)

914 to 1,523 m: 4 (2017)

under 914 m: 1 (2017)

AIRPORTS - WITH UNPAVED RUNWAYS:

total: 20 (2013)

1,524 to 2,437 m: 1 (2013)

914 to 1,523 m: 1 (2013)

under 914 m: 18 (2013)

HELIPORTS:

1 (2013)

PIPELINES:

27 km gas, 103 km oil (2013)

RAILWAYS:

total: 496 km (2014)

standard gauge: 354 km 1.435-m gauge (2014)

narrow gauge: 142 km 0.762-m gauge (2014)

country comparison to the world: 114

ROADWAYS:

total: 19,705 km (2002)

paved: 9,872 km (2002)

unpaved: 9,833 km (2002)

country comparison to the world: 111

MERCHANT MARINE:

total: 23 (2017)

by type: general cargo 2, other 21 (2017)

country comparison to the world: 135

PORTS AND TERMINALS:

major seaport(s): Puerto Haina, Puerto Plata, Santo Domingo

oil terminal(s): Punta Nizao oil terminal

LNG terminal(s) (import): Andres LNG terminal (Boca Chica)

MILITARY AND SECURITY :: DOMINICAN REPUBLIC

MILITARY EXPENDITURES:

0.64% of GDP (2016)

0.67% of GDP (2015)

0.67% of GDP (2014)

country comparison to the world: 136

MILITARY BRANCHES:

Army (Ejercito Nacional, EN), Navy (Marina de Guerra, MdG, includes naval infantry), Dominican Air Force (Fuerza Aerea Dominicana, FAD) (2017)

MILITARY SERVICE AGE AND OBLIGATION:

17-21 years of age for voluntary military service; recruits must have completed primary school and be Dominican Republic citizens; women may volunteer (2012)

TRANSNATIONAL ISSUES :: DOMINICAN REPUBLIC

DISPUTES - INTERNATIONAL:

Haitian migrants cross the porous border into the Dominican Republic to find workillegal migrants from the Dominican Republic cross the Mona Passage each year to Puerto Rico to find better work

REFUGEES AND INTERNALLY DISPLACED PERSONS:

stateless persons: 133,770 (2016); note - a September 2013 Constitutional Court ruling revoked the citizenship of those born after 1929 to immigrants without proper documentation, even though the constitution at the time automatically granted citizenship to children born in the Dominican Republic and the 2010 constitution provides that constitutional provisions cannot be applied retroactively; the decision overwhelmingly affected people of Haitian descent whose relatives had come to the Dominican Republic since the 1890s as a cheap source of labor for sugar plantations; a May 2014 law passed by the Dominican Congress regularizes the status of those with birth certificates but will require those without them to prove they were born in the Dominican Republic and to apply for naturalization; the government has issued documents to thousands of individuals who may claim citizenship under this law, but no official estimate has been released

note: revised estimate includes only individuals born to parents who were both born abroad; it does not include individuals born in the country to one Dominican-born and one foreign-born parent or subsequent generations of individuals of foreign descent; the estimate, as such, does not include all stateless persons (2015)

ILLICIT DRUGS:

transshipment point for South American drugs destined for the US and Europe; has become a transshipment point for ecstasy from the Netherlands and Belgium destined for US and Canada; substantial money laundering activity in particular by Colombian narcotics traffickers; significant amphetamine consumption

SOUTH AMERICA :: ECUADOR

INTRODUCTION :: ECUADOR

BACKGROUND:

What is now Ecuador formed part of the northern Inca Empire until the Spanish conquest in 1533. Quito became a seat of Spanish colonial government in 1563 and part of the Viceroyalty of New Granada in 1717. The territories of the Viceroyalty - New Granada (Colombia), Venezuela, and Quito - gained their independence between 1819 and 1822 and formed a federation known as Gran Colombia. When Quito withdrew in 1830, the traditional name was changed in favor of the "Republic of the Equator." Between 1904 and 1942, Ecuador lost territories in a series of conflicts with its neighbors. A border war with Peru that flared in 1995 was resolved in 1999. Although Ecuador marked 30 years of civilian governance in 2004, the period was marred by political instability. Protests in Quito contributed to the mid-term ouster of three of Ecuador's last four democratically elected presidents. In late 2008, voters approved a new constitution, Ecuador's 20th since gaining independence. General elections were held in April 2017, and voters elected President Lenin MORENO.

GEOGRAPHY :: ECUADOR

LOCATION:

Western South America, bordering the Pacific Ocean at the Equator, between Colombia and Peru

GEOGRAPHIC COORDINATES:

2 00 S, 77 30 W

MAP REFERENCES:

South America

AREA:

total: 283,561 sq km

land: 276,841 sq km

water: 6,720 sq km

note: includes Galapagos Islands

country comparison to the world: 75

AREA - COMPARATIVE:

slightly smaller than Nevada

LAND BOUNDARIES:

total: 2,237 km

border countries (2): Colombia 708 km, Peru 1529 km

COASTLINE:

2,237 km

MARITIME CLAIMS:

territorial sea: 200 nm

exclusive economic zone: 200 nm

continental shelf: 200 nm

note: Ecuador has declared its right to extend its continental shelf to 350nm measured from the baselines of the Galapagos Archipelago

CLIMATE:

tropical along coast, becoming cooler inland at higher elevations; tropical in Amazonian jungle lowlands

TERRAIN:

coastal plain (costa), inter-Andean central highlands (sierra), and flat to rolling eastern jungle (oriente)

ELEVATION:

mean elevation: 1,117 m

elevation extremes: 0 m lowest point: Pacific Ocean

6267 highest point: Chimborazo
note: because the earth is not a perfect sphere and has an equatorial bulge, the highest point on the planet farthest from its center is Mount Chimborazo not Mount Everest, which is merely the highest peak above sea level

NATURAL RESOURCES:

petroleum, fish, timber, hydropower

LAND USE:

agricultural land: 29.7% (2011 est.)

arable land: 4.7% (2011 est.) / permanent crops: 5.6% (2011 est.) / permanent pasture: 19.4% (2011 est.)

forest: 38.9% (2011 est.)

other: 31.4% (2011 est.)

IRRIGATED LAND:

15,000 sq km (2012)

POPULATION DISTRIBUTION:

nearly half of the population is concentrated in the interior in the Andean intermontane basins and valleys, with large concentrations also found along the western coastal strip; the rainforests of the east remain sparsely populated

NATURAL HAZARDS:

frequent earthquakes; landslides; volcanic activity; floods; periodic droughts

volcanism: volcanic activity concentrated along the Andes Mountains; Sangay (5,230 m), which erupted in 2010, is mainland Ecuador's most active volcano; other historically active volcanoes in the Andes include Antisana, Cayambe, Chacana, Cotopaxi, Guagua Pichincha, Reventador, Sumaco, and Tungurahua; Fernandina (1,476 m), a shield volcano that last erupted in 2009, is the most active of the many Galapagos volcanoes; other historically active Galapagos volcanoes include Wolf, Sierra Negra, Cerro Azul, Pinta, Marchena, and Santiago

ENVIRONMENT - CURRENT ISSUES:

deforestation; soil erosion; desertification; water pollution; pollution from oil production wastes in ecologically sensitive areas of the Amazon Basin and Galapagos Islands

ENVIRONMENT - INTERNATIONAL AGREEMENTS:

party to: Antarctic-Environmental Protocol, Antarctic Treaty, Biodiversity, Climate Change, Climate Change-Kyoto Protocol, Desertification, Endangered Species, Hazardous Wastes, Ozone Layer Protection, Ship Pollution, Tropical Timber 83, Tropical Timber 94, Wetlands

signed, but not ratified: none of the selected agreements

GEOGRAPHY - NOTE:

Cotopaxi in Andes is highest active volcano in world

PEOPLE AND SOCIETY :: ECUADOR

POPULATION:

16,498,502 (July 2018 est.)

country comparison to the world: 68

NATIONALITY:

noun: Ecuadorian(s)

adjective: Ecuadorian

ETHNIC GROUPS:

mestizo (mixed Amerindian and white) 71.9%, Montubio 7.4%, Amerindian 7%, white 6.1%, Afroecuadorian 4.3%, mulatto 1.9%, black 1%, other 0.4% (2010 est.)

LANGUAGES:

Spanish (Castilian) 93% (official), Quechua 4.1%, other indigenous 0.7%, foreign 2.2% (2010 est.)

note: (Quechua and Shuar are official languages of intercultural relations; other indigenous languages are in official use by indigenous peoples in the areas they inhabit)

RELIGIONS:

Roman Catholic 74%, Evangelical 10.4%, Jehovah's Witness 1.2%, other 6.4% (includes Mormon Buddhist, Jewish, Spiritualist, Muslim, Hindu, indigenous religions, African American religions, Pentecostal), atheist 7.9%, agnostic 0.1% (2012 est.)

note: data represent persons at least 16 years of age from five Ecuadoran cities

DEMOGRAPHIC PROFILE:

Ecuador's high poverty and income inequality most affect indigenous, mixed race, and rural populations. The government has increased its social spending to ameliorate these problems, but critics question the efficiency and implementation of its national development plan. Nevertheless, the conditional cash transfer program, which requires participants' children to attend school and have medical check-ups, has helped improve educational attainment and healthcare among poor children. Ecuador is stalled at above replacement level fertility and the population most likely will keep growing rather than stabilize.

An estimated 2 to 3 million Ecuadorians live abroad, but increased unemployment in key receiving countries - Spain, the United States, and Italy - is slowing emigration and increasing the likelihood of returnees to Ecuador. The first large-scale emigration of Ecuadorians occurred between 1980 and 2000, when an economic crisis drove Ecuadorians from southern provinces to New York City, where they had trade contacts. A second, nationwide wave of emigration in the late 1990s was caused by another economic downturn, political instability, and a currency crisis. Spain was the logical destination because of its shared language and the wide availability of low-skilled, informal jobs at a time when increased border surveillance made illegal migration to the US difficult. Ecuador has a small but growing immigrant population and is Latin America's top recipient of refugees; 98% are neighboring Colombians fleeing violence in their country.

AGE STRUCTURE:

0-14 years: 26.64% (male 2,242,148 /female 2,153,776)

15-24 years: 18.19% (male 1,526,300 /female 1,474,626)

25-54 years: 39.82% (male 3,207,692 /female 3,362,464)

55-64 years: 7.67% (male 615,769 /female 649,777)

65 years and over: 7.67% (male 599,221 /female 666,729) (2018 est.)

DEPENDENCY RATIOS:

total dependency ratio: 55.6 (2015 est.)

youth dependency ratio: 45.1 (2015 est.)

elderly dependency ratio: 10.4 (2015 est.)

potential support ratio: 9.6 (2015 est.)

MEDIAN AGE:

total: 28.1 years

male: 27.3 years

female: 28.8 years (2018 est.)

country comparison to the world: 141

POPULATION GROWTH RATE:

1.25% (2018 est.)

country comparison to the world: 87

BIRTH RATE:

17.6 births/1,000 population (2018 est.)

country comparison to the world: 96

DEATH RATE:

5.1 deaths/1,000 population (2018 est.)

country comparison to the world: 192

NET MIGRATION RATE:

0 migrant(s)/1,000 population (2017 est.)

country comparison to the world: 80

POPULATION DISTRIBUTION:

nearly half of the population is concentrated in the interior in the Andean intermontane basins and valleys, with large concentrations also found along the western coastal strip; the rainforests of the east remain sparsely populated

URBANIZATION:

urban population: 63.8% of total population (2018)

rate of urbanization: 1.66% annual rate of change (2015-20 est.)

MAJOR URBAN AREAS - POPULATION:

2.899 million Guayaquil, 1.822 million QUITO (capital) (2018)

SEX RATIO:

at birth: 1.04 male(s)/female (2017 est.)

0-14 years: 1.04 male(s)/female (2017 est.)

15-24 years: 1.03 male(s)/female (2017 est.)

25-54 years: 0.95 male(s)/female (2017 est.)

55-64 years: 0.96 male(s)/female (2017 est.)

65 years and over: 0.91 male(s)/female (2017 est.)

total population: 0.99 male(s)/female (2017 est.)

MATERNAL MORTALITY RATE:

64 deaths/100,000 live births (2015 est.)

country comparison to the world: 87

INFANT MORTALITY RATE:

total: 15.9 deaths/1,000 live births (2018 est.)

male: 18.8 deaths/1,000 live births (2018 est.)

female: 12.8 deaths/1,000 live births (2018 est.)

country comparison to the world: 97

LIFE EXPECTANCY AT BIRTH:

total population: 77.1 years (2018 est.)

male: 74.2 years (2018 est.)

female: 80.3 years (2018 est.)

country comparison to the world: 79

TOTAL FERTILITY RATE:

2.15 children born/woman (2018 est.)

country comparison to the world: 99

CONTRACEPTIVE PREVALENCE RATE:

80.1% (2007/12)

HEALTH EXPENDITURES:

9.2% of GDP (2014)

country comparison to the world: 35

PHYSICIANS DENSITY:

1.67 physicians/1,000 population (2011)

HOSPITAL BED DENSITY:

1.5 beds/1,000 population (2013)

DRINKING WATER SOURCE:

improved:

urban: 93.4% of population

rural: 75.5% of population

total: 86.9% of population

unimproved:

urban: 6.6% of population

rural: 24.5% of population

total: 13.1% of population (2015 est.)

SANITATION FACILITY ACCESS:

improved:

urban: 87% of population (2015 est.)

rural: 80.7% of population (2015 est.)

total: 84.7% of population (2015 est.)

unimproved:

urban: 13% of population (2015 est.)

rural: 19.3% of population (2015 est.)

total: 15.3% of population (2015 est.)

HIV/AIDS - ADULT PREVALENCE RATE:

0.3% (2017 est.)

country comparison to the world: 79

HIV/AIDS - PEOPLE LIVING WITH HIV/AIDS:

36,000 (2017 est.)

country comparison to the world: 67

HIV/AIDS - DEATHS:

<1000 (2017 est.)

MAJOR INFECTIOUS DISEASES:

degree of risk: high (2016)

food or waterborne diseases: bacterial diarrhea, hepatitis A, and typhoid fever (2016)

vectorborne diseases: dengue fever and malaria (2016)

note: active local transmission of Zika virus by Aedes species mosquitoes has been identified in this country (as of August 2016); it poses an important risk (a large number of cases possible) among US citizens if bitten by an infective mosquito; other less common ways to get Zika are through sex, via blood transfusion, or during pregnancy, in which the pregnant woman passes Zika virus to her fetus

OBESITY - ADULT PREVALENCE RATE:

19.9% (2016)

country comparison to the world: 107

CHILDREN UNDER THE AGE OF 5 YEARS UNDERWEIGHT:

5.1% (2014)

country comparison to the world: 81

EDUCATION EXPENDITURES:

5% of GDP (2015)

country comparison to the world: 76

LITERACY:

definition: age 15 and over can read and write (2016 est.)

total population: 94.4% (2016 est.)

male: 95.4% (2016 est.)

female: 93.3% (2016 est.)

SCHOOL LIFE EXPECTANCY (PRIMARY TO TERTIARY EDUCATION):

total: 15 years (2012)

male: 15 years (2012)

female: 16 years (2012)

UNEMPLOYMENT, YOUTH AGES 15-24:

total: 8.4% (2017 est.)

male: 6.6% (2017 est.)

female: 11.4% (2017 est.)

country comparison to the world: 137

GOVERNMENT :: ECUADOR

COUNTRY NAME:

conventional long form: Republic of Ecuador

conventional short form: Ecuador

local long form: Republica del Ecuador

local short form: Ecuador

etymology: the country's position on the globe, straddling the Equator, accounts for its Spanish name

GOVERNMENT TYPE:

presidential republic

CAPITAL:

name: Quito

geographic coordinates: 0 13 S, 78 30 W

time difference: UTC-5 (same time as Washington, DC, during Standard Time)

note: Ecuador has two time zones, including the Galapagos Islands (UTC-6)

ADMINISTRATIVE DIVISIONS:

24 provinces (provincias, singular - provincia); Azuay, Bolivar, Canar, Carchi, Chimborazo, Cotopaxi, El Oro, Esmeraldas, Galapagos, Guayas, Imbabura, Loja, Los Rios, Manabi, Morona-Santiago, Napo, Orellana, Pastaza, Pichincha, Santa Elena, Santo Domingo de los Tsachilas, Sucumbios, Tungurahua, Zamora-Chinchipe

INDEPENDENCE:

24 May 1822 (from Spain)

NATIONAL HOLIDAY:

Independence Day (independence of Quito), 10 August (1809)

CONSTITUTION:

history: many previous; latest approved 20 October 2008 (2018)

amendments: proposed by the president of the republic through a referendum, by public petition of at least 1% of registered voters, or by agreement of at least one-third of the National Assembly membership; passage requires two separate readings a year apart and approval by at least two-thirds majority vote of the Assembly, and approval by absolute majority in a referendum; amendments such as changes to the structure of the state, constraints on personal rights and guarantees, or constitutional amendment procedures are not allowed; amended 2011, 2015, last 2018; note - a 2015 constitutional amendment lifting presidential term limits was overturned by a February 2018 referendum (2018)

LEGAL SYSTEM:

civil law based on the Chilean civil code with modifications; traditional law in indigenous communities

INTERNATIONAL LAW ORGANIZATION PARTICIPATION:

has not submitted an ICJ jurisdiction declaration; accepts ICCt jurisdiction

CITIZENSHIP:

citizenship by birth: yes

citizenship by descent only: yes

dual citizenship recognized: no

residency requirement for naturalization: 3 years

SUFFRAGE:

18-65 years of age; universal and compulsory; 16-18, over 65, and other eligible voters, voluntary

EXECUTIVE BRANCH:

chief of state: President Lenin MORENO Garces (since 24 May 2017); Vice President Otto Ramon SONNENHOLZNER Sper (since 11 December 2018); note - Vice President Jorge GLAS Espinel (since 24 May 2013) was jailed for corruption and absent from office for more than 3 months, causing him to be constitutionally stripped of his office; Vice President Maria Alejandra VICUNA Munoz (since 6 January 2018) resigned from office 4 December 2018; president is both chief of state and head of government

head of government: President Lenin MORENO Garces (since 24 May 2017); Vice President Otto Ramon SONNENHOLZNER Sper (since 11 December 2018)

cabinet: Cabinet appointed by the president

elections/appointments: president and vice president directly elected on the same ballot by absolute majority popular vote in 2 rounds if needed for a 4-year term (eligible for a second term); election last held on 19 February 2017 with a runoff on 2 April 2017 (next to be held in 2021)

election results: Lenin MORENO Garces elected president in second round; percent of vote - Lenin MORENO Garces (Alianza PAIS Movement) 51.1%, Guillermo LASSO (CREO) 48.9%

LEGISLATIVE BRANCH:

description: unicameral National Assembly or Asamblea Nacional (137 seats; 116 members directly elected in single-seat constituencies by simple majority vote, 15 members directly elected in a single nationwide constituency by proportional representation vote, and 6 directly elected in multi-seat constituencies for Ecuadorians living abroad by simple majority vote; members serve 4-year terms)

elections: last held on 19 February 2017 (next to be held in 2021)

election results: percent of vote by party - PAIS 39.1%, CREO-SUMA 20.1%, PSC 15.9%, ID 3.8%, MUPP 2.7%, other 10.7; seats by party - PAIS 74, CREO-SUMA 34, PSC 15, ID 4, MUPP 4, PSP 2, Fuerza Ecuador 1, independent 3; note - defections by members of National Assembly are commonplace, resulting in frequent changes in the numbers of seats held by the various parties

JUDICIAL BRANCH:

highest courts: National Court of Justice or Corte Nacional de Justicia (consists of 21 judges including the chief justice and organized into 5 specialized chambers); Constitutional Court or Corte Constitucional (consists of 9 judges)

judge selection and term of office: justices of National Court of Justice elected by the Judiciary Council, a 9-member independent body of law professionals; judges elected for 9-year, non-renewable terms, with one-third of the membership renewed every 3 years; Constitutional Court judges appointed by the executive, legislative, and Citizen Participation branches of government; judges appointed for 9-year non-renewable terms with one-third of the membership renewed every 3 years

subordinate courts: Fiscal Tribunal; Election Dispute Settlement Courts, provincial courts (one for each province); cantonal courts

POLITICAL PARTIES AND LEADERS:

Alianza PAIS movement [Lenin Voltaire MORENO Garces]
Avanza Party or AVANZA [Ramiro GONZALEZ]
Creating Opportunities Movement or CREO [Guillermo LASSO]
Democratic Left or ID
Forward Ecuador Movement [Alvaro NOBOA]
Fuerza Ecuador [Abdala BUCARAM] (successor to Roldosist Party)
Pachakutik Plurinational Unity Movement or MUPP [Marlon Rene SANTI Gualinga]
Patriotic Society Party or PSP [Gilmar GUTIERREZ Borbua]
Popular Democracy Movement or MPD [Luis VILLACIS]
Social Christian Party or PSC [Pascual DEL CIOPPO]
Socialist Party [Patricio ZABRANO]
Society United for More Action or SUMA [Mauricio RODAS]

INTERNATIONAL ORGANIZATION PARTICIPATION:

CAN, CD, CELAC, FAO, G-11, G-77, IADB, IAEA, IBRD, ICAO, ICC (national committees), ICCt, ICRM, IDA, IFAD, IFC, IFRCS, IHO, ILO, IMF, IMO, Interpol, IOC, IOM, IPU, ISO, ITSO, ITU, ITUC (NGOs), LAES, LAIA, Mercosur (associate), MIGA, MINUSTAH, NAM, OAS, OPANAL, OPCW, OPEC, Pacific Alliance (observer), PCA, SICA (observer), UN, UNAMID, UNASUR, UNCTAD, UNESCO, UNHCR, UNIDO, Union Latina, UNISFA, UNMIL, UNMISS, UNOCI, UNWTO, UPU, WCO, WFTU (NGOs), WHO, WIPO, WMO, WTO

DIPLOMATIC REPRESENTATION IN THE US:

chief of mission: Ambassador Francisco Benjamin Esteban CARRION Mena (since 24 January 2018)

chancery: 2535 15th Street NW, Washington, DC 20009

telephone: [1] (202) 234-7200

FAX: [1] (202) 667-3482

consulate(s) general: Atlanta, Chicago, Houston, Los Angeles, Miami, Minneapolis, New Haven (CT), New Orleans, New York, Newark (NJ), Phoenix, San Francisco

DIPLOMATIC REPRESENTATION FROM THE US:

chief of mission: Ambassador Todd C. CHAPMAN (since 14 April 2016)

embassy: Avenida Avigiras E12-170 y Avenida Eloy Alfaro, Quito

mailing address: Avenida Guayacanes N52-205 y Avenida Avigiras

telephone: [593] (2) 398-5000

FAX: [593] (2) 398-5100

consulate(s) general: Guayaquil

FLAG DESCRIPTION:

three horizontal bands of yellow (top, double width), blue, and red with the coat of arms superimposed at the center of the flag; the flag retains the three main colors of the banner of Gran Colombia, the South American republic that broke up in 1830; the yellow color represents sunshine, grain, and mineral wealth, blue the sky, sea, and rivers, and red the blood of patriots spilled in the struggle for freedom and justice

note: similar to the flag of Colombia, which is shorter and does not bear a coat of arms

NATIONAL SYMBOL(S):

Andean condor; national colors: yellow, blue, red

NATIONAL ANTHEM:

name: "Salve, Oh Patria!" (We Salute You, Our Homeland)

lyrics/music: Juan Leon MERA/Antonio NEUMANE

note: adopted 1948; Juan Leon MERA wrote the lyrics in 1865; only the chorus and second verse are sung

ECONOMY :: ECUADOR

ECONOMY - OVERVIEW:

Ecuador is substantially dependent on its petroleum resources, which accounted for about a third of the country's export earnings in 2017. Remittances from overseas Ecuadorian are also important.

In 1999/2000, Ecuador's economy suffered from a banking crisis that lead to some reforms, including adoption of the US dollar as legal tender. Dollarization stabilized the economy, and positive growth returned in most of the years that followed. China has become Ecuador's largest foreign lender since 2008 and now accounts for 77.7% of the Ecuador's bilateral debt. Various economic policies under the CORREA administration, such as an announcement in 2017 that Ecuador would terminate 13 bilateral investment treaties - including one with the US, generated economic uncertainty and discouraged private investment.

Faced with a 2013 trade deficit of $1.1 billion, Ecuador imposed tariff surcharges from 5% to 45% on an estimated 32% of imports. Ecuador's economy fell into recession in 2015 and remained in recession in 2016. Declining oil prices and exports forced the CORREA administration to cut government oulays. Foreign investment in Ecuador is low as a result of the unstable regulatory environment and weak rule of law.

n April of 2017, Lenin MORENO was elected President of Ecuador by popular vote. His immediate challenge was to reengage the private sector to improve cash flow in the country. Ecuador's economy returned to positive, but sluggish, growth. In early 2018, the MORENO administration held a public referendum on seven economic and political issues in a move counter to CORREA-administration policies, reduce corruption, strengthen democracy, and revive employment and the economy. The referendum resulted in repeal of taxes associated with recovery from the earthquake of 2016, reduced restrictions on metal mining in the Yasuni Intangible Zone - a protected area, and several political reforms.

GDP (PURCHASING POWER PARITY):

$193 billion (2017 est.)

$188.6 billion (2016 est.)

$190.9 billion (2015 est.)

note: data are in 2017 dollars

country comparison to the world: 66

GDP (OFFICIAL EXCHANGE RATE):

$104.3 billion (2017 est.) (2017 est.)

GDP - REAL GROWTH RATE:

2.4% (2017 est.)

-1.2% (2016 est.)

0.1% (2015 est.)

country comparison to the world: 138

GDP - PER CAPITA (PPP):

$11,500 (2017 est.)

$11,400 (2016 est.)

$11,700 (2015 est.)

note: data are in 2017 dollars

country comparison to the world: 132

GROSS NATIONAL SAVING:

25.9% of GDP (2017 est.)

26.4% of GDP (2016 est.)

24.7% of GDP (2015 est.)

country comparison to the world: 51

GDP - COMPOSITION, BY END USE:

household consumption: 60.7% (2017 est.)

government consumption: 14.4% (2017 est.)

investment in fixed capital: 24.3% (2017 est.)

investment in inventories: 1% (2017 est.)

exports of goods and services: 20.8% (2017 est.)

imports of goods and services: -21.3% (2017 est.)

GDP - COMPOSITION, BY SECTOR OF ORIGIN:

agriculture: 6.7% (2017 est.)

industry: 32.9% (2017 est.)

services: 60.4% (2017 est.)

AGRICULTURE - PRODUCTS:

bananas, coffee, cocoa, rice, potatoes, cassava (manioc, tapioca), plantains, sugarcane; cattle, sheep, pigs, beef, pork, dairy products; fish, shrimp; balsa wood

INDUSTRIES:

petroleum, food processing, textiles, wood products, chemicals

INDUSTRIAL PRODUCTION GROWTH RATE:

-0.6% (2017 est.)

note: excludes oil refining

country comparison to the world: 173

LABOR FORCE:

8.086 million (2017 est.)

country comparison to the world: 62

LABOR FORCE - BY OCCUPATION:

agriculture: 26.1%

industry: 18.4%

services: 55.5% (2017 est.)

UNEMPLOYMENT RATE:

4.6% (2017 est.)

5.2% (2016 est.)

country comparison to the world: 66

POPULATION BELOW POVERTY LINE:

21.5% (December 2017 est.)

HOUSEHOLD INCOME OR CONSUMPTION BY PERCENTAGE SHARE:

lowest 10%: 35.4% (2012 est.)

highest 10%: 35.4% (2012 est.)

note: data are for urban households only

DISTRIBUTION OF FAMILY INCOME - GINI INDEX:

45.9 (December 2017)

48.5 (December 2017)

note: data are for urban households only

country comparison to the world: 36

BUDGET:

revenues: 33.43 billion (2017 est.)

expenditures: 38.08 billion (2017 est.)

TAXES AND OTHER REVENUES:

32% (of GDP) (2017 est.)

country comparison to the world: 69

BUDGET SURPLUS (+) OR DEFICIT (-):

-4.5% (of GDP) (2017 est.)

country comparison to the world: 164

PUBLIC DEBT:

45.4% of GDP (2017 est.)

43.2% of GDP (2016 est.)

country comparison to the world: 114

FISCAL YEAR:

calendar year

INFLATION RATE (CONSUMER PRICES):

0.4% (2017 est.)

1.7% (2016 est.)

country comparison to the world: 23

CENTRAL BANK DISCOUNT RATE:

8.17% (31 December 2011)

8.68% (31 December 2010)

country comparison to the world: 39

COMMERCIAL BANK PRIME LENDING RATE:

7.92% (31 December 2017 est.)

8.69% (31 December 2016 est.)

country comparison to the world: 111

STOCK OF NARROW MONEY:

$9.578 billion (31 December 2017 est.)

$9.281 billion (31 December 2016 est.)

country comparison to the world: 83

STOCK OF BROAD MONEY:

$9.578 billion (31 December 2017 est.)

$9.281 billion (31 December 2016 est.)

country comparison to the world: 85

STOCK OF DOMESTIC CREDIT:

$39.3 billion (31 December 2017 est.)

$35.56 billion (31 December 2016 est.)

country comparison to the world: 71

MARKET VALUE OF PUBLICLY TRADED SHARES:

$6.838 billion (31 December 2017 est.)

$6.065 billion (31 December 2016 est.)

$6.615 billion (31 December 2015 est.)

country comparison to the world: 79

CURRENT ACCOUNT BALANCE:

-$349 million (2017 est.)

$1.442 billion (2016 est.)

country comparison to the world: 109

EXPORTS:

$19.62 billion (2017 est.)

$16.8 billion (2016 est.)

country comparison to the world: 72

EXPORTS - PARTNERS:

US 31.5%, Vietnam 7.6%, Peru 6.7%, Chile 6.5%, Panama 4.9%, Russia 4.4%, China 4% (2017)

EXPORTS - COMMODITIES:

petroleum, bananas, cut flowers, shrimp, cacao, coffee, wood, fish

IMPORTS:

$19.31 billion (2017 est.)

$15.86 billion (2016 est.)

country comparison to the world: 79

IMPORTS - COMMODITIES:

industrial materials, fuels and lubricants, nondurable consumer goods

IMPORTS - PARTNERS:

US 22.8%, China 15.4%, Colombia 8.7%, Panama 6.4%, Brazil 4.4%, Peru 4.2% (2017)

RESERVES OF FOREIGN EXCHANGE AND GOLD:

$2.395 billion (31 December 2017 est.)

$4.259 billion (31 December 2016 est.)

country comparison to the world: 116

DEBT - EXTERNAL:

$39.29 billion (31 December 2017 est.)

$38.14 billion (31 December 2016 est.)

country comparison to the world: 77

STOCK OF DIRECT FOREIGN INVESTMENT - AT HOME:

$17.25 billion (31 December 2017 est.)

$16.63 billion (31 December 2016 est.)

country comparison to the world: 85

STOCK OF DIRECT FOREIGN INVESTMENT - ABROAD:

$6.33 billion (31 December 2012 est.)

country comparison to the world: 71

EXCHANGE RATES:

the US dollar became Ecuador's currency in 2001

ENERGY :: ECUADOR

ELECTRICITY ACCESS:

population without electricity: 500,000 (2013)

electrification - total population: 97% (2013)

electrification - urban areas: 100% (2013)

electrification - rural areas: 92% (2013)

ELECTRICITY - PRODUCTION:

26.5 billion kWh (2016 est.)

country comparison to the world: 71

ELECTRICITY - CONSUMPTION:

22.68 billion kWh (2016 est.)

country comparison to the world: 70

ELECTRICITY - EXPORTS:

211 million kWh (2015 est.)

country comparison to the world: 75

ELECTRICITY - IMPORTS:

82 million kWh (2016 est.)

country comparison to the world: 102

ELECTRICITY - INSTALLED GENERATING CAPACITY:

8.192 million kW (2016 est.)

country comparison to the world: 69

ELECTRICITY - FROM FOSSIL FUELS:

43% of total installed capacity (2016 est.)

country comparison to the world: 163

ELECTRICITY - FROM NUCLEAR FUELS:

0% of total installed capacity (2017 est.)

country comparison to the world: 81

ELECTRICITY - FROM HYDROELECTRIC PLANTS:

54% of total installed capacity (2017 est.)

country comparison to the world: 32

ELECTRICITY - FROM OTHER RENEWABLE SOURCES:

2% of total installed capacity (2017 est.)

country comparison to the world: 138

CRUDE OIL - PRODUCTION:

531,300 bbl/day (2017 est.)

country comparison to the world: 28

CRUDE OIL - EXPORTS:

383,500 bbl/day (2017 est.)

country comparison to the world: 22

CRUDE OIL - IMPORTS:

0 bbl/day (2015 est.)

country comparison to the world: 119

CRUDE OIL - PROVED RESERVES:

8.273 billion bbl (1 January 2018 est.)

country comparison to the world: 17

REFINED PETROLEUM PRODUCTS - PRODUCTION:

137,400 bbl/day (2015 est.)

country comparison to the world: 62

REFINED PETROLEUM PRODUCTS - CONSUMPTION:

265,000 bbl/day (2016 est.)

country comparison to the world: 48

REFINED PETROLEUM PRODUCTS - EXPORTS:

25,870 bbl/day (2015 est.)

country comparison to the world: 66

REFINED PETROLEUM PRODUCTS - IMPORTS:

153,900 bbl/day (2015 est.)

country comparison to the world: 40

NATURAL GAS - PRODUCTION:

477.8 million cu m (2017 est.)

country comparison to the world: 73

NATURAL GAS - CONSUMPTION:

453.1 million cu m (2017 est.)

country comparison to the world: 100

NATURAL GAS - EXPORTS:

0 cu m (2017 est.)

country comparison to the world: 97

NATURAL GAS - IMPORTS:

0 cu m (2017 est.)

country comparison to the world: 118

NATURAL GAS - PROVED RESERVES:

10.9 billion cu m (1 January 2018 est.)

country comparison to the world: 78

CARBON DIOXIDE EMISSIONS FROM CONSUMPTION OF ENERGY:

37.54 million Mt (2017 est.)

country comparison to the world: 69

COMMUNICATIONS :: ECUADOR

TELEPHONES - FIXED LINES:

total subscriptions: 2,415,204 (2017 est.)

subscriptions per 100 inhabitants: 15 (2017 est.)

country comparison to the world: 55

TELEPHONES - MOBILE CELLULAR:

total subscriptions: 13,881,562 (2017 est.)

subscriptions per 100 inhabitants: 85 (2017 est.)

country comparison to the world: 69

TELEPHONE SYSTEM:

general assessment: fixed-line service and sophisticated 4G LTE ultra-broadband network; much of the country's fixed-line structure is influenced by topographical challenges associated with the Andes Mountains; Ecuador has a small telecom market with a dominant mobile sector; the state-owned incumbent CNT dominates the fixed-line market, and therefore the DSL broadband market aswell (2018)

domestic: fixed-line services with digital networks provided by multiple telecommunications operators; fixed-line teledensity stands at about 15 per 100 persons; mobile-cellular use has surged and subscribership has reached 85 per 100 persons (2018)

international: country code - 593; landing points for the PAN-AM and South America-1 submarine cables that provide links to the west coast of South America, Panama, Colombia, Venezuela, and extending onward to Aruba and the US Virgin Islands in the Caribbean; in 2017, Alcatel completed a 6000km, submarine-cable system from Sarasota, Florida to Manta, Ecuador; satellite earth station - 1 Intelsat (Atlantic Ocean) (2018)

BROADCAST MEDIA:

about 60 media outlets are recognized as national; the Ecuadorian Government controls 12 national outlets and multiple radio stations; there are multiple TV networks and many local channels, as well as more than 300 radio stations; many TV and radio stations are privately owned; broadcast media is required by law to give the government free airtime to broadcast programs produced by the state; the Ecuadorian Government is the biggest advertiser and grants advertising contracts to outlets that provide favorable coverage; a 2011 antimonopoly law and the 2013 Communication Law limit ownership and investment in the media by non-media businesses (2018)

INTERNET COUNTRY CODE:

.ec

INTERNET USERS:

total: 8,693,739 (July 2016 est.)

percent of population: 54.1% (July 2016 est.)

country comparison to the world: 51

BROADBAND - FIXED SUBSCRIPTIONS:

total: 1,683,783 (2017 est.)

subscriptions per 100 inhabitants: 10 (2017 est.)

country comparison to the world: 58

TRANSPORTATION :: ECUADOR

NATIONAL AIR TRANSPORT SYSTEM:

number of registered air carriers: 7 (2015)

inventory of registered aircraft operated by air carriers: 35 (2015)

annual passenger traffic on registered air carriers: 5,762,485 (2015)

annual freight traffic on registered air carriers: 86,128,720 mt-km (2015)

CIVIL AIRCRAFT REGISTRATION COUNTRY CODE PREFIX:

HC (2016)

AIRPORTS:

432 (2013)

country comparison to the world: 20

AIRPORTS - WITH PAVED RUNWAYS:

total: 104 (2017)

over 3,047 m: 4 (2017)

2,438 to 3,047 m: 5 (2017)

1,524 to 2,437 m: 18 (2017)

914 to 1,523 m: 26 (2017)

under 914 m: 51 (2017)

AIRPORTS - WITH UNPAVED RUNWAYS:

total: 328 (2013)

914 to 1,523 m: 37 (2013)

under 914 m: 291 (2013)

HELIPORTS:

2 (2013)

PIPELINES:

485 km extra heavy crude, 123 km gas, 2131 km oil, 1526 km refined products (2017)

RAILWAYS:

total: 965 km (2017)

narrow gauge: 965 km 1.067-m gauge (2017)

note: passenger service limited to certain sections of track, mostly for tourist trains

country comparison to the world: 91

ROADWAYS:

total: 43,670 km (2007)

paved: 6,472 km (2007)

unpaved: 37,198 km (2007)

country comparison to the world: 84

WATERWAYS:

1,500 km (most inaccessible) (2012)

country comparison to the world: 52

MERCHANT MARINE:

total: 138 (2017)

by type: general cargo 6, oil tanker 37, other 95 (2017)

country comparison to the world: 76

PORTS AND TERMINALS:

major seaport(s): Esmeraldas, Manta, Puerto Bolivar

container port(s) (TEUs): Guayaquil (1,821,654) (2016)

river port(s): Guayaquil (Guayas)

MILITARY AND SECURITY :: ECUADOR

MILITARY EXPENDITURES:

1.7% of GDP (2017)

2.21% of GDP (2016)

2.44% of GDP (2015)

country comparison to the world: 65

MILITARY BRANCHES:

Ecuadorian Armed Forces: Ecuadorian Land Force (Fuerza Terrestre Ecuatoriana, FTE), Ecuadorian Navy (Fuerza Naval del Ecuador, FNE, includes Naval Infantry, Naval Aviation, Coast Guard), Ecuadorian Air Force (Fuerza Aerea Ecuatoriana, FAE) (2012)

MILITARY SERVICE AGE AND OBLIGATION:

18 years of age for selective conscript military service; conscription has been suspended; 18 years of age for voluntary military service; Air Force 18-22 years of age, Ecuadorian birth requirement; 1-year service obligation (2012)

MARITIME THREATS:

the International Maritime Bureau continues to report the territorial and offshore waters as at risk for piracy and armed robbery against ships; vessels, including commercial shipping and pleasure craft, have been attacked and hijacked both at anchor and while underway; crews have been robbed and stores or cargoes stolen; after several years with no incidents, two attacks were reported in 2017

TRANSNATIONAL ISSUES :: ECUADOR

DISPUTES - INTERNATIONAL:

organized illegal narcotics operations in Colombia penetrate across Ecuador's shared border, which thousands of Colombians also cross to escape the violence in their home country

REFUGEES AND INTERNALLY DISPLACED PERSONS:

refugees (country of origin): 101,161 (Colombia) (2016), 106,215 (Venezuela) (economic and political crisis; includes Venezuelans who have claimed asylum or have received alternative legal stay) (2018)

IDPs: 1,708 (earthquake April 2016) (2017)

ILLICIT DRUGS:

significant transit country for cocaine originating in Colombia and Peru, with much of the US-bound cocaine passing through Ecuadorian Pacific waters; importer of precursor chemicals used in production of illicit narcotics; attractive location for cash-placement by drug traffickers laundering money because of dollarization and weak anti-money-laundering regime; increased activity on the northern frontier by trafficking groups and Colombian insurgents

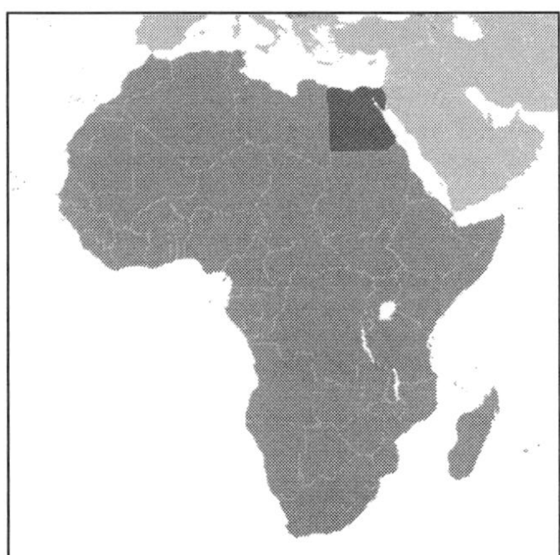

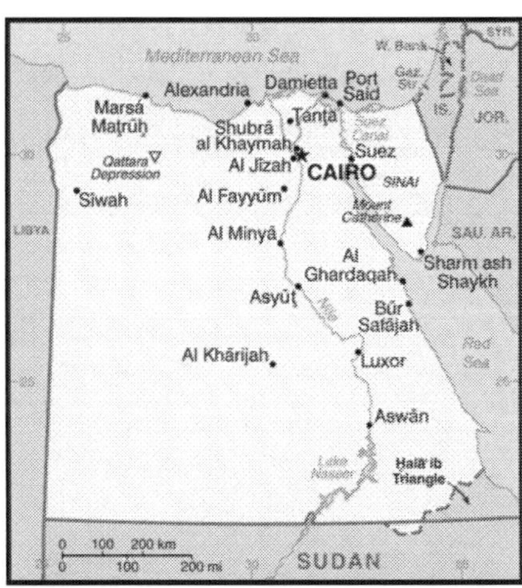

AFRICA :: EGYPT

INTRODUCTION :: EGYPT

BACKGROUND:

The regularity and richness of the annual Nile River flood, coupled with semi-isolation provided by deserts to the east and west, allowed for the development of one of the world's great civilizations. A unified kingdom arose circa 3200 B.C., and a series of dynasties ruled in Egypt for the next three millennia. The last native dynasty fell to the Persians in 341 B.C., who in turn were replaced by the Greeks, Romans, and Byzantines. It was the Arabs who introduced Islam and the Arabic language in the 7th century and who ruled for the next six centuries. A local military caste, the Mamluks took control about 1250 and continued to govern after the conquest of Egypt by the Ottoman Turks in 1517. Completion of the Suez Canal in 1869 elevated Egypt as an important world transportation hub. Ostensibly to protect its investments, Britain seized control of Egypt's government in 1882, but nominal allegiance to the Ottoman Empire continued until 1914. Partially independent from the UK in 1922, Egypt acquired full sovereignty from Britain in 1952. The completion of the Aswan High Dam in 1971 and the resultant Lake Nasser have reaffirmed the time-honored place of the Nile River in the agriculture and ecology of Egypt. A rapidly growing population (the largest in the Arab world), limited arable land, and dependence on the Nile all continue to overtax resources and stress society. The government has struggled to meet the demands of Egypt's population through economic reform and massive investment in communications and physical infrastructure.

Inspired by the 2010 Tunisian revolution, Egyptian opposition groups led demonstrations and labor strikes countrywide, culminating in President Hosni MUBARAK's ouster in 2011. Egypt's military assumed national leadership until a new parliament was in place in early 2012; later that same year, Muhammad MURSI won the presidential election. Following often violent protests throughout the spring of 2013 against MURSI's government and the Muslim Brotherhood, the Egyptian Armed Forces intervened and removed MURSI from power in July 2013 and replaced him with interim president Adly MANSOUR. In January 2014, voters approved a new constitution by referendum and in May 2014 elected former defense minister Abdelfattah ELSISI president. Egypt elected a new legislature in December 2015, its first parliament since 2012. ELSISI was reelected to a second four-year term in March 2018.

GEOGRAPHY :: EGYPT

LOCATION:

Northern Africa, bordering the Mediterranean Sea, between Libya and the Gaza Strip, and the Red Sea north of Sudan, and includes the Asian Sinai Peninsula

GEOGRAPHIC COORDINATES:

27 00 N, 30 00 E

MAP REFERENCES:

Africa

AREA:

total: 1,001,450 sq km

land: 995,450 sq km

water: 6,000 sq km

country comparison to the world: 31

AREA - COMPARATIVE:

more than eight times the size of Ohio; slightly more than three times the size of New Mexico

LAND BOUNDARIES:

total: 2,612 km

border countries (4): Gaza Strip 13 km, Israel 208 km, Libya 1115 km, Sudan 1276 km

COASTLINE:

2,450 km

MARITIME CLAIMS:

territorial sea: 12 nm

exclusive economic zone: 200 nm or the equidistant median line with Cyprus

contiguous zone: 24 nm

continental shelf: 200 nm

CLIMATE:

desert; hot, dry summers with moderate winters

TERRAIN:

vast desert plateau interrupted by Nile valley and delta

ELEVATION:

mean elevation: 321 m

elevation extremes: -133 m lowest point: Qattara Depression

2629 highest point: Mount Catherine

NATURAL RESOURCES:

petroleum, natural gas, iron ore, phosphates, manganese, limestone, gypsum, talc, asbestos, lead, rare earth elements, zinc

LAND USE:

agricultural land: 3.6% (2011 est.)

arable land: 2.8% (2011 est.) / permanent crops: 0.8% (2011 est.) / permanent pasture: 0% (2011 est.)

forest: 0.1% (2011 est.)

other: 96.3% (2011 est.)

IRRIGATED LAND:

36,500 sq km (2012)

POPULATION DISTRIBUTION:

approximately 95% of the population lives within 20 km of the Nile River and its delta; vast areas of the country remain sparsely populated or uninhabited

NATURAL HAZARDS:

periodic droughts; frequent earthquakes; flash floods; landslides; hot, driving windstorms called khamsin occur in spring; dust storms; sandstorms

ENVIRONMENT - CURRENT ISSUES:

agricultural land being lost to urbanization and windblown sands; increasing soil salination below Aswan High Dam; desertification; oil pollution threatening coral reefs, beaches, and marine habitats; other water pollution from agricultural pesticides, raw sewage, and industrial effluents; limited natural freshwater resources away from the Nile, which is the only perennial water source; rapid growth in population overstraining the Nile and natural resources

ENVIRONMENT - INTERNATIONAL AGREEMENTS:

party to: Biodiversity, Climate Change, Climate Change-Kyoto Protocol, Desertification, Endangered Species, Environmental Modification, Hazardous Wastes, Law of the Sea, Marine Dumping, Ozone Layer Protection, Ship Pollution, Tropical Timber 83, Tropical Timber 94, Wetlands

signed, but not ratified: none of the selected agreements

GEOGRAPHY - NOTE:

controls Sinai Peninsula, the only land bridge between Africa and remainder of Eastern Hemisphere; controls Suez Canal, a sea link between Indian Ocean and Mediterranean Sea; size, and juxtaposition to Israel, establish its major role in Middle Eastern geopolitics; dependence on upstream neighbors; dominance of Nile basin issues; prone to influxes of refugees from Sudan and the Palestinian territories

PEOPLE AND SOCIETY :: EGYPT

POPULATION:

99,413,317 (July 2018 est.)

country comparison to the world: 14

NATIONALITY:

noun: Egyptian(s)

adjective: Egyptian

ETHNIC GROUPS:

Egyptian 99.7%, other 0.3% (2006 est.)

note: data represent respondents by nationality

LANGUAGES:

Arabic (official), Arabic, English, and French widely understood by educated classes

RELIGIONS:

Muslim (predominantly Sunni) 90%, Christian (majority Coptic Orthodox, other Christians include Armenian Apostolic, Catholic, Maronite, Orthodox, and Anglican) 10% (2015 est.)

DEMOGRAPHIC PROFILE:

Egypt is the most populous country in the Arab world and the third most populous country in Africa, behind Nigeria and Ethiopia. Most of the country is desert, so about 95% of the population is concentrated in a narrow strip of fertile land along the Nile River, which represents only about 5% of Egypt's land area. Egypt's rapid population growth – 46% between 1994 and 2014 – stresses limited natural resources, jobs, housing, sanitation, education, and health care.

Although the country's total fertility rate (TFR) fell from roughly 5.3 children per woman in 1980 to just over 3 in the late 1990s, largely as a result of state-sponsored family planning programs, the population growth rate dropped more modestly because of decreased mortality rates and longer life expectancies. During the last decade, Egypt's TFR decline stalled for several years and then reversed, reaching 3.6 in 2011, and has plateaued the last few years. Contraceptive use has held steady at about 60%, while preferences for larger families and early marriage may have strengthened in the wake of the recent 2011 revolution. The large cohort of women of or nearing childbearing age will sustain high population growth for the foreseeable future (an effect called population momentum).

Nevertheless, post-MUBARAK governments have not made curbing population growth a priority. To increase contraceptive use and to prevent further overpopulation will require greater government commitment and substantial social change, including encouraging smaller families and better educating and empowering women. Currently, literacy, educational attainment, and labor force participation rates are much lower for women than men. In addition, the prevalence of violence against women, the lack of female political representation, and the perpetuation of the nearly universal practice of female genital cutting continue to keep women from playing a more significant role in Egypt's public sphere.

Population pressure, poverty, high unemployment, and the fragmentation of inherited land holdings have historically motivated Egyptians, primarily young men, to migrate internally from rural and smaller urban areas in the Nile Delta region and the poorer rural south to Cairo, Alexandria, and other urban centers in the north, while a much smaller number migrated to the Red Sea and Sinai areas. Waves of forced internal migration also resulted from the 1967 Arab-Israeli War and the floods caused by the completion of the Aswan High Dam in 1970. Limited numbers of students and professionals emigrated temporarily prior to the early 1970s, when economic problems and high unemployment pushed the Egyptian Government to lift restrictions on labor migration. At the same time, high oil revenues enabled Saudi Arabia, Iraq, and other Gulf states, as well as Libya and Jordan, to fund development projects, creating a demand for unskilled labor (mainly in construction), which attracted tens of thousands of young Egyptian men.

Between 1970 and 1974 alone, Egyptian migrants in the Gulf countries increased from approximately 70,000 to 370,000. Egyptian officials encouraged legal labor migration both to alleviate unemployment and to generate remittance income (remittances continue to be one of Egypt's largest sources of foreign currency and GDP). During the mid-1980s, however, depressed oil prices resulting from the Iran-Iraq War, decreased demand for low-skilled labor, competition from less costly South Asian workers, and efforts to replace foreign workers with locals significantly reduced Egyptian migration to the Gulf States. The number of Egyptian migrants dropped from a peak of almost 3.3 million in 1983 to about 2.2 million at the start of the 1990s, but numbers gradually recovered.

In the 2000s, Egypt began facilitating more labor migration through bilateral agreements, notably with Arab countries and Italy, but illegal migration to Europe through overstayed visas or maritime human smuggling via Libya also rose. The Egyptian Government estimated there were 6.5 million Egyptian migrants in 2009, with roughly 75% being temporary migrants in other Arab countries (Libya, Saudi Arabia, Jordan, Kuwait, and the United Arab Emirates) and 25% being predominantly permanent migrants in the West (US, UK, Italy, France, and Canada).

During the 2000s, Egypt became an increasingly important transit and destination country for economic migrants and asylum seekers, including Palestinians, East Africans, and South Asians and, more recently, Iraqis and Syrians. Egypt draws many refugees because of its resettlement programs with the West; Cairo has one of the largest urban refugee populations in the world. Many East African migrants are interned or live in temporary encampments along the Egypt-Israel border, and some have been shot and killed by Egyptian border guards.

AGE STRUCTURE:

0-14 years: 33.38% (male 17,177,977 /female 16,007,877)

15-24 years: 18.65% (male 9,551,309 /female 8,988,006)

25-54 years: 37.71% (male 19,053,300 /female 18,431,808)

55-64 years: 5.99% (male 2,956,535 /female 2,995,497)

65 years and over: 4.28% (male 2,058,217 /female 2,192,791) (2018 est.)

DEPENDENCY RATIOS:

total dependency ratio: 61.8 (2015 est.)

youth dependency ratio: 53.6 (2015 est.)

elderly dependency ratio: 8.2 (2015 est.)

potential support ratio: 12.2 (2015 est.)

MEDIAN AGE:

total: 23.9 years

male: 23.6 years

female: 24.3 years (2018 est.)

country comparison to the world: 167

POPULATION GROWTH RATE:

2.38% (2018 est.)

country comparison to the world: 28

BIRTH RATE:

28.8 births/1,000 population (2018 est.)

country comparison to the world: 42

DEATH RATE:

4.5 deaths/1,000 population (2018 est.)

country comparison to the world: 204

NET MIGRATION RATE:

-0.5 migrant(s)/1,000 population (2017 est.)

country comparison to the world: 123

POPULATION DISTRIBUTION:

approximately 95% of the population lives within 20 km of the Nile River and its delta; vast areas of the country remain sparsely populated or uninhabited

URBANIZATION:

urban population: 42.7% of total population (2018)

rate of urbanization: 1.86% annual rate of change (2015-20 est.)

MAJOR URBAN AREAS - POPULATION:

20.076 million CAIRO (capital), 5.086 million Alexandria (2018)

SEX RATIO:

at birth: 1.06 male(s)/female (2017 est.)

0-14 years: 1.07 male(s)/female (2017 est.)

15-24 years: 1.06 male(s)/female (2017 est.)

25-54 years: 1.03 male(s)/female (2017 est.)

55-64 years: 0.98 male(s)/female (2017 est.)

65 years and over: 0.82 male(s)/female (2017 est.)

total population: 1.05 male(s)/female (2017 est.)

MOTHER'S MEAN AGE AT FIRST BIRTH:

22.7 years (2014 est.)

note: median age at first birth among women 25-29

MATERNAL MORTALITY RATE:

33 deaths/100,000 live births (2015 est.)

country comparison to the world: 110

INFANT MORTALITY RATE:

total: 18.3 deaths/1,000 live births (2018 est.)

male: 19.5 deaths/1,000 live births (2018 est.)

female: 17 deaths/1,000 live births (2018 est.)

country comparison to the world: 85

LIFE EXPECTANCY AT BIRTH:

total population: 73.2 years (2018 est.)

male: 71.8 years (2018 est.)

female: 74.7 years (2018 est.)

country comparison to the world: 140

TOTAL FERTILITY RATE:

3.41 children born/woman (2018 est.)

country comparison to the world: 45

CONTRACEPTIVE PREVALENCE RATE:

58.5% (2014)

HEALTH EXPENDITURES:

5.6% of GDP (2014)

country comparison to the world: 118

PHYSICIANS DENSITY:

0.81 physicians/1,000 population (2014)

HOSPITAL BED DENSITY:

1.6 beds/1,000 population (2014)

DRINKING WATER SOURCE:

improved:

urban: 100% of population

rural: 99% of population

total: 99.4% of population

unimproved:

urban: 0% of population

rural: 1% of population

total: 0.6% of population (2015 est.)

SANITATION FACILITY ACCESS:

improved:

urban: 96.8% of population (2015 est.)

rural: 93.1% of population (2015 est.)

total: 94.7% of population (2015 est.)

unimproved:

urban: 3.2% of population (2015 est.)

rural: 6.9% of population (2015 est.)

total: 5.3% of population (2015 est.)

HIV/AIDS - ADULT PREVALENCE RATE:

<.1% (2017 est.)

HIV/AIDS - PEOPLE LIVING WITH HIV/AIDS:

16,000 (2017 est.)

country comparison to the world: 85

HIV/AIDS - DEATHS:

<500 (2017 est.)

MAJOR INFECTIOUS DISEASES:

degree of risk: intermediate (2016)

food or waterborne diseases: bacterial diarrhea, hepatitis A, and typhoid fever (2016)

water contact diseases: schistosomiasis (2016)

OBESITY - ADULT PREVALENCE RATE:

32% (2016)

country comparison to the world: 18

CHILDREN UNDER THE AGE OF 5 YEARS UNDERWEIGHT:

7% (2014)

country comparison to the world: 72

EDUCATION EXPENDITURES:

3.8% of GDP (2008)

country comparison to the world: 115

LITERACY:

definition: age 15 and over can read and write (2015 est.)

total population: 73.8% (2015 est.)

male: 82.2% (2015 est.)

female: 65.4% (2015 est.)

SCHOOL LIFE EXPECTANCY (PRIMARY TO TERTIARY EDUCATION):

total: 13 years (2014)

male: 13 years (2014)

female: 13 years (2014)

UNEMPLOYMENT, YOUTH AGES 15-24:

total: 30.8% (2016 est.)

male: 27.2% (2016 est.)

female: 38.5% (2016 est.)

country comparison to the world: 28

GOVERNMENT :: EGYPT

COUNTRY NAME:

conventional long form: Arab Republic of Egypt

conventional short form: Egypt

local long form: Jumhuriyat Misr al-Arabiyah

local short form: Misr

former: United Arab Republic (with Syria)

etymology: the English name "Egypt" derives from the ancient Greek name for the country "Aigyptos"; the Arabic name "Misr" can be traced to the ancient Akkadian "misru" meaning border or frontier

GOVERNMENT TYPE:

presidential republic

CAPITAL:

name: Cairo

geographic coordinates: 30 03 N, 31 15 E

time difference: UTC+2 (7 hours ahead of Washington, DC, during Standard Time)

ADMINISTRATIVE DIVISIONS:

27 governorates (muhafazat, singular - muhafazat); Ad Daqahliyah, Al Bahr al Ahmar (Red Sea), Al Buhayrah, Al Fayyum, Al Gharbiyah, Al Iskandariyah (Alexandria), Al Isma'iliyah (Ismailia), Al Jizah (Giza), Al Minufiyah, Al Minya, Al Qahirah (Cairo), Al Qalyubiyah, Al Uqsur (Luxor), Al Wadi al Jadid (New Valley), As Suways (Suez), Ash Sharqiyah, Aswan, Asyut, Bani Suwayf, Bur Sa'id (Port Said), Dumyat (Damietta), Janub Sina' (South Sinai), Kafr ash Shaykh, Matruh, Qina, Shamal Sina' (North Sinai), Suhaj

INDEPENDENCE:

28 February 1922 (from UK protectorate status; the revolution that began on 23 July 1952 led to a republic being declared on 18 June 1953 and all British troops withdrawn on 18 June 1956); note - it was ca. 3200 B.C. that the Two Lands of Upper (southern) and Lower (northern) Egypt were first united politically

NATIONAL HOLIDAY:

Revolution Day, 23 July (1952)

CONSTITUTION:

history: several previous; latest approved by a constitutional committee in December 2013, approved by referendum held on 14-15 January 2014, ratified by interim president on 19 January 2014 (2017)

amendments: proposed by the president of the republic or by one-fifth of the House of Representatives members; a decision to accept the proposal requires majority vote by House members; passage of amendment requires a two-thirds majority vote by House members and passage by majority vote in a referendum; articles of reelection of the president and principles of freedom not amendable unless the amendment "brings more guarantees" (2017)

LEGAL SYSTEM:

mixed legal system based on Napoleonic civil and penal law, Islamic religious law, and vestiges of colonial-era laws; judicial review of the constitutionality of laws by the Supreme Constitutional Court

INTERNATIONAL LAW ORGANIZATION PARTICIPATION:

accepts compulsory ICJ jurisdiction with reservations; non-party state to the ICCt

CITIZENSHIP:

citizenship by birth: no

citizenship by descent only: if the father was born in Egypt

dual citizenship recognized: only with prior permission from the government

residency requirement for naturalization: 10 years

SUFFRAGE:

18 years of age; universal and compulsory

EXECUTIVE BRANCH:

chief of state: President Abdelfattah ELSISI (since 8 June 2014)

head of government: Prime Minister Mostafa MADBOULY (since 7 June 2018); note - Prime Minister Sherif ISMAIL (since 12 September 2015) resigned 6 June 2018

cabinet: Cabinet ministers nominated by the executive authorities and approved by the House of Representtives

elections/appointments: president elected by absolute majority popular vote in 2 rounds if needed for a 4-year term (eligible for a second term); election last held on 26-28 March 2018 (next to be held in 2022); prime minister appointed by the president, approved by the House of Representatives

election results: Abdelfattah Said ELSISI relected president in first round; percent of valid votes case - Abdelfattah Said ELSISI (independent) 97.8%, Moussa Mostafa

MOUSSA (El Ghad Party) 2.3%; note - over 7% of ballots cast were deemed invalid

LEGISLATIVE BRANCH:

description: unicameral House of Representatives (Majlis Al-Nowaab); 596 seats; 448 members directly elected by individual candidacy system, 120 members - with quotas for women, youth, Christians and workers - elected in party-list constituencies by simple majority popular vote, and 28 members appointed by the president; member term 5 years; note - inaugural session held on 10 January 2016

elections: multi-phase election completed on 16 December 2015 (next to be held in 2020

election results: percent of vote by party - NA; seats by party -- Free Egyptians Party 65, Future of the Nation 53, New Wafd Party 36, Homeland's Protector Party 18, Republican People's Party 13, Congress Party 12, Al-Nour Party 11, Conservative Party 6, Democratic Peace Party 5, Egyptian National Movement 4, Egyptian Social Democratic Party 4, Modern Egypt Party 4, Freedom Party 3, My Homeland Egypt Party 3, Reform and Development Party 3, National Progressive Unionist Party 2, Arab Democratic Nasserist Party 1, El Serh El Masry el Hor 1, Revolutionary Guards Party 1, independent 351; composition - men 507, women 89, percent of women 14.9%

JUDICIAL BRANCH:

highest courts: Supreme Constitutional Court or SCC (consists of the court president and 10 justices); the SCC serves as the final court of arbitration on the constitutionality of laws and conflicts between lower courts regarding jurisdiction and rulings; Court of Cassation (CC) (consists of the court president and 550 judges organized in circuits with cases heard by panels of 5 judges); the CC is the highest appeals body for civil and criminal cases, also known as "ordinary justices"; Supreme Administrative Court (SAC) - consists of the court president and organized in circuits with cases heard by panels of 5 judges); the SAC is the highest court of the State Council

judge selection and term of office: under the 2014 constitution, all judges and justices selected by the Supreme Judiciary Council and appointed by the president of the Republic; judges appointed for life

subordinate courts: Courts of Appeal; Courts of First Instance; courts of limited jurisdiction; Family Court (established in 2004)

POLITICAL PARTIES AND LEADERS:

Al-Nour [Yunis MAKHYUN]
Arab Democratic Nasserist Party [Sayed Abdel GHANY]
Congress Party [Omar Al-Mokhtar SEMIDA]
Conservative Party [Akmal KOURTAM]
Democratic Peace Party [Ahmed FADALY]
Egyptian National Movement Party [Gen. Raouf EL SAYED]
Egyptian Social Democratic Party [Farid ZAHRAN]
El Ghad Party [Moussa Mostafa MOUSSA]
El Serh El Masry el Hor [Tarek Ahmed Abbas NADIM]
Freedom Party [Salah HASSABALAH]
Free Egyptians Party [Essam KHALIL]
Homeland's Protector Party [Lt. Gen. (retired) Galal AL-HARIDI]
Modern Egypt Party [Nabil DEIBIS]
Nation's Future Party (Mostaqbal Watan) [Mohamed Ashraf RASHAD]
My Homeland Egypt Party [Qadry ABU HUSSEIN]
National Progressive Unionist (Tagammu) Party [Sayed Abdel AAL]
Reform and Development Party [Mohamad Anwar al-SADAT]
Republican People's Party [Hazim AMR]
Wafd Party [Bahaa ABU SHOKA]Revolutionary Guards Party [Magdy EL-SHARIF]

INTERNATIONAL ORGANIZATION PARTICIPATION:

ABEDA, AfDB, AFESD, AMF, AU, BSEC (observer), CAEU, CD, CICA, COMESA, D-8, EBRD, FAO, G-15, G-24, G-77, IAEA, IBRD, ICAO, ICC (national committees), ICRM, IDA, IDB, IFAD, IFC, IFRCS, IHO, ILO, IMF, IMO, IMSO, Interpol, IOC, IOM, IPU, ISO, ITSO, ITU, LAS, MIGA, MINURSO, MINUSMA, MONUSCO, NAM, OAPEC, OAS (observer), OIC, OIF, OSCE (partner), PCA, UN, UNAMID, UNCTAD, UNESCO, UNHCR, UNIDO, UNMISS, UNOCI, UNRWA, UNWTO, UPU, WCO, WFTU (NGOs), WHO, WIPO, WMO, WTO

DIPLOMATIC REPRESENTATION IN THE US:

chief of mission: Ambassador Yasser REDA (since 19 September 2015)

chancery: 3521 International Court NW, Washington, DC 20008

telephone: [1] (202) 895-5400

FAX: [1] (202) 244-5131

consulate(s) general: Chicago, Houston, Los Angeles, New York

DIPLOMATIC REPRESENTATION FROM THE US:

chief of mission: Ambassador (vacant); Charge d'Affaires Thomas H. GOLDBERGER (since 30 June 2017)

embassy: 5 Tawfik Diab St., Garden City, Cairo

mailing address: Unit 64900, Box 15, APO AE 09839-4900; 5 Tawfik Diab Street, Garden City, Cairo

telephone: [20-2] 2797-3300

FAX: [20-2] 2797-3200

FLAG DESCRIPTION:

three equal horizontal bands of red (top), white, and black; the national emblem (a gold Eagle of Saladin facing the hoist side with a shield superimposed on its chest above a scroll bearing the name of the country in Arabic) centered in the white band; the band colors derive from the Arab Liberation flag and represent oppression (black), overcome through bloody struggle (red), to be replaced by a bright future (white)

note: similar to the flag of Syria, which has two green stars in the white band, Iraq, which has an Arabic inscription centered in the white band, and Yemen, which has a plain white band

NATIONAL SYMBOL(S):

golden eagle, white lotus; national colors: red, white, black

NATIONAL ANTHEM:

name: "Bilady, Bilady, Bilady" (My Homeland, My Homeland, My Homeland)

lyrics/music: Younis-al QADI/Sayed DARWISH

note: adopted 1979; the current anthem, less militaristic than the previous one, was created after the signing of the 1979 peace treaty with Israel; Sayed DARWISH, commonly considered the father of modern Egyptian music, composed the anthem

ECONOMY :: EGYPT

ECONOMY - OVERVIEW:

Occupying the northeast corner of the African continent, Egypt is bisected by the highly fertile Nile valley where most economic activity takes place.

Egypt's economy was highly centralized during the rule of former President Gamal Abdel NASSER but opened up considerably under former Presidents Anwar EL-SADAT and Mohamed Hosni MUBARAK. Agriculture, hydrocarbons, manufacturing, tourism, and other service sectors drove the country's relatively diverse economic activity.

Despite Egypt's mixed record for attracting foreign investment over the past two decades, poor living conditions and limited job opportunities have contributed to public discontent. These socioeconomic pressures were a major factor leading to the January 2011 revolution that ousted MUBARAK. The uncertain political, security, and policy environment since 2011 has restricted economic growth and failed to alleviate persistent unemployment, especially among the young.

In late 2016, persistent dollar shortages and waning aid from its Gulf allies led Cairo to turn to the IMF for a 3-year, $12 billion loan program. To secure the deal, Cairo floated its currency, introduced new taxes, and cut energy subsidies - all of which pushed inflation above 30% for most of 2017, a high that had not been seen in a generation. Since the currency float, foreign investment in Egypt's high interest treasury bills has risen exponentially, boosting both dollar availability and central bank reserves. Cairo will be challenged to obtain foreign and local investment in manufacturing and other sectors without a sustained effort to implement a range of business reforms.

GDP (PURCHASING POWER PARITY):

$1.204 trillion (2017 est.)

$1.155 trillion (2016 est.)

$1.107 trillion (2015 est.)

note: data are in 2017 dollars

country comparison to the world: 21

GDP (OFFICIAL EXCHANGE RATE):

$236.5 billion (2017 est.) (2017 est.)

GDP - REAL GROWTH RATE:

4.2% (2017 est.)

4.3% (2016 est.)

4.4% (2015 est.)

country comparison to the world: 71

GDP - PER CAPITA (PPP):

$12,700 (2017 est.)

$12,800 (2016 est.)

$12,400 (2015 est.)

note: data are in 2017 dollars

country comparison to the world: 124

GROSS NATIONAL SAVING:

9% of GDP (2017 est.)

9.1% of GDP (2016 est.)

10.6% of GDP (2015 est.)

country comparison to the world: 166

GDP - COMPOSITION, BY END USE:

household consumption: 86.8% (2017 est.)

government consumption: 10.1% (2017 est.)

investment in fixed capital: 14.8% (2017 est.)

investment in inventories: 0.5% (2017 est.)

exports of goods and services: 16.3% (2017 est.)

imports of goods and services: -28.5% (2017 est.)

GDP - COMPOSITION, BY SECTOR OF ORIGIN:

agriculture: 11.7% (2017 est.)

industry: 34.3% (2017 est.)

services: 54% (2017 est.)

AGRICULTURE - PRODUCTS:

cotton, rice, corn, wheat, beans, fruits, vegetables; cattle, water buffalo, sheep, goats

INDUSTRIES:

textiles, food processing, tourism, chemicals, pharmaceuticals, hydrocarbons, construction, cement, metals, light manufactures

INDUSTRIAL PRODUCTION GROWTH RATE:

3.5% (2017 est.)

country comparison to the world: 84

LABOR FORCE:

29.95 million (2017 est.)

country comparison to the world: 22

LABOR FORCE - BY OCCUPATION:

agriculture: 25.8%

industry: 25.1%

services: 49.1% (2015 est.)

UNEMPLOYMENT RATE:

12.2% (2017 est.)

12.7% (2016 est.)

country comparison to the world: 161

POPULATION BELOW POVERTY LINE:

27.8% (2016 est.)

HOUSEHOLD INCOME OR CONSUMPTION BY PERCENTAGE SHARE:

lowest 10%: 26.6% (2008)

highest 10%: 26.6% (2008)

DISTRIBUTION OF FAMILY INCOME - GINI INDEX:

31.8 (2015)

29.8 (2012)

country comparison to the world: 124

BUDGET:

revenues: 42.32 billion (2017 est.)

expenditures: 62.61 billion (2017 est.)

TAXES AND OTHER REVENUES:

17.9% (of GDP) (2017 est.)

country comparison to the world: 165

BUDGET SURPLUS (+) OR DEFICIT (-):

-8.6% (of GDP) (2017 est.)

country comparison to the world: 202

PUBLIC DEBT:

103% of GDP (2017 est.)

96.8% of GDP (2016 est.)

note: data cover central government debt and include debt instruments issued (or owned) by government entities other than the treasury; the data include treasury debt held by foreign entities; the data include debt issued by subnational entities, as well as intragovernmental debt; intragovernmental debt consists of treasury borrowings from surpluses in the social funds, such as for retirement, medical care, and unemployment; debt instruments for the social funds are sold at public auctions

country comparison to the world: 14

FISCAL YEAR:

1 July - 30 June

INFLATION RATE (CONSUMER PRICES):

23.5% (2017 est.)

10.2% (2016 est.)

country comparison to the world: 217

CENTRAL BANK DISCOUNT RATE:

19.25% (9 July 2017)

15.25% (3 November 2016)

country comparison to the world: 7

COMMERCIAL BANK PRIME LENDING RATE:

18.18% (31 December 2017 est.)

13.6% (31 December 2016 est.)

country comparison to the world: 20

STOCK OF NARROW MONEY:

$43.4 billion (31 December 2017 est.)

$34.51 billion (31 December 2016 est.)

country comparison to the world: 56

STOCK OF BROAD MONEY:

$43.4 billion (31 December 2017 est.)

$34.51 billion (31 December 2016 est.)

country comparison to the world: 56

STOCK OF DOMESTIC CREDIT:

$193.4 billion (31 December 2017 est.)

$178.7 billion (31 December 2016 est.)

country comparison to the world: 46

MARKET VALUE OF PUBLICLY TRADED SHARES:

$27.35 billion (30 December 2016 est.)

$25.07 billion (31 December 2015 est.)

$26.33 billion (31 December 2014 est.)

country comparison to the world: 59

CURRENT ACCOUNT BALANCE:

-$14.92 billion (2017 est.)

-$19.83 billion (2016 est.)

country comparison to the world: 196

EXPORTS:

$23.3 billion (2017 est.)

$20.02 billion (2016 est.)

country comparison to the world: 69

EXPORTS - PARTNERS:

UAE 10.9%, Italy 10%, US 7.4%, UK 5.7%, Turkey 4.4%, Germany 4.3%, India 4.3% (2017)

EXPORTS - COMMODITIES:

crude oil and petroleum products, fruits and vegetables, cotton, textiles, metal products, chemicals, processed food

IMPORTS:

$59.78 billion (2017 est.)

$57.84 billion (2016 est.)

country comparison to the world: 50

IMPORTS - COMMODITIES:

machinery and equipment, foodstuffs, chemicals, wood products, fuels

IMPORTS - PARTNERS:

China 7.9%, UAE 5.2%, Germany 4.8%, Saudi Arabia 4.6%, US 4.4%, Russia 4.3% (2017)

RESERVES OF FOREIGN EXCHANGE AND GOLD:

$35.89 billion (31 December 2017 est.)

$23.2 billion (31 December 2016 est.)

country comparison to the world: 47

DEBT - EXTERNAL:

$77.47 billion (31 December 2017 est.)

$62.38 billion (31 December 2016 est.)

country comparison to the world: 56

STOCK OF DIRECT FOREIGN INVESTMENT - AT HOME:

$106.6 billion (31 December 2017 est.)

$97.14 billion (31 December 2016 est.)

country comparison to the world: 45

STOCK OF DIRECT FOREIGN INVESTMENT - ABROAD:

$7.426 billion (31 December 2017 est.)

$7.257 billion (31 December 2016 est.)

country comparison to the world: 69

EXCHANGE RATES:

Egyptian pounds (EGP) per US dollar -

18.05 (2017 est.)

8.8 (2016 est.)

10.07 (2015 est.)

7.7133 (2014 est.)

7.08 (2013 est.)

ENERGY :: EGYPT

ELECTRICITY ACCESS:

population without electricity: 300,000 (2013)

electrification - total population: 99.6% (2013)

electrification - urban areas: 100% (2013)

electrification - rural areas: 99.3% (2013)

ELECTRICITY - PRODUCTION:

183.5 billion kWh (2016 est.)

country comparison to the world: 22

ELECTRICITY - CONSUMPTION:

159.7 billion kWh (2016 est.)

country comparison to the world: 23

ELECTRICITY - EXPORTS:

1.158 billion kWh (2015 est.)

country comparison to the world: 57

ELECTRICITY - IMPORTS:

54 million kWh (2016 est.)

country comparison to the world: 106

ELECTRICITY - INSTALLED GENERATING CAPACITY:

45.12 million kW (2016 est.)

country comparison to the world: 23

ELECTRICITY - FROM FOSSIL FUELS:

91% of total installed capacity (2016 est.)

country comparison to the world: 54

ELECTRICITY - FROM NUCLEAR FUELS:

0% of total installed capacity (2017 est.)

country comparison to the world: 82

ELECTRICITY - FROM HYDROELECTRIC PLANTS:

6% of total installed capacity (2017 est.)

country comparison to the world: 129

ELECTRICITY - FROM OTHER RENEWABLE SOURCES:

2% of total installed capacity (2017 est.)

country comparison to the world: 139

CRUDE OIL - PRODUCTION:

589,400 bbl/day (2017 est.)

country comparison to the world: 27

CRUDE OIL - EXPORTS:

246,500 bbl/day (2017 est.)

country comparison to the world: 29

CRUDE OIL - IMPORTS:

64,760 bbl/day (2015 est.)

country comparison to the world: 51

CRUDE OIL - PROVED RESERVES:

4.4 billion bbl (1 January 2018 est.)

country comparison to the world: 24

REFINED PETROLEUM PRODUCTS - PRODUCTION:

547,500 bbl/day (2015 est.)

country comparison to the world: 31

REFINED PETROLEUM PRODUCTS - CONSUMPTION:

878,000 bbl/day (2016 est.)

country comparison to the world: 25

REFINED PETROLEUM PRODUCTS - EXPORTS:

47,360 bbl/day (2015 est.)

country comparison to the world: 56

REFINED PETROLEUM PRODUCTS - IMPORTS:

280,200 bbl/day (2015 est.)

country comparison to the world: 26

NATURAL GAS - PRODUCTION:

50.86 billion cu m (2017 est.)

country comparison to the world: 16

NATURAL GAS - CONSUMPTION:

57.71 billion cu m (2017 est.)

country comparison to the world: 13

NATURAL GAS - EXPORTS:

212.4 million cu m (2017 est.)

country comparison to the world: 45

NATURAL GAS - IMPORTS:

7.079 billion cu m (2017 est.)

country comparison to the world: 29

NATURAL GAS - PROVED RESERVES:

2.186 trillion cu m (1 January 2018 est.)

country comparison to the world: 15

CARBON DIOXIDE EMISSIONS FROM CONSUMPTION OF ENERGY:

232.7 million Mt (2017 est.)

country comparison to the world: 30

COMMUNICATIONS :: EGYPT

TELEPHONES - FIXED LINES:

total subscriptions: 6,604,849 (2017 est.)

subscriptions per 100 inhabitants: 7 (2017 est.)

country comparison to the world: 24

TELEPHONES - MOBILE CELLULAR:

total subscriptions: 102,958,194 (2017 est.)

subscriptions per 100 inhabitants: 106 (2017 est.)

country comparison to the world: 16

TELEPHONE SYSTEM:

general assessment: largest fixed-line system in Africa and the Arab region; multiple mobile-cellular networks with a 100-percent penetration of the market; Telecom Egypt is mostly state owned; principal centers at Alexandria, Cairo, Al Mansurah, Ismailia, Suez, and Tanta are connected by coaxial cable and microwave radio relay; launch of LTE in late 2017 greatly helped the capabilities of mobile broadband services and will continue to do so for future development (2017)

domestic: fixed-line 7 per 100, mobile-cellular 106 per 100 (2017)

international: country code - 20; landing point for Aletar, the SEA-ME-WE-3 and SEA-ME-WE-4 submarine cable networks, Link Around the Globe (FLAG) Falcon and FLAG FEA; satellite earth stations - 4 (2 Intelsat - Atlantic Ocean and Indian Ocean, 1 Arabsat, and 1 Inmarsat); tropospheric scatter to Sudan; microwave radio relay to Israel; a participant in Medarabtel; MENA subsea cable came into commercial use in late 2015, augmenting the country's considerable international bandwidth (2017)

BROADCAST MEDIA:

mix of state-run and private broadcast media; state-run TV operates 2 national and 6 regional terrestrial networks, as well as a few satellite channels; dozens of private satellite channels and a large number of Arabic satellite channels are available for free; some limited satellite services are also available via subscription; state-run radio operates about 30 stations belonging to 8 networks (2018)

INTERNET COUNTRY CODE:

.eg

INTERNET USERS:

total: 37,122,537 (July 2016 est.)

percent of population: 39.2% (July 2016 est.)

country comparison to the world: 19

BROADBAND - FIXED SUBSCRIPTIONS:

total: 5,223,311 (2017 est.)

subscriptions per 100 inhabitants: 5 (2017 est.)

country comparison to the world: 28

COMMUNICATIONS - NOTE:

one of the largest and most famous libraries in the ancient world was the Great Library of Alexandria in Egypt (founded about 295 B.C., it may have survived in some form into the 5th century A.D.); seeking to resurrect the great center of learning and communication, the Egyptian Government in 2002 inaugurated the Bibliotheca Alexandrina, an Egyptian National Library on the site of the original Great Library, which commemorates the original archive and also serves as a center of cultural and scientific excellence

TRANSPORTATION :: EGYPT

NATIONAL AIR TRANSPORT SYSTEM:

number of registered air carriers: 14 (2015)

inventory of registered aircraft operated by air carriers: 101 (2015)

annual passenger traffic on registered air carriers: 10,159,464 (2015)

annual freight traffic on registered air carriers: 397,531,535 mt-km (2015)

CIVIL AIRCRAFT REGISTRATION COUNTRY CODE PREFIX:

SU (2016)

AIRPORTS:

83 (2013)

country comparison to the world: 65

AIRPORTS - WITH PAVED RUNWAYS:

total: 72 (2017)

over 3,047 m: 15 (2017)

2,438 to 3,047 m: 36 (2017)

1,524 to 2,437 m: 15 (2017)

under 914 m: 6 (2017)

AIRPORTS - WITH UNPAVED RUNWAYS:

total: 11 (2013)

2,438 to 3,047 m: 1 (2013)

1,524 to 2,437 m: 3 (2013)

914 to 1,523 m: 4 (2013)

under 914 m: 3 (2013)

HELIPORTS:

7 (2013)

PIPELINES:

486 km condensate, 74 km condensate/gas, 7986 km gas, 957 km liquid petroleum gas, 5225 km oil, 37 km oil/gas/water, 895 km refined products, 65 km water (2013)

RAILWAYS:

total: 5,085 km (2014)

standard gauge: 5,085 km 1.435-m gauge (62 km electrified) (2014)

country comparison to the world: 39

ROADWAYS:

total: 137,430 km (2010)

paved: 126,742 km (includes 838 km of expressways) (2010)

unpaved: 10,688 km (2010)

country comparison to the world: 39

WATERWAYS:

3,500 km (includes the Nile River, Lake Nasser, Alexandria-Cairo Waterway, and numerous smaller canals in Nile Delta; the Suez Canal (193.5 km including approaches) is navigable by oceangoing vessels drawing up to 17.68 m) (2011)

country comparison to the world: 29

MERCHANT MARINE:

total: 399 (2017)

by type: bulk carrier 14, container ship 8, general cargo 33, oil tanker 36, other 308 (2017)

country comparison to the world: 46

PORTS AND TERMINALS:

major seaport(s): Mediterranean Sea - Alexandria, Damietta, El Dekheila, Port Said

oil terminal(s): Ain Sukhna terminal, Sidi Kerir terminal

container port(s) (TEUs): Alexandria (1,633,600), Port Said (East) (3,035,900) (2016)

LNG terminal(s) (export): Damietta, Idku (Abu Qir Bay)

Gulf of Suez - Suez

MILITARY AND SECURITY :: EGYPT

MILITARY EXPENDITURES:

2-3% of GDP according to President ELSISI (March 2017)

1.67% of GDP (2016)

1.72% of GDP (2015)

1.69% of GDP (2014)

1.61% of GDP (2013)

country comparison to the world: 68

MILITARY BRANCHES:

Army, Navy, Air Force, Air Defense Forces (2018)

MILITARY SERVICE AGE AND OBLIGATION:

18-30 years of age for male conscript military service; service obligation - 18-36 months, followed by a 9-year reserve obligation; voluntary enlistment possible from age 15 (2017)

TERRORISM :: EGYPT

TERRORIST GROUPS - HOME BASED:

Harakat Sawa'd Misr (HASM):
aim(s): overthrow the Egyptian Government
area(s) of operation: Cairo, Nile Delta, Western Desert (April 2018)

Islamic State of Iraq and ash-Sham (ISIS)-Sinai:
aim(s): spread the ISIS caliphate by eliminating the Egyptian Government, destroying Israel, and establishing an Islamic emirate in the Sinai
area(s) of operation: operational throughout Egypt, primarily in North Sinai
note: formerly known as Ansar Bayt al-Maqdis; core ISIS refers to Egypt as its Wilayat Sinai (April 2018)

Liwa al-Thawra:
aim(s): overthrow the Egyptian Government
area(s) of operation: Nile Delta (April 2018)

TERRORIST GROUPS - FOREIGN BASED:

al-Qa'ida (AQ):
aim(s): overthrow the Egyptian Government and, ultimately, establish a pan-Islamic caliphate under a strict Salafi Muslim interpretation of sharia
area(s) of operation: maintains a longtime operational presence and established networks (April 2018)

Army of Islam (AOI):
aim(s): disrupt the Egyptian Government's efforts to provide security and, ultimately, establish an Islamic caliphate
area(s) of operation: operational mainly in Cairo and the Sinai Peninsula
note: associated with ISIS Sinai Province (formerly known as Ansar Bayt al-Maqdis); targets Israeli Government interests, sometimes in collaboration with the Mujahidin Shura Council in the Environs of Jerusalem (April 2018)

TRANSNATIONAL ISSUES :: EGYPT

DISPUTES - INTERNATIONAL:

Sudan claims but Egypt de facto administers security and economic development of Halaib region north of the 22nd parallel boundaryEgypt no longer shows its administration of the Bir Tawil trapezoid in Sudan on its mapsGazan breaches in the security wall with Egypt in January 2008 highlight difficulties in monitoring the Sinai borderSaudi Arabia claims Egyptian-administered islands of Tiran and Sanafir

REFUGEES AND INTERNALLY DISPLACED PERSONS:

refugees (country of origin): 70,027 (West Bank and Gaza Strip) (2016), 6,611 (Iraq) (refugees and asylum seekers), 6,561 (Somalia) (refugees and asylum seekers) (2017), 132,553 (Syria) (refugees and asylum seekers), 20,001 (Sudan) (refugees and asylum seekers), 11,769 (Ethiopia) (refugees and asylum seekers), 11,041 (Eritrea) (refugees and asylum seekers), 6,978 (South Sudan) (refugees and asylum seekers) (2018)

IDPs: 82,000 (2017)

stateless persons: 19 (2016)

TRAFFICKING IN PERSONS:

current situation: Egypt is a source, transit, and destination country for men, women, and children subjected to sex trafficking and forced labor; Egyptian children, including the large population of street children are vulnerable to forced labor in domestic service, begging and agriculture or may be victims of sex trafficking or child sex tourism, which occurs in Cairo, Alexandria, and Luxor; some Egyptian women and girls are sold into "temporary" or "summer" marriages with Gulf men, through the complicity of their parents or marriage brokers, and are exploited for prostitution or forced labor; Egyptian men are subject to forced labor in neighboring countries, while adults from South and Southeast Asia and East Africa – and increasingly Syrian refugees – are forced to work in domestic service, construction, cleaning, and begging in Egypt; women and girls, including migrants and refugees, from Asia, sub-Saharan Africa, and the Middle East are sex trafficked in Egypt; the Egyptian military cracked down on criminal group's smuggling, abducting, trafficking, and extorting African migrants in the Sinai Peninsula, but the practice has reemerged along Egypt's western border with Libya

tier rating: Tier 2 Watch List – Egypt does not fully comply with the minimum standards for the elimination of trafficking; however, it is making significant efforts to do so; the government gathered data nationwide on trafficking cases to better allocate and prioritize anti-trafficking efforts, but overall it did not demonstrate increased progress; prosecutions increased in 2014, but no offenders were convicted for the second consecutive year; fewer trafficking victims were identified in 2014, which represents a significant and ongoing decrease from the previous two reporting periods; the government relied on NGOs and international organizations to identify and refer victims to protective services, and focused on Egyptian victims and refused to provide some services to foreign victims, at times including shelter (2015)

ILLICIT DRUGS:

transit point for cannabis, heroin, and opium moving to Europe, Israel, and North Africa; transit stop for Nigerian drug couriers; concern as money laundering site due to lax enforcement of financial regulations

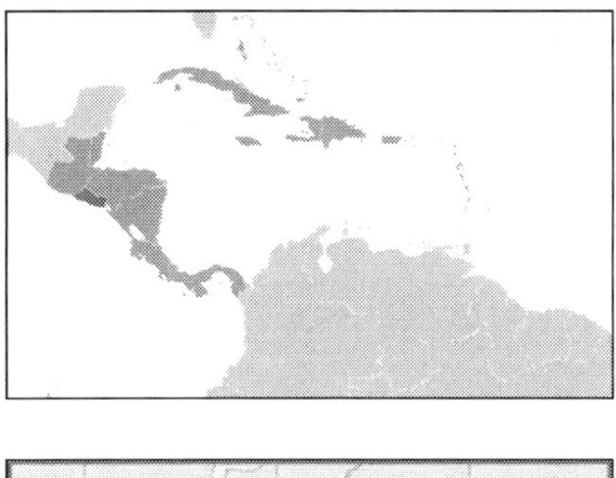

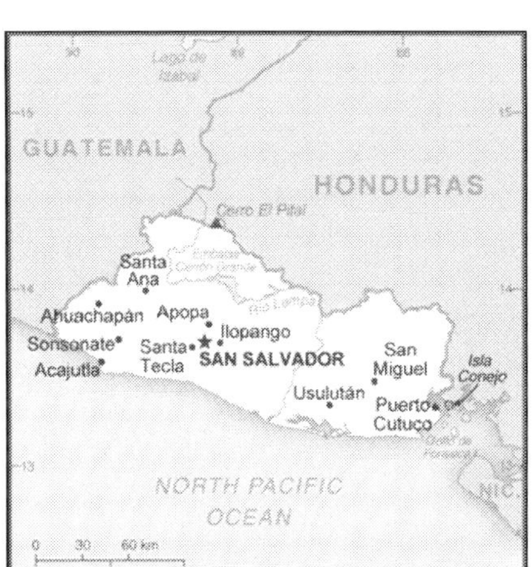

CENTRAL AMERICA :: EL SALVADOR

INTRODUCTION :: EL SALVADOR

BACKGROUND:

El Salvador achieved independence from Spain in 1821 and from the Central American Federation in 1839. A 12-year civil war, which cost about 75,000 lives, was brought to a close in 1992 when the government and leftist rebels signed a treaty that provided for military and political reforms. El Salvador is beset by one of the world's highest homicide rates and pervasive criminal gangs.

GEOGRAPHY :: EL SALVADOR

LOCATION:

Central America, bordering the North Pacific Ocean, between Guatemala and Honduras

GEOGRAPHIC COORDINATES:

13 50 N, 88 55 W

MAP REFERENCES:

Central America and the Caribbean

AREA:

total: 21,041 sq km

land: 20,721 sq km

water: 320 sq km

country comparison to the world: 153

AREA - COMPARATIVE:

about the same size as New Jersey

LAND BOUNDARIES:

total: 590 km

border countries (2): Guatemala 199 km, Honduras 391 km

COASTLINE:

307 km

MARITIME CLAIMS:

territorial sea: 12 nm

exclusive economic zone: 200 nm

contiguous zone: 24 nm

CLIMATE:

tropical; rainy season (May to October); dry season (November to April); tropical on coast; temperate in uplands

TERRAIN:

mostly mountains with narrow coastal belt and central plateau

ELEVATION:

mean elevation: 442 m

elevation extremes: 0 m lowest point: Pacific Ocean

2730 highest point: Cerro El Pital

NATURAL RESOURCES:

hydropower, geothermal power, petroleum, arable land

LAND USE:

agricultural land: 74.7% (2011 est.)

arable land: 33.1% (2011 est.) / permanent crops: 10.9% (2011 est.) / permanent pasture: 30.7% (2011 est.)

forest: 13.6% (2011 est.)

other: 11.7% (2011 est.)

IRRIGATED LAND:

452 sq km (2012)

POPULATION DISTRIBUTION:

athough it is the smallest country in land area in Central America, El Salvador has a population that is 18 times larger than Belize; at least 20% of the population lives abroad; high population density country-wide, with particular concentration around the capital of San Salvador

NATURAL HAZARDS:

known as the Land of Volcanoes; frequent and sometimes destructive earthquakes and volcanic activity; extremely susceptible to hurricanes

volcanism: significant volcanic activity; San Salvador (1,893 m), which last erupted in 1917, has the potential to cause major harm to the country's capital, which lies just below the volcano's slopes; San Miguel (2,130 m), which last erupted in 2002, is one of the most active volcanoes in the country; other historically active volcanoes include Conchaguita, Ilopango, Izalco, and Santa Ana

ENVIRONMENT - CURRENT ISSUES:

deforestation; soil erosion; water pollution; contamination of soils from disposal of toxic wastes

ENVIRONMENT - INTERNATIONAL AGREEMENTS:

party to: Biodiversity, Climate Change, Climate Change Kyoto Protocol, Desertification, Endangered Species, Hazardous Wastes, Ozone Layer Protection, Wetlands

signed, but not ratified: Law of the Sea

GEOGRAPHY - NOTE:

smallest Central American country and only one without a coastline on the Caribbean Sea

PEOPLE AND SOCIETY :: EL SALVADOR

POPULATION:

6,187,271 (July 2018 est.)

country comparison to the world: 109

NATIONALITY:

noun: Salvadoran(s)

adjective: Salvadoran

ETHNIC GROUPS:

mestizo 86.3%, white 12.7%, Amerindian 0.2% (includes Lenca, Kakawira, Nahua-Pipil), black 0.1%, other 0.6% (2007 est.)

LANGUAGES:

Spanish (official), Nawat (among some Amerindians)

RELIGIONS:

Roman Catholic 50%, Protestant 36%, other 2%, none 12% (2014 est.)

DEMOGRAPHIC PROFILE:

El Salvador is the smallest and most densely populated country in Central America. It is well into its demographic transition, experiencing slower population growth, a decline in its number of youths, and the gradual aging of its population. The increased use of family planning has substantially lowered El Salvador's fertility rate, from approximately 6 children per woman in the 1970s to replacement level today. A 2008 national family planning survey showed that female sterilization remained the most common contraception method in El Salvador - its sterilization rate is among the highest in Latin America and the Caribbean - but that the use of injectable contraceptives is growing. Fertility differences between rich and poor and urban and rural women are narrowing.

Salvadorans fled during the 1979 to 1992 civil war mainly to the United States but also to Canada and to neighboring Mexico, Guatemala, Honduras, Nicaragua, and Costa Rica. Emigration to the United States increased again in the 1990s and 2000s as a result of deteriorating economic conditions, natural disasters (Hurricane Mitch in 1998 and earthquakes in 2001), and family reunification. At least 20% of El Salvador's population lives abroad. The remittances they send home account for close to 20% of GDP, are the second largest source of external income after exports, and have helped reduce poverty.

AGE STRUCTURE:

0-14 years: 25.3% (male 802,813 /female 762,852)

15-24 years: 19.88% (male 619,550 /female 610,725)

25-54 years: 39.8% (male 1,143,226 /female 1,319,138)

55-64 years: 7.32% (male 198,513 /female 254,640)

65 years and over: 7.69% (male 208,817 /female 266,997) (2018 est.)

DEPENDENCY RATIOS:

total dependency ratio: 56.8 (2015 est.)

youth dependency ratio: 44.4 (2015 est.)

elderly dependency ratio: 12.4 (2015 est.)

potential support ratio: 8 (2015 est.)

MEDIAN AGE:

total: 27.6 years

male: 26.1 years

female: 29.1 years (2018 est.)

country comparison to the world: 143

POPULATION GROWTH RATE:

0.25% (2018 est.)

country comparison to the world: 177

BIRTH RATE:

16.1 births/1,000 population (2018 est.)

country comparison to the world: 111

DEATH RATE:

5.8 deaths/1,000 population (2018 est.)

country comparison to the world: 173

NET MIGRATION RATE:

-8 migrant(s)/1,000 population (2017 est.)

country comparison to the world: 205

POPULATION DISTRIBUTION:

athough it is the smallest country in land area in Central America, El Salvador has a population that is 18 times larger than Belize; at least 20% of the population lives abroad; high population density country-wide, with particular concentration around the capital of San Salvador

URBANIZATION:

urban population: 72% of total population (2018)

rate of urbanization: 1.57% annual rate of change (2015-20 est.)

MAJOR URBAN AREAS - POPULATION:

1.107 million SAN SALVADOR (capital) (2018)

SEX RATIO:

at birth: 1.05 male(s)/female (2017 est.)

0-14 years: 1.05 male(s)/female (2017 est.)

15-24 years: 1.01 male(s)/female (2017 est.)

25-54 years: 0.86 male(s)/female (2017 est.)

55-64 years: 0.8 male(s)/female (2017 est.)

65 years and over: 0.8 male(s)/female (2017 est.)

total population: 0.93 male(s)/female (2017 est.)

MOTHER'S MEAN AGE AT FIRST BIRTH:

20.8 years (2008 est.)

note: median age at first birth among women 25-29

MATERNAL MORTALITY RATE:

54 deaths/100,000 live births (2015 est.)

country comparison to the world: 91

INFANT MORTALITY RATE:

total: 16.3 deaths/1,000 live births (2018 est.)

male: 18.3 deaths/1,000 live births (2018 est.)

female: 14.1 deaths/1,000 live births (2018 est.)

country comparison to the world: 95

LIFE EXPECTANCY AT BIRTH:

total population: 75.1 years (2018 est.)

male: 71.8 years (2018 est.)

female: 78.6 years (2018 est.)

country comparison to the world: 114

TOTAL FERTILITY RATE:

1.84 children born/woman (2018 est.)

country comparison to the world: 146

CONTRACEPTIVE PREVALENCE RATE:

72% (2014)

HEALTH EXPENDITURES:

6.8% of GDP (2014)

country comparison to the world: 87

PHYSICIANS DENSITY:

1.92 physicians/1,000 population (2008)

HOSPITAL BED DENSITY:

1.3 beds/1,000 population (2014)

DRINKING WATER SOURCE:

improved:

urban: 97.5% of population

rural: 86.5% of population

total: 93.8% of population

unimproved:

urban: 2.5% of population

rural: 13.5% of population

total: 6.2% of population (2015 est.)

SANITATION FACILITY ACCESS:

improved:

urban: 82.4% of population (2015 est.)

rural: 60% of population (2015 est.)

total: 75% of population (2015 est.)

unimproved:

urban: 17.6% of population (2015 est.)

rural: 40% of population (2015 est.)

total: 25% of population (2015 est.)

HIV/AIDS - ADULT PREVALENCE RATE:

0.6% (2017 est.)

country comparison to the world: 58

HIV/AIDS - PEOPLE LIVING WITH HIV/AIDS:

25,000 (2017 est.)

country comparison to the world: 76

HIV/AIDS - DEATHS:

<1000 (2017 est.)

MAJOR INFECTIOUS DISEASES:

degree of risk: high (2016)

food or waterborne diseases: bacterial and protozoal diarrhea (2016)

vectorborne diseases: dengue fever (2016)

note: active local transmission of Zika virus by Aedes species mosquitoes has been identified in this country (as of August 2016); it poses an important risk (a large number of cases possible) among US citizens if bitten by an infective mosquito; other less common ways to get Zika are through sex, via blood transfusion, or during pregnancy, in which the pregnant woman passes Zika virus to her fetus

OBESITY - ADULT PREVALENCE RATE:

24.6% (2016)

country comparison to the world: 57

CHILDREN UNDER THE AGE OF 5 YEARS UNDERWEIGHT:

5% (2014)

country comparison to the world: 82

EDUCATION EXPENDITURES:

3.5% of GDP (2016)

country comparison to the world: 129

LITERACY:

definition: age 15 and over can read and write (2015 est.)

total population: 88% (2015 est.)

male: 90% (2015 est.)

female: 86.2% (2015 est.)

SCHOOL LIFE EXPECTANCY (PRIMARY TO TERTIARY EDUCATION):

total: 13 years (2014)

male: 13 years (2014)

female: 13 years (2014)

UNEMPLOYMENT, YOUTH AGES 15-24:

total: 9.8% (2016)

male: 9.6% (2016)

female: 10.1% (2016)

country comparison to the world: 128

GOVERNMENT :: EL SALVADOR

COUNTRY NAME:

conventional long form: Republic of El Salvador

conventional short form: El Salvador

local long form: Republica de El Salvador

local short form: El Salvador

etymology: name is an abbreviation of the original Spanish conquistador designation for the area "Provincia de Nuestro Senor Jesus Cristo, el Salvador del Mundo" (Province of Our Lord Jesus Christ, the Saviour of the World), which became simply "El Salvador" (The Savior)

GOVERNMENT TYPE:

presidential republic

CAPITAL:

name: San Salvador

geographic coordinates: 13 42 N, 89 12 W

time difference: UTC-6 (1 hour behind Washington, DC, during Standard Time)

ADMINISTRATIVE DIVISIONS:

14 departments (departamentos, singular - departamento); Ahuachapan, Cabanas, Chalatenango, Cuscatlan, La Libertad, La Paz, La Union, Morazan, San Miguel, San Salvador, San Vicente, Santa Ana, Sonsonate, Usulutan

INDEPENDENCE:

15 September 1821 (from Spain)

NATIONAL HOLIDAY:

Independence Day, 15 September (1821)

CONSTITUTION:

history: many previous; latest drafted 16 December 1983, enacted 23 December 1983 (2018)

amendments: proposals require agreement by absolute majority of the Legislative Assembly membership; passage requires at least two-thirds majority vote of the Assembly; constitutional articles on basic principles, and citizen rights and freedoms cannot be amended; amended many times, last in 2018 (2018)

LEGAL SYSTEM:

civil law system with minor common law influence; judicial review of legislative acts in the Supreme Court

INTERNATIONAL LAW ORGANIZATION PARTICIPATION:

has not submitted an ICJ jurisdiction declaration; non-party state to the ICCt

CITIZENSHIP:

citizenship by birth: yes

citizenship by descent only: yes

dual citizenship recognized: yes

residency requirement for naturalization: 5 years

SUFFRAGE:

18 years of age; universal

EXECUTIVE BRANCH:

chief of state: President Salvador SANCHEZ CEREN (since 1 June 2014); Vice President Salvador Oscar ORTIZ (since 1 June 2014); note - the president is both chief of state and head of government

head of government: President Salvador SANCHEZ CEREN (since 1 June 2014); Vice President Salvador Oscar ORTIZ (since 1 June 2014)

cabinet: Council of Ministers selected by the president

elections/appointments: president and vice president directly elected on the same ballot by absolute majority popular vote in 2 rounds if needed for a single 5-year term; election last held on 2 February 2014 with a runoff on 9 March 2014 (next to be held on 3 February 2019)

election results: Salvador SANCHEZ CEREN elected president in second round; percent of vote in first round - Salvador SANCHEZ CEREN (FMLN) 48.9%, Norman QUIJANO (ARENA) 39%, Antonio SACA (CN) 11.4%, other 0.7%; percent of vote in second round - Salvador SANCHEZ CEREN 50.1%, Norman QUIJANO 49.9%

LEGISLATIVE BRANCH:

description: unicameral Legislative Assembly or Asamblea Legislativa (84 seats; members directly elected in multi-seat constituencies and a single nationwide constituency by proportional representation vote to serve 3-year terms)

elections: last held on 4 March 2018 (next to be held in March 2021)

election results: percent of vote by party - ARENA 42.3%, FMLN 24.4%, GANA 11.5%, PCN 10.8%, PDC 3.2%, CD 0.9%, Independent 0.7%, other 6.2%; seats by party - ARENA 37, FMLN 23, GANA 11, PCN 8, PDC 3, CD 1, independent 1

JUDICIAL BRANCH:

highest courts: Supreme Court or Corte Suprema de Justicia (consists of 15 judges assigned to constitutional, civil, penal, and administrative conflict divisions)

judge selection and term of office: judges elected by the Legislative Assembly on the recommendation of both the National Council of the Judicature, an independent body elected by the Legislative Assembly, and the Bar Association; judges elected for 9-year terms, with renewal of one-third of membership every 3 years; consecutive reelection is allowed

subordinate courts: Appellate Courts; Courts of First Instance; Courts of Peace

POLITICAL PARTIES AND LEADERS:

Christian Democratic Party or PDC [Rodolfo Antonio PARKER Soto]
Democratic Change (Cambio Democratico) or CD [Douglas AVILES] (formerly United Democratic Center or CDU)
Farabundo Marti National Liberation Front or FMLN [Medardo GONZALEZ]
Great Alliance for National Unity or GANA [Jose Andres ROVIRA Caneles]
National Coalition Party or PCN [Manuel RODRIGUEZ]
Nationalist Republican Alliance or ARENA [Mauricio INTERIANO]

INTERNATIONAL ORGANIZATION PARTICIPATION:

BCIE, CACM, CD, CELAC, FAO, G-11, G-77, IADB, IAEA, IBRD, ICAO, ICC (national committees), ICRM, IDA, IFAD, IFC, IFRCS, ILO, IMF, IMO, Interpol, IOC, IOM, IPU, ISO (correspondent), ITSO, ITU, ITUC (NGOs), LAES, LAIA (observer), MIGA, MINURSO, MINUSTAH, NAM (observer), OAS, OPANAL, OPCW, Pacific Alliance (observer), PCA, Petrocaribe, SICA, UN, UNCTAD, UNESCO, UNIDO, UNIFIL, Union Latina, UNISFA, UNMISS, UNOCI, UNWTO, UPU, WCO, WFTU (NGOs), WHO, WIPO, WMO, WTO

DIPLOMATIC REPRESENTATION IN THE US:

chief of mission: Ambassador Claudia Ivette CANJURA de Centeno (since 17 June 2016)

chancery: 1400 16th Street NW, Suite 100, Washington, DC 20036

telephone: [1] (202) 595-7500

FAX: [1] (202) 232-1928

consulate(s) general: Atlanta, Boston, Brentwood (NY), Chicago, Dallas, Doral (FL), Houston, Las Vegas (NV), Los Angeles, McAllen (TX), New York, Nogales (AZ), San Francisco, Silver Spring (MD), Tucson (AZ), Washington, DC, Woodbridge (VA), Woodstock (GA)

consulate(s): Elizabeth (NJ), Newark (NJ), Seattle, Woodbridge (VA)

DIPLOMATIC REPRESENTATION FROM THE US:

chief of mission: Ambassador Jean Elizabeth MANES (since 29 March 2016)

embassy: Final Boulevard Santa Elena Sur, Antiguo Cuscatlan, La Libertad, San Salvador

mailing address: Unit 3450, APO AA 34023; 3450 San Salvador Place, Washington, DC 20521-3450

telephone: [503] 2501-2999

FAX: [503] 2501-2150

FLAG DESCRIPTION:

three equal horizontal bands of cobalt blue (top), white, and cobalt blue with the national coat of arms centered in the white band; the coat of arms features a round emblem encircled by the words REPUBLICA DE EL SALVADOR EN LA AMERICA CENTRAL; the banner is based on the former blue-white-blue flag of the Federal Republic of Central America; the blue bands symbolize the Pacific Ocean and the Caribbean Sea, while the white band represents the land between the two bodies of water, as well as peace and prosperity

note: similar to the flag of Nicaragua, which has a different coat of arms centered in the white band; also similar to the flag of Honduras, which has five blue stars arranged in an X pattern centered in the white band

NATIONAL SYMBOL(S):

turquoise-browed motmot (bird); national colors: blue, white

NATIONAL ANTHEM:

name: "Himno Nacional de El Salvador" (National Anthem of El Salvador)

lyrics/music: Juan Jose CANAS/Juan ABERLE

note: officially adopted 1953, in use since 1879; at 4:20 minutes, the anthem of El Salvador is one of the world's longest

ECONOMY :: EL SALVADOR

ECONOMY - OVERVIEW:

The smallest country in Central America geographically, El Salvador has the fourth largest economy in the region. With the global recession, real GDP contracted in 2009 and economic growth has since remained low, averaging less than 2% from 2010 to 2014, but recovered somewhat in 2015-17 with an average annual growth rate of 2.4%. Remittances accounted for approximately 18% of GDP in 2017 and were received by about a third of all households.

In 2006, El Salvador was the first country to ratify the Dominican Republic-Central American Free Trade Agreement, which has bolstered the export of processed foods, sugar, and ethanol, and supported investment in the apparel sector amid increased Asian competition. In September 2015, El Salvador kicked off a five-year $277 million second compact with the Millennium Challenge Corporation - a US Government agency aimed at stimulating economic growth and reducing poverty - to improve El Salvador's competitiveness and productivity in international markets.

The Salvadoran Government maintained fiscal discipline during reconstruction and rebuilding following earthquakes in 2001 and hurricanes in 1998 and 2005, but El Salvador's public debt, estimated at 59.3% of GDP in 2017, has been growing over the last several years.

GDP (PURCHASING POWER PARITY):

$51.17 billion (2017 est.)

$50.01 billion (2016 est.)

$48.75 billion (2015 est.)

note: data are in 2017 dollars

country comparison to the world: 109

GDP (OFFICIAL EXCHANGE RATE):

$24.81 billion (2017 est.) (2017 est.)

GDP - REAL GROWTH RATE:

2.3% (2017 est.)

2.6% (2016 est.)

2.4% (2015 est.)

country comparison to the world: 140

GDP - PER CAPITA (PPP):

$8,000 (2017 est.)

$7,900 (2016 est.)

$7,700 (2015 est.)

note: data are in 2017 dollars

country comparison to the world: 152

GROSS NATIONAL SAVING:

14.9% of GDP (2017 est.)

13% of GDP (2016 est.)

12.4% of GDP (2015 est.)

country comparison to the world: 137

GDP - COMPOSITION, BY END USE:

household consumption: 84.5% (2017 est.)

government consumption: 15.8% (2017 est.)

investment in fixed capital: 16.9% (2017 est.)

investment in inventories: 0% (2017 est.)

exports of goods and services: 27.6% (2017 est.)

imports of goods and services: -44.9% (2017 est.)

GDP - COMPOSITION, BY SECTOR OF ORIGIN:

agriculture: 12% (2017 est.)

industry: 27.7% (2017 est.)

services: 60.3% (2017 est.)

AGRICULTURE - PRODUCTS:

coffee, sugar, corn, rice, beans, oilseed, cotton, sorghum; beef, dairy products

INDUSTRIES:

food processing, beverages, petroleum, chemicals, fertilizer, textiles, furniture, light metals

INDUSTRIAL PRODUCTION GROWTH RATE:

3.6% (2017 est.)

country comparison to the world: 81

LABOR FORCE:

2.774 million (2017 est.)

country comparison to the world: 109

LABOR FORCE - BY OCCUPATION:

agriculture: 21%

industry: 20%

services: 58% (2011 est.)

UNEMPLOYMENT RATE:

7% (2017 est.)

6.9% (2016 est.)

note: data are official rates; but underemployment is high

country comparison to the world: 107

POPULATION BELOW POVERTY LINE:

32.7% (2016 est.)

HOUSEHOLD INCOME OR CONSUMPTION BY PERCENTAGE SHARE:

lowest 10%: 32.3% (2014 est.)

highest 10%: 32.3% (2014 est.)

DISTRIBUTION OF FAMILY INCOME - GINI INDEX:

36 (2016 est.)

38 (2014)

country comparison to the world: 90

BUDGET:

revenues: 5.886 billion (2017 est.)

expenditures: 6.517 billion (2017 est.)

TAXES AND OTHER REVENUES:

23.7% (of GDP) (2017 est.)

country comparison to the world: 123

BUDGET SURPLUS (+) OR DEFICIT (-):

-2.5% (of GDP) (2017 est.)

country comparison to the world: 114

PUBLIC DEBT:

67.9% of GDP (2017 est.)

66.4% of GDP (2016 est.)

note: El Salvador's total public debt includes non-financial public sector debt, financial public sector debt, and central bank debt

country comparison to the world: 54

FISCAL YEAR:

calendar year

INFLATION RATE (CONSUMER PRICES):

1% (2017 est.)

0.6% (2016 est.)

country comparison to the world: 51

COMMERCIAL BANK PRIME LENDING RATE:

6.47% (31 December 2017 est.)

6.37% (31 December 2016 est.)

country comparison to the world: 124

STOCK OF NARROW MONEY:

$3.653 billion (31 December 2017 est.)

$3.129 billion (31 December 2016 est.)

country comparison to the world: 114

STOCK OF BROAD MONEY:

$3.653 billion (31 December 2017 est.)

$3.129 billion (31 December 2016 est.)

country comparison to the world: 120

STOCK OF DOMESTIC CREDIT:

$14.22 billion (31 December 2017 est.)

$13.71 billion (31 December 2016 est.)

country comparison to the world: 100

MARKET VALUE OF PUBLICLY TRADED SHARES:

$2.64 billion (31 December 2017 est.)

$4.4 billion (31 December 2017 est.)

$3.816 billion (31 December 2017 est.)

country comparison to the world: 97

CURRENT ACCOUNT BALANCE:

-$501 million (2017 est.)

-$500 million (2016 est.)

country comparison to the world: 119

EXPORTS:

$4.662 billion (2017 est.)

$5.42 billion (2016 est.)

country comparison to the world: 113

EXPORTS - PARTNERS:

US 45.7%, Honduras 13.9%, Guatemala 13.5%, Nicaragua 6.7%, Costa Rica 4.6% (2017)

EXPORTS - COMMODITIES:

offshore assembly exports, coffee, sugar, textiles and apparel, ethanol, chemicals, electricity, iron and steel manufactures

IMPORTS:

$9.499 billion (2017 est.)

$8.954 billion (2016 est.)

country comparison to the world: 104

IMPORTS - COMMODITIES:

raw materials, consumer goods, capital goods, fuels, foodstuffs, petroleum, electricity

IMPORTS - PARTNERS:

US 36.7%, Guatemala 10.5%, China 8.7%, Mexico 7.4%, Honduras 6.7% (2017)

RESERVES OF FOREIGN EXCHANGE AND GOLD:

$3.567 billion (31 December 2017 est.)

$3.238 billion (31 December 2016 est.)

country comparison to the world: 104

DEBT - EXTERNAL:

$15.51 billion (31 December 2017 est.)

$16.32 billion (31 December 2016 est.)

country comparison to the world: 102

STOCK OF DIRECT FOREIGN INVESTMENT - AT HOME:

$10.28 billion (31 December 2017 est.)

$9.197 billion (31 December 2016 est.)

country comparison to the world: 96

STOCK OF DIRECT FOREIGN INVESTMENT - ABROAD:

$678.7 million (31 December 2017 est.)

$976.3 million (31 December 2016 est.)

country comparison to the world: 93

EXCHANGE RATES:

note: the US dollar is used as a medium of exchange and circulates freely in the economy

1 (2017 est.)

ENERGY :: EL SALVADOR

ELECTRICITY ACCESS:

population without electricity: 400,000 (2013)

electrification - total population: 94% (2013)

electrification - urban areas: 98% (2013)

electrification - rural areas: 86% (2013)

ELECTRICITY - PRODUCTION:

5.83 billion kWh (2016 est.)

country comparison to the world: 116

ELECTRICITY - CONSUMPTION:

5.928 billion kWh (2016 est.)

country comparison to the world: 116

ELECTRICITY - EXPORTS:

89.6 million kWh (2017 est.)

country comparison to the world: 82

ELECTRICITY - IMPORTS:

1.066 billion kWh (2016 est.)

country comparison to the world: 70

ELECTRICITY - INSTALLED GENERATING CAPACITY:

1.983 million kW (2016 est.)

country comparison to the world: 113

ELECTRICITY - FROM FOSSIL FUELS:

49% of total installed capacity (2016 est.)

country comparison to the world: 154

ELECTRICITY - FROM NUCLEAR FUELS:

0% of total installed capacity (2017 est.)

country comparison to the world: 83

ELECTRICITY - FROM HYDROELECTRIC PLANTS:

23% of total installed capacity (2017 est.)

country comparison to the world: 84

ELECTRICITY - FROM OTHER RENEWABLE SOURCES:

29% of total installed capacity (2017 est.)

country comparison to the world: 18

CRUDE OIL - PRODUCTION:

0 bbl/day (2017 est.)

country comparison to the world: 129

CRUDE OIL - EXPORTS:

0 bbl/day (2015 est.)

country comparison to the world: 117

CRUDE OIL - IMPORTS:

0 bbl/day (2015 est.)

country comparison to the world: 120

CRUDE OIL - PROVED RESERVES:

0 bbl (1 January 2018 est.)

country comparison to the world: 126

REFINED PETROLEUM PRODUCTS - PRODUCTION:

0 bbl/day (2015 est.)

country comparison to the world: 138

REFINED PETROLEUM PRODUCTS - CONSUMPTION:

52,000 bbl/day (2016 est.)

country comparison to the world: 103

REFINED PETROLEUM PRODUCTS - EXPORTS:

347 bbl/day (2015 est.)

country comparison to the world: 115

REFINED PETROLEUM PRODUCTS - IMPORTS:

49,280 bbl/day (2015 est.)

country comparison to the world: 82

NATURAL GAS - PRODUCTION:

0 cu m (2017 est.)

country comparison to the world: 126

NATURAL GAS - CONSUMPTION:

0 cu m (2017 est.)

country comparison to the world: 141

NATURAL GAS - EXPORTS:

0 cu m (2017 est.)

country comparison to the world: 98

NATURAL GAS - IMPORTS:

0 cu m (2017 est.)

country comparison to the world: 119

NATURAL GAS - PROVED RESERVES:

0 cu m (1 January 2017 est.)

country comparison to the world: 130

CARBON DIOXIDE EMISSIONS FROM CONSUMPTION OF ENERGY:

7.331 million Mt (2017 est.)

country comparison to the world: 124

COMMUNICATIONS :: EL SALVADOR

TELEPHONES - FIXED LINES:

total subscriptions: 677,599 (2017 est.)

subscriptions per 100 inhabitants: 11 (2017 est.)

country comparison to the world: 89

TELEPHONES - MOBILE CELLULAR:

total subscriptions: 9,982,186 (2017 est.)

subscriptions per 100 inhabitants: 162 (2017 est.)

country comparison to the world: 85

TELEPHONE SYSTEM:

general assessment: multiple mobile-cellular began rolling out Long Term Evolution (LTE) data services in late-2016; Internet usage grew almost 400% between 2007 and 2015; 6% of phones are fixed while 94% are mobile (2017)

domestic: nationwide microwave radio relay system; growth in fixed-line services 11 per 100, has slowed in the face of mobile-cellular competitionat at 162 per 100 (2017)

international: country code - 503; satellite earth station - 1 Intelsat (Atlantic Ocean); connected to Central American Microwave System (2017)

BROADCAST MEDIA:

multiple privately owned national terrestrial TV networks, supplemented by cable TV networks that carry international channels; hundreds of commercial radio broadcast stations and 1 government-owned radio broadcast station; transition to digital transmission to begin in 2018 along with adaptation of the Japanese-

Brazilian Digital Standard (ISDB-T) (2017)

INTERNET COUNTRY CODE:

.sv

INTERNET USERS:

total: 1,785,254 (July 2016 est.)

percent of population: 29% (July 2016 est.)

country comparison to the world: 118

BROADBAND - FIXED SUBSCRIPTIONS:

total: 442,727 (2017 est.)

subscriptions per 100 inhabitants: 7 (2017 est.)

country comparison to the world: 84

TRANSPORTATION :: EL SALVADOR

NATIONAL AIR TRANSPORT SYSTEM:

number of registered air carriers: 1 (2015)

inventory of registered aircraft operated by air carriers: 32 (2015)

annual passenger traffic on registered air carriers: 2,597,649 (2015)

annual freight traffic on registered air carriers: 13,873,884 mt-km (2015)

CIVIL AIRCRAFT REGISTRATION COUNTRY CODE PREFIX:

YS (2016)

AIRPORTS:

68 (2013)

country comparison to the world: 74

AIRPORTS - WITH PAVED RUNWAYS:

total: 5 (2017)

over 3,047 m: 1 (2017)

1,524 to 2,437 m: 1 (2017)

914 to 1,523 m: 2 (2017)

under 914 m: 1 (2017)

AIRPORTS - WITH UNPAVED RUNWAYS:

total: 63 (2013)

1,524 to 2,437 m: 1 (2013)

914 to 1,523 m: 11 (2013)

under 914 m: 51 (2013)

HELIPORTS:

2 (2013)

RAILWAYS:

total: 13 km (2014)

narrow gauge: 12.5 km 0.914-m gauge (2014)

country comparison to the world: 135

ROADWAYS:

total: 6,979 km (2016)

paved: 4,414 km (includes 341 km of expressways) (2016)

unpaved: 2,565 km (2016)

country comparison to the world: 146

WATERWAYS:

(Rio Lempa River is partially navigable by small craft) (2011)

MERCHANT MARINE:

total: 2 (2017)

by type: other 2 (2017)

country comparison to the world: 169

PORTS AND TERMINALS:

major seaport(s): Puerto Cutuco

oil terminal(s): Acajutla offshore terminal

MILITARY AND SECURITY :: EL SALVADOR

MILITARY EXPENDITURES:

0.87% of GDP (2016)

0.95% of GDP (2015)

0.93% of GDP (2014)

country comparison to the world: 127

MILITARY BRANCHES:

Salvadoran Armed Forces (Fuerza Armada de El Salvador, FAES): Salvadoran Army (Ejercito de El Salvador, ES), Salvadoran Navy (Fuerza Naval de El Salvador, FNES), Salvadoran Air Force (Fuerza Aerea Salvadorena, FAS) (2017)

MILITARY SERVICE AGE AND OBLIGATION:

18 years of age for selective compulsory military service; 16-22 years of age for voluntary male or female service; service obligation is 12 months, with 11 months for officers and NCOs (2012)

TRANSNATIONAL ISSUES :: EL SALVADOR

DISPUTES - INTERNATIONAL:

International Court of Justice (ICJ) ruled on the delimitation of "bolsones" (disputed areas) along the El Salvador-Honduras boundary, in 1992, with final agreement by the parties in 2006 after an Organization of American States survey and a further ICJ ruling in 2003the 1992 ICJ ruling advised a tripartite resolution to a maritime boundary in the Gulf of Fonseca advocating Honduran access to the PacificEl Salvador continues to claim tiny Conejo Island, not identified in the ICJ decision, off Honduras in the Gulf of Fonseca

REFUGEES AND INTERNALLY DISPLACED PERSONS:

IDPs: 71,500 (2017)

ILLICIT DRUGS:

transshipment point for cocaine; small amounts of marijuana produced for local consumption; significant use of cocaine

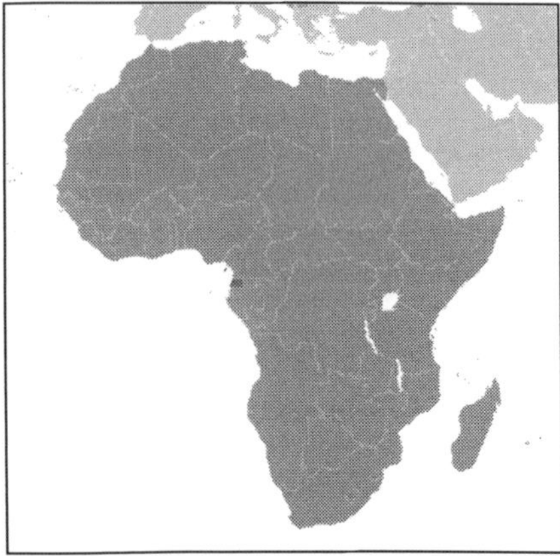

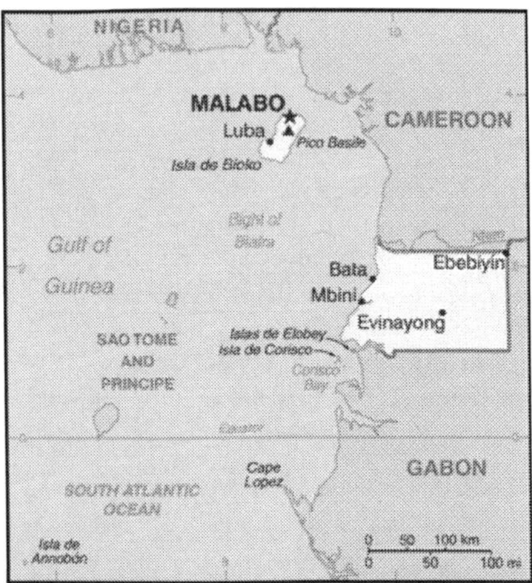

AFRICA :: EQUATORIAL GUINEA

INTRODUCTION :: EQUATORIAL GUINEA

BACKGROUND:

Equatorial Guinea gained independence in 1968 after 190 years of Spanish rule; it is one of the smallest countries in Africa consisting of a mainland territory and five inhabited islands. The capital of Malabo is located on the island of Bioko, approximately 25 km from the Cameroonian coastline in the Gulf of Guinea. Between 1968 and 1979, autocratic President Francisco MACIAS NGUEMA virtually destroyed all of the country's political, economic, and social institutions before being deposed by his nephew Teodoro OBIANG NGUEMA MBASOGO in a coup. President OBIANG has ruled since October 1979 and was reelected in 2016. Although nominally a constitutional democracy since 1991, presidential and legislative elections since 1996 have generally been labeled as flawed. The president exerts almost total control over the political system and has placed legal and bureaucratic barriers that prevent political opposition. Equatorial Guinea has experienced rapid economic growth due to the discovery of large offshore oil reserves, and in the last decade has become Sub-Saharan Africa's third largest oil exporter. Despite the country's economic windfall from oil production, resulting in a massive increase in government revenue in recent years, the drop in global oil prices has placed significant strain on the state budget. Equatorial Guinea continues to seek to diversify its economy and to increase foreign investment despite limited improvements in the population's living standards. Equatorial Guinea is the host of major regional and international conferences and continues to seek a greater role in regional affairs.

GEOGRAPHY :: EQUATORIAL GUINEA

LOCATION:

Central Africa, bordering the Bight of Biafra, between Cameroon and Gabon

GEOGRAPHIC COORDINATES:

2 00 N, 10 00 E

MAP REFERENCES:

Africa

AREA:

total: 28,051 sq km

land: 28,051 sq km

water: 0 sq km

country comparison to the world: 146

AREA - COMPARATIVE:

slightly smaller than Maryland

LAND BOUNDARIES:

total: 528 km

border countries (2): Cameroon 183 km, Gabon 345 km

COASTLINE:

296 km

MARITIME CLAIMS:

territorial sea: 12 nm

exclusive economic zone: 200 nm

CLIMATE:

tropical; always hot, humid

TERRAIN:

coastal plains rise to interior hills; islands are volcanic

ELEVATION:

mean elevation: 577 m

elevation extremes: 0 m lowest point: Atlantic Ocean

3008 highest point: Pico Basile

NATURAL RESOURCES:

petroleum, natural gas, timber, gold, bauxite, diamonds, tantalum, sand and gravel, clay

LAND USE:

agricultural land: 10.1% (2011 est.)

arable land: 4.3% (2011 est.) / permanent crops: 2.1% (2011 est.) / permanent pasture: 3.7% (2011 est.)

forest: 57.5% (2011 est.)

other: 32.4% (2011 est.)

IRRIGATED LAND:

NA

POPULATION DISTRIBUTION:

only two large cities over 30,000 people (Bata on the mainland, and the capital Malabo on the island of Bioko); small communities are scattered throughout the mainland and the five inhabited islands

NATURAL HAZARDS:

violent windstorms; flash floods

volcanism: Santa Isabel (3,007 m), which last erupted in 1923, is the country's only historically active volcano; Santa Isabel, along with two dormant volcanoes, form Bioko Island in the Gulf of Guinea

ENVIRONMENT - CURRENT ISSUES:

deforestation (forests are threatened by agricultural expansion, fires, and grazing); desertification; water pollution (tap water is non-potable); wildlife preservation

ENVIRONMENT - INTERNATIONAL AGREEMENTS:

party to: Biodiversity, Climate Change, Climate Change-Kyoto Protocol, Desertification, Endangered Species, Hazardous Wastes, Law of the Sea, Marine Dumping, Ozone Layer Protection, Ship Pollution, Wetlands

signed, but not ratified: none of the selected agreements

GEOGRAPHY - NOTE:

insular and continental regions widely separated; despite its name, no part of the Equator passes through Equatorial Guinea; the mainland part of the country is located just north of the Equator

PEOPLE AND SOCIETY :: EQUATORIAL GUINEA

POPULATION:

797,457 (July 2018 est.)

country comparison to the world: 164

NATIONALITY:

noun: Equatorial Guinean(s) or Equatoguinean(s)

adjective: Equatorial Guinean or Equatoguinean

ETHNIC GROUPS:

Fang 85.7%, Bubi 6.5%, Mdowe 3.6%, Annobon 1.6%, Bujeba 1.1%, other 1.4% (1994 census)

LANGUAGES:

Spanish (official) 67.6%, other (includes French (official), Fang, Bubi) 32.4% (1994 census)

RELIGIONS:

nominally Christian and predominantly Roman Catholic, pagan practices

DEMOGRAPHIC PROFILE:

Equatorial Guinea is one of the smallest and least populated countries in continental Africa and is the only independent African country where Spanish is an official language. Despite a boom in oil production in the 1990s, authoritarianism, corruption, and resource mismanagement have concentrated the benefits among a small elite. These practices have perpetuated income inequality and unbalanced development, such as low public spending on education and health care. Unemployment remains problematic because the oil-dominated economy employs a small labor force dependent on skilled foreign workers. The agricultural sector, Equatorial Guinea's main employer, continues to deteriorate because of a lack of investment and the migration of rural workers to urban areas. About three-quarters of the population lives below the poverty line.

Equatorial Guinea's large and growing youth population – about 60% are under the age of 25 – is particularly affected because job creation in the non-oil sectors is limited, and young people often do not have the skills needed in the labor market. Equatorial Guinean children frequently enter school late, have poor attendance, and have high dropout rates. Thousands of Equatorial Guineans fled across the border to Gabon in the 1970s to escape the dictatorship of MACIAS NGUEMA; smaller numbers have followed in the decades since. Continued inequitable economic growth and high youth unemployment increases the likelihood of ethnic and regional violence.

AGE STRUCTURE:

0-14 years: 39.46% (male 159,814 /female 154,860)

15-24 years: 19.8% (male 80,368 /female 77,515)

25-54 years: 32.34% (male 129,248 /female 128,664)

55-64 years: 4.46% (male 15,428 /female 20,176)

65 years and over: 3.94% (male 13,000 /female 18,384) (2018 est.)

DEPENDENCY RATIOS:

total dependency ratio: 67.5 (2015 est.)

youth dependency ratio: 62.7 (2015 est.)

elderly dependency ratio: 4.8 (2015 est.)

potential support ratio: 20.6 (2015 est.)

MEDIAN AGE:

total: 19.9 years

male: 19.5 years

female: 20.4 years (2018 est.)

country comparison to the world: 193

POPULATION GROWTH RATE:

2.41% (2018 est.)

country comparison to the world: 26

BIRTH RATE:

31.7 births/1,000 population (2018 est.)

country comparison to the world: 31

DEATH RATE:

7.6 deaths/1,000 population (2018 est.)

country comparison to the world: 102

NET MIGRATION RATE:

0 migrant(s)/1,000 population (2017 est.)

country comparison to the world: 81

POPULATION DISTRIBUTION:

only two large cities over 30,000 people (Bata on the mainland, and the capital Malabo on the island of Bioko); small communities are scattered throughout the mainland and the five inhabited islands

URBANIZATION:

urban population: 72.1% of total population (2018)

rate of urbanization: 4.28% annual rate of change (2015-20 est.)

MAJOR URBAN AREAS - POPULATION:

297,000 MALABO (capital) (2018)

SEX RATIO:

at birth: 1.03 male(s)/female (2017 est.)

0-14 years: 1.03 male(s)/female (2017 est.)

15-24 years: 1.04 male(s)/female (2017 est.)

25-54 years: 1 male(s)/female (2017 est.)

55-64 years: 0.76 male(s)/female (2017 est.)

65 years and over: 0.72 male(s)/female (2017 est.)

total population: 0.99 male(s)/female (2017 est.)

MATERNAL MORTALITY RATE:

342 deaths/100,000 live births (2015 est.)

country comparison to the world: 37

INFANT MORTALITY RATE:

total: 63.3 deaths/1,000 live births (2018 est.)

male: 64.4 deaths/1,000 live births (2018 est.)

female: 62.2 deaths/1,000 live births (2018 est.)

country comparison to the world: 12

LIFE EXPECTANCY AT BIRTH:

total population: 65 years (2018 est.)

male: 63.8 years (2018 est.)

female: 66.2 years (2018 est.)

country comparison to the world: 183

TOTAL FERTILITY RATE:

4.29 children born/woman (2018 est.)

country comparison to the world: 27

CONTRACEPTIVE PREVALENCE RATE:

12.6% (2011)

HEALTH EXPENDITURES:

3.8% of GDP (2014)

country comparison to the world: 165

HOSPITAL BED DENSITY:

2.1 beds/1,000 population (2010)

DRINKING WATER SOURCE:

improved:

urban: 72.5% of population

rural: 31.5% of population

total: 47.9% of population

unimproved:

urban: 27.5% of population

rural: 68.5% of population

total: 52.1% of population (2015 est.)

SANITATION FACILITY ACCESS:

improved:

urban: 79.9% of population (2015 est.)

rural: 71% of population (2015 est.)

total: 74.5% of population (2015 est.)

unimproved:

urban: 20.1% of population (2015 est.)

rural: 29% of population (2015 est.)

total: 25.5% of population (2015 est.)

HIV/AIDS - ADULT PREVALENCE RATE:

6.5% (2017 est.)

country comparison to the world: 10

HIV/AIDS - PEOPLE LIVING WITH HIV/AIDS:

53,000 (2017 est.)

country comparison to the world: 58

HIV/AIDS - DEATHS:

1,900 (2017 est.)

country comparison to the world: 52

MAJOR INFECTIOUS DISEASES:

degree of risk: very high (2016)

food or waterborne diseases: bacterial and protozoal diarrhea, hepatitis A, and typhoid fever (2016)

vectorborne diseases: malaria and dengue fever (2016)

animal contact diseases: rabies (2016)

OBESITY - ADULT PREVALENCE RATE:

8% (2016)

country comparison to the world: 156

CHILDREN UNDER THE AGE OF 5 YEARS UNDERWEIGHT:

5.6% (2010)

country comparison to the world: 79

LITERACY:

definition: age 15 and over can read and write (2015 est.)

total population: 95.3% (2015 est.)

male: 97.4% (2015 est.)

female: 93% (2015 est.)

GOVERNMENT :: EQUATORIAL GUINEA

COUNTRY NAME:

conventional long form: Republic of Equatorial Guinea

conventional short form: Equatorial Guinea

local long form: Republica de Guinea Ecuatorial/Republique de Guinee Equatoriale

local short form: Guinea Ecuatorial/Guinee Equatoriale

former: Spanish Guinea

etymology: the country is named for the Guinea region of West Africa that lies along the Gulf of Guinea and stretches north to the Sahel; the "equatorial" refers to the fact that the country lies just north of the Equator

GOVERNMENT TYPE:

presidential republic

CAPITAL:

name: Malabo; note - a new capital of Oyala is being built on the mainland near Djibloho; Malabo is on the island of Bioko

geographic coordinates: 3 45 N, 8 47 E

time difference: UTC+1 (6 hours ahead of Washington, DC, during Standard Time)

ADMINISTRATIVE DIVISIONS:

7 provinces (provincias, singular - provincia); Annobon, Bioko Norte, Bioko Sur, Centro Sur, Kie-Ntem, Litoral, Wele-Nzas

INDEPENDENCE:

12 October 1968 (from Spain)

NATIONAL HOLIDAY:

Independence Day, 12 October (1968)

CONSTITUTION:

history: previous 1968, 1973, 1982; approved by referendum 17 November 1991 (2017)

amendments: proposed by the president of the republic or supported by three-fourths of the membership in either house of the National Assembly; passage requires three-fourths majority vote by both houses of the Assembly and approval in a referendum if requested by the president; amended several times, last in 2012 (2017)

LEGAL SYSTEM:

mixed system of civil and customary law

INTERNATIONAL LAW ORGANIZATION PARTICIPATION:

accepts compulsory ICJ jurisdiction; accepts ICCt jurisdiction

CITIZENSHIP:

citizenship by birth: no

citizenship by descent only: at least one parent must be a citizen of Equatorial Guinea

dual citizenship recognized: no

residency requirement for naturalization: 10 years

SUFFRAGE:

18 years of age; universal

EXECUTIVE BRANCH:

chief of state: President Brig. Gen. (Ret.) Teodoro OBIANG Nguema Mbasogo (since 3 August 1979 when he seized power in a military coup); Vice President Teodoro OBIANG Nguema Mangue(since 2012)

head of government: Prime Minister Francisco Pascual Eyegue OBAMA Asue (since 23 June 2016); First Deputy Prime Minister Clemente Engonga NGUEMA Onguene (since 23 June 2016); Second Deputy Prime Minister Andres Jorge Mbomio Nsem ABUA (since 23 June 2016); Third Deputy Prime Minister Alfonso Nsue MOKUY (since 23 June 2016)

cabinet: Council of Ministers appointed by the president

elections/appointments: president directly elected by simple majority popular vote for a 7-year term (eligible for a second term); election last held on 24 April 2016 (next to be held in 2023); prime minister and deputy prime ministers appointed by the president

election results: Teodoro OBIANG Nguema Mbasogo reelected president; percent of vote - Teodoro OBIANG Nguema Mbasogo (PDGE) 93.5%, other 6.5%

LEGISLATIVE BRANCH:

description: bicameral National Assembly or Asemblea Nacional consists of:
Senate or Senado (70 seats; 55 members directly elected in multi-seat constituencies by closed party-list proportional representation vote and 15 appointed by the president)
Chamber of Deputies or Camara de los Diputados (100 seats; members directly elected in multi-seat constituencies by closed paryt-list proportional representation vote to serve 5-year terms)

elections:
Senate - last held on 12 November 2017 (next to be held in 2022)
Chamber of Deputies - last held on 12 November 2017 (next to be held in 2022)

election results:
Senate - percent of vote by party - NA; seats by party - PDGE 75
Chamber of Deputies - percent of vote by party - NA; seats by party - PDGE 99, CI 1

JUDICIAL BRANCH:

highest courts: Supreme Court of Justice (consists of the chief justice - who is also chief of state - and 9 judges and organized into civil, criminal, commercial, labor, administrative, and customary sections); Constitutional Court (consists of the court president and 4 members)

judge selection and term of office: Supreme Court judges appointed by the president for 5-year terms; Constitutional Court members appointed by the president, 2 of which are nominated by the Chamber of Deputies

subordinate courts: Court of Guarantees; military courts; Courts of Appeal; first instance tribunals; district and county tribunals

POLITICAL PARTIES AND LEADERS:

Convergence Party for Social Democracy or CPDS [Andres ESONO ONDO]
Democratic Party for Equatorial Guinea or PDGE [Teodoro OBIANG Nguema Mbasogo]
Electoral Coalition or EC
Front of Democratic Opposiiton or FOD (coalition includes CPDS, FDR, UP)
Popular Action of Equatorial Guinea or APGE [Carmelo MBA BACALE]
Popular Union or UP [Daniel MARTINEZ AYECABA]
not officially registered parties:
Democratic Republican Force or FDR [Guillermo NGUEMA ELA];
Citizens for Innovation or CI [Gabriel Nse Obiang OBONO];
Party for Progress of Equatorial Guinea or PPGE [Severo MOTO];
Union for the Center Right or UDC [Avelino MOCACHE MEAENGA]

INTERNATIONAL ORGANIZATION PARTICIPATION:

ACP, AfDB, AU, BDEAC, CEMAC, CPLP (associate), FAO, FZ, G-77, IBRD, ICAO, ICRM, IDA, IFAD, IFC, IFRCS, ILO, IMF, IMO, Interpol, IOC, IPU, ITSO, ITU, MIGA, NAM, OAS (observer), OIF, OPCW, UN, UNCTAD, UNESCO, UNIDO, UN Security Council (temporary), UNWTO, UPU, WHO, WIPO, WTO (observer)

DIPLOMATIC REPRESENTATION IN THE US:

chief of mission: Ambassador Miguel Ntutumu EVUNA ANDEME (since 23 February 2015)

chancery: 2020 16th Street NW, Washington, DC 20009

telephone: [1] (202) 518-5700

FAX: [1] (202) 518-5252

consulate(s) general: Houston

DIPLOMATIC REPRESENTATION FROM THE US:

chief of mission: Ambassador Julie FURUTA-TOY (since January 2016)

embassy: Carretera Malabo II, Malabo, Guinea Ecuatorial

mailing address: US Embassy Malabo, US Department of State, Washington, DC 20521-2520

telephone: [240] 333 09 57 41

FLAG DESCRIPTION:

three equal horizontal bands of green (top), white, and red, with a blue isosceles triangle based on the hoist side and the coat of arms centered in the white band; the coat of arms has six yellow six-pointed stars (representing the mainland and five offshore islands) above a gray shield bearing a silk-cotton tree and below which is a scroll with the motto UNIDAD, PAZ, JUSTICIA (Unity, Peace, Justice); green symbolizes the jungle and natural resources, blue represents the sea that connects the mainland to the islands, white stands for peace, and red recalls the fight for independence

NATIONAL SYMBOL(S):

silk cotton tree; national colors: green, white, red, blue

NATIONAL ANTHEM:

name: "Caminemos pisando la senda" (Let Us Tread the Path)

lyrics/music: Atanasio Ndongo MIYONO/Atanasio Ndongo MIYONO or Ramiro Sanchez LOPEZ (disputed)

note: adopted 1968

ECONOMY :: EQUATORIAL GUINEA

ECONOMY - OVERVIEW:

Exploitation of oil and gas deposits, beginning in the 1990s, has driven economic growth in Equatorial Guinea; a recent rebasing of GDP resulted in an upward revision of the size of the economy by approximately 30%. Forestry and farming are minor components of GDP. Although preindependence Equatorial Guinea counted on cocoa production for hard currency earnings, the neglect of the rural economy since independence has diminished the potential for agriculture-led growth. Subsistence farming is the dominant form of livelihood. Declining revenue from hydrocarbon production, high levels of infrastructure expenditures, lack of economic diversification, and corruption have pushed the economy into decline in recent years and limited improvements in the general population's living conditions. Equatorial Guinea's real GDP growth has been weak in recent years, averaging -0.5% per year from 2010 to 2014, because of a declining hydrocarbon sector. Inflation remained very low in 2016, down from an average of 4% in 2014.

As a middle income country, Equatorial Guinea is now ineligible for most low-income World Bank and the IMF funding. The government has been widely criticized for its lack of transparency and misuse of oil revenues and has attempted to address this issue by working toward compliance with the Extractive Industries Transparency Initiative. US foreign assistance to Equatorial Guinea is limited in part because of

US restrictions pursuant to the Trafficking Victims Protection Act.

Equatorial Guinea hosted two economic diversification symposia in 2014 that focused on attracting investment in five sectors: agriculture and animal ranching, fishing, mining and petrochemicals, tourism, and financial services. Undeveloped mineral resources include gold, zinc, diamonds, columbite-tantalite, and other base metals. In 2017 Equatorial Guinea signed a preliminary agreement with Ghana to sell liquefied natural gas (LNG); as oil production wanes, the government believes LNG could provide a boost to revenues, but it will require large investments and long lead times to develop.

GDP (PURCHASING POWER PARITY):

$31.52 billion (2017 est.)

$32.57 billion (2016 est.)

$35.62 billion (2015 est.)

note: data are in 2017 dollars

country comparison to the world: 130

GDP (OFFICIAL EXCHANGE RATE):

$12.49 billion (2017 est.) (2017 est.)

GDP - REAL GROWTH RATE:

-3.2% (2017 est.)

-8.6% (2016 est.)

-9.1% (2015 est.)

country comparison to the world: 213

GDP - PER CAPITA (PPP):

$37,400 (2017 est.)

$39,700 (2016 est.)

$44,600 (2015 est.)

note: data are in 2017 dollars

country comparison to the world: 52

GROSS NATIONAL SAVING:

6.1% of GDP (2017 est.)

3.6% of GDP (2016 est.)

8.5% of GDP (2015 est.)

country comparison to the world: 173

GDP - COMPOSITION, BY END USE:

household consumption: 50% (2017 est.)

government consumption: 21.8% (2017 est.)

investment in fixed capital: 10.2% (2017 est.)

investment in inventories: 0.1% (2017 est.)

exports of goods and services: 56.9% (2017 est.)

imports of goods and services: -39% (2017 est.)

GDP - COMPOSITION, BY SECTOR OF ORIGIN:

agriculture: 2.5% (2017 est.)

industry: 54.6% (2017 est.)

services: 42.9% (2017 est.)

AGRICULTURE - PRODUCTS:

coffee, cocoa, rice, yams, cassava (manioc, tapioca), bananas, palm oil nuts; livestock; timber

INDUSTRIES:

petroleum, natural gas, sawmilling

INDUSTRIAL PRODUCTION GROWTH RATE:

-6.9% (2017 est.)

country comparison to the world: 197

LABOR FORCE:

195,200 (2007 est.)

country comparison to the world: 175

UNEMPLOYMENT RATE:

8.6% (2014 est.)

22.3% (2009 est.)

country comparison to the world: 123

POPULATION BELOW POVERTY LINE:

44% (2011 est.)

HOUSEHOLD INCOME OR CONSUMPTION BY PERCENTAGE SHARE:

lowest 10%: NA

highest 10%: NA

BUDGET:

revenues: 2.114 billion (2017 est.)

expenditures: 2.523 billion (2017 est.)

TAXES AND OTHER REVENUES:

16.9% (of GDP) (2017 est.)

country comparison to the world: 173

BUDGET SURPLUS (+) OR DEFICIT (-):

-3.3% (of GDP) (2017 est.)

country comparison to the world: 141

PUBLIC DEBT:

37.4% of GDP (2017 est.)

43.3% of GDP (2016 est.)

country comparison to the world: 139

FISCAL YEAR:

calendar year

INFLATION RATE (CONSUMER PRICES):

0.7% (2017 est.)

1.4% (2016 est.)

country comparison to the world: 37

CENTRAL BANK DISCOUNT RATE:

8.5% (31 December 2010)

4.25% (31 December 2009)

country comparison to the world: 37

COMMERCIAL BANK PRIME LENDING RATE:

15% (31 December 2017 est.)

14% (31 December 2016 est.)

country comparison to the world: 39

STOCK OF NARROW MONEY:

$1.51 billion (31 December 2017 est.)

$1.467 billion (31 December 2016 est.)

country comparison to the world: 142

STOCK OF BROAD MONEY:

$1.51 billion (31 December 2017 est.)

$1.467 billion (31 December 2016 est.)

country comparison to the world: 150

STOCK OF DOMESTIC CREDIT:

$2.806 billion (31 December 2017 est.)

$2.254 billion (31 December 2016 est.)

country comparison to the world: 142

CURRENT ACCOUNT BALANCE:

-$738 million (2017 est.)

-$1.457 billion (2016 est.)

country comparison to the world: 132

EXPORTS:

$6.118 billion (2017 est.)

$5.042 billion (2016 est.)

country comparison to the world: 102

EXPORTS - PARTNERS:

China 28%, India 11.8%, South Korea 10.3%, Portugal 8.7%, US 6.9%, Spain 4.9% (2017)

EXPORTS - COMMODITIES:

petroleum products, timber

IMPORTS:

$2.577 billion (2017 est.)

$2.915 billion (2016 est.)

country comparison to the world: 156

IMPORTS - COMMODITIES:

petroleum sector equipment, other equipment, construction materials, vehicles

IMPORTS - PARTNERS:

Spain 20.5%, China 19.4%, US 13%, Cote dIvoire 6.2%, Netherlands 4.7% (2017)

RESERVES OF FOREIGN EXCHANGE AND GOLD:

$45.5 million (31 December 2017 est.)

$62.31 million (31 December 2016 est.)

country comparison to the world: 188

DEBT - EXTERNAL:

$1.211 billion (31 December 2017 est.)

$1.074 billion (31 December 2016 est.)

country comparison to the world: 163

STOCK OF DIRECT FOREIGN INVESTMENT - AT HOME:

(31 December 2009 est.)

EXCHANGE RATES:

Cooperation Financiere en Afrique Centrale francs (XAF) per US dollar -

605.3 (2017 est.)

593.01 (2016 est.)

593.01 (2015 est.)

591.45 (2014 est.)

494.42 (2013 est.)

ENERGY :: EQUATORIAL GUINEA

ELECTRICITY ACCESS:

population without electricity: 300,000 (2013)

electrification - total population: 66% (2013)

electrification - urban areas: 93% (2013)

electrification - rural areas: 48% (2013)

ELECTRICITY - PRODUCTION:

500 million kWh (2016 est.)

country comparison to the world: 166

ELECTRICITY - CONSUMPTION:

465 million kWh (2016 est.)

country comparison to the world: 171

ELECTRICITY - EXPORTS:

0 kWh (2016 est.)

country comparison to the world: 130

ELECTRICITY - IMPORTS:

0 kWh (2016 est.)

country comparison to the world: 144

ELECTRICITY - INSTALLED GENERATING CAPACITY:

331,000 kW (2016 est.)

country comparison to the world: 156

ELECTRICITY - FROM FOSSIL FUELS:

61% of total installed capacity (2016 est.)

country comparison to the world: 127

ELECTRICITY - FROM NUCLEAR FUELS:

0% of total installed capacity (2017 est.)

country comparison to the world: 84

ELECTRICITY - FROM HYDROELECTRIC PLANTS:

38% of total installed capacity (2017 est.)

country comparison to the world: 54

ELECTRICITY - FROM OTHER RENEWABLE SOURCES:

2% of total installed capacity (2017 est.)

country comparison to the world: 140

CRUDE OIL - PRODUCTION:

188,300 bbl/day (2017 est.)

country comparison to the world: 37

CRUDE OIL - EXPORTS:

308,700 bbl/day (2017 est.)

country comparison to the world: 26

CRUDE OIL - IMPORTS:

0 bbl/day (2015 est.)

country comparison to the world: 121

CRUDE OIL - PROVED RESERVES:

1.1 billion bbl (1 January 2018 est.)

country comparison to the world: 40

REFINED PETROLEUM PRODUCTS - PRODUCTION:

0 bbl/day (2015 est.)

country comparison to the world: 139

REFINED PETROLEUM PRODUCTS - CONSUMPTION:

5,200 bbl/day (2016 est.)

country comparison to the world: 176

REFINED PETROLEUM PRODUCTS - EXPORTS:

0 bbl/day (2015 est.)

country comparison to the world: 150

REFINED PETROLEUM PRODUCTS - IMPORTS:

5,094 bbl/day (2015 est.)

country comparison to the world: 171

NATURAL GAS - PRODUCTION:

6.069 billion cu m (2017 est.)

country comparison to the world: 46

NATURAL GAS - CONSUMPTION:

1.189 billion cu m (2017 est.)

country comparison to the world: 91

NATURAL GAS - EXPORTS:

4.878 billion cu m (2017 est.)

country comparison to the world: 30

NATURAL GAS - IMPORTS:

0 cu m (2017 est.)

country comparison to the world: 120

NATURAL GAS - PROVED RESERVES:

36.81 billion cu m (1 January 2018 est.)

country comparison to the world: 66

CARBON DIOXIDE EMISSIONS FROM CONSUMPTION OF ENERGY:

3.062 million Mt (2017 est.)

country comparison to the world: 148

COMMUNICATIONS :: EQUATORIAL GUINEA

TELEPHONES - FIXED LINES:

total subscriptions: 10,989 (July 2016 est.)

subscriptions per 100 inhabitants: 1 (July 2016 est.)

country comparison to the world: 193

TELEPHONES - MOBILE CELLULAR:

total subscriptions: 575,650 (July 2016 est.)

subscriptions per 100 inhabitants: 74 (July 2016 est.)

country comparison to the world: 167

TELEPHONE SYSTEM:

general assessment: digital fixed-line network in most major urban areas and decent mobile cellular coverage; 3G technology has allowed for estimated growth of 9.5% during 2016 -2021; mobile data will be the fastest-growing segment 2016-2021 (2017)

domestic: fixed-line density is about 1 per 100 persons; mobile-cellular subscribership has been increasing and in 2016 stood at about 70 percent (2017)

international: country code - 240; international communications from Bata and Malabo to African and European countries; satellite earth station 1 Intelsat (Indian Ocean) (2016)

BROADCAST MEDIA:

state maintains control of broadcast media with domestic broadcast media limited to 1 state-owned TV station, 1 private TV station owned by the president's eldest son, 1 state-owned radio station, and 1 private radio station owned by the president's eldest son; satellite TV service is available; transmissions of multiple international broadcasters are accessible (2013)

INTERNET COUNTRY CODE:

.gq

INTERNET USERS:

total: 180,597 (July 2016 est.)

percent of population: 23.8% (July 2016 est.)

country comparison to the world: 172

BROADBAND - FIXED SUBSCRIPTIONS:

total: 3,382 (2017 est.)

subscriptions per 100 inhabitants: less than 1 (2017 est.)

country comparison to the world: 181

TRANSPORTATION :: EQUATORIAL GUINEA

NATIONAL AIR TRANSPORT SYSTEM:

number of registered air carriers: 6 (2015)

inventory of registered aircraft operated by air carriers: 15 (2015)

annual passenger traffic on registered air carriers: 400,759 (2015)

annual freight traffic on registered air carriers: 461,650 mt-km (2015)

CIVIL AIRCRAFT REGISTRATION COUNTRY CODE PREFIX:

3C (2016)

AIRPORTS:

7 (2013)

country comparison to the world: 166

AIRPORTS - WITH PAVED RUNWAYS:

total: 6 (2017)

over 3,047 m: 1 (2017)

2,438 to 3,047 m: 2 (2017)

1,524 to 2,437 m: 1 (2017)

under 914 m: 2 (2017)

AIRPORTS - WITH UNPAVED RUNWAYS:

total: 1 (2013)

2,438 to 3,047 m: 1 (2013)

PIPELINES:

42 km condensate, 5 km condensate/gas, 79 km gas, 71 km oil (2013)

ROADWAYS:

total: 2,880 km (2000)

country comparison to the world: 168

MERCHANT MARINE:

total: 40 (2017)

by type: container ship 1, general cargo 7, oil tanker 8, other 24 (2017)

country comparison to the world: 123

PORTS AND TERMINALS:

major seaport(s): Bata, Luba, Malabo

LNG terminal(s) (export): Bioko Island

MILITARY AND SECURITY :: EQUATORIAL GUINEA

MILITARY EXPENDITURES:

0.18% of GDP (2016)

0.78% of GDP (2014)

country comparison to the world: 153

MILITARY BRANCHES:

Equatorial Guinea Armed Forces (FAGE): Equatorial Guinea National Guard (Guardia Nacional de Guinea Ecuatorial, GNGE (Army), Navy, Air Force (2013)

MILITARY SERVICE AGE AND OBLIGATION:

18 years of age for selective compulsory military service, although conscription is rare in practice; 2-year service obligation; women hold only administrative positions in the Navy (2013)

TRANSNATIONAL ISSUES :: EQUATORIAL GUINEA

DISPUTES - INTERNATIONAL:

in 2002, ICJ ruled on an equidistance settlement of Cameroon-Equatorial Guinea-Nigeria maritime boundary in the Gulf of Guinea, but a dispute between Equatorial Guinea and Cameroon over an island at the mouth of the Ntem River and imprecisely defined maritime coordinates in the ICJ decision delayed final delimitationUN urged Equatorial Guinea and Gabon to resolve the sovereignty dispute over Gabon-occupied Mbane and lesser islands and to create a maritime boundary in the hydrocarbon-rich Corisco Bay

TRAFFICKING IN PERSONS:

current situation: Equatorial Guinea is a source country for children subjected to sex trafficking and destination country for men, women, and children subjected to forced labor; Equatorial Guinean girls may be encouraged by their parents to engage in the sex trade in urban centers to receive groceries, gifts, housing, and money; children are also trafficked from nearby countries for work as domestic servants, market laborers, ambulant vendors, and launderers; women are trafficked to Equatorial Guinea from Cameroon, Benin, other neighboring countries, and China for forced labor or prostitution

tier rating: Tier 3 – Equatorial Guinea does not fully comply with the minimum standards on the elimination of trafficking and is not making significant efforts to do so; in 2014, the government made no efforts to investigate or prosecute any suspected trafficking offenders or to identify or protect victims, despite its 2004 law prohibiting all forms of trafficking and mandating the provision of services to victims; undocumented migrants continued to be deported without being screened to assess whether any were trafficking victims; authorities did not undertake any trafficking awareness campaigns, implement any programs to address forced child labor, or make any other efforts to prevent trafficking (2015)

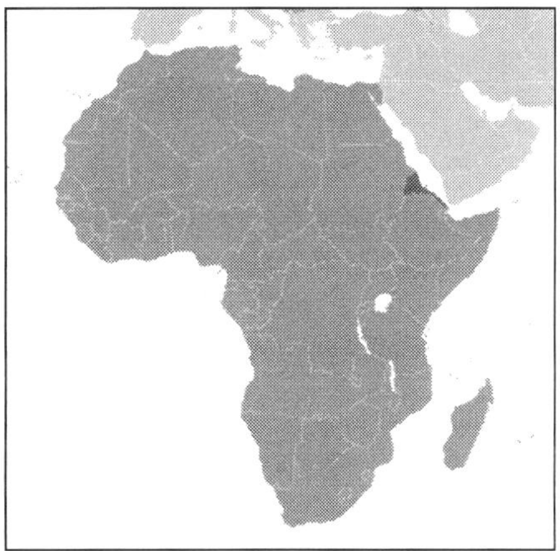

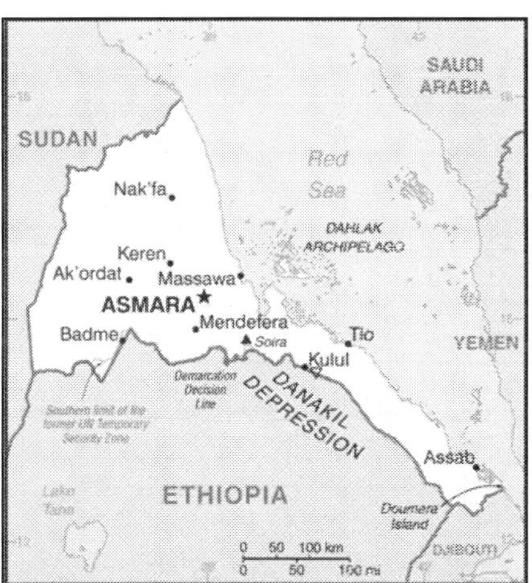

AFRICA :: ERITREA

INTRODUCTION :: ERITREA

BACKGROUND:

After independence from Italian colonial control in 1941 and 10 years of British administrative control, the UN established Eritrea as an autonomous region within the Ethiopian federation in 1952. Ethiopia's full annexation of Eritrea as a province 10 years later sparked a violent 30-year struggle for independence that ended in 1991 with Eritrean rebels defeating government forces. Eritreans overwhelmingly approved independence in a 1993 referendum. ISAIAS Afworki has been Eritrea's only president since independence; his rule, particularly since 2001, has been highly autocratic and repressive. His government has created a highly militarized society by pursuing an unpopular program of mandatory conscription into national service, sometimes of indefinite length. A two-and-a-half-year border war with Ethiopia that erupted in 1998 ended under UN auspices in December 2000. A UN peacekeeping operation was established that monitored a 25 km-wide Temporary Security Zone. The Eritrea-Ethiopia Boundary Commission (EEBC) created in April 2003 was tasked "to delimit and demarcate the colonial treaty border based on pertinent colonial treaties (1900, 1902, and 1908) and applicable international law." The EEBC on 30 November 2007 remotely demarcated the border, assigning the town of Badme to Eritrea, despite Ethiopia's maintaining forces there from the time of the 1998-2000 war. Eritrea insisted that the UN terminate its peacekeeping mission on 31 July 2008. Eritrea has accepted the EEBC's "virtual demarcation" decision and repeatedly called on Ethiopia to remove its troops. Ethiopia has not accepted the demarcation decision, and neither party has entered into meaningful dialogue to resolve the impasse. Eritrea is subject to several UN Security Council Resolutions (initially in 2009 and renewed annually) imposing an arms embargo and a travel ban and assets freeze on certain individuals, in view of evidence that it has supported armed opposition groups in the region.

GEOGRAPHY :: ERITREA

LOCATION:

Eastern Africa, bordering the Red Sea, between Djibouti and Sudan

GEOGRAPHIC COORDINATES:

15 00 N, 39 00 E

MAP REFERENCES:

Africa

AREA:

total: 117,600 sq km

land: 101,000 sq km

water: 16,600 sq km

country comparison to the world: 102

AREA - COMPARATIVE:

slightly larger than Pennsylvania

LAND BOUNDARIES:

total: 1,840 km

border countries (3): Djibouti 125 km, Ethiopia 1033 km, Sudan 682 km

COASTLINE:

2,234 km (mainland on Red Sea 1,151 km, islands in Red Sea 1,083 km)

MARITIME CLAIMS:

territorial sea: 12 nm

CLIMATE:

hot, dry desert strip along Red Sea coast; cooler and wetter in the central highlands (up to 61 cm of rainfall annually, heaviest June to September); semiarid in western hills and lowlands

TERRAIN:

dominated by extension of Ethiopian north-south trending highlands, descending on the east to a coastal desert plain, on the northwest to hilly terrain and on the southwest to flat-to-rolling plains

ELEVATION:

mean elevation: 853 m

elevation extremes: -75 m lowest point: near Kulul within the Danakil Depression

3018 highest point: Soira

NATURAL RESOURCES:

gold, potash, zinc, copper, salt, possibly oil and natural gas, fish

LAND USE:

agricultural land: 75.1% (2011 est.)

arable land: 6.8% (2011 est.) / permanent crops: 0% (2011 est.) / permanent pasture: 68.3% (2011 est.)

forest: 15.1% (2011 est.)

other: 9.8% (2011 est.)

IRRIGATED LAND:

210 sq km (2012)

POPULATION DISTRIBUTION:

density is highest in the center of the country in and around the cities of Asmara (capital) and Keren; smaller settlements exist in the north and south

NATURAL HAZARDS:

frequent droughts, rare earthquakes and volcanoes; locust swarms

volcanism: Dubbi (1,625 m), which last erupted in 1861, was the country's only historically active volcano until Nabro (2,218 m) came to life on 12 June 2011

ENVIRONMENT - CURRENT ISSUES:

deforestation; desertification; soil erosion; overgrazing

ENVIRONMENT - INTERNATIONAL AGREEMENTS:

party to: Biodiversity, Climate Change, Climate Change-Kyoto Protocol, Desertification, Endangered Species, Hazardous Wastes, Ozone Layer Protection

signed, but not ratified: none of the selected agreements

GEOGRAPHY - NOTE:

strategic geopolitical position along world's busiest shipping lanes; Eritrea retained the entire coastline of Ethiopia along the Red Sea upon de jure independence from Ethiopia on 24 May 1993

PEOPLE AND SOCIETY :: ERITREA

POPULATION:

5,970,646 (July 2018 est.)

country comparison to the world: 113

NATIONALITY:

noun: Eritrean(s)

adjective: Eritrean

ETHNIC GROUPS:

Tigrinya 55%, Tigre 30%, Saho 4%, Kunama 2%, Rashaida 2%, Bilen 2%, other (Afar, Beni Amir, Nera) 5% (2010 est.)

note: data represent Eritrea's nine recognized ethnic groups

LANGUAGES:

Tigrinya (official), Arabic (official), English (official), Tigre, Kunama, Afar, other Cushitic languages

RELIGIONS:

Muslim, Coptic Christian, Roman Catholic, Protestant

DEMOGRAPHIC PROFILE:

Eritrea is a persistently poor country that has made progress in some socioeconomic categories but not in others. Education and human capital formation are national priorities for facilitating economic development and eradicating poverty. To this end, Eritrea has made great strides in improving adult literacy – doubling the literacy rate over the last 20 years – in large part because of its successful adult education programs. The overall literacy rate was estimated to be almost 74% in 2015; more work needs to be done to raise female literacy and school attendance among nomadic and rural communities. Subsistence farming fails to meet the needs of Eritrea's growing population because of repeated droughts, dwindling arable land, overgrazing, soil erosion, and a shortage of farmers due to conscription and displacement. The government's emphasis on spending on defense over agriculture and its lack of foreign exchange to import food also contribute to food insecurity.

Eritrea has been a leading refugee source country since at least the 1960s, when its 30-year war for independence from Ethiopia began. Since gaining independence in 1993, Eritreans have continued migrating to Sudan, Ethiopia, Yemen, Egypt, or Israel because of a lack of basic human rights or political freedom, educational and job opportunities, or to seek asylum because of militarization. Eritrea's large diaspora has been a source of vital remittances, funding its war for independence and providing 30% of the country's GDP annually since it became independent.

In the last few years, Eritreans have increasingly been trafficked and held hostage by Bedouins in the Sinai Desert, where they are victims of organ harvesting, rape, extortion, and torture. Some Eritrean trafficking victims are kidnapped after being smuggled to Sudan or Ethiopia, while others are kidnapped from within or around refugee camps or crossing Eritrea's borders. Eritreans composed approximately 90% of the conservatively estimated 25,000-30,000 victims of Sinai trafficking from 2009-2013, according to a 2013 consultancy firm report.

AGE STRUCTURE:

0-14 years: 39.53% (male 1,186,749 /female 1,173,530)

15-24 years: 19.94% (male 592,365 /female 598,305)

25-54 years: 32.88% (male 965,405 /female 997,771)

55-64 years: 3.7% (male 96,967 /female 123,895)

65 years and over: 3.95% (male 97,816 /female 137,843) (2018 est.)

DEPENDENCY RATIOS:

total dependency ratio: 85 (2015 est.)

youth dependency ratio: 78.3 (2015 est.)

elderly dependency ratio: 6.8 (2015 est.)

potential support ratio: 14.8 (2015 est.)

MEDIAN AGE:

total: 19.9 years

male: 19.4 years

female: 20.4 years (2018 est.)

country comparison to the world: 194

POPULATION GROWTH RATE:

0.89% (2018 est.)

country comparison to the world: 123

BIRTH RATE:

29.1 births/1,000 population (2018 est.)

country comparison to the world: 40

DEATH RATE:

7.1 deaths/1,000 population (2018 est.)

country comparison to the world: 126

NET MIGRATION RATE:

-13.9 migrant(s)/1,000 population (2017 est.)

country comparison to the world: 215

POPULATION DISTRIBUTION:

density is highest in the center of the country in and around the cities of Asmara (capital) and Keren; smaller settlements exist in the north and south

URBANIZATION:

urban population: 40.1% of total population (2018)

rate of urbanization: 3.86% annual rate of change (2015-20 est.)

MAJOR URBAN AREAS - POPULATION:

896,000 ASMARA (capital) (2018)

SEX RATIO:

at birth: 1.02 male(s)/female (2017 est.)

0-14 years: 1.01 male(s)/female (2017 est.)

15-24 years: 0.99 male(s)/female (2017 est.)

25-54 years: 0.97 male(s)/female (2017 est.)

55-64 years: 0.74 male(s)/female (2017 est.)

65 years and over: 0.75 male(s)/female (2017 est.)

total population: 0.97 male(s)/female (2017 est.)

MOTHER'S MEAN AGE AT FIRST BIRTH:

21.3 years (2010 est.)

note: median age at first birth among women 25-29

MATERNAL MORTALITY RATE:

501 deaths/100,000 live births (2015 est.)

country comparison to the world: 20

INFANT MORTALITY RATE:

total: 44.4 deaths/1,000 live births (2018 est.)

male: 51.4 deaths/1,000 live births (2018 est.)

female: 37.3 deaths/1,000 live births (2018 est.)

country comparison to the world: 38

LIFE EXPECTANCY AT BIRTH:

total population: 65.6 years (2018 est.)

male: 63 years (2018 est.)

female: 68.2 years (2018 est.)

country comparison to the world: 180

TOTAL FERTILITY RATE:

3.9 children born/woman (2018 est.)

country comparison to the world: 37

CONTRACEPTIVE PREVALENCE RATE:

8.4% (2010)

HEALTH EXPENDITURES:

3.3% of GDP (2014)

country comparison to the world: 178

HOSPITAL BED DENSITY:

0.7 beds/1,000 population (2011)

DRINKING WATER SOURCE:

improved:

urban: 73.2% of population

rural: 53.3% of population

total: 57.8% of population

unimproved:

urban: 26.8% of population

rural: 46.7% of population

total: 42.2% of population (2015 est.)

SANITATION FACILITY ACCESS:

improved:

urban: 44.5% of population (2015 est.)

rural: 7.3% of population (2015 est.)

total: 15.7% of population (2015 est.)

unimproved:

urban: 55.5% of population (2015 est.)

rural: 92.7% of population (2015 est.)

total: 84.3% of population (2015 est.)

HIV/AIDS - ADULT PREVALENCE RATE:

0.6% (2017 est.)

country comparison to the world: 59

HIV/AIDS - PEOPLE LIVING WITH HIV/AIDS:

14,000 (2017 est.)

country comparison to the world: 90

HIV/AIDS - DEATHS:

<500 (2017 est.)

MAJOR INFECTIOUS DISEASES:

degree of risk: high (2016)

food or waterborne diseases: bacterial diarrhea, hepatitis A, and typhoid fever (2016)

vectorborne diseases: malaria and dengue fever (2016)

OBESITY - ADULT PREVALENCE RATE:

5% (2016)

country comparison to the world: 183

CHILDREN UNDER THE AGE OF 5 YEARS UNDERWEIGHT:

38.8% (2010)

country comparison to the world: 1

LITERACY:

definition: age 15 and over can read and write (2015 est.)

total population: 73.8% (2015 est.)

male: 82.4% (2015 est.)

female: 65.5% (2015 est.)

SCHOOL LIFE EXPECTANCY (PRIMARY TO TERTIARY EDUCATION):

total: 5 years (2014)

male: 6 years (2014)

female: 5 years (2014)

GOVERNMENT :: ERITREA

COUNTRY NAME:

conventional long form: State of Eritrea

conventional short form: Eritrea

local long form: Hagere Ertra

local short form: Ertra

former: Eritrea Autonomous Region in Ethiopia

etymology: the country name derives from the ancient Greek appellation "Erythra Thalassa" meaning Red Sea, which is the major water body bordering the country

GOVERNMENT TYPE:

presidential republic

CAPITAL:

name: Asmara (Asmera)

geographic coordinates: 15 20 N, 38 56 E

time difference: UTC+3 (8 hours ahead of Washington, DC, during Standard Time)

ADMINISTRATIVE DIVISIONS:

6 regions (zobatat, singular - zoba); Anseba, Debub (South), Debubawi K'eyih Bahri (Southern Red Sea), Gash Barka, Ma'akel (Central), Semenawi Keyih Bahri (Northern Red Sea)

INDEPENDENCE:

24 May 1993 (from Ethiopia)

NATIONAL HOLIDAY:

Independence Day, 24 May (1991)

CONSTITUTION:

history: ratified by the Constituent Assembly 23 May 1997 (not fully implemented); note - drafting of a new constitution, which began in 2014, but interrupted by the war, is expected to resume in 2019 (2018)

amendments: proposed by the president of Eritrea or by assent of at least one-half of the National Assembly membership; passage requires at least an initial three-quarters majority vote by the Assembly and, after one year, final passage by at least four-fifths majority vote by the Assembly (2018)

LEGAL SYSTEM:

mixed legal system of civil, customary, and Islamic religious law

INTERNATIONAL LAW ORGANIZATION PARTICIPATION:

has not submitted an ICJ jurisdiction declaration; non-party state to the ICCt

CITIZENSHIP:

citizenship by birth: no

citizenship by descent only: at least one parent must be a citizen of Eritrea

dual citizenship recognized: no

residency requirement for naturalization: 20 years

SUFFRAGE:

18 years of age; universal

EXECUTIVE BRANCH:

chief of state: President ISAIAS Afworki (since 8 June 1993); note - the president is both chief of state and head of government and is head of the State Council and National Assembly

head of government: President ISAIAS Afworki (since 8 June 1993)

cabinet: State Council appointed by the president

elections/appointments: president indirectly elected by the National Assembly for a 5-year term (eligible for a second term); the only election was held on 8 June 1993, following independence from Ethiopia (next election postponed indefinitely)

election results: ISAIAS Afworki elected president by the transitional National Assembly; percent of National Assembly vote - ISAIAS Afworki (PFDJ) 95%, other 5%

LEGISLATIVE BRANCH:

description: unicameral National Assembly (Hagerawi Baito) (150 seats; 75 members indirectly elected by the ruling party and 75 directly elected by simple majority vote; members serve 5-year terms)

elections: in May 1997, following the adoption of the new constitution, 75 members of the PFDJ Central Committee (the old Central Committee of the EPLF), 60 members of the 527-member Constituent Assembly, which had been established in 1997 to discuss and ratify the new constitution, and 15 representatives of Eritreans living abroad were formed into a Transitional National Assembly to serve as the country's legislative body until countrywide elections to form a National Assembly were held; although only 75 of 150 members of the Transitional National Assembly were elected, the constitution stipulates that once past the transition stage, all members of the National Assembly will be elected by secret ballot of all eligible voters; National Assembly elections scheduled for December 2001 were postponed indefinitely due to the war with Ethiopia

JUDICIAL BRANCH:

highest courts: High Court (consists of 20 judges and organized into civil, commercial, criminal, labor, administrative, and customary sections)

judge selection and term of office: High Court judges appointed by the president

subordinate courts: regional/zonal courts; community courts; special courts; sharia courts (for issues dealing with Muslim marriage, inheritance, and family); military courts

POLITICAL PARTIES AND LEADERS:

People's Front for Democracy and Justice or PFDJ [ISAIAS Afworki] (the only party recognized by the government)

INTERNATIONAL ORGANIZATION PARTICIPATION:

ACP, AfDB, AU, COMESA, FAO, G-77, IAEA, IBRD, ICAO, ICC (NGOs), IDA, IFAD, IFC, IFRCS (observer), ILO, IMF, IMO, Interpol, IOC, ISO (correspondent), ITU, ITUC (NGOs), LAS (observer), MIGA, NAM, OPCW, PCA, UN, UNCTAD, UNESCO, UNIDO, UNWTO, UPU, WCO, WFTU (NGOs), WHO, WIPO, WMO

DIPLOMATIC REPRESENTATION IN THE US:

chief of mission: Ambassador (vacant); Charge d'Affaires BERHANE Gebrehiwet Solomon (since 15 March 2011)

chancery: 1708 New Hampshire Avenue NW, Washington, DC 20009

telephone: [1] (202) 319-1991

FAX: [1] (202) 319-1304

DIPLOMATIC REPRESENTATION FROM THE US:

chief of mission: Ambassador (vacant); Charge d'Affaires Natalie E. BROWN (since September 2016)

embassy: 179 Ala Street, Asmara

mailing address: P.O. Box 211, Asmara

telephone: [291] (1) 120004

FAX: [291] (1) 127584

FLAG DESCRIPTION:

red isosceles triangle (based on the hoist side) dividing the flag into two right triangles; the upper triangle is green, the lower one is blue; a gold wreath encircling a gold olive branch is centered on the hoist side of the red triangle; green stands for the country's agriculture economy, red signifies the blood shed in the fight for freedom, and blue symbolizes the bounty of the sea; the wreath-olive branch symbol is similar to that on the first flag of Eritrea from 1952; the shape of the red triangle broadly mimics the shape of the country

note: one of several flags where a prominent component of the design reflects the shape of the country; other such flags are those of Bosnia and Herzegovina, Brazil, and Vanuatu

NATIONAL SYMBOL(S):

camel; national colors: green, red, blue

NATIONAL ANTHEM:

name: "Ertra, Ertra, Ertra" (Eritrea, Eritrea, Eritrea)

lyrics/music: SOLOMON Tsehaye Beraki/Isaac Abraham MEHAREZGI and ARON Tekle Tesfatsion

note: adopted 1993; upon independence from Ethiopia

ECONOMY :: ERITREA

ECONOMY - OVERVIEW:

Since formal independence from Ethiopia in 1993, Eritrea has faced many economic problems, including lack of financial resources and chronic drought. Eritrea has a command economy under the control of the sole political party, the People's Front for Democracy and Justice. Like the economies of many African nations, a large share of the population - nearly 80% in Eritrea - is engaged in subsistence agriculture, but the sector only produces a small share of the country's total output. Mining accounts for the lion's share of output.

The government has strictly controlled the use of foreign currency by limiting access and availability; new regulations in 2013 aimed at relaxing currency controls have had little economic effect. Few large private enterprises exist in Eritrea and most operate in conjunction with government partners, including a number of large international mining ventures, which began production in 2013. In late 2015, the Government of Eritrea introduced a new currency, retaining the name nakfa, and restricted the amount of hard currency individuals could withdraw from banks per month. The changeover has resulted in exchange fluctuations and the scarcity of hard currency available in the market.

While reliable statistics on Eritrea are difficult to obtain, erratic rainfall and the large percentage of the labor force tied up in military service continue to interfere with agricultural production and economic development. Eritrea's harvests generally cannot meet the food needs of the country without supplemental grain purchases. Copper, potash, and gold production are likely to continue to drive limited economic growth and government revenue over the next few years, but military spending will continue to compete with development and investment plans.

GDP (PURCHASING POWER PARITY):

$9.402 billion (2017 est.)

$8.953 billion (2016 est.)

$8.791 billion (2015 est.)

note: data are in 2017 dollars

country comparison to the world: 161

GDP (OFFICIAL EXCHANGE RATE):

$5.813 billion (2017 est.) (2017 est.)

GDP - REAL GROWTH RATE:

5% (2017 est.)

1.9% (2016 est.)

2.6% (2015 est.)

country comparison to the world: 49

GDP - PER CAPITA (PPP):

$1,600 (2017 est.)

$1,500 (2016 est.)

$1,500 (2015 est.)

note: data are in 2017 dollars

country comparison to the world: 217

GROSS NATIONAL SAVING:

5.5% of GDP (2017 est.)

6% of GDP (2016 est.)

6.8% of GDP (2015 est.)

country comparison to the world: 174

GDP - COMPOSITION, BY END USE:

household consumption: 80.9% (2017 est.)

government consumption: 24.3% (2017 est.)

investment in fixed capital: 6.4% (2017 est.)

investment in inventories: 0.1% (2017 est.)

exports of goods and services: 10.9% (2017 est.)

imports of goods and services: -22.5% (2017 est.)

GDP - COMPOSITION, BY SECTOR OF ORIGIN:

agriculture: 11.7% (2017 est.)

industry: 29.6% (2017 est.)

services: 58.7% (2017 est.)

AGRICULTURE - PRODUCTS:

sorghum, lentils, vegetables, corn, cotton, tobacco, sisal; livestock, goats; fish

INDUSTRIES:

food processing, beverages, clothing and textiles, light manufacturing, salt, cement

INDUSTRIAL PRODUCTION GROWTH RATE:

5.4% (2017 est.)

country comparison to the world: 52

LABOR FORCE:

2.71 million (2017 est.)

country comparison to the world: 111

LABOR FORCE - BY OCCUPATION:

agriculture: 80%

industry: 20% (2004 est.)

UNEMPLOYMENT RATE:

5.8% (2017 est.)

10% (2016 est.)

country comparison to the world: 87

POPULATION BELOW POVERTY LINE:

50% (2004 est.)

HOUSEHOLD INCOME OR CONSUMPTION BY PERCENTAGE SHARE:

lowest 10%: NA

highest 10%: NA

BUDGET:

revenues: 2.029 billion (2017 est.)

expenditures: 2.601 billion (2017 est.)

TAXES AND OTHER REVENUES:

34.9% (of GDP) (2017 est.)

country comparison to the world: 64

BUDGET SURPLUS (+) OR DEFICIT (-):

-9.8% (of GDP) (2017 est.)

country comparison to the world: 209

PUBLIC DEBT:

131.2% of GDP (2017 est.)

132.8% of GDP (2016 est.)

country comparison to the world: 6

FISCAL YEAR:

calendar year

INFLATION RATE (CONSUMER PRICES):

9% (2017 est.)

9% (2016 est.)

country comparison to the world: 201

COMMERCIAL BANK PRIME LENDING RATE:

NA

STOCK OF NARROW MONEY:

$3.084 billion (31 December 2017 est.)

$2.734 billion (31 December 2016 est.)

country comparison to the world: 121

STOCK OF BROAD MONEY:

$3.084 billion (31 December 2017 est.)

$2.734 billion (31 December 2016 est.)

country comparison to the world: 127

STOCK OF DOMESTIC CREDIT:

$5.787 billion (31 December 2017 est.)

$5.223 billion (31 December 2016 est.)

country comparison to the world: 127

CURRENT ACCOUNT BALANCE:

-$137 million (2017 est.)

-$105 million (2016 est.)

country comparison to the world: 90

EXPORTS:

$624.3 million (2017 est.)

$485.4 million (2016 est.)

country comparison to the world: 172

EXPORTS - PARTNERS:

China 62%, South Korea 28.3% (2017)

EXPORTS - COMMODITIES:

gold and other minerals, livestock, sorghum, textiles, food, small industry manufactures

IMPORTS:

$1.127 billion (2017 est.)

$1.048 billion (2016 est.)

country comparison to the world: 180

IMPORTS - COMMODITIES:

machinery, petroleum products, food, manufactured goods

IMPORTS - PARTNERS:

UAE 14.5%, China 13.2%, Saudi Arabia 13.2%, Italy 12.9%, Turkey 5.6%, South Africa 4.6% (2017)

RESERVES OF FOREIGN EXCHANGE AND GOLD:

$236.7 million (31 December 2017 est.)

$218.4 million (31 December 2016 est.)

country comparison to the world: 171

DEBT - EXTERNAL:

$792.7 million (31 December 2017 est.)

$875.6 million (31 December 2016 est.)

country comparison to the world: 170

EXCHANGE RATES:

nakfa (ERN) per US dollar -

15.38 (2017 est.)

15.375 (2016 est.)

15.375 (2015 est.)

15.375 (2014 est.)

15.375 (2013 est.)

ENERGY :: ERITREA

ELECTRICITY ACCESS:

population without electricity: 4.3 million (2013)

electrification - total population: 32% (2013)

electrification - urban areas: 86% (2013)

electrification - rural areas: 17% (2013)

ELECTRICITY - PRODUCTION:

415.9 million kWh (2016 est.)

country comparison to the world: 168

ELECTRICITY - CONSUMPTION:

353.9 million kWh (2016 est.)

country comparison to the world: 180

ELECTRICITY - EXPORTS:

0 kWh (2016 est.)

country comparison to the world: 131

ELECTRICITY - IMPORTS:

0 kWh (2016 est.)

country comparison to the world: 145

ELECTRICITY - INSTALLED GENERATING CAPACITY:

160,700 kW (2016 est.)

country comparison to the world: 172

ELECTRICITY - FROM FOSSIL FUELS:

99% of total installed capacity (2016 est.)

country comparison to the world: 23

ELECTRICITY - FROM NUCLEAR FUELS:

0% of total installed capacity (2017 est.)

country comparison to the world: 85

ELECTRICITY - FROM HYDROELECTRIC PLANTS:

0% of total installed capacity (2017 est.)

country comparison to the world: 169

ELECTRICITY - FROM OTHER RENEWABLE SOURCES:

1% of total installed capacity (2017 est.)

country comparison to the world: 152

CRUDE OIL - PRODUCTION:

0 bbl/day (2017 est.)

country comparison to the world: 130

CRUDE OIL - EXPORTS:

0 bbl/day (2015 est.)

country comparison to the world: 118

CRUDE OIL - IMPORTS:

0 bbl/day (2015 est.)

country comparison to the world: 122

CRUDE OIL - PROVED RESERVES:

0 bbl (1 January 2018 est.)

country comparison to the world: 127

REFINED PETROLEUM PRODUCTS - PRODUCTION:

0 bbl/day (2015 est.)

country comparison to the world: 140

REFINED PETROLEUM PRODUCTS - CONSUMPTION:

4,000 bbl/day (2016 est.)

country comparison to the world: 183

REFINED PETROLEUM PRODUCTS - EXPORTS:

0 bbl/day (2015 est.)

country comparison to the world: 151

REFINED PETROLEUM PRODUCTS - IMPORTS:

3,897 bbl/day (2015 est.)

country comparison to the world: 179

NATURAL GAS - PRODUCTION:

0 cu m (2017 est.)

country comparison to the world: 127

NATURAL GAS - CONSUMPTION:

0 cu m (2017 est.)

country comparison to the world: 142

NATURAL GAS - EXPORTS:

0 cu m (2017 est.)

country comparison to the world: 99

NATURAL GAS - IMPORTS:

0 cu m (2017 est.)

country comparison to the world: 121

NATURAL GAS - PROVED RESERVES:

0 cu m (1 January 2014 est.)

country comparison to the world: 131

CARBON DIOXIDE EMISSIONS FROM CONSUMPTION OF ENERGY:

597,100 Mt (2017 est.)

country comparison to the world: 182

COMMUNICATIONS :: ERITREA

TELEPHONES - FIXED LINES:

total subscriptions: 66,086 (July 2016 est.)

subscriptions per 100 inhabitants: 1 (July 2016 est.)

country comparison to the world: 152

TELEPHONES - MOBILE CELLULAR:

total subscriptions: 506,000 (July 2016 est.)

subscriptions per 100 inhabitants: 9 (July 2016 est.)

country comparison to the world: 171

TELEPHONE SYSTEM:

general assessment: woefully inadequate service provided by state-owned telecom monopoly; most fixed-line telephones are in Asmara; cell phone use only slowly increasing throughout the country; no data service; only about 3% of households having computers with 2% internet; untapped market ripe for competition; government telco working on roll-out of 3G network (2016)

domestic: fixed-line subscribership is less than 1 per 100 person and mobile-cellular 9 per 100 (2016)

international: country code - 291 (2016)

BROADCAST MEDIA:

government controls broadcast media with private ownership prohibited; 1 state-owned TV station; state-owned radio operates 2 networks; purchases of satellite dishes and subscriptions to international broadcast media are permitted (2007)

INTERNET COUNTRY CODE:

.er

INTERNET USERS:

total: 69,095 (July 2016 est.)

percent of population: 1.2% (July 2016 est.)

country comparison to the world: 182

BROADBAND - FIXED SUBSCRIPTIONS:

total: 600 (2017 est.)

subscriptions per 100 inhabitants: less than 1 (2017 est.)

country comparison to the world: 195

TRANSPORTATION :: ERITREA

NATIONAL AIR TRANSPORT SYSTEM:

number of registered air carriers: 1 (2015)

inventory of registered aircraft operated by air carriers: 1 (2015)

CIVIL AIRCRAFT REGISTRATION COUNTRY CODE PREFIX:

E3 (2016)

AIRPORTS:

13 (2013)

country comparison to the world: 152

AIRPORTS - WITH PAVED RUNWAYS:

total: 4 (2017)

over 3,047 m: 2 (2017)

2,438 to 3,047 m: 2 (2017)

AIRPORTS - WITH UNPAVED RUNWAYS:

total: 9 (2013)

over 3,047 m: 1 (2013)

2,438 to 3,047 m: 1 (2013)

1,524 to 2,437 m: 5 (2013)

914 to 1,523 m: 2 (2013)

HELIPORTS:

1 (2013)

RAILWAYS:

total: 306 km (2014)

narrow gauge: 306 km 0.950-m gauge (2014)

country comparison to the world: 121

ROADWAYS:

total: 4,010 km (2000)

paved: 874 km (2000)

unpaved: 3,136 km (2000)

country comparison to the world: 158

MERCHANT MARINE:

total: 9 (2017)

by type: general cargo 4, oil tanker 1, other 4 (2017)

country comparison to the world: 151

PORTS AND TERMINALS:

major seaport(s): Assab, Massawa

MILITARY AND SECURITY :: ERITREA

MILITARY BRANCHES:

Eritrean Armed Forces: Eritrean Ground Forces, Eritrean Navy, Eritrean Air Force (includes Air Defense Force) (2011)

MILITARY SERVICE AGE AND OBLIGATION:

18-40 years of age for male and female voluntary and compulsory military service; 16-month conscript service obligation (2012)

TRANSNATIONAL ISSUES :: ERITREA

DISPUTES - INTERNATIONAL:

Eritrea and Ethiopia agreed to abide by 2002 Ethiopia-Eritrea Boundary Commission's (EEBC) delimitation decision, but neither party responded to the revised line detailed in the November 2006 EEBC Demarcation StatementSudan accuses Eritrea of supporting eastern Sudanese rebel groupsin 2008, Eritrean troops moved across the border on Ras Doumera peninsula and occupied Doumera Island with undefined sovereignty in the Red Sea

TRAFFICKING IN PERSONS:

current situation: Eritrea is a source country for men, women, and children trafficked for the purposes of forced labor domestically and, to a lesser extent, sex and labor trafficking abroad; the country's national service program is often abused, with conscripts detained indefinitely and subjected to forced labor; Eritrean migrants, often fleeing national service, face strict exit control procedures and limited access to passports and visas, making them vulnerable to trafficking; Eritrean secondary school children are required to take part in public works projects during their summer breaks and must attend military and educational camp in their final year to obtain a high school graduation certificate and to gain access to higher education and some jobs; some Eritreans living in or near refugee camps, particularly in Sudan, are kidnapped by criminal groups and held for ransom in the Sinai Peninsula and Libya, where they are subjected to forced labor and abuse

tier rating: Tier 3 – Eritrea does not fully comply with the minimum standards for the elimination of trafficking and is not making significant efforts to do so; the government failed to investigate or prosecute any trafficking offenses or to identify or protect any victims; while the government continued to warn citizens of the dangers of human trafficking through awareness-raising events and poster campaigns, authorities lacked an understanding of the crime, conflating trafficking with transnational migration; Eritrea is not a party to the 2000 UN TIP Protocol (2015)

EUROPE :: ESTONIA

INTRODUCTION :: ESTONIA

BACKGROUND:

After centuries of Danish, Swedish, German, and Russian rule, Estonia attained independence in 1918. Forcibly incorporated into the USSR in 1940 - an action never recognized by the US and many other countries - it regained its freedom in 1991 with the collapse of the Soviet Union. Since the last Russian troops left in 1994, Estonia has been free to promote economic and political ties with the West. It joined both NATO and the EU in the spring of 2004, formally joined the OECD in late 2010, and adopted the euro as its official currency on 1 January 2011.

GEOGRAPHY :: ESTONIA

LOCATION:

Eastern Europe, bordering the Baltic Sea and Gulf of Finland, between Latvia and Russia

GEOGRAPHIC COORDINATES:

59 00 N, 26 00 E

MAP REFERENCES:

Europe

AREA:

total: 45,228 sq km

land: 42,388 sq km

water: 2,840 sq km

note: includes 1,520 islands in the Baltic Sea

country comparison to the world: 133

AREA - COMPARATIVE:

about twice the size of New Jersey

LAND BOUNDARIES:

total: 657 km

border countries (2): Latvia 333 km, Russia 324 km

COASTLINE:

3,794 km

MARITIME CLAIMS:

territorial sea: 12 nm

exclusive economic zone: limits as agreed to by Estonia, Finland, Latvia, Sweden, and Russia

CLIMATE:

maritime; wet, moderate winters, cool summers

TERRAIN:

marshy, lowlands; flat in the north, hilly in the south

ELEVATION:

mean elevation: 61 m

elevation extremes: 0 m lowest point: Baltic Sea

318 highest point: Suur Munamagi

NATURAL RESOURCES:

oil shale, peat, rare earth elements, phosphorite, clay, limestone, sand, dolomite, arable land, sea mud

LAND USE:

agricultural land: 22.2% (2011 est.)

arable land: 14.9% (2011 est.) / permanent crops: 0.1% (2011 est.) / permanent pasture: 7.2% (2011 est.)

forest: 52.1% (2011 est.)

other: 25.7% (2011 est.)

IRRIGATED LAND:

40 sq km (2012)

POPULATION DISTRIBUTION:

a fairly even distribution throughout most of the country, with urban areas attracting larger and denser populations

NATURAL HAZARDS:

sometimes flooding occurs in the spring

ENVIRONMENT - CURRENT ISSUES:

air polluted with sulfur dioxide from oil-shale burning power plants in northeast; however, the amounts of pollutants emitted to the air have fallen dramatically and the pollution load of wastewater at purification plants has decreased substantially due to improved technology and environmental monitoring; Estonia has more than 1,400 natural and manmade lakes, the smaller of which in agricultural areas need to be monitored; coastal seawater is polluted in certain locations

ENVIRONMENT - INTERNATIONAL AGREEMENTS:

party to: Air Pollution, Air Pollution-Nitrogen Oxides, Air Pollution-Persistent Organic Pollutants, Air Pollution-Sulfur 85, Air Pollution-Volatile Organic Compounds, Antarctic Treaty, Biodiversity, Climate Change, Climate Change-Kyoto Protocol, Endangered Species, Hazardous Wastes, Law of the Sea, Ozone Layer Protection, Ship Pollution, Wetlands

signed, but not ratified: none of the selected agreements

GEOGRAPHY - NOTE:

the mainland terrain is flat, boggy, and partly wooded; offshore lie more than 1,500 islands

PEOPLE AND SOCIETY :: ESTONIA

POPULATION:

1,244,288 (July 2018 est.)

country comparison to the world: 157

NATIONALITY:

noun: Estonian(s)

adjective: Estonian

ETHNIC GROUPS:

Estonian 68.7%, Russian 24.8%, Ukrainian 1.7%, Belarusian 1%, Finn 0.6%, other 1.6%, unspecified 1.6% (2011 est.)

LANGUAGES:

Estonian (official) 68.5%, Russian 29.6%, Ukrainian 0.6%, other 1.2%, unspecified 0.1% (2011 est.)

RELIGIONS:

Lutheran 9.9%, Orthodox 16.2%, other Christian (including Methodist, Seventh-Day Adventist, Roman Catholic, Pentecostal) 2.2%, other 0.9%, none 54.1%, unspecified 16.7% (2011 est.)

AGE STRUCTURE:

0-14 years: 16.3% (male 104,024 /female 98,757)

15-24 years: 8.8% (male 56,755 /female 52,711)

25-54 years: 41.07% (male 258,727 /female 252,304)

55-64 years: 13.63% (male 76,895 /female 92,759)

65 years and over: 20.2% (male 85,900 /female 165,456) (2018 est.)

DEPENDENCY RATIOS:

total dependency ratio: 53.7 (2015 est.)

youth dependency ratio: 24.8 (2015 est.)

elderly dependency ratio: 28.9 (2015 est.)

potential support ratio: 3.5 (2015 est.)

MEDIAN AGE:

total: 43 years

male: 39.7 years

female: 46.4 years (2018 est.)

country comparison to the world: 23

POPULATION GROWTH RATE:

-0.6% (2018 est.)

country comparison to the world: 224

BIRTH RATE:

9.9 births/1,000 population (2018 est.)

country comparison to the world: 193

DEATH RATE:

12.7 deaths/1,000 population (2018 est.)

country comparison to the world: 14

NET MIGRATION RATE:

-3.2 migrant(s)/1,000 population (2017 est.)

country comparison to the world: 177

POPULATION DISTRIBUTION:

a fairly even distribution throughout most of the country, with urban areas attracting larger and denser populations

URBANIZATION:

urban population: 68.9% of total population (2018)

rate of urbanization: 0.01% annual rate of change (2015-20 est.)

MAJOR URBAN AREAS - POPULATION:

437,000 TALLINN (capital) (2018)

SEX RATIO:

at birth: 1.05 male(s)/female (2017 est.)

0-14 years: 1.05 male(s)/female (2017 est.)

15-24 years: 1.08 male(s)/female (2017 est.)

25-54 years: 1.01 male(s)/female (2017 est.)

55-64 years: 0.81 male(s)/female (2017 est.)

65 years and over: 0.51 male(s)/female (2017 est.)

total population: 0.88 male(s)/female (2017 est.)

MOTHER'S MEAN AGE AT FIRST BIRTH:

26.6 years (2014 est.)

MATERNAL MORTALITY RATE:

9 deaths/100,000 live births (2015 est.)

country comparison to the world: 151

INFANT MORTALITY RATE:

total: 3.8 deaths/1,000 live births (2018 est.)

male: 3.7 deaths/1,000 live births (2018 est.)

female: 3.9 deaths/1,000 live births (2018 est.)

country comparison to the world: 192

LIFE EXPECTANCY AT BIRTH:

total population: 77 years (2018 est.)

male: 72.3 years (2018 est.)

female: 82 years (2018 est.)

country comparison to the world: 81

TOTAL FERTILITY RATE:

1.6 children born/woman (2018 est.)

country comparison to the world: 182

HEALTH EXPENDITURES:

6.4% of GDP (2014)

country comparison to the world: 95

PHYSICIANS DENSITY:

3.43 physicians/1,000 population (2015)

HOSPITAL BED DENSITY:

5 beds/1,000 population (2015)

DRINKING WATER SOURCE:

improved:

urban: 100% of population

rural: 99% of population

total: 99.6% of population

unimproved:

urban: 0% of population

rural: 1% of population

total: 0.4% of population (2015 est.)

SANITATION FACILITY ACCESS:

improved:

urban: 97.5% of population (2015 est.)

rural: 96.6% of population (2015 est.)

total: 97.2% of population (2015 est.)

unimproved:

urban: 2.5% of population (2015 est.)

rural: 3.4% of population (2015 est.)

total: 2.8% of population (2015 est.)

HIV/AIDS - ADULT PREVALENCE RATE:

0.7% (2017 est.)

country comparison to the world: 53

HIV/AIDS - PEOPLE LIVING WITH HIV/AIDS:

5,700 (2017 est.)

country comparison to the world: 114

HIV/AIDS - DEATHS:

<100 (2017 est.)

MAJOR INFECTIOUS DISEASES:

degree of risk: intermediate (2016)

vectorborne diseases: tickborne encephalitis (2016)

OBESITY - ADULT PREVALENCE RATE:

21.2% (2016)

country comparison to the world: 92

EDUCATION EXPENDITURES:

5.5% of GDP (2014)

country comparison to the world: 49

LITERACY:

definition: age 15 and over can read and write (2015 est.)

total population: 99.8% (2015 est.)

male: 99.8% (2015 est.)

female: 99.8% (2015 est.)

SCHOOL LIFE EXPECTANCY (PRIMARY TO TERTIARY EDUCATION):

total: 16 years (2015)

male: 16 years (2015)

female: 17 years (2015)

UNEMPLOYMENT, YOUTH AGES 15-24:

total: 13.4% (2016 est.)

male: 15.8% (2016 est.)

female: 10.6% (2016 est.)

country comparison to the world: 98

GOVERNMENT :: ESTONIA

COUNTRY NAME:

conventional long form: Republic of Estonia

conventional short form: Estonia

local long form: Eesti Vabariik

local short form: Eesti

former: Estonian Soviet Socialist Republic

etymology: the country name may derive from the Aesti, an ancient people who lived along the eastern Baltic Sea in the first centuries A.D.

GOVERNMENT TYPE:

parliamentary republic

CAPITAL:

name: Tallinn

geographic coordinates: 59 26 N, 24 43 E

time difference: UTC+2 (7 hours ahead of Washington, DC, during Standard Time)

daylight saving time: +1hr, begins last Sunday in March; ends last Sunday in October

ADMINISTRATIVE DIVISIONS:

15 counties (maakonnad, singular - maakond); Harjumaa (Tallinn), Hiiumaa (Kardla), Ida-Virumaa (Johvi), Jarvamaa (Paide), Jogevamaa (Jogeva), Laanemaa (Haapsalu), Laane-Virumaa (Rakvere), Parnumaa (Parnu), Polvamaa (Polva), Raplamaa (Rapla), Saaremaa (Kuressaare), Tartumaa (Tartu), Valgamaa (Valga), Viljandimaa (Viljandi), Vorumaa (Voru)

note: counties have the administrative center name following in parentheses

INDEPENDENCE:

20 August 1991 (declared);6 September 1991 (recognized by the Soviet Union)

NATIONAL HOLIDAY:

Independence Day, 24 February (1918); note - 24 February 1918 was the date Estonia declared its independence from Soviet Russia and established its statehood; 20 August 1991 was the date it declared its independence from the Soviet Union

CONSTITUTION:

history: several previous; latest adopted 28 June 1992 (2016)

amendments: proposed by at least one-fifth of Parliament members or by the president of the republic; passage requires three readings of the proposed amendment and a simple majority vote in two successive memberships of Parliament; passage of amendments to the "General Provisions" and "Amendment of the Constitution" chapters requires at least three-fifths majority vote by Parliament to conduct a referendum and majority vote in a referendum; amended several times, last in 2015 (2016)

LEGAL SYSTEM:

civil law system

INTERNATIONAL LAW ORGANIZATION PARTICIPATION:

accepts compulsory ICJ jurisdiction with reservations; accepts ICCt jurisdiction

CITIZENSHIP:

citizenship by birth: no

citizenship by descent only: at least one parent must be a citizen of Estonia

dual citizenship recognized: no

residency requirement for naturalization: 5 years

SUFFRAGE:

18 years of age; universal; age 16 for local elections

EXECUTIVE BRANCH:

chief of state: President Kersti KALJULAID (since 10 October 2016)

head of government: Juri RATAS (since 23 November 2016)

cabinet: Cabinet appointed by the prime minister, approved by Parliament

elections/appointments: president indirectly elected by Parliament for a 5-year term (eligible for a second term); if a candidate does not secure two-thirds of the votes after 3 rounds of balloting, then an electoral college consisting of Parliament members and local council members elects the president, choosing between the 2 candidates with the highest number of votes; election last held on 29-30 August 2016, but three rounds were inconclusive; two electoral college votes on 24 September 2016 were also indecisive, so the election passed back to Parliament; on 3 October the Parliament elected Kersti KALJULAID as president; prime minister nominated by the president and approved by Parliament

election results: Kersti KALJULAID elected president; Parliament vote - Kersti KALJULAID (independent) 81 of 98 votes; note - KALJULAID is Estonia's first female president

LEGISLATIVE BRANCH:

description: unicameral Parliament or Riigikogu (101 seats; members directly elected in multi-seat constituencies by proportional representation vote to serve 4-year terms)

elections: last held on 1 March 2015 (next to be held in March 2019)

election results: percent of vote by party - RE 27.7%, K 24.8%, SDE 15.2%, IRL 13.7%, EV 8.7%, EKRE 8.1%, other 1.8%; seats by party - RE 30, K 27, SDE 15, IRL 14, EV 8, EKRE 7; composition - men 77, women 24, percent of women 23.8%

JUDICIAL BRANCH:

highest courts: Supreme Court (consists of 19 justices including the chief justice and organized into civil, criminal, administrative, and constitutional review chambers)

judge selection and term of office: the chief justice is proposed by the president of the republic and appointed by the Riigikogu; other justices proposed by the chief justice and appointed by the Riigikogu; justices appointed for life

subordinate courts: circuit (appellate) courts; administrative, county, city, and specialized courts

POLITICAL PARTIES AND LEADERS:

Center Party of Estonia (Keskerakond) or K [Juri RATAS]
Estonian Conservative People's Party (Konservatiivne Rahvaerakond) or EKRE [Mart HELME]
Estonian Reform Party (Reformierakond) or RE [Kaja KALLAS]
Free Party or EV [Andres HERKEL]
Social Democratic Party or SDE [Jevgeni OSSINOVSKI]
Union of Pro Patria and Res Publica (Isamaa je Res Publica Liit) or IRL [Helir-Valdor SEEDER]

INTERNATIONAL ORGANIZATION PARTICIPATION:

Australia Group, BA, BIS, CBSS, CD, CE, EAPC, EBRD, ECB, EIB, EMU, ESA (cooperating state), EU, FAO, IAEA, IBRD, ICAO, ICC (national committees), ICCt, ICRM, IDA, IEA, IFAD, IFC, IFRCS, IHO, ILO, IMF, IMO, Interpol, IOC, IOM, IPU, ISO, ITSO, ITU, ITUC (NGOs), MIGA, MINUSMA, NATO, NIB, NSG, OAS (observer), OECD, OIF (observer), OPCW, OSCE, PCA, Schengen Convention, UN, UNCTAD, UNESCO, UNHCR, UNTSO, UPU, WCO, WHO, WIPO, WMO, WTO

DIPLOMATIC REPRESENTATION IN THE US:

chief of mission: Ambassador Jonatan VSEVIOV (since 17 September 2018)

chancery: 2131 Massachusetts Avenue NW, Washington, DC 20008

telephone: [1] (202) 588-0101

FAX: [1] (202) 588-0108

consulate(s) general: New York

DIPLOMATIC REPRESENTATION FROM THE US:

chief of mission: Ambassador James D. MELVILLE Jr. (since 8 December 2015)

embassy: Kentmanni 20, 15099 Tallinn

mailing address: use embassy street address

telephone: [372] 668-8100

FAX: [372] 668-8265

FLAG DESCRIPTION:

three equal horizontal bands of blue (top), black, and white; various interpretations are linked to the flag colors; blue represents faith, loyalty, and devotion, while also reminiscent of the sky, sea, and lakes of the country; black symbolizes the soil of the country and the dark past and suffering endured by the Estonian people; white refers to the striving towards enlightenment and virtue, and is the color of birch bark and snow, as well as summer nights illuminated by the midnight sun

NATIONAL SYMBOL(S):

barn swallow, cornflower; national colors: blue, black, white

NATIONAL ANTHEM:

name: "Mu isamaa, mu onn ja room" (My Native Land, My Pride and Joy)

lyrics/music: Johann Voldemar JANNSEN/Fredrik PACIUS

note: adopted 1920, though banned between 1940 and 1990 under Soviet occupation; the anthem, used in Estonia since 1869, shares the same melody as Finland's but has different lyrics

ECONOMY :: ESTONIA

ECONOMY - OVERVIEW:

Estonia, a member of the EU since 2004 and the euro zone since 2011, has a modern market-based economy and one of the higher per capita income levels in Central Europe and the Baltic region, but its economy is highly dependent on trade, leaving it vulnerable to external shocks. Estonia's successive governments have pursued a free market, pro-business economic agenda, and sound fiscal policies that have resulted in balanced budgets and the lowest debt-to-GDP ratio in the EU.

The economy benefits from strong electronics and telecommunications sectors and strong trade ties with Finland, Sweden, Germany, and Russia. The economy's 4.9% GDP growth in 2017 was the fastest in the past six years, leaving the Estonian economy in its best position since the financial crisis 10 years ago. For the first time in many years, labor productivity increased faster than labor costs in 2017. Inflation also rose in 2017 to 3.5% alongside increased global prices for food and energy, which make up a large share of Estonia's consumption.

Estonia is challenged by a shortage of labor, both skilled and unskilled, although the government has amended its immigration law to allow easier hiring of highly qualified foreign workers, and wage growth that outpaces productivity gains. The government is also pursuing efforts to boost productivity growth with a focus on innovations that emphasize technology start-ups and e-commerce.

GDP (PURCHASING POWER PARITY):

$41.65 billion (2017 est.)

$39.72 billion (2016 est.)

$38.92 billion (2015 est.)

note: data are in 2017 dollars

country comparison to the world: 115

GDP (OFFICIAL EXCHANGE RATE):

$25.97 billion (2017 est.) (2017 est.)

GDP - REAL GROWTH RATE:

4.9% (2017 est.)

2.1% (2016 est.)

1.7% (2015 est.)

country comparison to the world: 52

GDP - PER CAPITA (PPP):

$31,700 (2017 est.)

$30,200 (2016 est.)

$29,600 (2015 est.)

note: data are in 2017 dollars

country comparison to the world: 64

GROSS NATIONAL SAVING:

27% of GDP (2017 est.)

24.6% of GDP (2016 est.)

25.8% of GDP (2015 est.)

country comparison to the world: 44

GDP - COMPOSITION, BY END USE:

household consumption: 50.3% (2017 est.)

government consumption: 20.4% (2017 est.)

investment in fixed capital: 24% (2017 est.)

investment in inventories: 2.2% (2017 est.)

exports of goods and services: 77.2% (2017 est.)

imports of goods and services: -74% (2017 est.)

GDP - COMPOSITION, BY SECTOR OF ORIGIN:

agriculture: 2.8% (2017 est.)

industry: 29.2% (2017 est.)

services: 68.1% (2017 est.)

AGRICULTURE - PRODUCTS:

grain, potatoes, vegetables; livestock and dairy products; fish

INDUSTRIES:

food, engineering, electronics, wood and wood products, textiles; information technology, telecommunications

INDUSTRIAL PRODUCTION GROWTH RATE:

9.5% (2017 est.)

country comparison to the world: 17

LABOR FORCE:

670,200 (2017 est.)

country comparison to the world: 152

LABOR FORCE - BY OCCUPATION:

agriculture: 2.7%

industry: 20.5%

services: 76.8% (2017 est.)

UNEMPLOYMENT RATE:

5.8% (2017 est.)

6.8% (2016 est.)

country comparison to the world: 88

POPULATION BELOW POVERTY LINE:

21.1% (2016 est.)

HOUSEHOLD INCOME OR CONSUMPTION BY PERCENTAGE SHARE:

lowest 10%: 25.6% (2015)

highest 10%: 25.6% (2015)

DISTRIBUTION OF FAMILY INCOME - GINI INDEX:

34.8 (2015)

35.6 (2014)

country comparison to the world: 100

BUDGET:

revenues: 10.37 billion (2017 est.)

expenditures: 10.44 billion (2017 est.)

TAXES AND OTHER REVENUES:

39.9% (of GDP) (2017 est.)

country comparison to the world: 41

BUDGET SURPLUS (+) OR DEFICIT (-):

-0.3% (of GDP) (2017 est.)

country comparison to the world: 52

PUBLIC DEBT:

9% of GDP (2017 est.)

9.4% of GDP (2016 est.)

note: data cover general government debt and include debt instruments issued (or owned) by government entities, including sub-sectors of central government, state government, local government, and social security funds

country comparison to the world: 199

FISCAL YEAR:

calendar year

INFLATION RATE (CONSUMER PRICES):

3.7% (2017 est.)

0.8% (2016 est.)

country comparison to the world: 145

CENTRAL BANK DISCOUNT RATE:

0% (31 December 2017 est.)

0% (31 December 2016 est.)

country comparison to the world: 152

COMMERCIAL BANK PRIME LENDING RATE:

4.2% (31 December 2017 est.)

4.23% (31 December 2016 est.)

country comparison to the world: 163

STOCK OF NARROW MONEY:

$14.78 billion (31 December 2017 est.)

$11.8 billion (31 December 2016 est.)

note: see entry for the European Union for money supply for the entire euro area; the European Central Bank (ECB) controls monetary policy for the 18 members of the Economic and Monetary Union (EMU); individual members of the EMU do not control the quantity of money circulating within their own borders

country comparison to the world: 73

STOCK OF BROAD MONEY:

$14.78 billion (31 December 2017 est.)

$11.8 billion (31 December 2016 est.)

country comparison to the world: 74

STOCK OF DOMESTIC CREDIT:

$24.25 billion (31 December 2017 est.)

$20.97 billion (31 December 2016 est.)

country comparison to the world: 88

MARKET VALUE OF PUBLICLY TRADED SHARES:

$3.102 billion (31 December 2017 est.)

$2.407 billion (31 December 2016 est.)

$2.045 billion (31 December 2015 est.)

country comparison to the world: 92

CURRENT ACCOUNT BALANCE:

$809 million (2017 est.)

$443 million (2016 est.)

country comparison to the world: 54

EXPORTS:

$13.44 billion (2017 est.)

$12.36 billion (2016 est.)

country comparison to the world: 81

EXPORTS - PARTNERS:

Finland 16.2%, Sweden 13.5%, Latvia 9.2%, Russia 7.3%, Germany 6.9%, Lithuania 5.9% (2017)

EXPORTS - COMMODITIES:

machinery and electrical equipment 30%, food products and beverages 9%, mineral fuels 6%, wood and wood products 14%, articles of base metals 7%, furniture and bedding 11%, vehicles and parts 3%, chemicals 4% (2016 est.)

IMPORTS:

$14.42 billion (2017 est.)

$13.23 billion (2016 est.)

country comparison to the world: 91

IMPORTS - COMMODITIES:

machinery and electrical equipment 28%, mineral fuels 11%, food and food products 10%, vehicles 9%, chemical products 8%, metals 8% (2015 est.)

IMPORTS - PARTNERS:

Finland 14%, Germany 10.7%, Lithuania 8.9%, Sweden 8.5%, Latvia 8.2%, Poland 7.2%, Russia 6.7%, Netherlands 5.9%, China 4.7% (2017)

RESERVES OF FOREIGN EXCHANGE AND GOLD:

$345 million (31 December 2017 est.)

$352.2 million (31 December 2016 est.)

country comparison to the world: 164

DEBT - EXTERNAL:

$19.05 billion (31 December 2016 est.)

$18.3 billion (31 December 2015 est.)

country comparison to the world: 93

STOCK OF DIRECT FOREIGN INVESTMENT - AT HOME:

$27.05 billion (31 December 2017 est.)

$22.19 billion (31 December 2016 est.)

country comparison to the world: 73

STOCK OF DIRECT FOREIGN INVESTMENT - ABROAD:

$10.96 billion (31 December 2017 est.)

$9.396 billion (31 December 2016 est.)

country comparison to the world: 64

EXCHANGE RATES:

euros (EUR) per US dollar -

0.92 (2017 est.)

0.9 (2016 est.)

0.9214 (2015 est.)

0.885 (2014 est.)

0.7634 (2013 est.)

ENERGY :: ESTONIA

ELECTRICITY ACCESS:

electrification - total population: 100% (2016)

ELECTRICITY - PRODUCTION:

11.55 billion kWh (2016 est.)

country comparison to the world: 97

ELECTRICITY - CONSUMPTION:

8.795 billion kWh (2016 est.)

country comparison to the world: 102

ELECTRICITY - EXPORTS:

5.613 billion kWh (2016 est.)

country comparison to the world: 33

ELECTRICITY - IMPORTS:

3.577 billion kWh (2016 est.)

country comparison to the world: 46

ELECTRICITY - INSTALLED GENERATING CAPACITY:

2.578 million kW (2016 est.)

country comparison to the world: 106

ELECTRICITY - FROM FOSSIL FUELS:

72% of total installed capacity (2016 est.)

country comparison to the world: 103

ELECTRICITY - FROM NUCLEAR FUELS:

0% of total installed capacity (2017 est.)

country comparison to the world: 86

ELECTRICITY - FROM HYDROELECTRIC PLANTS:

0% of total installed capacity (2017 est.)

country comparison to the world: 170

ELECTRICITY - FROM OTHER RENEWABLE SOURCES:

28% of total installed capacity (2017 est.)

country comparison to the world: 22

CRUDE OIL - PRODUCTION:

0 bbl/day (2017 est.)

country comparison to the world: 131

CRUDE OIL - EXPORTS:

0 bbl/day (2015 est.)

country comparison to the world: 119

CRUDE OIL - IMPORTS:

0 bbl/day (2017 est.)

country comparison to the world: 123

CRUDE OIL - PROVED RESERVES:

0 bbl (1 January 2018 est.)

country comparison to the world: 128

REFINED PETROLEUM PRODUCTS - PRODUCTION:

0 bbl/day (2017 est.)

country comparison to the world: 141

REFINED PETROLEUM PRODUCTS - CONSUMPTION:

28,300 bbl/day (2017 est.)

country comparison to the world: 121

REFINED PETROLEUM PRODUCTS - EXPORTS:

27,150 bbl/day (2017 est.)

country comparison to the world: 64

REFINED PETROLEUM PRODUCTS - IMPORTS:

35,520 bbl/day (2017 est.)

country comparison to the world: 95

NATURAL GAS - PRODUCTION:

0 cu m (2017 est.)

country comparison to the world: 128

NATURAL GAS - CONSUMPTION:

481.4 million cu m (2017 est.)

country comparison to the world: 98

NATURAL GAS - EXPORTS:

0 cu m (2017 est.)

country comparison to the world: 100

NATURAL GAS - IMPORTS:

481.4 million cu m (2017 est.)

country comparison to the world: 67

NATURAL GAS - PROVED RESERVES:

0 cu m (2016 est.)

country comparison to the world: 132

CARBON DIOXIDE EMISSIONS FROM CONSUMPTION OF ENERGY:

5.306 million Mt (2017 est.)

country comparison to the world: 133

COMMUNICATIONS :: ESTONIA

TELEPHONES - FIXED LINES:

total subscriptions: 362,117 (2017 est.)

subscriptions per 100 inhabitants: 29 (2017 est.)

country comparison to the world: 107

TELEPHONES - MOBILE CELLULAR:

total subscriptions: 1,904,425 (2017 est.)

subscriptions per 100 inhabitants: 152 (2017 est.)

country comparison to the world: 151

TELEPHONE SYSTEM:

general assessment: range of regulatory measures comptition and foreign investment in the form of joint business ventures greatly improved telephone service with a wide range of high-quality voice, data, and Internet services available; one of the most advanced mobile markets in Europe; 5G trials for further growth commercially available by 2020; highest broadband penetration in Europe (2017)

domestic: 29 per 100 for fixed-line and 152 per 100 for mobile-cellular; substantial fiber-optic cable systems carry telephone, TV, and radio traffic in the digital mode; Internet services are widely available; schools and libraries are connected to the Internet, a large percentage of the population files income tax returns online, and online voting - in local and parliamentary elections - has climbed steadily since first introduced in 2005; 85% of Estonian households have broadband access (2017)

international: country code - 372; fiber-optic cables to Finland, Sweden, Latvia, and Russia provide worldwide packet-switched service; 2 international switches are located in Tallinn (2016)

BROADCAST MEDIA:

the publicly owned broadcaster, Eesti Rahvusringhaaling (ERR), operates 3 TV channels and 5 radio networks; growing number of private commercial radio stations broadcasting nationally, regionally, and locally; fully transitioned to digital television in 2010; national private TV channels expanding service; a range of channels are aimed at Russian-speaking viewers; in 2016, there were 42 on-demand services available in Estonia, including 19 pay TVOD and SVOD services; roughly 85% of households accessed digital television services (2016)

INTERNET COUNTRY CODE:

.ee

INTERNET USERS:

total: 1,097,921 (July 2016 est.)

percent of population: 87.2% (July 2016 est.)

country comparison to the world: 132

BROADBAND - FIXED SUBSCRIPTIONS:

total: 404,682 (2017 est.)

subscriptions per 100 inhabitants: 32 (2017 est.)

country comparison to the world: 87

TRANSPORTATION :: ESTONIA

NATIONAL AIR TRANSPORT SYSTEM:

number of registered air carriers: 3 (2015)

inventory of registered aircraft operated by air carriers: 14 (2015)

annual passenger traffic on registered air carriers: 512,388 (2015)

annual freight traffic on registered air carriers: 870,362 mt-km (2015)

CIVIL AIRCRAFT REGISTRATION COUNTRY CODE PREFIX:

ES (2016)

AIRPORTS:

18 (2013)

country comparison to the world: 140

AIRPORTS - WITH PAVED RUNWAYS:

total: 13 (2017)

over 3,047 m: 2 (2017)

2,438 to 3,047 m: 8 (2017)

1,524 to 2,437 m: 2 (2017)

914 to 1,523 m: 1 (2017)

AIRPORTS - WITH UNPAVED RUNWAYS:

total: 5 (2013)

1,524 to 2,437 m: 1 (2013)

914 to 1,523 m: 1 (2013)

under 914 m: 3 (2013)

HELIPORTS:

1 (2012)

PIPELINES:

2360 km gas (2016)

RAILWAYS:

total: 2,146 km (2016)

broad gauge: 2,146 km 1.520-m and 1.524-m gauge (132 km electrified) (2016)

note: includes 1,510 km public and 636 km non-public railway

country comparison to the world: 72

ROADWAYS:

total: 58,412 km (includes urban roads) (2011)

paved: 10,427 km (includes 115 km of expressways) (2011)

unpaved: 47,985 km (2011)

country comparison to the world: 73

WATERWAYS:

335 km (320 km are navigable year-round) (2011)

country comparison to the world: 90

MERCHANT MARINE:

total: 78 (2017)

by type: general cargo 7, oil tanker 5, other 66 (2017)

country comparison to the world: 98

PORTS AND TERMINALS:

major seaport(s): Kuivastu, Kunda, Muuga, Parnu Reid, Sillamae, Tallinn

MILITARY AND SECURITY :: ESTONIA

MILITARY EXPENDITURES:

2.17% of GDP (2016)

2.09% of GDP (2015)

1.95% of GDP (2014)

country comparison to the world: 48

MILITARY BRANCHES:

Estonian Defense Forces (Eesti Kaitsevagi): Ground Forces (Maavagi), Navy (Merevagi), Air Force (Ohuvagi), Reserves (Kaitseliit) (2016)

MILITARY SERVICE AGE AND OBLIGATION:

18-27 for compulsory military or governmental service, conscript service requirement 8-11 months depending on education; NCOs, reserve officers, and specialists serve 11 months (2016)

TRANSNATIONAL ISSUES :: ESTONIA

DISPUTES - INTERNATIONAL:

Russia and Estonia in May 2005 signed a technical border agreement, but Russia in June 2005 recalled its signature after the Estonian parliament added to its domestic ratification act a historical preamble referencing the Soviet occupation and Estonia's pre-war borders under the 1920 Treaty of TartuRussia contends that the preamble allows Estonia to make territorial claims on Russia in the future, while Estonian officials deny that the preamble has any legal impact on the treaty textRussia demands better treatment of the Russian-speaking population in Estoniaas a member state that forms part of the EU's external border, Estonia implements strict Schengen border rules with Russia

REFUGEES AND INTERNALLY DISPLACED PERSONS:

stateless persons: 80,314 (2017); note - following independence in 1991, automatic citizenship was restricted to those who were Estonian citizens prior to the 1940 Soviet occupation and their descendants; thousands of ethnic Russians remained stateless when forced to choose between passing Estonian language and citizenship tests or applying for Russian citizenship; one reason for demurring on Estonian citizenship was to retain the right of visa-free travel to Russia; stateless residents can vote in local elections but not general elections; stateless parents who have been lawful residents of Estonia for at least five years can apply for citizenship for their children before they turn 15 years old

ILLICIT DRUGS:

growing producer of synthetic drugs; increasingly important transshipment zone for cannabis, cocaine, opiates, and synthetic drugs since joining the European Union and the Schengen Accord; potential money laundering related to organized crime and drug trafficking is a concern, as is possible use of the gambling sector to launder funds; major use of opiates and ecstasy

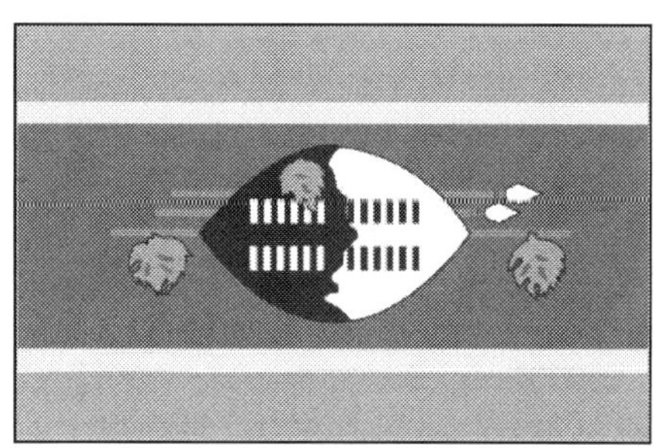

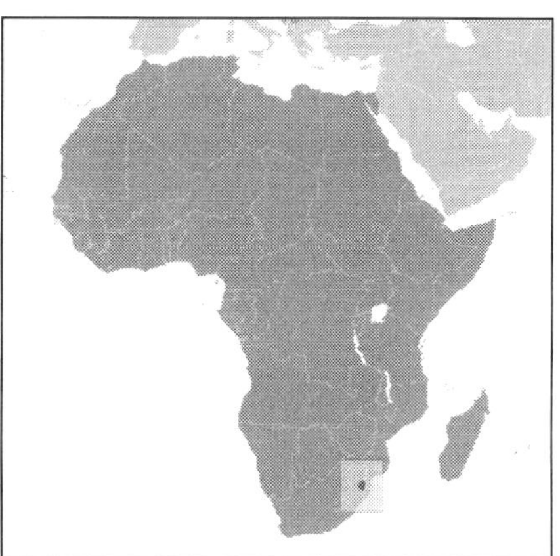

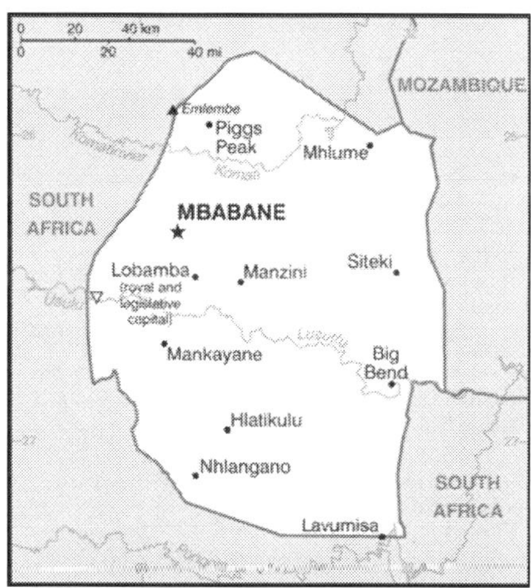

AFRICA :: ESWATINI

INTRODUCTION :: ESWATINI

BACKGROUND:

Autonomy for the Swazis of southern Africa was guaranteed by the British in the late 19th century; independence was granted in 1968. Student and labor unrest during the 1990s pressured King MSWATI III to grudgingly allow political reform and greater democracy, although he has backslid on these promises in recent years. A constitution came into effect in 2006, but the legal status of political parties was not defined and their status remains unclear. Eswatini has surpassed Botswana as the country with the world's highest known HIV/AIDS prevalence rate.

GEOGRAPHY :: ESWATINI

LOCATION:

Southern Africa, between Mozambique and South Africa

GEOGRAPHIC COORDINATES:

26 30 S, 31 30 E

MAP REFERENCES:

Africa

AREA:

total: 17,364 sq km

land: 17,204 sq km

water: 160 sq km

country comparison to the world: 159

AREA - COMPARATIVE:

slightly smaller than New Jersey

LAND BOUNDARIES:

total: 546 km

border countries (2): Mozambique 108 km, South Africa 438 km

COASTLINE:

0 km (landlocked)

MARITIME CLAIMS:

none (landlocked)

CLIMATE:

varies from tropical to near temperate

TERRAIN:

mostly mountains and hills; some moderately sloping plains

ELEVATION:

mean elevation: 305 m

elevation extremes: 21 m lowest point: Great Usutu River

1,862 m highest point: Emlembe

NATURAL RESOURCES:

asbestos, coal, clay, cassiterite, hydropower, forests, small gold and diamond deposits, quarry stone, and talc

LAND USE:

agricultural land: 68.3% (2011 est.)

arable land: 9.8% (2011 est.) / permanent crops: 0.8% (2011 est.) / permanent pasture: 57.7% (2011 est.)

forest: 31.7% (2011 est.)

other: 0% (2011 est.)

IRRIGATED LAND:

500 sq km (2012)

POPULATION DISTRIBUTION:

because of its mountainous terrain, the population distribution is uneven throughout the country, concentrating primarily in valleys and plains

NATURAL HAZARDS:

drought

ENVIRONMENT - CURRENT ISSUES:

limited supplies of potable water; wildlife populations being depleted because of excessive hunting; population growth, deforestation, and overgrazing lead to soil erosion and soil degradation

ENVIRONMENT - INTERNATIONAL AGREEMENTS:

party to: Biodiversity, Climate Change, Climate Change-Kyoto Protocol, Desertification, Endangered Species, Hazardous Wastes, Ozone Layer Protection

signed, but not ratified: Law of the Sea

GEOGRAPHY - NOTE:

landlocked; almost completely surrounded by South Africa

PEOPLE AND SOCIETY :: ESWATINI

POPULATION:

1,087,200 (July 2018 est.)

note: estimates for this country explicitly take into account the effects of excess mortality due to AIDS; this can result in lower life expectancy, higher infant mortality, higher death rates, lower population growth rates, and changes in the distribution of population by age and sex than would otherwise be expected

country comparison to the world: 160

NATIONALITY:

noun: Swazi(s)

adjective: Swazi

ETHNIC GROUPS:

African 97%, European 3%

LANGUAGES:

English (official, used for government business), siSwati (official)

RELIGIONS:

Christian 90% (Zionist - a blend of Christianity and indigenous ancestral worship - 40%, Roman Catholic 20%, other 30% - includes Anglican, Methodist, Mormon, Jehovah's Witness), Muslim 2%, other 8% (includes Baha'i, Buddhist, Hindu, indigenous religionist, Jewish) (2015 est.)

DEMOGRAPHIC PROFILE:

Eswatini, a small, predominantly rural, landlocked country surrounded by South Africa and Mozambique, suffers from severe poverty and the world's highest HIV/AIDS prevalence rate. A weak and deteriorating economy, high unemployment, rapid population growth, and an uneven distribution of resources all combine to worsen already persistent poverty and food insecurity, especially in rural areas. Erratic weather (frequent droughts and intermittent heavy rains and flooding), overuse of small plots, the overgrazing of cattle, and outdated agricultural practices reduce crop yields and further degrade the environment, exacerbating Eswatini's poverty and subsistence problems. Eswatini's extremely high HIV/AIDS prevalence rate – more than 28% of adults have the disease – compounds these issues. Agricultural production has declined due to HIV/AIDS, as the illness causes households to lose manpower and to sell livestock and other assets to pay for medicine and funerals.

Swazis, mainly men from the country's rural south, have been migrating to South Africa to work in coal, and later gold, mines since the late 19th century. Although the number of miners abroad has never been high in absolute terms because of Eswatini's small population, the outflow has had important social and economic repercussions. The peak of mining employment in South Africa occurred during the 1980s. Cross-border movement has accelerated since the 1990s, as increasing unemployment has pushed more Swazis to look for work in South Africa (creating a "brain drain" in the health and educational sectors); southern Swazi men have continued to pursue mining, although the industry has downsized. Women now make up an increasing share of migrants and dominate cross-border trading in handicrafts, using the proceeds to purchase goods back in Eswatini. Much of today's migration, however, is not work-related but focuses on visits to family and friends, tourism, and shopping.

AGE STRUCTURE:

0-14 years: 34.41% (male 186,747 /female 187,412)

15-24 years: 19.31% (male 99,192 /female 110,770)

25-54 years: 38.22% (male 193,145 /female 222,405)

55-64 years: 4.28% (male 19,915 /female 26,663)

65 years and over: 3.77% (male 15,470 /female 25,481) (2018 est.)

DEPENDENCY RATIOS:

total dependency ratio: 68.8 (2015 est.)

youth dependency ratio: 63.5 (2015 est.)

elderly dependency ratio: 5.2 (2015 est.)

potential support ratio: 19.1 (2015 est.)

MEDIAN AGE:

total: 23.2 years

male: 22.2 years

female: 24 years (2018 est.)

country comparison to the world: 175

POPULATION GROWTH RATE:

0.82% (2018 est.)

country comparison to the world: 128

BIRTH RATE:

25.8 births/1,000 population (2018 est.)

country comparison to the world: 48

DEATH RATE:

10.7 deaths/1,000 population (2018 est.)

country comparison to the world: 24

NET MIGRATION RATE:

0 migrant(s)/1,000 population (2017 est.)

country comparison to the world: 82

POPULATION DISTRIBUTION:

because of its mountainous terrain, the population distribution is uneven throughout the country, concentrating primarily in valleys and plains

URBANIZATION:

urban population: 23.8% of total population (2018)

rate of urbanization: 2.46% annual rate of change (2015-20 est.)

MAJOR URBAN AREAS - POPULATION:

68,000 MBABANE (capital) (2018)

SEX RATIO:

at birth: 1.02 male(s)/female (2017 est.)

0-14 years: 1.02 male(s)/female (2017 est.)

15-24 years: 1.02 male(s)/female (2017 est.)

25-54 years: 1.08 male(s)/female (2017 est.)

55-64 years: 0.66 male(s)/female (2017 est.)

65 years and over: 0.64 male(s)/female (2017 est.)

total population: 1 male(s)/female (2017 est.)

MATERNAL MORTALITY RATE:

389 deaths/100,000 live births (2015 est.)

country comparison to the world: 29

INFANT MORTALITY RATE:

total: 46.6 deaths/1,000 live births (2018 est.)

male: 51.4 deaths/1,000 live births (2018 est.)

female: 41.7 deaths/1,000 live births (2018 est.)

country comparison to the world: 33

LIFE EXPECTANCY AT BIRTH:

total population: 57.2 years

male: 55.1 years

female: 59.3 years (2018 est.)

country comparison to the world: 215

TOTAL FERTILITY RATE:

2.63 children born/woman (2018 est.)

country comparison to the world: 68

CONTRACEPTIVE PREVALENCE RATE:

66.1% (2014)

HEALTH EXPENDITURES:

9.3% of GDP (2014)

country comparison to the world: 34

PHYSICIANS DENSITY:

0.15 physicians/1,000 population (2009)

HOSPITAL BED DENSITY:

2.1 beds/1,000 population (2011)

DRINKING WATER SOURCE:

improved:

urban: 93.6% of population

rural: 68.9% of population

total: 74.1% of population

unimproved:

urban: 6.4% of population

rural: 31.1% of population

total: 25.9% of population (2015 est.)

SANITATION FACILITY ACCESS:

improved:

urban: 63.1% of population (2015 est.)

rural: 56% of population (2015 est.)

total: 57.5% of population (2015 est.)

unimproved:

urban: 36.9% of population (2015 est.)

rural: 44% of population (2015 est.)

total: 42.5% of population (2015 est.)

HIV/AIDS - ADULT PREVALENCE RATE:

27.4% (2017 est.)

country comparison to the world: 1

HIV/AIDS - PEOPLE LIVING WITH HIV/AIDS:

210,000 (2017 est.)

country comparison to the world: 28

HIV/AIDS - DEATHS:

3,500 (2017 est.)

country comparison to the world: 36

MAJOR INFECTIOUS DISEASES:

degree of risk: intermediate (2016)

food or waterborne diseases: bacterial diarrhea, hepatitis A, and typhoid fever (2016)

vectorborne diseases: malaria (2016)

water contact diseases: schistosomiasis (2016)

OBESITY - ADULT PREVALENCE RATE:

16.5% (2016)

country comparison to the world: 124

CHILDREN UNDER THE AGE OF 5 YEARS UNDERWEIGHT:

5.8% (2014)

country comparison to the world: 77

EDUCATION EXPENDITURES:

7.1% of GDP (2014)

country comparison to the world: 20

LITERACY:

definition: age 15 and over can read and write (2015 est.)

total population: 87.5% (2015 est.)

male: 87.4% (2015 est.)

female: 87.5% (2015 est.)

SCHOOL LIFE EXPECTANCY (PRIMARY TO TERTIARY EDUCATION):

total: 11 years (2013)

male: 12 years (2013)

female: 11 years (2013)

GOVERNMENT :: ESWATINI

COUNTRY NAME:

conventional long form: Kingdom of Eswatini

conventional short form: Eswatini

local long form: Umbuso weSwatini

local short form: Eswatini

etymology: the country name derives from 19th century King MSWATI II, under whose rule Swazi territory was expanded and unified

note: pronounced ay-swatini

GOVERNMENT TYPE:

constitutional monarchy

CAPITAL:

name: Mbabane (administrative capital); Lobamba (royal and legislative capital)

geographic coordinates: 26 19 S, 31 08 E

time difference: UTC+2 (7 hours ahead of Washington, DC, during Standard Time)

ADMINISTRATIVE DIVISIONS:

4 regions; Hhohho, Lubombo, Manzini, Shiselweni

INDEPENDENCE:

6 September 1968 (from the UK)

NATIONAL HOLIDAY:

Independence Day (Somhlolo Day), 6 September (1968)

CONSTITUTION:

history: previous 1968, 1978; latest signed by the king 26 July 2005, effective 8 February 2006 (2017)

amendments: proposed at a joint sitting of both houses of Parliament; passage requires majority vote by both houses and/or majority vote in a referendum, and assent by the king; passage of amendments affecting "specially entrenched" constitutional provisions requires at least three-fourths majority vote by both houses, passage by simple majority vote in a referendum, and assent by the king; passage of "entrenched" provisions requires at least two-thirds majority vote of both houses, passage in a referendum, and assent by the king (2017)

LEGAL SYSTEM:

mixed legal system of civil, common, and customary law

INTERNATIONAL LAW ORGANIZATION PARTICIPATION:

accepts compulsory ICJ jurisdiction with reservations; non-party state to the ICCt

CITIZENSHIP:

citizenship by birth: no

citizenship by descent only: both parents must be citizens of Eswatini

dual citizenship recognized: no

residency requirement for naturalization: 5 years

SUFFRAGE:

18 years of age

EXECUTIVE BRANCH:

chief of state: King MSWATI III (since 25 April 1986)

head of government: Prime Minister Ambrose Mandvulo DLAMINI (since 29 October 2018); Deputy Prime Minister Paul DLAMINI (since 2013)

cabinet: Cabinet recommended by the prime minister, confirmed by the monarch; at least one-half of the cabinet membership must be appointed from among elected members of the House of Assembly

elections/appointments: the monarchy is hereditary; prime minister appointed by the monarch from among members of the House of Assembly

LEGISLATIVE BRANCH:

description: bicameral Parliament (Libandla) consists of:
Senate (30 seats; 20 members appointed by the monarch and 10 indirectly elected by simple majority vote by the House of Assembly; members serve 5-year terms) House of Assembly (65 seats; 55 members directly elected in single-seat constituencies or tinkhundla by absolute majority vote in 2 rounds if needed, 10 members appointed by the monarch; members serve 5-year terms)

elections:
House of Assembly - last held on 24 August 2013 with a runoff on 20 September 2013 (tenetavely on 30 September 2018)

election results:
House of Assembly - percent of vote by party - NA; seats by party - independent 59

JUDICIAL BRANCH:

highest courts: the Supreme Court of the Judicature comprising the Supreme Court (consists of the chief justice and at least 6 justices) and the High Court (consists of the chief justice - ex officio - and at least 12 justices); note - the Supreme Court has jurisdiction in all constitutional matters

judge selection and term of office: justices of the Supreme Court of the Judicature appointed by the monarch on the advice of the Judicial Service Commission or JSC, a judicial advisory body consisting of the Supreme Court Chief Justice, 4 members appointed by the monarch, and the JSC head; justices of both courts eligible for retirement at age 65 with mandatory retirement at age 75 for Supreme Court justices and at age 70 for High Court justices

subordinate courts: magistrates' courts; National Swazi Courts for administering customary/traditional laws (jurisdiction restricted to customary law for Swazi citizens)

note: the national constitution as amended in 2006 shifted judicial power from the monarch and vested it exclusively in the judiciary

POLITICAL PARTIES AND LEADERS:

the status of political parties, previously banned, is unclear under the 2006 constitution; the following are considered political associations:
African United Democratic Party or AUDP [Sibusiso DLAMINI]
Ngwane National Liberatory Congress or NNLC [Dr. Alvit DLAMINI]
People's United Democratic Movement or PUDEMO [Mario MASUKU]
Swazi Democratic Party or SWADEPA [Jan SITHOLE]

INTERNATIONAL ORGANIZATION PARTICIPATION:

ACP, AfDB, AU, C, COMESA, FAO, G-77, IAEA, IBRD, ICAO, ICRM, IDA, IFAD, IFC, IFRCS, ILO, IMF, IMO, Interpol, IOC, IOM, ISO (correspondent), ITSO, ITU, ITUC (NGOs), MIGA, NAM, OPCW, PCA, SACU, SADC, UN, UNCTAD, UNESCO, UNIDO, UNWTO, UPU, WCO, WHO, WIPO, WMO, WTO

DIPLOMATIC REPRESENTATION IN THE US:

chief of mission: Ambassador Njabuliso Busisiwe Sikhulile GWEBU (since 24 April 2017)

chancery: 1712 New Hampshire Avenue, NW, Washington, DC 20009

telephone: [1] (202) 234-5002

FAX: [1] (202) 234-8254

DIPLOMATIC REPRESENTATION FROM THE US:

chief of mission: Ambassador Lisa J. PETERSON (since February 2016)

embassy: corner of MR 103 and Cultural Center Drive, Ezulwini

mailing address: P.O. Box D202, The Gables, H106

telephone: [268] 2417-9000

FAX: [268] 2416-3344

FLAG DESCRIPTION:

three horizontal bands of blue (top), red (triple width), and blue; the red band is edged in yellow; centered in the red band is a large black and white shield covering two spears and a staff decorated with feather tassels, all placed horizontally; blue stands for peace and stability, red represents past struggles, and yellow the mineral resources of the country; the shield, spears, and staff symbolize protection from the country's enemies, while the black and white of the shield are meant to portray black and white people living in peaceful coexistence

NATIONAL SYMBOL(S):

lion, elephant; national colors: blue, yellow, red

NATIONAL ANTHEM:

name: "Nkulunkulu Mnikati wetibusiso temaSwati" (Oh God, Bestower of the Blessings of the Swazi)

lyrics/music: Andrease Enoke Fanyana SIMELANE/David Kenneth RYCROFT

note: adopted 1968; uses elements of both ethnic Swazi and Western music styles

ECONOMY :: ESWATINI

ECONOMY - OVERVIEW:

A small, landlocked kingdom, Eswatini is bordered in the north, west and south by the Republic of South Africa and by Mozambique in the east. Eswatini depends on South Africa for a majority of its exports and imports. Eswatini's currency is pegged to the South African rand, effectively relinquishing Eswatini's monetary policy to South Africa. The government is dependent on customs duties from the Southern African Customs Union (SACU) for almost half of its revenue. Eswatini is a lower middle income country. As of 2017, more than one-quarter of the adult population was infected by HIV/AIDS; Eswatini has the world's highest HIV prevalence rate, a financial strain and source of economic instability.

The manufacturing sector diversified in the 1980s and 1990s, but manufacturing has grown little in the last decade. Sugar and soft drink concentrate are the largest foreign exchange earners, although a drought in 2015-16 decreased sugar production and exports. Overgrazing, soil depletion, drought, and floods are persistent problems. Mining has declined in importance in recent years. Coal, gold, diamond, and quarry stone mines are small scale, and the only iron ore mine closed in 2014. With an estimated 28% unemployment rate, Eswatini's need to increase the number and size of small and medium enterprises and to attract foreign direct investment is acute.

Eswatini's national development strategy, which expires in 2022, prioritizes increases in infrastructure, agriculture production, and economic diversification, while aiming to reduce poverty and government spending. Eswatini's revenue from SACU receipts are likely to continue to decline as South Africa pushes for a new distribution scheme, making it harder for the government to maintain fiscal balance without introducing new sources of revenue.

GDP (PURCHASING POWER PARITY):

$11.6 billion (2017 est.)

$11.41 billion (2016 est.)

$11.26 billion (2015 est.)

note: data are in 2017 dollars

country comparison to the world: 157

GDP (OFFICIAL EXCHANGE RATE):

$4.417 billion (2017 est.) (2017 est.)

GDP - REAL GROWTH RATE:

1.6% (2017 est.)

1.4% (2016 est.)

0.4% (2015 est.)

country comparison to the world: 168

GDP - PER CAPITA (PPP):

$10,100 (2017 est.)

$10,100 (2016 est.)

$10,100 (2015 est.)

note: data are in 2017 dollars

country comparison to the world: 139

GROSS NATIONAL SAVING:

25.4% of GDP (2017 est.)

29.7% of GDP (2016 est.)

23.3% of GDP (2015 est.)

country comparison to the world: 59

GDP - COMPOSITION, BY END USE:

household consumption: 64% (2017 est.)

government consumption: 21.3% (2017 est.)

investment in fixed capital: 13.4% (2017 est.)

investment in inventories: -0.1% (2017 est.)

exports of goods and services: 47.9% (2017 est.)

imports of goods and services: -46.3% (2017 est.)

GDP - COMPOSITION, BY SECTOR OF ORIGIN:

agriculture: 6.5% (2017 est.)

industry: 45% (2017 est.)

services: 48.6% (2017 est.)

AGRICULTURE - PRODUCTS:

sugarcane, corn, cotton, citrus, pineapples, cattle, goats

INDUSTRIES:

soft drink concentrates, coal, forestry, sugar processing, textiles, and apparel

INDUSTRIAL PRODUCTION GROWTH RATE:

5.6% (2017 est.)

country comparison to the world: 48

LABOR FORCE:

427,900 (2016 est.)

country comparison to the world: 157

LABOR FORCE - BY OCCUPATION:

agriculture: 10.7%

industry: 30.4%

services: 58.9% (2014 est.)

UNEMPLOYMENT RATE:

28% (2014 est.)

28% (2013 est.)

country comparison to the world: 203

POPULATION BELOW POVERTY LINE:

63% (2010 est.)

HOUSEHOLD INCOME OR CONSUMPTION BY PERCENTAGE SHARE:

lowest 10%: 40.1% (2010 est.)

highest 10%: 40.1% (2010 est.)

DISTRIBUTION OF FAMILY INCOME - GINI INDEX:

50.4 (2001)

country comparison to the world: 16

BUDGET:

revenues: 1.263 billion (2017 est.)

expenditures: 1.639 billion (2017 est.)

TAXES AND OTHER REVENUES:

28.6% (of GDP) (2017 est.)

country comparison to the world: 94

BUDGET SURPLUS (+) OR DEFICIT (-):

-8.5% (of GDP) (2017 est.)

country comparison to the world: 201

PUBLIC DEBT:

28.4% of GDP (2017 est.)

25.5% of GDP (2016 est.)

country comparison to the world: 168

FISCAL YEAR:

1 April - 31 March

INFLATION RATE (CONSUMER PRICES):

6.2% (2017 est.)

7.8% (2016 est.)

country comparison to the world: 188

CENTRAL BANK DISCOUNT RATE:

7.25% (31 December 2016)

6.5% (31 December 2015)

country comparison to the world: 43

COMMERCIAL BANK PRIME LENDING RATE:

10.75% (31 December 2017 est.)

10.25% (31 December 2016 est.)

country comparison to the world: 77

STOCK OF NARROW MONEY:

$554.3 million (31 December 2017 est.)

$439 million (31 December 2016 est.)

country comparison to the world: 168

STOCK OF BROAD MONEY:

$554.3 million (31 December 2017 est.)

$439 million (31 December 2016 est.)

country comparison to the world: 172

STOCK OF DOMESTIC CREDIT:

$1.144 billion (31 December 2017 est.)

$891.3 million (31 December 2016 est.)

country comparison to the world: 166

MARKET VALUE OF PUBLICLY TRADED SHARES:

$203.1 million (31 December 2007)

$199.9 million (31 December 2006)

NA

country comparison to the world: 117

CURRENT ACCOUNT BALANCE:

$604 million (2017 est.)

$642 million (2016 est.)

country comparison to the world: 55

EXPORTS:

$1.83 billion (2017 est.)

$1.577 billion (2016 est.)

country comparison to the world: 146

EXPORTS - PARTNERS:

South Africa 94% (2017)

EXPORTS - COMMODITIES:

soft drink concentrates, sugar, timber, cotton yarn, refrigerators, citrus, and canned fruit

IMPORTS:

$1.451 billion (2017 est.)

$1.266 billion (2016 est.)

country comparison to the world: 174

IMPORTS - COMMODITIES:

motor vehicles, machinery, transport equipment, foodstuffs, petroleum products, chemicals

IMPORTS - PARTNERS:

South Africa 81.6%, China 5.2% (2017)

RESERVES OF FOREIGN EXCHANGE AND GOLD:

$563.1 million (31 December 2017 est.)

$564.4 million (31 December 2016 est.)

country comparison to the world: 147

DEBT - EXTERNAL:

$526.3 million (31 December 2017 est.)

$468.9 million (31 December 2016 est.)

country comparison to the world: 178

STOCK OF DIRECT FOREIGN INVESTMENT - AT HOME:

NA

STOCK OF DIRECT FOREIGN INVESTMENT - ABROAD:

NA

EXCHANGE RATES:

emalangeni per US dollar -

14.44 (2017 est.)

14.6924 (2016 est.)

14.6924 (2015 est.)

12.7581 (2014 est.)

10.8469 (2013 est.)

ENERGY :: ESWATINI

ELECTRICITY ACCESS:

population without electricity: 900,000 (2013)

electrification - total population: 27% (2013)

electrification - urban areas: 40% (2013)

electrification - rural areas: 24% (2013)

ELECTRICITY - PRODUCTION:

381 million kWh (2016 est.)

country comparison to the world: 173

ELECTRICITY - CONSUMPTION:

1.431 billion kWh (2016 est.)

country comparison to the world: 149

ELECTRICITY - EXPORTS:

0 kWh (2016)

country comparison to the world: 132

ELECTRICITY - IMPORTS:

1.077 billion kWh (2016 est.)

country comparison to the world: 69

ELECTRICITY - INSTALLED GENERATING CAPACITY:

295,900 kW (2016 est.)

country comparison to the world: 160

ELECTRICITY - FROM FOSSIL FUELS:

39% of total installed capacity (2016 est.)

country comparison to the world: 172

ELECTRICITY - FROM NUCLEAR FUELS:

0% of total installed capacity (2017 est.)

country comparison to the world: 87

ELECTRICITY - FROM HYDROELECTRIC PLANTS:

20% of total installed capacity (2017 est.)

country comparison to the world: 87

ELECTRICITY - FROM OTHER RENEWABLE SOURCES:

41% of total installed capacity (2017 est.)

country comparison to the world: 6

CRUDE OIL - PRODUCTION:

0 bbl/day (2017 est.)

country comparison to the world: 132

CRUDE OIL - EXPORTS:

0 bbl/day (2015 est.)

country comparison to the world: 120

CRUDE OIL - IMPORTS:

0 bbl/day (2015 est.)

country comparison to the world: 124

CRUDE OIL - PROVED RESERVES:

0 bbl (1 January 2018)

country comparison to the world: 129

REFINED PETROLEUM PRODUCTS - PRODUCTION:

0 bbl/day (2015 est.)

country comparison to the world: 142

REFINED PETROLEUM PRODUCTS - CONSUMPTION:

5,300 bbl/day (2016 est.)

country comparison to the world: 175

REFINED PETROLEUM PRODUCTS - EXPORTS:

0 bbl/day (2015 est.)

country comparison to the world: 152

REFINED PETROLEUM PRODUCTS - IMPORTS:

5,279 bbl/day (2015 est.)

country comparison to the world: 169

NATURAL GAS - PRODUCTION:

0 cu m (2017 est.)

country comparison to the world: 129

NATURAL GAS - CONSUMPTION:

0 cu m (2017 est.)

country comparison to the world: 143

NATURAL GAS - EXPORTS:

0 cu m (2017 est.)

country comparison to the world: 101

NATURAL GAS - IMPORTS:

0 cu m (2017 est.)

country comparison to the world: 122

NATURAL GAS - PROVED RESERVES:

0 cu m (1 January 2014 est.)

country comparison to the world: 133

CARBON DIOXIDE EMISSIONS FROM CONSUMPTION OF ENERGY:

1.14 million Mt (2017 est.)

country comparison to the world: 166

COMMUNICATIONS :: ESWATINI

TELEPHONES - FIXED LINES:

total subscriptions: 42,000 (July 2016 est.)

subscriptions per 100 inhabitants: 3 (July 2016 est.)

country comparison to the world: 160

TELEPHONES - MOBILE CELLULAR:

total subscriptions: 995,000 (July 2016 est.)

subscriptions per 100 inhabitants: 68 (July 2016 est.)

country comparison to the world: 160

TELEPHONE SYSTEM:

general assessment: earlier government monopoly in telecommunicatioons hendered its growth; new regulatory authority estabished in 2013 has aided in the telecome sector; 2G, 3G and LTE services (2017)

domestic: Eswatini recently awarded a second mobile-cellular service; communication infrastructure has a geographic coverage of about 90% and a rising subscriber base; fixed-line stands at 3 per 100 and mobile-cellular teledensity roughly 68 telephones per 100 persons; telephone system consists of carrier-equipped, open-wire lines and low-capacity, microwave radio relay (2017)

international: country code - 268; satellite earth station - 1 Intelsat (Atlantic Ocean) (2017)

BROADCAST MEDIA:

1 state-owned TV station; satellite dishes are able to access South African providers; state-owned radio network with 3 channels; 1 private radio station (2017)

INTERNET COUNTRY CODE:

.sz

INTERNET USERS:

total: 414,724 (July 2016 est.)

percent of population: 28.6% (July 2016 est.)

country comparison to the world: 153

BROADBAND - FIXED SUBSCRIPTIONS:

total: 7,000 (2017 est.)

subscriptions per 100 inhabitants: less than 1 (2017 est.)

country comparison to the world: 173

TRANSPORTATION :: ESWATINI

NATIONAL AIR TRANSPORT SYSTEM:

number of registered air carriers: 1 (2015)

inventory of registered aircraft operated by air carriers: 1 (2015)

annual passenger traffic on registered air carriers: 89,791 (2015)

annual freight traffic on registered air carriers: 0 mt-km (2015)

CIVIL AIRCRAFT REGISTRATION COUNTRY CODE PREFIX:

3 (2016)

AIRPORTS:

14 (2013)

country comparison to the world: 148

AIRPORTS - WITH PAVED RUNWAYS:

total: 2 (2013)

over 3,047 m: 1 (2013)

2,438 to 3,047 m: 1 (2013)

AIRPORTS - WITH UNPAVED RUNWAYS:

total: 12 (2013)

914 to 1,523 m: 5 (2013)

under 914 m: 7 (2013)

RAILWAYS:

total: 301 km (2014)

narrow gauge: 301 km 1.067-m gauge (2014)

country comparison to the world: 122

ROADWAYS:

total: 3,594 km (2002)

paved: 1,078 km (2002)

unpaved: 2,516 km (2002)

country comparison to the world: 160

MILITARY AND SECURITY :: ESWATINI

MILITARY EXPENDITURES:

1.81% of GDP (2016)

1.78% of GDP (2015)

1.81% of GDP (2014)

country comparison to the world: 61

MILITARY BRANCHES:

Umbutfo Swaziland Defense Force (USDF): Ground Force (includes Air Wing (no operational aircraft)) (2013)

MILITARY SERVICE AGE AND OBLIGATION:

18-30 years of age for male and female voluntary military service; no conscription; compulsory HIV testing required, only HIV-negative applicants accepted (2012)

TRANSNATIONAL ISSUES :: ESWATINI

DISPUTES - INTERNATIONAL:

in 2006, Swazi king advocated resorting to ICJ to claim parts of Mpumalanga and KwaZulu-Natal from South Africa

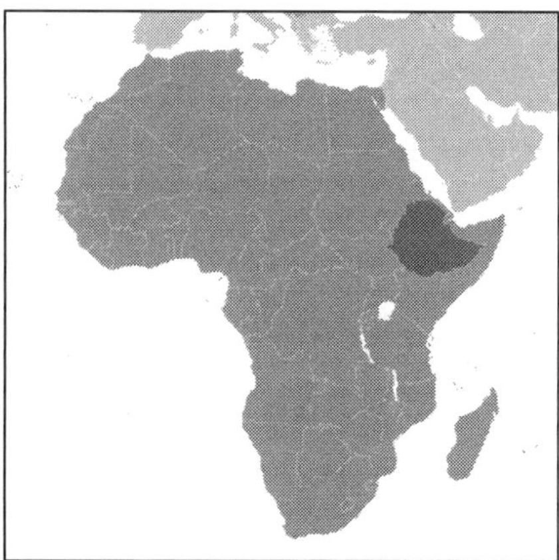

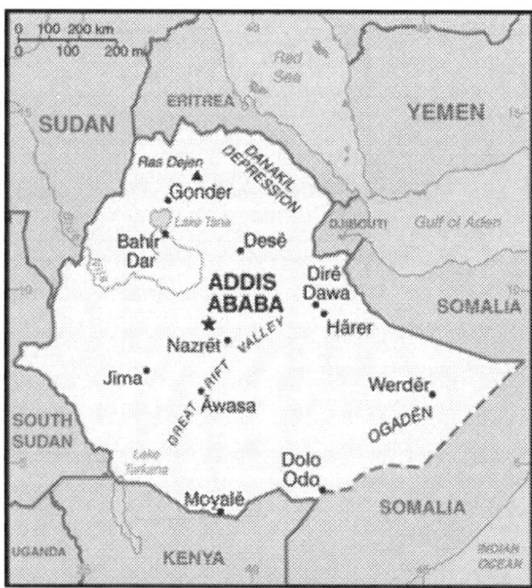

AFRICA :: ETHIOPIA

INTRODUCTION :: ETHIOPIA

BACKGROUND:

Unique among African countries, the ancient Ethiopian monarchy maintained its freedom from colonial rule with the exception of a short-lived Italian occupation from 1936-41. In 1974, a military junta, the Derg, deposed Emperor Haile SELASSIE (who had ruled since 1930) and established a socialist state. Torn by bloody coups, uprisings, wide-scale drought, and massive refugee problems, the regime was finally toppled in 1991 by a coalition of rebel forces, the Ethiopian People's Revolutionary Democratic Front. A constitution was adopted in 1994, and Ethiopia's first multiparty elections were held in 1995. A border war with Eritrea in the late 1990s ended with a peace treaty in December 2000. In November 2007, the Eritrea-Ethiopia Border Commission (EEBC) issued specific coordinates as virtually demarcating the border and pronounced its work finished. Alleging that the EEBC acted beyond its mandate in issuing the coordinates, Ethiopia has not accepted them and has not withdrawn troops from previously contested areas pronounced by the EEBC as belonging to Eritrea. In August 2012, longtime leader Prime Minister MELES Zenawi died in office and was replaced by his Deputy Prime Minister HAILEMARIAM Desalegn, marking the first peaceful transition of power in decades.

GEOGRAPHY :: ETHIOPIA

LOCATION:

Eastern Africa, west of Somalia

GEOGRAPHIC COORDINATES:

8 00 N, 38 00 E

MAP REFERENCES:

Africa

AREA:

total: 1,104,300 sq km

land: 1 million sq km

water: 104,300 sq km

country comparison to the world: 28

AREA - COMPARATIVE:

slightly less than twice the size of Texas

LAND BOUNDARIES:

total: 5,925 km

border countries (6): Djibouti 342 km, Eritrea 1033 km, Kenya 867 km, Somalia 1640 km, South Sudan 1299 km, Sudan 744 km

COASTLINE:

0 km (landlocked)

MARITIME CLAIMS:

none (landlocked)

CLIMATE:

tropical monsoon with wide topographic-induced variation

TERRAIN:

high plateau with central mountain range divided by Great Rift Valley

ELEVATION:

mean elevation: 1,330 m

elevation extremes: -125 m lowest point: Danakil Depression

4550 highest point: Ras Dejen

NATURAL RESOURCES:

small reserves of gold, platinum, copper, potash, natural gas, hydropower

LAND USE:

agricultural land: 36.3% (2011 est.)

arable land: 15.2% (2011 est.) / permanent crops: 1.1% (2011 est.) / permanent pasture: 20% (2011 est.)

forest: 12.2% (2011 est.)

other: 51.5% (2011 est.)

IRRIGATED LAND:

2,900 sq km (2012)

POPULATION DISTRIBUTION:

highest density is found in the highlands of the north and middle areas of the country, particularly around the centrally located capital city of Addis Ababa; the far east and southeast are sparsely populated

NATURAL HAZARDS:

geologically active Great Rift Valley susceptible to earthquakes, volcanic eruptions; frequent droughts

volcanism: volcanic activity in the Great Rift Valley; Erta Ale (613 m), which has caused frequent lava flows in recent years, is the country's most active volcano; Dabbahu became active in 2005, forcing evacuations; other historically active volcanoes include Alayta, Dalaffilla, Dallol, Dama Ali, Fentale, Kone, Manda Hararo, and Manda-Inakir

ENVIRONMENT - CURRENT ISSUES:

deforestation; overgrazing; soil erosion; desertification; loss of biodiversity; water shortages in some areas from water-intensive farming and poor management; industrial pollution and pesticides contribute to air, water, and soil pollution

ENVIRONMENT - INTERNATIONAL AGREEMENTS:

party to: Biodiversity, Climate Change, Climate Change-Kyoto Protocol, Desertification, Endangered Species, Hazardous Wastes, Ozone Layer Protection

signed, but not ratified: Environmental Modification, Law of the Sea

GEOGRAPHY - NOTE:

landlocked - entire coastline along the Red Sea was lost with the de jure independence of Eritrea on 24 May 1993; Ethiopia is, therefore, the most populous landlocked country in the world; the Blue Nile, the chief headstream of the Nile by water volume, rises in T'ana Hayk (Lake Tana) in northwest Ethiopia; three major crops are believed to have originated in Ethiopia: coffee, grain sorghum, and castor bean

PEOPLE AND SOCIETY :: ETHIOPIA

POPULATION:

108,386,391 (July 2018 est.)

note: estimates for this country explicitly take into account the effects of excess mortality due to AIDS; this can result in lower life expectancy, higher infant mortality, higher death rates, lower population growth rates, and changes in the distribution of population by age and sex than would otherwise be expected

country comparison to the world: 12

NATIONALITY:

noun: Ethiopian(s)

adjective: Ethiopian

ETHNIC GROUPS:

Oromo 34.4%, Amhara (Amara) 27%, Somali (Somalie) 6.2%, Tigray (Tigrinya) 6.1%, Sidama 4%, Gurage 2.5%, Welaita 2.3%, Hadiya 1.7%, Afar (Affar) 1.7%, Gamo 1.5%, Gedeo 1.3%, Silte 1.3%, Kefficho 1.2%, other 8.8% (2007 est.)

LANGUAGES:

Oromo (official working language in the State of Oromiya) 33.8%, Amharic (official national language) 29.3%, Somali (official working language of the State of Sumale) 6.2%, Tigrigna (Tigrinya) (official working language of the State of Tigray) 5.9%, Sidamo 4%, Wolaytta 2.2%, Gurage 2%, Afar (official working language of the State of Afar) 1.7%, Hadiyya 1.7%, Gamo 1.5%, Gedeo 1.3%, Opuuo 1.2%, Kafa 1.1%, other 8.1%, English (major foreign language taught in schools), Arabic (2007 est.)

RELIGIONS:

Ethiopian Orthodox 43.5%, Muslim 33.9%, Protestant 18.5%, traditional 2.7%, Catholic 0.7%, other 0.6% (2007 est.)

DEMOGRAPHIC PROFILE:

Ethiopia is a predominantly agricultural country – more than 80% of the population lives in rural areas – that is in the early stages of demographic transition. Infant, child, and maternal mortality have fallen sharply over the past decade, but the total fertility rate has declined more slowly and the population continues to grow. The rising age of marriage and the increasing proportion of women remaining single have contributed to fertility reduction. While the use of modern contraceptive methods among married women has increased significantly from 6 percent in 2000 to 27 percent in 2012, the overall rate is still quite low.

Ethiopia's rapid population growth is putting increasing pressure on land resources, expanding environmental degradation, and raising vulnerability to food shortages. With more than 40 percent of the population below the age of 15 and a fertility rate of over 5 children per woman (and even higher in rural areas), Ethiopia will have to make further progress in meeting its family planning needs if it is to achieve the age structure necessary for reaping a demographic dividend in the coming decades.

Poverty, drought, political repression, and forced government resettlement have driven Ethiopia's internal and external migration since the 1960s. Before the 1974 revolution, only small numbers of the Ethiopian elite went abroad to study and then returned home, but under the brutal Derg regime thousands fled the country, primarily as refugees. Between 1982 and 1991 there was a new wave of migration to the West for family reunification. Since the defeat of the Derg in 1991, Ethiopians have migrated to escape violence among some of the country's myriad ethnic groups or to pursue economic opportunities. Internal and international trafficking of women and children for domestic work and prostitution is a growing problem.

AGE STRUCTURE:

0-14 years: 43.21% (male 23,494,593 /female 23,336,508)

15-24 years: 20.18% (male 10,857,968 /female 11,011,100)

25-54 years: 29.73% (male 15,978,384 /female 16,247,086)

55-64 years: 3.92% (male 2,059,129 /female 2,185,814)

65 years and over: 2.97% (male 1,445,547 /female 1,770,262) (2018 est.)

DEPENDENCY RATIOS:

total dependency ratio: 82.1 (2015 est.)

youth dependency ratio: 75.8 (2015 est.)

elderly dependency ratio: 6.3 (2015 est.)

potential support ratio: 15.8 (2015 est.)

MEDIAN AGE:

total: 18 years

male: 17.8 years

female: 18.2 years (2018 est.)

country comparison to the world: 213

POPULATION GROWTH RATE:

2.83% (2018 est.)

country comparison to the world: 11

BIRTH RATE:

36 births/1,000 population (2018 est.)

country comparison to the world: 17

DEATH RATE:

7.5 deaths/1,000 population (2018 est.)

country comparison to the world: 110

NET MIGRATION RATE:

-0.2 migrant(s)/1,000 population (2017 est.)

country comparison to the world: 107

POPULATION DISTRIBUTION:

highest density is found in the highlands of the north and middle areas of the country, particularly around the centrally located capital city of Addis Ababa; the far east and southeast are sparsely populated

URBANIZATION:

urban population: 20.8% of total population (2018)

rate of urbanization: 4.63% annual rate of change (2015-20 est.)

MAJOR URBAN AREAS - POPULATION:

4.4 million ADDIS ABABA (capital) (2018)

SEX RATIO:

at birth: 1.02 male(s)/female (2017 est.)

0-14 years: 1.01 male(s)/female (2017 est.)

15-24 years: 0.99 male(s)/female (2017 est.)

25-54 years: 0.99 male(s)/female (2017 est.)

55-64 years: 0.95 male(s)/female (2017 est.)

65 years and over: 0.82 male(s)/female (2017 est.)

total population: 0.99 male(s)/female (2017 est.)

MOTHER'S MEAN AGE AT FIRST BIRTH:

20 years (2016 est.)

note: median age at first birth among women 25-29

MATERNAL MORTALITY RATE:

353 deaths/100,000 live births (2015 est.)

country comparison to the world: 34

INFANT MORTALITY RATE:

total: 48.3 deaths/1,000 live births (2018 est.)

male: 55.3 deaths/1,000 live births (2018 est.)

female: 41 deaths/1,000 live births (2018 est.)

country comparison to the world: 31

LIFE EXPECTANCY AT BIRTH:

total population: 63 years

male: 60.5 years

female: 65.5 years (2018 est.)

country comparison to the world: 197

TOTAL FERTILITY RATE:

4.91 children born/woman (2018 est.)

country comparison to the world: 15

CONTRACEPTIVE PREVALENCE RATE:

36.5% (2017)

HEALTH EXPENDITURES:

4.9% of GDP (2014)

country comparison to the world: 144

PHYSICIANS DENSITY:

0.03 physicians/1,000 population (2009)

HOSPITAL BED DENSITY:

0.3 beds/1,000 population (2015)

DRINKING WATER SOURCE:

improved:

urban: 93.1% of population

rural: 48.6% of population

total: 57.3% of population

unimproved:

urban: 6.9% of population

rural: 51.4% of population

total: 42.7% of population (2015 est.)

SANITATION FACILITY ACCESS:

improved:

urban: 27.2% of population (2015 est.)

rural: 28.2% of population (2015 est.)

total: 28% of population (2015 est.)

unimproved:

urban: 72.8% of population (2015 est.)

rural: 71.8% of population (2015 est.)

total: 72% of population (2015 est.)

HIV/AIDS - ADULT PREVALENCE RATE:

0.9% (2017 est.)

country comparison to the world: 47

HIV/AIDS - PEOPLE LIVING WITH HIV/AIDS:

610,000 (2017 est.)

country comparison to the world: 14

HIV/AIDS - DEATHS:

15,000 (2017 est.)

country comparison to the world: 16

MAJOR INFECTIOUS DISEASES:

degree of risk: very high (2016)

food or waterborne diseases: bacterial and protozoal diarrhea, hepatitis A, and typhoid fever (2016)

vectorborne diseases: malaria and dengue fever (2016)

water contact diseases: schistosomiasis (2016)

animal contact diseases: rabies (2016)

respiratory diseases: meningococcal meningitis (2016)

OBESITY - ADULT PREVALENCE RATE:

4.5% (2016)

country comparison to the world: 185

CHILDREN UNDER THE AGE OF 5 YEARS UNDERWEIGHT:

23.6% (2016)

country comparison to the world: 20

EDUCATION EXPENDITURES:

4.5% of GDP (2013)

country comparison to the world: 94

LITERACY:

definition: age 15 and over can read and write (2015 est.)

total population: 49.1% (2015 est.)

male: 57.2% (2015 est.)

female: 41.1% (2015 est.)

SCHOOL LIFE EXPECTANCY (PRIMARY TO TERTIARY EDUCATION):

total: 8 years (2012)

male: 9 years (2012)

female: 8 years (2012)

UNEMPLOYMENT, YOUTH AGES 15-24:

total: 25.2% (2016 est.)

male: 17.1% (2016 est.)

female: 30.9% (2016 est.)

country comparison to the world: 46

GOVERNMENT :: ETHIOPIA

COUNTRY NAME:

conventional long form: Federal Democratic Republic of Ethiopia

conventional short form: Ethiopia

local long form: Ityop'iya Federalawi Demokrasiyawi Ripeblik

local short form: Ityop'iya

former: Abyssinia, Italian East Africa

abbreviation: FDRE

etymology: the country name derives from the Greek word "Aethiopia," which in classical times referred to lands south of Egypt in the Upper Nile region

GOVERNMENT TYPE:

federal parliamentary republic

CAPITAL:

name: Addis Ababa

geographic coordinates: 9 02 N, 38 42 E

time difference: UTC+3 (8 hours ahead of Washington, DC, during Standard Time)

ADMINISTRATIVE DIVISIONS:

9 ethnically based regional states (kililoch, singular - kilil) and 2 self-governing administrations* (astedaderoch, singular - astedader); Adis Abeba* (Addis Ababa), Afar, Amara (Amhara), Binshangul Gumuz, Dire Dawa*, Gambela Hizboch (Gambela Peoples), Hareri Hizb (Harari People), Oromiya (Oromia),

Sumale (Somali), Tigray, Ye Debub Biheroch Bihereseboch na Hizboch (Southern Nations, Nationalities and Peoples)

INDEPENDENCE:

oldest independent country in Africa and one of the oldest in the world - at least 2,000 years (may be traced to the Aksumite Kingdom, which coalesced in the first century B.C.)

NATIONAL HOLIDAY:

Derg Downfall Day (defeat of MENGISTU regime), 28 May (1991)

CONSTITUTION:

history: several previous; latest drafted June 1994, adopted 8 December 1994, entered into force 21 August 1995 (2017)

amendments: proposals submitted for discussion require two-thirds majority approval in either house of Parliament or majority approval of one-third of the State Councils; passage of amendments other than constitutional articles on fundamental rights and freedoms and the initiation and amendment of the constitution requires two-thirds majority vote in a joint session of Parliament and majority vote by two-thirds of the State Councils; passage of amendments affecting rights and freedoms and amendment procedures requires two-thirds majority vote in each house of Parliament and majority vote by all the State Councils (2017)

LEGAL SYSTEM:

civil law system

INTERNATIONAL LAW ORGANIZATION PARTICIPATION:

has not submitted an ICJ jurisdiction declaration; non-party state to the ICCt

CITIZENSHIP:

citizenship by birth: no

citizenship by descent only: at least one parent must be a citizen of Ethiopia

dual citizenship recognized: no

residency requirement for naturalization: 4 years

SUFFRAGE:

18 years of age; universal

EXECUTIVE BRANCH:

chief of state: President SAHLE-WORK Zewde (since 25 October 2018)

head of government: Prime Minister ABIY Ahmed (since 2 April 2018); Deputy Prime Minister DEMEKE Mekonnen Hassen (since 29 November 2012); note - Prime Minister HAILEMARIAM Desalegn (since 21 September 2012) resigned on 15 February 2018

cabinet: Council of Ministers selected by the prime minister and approved by the House of People's Representatives

elections/appointments: president indirectly elected by both chambers of Parliament for a 6-year term (eligible for a second term); election last held on 7 October 2013 (next to be held in October 2019); prime minister designated by the majority party following legislative elections

election results: SAHLE-WORK Zewde elected president; Parliament vote - 659 (unanimous)

note: SAHLE-WORK Zewde is the first female elected head of state in Ethiopia; she is currently the only female president in Africa

LEGISLATIVE BRANCH:

description: bicameral Parliament consists of:
House of Federation or Yefedereshein Mikir Bete (153 seats; members indirectly elected by state assemblies to serve 5-year terms)
House of People's Representatives or Yehizb Tewokayoch Mekir Bete (547 seats; members directly elected in single-seat constituencies by simple majority vote; 22 seats reserved for minorities; all members serve 5-year terms)

elections:
House of People's Representatives - last held on 24 May 2015 (next to be held in 2020)

election results:
House of Representatives - percent of vote by party/coalition - NA; seats by party/coalition - EPRDF 501, SPDP 24, BGPDUP 9, ANDP 8, GPUDM 3, APDO 1, HNL 1

note: House of Federation is responsible for interpreting the constitution and federal-regional issues and the House of People's Representatives is responsible for passing legislation

JUDICIAL BRANCH:

highest courts: Federal Supreme Court (consists of 11 judges); note - the House of Federation has jurisdiction for all constitutional issues

judge selection and term of office: president and vice president of Federal Supreme Court recommended by the prime minister and appointed by the House of People's Representatives; other Supreme Court judges nominated by the Federal Judicial Administrative Council (a 10-member body chaired by the president of the Federal Supreme Court) and appointed by the House of People's Representatives; judges serve until retirement at age 60

subordinate courts: federal high courts and federal courts of first instance; state court systems (mirror structure of federal system); sharia courts and customary and traditional courts

POLITICAL PARTIES AND LEADERS:

Afar National Democratic Party or ANDP [Taha AHMED]
Argoba People Democratic Organization or APDO
Amhara National Democratic Movement or ANDM [Demeke MEKONNEN]
Benishangul Gumuz People's Democratic Unity Party or BGPDUP
Blue Party (Semayawi Party) [Solomon TESSEMA, spokesman]
Ethiopian Federal Democratic Unity Forum or MEDREK or FORUM [Beyene PETROS] (includes ESD-SCUP, OFC, SLM, UTDS)
Ethiopian People's Revolutionary Democratic Front or EPRDF [ABIY Ahmed] (includes ANDM, OPDO, SEPDM, TPLF)
Ethiopian Social Democracy-Sothern Coalition Unity Party or ESD-SCUP
Gambella Peoples Unity Democratic Movement or GPUDM
Harari National League or HNL [Murad ABDULHADI]
Oromo Fderalist Congress or OFC
Oromo People's Democratic Organization or OPDO [ABIY Ahmed]
Sidama Liberaton Movement or SLM
Somali People's Democratic Party or SPDP
Southern Ethiopian People's Democratic Movement or SEPDM [Muferiat KAMIL]
Tigray People's Liberation Front or TPLF [Meles ZENAWI]
Union of Tigraians for Democracy & Soveignty or UTDS

INTERNATIONAL ORGANIZATION PARTICIPATION:

ACP, AfDB, AU, COMESA, EITI (candidate country), FAO, G-24, G-77, IAEA, IBRD, ICAO, ICRM, IDA, IFAD, IFC, IFRCS, IGAD, ILO, IMF, IMO, Interpol, IOC, IOM, IPU, ISO, ITSO, ITU, ITUC (NGOs), MIGA, NAM, OPCW, PCA, UN, UNAMID,

UNCTAD, UNESCO, UNHCR, UNIDO, UNISFA, UNMIL, UN Security Council (temporary), UNOCI, UNWTO, UPU, WCO, WFTU (NGOs), WHO, WIPO, WMO, WTO (observer)

DIPLOMATIC REPRESENTATION IN THE US:

chief of mission: Ambassador Kassa TEKLEBERHAN Gebrehiwet (since 24 January 2018)

chancery: 3506 International Drive NW, Washington, DC 20008

telephone: [1] (202) 364-1200

FAX: [1] (202) 587-0195

consulate(s) general: Los Angeles, Seattle

consulate(s): Houston, New York

DIPLOMATIC REPRESENTATION FROM THE US:

chief of mission: Ambassador Michael RAYNOR (since 3 October 2017)

embassy: Entoto Street, Addis Ababa

mailing address: P.O. Box 1014, Addis Ababa

telephone: [251] 11 130-6000

FAX: [251] 11 124-2401

FLAG DESCRIPTION:

three equal horizontal bands of green (top), yellow, and red, with a yellow pentagram and single yellow rays emanating from the angles between the points on a light blue disk centered on the three bands; green represents hope and the fertility of the land, yellow symbolizes justice and harmony, while red stands for sacrifice and heroism in the defense of the land; the blue of the disk symbolizes peace and the pentagram represents the unity and equality of the nationalities and peoples of Ethiopia

note: Ethiopia is the oldest independent country in Africa, and the three main colors of her flag (adopted ca. 1895) were so often appropriated by other African countries upon independence that they became known as the Pan-African colors; the emblem in the center of the current flag was added in 1996

NATIONAL SYMBOL(S):

Abyssinian lion (traditional), yellow pentagram with five rays of light on a blue field (promoted by current government); national colors: green, yellow, red

NATIONAL ANTHEM:

name: "Whedefit Gesgeshi Woud Enat Ethiopia" (March Forward, Dear Mother Ethiopia)

lyrics/music: DEREJE Melaku Mengesha/SOLOMON Lulu

note: adopted 1992

ECONOMY :: ETHIOPIA

ECONOMY - OVERVIEW:

Ethiopia - the second most populous country in Africa - is a one-party state with a planned economy. For more than a decade before 2016, GDP grew at a rate between 8% and 11% annually – one of the fastest growing states among the 188 IMF member countries. This growth was driven by government investment in infrastructure, as well as sustained progress in the agricultural and service sectors. More than 70% of Ethiopia's population is still employed in the agricultural sector, but services have surpassed agriculture as the principal source of GDP.

Ethiopia has the lowest level of income-inequality in Africa and one of the lowest in the world, with a Gini coefficient comparable to that of the Scandinavian countries. Yet despite progress toward eliminating extreme poverty, Ethiopia remains one of the poorest countries in the world, due both to rapid population growth and a low starting base. Changes in rainfall associated with world-wide weather patterns resulted in the worst drought in 30 years in 2015-16, creating food insecurity for millions of Ethiopians.

The state is heavily engaged in the economy. Ongoing infrastructure projects include power production and distribution, roads, rails, airports and industrial parks. Key sectors are state-owned, including telecommunications, banking and insurance, and power distribution. Under Ethiopia's constitution, the state owns all land and provides long-term leases to tenants. Title rights in urban areas, particularly Addis Ababa, are poorly regulated, and subject to corruption.

Ethiopia's foreign exchange earnings are led by the services sector - primarily the state-run Ethiopian Airlines - followed by exports of several commodities. While coffee remains the largest foreign exchange earner, Ethiopia is diversifying exports, and commodities such as gold, sesame, khat, livestock and horticulture products are becoming increasingly important. Manufacturing represented less than 8% of total exports in 2016, but manufacturing exports should increase in future years due to a growing international presence.

The banking, insurance, telecommunications, and micro-credit industries are restricted to domestic investors, but Ethiopia has attracted roughly $8.5 billion in foreign direct investment (FDI), mostly from China, Turkey, India and the EU; US FDI is $567 million. Investment has been primarily in infrastructure, construction, agriculture/horticulture, agricultural processing, textiles, leather and leather products.

To support industrialization in sectors where Ethiopia has a comparative advantage, such as textiles and garments, leather goods, and processed agricultural products, Ethiopia plans to increase installed power generation capacity by 8,320 MW, up from a capacity of 2,000 MW, by building three more major dams and expanding to other sources of renewable energy. In 2017, the government devalued the birr by 15% to increase exports and alleviate a chronic foreign currency shortage in the country.

GDP (PURCHASING POWER PARITY):

$200.6 billion (2017 est.)

$181 billion (2016 est.)

$167.6 billion (2015 est.)

note: data are in 2017 dollars

country comparison to the world: 64

GDP (OFFICIAL EXCHANGE RATE):

$80.87 billion (2017 est.) (2017 est.)

GDP - REAL GROWTH RATE:

10.9% (2017 est.)

8% (2016 est.)

10.4% (2015 est.)

country comparison to the world: 5

GDP - PER CAPITA (PPP):

$2,200 (2017 est.)

$2,000 (2016 est.)

$1,900 (2015 est.)

note: data are in 2017 dollars

country comparison to the world: 204

GROSS NATIONAL SAVING:

32.1% of GDP (2017 est.)

32.7% of GDP (2016 est.)

32.4% of GDP (2015 est.)

country comparison to the world: 26

GDP - COMPOSITION, BY END USE:

household consumption: 69.6% (2017 est.)

government consumption: 10% (2017 est.)

investment in fixed capital: 43.5% (2017 est.)

investment in inventories: -0.1% (2017 est.)

exports of goods and services: 8.1% (2017 est.)

imports of goods and services: -31.2% (2017 est.)

GDP - COMPOSITION, BY SECTOR OF ORIGIN:

agriculture: 34.8% (2017 est.)

industry: 21.6% (2017 est.)

services: 43.6% (2017 est.)

AGRICULTURE - PRODUCTS:

cereals, coffee, oilseed, cotton, sugarcane, vegetables, khat, cut flowers; hides, cattle, sheep, goats; fish

INDUSTRIES:

food processing, beverages, textiles, leather, garments, chemicals, metals processing, cement

INDUSTRIAL PRODUCTION GROWTH RATE:

10.5% (2017 est.)

country comparison to the world: 13

LABOR FORCE:

52.82 million (2017 est.)

country comparison to the world: 13

LABOR FORCE - BY OCCUPATION:

agriculture: 72.7%

industry: 7.4%

services: 19.9% (2013 est.)

UNEMPLOYMENT RATE:

17.5% (2012 est.)

18% (2011 est.)

country comparison to the world: 180

POPULATION BELOW POVERTY LINE:

29.6% (2014 est.)

HOUSEHOLD INCOME OR CONSUMPTION BY PERCENTAGE SHARE:

lowest 10%: 25.6% (2005)

highest 10%: 25.6% (2005)

DISTRIBUTION OF FAMILY INCOME - GINI INDEX:

33 (2011)

30 (2000)

country comparison to the world: 114

BUDGET:

revenues: 11.24 billion (2017 est.)

expenditures: 13.79 billion (2017 est.)

TAXES AND OTHER REVENUES:

13.9% (of GDP) (2017 est.)

country comparison to the world: 203

BUDGET SURPLUS (+) OR DEFICIT (-):

-3.2% (of GDP) (2017 est.)

country comparison to the world: 139

PUBLIC DEBT:

54.2% of GDP (2017 est.)

53.2% of GDP (2016 est.)

country comparison to the world: 83

FISCAL YEAR:

8 July - 7 July

INFLATION RATE (CONSUMER PRICES):

9.9% (2017 est.)

7.3% (2016 est.)

country comparison to the world: 203

CENTRAL BANK DISCOUNT RATE:

NA

COMMERCIAL BANK PRIME LENDING RATE:

13.5% (31 December 2017 est.)

12.2% (31 December 2016 est.)

country comparison to the world: 54

STOCK OF NARROW MONEY:

$9.042 billion (31 December 2017 est.)

$8.757 billion (31 December 2016 est.)

country comparison to the world: 85

STOCK OF BROAD MONEY:

$9.042 billion (31 December 2017 est.)

$8.757 billion (31 December 2016 est.)

country comparison to the world: 87

STOCK OF DOMESTIC CREDIT:

$27.66 billion (31 December 2017 est.)

$25.78 billion (31 December 2016 est.)

country comparison to the world: 84

MARKET VALUE OF PUBLICLY TRADED SHARES:

NA

CURRENT ACCOUNT BALANCE:

-$6.551 billion (2017 est.)

-$6.574 billion (2016 est.)

country comparison to the world: 187

EXPORTS:

$3.23 billion (2017 est.)

$2.814 billion (2016 est.)

country comparison to the world: 127

EXPORTS - PARTNERS:

Sudan 23.3%, Switzerland 10.2%, China 8.1%, Somalia 6.6%, Netherlands 6.2%, US 4.7%, Germany 4.7%, Saudi Arabia 4.6%, UK 4.6% (2017)

EXPORTS - COMMODITIES:

coffee (27%, by value), oilseeds (17%), edible vegetables including khat (17%), gold (13%), flowers (7%), live animals (7%), raw leather products (3%), meat products (3%)

IMPORTS:

$15.59 billion (2017 est.)

$14.69 billion (2016 est.)

country comparison to the world: 89

IMPORTS - COMMODITIES:

machinery and aircraft (14%, by value), metal and metal products, (14%), electrical materials, (13%), petroleum products (12%), motor vehicles, (10%), chemicals and fertilizers (4%)

IMPORTS - PARTNERS:

China 24.1%, Saudi Arabia 10.1%, India 6.4%, Kuwait 5.3%, France 5.2% (2017)

RESERVES OF FOREIGN EXCHANGE AND GOLD:

$3.013 billion (31 December 2017 est.)

$3.022 billion (31 December 2016 est.)

country comparison to the world: 110

DEBT - EXTERNAL:

$26.05 billion (31 December 2017 est.)

$24.82 billion (31 December 2016 est.)

country comparison to the world: 87

STOCK OF DIRECT FOREIGN INVESTMENT - AT HOME:

(31 December 2009 est.)

EXCHANGE RATES:

birr (ETB) per US dollar -

25 (2017 est.)

21.732 (2016 est.)

21.732 (2015 est.)

21.55 (2014 est.)

19.8 (2013 est.)

ENERGY :: ETHIOPIA

ELECTRICITY ACCESS:

population without electricity: 71.2 million (2013)

electrification - total population: 24% (2013)

electrification - urban areas: 85% (2013)

electrification - rural areas: 10% (2013)

ELECTRICITY - PRODUCTION:

11.15 billion kWh (2016 est.)

country comparison to the world: 99

ELECTRICITY - CONSUMPTION:

9.062 billion kWh (2016 est.)

country comparison to the world: 100

ELECTRICITY - EXPORTS:

166 million kWh (2015 est.)

country comparison to the world: 78

ELECTRICITY - IMPORTS:

0 kWh (2016 est.)

country comparison to the world: 146

ELECTRICITY - INSTALLED GENERATING CAPACITY:

2.784 million kW (2016 est.)

country comparison to the world: 99

ELECTRICITY - FROM FOSSIL FUELS:

3% of total installed capacity (2016 est.)

country comparison to the world: 207

ELECTRICITY - FROM NUCLEAR FUELS:

0% of total installed capacity (2017 est.)

country comparison to the world: 88

ELECTRICITY - FROM HYDROELECTRIC PLANTS:

86% of total installed capacity (2017 est.)

country comparison to the world: 11

ELECTRICITY - FROM OTHER RENEWABLE SOURCES:

11% of total installed capacity (2017 est.)

country comparison to the world: 76

CRUDE OIL - PRODUCTION:

0 bbl/day (2017 est.)

country comparison to the world: 133

CRUDE OIL - EXPORTS:

0 bbl/day (2015 est.)

country comparison to the world: 121

CRUDE OIL - IMPORTS:

0 bbl/day (2015 est.)

country comparison to the world: 125

CRUDE OIL - PROVED RESERVES:

428,000 bbl (1 January 2018 est.)

country comparison to the world: 98

REFINED PETROLEUM PRODUCTS - PRODUCTION:

0 bbl/day (2017 est.)

country comparison to the world: 143

REFINED PETROLEUM PRODUCTS - CONSUMPTION:

74,000 bbl/day (2016 est.)

country comparison to the world: 89

REFINED PETROLEUM PRODUCTS - EXPORTS:

0 bbl/day (2015 est.)

country comparison to the world: 153

REFINED PETROLEUM PRODUCTS - IMPORTS:

69,970 bbl/day (2015 est.)

country comparison to the world: 67

NATURAL GAS - PRODUCTION:

0 cu m (2017 est.)

country comparison to the world: 130

NATURAL GAS - CONSUMPTION:

0 cu m (2017 est.)

country comparison to the world: 144

NATURAL GAS - EXPORTS:

0 cu m (2017 est.)

country comparison to the world: 102

NATURAL GAS - IMPORTS:

0 cu m (2017 est.)

country comparison to the world: 123

NATURAL GAS - PROVED RESERVES:

24.92 billion cu m (1 January 2018 est.)

country comparison to the world: 72

CARBON DIOXIDE EMISSIONS FROM CONSUMPTION OF ENERGY:

12.18 million Mt (2017 est.)

country comparison to the world: 99

COMMUNICATIONS :: ETHIOPIA

TELEPHONES - FIXED LINES:

total subscriptions: 1.181 million (2017 est.)

subscriptions per 100 inhabitants: 1 (2017 est.)

country comparison to the world: 70

TELEPHONES - MOBILE CELLULAR:

total subscriptions: 62.617 million

subscriptions per 100 inhabitants: 59 (2017 est.)

country comparison to the world: 24

TELEPHONE SYSTEM:

general assessment: Ethio Telecom maintains a monopoly over telecommunication services; open-wire, microwave radio relay; radio communication in the HF, VHF, and UHF frequencies; mobile broadband services via 3G and LTE networks; 2 domestic satellites provide the national trunk service; international Internet bandwidth increased 56% in 2016 to reach 35 Gb/s (2017)

domestic: fixed-line subscriptions at 1 per 100 while mobile-cellular stands at 59 per 100; the number of mobile telephones is increasing steadily (2017)

international: country code - 251; open-wire to Sudan and Djibouti; microwave radio relay to Kenya and Djibouti; satellite earth stations - 3 Intelsat (1 Atlantic Ocean and 2 Pacific Ocean) (2016)

BROADCAST MEDIA:

6 public TV stations broadcasting nationally and 10 public radio broadcasters; 7 private radio stations and 19 community radio stations (2017)

INTERNET COUNTRY CODE:

.et

INTERNET USERS:

total: 15,731,741 (July 2016 est.)

percent of population: 15.4% (July 2016 est.)

country comparison to the world: 38

BROADBAND - FIXED SUBSCRIPTIONS:

total: 580,120 (2017 est.)

subscriptions per 100 inhabitants: 1 (2017 est.)

country comparison to the world: 79

TRANSPORTATION :: ETHIOPIA

NATIONAL AIR TRANSPORT SYSTEM:

number of registered air carriers: 1 (2015)

inventory of registered aircraft operated by air carriers: 75 (2015)

annual passenger traffic on registered air carriers: 7,074,779 (2015)

annual freight traffic on registered air carriers: 1,228,738,320 mt-km (2015)

CIVIL AIRCRAFT REGISTRATION COUNTRY CODE PREFIX:

ET (2016)

AIRPORTS:

57 (2013)

country comparison to the world: 83

AIRPORTS - WITH PAVED RUNWAYS:

total: 17 (2017)

over 3,047 m: 3 (2017)

2,438 to 3,047 m: 8 (2017)

1,524 to 2,437 m: 4 (2017)

under 914 m: 2 (2017)

AIRPORTS - WITH UNPAVED RUNWAYS:

total: 40 (2013)

2,438 to 3,047 m: 3 (2013)

1,524 to 2,437 m: 9 (2013)

914 to 1,523 m: 20 (2013)

under 914 m: 8 (2013)

RAILWAYS:

total: 659 km (Ethiopian segment of the 756 km Addis Ababa-Djibouti railroad) (2017)

standard gauge: 659 km 1.435-m gauge (2017)

note: electric railway with redundant power supplies; under joint control of Djibouti and Ethiopia and managed by a Chinese contractor

country comparison to the world: 105

ROADWAYS:

total: 110,414 km (2015)

paved: 14,354 km (2015)

unpaved: 96,060 km (2015)

country comparison to the world: 44

MERCHANT MARINE:

total: 11 (2017)

by type: general cargo 9, oil tanker 2 (2017)

country comparison to the world: 146

PORTS AND TERMINALS:

Ethiopia is landlocked and uses the ports of Djibouti in Djibouti and Berbera in Somalia

MILITARY AND SECURITY :: ETHIOPIA

MILITARY EXPENDITURES:

0.67% of GDP (2016)

0.71% of GDP (2015)

0.77% of GDP (2014)

country comparison to the world: 134

MILITARY BRANCHES:

Ethiopian National Defense Force (ENDF): Ground Forces, Ethiopian Air Force (Ye Ityopya Ayer Hayl, ETAF) (2013)

MILITARY SERVICE AGE AND OBLIGATION:

18 years of age for voluntary military service; no compulsory military service, but the military can conduct callups when necessary and compliance is compulsory (2012)

TERRORISM :: ETHIOPIA

TERRORIST GROUPS - HOME BASED:

al-Shabaab:
aim(s): punish Ethiopia for participating in the African Union Mission in Somalia; compel Ethiopia to withdraw troops from Somalia
area(s) of operation: aspires to conduct attacks in Addis Ababa; no permanent presence (April 2018)

TERRORIST GROUPS - FOREIGN BASED:

al-Shabaab:
aim(s): punish Ethiopia for participating in the African Union Mission in Somalia; compel Ethiopia to withdraw troops from Somalia
area(s) of operation: aspires to conduct attacks in Addis Ababa; no permanent presence (April 2018)

TRANSNATIONAL ISSUES :: ETHIOPIA

DISPUTES - INTERNATIONAL:

Eritrea and Ethiopia agreed to abide by the 2002 Eritrea-Ethiopia Boundary Commission's (EEBC) delimitation decision, but neither party responded to the revised line detailed in the November 2006 EEBC Demarcation Statementthe undemarcated former British administrative line has little meaning as a political separation to rival clans within Ethiopia's Ogaden and southern Somalia's Oromo regionEthiopian forces invaded southern Somalia and routed Islamist courts from Mogadishu in January 2007"Somaliland" secessionists provide port facilities in Berbera and trade ties to landlocked Ethiopiacivil unrest in eastern Sudan has hampered efforts to demarcate the porous boundary with Ethiopia

REFUGEES AND INTERNALLY DISPLACED PERSONS:

refugees (country of origin): 422,240 (South Sudan) (refugees and asylum seekers), 257,283 (Somalia) (refugees and asylum seekers), 173,879 (Eritrea) (refugees and asylum seekers), 44,620 (Sudan) (refugees and asylum seekers) (2018)

IDPs: 2,075,278 (includes conflict- and climate-induced IDPs; border war with Eritrea from 1998-2000; ethnic clashes; and ongoing fighting between the Ethiopian military and separatist rebel groups in the Somali and Oromia regions; natural disasters; intercommunal violence; most IDPs live in Sumale state) (2018)

ILLICIT DRUGS:

transit hub for heroin originating in Southwest and Southeast Asia and destined for Europe, as well as cocaine destined for markets in southern Africa; cultivates qat (khat) for local use and regional export, principally to Djibouti and Somalia (legal in all three countries); the lack of a well-developed financial system limits the country's utility as a money laundering center

INTRODUCTION :: EUROPEAN UNION

PRELIMINARY STATEMENT:

The evolution of what is today the European Union (EU) from a regional economic agreement among six neighboring states in 1951 to today's hybrid intergovernmental and supranational organization of 28 countries across the European continent stands as an unprecedented phenomenon in the annals of history. Dynastic unions for territorial consolidation were long the norm in Europe; on a few occasions even country-level unions were arranged - the Polish-Lithuanian Commonwealth and the Austro-Hungarian Empire were examples. But for such a large number of nation-states to cede some of their sovereignty to an overarching entity is unique.

Although the EU is not a federation in the strict sense, it is far more than a free-trade association such as ASEAN, NAFTA, or Mercosur, and it has certain attributes associated with independent nations: its own flag, currency (for some members), and law-making abilities, as well as diplomatic representation and a common foreign and security policy in its dealings with external partners.

Thus, inclusion of basic intelligence on the EU has been deemed appropriate as a separate entity in The World Factbook. However, because of the EU's special status, this description is placed after the regular country entries.

BACKGROUND:

Following the two devastating World Wars in the first half of the 20th century, a number of far-sighted European leaders in the late 1940s sought a response to the overwhelming desire for peace and reconciliation on the continent. In 1950, the French Foreign Minister Robert SCHUMAN proposed pooling the production of coal and steel in Western Europe and setting up an organization for that purpose that would bring France and the Federal Republic of Germany together and would be open to other countries as well. The following year, the European Coal and Steel Community (ECSC) was set up when six members - Belgium, France, West Germany, Italy, Luxembourg, and the Netherlands - signed the Treaty of Paris.

The ECSC was so successful that within a few years the decision was made to integrate other elements of the countries' economies. In 1957, envisioning an "ever closer union," the Treaties of Rome created the European Economic Community (EEC) and the European Atomic Energy Community (Euratom), and the six member states undertook to eliminate trade barriers among themselves by forming a common market. In 1967, the institutions of all three communities were formally merged into the European Community (EC), creating a single Commission, a single Council of Ministers, and the body known today as the European Parliament. Members of the European Parliament were initially selected by national parliaments, but in 1979 the first direct elections were undertaken and have been held every five years since.

In 1973, the first enlargement of the EC took place with the addition of Denmark, Ireland, and the UK. The 1980s saw further membership expansion with Greece joining in 1981 and Spain and Portugal in 1986. The 1992 Treaty of Maastricht laid the basis for further forms of cooperation in foreign and defense policy, in judicial and internal affairs, and in the creation of an economic and monetary union - including a common currency. This further integration created the European Union (EU), at the time standing alongside the EC. In 1995, Austria, Finland, and Sweden joined the EU/EC, raising the membership total to 15.

A new currency, the euro, was launched in world money markets on 1 January 1999; it became the unit of exchange for all EU member states except Denmark, Sweden, and the UK. In 2002, citizens of those 12 countries began using euro banknotes and coins. Ten new countries joined the EU in 2004 - Cyprus, the Czech Republic, Estonia, Hungary, Latvia, Lithuania, Malta, Poland, Slovakia, and Slovenia. Bulgaria and Romania joined in 2007 and Croatia in 2013, bringing the current membership to 28. (Seven of these new countries - Cyprus, Estonia, Latvia, Lithuania, Malta, Slovakia, and Slovenia - have now adopted the euro, bringing total euro-zone membership to 19.)

In an effort to ensure that the EU could function efficiently with an expanded membership, the Treaty of Nice (concluded in 2000; entered into force in 2003) set forth rules to streamline the size and procedures of EU institutions. An effort to establish a "Constitution for Europe," growing out of a Convention held in 2002-2003, foundered when it was rejected in referenda in France and the Netherlands in 2005. A subsequent effort in 2007 incorporated many of the features of the rejected draft Constitutional Treaty while also making a number of substantive and symbolic changes. The new treaty, referred to as the Treaty of Lisbon, sought to amend existing treaties rather than replace them. The treaty was approved at the EU intergovernmental conference of the then 27 member states held in Lisbon in December 2007, after which the process of national ratifications began. In October 2009, an Irish referendum approved the Lisbon Treaty (overturning a previous rejection) and cleared the way for an ultimate unanimous endorsement. Poland and the Czech Republic ratified soon after. The Lisbon Treaty came into force on 1 December 2009 and the EU officially replaced and succeeded the EC. The Treaty's provisions are part of the basic consolidated versions of the Treaty on European Union (TEU) and the Treaty on the Functioning of the European Union (TFEU) now governing what remains a very specific integration project.

Frustrated by a remote bureaucracy in Brussels and massive migration into the country, UK citizens on 23 June 2016 narrowly voted to leave the EU. The so-called "Brexit" will take several years to carry out, but could embolden skeptics of EU membership in other member states. The EU and UK are negotiating a transition period from March 2019, when the UK ends its membership in the EU, to December 2020.

GEOGRAPHY :: EUROPEAN UNION

LOCATION:

Europe between the North Atlantic Ocean in the west and Russia, Belarus, and Ukraine to the east

MAP REFERENCES:

Europe

AREA:

total: 4,479,968 sq km

rank by area (sq km):
1. France (includes five overseas regions) 643,801
2. Spain 505,370
3. Sweden 450,295
4. Germany 357,022
5. Finland 338,145
6. Poland 312,685
7. Italy 301,340
8. United Kingdom (includes Gibraltar) 243,617
9. Romania 238,391
10. Greece 131,957
11. Bulgaria 110,879
12. Hungary 93,028
13. Portugal 92,090
14. Austria 83,871
15. Czechia 78,867
16. Ireland 70,273
17. Lithuania 65,300
18. Latvia 64,589
19. Croatia 56,594
20. Slovakia 49,035
21. Estonia 45,228
22. Denmark 43,094
23. Netherlands 41,543
24. Belgium 30,528
25. Slovenia 20,273
26. Cyprus 9,251
27. Luxembourg 2,586
28. Malta 316

AREA - COMPARATIVE:

less than one-half the size of the US

LAND BOUNDARIES:

total: 13,271 km

border countries (17): Albania 212 km, Andorra 118 km, Belarus 1176 km, Bosnia and Herzegovina 956 km, Holy See 3 km, Liechtenstein 34 km, Macedonia 396 km, Moldova 683 km, Monaco 6 km, Montenegro 19 km, Norway 2375 km, Russia 2435 km, San Marino 37 km, Serbia 1353 km, Switzerland 1729 km, Turkey 415 km, Ukraine 1324 km

note: data for European continent only

COASTLINE:

65,992.9 km

CLIMATE:

cold temperate; potentially subarctic in the north to temperate; mild wet winters; hot dry summers in the south

TERRAIN:

fairly flat along Baltic and Atlantic coasts; mountainous in the central and southern areas

ELEVATION:

-7 m lowest point: Lammefjord, Denmark

-7 Zuidplaspolder, Netherlands 4810 highest point: Mont Blanc

NATURAL RESOURCES:

iron ore, natural gas, petroleum, coal, copper, lead, zinc, bauxite, uranium, potash, salt, hydropower, arable land, timber, fish

IRRIGATED LAND:

154,539.82 sq km (2011 est.)

POPULATION DISTRIBUTION:

population distribution varies considerably from country to country, but tends to follow a pattern of coastal and river settlement, with urban agglomerations forming large hubs facilitating large scale housing, industry, and commerce; the area in and around the Netherlands, Belgium, and Luxembourg (known collectively as Benelux), is the most densely populated area in the EU

NATURAL HAZARDS:

flooding along coasts; avalanches in mountainous area; earthquakes in the south; volcanic eruptions in Italy; periodic droughts in Spain; ice floes in the Baltic

ENVIRONMENT - CURRENT ISSUES:

various forms of air, soil, and water pollution; see individual country entries

ENVIRONMENT - INTERNATIONAL AGREEMENTS:

party to: Air Pollution, Air Pollution-Nitrogen Oxides, Air Pollution-Persistent Organic Pollutants, Air Pollution-Sulphur 94, Antarctic-Marine Living Resources, Biodiversity, Climate Change, Climate Change-Kyoto Protocol, Desertification, Hazardous Wastes, Law of the Sea, Ozone Layer Protection, Tropical Timber 83, Tropical Timber 94

signed, but not ratified: Air Pollution-Volatile Organic Compounds

PEOPLE AND SOCIETY :: EUROPEAN UNION

POPULATION.

517,111,329 (July 2018 est.)

rank by population: Germany - 80,457,737 France - 67,364,357 United Kingdom - 65,105,246 Italy - 62,246,674 Spain - 49,331,076 Poland - 38,420,687 Romania - 21,457,116 Netherlands - 17,151,228 Belgium - 11,570,762 Greece - 10,761,523 Czechia - 10,686,269 Portugal - 10,355,493 Sweden - 10,040,995 Hungary - 9,825,704 Austria - 8,793,370 Bulgaria - 7,057,504 Denmark - 5,809,502 Finland - 5,537,364 Slovakia - 5,445,040 Ireland - 5,068,050 Croatia - 4,270,480 Lithuania - 2,793,284 Slovenia - 2,102,126 Latvia - 1,923,559 Estonia - 1,244,288 Cyprus - 1,237,088

Luxembourg - 605,764 Malta - 449,043 (July 2018 est.)

LANGUAGES:

Bulgarian, Croatian, Czech, Danish, Dutch, English, Estonian, Finnish, French, German, Greek, Hungarian, Irish, Italian, Latvian, Lithuanian, Maltese, Polish, Portuguese, Romanian, Slovak, Slovene, Spanish, Swedish (2012)

note: only the 24 official languages are listed; German, the major language of Germany, Austria, and Switzerland, is the most widely spoken mother tongue - about 16% of the EU population; English is the most widely spoken foreign language - about 38% of the EU population is conversant with it

RELIGIONS:

Roman Catholic 48%, Protestant 12%, Orthodox 8%, other Christian 4%, Muslim 2%, other 1% (includes Jewish, Sikh, Buddhist, Hindu), atheist 7%, non-believer/agnostic 16%, unspecified 2% (2012 est.)

AGE STRUCTURE:

0-14 years: 15.43% (male 40,905,648/female 38,860,151)

15-24 years: 10.62% (male 28,085,190/female 26,851,677)

25-54 years: 41.17% (male 107,404,085/female 105,480,809)

55-64 years: 13.14% (male 33,083,278/female 34,885,100)

65 years and over: 19.64% (male 43,673,572/female 57,881,819) (2018 est.)

MEDIAN AGE:

total: 43.2 years

male: 41.8 years

female: 44.6 years (2018 est.)

POPULATION GROWTH RATE:

0.19% (2018 est.)

BIRTH RATE:

9.9 births/1,000 population (2018 est.)

DEATH RATE:

10.4 deaths/1,000 population (2018 est.)

NET MIGRATION RATE:

2.4 migrant(s)/1,000 population (2018 est.)

POPULATION DISTRIBUTION:

population distribution varies considerably from country to country, but tends to follow a pattern of coastal and river settlement, with urban agglomerations forming large hubs facilitating large scale housing, industry, and commerce; the area in and around the Netherlands, Belgium, and Luxembourg (known collectively as Benelux), is the most densely populated area in the EU

SEX RATIO:

at birth: 1.06 male(s)/female

0-14 years: 1.05 male(s)/female

15-24 years: 1.05 male(s)/female

25-54 years: 1.02 male(s)/female

55-64 years: 0.95 male(s)/female

65 years and over: 0.75 male(s)/female

total population: 0.96 male(s)/female (2018 est.)

INFANT MORTALITY RATE:

total: 3.9 deaths/1,000 live births (2017 est.)

male: 4.2 deaths/1,000 live births (2017 est.)

female: 3.5 deaths/1,000 live births (2017 est.)

LIFE EXPECTANCY AT BIRTH:

total population: 80.7 years

male: 77.9 years

female: 83.6 years (2018 est.)

TOTAL FERTILITY RATE:

1.62 children born/woman (2018 est.)

HIV/AIDS - ADULT PREVALENCE RATE:

note - see individual entries of member states

HIV/AIDS - PEOPLE LIVING WITH HIV/AIDS:

note - see individual entries of member states

HIV/AIDS - DEATHS:

note - see individual entries of member states

UNEMPLOYMENT, YOUTH AGES 15-24:

total: 21% (2016 est.)

male: 21.3% (2016 est.)

female: 20.8% (2016 est.)

GOVERNMENT :: EUROPEAN UNION

UNION NAME:

conventional long form: European Union

abbreviation: EU

POLITICAL STRUCTURE:

a hybrid and unique intergovernmental and supranational organization

CAPITAL:

name: Brussels (Belgium), Strasbourg (France), Luxembourg, Frankfurt (Germany); note - the European Council, a gathering of the EU heads of state and/or government, and the Council of the European Union, a ministerial-level body of ten formations, meet in Brussels, Belgium, except for Council meetings held in Luxembourg in April, June, and October; the European Parliament meets in Brussels and Strasbourg, France, and has administrative offices in Luxembourg; the Court of Justice of the European Union is located in Luxembourg; and the European Central Bank is located in Frankfurt, Germany

geographic coordinates: (Brussels) 50 50 N, 4 20 E

time difference: UTC+1 (6 hours ahead of Washington, DC, during Standard Time)

daylight saving time: +1hr, begins last Sunday in March; ends last Sunday in October

note: the 28 European Union countries spread across three time zones; a proposal has been put forward to do away with daylight savings time in all EU countries

MEMBER STATES:

28 countries: Austria, Belgium, Bulgaria, Croatia, Cyprus, Czech Republic, Denmark, Estonia, Finland, France, Germany, Greece, Hungary, Ireland, Italy, Latvia, Lithuania, Luxembourg, Malta, Netherlands, Poland, Portugal, Romania, Slovakia, Slovenia, Spain, Sweden, UK; note - candidate countries: Albania, Macedonia, Montenegro, Serbia, Turkey

there are 25 OCTs (1 with Denmark [Greenland], 6 with France [French Polynesia; French Southern and Antarctic Lands; New Caledonia; Saint Barthelemy; Saint Pierre and Miquelon; Wallis and Futuna], 6 with the Netherlands [Aruba, Bonaire, Curacao, Saba, Sint Eustatius, Sint Maarten], and 12 with the UK [Anguilla; Bermuda; British Antarctic Territory; British Indian Ocean Territory; British Virgin Islands; Cayman Islands; Falkland Islands; Montserrat; Pitcairn Islands; Saint Helena, Ascension, and Tristan da

Cunha; South Georgia and the South Sandwich Islands; Turks and Caicos Islands]), of which 22 have joined the Overseas Countries and Territories Association (OCTA); the 3 OCTs that are not part of OCTA (British Antarctic Territory, British Indian Ocean Territory, South Georgia and the South Sandwich Islands) do not have a permanent population

note: there are non-European overseas countries and territories (OCTs) having special relations with Denmark, France, the Netherlands, and the UK (list is annexed to the Treaty on the Functioning of the European Union), that are associated with the Union to promote their economic and social development; member states apply to their trade with OCTs the same treatment as they accord each other pursuant to the treaties; OCT nationals are in principle EU citizens, but these countries are neither part of the EU, nor subject to the EU

INDEPENDENCE:

7 February 1992 (Maastricht Treaty signed establishing the European Union); 1 November 1993 (Maastricht Treaty entered into force)

note: the Treaties of Rome, signed on 25 March 1957 and subsequently entered into force on 1 January 1958, created the European Economic Community and the European Atomic Energy Community; a series of subsequent treaties have been adopted to increase efficiency and transparency, to prepare for new member states, and to introduce new areas of cooperation - such as a single currency; the Treaty of Lisbon, signed on 13 December 2007 and entered into force on 1 December 2009 is the most recent of these treaties and is intended to make the EU more democratic, more efficient, and better able to address global problems with one voice

NATIONAL HOLIDAY:

Europe Day (also known as Schuman Day), 9 May (1950); note - the day in 1950 that Robert SCHUMAN proposed the creation of what became the European Coal and Steel Community, the progenitor of today's European Union, with the aim of achieving a united Europe

CONSTITUTION:

history: none; note - the EU legal order relies primarily on two consolidated texts encompassing all provisions as amended from a series of past treaties: the Treaty on European Union (TEU), as modified by the 2009 Lisbon Treaty states in Article 1 that "the HIGH CONTRACTING PARTIES establish among themselves a EUROPEAN UNION ... on which the Member States confer competences to attain objectives they have in common"; Article 1 of the TEU states further that the EU is "founded on the present Treaty and on the Treaty on the Functioning of the European Union (hereinafter referred to as 'the Treaties')," both possessing the same legal value; Article 6 of the TEU provides that a separately adopted Charter of Fundamental Rights of the European Union "shall have the same legal value as the Treaties" (2016)

amendments: European Union treaties can be amended in several ways: 1) Ordinary Revision Procedure (for key amendments to the treaties); initiated by an EU country's government, by the EU Parliament, or by the EU Commission; following adoption of the proposal by the European Council, a convention is formed of national government representatives to review the proposal and subsequently a conference of government representatives also reviews the proposal; passage requires ratification by all EU countries; 2) Simplified Revision Procedure (for amendment of EU internal policies and actions); passage of a proposal requires unanimous European Council vote following European Council consultation with the EU Commission, the European Council, and the European Parliament, and requires ratification by all EU countries; 3) Passerelle Clause (allows the alteration of a legislative procedure without a formal amendment of the treaties); 4) Flexibility Clause (permits the EU to decide in subject areas not covered by the EU treaties); note - the Treaty of Lisbon (signed in December 2007 and effective in December 2009) amended the two treaties that formed the EU - the Maastricht Treaty (1993) and the Treaty of Rome (1958), known in updated form as the Treaty on the Functioning of the European Union (2007) (2016)

LEGAL SYSTEM:

unique supranational law system in which, according to an interpretive declaration of member-state governments appended to the Treaty of Lisbon, "the Treaties and the law adopted by the Union on the basis of the Treaties have primacy over the law of Member States" under conditions laid down in the case law of the Court of Justice; key principles of EU law include fundamental rights as guaranteed by the Charter of Fundamental Rights and as resulting from constitutional traditions common to the EU's 28-member states; EU law is divided into 'primary' and 'secondary' legislation; primary legislation is derived from the consolidated versions of the Treaty on European Union and the Treaty on the Functioning of the European Union and are the basis for all EU action; secondary legislation - which includes directives, regulations, and decisions - is derived from the principles and objectives set out in the treaties

SUFFRAGE:

18 years of age (16 years in Austria); universal; voting for the European Parliament is permitted in each member state

EXECUTIVE BRANCH:

the European Council: brings together heads of state and government, along with the president of the European Commission, and meets at least four times a year; its aim is to provide the impetus for the development of the Union and to issue general policy guidelines; the Treaty of Lisbon established the position of "permanent" (full-time) president of the European Council; leaders of the EU member states appoint the president for a 2 1/2 year term, renewable once; the president's responsibilities include chairing the EU summits and providing policy and organizational continuity; the current president is Donald TUSK (Poland), since 1 December 2014, succeeding Herman VAN ROMPUY (Belgian; 2009-14)

the Council of the European Union: consists of ministers of each EU member state and meets regularly in 10 different configurations depending on the subject matter; it conducts policymaking and coordinating functions as well as legislative functions; ministers of EU member states chair meetings of the Council of the EU based on a 6-month rotating presidency except for the meetings of EU Foreign Ministers in the Foreign Affairs Council that are chaired by the High Representative for Foreign Affairs and Security Policy

the European Commission: headed by a College of Commissioners comprised of 28 members (one from each member country) including the president; each commissioner is responsible for one or more policy areas; the Commission's main responsibilities include the sole right to initiate EU legislation (except for foreign and security/defense policy), promoting the general interest of the EU, acting as "guardian of the Treaties" by monitoring the application of EU law, implementing/executing the EU budget, managing programs, negotiating on the EU's behalf in core policy areas such as trade, and ensuring the Union's external representation in some policy areas; its current president is Jean-Claude JUNCKER (Luxembourg) elected on 15 July 2014 (took office on 1 November 2014); the president of the European Commission is nominated by the European Council and formally "elected" by the European Parliament; the Commission president allocates specific responsibilities among the members of the College (appointed by common accord of the member state governments in consultation with the president-elect); the European Parliament confirms the entire Commission for a 5-year term; President JUNCKER reorganized the structure of the College around clusters or project teams coordinated by 7 vice presidents in line with the current Commission's main political priorities and appointed Frans TIMMERMANS (Netherlands) to act as his first vice president; the confirmation process for the next Commission expected be held in the fall of 2019

under the EU treaties there are three distinct institutions, each of which conducts functions that may be regarded as executive in nature:

note: for external representation and foreign policy making, leaders of the EU member states appointed Federica MOGHERINI (Italy) as the High Representative of the European Union for Foreign Affairs and Security Policy; MOGHERINI took office on 1 November 2014, succeeding Catherine ASHTON (UK) (2009-14); the High Representative's concurrent appointment as Vice President of the European Commission endows the position with the policymaking influence of the Council of the EU and the budgetary influence (subject to Council's approval) of the Council of the EU and the budgetary/management influence of the European Commission; the High Representative helps develop and implement the EU's Common Foreign and Security Policy and Common Security and Defense Policy component, chairs the Foreign Affairs Council, represents and acts for the Union in many international contexts, and oversees the European External Action Service, the diplomatic corps of the EU, established on 1 December 2010

LEGISLATIVE BRANCH:

description: two legislative bodies consisting of the Council of the European Union (28 seats; ministers representing the 28 member states) and the European Parliament (751 seats; seats allocated among member states roughly in proportion to population size; members elected by proportional representation to serve 5-year terms); note - the European Parliament President, Antonio TAJANI (Italian center-right), was elected in January 2017 by a majority of fellow members of the European Parliament (MEPs) and represents the Parliament within the EU and internationally; the Council of the EU and the MEPs share responsibilities for adopting the bulk of EU legislation, normally acting in co-decision on Commission proposals (but not in the area of Common Foreign and Security Policy, which is governed by consensus of the EU member state governments)

elections: last held on 22-25 May 2014 (next to be held 23-26 May 2019)

election results: percent of vote - EPP 29.4%, S&D 25.4%, ECR 9.3%, ALDE 8.9%, GUE/NGL 6.9%, Greens/EFA 6.7%, EFD 6.4%, independent 6.9%; seats by party - EPP 221, S&D 191, ECR 70, ALDE 67, GUE/NGL 52, Greens/EFA 50, EFD 48, independent 52

JUDICIAL BRANCH:

highest courts: European Court of Justice or ECJ (consists of 28 judges - 1 from each member state); the court may sit as a full court, in a "Grand Chamber" of 13 judges in special cases but usually in chambers of 3 to 5 judges

judge selection and term of office: judges appointed by the common consent of the member states to serve 6-year renewable terms

subordinate courts: General Court; Civil Service Tribunal

note: the ECJ is the supreme judicial authority of the EU; ECJ ensures that EU law is interpreted and applied uniformly throughout the EU, resolves disputed issues among the EU institutions and with member states, issues opinions on questions of EU law referred by member state courts

POLITICAL PARTIES AND LEADERS:

Alliance of Liberals and Democrats for Europe or ALDE [Guy VERHOFSTADT]
European United Left-Nordic Green Left or GUE/NGL [Gabriele ZIMMER]
Europe of Freedom and Direct Democracy or EFDD [Nigel FARAGE]
Europe of Nations and Freedom or ENF or ENL [Nicolas BAY and Marcel DE GRAAFF]
European Conservatives and Reformists or ECR [Syed KAMALL]
European Greens/European Free Alliance or Greens/EFA [Ska KELLER and Philippe LAMBERTS]
European People's Party or EPP [Joseph DAUL]
Progressive Alliance of Socialists and Democrats or S&D [Udo BULLMANN]

INTERNATIONAL ORGANIZATION PARTICIPATION:

ARF, ASEAN (dialogue member), Australian Group, BIS, BSEC (observer), CBSS, CERN, EBRD, FAO, FATF, G-8, G-10, G-20, IDA, IEA, IGAD (partners), LAIA (observer), NSG (observer), OAS (observer), OECD, PIF (partner), SAARC (observer), SICA (observer), UN (observer), UNRWA (observer), WCO, WTO, ZC (observer)

DIPLOMATIC REPRESENTATION IN THE US:

chief of mission: Ambassador David O'SULLIVAN (since 18 November 2014)

chancery: 2175 K Street, NW, Suite 800, Washington, DC 20037

telephone: [1] (202) 862-9500

FAX: [1] (202) 429-1766

DIPLOMATIC REPRESENTATION FROM THE US:

chief of mission: Ambassador Gordon SONDLAND (since 9 July 2018)

embassy: 13 Zinnerstraat/Rue Zinner, B-1000 Brussels

mailing address: use embassy street address

telephone: [32] (2) 811-4100

FAX: [32] (2) 811-5154

FLAG DESCRIPTION:

a blue field with 12 five-pointed gold stars arranged in a circle in the center; blue represents the sky of the Western world, the stars are the peoples of Europe in a circle, a symbol of unity; the number of stars is fixed

NATIONAL SYMBOL(S):

a circle of 12, five-pointed, golden yellow stars on a blue field; union colors: blue, yellow

NATIONAL ANTHEM:

name: Ode to Joy

lyrics/music: no lyrics/Ludwig VAN BEETHOVEN, arranged by Herbert VON KARAJAN

note: official EU anthem since 1985; the anthem is meant to represent all of Europe rather than just the organization, conveying ideas of peace, freedom, and unity

ECONOMY :: EUROPEAN UNION

ECONOMY - OVERVIEW:

The 28 member states that make up the EU have adopted an internal single market with free movement of goods, services, capital, and labor. The EU, which is also a customs union, aims to bolster Europe's trade position and its political and economic weight in international affairs.

Despite great differences in per capita income among member states (from $28,000 to $109,000) and in national attitudes toward issues like inflation, debt, and foreign trade, the EU has achieved a high degree of coordination of monetary and fiscal policies. A common currency – the euro – circulates among 19 of the member states that make up the European Economic and Monetary Union (EMU). Eleven member states introduced the euro as their common currency on 1 January 1999 (Greece did so two years later). Since 2004, 13 states acceded to the EU. Of the 13, Slovenia (2007), Cyprus and Malta (2008), Slovakia (2009), Estonia (2011), Latvia (2014), and Lithuania (2015) have adopted the euro; 7 other member states - excluding the UK and Denmark, which have formal opt-outs - are required by EU treaties to adopt the common currency upon meeting fiscal and monetary convergence criteria.

The EU economy posted moderate GDP growth for 2014 through 2017, capping five years of sustained growth since the 2008-09 global economic crisis and the ensuing sovereign debt crisis in the euro zone in 2011. However, the bloc's recovery has been uneven. Some EU member states (Czechia, Ireland, Malta, Romania, Sweden, and Spain) have recorded strong growth, others (Italy and the UK) are experiencing modest expansion and some (Greece) have only recently shaken off recession. Only Greece remains under an EU rescue program (due to end in August 2018), while Cyprus, Ireland, Portugal, and Spain have successfully concluded their agreements. Overall, the EU's recovery has been buoyed by lower commodities prices and accommodative monetary policy, which has lowered interest rates and stimulated demand. The euro zone, which makes up about 70% of the total EU economy, is also performing well, achieving a growth rate not seen in a decade. In October 2017 the European Central Bank (ECB) announced it would extend its bond-buying program through September 2018, and possibly beyond that date, to keep the euro zone recovery on track. The ECB's efforts to spur more lending and investment through its asset-buying program, negative interest rates, and long-term loan refinancing programs have not yet raised inflation in line with the ECB's statutory target of just under 2%.

Despite its performance, high unemployment in some member states, high levels of public and private debt, muted productivity, an incomplete single market in services, and an aging population remain sources of potential drag on the EU's future growth. Moreover, the EU economy remains vulnerable to a slowdown of global trade and bouts of political and financial turmoil. In June 2016, the UK voted to withdraw from the EU, the first member country ever to attempt to secede. Continued uncertainty about the implications of the UK's exit from the EU (set for March 2019) could hurt consumer and investor confidence and dampen EU growth, particularly if trade and cross-border investment significantly declines. Political disagreements between EU member states on reforms to fiscal and economic policy also may impair the EU's ability to bolster its crisis-prevention and resolution mechanisms. International investors' fears of a broad dissolution of the single currency area have largely dissipated, but these concerns could resurface if elected leaders implement policies that contravene euro-zone budget or banking rules. State interventions in ailing banks, including rescue of banks in Italy and resolution of banks in Spain, have eased financial vulnerabilities in the European banking sector even though some banks are struggling with low profitability and a large stock of bad loans, fragilities that could precipitate localized crises. Externally, the EU has continued to pursue comprehensive free trade agreements to expand EU external market share, particularly with Asian countries; EU and Japanese leaders reached a political-level agreement on a free trade agreement in July 2017, and agreement with Mexico in April 2018 on updates to an existing free trade agreement.

GDP (PURCHASING POWER PARITY):

$20.85 trillion (2017 est.)

$20.38 trillion (2016 est.)

$19.98 trillion (2015 est.)

note: data are in 2017 dollars

GDP (OFFICIAL EXCHANGE RATE):

$17.11 trillion (2017 est.) (2017 est.)

GDP - REAL GROWTH RATE:

2.3% (2017 est.)

2% (2016 est.)

2.3% (2015 est.)

GDP - PER CAPITA (PPP):

$40,900 (2017 est.)

$39,400 (2016 est.)

$38,200 (2015 est.)

note: data are in 2017 dollars

GROSS NATIONAL SAVING:

22.7% of GDP (2017 est.)

22.2% of GDP (2016 est.)

22% of GDP (2015 est.)

GDP - COMPOSITION, BY END USE:

household consumption: 54.4% (2016 est.)

government consumption: 20.4% (2016 est.)

investment in fixed capital: 19.8% (2016 est.)

investment in inventories: 0.4% (2016 est.)

exports of goods and services: 43.9% (2016 est.)

imports of goods and services: -40.5% (2016 est.)

GDP - COMPOSITION, BY SECTOR OF ORIGIN:

agriculture: 1.6% (2017 est.)

industry: 25.1% (2017 est.)

services: 70.9% (2017 est.)

AGRICULTURE - PRODUCTS:

wheat, barley, oilseeds, sugar beets, wine, grapes; dairy products, cattle, sheep, pigs, poultry; fish

INDUSTRIES:

among the world's largest and most technologically advanced regions, the EU industrial base includes: ferrous and non-ferrous metal production and processing, metal products, petroleum, coal, cement, chemicals, pharmaceuticals, aerospace, rail transportation equipment, passenger and commercial vehicles, construction equipment, industrial equipment, shipbuilding, electrical power equipment, machine tools and automated manufacturing systems, electronics and telecommunications equipment, fishing, food and beverages, furniture, paper, textiles

INDUSTRIAL PRODUCTION GROWTH RATE:

3.5% (2017 est.)

LABOR FORCE:

238.9 million (2016 est.)

LABOR FORCE - BY OCCUPATION:

agriculture: 5%

industry: 21.9%

services: 73.1% (2014 est.)

UNEMPLOYMENT RATE:

8.6% (2016 est.)

9.4% (2015 est.)

POPULATION BELOW POVERTY LINE:

9.8% (2013 est.)

note: see individual country entries of member states

HOUSEHOLD INCOME OR CONSUMPTION BY PERCENTAGE SHARE:

lowest 10%: 23.8% (2016 est.)

highest 10%: 23.8% (2016 est.)

DISTRIBUTION OF FAMILY INCOME - GINI INDEX:

30.8 (2016 est.)

31 (2015 est.)

TAXES AND OTHER REVENUES:

45.2% (of GDP) (2014)

BUDGET SURPLUS (+) OR DEFICIT (-):

-3% (of GDP) (2014)

PUBLIC DEBT:

86.8% of GDP (2014)

85.5% of GDP (2013)

FISCAL YEAR:

NA

INFLATION RATE (CONSUMER PRICES):

1.5% (2017 est.)

1.1% (2016 est.)

CENTRAL BANK DISCOUNT RATE:

0% (31 December 2017 est.)

0% (31 December 2016 est.)

note: this is the European Central Bank's rate on the marginal lending facility, which offers overnight credit to banks in the euro area

COMMERCIAL BANK PRIME LENDING RATE:

0.25% (31 December 2017 est.)

0.25% (31 December 2016 est.)

STOCK OF NARROW MONEY:

$8.775 trillion (31 December 2017 est.)

$13.13 trillion (31 December 2016 est.)

note: this is the quantity of money, M1, for the euro area, converted into US dollars at the exchange rate for the date indicated; it excludes the stock of money carried by non-euro-area members of the European Union, e.g., UK pounds, Danish kroner, and Czech koruny

STOCK OF BROAD MONEY:

$8.138 trillion (31 December 2017 est.)

$12.62 trillion (31 December 2016 est.)

note: this is the quantity of broad money for the euro area, converted into US dollars at the exchange rate for the date indicated; it excludes the stock of broad money carried by non-euro-area members of the European Union

STOCK OF DOMESTIC CREDIT:

$22.74 trillion (31 December 2016 est.)

$22.92 trillion (31 December 2015 est.)

note: this figure refers to the euro area only; it excludes credit data for non-euro-area members of the EU

MARKET VALUE OF PUBLICLY TRADED SHARES:

$7.185 trillion (31 December 2014 est.)

$7.932 trillion (31 December 2013 est.)

$10.4 trillion (31 December 2012 est.)

CURRENT ACCOUNT BALANCE:

$404.9 billion (2017 est.)

$359.7 billion (2016 est.)

EXPORTS:

$1.929 trillion (2016 est.)

$1.985 trillion (2015 est.)

note: external exports, excluding intra-EU trade

EXPORTS - PARTNERS:

United States 20.7%, China 9.6%, Switzerland 8.1%, Turkey 4.4%, Russia 4.1% (2016 est.)

EXPORTS - COMMODITIES:

machinery, motor vehicles, pharmaceuticals and other chemicals, fuels, aircraft, plastics, iron and steel, wood pulp and paper products, alcoholic beverages, furniture

IMPORTS:

$1.895 trillion (2016 est.)

$1.92 trillion (2015 est.)

note: external imports, excluding intra-EU trade

IMPORTS - COMMODITIES:

fuels and crude oil, machinery, vehicles, pharmaceuticals and other chemicals, precious gemstones, textiles, aircraft, plastics, metals, ships

IMPORTS - PARTNERS:

China 20.1%, United States 14.5%, Switzerland 7.1%, Russia 6.3% (2016 est.)

RESERVES OF FOREIGN EXCHANGE AND GOLD:

$740.9 billion (31 December 2014 est.)

$746.9 billion (31 December 2013)

note: data are for the European Central Bank

DEBT - EXTERNAL:

$29.27 trillion (31 December 2016 est.)

$28.68 trillion (31 December 2015 est.)

STOCK OF DIRECT FOREIGN INVESTMENT - AT HOME:

$6.938 trillion (31 December 2016 est.)

$6.482 trillion (31 December 2015 est.)

STOCK OF DIRECT FOREIGN INVESTMENT - ABROAD:

$8.411 trillion (31 December 2016 est.)

$7.649 trillion (31 December 2015 est.)

EXCHANGE RATES:

euros per US dollar -

0.885 (2017 est.)

0.903 (2016 est.)

0.9214 (2015 est.)

0.885 (2014 est.)

0.7634 (2013 est.)

ENERGY :: EUROPEAN UNION

ELECTRICITY - PRODUCTION:

3.043 trillion kWh (2015 est.)

ELECTRICITY - CONSUMPTION:

2.845 trillion kWh (2015 est.)

ELECTRICITY - EXPORTS:

390 billion kWh (2015 est.)

ELECTRICITY - IMPORTS:

397 billion kWh (2015 est.)

ELECTRICITY - INSTALLED GENERATING CAPACITY:

975 million kW (2015 est.)

ELECTRICITY - FROM FOSSIL FUELS:

44% of total installed capacity (2015 est.)

ELECTRICITY - FROM NUCLEAR FUELS:

12% of total installed capacity (2015 est.)

ELECTRICITY - FROM HYDROELECTRIC PLANTS:

11% of total installed capacity (2015 est.)

ELECTRICITY - FROM OTHER RENEWABLE SOURCES:

44% of total installed capacity (2015 est.)

CRUDE OIL - PRODUCTION:

1.488 million bbl/day (2016 est.)

CRUDE OIL - PROVED RESERVES:

5.1 billion bbl (2016 est.)

REFINED PETROLEUM PRODUCTS - PRODUCTION:

11.66 million bbl/day (2016 est.)

REFINED PETROLEUM PRODUCTS - CONSUMPTION:

12.89 million bbl/day (2015 est.)

REFINED PETROLEUM PRODUCTS - EXPORTS:

2.196 million bbl/day (2017 est.)

REFINED PETROLEUM PRODUCTS - IMPORTS:

8.613 million bbl/day (2017 est.)

NATURAL GAS - PRODUCTION:

118.2 billion cu m (2016 est.)

NATURAL GAS - CONSUMPTION:

428.8 billion cu m (2016 est.)

NATURAL GAS - EXPORTS:

93.75 billion cu m (2010 est.)

NATURAL GAS - IMPORTS:

420.6 billion cu m (2010 est.)

NATURAL GAS - PROVED RESERVES:

1.3 trillion cu m (1 January 2017 est.)

CARBON DIOXIDE EMISSIONS FROM CONSUMPTION OF ENERGY:

3.475 billion Mt (2015 est.)

COMMUNICATIONS :: EUROPEAN UNION

TELEPHONES - FIXED LINES:

total subscriptions: 210,621,546 (2017 est.)

subscriptions per 100 inhabitants: 4 (2017 est.)

TELEPHONES - MOBILE CELLULAR:

total subscriptions: 625,000,799 (2017 est.)

subscriptions per 100 inhabitants: 12 (2017 est.)

TELEPHONE SYSTEM:

note - see individual country entries of member states

INTERNET COUNTRY CODE:

.eu; note - see country entries of member states for individual country codes

INTERNET USERS:

398.1 million (July 2016 est.)

BROADBAND - FIXED SUBSCRIPTIONS:

total: 174,634,171

subscriptions per 100 inhabitants: 3

TRANSPORTATION :: EUROPEAN UNION

AIRPORTS:

3 (2013)

AIRPORTS - WITH PAVED RUNWAYS:

total: 1,882 (2017)

over 3,047 m: 120 (2017)

2,438 to 3,047 m: 341 (2017)

1,524 to 2,437 m: 507 (2017)

914 to 1,523 m: 425 (2017)

under 914 m: 489 (2017)

AIRPORTS - WITH UNPAVED RUNWAYS:

total: 1,244 (2013)

over 3,047 m: 1 (2013)

2,438 to 3,047 m: 1 (2013)

1,524 to 2,437 m: 15 (2013)

914 to 1,523 m: 245 (2013)

under 914 m: 982 (2013)

HELIPORTS:

90 (2013)

RAILWAYS:

total: 230,548 km (2013)

ROADWAYS:

total: 10,582,653 km (2013)

WATERWAYS:

53,384 km (2013)

PORTS AND TERMINALS:

major port(s): Antwerp (Belgium), Barcelona (Spain), Braila (Romania), Bremen (Germany), Burgas (Bulgaria), Constanta (Romania), Copenhagen (Denmark), Galati (Romania), Gdansk (Poland), Hamburg (Germany), Helsinki (Finland), Las Palmas (Canary Islands, Spain), Le Havre (France), Lisbon (Portugal), London (UK), Marseille (France), Naples (Italy), Peiraiefs or Piraeus (Greece), Riga (Latvia), Rotterdam (Netherlands), Split (Croatia), Stockholm (Sweden), Talinn (Estonia), Tulcea (Romania), Varna (Bulgaria)

MILITARY AND SECURITY :: EUROPEAN UNION

MILITARY EXPENDITURES:

1.52% of GDP (2016)

1.51% of GDP (2015)

1.52% of GDP (2014)

MILITARY - NOTE:

the current five-nation Eurocorps, formally established in 1992 and activated the following year, began in 1987 as a French-German Brigade; Belgium (1993), Spain (1994), and Luxembourg (1996) joined over the next few years; five additional countries participate in Eurocorps as associated nations: Greece, Poland, and Turkey (since 2002), Italy and Romania (joined in 2009 and 2016 respectively); Eurocorps consists of approximately 1,000 troops at its headquarters in Strasbourg, France and the 5,000-man Franco-German Brigade; Eurocorps has deployed troops and police on NATO peacekeeping missions to Bosnia-Herzegovina (1998-2000), Kosovo (2000), and Afghanistan (2004-05 and 2012); Eurocorps has been involved in EU operations to Mali (2015) and the Central African Republic (2016-17) (2018)

TRANSNATIONAL ISSUES :: EUROPEAN UNION

DISPUTES - INTERNATIONAL:

as a political union, the EU has no border disputes with neighboring countries, but Estonia has no land boundary agreements with Russia, Slovenia disputes its land and maritime boundaries with Croatia, and Spain has territorial and maritime disputes with Morocco and with the UK over Gibraltarthe EU has set up a Schengen area - consisting of 22 EU member states that have signed the convention implementing the Schengen agreements or "acquis" (1985 and 1990) on the free movement of persons and the harmonization of border controls in Europethese agreements became incorporated into EU law with the implementation of the 1997 Treaty of Amsterdam on 1 May 1999in addition, non-EU states Iceland and Norway (as part of the Nordic Union) have been included in the Schengen area since 1996 (full members in 2001), Switzerland since 2008, and Liechtenstein since 2011 bringing the total current membership to 26the UK (since 2000) and Ireland (since 2002) take part in only some aspects of the Schengen area, especially with respect to police and criminal mattersnine of the 13 new member states that joined the EU since 2004 joined Schengen on 21 December 2007; of the four remaining EU states, Romania, Bulgaria, and Croatia are obligated to eventually join, while Cyprus' entry is held up by the ongoing Cyprus dispute

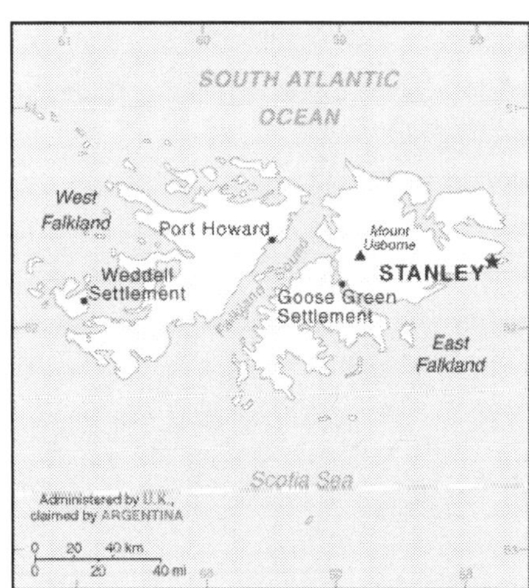

SOUTH AMERICA :: FALKLAND ISLANDS (ISLAS MALVINAS)

INTRODUCTION :: FALKLAND ISLANDS (ISLAS MALVINAS)

BACKGROUND:

Although first sighted by an English navigator in 1592, the first landing (English) did not occur until almost a century later in 1690, and the first settlement (French) was not established until 1764. The colony was turned over to Spain two years later and the islands have since been the subject of a territorial dispute, first between Britain and Spain, then between Britain and Argentina. The UK asserted its claim to the islands by establishing a naval garrison there in 1833. Argentina invaded the islands on 2 April 1982. The British responded with an expeditionary force that landed seven weeks later and after fierce fighting forced an Argentine surrender on 14 June 1982. With hostilities ended and Argentine forces withdrawn, UK administration resumed. In response to renewed calls from Argentina for Britain to relinquish control of the islands, a referendum was held in March 2013, which resulted in 99.8% of the population voting to remain a part of the UK.

GEOGRAPHY :: FALKLAND ISLANDS (ISLAS MALVINAS)

LOCATION:

Southern South America, islands in the South Atlantic Ocean, about 500 km east of southern Argentina

GEOGRAPHIC COORDINATES:

51 45 S, 59 00 W

MAP REFERENCES:

South America

AREA:

total: 12,173 sq km

land: 12,173 sq km

water: 0 sq km

note: includes the two main islands of East and West Falkland and about 200 small islands

country comparison to the world: 164

AREA - COMPARATIVE:

slightly smaller than Connecticut

LAND BOUNDARIES:

0 km

COASTLINE:

1,288 km

MARITIME CLAIMS:

territorial sea: 12 nm

continental shelf: 200 nm

exclusive fishing zone: 200 nm

CLIMATE:

cold marine; strong westerly winds, cloudy, humid; rain occurs on more than half of days in year; average annual rainfall is 60 cm in Stanley; occasional snow all year, except in January and February, but typically does not accumulate

TERRAIN:

rocky, hilly, mountainous with some boggy, undulating plains

ELEVATION:

0 m lowest point: Atlantic Ocean

705 highest point: Mount Usborne

NATURAL RESOURCES:

fish, squid, wildlife, calcified seaweed, sphagnum moss

LAND USE:

agricultural land: 92.4% (2011 est.)

arable land: 0% (2011 est.) / permanent crops: 0% (2011 est.) / permanent pasture: 92.4% (2011 est.)

forest: 0% (2011 est.)

other: 7.6% (2011 est.)

IRRIGATED LAND:

NA

POPULATION DISTRIBUTION:

a very small population, with most residents living in and around Stanley

NATURAL HAZARDS:

strong winds persist throughout the year

ENVIRONMENT - CURRENT ISSUES:

overfishing by unlicensed vessels is a problem; reindeer - introduced to the islands in 2001 from South Georgia - are part of a farming effort to produce specialty meat and diversify the islands' economy; this is the only commercial reindeer herd in the world unaffected by the 1986 Chornobyl disaster; grazing threatens important habitats including tussac grass and its ecosystem with penguins and sea lions; soil erosion from fires

GEOGRAPHY - NOTE:

deeply indented coast provides good natural harbors; short growing season

PEOPLE AND SOCIETY :: FALKLAND ISLANDS (ISLAS MALVINAS)

POPULATION:

3,198 (2016 est.)

note: data include all persons usually resident in the islands at the time of the 2016 census

country comparison to the world: 229

NATIONALITY:

noun: Falkland Islander(s)

adjective: Falkland Island

ETHNIC GROUPS:

Falkland Islander 48.3%, British 23.1%, St. Helenian 7.5%, Chilean 4.6%, mixed 6%, other 8.5%, unspecified 2% (2016 est.)

LANGUAGES:

English 89%, Spanish 7.7%, other 3.3% (2006 est.)

RELIGIONS:

Christian 57.1%, other 1.6%, none 35.4%, unspecified 6% (2016 est.)

POPULATION GROWTH RATE:

0.01% (2014 est.)

country comparison to the world: 189

BIRTH RATE:

10.9 births/1,000 population (2012 est.)

country comparison to the world: 179

DEATH RATE:

4.9 deaths/1,000 population (2012 est.)

country comparison to the world: 196

NET MIGRATION RATE:

NA

POPULATION DISTRIBUTION:

a very small population, with most residents living in and around Stanley

URBANIZATION:

urban population: 77.7% of total population (2018)

rate of urbanization: 0.76% annual rate of change (2015-20 est.)

MAJOR URBAN AREAS - POPULATION:

2,000 STANLEY (capital) (2018)

SEX RATIO:

1.12 male(s)/female (2016 est.)

note: sex ratio is somewhat skewed by the high proportion of males at the Royal Air Force station, Mount Pleasant Airport (MPA); excluding MPA, the sex ratio of the total population would be 1.04

INFANT MORTALITY RATE:

total: NA

male: NA

female: NA

LIFE EXPECTANCY AT BIRTH:

total population: 77.9 (2017 est.)

male: 75.6 (2017 est.)

female: 79.6 (2017 est.)

TOTAL FERTILITY RATE:

NA

HIV/AIDS - ADULT PREVALENCE RATE:

NA

HIV/AIDS - PEOPLE LIVING WITH HIV/AIDS:

NA

HIV/AIDS - DEATHS:

NA

GOVERNMENT :: FALKLAND ISLANDS (ISLAS MALVINAS)

COUNTRY NAME:

conventional long form: none

conventional short form: Falkland Islands (Islas Malvinas)

etymology: the archipelago takes its name from the Falkland Sound, the strait separating the two main islands; the channel itself was named after the Viscount of Falkland who sponsored an expedition to the islands in 1690; the Spanish name for the archipelago derives from the French "Iles Malouines," the name applied to the islands by French explorer Louis-Antoine de BOUGAINVILLE in 1764

DEPENDENCY STATUS:

overseas territory of the UK; also claimed by Argentina

GOVERNMENT TYPE:

parliamentary democracy (Legislative Assembly); self-governing overseas territory of the UK

CAPITAL:

name: Stanley

geographic coordinates: 51 42 S, 57 51 W

time difference: UTC-4 (1 hour ahead of Washington, DC, during Standard Time)

ADMINISTRATIVE DIVISIONS:

none (overseas territory of the UK; also claimed by Argentina)

INDEPENDENCE:

none (overseas territory of the UK; also claimed by Argentina)

NATIONAL HOLIDAY:

Liberation Day, 14 June (1982)

CONSTITUTION:

previous 1985; latest entered into force 1 January 2009 (The Falkland Islands Constitution Order 2008) (2018)

LEGAL SYSTEM:

English common law and local statutes

CITIZENSHIP:

see United Kingdom

SUFFRAGE:

18 years of age; universal

EXECUTIVE BRANCH:

chief of state: Queen ELIZABETH II (since 6 February 1952); represented by Governor Nigel PHILLIPS (since 12 September 2017)

head of government: Chief Executive Barry ROWLAND (since 3 October 2016)

cabinet: Executive Council elected by the Legislative Council

elections/appointments: the monarchy is hereditary; governor appointed by the monarch; chief executive appointed by the governor

LEGISLATIVE BRANCH:

description: unicameral Legislative Assembly, formerly the Legislative Council (10 seats; 8 members directly elected by majority vote and 2 appointed ex-officio members - the chief executive, appointed by the governor, and the financial secretary; members serve 4-year terms)

elections: last held on 9 November 2017 (next to be held in November 2021)

election results: percent of vote - NA; seats - independent 8

JUDICIAL BRANCH:

highest courts: Court of Appeal (consists of the court president, the chief justice as an ex officio, non-resident member, and 2 justices of appeal); Supreme Court (consists of the chief justice); note - appeals beyond the Court of Appeal are referred to the Judicial Committee of the Privy Council (in London)

judge selection and term of office: all justices appointed by the governor; tenure specified in each justice's instrument of appointment

subordinate courts: Magistrate's Court (senior magistrate presides over civil and criminal divisions); Court of Summary Jurisdiction

POLITICAL PARTIES AND LEADERS:

none; all independents

INTERNATIONAL ORGANIZATION PARTICIPATION:

UPU

DIPLOMATIC REPRESENTATION IN THE US:

none (overseas territory of the UK)

DIPLOMATIC REPRESENTATION FROM THE US:

none (overseas territory of the UK; also claimed by Argentina)

FLAG DESCRIPTION:

blue with the flag of the UK in the upper hoist-side quadrant and the Falkland Island coat of arms centered on the outer half of the flag; the coat of arms contains a white ram (sheep raising was once the major economic activity) above the sailing ship Desire (whose crew discovered the islands) with a scroll at the bottom bearing the motto DESIRE THE RIGHT

NATIONAL SYMBOL(S):

ram

NATIONAL ANTHEM:

name: Song of the Falklands"

lyrics/music: Christopher LANHAM

note: adopted 1930s; the song is the local unofficial anthem; as a territory of the United Kingdom, "God Save the Queen" is official (see United Kingdom)

ECONOMY :: FALKLAND ISLANDS (ISLAS MALVINAS)

ECONOMY - OVERVIEW:

The economy was formerly based on agriculture, mainly sheep farming, but fishing and tourism currently comprise the bulk of economic activity. In 1987, the government began selling fishing licenses to foreign trawlers operating within the Falkland Islands' exclusive fishing zone. These license fees net more than $40 million per year, which help support the island's health, education, and welfare system. The waters around the Falkland Islands are known for their squid, which account for around 75% of the annual 200,000-ton catch.

Dairy farming supports domestic consumption; crops furnish winter fodder. Foreign exchange earnings come from shipments of high-grade wool to the UK and from the sale of postage stamps and coins.

Tourism, especially ecotourism, is increasing rapidly, with about 69,000 visitors in 2009 and adds approximately $5.5 million to the Falkland's annual GDP. The British military presence also provides a sizable economic boost. The islands are now self-financing except for defense.

In 1993, the British Geological Survey announced a 200-mile oil exploration zone around the islands, and early seismic surveys suggest substantial reserves capable of producing 500,000 barrels per day. Political tensions between the UK and Argentina remain high following the start of oil drilling activities in the waters. In May 2010 the first commercial oil discovery was made, signaling the potential for the development of a long term hydrocarbon industry in the Falkland Islands.

GDP (PURCHASING POWER PARITY):

$206.4 million (2015 est.)

$164.5 million (2014 est.)

$167.5 million (2013 est.)

country comparison to the world: 220

GDP (OFFICIAL EXCHANGE RATE):

$206.4 million (2015 est.) (2015 est.)

GDP - REAL GROWTH RATE:

25.5% (2015 est.)

-1.8% (2014 est.)

-20.4% (2013 est.)

country comparison to the world: 3

GDP - PER CAPITA (PPP):

$70,800 (2015 est.)

$63,000 (2014 est.)

country comparison to the world: 12

GDP - COMPOSITION, BY SECTOR OF ORIGIN:

agriculture: 41% (2015 est.)

industry: 20.6% NA (2015 est.)

services: 38.4% NA (2015 est.)

AGRICULTURE - PRODUCTS:

fodder and vegetable crops; venison, sheep, dairy products; fish, squid

INDUSTRIES:

fish and wool processing; tourism

INDUSTRIAL PRODUCTION GROWTH RATE:

NA

LABOR FORCE:

1,850 (2016 est.)

country comparison to the world: 227

LABOR FORCE - BY OCCUPATION:

agriculture: 41%

industry: 24.5%

services: 34.5% (2015 est.)

UNEMPLOYMENT RATE:

1% (2016 est.)

country comparison to the world: 8

POPULATION BELOW POVERTY LINE:

NA

HOUSEHOLD INCOME OR CONSUMPTION BY PERCENTAGE SHARE:

lowest 10%: NA

highest 10%: NA

DISTRIBUTION OF FAMILY INCOME - GINI INDEX:

36 (2015)

country comparison to the world: 91

BUDGET:

revenues: 67.1 million (FY09/10)

expenditures: 75.3 million (FY09/10)

TAXES AND OTHER REVENUES:

32.5% (of GDP) (FY09/10)

country comparison to the world: 66

BUDGET SURPLUS (+) OR DEFICIT (-):

-4% (of GDP) (FY09/10)

country comparison to the world: 156

PUBLIC DEBT:

0% of GDP (2015 est.)

country comparison to the world: 209

FISCAL YEAR:

1 April - 31 March

INFLATION RATE (CONSUMER PRICES):

1.4% (2014 est.)

country comparison to the world: 77

EXPORTS:

$257.3 million (2015 est.)

$125 million (2004 est.)

country comparison to the world: 187

EXPORTS - PARTNERS:

Spain 74.4%, Namibia 10.4%, US 5% (2017)

EXPORTS - COMMODITIES:

wool, hides, meat, venison, fish, squid

IMPORTS:

$90 million (2004 est.)

country comparison to the world: 217

IMPORTS - COMMODITIES:

fuel, food and drink, building materials, clothing

IMPORTS - PARTNERS:

UK 47.8%, Spain 28.4%, Greece 10.2%, Netherlands 5.7%, Cote dIvoire 4.3% (2017)

DEBT - EXTERNAL:

$0 (2017 est.)

$0 (2016 est.)

country comparison to the world: 205

STOCK OF DIRECT FOREIGN INVESTMENT - AT HOME:

(31 December 2009 est.)

EXCHANGE RATES:

Falkland pounds (FKP) per US dollar -

0.7836 (2017 est.)

0.6542 (2016 est.)

0.6542 (2015)

0.6542 (2014 est.)

0.6391 (2013 est.)

ENERGY :: FALKLAND ISLANDS (ISLAS MALVINAS)

ELECTRICITY - PRODUCTION:

19 million kWh (2016 est.)

country comparison to the world: 213

ELECTRICITY - CONSUMPTION:

17.67 million kWh (2016 est.)

country comparison to the world: 213

ELECTRICITY - EXPORTS:

0 kWh (2016 est.)

country comparison to the world: 133

ELECTRICITY - IMPORTS:

0 kWh (2016 est.)

country comparison to the world: 147

ELECTRICITY - INSTALLED GENERATING CAPACITY:

12,100 kW (2016 est.)

country comparison to the world: 208

ELECTRICITY - FROM FOSSIL FUELS:

74% of total installed capacity (2016 est.)

country comparison to the world: 96

ELECTRICITY - FROM NUCLEAR FUELS:

0% of total installed capacity (2017 est.)

country comparison to the world: 89

ELECTRICITY - FROM HYDROELECTRIC PLANTS:

0% of total installed capacity (2017 est.)

country comparison to the world: 171

ELECTRICITY - FROM OTHER RENEWABLE SOURCES:

26% of total installed capacity (2017 est.)

country comparison to the world: 26

CRUDE OIL - PRODUCTION:

0 bbl/day (2017 est.)

country comparison to the world: 134

CRUDE OIL - EXPORTS:

0 bbl/day (2015 est.)

country comparison to the world: 122

CRUDE OIL - IMPORTS:

0 bbl/day (2015 est.)

country comparison to the world: 126

CRUDE OIL - PROVED RESERVES:

0 bbl (1 January 2018 est.)

country comparison to the world: 130

REFINED PETROLEUM PRODUCTS - PRODUCTION:

0 bbl/day (2017 est.)

country comparison to the world: 144

REFINED PETROLEUM PRODUCTS - CONSUMPTION:

290 bbl/day (2016 est.)

country comparison to the world: 213

REFINED PETROLEUM PRODUCTS - EXPORTS:

0 bbl/day (2015 est.)

country comparison to the world: 154

REFINED PETROLEUM PRODUCTS - IMPORTS:

286 bbl/day (2015 est.)

country comparison to the world: 209

NATURAL GAS - PRODUCTION:

0 cu m (2017 est.)

country comparison to the world: 131

NATURAL GAS - CONSUMPTION:

0 cu m (2017 est.)

country comparison to the world: 145

NATURAL GAS - EXPORTS:

0 cu m (2017 est.)

country comparison to the world: 103

NATURAL GAS - IMPORTS:

0 cu m (2017 est.)

country comparison to the world: 124

NATURAL GAS - PROVED RESERVES:

0 cu m (1 January 2014 est.)

country comparison to the world: 134

CARBON DIOXIDE EMISSIONS FROM CONSUMPTION OF ENERGY:

44,070 Mt (2017 est.)

country comparison to the world: 211

COMMUNICATIONS :: FALKLAND ISLANDS (ISLAS MALVINAS)

TELEPHONES - FIXED LINES:

total subscriptions: 2,255 (July 2016 est.)

subscriptions per 100 inhabitants: 77 (July 2016 est.)

country comparison to the world: 212

TELEPHONES - MOBILE CELLULAR:

total subscriptions: 4,674 (July 2016 est.)

subscriptions per 100 inhabitants: 146 (July 2016 est.)

country comparison to the world: 215

TELEPHONE SYSTEM:

general assessment: government-operated radiotelephone and private VHF/CB radiotelephone networks provide effective service to almost all points on both islands

domestic: fixed-line subscriptions 77 per 100, 146 per 100 for mobile-cellular (2015)

international: country code - 500; satellite earth station - 1 Intelsat

(Atlantic Ocean) with links through London to other countries (2015)

BROADCAST MEDIA:

TV service provided by a multi-channel service provider; radio services provided by the public broadcaster, Falkland Islands Radio Service, broadcasting on both AM and FM frequencies, and by the British Forces Broadcasting Service (BFBS) (2007)

INTERNET COUNTRY CODE:

.fk

INTERNET USERS:

total: 3,000 (July 2016 est.)

percent of population: 98.3% (July 2016 est.)

country comparison to the world: 219

BROADBAND - FIXED SUBSCRIPTIONS:

total: 1,610 (2017 est.)

subscriptions per 100 inhabitants: 50 (2017 est.)

country comparison to the world: 186

TRANSPORTATION :: FALKLAND ISLANDS (ISLAS MALVINAS)

NATIONAL AIR TRANSPORT SYSTEM:

number of registered air carriers: 1 (2015)

inventory of registered aircraft operated by air carriers: 5 (2015)

CIVIL AIRCRAFT REGISTRATION COUNTRY CODE PREFIX:

VP-F (2016)

AIRPORTS:

7 (2013)

country comparison to the world: 167

AIRPORTS - WITH PAVED RUNWAYS:

total: 2 (2017)

2,438 to 3,047 m: 1 (2017)

914 to 1,523 m: 1 (2017)

AIRPORTS - WITH UNPAVED RUNWAYS:

total: 5 (2013)

under 914 m: 5 (2013)

ROADWAYS:

total: 440 km (2008)

paved: 50 km (2008)

unpaved: 390 km (2008)

country comparison to the world: 199

MERCHANT MARINE:

total: 3 (2017)

by type: general cargo 1, other 2 (2017)

country comparison to the world: 167

PORTS AND TERMINALS:

major seaport(s): Stanley

MILITARY AND SECURITY :: FALKLAND ISLANDS (ISLAS MALVINAS)

MILITARY BRANCHES:

no regular military forces

MILITARY - NOTE:

defense is the responsibility of the UK

TRANSNATIONAL ISSUES :: FALKLAND ISLANDS (ISLAS MALVINAS)

DISPUTES - INTERNATIONAL:

Argentina, which claims the islands in its constitution and briefly occupied them by force in 1982, agreed in 1995 to no longer seek settlement by forceUK continues to reject Argentine requests for sovereignty talks

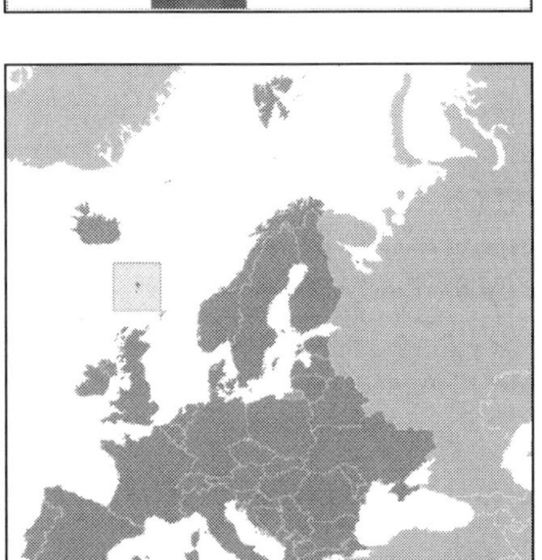

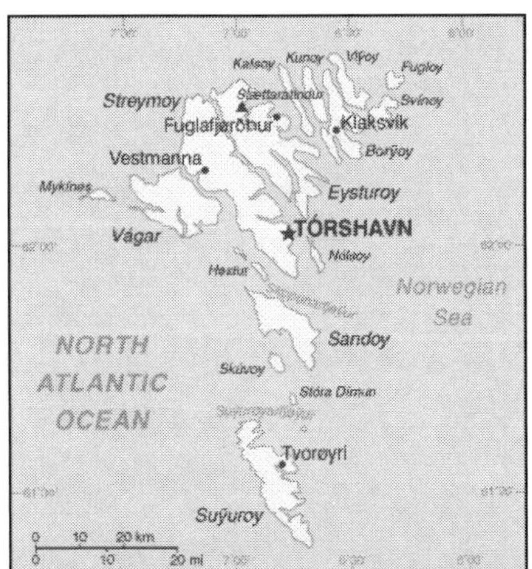

EUROPE :: FAROE ISLANDS

INTRODUCTION :: FAROE ISLANDS

BACKGROUND:

The population of the Faroe Islands is largely descended from Viking settlers who arrived in the 9th century. The islands have been connected politically to Denmark since the 14th century. A high degree of self-government was granted the Faroese in 1948, who have autonomy over most internal affairs while Denmark is responsible for justice, defense, and foreign affairs. The Faroe Islands are not part of the European Union.

GEOGRAPHY :: FAROE ISLANDS

LOCATION:

Northern Europe, island group between the Norwegian Sea and the North Atlantic Ocean, about halfway between Iceland and Norway

GEOGRAPHIC COORDINATES:

62 00 N, 7 00 W

MAP REFERENCES:

Europe

AREA:

total: 1,393 sq km

land: 1,393 sq km

water: 0 sq km (some lakes and streams)

country comparison to the world: 183

AREA - COMPARATIVE:

eight times the size of Washington, DC

LAND BOUNDARIES:

0 km

COASTLINE:

1,117 km

MARITIME CLAIMS:

territorial sea: 12 nm

continental shelf: 200 nm or agreed boundaries or median line

exclusive fishing zone: 200 nm or agreed boundaries or median line

CLIMATE:

mild winters, cool summers; usually overcast; foggy, windy

TERRAIN:

rugged, rocky, some low peaks; cliffs along most of coast

ELEVATION:

0 m lowest point: Atlantic Ocean

882 highest point: Slaettaratindur

NATURAL RESOURCES:

fish, whales, hydropower, possible oil and gas

LAND USE:

agricultural land: 2.1% (2011 est.)

arable land: 2.1% (2011 est.) / permanent crops: 0% (2011 est.) / permanent pasture: 0% (2011 est.)

forest: 0.1% (2011 est.)

other: 97.8% (2011 est.)

POPULATION DISTRIBUTION:

the island of Streymoy is by far the most populous with over 40% of the population; it has approximately twice as many inhabitants as Eysturoy, the second most populous island; seven of the inhabited islands have fewer than 100 people

NATURAL HAZARDS:

strong winds and heavy rains can occur throughout the year

ENVIRONMENT - CURRENT ISSUES:

coastal erosion, landslides and rockfalls, flash flooding, wind storms; oil spills

ENVIRONMENT - INTERNATIONAL AGREEMENTS:

party to: Marine Dumping - associate member to the London Convention and Ship Pollution

GEOGRAPHY - NOTE:

archipelago of 17 inhabited islands and one uninhabited island, and a few uninhabited islets; strategically located along important sea lanes in northeastern Atlantic; precipitous terrain limits habitation to small coastal lowlands

PEOPLE AND SOCIETY :: FAROE ISLANDS

POPULATION:

51,018 (July 2018 est.)

country comparison to the world: 210

NATIONALITY:

noun: Faroese (singular and plural)

adjective: Faroese

ETHNIC GROUPS:

Faroese 87.6% (Scandinavian and Anglo-Saxon descent), Danish 7.8%, other 4.6% (includes Icelandic, Norwegian, Filipino, Greenlandic, Thai, British) (2018 est.)

note: data represent respondents by country of birth

LANGUAGES:

Faroese 93.8% (derived from Old Norse), Danish 3.2%, other 3% (2011 est.)

RELIGIONS:

Christian 89.3% (predominantly Evangelical Lutheran), other 0.7%, more than one religion 0.2%, none 3.8%, unspecified 6% (2011 est.)

AGE STRUCTURE:

0-14 years: 19.79% (male 5,220 /female 4,878)

15-24 years: 14.17% (male 3,714 /female 3,515)

25-54 years: 37.24% (male 10,280 /female 8,718)

55-64 years: 11.82% (male 3,094 /female 2,934)

65 years and over: 16.98% (male 4,194 /female 4,471) (2018 est.)

MEDIAN AGE:

total: 37.6 years

male: 37.1 years

female: 38.2 years (2018 est.)

country comparison to the world: 66

POPULATION GROWTH RATE:

0.58% (2018 est.)

country comparison to the world: 149

BIRTH RATE:

14.5 births/1,000 population (2018 est.)

country comparison to the world: 131

DEATH RATE:

8.8 deaths/1,000 population (2018 est.)

country comparison to the world: 68

NET MIGRATION RATE:

0 migrant(s)/1,000 population (2017 est.)

country comparison to the world: 83

POPULATION DISTRIBUTION:

the island of Streymoy is by far the most populous with over 40% of the population; it has approximately twice as many inhabitants as Eysturoy, the second most populous island; seven of the inhabited islands have fewer than 100 people

URBANIZATION:

urban population: 42.1% of total population (2018)

rate of urbanization: 0.74% annual rate of change (2015-20 est.)

MAJOR URBAN AREAS - POPULATION:

21,000 TORSHAVN (capital) (2018)

SEX RATIO:

at birth: 1.07 male(s)/female (2017 est.)

0-14 years: 1.07 male(s)/female (2017 est.)

15-24 years: 1.05 male(s)/female (2017 est.)

25-54 years: 1.18 male(s)/female (2017 est.)

55-64 years: 1.06 male(s)/female (2017 est.)

65 years and over: 0.94 male(s)/female (2017 est.)

total population: 1.08 male(s)/female (2017 est.)

INFANT MORTALITY RATE:

total: 5.3 deaths/1,000 live births (2018 est.)

male: 5.6 deaths/1,000 live births (2018 est.)

female: 5 deaths/1,000 live births (2018 est.)

country comparison to the world: 173

LIFE EXPECTANCY AT BIRTH:

total population: 80.6 years (2018 est.)

male: 78.1 years (2018 est.)

female: 83.3 years (2018 est.)

country comparison to the world: 42

TOTAL FERTILITY RATE:

2.34 children born/woman (2018 est.)

country comparison to the world: 85

PHYSICIANS DENSITY:

2.63 physicians/1,000 population (2014)

HOSPITAL BED DENSITY:

4.1 beds/1,000 population (2015)

HIV/AIDS - ADULT PREVALENCE RATE:

NA

HIV/AIDS - PEOPLE LIVING WITH HIV/AIDS:

NA

HIV/AIDS - DEATHS:

NA

GOVERNMENT :: FAROE ISLANDS

COUNTRY NAME:

conventional long form: none

conventional short form: Faroe Islands

local long form: none

local short form: Foroyar

etymology: the archipelago's name may derive from the Old Norse word "faer," meaning sheep

DEPENDENCY STATUS:

part of the Kingdom of Denmark; self-governing overseas administrative division of Denmark since 1948

GOVERNMENT TYPE:

parliamentary democracy (Faroese Parliament); part of the Kingdom of Denmark

CAPITAL:

name: Torshavn

geographic coordinates: 62 00 N, 6 46 W

time difference: UTC 0 (5 hours ahead of Washington, DC, during Standard Time)

daylight saving time: +1hr, begins last Sunday in March; ends last Sunday in October

ADMINISTRATIVE DIVISIONS:

part of the Kingdom of Denmark; self-governing overseas administrative division of Denmark; there are 29 first-order municipalities (kommunur, singular - kommuna) Eidhis, Eystur, Famjins, Fuglafjardhar, Fugloyar, Hovs, Husavikar, Hvalbiar, Hvannasunds, Klaksvikar, Kunoyar, Kvivik, Nes, Porkeris, Runavikar, Sands, Sjovar, Skalavikar, Skopunar, Skuvoyar, Sorvags, Sumbiar, Sunda, Torshavnar, Tvoroyrar, Vaga, Vags, Vestmanna, Vidhareidhis

INDEPENDENCE:

none (part of the Kingdom of Denmark; self-governing overseas administrative division of Denmark)

NATIONAL HOLIDAY:

Olaifest (Olavsoka) (commemorates the death in battle of King OLAF II of Norway, later St. OLAF), 29 July (1030)

CONSTITUTION:

history: 5 June 1953 (Danish Constitution), 23 March 1948 (Home Rule Act), and 24 June 2005 (Takeover Act) serve as the Faroe Islands constitutional position in the Unity of the Realm (2016)

amendments: see entry for Denmark (2016)

LEGAL SYSTEM:

the laws of Denmark, where applicable, apply

CITIZENSHIP:

see Denmark

SUFFRAGE:

18 years of age; universal

EXECUTIVE BRANCH:

chief of state: Queen MARGRETHE II of Denmark (since 14 January 1972), represented by High Commissioner Dan Michael KNUDSEN, chief administrative officer (since 1 January 2008)

head of government: Prime Minister Aksel V. JOHANNESEN (since 15 September 2015)

cabinet: Landsstyri appointed by the prime minister

elections/appointments: the monarchy is hereditary; high commissioner appointed by the monarch; following legislative elections, the leader of the majority party or majority coalition usually elected prime minister by the Faroese Parliament; election last held on 1 September 2015 (next to be held in 2019)

election results: Aksel V. JOHANNESEN elected prime minister; Parliament vote - NA

LEGISLATIVE BRANCH:

description: unicameral Faroese Parliament or Logting (33 seats; members directly elected in a single nationwide constituency by proportional representation vote; members serve 4-year terms)

elections: last held on 1 September 2015 (next to be held no later than October 2019)

election results: percent of vote by party - JF 25.1%, Republic 20.7%, People's Party, 18.9%, Union Party 18.7%, Progressive Party 7%, Center Party 5.5%, New Self-Government Party 4.1%; seats by party - JF 8, Republic 7, People's Party 6, Union Party 6, Center Party 2, Progressive Party 2, New Self-Government Party 2; composition - men 23, women 10, percent of women 30.3%

note: election for 2 seats in the Danish Parliament was last held on 18 June 2015 (next to be held no later than June 2019); percent of vote by party - NA; seats by party - Social Democratic Party 1, Republican Party 1

JUDICIAL BRANCH:

highest courts: Faroese Court or Raett (Rett - Danish) decides both civil and criminal cases; the Court is part of the Danish legal system

subordinate courts: Court of the First Instance or Tribunal de Premiere Instance; Court of Administrative Law or Tribunal Administratif; Mixed Commercial Court; Land Court

POLITICAL PARTIES AND LEADERS:

Center Party (Midflokkurin) [Jenis av RANA]
New Self-Government Party (Nytt Sjalvstyri) [Jogvan SKORHEIM] (formerly Self-Government Party) (Sjalvstyrisflokkurin)
People's Party (Folkaflokkurin) [Jorgen NICLASEN]
Progressive Party (Framsokn) [Poul MICHELSEN]
Republic (Tjodveldi) [Hogni HOYDAL] (formerly the Republican Party)
Social Democratic Party (Javnadarflokkurin) or JF [Aksel V. JOHANNESEN]
Union Party (Sambandsflokkurin) [Bardur a STEIG NIELSEN]

INTERNATIONAL ORGANIZATION PARTICIPATION:

Arctic Council, IMO (associate), NC, NIB, UNESCO (associate), UPU

DIPLOMATIC REPRESENTATION IN THE US:

none (self-governing overseas administrative division of Denmark)

DIPLOMATIC REPRESENTATION FROM THE US:

none (self-governing overseas administrative division of Denmark)

FLAG DESCRIPTION:

white with a red cross outlined in blue extending to the edges of the flag; the vertical part of the cross is shifted toward the hoist side in the style of the Dannebrog (Danish flag); referred to as Merkid, meaning "the banner" or "the mark," the flag resembles those of neighboring Iceland and Norway, and uses the same three colors - but in a different sequence; white represents the clear Faroese sky, as well as the foam of the waves; red and blue are traditional Faroese colors

note: the blue on the flag is a lighter blue (azure) than that found on the flags of Iceland or Norway

NATIONAL SYMBOL(S):

ram; national colors: red, white, blue

NATIONAL ANTHEM:

name: "Mitt alfagra land" (My Fairest Land)

lyrics/music: Simun av SKAROI/Peter ALBERG

note: adopted 1948; the anthem is also known as "Tu alfagra land mitt" (Thou Fairest Land of Mine); as a self-governing overseas administrative division of Denmark, the Faroe Islands are permitted their own national anthem

ECONOMY :: FAROE ISLANDS

ECONOMY - OVERVIEW:

The Faroese economy has experienced a period of significant growth since 2011, due to higher fish prices and increased salmon farming and catches in the pelagic fisheries. Fishing has been the main source of income for the Faroe Islands since the late 19th century, but dependence on fishing makes the economy vulnerable to price fluctuations. Nominal GDP, measured in current prices, grew 5.6% in 2015 and 6.8% in 2016. GDP growth was forecast at 6.2% in 2017, slowing to 0.5% in 2018, due to lower fisheries quotas, higher oil prices and fewer farmed salmon combined with lower salmon prices. The fisheries sector accounts for about 97% of exports, and half of GDP. Unemployment is low, estimated at 2.1% in early 2018. Aided by an annual subsidy from Denmark, which amounts to about 11% of Faroese GDP , Faroese have a standard of living equal to that of Denmark. The Faroe Islands have bilateral free trade agreements with the EU, Iceland, Norway, Switzerland, and Turkey.

For the first time in 8 years, the Faroe Islands managed to generate a public budget surplus in 2016, a trend which continued in 2017. The local government intends to use this to reduce public debt, which reached 38% of GDP in 2015. A fiscal sustainability analysis of the Faroese economy shows that a long-term tightening of fiscal policy of 5% of GDP is required for fiscal sustainability.

Increasing public infrastructure investments are likely to lead to continued growth in the short term, and the Faroese economy is becoming somewhat more diversified. Growing industries include financial services, petroleum-related businesses, shipping, maritime manufacturing services, civil aviation, IT, telecommunications, and tourism.

GDP (PURCHASING POWER PARITY):

$2.001 billion (2014 est.)

$1.89 billion (2013 est.)

$1.608 billion (2012 est.)

country comparison to the world: 197

GDP (OFFICIAL EXCHANGE RATE):

$2.765 billion (2014 est.) (2014 est.)

GDP - REAL GROWTH RATE:

5.9% (2017 est.)

7.5% (2016 est.)

2.4% (2015 est.)

country comparison to the world: 35

GDP - PER CAPITA (PPP):

$40,000 (2014 est.)

country comparison to the world: 45

GROSS NATIONAL SAVING:

25.7% of GDP (2012 est.)

25.2% of GDP (2011 est.)

25.9% of GDP (2010 est.)

country comparison to the world: 53

GDP - COMPOSITION, BY END USE:

household consumption: 52% (2013)

government consumption: 29.6% (2013)

investment in fixed capital: 18.4% (2013)

GDP - COMPOSITION, BY SECTOR OF ORIGIN:

agriculture: 18% (2013 est.)

industry: 39% (2013 est.)

services: 43% (2013 est.)

AGRICULTURE - PRODUCTS:

milk, potatoes, vegetables, sheep, salmon, herring, mackerel and other fish

INDUSTRIES:

fishing, fish processing, tourism, small ship repair and refurbishment, handicrafts

INDUSTRIAL PRODUCTION GROWTH RATE:

3.4% (2009 est.)

country comparison to the world: 91

LABOR FORCE:

27,540 (2017 est.)

country comparison to the world: 206

LABOR FORCE - BY OCCUPATION:

agriculture: 15%

industry: 15%

services: 70% (December 2016 est.)

UNEMPLOYMENT RATE:

2.2% (2017 est.)

3.4% (2016 est.)

country comparison to the world: 20

POPULATION BELOW POVERTY LINE:

10% (2015 est.)

HOUSEHOLD INCOME OR CONSUMPTION BY PERCENTAGE SHARE:

lowest 10%: NA

highest 10%: NA

DISTRIBUTION OF FAMILY INCOME - GINI INDEX:

22.7 (2013 est.)

21.6 (2011 est.)

country comparison to the world: 157

BUDGET:

revenues: 835.6 million (2014 est.)

expenditures: 883.8 million (2014)

note: Denmark supplies the Faroe Islands with almost one-third of its public funds

TAXES AND OTHER REVENUES:

30.2% (of GDP) (2014 est.)

country comparison to the world: 76

BUDGET SURPLUS (+) OR DEFICIT (-):

-1.7% (of GDP) (2014 est.)

country comparison to the world: 95

PUBLIC DEBT:

35% of GDP (2014 est.)

country comparison to the world: 152

FISCAL YEAR:

calendar year

INFLATION RATE (CONSUMER PRICES):

-0.3% (2016)

-1.7% (2015)

country comparison to the world: 8

EXPORTS:

$1.184 billion (2016 est.)

$1.019 billion (2015 est.)

country comparison to the world: 153

EXPORTS - PARTNERS:

Russia 26.4%, UK 14.1%, Germany 8.4%, China 7.9%, Spain 6.8%, Denmark 6.2%, US 4.7%, Poland 4.4%, Norway 4.1% (2017)

EXPORTS - COMMODITIES:

fish and fish products (97%) (2017 est.)

IMPORTS:

$978.4 million (2016 est.)

$906.1 million (2015 est.)

country comparison to the world: 185

IMPORTS - COMMODITIES:

goods for household consumption, machinery and transport equipment, fuels, raw materials and semi-manufactures, cars

IMPORTS - PARTNERS:

Denmark 33%, China 10.7%, Germany 7.6%, Poland 6.8%, Norway 6.7%, Ireland 5%, Chile 4.3% (2017)

DEBT - EXTERNAL:

$387.6 million (2012)

$274.5 million (2010)

country comparison to the world: 182

STOCK OF DIRECT FOREIGN INVESTMENT - AT HOME:

NA

EXCHANGE RATES:

Danish kroner (DKK) per US dollar -

6.586 (2017 est.)

6.7269 (2016 est.)

6.7269 (2015 est.)

6.7236 (2014 est.)

5.6125 (2013 est.)

ENERGY :: FAROE ISLANDS

ELECTRICITY ACCESS:

electrification - total population: 100% (2016)

ELECTRICITY - PRODUCTION:

307 million kWh (2016 est.)

country comparison to the world: 180

ELECTRICITY - CONSUMPTION:

285.5 million kWh (2016 est.)

country comparison to the world: 185

ELECTRICITY - EXPORTS:

0 kWh (2016 est.)

country comparison to the world: 134

ELECTRICITY - IMPORTS:

0 kWh (2016 est.)

country comparison to the world: 148

ELECTRICITY - INSTALLED GENERATING CAPACITY:

128,300 kW (2016 est.)

country comparison to the world: 176

ELECTRICITY - FROM FOSSIL FUELS:

54% of total installed capacity (2016 est.)

country comparison to the world: 142

ELECTRICITY - FROM NUCLEAR FUELS:

0% of total installed capacity (2017 est.)

country comparison to the world: 90

ELECTRICITY - FROM HYDROELECTRIC PLANTS:

31% of total installed capacity (2017 est.)

country comparison to the world: 66

ELECTRICITY - FROM OTHER RENEWABLE SOURCES:

16% of total installed capacity (2017 est.)

country comparison to the world: 52

CRUDE OIL - PRODUCTION:

0 bbl/day (2017 est.)

country comparison to the world: 135

CRUDE OIL - EXPORTS:

0 bbl/day (2015 est.)

country comparison to the world: 123

CRUDE OIL - IMPORTS:

0 bbl/day (2015 est.)

country comparison to the world: 127

CRUDE OIL - PROVED RESERVES:

0 bbl (1 January 2018 est.)

country comparison to the world: 131

REFINED PETROLEUM PRODUCTS - PRODUCTION:

0 bbl/day (2015 est.)

country comparison to the world: 145

REFINED PETROLEUM PRODUCTS - CONSUMPTION:

4,600 bbl/day (2016 est.)

country comparison to the world: 180

REFINED PETROLEUM PRODUCTS - EXPORTS:

0 bbl/day (2015 est.)

country comparison to the world: 155

REFINED PETROLEUM PRODUCTS - IMPORTS:

4,555 bbl/day (2015 est.)

country comparison to the world: 174

NATURAL GAS - PRODUCTION:

0 cu m (2017 est.)

country comparison to the world: 132

NATURAL GAS - CONSUMPTION:

0 cu m (2017 est.)

country comparison to the world: 146

NATURAL GAS - EXPORTS:

0 cu m (2017 est.)

country comparison to the world: 104

NATURAL GAS - IMPORTS:

0 cu m (2017 est.)

country comparison to the world: 125

NATURAL GAS - PROVED RESERVES:

0 cu m (1 January 2014 est.)

country comparison to the world: 135

CARBON DIOXIDE EMISSIONS FROM CONSUMPTION OF ENERGY:

739,300 Mt (2017 est.)

country comparison to the world: 176

COMMUNICATIONS :: FAROE ISLANDS

TELEPHONES - FIXED LINES:

total subscriptions: 20,193 (July 2016 est.)

subscriptions per 100 inhabitants: 46 (July 2016 est.)

country comparison to the world: 177

TELEPHONES - MOBILE CELLULAR:

total subscriptions: 54,487 (July 2016 est.)

subscriptions per 100 inhabitants: 107 (July 2016 est.)

country comparison to the world: 200

TELEPHONE SYSTEM:

general assessment: good international communications; good domestic facilities (2015)

domestic: conversion to digital system completed in 1998; both NMT (analog) and GSM (digital) mobile telephone systems are installed (2015)

international: country code - 298; satellite earth stations - 1 Orion; 1 fiber-optic submarine cable to the Shetland Islands, linking the Faroe Islands with Denmark and Iceland; fiber-optic submarine cable connection to Canada-Europe cable (2015)

BROADCAST MEDIA:

1 publicly owned TV station; the Faroese telecommunications company distributes local and international channels through its digital terrestrial network; publicly owned radio station supplemented by 3 privately owned stations broadcasting over multiple frequencies (2015)

INTERNET COUNTRY CODE:

.fo

INTERNET USERS:

total: 47,988 (July 2016 est.)

percent of population: 95.1% (July 2016 est.)

country comparison to the world: 196

BROADBAND - FIXED SUBSCRIPTIONS:

total: 17,973 (2017 est.)

subscriptions per 100 inhabitants: 35 (2017 est.)

country comparison to the world: 153

TRANSPORTATION :: FAROE ISLANDS

NATIONAL AIR TRANSPORT SYSTEM:

number of registered air carriers: 1 (registered in Denmark) (2015)

inventory of registered aircraft operated by air carriers: 3 (registered in Denmark) (2015)

CIVIL AIRCRAFT REGISTRATION COUNTRY CODE PREFIX:

OY-H (2016)

AIRPORTS:

1 (2013)

country comparison to the world: 220

AIRPORTS - WITH PAVED RUNWAYS:

total: 1 (2017)

1,524 to 2,437 m: 1 (2017)

ROADWAYS:

total: 960 km (2017)

note: those islands not commected by roads (bridges or tunnels) are connected by seven different ferry links operated by the nationally owned company SSL

country comparison to the world: 187

MERCHANT MARINE:

total: 96 (2017)

by type: container ship 2, general cargo 41, oil tanker 1, other 52 (2017)

country comparison to the world: 88

PORTS AND TERMINALS:

major seaport(s): Fuglafjordur, Torshavn, Vagur

MILITARY AND SECURITY :: FAROE ISLANDS

MILITARY BRANCHES:

no regular military forces or conscription; the Government of Denmark has responsibility for defense; as such, the Danish military's Joint Arctic Command in Nuuk, Greenland is responsible for territorial defense of the Faroe Islands; the Joint Arctic Command has a contact element in the capital of Torshavn (2017)

MILITARY - NOTE:

defense is the responsibility of Denmark

DISPUTES - INTERNATIONAL:

because anticipated offshore hydrocarbon resources have not been realized, earlier Faroese proposals for full independence have been deferredIceland, the UK, and Ireland dispute Denmark's claim to UNCLOS that the Faroe Islands' continental shelf extends beyond 200 nm

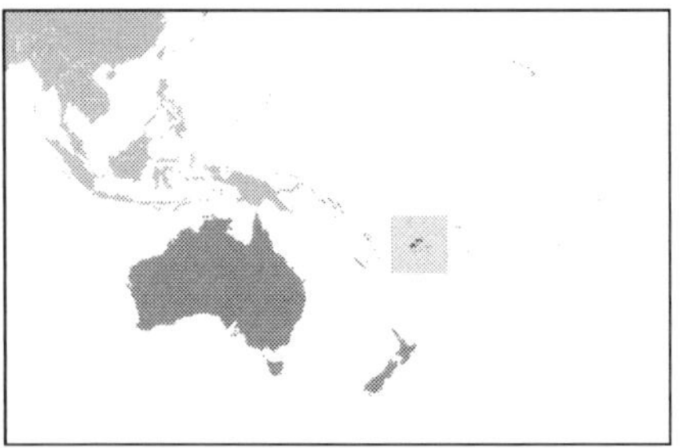

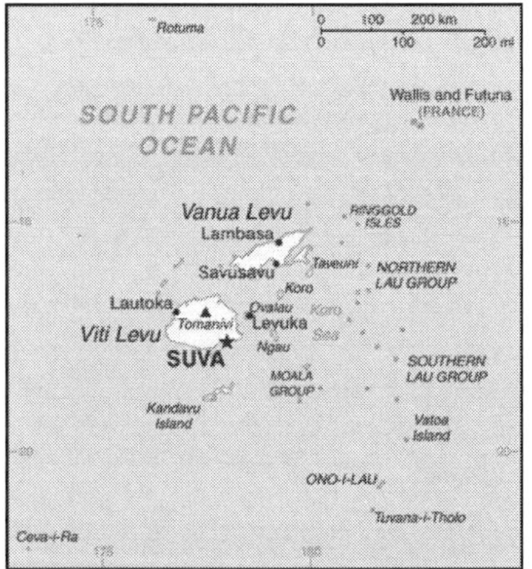

INTRODUCTION :: FIJI

BACKGROUND:

Fiji became independent in 1970 after nearly a century as a British colony. Democratic rule was interrupted by two military coups in 1987 caused by concern over a government perceived as dominated by the Indian community (descendants of contract laborers brought to the islands by the British in the 19th century). The coups and a 1990 constitution that cemented native Melanesian control of Fiji led to heavy Indian emigration; the population loss resulted in economic difficulties, but ensured that Melanesians became the majority. A new constitution enacted in 1997 was more equitable. Free and peaceful elections in 1999 resulted in a government led by an Indo-Fijian, but a civilian-led coup in 2000 ushered in a prolonged period of political turmoil. Parliamentary elections held in 2001 provided Fiji with a democratically elected government led by Prime Minister Laisenia QARASE. Reelected in May 2006, QARASE was ousted in a December 2006 military coup led by Commodore Voreqe BAINIMARAMA, who initially appointed himself acting president but in January 2007 became interim prime minister. Following years of political turmoil, long-delayed legislative elections were held in September 2014 that were deemed "credible" by international observers and that resulted in BAINIMARAMA being reelected.

GEOGRAPHY :: FIJI

LOCATION:

Oceania, island group in the South Pacific Ocean, about two-thirds of the way from Hawaii to New Zealand

GEOGRAPHIC COORDINATES:

18 00 S, 175 00 E

MAP REFERENCES:

Oceania

AREA:

total: 18,274 sq km

land: 18,274 sq km

water: 0 sq km

country comparison to the world: 157

AREA - COMPARATIVE:

slightly smaller than New Jersey

LAND BOUNDARIES:

0 km

COASTLINE:

1,129 km

MARITIME CLAIMS:

territorial sea: 12 nm

exclusive economic zone: 200 nm

contiguous zone: 24 nm

continental shelf: 200-m depth or to the depth of exploitation

measured from claimed archipelagic straight baselines

CLIMATE:

tropical marine; only slight seasonal temperature variation

TERRAIN:

mostly mountains of volcanic origin

ELEVATION:

0 m lowest point: Pacific Ocean

1324 highest point: Tomanivi

NATURAL RESOURCES:

timber, fish, gold, copper, offshore oil potential, hydropower

LAND USE:

agricultural land: 23.3% (2011 est.)

arable land: 9% (2011 est.) / permanent crops: 4.7% (2011 est.) / permanent pasture: 9.6% (2011 est.)

forest: 55.7% (2011 est.)

other: 21% (2011 est.)

IRRIGATED LAND:

40 sq km (2012)

POPULATION DISTRIBUTION:

approximately 70% of the population lives on the island of Viti Levu; roughly half of the population lives in urban areas

NATURAL HAZARDS:

cyclonic storms can occur from November to January

ENVIRONMENT - CURRENT ISSUES:

the widespread practice of waste incineration is a major contributor to air pollution in the country, as are vehicle emissions in urban areas; deforestation and soil erosion are significant problems; a contributory factor to erosion is clearing of land by bush burning, a widespread practie that threatens biodiversity

ENVIRONMENT - INTERNATIONAL AGREEMENTS:

party to: Biodiversity, Climate Change, Climate Change-Kyoto Protocol, Desertification, Endangered Species, Law of the Sea, Marine Life Conservation, Ozone Layer Protection, Tropical Timber 83, Tropical Timber 94, Wetlands

signed, but not ratified: none of the selected agreements

GEOGRAPHY - NOTE:

includes 332 islands; approximately 110 are inhabited

PEOPLE AND SOCIETY :: FIJI

POPULATION:

926,276 (July 2018 est.)

country comparison to the world: 161

NATIONALITY:

noun: Fijian(s)

adjective: Fijian

ETHNIC GROUPS:

iTaukei 56.8% (predominantly Melanesian with a Polynesian admixture), Indian 37.5%, Rotuman 1.2%, other 4.5% (European, part European, other Pacific Islanders, Chinese) (2007 est.)

note: a 2010 law replaces 'Fijian' with 'iTaukei' when referring to the original and native settlers of Fiji

LANGUAGES:

English (official), Fijian (official), Hindustani

RELIGIONS:

Protestant 45% (Methodist 34.6%, Assembly of God 5.7%, Seventh Day Adventist 3.9%, and Anglican 0.8%), Hindu 27.9%, other Christian 10.4%, Roman Catholic 9.1%, Muslim 6.3%, Sikh 0.3%, other 0.3%, none 0.8% (2007 est.)

AGE STRUCTURE:

0-14 years: 27.45% (male 129,962 /female 124,305)

15-24 years: 15.91% (male 75,165 /female 72,219)

25-54 years: 41.05% (male 194,743 /female 185,469)

55-64 years: 8.79% (male 41,286 /female 40,167)

65 years and over: 6.8% (male 28,924 /female 34,036) (2018 est.)

DEPENDENCY RATIOS:

total dependency ratio: 52.8 (2015 est.)

youth dependency ratio: 43.9 (2015 est.)

elderly dependency ratio: 8.9 (2015 est.)

potential support ratio: 11.2 (2015 est.)

MEDIAN AGE:

total: 29.2 years

male: 29 years

female: 29.4 years (2018 est.)

country comparison to the world: 126

POPULATION GROWTH RATE:

0.56% (2018 est.)

country comparison to the world: 151

BIRTH RATE:

18.2 births/1,000 population (2018 est.)

country comparison to the world: 91

DEATH RATE:

6.2 deaths/1,000 population (2018 est.)

country comparison to the world: 156

NET MIGRATION RATE:

-6.5 migrant(s)/1,000 population (2017 est.)

country comparison to the world: 200

POPULATION DISTRIBUTION:

approximately 70% of the population lives on the island of Viti Levu; roughly half of the population lives in urban areas

URBANIZATION:

urban population: 56.2% of total population (2018)

rate of urbanization: 1.62% annual rate of change (2015-20 est.)

MAJOR URBAN AREAS - POPULATION:

178,000 SUVA (capital) (2018)

SEX RATIO:

at birth: 1.05 male(s)/female (2017 est.)

0-14 years: 1.05 male(s)/female (2017 est.)

15-24 years: 1.04 male(s)/female (2017 est.)

25-54 years: 1.05 male(s)/female (2017 est.)

55-64 years: 1.03 male(s)/female (2017 est.)

65 years and over: 0.85 male(s)/female (2017 est.)

total population: 1.03 male(s)/female (2017 est.)

MATERNAL MORTALITY RATE:

30 deaths/100,000 live births (2015 est.)

country comparison to the world: 113

INFANT MORTALITY RATE:

total: 9.3 deaths/1,000 live births (2018 est.)

male: 10.2 deaths/1,000 live births (2018 est.)

female: 8.2 deaths/1,000 live births (2018 est.)

country comparison to the world: 142

LIFE EXPECTANCY AT BIRTH:

total population: 73.2 years (2018 est.)

male: 70.5 years (2018 est.)

female: 76 years (2018 est.)

country comparison to the world: 141

TOTAL FERTILITY RATE:

2.37 children born/woman (2018 est.)

country comparison to the world: 82

HEALTH EXPENDITURES:

4.5% of GDP (2014)

country comparison to the world: 156

PHYSICIANS DENSITY:

0.84 physicians/1,000 population (2015)

HOSPITAL BED DENSITY:

2.3 beds/1,000 population (2011)

DRINKING WATER SOURCE:

improved:

urban: 99.5% of population

rural: 91.2% of population

total: 95.7% of population

unimproved:

urban: 0.5% of population

rural: 8.8% of population

total: 4.3% of population (2015 est.)

SANITATION FACILITY ACCESS:

improved:

urban: 93.4% of population (2015 est.)

rural: 88.4% of population (2015 est.)

total: 91.1% of population (2015 est.)

unimproved:

urban: 6.6% of population (2015 est.)

rural: 11.6% of population (2015 est.)

total: 8.9% of population (2015 est.)

HIV/AIDS - ADULT PREVALENCE RATE:

0.1% (2016 est.)

country comparison to the world: 111

HIV/AIDS - PEOPLE LIVING WITH HIV/AIDS:

<1000 (2016 est.)

HIV/AIDS - DEATHS:

<100 (2016 est.)

MAJOR INFECTIOUS DISEASES:

note: active local transmission of Zika virus by Aedes species mosquitoes has been identified in this country (as of August 2016); it poses an important risk (a large number of cases possible) among US citizens if bitten by an infective mosquito; other less common ways to get Zika are through sex, via blood transfusion, or during pregnancy, in which the pregnant woman passes Zika virus to her fetus

OBESITY - ADULT PREVALENCE RATE:

30.2% (2016)

country comparison to the world: 24

EDUCATION EXPENDITURES:

3.9% of GDP (2013)

country comparison to the world: 113

UNEMPLOYMENT, YOUTH AGES 15-24:

total: 15.4% (2016 est.)

male: 11.9% (2016 est.)

female: 22.4% (2016 est.)

country comparison to the world: 85

GOVERNMENT :: FIJI

COUNTRY NAME:

conventional long form: Republic of Fiji

conventional short form: Fiji

local long form: Republic of Fiji/Matanitu ko Viti

local short form: Fiji/Viti

etymology: the Fijians called their home Viti, but the neighboring Tongans called it Fisi, and in the Anglicized spelling of the Tongan pronunciation - promulgated by explorer Captain James COOK - the designation became Fiji

GOVERNMENT TYPE:

parliamentary republic

CAPITAL:

name: Suva (on Viti Levu)

geographic coordinates: 18 08 S, 178 25 E

time difference: UTC+12 (17 hours ahead of Washington, DC, during Standard Time)

daylight saving time: +1hr, begins first Sunday in November; ends second Sunday in January

ADMINISTRATIVE DIVISIONS:

14 provinces and 1 dependency*; Ba, Bua, Cakaudrove, Kadavu, Lau, Lomaiviti, Macuata, Nadroga and Navosa, Naitasiri, Namosi, Ra, Rewa, Rotuma*, Serua, Tailevu

INDEPENDENCE:

10 October 1970 (from the UK)

NATIONAL HOLIDAY:

Fiji (Independence) Day, 10 October (1970)

CONSTITUTION:

several previous; latest signed into law September 2013 (2017)

LEGAL SYSTEM:

common law system based on the English model

INTERNATIONAL LAW ORGANIZATION PARTICIPATION:

has not submitted an ICJ jurisdiction declaration; accepts ICCt jurisdiction

CITIZENSHIP:

citizenship by birth: no

citizenship by descent only: at least one parent must be a citizen of Fiji

dual citizenship recognized: yes

residency requirement for naturalization: at least 5 years residency out of the 10 years preceding application

SUFFRAGE:

18 years of age; universal

EXECUTIVE BRANCH:

chief of state: President Jioji Konousi KONROTE (since 12 November 2015)

head of government: Prime Minister Voreqe "Frank" BAINIMARAMA (since 22 September 2014)

cabinet: Cabinet appointed by the prime minister from among members of Parliament and is responsible to Parliament

elections/appointments: president elected by Parliament for a 3-year term (eligible for a second term); election last held on 31 August 2018 (next to be held in 2021); prime minister appointed by the president

election results: Jioji Konousi KONROTE reelected president (unopposed)

LEGISLATIVE BRANCH:

description: unicameral Parliament (51 seats; members directly elected in a nationwide, multi-seat constituency by open-list proportional representation vote to serve 4-year terms)

elections: last held on 14 November 2018 (next to be held in 2022)

election results: percent of vote by party - FijiFirst 50%, SODELPA 39.6%, NFP 7.4%; seats by party - FijiFirst 27, SODELPA 21, NFP 3; composition - men 41, women 10, percent of women 19.6%

JUDICIAL BRANCH:

highest courts: Supreme Court (consists of the chief justice, all justices of the Court of Appeal, and judges appointed specifically as Supreme Court judges); Court of Appeal (consists of the court president, all puisne judges of the High Court, and judges specifically appointed to the Court of Appeal); High Court (chaired by the chief justice and includes a minimum of 10 puisne judges; High Court organized into civil, criminal, family, employment, and tax divisions)

judge selection and term of office: chief justice appointed by the president of Fiji on the advice of the prime minister following consultation with the parliamentary leader of the opposition; judges of the Supreme Court, the president of the Court of Appeal, the justices of the Court of Appeal, and puisne judges of the High Court appointed by the president of Fiji upon the nomination of the Judicial Service Commission after consulting with the cabinet minister and the committee of the House of Representatives responsible for the administration of justice; the chief justice, Supreme Court judges and justices of Appeal generally required to retire at age 70 but may be waived for one or more sessions of the court; puisne judges appointed for not less than 4 years nor more than 7 years with mandatory retirement at age 65

subordinate courts: Magistrates' Court (organized into civil, criminal, juvenile, and small claims divisions)

POLITICAL PARTIES AND LEADERS:

FijiFirst [Veroqe "Frank" BAINIMARAMA]
Fiji Labor Party or FLP [Mahendra CHAUDHRY]
Fiji United Freedon Party or FUFP [Jagath KARUNARATNE]
National Federation Party or NFP [Biman PRASAD] (primarily Indian)
Peoples Democratic Party or PDP [Lynda TABUYA]
Social Democratic Liberal Party or SODELPA
Unity Fiji [Adi QORO]

INTERNATIONAL ORGANIZATION PARTICIPATION:

ACP, ADB, AOSIS, C, CP, FAO, G-77, IAEA, IBRD, ICAO, ICCt, ICRM, IDA, IFAD, IFC, IFRCS, IHO, ILO, IMF, IMO, Interpol, IOC, IOM, ISO, ITSO, ITU, ITUC (NGOs), MIGA, OPCW, PCA, PIF, Sparteca (suspended), SPC, UN, UNCTAD,

UNDOF, UNESCO, UNIDO, UNMISS, UNWTO, UPU, WCO, WFTU (NGOs), WHO, WIPO, WMO, WTO

DIPLOMATIC REPRESENTATION IN THE US:

chief of mission: Ambassador Solo MARA (since 28 January 2016)

chancery: 2000 M Street NW, Suite 710, Washington, DC 20036

telephone: [1] (202) 466-8320

FAX: [1] (202) 466-8325

DIPLOMATIC REPRESENTATION FROM THE US:

chief of mission: Ambassador Judith CEFKIN (since 3 February 2015); note - also accredited to Kiribati, Nauru, Tonga, and Tuvalu

embassy: 158 Princes Rd, Tamavua

mailing address: P. O. Box 218, Suva

telephone: [679] 331-4466

FAX: [679] 330-8685

FLAG DESCRIPTION:

light blue with the flag of the UK in the upper hoist-side quadrant and the Fijian shield centered on the outer half of the flag; the blue symbolizes the Pacific Ocean and the Union Jack reflects the links with Great Britain; the shield - taken from Fiji's coat of arms - depicts a yellow lion, holding a coconut pod between its paws, above a white field quartered by the cross of Saint George; the four quarters depict stalks of sugarcane, a palm tree, a banana bunch, and a white dove of peace

NATIONAL SYMBOL(S):

Fijian canoe; national color: light blue

NATIONAL ANTHEM:

name: God Bless Fiji

lyrics/music: Michael Francis Alexander PRESCOTT/C. Austin MILES (adapted by Michael Francis Alexander PRESCOTT)

note: adopted 1970; known in Fijian as "Meda Dau Doka" (Let Us Show Pride); adapted from the hymn, "Dwelling in Beulah Land," the anthem's English lyrics are generally sung, although they differ in meaning from the official Fijian lyrics

ECONOMY :: FIJI

ECONOMY - OVERVIEW:

Fiji, endowed with forest, mineral, and fish resources, is one of the most developed and connected of the Pacific island economies. Earnings from the tourism industry, with an estimated 842,884 tourists visiting in 2017, and remittances from Fijian's working abroad are the country's largest foreign exchange earners.

Bottled water exports to the US is Fiji's largest domestic export. Fiji's sugar sector remains a significant industry and a major export, but crops and one of the sugar mills suffered damage during Cyclone Winston in 2016. Fiji's trade imbalance continues to widen with increased imports and sluggish performance of domestic exports.

The return to parliamentary democracy and successful elections in September 2014 improved investor confidence, but increasing bureaucratic regulation, new taxes, and lack of consultation with relevant stakeholders brought four consecutive years of decline for Fiji on the World Bank Ease of Doing Business index. Private sector investment in 2017 approached 20% of GDP, compared to 13% in 2013.

GDP (PURCHASING POWER PARITY):

$8.629 billion (2017 est.)

$8.376 billion (2016 est.)

$8.321 billion (2015 est.)

note: data are in 2017 dollars

country comparison to the world: 163

GDP (OFFICIAL EXCHANGE RATE):

$4.891 billion (2017 est.) (2017 est.)

GDP - REAL GROWTH RATE:

3% (2017 est.)

0.7% (2016 est.)

3.8% (2015 est.)

country comparison to the world: 113

GDP - PER CAPITA (PPP):

$9,800 (2017 est.)

$9,600 (2016 est.)

$9,600 (2015 est.)

note: data are in 2017 dollars

country comparison to the world: 140

GROSS NATIONAL SAVING:

12.7% of GDP (2017 est.)

13.4% of GDP (2016 est.)

16.1% of GDP (2015 est.)

country comparison to the world: 146

GDP - COMPOSITION, BY END USE:

household consumption: 81.3% (2017 est.)

government consumption: 24.4% (2017 est.)

investment in fixed capital: 16.9% (2017 est.)

investment in inventories: 0% (2017 est.)

exports of goods and services: 29% (2017 est.)

imports of goods and services: -51.6% (2017 est.)

GDP - COMPOSITION, BY SECTOR OF ORIGIN:

agriculture: 13.5% (2017 est.)

industry: 17.4% (2017 est.)

services: 69.1% (2017 est.)

AGRICULTURE - PRODUCTS:

sugarcane, copra, ginger, tropical fruits, vegetables; beef, pork, chicken, fish

INDUSTRIES:

tourism, sugar processing, clothing, copra, gold, silver, lumber

INDUSTRIAL PRODUCTION GROWTH RATE:

2.8% (2017 est.)

country comparison to the world: 108

LABOR FORCE:

353,100 (2017 est.)

country comparison to the world: 161

LABOR FORCE - BY OCCUPATION:

agriculture: 44.2%

industry: 14.3%

services: 41.6% (2011)

UNEMPLOYMENT RATE:

4.5% (2017 est.)

5.5% (2016 est.)

country comparison to the world: 63

POPULATION BELOW POVERTY LINE:

31% (2009 est.)

HOUSEHOLD INCOME OR CONSUMPTION BY PERCENTAGE SHARE:

lowest 10%: 34.9% (2009 est.)

highest 10%: 34.9% (2009 est.)

BUDGET:

revenues: 1.454 billion (2017 est.)

expenditures: 1.648 billion (2017 est.)

TAXES AND OTHER REVENUES:

29.7% (of GDP) (2017 est.)

country comparison to the world: 80

BUDGET SURPLUS (+) OR DEFICIT (-):

-4% (of GDP) (2017 est.)

country comparison to the world: 157

PUBLIC DEBT:

48.9% of GDP (2017 est.)

47.5% of GDP (2016 est.)

country comparison to the world: 106

FISCAL YEAR:

calendar year

INFLATION RATE (CONSUMER PRICES):

3.4% (2017 est.)

3.9% (2016 est.)

country comparison to the world: 140

CENTRAL BANK DISCOUNT RATE:

1.75% (31 December 2010)

3% (31 December 2009)

country comparison to the world: 122

COMMERCIAL BANK PRIME LENDING RATE:

5.74% (31 December 2017 est.)

5.85% (31 December 2016 est.)

country comparison to the world: 129

STOCK OF NARROW MONEY:

$2.272 billion (31 December 2017 est.)

$1.994 billion (31 December 2016 est.)

country comparison to the world: 132

STOCK OF BROAD MONEY:

$2.272 billion (31 December 2017 est.)

$1.994 billion (31 December 2016 est.)

country comparison to the world: 140

STOCK OF DOMESTIC CREDIT:

$3.607 billion (31 December 2017 est.)

$3.295 billion (31 December 2016 est.)

country comparison to the world: 135

MARKET VALUE OF PUBLICLY TRADED SHARES:

$452.5 million (31 December 2012 est.)

$392.2 million (31 December 2011 est.)

$418.8 million (31 December 2010 est.)

country comparison to the world: 113

CURRENT ACCOUNT BALANCE:

-$277 million (2017 est.)

-$131 million (2016 est.)

country comparison to the world: 101

EXPORTS:

$908.2 million (2017 est.)

$709 million (2016 est.)

country comparison to the world: 164

EXPORTS - PARTNERS:

US 20.8%, Australia 14.9%, NZ 7.7%, Tonga 5%, Vanuatu 4.6%, China 4.5%, Spain 4.3%, UK 4.3%, Kiribati 4.1% (2017)

EXPORTS - COMMODITIES:

fuel, including oil, fish, beverages, gems, sugar, garments, gold, timber, fish, molasses, coconut oil, mineral water

IMPORTS:

$1.911 billion (2017 est.)

$1.761 billion (2016 est.)

country comparison to the world: 168

IMPORTS - COMMODITIES:

manufactured goods, machinery and transport equipment, petroleum products, food and beverages, chemicals, tobacco

IMPORTS - PARTNERS:

Australia 19.2%, NZ 17.2%, Singapore 17%, China 13.8% (2017)

RESERVES OF FOREIGN EXCHANGE AND GOLD:

$1.116 billion (31 December 2017 est.)

$908.6 million (31 December 2016 est.)

country comparison to the world: 130

DEBT - EXTERNAL:

$1.022 billion (31 December 2017 est.)

$696.4 million (31 December 2016 est.)

country comparison to the world: 166

STOCK OF DIRECT FOREIGN INVESTMENT - AT HOME:

$4.342 billion (31 December 2017 est.)

$4.022 billion (31 December 2016 est.)

country comparison to the world: 108

STOCK OF DIRECT FOREIGN INVESTMENT - ABROAD:

$117.1 million (31 December 2017 est.)

$115.1 million (31 December 2016 est.)

country comparison to the world: 110

EXCHANGE RATES:

Fijian dollars (FJD) per US dollar -

2.075 (2017 est.)

2.0947 (2016 est.)

2.0947 (2015 est.)

2.0976 (2014 est.)

1.8874 (2013 est.)

ENERGY :: FIJI

ELECTRICITY ACCESS:

population without electricity: 375,274 (2012)

electrification - total population: 59% (2012)

electrification - urban areas: 72% (2012)

electrification - rural areas: 45% (2012)

ELECTRICITY - PRODUCTION:

914 million kWh (2016 est.)

country comparison to the world: 155

ELECTRICITY - CONSUMPTION:

850 million kWh (2016 est.)

country comparison to the world: 159

ELECTRICITY - EXPORTS:

0 kWh (2016 est.)

country comparison to the world: 135

ELECTRICITY - IMPORTS:

0 kWh (2016 est.)

country comparison to the world: 149

ELECTRICITY - INSTALLED GENERATING CAPACITY:

338,000 kW (2016 est.)

country comparison to the world: 154

ELECTRICITY - FROM FOSSIL FUELS:

34% of total installed capacity (2016 est.)

country comparison to the world: 181

ELECTRICITY - FROM NUCLEAR FUELS:

0% of total installed capacity (2017 est.)

country comparison to the world: 91

ELECTRICITY - FROM HYDROELECTRIC PLANTS:

38% of total installed capacity (2017 est.)

country comparison to the world: 55

ELECTRICITY - FROM OTHER RENEWABLE SOURCES:

27% of total installed capacity (2017 est.)

country comparison to the world: 24

CRUDE OIL - PRODUCTION:

0 bbl/day (2017 est.)

country comparison to the world: 136

CRUDE OIL - EXPORTS:

0 bbl/day (2015 est.)

country comparison to the world: 124

CRUDE OIL - IMPORTS:

0 bbl/day (2015 est.)

country comparison to the world: 128

CRUDE OIL - PROVED RESERVES:

0 bbl (1 January 2018 est.)

country comparison to the world: 132

REFINED PETROLEUM PRODUCTS - PRODUCTION:

0 bbl/day (2015 est.)

country comparison to the world: 146

REFINED PETROLEUM PRODUCTS - CONSUMPTION:

16,000 bbl/day (2016 est.)

country comparison to the world: 151

REFINED PETROLEUM PRODUCTS - EXPORTS:

0 bbl/day (2015 est.)

country comparison to the world: 156

REFINED PETROLEUM PRODUCTS - IMPORTS:

17,460 bbl/day (2015 est.)

country comparison to the world: 131

NATURAL GAS - PRODUCTION:

0 cu m (2017 est.)

country comparison to the world: 133

NATURAL GAS - CONSUMPTION:

0 cu m (2017 est.)

country comparison to the world: 147

NATURAL GAS - EXPORTS:

0 cu m (2017 est.)

country comparison to the world: 105

NATURAL GAS - IMPORTS:

0 cu m (2017 est.)

country comparison to the world: 126

NATURAL GAS - PROVED RESERVES:

0 cu m (1 January 2014 est.)

country comparison to the world: 136

CARBON DIOXIDE EMISSIONS FROM CONSUMPTION OF ENERGY:

2.369 million Mt (2017 est.)

country comparison to the world: 155

COMMUNICATIONS :: FIJI

TELEPHONES - FIXED LINES:

total subscriptions: 75,952 (2017 est.)

subscriptions per 100 inhabitants: 8 (2017 est.)

country comparison to the world: 147

TELEPHONES - MOBILE CELLULAR:

total subscriptions: 1,033,915 (2017 est.)

subscriptions per 100 inhabitants: 112 (2017 est.)

country comparison to the world: 159

TELEPHONE SYSTEM:

general assessment: modern local, interisland, and international (wire/radio integrated) public and special-purpose telephone, telegraph, and teleprinter facilities; regional radio communications center; subject to occasional devastating cyclones; Fiji is a leader in the Pacific region in terms of development of its ICT sector and investment in telecoms infrastructure; initial progress towards 5G readiness (2017)

domestic: telephone or radio telephone links to almost all inhabited islands; most towns and large villages have automatic telephone exchanges and direct dialing; fixed-line 8 per 100 persons and mobile-cellular teledensity roughly 112 per 100 persons (2017)

international: country code - 679; access to important cable links between US and Canada, as well as between NZ and Australia; satellite earth stations - 2 Inmarsat (Pacific Ocean); 2018 Fijian government to implement cable to connect the two major islands via submarine cable system (2017)

BROADCAST MEDIA:

Fiji TV, a publicly traded company, operates a free-to-air channel; Digicel Fiji operates the Sky Fiji and Sky Pacific multi-channel pay-TV services; state-owned commercial company, Fiji Broadcasting Corporation, Ltd, operates 6 radio stations - 2 public broadcasters and 4 commercial broadcasters with multiple repeaters; 5 radio stations with repeaters operated by Communications Fiji, Ltd; transmissions of multiple international broadcasters are available (2017)

INTERNET COUNTRY CODE:

.fj

INTERNET USERS:

total: 425,680 (July 2016 est.)

percent of population: 46.5% (July 2016 est.)

country comparison to the world: 152

BROADBAND - FIXED SUBSCRIPTIONS:

total: 12,135 (2017 est.)

subscriptions per 100 inhabitants: 1 (2017 est.)

country comparison to the world: 167

TRANSPORTATION :: FIJI

NATIONAL AIR TRANSPORT SYSTEM:

number of registered air carriers: 2 (2015)

inventory of registered aircraft operated by air carriers: 12 (2015)

annual passenger traffic on registered air carriers: 1,336,976 (2015)

annual freight traffic on registered air carriers: 83,686,504 mt-km (2015)

CIVIL AIRCRAFT REGISTRATION COUNTRY CODE PREFIX:

DQ (2016)

AIRPORTS:

28 (2013)

country comparison to the world: 121

AIRPORTS - WITH PAVED RUNWAYS:

total: 4 (2017)

over 3,047 m: 1 (2017)

1,524 to 2,437 m: 1 (2017)

914 to 1,523 m: 2 (2017)

AIRPORTS - WITH UNPAVED RUNWAYS:

total: 24 (2013)

914 to 1,523 m: 5 (2013)

under 914 m: 19 (2013)

RAILWAYS:

total: 597 km (2008)

narrow gauge: 597 km 0.600-m gauge (2008)

note: belongs to the government-owned Fiji Sugar Corporation; used to haul sugarcane during the harvest season, which runs from May to December

country comparison to the world: 109

ROADWAYS:

total: 3,440 km (2011)

paved: 1,686 km (2011)

unpaved: 1,754 km (2011)

country comparison to the world: 163

WATERWAYS:

203 km (122 km are navigable by motorized craft and 200-metric-ton barges) (2012)

country comparison to the world: 97

MERCHANT MARINE:

total: 68 (2017)

by type: bulk carrier 6, general cargo 25, oil tanker 2, other 35 (2017)

country comparison to the world: 103

PORTS AND TERMINALS:

major seaport(s): Lautoka, Levuka, Suva

MILITARY AND SECURITY :: FIJI

MILITARY EXPENDITURES:

0.98% of GDP (2016)

1.07% of GDP (2015)

1.03% of GDP (2014)

country comparison to the world: 116

MILITARY BRANCHES:

Republic of Fiji Military Forces (RFMF): Land Forces, Naval Forces (2011)

MILITARY SERVICE AGE AND OBLIGATION:

18 years of age for voluntary military service; mandatory retirement at age 55 (2013)

TRANSNATIONAL ISSUES :: FIJI

DISPUTES - INTERNATIONAL:

none

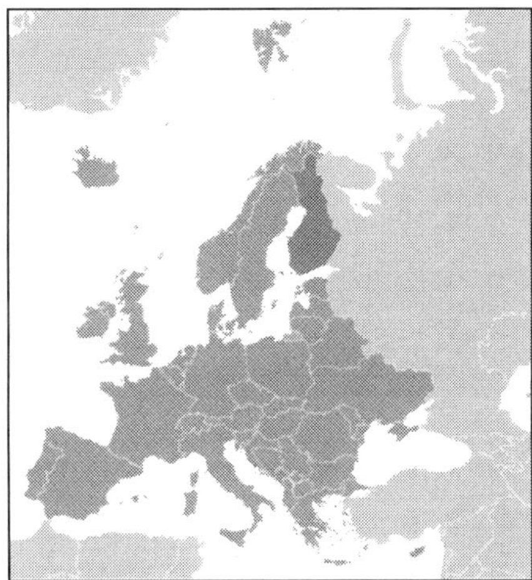

EUROPE :: FINLAND

INTRODUCTION :: FINLAND

BACKGROUND:

Finland was a province and then a grand duchy under Sweden from the 12th to the 19th centuries, and an autonomous grand duchy of Russia after 1809. It gained complete independence in 1917. During World War II, Finland successfully defended its independence through cooperation with Germany and resisted subsequent invasions by the Soviet Union - albeit with some loss of territory. In the subsequent half century, Finland transformed from a farm/forest economy to a diversified modern industrial economy; per capita income is among the highest in Western Europe. A member of the EU since 1995, Finland was the only Nordic state to join the euro single currency at its initiation in January 1999. In the 21st century, the key features of Finland's modern welfare state are high quality education, promotion of equality, and a national social welfare system - currently challenged by an aging population and the fluctuations of an export-driven economy.

GEOGRAPHY :: FINLAND

LOCATION:

Northern Europe, bordering the Baltic Sea, Gulf of Bothnia, and Gulf of Finland, between Sweden and Russia

GEOGRAPHIC COORDINATES:

64 00 N, 26 00 E

MAP REFERENCES:

Europe

AREA:

total: 338,145 sq km

land: 303,815 sq km

water: 34,330 sq km

country comparison to the world: 66

AREA - COMPARATIVE:

slightly more than two times the size of Georgia; slightly smaller than Montana

LAND BOUNDARIES:

total: 2,563 km

border countries (3): Norway 709 km, Sweden 545 km, Russia 1309 km

COASTLINE:

1,250 km

MARITIME CLAIMS:

territorial sea: 12 nm (in the Gulf of Finland - 3 nm)

contiguous zone: 24 nm

continental shelf: 200 m depth or to the depth of exploitation

exclusive fishing zone: 12 nm; extends to continental shelf boundary with Sweden, Estonia, and Russia

CLIMATE:

cold temperate; potentially subarctic but comparatively mild because of moderating influence of the North Atlantic Current, Baltic Sea, and more than 60,000 lakes

TERRAIN:

mostly low, flat to rolling plains interspersed with lakes and low hills

ELEVATION:

mean elevation: 164 m

elevation extremes: 0 m lowest point: Baltic Sea

1328 highest point: Halti (alternatively Haltia, Haltitunturi, Haltiatunturi)

NATURAL RESOURCES:

timber, iron ore, copper, lead, zinc, chromite, nickel, gold, silver, limestone

LAND USE:

agricultural land: 7.5% (2011 est.)

arable land: 7.4% (2011 est.) / permanent crops: 0% (2011 est.) / permanent pasture: 0.1% (2011 est.)

forest: 72.9% (2011 est.)

other: 19.6% (2011 est.)

IRRIGATED LAND:

690 sq km (2012)

POPULATION DISTRIBUTION:

the vast majority of people are found in the south; the northern interior areas remain sparsely poplulated

NATURAL HAZARDS:

severe winters in the north

ENVIRONMENT - CURRENT ISSUES:

limited air pollution in urban centers; some water pollution from industrial wastes, agricultural chemicals; habitat loss threatens wildlife populations

ENVIRONMENT - INTERNATIONAL AGREEMENTS:

party to: Air Pollution, Air Pollution-Nitrogen Oxides, Air Pollution-Persistent Organic Pollutants, Air Pollution-Sulfur 85, Air Pollution-Sulfur 94, Air Pollution-Volatile Organic Compounds, Antarctic-Environmental Protocol, Antarctic-Marine Living Resources, Antarctic Treaty, Biodiversity, Climate Change, Climate Change-Kyoto Protocol, Desertification, Endangered Species, Environmental Modification, Hazardous Wastes, Law of the Sea, Marine Dumping, Marine Life Conservation, Ozone Layer Protection, Ship Pollution, Tropical Timber 83, Tropical Timber 94, Wetlands, Whaling

signed, but not ratified: none of the selected agreements

GEOGRAPHY - NOTE:

long boundary with Russia; Helsinki is northernmost national capital on European continent; population concentrated on small southwestern coastal plain

PEOPLE AND SOCIETY :: FINLAND

POPULATION:

5,537,364 (July 2018 est.)

country comparison to the world: 117

NATIONALITY:

noun: Finn(s)

adjective: Finnish

ETHNIC GROUPS:

Finn, Swede, Russian, Estonian, Romani, Sami

LANGUAGES:

Finnish (official) 87.9%, Swedish (official) 5.2%, Russian 1.4%, other 5.5% (2017 est.)

RELIGIONS:

Lutheran 70.9%, Greek Orthodox 1.1%, other 1.7%, unspecified 26.3% (2017 est.)

AGE STRUCTURE:

0-14 years: 16.44% (male 465,298 /female 445,186)

15-24 years: 11.21% (male 317,500 /female 303,326)

25-54 years: 37.64% (male 1,064,751 /female 1,019,748)

55-64 years: 13.19% (male 359,434 /female 370,993)

65 years and over: 21.51% (male 519,775 /female 671,353) (2018 est.)

DEPENDENCY RATIOS:

total dependency ratio: 57.9 (2015 est.)

youth dependency ratio: 25.9 (2015 est.)

elderly dependency ratio: 32 (2015 est.)

potential support ratio: 3.1 (2015 est.)

MEDIAN AGE:

total: 42.6 years

male: 41 years

female: 44.3 years (2018 est.)

country comparison to the world: 27

POPULATION GROWTH RATE:

0.33% (2018 est.)

country comparison to the world: 167

BIRTH RATE:

10.7 births/1,000 population (2018 est.)

country comparison to the world: 183

DEATH RATE:

10.1 deaths/1,000 population (2018 est.)

country comparison to the world: 35

NET MIGRATION RATE:

2.9 migrant(s)/1,000 population (2017 est.)

country comparison to the world: 35

POPULATION DISTRIBUTION:

the vast majority of people are found in the south; the northern interior areas remain sparsely poplulated

URBANIZATION:

urban population: 85.4% of total population (2018)

rate of urbanization: 0.42% annual rate of change (2015-20 est.)

MAJOR URBAN AREAS - POPULATION:

1.279 million HELSINKI (capital) (2018)

SEX RATIO:

at birth: 1.05 male(s)/female (2017 est.)

0-14 years: 1.05 male(s)/female (2017 est.)

15-24 years: 1.04 male(s)/female (2017 est.)

25-54 years: 1.04 male(s)/female (2017 est.)

55-64 years: 0.97 male(s)/female (2017 est.)

65 years and over: 0.76 male(s)/female (2017 est.)

total population: 0.97 male(s)/female (2017 est.)

MOTHER'S MEAN AGE AT FIRST BIRTH:

28.8 years (2015 est.)

MATERNAL MORTALITY RATE:

3 deaths/100,000 live births (2015 est.)

country comparison to the world: 181

INFANT MORTALITY RATE:

total: 2.5 deaths/1,000 live births (2018 est.)

male: 2.7 deaths/1,000 live births (2018 est.)

female: 2.4 deaths/1,000 live births (2018 est.)

country comparison to the world: 218

LIFE EXPECTANCY AT BIRTH:

total population: 81.1 years (2018 est.)

male: 78.1 years (2018 est.)

female: 84.2 years (2018 est.)

country comparison to the world: 33

TOTAL FERTILITY RATE:

1.75 children born/woman (2018 est.)

country comparison to the world: 160

CONTRACEPTIVE PREVALENCE RATE:

85.5% (2015)

note: percent of women aged 18-49

HEALTH EXPENDITURES:

9.7% of GDP (2014)

country comparison to the world: 27

PHYSICIANS DENSITY:

3.2 physicians/1,000 population (2014)

HOSPITAL BED DENSITY:

4.4 beds/1,000 population (2015)

DRINKING WATER SOURCE:

improved:

urban: 100% of population

rural: 100% of population

total: 100% of population

unimproved:

urban: 0% of population

rural: 0% of population

total: 0% of population (2015 est.)

SANITATION FACILITY ACCESS:

improved:

urban: 99.4% of population (2015 est.)

rural: 88% of population (2015 est.)

total: 97.6% of population (2015 est.)

unimproved:

urban: 0.6% of population (2015 est.)

rural: 12% of population (2015 est.)

total: 2.4% of population (2015 est.)

HIV/AIDS - ADULT PREVALENCE RATE:

NA

HIV/AIDS - PEOPLE LIVING WITH HIV/AIDS:

NA

HIV/AIDS - DEATHS:

NA

OBESITY - ADULT PREVALENCE RATE:

22.2% (2016)

country comparison to the world: 80

EDUCATION EXPENDITURES:

7.2% of GDP (2014)

country comparison to the world: 17

SCHOOL LIFE EXPECTANCY (PRIMARY TO TERTIARY EDUCATION):

total: 19 years (2015)

male: 19 years (2015)

female: 20 years (2015)

UNEMPLOYMENT, YOUTH AGES 15-24:

total: 20.1% (2016 est.)

male: 21.8% (2016 est.)

female: 18.6% (2016 est.)

country comparison to the world: 65

GOVERNMENT :: FINLAND

COUNTRY NAME:

conventional long form: Republic of Finland

conventional short form: Finland

local long form: Suomen tasavalta/Republiken Finland

local short form: Suomi/Finland

etymology: name may derive from the ancient Fenni peoples who are first described as living in northeastern Europe in the first centuries A.D.

GOVERNMENT TYPE:

parliamentary republic

CAPITAL:

name: Helsinki

geographic coordinates: 60 10 N, 24 56 E

time difference: UTC+2 (7 hours ahead of Washington, DC, during Standard Time)

daylight saving time: +1hr, begins last Sunday in March; ends last Sunday in October

ADMINISTRATIVE DIVISIONS:

19 regions (maakunnat, singular - maakunta (Finnish); landskapen, singular - landskapet (Swedish)); Aland (Swedish), Ahvenanmaa (Finnish); Etela-Karjala (Finnish), Sodra Karelen (Swedish) [South Karelia]; Etela-Pohjanmaa (Finnish), Sodra Osterbotten (Swedish) [South Ostrobothnia]; Etela-Savo (Finnish), Sodra Savolax (Swedish) [South Savo]; Kanta-Hame (Finnish), Egentliga Tavastland (Swedish); Kainuu (Finnish), Kajanaland (Swedish); Keski-Pohjanmaa (Finnish), Mellersta Osterbotten (Swedish) [Central Ostrobothnia]; Keski-Suomi (Finnish), Mellersta Finland (Swedish) [Central Finland]; Kymenlaakso (Finnish), Kymmenedalen (Swedish); Lappi (Finnish), Lappland (Swedish); Paijat-Hame (Finnish), Paijanne-Tavastland (Swedish); Pirkanmaa (Finnish), Birkaland (Swedish) [Tampere]; Pohjanmaa (Finnish), Osterbotten (Swedish) [Ostrobothnia]; Pohjois-Karjala (Finnish), Norra Karelen (Swedish) [North Karelia]; Pohjois-Pohjanmaa (Finnish), Norra Osterbotten (Swedish) [North Ostrobothnia]; Pohjois-Savo (Finnish), Norra Savolax (Swedish) [North Savo]; Satakunta (Finnish and Swedish); Uusimaa (Finnish), Nyland (Swedish) [Newland]; Varsinais-Suomi (Finnish), Egentliga Finland (Swedish) [Southwest Finland]

INDEPENDENCE:

6 December 1917 (from Russia)

NATIONAL HOLIDAY:

Independence Day, 6 December (1917)

CONSTITUTION:

history: previous 1906, 1919; latest drafted 17 June 1997, approved by Parliament 11 June 1999, entered into force 1 March 2000 (2016)

amendments: proposed by Parliament; passage normally requires simple majority vote in two readings in the first parliamentary session and at least two-thirds majority vote in a single reading by the newly elected Parliament; proposals declared "urgent" by five-sixths of Parliament members can be passed by at least two-thirds majority vote in the first parliamentary session only; amended several times, last in 2012 (2016)

LEGAL SYSTEM:

civil law system based on the Swedish model

INTERNATIONAL LAW ORGANIZATION PARTICIPATION:

accepts compulsory ICJ jurisdiction with reservations; accepts ICCt jurisdiction

CITIZENSHIP:

citizenship by birth: no

citizenship by descent only: at least one parent must be a citizen of Finland

dual citizenship recognized: yes

residency requirement for naturalization: 6 years

SUFFRAGE:

18 years of age; universal

EXECUTIVE BRANCH:

chief of state: President Sauli NIINISTO (since 1 March 2012)

head of government: Prime Minister Juha SIPILA (since 28 May 2015)

cabinet: Council of State or Valtioneuvosto appointed by the president, responsible to Parliament

elections/appointments: president directly elected by absolute majority popular vote in 2 rounds if needed for a 6-year term (eligible for a second term); election last held on 28 January 2018 (next to be held in January 2024); prime minister appointed by Parliament

election results: Sauli NIINISTO reelected president; percent of vote Sauli NIINISTO (independent) 62.7%, Pekka HAAVISTO (Vihr) 12.4%, Laura HUHTASAARI (PS) 6.9%, Paavo VAYRYNEN (independent) 6.2%, Matti VANHANEN (Kesk) 4.1%, other 7.7%

LEGISLATIVE BRANCH:

description: unicameral Parliament or Eduskunta (200 seats; 199 members directly elected in single- and multi-seat constituencies by proportional representation vote and 1 member in the province of Aland directly elected by simple majority vote; members serve 4-year terms)

elections: last held on 19 April 2015 (next to be held by April 2019)

election results: percent of vote by party/coalition - Kesk 21.1%, PS 17.6%, Kok 18.2%, SDP 16.5%, Vihr 8.5%, Vas 7.1%, SFP 4.9%, KD 3.5%, other 2.6%; seats by party/coalition - Kesk 49, PS 38, Kok 37, SDP 34, Vihr 15, Vas 12, SFP 9, KD 5, Aland Coalition 1; composition men 117, women 83, percent of women 41.5%

JUDICIAL BRANCH:

highest courts: Supreme Court or Korkein Oikeus (consists of the court president and 18 judges); Supreme Administrative Court (consists of 21 judges including the court president and organized into 3 chambers); note - Finland has a dual judicial system - courts with civil and criminal jurisdiction and administrative courts with jurisdiction for litigation between individuals and administrative organs of the state and communities

judge selection and term of office: Supreme Court and Supreme Administrative Court judges appointed by the president of the republic; judges serve until mandatory retirement at age 65

subordinate courts: 6 Courts of Appeal; 8 regional administrative courts; 27 district courts; special courts for issues relating to markets, labor, insurance, impeachment, land, tenancy, and water rights

POLITICAL PARTIES AND LEADERS:

Aland Coalition (a coalition of several political parties on the Aland Islands)
Center Party or Kesk [Juha SIPILA]
Christian Democrats or KD [Sari ESSAYAH]
Finns Party or PS [Jussi HALLA-AHO]
Green League or Vihr [Ville NIINISTO]
Left Alliance or Vas [Li ANDERSSON]]
National Coalition Party or Kok [Petteri ORPO]
Social Democratic Party or SDP [Antti RINNE]
Swedish People's Party or SFP [Anna-Maja HENRIKSSON]

INTERNATIONAL ORGANIZATION PARTICIPATION:

ADB (nonregional member), AfDB (nonregional member), Arctic Council, Australia Group, BIS, CBSS, CD, CE, CERN, EAPC, EBRD, ECB, EIB, EITI (implementing country), EMU, ESA, EU, FAO, FATF, G-9, IADB, IAEA, IBRD, ICAO, ICC (national committees), ICCt, ICRM, IDA, IEA, IFAD, IFC, IFRCS, IHO, ILO, IMF, IMO, IMSO, Interpol, IOC, IOM, IPU, ISO, ITSO, ITU, ITUC (NGOs), MIGA, MINUSMA, NC, NEA, NIB, NSG, OAS (observer), OECD, OPCW, OSCE, Pacific Alliance (observer), Paris Club, PCA, PFP, Schengen Convention, UN, UNCTAD, UNESCO, UNHCR, UNIDO, UNIFIL, UNMIL, UNMOGIP, UNRWA, UNTSO, UPU, WCO, WFTU (NGOs), WHO, WIPO, WMO, WTO, ZC

DIPLOMATIC REPRESENTATION IN THE US:

chief of mission: Ambassador Kirsti KAUPPI (since 17 September 2015)

chancery: 3301 Massachusetts Avenue NW, Washington, DC 20008

telephone: [1] (202) 298-5800

FAX: [1] (202) 298-6030

consulate(s) general: Los Angeles, New York

DIPLOMATIC REPRESENTATION FROM THE US:

chief of mission: Ambassador Robert "Bob" Frank PENCE (since 24 May 2018) (2018)

embassy: Itainen Puistotie 14B, 00140 Helsinki

mailing address: APO AE 09723

telephone: [358] (9) 6162-50

FAX: [358] (9) 6162-5135

FLAG DESCRIPTION:

white with a blue cross extending to the edges of the flag; the vertical part of the cross is shifted to the hoist side in the style of the Dannebrog (Danish flag); the blue represents the thousands of lakes scattered across the country, while the white is for the snow that covers the land in winter

NATIONAL SYMBOL(S):

lion; national colors: blue, white

NATIONAL ANTHEM:

name: "Maamme" (Our Land)

lyrics/music: Johan Ludvig RUNEBERG/Fredrik PACIUS

note: in use since 1848; although never officially adopted by law, the anthem has been popular since it was first sung by a student group in 1848; Estonia's anthem uses the same melody as that of Finland

ECONOMY :: FINLAND

ECONOMY - OVERVIEW:

Finland has a highly industrialized, largely free-market economy with per capita GDP almost as high as that of Austria and the Netherlands and slightly above that of Germany and Belgium. Trade is important, with exports accounting for over one-third of GDP in recent years. The government is open to, and actively takes steps to attract, foreign direct investment.

Finland is historically competitive in manufacturing, particularly in the wood, metals, engineering, telecommunications, and electronics industries. Finland excels in export of technology as well as promotion of startups in the information and communications technology, gaming, cleantech, and biotechnology sectors. Except for timber and several minerals, Finland depends on imports of raw materials, energy, and some components for manufactured goods. Because of the cold climate, agricultural development is limited to maintaining self-sufficiency in basic products. Forestry, an important export industry, provides a secondary occupation for the rural population.

Finland had been one of the best performing economies within the EU before 2009 and its banks and financial markets avoided the worst of global financial crisis. However, the world slowdown hit exports and domestic demand hard in that year, causing Finland's economy to contract from 2012 to 2014. The recession affected general government finances and the debt ratio. The economy returned to growth in 2016, posting a 1.9% GDP increase before growing an estimated 3.3% in 2017, supported by a strong increase in investment, private consumption, and net exports. Finnish economists expect GDP to grow a rate of 2-3% in the next few years.

Finland's main challenges will be reducing high labor costs and boosting demand for its exports. In June 2016, the government enacted a Competitiveness Pact aimed at reducing labor costs, increasing hours worked, and introducing more flexibility into the wage bargaining system. As a result, wage growth was nearly flat in 2017. The Government was also seeking to reform the health care system and social services. In the long term, Finland must address a rapidly aging population and decreasing productivity in traditional industries that threaten competitiveness, fiscal sustainability, and economic growth.

GDP (PURCHASING POWER PARITY):

$244.9 billion (2017 est.)

$238.2 billion (2016 est.)

$232.4 billion (2015 est.)

note: data are in 2017 dollars

country comparison to the world: 62

GDP (OFFICIAL EXCHANGE RATE):

$252.8 billion (2017 est.) (2017 est.)

GDP - REAL GROWTH RATE:

2.8% (2017 est.)

2.5% (2016 est.)

0.1% (2015 est.)

country comparison to the world: 122

GDP - PER CAPITA (PPP):

$44,500 (2017 est.)

$43,400 (2016 est.)

$42,500 (2015 est.)

note: data are in 2017 dollars

country comparison to the world: 38

GROSS NATIONAL SAVING:

23.3% of GDP (2017 est.)

21.7% of GDP (2016 est.)

20% of GDP (2015 est.)

country comparison to the world: 73

GDP - COMPOSITION, BY END USE:

household consumption: 54.4% (2017 est.)

government consumption: 22.9% (2017 est.)

investment in fixed capital: 22.1% (2017 est.)

investment in inventories: 0.4% (2017 est.)

exports of goods and services: 38.5% (2017 est.)

imports of goods and services: -38.2% (2017 est.)

GDP - COMPOSITION, BY SECTOR OF ORIGIN:

agriculture: 2.7% (2017 est.)

industry: 28.2% (2017 est.)

services: 69.1% (2017 est.)

AGRICULTURE - PRODUCTS:

barley, wheat, sugar beets, potatoes; dairy cattle; fish

INDUSTRIES:

metals and metal products, electronics, machinery and scientific instruments, shipbuilding, pulp and paper, foodstuffs, chemicals, textiles, clothing

INDUSTRIAL PRODUCTION GROWTH RATE:

6.2% (2017 est.)

country comparison to the world: 39

LABOR FORCE:

2.473 million (2017 est.)

country comparison to the world: 115

LABOR FORCE - BY OCCUPATION:

agriculture: 4%

industry: 20.7%

services: 75.3% (2017 est.)

UNEMPLOYMENT RATE:

8.5% (2017 est.)

8.8% (2016 est.)

country comparison to the world: 121

HOUSEHOLD INCOME OR CONSUMPTION BY PERCENTAGE SHARE:

lowest 10%: 45.2% (2013)

highest 10%: 45.2% (2013)

DISTRIBUTION OF FAMILY INCOME - GINI INDEX:

27.2 (2016)

22.2 (1995)

country comparison to the world: 144

BUDGET:

revenues: 134.2 billion (2017 est.)

expenditures: 135.6 billion (2017 est.)

note: Central Government Budget data; these numbers represent a significant reduction from previous official reporting

TAXES AND OTHER REVENUES:

53.1% (of GDP) (2017 est.)

country comparison to the world: 11

BUDGET SURPLUS (+) OR DEFICIT (-):

-0.6% (of GDP) (2017 est.)

country comparison to the world: 64

PUBLIC DEBT:

61.3% of GDP (2017 est.)

62.9% of GDP (2016 est.)

note: data cover general government debt and include debt instruments issued (or owned) by government entities other than the treasury; the data include treasury debt held by foreign entities; the data include debt issued by subnational entities, as well as intragovernmental debt; intragovernmental debt consists of treasury borrowings from surpluses in the social funds, such as for retirement, medical care, and unemployment; debt instruments for the social funds are not sold at public auctions

country comparison to the world: 72

FISCAL YEAR:

calendar year

INFLATION RATE (CONSUMER PRICES):

0.8% (2017 est.)

0.4% (2016 est.)

country comparison to the world: 41

CENTRAL BANK DISCOUNT RATE:

1.25% (31 December 2017)

0% (31 December 2010)

note: this is the European Central Bank's rate on the marginal lending facility, which offers overnight credit to banks in the euro area

country comparison to the world: 131

COMMERCIAL BANK PRIME LENDING RATE:

1.61% (31 December 2017 est.)

1.79% (31 December 2016 est.)

country comparison to the world: 188

STOCK OF NARROW MONEY:

$152.6 billion (31 December 2017 est.)

$124 billion (31 December 2016 est.)

note: see entry for the European Union for money supply for the entire euro area; the European Central Bank (ECB) controls monetary policy for the 18 members of the Economic and Monetary Union (EMU); individual members of the EMU do not control the quantity of money circulating within their own borders

country comparison to the world: 28

STOCK OF BROAD MONEY:

$152.6 billion (31 December 2017 est.)

$124 billion (31 December 2016 est.)

country comparison to the world: 28

STOCK OF DOMESTIC CREDIT:

$323.9 billion (31 December 2017 est.)

$351.6 billion (31 December 2016 est.)

country comparison to the world: 34

MARKET VALUE OF PUBLICLY TRADED SHARES:

$231 billion (31 December 2016 est.)

$207.5 billion (31 December 2015 est.)

$208.7 billion (31 December 2014 est.)

country comparison to the world: 32

CURRENT ACCOUNT BALANCE:

$1.806 billion (2017 est.)

-$819 million (2016 est.)

country comparison to the world: 42

EXPORTS:

$67.73 billion (2017 est.)

$51.9 billion (2016 est.)

country comparison to the world: 43

EXPORTS - PARTNERS:

Germany 14.2%, Sweden 10.1%, US 7%, Netherlands 6.8%, China 5.7%, Russia 5.7%, UK 4.5% (2017)

EXPORTS - COMMODITIES:

electrical and optical equipment, machinery, transport equipment, paper and pulp, chemicals, basic metals; timber

IMPORTS:

$65.26 billion (2017 est.)

$58.18 billion (2016 est.)

country comparison to the world: 47

IMPORTS - COMMODITIES:

foodstuffs, petroleum and petroleum products, chemicals, transport equipment, iron and steel, machinery, computers, electronic industry products, textile yarn and fabrics, grains

IMPORTS - PARTNERS:

Germany 17.7%, Sweden 15.8%, Russia 13.1%, Netherlands 8.7% (2017)

RESERVES OF FOREIGN EXCHANGE AND GOLD:

$10.51 billion (31 December 2017 est.)

$11.2 billion (31 December 2016 est.)

country comparison to the world: 73

DEBT - EXTERNAL:

$150.6 billion (31 December 2016 est.)

$147.8 billion (31 December 2015 est.)

country comparison to the world: 42

STOCK OF DIRECT FOREIGN INVESTMENT - AT HOME:

$135.2 billion (31 December 2017 est.)

$84.8 billion (31 December 2016 est.)

country comparison to the world: 40

STOCK OF DIRECT FOREIGN INVESTMENT - ABROAD:

$185.6 billion (31 December 2017 est.)

$116.7 billion (2016 est.)

country comparison to the world: 29

EXCHANGE RATES:

euros (EUR) per US dollar -

0.885 (2017 est.)

0.903 (2016 est.)

0.9214 (2015 est.)

0.885 (2014 est.)

0.7634 (2013 est.)

ENERGY :: FINLAND

ELECTRICITY ACCESS:

electrification - total population: 100% (2016)

ELECTRICITY - PRODUCTION:

66.54 billion kWh (2016 est.)

country comparison to the world: 43

ELECTRICITY - CONSUMPTION:

82.79 billion kWh (2016 est.)

country comparison to the world: 35

ELECTRICITY - EXPORTS:

3.159 billion kWh (2016 est.)

country comparison to the world: 43

ELECTRICITY - IMPORTS:

22.11 billion kWh (2016 est.)

country comparison to the world: 8

ELECTRICITY - INSTALLED GENERATING CAPACITY:

16.27 million kW (2016 est.)

country comparison to the world: 50

ELECTRICITY - FROM FOSSIL FUELS:

41% of total installed capacity (2016 est.)

country comparison to the world: 165

ELECTRICITY - FROM NUCLEAR FUELS:

17% of total installed capacity (2017 est.)

country comparison to the world: 12

ELECTRICITY - FROM HYDROELECTRIC PLANTS:

20% of total installed capacity (2017 est.)

country comparison to the world: 88

ELECTRICITY - FROM OTHER RENEWABLE SOURCES:

23% of total installed capacity (2017 est.)

country comparison to the world: 30

CRUDE OIL - PRODUCTION:

0 bbl/day (2017 est.)

country comparison to the world: 137

CRUDE OIL - EXPORTS:

0 bbl/day (2015 est.)

country comparison to the world: 125

CRUDE OIL - IMPORTS:

236,700 bbl/day (2017 est.)

country comparison to the world: 27

CRUDE OIL - PROVED RESERVES:

0 bbl (1 January 2018 est.)

country comparison to the world: 133

REFINED PETROLEUM PRODUCTS - PRODUCTION:

310,600 bbl/day (2017 est.)

country comparison to the world: 40

REFINED PETROLEUM PRODUCTS - CONSUMPTION:

217,100 bbl/day (2017 est.)

country comparison to the world: 55

REFINED PETROLEUM PRODUCTS - EXPORTS:

166,200 bbl/day (2017 est.)

country comparison to the world: 34

REFINED PETROLEUM PRODUCTS - IMPORTS:

122,200 bbl/day (2017 est.)

country comparison to the world: 48

NATURAL GAS - PRODUCTION:

0 cu m (2017 est.)

country comparison to the world: 134

NATURAL GAS - CONSUMPTION:

2.35 billion cu m (2017 est.)

country comparison to the world: 81

NATURAL GAS - EXPORTS:

4 million cu m (2017 est.)

country comparison to the world: 54

NATURAL GAS - IMPORTS:

2.322 billion cu m (2017 est.)

country comparison to the world: 49

NATURAL GAS - PROVED RESERVES:

NA cu m (1 January 2016 est.)

CARBON DIOXIDE EMISSIONS FROM CONSUMPTION OF ENERGY:

46.01 million Mt (2017 est.)

country comparison to the world: 64

COMMUNICATIONS :: FINLAND

TELEPHONES - FIXED LINES:

total subscriptions: 378,200 (2017 est.)

subscriptions per 100 inhabitants: 7 (2017 est.)

country comparison to the world: 104

TELEPHONES - MOBILE CELLULAR:

total subscriptions: 7,307,800 (2017 est.)

subscriptions per 100 inhabitants: 132 (2017 est.)

country comparison to the world: 104

TELEPHONE SYSTEM:

general assessment: modern system with excellent service; one of the most progressive in Europe; one of the highest broadband and mobile penetrations rates in the region; forefront in testing 5G networks; for 2025 and 2030 FttP (fiber to the home) and DOCSIS3.1 (new generation of cable services for high speed connections) technologies (2017)

domestic: digital fiber-optic, fixed-line 7 per 100 subscription; 132 per 100 mobile-cellular; network and an extensive mobile-cellular network provide domestic needs (2017)

international: country code - 358; submarine cables provide links to Estonia and Sweden; satellite earth stations - access to Intelsat transmission service via a Swedish satellite earth station, 1 Inmarsat (Atlantic and Indian Ocean regions); note - Finland shares the Inmarsat earth station with the other Nordic countries (Denmark, Iceland, Norway, and Sweden) (2015)

BROADCAST MEDIA:

a mix of 3 publicly operated TV stations and numerous privately owned TV stations; several free and special-interest pay-TV channels; cable and satellite multi-channel subscription services are available; all TV signals are broadcast digitally; Internet television, such as Netflix and others, is available; public broadcasting maintains a network of 13 national and 25 regional radio stations; a large number of private radio broadcasters and access to Internet radio (2017)

INTERNET COUNTRY CODE:

.finote - Aland Islands assigned .ax

INTERNET USERS:

total: 4,822,132 (July 2016 est.)

percent of population: 87.7% (July 2016 est.)

country comparison to the world: 77

BROADBAND - FIXED SUBSCRIPTIONS:

total: 1,709,400 (2017 est.)

subscriptions per 100 inhabitants: 31 (2017 est.)

country comparison to the world: 56

TRANSPORTATION :: FINLAND

NATIONAL AIR TRANSPORT SYSTEM:

number of registered air carriers: 3 (2015)

inventory of registered aircraft operated by air carriers: 73 (2015)

annual passenger traffic on registered air carriers: 9,972,333 (2015)

annual freight traffic on registered air carriers: 713.484 million mt-km (2015)

CIVIL AIRCRAFT REGISTRATION COUNTRY CODE PREFIX:

OH (2016)

AIRPORTS:

148 (2013)

country comparison to the world: 39

AIRPORTS - WITH PAVED RUNWAYS:

total: 74 (2017)

over 3,047 m: 3 (2017)

2,438 to 3,047 m: 26 (2017)

1,524 to 2,437 m: 10 (2017)

914 to 1,523 m: 21 (2017)

under 914 m: 14 (2017)

AIRPORTS - WITH UNPAVED RUNWAYS:

total: 74 (2013)

914 to 1,523 m: 3 (2013)

under 914 m: 71 (2013)

PIPELINES:

1288 km gas transmission pipes, 1976 km distribution pipes (2016)

RAILWAYS:

total: 5,926 km (2016)

broad gauge: 5,926 km 1.524-m gauge (3,270 km electrified) (2016)

country comparison to the world: 32

ROADWAYS:

total: 454,000 km (2012)

highways: 78,000 km (50,000 paved, including 700 km of expressways; 28,000 unpaved) (2012)

private and forest roads: 350,000 km (2012)

urban: 26,000 km (2012)

country comparison to the world: 16

WATERWAYS:

8,000 km (includes Saimaa Canal system of 3,577 km; southern part leased from Russia; water transport used frequently in the summer and widely replaced with sledges on the ice in winter; there are 187,888 lakes in Finland that cover 31,500 km); Finland also maintains 8,200 km of coastal fairways (2013)

country comparison to the world: 17

MERCHANT MARINE:

total: 267 (2017)

by type: bulk carrier 7, container ship 1, general cargo 92, oil tanker 5, other 162 (2017)

country comparison to the world: 57

PORTS AND TERMINALS:

major seaport(s): Helsinki, Kotka, Naantali, Porvoo, Raahe, Rauma

MILITARY AND SECURITY :: FINLAND

MILITARY EXPENDITURES:

1.23% of GDP (2018)

1.26% of GDP (2017)

1.31% of GDP (2016)

1.29% of GDP (2015)

1.3% of GDP (2014)

country comparison to the world: 95

MILITARY BRANCHES:

Finnish Defense Forces (FDF): Army (Puolustusvoimat), Navy (Merivoimat, includes Coastal Defense Forces), Air Force (Ilmavoimat) (2016)

MILITARY SERVICE AGE AND OBLIGATION:

all Finnish men are called-up for military service the year they turn 18; at 18, women may volunteer for military service; service obligation 6-12 months; individuals enter the reserve upon completing their initial obligation; military obligation to age 60 (2016)

TRANSNATIONAL ISSUES :: FINLAND

DISPUTES - INTERNATIONAL:

various groups in Finland advocate restoration of Karelia and other areas ceded to the former Soviet Union, but the Finnish Government asserts no territorial demands

REFUGEES AND INTERNALLY DISPLACED PERSONS:

refugees (country of origin): 6,781 (Iraq) (2016)

stateless persons: 2,749 (2017)

INTRODUCTION :: FRANCE

BACKGROUND:

France today is one of the most modern countries in the world and is a leader among European nations. It plays an influential global role as a permanent member of the United Nations Security Council, NATO, the G-7, the G-20, the EU, and other multilateral organizations. France rejoined NATO's integrated military command structure in 2009, reversing DE GAULLE's 1966 decision to withdraw French forces from NATO. Since 1958, it has constructed a hybrid presidential-parliamentary governing system resistant to the instabilities experienced in earlier, more purely parliamentary administrations. In recent decades, its reconciliation and cooperation with Germany have proved central to the economic integration of Europe, including the introduction of a common currency, the euro, in January 1999. In the early 21st century, five French overseas entities - French Guiana, Guadeloupe, Martinique, Mayotte, and Reunion - became French regions and were made part of France proper.

GEOGRAPHY :: FRANCE

LOCATION:

metropolitan France: Western Europe, bordering the Bay of Biscay and English Channel, between Belgium and Spain, southeast of the UK; bordering the Mediterranean Sea, between Italy and Spain;

French Guiana: Northern South America, bordering the North Atlantic Ocean, between Brazil and Suriname;

Guadeloupe: Caribbean, islands between the Caribbean Sea and the North Atlantic Ocean, southeast of Puerto Rico;

Martinique: Caribbean, island between the Caribbean Sea and North Atlantic Ocean, north of Trinidad and Tobago;

Mayotte: Southern Indian Ocean, island in the Mozambique Channel, about halfway between northern Madagascar and northern Mozambique;

Reunion: Southern Africa, island in the Indian Ocean, east of Madagascar

GEOGRAPHIC COORDINATES:

metropolitan France: 46 00 N, 2 00 E;

French Guiana: 4 00 N, 53 00 W;

Guadeloupe: 16 15 N, 61 35 W;

Martinique: 14 40 N, 61 00 W;

Mayotte: 12 50 S, 45 10 E;

Reunion: 21 06 S, 55 36 E

MAP REFERENCES:

metropolitan France: Europe;

French Guiana: South America;

Guadeloupe: Central America and the Caribbean;

Martinique: Central America and the Caribbean;

Mayotte: Africa;

Reunion: World

AREA:

total: 643,801 sq km

land: 640,427 sq km

water: 3,374 sq km

551,500 sq km (metropolitan France)
549,970 sq km (metropolitan France)
1,530 sq km (metropolitan France)
note: the first numbers include the overseas regions of French Guiana, Guadeloupe, Martinique, Mayotte, and Reunion

country comparison to the world: 44

AREA - COMPARATIVE:

slightly more than four times the size of Georgia; slightly less than the size of Texas

LAND BOUNDARIES:

border countries (8): Andorra 55 km, Belgium 556 km, Germany 418 km, Italy 476 km, Luxembourg 69 km, Monaco 6 km, Spain 646 km, Switzerland 525 km

metropolitan France - total: 2751

French Guiana - total: 1205

COASTLINE:

4,853 km

metropolitan France: 3,427 km

MARITIME CLAIMS:

territorial sea: 12 nm

exclusive economic zone: 200 nm (does not apply to the Mediterranean Sea)

contiguous zone: 24 nm

continental shelf: 200-m depth or to the depth of exploitation

CLIMATE:

metropolitan France: generally cool winters and mild summers, but mild winters and hot summers along the Mediterranean; occasional strong, cold, dry, north-to-northwesterly wind known as mistral;

French Guiana: tropical; hot, humid; little seasonal temperature variation;

Guadeloupe and Martinique: subtropical tempered by trade winds; moderately high humidity; rainy season (June to October); vulnerable to devastating cyclones (hurricanes) every eight years on average;

Mayotte: tropical; marine; hot, humid, rainy season during northeastern monsoon (November to May); dry season is cooler (May to November);

Reunion: tropical, but temperature moderates with elevation; cool and dry (May to November), hot and rainy (November to April)

TERRAIN:

metropolitan France: mostly flat plains or gently rolling hills in north and west; remainder is mountainous, especially Pyrenees in south, Alps in east;

French Guiana: low-lying coastal plains rising to hills and small mountains;

Guadeloupe: Basse-Terre is volcanic in origin with interior mountains; Grande-Terre is low limestone formation; most of the seven other islands are volcanic in origin;

Martinique: mountainous with indented coastline; dormant volcano;

Mayotte: generally undulating, with deep ravines and ancient volcanic peaks;

Reunion: mostly rugged and mountainous; fertile lowlands along coast

ELEVATION:

mean elevation: 375 m

elevation extremes: -2 m lowest point: Rhone River delta

4810 highest point: Mont Blanc
note: to assess the possible effects of climate change on the ice and snow cap of Mont Blanc, its surface and peak have been extensively measured in recent years; these new peak measurements have exceeded the traditional height of 4,807 m and have varied between 4,808 m and 4,811 m; the actual rock summit is 4,792 m and is 40 m away from the ice-covered summit

NATURAL RESOURCES:

metropolitan France, coal, iron ore, bauxite, zinc, uranium, antimony, arsenic, potash, feldspar, fluorspar, gypsum, timber, arable land, fish, French Guiana, gold deposits, petroleum, kaolin, niobium, tantalum, clay

LAND USE:

agricultural land: 52.7% (2011 est.)

arable land: 33.4% (2011 est.) / permanent crops: 1.8% (2011 est.) / permanent pasture: 17.5% (2011 est.)

forest: 29.2% (2011 est.)

other: 18.1% (2011 est.)

IRRIGATED LAND:

26,420 sq km 26,950 sq km (2012)

metropolitan France: 26,000 sq km (2012)

POPULATION DISTRIBUTION:

much of the population is concentrated in the north and southeast; although there are many urban agglomerations throughout the country, Paris is by far the largest city, with Lyon ranked a distant second

NATURAL HAZARDS:

metropolitan France: flooding; avalanches; midwinter windstorms; drought; forest fires in south near the Mediterranean;

overseas departments: hurricanes (cyclones); flooding;

volcanism: Montagne Pelee (1,394 m) on the island of Martinique in the Caribbean is the most active volcano of the Lesser Antilles arc, it last erupted in 1932; a catastrophic eruption in May 1902 destroyed the city of St. Pierre, killing an estimated 30,000 people;; La Soufriere (1,467 m) on the island of Guadeloupe in the Caribbean last erupted from July 1976 to March 1977;; these volcanoes are part of the volcanic island arc of the Lesser Antilles that extends from Saba in the north to Grenada in the south

ENVIRONMENT - CURRENT ISSUES:

some forest damage from acid rain; air pollution from industrial and vehicle emissions; water pollution from urban wastes, agricultural runoff

ENVIRONMENT - INTERNATIONAL AGREEMENTS:

party to: Air Pollution, Air Pollution-Nitrogen Oxides, Air Pollution-Persistent Organic Pollutants, Air Pollution-Sulfur 85, Air Pollution-Sulfur 94, Air Pollution-Volatile Organic Compounds, Antarctic-Environmental Protocol, Antarctic-Marine Living Resources, Antarctic Seals, Antarctic Treaty, Biodiversity, Climate Change, Climate Change-Kyoto Protocol, Desertification, Endangered Species, Hazardous Wastes, Law of the Sea, Marine Dumping, Marine Life Conservation, Ozone Layer Protection, Ship Pollution, Tropical Timber 83, Tropical Timber 94, Wetlands, Whaling

signed, but not ratified: none of the selected agreements

GEOGRAPHY - NOTE:

largest West European nation; most major French rivers - the Meuse, Seine, Loire, Charente, Dordogne, and Garonne - flow northward or westward into the Atlantic Ocean, only the Rhone flows southward into the Mediterranean Sea

PEOPLE AND SOCIETY :: FRANCE

POPULATION:

67,364,357 (July 2018 est.)

note: the above figure is for metropolitan France and five overseas regions; the metropolitan France population is 62,814,233

country comparison to the world: 21

NATIONALITY:

noun: Frenchman(men), Frenchwoman(women)

adjective: French

ETHNIC GROUPS:

Celtic and Latin with Teutonic, Slavic, North African, Indochinese, Basque minorities

note: overseas departments: black, white, mulatto, East Indian, Chinese, Amerindian

LANGUAGES:

French (official) 100%, French (official) declining regional dialects and languages (Provencal, Breton, Alsatian, Corsican, Catalan, Basque, Flemish, Occitan, Picard)

note: overseas departments: French, Creole patois, Mahorian (a Swahili dialect)

RELIGIONS:

Christian (overwhelmingly Roman Catholic) 63-66%, Muslim 7-9%, Buddhist 0.5-0.75%, Jewish 0.5-0.75%, other 0.5-1.0%, none 23-28% (2015 est.)

note: France maintains a tradition of secularism and has not officially collected data on religious affiliation since the 1872 national census, which complicates assessments of France's religious composition; an 1872 law prohibiting state authorities from collecting data on individuals' ethnicity or religious beliefs was reaffirmed by a 1978 law emphasizing the prohibition of the collection or exploitation of personal data revealing an individual's race, ethnicity, or political, philosophical, or religious opinions; a 1905 law codified France's separation of church and state

AGE STRUCTURE:

0-14 years: 18.48% (male 6,366,789 /female 6,082,729)

15-24 years: 11.8% (male 4,065,780 /female 3,884,488)

25-54 years: 37.48% (male 12,731,825 /female 12,515,501)

55-64 years: 12.42% (male 4,035,073 /female 4,331,751)

65 years and over: 19.82% (male 5,781,410 /female 7,569,011) (2018 est.)

DEPENDENCY RATIOS:

total dependency ratio: 59.2 (2015 est.)

youth dependency ratio: 29.1 (2015 est.)

elderly dependency ratio: 30.2 (2015 est.)

potential support ratio: 3.3 (2015 est.)

MEDIAN AGE:

total: 41.5 years

male: 39.7 years

female: 43.2 years (2018 est.)

country comparison to the world: 40

POPULATION GROWTH RATE:

0.37% (2018 est.)

country comparison to the world: 166

BIRTH RATE:

12.1 births/1,000 population (2018 est.)

country comparison to the world: 162

DEATH RATE:

9.4 deaths/1,000 population (2018 est.)

country comparison to the world: 51

NET MIGRATION RATE:

1.1 migrant(s)/1,000 population (2017 est.)

country comparison to the world: 56

POPULATION DISTRIBUTION:

much of the population is concentrated in the north and southeast; although there are many urban agglomerations throughout the country, Paris is by far the largest city, with Lyon ranked a distant second

URBANIZATION:

urban population: 80.4% of total population (2018)

rate of urbanization: 0.72% annual rate of change (2015-20 est.)

MAJOR URBAN AREAS - POPULATION:

10.901 million PARIS (capital), 1.69 million Lyon, 1.599 million Marseille-Aix-en-Provence, 1.054 million Lille, 997,000 Toulouse, 945,000 Bordeaux (2018)

SEX RATIO:

at birth: 1.05 male(s)/female (2017 est.)

0-14 years: 1.05 male(s)/female (2017 est.)

15-24 years: 1.05 male(s)/female (2017 est.)

25-54 years: 1.01 male(s)/female (2017 est.)

55-64 years: 0.93 male(s)/female (2017 est.)

65 years and over: 0.75 male(s)/female (2017 est.)

total population: 0.96 male(s)/female (2017 est.)

MOTHER'S MEAN AGE AT FIRST BIRTH:

28.1 years (2010 est.)

MATERNAL MORTALITY RATE:

8 deaths/100,000 live births (2015 est.)

country comparison to the world: 157

INFANT MORTALITY RATE:

total: 3.2 deaths/1,000 live births (2018 est.)

male: 3.5 deaths/1,000 live births (2018 est.)

female: 2.9 deaths/1,000 live births (2018 est.)

country comparison to the world: 209

LIFE EXPECTANCY AT BIRTH:

total population: 82 years (2018 est.)

male: 78.9 years (2018 est.)

female: 85.3 years (2018 est.)

country comparison to the world: 19

TOTAL FERTILITY RATE:

2.06 children born/woman (2018 est.)

country comparison to the world: 106

CONTRACEPTIVE PREVALENCE RATE:

78.4% (2010/11)

HEALTH EXPENDITURES:

11.5% of GDP (2014)

country comparison to the world: 8

PHYSICIANS DENSITY:

3.24 physicians/1,000 population (2016)

HOSPITAL BED DENSITY:

6.5 beds/1,000 population (2013)

DRINKING WATER SOURCE:

improved:

urban: 100% of population

rural: 100% of population

total: 100% of population

unimproved:

urban: 0% of population

rural: 0% of population

total: 0% of population (2015 est.)

SANITATION FACILITY ACCESS:

improved:

urban: 98.6% of population (2015 est.)

rural: 98.9% of population (2015 est.)

total: 98.7% of population (2015 est.)

unimproved:

urban: 1.4% of population (2015 est.)

rural: 1.1% of population (2015 est.)

total: 1.3% of population (2015 est.)

HIV/AIDS - ADULT PREVALENCE RATE:

0.5% (2017 est.)

country comparison to the world: 66

HIV/AIDS - PEOPLE LIVING WITH HIV/AIDS:

200,000 (2017 est.)

country comparison to the world: 29

HIV/AIDS - DEATHS:

<500 (2017 est.)

OBESITY - ADULT PREVALENCE RATE:

21.6% (2016)

country comparison to the world: 87

EDUCATION EXPENDITURES:

5.5% of GDP (2014)

country comparison to the world: 50

SCHOOL LIFE EXPECTANCY (PRIMARY TO TERTIARY EDUCATION):

total: 16 years (2014)

male: 16 years (2014)

female: 17 years (2014)

UNEMPLOYMENT, YOUTH AGES 15-24:

total: 24.6% (2016 est.)

male: 25.1% (2016 est.)

female: 24.1% (2016 est.)

country comparison to the world: 47

GOVERNMENT :: FRANCE

COUNTRY NAME:

conventional long form: French Republic

conventional short form: France

local long form: Republique francaise

local short form: France

etymology: name derives from the Latin "Francia" meaning "Land of the Franks"; the Franks were a group of Germanic tribes located along the middle and lower Rhine River in the 3rd century A.D. who merged with Gallic-Roman populations in succeeding centuries and to whom they passed on their name

GOVERNMENT TYPE:

semi-presidential republic

CAPITAL:

name: Paris

geographic coordinates: 48 52 N, 2 20 E

time difference: UTC+1 (6 hours ahead of Washington, DC, during Standard Time)

daylight saving time: +1hr, begins last Sunday in March; ends last Sunday in October

note: applies to metropolitan France only; for its overseas regions the time difference is UTC-4 for Guadeloupe and Martinique, UTC-3 for French Guiana, UTC+3 for Mayotte, and UTC+4 for Reunion

ADMINISTRATIVE DIVISIONS:

18 regions (regions, singular - region); Auvergne-Rhone-Alpes, Bourgogne-Franche-Comte (Burgundy-Free County), Bretagne (Brittany), Centre-Val de Loire (Center-Loire Valley), Corse (Corsica), Grand Est (Grand East), Guadeloupe, Guyane (French Guiana), Hauts-de-France (Upper France), Ile-de-France, Martinique, Mayotte, Normandie (Normandy), Nouvelle-Aquitaine (New Aquitaine), Occitanie (Occitania), Pays de la Loire (Lands of the Loire), Provence-Alpes-Cote d'Azur, Reunion

note: France is divided into 13 metropolitan regions (including the "collectivity" of Corse or Corsica) and 5 overseas regions (French Guiana, Guadeloupe, Martinique, Mayotte, and Reunion) and is subdivided into 96 metropolitan departments and 5 overseas departments (which are the same as the overseas regions)

DEPENDENT AREAS:

Clipperton Island, French Polynesia, French Southern and Antarctic Lands, New Caledonia, Saint Barthelemy, Saint Martin, Saint Pierre and Miquelon, Wallis and Futuna

note: the US Government does not recognize claims to Antarctica; New Caledonia has been considered a "sui generis" collectivity of France since 1998, a unique status falling between that of an independent country and a French overseas department

INDEPENDENCE:

no official date of independence: 486 (Frankish tribes unified under Merovingian kingship);10 August 843 (Western Francia established from the division of the Carolingian Empire);14 July 1789 (French monarchy overthrown);22 September 1792 (First French Republic founded);4 October 1958 (Fifth French Republic established)

NATIONAL HOLIDAY:

Fete de la Federation, 14 July (1790); note - although often incorrectly referred to as Bastille Day, the celebration actually commemorates the holiday held on the first anniversary of the storming of the Bastille (on 14 July 1789) and the establishment of a constitutional monarchy; other names for the holiday are Fete Nationale (National Holiday) and quatorze juillet (14th of July)

CONSTITUTION:

history: many previous; latest effective 4 October 1958 (2018)

amendments: proposed by the president of the republic (upon recommendation of the prime minister and Parliament) or by Parliament; proposals submitted by Parliament members require passage by both houses followed by approval in a referendum; passage of proposals submitted by the government can bypass a referendum if submitted by the president to Parliament and passed by at least three-fifths majority vote by Parliament's National Assembly; amended many times, last in 2008; note - in May 2018, the prime minister submitted a bill to the National Assembly to amend several provisions of the constitution (2018)

LEGAL SYSTEM:

civil law; review of administrative but not legislative acts

INTERNATIONAL LAW ORGANIZATION PARTICIPATION:

has not submitted an ICJ jurisdiction declaration; accepts ICCt jurisdiction

CITIZENSHIP:

citizenship by birth: no

citizenship by descent only: at least one parent must be a citizen of France

dual citizenship recognized: yes

residency requirement for naturalization: 5 years

SUFFRAGE:

18 years of age; universal

EXECUTIVE BRANCH:

chief of state: President Emmanuel MACRON (since 14 May 2017)

head of government: Prime Minister Edouard PHILIPPE (since 15 May 2017)

cabinet: Council of Ministers appointed by the president at the suggestion of the prime minister

elections/appointments: president directly elected by absolute majority popular vote in 2 rounds if needed for a 5-year term (eligible for a second term); election last held on 23 April with a runoff on 7 May 2017 (next to be held in April 2022); prime minister appointed by the president

election results: Emmanuel MACRON elected president in second round; percent of vote in first round - Emmanuel MACRON (EM) 24.%, Marine LE PEN (FN) 21.3%, Francois FILLON (LR) 20.%, Jean-Luc MELENCHON (FI) 19.6%, Benoit HAMON (PS) 6.4%, other 8.7%; percent of vote in second round - MACRON 66.1%, LE PEN 33.9%

LEGISLATIVE BRANCH:

description: bicameral Parliament or Parlement consists of:
Senate or Senat (348 seats - 328 for metropolitan France and overseas departments and regions of Guadeloupe, Martinque, French

Guiana, Reunion, and Mayotte, 2 for New Caledonia, 2 for French Polynesia, 1 for Saint-Pierre and Miquelon, 1 for Saint-Barthelemy, 1 for Saint-Martin, 1 for Wallis and Futuna, and 12 for French nationals abroad; members indirectly elected by departmental electoral colleges using absolute majority vote in 2 rounds if needed for departments with 1-3 members and proportional representation vote in departments with 4 or more members; members serve 6-year terms with one-half of the membership renewed every 3 years)
National Assembly or Assemblee Nationale (577 seats - 556 for metropolitan France, 10 for overseas departments, and 11 for citizens abroad; members directly elected by absolute majority vote in 2 rounds if needed to serve 5-year terms)

elections:
Senate - last held on 24 September 2017 (next to be held on 24 September 2020)
National Assembly - last held on 11 and 18 June 2017 (next to be held in June 2022)

election results:
Senate - percent of vote by party - NA; seats by party - LR 146, SOC 78, UC 49, REM 21, CRC 21, other 33
National Assembly - percent of vote by party first round - REM 28.2%, LR 15.8%, FN 13.2%, FI 11%, PS 7.4%, other 24.4%; percent of vote by party second round - REM 43.1%, LR 22.2%, FN 8.8%, MoDEM 6.1%, PS 5.7%, FI 4.9%, other 9.2%; seats by party - EM 308, LR 112, MoDEM 42, PS 29, UDI 18, FI 17, PCF 10, FN 8, other 33

JUDICIAL BRANCH:

highest courts: Court of Cassation or Cour de Cassation (consists of the court president, 6 divisional presiding judges, 120 trial judges, and 70 deputy judges organized into 6 divisions - 3 civil, 1 commercial, 1 labor, and 1 criminal); Constitutional Council (consists of 9 members)

judge selection and term of office: Court of Cassation judges appointed by the president of the republic from nominations from the High Council of the Judiciary, presided over by the Court of Cassation and 15 appointed members; judges appointed for life; Constitutional Council members - 3 appointed by the president of the republic and 3 each by the National Assembly and Senate presidents; members serve 9-year, non-renewable terms with one-third of the membership renewed every 3 years

subordinate courts: appellate courts or Cour d'Appel; regional courts or Tribunal de Grande Instance; first instance courts or Tribunal d'instance; administrative courts

note: in April 2018, the French Government announced its intention to reform the country's judicial system

POLITICAL PARTIES AND LEADERS:

Democratic Movement or MoDEM [Francois BAYROU]
Europe Ecology - The Greens or EELV [David CORMAND]
French Communist Party or PCF [Pierre LAURENT]
La France Insoumise or FI [Jean-Luc MELENCHON]
Left Front Coalition or FDG [Jean-Luc MELENCHON]
Left Party or PG [linked with the movement La France Insoumise or FI [Jean-Luc MELENCHON]]
Left Radical Party or PRG [Sylvia PINEL] (formerly Radical Socialist Party or PRS and the Left Radical Movement or MRG)
Movement for France or MPF [Philippe DE VILLIERS]
National Rally or RN [Marine LE PEN] (formerly National Front or FN)
New Anticapitalist Party or NPA [collective leadership; Christine POUPIN, main spokesperson; Philippe POUTOU, presidential candidate]
Rally for France or RPF [Igor KUREK]
Republican and Citizen Movement or MRC [Jean-Luc LAURENT]
Socialist Party or PS [Rachid TEMAL, interim leader]
Stand Up France (Debout La France) [Nicolas DUPONT-AIGNAN]
The Centrists [Herve MORIN] (formerly new Center or NC)
The Republic on the Move (La Republique en Marche) or REM [Christophe CASTANER]
The Republicans or LR [Laurent WAUQUIEZ] (formerly Union for a Popular Movement or UMP)
Union des Democrates et Independants or UDI [Jean-Christohe LAGARDE] and Democratic Movement or MoDem [Francois BAYROU] (previously Union for French Democracy or UDF); together known as UDI-Modem; Radical Party [Laurent HENART] is a member of UDI)
United Republic or RS [Dominique DE VILLEPIN]
Worker's Struggle (Lutte Ouvriere) or LO [Nathalie ARTHAUD, Arlette LAGUILLER, spokespersons] (also known as Communist Union)

INTERNATIONAL ORGANIZATION PARTICIPATION:

ADB (nonregional member), AfDB (nonregional member), Arctic Council (observer), Australia Group, BDEAC, BIS, BSEC (observer), CBSS (observer), CE, CERN, EAPC, EBRD, ECB, EIB, EITI (implementing country), EMU, ESA, EU, FAO, FATF, FZ, G-5, G-7, G-8, G-10, G-20, IADB, IAEA, IBRD, ICAO, ICC (national committees), ICCt, ICRM, IDA, IEA, IFAD, IFC, IFRCS, IGAD (partners), IHO, ILO, IMF, IMO, IMSO, InOC, Interpol, IOC, IOM, IPU, ISO, ITSO, ITU, ITUC (NGOs), MIGA, MINURSO, MINUSMA, MINUSTAH, MONUSCO, NATO, NEA, NSG, OAS (observer), OECD, OIF, OPCW, OSCE, Pacific Alliance (observer), Paris Club, PCA, PIF (partner), Schengen Convention, SELEC (observer), SPC, UN, UNCTAD, UNESCO, UNHCR, UNIDO, UNIFIL, Union Latina, UNMIL, UNOCI, UNRWA, UN Security Council (permanent), UNTSO, UNWTO, UPU, WCO, WFTU (NGOs), WHO, WIPO, WMO, WTO, ZC

DIPLOMATIC REPRESENTATION IN THE US:

chief of mission: Ambassador Gerard Roger ARAUD (since 18 September 2014)

chancery: 4101 Reservoir Road NW, Washington, DC 20007

telephone: [1] (202) 944-6000

FAX: [1] (202) 944-6166

consulate(s) general: Atlanta, Boston, Chicago, Houston, Los Angeles, Miami, New Orleans, New York, San Francisco, Washington DC

DIPLOMATIC REPRESENTATION FROM THE US:

chief of mission: Ambassador Jamie D. McCOURT (since 18 December 2017); note - also accredited to Monaco

embassy: 2 Avenue Gabriel, 75382 Paris Cedex 08

mailing address: PSC 116, APO AE 09777

telephone: [33] (1) 43-12-22-22

FAX: [33] (1) 42 66 97 83

consulate(s) general: Marseille, Strasbourg

consulate(s): Bordeaux, Lyon, Rennes, Toulouse

FLAG DESCRIPTION:

three equal vertical bands of blue (hoist side), white, and red; known as the "Le drapeau tricolore" (French Tricolor), the origin of the flag dates to 1790 and the French Revolution when the "ancient French color" of white was combined with the blue and red colors of the Parisian militia; the official flag for all French dependent areas

note: the design and/or colors are similar to a number of other flags, including those of Belgium, Chad, Cote d'Ivoire, Ireland, Italy, Luxembourg, and Netherlands

NATIONAL SYMBOL(S):

Gallic rooster, fleur-de-lis, Marianne (female personification); national colors: blue, white, red

NATIONAL ANTHEM:

name: "La Marseillaise" (The Song of Marseille)

lyrics/music: Claude-Joseph ROUGET de Lisle

note: adopted 1795, restored 1870; originally known as "Chant de Guerre pour l'Armee du Rhin" (War Song for the Army of the Rhine), the National Guard of Marseille made the song famous by singing it while marching into Paris in 1792 during the French Revolutionary Wars

ECONOMY :: FRANCE

ECONOMY - OVERVIEW:

The French economy is diversified across all sectors. The government has partially or fully privatized many large companies, including Air France, France Telecom, Renault, and Thales. However, the government maintains a strong presence in some sectors, particularly power, public transport, and defense industries. France is the most visited country in the world with 89 million foreign tourists in 2017. France's leaders remain committed to a capitalism in which they maintain social equity by means of laws, tax policies, and social spending that mitigate economic inequality.

France's real GDP grew by 1.9% in 2017, up from 1.2% the year before. The unemployment rate (including overseas territories) increased from 7.8% in 2008 to 10.2% in 2015, before falling to 9.0% in 2017. Youth unemployment in metropolitan France decreased from 24.6% in the fourth quarter of 2014 to 20.6% in the fourth quarter of 2017.

France's public finances have historically been strained by high spending and low growth. In 2017, the budget deficit improved to 2.7% of GDP, bringing it in compliance with the EU-mandated 3% deficit target. Meanwhile, France's public debt rose from 89.5% of GDP in 2012 to 97% in 2017.

Since entering office in May 2017, President Emmanuel MACRON launched a series of economic reforms to improve competitiveness and boost economic growth. President MACRON campaigned on reforming France's labor code and in late 2017 implemented a range of reforms to increase flexibility in the labor market by making it easier for firms to hire and fire and simplifying negotiations between employers and employees. In addition to labor reforms, President MACRON's 2018 budget cuts public spending, taxes, and social security contributions to spur private investment and increase purchasing power. The government plans to gradually reduce corporate tax rate for businesses from 33.3% to 25% by 2022.

GDP (PURCHASING POWER PARITY):

$2.856 trillion (2017 est.)

$2.791 trillion (2016 est.)

$2.761 trillion (2015 est.)

note: data are in 2017 dollars

country comparison to the world: 10

GDP (OFFICIAL EXCHANGE RATE):

$2.588 trillion (2017 est.) (2017 est.)

GDP - REAL GROWTH RATE:

2.3% (2017 est.)

1.1% (2016 est.)

1% (2015 est.)

country comparison to the world: 141

GDP - PER CAPITA (PPP):

$44,100 (2017 est.)

$43,200 (2016 est.)

$42,900 (2015 est.)

note: data are in 2017 dollars

country comparison to the world: 40

GROSS NATIONAL SAVING:

22.9% of GDP (2017 est.)

21.9% of GDP (2016 est.)

22.3% of GDP (2015 est.)

country comparison to the world: 77

GDP - COMPOSITION, BY END USE:

household consumption: 54.1% (2017 est.)

government consumption: 23.6% (2017 est.)

investment in fixed capital: 22.5% (2017 est.)

investment in inventories: 0.9% (2017 est.)

exports of goods and services: 30.9% (2017 est.)

imports of goods and services: -32% (2017 est.)

GDP - COMPOSITION, BY SECTOR OF ORIGIN:

agriculture: 1.7% (2017 est.)

industry: 19.5% (2017 est.)

services: 78.8% (2017 est.)

AGRICULTURE - PRODUCTS:

wheat, cereals, sugar beets, potatoes, wine grapes; beef, dairy products; fish

INDUSTRIES:

machinery, chemicals, automobiles, metallurgy, aircraft, electronics; textiles, food processing; tourism

INDUSTRIAL PRODUCTION GROWTH RATE:

2% (2017 est.)

country comparison to the world: 130

LABOR FORCE:

30.68 million (2017 est.)

country comparison to the world: 20

LABOR FORCE - BY OCCUPATION:

agriculture: 2.8% (2016 est.)

industry: 20% (2016 est.)

services: 77.2% (2016 est.)

UNEMPLOYMENT RATE:

9.4% (2017 est.)

10.1% (2016 est.)

note: includes overseas territories

country comparison to the world: 136

POPULATION BELOW POVERTY LINE:

14.2% (2015 est.)

HOUSEHOLD INCOME OR CONSUMPTION BY PERCENTAGE SHARE:

lowest 10%: 25.4% (2013)

highest 10%: 25.4% (2013)

DISTRIBUTION OF FAMILY INCOME - GINI INDEX:

29.3 (2016)

29.2 (2015)

country comparison to the world: 137

BUDGET:

revenues: 1.392 trillion (2017 est.)

expenditures: 1.459 trillion (2017 est.)

TAXES AND OTHER REVENUES:

53.8% (of GDP) (2017 est.)

country comparison to the world: 10

BUDGET SURPLUS (+) OR DEFICIT (-):

-2.6% (of GDP) (2017 est.)

country comparison to the world: 116

PUBLIC DEBT:

96.8% of GDP (2017 est.)

96.6% of GDP (2016 est.)

note: data cover general government debt and include debt instruments issued (or owned) by government entities other than the treasury; the data include treasury debt held by foreign entities; the data include debt issued by subnational entities, as well as intragovernmental debt; intragovernmental debt consists of treasury borrowings from surpluses in the social funds, such as for retirement, medical care, and unemployment; debt instruments for the social funds are not sold at public auctions

country comparison to the world: 20

FISCAL YEAR:

calendar year

INFLATION RATE (CONSUMER PRICES):

1.2% (2017 est.)

0.3% (2016 est.)

country comparison to the world: 64

CENTRAL BANK DISCOUNT RATE:

0% (31 December 2016)

0.05% (31 December 2015)

note: this is the European Central Bank's rate on the marginal lending facility, which offers overnight credit to banks in the euro area

country comparison to the world: 153

COMMERCIAL BANK PRIME LENDING RATE:

1.29% (31 December 2017 est.)

1.6% (31 December 2016 est.)

country comparison to the world: 193

STOCK OF NARROW MONEY:

$1.465 trillion (31 December 2017 est.)

$1.139 trillion (31 December 2016 est.)

note: see entry for the European Union for money supply for the entire euro area; the European Central Bank (ECB) controls monetary policy for the 18 members of the Economic and Monetary Union (EMU); individual members of the EMU do not control the quantity of money circulating within their own borders

country comparison to the world: 5

STOCK OF BROAD MONEY:

$1.465 trillion (31 December 2017 est.)

$1.139 trillion (31 December 2016 est.)

country comparison to the world: 5

STOCK OF DOMESTIC CREDIT:

$4.334 trillion (31 December 2017 est.)

$3.646 trillion (31 December 2016 est.)

country comparison to the world: 5

MARKET VALUE OF PUBLICLY TRADED SHARES:

$1.591 trillion (31 March 2017 est.)

$2.088 trillion (31 December 2015 est.)

$2.086 trillion (31 December 2014 est.)

country comparison to the world: 8

CURRENT ACCOUNT BALANCE:

-$14.83 billion (2017 est.)

-$18.55 billion (2016 est.)

country comparison to the world: 195

EXPORTS:

$549.9 billion (2017 est.)

$507 billion (2016 est.)

country comparison to the world: 7

EXPORTS - PARTNERS:

Germany 14.8%, Spain 7.7%, Italy 7.5%, US 7.2%, Belgium 7%, UK 6.7% (2017)

EXPORTS - COMMODITIES:

machinery and transportation equipment, aircraft, plastics, chemicals, pharmaceutical products, iron and steel, beverages

IMPORTS:

$601.7 billion (2017 est.)

$536.7 billion (2016 est.)

country comparison to the world: 6

IMPORTS - COMMODITIES:

machinery and equipment, vehicles, crude oil, aircraft, plastics, chemicals

IMPORTS - PARTNERS:

Germany 18.5%, Belgium 10.2%, Netherlands 8.3%, Italy 7.9%, Spain 7.1%, UK 5.3%, US 5.2%, China 5.1% (2017)

RESERVES OF FOREIGN EXCHANGE AND GOLD:

$156.4 billion (31 December 2017 est.)

$138.2 billion (31 December 2015 est.)

country comparison to the world: 15

DEBT - EXTERNAL:

$5.36 trillion (31 March 2016 est.)

$5.25 trillion (31 March 2015 est.)

country comparison to the world: 3

STOCK OF DIRECT FOREIGN INVESTMENT - AT HOME:

$858.3 billion (31 December 2017 est.)

$807.4 billion (31 December 2016 est.)

country comparison to the world: 12

STOCK OF DIRECT FOREIGN INVESTMENT - ABROAD:

$1.429 trillion (31 December 2017 est.)

$1.259 trillion (31 December 2016 est.)

country comparison to the world: 9

EXCHANGE RATES:

euros (EUR) per US dollar -

0.885 (2017 est.)

0.903 (2016 est.)

0.9214 (2015 est.)

0.885 (2014 est.)

0.7634 (2013 est.)

ENERGY :: FRANCE

ELECTRICITY ACCESS:

electrification - total population: 100% (2016)

ELECTRICITY - PRODUCTION:

529.1 billion kWh (2016 est.)

country comparison to the world: 9

ELECTRICITY - CONSUMPTION:

450.8 billion kWh (2016 est.)

country comparison to the world: 10

ELECTRICITY - EXPORTS:

61.41 billion kWh (2016 est.)

country comparison to the world: 3

ELECTRICITY - IMPORTS:

19.9 billion kWh (2016 est.)

country comparison to the world: 10

ELECTRICITY - INSTALLED GENERATING CAPACITY:

130.8 million kW (2016 est.)

country comparison to the world: 9

ELECTRICITY - FROM FOSSIL FUELS:

17% of total installed capacity (2016 est.)

country comparison to the world: 198

ELECTRICITY - FROM NUCLEAR FUELS:

50% of total installed capacity (2017 est.)

country comparison to the world: 1

ELECTRICITY - FROM HYDROELECTRIC PLANTS:

15% of total installed capacity (2017 est.)

country comparison to the world: 102

ELECTRICITY - FROM OTHER RENEWABLE SOURCES:

19% of total installed capacity (2017 est.)

country comparison to the world: 42

CRUDE OIL - PRODUCTION:

15,170 bbl/day (2017 est.)

country comparison to the world: 70

CRUDE OIL - EXPORTS:

0 bbl/day (2015 est.)

country comparison to the world: 126

CRUDE OIL - IMPORTS:

1.147 million bbl/day (2017 est.)

country comparison to the world: 9

CRUDE OIL - PROVED RESERVES:

65.97 million bbl (1 January 2018 est.)

country comparison to the world: 75

REFINED PETROLEUM PRODUCTS - PRODUCTION:

1.311 million bbl/day (2017 est.)

country comparison to the world: 15

REFINED PETROLEUM PRODUCTS - CONSUMPTION:

1.705 million bbl/day (2017 est.)

country comparison to the world: 13

REFINED PETROLEUM PRODUCTS - EXPORTS:

440,600 bbl/day (2017 est.)

country comparison to the world: 19

REFINED PETROLEUM PRODUCTS - IMPORTS:

886,800 bbl/day (2017 est.)

country comparison to the world: 8

NATURAL GAS - PRODUCTION:

16.99 million cu m (2017 est.)

country comparison to the world: 90

NATURAL GAS - CONSUMPTION:

41.88 billion cu m (2017 est.)

country comparison to the world: 24

NATURAL GAS - EXPORTS:

6.031 billion cu m (2017 est.)

country comparison to the world: 26

NATURAL GAS - IMPORTS:

48.59 billion cu m (2017 est.)

country comparison to the world: 10

NATURAL GAS - PROVED RESERVES:

8.41 billion cu m (1 January 2018 est.)

country comparison to the world: 81

CARBON DIOXIDE EMISSIONS FROM CONSUMPTION OF ENERGY:

341.2 million Mt (2017 est.)

country comparison to the world: 22

COMMUNICATIONS :: FRANCE

TELEPHONES - FIXED LINES:

total subscriptions: 38.687 million (2017 est.)

subscriptions per 100 inhabitants: 58 (2017 est.)

country comparison to the world: 6

TELEPHONES - MOBILE CELLULAR:

total subscriptions: 69.017 million (2017 est.)

subscriptions per 100 inhabitants: 103 (2017 est.)

country comparison to the world: 22

TELEPHONE SYSTEM:

general assessment: extensive cable and microwave radio relay; extensive use of fiber-optic cable; domestic satellite system; highly developed; 3rd largest in Europe; broadband subscriber rate remains strong at 4% (2017)

domestic: 58 per 100 persons for fixed-line and 103 per 100 for mobile-cellular subscriptions (2017)

international: country code - 33; numerous submarine cables provide links throughout Europe, Asia, Australia, the Middle East, and US; satellite earth stations - more than 3 (2 Intelsat (with total of 5 antennas - 2 for Indian Ocean and 3 for Atlantic Ocean), NA Eutelsat, 1 Inmarsat - Atlantic Ocean region); HF radiotelephone communications with more than 20 countries (2015)

overseas departments: country codes: French Guiana - 594; Guadeloupe - 590; Martinique - 596; Mayotte - 262; Reunion - 262; ACE submarine cable connecting France with African markets extended (2015)

BROADCAST MEDIA:

a mix of both publicly operated and privately owned TV stations; state-owned France television stations operate 4 networks, one of which is a network of regional stations, and has part-interest in several thematic cable/satellite channels and international channels; a large number of privately owned regional and local TV stations; multi-channel satellite and cable services provide a large number of channels; public broadcaster Radio France operates 7 national networks, a series of regional networks, and operates services for overseas territories and foreign audiences; Radio France Internationale, under the Ministry of Foreign Affairs, is a leading international broadcaster; a large number of commercial FM stations, with many of them consolidating into commercial networks (2008)

INTERNET COUNTRY CODE:

metropolitan France - .fr; French Guiana - .gf; Guadeloupe - .gp; Martinique - .mq; Mayotte - .yt; Reunion - .re

INTERNET USERS:

total: 57,226,585 (July 2016 est.)

percent of population: 85.6% (July 2016 est.)

country comparison to the world: 11

BROADBAND - FIXED SUBSCRIPTIONS:

total: 28.429 million (2017 est.)

subscriptions per 100 inhabitants: 42 (2017 est.)

country comparison to the world: 7

TRANSPORTATION :: FRANCE

NATIONAL AIR TRANSPORT SYSTEM:

number of registered air carriers: 30 (2015)

inventory of registered aircraft operated by air carriers: 485 (2015)

annual passenger traffic on registered air carriers: 65,039,503 (2015)

annual freight traffic on registered air carriers: 4,098,310,000 mt-km (2015)

CIVIL AIRCRAFT REGISTRATION COUNTRY CODE PREFIX:

F (2016)

AIRPORTS:

464 (2013)

country comparison to the world: 17

AIRPORTS - WITH PAVED RUNWAYS:

total: 294 (2017)

over 3,047 m: 14 (2017)

2,438 to 3,047 m: 25 (2017)

1,524 to 2,437 m: 97 (2017)

914 to 1,523 m: 83 (2017)

under 914 m: 75 (2017)

AIRPORTS - WITH UNPAVED RUNWAYS:

total: 170 (2013)

1,524 to 2,437 m: 1 (2013)

914 to 1,523 m: 64 (2013)

under 914 m: 105 (2013)

HELIPORTS:

1 (2013)

PIPELINES:

15322 km gas, 2939 km oil, 5084 km refined products (2013)

RAILWAYS:

total: 29,640 km (2014)

standard gauge: 29,473 km 1.435-m gauge (15,561 km electrified) (2014)

narrow gauge: 167 km 1.000-m gauge (63 km electrified) (2014)

country comparison to the world: 10

ROADWAYS:

total: 1,028,446 km (metropolitan France) (2010)

paved: 1,028,446 km (includes 11,416 km of expressways) (2010)

note: not included are 5,100 km of roadways in overseas departments

country comparison to the world: 8

WATERWAYS:

metropolitan France: 8,501 km (1,621 km navigable by craft up to 3,000 metric tons) (2010)

MERCHANT MARINE:

total: 555 (2017)

by type: container ship 24, general cargo 72, oil tanker 28, other 431 (2017)

note: includes Monaco

country comparison to the world: 37

PORTS AND TERMINALS:

major seaport(s): Brest, Calais, Dunkerque, Le Havre, Marseille, Nantes,

container port(s) (TEUs): Le Havre (2,510,000) (2016)

LNG terminal(s) (import): Fos Cavaou, Fos Tonkin, Montoir de Bretagne

river port(s): Paris, Rouen (Seine)

cruise/ferry port(s): Calais, Cherbourg, Le Havre

Strasbourg (Rhine) Bordeaux (Garronne)

MILITARY AND SECURITY :: FRANCE

MILITARY EXPENDITURES:

2.26% of GDP (2016)

2.27% of GDP (2015)

2.23% of GDP (2014)

2.22% of GDP (2013)

2.24% of GDP (2012)

country comparison to the world: 43

MILITARY BRANCHES:

Army (Armee de Terre; includes Marines, Foreign Legion, Army Light Aviation), Navy (Marine Nationale), Air Force (Armee de l'Air (AdlA); includes Air Defense) (2011)

MILITARY SERVICE AGE AND OBLIGATION:

18-25 years of age for male and female voluntary military service; no conscription; 1-year service obligation; women serve in noncombat posts (2013)

TERRORISM :: FRANCE

TERRORIST GROUPS - FOREIGN BASED:

Basque Fatherland and Liberty (ETA):
aim(s): establish an independent Basque homeland based on Marxist principles in what is now southwestern France and northern Spain
area(s) of operation: maintains a presence in the southwest (April 2018)

TRANSNATIONAL ISSUES :: FRANCE

DISPUTES - INTERNATIONAL:

Madagascar claims the French territories of Bassas da India, Europa Island, Glorioso Islands, and Juan de Nova IslandComoros claims MayotteMauritius claims Tromelin Islandterritorial dispute between Suriname and the French overseas department of French GuianaFrance asserts a territorial claim in Antarctica (Adelie Land)France and Vanuatu claim Matthew and Hunter Islands, east of New Caledonia

REFUGEES AND INTERNALLY DISPLACED PERSONS:

refugees (country of origin): 24,326 (Sri Lanka), 15,232 (Russia), 15,037 (Democratic Republic of the Congo), 13,154 (Serbia and Kosovo), 11,566 (Cambodia), 10,615 (Turkey), 8,991 (Syria), 8,008 (Vietnam), 7,685 (Afghanistan), 7,049 (Sudan), 6,841 (Laos), 6,823 (Guinea), 6,043 (Iraq), 5,183 (Mauritania) (2016)

stateless persons: 1,425 (2017)

ILLICIT DRUGS:

metropolitan France: transshipment point for South American cocaine, Southwest Asian heroin, and European synthetics;

French Guiana: small amount of marijuana grown for local consumption; minor transshipment point to Europe;

Martinique: transshipment point for cocaine and marijuana bound for the US and Europe

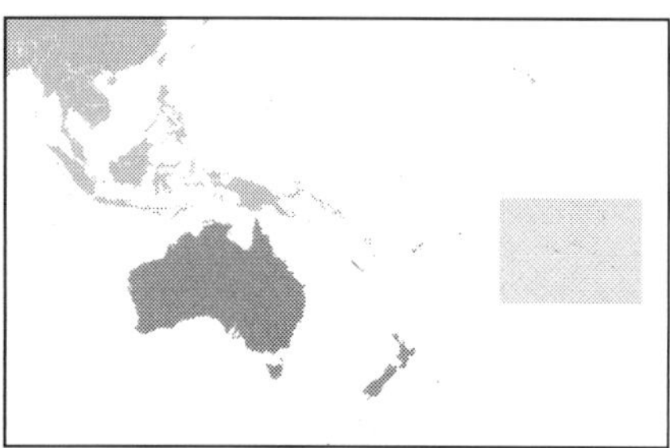

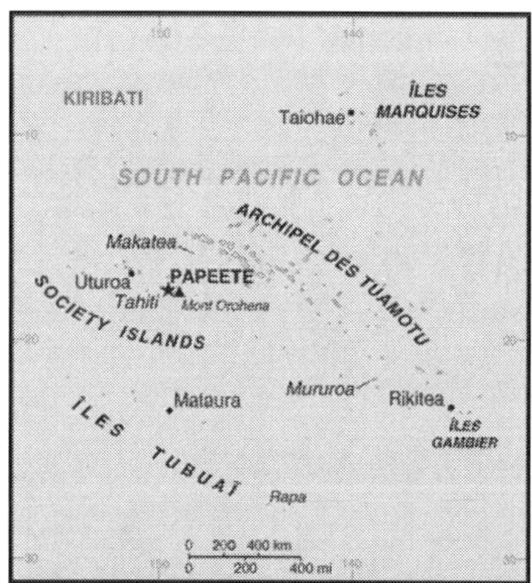

AUSTRALIA - OCEANIA :: FRENCH POLYNESIA

INTRODUCTION :: FRENCH POLYNESIA

BACKGROUND:

The French annexed various Polynesian island groups during the 19th century. In 1966, the French Government began testing nuclear weapons on the uninhabited Mururoa Atoll; following mounting opposition, the tests were moved underground in 1975. In September 1995, France stirred up widespread protests by resuming nuclear testing after a three-year moratorium. The tests were halted in January 1996. In recent years, French Polynesia's autonomy has been considerably expanded.

GEOGRAPHY :: FRENCH POLYNESIA

LOCATION:

Oceania, five archipelagoes (Archipel des Tuamotu, Iles Gambier, Iles Marquises, Iles Tubuai, Society Islands) in the South Pacific Ocean about halfway between South America and Australia

GEOGRAPHIC COORDINATES:

15 00 S, 140 00 W

MAP REFERENCES:

Oceania

AREA:

total: 4,167 sq km (118 islands and atolls; 67 are inhabited)

land: 3,827 sq km

water: 340 sq km

country comparison to the world: 175

AREA - COMPARATIVE:

slightly less than one-third the size of Connecticut

LAND BOUNDARIES:

0 km

COASTLINE:

2,525 km

MARITIME CLAIMS:

territorial sea: 12 nm

exclusive economic zone: 200 nm

CLIMATE:

tropical, but moderate

TERRAIN:

mixture of rugged high islands and low islands with reefs

ELEVATION:

0 m lowest point: Pacific Ocean

2241 highest point: Mont Orohena

NATURAL RESOURCES:

timber, fish, cobalt, hydropower

LAND USE:

agricultural land: 12.5% (2011 est.)

arable land: 0.7% (2011 est.) / permanent crops: 6.3% (2011 est.) / permanent pasture: 5.5% (2011 est.)

forest: 43.7% (2011 est.)

other: 43.8% (2011 est.)

IRRIGATED LAND:

10 sq km (2012)

POPULATION DISTRIBUTION:

the majority of the population lives in the Society Islands, one of five archipelagos that includes the most populous island - Tahiti - with approximately 70% of the nation's population

NATURAL HAZARDS:

occasional cyclonic storms in January

ENVIRONMENT - CURRENT ISSUES:

sea level rise; extreme weather events (cyclones, storms, and tsunamis producing floods, landslides, erosion, and reef damage); droughts; fresh water scarcity

GEOGRAPHY - NOTE:

includes five archipelagoes: four volcanic (Iles Gambier, Iles Marquises, Iles Tubuai, Society Islands) and one coral (Archipel des Tuamotu); the Tuamotu Archipelago forms the largest group of atolls in the world - 78 in total, 48 inhabited; Makatea in the Tuamotu Archipelago is one of the three great phosphate rock islands in the Pacific Ocean - the others are Banaba (Ocean Island) in Kiribati and Nauru

PEOPLE AND SOCIETY :: FRENCH POLYNESIA

POPULATION:

290,373 (July 2018 est.)

country comparison to the world: 181

NATIONALITY:

noun: French Polynesian(s)

adjective: French Polynesian

ETHNIC GROUPS:

Polynesian 78%, Chinese 12%, local French 6%, metropolitan French 4%

LANGUAGES:

French (official) 70%, Polynesian (official) 28.2%, other 1.8% (2012 est.)

RELIGIONS:

Protestant 54%, Roman Catholic 30%, other 10%, no religion 6%

AGE STRUCTURE:

0-14 years: 22.21% (male 33,165 /female 31,322)

15-24 years: 15.37% (male 23,232 /female 21,405)

25-54 years: 44.4% (male 66,074 /female 62,854)

55-64 years: 9.72% (male 14,503 /female 13,719)

65 years and over: 8.3% (male 11,634 /female 12,465) (2018 est.)

DEPENDENCY RATIOS:

total dependency ratio: 45.3 (2015 est.)

youth dependency ratio: 34.8 (2015 est.)

elderly dependency ratio: 10.5 (2015 est.)

potential support ratio: 9.5 (2015 est.)

MEDIAN AGE:

total: 32.4 years

male: 32.1 years

female: 32.6 years (2018 est.)

country comparison to the world: 101

POPULATION GROWTH RATE:

0.85% (2018 est.)

country comparison to the world: 125

BIRTH RATE:

14.5 births/1,000 population (2018 est.)

country comparison to the world: 132

DEATH RATE:

5.3 deaths/1,000 population (2018 est.)

country comparison to the world: 184

NET MIGRATION RATE:

-0.8 migrant(s)/1,000 population (2017 est.)

country comparison to the world: 131

POPULATION DISTRIBUTION:

the majority of the population lives in the Society Islands, one of five archipelagos that includes the most populous island - Tahiti - with approximately 70% of the nation's population

URBANIZATION:

urban population: 61.8% of total population (2018)

rate of urbanization: 1.01% annual rate of change (2015-20 est.)

MAJOR URBAN AREAS - POPULATION:

136,000 PAPEETE (capital) (2018)

SEX RATIO:

at birth: 1.05 male(s)/female (2017 est.)

0-14 years: 1.06 male(s)/female (2017 est.)

15-24 years: 1.08 male(s)/female (2017 est.)

25-54 years: 1.05 male(s)/female (2017 est.)

55-64 years: 1.06 male(s)/female (2017 est.)

65 years and over: 0.94 male(s)/female (2017 est.)

total population: 1.05 male(s)/female (2017 est.)

INFANT MORTALITY RATE:

total: 4.6 deaths/1,000 live births (2018 est.)

male: 5.1 deaths/1,000 live births (2018 est.)

female: 4.1 deaths/1,000 live births (2018 est.)

country comparison to the world: 179

LIFE EXPECTANCY AT BIRTH:

total population: 77.5 years (2018 est.)

male: 75.2 years (2018 est.)

female: 80 years (2018 est.)

country comparison to the world: 72

TOTAL FERTILITY RATE:

1.87 children born/woman (2018 est.)

country comparison to the world: 139

PHYSICIANS DENSITY:

2.13 physicians/1,000 population (2009)

DRINKING WATER SOURCE:

improved:

urban: 100% of population

rural: 100% of population

total: 100% of population

unimproved:

urban: 0% of population

rural: 0% of population

total: 0% of population (2015 est.)

SANITATION FACILITY ACCESS:

improved:

urban: 98.5% of population (2015 est.)

rural: 98.5% of population (2015 est.)

total: 98.5% of population (2015 est.)

unimproved:

urban: 1.5% of population (2015 est.)

rural: 1.5% of population (2015 est.)

total: 1.5% of population (2015 est.)

HIV/AIDS - ADULT PREVALENCE RATE:

NA

HIV/AIDS - PEOPLE LIVING WITH HIV/AIDS:

NA

HIV/AIDS - DEATHS:

NA

UNEMPLOYMENT, YOUTH AGES 15-24:

total: 56.7% (2012 est.)

male: 54.5% (2012 est.)

female: 59.7% (2012 est.)

country comparison to the world: 2

GOVERNMENT :: FRENCH POLYNESIA

COUNTRY NAME:

conventional long form: Overseas Lands of French Polynesia

conventional short form: French Polynesia

local long form: Pays d'outre-mer de la Polynesie Francaise

local short form: Polynesie Francaise

former: Establishments in Oceania, French Establishments in Oceania

etymology: the term "Polynesia" is an 18th-century construct composed of two Greek words, "poly" (many) and "nesoi" (islands), and refers to the more than 1,000 islands scattered over the central and southern Pacific Ocean

DEPENDENCY STATUS:

overseas lands of France; overseas territory of France from 1946-2003; overseas collectivity of France since 2003, though it is often referred to as an overseas country due to its degree of autonomy

GOVERNMENT TYPE:

parliamentary democracy (Assembly of French Polynesia); an overseas collectivity of France

CAPITAL:

name: Papeete (located on Tahiti)

geographic coordinates: 17 32 S, 149 34 W

time difference: UTC-10 (5 hours behind Washington, DC, during Standard Time)

ADMINISTRATIVE DIVISIONS:

5 administrative subdivisions (subdivisions administratives, singular - subdivision administrative): Iles Australes (Austral Islands), Iles du Vent (Windward Islands), Iles Marquises (Marquesas Islands), Iles Sous-le-Vent (Leeward Islands), Iles Tuamotu-Gambier; note - the Leeward Islands and the Windward Islands together make up the Society Islands (Iles de la Societe)

INDEPENDENCE:

none (overseas lands of France)

NATIONAL HOLIDAY:

Fete de la Federation, 14 July (1790); note - the local holiday is Internal Autonomy Day, 29 June (1880)

CONSTITUTION:

history: 4 October 1958 (French Constitution)

amendments: French constitution amendment procedures apply

LEGAL SYSTEM:

the laws of France, where applicable, apply

CITIZENSHIP:

see France

SUFFRAGE:

18 years of age; universal

EXECUTIVE BRANCH:

chief of state: President Emmanuel MACRON (since 14 May 2017), represented by High Commissioner of the Republic Rene BIDALL (since 30 May 2016)

head of government: President of French Polynesia Edouard FRITCH (since 12 September 2014)

cabinet: Council of Ministers approved by the Assembly from a list of its members submitted by the president

elections/appointments: French president directly elected by absolute majority popular vote in 2 rounds if needed for a 5-year term (eligible for a second term); high commissioner appointed by the French president on the advice of the French Ministry of Interior; French Polynesia president indirectly elected by Assembly of French Polynesia for a 5-year term (no term limits)

LEGISLATIVE BRANCH:

description: unicameral Assembly of French Polynesia or Assemblee de la Polynesie Francaise (57 seats; elections held in 2 rounds; in the second round, 38 members directly elected in multi-seat constituencies by a closed-list proportional representation vote; the party receiving the most votes gets an additional 19 seats; members serve 5-year terms)
French Polynesia indirectly elects 2 senators to the French Senate via an electoral college by absolute majority vote for 6-year terms with one-half the membership renewed every 3 years and directly elects 3 deputies to the French National Assembly by absolute majority vote in 2 rounds if needed for 5-year terms

elections:

Assembly of French Polynesia - last held on 22 April 2018 and 6 May 2018 (next to be held in 2023)
French Senate - last held in September 2017 (next to be held In September 2020)
French National Assembly - last held in 2 rounds on 3 and 17 June 2017 (next to be held in 2022)

election results:

Assembly of French Polynesia - percent of vote by party - Tapura Huiraatira 45.1%, Popular Rally 29.3%, Tavini Huiraatira 25.6%; seats by party - Tapura Huiraatira 38, Popular Rally 11, Tavini Huiraatira 8; composition - men 27, women 30, percent of women 52.6%
French Senate - percent of vote by party - NA; seats by party - Popular Rally 1, People's Servant Party 1; composition - men 246, women 102, percent of women 29.3%
French National Assembly - percent of vote by party - NA; seats by party - Tapura Huiractura 2, Tavini Huiraatura 1; composition - men 353, women 224, percent of women 38.8%; note - total Parliament percent of women 20%

JUDICIAL BRANCH:

highest courts: Court of Appeal or Cour d'Appel (composition NA); note - appeals beyond the French Polynesia Court of Appeal are heard by the Court of Cassation (in Paris)

judge selection and term of office: judges assigned from France normally for 3 years

subordinate courts: Court of the First Instance or Tribunal de Premiere Instance; Court of Administrative Law or Tribunal Administratif

POLITICAL PARTIES AND LEADERS:

A Tia Porinetia [Teva ROHFRITSCH]
Alliance for a New Democracy or ADN (includes The New Star [Philip SCHYLE], This Country is Yours [Nicole BOUTEAU])
New Fatherland Party (Ai'a Api) [Emile VERNAUDON]
Our Home alliance
People's Servant Party (Tavini Huiraatira) [Oscar TEMARU]
Popular Rally (Tahoeraa Huiraatira) [Gaston FLOSSE]
Tapura Huiraatira [Edouard FRITICH]
Tavini Huiraatira [James CHANCELOR]
Union for Democracy alliance or UPD [Oscar TEMARU]

INTERNATIONAL ORGANIZATION PARTICIPATION:

ITUC (NGOs), PIF (associate member), SPC, UPU, WMO

DIPLOMATIC REPRESENTATION IN THE US:

none (overseas lands of France)

DIPLOMATIC REPRESENTATION FROM THE US:

none (overseas lands of France)

FLAG DESCRIPTION:

two red horizontal bands encase a wide white band in a 1:2:1 ratio; centered on the white band is a disk with a blue and white wave pattern depicting the sea on the lower half and a gold and white ray pattern depicting the sun on the upper half; a Polynesian canoe rides on the wave pattern; the canoe has a crew of five represented by five stars that symbolize the five island groups; red and white are traditional Polynesian colors

note: identical to the red-white-red flag of Tahiti, the largest and most populous of the islands in French Polynesia, but which has no emblem in the white band; the flag of France is used for official occasions

NATIONAL SYMBOL(S):

outrigger canoe, Tahitian gardenia (Gardenia taitensis) flower; national colors: red, white

NATIONAL ANTHEM:

name: "Ia Ora 'O Tahiti Nui" (Long Live Tahiti Nui)

lyrics/music: Maeva BOUGES, Irmine TEHEI, Angele TEROROTUA, Johanna NOUVEAU, Patrick AMARU, Louis MAMATUI, and Jean-Pierre CELESTIN (the compositional group created both the lyrics and music)

note: adopted 1993; serves as a local anthem; as a territory of France, "La Marseillaise" is official (see France)

GOVERNMENT - NOTE:

under certain acts of France, French Polynesia has acquired autonomy in all areas except those relating to police, monetary policy, tertiary education, immigration, and defense and foreign affairs; the duties of its president are fashioned after those of the French prime minister

ECONOMY :: FRENCH POLYNESIA

ECONOMY - OVERVIEW:

Since 1962, when France stationed military personnel in the region, French Polynesia has changed from a subsistence agricultural economy to one in which a high proportion of the work force is either employed by the military or supports the tourist industry. With the halt of French nuclear testing in 1996, the military contribution to the economy fell sharply.

After growing at an average yearly rate of 4.2% from 1997-2007, the economic and financial crisis in 2008 marked French Polynesia's entry into recession. However, since 2014, French Polynesia has shown signs of recovery. Business turnover reached 1.8% year-on-year in September 2016, tourism increased 1.8% in 2015, and GDP grew 2.0% in 2015.

French Polynesia's tourism-dominated service sector accounted for 85% of total value added for the economy in 2012. Tourism employs 17% of the workforce. Pearl farming is the second biggest industry, accounting for 54% of exports in 2015; however, the output has decreased to 12.5 tons – the lowest level since 2008. A small manufacturing sector predominantly processes commodities from French Polynesia's primary sector - 8% of total economy in 2012 - including agriculture and fishing.

France has agreed to finance infrastructure, marine businesses, and cultural and ecological sites at roughly $80 million per year between 2015 and 2020. Japan, the US, and China are French Polynesia's three largest trade partners.

GDP (PURCHASING POWER PARITY):

$5.49 billion (2015 est.)

$5.383 billion (2014 est.)

$6.963 billion (2010 est.)

country comparison to the world: 177

GDP (OFFICIAL EXCHANGE RATE):

$4.795 billion (2015 est.) (2015 est.)

GDP - REAL GROWTH RATE:

2% (2015 est.)

-2.7% (2014 est.)

-2.5% (2010 est.)

country comparison to the world: 150

GDP - PER CAPITA (PPP):

$17,000 (2015 est.)

$20,100 (2014 est.)

$22,700 (2010)

country comparison to the world: 103

GDP - COMPOSITION, BY END USE:

household consumption: 66.9% (2014 est.)

government consumption: 33.6% (2014 est.)

investment in fixed capital: 19.4% (2014 est.)

investment in inventories: 0.1% (2014 est.)

exports of goods and services: 17.5% (2014 est.)

imports of goods and services: -37.5% (2014 est.)

GDP - COMPOSITION, BY SECTOR OF ORIGIN:

agriculture: 2.5% (2009)

industry: 13% (2009)

services: 84.5% (2009)

AGRICULTURE - PRODUCTS:

coconuts, vanilla, vegetables, fruits, coffee; poultry, beef, dairy products; fish

INDUSTRIES:

tourism, pearls, agricultural processing, handicrafts, phosphates

INDUSTRIAL PRODUCTION GROWTH RATE:

NA

LABOR FORCE:

126,300 (2016 est.)

country comparison to the world: 179

LABOR FORCE - BY OCCUPATION:

agriculture: 13%

industry: 19%

services: 68% (2013 est.)

UNEMPLOYMENT RATE:

21.8% (2012)

11.7% (2010)

country comparison to the world: 190

POPULATION BELOW POVERTY LINE:

19.7% (2009 est.)

HOUSEHOLD INCOME OR CONSUMPTION BY PERCENTAGE SHARE:

lowest 10%: NA

highest 10%: NA

BUDGET:

revenues: 1.891 billion (2012)

expenditures: 1.833 billion (2011)

TAXES AND OTHER REVENUES:

39.4% (of GDP) (2012)

country comparison to the world: 46

BUDGET SURPLUS (+) OR DEFICIT (-):

1.2% (of GDP) (2012)

country comparison to the world: 28

FISCAL YEAR:

calendar year

INFLATION RATE (CONSUMER PRICES):

0% (2015 est.)

0.3% (2014 est.)

country comparison to the world: 10

STOCK OF BROAD MONEY:

$3.81 billion (2015 est.)

country comparison to the world: 118

MARKET VALUE OF PUBLICLY TRADED SHARES:

NA

CURRENT ACCOUNT BALANCE:

$207.7 million (2014 est.)

$158.8 million (2013 est.)

country comparison to the world: 58

EXPORTS:

$1.245 billion (2014 est.)

$1.168 billion (2013 est.)

country comparison to the world: 152

EXPORTS - PARTNERS:

Japan 23.1%, Hong Kong 21.5%, Kyrgyzstan 15.9%, US 15.9%, France 12.4% (2017)

EXPORTS - COMMODITIES:

cultured pearls, coconut products, mother-of-pearl, vanilla, shark meat

IMPORTS:

$2.235 billion (2014 est.)

$2.271 billion (2013 est.)

country comparison to the world: 162

IMPORTS - COMMODITIES:

fuels, foodstuffs, machinery and equipment

IMPORTS - PARTNERS:

France 27.9%, South Korea 12.1%, US 10.1%, China 7.3%, NZ 6.7%, Singapore 4.2% (2017)

DEBT - EXTERNAL:

NA

STOCK OF DIRECT FOREIGN INVESTMENT - AT HOME:

$905 million (2015 est.)

$822.3 million (2014 est.)

country comparison to the world: 124

STOCK OF DIRECT FOREIGN INVESTMENT - ABROAD:

$349.3 million (2015)

$310.8 million (2014 est.)

country comparison to the world: 101

EXCHANGE RATES:

Comptoirs Francais du Pacifique francs (XPF) per US dollar -

110.2 (2017 est.)

107.84 (2016 est.)

107.84 (2015 est.)

89.85 (2014 est.)

90.56 (2013 est.)

ENERGY :: FRENCH POLYNESIA

ELECTRICITY ACCESS:

population without electricity: 116,981 (2012)

electrification - total population: 59% (2012)

electrification - urban areas: 72% (2012)

electrification - rural areas: 45% (2012)

ELECTRICITY - PRODUCTION:

677.3 million kWh (2016 est.)

country comparison to the world: 158

ELECTRICITY - CONSUMPTION:

629.9 million kWh (2016 est.)

country comparison to the world: 164

ELECTRICITY - EXPORTS:

0 kWh (2016 est.)

country comparison to the world: 136

ELECTRICITY - IMPORTS:

0 kWh (2016 est.)

country comparison to the world: 150

ELECTRICITY - INSTALLED GENERATING CAPACITY:

253,000 kW (2016 est.)

country comparison to the world: 163

ELECTRICITY - FROM FOSSIL FUELS:

70% of total installed capacity (2016 est.)

country comparison to the world: 108

ELECTRICITY - FROM NUCLEAR FUELS:

0% of total installed capacity (2017 est.)

country comparison to the world: 92

ELECTRICITY - FROM HYDROELECTRIC PLANTS:

19% of total installed capacity (2017 est.)

country comparison to the world: 89

ELECTRICITY - FROM OTHER RENEWABLE SOURCES:

11% of total installed capacity (2017 est.)

country comparison to the world: 77

CRUDE OIL - PRODUCTION:

0 bbl/day (2017 est.)

country comparison to the world: 138

CRUDE OIL - EXPORTS:

0 bbl/day (2015 est.)

country comparison to the world: 127

CRUDE OIL - IMPORTS:

0 bbl/day (2015 est.)

country comparison to the world: 129

CRUDE OIL - PROVED RESERVES:

0 bbl (1 January 2018 est.)

country comparison to the world: 134

REFINED PETROLEUM PRODUCTS - PRODUCTION:

0 bbl/day (2015 est.)

country comparison to the world: 147

REFINED PETROLEUM PRODUCTS - CONSUMPTION:

6,600 bbl/day (2016 est.)

country comparison to the world: 168

REFINED PETROLEUM PRODUCTS - EXPORTS:

0 bbl/day (2015 est.)

country comparison to the world: 157

REFINED PETROLEUM PRODUCTS - IMPORTS:

6,785 bbl/day (2015 est.)

country comparison to the world: 160

NATURAL GAS - PRODUCTION:

0 cu m (2017 est.)

country comparison to the world: 135

NATURAL GAS - CONSUMPTION:

0 cu m (2017 est.)

country comparison to the world: 148

NATURAL GAS - EXPORTS:

0 cu m (2017 est.)

country comparison to the world: 106

NATURAL GAS - IMPORTS:

0 cu m (2017 est.)

country comparison to the world: 127

NATURAL GAS - PROVED RESERVES:

0 cu m (1 January 2014 est.)

country comparison to the world: 137

CARBON DIOXIDE EMISSIONS FROM CONSUMPTION OF ENERGY:

1.03 million Mt (2017 est.)

country comparison to the world: 168

COMMUNICATIONS :: FRENCH POLYNESIA

TELEPHONES - FIXED LINES:

total subscriptions: 60,530 (July 2016 est.)

subscriptions per 100 inhabitants: 33 (July 2016 est.)

country comparison to the world: 154

TELEPHONES - MOBILE CELLULAR:

total subscriptions: 280,111 (July 2016 est.)

subscriptions per 100 inhabitants: 97 (July 2016 est.)

country comparison to the world: 178

TELEPHONE SYSTEM:

general assessment: one of the most advanced telecom infrastructures for the Pacific islands region; 85% mobile broadband coverage (2017)

domestic: fixed-line subscriptions 33 per 100 persons and mobile-cellular density is roughly 97 per 100 persons (2017)

international: country code - 689; satellite earth station - 1 Intelsat (Pacific Ocean); international submarine cables depolyed in 2010 and more cables after 2016 (2017)

BROADCAST MEDIA:

French public overseas broadcaster Reseau Outre-Mer provides 2 TV channels and 1 radio station; 1 government-owned TV station; a small number of privately owned radio stations (2018)

INTERNET COUNTRY CODE:

.pf

INTERNET USERS:

total: 195,275 (July 2016 est.)

percent of population: 68.4% (July 2016 est.)

country comparison to the world: 171

BROADBAND - FIXED SUBSCRIPTIONS:

total: 55,443 (2017 est.)

subscriptions per 100 inhabitants: 19 (2017 est.)

country comparison to the world: 129

TRANSPORTATION :: FRENCH POLYNESIA

NATIONAL AIR TRANSPORT SYSTEM:

number of registered air carriers: 2 (registered in France) (2015)

inventory of registered aircraft operated by air carriers: 21 (registered in France) (2015)

CIVIL AIRCRAFT REGISTRATION COUNTRY CODE PREFIX:

F-OH (2016)

AIRPORTS:

54 (2013)

country comparison to the world: 87

AIRPORTS - WITH PAVED RUNWAYS:

total: 45 (2017)

over 3,047 m: 2 (2017)

1,524 to 2,437 m: 5 (2017)

914 to 1,523 m: 33 (2017)

under 914 m: 5 (2017)

AIRPORTS - WITH UNPAVED RUNWAYS:

total: 9 (2013)

914 to 1,523 m: 4 (2013)

under 914 m: 5 (2013)

HELIPORTS:

1 (2013)

ROADWAYS:

total: 2,590 km (1999)

paved: 1,735 km (1999)

unpaved: 855 km (1999)

country comparison to the world: 171

MERCHANT MARINE:

total: 17 (2017)

by type: general cargo 8, other 9 (2017)

country comparison to the world: 142

PORTS AND TERMINALS:

major seaport(s): Papeete

MILITARY AND SECURITY :: FRENCH POLYNESIA

MILITARY BRANCHES:

no regular military forces (2011)

MILITARY - NOTE:

defense is the responsibility of France

TRANSNATIONAL ISSUES :: FRENCH POLYNESIA

DISPUTES - INTERNATIONAL:

none

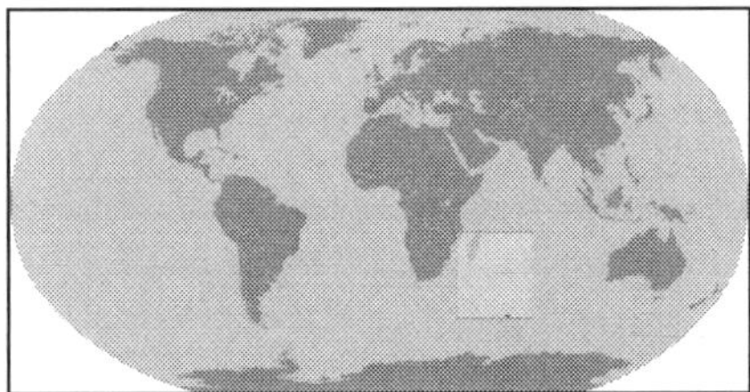

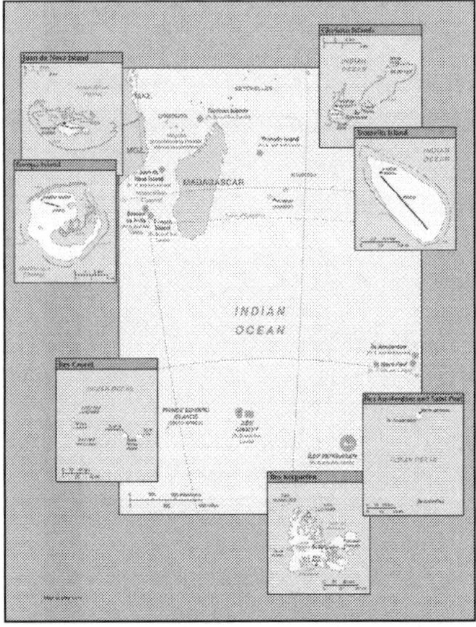

ANTARCTICA :: FRENCH SOUTHERN AND ANTARCTIC LANDS

INTRODUCTION :: FRENCH SOUTHERN AND ANTARCTIC LANDS

BACKGROUND:

In February 2007, the Iles Eparses became an integral part of the French Southern and Antarctic Lands (TAAF). The Southern Lands are now divided into five administrative districts, two of which are archipelagos, Iles Crozet and Iles Kerguelen; the third is a district composed of two volcanic islands, Ile Saint-Paul and Ile Amsterdam; the fourth, Iles Eparses, consists of five scattered tropical islands around Madagascar. They contain no permanent inhabitants and are visited only by researchers studying the native fauna, scientists at the various scientific stations, fishermen, and military personnel. The fifth district is the Antarctic portion, which consists of "Adelie Land," a thin slice of the Antarctic continent discovered and claimed by the French in 1840.

Ile Amsterdam: Discovered but not named in 1522 by the Spanish, the island subsequently received the appellation of Nieuw Amsterdam from a Dutchman; it was claimed by France in 1843. A short-lived attempt at cattle farming began in 1871. A French meteorological station established on the island in 1949 is still in use.;

Ile Saint Paul: Claimed by France since 1893, the island was a fishing industry center from 1843 to 1914. In 1928, a spiny lobster cannery was established, but when the company went bankrupt in 1931, seven workers were abandoned. Only two survived until 1934 when rescue finally arrived.;

Iles Crozet: A large archipelago formed from the Crozet Plateau, Iles Crozet is divided into two main groups: L'Occidental (the West), which includes Ile aux Cochons, Ilots des Apotres, Ile des Pingouins, and the reefs Brisants de l'Heroine; and L'Oriental (the East), which includes Ile d'Est and Ile de la Possession (the largest island of the Crozets). Discovered and claimed by France in 1772, the islands were used for seal hunting and as a base for whaling. Originally administered as a dependency of Madagascar, they became part of the TAAF in 1955.;

Iles Kerguelen: This island group, discovered in 1772, consists of one large island (Ile Kerguelen) and about 300 smaller islands. A permanent group of 50 to 100 scientists resides at the main base at Port-aux-Francais.;

Adelie Land: The only non-insular district of the TAAF is the Antarctic claim known as "Adelie Land." The US Government does not recognize it as a French dependency.;

Bassas da India: A French possession since 1897, this atoll is a volcanic rock surrounded by reefs and is awash at high tide.;

Europa Island: This heavily wooded island has been a French possession since 1897; it is the site of a small military garrison that staffs a weather station.;

Glorioso Islands: A French possession since 1892, the Glorioso Islands are composed of two lushly vegetated coral islands (Ile Glorieuse and Ile du Lys) and three rock islets. A military garrison operates a weather and radio station on Ile Glorieuse.;

Juan de Nova Island: Named after a famous 15th-century Spanish navigator and explorer, the island has been a French possession since 1897. It has been exploited for its guano and phosphate. Presently a small military garrison oversees a meteorological station.;

Tromelin Island: First explored by the French in 1776, the island came under the jurisdiction of Reunion in 1814. At present, it serves as a sea turtle sanctuary and is the site of an important meteorological station.

GEOGRAPHY :: FRENCH SOUTHERN AND ANTARCTIC LANDS

LOCATION:

southeast and east of Africa, islands in the southern Indian Ocean, some near Madagascar and others about equidistant between Africa, Antarctica, and Australia; note - French Southern and Antarctic Lands include Ile Amsterdam, Ile Saint-Paul, Iles Crozet, Iles Kerguelen, Bassas da India, Europa Island, Glorioso Islands, Juan de Nova Island, and Tromelin Island in the southern Indian Ocean, along with the French-claimed sector of Antarctica, "Adelie Land"; the US does not recognize the French claim to "Adelie Land"

GEOGRAPHIC COORDINATES:

Ile Amsterdam (Ile Amsterdam et Ile Saint-Paul): 37 50 S, 77 32 E;

Ile Saint-Paul (Ile Amsterdam et Ile Saint-Paul): 38 72 S, 77 53 E;

Iles Crozet: 46 25 S, 51 00 E;

Iles Kerguelen: 49 15 S, 69 35 E;

Bassas da India (Iles Eparses): 21 30 S, 39 50 E;

Europa Island (Iles Eparses): 22 20 S, 40 22 E;

Glorioso Islands (Iles Eparses): 11 30 S, 47 20 E;

Juan de Nova Island (Iles Eparses): 17 03 S, 42 45 E;

Tromelin Island (Iles Eparses): 15 52 S, 54 25 E

MAP REFERENCES:

Antarctic RegionAfrica

AREA:

Ile Amsterdam (Ile Amsterdam et Ile Saint-Paul): total - 55 sq km; land - 55 sq km; water - 0 sq km
Ile Saint-Paul (Ile Amsterdam et Ile Saint-Paul): total - 7 sq km; land - 7 sq km; water - 0 sq km
Iles Crozet: total - 352 sq km; land - 352 sq km; water - 0 sq km
Iles Kerguelen: total - 7,215 sq km; land - 7,215 sq km; water - 0 sq km
Bassas da India (Iles Eparses): total - 80 sq km; land - 0.2 sq km; water - 79.8 sq km (lagoon)
Europa Island (Iles Eparses): total - 28 sq km; land - 28 sq km; water - 0 sq km
Glorioso Islands (Iles Eparses): total - 5 sq km; land - 5 sq km; water - 0 sq km
Juan de Nova Island (Iles Eparses): total - 4.4 sq km; land - 4.4 sq km; water - 0 sq km
Tromelin Island (Iles Eparses): total - 1 sq km; land - 1 sq km; water - 0 sq km
note: excludes "Adelie Land" claim of about 500,000 sq km in Antarctica that is not recognized by the US

AREA - COMPARATIVE:

Ile Amsterdam (Ile Amsterdam et Ile Saint-Paul): less than one-half the size of Washington, DC;

Ile Saint-Paul (Ile Amsterdam et Ile Saint-Paul): more than 10 times the size of the National Mall in Washington, DC;

Iles Crozet: about twice the size of Washington, DC;

Iles Kerguelen: slightly larger than Delaware;

Bassas da India (Iles Eparses): land area about one-third the size of the National Mall in Washington, DC;

Europa Island (Iles Eparses): about one-sixth the size of Washington, DC;

Glorioso Islands (Iles Eparses): about eight times the size of the National Mall in Washington, DC;

Juan de Nova Island (Iles Eparses): about seven times the size of the National Mall in Washington, DC;

Tromelin Island (Iles Eparses): about 1.7 times the size of the National Mall in Washington, DC

LAND BOUNDARIES:

0 km

COASTLINE:

Ile Amsterdam (Ile Amsterdam et Ile Saint-Paul): 28 km
Ile Saint-Paul (Ile Amsterdam et Ile Saint-Paul):
Iles Kerguelen: 2,800 km
Bassas da India (Iles Eparses): 35.2 km
Europa Island (Iles Eparses): 22.2 km
Glorioso Islands (Iles Eparses): 35.2 km
Juan de Nova Island (Iles Eparses): 24.1 km
Tromelin Island (Iles Eparses): 3.7 km

MARITIME CLAIMS:

territorial sea: 12 nm

exclusive economic zone: 200 nm from Iles Kerguelen and Iles Eparses (does not include the rest of French Southern and Antarctic Lands); Juan de Nova Island and Tromelin Island claim a continental shelf of 200-m depth or to the depth of exploitation

CLIMATE:

Ile Amsterdam et Ile Saint-Paul: oceanic with persistent westerly winds and high humidity;

Iles Crozet: windy, cold, wet, and cloudy;

Iles Kerguelen: oceanic, cold, overcast, windy;

Iles Eparses: tropical

TERRAIN:

Ile Amsterdam (Ile Amsterdam et Ile Saint-Paul): a volcanic island with steep coastal cliffs; the center floor of the volcano is a large plateau;

Ile Saint-Paul (Ile Amsterdam et Ile Saint-Paul): triangular in shape, the island is the top of a volcano, rocky with steep cliffs on the eastern side; has active thermal springs;

Iles Crozet: a large archipelago formed from the Crozet Plateau is divided into two groups of islands;

Iles Kerguelen: the interior of the large island of Ile Kerguelen is composed of high mountains, hills, valleys, and plains with peninsulas stretching off its coasts;

Bassas da India (Iles Eparses): atoll, awash at high tide; shallow (15 m) lagoon;

Europa Island, Glorioso Islands, Juan de Nova Island: low, flat, and sandy;

Tromelin Island (Iles Eparses): low, flat, sandy; likely volcanic seamount

ELEVATION:

0 m lowest point: Indian Ocean

867 highest point: Mont de la Dives on Ile Amsterdam (Ile Amsterdam et Ile Saint-Paul) 272 unnamed location on Ile Saint-Paul (Ile Amsterdam et Ile Saint-Paul) 1090 Pic Marion-Dufresne in Iles Crozet 1850 Mont Ross in Iles Kerguelen 2.4 unnamed location on Bassas de India (Iles Eparses) 24 unnamed location on Europa Island (Iles Eparses) 12 unnamed location on Glorioso Islands (Iles Eparses) 10 unnamed location on Juan de Nova Island (Iles Eparses) 7 unnamed location on Tromelin Island (Iles Eparses)

NATURAL RESOURCES:

fish, crayfish, note, Glorioso Islands and Tromelin Island (Iles Eparses) have guano, phosphates, and coconuts

NATURAL HAZARDS:

Ile Amsterdam and Ile Saint-Paul are inactive volcanoes; Iles Eparses subject to periodic cyclones; Bassas da India is a maritime hazard since it is under water for a period of three hours prior to and following the high tide and surrounded by reefs

volcanism: Reunion Island - Piton de la Fournaise (2,632 m), which has erupted many times in recent years including 2010, 2015, and 2017, is one of the world's most active volcanoes; although rare, eruptions outside the volcano's caldera could threaten nearby cities

ENVIRONMENT - CURRENT ISSUES:

introduction of foreign species on Iles Crozet has caused severe damage to the original ecosystem; overfishing of Patagonian toothfish around Iles Crozet and Iles Kerguelen

GEOGRAPHY - NOTE:

islands' component is widely scattered across remote locations in the southern Indian Ocean

Bassas da India (Iles Eparses): atoll is a circular reef atop a long-extinct, submerged volcano;

Europa Island and Juan de Nova Island (Iles Eparses): wildlife sanctuary for seabirds and sea turtles;

Glorioso Island (Iles Eparses): islands and rocks are surrounded by an extensive reef system;

Tromelin Island (Iles Eparses): climatologically important location for forecasting cyclones in the western Indian Ocean; wildlife sanctuary (seabirds, tortoises)

PEOPLE AND SOCIETY :: FRENCH SOUTHERN AND ANTARCTIC LANDS

POPULATION:

no indigenous inhabitants

Ile Amsterdam (Ile Amsterdam et Ile Saint-Paul): uninhabited but has a meteorological station
Ile Saint-Paul (Ile Amsterdam et Ile Saint-Paul): uninhabited but is frequently visited by fishermen and has a scientific research cabin for short stays
Iles Crozet: uninhabited except for 18 to 30 people staffing the Alfred Faure research station on Ile del la Possession
Iles Kerguelen: 50 to 100 scientists are located at the main base at Port-aux-Francais on Ile Kerguelen
Bassas da India (Iles Eparses): uninhabitable
Europa Island, Glorioso Islands, Juan de Nova Island (Iles Eparses): a small French military garrison and a few meteorologists on each possession; visited by scientists
Tromelin Island (Iles Eparses): uninhabited, except for visits by scientists

GOVERNMENT :: FRENCH SOUTHERN AND ANTARCTIC LANDS

COUNTRY NAME:

conventional long form: Territory of the French Southern and Antarctic Lands

conventional short form: French Southern and Antarctic Lands

local long form: Territoire des Terres Australes et Antarctiques Francaises

local short form: Terres Australes et Antarctiques Francaises

abbreviation: TAAF

etymology: self-descriptive name specifying the territories' affiliation and location in the Southern Hemisphere

DEPENDENCY STATUS:

overseas territory of France since 1955

note: note

ADMINISTRATIVE DIVISIONS:

none (overseas territory of France); there are no first-order administrative divisions as defined by the US Government, but there are 5 administrative districts named Iles Crozet, Iles Eparses, Iles Kerguelen, Ile Saint-Paul et Ile Amsterdam; the fifth district is the "Adelie Land" claim in Antarctica that is not recognized by the US

LEGAL SYSTEM:

the laws of France, where applicable, apply

CITIZENSHIP:

see France

EXECUTIVE BRANCH:

President Emmanuel MACRON (since 14 May 2017), represented by Prefect Cecile POZZO DI BORGO (since 13 October 2014)

INTERNATIONAL ORGANIZATION PARTICIPATION:

UPU

DIPLOMATIC REPRESENTATION IN THE US:

none (overseas territory of France)

DIPLOMATIC REPRESENTATION FROM THE US:

none (overseas territory of France)

FLAG DESCRIPTION:

the flag of France is used

NATIONAL ANTHEM:

note: as a territory of France, "La Marseillaise" is official (see France)

ECONOMY :: FRENCH SOUTHERN AND ANTARCTIC LANDS

ECONOMY - OVERVIEW:

Economic activity is limited to servicing meteorological and geophysical research stations, military bases, and French and other fishing fleets. The fish catches landed on Iles Kerguelen by foreign ships are exported to France and Reunion.

COMMUNICATIONS :: FRENCH SOUTHERN AND ANTARCTIC LANDS

INTERNET COUNTRY CODE:

.tf

COMMUNICATIONS - NOTE:

has one or more meteorological stations on each possession

TRANSPORTATION :: FRENCH SOUTHERN AND ANTARCTIC LANDS

AIRPORTS:

4 (2013)

country comparison to the world: 187

PORTS AND TERMINALS:

none; offshore anchorage only

MILITARY AND SECURITY :: FRENCH SOUTHERN AND ANTARCTIC LANDS

MILITARY - NOTE:

defense is the responsibility of France

TRANSNATIONAL ISSUES :: FRENCH SOUTHERN AND ANTARCTIC LANDS

DISPUTES - INTERNATIONAL:

French claim to "Adelie Land" in Antarctica is not recognized by the US

Bassas da India, Europa Island, Glorioso Islands, Juan de Nova Island (Iles Eparses): claimed by Madagascar;

the vegetated drying cays of Banc du Geyser, which were claimed by Madagascar in 1976, also fall within the EEZ claims of the Comoros and France (Glorioso Islands);

Tromelin Island (Iles Eparses): claimed by Mauritius

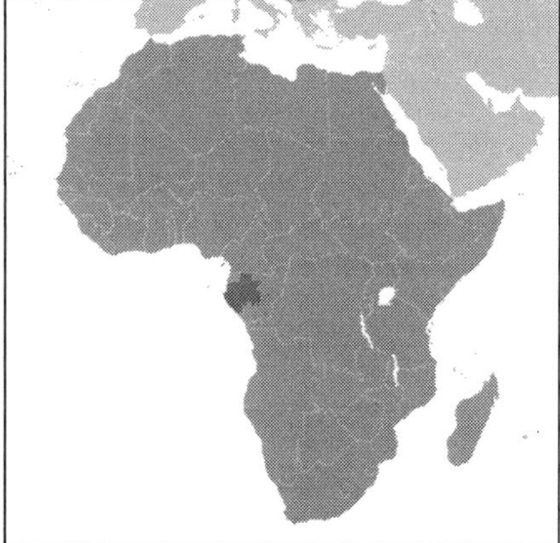

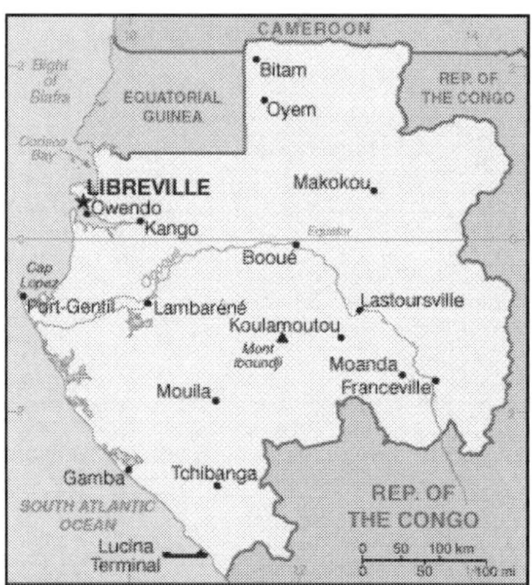

AFRICA :: GABON

INTRODUCTION :: GABON

BACKGROUND:

Following, independence from France in 1960, El Hadj Omar BONGO Ondimba - one of the longest-ruling heads of state in the world - dominated the country's political scene for four decades (1967-2009). President BONGO introduced a nominal multiparty system and a new constitution in the early 1990s. However, allegations of electoral fraud during local elections in December 2002 and the presidential election in 2005 exposed the weaknesses of formal political structures in Gabon. Following President BONGO's death in 2009, a new election brought his son, Ali BONGO Ondimba, to power. Despite constrained political conditions, Gabon's small population, abundant natural resources, and considerable foreign support have helped make it one of the more stable African countries.

President Ali BONGO Ondimba's controversial August 2016 reelection sparked unprecedented opposition protests that resulted in the burning of the parliament building. The election was contested by the opposition after fraudulent results were flagged by international election observers. Gabon's Constitutional Court reviewed the election results but ruled in favor of President BONGO, upholding his win and extending his mandate to 2023.

GEOGRAPHY :: GABON

LOCATION:

Central Africa, bordering the Atlantic Ocean at the Equator, between Republic of the Congo and Equatorial Guinea

GEOGRAPHIC COORDINATES:

1 00 S, 11 45 E

MAP REFERENCES:

Africa

AREA:

total: 267,667 sq km

land: 257,667 sq km

water: 10,000 sq km

country comparison to the world: 78

AREA - COMPARATIVE:

slightly smaller than Colorado

LAND BOUNDARIES:

total: 3,261 km

border countries (3): Cameroon 349 km, Republic of the Congo 2567 km, Equatorial Guinea 345 km

COASTLINE:

885 km

MARITIME CLAIMS:

territorial sea: 12 nm

exclusive economic zone: 200 nm

contiguous zone: 24 nm

CLIMATE:

tropical; always hot, humid

TERRAIN:

narrow coastal plain; hilly interior; savanna in east and south

ELEVATION:

mean elevation: 377 m

elevation extremes: 0 m lowest point: Atlantic Ocean

1575 highest point: Mont Iboundji

NATURAL RESOURCES:

petroleum, natural gas, diamond, niobium, manganese, uranium, gold, timber, iron ore, hydropower

LAND USE:

agricultural land: 19% (2011 est.)

arable land: 1.2% (2011 est.) / permanent crops: 0.6% (2011 est.) / permanent pasture: 17.2% (2011 est.)

forest: 81% (2011 est.)

other: 0% (2011 est.)

IRRIGATED LAND:

40 sq km (2012)

POPULATION DISTRIBUTION:

the relatively small population is spread in pockets throughout the country; the largest urban center is the capital of Libreville, located along the Atlantic coast in the northwest

NATURAL HAZARDS:

none

ENVIRONMENT - CURRENT ISSUES:

deforestation (the forests that cover three-quarters of the country are threatened by excessive logging); burgeoning population exacerbating disposal of solid waste; oil industry contributing to water pollution; wildlife poaching

ENVIRONMENT - INTERNATIONAL AGREEMENTS:

party to: Biodiversity, Climate Change, Climate Change-Kyoto Protocol, Desertification, Endangered Species, Hazardous Wastes, Law of the Sea, Marine Dumping, Ozone Layer Protection, Ship Pollution, Tropical Timber 83, Tropical Timber 94, Wetlands, Whaling

signed, but not ratified: none of the selected agreements

GEOGRAPHY - NOTE:

a small population and oil and mineral reserves have helped Gabon become one of Africa's wealthier countries; in general, these circumstances have allowed the country to maintain and conserve its pristine rain forest and rich biodiversity

PEOPLE AND SOCIETY :: GABON

POPULATION:

2,119,036 (July 2018 est.)

note: estimates for this country explicitly take into account the effects of excess mortality due to AIDS; this can result in lower life expectancy, higher infant mortality, higher death rates, lower population growth rates, and changes in the distribution of population by age and sex than would otherwise be expected

country comparison to the world: 145

NATIONALITY:

noun: Gabonese (singular and plural)

adjective: Gabonese

ETHNIC GROUPS:

Gabonese-born 80.1% (includes Fang 23.2%, Shira-Punu/Vili 18.9%, Nzabi-Duma 11.3%, Mbede-Teke 6.9%, Myene 5%, Kota-Kele 4.9%, Okande-Tsogo 2.1%, Pygmy .3%, other 7.5%), Cameroonian 4.6%, Malian 2.4%, Beninese 2.1%, acquired Gabonese nationality 1.6%, Togolese 1.6%, Senegalese 1.1%, Congolese (Brazzaville) 1%, other 5.5% (includes Congolese (Kinshasa), Equatorial Guinean, Nigerian) (2012)

LANGUAGES:

French (official), Fang, Myene, Nzebi, Bapounou/Eschira, Bandjabi

RELIGIONS:

Roman Catholic 42.3%, Protestant 12.3%, other Christian 27.4%, Muslim 9.8%, animist 0.6%, other 0.5%, none/no answer 7.1% (2012 est.)

DEMOGRAPHIC PROFILE:

Gabon's oil revenues have given it one of the highest per capita income levels in sub-Saharan Africa, but the wealth is not evenly distributed and poverty is widespread. Unemployment is especially prevalent among the large youth population; more than 60% of the population is under the age of 25. With a fertility rate still averaging more than 4 children per woman, the youth population will continue to grow and further strain the mismatch between Gabon's supply of jobs and the skills of its labor force.

Gabon has been a magnet to migrants from neighboring countries since the 1960s because of the discovery of oil, as well as the country's political stability and timber, mineral, and natural gas resources. Nonetheless, income inequality and high unemployment have created slums in Libreville full of migrant workers from Senegal, Nigeria, Cameroon, Benin, Togo, and elsewhere in West Africa. In 2011, Gabon declared an end to refugee status for 9,500 remaining Congolese nationals to whom it had granted asylum during the Republic of the Congo's civil war between 1997 and 2003. About 5,400 of these refugees received permits to reside in Gabon.

AGE STRUCTURE:

0-14 years: 37.45% (male 405,676 /female 387,900)

15-24 years: 22.08% (male 245,490 /female 222,343)

25-54 years: 31.6% (male 355,348 /female 314,344)

55-64 years: 4.96% (male 54,679 /female 50,356)

65 years and over: 3.91% (male 40,721 /female 42,179) (2018 est.)

DEPENDENCY RATIOS:

total dependency ratio: 67.4 (2015 est.)

youth dependency ratio: 59.9 (2015 est.)

elderly dependency ratio: 7.6 (2015 est.)

potential support ratio: 13.2 (2015 est.)

MEDIAN AGE:

total: 20.5 years

male: 20.8 years

female: 20.2 years (2018 est.)

country comparison to the world: 187

POPULATION GROWTH RATE:

2.73% (2018 est.)

country comparison to the world: 15

BIRTH RATE:

26.5 births/1,000 population (2018 est.)

country comparison to the world: 46

DEATH RATE:

6.2 deaths/1,000 population (2018 est.)

country comparison to the world: 157

NET MIGRATION RATE:

-2 migrant(s)/1,000 population (2017 est.)

country comparison to the world: 161

POPULATION DISTRIBUTION:

the relatively small population is spread in pockets throughout the country; the largest urban center is the capital of Libreville, located along the Atlantic coast in the northwest

URBANIZATION:

urban population: 89.4% of total population (2018)

rate of urbanization: 2.61% annual rate of change (2015-20 est.)

MAJOR URBAN AREAS - POPULATION:

813,000 LIBREVILLE (capital) (2018)

SEX RATIO:

at birth: 1.02 male(s)/female (2017 est.)

0-14 years: 1.01 male(s)/female (2017 est.)

15-24 years: 1 male(s)/female (2017 est.)

25-54 years: 1 male(s)/female (2017 est.)

55-64 years: 0.93 male(s)/female (2017 est.)

65 years and over: 0.75 male(s)/female (2017 est.)

total population: 0.99 male(s)/female (2017 est.)

MOTHER'S MEAN AGE AT FIRST BIRTH:

20.3 years (2012 est.)

note: median age at first birth among women 25-29

MATERNAL MORTALITY RATE:

291 deaths/100,000 live births (2015 est.)

country comparison to the world: 42

INFANT MORTALITY RATE:

total: 32.9 deaths/1,000 live births (2018 est.)

male: 36.4 deaths/1,000 live births (2018 est.)

female: 29.3 deaths/1,000 live births (2018 est.)

country comparison to the world: 56

LIFE EXPECTANCY AT BIRTH:

total population: 68 years (2018 est.)

male: 66.3 years (2018 est.)

female: 69.6 years (2018 est.)

country comparison to the world: 169

TOTAL FERTILITY RATE:

3.52 children born/woman (2018 est.)

country comparison to the world: 42

CONTRACEPTIVE PREVALENCE RATE:

31.1% (2012)

HEALTH EXPENDITURES:

3.4% of GDP (2014)

country comparison to the world: 175

PHYSICIANS DENSITY:

0.41 physicians/1,000 population (2016)

HOSPITAL BED DENSITY:

6.3 beds/1,000 population (2010)

DRINKING WATER SOURCE:

improved:

urban: 97.2% of population

rural: 66.7% of population

total: 93.2% of population

unimproved:

urban: 2.8% of population

rural: 33.3% of population

total: 6.8% of population (2015 est.)

SANITATION FACILITY ACCESS:

improved:

urban: 43.4% of population (2015 est.)

rural: 31.5% of population (2015 est.)

total: 41.9% of population (2015 est.)

unimproved:

urban: 56.6% of population (2015 est.)

rural: 68.5% of population (2015 est.)

total: 58.1% of population (2015 est.)

HIV/AIDS - ADULT PREVALENCE RATE:

4.2% (2017 est.)

country comparison to the world: 14

HIV/AIDS - PEOPLE LIVING WITH HIV/AIDS:

56,000 (2017 est.)

country comparison to the world: 57

HIV/AIDS - DEATHS:

1,300 (2017 est.)

country comparison to the world: 60

MAJOR INFECTIOUS DISEASES:

degree of risk: very high (2016)

food or waterborne diseases: bacterial diarrhea, hepatitis A, and typhoid fever (2016)

vectorborne diseases: malaria and dengue fever (2016)

water contact diseases: schistosomiasis (2016)

animal contact diseases: rabies (2016)

OBESITY - ADULT PREVALENCE RATE:

15% (2016)

country comparison to the world: 127

CHILDREN UNDER THE AGE OF 5 YEARS UNDERWEIGHT:

6.5% (2012)

country comparison to the world: 74

EDUCATION EXPENDITURES:

2.7% of GDP (2014)

country comparison to the world: 159

LITERACY:

definition: age 15 and over can read and write (2015 est.)

total population: 83.2% (2015 est.)

male: 85.3% (2015 est.)

female: 81% (2015 est.)

UNEMPLOYMENT, YOUTH AGES 15-24:

total: 35.7% (2010 est.)

male: 30.5% (2010 est.)

female: 41.9% (2010 est.)

country comparison to the world: 21

GOVERNMENT :: GABON

COUNTRY NAME:

conventional long form: Gabonese Republic

conventional short form: Gabon

local long form: Republique Gabonaise

local short form: Gabon

etymology: name originates from the Portuguese word "gabao" meaning "cloak," which is roughly the shape that the early explorers gave to the estuary of the Komo River by the capital of Libreville

GOVERNMENT TYPE:

presidential republic

CAPITAL:

name: Libreville

geographic coordinates: 0 23 N, 9 27 E

time difference: UTC+1 (6 hours ahead of Washington, DC, during Standard Time)

ADMINISTRATIVE DIVISIONS:

9 provinces; Estuaire, Haut-Ogooue, Moyen-Ogooue, Ngounie, Nyanga, Ogooue-Ivindo, Ogooue-Lolo, Ogooue-Maritime, Woleu-Ntem

INDEPENDENCE:

17 August 1960 (from France)

NATIONAL HOLIDAY:

Independence Day, 17 August (1960)

CONSTITUTION:

history: previous 1961; latest drafted May 1990, adopted 15 March 1991, promulgated 26 March 1991 (2017)

amendments: proposed by the president of the republic, by the Council of Ministers, or by one-third of either house of Parliament; passage requires Constitutional Court evaluation, at least two-thirds majority vote of two-thirds of the Parliament membership convened in joint session, and approval in a referendum; constitutional articles on Gabon's democratic form of government cannot be amended; amended several times, last in 2011 (2017)

LEGAL SYSTEM:

mixed legal system of French civil law and customary law

INTERNATIONAL LAW ORGANIZATION PARTICIPATION:

has not submitted an ICJ jurisdiction declaration; accepts ICCt jurisdiction

CITIZENSHIP:

citizenship by birth: no

citizenship by descent only: at least one parent must be a citizen of Gabon

dual citizenship recognized: no

residency requirement for naturalization: 10 years

SUFFRAGE:

18 years of age; universal

EXECUTIVE BRANCH:

chief of state: President Ali BONGO Ondimba (since 16 October 2009)

head of government: Prime Minister Emmanuel ISSOZE-NGONDET (since 3 May 2018); note - Prime Minister Emmanuel ISSOZE-NGONDET (since 29 September 2016) resigned on 1 May 2018, after the constitutional court dissolved the National Assembly and ordered his resignation when elections failed to be held by 30 April 2018; reinstated by President Ali BONGO

cabinet: Council of Ministers appointed by the prime minister in consultation with the president

elections/appointments: president directly elected by simple majority popular vote for a 7-year term (no term limits); election last held on 27 August 2016 (next to be held in August 2023); prime minister appointed by the president

election results: Ali BONGO Ondimba reelected president; percent of vote - Ali BONGO Ondimba (PDG) 49.8%, Jean PING (UFC) 48.2%, other 2.0%

LEGISLATIVE BRANCH:

description: bicameral Parliament or Parlement consists of:
Senate or Senat (102 seats; members indirectly elected by municipal councils and departmental assemblies by absolute majority vote in 2 rounds if needed; members serve 6-year terms)
National Assembly or Assemblee Nationale (120 seats; members elected in single-seat constituencies by absolute majority vote in 2 rounds if needed; members serve 5-year terms)

elections:
Senate - last held on 13 December 2014 (next to be held in January 2020)
National Assembly - first round last held on 6 October 2018; next round scheduled for 27 October 2018

election results:
Senate - percent of vote by party - NA; seats by party - PDG 81, CLR 7, PSD 2, ADERE-UPG 1, UPG 1, PGCI 1, independent 7
National Assembly - percent of vote by party - NA; seats by party - PDG 113, RPG 3, other 4

JUDICIAL BRANCH:

highest courts: Supreme Court (consists of 4 permanent specialized supreme courts - Supreme Court or Cour de Cassation, Administrative Supreme Court or Conseil d'Etat, Accounting Supreme Court or Cour des Comptes, Constitutional Court or Cour Constitutionnelle - and the non-permanent Court of State Security, initiated only for cases of high treason by the president and criminal activity by executive branch officials)

judge selection and term of office: appointment and tenure of Supreme, Administrative, Accounting, and State Security courts NA; Constitutional Court judges appointed - 3 by the national president, 3 by the president of the Senate, and 3 by the president of the National Assembly; judges serve 7-year, single renewable terms

subordinate courts: Courts of Appeal; county courts; military courts

POLITICAL PARTIES AND LEADERS:

Circle of Liberal Reformers or CLR [Gen. Jean-Boniface ASSELE]
Democratic and Republican Alliance or ADERE [DIDJOB Divungui di Ndinge]
Gabonese Democratic Party or PDG [Ali BONGO Ondimba]
Independent Center Party of Gabon or PGCI [Luccheri GAHILA]
Rally for Gabon or RPG
Social Democratic Party or PSD [Pierre Claver MAGANGA-MOUSSAVOU]
Union for the New Republic or UPRN [Louis Gaston MAYILA]
Union of Gabonese People or UPG [Richard MOULOMBA]
Union of Forces for Change or UFC [Jean PING]

INTERNATIONAL ORGANIZATION PARTICIPATION:

ACP, AfDB, AU, BDEAC, CEMAC, FAO, FZ, G-24, G-77, IAEA, IBRD, ICAO, ICCt, ICRM, IDA, IDB, IFAD, IFC, IFRCS, ILO, IMF, IMO, IMSO, Interpol, IOC, IOM, IPU, ISO, ITSO, ITU, ITUC (NGOs), MIGA, NAM, OIC, OIF, OPCW, UN, UNCTAD, UNESCO, UNIDO, UNWTO, UPU, WCO, WHO, WIPO, WMO, WTO

DIPLOMATIC REPRESENTATION IN THE US:

chief of mission: Ambassador Michael MOUSSA-ADAMO (since September 9, 2011)

chancery: 2034 20th Street NW, Suite 200, Washington, DC 20009

telephone: [1] (202) 797-1000

FAX: [1] (301) 332-0668

DIPLOMATIC REPRESENTATION FROM THE US:

chief of mission: Ambassador Joel DANIES (since 22 MARCH 2018); note - also accredited to Sao Tome and Principe

embassy: Boulevard du Bord de Mer, Libreville

mailing address: Centre Ville, B. P. 4000, Libreville; pouch: 2270 Libreville Place, Washington, DC 20521-2270

telephone: [241] 01-45-71-00

FAX: [241] 01-74-55-07

FLAG DESCRIPTION:

three equal horizontal bands of green (top), yellow, and blue; green represents the country's forests and natural resources, gold represents the equator (which transects Gabon) as well as the sun, blue represents the sea

NATIONAL SYMBOL(S):

black panther; national colors: green, yellow, blue

NATIONAL ANTHEM:

name: "La Concorde" (The Concorde)

lyrics/music: Georges Aleka DAMAS

note: adopted 1960

ECONOMY :: GABON

ECONOMY - OVERVIEW:

Gabon enjoys a per capita income four times that of most sub-Saharan African nations, but because of high income inequality, a large proportion of the population remains poor. Gabon relied on timber and manganese exports until oil was discovered offshore in the early 1970s. From 2010 to 2016, oil accounted for approximately 80% of Gabon's exports, 45% of its GDP, and 60% of its state budget revenues.

Gabon faces fluctuating international prices for its oil, timber, and manganese exports. A rebound of oil prices from 2001 to 2013 helped growth, but declining production, as some fields passed their peak production, has hampered Gabon from fully realizing potential gains. GDP grew nearly 6% per year over the 2010-14 period, but slowed significantly from 2014 to just 1% in 2017 as oil prices declined. Low oil prices also weakened government revenue and negatively affected the trade and current account balances. In the wake of lower revenue, Gabon signed a 3-year agreement with the IMF in June 2017.

Despite an abundance of natural wealth, poor fiscal management and over-reliance on oil has stifled the economy. Power cuts and water shortages are frequent. Gabon is reliant on imports and the government heavily subsidizes commodities, including food, but will be hard pressed to tamp down public frustration with unemployment and corruption.

GDP (PURCHASING POWER PARITY):

$36.66 billion (2017 est.)

$36.5 billion (2016 est.)

$35.75 billion (2015 est.)

note: data are in 2017 dollars

country comparison to the world: 123

GDP (OFFICIAL EXCHANGE RATE):

$14.93 billion (2017 est.) (2017 est.)

GDP - REAL GROWTH RATE:

0.5% (2017 est.)

2.1% (2016 est.)

3.9% (2015 est.)

country comparison to the world: 191

GDP - PER CAPITA (PPP):

$18,100 (2017 est.)

$18,400 (2016 est.)

$18,500 (2015 est.)

note: data are in 2017 dollars

country comparison to the world: 97

GROSS NATIONAL SAVING:

25.6% of GDP (2017 est.)

24.3% of GDP (2016 est.)

29.2% of GDP (2015 est.)

country comparison to the world: 55

GDP - COMPOSITION, BY END USE:

household consumption: 37.6% (2017 est.)

government consumption: 14.1% (2017 est.)

investment in fixed capital: 29% (2017 est.)

investment in inventories: -0.6% (2016 est.)

exports of goods and services: 46.7% (2017 est.)

imports of goods and services: -26.8% (2017 est.)

GDP - COMPOSITION, BY SECTOR OF ORIGIN:

agriculture: 5% (2017 est.)

industry: 44.7% (2017 est.)

services: 50.4% (2017 est.)

AGRICULTURE - PRODUCTS:

cocoa, coffee, sugar, palm oil, rubber; cattle; okoume (a tropical softwood); fish

INDUSTRIES:

petroleum extraction and refining; manganese, gold; chemicals, ship repair, food and beverages, textiles, lumbering and plywood, cement

INDUSTRIAL PRODUCTION GROWTH RATE:

1.8% (2017 est.)

country comparison to the world: 135

LABOR FORCE:

557,800 (2017 est.)

country comparison to the world: 155

LABOR FORCE - BY OCCUPATION:

agriculture: 64%

industry: 12%

services: 24% (2005 est.)

UNEMPLOYMENT RATE:

28% (2015 est.)

20.4% (2014 est.)

country comparison to the world: 204

POPULATION BELOW POVERTY LINE:

34.3% (2015 est.)

HOUSEHOLD INCOME OR CONSUMPTION BY PERCENTAGE SHARE:

lowest 10%: 32.7% (2005)

highest 10%: 32.7% (2005)

DISTRIBUTION OF FAMILY INCOME - GINI INDEX:

42.2 (2005 est.)

country comparison to the world: 52

BUDGET:

revenues: 2.634 billion (2017 est.)

expenditures: 2.914 billion (2017 est.)

TAXES AND OTHER REVENUES:

17.6% (of GDP) (2017 est.)

country comparison to the world: 167

BUDGET SURPLUS (+) OR DEFICIT (-):

-1.9% (of GDP) (2017 est.)

country comparison to the world: 101

PUBLIC DEBT:

62.7% of GDP (2017 est.)

64.2% of GDP (2016 est.)

country comparison to the world: 68

FISCAL YEAR:

calendar year

INFLATION RATE (CONSUMER PRICES):

2.7% (2017 est.)

2.1% (2016 est.)

country comparison to the world: 125

CENTRAL BANK DISCOUNT RATE:

3% (31 December 2010)

4.25% (31 December 2009)

country comparison to the world: 110

COMMERCIAL BANK PRIME LENDING RATE:

15% (31 December 2017 est.)

14% (31 December 2016 est.)

country comparison to the world: 40

STOCK OF NARROW MONEY:

$2.357 billion (31 December 2017 est.)

$2.053 billion (31 December 2016 est.)

country comparison to the world: 130

STOCK OF BROAD MONEY:

$2.357 billion (31 December 2017 est.)

$2.053 billion (31 December 2016 est.)

country comparison to the world: 138

STOCK OF DOMESTIC CREDIT:

$2.91 billion (31 December 2017 est.)

$3.097 billion (31 December 2016 est.)

country comparison to the world: 141

MARKET VALUE OF PUBLICLY TRADED SHARES:

NA

CURRENT ACCOUNT BALANCE:

-$725 million (2017 est.)

-$1.389 billion (2016 est.)

country comparison to the world: 131

EXPORTS:

$5.564 billion (2017 est.)

$4.364 billion (2016 est.)

country comparison to the world: 107

EXPORTS - PARTNERS:

China 36.4%, US 10%, Ireland 8.5%, Netherlands 6.3%, South Korea 5.1%, Australia 5%, Italy 4.6% (2017)

EXPORTS - COMMODITIES:

crude oil, timber, manganese, uranium

IMPORTS:

$2.829 billion (2017 est.)

$2.652 billion (2016 est.)

country comparison to the world: 151

IMPORTS - COMMODITIES:

machinery and equipment, foodstuffs, chemicals, construction materials

IMPORTS - PARTNERS:

France 23.6%, Belgium 19.6%, China 15.2% (2017)

RESERVES OF FOREIGN EXCHANGE AND GOLD:

$981.6 million (31 December 2017 est.)

$804.1 million (31 December 2016 est.)

country comparison to the world: 133

DEBT - EXTERNAL:

$6.49 billion (31 December 2017 est.)

$5.321 billion (31 December 2016 est.)

country comparison to the world: 127

EXCHANGE RATES:

Cooperation Financiere en Afrique Centrale francs (XAF) per US dollar -

605.3 (2017 est.)

593.01 (2016 est.)

593.01 (2015 est.)

591.45 (2014 est.)

494.42 (2013 est.)

ENERGY :: GABON

ELECTRICITY ACCESS:

population without electricity: 200,000 (2013)

electrification - total population: 89% (2013)

electrification - urban areas: 97% (2013)

electrification - rural areas: 38% (2013)

ELECTRICITY - PRODUCTION:

2.244 billion kWh (2016 est.)

country comparison to the world: 137

ELECTRICITY - CONSUMPTION:

2.071 billion kWh (2016 est.)

country comparison to the world: 143

ELECTRICITY - EXPORTS:

0 kWh (2016 est.)

country comparison to the world: 137

ELECTRICITY - IMPORTS:

344 million kWh (2016 est.)

country comparison to the world: 85

ELECTRICITY - INSTALLED GENERATING CAPACITY:

671,000 kW (2016 est.)

country comparison to the world: 137

ELECTRICITY - FROM FOSSIL FUELS:

51% of total installed capacity (2016 est.)

country comparison to the world: 148

ELECTRICITY - FROM NUCLEAR FUELS:

0% of total installed capacity (2017 est.)

country comparison to the world: 93

ELECTRICITY - FROM HYDROELECTRIC PLANTS:

49% of total installed capacity (2017 est.)

country comparison to the world: 41

ELECTRICITY - FROM OTHER RENEWABLE SOURCES:

0% of total installed capacity (2017 est.)

country comparison to the world: 186

CRUDE OIL - PRODUCTION:

198,800 bbl/day (2017 est.)

country comparison to the world: 35

CRUDE OIL - EXPORTS:

214,200 bbl/day (2017 est.)

country comparison to the world: 30

CRUDE OIL - IMPORTS:

0 bbl/day (2015 est.)

country comparison to the world: 130

CRUDE OIL - PROVED RESERVES:

2 billion bbl (1 January 2018 est.)

country comparison to the world: 34

REFINED PETROLEUM PRODUCTS - PRODUCTION:

16,580 bbl/day (2017 est.)

country comparison to the world: 91

REFINED PETROLEUM PRODUCTS - CONSUMPTION:

24,000 bbl/day (2016 est.)

country comparison to the world: 129

REFINED PETROLEUM PRODUCTS - EXPORTS:

4,662 bbl/day (2015 est.)

country comparison to the world: 91

REFINED PETROLEUM PRODUCTS - IMPORTS:

10,680 bbl/day (2015 est.)

country comparison to the world: 146

NATURAL GAS - PRODUCTION:

401 million cu m (2017 est.)

country comparison to the world: 74

NATURAL GAS - CONSUMPTION:

401 million cu m (2017 est.)

country comparison to the world: 101

NATURAL GAS - EXPORTS:

0 cu m (2017 est.)

country comparison to the world: 107

NATURAL GAS - IMPORTS:

0 cu m (2017 est.)

country comparison to the world: 128

NATURAL GAS - PROVED RESERVES:

28.32 billion cu m (1 January 2018 est.)

country comparison to the world: 69

CARBON DIOXIDE EMISSIONS FROM CONSUMPTION OF ENERGY:

4.293 million Mt (2017 est.)

country comparison to the world: 137

COMMUNICATIONS :: GABON

TELEPHONES - FIXED LINES:

total subscriptions: 21,235 (2017 est.)

subscriptions per 100 inhabitants: 1 (2017 est.)

country comparison to the world: 175

TELEPHONES - MOBILE CELLULAR:

total subscriptions: 2,663,243 (2017 est.)

subscriptions per 100 inhabitants: 150 (2017 est.)

country comparison to the world: 142

TELEPHONE SYSTEM:

general assessment: adequate system of cable, microwave radio relay, tropospheric scatter, radiotelephone communication stations, and a domestic satellite system with 12 earth stations; competition among telecoms, independent regulatory authority and reduction in cost connecting makes for strong telecommunications (2017)

domestic: fixed-line is 1 per 100 subscriptions; a growing mobile cellular network with multiple providers is making telephone service more widely available with mobile cellular teledensity at 150 per 100 persons (2017)

international: country code - 241; landing point for the SAT-3/WASC fiber-optic submarine cable that provides connectivity to Europe and Asia; satellite earth stations - 3 Intelsat (Atlantic Ocean); sufficient international bandwidth on the SAT-3/WASC/SAFE submarine cable and ACE submarine cable; Airtel Gabon opens submarine link between Libreville and Port-Gentil (2017)

BROADCAST MEDIA:

state owns and operates 2 TV stations and 2 radio broadcast stations; a few private radio and TV stations; transmissions of at least 2 international broadcasters are accessible; satellite service subscriptions are available (2007)

INTERNET COUNTRY CODE:

.ga

INTERNET USERS:

total: 835,408 (July 2016 est.)

percent of population: 48.1% (July 2016 est.)

country comparison to the world: 138

BROADBAND - FIXED SUBSCRIPTIONS:

total: 14,967 (2017 est.)

subscriptions per 100 inhabitants: 1 (2017 est.)

country comparison to the world: 162

TRANSPORTATION :: GABON

NATIONAL AIR TRANSPORT SYSTEM:

number of registered air carriers: 5 (2015)

inventory of registered aircraft operated by air carriers: 7 (2015)

annual passenger traffic on registered air carriers: 137,331 (2015)

annual freight traffic on registered air carriers: 0 mt-km (2015)

CIVIL AIRCRAFT REGISTRATION COUNTRY CODE PREFIX:

TR (2016)

AIRPORTS:

44 (2013)

country comparison to the world: 97

AIRPORTS - WITH PAVED RUNWAYS:

total: 14 (2017)

over 3,047 m: 1 (2017)

2,438 to 3,047 m: 2 (2017)

1,524 to 2,437 m: 9 (2017)

914 to 1,523 m: 1 (2017)

under 914 m: 1 (2017)

AIRPORTS - WITH UNPAVED RUNWAYS:

total: 30 (2013)

1,524 to 2,437 m: 7 (2013)

914 to 1,523 m: 9 (2013)

under 914 m: 14 (2013)

PIPELINES:

807 km gas, 1639 km oil, 3 km water (2013)

RAILWAYS:

total: 649 km (2014)

standard gauge: 649 km 1.435-m gauge (2014)

country comparison to the world: 106

ROADWAYS:

total: 9,170 km (2007)

paved: 1,097 km (2007)

unpaved: 8,073 km (2007)

country comparison to the world: 140

WATERWAYS:

1,600 km (310 km on Ogooue River) (2010)

country comparison to the world: 48

MERCHANT MARINE:

total: 27 (2017)

by type: general cargo 11, oil tanker 1, other 15 (2017)

country comparison to the world: 131

PORTS AND TERMINALS:

major seaport(s): Libreville, Owendo, Port-Gentil

oil terminal(s): Gamba, Lucina

MILITARY AND SECURITY :: GABON

MILITARY EXPENDITURES:

1.43% of GDP (2016)

1.19% of GDP (2015)

1.14% of GDP (2014)

1.6% of GDP (2013)

1.62% of GDP (2012)

country comparison to the world: 80

MILITARY BRANCHES:

Gabonese Defense Forces (Forces de Defense Gabonaise): Land Force (Force Terrestre), Gabonese Navy (Marine Gabonaise), Gabonese Air Forces (Forces Aerienne Gabonaises, FAG) (2012)

MILITARY SERVICE AGE AND OBLIGATION:

20 years of age for voluntary military service; no conscription (2012)

TRANSNATIONAL ISSUES :: GABON

DISPUTES - INTERNATIONAL:

UN urges Equatorial Guinea and Gabon to resolve the sovereignty dispute over Gabon-occupied Mbane Island and lesser islands and to establish a maritime boundary in hydrocarbon-rich Corisco Bay

TRAFFICKING IN PERSONS:

current situation: Gabon is primarily a destination and transit country for adults and children from West and Central African countries subjected to forced labor and sex trafficking; boys are forced to work as street vendors, mechanics, or in the fishing sector, while girls are subjected to domestic servitude or forced to work in markets or roadside restaurants; West African women are forced into domestic servitude or prostitution; men are reportedly forced to work on cattle farms; some foreign adults end up in forced labor in Gabon after initially seeking the help of human smugglers to help them migrate clandestinely; traffickers operate in loose, ethnic-based criminal networks, with female traffickers recruiting and facilitating the transport of victims from source countries; in some cases, families turn child victims over to traffickers, who promise paid jobs in Gabon

tier rating: Tier 2 Watch List – Gabon does not fully comply with the minimum standards for the elimination of trafficking; however, it is making significant efforts to do so; Gabon's existing laws do not prohibit all forms of trafficking, and the government failed to pass a legal amendment drafted in 2013 to criminalize the trafficking of adults; anti-trafficking law enforcement decreased in 2014, dropping from 50 investigations to 16, and the only defendant to face prosecution fled the country; government efforts to identify and refer victims to protective services declined from 50 child victims in 2013 to just 3 in 2014, none of whom was referred to a care facility; the government provided support to four centers offering services to orphans and vulnerable children – 14 child victims identified by an NGO received government assistance; no adult victims have been identified since 2009 (2015)

Made in the USA
Coppell, TX
30 June 2021